Stephen Walther

ASP.NET 3.5

UNLEASHED

 800 East 96th Street, Indianapolis, Indiana 46240 USA

ASP.NET 3.5 Unleashed

ISBN-13: 978-0-672-33011-7
ISBN-10: 0-672-33011-3

Library of Congress Cataloging-in-Publication Data

Walther, Stephen.
  ASP.NET 3.5 unleashed / Stephen Walther.
      p. cm.
  Includes index.
  ISBN 0-672-33011-3
  1. Active server pages. 2. Web sites—Design. 3. Web site development. 4. Microsoft .NET. I. Title.
TK5105.8885.A26W3516 2007
005.2'76—dc22
                                2007046046

Printed in the United States on America

Third Printing: October 2008

Trademarks

Warning and Disclaimer

Bulk Sales

Sams Publishing offers excellent discounts on this book when ordered in quantity for bulk purchases or special sales. For more information, please contact

> **U.S. Corporate and Government Sales**
> **1-800-382-3419**
> **corpsales@pearsontechgroup.com**

For sales outside of the U.S., please contact

> **International Sales**
> **international@pearsoned.com**

Editor-in-Chief
Karen Gettman

Senior Acquisitions Editor
Neil Rowe

Development Editor
Mark Renfrow

Managing Editor
Gina Kanouse

Project Editors
Lori Lyons
Anne Goebel

Copy Editor
Bart Reed

Indexer
Erika Millen

Proofreaders
Watercrest Publishing
San Dee Phillips

Technical Editor
Todd Meister

Publishing Coordinator
Cindy Teeters

Multimedia Developer
Dan Scherf

Book Designer
Gary Adair

Composition
Jake McFarland

Contents at a Glance

Table of Contents

About the Author

Stephen Walther is a Microsoft Software Legend, a Microsoft ASP.NET MVP, and a member of the INETA Speaker's Bureau. He has spoken at a number of major conferences, including Microsoft TechEd, Microsoft DevDays, and ASP.NET Connections.

He wrote several ASP.NET best-practice applications for Microsoft. He was the lead developer of the ASP.NET Community Starter Kit and the Issue Tracker Starter Kit.

His company, Superexpert ASP.NET Training (www.SuperexpertTraining.com), has provided ASP.NET training to companies and organizations across the United States, including NASA, the National Science Foundation, the U.S. House of Representatives, Boeing, Lockheed Martin, Verizon, and Microsoft.

Dedication

This book is dedicated to my wife, Ruth Walther,
who is my favorite person in the world.

Acknowledgments

I want to thank a number of people at Microsoft for taking the time to answer my questions about ASP.NET: Scott Guthrie, Susan Chory, Bradley Millington, Mike Harder, Andres Sanabria, Nikhil Kothari, Matthew Gibbs, Rob Howard, and Stefan Schackow.

I also want to thank Neil Rowe for all the support and encouragement that he gave me while I was writing this book. I really appreciate the work that Mark Renfrow, Lori Lyons, Anne Goebel, and Jake McFarland performed when putting together the book to meet a very tight deadline.

Finally, I want to thank Scott Cate for fixing the regular expressions in the first edition of this book. I want to thank Paul Litwin for reviewing the chapter on the ObjectDataSource control. And, I want to thank Dan Wahlin for agreeing with me about the UpdatePanel.

We Want to Hear from You!

As the reader of this book, *you* are our most important critic and commentator. We value your opinion and want to know what we're doing right, what we could do better, what areas you'd like to see us publish in, and any other words of wisdom you're willing to pass our way.

As a senior acquisitions editor for Sams Publishing, I welcome your comments. You can email or write me directly to let me know what you did or didn't like about this book—as well as what we can do to make our books better.

Please note that I cannot help you with technical problems related to the topic of this book. We do have a User Services group, however, where I will forward specific technical questions related to the book.

When you write, please be sure to include this book's title and author as well as your name, email address, and phone number. I will carefully review your comments and share them with the author and editors who worked on the book.

Email: feedback@samspublishing.com

Mail: Neil Rowe
Senior Acquisitions Editor
Sams Publishing
800 East 96th Street
Indianapolis, IN 46240 USA

For more information about this book or another Sams Publishing title, visit our website at www.informit.com/title/9780672330117.

Reader Services

Visit our website and register this book at www.informit.com/title/9780672330117 for convenient access to any updates, downloads, or errata that might be available for this book.

Introduction

ASP.NET is Microsoft's flagship technology for building highly interactive, highly scalable websites. Some of the largest websites hosted on the Internet were built with the ASP.NET Framework, including Dell (www.Dell.com), MySpace (www.MySpace.com), and Microsoft (www.Microsoft.com). If you need to build a highly interactive website that can scale to handle thousands of simultaneous users, then ASP.NET is the technology to use.

Who Should Read This Book?

ASP.NET 3.5 Unleashed is intended for professional programmers who need to create a website. This book is a comprehensive reference for building a website with ASP.NET 3.5. The CD that accompanies this book contains hundreds of code samples that you can start using immediately while building your website.

If you are new to building websites with ASP.NET, you can use this book to teach yourself everything you need to know to build a website with the ASP.NET Framework. If you are an experienced ASP.NET developer, you can use this book to learn about the new features of ASP.NET 3.5.

The final part of this book contains a complete sample application written with ASP.NET 3.5: a code sample site. All the code for this application is included on the CD that accompanies this book. (The source is in both C# and VB.NET.)

What Do You Need to Know Before You Read This Book?

This book assumes that you know either the C# or Visual Basic .NET programming language. If you are completely new to the .NET Framework, then I recommend you read an introductory book on either C# or Visual Basic .NET before reading this book.

In the body of the book, all the code samples are presented in C#. However, this was not intended as any kind of insult to VB.NET programmers. The CD that accompanies this book includes every code sample translated into the VB.NET programming language.

To get the most from the database chapters, you should have some experience working with a database, such as Microsoft SQL Server, Oracle, or Microsoft Access.

Changes to This Book

This edition of the book reflects three important transitions in the ASP.NET Framework.

First (and most obviously), unlike the previous editions of this book, all the code samples in the body of this edition of the book are written in the C# programming language. There are now more professional C# developers than Visual Basic .NET developers. The book has been updated to reflect this important transition. If your preference is Visual Basic, Visual Basic .NET versions of all code samples are included on the CD that accompanies this book.

Second, this edition of the book includes a new chapter that covers Microsoft LINQ to SQL in detail. LINQ to SQL is a new query language that enables you to access a database without writing any SQL. The chapter examines LINQ to SQL from an ASP.NET perspective (see Chapter 18, "Data Access with LINQ to SQL").

This edition of the book also includes a new chapter on the two new data access controls introduced with the ASP.NET 3.5 Framework: the ListView and DataPager controls. The ListView control is a more flexible version of the GridView control (see Chapter 14, "Using the ListView and DataPager Controls").

The third important transition in the ASP.NET 3.5 Framework concerns AJAX. The Microsoft AJAX Extensions for ASP.NET are integrated into the ASP.NET 3.5 Framework. AJAX represents a transition from using server-side technologies to using client-side technologies when building web applications.

Ajax represents a fundamental shift in the way that developers build websites. Users are no longer satisfied with slow, noninteractive web applications built with server-side technologies. They want highly responsive and interactive web applications that behave more like desktop applications.

This book includes three chapters devoted to the very important topic of Ajax. You learn how to take advantage of Microsoft's server-side Ajax framework to retrofit existing ASP.NET applications with Ajax functionality. You also learn how to take advantage of Microsoft's client-side Ajax framework to build the web applications of the future: pure client-side Ajax applications (see Part IX of this book, "ASP.NET AJAX").

The final chapter of this book contains a completely new sample application written with LINQ to SQL and server-side Ajax. The sample application demonstrates how you can take advantage of these new technologies when building real-world web applications (see Chapter 34, "Building a Code Sample Website").

How This Book Is Organized

Although I encourage you to read this book from start to finish, reading chapter by chapter, I realize that not everyone has time to do so. If necessary, you can use this book solely as a reference and jump to a chapter only when the need arises. It may be helpful, therefore, to have an idea of the overall organization of this book.

▸ **Part I: Building ASP.NET Pages**—The chapters in this part provide you with an overview of the basic controls included in the ASP.NET Framework. You learn how to build interactive Web Forms with the form controls. You also learn how to validate form data with the validation controls. Finally, you learn how to upload files and display interactive calendars and wizards with the rich controls.

▸ **Part II: Designing ASP.NET Websites**—The chapters in this part discuss how you can create a common layout and style for the pages in your website. You learn how to use Master Pages to share content across multiple pages. You also learn how to use Themes to create a consistent page style.

▸ **Part III: Performing Data Access**—The chapters in this part focus on data access. You learn how to use the `ListView` and `GridView` controls to display, page, sort, and edit a set of database records. You learn how to use the `DetailsView` and `FormView` controls to display and edit a single database record at a time.

▸ **Part IV: Building Components**—The chapters in this part focus on building custom components. You learn how to design and create multitiered applications. You also learn how to build data access components by taking advantage of both LINQ to SQL and ADO.NET.

▸ **Part V: Site Navigation**—The chapters in this part discuss the various navigation controls included in the ASP.NET Framework, such as the `TreeView` and `Menu` controls. You learn how to use these controls with a Site Map in order to allow users to easily navigate a website. You also learn how to use the `VirtualPathProvider` class to abstract a website from the file system. For example, you learn how to store the pages in a website in a Microsoft SQL Server database.

▸ **Part VI: Security**—The chapters in this part focus on the Login controls and Membership API. You learn how to create a user registration and authentication system. You learn how to store Membership information in either a SQL Server database or Active Directory.

▸ **Part VII: Building ASP.NET Applications**—These chapters discuss a variety of topics related to building ASP.NET applications. For example, you learn how to improve the performance of your ASP.NET applications by taking advantage of caching. You also learn how to localize your ASP.NET applications so that they can be easily translated and presented in multiple human languages.

▶ **Part VIII: Custom Control Building**—The chapters in this part concentrate on extending the ASP.NET Framework with custom controls. For example, you learn how to create custom data access controls that work like the `ListView` and `GridView` controls.

▶ **Part IX: ASP.NET AJAX**—These chapters focus on using Ajax in an ASP.NET application. The first two chapters discuss the Microsoft server-side Ajax controls. You learn how to use the `UpdatePanel` control and the ASP.NET AJAX Control Toolkit. In the last chapter, you learn how to build pure client-side Ajax applications with the Microsoft AJAX Library.

▶ **Part X: Sample Application**—The last part of this book contains a single chapter that describes a sample application. You learn how to build a code sample website with the ASP.NET Framework that takes advantage of new ASP.NET 3.5 features, such as LINQ to SQL and the AJAX Extensions to ASP.NET.

PART I

Building ASP.NET Pages

IN THIS PART

CHAPTER 1

Overview of the ASP.NET Framework

Let's start by building a simple ASP.NET page.

> **NOTE**
>
> For information on installing ASP.NET, see the last section of this chapter.

If you are using Visual Web Developer or Visual Studio, you first need to create a new website. Start Visual Web Developer and select the menu option File, New Web Site. The New Web Site dialog box appears (see Figure 1.1). Enter the folder where you want your new website to be created in the Location field and click the OK button.

> **NOTE**
>
> When you create a new website, you might receive an error message warning you that you need to enable script debugging in Internet Explorer. You'll want to enable script debugging to build Ajax applications. We discuss Ajax in Part IX of this book, "ASP.NET AJAX."

After you create a new website, you can add an ASP.NET page to it. Select the menu option Web Site, Add New Item. Select Web Form and enter the value `FirstPage.aspx` in the Name field. Make sure that both the `Place Code in Separate File` and `Select Master Page` check boxes are unchecked, and click the Add button to create the new ASP.NET page (see Figure 1.2).

The code for the first ASP.NET page is contained in Listing 1.1.

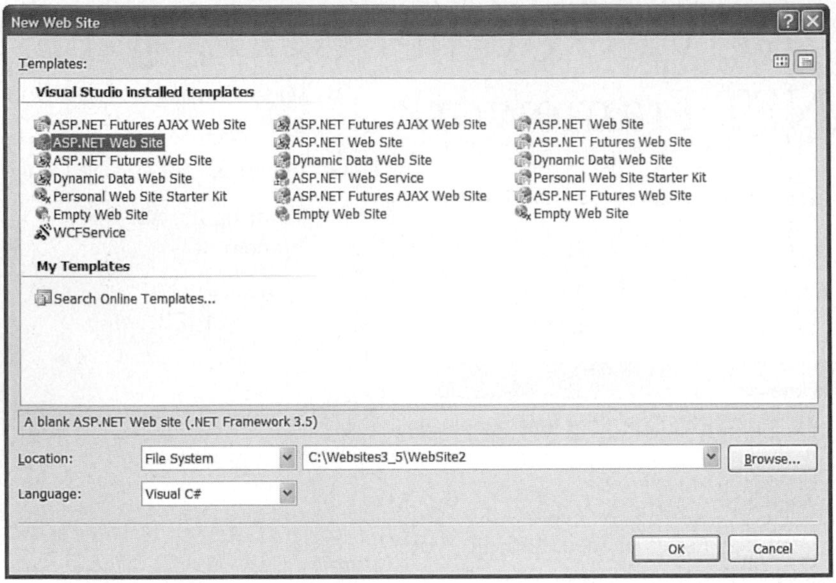

FIGURE 1.1   Creating a new website.

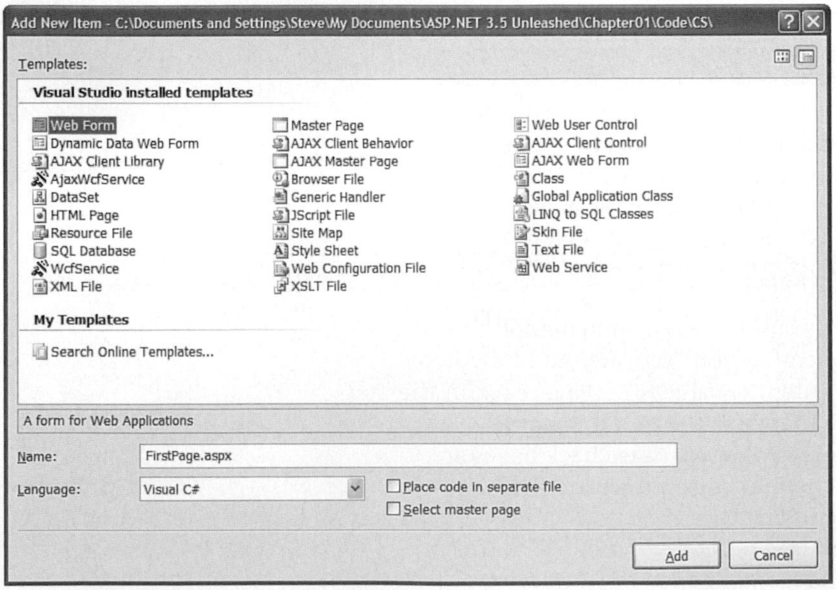

FIGURE 1.2   Adding a new ASP.NET page.

LISTING 1.1 `FirstPage.aspx`

```
<%@ Page Language="C#" %>
<!DOCTYPE html PUBLIC "-//W3C//DTD XHTML 1.0 Transitional//EN"
"http://www.w3.org/TR/xhtml1/DTD/xhtml1-transitional.dtd">
<script runat="server">

    void Page_Load()
    {
        lblServerTime.Text = DateTime.Now.ToString();
    }

</script>
<html xmlns="http://www.w3.org/1999/xhtml" >
<head>
    <title>First Page</title>
</head>
<body>
    <form id="form1" runat="server">
    <div>

    Welcome to ASP.NET 3.5! The current date and time is:

    <asp:Label
        id="lblServerTime"
        Runat="server" />

    </div>
    </form>
</body>
</html>
```

> **NOTE**
>
> The CD that accompanies this book contains both C# and VB.NET versions of all the
> code samples. The code samples are also posted online at www.Superexpert.com. Go
> to the Books section of the website and you can view the listings for each chapter and
> try the listings "live."

The ASP.NET page in Listing 1.1 displays a brief message and the server's current date and
time. You can view the page in Listing 1.1 in a browser by right-clicking the page and
selecting View in Browser (see Figure 1.3).

FIGURE 1.3   Viewing `FirstPage.aspx` in a browser.

The page in Listing 1.1 is an extremely simple page. However, it does illustrate the most common elements of an ASP.NET page. The page contains a directive, a code declaration block, and a page render block.

The first line, in Listing 1.1, contains a directive. It looks like this:

```
<%@ Page Language="C#" %>
```

A directive always begins with the special characters <%@ and ends with the characters %>. Directives are used primarily to provide the compiler with the information it needs to compile the page.

For example, the directive in Listing 1.1 indicates that the code contained in the page is C# code. The page is compiled by the C# compiler and not another compiler such as the Visual Basic .NET (VB.NET) compiler.

The next part of the page begins with the opening <script runat="server"> tag and ends with the closing </script> tag. The <script> tag contains something called the *code declaration block*.

The code declaration block contains all the methods used in the page. It contains all the page's functions and subroutines. The code declaration block in Listing 1.1 includes a single method named Page_Load(), which looks like this:

```
void Page_Load()
{
    lblServerTime.Text = DateTime.Now.ToString();
}
```

This method assigns the current date and time to the Text property of a Label control contained in the body of the page named lblServerTime.

The Page_Load() method is an example of an event handler. This method handles the Page Load event. Each and every time the page loads, the method automatically executes and assigns the current date and time to the Label control.

The final part of the page is called the *page render block*. The page render block contains everything that is rendered to the browser. In Listing 1.1, the render block includes everything between the opening and closing <html> tags.

The majority of the page render block consists of everyday HTML. For example, the page contains the standard HTML <head> and <body> tags. In Listing 1.1, there are two special things contained in the page render block.

First, notice that the page contains a <form> tag that looks like this:

```
<form id="form1" runat="server">
```

This is an example of an ASP.NET control. Because the tag includes a runat="server" attribute, the tag represents an ASP.NET control that executes on the server.

ASP.NET pages are often called *web form* pages because they almost always contain a server-side form element.

The page render block also contains a Label control. The Label control is declared with the <asp:Label> tag. In Listing 1.1, the Label control is used to display the current date and time.

Controls are the heart of the ASP.NET framework. Most of the ink contained in this book is devoted to describing the properties and features of the ASP.NET controls.

Controls are discussed in more detail shortly. However, first you need to understand the .NET Framework.

> **NOTE**
>
> By default, ASP.NET pages are compatible with the XHTML 1.0 Transitional standard. You'll notice that the page in Listing 1.1 includes an XHTML 1.0 Transitional DOCTYPE. For details on how the ASP.NET framework complies with both XHTML and accessibility standards, see my article at the Microsoft MSDN website (msdn.Microsoft.com), entitled "Building ASP.NET 2.0 Web Sites Using Web Standards."

ASP.NET and the .NET Framework

ASP.NET is part of the Microsoft .NET Framework. To build ASP.NET pages, you need to take advantage of the features of the .NET Framework. The .NET Framework consists of two parts: the Framework Class Library and the Common Language Runtime.

Understanding the Framework Class Library

The .NET Framework contains thousands of classes that you can use when building an application. The Framework Class Library was designed to make it easier to perform the most common programming tasks. Here are just a few examples of the classes in the framework:

▶ **File** class—Enables you to represent a file on your hard drive. You can use the File class to check whether a file exists, create a new file, delete a file, and perform many other file-related tasks.

▶ **Graphics** class—Enables you to work with different types of images such as GIF, PNG, BMP, and JPEG images. You can use the Graphics class to draw rectangles, arcs, ellipsis, and other elements on an image.

▶ **Random** class—Enables you to generate a random number.

▶ **SmtpClient** class—Enables you to send email. You can use the SmtpClient class to send emails that contain attachments and HTML content.

These are only four examples of classes in the Framework. The .NET Framework contains almost 13,000 classes you can use when building applications.

You can view all the classes contained in the Framework by opening the Microsoft .NET Framework SDK documentation and expanding the Class Library node (see Figure 1.4). If you don't have the SDK documentation installed on your computer, then see the last section of this chapter.

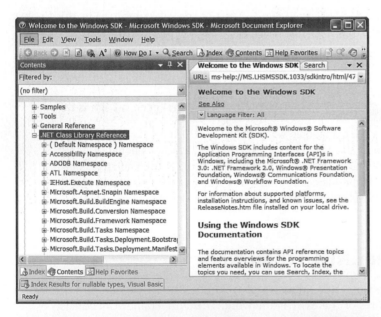

FIGURE 1.4   Opening the Microsoft .NET Framework SDK Documentation.

NOTE

The Microsoft .NET Framework 2.0 includes 18,619 types; 12,909 classes; 401,759 public methods; 93,105 public properties; and 30,546 public events. The .NET Framework 3.0 and 3.5 build on top of this base set of types with even more classes.

Each class in the Framework can include properties, methods, and events. The properties, methods, and events exposed by a class are the members of a class. For example, here is a partial list of the members of the SmtpClient class:

- ▶ Properties

    - ▶ **Host**—The name or IP address of your email server

    - ▶ **Port**—The number of the port to use when sending an email message

- ▶ Methods

    - ▶ **Send**—Enables you to send an email message synchronously

    - ▶ **SendAsync**—Enables you to send an email message asynchronously

- ▶ Events

    - ▶ **SendCompleted**—Raised when an asynchronous send operation completes

If you know the members of a class, then you know everything that you can do with a class. For example, the SmtpClient class includes two properties named Host and Port, which enable you to specify the email server and port to use when sending an email message.

The SmtpClient class also includes two methods you can use to send an email: Send() and SendAsync(). The Send method blocks further program execution until the send operation is completed. The SendAsync() method, on the other hand, sends the email asynchronously. Unlike the Send() method, the SendAsync() method does not wait to check whether the send operation was successful.

Finally, the SmtpClient class includes an event named SendCompleted, which is raised when an asynchronous send operation completes. You can create an event handler for the SendCompleted event that displays a message when the email has been successfully sent.

The page in Listing 1.2 sends an email by using the SmtpClient class and calling its Send() method.

LISTING 1.2 SendMail.aspx

```
<%@ Page Language="C#" %>
<%@ Import Namespace="System.Net.Mail" %>
<!DOCTYPE html PUBLIC "-//W3C//DTD XHTML 1.0 Transitional//EN"
"http://www.w3.org/TR/xhtml1/DTD/xhtml1-transitional.dtd">
<script runat="server">

    void Page_Load()
    {
        SmtpClient client = new SmtpClient();
        client.Host = "localhost";
        client.Port = 25;
        client.Send("steve@somewhere", "steve@superexpert.com",
            "Let's eat lunch!", "Lunch at the Steak House?");
```

LISTING 1.2   Continued

```
    }

</script>
<html xmlns="http://www.w3.org/1999/xhtml" >
<head id="Head1" runat="server">
    <title>Send Mail</title>
</head>
<body>
    <form id="form1" runat="server">
    <div>

    Email sent!

    </div>
    </form>
</body>
</html>
```

The page in Listing 1.2 calls the SmtpClient Send() method to send the email. The first parameter is the from: address; the second parameter is the to: address; the third parameter is the subject; and the final parameter is the body of the email.

> **WARNING**
>
> The page in Listing 1.2 sends the email by using the local SMTP Server. If your SMTP Server is not enabled, then you'll receive the error An existing connection was forcibly closed by the remote host. You can enable your local SMTP Server by opening Internet Information Services, right-clicking Default SMTP Virtual Server, and selecting Start.

Understanding Namespaces   There are almost 13,000 classes in the .NET Framework. This is an overwhelming number. If Microsoft simply jumbled all the classes together, then you would never find anything. Fortunately, Microsoft divided the classes in the Framework into separate namespaces.

A *namespace* is simply a category. For example, all the classes related to working with the file system are located in the System.IO namespace. All the classes for working a Microsoft SQL Server database are located in the System.Data.SqlClient namespace.

Before you can use a class in a page, you must indicate the namespace associated with the class. There are multiple ways of doing this.

First, you can fully qualify a class name with its namespace. For example, because the `File` class is contained in the `System.IO` namespace, you can use the following statement to check whether a file exists:

```
System.IO.File.Exists("SomeFile.txt")
```

Specifying a namespace each and every time you use a class can quickly become tedious (it involves a lot of typing). A second option is to import a namespace.

You can add an `<%@ Import %>` directive to a page to import a particular namespace. In Listing 1.2, we imported the `System.Net.Mail` namespace because the `SmtpClient` is part of this namespace. The page in Listing 1.2 includes the following directive near the very top of the page:

```
<%@ Import Namespace="System.Net.Mail" %>
```

After you import a particular namespace, you can use all the classes in that namespace without qualifying the class names.

Finally, if you discover that you are using a namespace in multiple pages in your application, then you can configure all the pages in your application to recognize the namespace.

NOTE

A web configuration file is a special type of file that you can add to your application to configure your application. Be aware that the file is an XML file and, therefore, all the tags contained in the file are case sensitive. You can add a web configuration file to your application by selecting Web Site, Add New Item and selecting Web Configuration File. Chapter 28, "Configuring Applications," discusses web configuration files in detail.

If you add the web configuration file in Listing 1.3 to your application, then you do not need to import the `System.Net.Mail` namespace in a page to use the classes from this namespace. For example, if you include the `Web.config` file in your project, you can remove the `<%@ Import %>` directive from the page in Listing 1.2.

LISTING 1.3 `Web.Config`

```
<configuration>
    <system.web>
      <pages>
        <namespaces>
          <add namespace="System.Net.Mail"/>
        </namespaces>
      </pages>
    </system.web>
</configuration>
```

You don't have to import every namespace. The ASP.NET Framework gives you the most commonly used namespaces for free. These namespaces are as follows:

- ▶ System
- ▶ System.Collections
- ▶ System.Collections.Specialized
- ▶ System.Configuration
- ▶ System.Text
- ▶ System.Text.RegularExpressions
- ▶ System.Web
- ▶ System.Web.Caching
- ▶ System.Web.SessionState
- ▶ System.Web.Security
- ▶ System.Web.Profile
- ▶ System.Web.UI
- ▶ System.Web.UI.WebControls
- ▶ System.Web.UI.WebControls.WebParts
- ▶ System.Web.UI.HTMLControls

The default namespaces are listed inside the pages element in the root web configuration file located at the following path:

\WINDOWS\Microsoft.NET\Framework\v2.0.50727\CONFIG\Web.Config

Understanding Assemblies   An assembly is the actual .dll file on your hard drive where the classes in the .NET Framework are stored. For example, all the classes contained in the ASP.NET Framework are located in an assembly named System.Web.dll.

More accurately, an assembly is the primary unit of deployment, security, and version control in the .NET Framework. Because an assembly can span multiple files, an assembly is often referred to as a "logical" dll.

There are two types of assemblies: private and shared. A private assembly can be used by only a single application. A shared assembly, on the other hand, can be used by all applications located on the same server.

Shared assemblies are located in the Global Assembly Cache (GAC). For example, the System.Web.dll assembly and all the other assemblies included with the .NET Framework are located in the Global Assembly Cache.

1

Before you can use a class contained in an assembly in your application, you must add a reference to the assembly. By default, an ASP.NET application references the most common assemblies contained in the Global Assembly Cache:

- ► `mscorlib.dll`
- ► `System.dll`
- ► `System.Configuration.dll`
- ► `System.Web.dll`
- ► `System.Data.dll`
- ► `System.Web.Services.dll`
- ► `System.Xml.dll`
- ► `System.Drawing.dll`
- ► `System.EnterpriseServices.dll`
- ► `System.Web.Mobile.dll`

In addition, websites built to target the .NET Framework 3.5 also reference the following assemblies:

- ► System.Web.Extensions
- ► System.Xml.Linq
- ► System.Data.DataSetExtensions

To use any particular class in the .NET Framework, you must do two things. First, your application must reference the assembly that contains the class. Second, your application must import the namespace associated with the class.

In most cases, you won't worry about referencing the necessary assembly because the most common assemblies are referenced automatically. However, if you need to use a specialized assembly, you need to add a reference explicitly to the assembly. For example, if you need to interact with Active Directory by using the classes in the System.DirectoryServices namespace, then you will need to add a reference to the System.DirectoryServices.dll assembly to your application.

Each class entry in the .NET Framework SDK documentation lists the assembly and namespace associated with the class. For example, if you look up the `MessageQueue` class in the documentation, you'll discover that this class is located in the `System.Messaging` namespace located in the `System.Messaging.dll` assembly.

If you are using Visual Web Developer, you can add a reference to an assembly explicitly by selecting the menu option Web Site, Add Reference, and selecting the name of the assembly that you need to reference. For example, adding a reference to the `System.Messaging.dll` assembly results in the web configuration file in Listing 1.4 being added to your application.

LISTING 1.4   `Web.Config`

```
<configuration>
<system.web>
  <compilation>
  <assemblies>
  <add
    assembly="System.Messaging, Version=2.0.0.0,
    Culture=neutral, PublicKeyToken=B03F5F7F11D50A3A"/>
  </assemblies>
  </compilation>
</system.web>
</configuration>
```

If you prefer not to use Visual Web Developer, then you can add the reference to the `System.Messaging.dll` assembly by creating the file in Listing 1.4 by hand.

Understanding the Common Language Runtime

The second part of the .NET Framework is the Common Language Runtime (CLR). The Common Language Runtime is responsible for executing your application code.

When you write an application for the .NET Framework with a language such as C# or Visual Basic .NET, your source code is never compiled directly into machine code. Instead, the C# or Visual Basic compiler converts your code into a special language named MSIL (Microsoft Intermediate Language).

MSIL looks very much like an object-oriented assembly language. However, unlike a typical assembly language, it is not CPU specific. MSIL is a low-level and platform-independent language.

When your application actually executes, the MSIL code is "just-in-time" compiled into machine code by the JITTER (the Just-In-Time compiler). Normally, your entire application is not compiled from MSIL into machine code. Instead, only the methods that are actually called during execution are compiled.

In reality, the .NET Framework understands only one language: MSIL. However, you can write applications using languages such as Visual Basic .NET and C# for the .NET Framework because the .NET Framework includes compilers for these languages that enable you to compile your code into MSIL.

You can write code for the .NET Framework using any one of dozens of different languages, including the following:

- ▶ Ada
- ▶ Apl
- ▶ Caml
- ▶ COBOL
- ▶ Eiffel
- ▶ Forth
- ▶ Fortran
- ▶ JavaScript
- ▶ Oberon
- ▶ PERL
- ▶ Pascal
- ▶ PHP
- ▶ Python
- ▶ RPG
- ▶ Scheme
- ▶ Small Talk

The vast majority of developers building ASP.NET applications write the applications in either C# or Visual Basic .NET. Many of the other .NET languages in the preceding list are academic experiments.

Once upon a time, if you wanted to become a developer, you concentrated on becoming proficient at a particular language. For example, you became a C++ programmer, a COBOL programmer, or a Visual Basic Programmer.

When it comes to the .NET Framework, however, knowing a particular language is not particularly important. The choice of which language to use when building a .NET application is largely a preference choice. If you like case-sensitivity and curly braces, then you should use the C# programming language. If you want to be lazy about casing and you don't like semicolons, then write your code with Visual Basic .NET.

All the real action in the .NET Framework happens in the Framework Class Library. If you want to become a good programmer using Microsoft technologies, you need to learn how to use the methods, properties, and events of the 13,000 classes included in the Framework. From the point of view of the .NET Framework, it doesn't matter whether you are using these classes from a Visual Basic .NET or C# application.

NOTE

All the code samples in this book were written in both C# and Visual Basic .NET. The VB.NET code samples are included on the CD that accompanies this book and at the Superexpert website (www.Superexpert.com).

Understanding ASP.NET Controls

ASP.NET controls are the heart of the ASP.NET Framework. An ASP.NET control is a .NET class that executes on the server and renders certain content to the browser.

For example, in the first ASP.NET page created at the beginning of this chapter, a Label control was used to display the current date and time. The ASP.NET framework includes over 70 controls, which enable you to do everything from displaying a list of database records to displaying a randomly rotating banner advertisement.

In this section, you are provided with an overview of the controls included in the ASP.NET Framework. You also learn how to handle events that are raised by controls and how to take advantage of View State.

Overview of ASP.NET Controls

The ASP.NET Framework contains over 70 controls. These controls can be divided into eight groups:

▶ **Standard Controls**—The standard controls enable you to render standard form elements such as buttons, input fields, and labels. We examine these controls in detail in the following chapter, "Using the Standard Controls."

▶ **Validation Controls**—The validation controls enable you to validate form data before you submit the data to the server. For example, you can use a RequiredFieldValidator control to check whether a user entered a value for a required input field. These controls are discussed in Chapter 3, "Using the Validation Controls."

▶ **Rich Controls**—The rich controls enable you to render things such as calendars, file upload buttons, rotating banner advertisements, and multi-step wizards. These controls are discussed in Chapter 4, "Using the Rich Controls."

▶ **Data Controls**—The data controls enable you to work with data such as database data. For example, you can use these controls to submit new records to a database table or display a list of database records. These controls are discussed in detail in Part III of this book, "Performing Data Access."

▶ **Navigation Controls**—The navigation controls enable you to display standard navigation elements such as menus, tree views, and bread crumb trails. These controls are discussed in Chapter 19, "Using the Navigation Controls."

▶ **Login Controls**—The login controls enable you to display login, change password, and registration forms. These controls are discussed in Chapter 22, "Using the Login Controls."

▶ **HTML Controls**—The HTML controls enable you to convert any HTML tag into a server-side control. We discuss this group of controls in the next section of this chapter.

With the exception of the HTML controls, you declare and use all the ASP.NET controls in a page in exactly the same way. For example, if you want to display a text input field in a page, then you can declare a TextBox control like this:

```
<asp:TextBox id="TextBox1" runat="Server" />
```

This control declaration looks like the declaration for an HTML tag. Remember, however, unlike an HTML tag, a control is a .NET class that executes on the server and not in the web browser.

When the TextBox control is rendered to the browser, it renders the following content:

```
<input name="TextBox1" type="text" id="TextBox1" />
```

The first part of the control declaration, the asp: prefix, indicates the namespace for the control. All the standard ASP.NET controls are contained in the System.Web.UI. WebControls namespace. The prefix asp: represents this namespace.

Next, the declaration contains the name of the control being declared. In this case, a TextBox control is being declared.

This declaration also includes an ID attribute. You use the ID to refer to the control in the page within your code. Every control must have a unique ID.

NOTE

You should always assign an ID attribute to every control even when you don't need to program against it. If you don't provide an ID attribute, then certain features of the ASP.NET Framework (such as two-way databinding) won't work.

The declaration also includes a runat="Server" attribute. This attribute marks the tag as representing a server-side control. If you neglect to include this attribute, then the TextBox tag would be passed, without being executed, to the browser. The browser would simply ignore the tag.

Finally, notice that the tag ends with a forward slash. The forward slash is shorthand for creating a closing </asp:TextBox> tag. You can, if you prefer, declare the TextBox control like this:

```
<asp:TextBox id="TextBox1" runat="server"></asp:TextBox>
```

In this case, the opening tag does not contain a forward slash and an explicit closing tag is included.

Understanding HTML Controls

You declare HTML controls in a different way than you declare standard ASP.NET controls. The ASP.NET Framework enables you to take any HTML tag (real or imaginary) and add a `runat="server"` attribute to the tag. The `runat="server"` attribute converts the HTML tag into a server-side ASP.NET control.

For example, the page in Listing 1.5 contains a <span> tag, which has been converted into an ASP.NET control.

LISTING 1.5   HtmlControls.aspx

```
<%@ Page Language="C#" %>
<!DOCTYPE html PUBLIC "-//W3C//DTD XHTML 1.0 Transitional//EN"
"http://www.w3.org/TR/xhtml1/DTD/xhtml1-transitional.dtd">
<script runat="server">

    void Page_Load()
    {
        spanNow.InnerText = DateTime.Now.ToString("T");
    }

</script>
<html xmlns="http://www.w3.org/1999/xhtml" >
<head id="Head1" runat="server">
    <title>HTML Controls</title>
</head>
<body>
    <form id="form1" runat="server">
    <div>

    At the tone, the time will be:
    <span id="spanNow" runat="server" />

    </div>
    </form>
</body>
</html>
```

Notice that the <span> tag in Listing 1.5 looks just like a normal HTML <span> tag except for the addition of the `runat="server"` attribute.

Because the <span> tag in Listing 1.5 is a server-side HTML control, you can program against it. In Listing 1.5, the current date and time are assigned to the <span> tag in the Page_Load() method.

The HTML controls are included in the ASP.NET Framework to make it easier to convert existing HTML pages to use the ASP.NET Framework. I rarely use the HTML controls in this book because, in general, the standard ASP.NET controls provide all the same functionality and more.

Understanding and Handling Control Events

The majority of the ASP.NET controls support one or more events. For example, the ASP.NET Button control supports the Click event. The Click event is raised on the server after you click the button rendered by the Button control in the browser.

The page in Listing 1.6 illustrates how you can write code that executes when a user clicks the button rendered by the Button control (in other words, it illustrates how you can create a Click event handler).

LISTING 1.6   ShowButtonClick.aspx

```
<%@ Page Language="C#" %>
<!DOCTYPE html PUBLIC "-//W3C//DTD XHTML 1.0 Transitional//EN"
"http://www.w3.org/TR/xhtml1/DTD/xhtml1-transitional.dtd">
<script runat="server">

    protected void btnSubmit_Click(object sender, EventArgs e)
    {
        Label1.Text = "Thanks!";
    }
</script>
<html xmlns="http://www.w3.org/1999/xhtml" >
<head id="Head1" runat="server">
    <title>Show Button Click</title>
</head>
<body>
    <form id="form1" runat="server">
    <div>

    <asp:Button
        id="btnSubmit"
        Text="Click Here"
        OnClick="btnSubmit_Click"
        Runat="server" />

    <br /><br />
```

LISTING 1.6   Continued

```
    <asp:Label
        id="Label1"
        Runat="server" />

    </div>
    </form>
</body>
</html>
```

Notice that the Button control in Listing 1.6 includes an OnClick attribute. This attribute points to a subroutine named btnSubmit_Click(). The btnSubmit_Click() subroutine is the handler for the Button Click event. This subroutine executes whenever you click the button (see Figure 1.5).

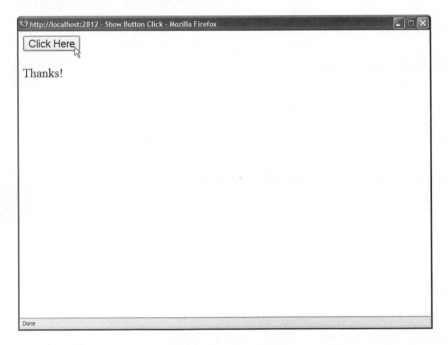

FIGURE 1.5   Raising a Click event.

You can add an event handler automatically to a control in multiple ways when using Visual Web Developer. In Source view, add a handler by selecting a control from the top-left drop-down list and selecting an event from the top-right drop-down list. The event handler code is added to the page automatically (see Figure 1.6).

In Design view, you can double-click a control to add a handler for the control's default event. Double-clicking a control switches you to Source view and adds the event handler.

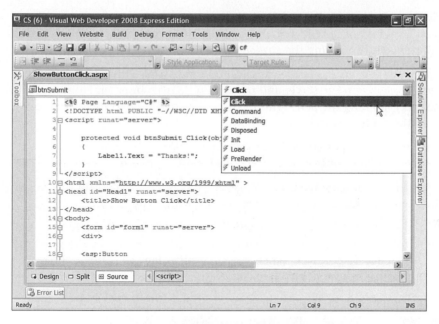

FIGURE 1.6   Adding an event handler from Source view.

Finally, from Design view, after selecting a control on the designer surface you can add an event handler from the Properties window by clicking the Events button (the lightning bolt) and double-clicking next to the name of any of the events (see Figure 1.7).

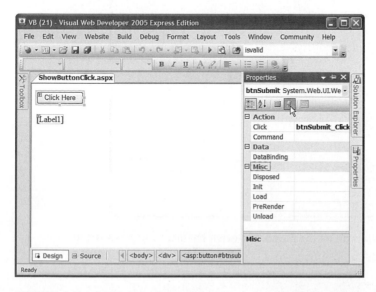

FIGURE 1.7   Adding an event handler from the Properties window.

It is important to understand that all ASP.NET control events happen on the server. For example, the Click event is not raised when you actually click a button. The Click event is not raised until the page containing the Button control is posted back to the server.

The ASP.NET Framework is a server-side web application framework. The .NET Framework code that you write executes on the server and not within the web browser. From the perspective of ASP.NET, nothing happens until the page is posted back to the server and can execute within the context of the .NET Framework.

Notice that two parameters are passed to the btnSubmit_Click() handler in Listing 1.6. All event handlers for ASP.NET controls have the same general signature.

The first parameter, the object parameter named sender, represents the control that raised the event. In other words, it represents the Button control which you clicked.

You can wire multiple controls in a page to the same event handler and use this first parameter to determine the particular control that raised the event. For example, the page in Listing 1.7 includes two Button controls. When you click either Button control, the text displayed by the Button control is updated (see Figure 1.8).

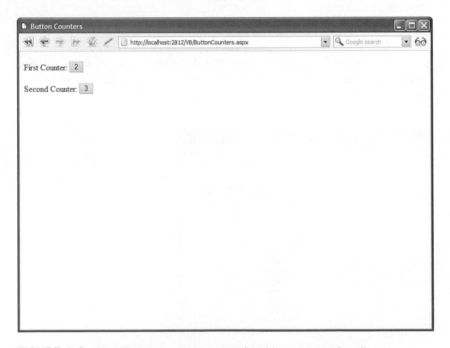

FIGURE 1.8   Handling two Button controls with one event handler.

LISTING 1.7   ButtonCounters.aspx

```
<%@ Page Language="C#" %>
<!DOCTYPE html PUBLIC "-//W3C//DTD XHTML 1.0 Transitional//EN"
"http://www.w3.org/TR/xhtml1/DTD/xhtml1-transitional.dtd">
<script runat="server">

    protected void Button_Click(object sender, EventArgs e)
    {
        Button btn = (Button)sender;
        btn.Text = (Int32.Parse(btn.Text) + 1).ToString();
    }
</script>
<html xmlns="http://www.w3.org/1999/xhtml" >
<head id="Head1" runat="server">
    <title>Button Counters</title>
</head>
<body>
    <form id="form1" runat="server">
    <div>

    First Counter:
    <asp:Button
        id="Button1"
        Text="0"
        OnClick="Button_Click"
        Runat="server" />

    <br /><br />

    Second Counter:
    <asp:Button
        id="Button2"
        Text="0"
        OnClick="Button_Click"
        Runat="server" />

    </div>
    </form>
</body>
</html>
```

The second parameter passed to the Click event handler, the EventArgs parameter named e, represents any additional event information associated with the event. No additional event information is associated with clicking a button, so this second parameter does not represent anything useful in either Listing 1.6 or Listing 1.7.

When you click an ImageButton control instead of a Button control, on the other hand, additional event information is passed to the event handler. When you click an ImageButton control, the X and Y coordinates of where you clicked are passed to the handler.

The page in Listing 1.8 contains an ImageButton control that displays a picture. When you click the picture, the X and Y coordinates of the spot you clicked are displayed in a Label control (see Figure 1.9).

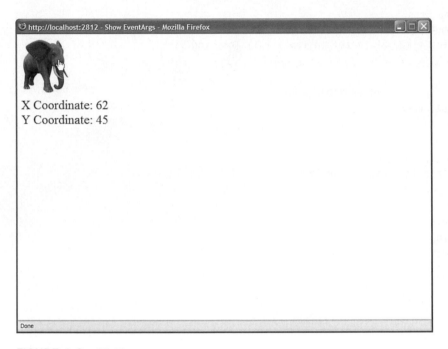

FIGURE 1.9   Clicking an ImageButton.

LISTING 1.8   ShowEventArgs.aspx

```
<%@ Page Language="C#" %>
<!DOCTYPE html PUBLIC "-//W3C//DTD XHTML 1.0 Transitional//EN"
"http://www.w3.org/TR/xhtml1/DTD/xhtml1-transitional.dtd">
<script runat="server">

    protected void btnElephant_Click(object sender, ImageClickEventArgs e)
    {
        lblX.Text = e.X.ToString();
        lblY.Text = e.Y.ToString();
    }
</script>
```

```
<html xmlns="http://www.w3.org/1999/xhtml" >
<head id="Head1" runat="server">
    <title>Show EventArgs</title>
</head>
<body>
    <form id="form1" runat="server">
    <div>

    <asp:ImageButton
        id="btnElephant"
        ImageUrl="Elephant.jpg"
        Runat="server" OnClick="btnElephant_Click" />

    <br />
    X Coordinate:
    <asp:Label
        id="lblX"
        Runat="server" />
    <br />
    Y Coordinate:
    <asp:Label
        id="lblY"
        Runat="server" />

    </div>
    </form>
</body>
</html>
```

Notice that the second parameter passed to the `btnElephant_Click()` method is an `ImageClickEventArgs` parameter. Whenever the second parameter is not the default `EventArgs` parameter, you know that additional event information is being passed to the handler.

Understanding View State

The HTTP protocol, the fundamental protocol of the World Wide Web, is a stateless protocol. Each time you request a web page from a website, from the website's perspective, you are a completely new person.

The ASP.NET Framework, however, manages to transcend this limitation of the HTTP protocol. For example, if you assign a value to a `Label` control's `Text` property, the `Label` control retains this value across multiple page requests.

Consider the page in Listing 1.9. This page contains a Button control and a Label control. Each time you click the Button control, the value displayed by the Label control is incremented by 1 (see Figure 1.10). How does the Label control preserve its value across postbacks to the web server?

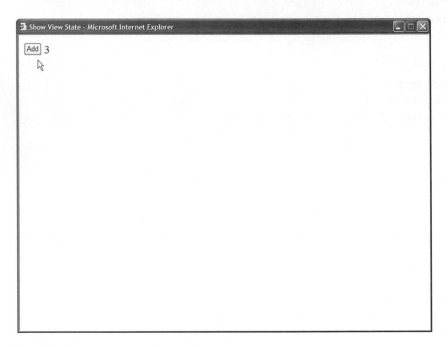

FIGURE 1.10   Preserving state between postbacks.

LISTING 1.9   ShowViewState.aspx

```
<%@ Page Language="C#" %>
<!DOCTYPE html PUBLIC "-//W3C//DTD XHTML 1.0 Transitional//EN"
"http://www.w3.org/TR/xhtml1/DTD/xhtml1-transitional.dtd">
<script runat="server">

    protected void btnAdd_Click(object sender, EventArgs e)
    {
        lblCounter.Text = (Int32.Parse(lblCounter.Text) + 1).ToString();
    }
</script>
<html xmlns="http://www.w3.org/1999/xhtml" >
<head id="Head1" runat="server">
    <title>Show View State</title>
</head>
<body>
    <form id="form1" runat="server">
```

```
    <div>

    <asp:Button
        id="btnAdd"
        Text="Add"
        OnClick="btnAdd_Click"
        Runat="server" />

    <asp:Label
        id="lblCounter"
        Text="0"
        Runat="server" />

    </div>
    </form>
</body>
</html>
```

The ASP.NET Framework uses a trick called View State. If you open the page in Listing 1.9 in your browser and select View Source, you'll notice that the page includes a hidden form field named __VIEWSTATE that looks like this:

```
<input type="hidden" name="__VIEWSTATE" id="__
  VIEWSTATE" value="/wEPDwUKLTc2ODE1OTYxNw9kFgICBA9kFgIC
  Aw8PFgIeBFR1eHQFATFkZGT3tMnThg9KZpGak55p367vfInj1w==" />
```

This hidden form field contains the value of the Label control's Text property (and the values of any other control properties that are stored in View State). When the page is posted back to the server, the ASP.NET Framework rips apart this string and re-creates the values of all the properties stored in View State. In this way, the ASP.NET Framework preserves the state of control properties across postbacks to the web server.

By default, View State is enabled for every control in the ASP.NET Framework. If you change the background color of a Calendar control, the new background color is remembered across postbacks. If you change the selected item in a DropDownList, the selected item is remembered across postbacks. The values of these properties are automatically stored in View State.

View State is a good thing, but sometimes it can be too much of a good thing. The __VIEWSTATE hidden form field can become very large. Stuffing too much data into View State can slow down the rendering of a page because the contents of the hidden field must be pushed back and forth between the web server and web browser.

You can determine how much View State each control contained in a page is consuming by enabling tracing for a page (see Figure 1.11). The page in Listing 1.10 includes a Trace="true" attribute in its <%@ Page %> directive, which enables tracing.

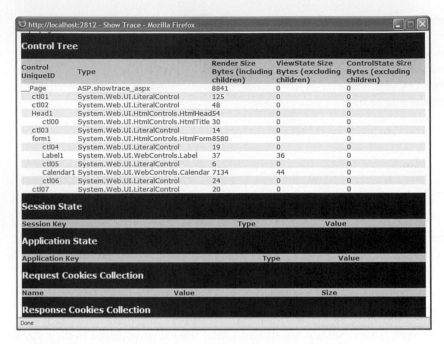

FIGURE 1.11   Viewing View State size for each control.

LISTING 1.10   ShowTrace.aspx

```
<%@ Page Language="C#" Trace="true" %>
<!DOCTYPE html PUBLIC "-//W3C//DTD XHTML 1.0 Transitional//EN"
"http://www.w3.org/TR/xhtml1/DTD/xhtml1-transitional.dtd">
<script runat="server">

    void Page_Load()
    {
        Label1.Text = "Hello World!";
        Calendar1.TodaysDate = DateTime.Now;
    }

</script>
<html xmlns="http://www.w3.org/1999/xhtml" >
<head id="Head1" runat="server">
    <title>Show Trace</title>
</head>
<body>
    <form id="form1" runat="server">
    <div>

    <asp:Label
```

```
            id="Label1"
            Runat="server" />
        <asp:Calendar
            id="Calendar1"
            TodayDayStyle-BackColor="Yellow"
            Runat="server" />

    </div>
    </form>
</body>
</html>
```

When you open the page in Listing 1.10, additional information about the page is appended to the bottom of the page. The Control Tree section displays the amount of View State used by each ASP.NET control contained in the page.

Every ASP.NET control includes a property named EnableViewState. If you set this property to the value False, then View State is disabled for the control. In that case, the values of the control properties are not remembered across postbacks to the server.

For example, the page in Listing 1.11 contains two Label controls and a Button control. The first Label has View State disabled and the second Label has View State enabled. When you click the button, only the value of the second Label control is incremented past 1.

LISTING 1.11 DisableViewState.aspx

```
<%@ Page Language="C#" %>
<!DOCTYPE html PUBLIC "-//W3C//DTD XHTML 1.0 Transitional//EN"
"http://www.w3.org/TR/xhtml1/DTD/xhtml1-transitional.dtd">
<script runat="server">

    protected void btnAdd_Click(object sender, EventArgs e)
    {
        Label1.Text = (Int32.Parse(Label1.Text) + 1).ToString();
        Label2.Text = (Int32.Parse(Label2.Text) + 1).ToString();
    }
</script>
<html xmlns="http://www.w3.org/1999/xhtml" >
<head id="Head1" runat="server">
    <title>Disable View State</title>
</head>
<body>
    <form id="form1" runat="server">
    <div>
```

LISTING 1.11   Continued

```
    Label 1:
    <asp:Label
        id="Label1"
        EnableViewState="false"
        Text="0"
        Runat="server" />

    <br />

    Label 2:
    <asp:Label
        id="Label2"
        Text="0"
        Runat="server" />

    <br /><br />

    <asp:Button
        id="btnAdd"
        Text="Add"
        OnClick="btnAdd_Click"
        Runat="server" />

    </div>
    </form>
</body>
</html>
```

Sometimes, you might want to disable View State even when you aren't concerned with the size of the __VIEWSTATE hidden form field. For example, if you are using a Label control to display a form validation error message, you might want to start from scratch each time the page is submitted. In that case, simply disable View State for the Label control.

> **NOTE**
>
> The ASP.NET Framework version 2.0 introduced a new feature called Control State. Control State is similar to View State except that it is used to preserve only critical state information. For example, the GridView control uses Control State to store the selected row. Even if you disable View State, the GridView control remembers which row is selected.

Understanding ASP.NET Pages

This section examines ASP.NET pages in more detail. You learn about dynamic compilation and code-behind files. We also discuss the events supported by the Page class.

Understanding Dynamic Compilation

Strangely enough, when you create an ASP.NET page, you are actually creating the source code for a .NET class. You are creating a new instance of the System.Web.UI.Page class. The entire contents of an ASP.NET page, including all script and HTML content, are compiled into a .NET class.

When you request an ASP.NET page, the ASP.NET Framework checks for a .NET class that corresponds to the page. If a corresponding class does not exist, the Framework automatically compiles the page into a new class and stores the compiled class (the assembly) in the Temporary ASP.NET Files folder located at the following path:

```
\WINDOWS\Microsoft.NET\Framework\v2.0.50727\Temporary ASP.NET Files
```

The next time anyone requests the same page in the future, the page is not compiled again. The previously compiled class is executed and the results are returned to the browser.

Even if you unplug your web server, move to Borneo for three years, and start up your web server again, the next time someone requests the same page, the page does not need to be re-compiled. The compiled class is preserved in the Temporary ASP.NET Files folder until the source code for your application is modified.

When the class is added to the Temporary ASP.NET Files folder, a file dependency is created between the class and the original ASP.NET page. If the ASP.NET page is modified in any way, the corresponding .NET class is automatically deleted. The next time someone requests the page, the Framework automatically compiles the modified page source into a new .NET class.

This process is called *dynamic compilation*. Dynamic compilation enables ASP.NET applications to support thousands of simultaneous users. Unlike an ASP Classic page, for example, an ASP.NET page does not need to be parsed and compiled each and every time it is requested. An ASP.NET page is compiled only when an application is modified.

NOTE

You can precompile an entire ASP.NET application by using the aspnet_compiler.exe command-line tool. If you precompile an application, users don't experience the compilation delay resulting from the first page request.

In case you are curious, I've included the source code for the class that corresponds to the FirstPage.aspx page in Listing 1.12 (I've cleaned up the code and made it shorter to save space). I copied this file from the Temporary ASP.NET Files folder after enabling debugging for the application.

NOTE

You can disable dynamic compilation for a single page, the pages in a folder, or an entire website with the `CompilationMode` attribute. When the `CompilationMode` attribute is used with the `<%@ Page %>` directive, it enables you to disable dynamic compilation for a single page. When the `compilationMode` attribute is used with the pages element in a web configuration file, it enables you to disable dynamic compilation for an entire folder or application.

Disabling compilation is useful when you have thousands of pages in a website and you don't want to load too many assemblies into memory. When the `CompilationMode` attribute is set to the value `Never`, the page is never compiled and an assembly is never generated for the page. The page is interpreted at runtime.

You cannot disable compilation for pages that include server-side code. In particular, a no compile page cannot include a server-side `<script>...</script>` block. On the other hand, a no compile page can contain ASP.NET controls and databinding expressions.

LISTING 1.12   `FirstPage.aspx` Source

```
namespace ASP
{
    using System.Web.Profile;
    using System.Text.RegularExpressions;
    using System.Web.Caching;
    using System.Configuration;
    using System.Collections.Specialized;
    using System.Web.UI.WebControls.WebParts;
    using System.Web.UI.HtmlControls;
    using System.Web.UI.WebControls;
    using System.Web.UI;
    using System.Collections;
    using System;
    using System.Web.Security;
    using System.Web;
    using System.Web.SessionState;
    using System.Text;


    [System.Runtime.CompilerServices.CompilerGlobalScopeAttribute()]
    public class firstpage_aspx : global::System.Web.UI.Page,
    ➥System.Web.SessionState.IRequiresSessionState, System.Web.IHttpHandler
    {
        protected global::System.Web.UI.WebControls.Label lblServerTime;
        protected global::System.Web.UI.HtmlControls.HtmlForm form1;
```

```
private static bool @__initialized;
private static object @__fileDependencies;

void Page_Load()
{
    lblServerTime.Text = DateTime.Now.ToString();
}

public firstpage_aspx()
{
    string[] dependencies;
    ((global::System.Web.UI.Page)(this)).AppRelativeVirtualPath =
    ➥"~/FirstPage.aspx";
    if ((global::ASP.firstpage_aspx.@__initialized == false))
    {
        dependencies = new string[1];
        dependencies[0] = "~/FirstPage.aspx";
        global::ASP.firstpage_aspx.@__fileDependencies =
        ➥this.GetWrappedFileDependencies(dependencies);
        global::ASP.firstpage_aspx.@__initialized = true;
    }
    this.Server.ScriptTimeout = 30000000;
}

protected System.Web.Profile.DefaultProfile Profile
{
    get
    {
        return ((System.Web.Profile.DefaultProfile)(this.Context.Profile));
    }
}

protected System.Web.HttpApplication ApplicationInstance
{
    get
    {
        return ((System.Web.HttpApplication)(this.Context.
        ➥ApplicationInstance));
    }
}

private global::System.Web.UI.WebControls.Label
➥@__BuildControllblServerTime()
{
...code...
}
```

LISTING 1.12   Continued

```
    private global::System.Web.UI.HtmlControls.HtmlForm @__BuildControlform1()
    {
    ...code...
    }

    private void @__BuildControlTree(firstpage_aspx @__ctrl)
    {
    ...code...
    }

    protected override void FrameworkInitialize()
    {
        base.FrameworkInitialize();
        this.@__BuildControlTree(this);
        this.AddWrappedFileDependencies(global::ASP.firstpage_aspx.
    ➥@__fileDependencies);
        this.Request.ValidateInput();
    }

    public override int GetTypeHashCode()
    {
        return 579569163;
    }

    public override void ProcessRequest(System.Web.HttpContext context)
    {
        base.ProcessRequest(context);
    }
    }
}
```

The class in Listing 1.12 inherits from the `System.Web.UI.Page` class. The `ProcessRequest()` method is called by the ASP.NET Framework when the page is displayed. This method builds the page's control tree, which is the subject of the next section.

Understanding Control Trees

In the previous section, you learned that an ASP.NET page is really the source code for a .NET class. Alternatively, you can think of an ASP.NET page as a bag of controls. More accurately, because some controls might contain child controls, you can think of an ASP.NET page as a control tree.

For example, the page in Listing 1.13 contains a `DropDownList` control and a `Button` control. Furthermore, because the `<%@ Page %>` directive has the `Trace="true"` attribute, tracing is enabled for the page.

LISTING 1.13   ShowControlTree.aspx

```
<%@ Page Language="C#" Trace="true" %>
<!DOCTYPE html PUBLIC "-//W3C//DTD XHTML 1.0 Transitional//EN"
"http://www.w3.org/TR/xhtml1/DTD/xhtml1-transitional.dtd">
<html xmlns="http://www.w3.org/1999/xhtml" >
<head id="Head1" runat="server">
    <title>Show Control Tree</title>
</head>
<body>
    <form id="form1" runat="server">
    <div>

    <asp:DropDownList
        id="DropDownList1"
        Runat="server">
        <asp:ListItem Text="Oranges" />
        <asp:ListItem Text="Apples" />
    </asp:DropDownList>

    <asp:Button
        id="Button1"
        Text="Submit"
        Runat="server" />

    </div>
    </form>
</body>
</html>
```

When you open the page in Listing 1.12 in your browser, you can see the control tree for the page appended to the bottom of the page. It looks like this:

```
__Page ASP.showcontroltree_aspx
    ctl02 System.Web.UI.LiteralControl
    ctl00 System.Web.UI.HtmlControls.HtmlHead
        ctl01 System.Web.UI.HtmlControls.HtmlTitle
    ctl03 System.Web.UI.LiteralControl
    form1 System.Web.UI.HtmlControls.HtmlForm
        ctl04 System.Web.UI.LiteralControl
        DropDownList1 System.Web.UI.WebControls.DropDownList
        ctl05 System.Web.UI.LiteralControl
        Button1 System.Web.UI.WebControls.Button
        ctl06 System.Web.UI.LiteralControl
    ctl07
```

The root node in the control tree is the page itself. The page has an ID of __Page. The page class contains all the other controls in its child controls collection.

The control tree also contains an instance of the HtmlForm class named form1. This control is the server-side form tag contained in the page. It contains all the other form controls—the DropDownList and Button controls—as child controls.

Notice that there are several LiteralControl controls interspersed between the other controls in the control tree. What are these controls?

Remember that everything in an ASP.NET page is converted into a .NET class, including any HTML or plain text content in a page. The LiteralControl class represents the HTML content in the page (including any carriage returns between tags).

> **NOTE**
>
> Normally, you refer to a control in a page by its ID. However, there are situations in which this is not possible. In those cases, you can use the FindControl() method of the Control class to retrieve a control with a particular ID. The FindControl() method is similar to the JavaScript getElementById() method.

Using Code-Behind Pages

The ASP.NET Framework (and Visual Web Developer) enables you to create two different types of ASP.NET pages. You can create both single-file and two-file ASP.NET pages.

All the code samples in this book are written as single-file ASP.NET pages. In a single-file ASP.NET page, a single file contains both the page code and page controls. The page code is contained in a <script runat="server"> tag.

As an alternative to a single-file ASP.NET page, you can create a two-file ASP.NET page. A two-file ASP.NET page is normally referred to as a *code-behind* page. In a code-behind page, the page code is contained in a separate file.

> **NOTE**
>
> Code-behind pages work in a different way after the ASP.NET 2.0 Framework than they did in the ASP.NET 1.x Framework. In ASP.NET 1.x, the two halves of a code-behind page were related by inheritance. After the ASP.NET 2.0 Framework, the two halves of a code-behind page are related by a combination of partial classes and inheritance.

For example, Listing 1.14 and Listing 1.15 contain the two halves of a code-behind page.

VISUAL WEB DEVELOPER NOTE

When using Visual Web Developer, you create a code-behind page by selecting Web Site, Add New Item, selecting the Web Form Item, and checking the Place Code in Separate File check box before adding the page.

LISTING 1.14   FirstPageCodeBehind.aspx

```
<%@ Page Language="C#" AutoEventWireup="true" CodeFile="FirstPageCodeBehind.
➥aspx.cs" Inherits="FirstPageCodeBehind" %>
<!DOCTYPE html PUBLIC "-//W3C//DTD XHTML 1.0 Transitional//EN"
"http://www.w3.org/TR/xhtml1/DTD/xhtml1-transitional.dtd">
<html xmlns="http://www.w3.org/1999/xhtml" >
<head id="Head1" runat="server">
    <title>First Page Code-Behind</title>
</head>
<body>
    <form id="form1" runat="server">
    <div>

    <asp:Button
        id="Button1"
        Text="Click Here"
        OnClick="Button1_Click"
        Runat="server" />

    <br /><br />

    <asp:Label
        id="Label1"
        Runat="server" />

    </div>
    </form>
</body>
</html>
```

LISTING 1.15   FirstPageCodeBehind.aspx.cs

```
using System;
using System.Data;
using System.Configuration;
using System.Collections;
using System.Web;
```

LISTING 1.15   Continued

```
using System.Web.Security;
using System.Web.UI;
using System.Web.UI.WebControls;
using System.Web.UI.WebControls.WebParts;
using System.Web.UI.HtmlControls;

public partial class FirstPageCodeBehind : System.Web.UI.Page
{
    protected void Page_Load(object sender, EventArgs e)
    {
        Label1.Text = "Click the Button";
    }

    protected void Button1_Click(object sender, EventArgs e)
    {
        Label1.Text = "Thanks!";
    }
}
```

The page in Listing 1.14 is called the *presentation page*. It contains a Button control and a Label control. However, the page does not contain any code. All the code is contained in the code-behind file.

VISUAL WEB DEVELOPER NOTE

You can flip to the code-behind file for a page by right-clicking a page and selecting View Code.

The code-behind file in Listing 1.15 contains the Page_Load() and Button1_Click() handlers. The code-behind file in Listing 1.15 does not contain any controls.

Notice that the page in Listing 1.14 includes both a CodeFile and Inherits attribute in its <%@ Page %> directive. These attributes link the page to its code-behind file.

How Code-Behind Works: The Ugly Details   In the previous version of the ASP.NET Framework (ASP.NET 1.x), two classes were generated by a code-behind page. One class corresponded to the presentation page and one class corresponded to the code-behind file. These classes were related to one another through class inheritance. The presentation page class inherited from the code-behind file class.

The problem with this method of associating presentation pages with their code-behind files was that it was very brittle. Inheritance is a one-way relationship. Anything that is true of the mother is true of the daughter, but not the other way around. Any control that you declared in the presentation page was required to be declared in the code-behind file. Furthermore, the control had to be declared with exactly the same ID. Otherwise, the inheritance relationship would be broken and events raised by a control could not be handled in the code-behind file.

In the beta version of ASP.NET 2.0, a completely different method of associating presentation pages with their code-behind files was used. This new method was far less brittle. The two halves of a code-behind page were no longer related through inheritance, but through a new technology supported by the .NET 2.0 Framework called *partial classes*.

NOTE

Partial classes are discussed in Chapter 15, "Building Components."

Partial classes enable you to declare a class in more than one physical file. When the class gets compiled, one class is generated from all the partial classes. Any members of one partial class—including any private fields, methods, and properties—are accessible to any other partial classes of the same class. This makes sense because partial classes are combined eventually to create one final class.

The advantage of using partial classes is that you don't need to worry about declaring a control in both the presentation page and code-behind file. Anything that you declare in the presentation page is available automatically in the code-behind file, and anything you declare in the code-behind file is available automatically in the presentation page.

The beta version of the ASP.NET 2.0 Framework used partial classes to relate a presentation page with its code-behind file. However, certain advanced features of the ASP.NET 1.x Framework were not compatible with using partial classes. To support these advanced features, a more complex method of associating presentation pages with code-behind files is used in the final release of the ASP.NET 2.0 Framework.

NOTE

The ASP.NET 1.x Framework enabled you to create a custom base Page class and inherit every ASP.NET page in an application from the custom Page class. Relating pages and code-behind files with partial classes conflicted with inheriting from a custom base Page class. In the final release of the ASP.NET 2.0 Framework, you can once again create custom base Page classes. For a sample of a custom base Page class, see the final section of Chapter 5, "Designing Websites with Master Pages."

The final release of the ASP.NET 2.0 Framework uses a combination of inheritance and partial classes to relate presentation pages and code-behind files. The ASP.NET 2.0 Framework generates three classes whenever you create a code-behind page.

The first two classes correspond to the presentation page. For example, when you create the FirstPageCodeBehind.aspx page, the following two classes are generated automatically in the Temporary ASP.NET Files folder:

```
public partial class FirstPageCodeBehind
{
    protected System.Web.UI.WebControls.Button Button1;
    protected System.Web.UI.WebControls.Label Label1;

    ... additional code ...
}

public class firstpagecodebehind_aspx : FirstPageCodeBehind
{
    ... additional code ...
}
```

A third class is generated that corresponds to the code-behind file. Corresponding to the FirstPageCodeBehind.aspx.cs file, the following class is generated:

```
public partial class FirstPageCodeBehind : System.Web.UI.Page
{
    protected void Page_Load(object sender, EventArgs e)
    {
        Label1.Text = "Click the Button";
    }

    protected void Button1_Click(object sender, EventArgs e)
    {
        Label1.Text = "Thanks!";
    }
}
```

The firstpagecodebehind_aspx class is executed when the FirstPageCodeBehind.aspx page is requested from a browser. This class inherits from the FirstPageCodeBehind class. The FirstPageCodeBehind class is a partial class. It gets generated twice: once by the presentation page and once by the code-behind file.

The final release of the ASP.NET 2.0 Framework uses a combination of partial classes and inheritance to relate presentation pages and code-behind files. Because the page and code-behind classes are partial classes, unlike the previous version of ASP.NET, you no longer need to declare controls in both the presentation and code-behind page. Any control declared in the presentation page is accessible in the code-behind file automatically. Because the page class inherits from the code-behind class, the ASP.NET 2.0 Framework continues to support advanced features of the ASP.NET 1.x Framework such as custom base Page classes.

Deciding Between Single-File and Code-Behind Pages   So, when should you use single-file ASP.NET pages and when should you use code-behind pages? This decision is a preference choice. There are intense arguments over this topic contained in blogs spread across the Internet.

I've heard it argued that code-behind pages are superior to single-file pages because code-behind pages enable you to more cleanly separate your user interface from your application logic. The problem with this argument is that the normal justification for separating your user interface from your application logic is code reuse. Building code-behind pages really doesn't promote code reuse. A better way to reuse application logic across multiple pages is to build separate component libraries. (Part IV of this book explores this topic.)

My personal preference is to build ASP.NET applications using single-file ASP.NET pages because this approach requires managing fewer files. However, I've built many applications using the code-behind model (such as some of the ASP.NET Starter Kits) without suffering dire consequences.

NOTE

The first versions of Visual Studio did not support building single-file ASP.NET pages. If you wanted to create single-file ASP.NET pages in the previous version of ASP.NET, you had to use an alternate development environment such as Web Matrix or Notepad.

Handling Page Events

Whenever you request an ASP.NET page, a particular set of events is raised in a particular sequence. This sequence of events is called the *page execution lifecycle*.

For example, we have already used the Page Load event in previous code samples in this chapter. You normally use the Page Load event to initialize the properties of controls contained in a page. However, the Page Load event is only one event supported by the Page class.

Here is the sequence of events that are raised whenever you request a page:

1. PreInit
2. Init
3. InitComplete
4. PreLoad
5. Load
6. LoadComplete
7. PreRender
8. PreRenderComplete
9. SaveStateComplete
10. Unload

Why so many events? Different things happen and different information is available at different stages in the page execution lifecycle.

For example, View State is not loaded until after the InitComplete event. Data posted to the server from a form control, such as a TextBox control, is also not available until after this event.

Ninety-nine percent of the time, you won't handle any of these events except for the Load and the PreRender events. The difference between these two events is that the Load event happens before any control events and the PreRender event happens after any control events.

The page in Listing 1.16 illustrates the difference between the Load and PreRender events. The page contains three event handlers: one for the Load event, one for the Button Click event, and one for the PreRender event. Each handler adds a message to a Label control (see Figure 1.12).

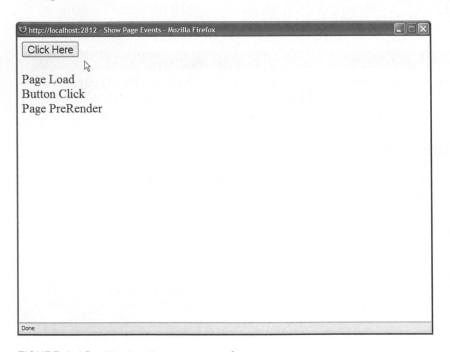

FIGURE 1.12   Viewing the sequence of page events.

LISTING 1.16   ShowPageEvents.aspx

```
<%@ Page Language="C#" %>
<!DOCTYPE html PUBLIC "-//W3C//DTD XHTML 1.0 Transitional//EN"
"http://www.w3.org/TR/xhtml1/DTD/xhtml1-transitional.dtd">
<script runat="server">

    void Page_Load(object sender, EventArgs e)
    {
        Label1.Text = "Page Load";
    }

    void Button1_Click(object sender, EventArgs e)
    {
```

```
                Label1.Text += "<br />Button Click";
        }

        void Page_PreRender()
        {
            Label1.Text += "<br />Page PreRender";
        }
</script>
<html xmlns="http://www.w3.org/1999/xhtml" >
<head id="Head1" runat="server">
    <title>Show Page Events</title>
</head>
<body>
    <form id="form1" runat="server">
    <div>

    <asp:Button
        id="Button1"
        Text="Click Here"
        OnClick="Button1_Click"
        Runat="server" />

    <br /><br />

    <asp:Label
        id="Label1"
        Runat="server" />

    </div>
    </form>
</body>
</html>
```

When you click the Button control, the Click event does not happen on the server until after the Load event and before the PreRender event.

The other thing you should notice about the page in Listing 1.16 is the way the event handlers are wired to the Page events. ASP.NET pages support a feature named AutoEventWireUp, which is enabled by default. If you name a subroutine Page_Load(), the subroutine automatically handles the Page Load event; if you name a subroutine Page_PreRender(), the subroutine automatically handles the Page PreRender event, and so on.

> **WARNING**
>
> AutoEventWireUp does not work for every page event. For example, it does not work for the Page_InitComplete() event.

Using the Page.IsPostBack Property

The Page class includes a property called the IsPostBack property, which you can use to detect whether the page has already been posted back to the server.

Because of View State, when you initialize a control property, you do not want to initialize the property every time a page loads. Because View State saves the state of control properties across page posts, you typically initialize a control property only once, when the page first loads.

In fact, many controls don't work correctly if you re-initialize the properties of the control with each page load. In these cases, you must use the IsPostBack property to detect whether or not the page has been posted.

The page in Listing 1.17 illustrates how you can use the Page.IsPostBack property when adding items to a DropDownList control.

LISTING 1.17   ShowIsPostBack.aspx

```
<%@ Page Language="C#" %>
<!DOCTYPE html PUBLIC "-//W3C//DTD XHTML 1.0 Transitional//EN"
"http://www.w3.org/TR/xhtml1/DTD/xhtml1-transitional.dtd">
<script runat="server">

    void Page_Load()
    {
        if (!Page.IsPostBack)
        {
            // Create collection of items
            ArrayList items = new ArrayList();
            items.Add("Apples");
            items.Add("Oranges");

            // Bind to DropDownList
            DropDownList1.DataSource = items;
            DropDownList1.DataBind();
        }
    }

    protected void Button1_Click(object sender, EventArgs e)
    {
```

```
            Label1.Text = DropDownList1.SelectedItem.Text;
        }
</script>
<html xmlns="http://www.w3.org/1999/xhtml" >
<head id="Head1" runat="server">
    <title>Show IsPostBack</title>
</head>
<body>
    <form id="form1" runat="server">
    <div>

    <asp:DropDownList
        id="DropDownList1"
        Runat="server" />

    <asp:Button
        id="Button1"
        Text="Select"
        OnClick="Button1_Click"
        Runat="server" />

    <br /><br />

    You selected:
    <asp:Label
        id="Label1"
        Runat="server" />

    </div>
    </form>
</body>
</html>
```

In Listing 1.17, the code in the Page_Load() event handler executes only once when the page first loads. When you post the page again, the IsPostBack property returns True and the code contained in the Page_Load() handler is skipped.

If you remove the IsPostBack check from the Page_Load() method, then you get a strange result. The DropDownList always displays its first item as the selected item. Binding the DropDownList to a collection of items re-initializes the DropDownList control. Therefore, you want to bind the DropDownList control only once, when the page first loads.

Debugging and Tracing ASP.NET Pages

The sad fact of life is that you spend the majority of your development time when building applications debugging the application.

In this section, you learn how to get detailed error messages when developing ASP.NET pages. You also learn how you can display custom trace messages that you can use when debugging a page.

Debugging ASP.NET Pages   If you need to view detailed error messages when you execute a page, you need to enable debugging for either the page or your entire application. You can enable debugging for a page by adding a `Debug="true"` attribute to the `<%@ Page %>` directive. For example, the page in Listing 1.18 has debugging enabled.

LISTING 1.18   ShowError.aspx

```
<%@ Page Language="C#" Debug="true" %>
<!DOCTYPE html PUBLIC "-//W3C//DTD XHTML 1.0 Transitional//EN"
"http://www.w3.org/TR/xhtml1/DTD/xhtml1-transitional.dtd">
<script runat="server">

    void Page_Load()
    {
        int zero = 0;
        Label1.Text = (1 / zero).ToString();
    }

</script>
<html xmlns="http://www.w3.org/1999/xhtml" >
<head id="Head1" runat="server">
    <title>Show Error</title>
</head>
<body>
    <form id="form1" runat="server">
    <div>

    <asp:Label
        id="Label1"
        Runat="server" />

    </div>
    </form>
</body>
</html>
```

WARNING

Make sure that you disable debugging before placing your application into production. When an application is compiled in debug mode, the compiler can't make certain performance optimizations.

When you open the page in Listing 1.18 in your web browser, a detailed error message is displayed (see Figure 1.13).

FIGURE 1.13   Viewing a detailed error message.

Rather than enable debugging for a single page, you can enable debugging for an entire application by adding the web configuration file in Listing 1.19 to your application.

LISTING 1.19   Web.Config

```
<configuration>
<system.web>
  <compilation debug="true" />
</system.web>
</configuration>
```

When debugging an ASP.NET application located on a remote web server, you need to disable custom errors. For security reasons, by default, the ASP.NET Framework doesn't display error messages when you request a page from a remote machine. When custom errors are enabled, you don't see errors on a remote machine. The modified web configuration file in Listing 1.20 disables custom errors.

LISTING 1.20   Modified Web.Config

```
<configuration>
<system.web>
  <compilation debug="true" />
```

LISTING 1.20   Continued

```
  <customErrors mode="Off" />
</system.web>
</configuration>
```

WARNING

For security and performance reasons, don't put websites into production with debug enabled, custom errors disabled, or trace enabled. On your production server, add the following element inside the system.web section of your machine.config file:

<deployment retail="true"/>

Adding this element disables debug mode, enables remote custom errors, and disables trace. You should add this element to the machine.config file located on all of your production servers.

Debugging Pages with Visual Web Developer   If you are using Visual Web Developer, then you can display compilation error messages by performing a build on a page or an entire website. Select the menu option Build, Build Page or the menu option Build, Build Web Site. A list of compilation error messages and warnings appears in the Error List window (see Figure 1.14). You can double-click any of the errors to navigate directly to the code that caused the error.

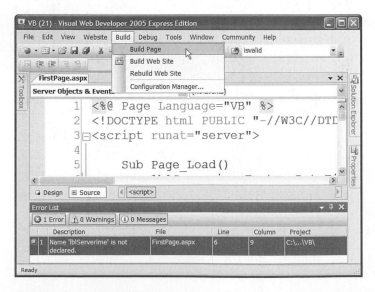

FIGURE 1.14   Performing a build in Visual Web Developer.

If you need to perform more advanced debugging, you can use the Visual Web Developer's debugger. The debugger enables you to set breakpoints and step line by line through your code.

You set a breakpoint by double-clicking the left-most column in Source view. When you add a breakpoint, a red circle appears (see Figure 1.15).

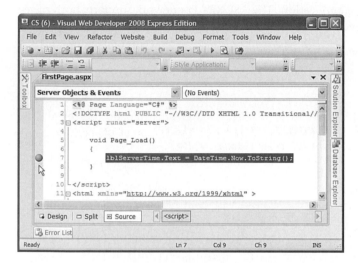

FIGURE 1.15   Setting a breakpoint.

After you set a breakpoint, run your application by selecting the menu option Debug, Start Debugging. Execution stops when the breakpoint is hit. At that point, you can hover your mouse over any variable or control property to view the current value of the variable or control property.

NOTE

You can designate one of the pages in your application as the Start Page. That way, whenever you run your application, the Start Page is executed regardless of the page that you have open. Set the Start Page by right-clicking a page in the Solution Explorer window and selecting the menu option Set As Start Page.

After you hit a breakpoint, you can continue execution by selecting Step Into, Step Over, or Step Out from the Debug menu or the toolbar. Here's an explanation of each of these options:

▶ **Step Into**—Executes the next line of code.

▶ **Step Over**—Executes the next line of code without leaving the current method.

▶ **Step Out**—Executes the next line of code and returns to the method that called the current method.

When you are finished debugging a page, you can continue, stop, or restart your application by selecting a particular option from the Debug menu or the toolbar.

Tracing Page Execution

If you want to output trace messages while a page executes, then you can enable tracing for a particular page or an entire application. The ASP.NET Framework supports both page-level tracing and application-level tracing.

The page in Listing 1.21 illustrates how you can take advantage of page-level tracing.

LISTING 1.21   PageTrace.aspx

```
<%@ Page Language="C#" Trace="true" %>
<!DOCTYPE html PUBLIC "-//W3C//DTD XHTML 1.0 Transitional//EN"
"http://www.w3.org/TR/xhtml1/DTD/xhtml1-transitional.dtd">
<script runat="server">

    void Page_Load()
    {
        for (int counter = 0; counter < 10; counter++)
        {
            ListBox1.Items.Add("item " + counter.ToString());
            Trace.Warn("counter=" + counter.ToString());
        }
    }

</script>
<html xmlns="http://www.w3.org/1999/xhtml" >
<head id="Head1" runat="server">
    <title>Page Trace</title>
</head>
<body>
    <form id="form1" runat="server">
    <div>

    <asp:ListBox
        id="ListBox1"
        Runat="server" />

    </div>
    </form>
</body>
</html>
```

Notice that the <%@ Page %> directive in Listing 1.21 includes a trace="true" attribute. This attribute enables tracing and causes a Trace Information section to be appended to the bottom of the page (see Figure 1.16).

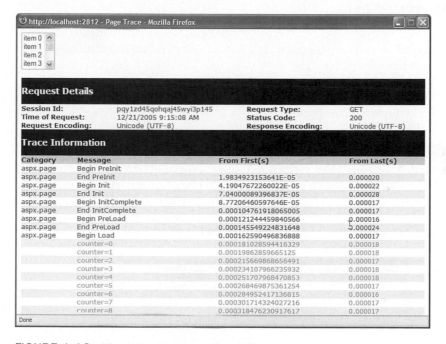

FIGURE 1.16   Viewing page trace information.

Notice, furthermore, that the Page_Load() handler uses the Trace.Warn() method to write messages to the Trace Information section. You can output any string to the Trace Information section that you please. In Listing 1.21, the current value of a variable named counter is displayed.

You'll want to take advantage of page tracing when you need to determine exactly what is happening when a page executes. You can call the Trace.Warn() method wherever you need in your code. Because the Trace Information section appears even when there is an error in your page, you can use tracing to diagnose the causes of any page errors.

One disadvantage of page tracing is that everyone in the world gets to see your trace information. You can get around this problem by taking advantage of application-level tracing. When application-level tracing is enabled, trace information appears only when you request a special page named Trace.axd.

To enable application-level tracing, you need to add the web configuration file in Listing 1.22 to your application.

LISTING 1.22 `Web.Config`

```
<configuration>
<system.web>
    <trace enabled="true" />
</system.web>
</configuration>
```

After you add the `Web.Config` file in Listing 1.22 to your application, you can request the `Trace.axd` page in your browser. The last 10 page requests made after application-level tracing is enabled are displayed (see Figure 1.17).

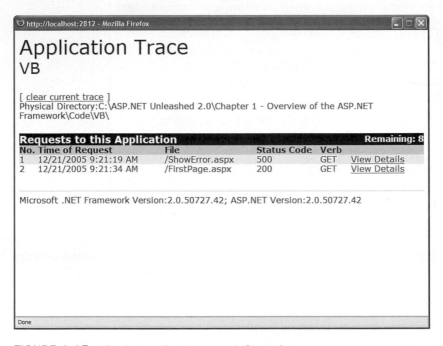

FIGURE 1.17   Viewing application trace information.

WARNING

By default, the `Trace.axd` page cannot be requested from a remote machine. If you need to access the `Trace.axd` page remotely, you need to add a `localOnly="false"` attribute to the trace element in the web configuration file.

If you click the View Details link next to any of the listed page requests, you can view all the trace messages outputted by the page. Messages written with the `Trace.Warn()` method are displayed by the `Trace.axd` page even when page-level tracing is disabled.

> **NOTE**
>
> You can use the new `writeToDiagnosticsTrace` attribute of the `trace` element to write all trace messages to the Output window of Visual Web Developer when you run an application. You can use the new `mostRecent` attribute to display the last 10 page requests rather than the 10 page requests after tracing was enabled.

> **WARNING**
>
> If you don't enable the `mostRecent` attribute when application level tracing is enabled, tracing will stop after 10 pages.

Installing the ASP.NET Framework

The easiest way to install the ASP.NET Framework is to install Visual Web Developer Express. You can download the latest version of Visual Web Developer from www.ASP.net, which is the official Microsoft ASP.NET website.

Installing Visual Web Developer Express also installs the following components:

▶ Microsoft .NET Framework version 3.5

▶ SQL Server Express

Visual Web Developer Express is compatible with the following operating systems:

▶ Windows 2000 Service Pack 4

▶ Windows XP Service Pack 2

▶ Windows Server 2003 Service Pack 1

▶ Windows x64 editions

▶ Windows Vista

I strongly recommend that you also download the .NET Framework SDK (Software Development Kit). The SDK includes additional documentation, sample code, and tools for building ASP.NET applications. You can download the SDK from the Microsoft MSDN website located at msdn.microsoft.com. The .NET Framework 3.5 SDK is included as part of the Microsoft Windows SDK for Windows Server 2008.

You can install Visual Web Developer Express on a computer that already has Visual Studio 2005 or Visual Web Developer 2005 installed. Different versions of the development environments can co-exist peacefully.

Furthermore, the same web server can serve ASP.NET 1.1 pages, ASP.NET 2.0 pages, ASP.NET 3.0 pages, and ASP.NET 3.5 pages. Each version of the .NET Framework is installed in the following folder:

```
C:\WINDOWS\Microsoft.NET\Framework
```

For example, on my computer, I have the following five versions of the .NET Framework installed (version 1.0, version 1.1, version 2.0, version 3.0, and version 3.5):

```
C:\WINDOWS\Microsoft.NET\Framework\v1.0.3705
C:\WINDOWS\Microsoft.NET\Framework\v1.1.4322
C:\WINDOWS\Microsoft.NET\Framework\v2.0.50727
C:\WINDOWS\Microsoft.NET\Framework\v3.0
C:\WINDOWS\Microsoft.NET\Framework\v3.5
```

The first three folders include a command-line tool named aspnet_regiis.exe. You can use this tool to associate a particular virtual directory on your machine with a particular version of the .NET Framework.

For example, executing the following command from a command prompt located in the v1.0.3705, v1.1.4322, or v2.0.50727 folders enables the 1.0, 1.1, or 2.0 version of ASP.NET for a virtual directory named MyApplication:

```
aspnet_regiis -s W3SVC/1/ROOT/MyApplication
```

By executing the aspnet_regiis.exe tool located in the different .NET Framework version folders, you can map a particular virtual directory to any version of the ASP.NET Framework.

The .NET Frameworks 3.0 and 3.5 work differently than earlier versions. The 3.0 and 3.5 versions build on top of the existing .NET Framework 2.0. To use these versions of the .NET Framework, you need to add the correct assembly references to your website and use the correct versions of the C# or VB.NET compilers. You reference these assemblies and configure the compiler within your application's web.config file. When you create a new website in Visual Web Developer, the necessary configuration settings are included in your web.config file automatically.

You also have the option of targeting a particular version of the .NET Framework. To do this, select the menu option Website, Start Options and select the Build tab. You can choose to target the .NET Framework 2.0, .NET Framework 3.0, or .NET Framework 3.5 (see Figure 1.18).

NOTE

If you load an existing ASP.NET 2.0 website into Visual Web Developer 2008, Visual Web Developer will prompt you to upgrade the website to ASP.NET 3.5. When Visual Web Developer upgrades your website, it modifies your web.config file.

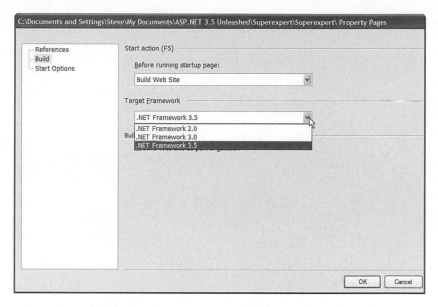

FIGURE 1.18   Targeting a particular version of the .NET Framework.

Summary

In this chapter, you were introduced to the ASP.NET 3.5 Framework. First, we built a simple ASP.NET page. You learned about the three main elements of an ASP.NET page: directives, code declaration blocks, and page render blocks.

Next, we discussed the .NET Framework. You learned about the 13,000 classes contained in the Framework Class Library and you learned about the features of the Common Language Runtime.

You also were provided with an overview of ASP.NET controls. You learned about the different groups of controls included in the .NET Framework. You also learned how to handle control events and take advantage of View State.

We also discussed ASP.NET pages. You learned how ASP.NET pages are dynamically compiled when they are first requested. We also examined how you can divide a single-file ASP.NET page into a code-behind page. You learned how to debug and trace the execution of an ASP.NET page.

At the end of the chapter, we covered installation issues in getting the ASP.NET Framework up and running. You learned how to map different Virtual Directories to different versions of the ASP.NET Framework. You also learned how to target different versions of the .NET Framework in your web configuration file.

CHAPTER 2

Using the Standard Controls

In this chapter, you learn how to use the core controls contained in the ASP.NET 3.5 Framework. These are controls that you'll use in just about any ASP.NET application that you build.

You learn how to display information to users by using the Label and Literal controls. You learn how to accept user input with the TextBox, CheckBox, and RadioButton controls. You also learn how to submit forms with the button controls.

At the end of this chapter, you learn how to group form fields with the Panel control. Finally, you learn how to link from one page to another with the HyperLink control.

Displaying Information

The ASP.NET Framework includes two controls you can use to display text in a page: the Label control and the Literal control. Whereas the Literal control simply displays text, the Label control supports several additional formatting properties.

Using the Label Control

Whenever you need to modify the text displayed in a page dynamically, you can use the Label control. For example, the page in Listing 2.1 dynamically modifies the value of a Label control's Text property to display the current time (see Figure 2.1).

FIGURE 2.1   Displaying the time with a `Label` control.

LISTING 2.1   ShowLabel.aspx

```
<%@ Page Language="C#" %>
<!DOCTYPE html PUBLIC "-//W3C//DTD XHTML 1.0 Transitional//EN"
"http://www.w3.org/TR/xhtml1/DTD/xhtml1-transitional.dtd">
<script runat="server">

    void Page_Load()
    {
        lblTime.Text = DateTime.Now.ToString("T");
    }
</script>
<html xmlns="http://www.w3.org/1999/xhtml" >
<head id="Head1" runat="server">
    <title>Show Label</title>
</head>
<body>
    <form id="form1" runat="server">
    <div>

    <asp:Label
        id="lblTime"
        Runat="server" />
```

```
        </div>
        </form>
</body>
</html>
```

Any string that you assign to the `Label` control's `Text` property is displayed by the `Label` when the control is rendered. You can assign simple text to the `Text` property or you can assign HTML content.

As an alternative to assigning text to the `Text` property, you can place the text between the `Label` control's opening and closing tags. Any text that you place before the opening and closing tags gets assigned to the `Text` property.

By default, a `Label` control renders its contents in an HTML `<span>` tag. Whatever value you assign to the `Text` property is rendered to the browser enclosed in a `<span>` tag.

The `Label` control supports several properties you can use to format the text displayed by the `Label` (this is not a complete list):

- ▶ **BackColor**—Enables you to change the background color of the label.
- ▶ **BorderColor**—Enables you to set the color of a border rendered around the label.
- ▶ **BorderStyle**—Enables you to display a border around the label. Possible values are `NotSet`, `None`, `Dotted`, `Dashed`, `Solid`, `Double`, `Groove`, `Ridge`, `Inset`, and `Outset`.
- ▶ **BorderWidth**—Enables you to set the size of a border rendered around the label.
- ▶ **CssClass**—Enables you to associate a Cascading Style Sheet class with the label.
- ▶ **Font**—Enables you to set the label's font properties.
- ▶ **ForeColor**—Enables you to set the color of the content rendered by the label.
- ▶ **Style**—Enables you to assign style attributes to the label.
- ▶ **ToolTip**—Enables you to set a label's `title` attribute. (In Microsoft Internet Explorer, the `title` attribute is displayed as a floating tooltip.)

In general, I recommend that you avoid using the formatting properties and take advantage of Cascading Style Sheets to format the rendered output of the `Label` control. The page in Listing 2.2 contains two `Label` controls: The first is formatted with properties and the second is formatted with a Cascading Style Sheet (see Figure 2.2).

LISTING 2.2   `FormatLabel.aspx`

```
<%@ Page Language="C#" %>
<!DOCTYPE html PUBLIC "-//W3C//DTD XHTML 1.0 Transitional//EN"
  "http://www.w3.org/TR/xhtml1/DTD/xhtml1-transitional.dtd">
<html xmlns="http://www.w3.org/1999/xhtml" >
<head id="Head1" runat="server">
    <style type="text/css">
```

LISTING 2.2   Continued

```
        div
        {
            padding:10px;
        }
        .labelStyle
        {
            color:red;
            background-color:yellow;
            border:Solid 2px Red;
        }
    </style>
    <title>Format Label</title>
</head>
<body>
    <form id="form1" runat="server">
    <div>

    <asp:Label
        id="lblFirst"
        Text="First Label"
        ForeColor="Red"
        BackColor="Yellow"
        BorderStyle="Solid"
        BorderWidth="2"
        BorderColor="red"
        Runat="server" />

    <br /><br />

    <asp:Label
        id="lblSecond"
        Text="Second Label"
        CssClass="labelStyle"
        Runat="server" />

    </div>
    </form>
</body>
</html>
```

You should use a Label control when labeling the fields in an HTML form. The Label
control includes a property named the AssociatedControlID property. You can set this
property to point at an ASP.NET control that represents a form field.

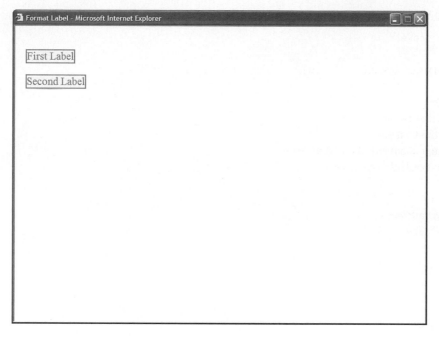

FIGURE 2.2   Formatting a label.

For example, the page in Listing 2.3 contains a simple form that contains fields for entering a first and last name. Label controls are used to label the two TextBox controls.

LISTING 2.3   LabelForm.aspx

```
<%@ Page Language="C#" %>
<!DOCTYPE html PUBLIC "-//W3C//DTD XHTML 1.0 Transitional//EN"
"http://www.w3.org/TR/xhtml1/DTD/xhtml1-transitional.dtd">
<html xmlns="http://www.w3.org/1999/xhtml" >
<head id="Head1" runat="server">
    <title>Label Form</title>
</head>
<body>
    <form id="form1" runat="server">
    <div>

    <asp:Label
        id="lblFirstName"
        Text="First Name:"
        AssociatedControlID="txtFirstName"
        Runat="server" />
    <br />
    <asp:TextBox
        id="txtFirstName"
```

LISTING 2.3 Continued

```
        Runat="server" />

    <br /><br />

    <asp:Label
        id="lblLastName"
        Text="Last Name:"
        AssociatedControlID="txtLastName"
        Runat="server" />
    <br />
    <asp:TextBox
        id="txtLastName"
        Runat="server" />

    </div>
    </form>
</body>
</html>
```

When you provide a Label control with an AssociatedControlID property, the Label control is rendered as an HTML <label> tag instead of an HTML <span> tag. For example, if you select View Source on your web browser, you'll see that the first Label in Listing 2.3 renders the following content to the browser:

```
<label for="txtFirstName" id="lblFirstName">First Name:</label>
```

Always use a Label control with an AssociatedControlID property when labeling form fields. This is important when you need to make your website accessible to persons with disabilities. If someone is using an assistive device, such as a screen reader, to interact with your website, the AssociatedControlID property enables the assistive device to associate the correct label with the correct form field.

A side benefit of using the AssociatedControlID property is that clicking a label when this property is set automatically changes the form focus to the associated form input field.

WEB STANDARDS NOTE

Both the WCAG 1.0 and Section 508 accessibility guidelines require you to use the <label for> tag when labeling form fields. For more information, see http://www.w3. org/wai and http://www.Section508.gov.

Using the Literal Control

The Literal control is similar to the Label control. You can use the Literal control to display text or HTML content in a browser. However, unlike the Label control, the Literal control does not render its content inside of a <span> tag.

For example, the page in Listing 2.4 uses a Literal control in the page's <head> tag to dynamically modify the title displayed in the browser title bar. The current date is displayed in the Literal control (see Figure 2.3).

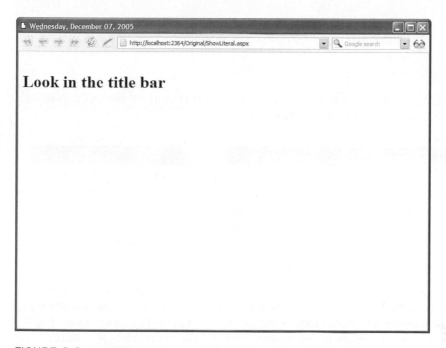

FIGURE 2.3   Modifying the browser title with a Literal control.

LISTING 2.4   ShowLiteral.aspx

```
<%@ Page Language="C#" %>
<!DOCTYPE html PUBLIC "-//W3C//DTD XHTML 1.0 Transitional//EN"
"http://www.w3.org/TR/xhtml1/DTD/xhtml1-transitional.dtd">
<script runat="server">
    void Page_Load()
    {
        ltlTitle.Text = DateTime.Now.ToString("D");
    }
</script>
<html xmlns="http://www.w3.org/1999/xhtml" >
<head>
    <title><asp:Literal id="ltlTitle" Runat="Server" /></title>
</head>
<body>
    <form id="form1" runat="server">
    <div>
```

LISTING 2.4   Continued

```
    <h1>Look in the title bar</h1>

    </div>
    </form>
</body>
</html>
```

If you used a Label control in Listing 2.4 instead of a Literal control, the uninterpreted <span> tags would appear in the browser title bar.

> **NOTE**
>
> The page in Listing 2.4 uses a format specifier to format the date before assigning the date to the Label control. The D format specifier causes the date to be formatted in a long format. You can use several standard format specifiers with the ToString() method to format dates, times, currency amounts, and numbers. For a list of these format specifiers, look up the Format Specifiers topic in the index of the Microsoft .NET Framework SDK Documentation.

Because the contents of a Literal control are not contained in a <span> tag, the Literal control does not support any of the formatting properties supported by the <span> tag. For example, the Literal control does not support either the CssClass or BackColor properties.

The Literal control does support one property that is not supported by the Label control: the Mode property. The Mode property enables you to encode HTML content. The Mode property accepts any of the following three values:

▶ **PassThrough**—Displays the contents of the control without encoding.

▶ **Encode**—Displays the contents of the control after HTML encoding the content.

▶ **Transform**—Displays the contents of the control after stripping markup that is not supported by the requesting device.

For example, the page in Listing 2.5 contains three Literal controls that are set to the three possible values of the Mode property (see Figure 2.4).

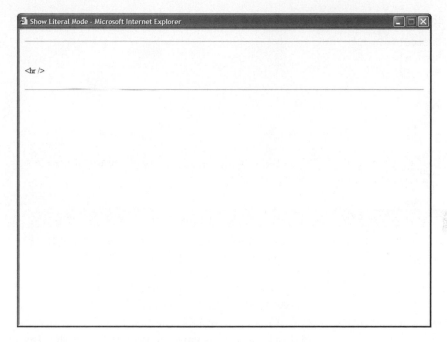

FIGURE 2.4   Three values of the Literal control's Mode property.

LISTING 2.5   ShowLiteralMode.aspx

```
<%@ Page Language="C#" %>
<!DOCTYPE html PUBLIC "-//W3C//DTD XHTML 1.0 Transitional//EN"
"http://www.w3.org/TR/xhtml1/DTD/xhtml1-transitional.dtd">
<html xmlns="http://www.w3.org/1999/xhtml" >
<head id="Head1" runat="server">
    <title>Show Literal Mode</title>
</head>
<body>
    <form id="form1" runat="server">
    <div>

    <asp:Literal
        id="ltlFirst"
        Mode="PassThrough"
        Text="<hr />"
        Runat="server" />

    <br /><br />

    <asp:Literal
        id="ltlSecond"
```

LISTING 2.5   Continued

```
        Mode="Encode"
        Text="<hr />"
        Runat="server" />

    <br /><br />

    <asp:Literal
        id="ltlThird"
        Mode="Transform"
        Text="<hr />"
        Runat="server" />

    </div>
    </form>
</body>
</html>
```

When you request the page in Listing 2.5 with a web browser, the first `Literal` control displays a horizontal rule, the second `Literal` control displays the uninterpreted `<hr />` tag, and the final `Literal` control displays another horizontal rule. If you requested the page from a device (such as a WML cell phone) that does not support the `<hr>` tag, the third `<hr />` tag would be stripped.

Accepting User Input

The ASP.NET Framework includes several controls that you can use to gather user input. In this section, you learn how to use the `TextBox`, `CheckBox`, and `RadioButton` controls. These controls correspond to the standard types of HTML input tags.

Using the `TextBox` Control

The `TextBox` control can be used to display three different types of input fields depending on the value of its `TextMode` property. The `TextMode` property accepts the following three values:

- ▶ **`SingleLine`**—Displays a single-line input field.

- ▶ **`MultiLine`**—Displays a multi-line input field.

- ▶ **`Password`**—Displays a single-line input field in which the text is hidden.

The page in Listing 2.6 contains three `TextBox` controls that illustrate all three of the `TextMode` values (see Figure 2.5).

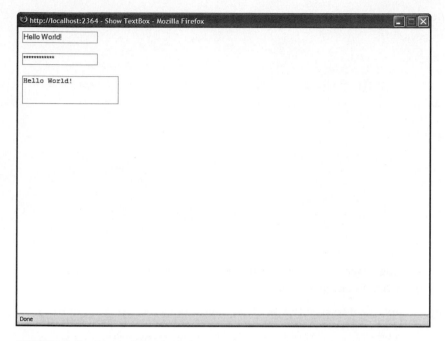

FIGURE 2.5   Displaying TextBox controls with different values for TextMode.

LISTING 2.6   ShowTextBox.aspx

```
<%@ Page Language="C#" %>
<!DOCTYPE html PUBLIC "-//W3C//DTD XHTML 1.0 Transitional//EN"
"http://www.w3.org/TR/xhtml1/DTD/xhtml1-transitional.dtd">
<html xmlns="http://www.w3.org/1999/xhtml" >
<head id="Head1" runat="server">
    <title>Show TextBox</title>
</head>
<body>
    <form id="form1" runat="server">
    <div>

    <asp:TextBox
        id="txtUserName"
        TextMode="SingleLine"
        Runat="server" />

    <br /><br />

    <asp:TextBox
        id="txtPassword"
        TextMode="Password"
```

LISTING 2.6   Continued

```
        Runat="server" />

    <br /><br />

    <asp:TextBox
        id="txtComments"
        TextMode="MultiLine"
        Runat="server" />

    </div>
    </form>
</body>
</html>
```

You can use the following properties to control the rendering characteristics of the TextBox control (this is not a complete list):

▶ **AccessKey**—Enables you to specify a key that navigates to the TextBox control.

▶ **AutoCompleteType**—Enables you to associate an AutoComplete class with the TextBox control.

▶ **AutoPostBack**—Enables you to post the form containing the TextBox back to the server automatically when the contents of the TextBox is changed.

▶ **Columns**—Enables you to specify the number of columns to display.

▶ **Enabled**—Enables you to disable the text box.

▶ **MaxLength**—Enables you to specify the maximum length of data that a user can enter in a text box (does not work when TextMode is set to Multiline).

▶ **ReadOnly**—Enables you to prevent users from changing the text in a text box.

▶ **Rows**—Enables you to specify the number of rows to display.

▶ **TabIndex**—Enables you to specify the tab order of the text box.

▶ **Wrap**—Enables you to specify whether text word-wraps when the TextMode is set to Multiline.

The TextBox control also supports the following method:

▶ **Focus**—Enables you to set the initial form focus to the text box.

And, the TextBox control supports the following event:

▶ **TextChanged**—Raised on the server when the contents of the text box are changed.

When the AutoPostBack property has the value True, the form containing the TextBox is automatically posted back to the server when the contents of the TextBox changes. For example, the page in Listing 2.7 contains a simple search form. If you modify the contents of the text box and tab out of the TextBox control, the form is automatically posted back to the server and the contents of the TextBox are displayed (see Figure 2.6).

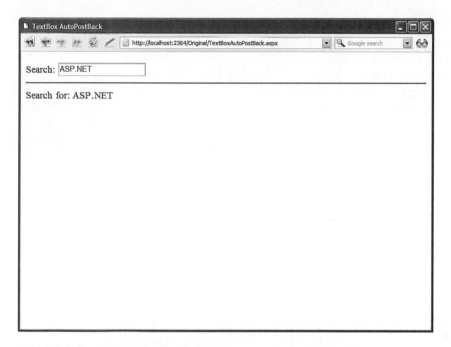

FIGURE 2.6   Reloading a form automatically when the contents of a form field change.

LISTING 2.7   TextBoxAutoPostBack.aspx

```
<%@ Page Language="C#" %>
<!DOCTYPE html PUBLIC "-//W3C//DTD XHTML 1.0 Transitional//EN"
"http://www.w3.org/TR/xhtml1/DTD/xhtml1-transitional.dtd">
<script runat="server">

    protected void txtSearch_TextChanged(object sender, EventArgs e)
    {
        lblSearchResults.Text = "Search for: " + txtSearch.Text;
    }
</script>
<html xmlns="http://www.w3.org/1999/xhtml" >
<head id="Head1" runat="server">
    <title>TextBox AutoPostBack</title>
</head>
<body>
    <form id="form1" runat="server">
    <div>
```

LISTING 2.7   Continued

```
    <asp:Label
        id="lblSearch"
        Text="Search:"
        Runat="server" />
    <asp:TextBox
        id="txtSearch"
        AutoPostBack="true"
        OnTextChanged="txtSearch_TextChanged"
        Runat="server" />

    <hr />

    <asp:Label
        id="lblSearchResults"
        Runat="server" />

    </div>
    </form>
</body>
</html>
```

In Listing 2.7, the `TextBox` control's `TextChanged` event is handled. This event is raised on the server when the contents of the `TextBox` have been changed. You can handle this event even when you don't use the `AutoPostBack` property.

WEB STANDARDS NOTE

You should avoid using the `AutoPostBack` property for accessibility reasons. Creating a page that automatically reposts the server can be very confusing to someone using an assistive device such as a screen reader. If you insist on using the `AutoPostBack` property, you should include a value for the `ToolTip` property that warns the user that the page will be reloaded.

Notice that the `TextBox` control also includes a property that enables you to associate the `TextBox` with a particular `AutoComplete` class. When `AutoComplete` is enabled, the user does not need to re-enter common information—such as a first name, last name, or phone number—in a form field. If the user has not disabled `AutoComplete` on his browser, then his browser prompts him to enter the same value that he entered previously for the form field (even if the user entered the value for a form field at a different website).

NOTE

You can disable auto-complete by adding an `AutoComplete="Off"` attribute to the TextBox. This is useful when you want to use the ASP.NET AJAX Control Toolkit AutoComplete control, and you don't want the browser auto-complete to interfere with the Ajax auto-complete.

For example, the page in Listing 2.8 asks for your first name, last name, and phone number. Each `TextBox` control is associated with a particular `AutoComplete` class. The `AutoComplete` class specifies the type of information associated with the form field. After you complete the form once, if you return to the same form in the future, you are prompted to enter the same responses (see Figure 2.7).

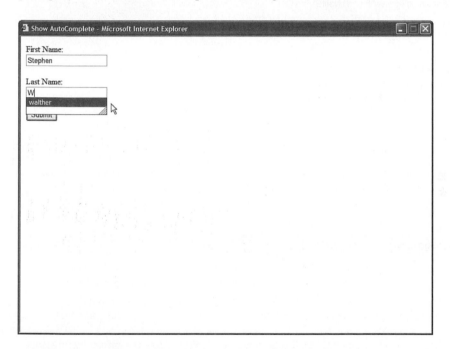

FIGURE 2.7   Using `AutoComplete` with the `TextBox` control.

LISTING 2.8   `ShowAutoComplete.aspx`

```
<%@ Page Language="C#" %>
<!DOCTYPE html PUBLIC "-//W3C//DTD XHTML 1.0 Transitional//EN"
"http://www.w3.org/TR/xhtml1/DTD/xhtml1-transitional.dtd">
<html xmlns="http://www.w3.org/1999/xhtml" >
<head id="Head1" runat="server">
    <title>Show AutoComplete</title>
</head>
<body>
```

LISTING 2.8   Continued

```
<form id="form1" runat="server">
<div>

<asp:Label
    id="lblFirstName"
    Text="First Name:"
    AssociatedControlID="txtFirstName"
    Runat="server" />
<br />
<asp:TextBox
    id="txtFirstName"
    AutoCompleteType="FirstName"
    Runat="server" />
<br /><br />
<asp:Label
    id="lblLastname"
    Text="Last Name:"
    AssociatedControlID="txtLastName"
    Runat="server" />
<br />
<asp:TextBox
    id="txtLastName"
    AutoCompleteType="LastName"
    Runat="server" />
<br /><br />
<asp:Button
    id="btnSubmit"
    Text="Submit"
    Runat="server" />

</div>
</form>
</body>
</html>
```

NOTE

When using Internet Explorer, you can configure AutoComplete by selecting Tools, Internet Options, Content, and clicking the AutoComplete button. The ASP.NET Framework does not support AutoComplete for other browsers such as FireFox or Opera.

Finally, the TextBox control supports the Focus() method. You can use the Focus() method to shift the initial form focus to a particular TextBox control. By default, no form field has focus when a page first opens. If you want to make it easier for users to complete a form, you can set the focus automatically to a particular TextBox control contained in a form.

For example, the page in Listing 2.9 sets the focus to the first of two form fields.

LISTING 2.9   TextBoxFocus.aspx

```
<%@ Page Language="C#" %>
<!DOCTYPE html PUBLIC "-//W3C//DTD XHTML 1.0 Transitional//EN"
"http://www.w3.org/TR/xhtml1/DTD/xhtml1-transitional.dtd">
<script runat="server">

    void Page_Load()
    {
        txtFirstName.Focus();
    }

</script>
<html xmlns="http://www.w3.org/1999/xhtml" >
<head id="Head1" runat="server">
    <title>TextBox Focus</title>
</head>
<body>
    <form id="form1" runat="server">
    <div>

    <asp:Label
        id="lblFirstName"
        Text="First Name:"
        AssociatedControlID="txtFirstName"
        Runat="server" />
    <br />
    <asp:TextBox
        id="txtFirstName"
        AutoCompleteType="FirstName"
        Runat="server" />
    <br /><br />
    <asp:Label
        id="lblLastname"
        Text="Last Name:"
        AssociatedControlID="txtLastName"
        Runat="server" />
    <br />
    <asp:TextBox
        id="txtLastName"
        AutoCompleteType="LastName"
```

LISTING 2.9   Continued

```
        Runat="server" />
    <br /><br />
    <asp:Button
        id="btnSubmit"
        Text="Submit"
        Runat="server" />

    </div>
    </form>
</body>
</html>
```

In Listing 2.9, the Page_Load() event handler sets the form focus to the txtFirstName TextBox control.

NOTE

You can also set the form focus by setting either the Page.SetFocus() method or the server-side HtmlForm control's DefaultFocus property.

Using the CheckBox Control

The CheckBox control enables you to display, well, a check box. The page in Listing 2.10 illustrates how you can use the CheckBox control in a newsletter signup form (see Figure 2.8).

LISTING 2.10   ShowCheckBox.aspx

```
<%@ Page Language="C#" %>
<!DOCTYPE html PUBLIC "-//W3C//DTD XHTML 1.0 Transitional//EN"
"http://www.w3.org/TR/xhtml1/DTD/xhtml1-transitional.dtd">
<script runat="server">

    protected void btnSubmit_Click(object sender, EventArgs e)
    {
        lblResult.Text = chkNewsletter.Checked.ToString();
    }
</script>
<html xmlns="http://www.w3.org/1999/xhtml" >
<head id="Head1" runat="server">
    <title>Show CheckBox</title>
</head>
<body>
    <form id="form1" runat="server">
    <div>
```

```
    <asp:CheckBox
        id="chkNewsletter"
        Text="Receive Newsletter?"
        Runat="server" />
    <br />
    <asp:Button
        id="btnSubmit"
        Text="Submit"
        OnClick="btnSubmit_Click"
        Runat="server" />
    <hr />

    <asp:Label
        id="lblResult"
        Runat="server" />

    </div>
    </form>
</body>
</html>
```

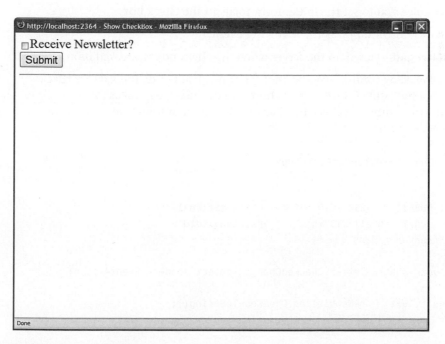

FIGURE 2.8   Displaying a CheckBox control.

In Listing 2.10, the `Checked` property is used to determine whether the user has checked the check box.

Notice that the `CheckBox` includes a `Text` property that is used to label the `CheckBox`. If you use this property, then the proper (accessibility standards-compliant) HTML `<label>` tag is generated for the `TextBox`.

The `CheckBox` control supports the following properties (this is not a complete list):

- **AccessKey**—Enables you to specify a key that navigates to the `TextBox` control.
- **AutoPostBack**—Enables you to post the form containing the CheckBox back to the server automatically when the `CheckBox` is checked or unchecked.
- **Checked**—Enables you to get or set whether the `CheckBox` is checked.
- **Enabled**—Enables you to disable the `TextBox`.
- **TabIndex**—Enables you to specify the tab order of the check box.
- **Text**—Enables you to provide a label for the check box.
- **TextAlign**—Enables you to align the label for the check box. Possible values are Left and Right.

The `CheckBox` control also supports the following method:

- **Focus**—Enables you to set the initial form focus to the check box.

And, the `CheckBox` control supports the following event:

- **CheckedChanged**—Raised on the server when the check box is checked or unchecked.

Notice that the `CheckBox` control, like the `TextBox` control, supports the `AutoPostBack` property. The page in Listing 2.11 illustrates how you can use the `AutoPostBack` property to post the form containing the check box back to the server automatically when the check box is checked or unchecked.

LISTING 2.11   `CheckBoxAutoPostBack.aspx`

```
<%@ Page Language="C#" %>
<!DOCTYPE html PUBLIC "-//W3C//DTD XHTML 1.0 Transitional//EN"
"http://www.w3.org/TR/xhtml1/DTD/xhtml1-transitional.dtd">
<script runat="server">

    protected void chkNewsletter_CheckedChanged(object sender, EventArgs e)
    {
        lblResult.Text = chkNewsletter.Checked.ToString();
    }
</script>

<html xmlns="http://www.w3.org/1999/xhtml" >
<head id="Head1" runat="server">
```

```
    <title>CheckBox AutoPostBack</title>
</head>
<body>
    <form id="form1" runat="server">
    <div>

    <asp:CheckBox
        id="chkNewsletter"
        Text="Receive Newsletter?"
        AutoPostBack="true"
        OnCheckedChanged="chkNewsletter_CheckedChanged"
        Runat="server" />
    <hr />

    <asp:Label
        id="lblResult"
        Runat="server" />

    </div>
    </form>
</body>
</html>
```

> **NOTE**
>
> The ASP.NET Framework also includes the `CheckBoxList` control that enables you to display a list of check boxes automatically. This control is discussed in detail in Chapter 10, "Using List Controls."

Using the RadioButton Control

You always use the `RadioButton` control in a group. Only one radio button in a group of `RadioButton` controls can be checked at a time.

For example, the page in Listing 2.12 contains three RadioButton controls (see Figure 2.9).

LISTING 2.12   ShowRadioButton.aspx

```
<%@ Page Language="C#" %>
<!DOCTYPE html PUBLIC "-//W3C//DTD XHTML 1.0 Transitional//EN"
"http://www.w3.org/TR/xhtml1/DTD/xhtml1-transitional.dtd">
<script runat="server">

    protected void btnSubmit_Click(object sender, EventArgs e)
    {
```

LISTING 2.12   Continued

```
            if (rdlMagazine.Checked)
                lblResult.Text = rdlMagazine.Text;
            if (rdlTelevision.Checked)
                lblResult.Text = rdlTelevision.Text;
            if (rdlOther.Checked)
                lblResult.Text = rdlOther.Text;
        }
</script>
<html xmlns="http://www.w3.org/1999/xhtml" >
<head id="Head1" runat="server">
    <title>Show RadioButton</title>
</head>
<body>
    <form id="form1" runat="server">
    <div>

    How did you hear about our Website?

    <ul>
        <li>
        <asp:RadioButton
            id="rdlMagazine"
            Text="Magazine Article"
            GroupName="Source"
            Runat="server" />
        </li>
        <li>
        <asp:RadioButton
            id="rdlTelevision"
            Text="Television Program"
            GroupName="Source"
            Runat="server" />
        </li>
        <li>
        <asp:RadioButton
            id="rdlOther"
            Text="Other Source"
            GroupName="Source"
            Runat="server" />
        </li>
    </ul>

    <asp:Button
        id="btnSubmit"
```

```
        Text="Submit"
        Runat="server" OnClick="btnSubmit_Click" />

    <hr />

    <asp:Label
        id="lblResult"
        Runat="server" />

    </div>
    </form>
</body>
</html>
```

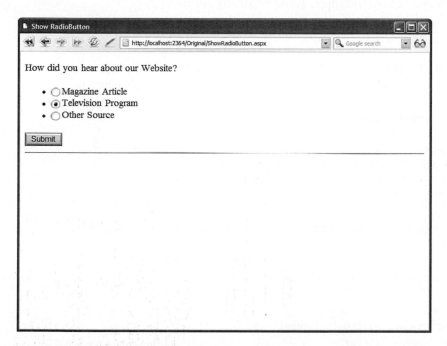

FIGURE 2.9 Displaying RadioButton.

The RadioButton controls in Listing 2.12 are grouped together with the RadioButton control's GroupName property. Only one of the three RadioButton controls can be checked at a time.

The RadioButton control supports the following properties (this is not a complete list):

▶ **AccessKey**—Enables you to specify a key that navigates to the RadioButton control.

▶ **AutoPostBack**—Enables you to post the form containing the RadioButton back to the server automatically when the radio button is checked or unchecked.

▶ **Checked**—Enables you to get or set whether the `RadioButton` control is checked.

▶ **Enabled**—Enables you to disable the `RadioButton`.

▶ **GroupName**—Enables you to group `RadioButton` controls.

▶ **TabIndex**—Enables you to specify the tab order of the `RadioButton` control.

▶ **Text**—Enables you to label the `RadioButton` control.

▶ **TextAlign**—Enables you to align the `RadioButton` label. Possible values are `Left` and `Right`.

The `RadioButton` control supports the following method:

▶ **Focus**—Enables you to set the initial form focus to the `RadionButton` control.

Finally, the `RadioButton` control supports the following event:

▶ **CheckedChanged**—Raised on the server when the `RadioButton` is checked or unchecked.

The page in Listing 2.13 demonstrates how you can use the `AutoPostBack` property with a group of `RadioButton` controls and detect which `RadioButton` control is selected.

LISTING 2.13   `RadioButtonAutoPostBack.aspx`

```
<%@ Page Language="C#" %>
<!DOCTYPE html PUBLIC "-//W3C//DTD XHTML 1.0 Transitional//EN"
"http://www.w3.org/TR/xhtml1/DTD/xhtml1-transitional.dtd">
<script runat="server">

    protected void RadioButton_CheckedChanged(object sender, EventArgs e)
    {
        RadioButton selectedRadioButton = (RadioButton)sender;
        lblResult.Text = selectedRadioButton.Text;
    }
</script>
<html xmlns="http://www.w3.org/1999/xhtml" >
<head id="Head1" runat="server">
    <title>RadioButton AutoPostBack</title>
</head>
<body>
    <form id="form1" runat="server">
    <div>

    How did you hear about our Website?

    <ul>
        <li>
```

```
            <asp:RadioButton
                id="rdlMagazine"
                Text="Magazine Article"
                GroupName="Source"
                AutoPostBack="true"
                OnCheckedChanged="RadioButton_CheckedChanged"
                Runat="server" />
        </li>
        <li>
            <asp:RadioButton
                id="rdlTelevision"
                Text="Television Program"
                GroupName="Source"
                AutoPostBack="true"
                OnCheckedChanged="RadioButton_CheckedChanged"
                Runat="server" />
        </li>
        <li>
            <asp:RadioButton
                id="rdlOther"
                Text="Other Source"
                GroupName="Source"
                AutoPostBack="true"
                OnCheckedChanged="RadioButton_CheckedChanged"
                Runat="server" />
        </li>
    </ul>

    <hr />

    <asp:Label
        id="lblResult"
        Runat="server" />

    </div>
    </form>
</body>
</html>
```

In Listing 2.13, when you select a RadioButton control, the page is automatically posted back to the server, and the value of the Text property of the selected RadioButton control is displayed. Notice that all three of the RadioButton controls are associated with the same CheckedChanged event handler. The first parameter passed to the handler represents the particular RadioButton that was changed.

> **NOTE**
>
> The ASP.NET Framework also includes the `RadioButtonList` control, which enables you to display a list of radio buttons automatically. This control is discussed in detail in Chapter 10, "Using List Controls."

Submitting Form Data

The ASP.NET Framework includes three controls you can use to submit a form to the server: the `Button`, `LinkButton`, and `ImageButton` controls. These controls have the same function, but each control has a distinct appearance.

In this section, you learn how to use each of these three types of buttons in a page. Next, you learn how to associate client-side scripts with server-side `Button` controls. You also learn how to use a button control to post a form to a page other than the current page. Finally, you learn how to handle a button control's Command event.

Using the `Button` Control

The `Button` control renders a push button that you can use to submit a form to the server. For example, the page in Listing 2.14 contains a `Button` control. When you click the Button control, the time displayed by a `Label` control is updated (see Figure 2.10).

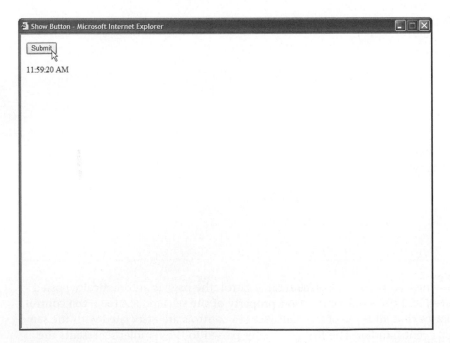

FIGURE 2.10   Displaying a `Button` control.

LISTING 2.14 ShowButton.aspx

```
<%@ Page Language="C#" %>
<!DOCTYPE html PUBLIC "-//W3C//DTD XHTML 1.0 Transitional//EN"
"http://www.w3.org/TR/xhtml1/DTD/xhtml1-transitional.dtd">
<script runat="server">

    protected void btnSubmit_Click(object sender, EventArgs e)
    {
        lblTime.Text = DateTime.Now.ToString("T");
    }
</script>
<html xmlns="http://www.w3.org/1999/xhtml" >
<head id="Head1" runat="server">
    <title>Show Button</title>
</head>
<body>
    <form id="form1" runat="server">
    <div>

    <asp:Button
        id="btnSubmit"
        Text="Submit"
        OnClick="btnSubmit_Click"
        Runat="server" />

    <br /><br />

    <asp:Label
        id="lblTime"
        Runat="server" />

    </div>
    </form>
</body>
</html>
```

The Button control supports the following properties (this is not a complete list):

▶ **AccessKey**—Enables you to specify a key that navigates to the Button control.

▶ **CommandArgument**—Enables you to specify a command argument that is passed to the Command event.

▶ **CommandName**—Enables you to specify a command name that is passed to the Command event.

▶ **Enabled**—Enables you to disable the `Button` control.

▶ **OnClientClick**—Enables you to specify a client-side script that executes when the button is clicked.

▶ **PostBackUrl**—Enables you to post a form to a particular page.

▶ **TabIndex**—Enables you to specify the tab order of the `Button` control.

▶ **Text**—Enables you to label the `Button` control.

▶ **UseSubmitBehavior**—Enables you to use JavaScript to post a form.

The `Button` control also supports the following method:

▶ **Focus**—Enables you to set the initial form focus to the `Button` control.

The `Button` control also supports the following two events:

▶ **Click**—Raised when the `Button` control is clicked.

▶ **Command**—Raised when the Button control is clicked. The `CommandName` and `CommandArgument` are passed to this event.

Using the `LinkButton` Control

The `LinkButton` control, like the `Button` control, enables you to post a form to the server. Unlike a `Button` control, however, the `LinkButton` control renders a link instead of a push button.

The page in Listing 2.15 contains a simple form. The form includes a `LinkButton` control that enables you to submit the form to the server and display the contents of the form fields (see Figure 2.11).

LISTING 2.15   ShowLinkButton.aspx

```
<%@ Page Language="C#" %>
<!DOCTYPE html PUBLIC "-//W3C//DTD XHTML 1.0 Transitional//EN"
"http://www.w3.org/TR/xhtml1/DTD/xhtml1-transitional.dtd">
<script runat="server">

    protected void lnkSubmit_Click(object sender, EventArgs e)
    {
        lblResults.Text = "First Name: " + txtFirstName.Text;
        lblResults.Text += "<br />Last Name: " + txtLastName.Text;
    }
</script>
<html xmlns="http://www.w3.org/1999/xhtml" >
<head id="Head1" runat="server">
    <title>Show LinkButton</title>
</head>
```

```
<body>
    <form id="form1" runat="server">
    <div>

    <asp:Label
        id="lblFirstName"
        Text="First Name:"
        AssociatedControlID="txtFirstName"
        Runat="server" />
    <br />
    <asp:TextBox
        id="txtFirstName"
        Runat="server" />
    <br /><br />
    <asp:Label
        id="lblLastName"
        Text="Last Name:"
        AssociatedControlID="txtLastName"
        Runat="server" />
    <br />
    <asp:TextBox
        id="txtLastName"
        Runat="server" />
    <br /><br />
    <asp:LinkButton
        id="lnkSubmit"
        Text="Submit"
        OnClick="lnkSubmit_Click"
        Runat="server" />

    <br /><br />

    <asp:Label
        id="lblResults"
        Runat="server" />

    </div>
    </form>
</body>
</html>
```

Behind the scenes, the LinkButton control uses JavaScript to post the form back to the server. The hyperlink rendered by the LinkButton control looks like this:

```
<a id="lnkSubmit" href="javascript:__doPostBack('lnkSubmit','')">Submit</a>
```

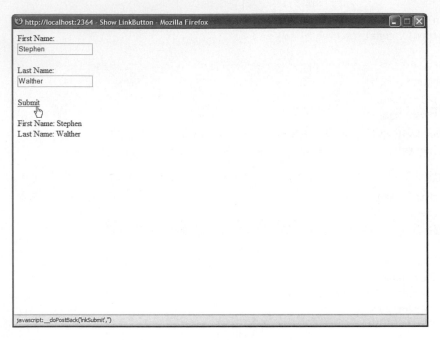

FIGURE 2.11   Displaying a LinkButton control.

Clicking the LinkButton invokes the JavaScript __doPostBack() method, which posts the form to the server. When the form is posted, the values of all the other form fields in the page are also posted to the server.

The LinkButton control supports the following properties (this is not a complete list):

▶ **AccessKey**—Enables you to specify a key that navigates to the Button control.

▶ **CommandArgument**—Enables you to specify a command argument that is passed to the Command event.

▶ **CommandName**—Enables you to specify a command name that is passed to the Command event.

▶ **Enabled**—Enables you to disable the LinkButton control.

▶ **OnClientClick**—Enables you to specify a client-side script that executes when the LinkButton is clicked.

▶ **PostBackUrl**—Enables you to post a form to a particular page.

▶ **TabIndex**—Enables you to specify the tab order of the LinkButton control.

▶ **Text**—Enables you to label the LinkButton control.

The LinkButton control also supports the following method:

▶ **Focus**—Enables you to set the initial form focus to the LinkButton control.

The LinkButton control also supports the following two events:

► **Click**—Raised when the LinkButton control is clicked.

► **Command**—Raised when the LinkButton control is clicked. The CommandName and CommandArgument are passed to this event.

Using the ImageButton Control

The ImageButton control, like the Button and LinkButton controls, enables you to post a form to the server. However, the ImageButton control always displays an image.

The page in Listing 2.16 contains an ImageButton control that posts a simple form back to the server (see Figure 2.12).

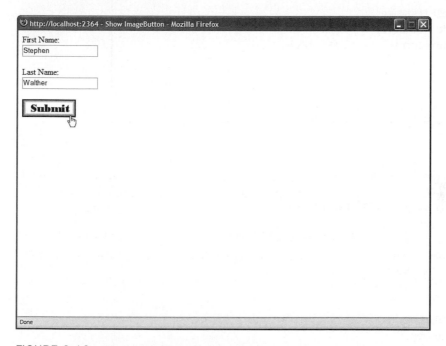

FIGURE 2.12   Displaying an ImageButton control.

LISTING 2.16   ShowImageButton.aspx

```
<%@ Page Language="C#" %>
<!DOCTYPE html PUBLIC "-//W3C//DTD XHTML 1.0 Transitional//EN"
"http://www.w3.org/TR/xhtml1/DTD/xhtml1-transitional.dtd">
<script runat="server">

    protected void btnSubmit_Click(object sender, ImageClickEventArgs e)
    {
        lblResults.Text = "First Name: " + txtFirstName.Text;
        lblResults.Text += "<br />Last Name: " + txtLastName.Text;
```

LISTING 2.16   Continued

```
        }
</script>
<html xmlns="http://www.w3.org/1999/xhtml" >
<head id="Head1" runat="server">
    <title>Show ImageButton</title>
</head>
<body>
    <form id="form1" runat="server">
    <div>

    <asp:Label
        id="lblFirstName"
        Text="First Name:"
        AssociatedControlID="txtFirstName"
        Runat="server" />
    <br />
    <asp:TextBox
        id="txtFirstName"
        Runat="server" />
    <br /><br />
    <asp:Label
        id="lblLastName"
        Text="Last Name:"
        AssociatedControlID="txtLastName"
        Runat="server" />
    <br />
    <asp:TextBox
        id="txtLastName"
        Runat="server" />
    <br /><br />
    <asp:ImageButton
        id="btnSubmit"
        ImageUrl="Submit.gif"
        AlternateText="Submit Form"
        Runat="server" OnClick="btnSubmit_Click" />

    <br /><br />
    <asp:Label
        id="lblResults"
        Runat="server" />

    </div>
    </form>
</body>
</html>
```

The ImageButton in Listing 2.16 includes both an ImageUrl and AlternateText property. The ImageUrl contains the path to the image that the ImageButton displays. The AlternateText property is used to provide alternate text for the image used by screen readers and text-only browsers.

WEB STANDARDS NOTE

Always include alternate text for any image. The accessibility guidelines require it. Furthermore, remember that some people turn off images in their browsers for a faster surfing experience.

Notice that the event handler for an Image control's Click event is different than that for the other button controls. The second parameter passed to the event handler is an instance of the ImageClickEventArgs class. This class has the following properties:

▶ **X**—The x coordinate relative to the image the user clicked.

▶ **Y**—The y coordinate relative to the image the user clicked.

You can use the ImageButton control to create a simple image map. For example, the page in Listing 2.17 contains an ImageButton that displays an image of a target. If you click the center of the target, then a success message is displayed (see Figure 2.13).

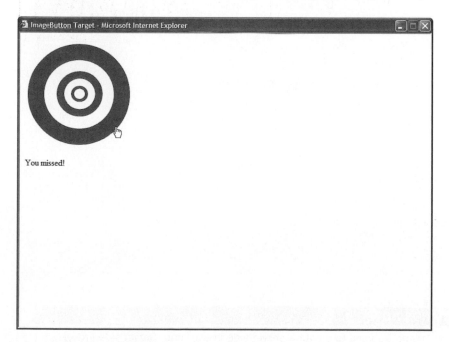

FIGURE 2.13   Retrieving X and Y coordinates from an ImageButton.

LISTING 2.17   `ImageButtonTarget.aspx`

```
<%@ Page Language="C#" %>
<!DOCTYPE html PUBLIC "-//W3C//DTD XHTML 1.0 Transitional//EN"
"http://www.w3.org/TR/xhtml1/DTD/xhtml1-transitional.dtd">
<script runat="server">

    protected void btnTarget_Click(object sender, ImageClickEventArgs e)
    {
        if ((e.X > 90 && e.X < 110) && (e.Y > 90 && e.Y < 110))
            lblResult.Text = "You hit the target!";
        else
            lblResult.Text = "You missed!";
    }
</script>
<html xmlns="http://www.w3.org/1999/xhtml" >
<head id="Head1" runat="server">
    <title>ImageButton Target</title>
</head>
<body>
    <form id="form1" runat="server">
    <div>

    <asp:ImageButton
        id="btnTarget"
        ImageUrl="Target.gif"
        Runat="server" OnClick="btnTarget_Click" />

    <br /><br />

    <asp:Label
        id="lblResult"
        Runat="server" />

    </div>
    </form>
</body>
</html>
```

WEB STANDARDS NOTE

The `ImageButton` can be used to create a server-side image map. Server-side image maps are not accessible to persons with disabilities. A better method for creating an `ImageMap` is to use the `ImageMap` control, which enables you to create a client-side image map. The `ImageMap` control is discussed in the next section of this chapter.

The ImageButton control supports the following properties (this is not a complete list):

- ▸ **AccessKey**—Enables you to specify a key that navigates to the ImageButton control.

- ▸ **AlternateText**—Enables you to provide alternate text for the image (required for accessibility).

- ▸ **DescriptionUrl**—Enables you to provide a link to a page that contains a detailed description of the image (required to make a complex image accessible).

- ▸ **CommandArgument**—Enables you to specify a command argument that is passed to the Command event.

- ▸ **CommandName**—Enables you to specify a command name that is passed to the Command event.

- ▸ **Enabled**—Enables you to disable the ImageButton control.

- ▸ **GenerateEmptyAlternateText**—Enables you to set the AlternateText property to an empty string.

- ▸ **ImageAlign**—Enables you to align the image relative to other HTML elements in the page. Possible values are AbsBottom, AbsMiddle, Baseline, Bottom, Left, Middle, NotSet, Right, TextTop, and Top.

- ▸ **ImageUrl**—Enables you to specify the URL to the image.

- ▸ **OnClientClick**—Enables you to specify a client-side script that executes when the ImageButton is clicked.

- ▸ **PostBackUrl**—Enables you to post a form to a particular page.

- ▸ **TabIndex**—Enables you to specify the tab order of the ImageButton control.

The ImageButton control also supports the following method:

- ▸ **Focus**—Enables you to set the initial form focus to the ImageButton control.

The ImageButton control also supports the following two events:

- ▸ **Click**—Raised when the ImageButton control is clicked.

- ▸ **Command**—Raised when the ImageButton control is clicked. The CommandName and CommandArgument are passed to this event.

Using Client Scripts with Button Controls

All three Button controls support an OnClientClick property. You can use this property to execute any client-side code that you need when a button is clicked. The page in Listing 2.18 illustrates how you can use the OnClientClick property to display a confirmation dialog box (see Figure 2.14).

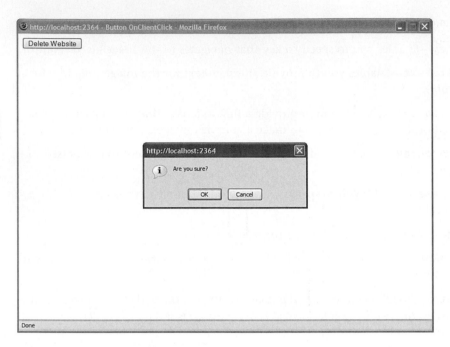

FIGURE 2.14   Displaying a client-side confirmation dialog box.

LISTING 2.18   ButtonOnClientClick.aspx

```
<%@ Page Language="C#" %>
<!DOCTYPE html PUBLIC "-//W3C//DTD XHTML 1.0 Transitional//EN"
"http://www.w3.org/TR/xhtml1/DTD/xhtml1-transitional.dtd">
<script runat="server">

    protected void btnDelete_Click(object sender, EventArgs e)
    {
        lblResult.Text = "All pages deleted!";
    }
</script>
<html xmlns="http://www.w3.org/1999/xhtml" >
<head id="Head1" runat="server">
    <title>Button OnClientClick</title>
</head>
<body>
    <form id="form1" runat="server">
    <div>

    <asp:Button
        id="btnDelete"
        Text="Delete Website"
```

```
            OnClick="btnDelete_Click"
            OnClientClick="return confirm('Are you sure?');"
            Runat="server" />

        <br /><br />

        <asp:Label
            id="lblResult"
            Runat="server" />

    </div>
    </form>
</body>
</html>
```

In Listing 2.18, the Button control includes an OnClientClick property, which executes a JavaScript script when you click the button on the client. The script displays a confirmation dialog box. If the confirmation box returns False, then the button click is canceled and the form containing the button is not posted to the server.

Because the button controls, like most ASP.NET controls, support expando attributes, you can handle other client-side events simply by adding an arbitrary attribute to the control. If the ASP.NET Framework does not recognize an attribute declared on a button control, the framework simply passes the attribute to the browser.

For example, the page in Listing 2.19 contains a button control that includes onmouseover and onmouseout attributes. When you hover your mouse over the button, the text displayed in the button is changed.

LISTING 2.19   ButtonExpando.aspx

```
<%@ Page Language="C#" %>
<!DOCTYPE html PUBLIC "-//W3C//DTD XHTML 1.0 Transitional//EN"
"http://www.w3.org/TR/xhtml1/DTD/xhtml1-transitional.dtd">
<html xmlns="http://www.w3.org/1999/xhtml" >
<head id="Head1" runat="server">
    <title>Button Expando</title>
</head>
<body>
    <form id="form1" runat="server">
    <div>

    <asp:Button
        id="btnSubmit"
        Text="Submit"
        onmouseover="this.value='Click Here!'"
```

LISTING 2.19   Continued

```
            onmouseout="this.value='Submit'"
            Runat="server" />


    </div>
    </form>
</body>
</html>
```

NOTE

You'll get green squiggly warnings under expando attributes in Visual Web Developer—but these warnings can be safely ignored.

Performing Cross-Page Posts

By default, if you click a button control, the page containing the control is posted back to itself and the same page is reloaded. However, you can use the `PostBackUrl` property to post form data to another page.

For example, the page in Listing 2.20 includes a search form. The `Button` control in the page posts the form to another page named `ButtonSearchResults.aspx`. The `ButtonSearchResults.aspx` page is contained in Listing 2.21.

LISTING 2.20   `ButtonSearch.aspx`

```
<%@ Page Language="C#" %>
<!DOCTYPE html PUBLIC "-//W3C//DTD XHTML 1.0 Transitional//EN"
"http://www.w3.org/TR/xhtml1/DTD/xhtml1-transitional.dtd">
<html xmlns="http://www.w3.org/1999/xhtml" >
<head id="Head1" runat="server">
    <title>Button Search</title>
</head>
<body>
    <form id="form1" runat="server">
    <div>

    <asp:Label
        id="lblSearch"
        Text="Search:"
        Runat="server" />
    <asp:TextBox
        id="txtSearch"
```

```
        Runat="server" />
    <asp:Button
        id="btnSearch"
        Text="Go!"
        PostBackUrl="ButtonSearchResults.aspx"
        Runat="server" />
    </div>
    </form>
</body>
</html>
```

LISTING 2.21 ButtonSearchResults.aspx

```
<%@ Page Language="C#" %>
<!DOCTYPE html PUBLIC "-//W3C//DTD XHTML 1.0 Transitional//EN"
"http://www.w3.org/TR/xhtml1/DTD/xhtml1-transitional.dtd">
<script runat="server">

    void Page_Load()
    {
        if (PreviousPage != null)
        {
            TextBox txtSearch = (TextBox)PreviousPage.FindControl("txtSearch");
            lblSearch.Text = String.Format("Search For: {0}", txtSearch.Text);
        }
    }

</script>
<html xmlns="http://www.w3.org/1999/xhtml" >
<head id="Head1" runat="server">
    <title>Button Search Results</title>
</head>
<body>
    <form id="form1" runat="server">
    <div>

    <asp:Label
        id="lblSearch"
        Runat="server" />

    </div>
    </form>
</body>
</html>
```

In the Page_Load event handler in Listing 2.21, the PreviousPage property is used to get a reference to the previous page (the ButtonSearch.aspx page in Listing 2.20). Next, the FindControl() method is used to retrieve the txtSearch TextBox control from the previous page. Finally, the value entered into the TextBox is displayed in a label on the page.

As an alternative to using the FindControl() method to retrieve a particular control from the previous page, you can expose the control through a page property. The page in Listing 2.22 exposes the txtSearch TextBox through a property named SearchString. The page posts the form data to a page named ButtonSearchResultsTyped.aspx, contained in Listing 2.23.

LISTING 2.22   ButtonSearchTyped.aspx

```
<%@ Page Language="C#" %>
<!DOCTYPE html PUBLIC "-//W3C//DTD XHTML 1.0 Transitional//EN"
"http://www.w3.org/TR/xhtml1/DTD/xhtml1-transitional.dtd">
<script runat="server">

    public string SearchString
    {
        get { return txtSearch.Text; }
    }

</script>
<html xmlns="http://www.w3.org/1999/xhtml" >
<head id="Head1" runat="server">
    <title>Button Search Typed</title>
</head>
<body>
    <form id="form1" runat="server">
    <div>

    <asp:Label
        id="lblSearch"
        Text="Search:"
        Runat="server" />
    <asp:TextBox
        id="txtSearch"
        Runat="server" />
    <asp:Button
        id="btnSearch"
        Text="Go!"
        PostBackUrl="ButtonSearchResultsTyped.aspx"
```

```
            Runat="server" />
        </div>
        </form>
</body>
</html>
```

LISTING 2.23 ButtonSearchResultsTyped.aspx

```
<%@ Page Language="C#" %>
<%@ PreviousPageType VirtualPath="~/ButtonSearchTyped.aspx" %>
<!DOCTYPE html PUBLIC "-//W3C//DTD XHTML 1.0 Transitional//EN"
"http://www.w3.org/TR/xhtml1/DTD/xhtml1-transitional.dtd">
<script runat="server">

    void Page_Load()
    {
        if (Page.PreviousPage != null)
        {
            lblSearch.Text = String.Format("Search For: {0}", PreviousPage.Search-
String);
        }
    }

</script>
<html xmlns="http://www.w3.org/1999/xhtml" >
<head id="Head1" runat="server">
    <title>Button Search Results Typed</title>
</head>
<body>
    <form id="form1" runat="server">
    <div>

    <asp:Label
        id="lblSearch"
        Runat="server" />

    </div>
    </form>
</body>
</html>
```

Notice that the page in Listing 2.23 includes a `<%@ PreviousPageType %>` directive. This directive casts the value returned by the `PreviousPage` property as an instance of the `ButtonSearchTyped` class. Without this directive, the `PreviousPage` property would return the previous page as an instance of the generic `Page` class.

You can use either method when performing cross-page posts. The first method provides you with an untyped method of retrieving values from the previous page, and the second method provides you with a typed method.

Specifying a Default Button

You can specify a default button for a form by using the `DefaultButton` property of the server-side `Form` control. If you specify a default button, then pressing the keyboard Enter key invokes the button.

For example, the page in Listing 2.24 contains a simple search form. The `<form>` tag sets the `btnSearch` Button control as the default button on the page.

LISTING 2.24   `ButtonDefaultButton.aspx`

```
<%@ Page Language="C#" %>
<!DOCTYPE html PUBLIC "-//W3C//DTD XHTML 1.0 Transitional//EN"
"http://www.w3.org/TR/xhtml1/DTD/xhtml1-transitional.dtd">
<script runat="server">

    protected void btnSearch_Click(object sender, EventArgs e)
    {
        lblResult.Text = "Search for: " + txtSearch.Text;
    }
</script>
<html xmlns="http://www.w3.org/1999/xhtml" >
<head id="Head1" runat="server">
    <title>Button Default Button</title>
</head>
<body>
    <form id="form1" defaultbutton="btnSearch" runat="server">
    <div>

    <asp:Label
        id="lblSearch"
        Text="Search:"
        AssociatedControlID="txtSearch"
        Runat="server" />
    <asp:TextBox
```

```
            id="txtSearch"
            Runat="server" />
    <asp:Button
            id="btnSearch"
            Text="Search"
            OnClick="btnSearch_Click"
            Runat="server" />
    <asp:Button
            id="btnCancel"
            Text="Cancel"
            Runat="server" />

    <hr />

    <asp:Label
            id="lblResult"
            Runat="server" />

    </div>
    </form>
</body>
</html>
```

If you open the page in Listing 2.24, type a search phrase, and hit the keyboard Enter key, the form is submitted to the server. Pressing the Enter key causes the btnSearch_Click event handler to execute because the btnSearch button is the default button on the page.

NOTE

You can also specify a DefaultButton with a Panel control. The Panel control is discussed later in this chapter.

Handling the Command Event

All three Button controls support both the Click event and the Command event. The difference between these events is that you can pass a command name and command argument to a Command event handler but not to a Click event handler.

For example, the page in Listing 2.25 contains two Button controls and a BulletedList control. When you click the first button, the items displayed by the BulletedList control are sorted in ascending order, and when you click the second button, the items displayed by the BulletedList control are sorted in descending order (see Figure 2.15).

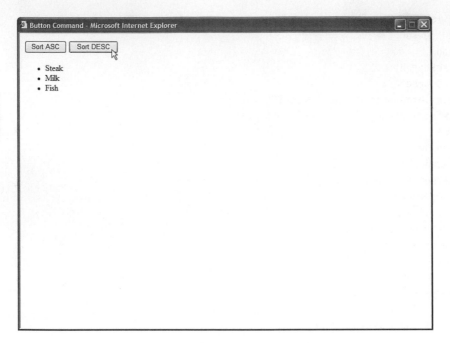

FIGURE 2.15   Handling the Command event.

LISTING 2.25   ButtonCommand.aspx

```
<%@ Page Language="C#" %>
<%@ Import Namespace="System.Collections.Generic" %>
<!DOCTYPE html PUBLIC "-//W3C//DTD XHTML 1.0 Transitional//EN"
"http://www.w3.org/TR/xhtml1/DTD/xhtml1-transitional.dtd">
<script runat="server">

    private List<String> groceries = new List<String>();

    void Page_Load()
    {
        groceries.Add("Milk");
        groceries.Add("Steak");
        groceries.Add("Fish");
    }

    protected void Sort_Command(object sender, CommandEventArgs e)
    {
        if (e.CommandName == "Sort")
        {
            switch (e.CommandArgument.ToString())
```

```
            {
                case "ASC":
                    groceries.Sort(SortASC);
                    break;
                case "DESC":
                    groceries.Sort(SortDESC);
                    break;
            }
        }
    }

    void Page_PreRender()
    {
        bltGroceries.DataSource = groceries;
        bltGroceries.DataBind();
    }

    int SortASC(string x, string y)
    {
        return String.Compare(x, y);
    }

    int SortDESC(string x, string y)
    {
        return String.Compare(x, y) * -1;
    }

</script>
<html xmlns="http://www.w3.org/1999/xhtml" >
<head id="Head1" runat="server">
    <title>Button Command</title>
</head>
<body>
    <form id="form1" runat="server">
    <div>

    <asp:Button
        id="btnSortAsc"
        Text="Sort ASC"
        CommandName-"Sort"
        CommandArgument="ASC"
        OnCommand="Sort_Command"
        Runat="server" />

    <asp:Button
        id="btnSortDESC"
```

LISTING 2.25   Continued

```
            Text="Sort DESC"
            CommandName="Sort"
            CommandArgument="DESC"
            OnCommand="Sort_Command"
            Runat="server" />

        <br /><br />

        <asp:BulletedList
            id="bltGroceries"
            Runat="server" />



    </div>
    </form>
</body>
</html>
```

Both `Button` controls include `CommandName` and `CommandArgument` properties. Furthermore, both `Button` controls are wired to the same `Sort_Command()` event handler. This event handler checks the `CommandName` and `CommandArgument` properties when determining how the elements in the `BulletedList` should be sorted.

Displaying Images

The ASP.NET framework includes two controls for displaying images: the `Image` and `ImageMap` controls. The `Image` control simply displays an image. The `ImageMap` control enables you to create a client-side, clickable, image map.

Using the `Image` Control

The page in Listing 2.26 randomly displays one of three images. The image is displayed by setting the `ImageUrl` property of the `Image` control contained in the body of the page.

LISTING 2.26   ShowImage.aspx

```
<%@ Page Language="C#" %>
<!DOCTYPE html PUBLIC "-//W3C//DTD XHTML 1.0 Transitional//EN"
"http://www.w3.org/TR/xhtml1/DTD/xhtml1-transitional.dtd">
<script runat="server">
```

```
    void Page_Load()
    {
        Random rnd = new Random();
        switch (rnd.Next(3))
        {
            case 0:
                imgRandom.ImageUrl = "Picture1.gif";
                imgRandom.AlternateText = "Picture 1";
                break;
            case 1:
                imgRandom.ImageUrl = "Picture2.gif";
                imgRandom.AlternateText = "Picture 2";
                break;
            case 2:
                imgRandom.ImageUrl = "Picture3.gif";
                imgRandom.AlternateText = "Picture 3";
                break;
        }
    }

</script>
<html xmlns="http://www.w3.org/1999/xhtml" >
<head id="Head1" runat="server">
    <title>Show Image</title>
</head>
<body>
    <form id="form1" runat="server">
    <div>

    <asp:Image
        id="imgRandom"
        Runat="server" />

    </div>
    </form>
</body>
</html>
```

The Image control supports the following properties (this is not a complete list):

▶ **AlternateText**—Enables you to provide alternate text for the image (required for accessibility).

▶ **DescriptionUrl**—Enables you to provide a link to a page that contains a detailed description of the image (required to make a complex image accessible).

▶ **GenerateEmptyAlternateText**—Enables you to set the `AlternateText` property to an empty string.

▶ **ImageAlign**—Enables you to align the image relative to other HTML elements in the page. Possible values are `AbsBottom`, `AbsMiddle`, `Baseline`, `Bottom`, `Left`, `Middle`, `NotSet`, `Right`, `TextTop`, and `Top`.

▶ **ImageUrl**—Enables you to specify the URL to the image.

The `Image` control supports three methods for supplying alternate text. If an image represents page content, then you should supply a value for the `AlternateText` property. For example, if you have an image for your company's logo, then you should assign the text "My Company Logo" to the `AlternateText` property.

If an `Image` control represents something really complex—such as a bar chart, pie graph, or company organizational chart—then you should supply a value for the `DescriptionUrl` property. The `DescriptionUrl` property links to a page that contains a long textual description of the image.

Finally, if the image is used purely for decoration (it expresses no content), then you should set the `GenerateEmptyAlternateText` property to the value `True`. When this property has the value `True`, then an `alt=""` attribute is included in the rendered `<img>` tag. Screen readers know to ignore images with empty `alt` attributes.

Using the `ImageMap` Control

The `ImageMap` control enables you to create a client-side image map. An image map displays an image. When you click different areas of the image, things happen.

For example, you can use an image map as a fancy navigation bar. In that case, clicking different areas of the image map navigates to different pages in your website.

You also can use an image map as an input mechanism. For example, you can click different product images to add a particular product to a shopping cart.

An `ImageMap` control is composed out of instances of the `HotSpot` class. A `HotSpot` defines the clickable regions in an image map. The ASP.NET framework ships with three `HotSpot` classes:

▶ **CircleHotSpot**—Enables you to define a circular region in an image map.

▶ **PolygonHotSpot**—Enables you to define an irregularly shaped region in an image map.

▶ **RectangleHotSpot**—Enables you to define a rectangular region in an image map.

The page in Listing 2.27 contains a navigation bar created with an `ImageMap` control. The `ImageMap` contains three `RectangleHotSpots` that delimit the three buttons displayed by the navigation bar (see Figure 2.16).

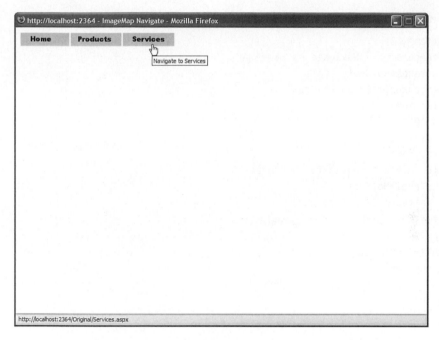

FIGURE 2.16   Navigating with an ImageMap control.

LISTING 2.27   ImageMapNavigate.aspx

```
<%@ Page Language="C#" %>
<!DOCTYPE html PUBLIC "-//W3C//DTD XHTML 1.0 Transitional//EN"
"http://www.w3.org/TR/xhtml1/DTD/xhtml1-transitional.dtd">
<html xmlns="http://www.w3.org/1999/xhtml" >
<head id="Head1" runat="server">
    <title>ImageMap Navigate</title>
</head>
<body>
    <form id="form1" runat="server">
    <div>

    <asp:ImageMap
        id="mapNavigate"
        ImageUrl="ImageBar.jpg"
        Runat="server">
        <asp:RectangleHotSpot
            NavigateUrl="Home.aspx"
            Left="0"
            Top="0"
            Right="100"
```

LISTING 2.27   Continued

```
            Bottom="50"
            AlternateText="Navigate to Home" />
        <asp:RectangleHotSpot
            NavigateUrl="Products.aspx"
            Left="100"
            Top="0"
            Right="200"
            Bottom="50"
            AlternateText="Navigate to Products" />
        <asp:RectangleHotSpot
            NavigateUrl="Services.aspx"
            Left="200"
            Top="0"
            Right="300"
            Bottom="50"
            AlternateText="Navigate to Services" />
    </asp:ImageMap>

    </div>
    </form>
</body>
</html>
```

Each `RectangleHotSpot` includes `Left`, `Top`, `Right`, and `Bottom` properties that describe the area of the rectangle. Each `RectangleHotSpot` also includes a `NavigateUrl` property that contains the URL to which the region of the image map links.

Rather than use an image map to link to different pages, you can use it to post back to the same page. For example, the page in Listing 2.28 uses an `ImageMap` control to display a menu. When you click different menu items represented by different regions of the image map, the text contained in the `TextBox` control is changed (see Figure 2.17).

LISTING 2.28   `ImageMapPostBack.aspx`

```
<%@ Page Language="C#" %>
<!DOCTYPE html PUBLIC "-//W3C//DTD XHTML 1.0 Transitional//EN"
"http://www.w3.org/TR/xhtml1/DTD/xhtml1-transitional.dtd">
<script runat="server">

    protected void mapMenu_Click(object sender, ImageMapEventArgs e)
    {
        switch (e.PostBackValue)
        {
            case "ToUpper":
                txtText.Text = txtText.Text.ToUpper();
```

```
                    break;
            case "ToLower":
                txtText.Text = txtText.Text.ToLower();
                break;
            case "Erase":
                txtText.Text = String.Empty;
                break;
        }
    }
</script>
<html xmlns="http://www.w3.org/1999/xhtml" >
<head id="Head1" runat="server">
    <title>ImageMap PostBack</title>
</head>
<body>
    <form id="form1" runat="server">
    <div>

    <asp:ImageMap
        id="mapMenu"
        ImageUrl="MenuBar.gif"
        HotSpotMode="PostBack"
        Runat="server" OnClick="mapMenu_Click">
        <asp:RectangleHotSpot
            PostBackValue="ToUpper"
            Left="0"
            Top="0"
            Right="100"
            Bottom="30"
            AlternateText="To Uppercase" />
        <asp:RectangleHotSpot
            PostBackValue="ToLower"
            Left="100"
            Top="0"
            Right="200"
            Bottom="30"
            AlternateText="To Uppercase" />
        <asp:RectangleHotSpot
            PostBackValue="Erase"
            Left="200"
            Top="0"
            Right="300"
            Bottom="30"
            AlternateText="To Uppercase" />
    </asp:ImageMap>
```

LISTING 2.28   Continued

```
    <br />

    <asp:TextBox
        id="txtText"
        TextMode="MultiLine"
        Columns="40"
        Rows="5"
        Runat="server" />

    </div>
    </form>
</body>
</html>
```

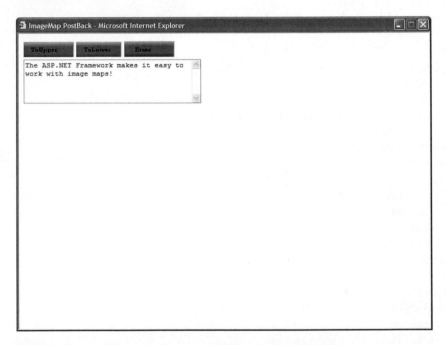

FIGURE 2.17   Posting back to the server with an ImageMap control.

Notice that the ImageMap control has its HotSpotMode property set to the value PostBack. Also, the ImageMap is wired to a Click event handler named mapMenu_Click.

Each HotSpot contained in the ImageMap control has a PostBackValue property. The mapMenu_Click handler reads the PostBackValue from the region clicked and modifies the text displayed by the TextBox control.

The `ImageMap` control supports the following properties (this is not a complete list):

- ▶ **AccessKey**—Enables you to specify a key that navigates to the `ImageMap` control.

- ▶ **AlternateText**—Enables you to provide alternate text for the image (required for accessibility).

- ▶ **DescriptionUrl**—Enables you to provide a link to a page which contains a detailed description of the image (required to make a complex image accessible).

- ▶ **GenerateEmptyAlternateText**—Enables you to set the `AlternateText` property to an empty string.

- ▶ **HotSpotMode**—Enables you to specify the behavior of the image map when you click a region. Possible values are `Inactive`, `Navigate`, `NotSet`, and `PostBack`.

- ▶ **HotSpots**—Enables you to retrieve the collection of `HotSpots` contained in the `ImageMap` control.

- ▶ **ImageAlign**—Enables you to align the image map with other HTML elements in the page. Possible values are `AbsBottom`, `AbsMiddle`, `Baseline`, `Bottom`, `Left`, `Middle`, `NotSet`, `Right`, `TextTop`, and `Top`.

- ▶ **ImageUrl**—Enables you to specify the URL to the image.

- ▶ **TabIndex**—Enables you to specify the tab order of the `ImageMap` control.

- ▶ **Target**—Enables you to open a page in a new window.

The `ImageMap` control also supports the following method:

- ▶ **Focus**—Enables you to set the initial form focus to the `ImageMap` control.

Finally, the `ImageMap` control supports the following event:

- ▶ **Click**—Raised when you click a region of the `ImageMap` and the `HotSpotMode` property is set to the value `PostBack`.

Using the `Panel` Control

The `Panel` control enables you to work with a group of ASP.NET controls.

For example, you can use a `Panel` control to hide or show a group of ASP.NET controls. The page in Listing 2.29 contains a list of `RadioButton` controls that can be used to select your favorite programming language. The last `RadioButton` is labeled `Other`. If you select the `Other` radio button, the contents of a `Panel` control are revealed (see Figure 2.18).

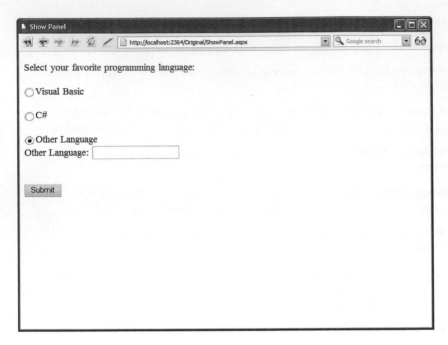

FIGURE 2.18 Hiding and displaying controls with the `Panel` control.

LISTING 2.29 `ShowPanel.aspx`

```
<%@ Page Language="C#" %>
<!DOCTYPE html PUBLIC "-//W3C//DTD XHTML 1.0 Transitional//EN"
"http://www.w3.org/TR/xhtml1/DTD/xhtml1-transitional.dtd">
<script runat="server">

    protected void btnSubmit_Click(object sender, EventArgs e)
    {
        if (rdlOther.Checked)
            pnlOther.Visible = true;
        else
            pnlOther.Visible = false;
    }
</script>
<html xmlns="http://www.w3.org/1999/xhtml" >
<head id="Head1" runat="server">
    <title>Show Panel</title>
</head>
<body>
    <form id="form1" runat="server">
    <div>

    Select your favorite programming language:
```

```
        <br /><br />
        <asp:RadioButton
            id="rdlVisualBasic"
            GroupName="language"
            Text="Visual Basic"
            Runat="server" />
        <br /><br />
        <asp:RadioButton
            id="rdlCSharp"
            GroupName="language"
            Text="C#"
            Runat="server" />
        <br /><br />
        <asp:RadioButton
            id="rdlOther"
            GroupName="language"
            Text="Other Language"
            Runat="server" />
        <br />
        <asp:Panel
            id="pnlOther"
            Visible="false"
            Runat="server">

            <asp:Label
                id="lblOther"
                Text="Other Language:"
                AssociatedControlID="txtOther"
                Runat="server" />
            <asp:TextBox
                id="txtOther"
                Runat="server" />

        </asp:Panel>

        <br /><br />

        <asp:Button
            id="btnSubmit"
            Text="Submit"
            Runat="server" OnClick="btnSubmit_Click" />

    </div>
    </form>
</body>
</html>
```

Notice that the Panel control is declared with a Visible property that has the value False. Because the Visible property is set to the value False, the Panel control and any controls contained in the Panel control are not rendered when the page is requested.

If you select the RadioButton control labeled Other, then the Visible property is set to the value True and the contents of the Panel control are displayed.

NOTE

Every control in the ASP.NET framework supports the Visible property. When Visible is set to the value False, the control does not render its contents.

The Panel control supports the following properties (this is not a complete list):

▸ **DefaultButton**—Enables you to specify the default button in a Panel. The default button is invoked when you press the Enter button.

▸ **Direction**—Enables you to get or set the direction in which controls that display text are rendered. Possible values are NotSet, LeftToRight, and RightToLeft.

▸ **GroupingText**—Enables you to render the Panel control as a fieldset with a particular legend.

▸ **HorizontalAlign**—Enables you to specify the horizontal alignment of the contents of the Panel. Possible values are Center, Justify, Left, NotSet, and Right.

▸ **ScrollBars**—Enables you to display scrollbars around the panel's contents. Possible values are Auto, Both, Horizontal, None, and Vertical.

By default, a Panel control renders a <div> tag around its contents. If you set the GroupingText property, however, the Panel control renders a <fieldset> tag. The value that you assign to the GroupingText property appears in the <fieldset> tag's <legend> tag. Listing 2.30 demonstrates how you can use the GroupingText property (see Figure 2.19).

LISTING 2.30   PanelGroupingText.aspx

```
<%@ Page Language="C#" %>
<!DOCTYPE html PUBLIC "-//W3C//DTD XHTML 1.0 Transitional//EN"
"http://www.w3.org/TR/xhtml1/DTD/xhtml1-transitional.dtd">
<html xmlns="http://www.w3.org/1999/xhtml" >
<head id="Head1" runat="server">
    <title>Panel Grouping Text</title>
</head>
<body>
    <form id="form1" runat="server">
    <div>
```

```
<asp:Panel
    id="pnlContact"
    GroupingText="Contact Information"
    Runat="server">

<asp:Label
    id="lblFirstName"
    Text="First Name:"
    AssociatedControlID="txtFirstName"
    Runat="server" />
<br />
<asp:TextBox
    id="txtFirstName"
    AutoCompleteType="FirstName"
    Runat="server" />
<br /><br />
<asp:Label
    id="lblLastname"
    Text="Last Name:"
    AssociatedControlID="txtLastName"
    Runat="server" />
<br />
<asp:TextBox
    id="txtLastName"
    AutoCompleteType="LastName"
    Runat="server" />
<br /><br />
<asp:Button
    id="btnSubmit"
    Text="Submit"
    Runat="server" />

</asp:Panel>

</div>
</form>
</body>
</html>
```

WEB STANDARDS NOTE

According to the accessibility guidelines, you should use `<fieldset>` tags when grouping related form fields in long forms.

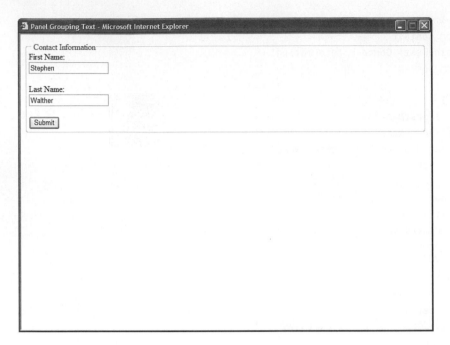

FIGURE 2.19   Setting the GroupingText property.

The ScrollBars property enables you to display scrollbars around a panel's contents. For example, the page in Listing 2.31 contains a Panel control that contains a BulletedList control that displays 100 items. The panel is configured to scroll when its contents overflow its width or height (see Figure 2.20).

LISTING 2.31   PanelScrollBars.aspx

```
<%@ Page Language="C#" %>
<!DOCTYPE html PUBLIC "-//W3C//DTD XHTML 1.0 Transitional//EN"
"http://www.w3.org/TR/xhtml1/DTD/xhtml1-transitional.dtd">
<script runat="server">

    void Page_Load()
    {
        for (int i = 0; i < 100; i++)
            bltList.Items.Add("Item " + i.ToString());
    }

</script>
<html xmlns="http://www.w3.org/1999/xhtml" >
<head id="Head1" runat="server">
    <style type="text/css">
        html
```

```
        {
            background-color:silver;
        }
        .contents
        {
            background-color:white;
            width:200px;
            height:200px;
        }
    </style>
    <title>Panel ScrollBars</title>
</head>
<body>
    <form id="form1" runat="server">
    <div>

    <asp:Panel
        id="pnlContent"
        ScrollBars="Auto"
        CssClass="contents"
        Runat="server">
        <asp:BulletedList
            id="bltList"
            Runat="server" />
    </asp:Panel>

    </div>
    </form>
</body>
</html>
```

2

WEB STANDARDS NOTE

Don't use the values `Horizontal` or `Vertical` with the `ScrollBars` property when you want the scrollbars to appear in browsers other than Microsoft Internet Explorer. If you want the scrollbars to appear in `FireFox` and `Opera`, use either the value `Auto` or `Both`.

When enabling scrollbars with the `Panel` control, you must specify a particular width and height to display the scrollbars. In Listing 2.31, the width and height are specified in a Cascading Style Sheet class. Alternatively, you can specify the width and height with the `Panel` control's `Width` and `Height` properties.

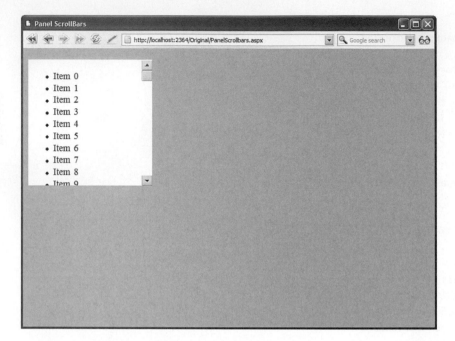

FIGURE 2.20   Displaying scrollbars with a Panel control.

Using the HyperLink Control

The HyperLink control enables you to create a link to a page. Unlike the LinkButton control, the HyperLink control does not submit a form to a server.

For example, the page in Listing 2.32 displays a hyperlink that randomly links to a page in your application.

LISTING 2.32   ShowHyperLink.aspx

```
<%@ Page Language="C#" %>
<%@ Import Namespace="System.IO" %>
<!DOCTYPE html PUBLIC "-//W3C//DTD XHTML 1.0 Transitional//EN"
"http://www.w3.org/TR/xhtml1/DTD/xhtml1-transitional.dtd">
<script runat="server">

    void Page_Load()
    {
        lnkRandom.NavigateUrl = GetRandomFile();
    }

    string GetRandomFile()
    {
```

```
        string[] files = Directory.GetFiles(MapPath(Request.ApplicationPath),
        ➥"*.aspx");
        Random rnd = new Random();
        string rndFile = files[rnd.Next(files.Length)];
        return Path.GetFileName(rndFile);
    }

</script>
<html xmlns="http://www.w3.org/1999/xhtml" >
<head id="Head1" runat="server">
    <title>Show HyperLink</title>
</head>
<body>
    <form id="form1" runat="server">
    <div>

    <asp:HyperLink
        id="lnkRandom"
        Text="Random Link"
        Runat="server" />

    </div>
    </form>
</body>
</html>
```

In the Page_Load event handler in Listing 2.32, a random file name from the current application is assigned to the NavigateUrl property of the HyperLink control.

The HyperLink control supports the following properties (this is not a complete list):

▶ **Enabled**—Enables you to disable the hyperlink.

▶ **ImageUrl**—Enables you to specify an image for the hyperlink.

▶ **NavigateUrl**—Enables you to specify the URL represented by the hyperlink.

▶ **Target**—Enables you to open a new window.

▶ **Text**—Enables you to label the hyperlink.

Notice that you can specify an image for the HyperLink control by setting the ImageUrl property. If you set both the Text and ImageUrl properties, then the ImageUrl property takes precedence.

Summary

In this chapter, you were introduced to the core controls of the ASP.NET 3.5 framework. You learned how to display information using the Label and Literal controls. You also learned how to accept user input using the TextBox, CheckBox, and RadioButton controls.

In the second part of this chapter, you learned how to use the different button controls—the Button, LinkButton, and ImageButton controls—to submit a form. You learned how to post forms between pages. You also learned how to set a default button.

Finally, we discussed the Panel and HyperLink controls. You learned how to hide and display a group of controls with the Panel control. You also learned how to create dynamic links with the HyperLink control.

CHAPTER 3

Using the Validation Controls

In this chapter, you learn how to validate form fields when a form is submitted to the web server. You can use the validation controls to prevent users from submitting the wrong type of data into a database table. For example, you can use validation controls to prevent a user from submitting the value "Apple" for a birth date field.

In the first part of this chapter, you are provided with an overview of the standard validation controls included in the ASP.NET 3.5 Framework. You learn how to control how validation errors are displayed, how to highlight validation error messages, and how to use validation groups. You are provided with sample code for using each of the standard validation controls.

Next, we extend the basic validation controls with our own custom validation controls. For example, you learn how to create an AjaxValidator control that enables you to call a server-side validation function from the client.

Overview of the Validation Controls

Six validation controls are included in the ASP.NET 3.5 Framework:

▶ **RequiredFieldValidator**—Enables you to require a user to enter a value in a form field.

▶ **RangeValidator**—Enables you to check whether a value falls between a certain minimum and maximum value.

▶ **CompareValidator**—Enables you to compare a value against another value or perform a data type check.

▶ **RegularExpressionValidator**—Enables you to compare a value against a regular expression.

▶ **CustomValidator**—Enables you to perform custom validation.

▶ **ValidationSummary**—Enables you to display a summary of all validation errors in a page.

You can associate the validation controls with any of the form controls included in the ASP.NET Framework. For example, if you want to require a user to enter a value into a TextBox control, then you can associate a RequiredFieldValidator control with the TextBox control.

> **NOTE**
>
> Technically, you can use the validation controls with any control that is decorated with the ValidationProperty attribute.

The page in Listing 3.1 contains a simple order entry form. It contains three TextBox controls that enable you to enter a product name, product price, and product quantity. Each of the form fields are validated with the validation controls.

LISTING 3.1 OrderForm.aspx

```
<%@ Page Language="C#" %>
<!DOCTYPE html PUBLIC "-//W3C//DTD XHTML 1.0 Transitional//EN"
"http://www.w3.org/TR/xhtml1/DTD/xhtml1-transitional.dtd">
<script runat="server">

    void btnSubmit_Click(Object sender, EventArgs e)
    {
        if (Page.IsValid)
        {
            lblResult.Text = @"<br />Product: " + txtProductName.Text
                + "<br />Price: " + txtProductPrice.Text
                + "<br />Quantity: " + txtProductQuantity.Text;
        }
    }
</script>
<html xmlns="http://www.w3.org/1999/xhtml" >
<head id="Head1" runat="server">
    <title>Order Form</title>
</head>
<body>
```

```
<form id="form1" runat="server">
<div>

<fieldset>
<legend>Product Order Form</legend>

<asp:Label
    id="lblProductName"
    Text="Product Name:"
    AssociatedControlID="txtProductName"
    Runat="server" />
<br />
<asp:TextBox
    id="txtProductName"
    Runat="server" />
<asp:RequiredFieldValidator
    id="reqProductName"
    ControlToValidate="txtProductName"
    Text="(Required)"
    Runat="server" />

<br /><br />

<asp:Label
    id="lblProductPrice"
    Text="Product Price:"
    AssociatedControlID="txtProductPrice"
    Runat="server" />
<br />
<asp:TextBox
    id="txtProductPrice"
    Columns="5"
    Runat="server" />
<asp:RequiredFieldValidator
    id="reqProductPrice"
    ControlToValidate="txtProductPrice"
    Text="(Required)"
    Display="Dynamic"
    Runat="server" />
<asp:CompareValidator
    id="cmpProductPrice"
    ControlToValidate="txtProductPrice"
    Text="(Invalid Price)"
    Operator="DataTypeCheck"
    Type="Currency"
    Runat="server" />
```

LISTING 3.1   Continued

```
    <br /><br />

    <asp:Label
        id="lblProductQuantity"
        Text="Product Quantity:"
        AssociatedControlID="txtProductQuantity"
        Runat="server" />
    <br />
    <asp:TextBox
        id="txtProductQuantity"
        Columns="5"
        Runat="server" />
    <asp:RequiredFieldValidator
        id="reqProductQuantity"
        ControlToValidate="txtProductQuantity"
        Text="(Required)"
        Display="Dynamic"
        Runat="server" />
    <asp:CompareValidator
        id="CompareValidator1"
        ControlToValidate="txtProductQuantity"
        Text="(Invalid Quantity)"
        Operator="DataTypeCheck"
        Type="Integer"
        Runat="server" />

    <br /><br />

    <asp:Button
        id="btnSubmit"
        Text="Submit Product Order"
        OnClick="btnSubmit_Click"
        Runat="server" />

    </fieldset>

    <asp:Label
        id="lblResult"
        Runat="server" />


    </div>
    </form>
</body>
</html>
```

A separate `RequiredFieldValidator` control is associated with each of the three form fields. If you attempt to submit the form in Listing 3.1 without entering a value for a field, then a validation error message is displayed (see Figure 3.1).

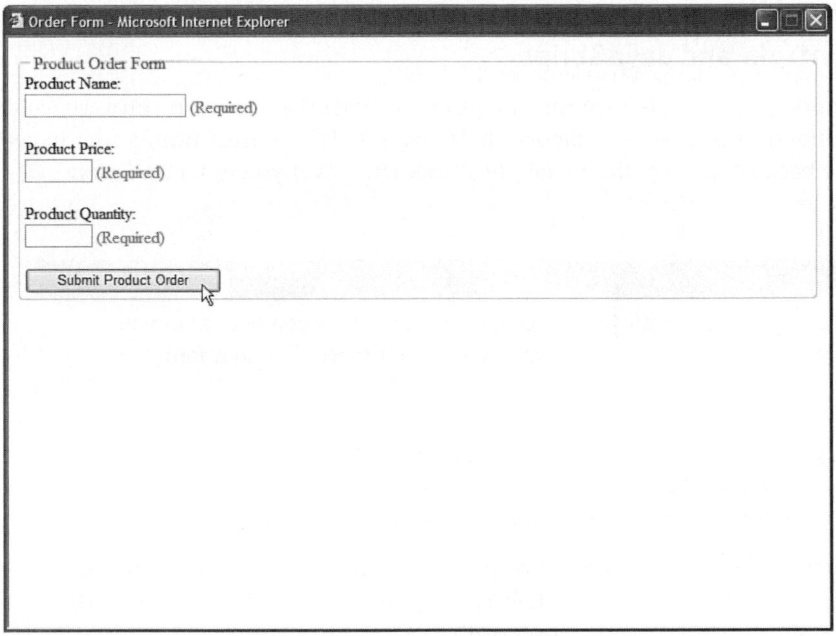

FIGURE 3.1   Displaying a validation error message.

Each `RequiredFieldValidator` is associated with a particular control through its `ControlToValidate` property. This property accepts the name of the control to validate on the page.

`CompareValidator` controls are associated with the `txtProductPrice` and `txtProductQuantity` TextBox controls. The first `CompareValidator` is used to check whether the `txtProductPrice` text field contains a currency value, and the second `CompareValidator` is used to check whether the `txtProductQuantity` text field contains an integer value.

Notice that there is nothing wrong with associating more than one validation control with a form field. If you need to make a form field required and check the data type entered into the form field, then you need to associate both a `RequiredFieldValidator` and `CompareValidator` control with the form field.

Finally, notice that the `Page.IsValid` property is checked in the `Page_Load()` handler before the form data is displayed. When using the validation controls, you should always check the `Page.IsValid` property before doing anything with the data submitted to a page. This property returns the value `true` when, and only when, there are no validation errors on the page.

Validation Controls and JavaScript

By default, the validation controls perform validation on both the client (the browser) and the server. The validation controls use client-side JavaScript. This is great from a user experience perspective because you get immediate feedback whenever you enter an invalid value into a form field.

> **NOTE**
>
> The `RequiredFieldValidator` will not perform client-side validation until after you attempt to submit a form at least once or you enter and remove data in a form field.

Client-side JavaScript is supported on any uplevel browser. Supported browsers include Internet Explorer, Firefox, and Opera. This is a change from the previous version of ASP.NET, which supported only Internet Explorer as an uplevel browser.

You can use the validation controls with browsers that do not support JavaScript (or do not have JavaScript enabled). If a browser does not support JavaScript, the form must be posted back to the server before a validation error message is displayed.

Even when validation happens on the client, validation is still performed on the server. This is done for security reasons. If someone creates a fake form and submits the form data to your web server, the person still won't be able to submit invalid data.

If you prefer, you can disable client-side validation for any of the validation controls by assigning the value `False` to the validation control's `EnableClientScript` property.

Using `Page.IsValid`

As mentioned earlier, you should always check the `Page.IsValid` property when working with data submitted with a form that contains validation controls. Each of the validation controls includes an `IsValid` property that returns the value `True` when there is not a validation error. The `Page.IsValid` property returns the value `True` when the `IsValid` property for all of the validation controls in a page returns the value `True`.

It is easy to forget to check the `Page.IsValid` property. When you use an uplevel browser that supports JavaScript with the validation controls, you are prevented from submitting a form back to the server when there are validation errors. However, if someone requests a page using a browser that does not support JavaScript, the page is submitted back to the server even when there are validation errors.

For example, if you request the page in Listing 3.1 with a browser that does not support JavaScript and submit the form without entering form data, then the `btnSubmit_Click()`

handler executes on the server. The `Page.IsValid` property is used in Listing 3.1 to prevent downlevel browsers from displaying invalid form data.

> **WARNING**
>
> Unfortunately, I've made the mistake of forgetting to include a check of the `Page.IsValid` property several times when building applications. Because you do not normally develop a web application with a downlevel browser, you won't notice the problem described in this section until you start getting invalid data in your database tables.

Setting the Display Property

All the validation controls include a `Display` property that determines how the validation error message is rendered. This property accepts any of the following three possible values:

- ▶ Static
- ▶ Dynamic
- ▶ None

By default, the `Display` property has the value `Static`. When the `Display` property has this value, the validation error message rendered by the validation control looks like this:

```
<span id="reqProductName" style="color:Red;visibility:hidden;">(Required)</span>
```

Notice that the error message is rendered in a <span> tag that includes a Cascading Style Sheet style attribute that sets the visibility of the <span> tag to `hidden`.

If, on the other hand, you set the `Display` property to the value `Dynamic`, the error message is rendered like this:

```
<span id="reqProductName" style="color:Red;display:none;">(Required)</span>
```

In this case, a Cascading Style Sheet `display` attribute hides the contents of the <span> tag.

Both the visibility and display attributes can be used to hide text in a browser. However, text hidden with the `visibility` attribute still occupies screen real estate. Text hidden with the `display` attribute, on the other hand, does not occupy screen real estate.

In general, you should set a validation control's `Display` property to the value `Dynamic`. That way, if other content is displayed next to the validation control, the content is not pushed to the right. All modern browsers (Internet Explorer, Firefox, and Opera) support the Cascading Style Sheet `display` attribute.

The third possible value of the `Display` property is `None`. If you prefer, you can prevent the individual validation controls from displaying an error message and display the error messages with a `ValidationSummary` control. You learn how to use the `ValidationSummary` control later in this chapter.

Highlighting Validation Errors

When a validation control displays a validation error, the control displays the value of its Text property. Normally, you assign a simple text string, such as "(Required)" to the Text property. However, the Text property accepts any HTML string.

For example, the page in Listing 3.2 displays an image when you submit the form without entering a value for the First Name text field (see Figure 3.2).

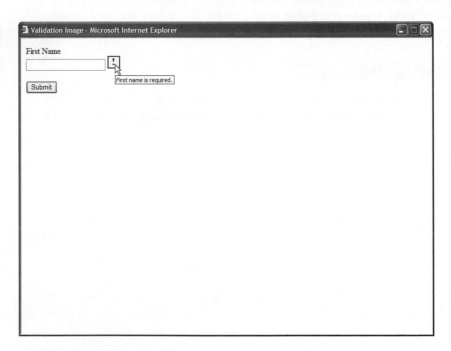

FIGURE 3.2   Displaying an image for a validation error.

LISTING 3.2   ValidationImage.aspx

```
<%@ Page Language="C#" %>
<!DOCTYPE html PUBLIC "-//W3C//DTD XHTML 1.0 Transitional//EN"
"http://www.w3.org/TR/xhtml1/DTD/xhtml1-transitional.dtd">
<html xmlns="http://www.w3.org/1999/xhtml" >
<head id="Head1" runat="server">
    <title>Validation Image</title>
</head>
<body>
    <form id="form1" runat="server">
    <div>

    <asp:Label
```

```
        id="lblFirstName"
        Text="First Name"
        AssociatedControlID="txtFirstName"
        Runat="server" />
    <br />
    <asp:TextBox
        id="txtFirstName"
        Runat="server" />
    <asp:RequiredFieldValidator
        id="reqFirstName"
        ControlToValidate="txtFirstName"
        Text="<img src='Error.gif' alt='First name is required.' />"
        Runat="server" />

    <br /><br />

    <asp:Button
        id="btnSubmit"
        Text="Submit"
        Runat="server" />

    </div>
    </form>
</body>
</html>
```

In Listing 3.2, the Text property contains an HTML <img> tag. When there is a validation error, the image represented by the <img> tag is displayed.

Another way that you can emphasize errors is to take advantage of the SetFocusOnError property that is supported by all the validation controls. When this property has the value True, the form focus is automatically shifted to the control associated with the validation control when there is a validation error.

For example, the page in Listing 3.3 contains two TextBox controls that are both validated with RequiredFieldValidator controls. Both RequiredFieldValidator controls have their SetFocusOnError properties enabled. If you provide a value for the first text field and not the second text field and submit the form, the form focus automatically shifts to the second form field.

LISTING 3.3   ShowSetFocusOnError.aspx

```
<%@ Page Language="C#" %>
<!DOCTYPE html PUBLIC "-//W3C//DTD XHTML 1.0 Transitional//EN"
"http://www.w3.org/TR/xhtml1/DTD/xhtml1-transitional.dtd">
<html xmlns="http://www.w3.org/1999/xhtml" >
<head id="Head1" runat="server">
```

LISTING 3.3   Continued

```
    <title>Show SetFocusOnError</title>
</head>
<body>
    <form id="form1" runat="server">
    <div>

    <asp:Label
        id="lblFirstName"
        Text="First Name"
        AssociatedControlID="txtFirstName"
        Runat="server" />
    <br />
    <asp:TextBox
        id="txtFirstName"
        Runat="server" />
    <asp:RequiredFieldValidator
        id="reqFirstName"
        ControlToValidate="txtFirstName"
        Text="(Required)"
        SetFocusOnError="true"
        Runat="server" />

    <br /><br />

    <asp:Label
        id="lblLastName"
        Text="Last Name"
        AssociatedControlID="txtLastName"
        Runat="server" />
    <br />
    <asp:TextBox
        id="txtLastname"
        Runat="server" />
    <asp:RequiredFieldValidator
        id="reqLastName"
        ControlToValidate="txtLastName"
        Text="(Required)"
        SetFocusOnError="true"
        Runat="server" />

     <br /><br />

     <asp:Button
        id="btnSubmit"
```

```
         Text="Submit"
         Runat="server" />

   </div>
   </form>
</body>
</html>
```

Finally, if you want to really emphasize the controls associated with a validation error, then you can take advantage of the Page.Validators property. This property exposes the collection of all the validation controls in a page. In Listing 3.4, the Page.Validators property is used to highlight each control that has a validation error (see Figure 3.3).

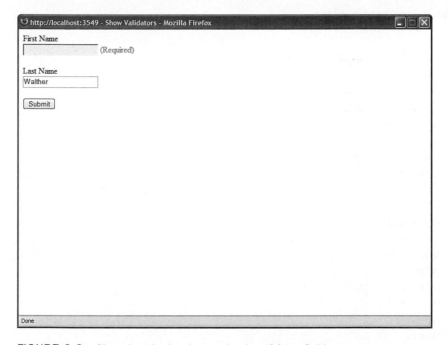

FIGURE 3.3   Changing the background color of form fields.

LISTING 3.4   ShowValidators.aspx

```
<%@ Page Language="C#" %>
<!DOCTYPE html PUBLIC "-//W3C//DTD XHTML 1.0 Transitional//EN"
"http://www.w3.org/TR/xhtml1/DTD/xhtml1-transitional.dtd">
<script runat="server">

    void Page_PreRender()
    {
        foreach (BaseValidator valControl in Page.Validators)
```

LISTING 3.4   Continued

```
        {
            WebControl assControl = (WebControl)Page.FindControl
            ➥(valControl.ControlToValidate);
            if (!valControl.IsValid)
                assControl.BackColor = System.Drawing.Color.Yellow;
            else
                assControl.BackColor = System.Drawing.Color.White;
        }
    }
</script>
<html xmlns="http://www.w3.org/1999/xhtml" >
<head id="Head1" runat="server">
    <title>Show Validators</title>
</head>
<body>
    <form id="form1" runat="server">
    <div>

    <asp:Label
        id="lblFirstName"
        Text="First Name"
        AssociatedControlID="txtFirstName"
        Runat="server" />
    <br />
    <asp:TextBox
        id="txtFirstName"
        Runat="server" />
    <asp:RequiredFieldValidator
        id="reqFirstName"
        ControlToValidate="txtFirstName"
        Text="(Required)"
        EnableClientScript="false"
        Runat="server" />

    <br /><br />

    <asp:Label
        id="lblLastName"
        Text="Last Name"
        AssociatedControlID="txtLastName"
        Runat="server" />
    <br />
    <asp:TextBox
        id="txtLastname"
```

```
            Runat="server" />
      <asp:RequiredFieldValidator
          id="reqLastName"
          ControlToValidate="txtLastName"
          Text="(Required)"
          EnableClientScript="false"
          Runat="server" />

      <br /><br />

      <asp:Button
          id="btnSubmit"
          Text="Submit"
          Runat="server" />

      </div>
      </form>
</body>
</html>
```

The `Page.Validators` property is used in the `Page_PreRender()` handler. The `IsValid` property is checked for each control in the `Page.Validators` collection. If `IsValid` returns `False`, then the control being validated by the validation control is highlighted with a yellow background color.

Using Validation Groups

In the first version of the ASP.NET Framework, there was no easy way to add two forms to the same page. If you added more than one form to a page, and both forms contained validation controls, then the validation controls in both forms were evaluated regardless of which form you submitted.

For example, imagine that you wanted to create a page that contained both a login and registration form. The login form appeared in the left column and the registration form appeared in the right column. If both forms included validation controls, then submitting the login form caused any validation controls contained in the registration form to be evaluated.

After the ASP.NET 2.0 Framework, you no longer face this limitation. The ASP.NET 2.0 Framework introduces the idea of validation groups. A validation group enables you to group related form fields together.

For example, the page in Listing 3.5 contains both a login and registration form and both forms contain independent sets of validation controls.

LISTING 3.5   ShowValidationGroups.aspx

```
<%@ Page Language="C#" %>
<!DOCTYPE html PUBLIC "-//W3C//DTD XHTML 1.0 Transitional//EN"
"http://www.w3.org/TR/xhtml1/DTD/xhtml1-transitional.dtd">
<script runat="server">

    void btnLogin_Click(Object sender, EventArgs e)
    {
        if (Page.IsValid)
            lblLoginResult.Text = "Log in successful!";
    }

    void btnRegister_Click(Object sender, EventArgs e)
    {
        if (Page.IsValid)
            lblRegisterResult.Text = "Registration successful!";
    }
</script>
<html xmlns="http://www.w3.org/1999/xhtml" >
<head id="Head1" runat="server">
    <style type="text/css">
        html
        {
            background-color:silver;
        }
        .column
        {
            float:left;
            width:300px;
            margin-left:10px;
            background-color:white;
            border:solid 1px black;
            padding:10px;
        }

    </style>
    <title>Show Validation Groups</title>
</head>
<body>
    <form id="form1" runat="server">

    <div class="column">
    <fieldset>
    <legend>Login</legend>
    <p>
```

```
Please log in to our Website.
</p>
<asp:Label
    id="lblUserName"
    Text="User Name:"
    AssociatedControlID="txtUserName"
    Runat="server" />
<br />
<asp:TextBox
    id="txtUserName"
    Runat="server" />
<asp:RequiredFieldValidator
    id="reqUserName"
    ControlToValidate="txtUserName"
    Text="(Required)"
    ValidationGroup="LoginGroup"
    Runat="server" />
<br /><br />
<asp:Label
    id="lblPassword"
    Text="Password:"
    AssociatedControlID="txtPassword"
    Runat="server" />
<br />
<asp:TextBox
    id="txtPassword"
    TextMode="Password"
    Runat="server" />
<asp:RequiredFieldValidator
    id="reqPassword"
    ControlToValidate="txtPassword"
    Text="(Required)"
    ValidationGroup="LoginGroup"
    Runat="server" />
<br /><br />
<asp:Button
    id="btnLogin"
    Text="Login"
    ValidationGroup="LoginGroup"
    Runat="server" OnClick="btnLogin_Click" />
</fieldset>

<asp:Label
    id="lblLoginResult"
    Runat="server" />
```

3

LISTING 3.5   Continued

```
    </div>

    <div class="column">
    <fieldset>
    <legend>Register</legend>
    <p>
    If you do not have a User Name, please
    register at our Website.
    </p>
    <asp:Label
        id="lblFirstName"
        Text="First Name:"
        AssociatedControlID="txtFirstName"
        Runat="server" />
    <br />
    <asp:TextBox
        id="txtFirstName"
        Runat="server" />
    <asp:RequiredFieldValidator
        id="reqFirstName"
        ControlToValidate="txtFirstName"
        Text="(Required)"
        ValidationGroup="RegisterGroup"
        Runat="server" />
    <br /><br />
    <asp:Label
        id="lblLastName"
        Text="Last Name:"
        AssociatedControlID="txtLastName"
        Runat="server" />
    <br />
    <asp:TextBox
        id="txtLastName"
        Runat="server" />
    <asp:RequiredFieldValidator
        id="reqLastName"
        ControlToValidate="txtLastName"
        Text="(Required)"
        ValidationGroup="RegisterGroup"
        Runat="server" />
    <br /><br />
    <asp:Button
        id="btnRegister"
        Text="Register"
        ValidationGroup="RegisterGroup"
```

```
        Runat="server" OnClick="btnRegister_Click" />
    </fieldset>

    <asp:Label
        id="lblRegisterResult"
        Runat="server" />

    </div>

    </form>
</body>
</html>
```

Notice that the validation controls and the button controls all include `ValidationGroup` properties. The controls associated with the login form all have the value `"LoginGroup"` assigned to their `ValidationGroup` properties. The controls associated with the register form all have the value `"RegisterGroup"` assigned to their `ValidationGroup` properties.

Because the form fields are grouped into different validation groups, you can submit the two forms independently. Submitting the Login form does not trigger the validation controls in the Register form (see Figure 3.4).

You can assign any string to the `ValidationGroup` property. The only purpose of the string is to associate different controls in a form together into different groups.

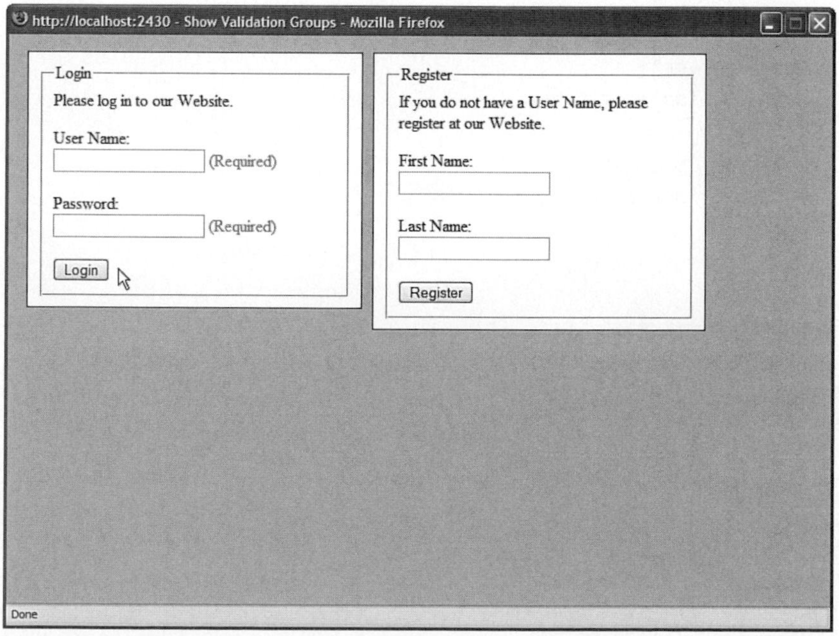

FIGURE 3.4   Using validation groups.

NOTE

Using validation groups is particularly important when working with Web Parts because multiple Web Parts with different forms might be added to the same page.

Disabling Validation

All the button controls—the `Button`, `LinkButton`, and `ImageButton` control—include a `CausesValidation` property. If you assign the value `False` to this property, then clicking the button bypasses any validation in the page.

Bypassing validation is useful when creating a Cancel button. For example, the page in Listing 3.6 includes a Cancel button that redirects the user back to the `Default.aspx` page.

LISTING 3.6   ShowDisableValidation.aspx

```
<%@ Page Language="C#" %>
<!DOCTYPE html PUBLIC "-//W3C//DTD XHTML 1.0 Transitional//EN"
"http://www.w3.org/TR/xhtml1/DTD/xhtml1-transitional.dtd">
<script runat="server">

    void btnCancel_Click(Object sender, EventArgs e)
    {
        Response.Redirect("~/Default.aspx");
    }
</script>
<html xmlns="http://www.w3.org/1999/xhtml" >
<head id="Head1" runat="server">
    <title>Show Disable Validation</title>
</head>
<body>
    <form id="form1" runat="server">
    <div>

    <asp:Label
        id="lblFirstName"
        Text="First Name:"
        AssociatedControlID="txtFirstName"
        Runat="server" />
    <asp:TextBox
        id="txtFirstName"
        Runat="server" />
    <asp:RequiredFieldValidator
        id="reqFirstName"
        ControlToValidate="txtFirstName"
        Text="(Required)"
        Runat="server" />
```

```
            <br /><br />
            <asp:Button
                id="btnSubmit"
                Text="Submit"
                Runat="server" />
            <asp:Button
                id="btnCancel"
                Text="Cancel"
                OnClick="btnCancel_Click"
                CausesValidation="false"
                Runat="server" />

            </div>
            </form>
</body>
</html>
```

Notice that the Cancel button in Listing 3.6 includes the CausesValidation property with the value False. If the button did not include this property, then the RequiredFieldValidator control would prevent you from submitting the form when you clicked the Cancel button.

Using the RequiredFieldValidator Control

The RequiredFieldValidator control enables you to require a user to enter a value into a form field before submitting the form. You must set two important properties when using the RequiredFieldValdiator control:

▶ **ControlToValidate**—The ID of the form field being validated.

▶ **Text**—The error message displayed when validation fails.

The page in Listing 3.7 illustrates how you can use the RequiredFieldValidator control to require a user to enter both a first and last name (see Figure 3.5).

LISTING 3.7   ShowRequiredFieldValidator.aspx

```
<%@ Page Language="C#" %>
<!DOCTYPE html PUBLIC "-//W3C//DTD XHTML 1.0 Transitional//EN"
"http://www.w3.org/TR/xhtml1/DTD/xhtml1-transitional.dtd">
<html xmlns="http://www.w3.org/1999/xhtml" >
<head id="Head1" runat="server">
    <title>Show RequiredFieldValidator</title>
</head>
<body>
    <form id="form1" runat="server">
    <div>
```

LISTING 3.7   Continued

```
    <asp:Label
        id="lblFirstName"
        Text="First Name:"
        AssociatedControlID="txtFirstName"
        Runat="server" />
    <br />
    <asp:TextBox
        id="txtFirstName"
        Runat="server" />
    <asp:RequiredFieldValidator
        id="reqFirstName"
        ControlToValidate="txtFirstName"
        Text="(Required)"
        Runat="server" />

    <br /><br />

    <asp:Label
        id="lblLastName"
        Text="Last Name:"
        AssociatedControlID="txtLastName"
        Runat="server" />
    <br />
    <asp:TextBox
        id="txtLastName"
        Runat="server" />
    <asp:RequiredFieldValidator
        id="reqLastName"
        ControlToValidate="txtLastName"
        Text="(Required)"
        Runat="server" />

    <br /><br />

    <asp:Button
        id="btnSubmit"
        Text="Submit"
        Runat="server" />

    </div>
    </form>
</body>
</html>
```

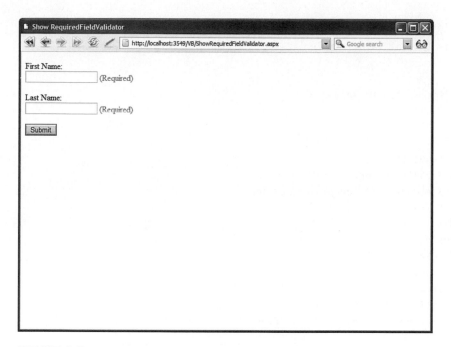

FIGURE 3.5   Requiring a user to enter form field values.

By default, the RequiredFieldValidator checks for a nonempty string (spaces don't count). If you enter anything into the form field associated with the RequiredFieldValidator, then the RequiredFieldValidator does not display its validation error message.

You can use the RequiredFieldValidator control's InitialValue property to specify a default value other than an empty string. For example, the page in Listing 3.8 uses a RequiredFieldValidator to validate a DropDownList control (see Figure 3.6).

LISTING 3.8   ShowInitialValue.aspx

```
<%@ Page Language="C#" %>
<!DOCTYPE html PUBLIC "-//W3C//DTD XHTML 1.0 Transitional//EN"
"http://www.w3.org/TR/xhtml1/DTD/xhtml1-transitional.dtd">
<script runat="server">

    void btnSubmit_Click(Object sender, EventArgs e)
    {
        if (Page.IsValid)
            lblResult.Text = dropFavoriteColor.SelectedValue;
    }
</script>
<html xmlns="http://www.w3.org/1999/xhtml" >
<head id="Head1" runat="server">
```

LISTING 3.8   Continued

```
    <title>Show Initial Value</title>
</head>
<body>
    <form id="form1" runat="server">
    <div>

    <asp:Label
        id="lblFavoriteColor"
        Text="Favorite Color:"
        AssociatedControlID="dropFavoriteColor"
        Runat="server" />
    <br />
    <asp:DropDownList
        id="dropFavoriteColor"
        Runat="server">
        <asp:ListItem Text="Select Color" Value="none" />
        <asp:ListItem Text="Red" Value="Red" />
        <asp:ListItem Text="Blue" Value="Blue" />
        <asp:ListItem Text="Green" Value="Green" />
    </asp:DropDownList>
    <asp:RequiredFieldValidator
        id="reqFavoriteColor"
        Text="(Required)"
        InitialValue="none"
        ControlToValidate="dropFavoriteColor"
        Runat="server" />

    <br /><br />

    <asp:Button
        id="btnSubmit"
        Text="Submit"
        Runat="server" OnClick="btnSubmit_Click" />

    <hr />

    <asp:Label
        id="lblResult"
        Runat="server" />

    </div>
    </form>
</body>
</html>
```

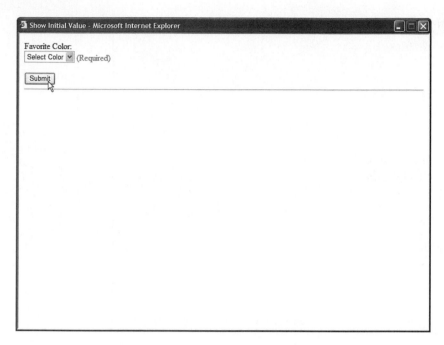

FIGURE 3.6   Using a RequiredFieldValidator with a DropDownList control.

The first list item displayed by the DropDownList control displays the text "Select Color".
If you submit the form without selecting a color from the DropDownList control, then a
validation error message is displayed.

Notice that the RequiredFieldValidator control includes an InitialValue property. The
value of the first list from the DropDownList control is assigned to this property.

Using the RangeValidator Control

The RangeValidator control enables you to check whether the value of a form field falls
between a certain minimum and maximum value. You must set five properties when
using this control:

- ▶ **ControlToValidate**—The ID of the form field being validated.

- ▶ **Text**—The error message displayed when validation fails.

- ▶ **MinimumValue**—The minimum value of the validation range.

- ▶ **MaximumValue**—The maximum value of the validation range.

- ▶ **Type**—The type of comparison to perform. Possible values are String, Integer,
  Double, Date, and Currency.

For example, the page in Listing 3.9 includes a RangeValidator that validates an age form
field. If you do not enter an age between 5 and 100, then a validation error is displayed
(see Figure 3.7).

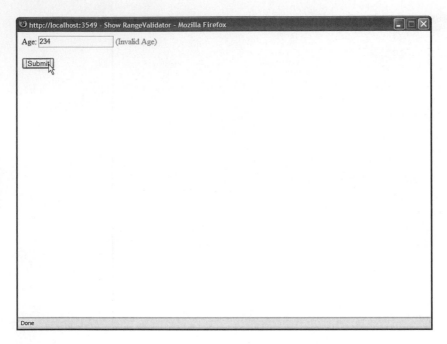

FIGURE 3.7   Validating a form field against a range of values.

LISTING 3.9   `ShowRangeValidator.aspx`

```
<%@ Page Language="C#" %>
<!DOCTYPE html PUBLIC "-//W3C//DTD XHTML 1.0 Transitional//EN"
"http://www.w3.org/TR/xhtml1/DTD/xhtml1-transitional.dtd">
<html xmlns="http://www.w3.org/1999/xhtml" >
<head id="Head1" runat="server">
    <title>Show RangeValidator</title>
</head>
<body>
    <form id="form1" runat="server">
    <div>

    <asp:Label
        id="lblAge"
        Text="Age:"
        AssociatedControlID="txtAge"
        Runat="server" />
    <asp:TextBox
        id="txtAge"
        Runat="server" />
    <asp:RangeValidator
```

```
            id="reqAge"
            ControlToValidate="txtAge"
            Text="(Invalid Age)"
            MinimumValue="5"
            MaximumValue="100"
            Type="Integer"
            Runat="server" />

    <br /><br />

    <asp:Button
         id="btnSubmit"
         Text="Submit"
         Runat="server" />

    </div>
    </form>
</body>
</html>
```

If you submit the form in Listing 3.9 with an age less than 5 or greater than 100, then the validation error message is displayed. The validation message is also displayed if you enter a value that is not a number. If the value entered into the form field cannot be converted into the data type represented by the `RangeValidator` control's `Type` property, then the error message is displayed.

If you don't enter any value into the age field and submit the form, no error message is displayed. If you want to require a user to enter a value, you must associate a `RequiredFieldValidator` with the form field.

Don't forget to set the `Type` property when using the `RangeValidator` control. By default, the `Type` property has the value `String`, and the `RangeValidator` performs a string comparison to determine whether a values falls between the minimum and maximum value.

Using the `CompareValidator` Control

The `CompareValidator` control enables you to perform three different types of validation tasks. You can use the `CompareValidator` to perform a data type check. In other words, you can use the control to determine whether a user has entered the proper type of value into a form field, such as a date in a birth date field.

You also can use the `CompareValidator` to compare the value entered into a form field against a fixed value. For example, if you are building an auction website, you can use the `CompareValidator` to check whether a new minimum bid is greater than the previous minimum bid.

Finally, you can use the CompareValidator to compare the value of one form field against another. For example, you use the CompareValidator to check whether the value entered into the meeting start date is less than the value entered into the meeting end date.

The CompareValidator has six important properties:

- ▶ **ControlToValidate**—The ID of the form field being validated.

- ▶ **Text**—The error message displayed when validation fails.

- ▶ **Type**—The type of value being compared. Possible values are String, Integer, Double, Date, and Currency.

- ▶ **Operator**—The type of comparison to perform. Possible values are DataTypeCheck, Equal, GreaterThan, GreaterThanEqual, LessThan, LessThanEqual, and NotEqual.

- ▶ **ValueToCompare**—The fixed value against which to compare.

- ▶ **ControlToCompare**—The ID of a control against which to compare.

The page in Listing 3.10 illustrates how you can use the CompareValidator to perform a data type check. The page contains a birth date field. If you enter a value that is not a date, then the validation error message is displayed (see Figure 3.8).

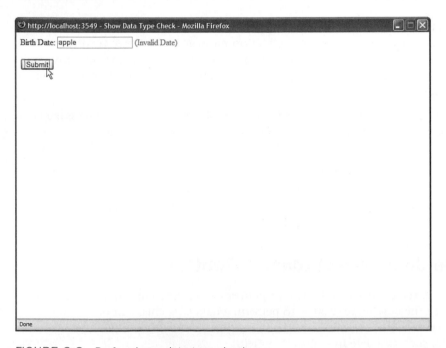

FIGURE 3.8   Performing a data type check.

LISTING 3.10   `ShowDataTypeCheck.aspx`

```
<%@ Page Language="C#" %>
<!DOCTYPE html PUBLIC "-//W3C//DTD XHTML 1.0 Transitional//EN"
"http://www.w3.org/TR/xhtml1/DTD/xhtml1-transitional.dtd">
<html xmlns="http://www.w3.org/1999/xhtml" >
<head id="Head1" runat="server">
    <title>Show Data Type Check</title>
</head>
<body>
    <form id="form1" runat="server">
    <div>

    <asp:Label
        id="lblBirthDate"
        Text="Birth Date:"
        AssociatedControlID="txtBirthDate"
        Runat="server" />
    <asp:TextBox
        id="txtBirthDate"
        Runat="server" />
    <asp:CompareValidator
        id="cmpBirthDate"
        Text="(Invalid Date)"
        ControlToValidate="txtBirthDate"
        Type="Date"
        Operator="DataTypeCheck"
        Runat="server" />

    <br /><br />

    <asp:Button
        id="btnSubmit"
        Text="Submit"
        Runat="server" />

    </div>
    </form>
</body>
</html>
```

Notice that the page in Listing 3.10 contains a `CompareValidator` control. Its `Type` property has the value `Date`, and its `Operator` property has the value `DataTypeCheck`. If you enter a value other than a date into the birth date field, the validation error message is displayed.

WARNING

An important limitation of the `CompareValidator` concerns how it performs a data type check. You cannot enter a long date into the form in Listing 3.10 (for example, December 25, 1966). You must enter a short date (for example, 12/25/1966). When validating currency amounts, you cannot enter the currency symbol. If these limitations concern you, you can use either the `RegularExpression` or `CustomValidator` controls to perform a more flexible data type check.

You can also use the `CompareValidator` to perform a comparison against a fixed value. For example, the page in Listing 3.11 uses a `CompareValidator` to check whether a date entered into a form field is greater than the current date (see Figure 3.9).

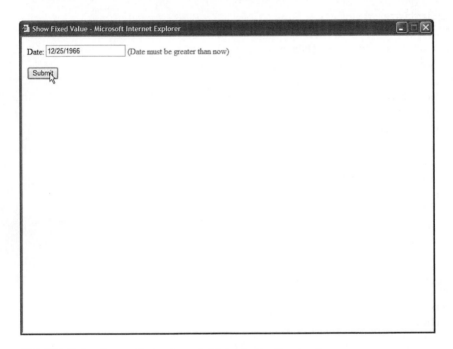

FIGURE 3.9   Comparing a form field against a fixed value.

LISTING 3.11   `ShowFixedValue.aspx`

```
<%@ Page Language="C#" %>
<!DOCTYPE html PUBLIC "-//W3C//DTD XHTML 1.0 Transitional//EN"
"http://www.w3.org/TR/xhtml1/DTD/xhtml1-transitional.dtd">
<script runat="server">

    void Page_Load()
    {
```

```
                cmpDate.ValueToCompare = DateTime.Now.ToString("d");
        }
</script>
<html xmlns="http://www.w3.org/1999/xhtml" >
<head id="Head1" runat="server">
    <title>Show Fixed Value</title>
</head>
<body>
    <form id="form1" runat="server">
    <div>

    <asp:Label
        id="lblDate"
        Text="Date:"
        AssociatedControlID="txtDate"
        Runat="server" />
    <asp:TextBox
        id="txtDate"
        Runat="server" />
    <asp:CompareValidator
        id="cmpDate"
        Text="(Date must be greater than now)"
        ControlToValidate="txtDate"
        Type="Date"
        Operator="GreaterThan"
        Runat="server" />

    <br /><br />

    <asp:Button
        id="btnSubmit"
        Text="Submit"
        Runat="server" />

    </div>
    </form>
</body>
</html>
```

Finally, you can use a `CompareValidator` to compare the value of one form field against another form field. The page in Listing 3.12 contains a meeting start date and meeting end date field. If you enter a value into the first field that is greater than the second field, a validation error is displayed (see Figure 3.10).

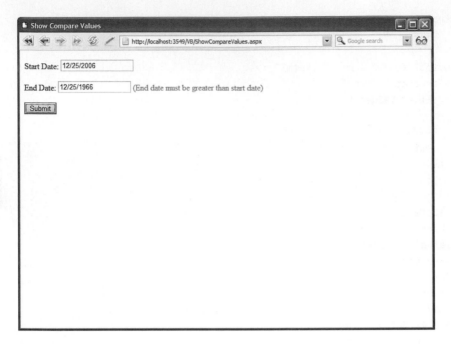

FIGURE 3.10   Comparing two form fields.

LISTING 3.12   ShowCompareValues.aspx

```
<%@ Page Language="C#" %>
<!DOCTYPE html PUBLIC "-//W3C//DTD XHTML 1.0 Transitional//EN"
"http://www.w3.org/TR/xhtml1/DTD/xhtml1-transitional.dtd">
<html xmlns="http://www.w3.org/1999/xhtml" >
<head id="Head1" runat="server">
    <title>Show Compare Values</title>
</head>
<body>
    <form id="form1" runat="server">
    <div>

    <asp:Label
        id="lblStartDate"
        Text="Start Date:"
        Runat="server" />
    <asp:TextBox
        id="txtStartDate"
        Runat="server" />
```

```
    <br /><br />

    <asp:Label
        id="lblEndDate"
        Text="End Date:"
        Runat="server" />
    <asp:TextBox
        id="txtEndDate"
        Runat="server" />
    <asp:CompareValidator
        id="cmpDate"
        Text="(End date must be greater than start date)"
        ControlToValidate="txtEndDate"
        ControlToCompare="txtStartDate"
        Type="Date"
        Operator="GreaterThan"
        Runat="server" />

    <br /><br />

    <asp:Button
        id="btnSubmit"
        Text="Submit"
        Runat="server" />

    </div>
    </form>
</body>
</html>
```

Just like the RangeValidator, the CompareValidator does not display an error if you don't enter a value into the form field being validated. If you want to require that a user enter a value, then you must associate a RequiredFieldValidator control with the field.

Using the RegularExpressionValidator Control

The RegularExpressionValidator control enables you to compare the value of a form field against a regular expression. You can use a regular expression to represent string patterns such as email addresses, Social Security numbers, phone numbers, dates, currency amounts, and product codes.

For example, the page in Listing 3.13 enables you to validate an email address (see Figure 3.11).

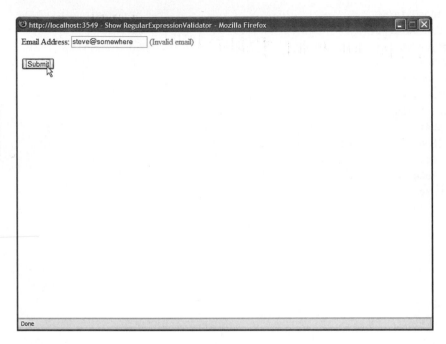

FIGURE 3.11   Validating an email address.

LISTING 3.13   ShowRegularExpressionValidator.aspx

```
<%@ Page Language="C#" %>
<!DOCTYPE html PUBLIC "-//W3C//DTD XHTML 1.0 Transitional//EN"
"http://www.w3.org/TR/xhtml1/DTD/xhtml1-transitional.dtd">
<html xmlns="http://www.w3.org/1999/xhtml" >
<head id="Head1" runat="server">
    <title>Show RegularExpressionValidator</title>
</head>
<body>
    <form id="form1" runat="server">
    <div>

    <asp:Label
        id="lblEmail"
        Text="Email Address:"
        AssociatedControlID="txtEmail"
        Runat="server" />
    <asp:TextBox
        id="txtEmail"
```

```
        Runat="server" />
    <asp:RegularExpressionValidator
        id="regEmail"
        ControlToValidate="txtEmail"
        Text="(Invalid email)"
        ValidationExpression="\w+([-+.']\w+)*@\w+([-.]\w+)*\.\w+([-.]\w+)*"
        Runat="server" />

    <br /><br />

    <asp:Button
        id="btnSubmit"
        Text="Submit"
        Runat="server" />

    </div>
    </form>
</body>
</html>
```

The regular expression is assigned to the `RegularExpressionValidator` control's `ValidationExpression` property. It looks like this:

```
\w+([-+.']\w+)*@\w+([-.]\w+)*\.\w+([-.]\w+)*
```

Regular expressions are not fun to read. This pattern matches a simple email address. The `\w` expression represents any non-whitespace character. Therefore, roughly, this regular expression matches an email address that contains non-whitespace characters, followed by an @ sign, followed by non-whitespace characters, followed by a period, followed by more non-whitespace characters.

NOTE

There are huge collections of regular expression patterns living on the Internet. My favorite website for finding regular expressions is http://regexlib.com/.

Just like the other validation controls, the `RegularExpressionValidator` doesn't validate a form field unless the form field contains a value. To make a form field required, you must associate a `RequiredFieldValidator` control with the form field.

VISUAL WEB DEVELOPER NOTE

If you open the property sheet for a `RegularExpressionValidator` control in Design view and select the `ValidationExpression` property, you can view a number of canned regular expressions. Visual Web Developer includes regular expressions for patterns such as email addresses, phone numbers, and Social Security numbers.

Using the `CustomValidator` Control

If none of the other validation controls perform the type of validation that you need, you can always use the `CustomValidator` control. You can associate a custom validation function with the `CustomValidator` control.

The `CustomValidator` control has three important properties:

- ▶ **`ControlToValidate`**—The ID of the form field being validated.

- ▶ **`Text`**—The error message displayed when validation fails.

- ▶ **`ClientValidationFunction`**—The name of a client-side function used to perform client-side validation.

The `CustomValidator` also supports one event:

- ▶ **`ServerValidate`**—This event is raised when the `CustomValidator` performs validation.

You associate your custom validation function with the `CustomValidator` control by handling the `ServerValidate` event.

For example, imagine that you want to validate the length of a string entered into a form field. You want to ensure that a user does not enter more than 10 characters into a multiline `TextBox` control. The page in Listing 3.14 contains an event handler for a `CustomValidator` control's `ServerValidate` event, which checks the string's length.

LISTING 3.14   ShowCustomValidator.aspx

```
<%@ Page Language="C#" %>
<!DOCTYPE html PUBLIC "-//W3C//DTD XHTML 1.0 Transitional//EN"
"http://www.w3.org/TR/xhtml1/DTD/xhtml1-transitional.dtd">
<script runat="server">

    void valComments_ServerValidate(Object source, ServerValidateEventArgs args)
    {
        if (args.Value.Length > 10)
            args.IsValid = false;
        else
            args.IsValid = true;
    }
</script>
<html xmlns="http://www.w3.org/1999/xhtml" >
<head id="Head1" runat="server">
    <title>Show CustomValidator</title>
</head>
<body>
    <form id="form1" runat="server">
    <div>
```

```
<asp:Label
    id="lblComments"
    Text="Comments:"
    AssociatedControlID="txtComments"
    Runat="server" />
<br />
<asp:TextBox
    id="txtComments"
    TextMode="MultiLine"
    Columns="30"
    Rows="5"
    Runat="server" />
<asp:CustomValidator
    id="valComments"
    ControlToValidate="txtComments"
    Text="(Comments must be less than 10 characters)"
    OnServerValidate="valComments_ServerValidate"
    Runat="server" />

<br /><br />

<asp:Button
    id="btnSubmit"
    Text="Submit"
    Runat="server" />

    </div>
    </form>
</body>
</html>
```

The second parameter passed to the ServerValidate event handler is an instance of the ServerValidateEventArgs class. This class has two properties:

▶ **Value**—Represents the value of the form field being validated.

▶ **IsValid**—Represents whether validation fails or succeeds.

▶ **ValidateEmptyText**—Represents whether validation is performed when the form field being validated does not contain a value.

In Listing 3.14, if the string represented by the Value property is longer than 10 characters, then the value False is assigned to the IsValid property and validation fails. Otherwise, the value True is assigned to the IsValid property and the input field passes the validation check (see Figure 3.12).

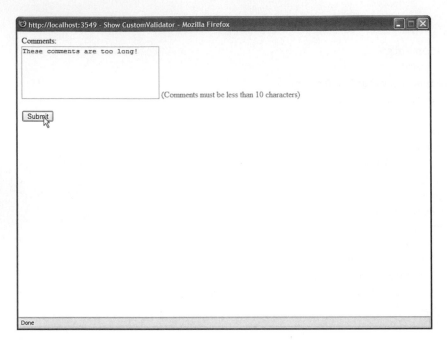

FIGURE 3.12   Validating field length with the `CustomValidator` control.

The `ServerValidate` event handler in Listing 3.14 is a server-side function. Therefore, validation does not occur until the page is posted back to the web server. If you want to perform validation on both the client (browser) and server, then you need to supply a client-side validation function.

WARNING

If you don't associate a client validation function with a `CustomValidator` control, then the `CustomValidator` doesn't render an error message until you post the page back to the server. Because the other validation controls prevent a page from being posted if the page contains any validation errors, you won't see the error message rendered by the `CustomValidator` control until you pass every other validation check in a page.

The page in Listing 3.15 illustrates how you can associate a client-side validation function with the `CustomValidator` control. This page also checks the length of the string entered into a `TextBox` control. However, it checks the length on both the browser and server.

LISTING 3.15   ShowCustomValidatorJS.aspx

```
<%@ Page Language="C#" %>
<!DOCTYPE html PUBLIC "-//W3C//DTD XHTML 1.0 Transitional//EN"
"http://www.w3.org/TR/xhtml1/DTD/xhtml1-transitional.dtd">
```

```
<script runat="server">

    void valComments_ServerValidate(Object source, ServerValidateEventArgs args)
    {
        if (args.Value.Length > 10)
            args.IsValid = false;
        else
            args.IsValid = true;
    }
</script>
<html xmlns="http://www.w3.org/1999/xhtml" >
<head id="Head1" runat="server">
    <script type="text/javascript">

    function valComments_ClientValidate(source, args)
    {
        if (args.Value.length > 10)
            args.IsValid = false;
        else
            args.IsValid = true;
    }

    </script>
    <title>Show CustomValidator with JavaScript</title>
</head>
<body>
    <form id="form1" runat="server">
    <div>

    <asp:Label
        id="lblComments"
        Text="Comments:"
        AssociatedControlID="txtComments"
        Runat="server" />
    <br />
    <asp:TextBox
        id="txtComments"
        TextMode="MultiLine"
        Columns="30"
        Rows="5"
        Runat="server" />
    <asp:CustomValidator
        id="valComments"
        ControlToValidate="txtComments"
        Text="(Comments must be less than 10 characters)"
        OnServerValidate="valComments_ServerValidate"
```

LISTING 3.15   Continued

```
        ClientValidationFunction="valComments_ClientValidate"
        Runat="server" />

    <br /><br />

    <asp:Button
        id="btnSubmit"
        Text="Submit"
        Runat="server" />

    </div>
    </form>
</body>
</html>
```

Notice that the CustomValidator control in Listing 3.15 includes a ClientValidationFunction property. This property contains the name of a JavaScript function defined in the page's <head> tag.

The JavaScript validation function accepts the same two parameters as the server-side validation function. The first parameter represents the CustomValidator control, and the second parameter represents an object that includes both a Value and an IsValid property. The client-side function is nearly identical to the server-side function (with the important difference that it is written in JavaScript).

Unlike the RangeValidator, CompareValidator, and RegularExpressionValidator controls, you can validate a form field with the CustomValidator control even when the form field is left blank. The CustomValidator control includes a property named the ValidateEmptyText property. You can use this property to cause the CustomValidator control to validate a form field even when the user hasn't entered a value into the form field. For example, the page in Listing 3.16 contains a TextBox that requires a product code that contains exactly four characters.

LISTING 3.16   ShowValidateEmptyText.aspx

```
<%@ Page Language="C#" %>
<!DOCTYPE html PUBLIC "-//W3C//DTD XHTML 1.0 Transitional//EN"
"http://www.w3.org/TR/xhtml1/DTD/xhtml1-transitional.dtd">
<script runat="server">

    void valProductCode_ServerValidate(Object source, ServerValidateEventArgs args)
    {
        if (args.Value.Length == 4)
            args.IsValid = true;
```

```
        else
             args.IsValid = false;
    }
</script>
<html xmlns="http://www.w3.org/1999/xhtml" >
<head id="Head1" runat="server">
    <title>Show Validate Empty Text</title>
</head>
<body>
    <form id="form1" runat="server">
    <div>

    <asp:Label
        id="lblProductCode"
        Text="Product Code:"
        AssociatedControlID="txtProductCode"
        Runat="server" />
    <br />
    <asp:TextBox
        id="txtProductCode"
        Runat="server" />
    <asp:CustomValidator
        id="valProductCode"
        ControlToValidate="txtProductCode"
        Text="(Invalid product code)"
        ValidateEmptyText="true"
        OnServerValidate="valProductCode_ServerValidate"
        Runat="server" />

    <br /><br />

    <asp:Button
        id="btnSubmit"
        Text="Submit"
        Runat="server" />

    </div>
    </form>
</body>
</html>
```

Notice that the CustomValidator control in Listing 3.16 includes a ValidateEmptyText property which has the value True. If the ValidateEmptyText property was not included, and you submitted the form without entering any data, then no validation error would be displayed.

Finally, unlike the other validation controls, you are not required to associate the CustomValidator control with any form field. In other words, you don't need to include a ControlToValidate property.

For example, the page in Listing 3.17 contains a timed test. If you don't answer the question within five seconds, then the CustomValidator control displays a validation error message (see Figure 3.13).

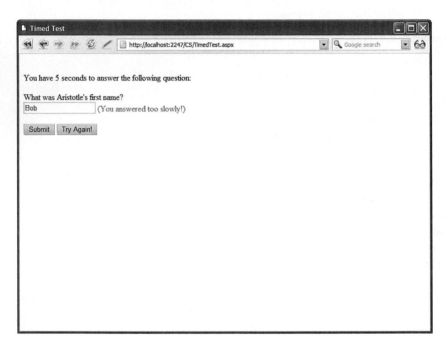

FIGURE 3.13   Performing validation against no particular field.

LISTING 3.17   TimedTest.aspx

```
<%@ Page Language="C#" %>
<!DOCTYPE html PUBLIC "-//W3C//DTD XHTML 1.0 Transitional//EN"
"http://www.w3.org/TR/xhtml1/DTD/xhtml1-transitional.dtd">
<script runat="server">

    void Page_Load()
    {
        if (!Page.IsPostBack)
            ResetStartTime();
    }

    void btnAgain_Click(Object sender, EventArgs e)
    {
```

```
            ResetStartTime();
        }

        void ResetStartTime()
        {
            Session["StartTime"] = DateTime.Now;
        }


        void valAnswer_ServerValidate(Object source, ServerValidateEventArgs args)
        {
            DateTime startTime = (DateTime)Session["StartTime"];
            if (startTime.AddSeconds(5) > DateTime.Now)
                args.IsValid = true;
            else
                args.IsValid = false;
        }
</script>
<html xmlns="http://www.w3.org/1999/xhtml" >
<head id="Head1" runat="server">
    <title>Timed Test</title>
</head>
<body>
    <form id="form1" runat="server">
    <div>


    <p>
    You have 5 seconds to answer the following question:
    </p>

    <asp:Label
        id="lblQuestion"
        Text="What was Aristotle's first name?"
        AssociatedControlID="txtAnswer"
        Runat="server" />
    <br />
    <asp:TextBox
        id="txtAnswer"
        Runat="server" />
    <asp:CustomValidator
        id="valAnswer"
        Text="(You answered too slowly!)"
        OnServerValidate="valAnswer_ServerValidate"
        Runat="server"   />

    <br /><br />
```

LISTING 3.17   Continued

```
    <asp:Button
        id="btnSubmit"
        Text="Submit"
        Runat="server" />

    <asp:Button
        id="btnAgain"
        Text="Try Again!"
        CausesValidation="false"
        OnClick="btnAgain_Click"
        Runat="server" />

    </div>
    </form>
</body>
</html>
```

Using the `ValidationSummary` Control

The `ValidationSummary` control enables you to display a list of all the validation errors in a page in one location. This control is particularly useful when working with large forms. If a user enters the wrong value for a form field located toward the end of the page, then the user might never see the error message. If you use the `ValidationSummary` control, however, you can always display a list of errors at the top of the form.

You might have noticed that each of the validation controls includes an `ErrorMessage` property. We have not been using the `ErrorMessage` property to represent the validation error message. Instead, we have used the `Text` property.

The distinction between the `ErrorMessage` and `Text` property is that any message that you assign to the `ErrorMessage` property appears in the `ValidationSummary` control, and any message that you assign to the `Text` property appears in the body of the page. Normally, you want to keep the error message for the `Text` property short (for example, `"Required!"`). The message assigned to the `ErrorMessage` property, on the other hand, should identify the form field that has the error (for example, `"First name is required!"`).

> **NOTE**
>
> If you don't assign a value to the `Text` property, then the value of the `ErrorMessage` property is displayed in both the `ValidationSummary` control and the body of the page.

The page in Listing 3.18 illustrates how you can use the `ValidationSummary` control to display a summary of error messages (see Figure 3.14).

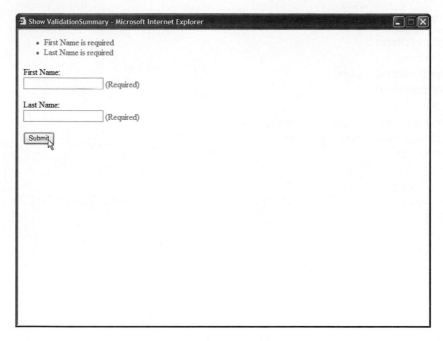

FIGURE 3.14   Displaying a validation summary.

LISTING 3.18   ShowValidationSummary.aspx

```
<%@ Page Language="C#" %>
<!DOCTYPE html PUBLIC "-//W3C//DTD XHTML 1.0 Transitional//EN"
"http://www.w3.org/TR/xhtml1/DTD/xhtml1-transitional.dtd">
<html xmlns="http://www.w3.org/1999/xhtml" >
<head id="Head1" runat="server">
    <title>Show ValidationSummary</title>
</head>
<body>
    <form id="form1" runat="server">
    <div>

    <asp:ValidationSummary
        id="ValidationSummary1"
        Runat="server" />

    <asp:Label
        id="lblFirstName"
        Text="First Name:"
        AssociatedControlID="txtFirstName"
        Runat="server" />
    <br />
    <asp:TextBox
```

LISTING 3.18   Continued

```
            id="txtFirstName"
            Runat="server" />
    <asp:RequiredFieldValidator
            id="reqFirstName"
            Text="(Required)"
            ErrorMessage="First Name is required"
            ControlToValidate="txtFirstName"
            Runat="server" />

    <br /><br />

    <asp:Label
            id="lblLastName"
            Text="Last Name:"
            AssociatedControlID="txtLastName"
            Runat="server" />
    <br />
    <asp:TextBox
            id="txtLastName"
            Runat="server" />
    <asp:RequiredFieldValidator
            id="reqLastName"
            Text="(Required)"
            ErrorMessage="Last Name is required"
            ControlToValidate="txtLastName"
            Runat="server" />

    <br /><br />

    <asp:Button
            id="btnSubmit"
            Text="Submit"
            Runat="server" />

    </div>
    </form>
</body>
</html>
```

If you submit the form in Listing 3.18 without entering a value for the first and last name, then validation error messages appear in both the body of the page and in the ValidationSummary control.

The ValidationSummary control supports the following properties:

- ▶ **DisplayMode**—Enables you to specify how the error messages are formatted. Possible values are BulletList, List, and SingleParagraph.

- ▶ **HeaderText**—Enables you to display header text above the validation summary.

- ▶ **ShowMessageBox**—Enables you to display a popup alert box.

- ▶ **ShowSummary**—Enables you to hide the validation summary in the page.

If you set the ShowMessageBox property to the value True and the ShowSummary property to the value False, then you can display the validation summary only within a popup alert box. For example, the page in Listing 3.19 displays a validation summary in an alert box (see Figure 3.15).

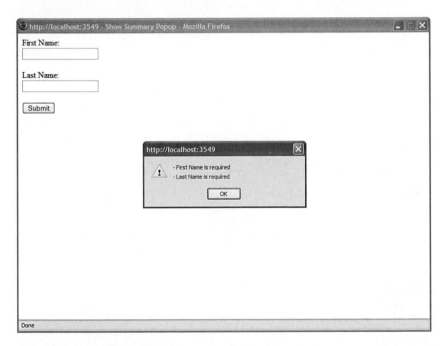

FIGURE 3.15   Displaying a validation summary in an alert box.

LISTING 3.19   ShowSummaryPopup.aspx

```
<%@ Page Language="C#" %>
<!DOCTYPE html PUBLIC "-//W3C//DTD XHTML 1.0 Transitional//EN"
"http://www.w3.org/TR/xhtml1/DTD/xhtml1-transitional.dtd">
<html xmlns="http://www.w3.org/1999/xhtml" >
<head id="Head1" runat="server">
    <title>Show Summary Popup</title>
</head>
```

LISTING 3.19   Continued

```
<body>
    <form id="form1" runat="server">
    <div>

    <asp:ValidationSummary
        id="ValidationSummary1"
        ShowMessageBox="true"
        ShowSummary="false"
        Runat="server" />

    <asp:Label
        id="lblFirstName"
        Text="First Name:"
        AssociatedControlID="txtFirstName"
        Runat="server" />
    <br />
    <asp:TextBox
        id="txtFirstName"
        Runat="server" />
    <asp:RequiredFieldValidator
        id="reqFirstName"
        ErrorMessage="First Name is required"
        ControlToValidate="txtFirstName"
        Display="None"
        Runat="server" />

    <br /><br />

    <asp:Label
        id="lblLastName"
        Text="Last Name:"
        AssociatedControlID="txtLastName"
        Runat="server" />
    <br />
    <asp:TextBox
        id="txtLastName"
        Runat="server" />
    <asp:RequiredFieldValidator
        id="reqLastName"
        ErrorMessage="Last Name is required"
        ControlToValidate="txtLastName"
        Display="None"
        Runat="server" />
```

```
    <br /><br />

    <asp:Button
        id="btnSubmit"
        Text="Submit"
        Runat="server" />

    </div>
    </form>
</body>
</html>
```

Notice that both of the RequiredFieldValidator controls have their Display properties set to the value None. The validation error messages appear only in the alert box.

Creating Custom Validation Controls

In this final section, you learn how to create custom validation controls. We create two custom controls. First we create a LengthValidator control that enables you to validate the length of an entry in a form field. Next, we create an AjaxValidator control. The AjaxValidator control performs validation on the client by passing information back to a custom function defined on the server.

You create a new validation control by deriving a new control from the BaseValidator class. As its name implies, the BaseValidator class is the base class for all the validation controls, including the RequiredFieldValidator and RegularExpressionValidator controls.

The BaseValidator class is a MustInherit (abstract) class, which requires you to implement a single method:

▶ **EvaluateIsValid**—Returns true when the form field being validated is valid.

The BaseValidator class also includes several other methods that you can override or otherwise use. The most useful of these methods is the following:

▶ **GetControlValidationValue**—Enables you to retrieve the value of the control being validated.

When you create a custom validation control, you override the EvaluateIsValid() method and, within the EvaluateIsValid() method, you call GetControlValidationValue to get the value of the form field being validated.

Creating a LengthValidator Control

To illustrate the general technique for creating a custom validation control, in this section we will create an extremely simple one. It's a LengthValidator control, which enables you to validate the length of a form field.

The code for the LengthValidator control is contained in Listing 3.20.

LISTING 3.20   LengthValidator.cs

```csharp
using System;
using System.Web.UI;
using System.Web.UI.WebControls;

namespace myControls
{
    /// <summary>
    /// Validates the length of an input field
    /// </summary>
    public class LengthValidator : BaseValidator
    {
        int _maximumLength = 0;

        public int MaximumLength
        {
            get { return _maximumLength; }
            set { _maximumLength = value; }
        }

        protected override bool EvaluateIsValid()
        {
            String value = this.GetControlValidationValue(this.ControlToValidate);
            if (value.Length > _maximumLength)
                return false;
            else
                return true;
        }
    }
}
```

Listing 3.20 contains a class that inherits from the BaseValidator class. The new class overrides the EvaluateIsValid method. The value from the control being validated is retrieved with the help of the GetControlValidationValue() method, and the length of the value is compared against the MaximumLength property.

NOTE

To use the class in Listing 3.20, you need to add the class to your application's App_Code folder. Any class added to this special folder is automatically compiled by the ASP.NET Framework.

The page in Listing 3.21 uses the LengthValidator control to validate the length of a comment input field (see Figure 3.16).

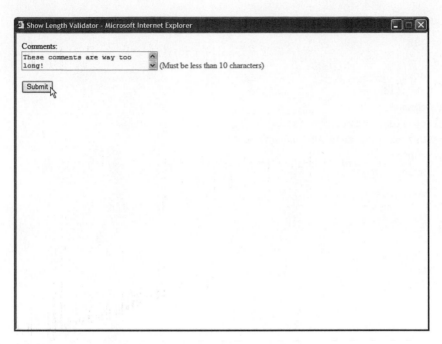

FIGURE 3.16   Validating the length of a field with the LengthValidator control.

LISTING 3.21   ShowLengthValidator.aspx

```
<%@ Page Language="C#" %>
<%@ Register TagPrefix="custom" Namespace="myControls" %>
<!DOCTYPE html PUBLIC "-//W3C//DTD XHTML 1.0 Transitional//EN"
"http://www.w3.org/TR/xhtml1/DTD/xhtml1-transitional.dtd">
<html xmlns="http://www.w3.org/1999/xhtml" >
<head id="Head1" runat="server">
    <title>Show Length Validator</title>
</head>
<body>
    <form id="form1" runat="server">
    <div>

    <asp:Label
        id="lblComments"
        Text="Comments:"
        AssociatedControlID="txtComments"
        Runat="server" />
    <br />
    <asp:TextBox
        id="txtComments"
        TextMode="MultiLine"
```

LISTING 3.21   Continued

```
            Columns="30"
            Rows="2"
            Runat="server" />
        <custom:LengthValidator
            id="valComments"
            ControlToValidate="txtComments"
            Text="(Must be less than 10 characters)"
            MaximumLength="10"
            Runat="server" />

        <br /><br />

        <asp:Button
            id="btnSubmit"
            Text="Submit"
            Runat="server" />

        </div>
        </form>
</body>
</html>
```

Notice that the LengthValidator is registered at the top of the page with the <%@ Register %> directive. If you need to use the control in multiple pages in your application, then you can alternatively register the control in the <pages> section of your application's web configuration file.

Creating an AjaxValidator Control

In this section, we are going to create an extremely useful control named the AjaxValidator control. Like the CustomValidator control, the AjaxValidator control enables you to create a custom server-side validation function. Unlike the CustomValidator control, however, the AjaxValidator control enables you to call the custom validation function from the browser.

The AjaxValidator control uses AJAX (Asynchronous JavaScript and XML) to call the server-side validation function from the client. The advantage of using AJAX is that no postback to the server is apparent to the user.

For example, imagine that you are creating a website registration form and you need to validate a User Name field. You want to make sure that the User Name entered does not already exist in the database. The AjaxValidator enables you to call a server-side validation function from the client to check whether the User Name is unique in the database.

The code for the `AjaxValidator` control is contained in Listing 3.22.

LISTING 3.22 AjaxValidator.cs

```csharp
using System;
using System.Web;
using System.Web.UI;
using System.Web.UI.WebControls;

namespace myControls
{
    /// <summary>
    /// Enables you to perform custom validation on both the client and server
    /// </summary>
    public class AjaxValidator : BaseValidator, ICallbackEventHandler
    {
        public event ServerValidateEventHandler ServerValidate;

        string _controlToValidateValue;

        protected override void OnPreRender(EventArgs e)
        {
            String eventRef = Page.ClientScript.GetCallbackEventReference
              (
                this,
                "",
                "",
                ""
              );

            // Register include file
            String includeScript =
                Page.ResolveClientUrl("~/ClientScripts/AjaxValidator.js");
            Page.ClientScript.RegisterClientScriptInclude("AjaxValidator",
                includeScript);

            // Register startup script
            String startupScript = String.Format("document.getElementById('{0}')
➥.evaluationfunction = 'AjaxValidatorEvaluateIsValid';", this.ClientID);
            Page.ClientScript.RegisterStartupScript(this.GetType(),
➥"AjaxValidator", startupScript, true);

            base.OnPreRender(e);
        }
```

LISTING 3.22   Continued

```csharp
/// <summary>
/// Only do the AJAX on browsers that support it
/// </summary>
protected override bool DetermineRenderUplevel()
{
    return Context.Request.Browser.SupportsCallback;
}


/// <summary>
/// Server method called by client AJAX call
/// </summary>
public string GetCallbackResult()
{
    return ExecuteValidationFunction(_controlToValidateValue).ToString();
}


/// <summary>
/// Return callback result to client
/// </summary>
public void RaiseCallbackEvent(string eventArgument)
{
    _controlToValidateValue = eventArgument;
}


/// <summary>
/// Server-side method for validation
/// </summary>
protected override bool EvaluateIsValid()
{
    string controlToValidateValue = this.GetControlValidationValue
    ➥(this.ControlToValidate);
    return ExecuteValidationFunction(controlToValidateValue);
}


/// <summary>
/// Performs the validation for both server and client
/// </summary>
private bool ExecuteValidationFunction(String controlToValidateValue)
{
    ServerValidateEventArgs args = new ServerValidateEventArgs
    ➥(controlToValidateValue, this.IsValid);
    if (ServerValidate != null)
        ServerValidate(this, args);
    return args.IsValid;
}
```

```
        }

    }

}
```

The control in Listing 3.22 inherits from the BaseValidator class. It also implements the ICallbackEventHandler interface. The ICallbackEventHandler interface defines two methods that are called on the server when an AJAX request is made from the client.

In the OnPreRender() method, a JavaScript include file and startup script are registered. The JavaScript include file contains the client-side functions that are called when the AjaxValidator validates a form field on the client. The startup script associates the client-side AjaxValidatorEvaluateIsValid() function with the AjaxValidator control. The client-side validation framework automatically calls this JavaScript function when performing validation.

The JavaScript functions used by the AjaxValidator control are contained in Listing 3.23.

LISTING 3.23 AjaxValidator.js

```javascript
// Performs AJAX call back to server
function AjaxValidatorEvaluateIsValid(val)
{
    var value = ValidatorGetValue(val.controltovalidate);
    WebForm_DoCallback(val.id, value, AjaxValidatorResult, val,
AjaxValidatorError, true);
    return true;
}

// Called when result is returned from server
function AjaxValidatorResult(returnValue, context)
{
    if (returnValue == 'True')
        context.isvalid = true;
    else
        context.isvalid = false;
    ValidatorUpdateDisplay(context);
}

// If there is an error, show it
function AjaxValidatorError(message)
{
    alert('Error: ' + message);
}
```

The `AjaxValidatorEvaluateIsValid()` JavaScript method initiates an AJAX call by calling the `WebForm_DoCallback()` method. This method calls the server-side validation function associated with the `AjaxValidator` control. When the AJAX call completes, the `AjaxValidatorResult()` method is called. This method updates the display of the validation control on the client.

The page in Listing 3.24 illustrates how you can use the `AjaxValidator` control. This page handles the `AjaxValidator` control's `ServerValidate` event to associate a custom validation function with the control.

The page in Listing 3.24 contains a form that includes fields for entering a username and favorite color. When you submit the form, the values of these fields are inserted into a database table named Users.

In Listing 3.24, the validation function checks whether a username already exists in the database. If you enter a username that already exists, a validation error message is displayed. The message is displayed in the browser before you submit the form back to the server (see Figure 3.17).

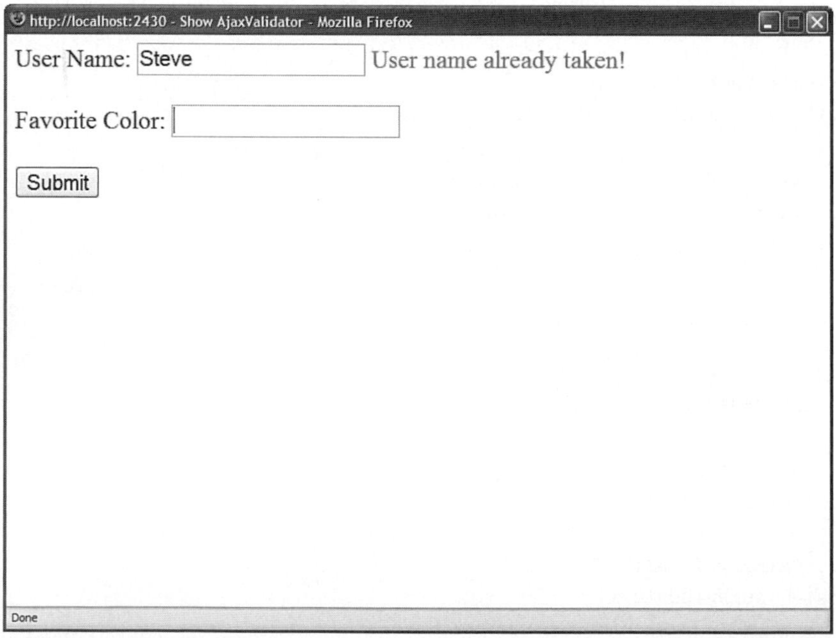

FIGURE 3.17   Using the `AjaxValidator` to check whether a username is unique.

It is important to realize that you can associate any server-side validation function with the `AjaxValidator`. You can perform a database lookup, call a web service, or perform a complex mathematical function. Whatever function you define on the server is automatically called on the client.

LISTING 3.24   ShowAjaxValidator.aspx

```
<%@ Page Language="C#" %>
<%@ Register TagPrefix="custom" Namespace="myControls" %>
<%@ Import Namespace="System.Data.SqlClient" %>
<%@ Import Namespace="System.Web.Configuration" %>
<!DOCTYPE html PUBLIC "-//W3C//DTD XHTML 1.0 Transitional//EN"
"http://www.w3.org/TR/xhtml1/DTD/xhtml1-transitional.dtd">
<script runat="server">

    /// <summary>
    /// Validation function that is called on both the client and server
    /// </summary>
    protected void AjaxValidator1_ServerValidate(object source,
    ➥ServerValidateEventArgs args)
    {
        if (UserNameExists(args.Value))
            args.IsValid = false;
        else
            args.IsValid = true;
    }


    /// <summary>
    /// Returns true when user name already exists
    /// in Users database table
    /// </summary>
    private bool UserNameExists(string userName)
    {
        string conString = WebConfigurationManager.ConnectionStrings
        ➥["UsersDB"].ConnectionString;
        SqlConnection con = new SqlConnection(conString);
        SqlCommand cmd = new SqlCommand("SELECT COUNT(*)
        ➥ FROM Users WHERE UserName=@UserName", con);
        cmd.Parameters.AddWithValue("@UserName", userName);
        bool result = false;
        using (con)
        {
            con.Open();
            int count = (int)cmd.ExecuteScalar();
            if (count > 0)
                result = true;
        }
        return result;
    }

    /// <summary>
```

LISTING 3.24   Continued

```
    /// Insert new user name to Users database table
    /// </summary>
    protected void btnSubmit_Click(object sender, EventArgs e)
    {
        string conString = WebConfigurationManager.ConnectionStrings
        ➥["UsersDB"].ConnectionString;
        SqlConnection con = new SqlConnection(conString);
        SqlCommand cmd = new SqlCommand("INSERT Users (UserName,FavoriteColor)
        ➥VALUES (@UserName,@FavoriteColor)", con);
        cmd.Parameters.AddWithValue("@UserName", txtUserName.Text);
        cmd.Parameters.AddWithValue("@FavoriteColor", txtFavoriteColor.Text);
        using (con)
        {
            con.Open();
            cmd.ExecuteNonQuery();
        }
        txtUserName.Text = String.Empty;
        txtFavoriteColor.Text = String.Empty;
    }
</script>
<html xmlns="http://www.w3.org/1999/xhtml" >
<head runat="server">
    <title>Show AjaxValidator</title>
</head>
<body>
    <form id="form1" runat="server">
    <div>

    <asp:Label
        id="lblUserName"
        Text="User Name:"
        AssociatedControlID="txtUserName"
        Runat="server" />
    <asp:TextBox
        id="txtUserName"
        Runat="server" />
    <custom:AjaxValidator
        id="AjaxValidator1"
        ControlToValidate="txtUserName"
        Text="User name already taken!"
        OnServerValidate="AjaxValidator1_ServerValidate"
        Runat="server" />
```

```
        <br /><br />
        <asp:Label
            id="lblFavoriteColor"
            Text="Favorite Color:"
            AssociatedControlID="txtFavoriteColor"
            Runat="server" />
        <asp:TextBox
            id="txtFavoriteColor"
            Runat="server" />

        <br /><br />
        <asp:Button
            id="btnSubmit"
            Text="Submit"
            Runat="server" OnClick="btnSubmit_Click" />

    </div>
    </form>
</body>
</html>
```

Summary

In this chapter, you learned how to perform form validation with the ASP.NET 3.5 Framework. First, you were provided with an overview of all the standard validation controls. You learned how to highlight validation error messages and how to take advantage of validation groups to simulate multiple forms in a single page.

In the final section of this chapter, you learned how to create custom validation controls by deriving new controls from the `BaseValidator` control. You saw the creation of a custom `LengthValidator` and `AjaxValidator` control.

CHAPTER 4

Using the Rich Controls

In previous chapters, we examined the ASP.NET controls that you will use in just about any application. In this chapter, we examine a more specialized set of controls known collectively as the *rich controls*.

In the first section, you learn how to accept file uploads at your website. For example, you learn how to enable users to upload images, Microsoft Word documents, or Microsoft Excel spreadsheets.

Next, you learn how to work with the Calendar control. You can use the Calendar control as a date picker. You can also use the Calendar control to display upcoming events (such as a meeting schedule).

In this chapter, we also discuss the AdRotator control. This control enables you to display banner advertisements randomly on your website. The control enables you to store a list of advertisements in an XML file or a database table.

Next, you will learn about the MultiView control. This control enables you to hide and display areas of content on a page. You learn how to use this control to divide a page into different tabs.

Finally, you will learn about the Wizard control, which enables you to display multi-step forms. This control is useful when you need to divide a long form into multiple sub-forms.

Accepting File Uploads

The FileUpload control enables users to upload files to your web application. After the file is uploaded, you can store the file anywhere you please. Normally, you store the file either on the file system or in a database. This section explores both options.

The `FileUpload` control supports the following properties (this is not a complete list):

- **Enabled**—Enables you to disable the `FileUpload` control.
- **FileBytes**—Enables you to get the uploaded file contents as a byte array.
- **FileContent**—Enables you to get the uploaded file contents as a stream.
- **FileName**—Enables you to get the name of the file uploaded.
- **HasFile**—Returns `True` when a file has been uploaded.
- **PostedFile**—Enables you to get the uploaded file wrapped in the `HttpPostedFile` object.

The `FileUpload` control also supports the following methods:

- **Focus**—Enables you to shift the form focus to the `FileUpload` control.
- **SaveAs**—Enables you to save the uploaded file to the file system.

The `FileUpload` control's `PostedFile` property enables you to retrieve the uploaded file wrapped in an `HttpPostedFile` object. This object exposes additional information about the uploaded file.

The `HttpPostedFile` class has the following properties (this is not a complete list):

- **ContentLength**—Enables you to get the size of the uploaded file in bytes.
- **ContentType**—Enables you to get the MIME type of the uploaded file.
- **FileName**—Enables you to get the name of the uploaded file.
- **InputStream**—Enables you to retrieve the uploaded file as a stream.

The `HttpPostedFile` class also supports the following method:

- **SaveAs**—Enables you to save the uploaded file to the file system.

Notice that there is some redundancy here. For example, you can get the name of the uploaded file by using either the `FileUpload.FileName` property or the `HttpPostedFile.FileName` property. You can save a file by using either the `FileUpload.SaveAs()` method or the `HttpPostedFile.SaveAs()` method.

> **NOTE**
>
> Adding a `FileUpload` control to a page automatically adds a `enctype="multipart/form-data"` attribute to the server-side `<form>` tag.

Saving Files to the File System

The page in Listing 4.1 illustrates how you can upload images to an application by using the `FileUpload` control.

LISTING 4.1 `FileUploadFile.aspx`

```
<%@ Page Language="C#" %>
<%@ Import Namespace="System.IO" %>
<!DOCTYPE html PUBLIC "-//W3C//DTD XHTML 1.0 Transitional//EN"
"http://www.w3.org/TR/xhtml1/DTD/xhtml1-transitional.dtd">
<script runat="server">

    protected void btnAdd_Click(object sender, EventArgs e)
    {
        if (upImage.HasFile)
        {
            if (CheckFileType(upImage.FileName))
            {
                String filePath = "~/UploadImages/" + upImage.FileName;
                upImage.SaveAs(MapPath(filePath));
            }
        }
    }

    bool CheckFileType(string fileName)
    {
        string ext = Path.GetExtension(fileName);
        switch (ext.ToLower())
        {
            case ".gif":
                return true;
            case ".png":
                return true;
            case ".jpg":
                return true;
            case ".jpeg":
                return true;
            default:
                return false;
        }
    }

    void Page_PreRender()
    {
        string upFolder = MapPath("~/UploadImages/");
```

LISTING 4.1   Continued

```
            DirectoryInfo dir = new DirectoryInfo(upFolder);
            dlstImages.DataSource = dir.GetFiles();
            dlstImages.DataBind();
    }
</script>
<html xmlns="http://www.w3.org/1999/xhtml" >
<head id="Head1" runat="server">
    <title>FileUpload File</title>
</head>
<body>
    <form id="form1" runat="server">
    <div>

    <asp:Label
        id="lblImageFile"
        Text="Image File:"
        AssociatedControlID="upImage"
        Runat="server" />

    <asp:FileUpload
        id="upImage"
        Runat="server" />

    <br /><br />

    <asp:Button
        id="btnAdd"
        Text="Add Image"
        OnClick="btnAdd_Click"
        Runat="server" />

    <hr />

    <asp:DataList
        id="dlstImages"
        RepeatColumns="3"
        runat="server">
        <ItemTemplate>
        <asp:Image ID="Image1"
            ImageUrl='<%# Eval("Name", "~/UploadImages/{0}") %>'
            style="width:200px"
            Runat="server" />
        <br />
        <%# Eval("Name") %>
        </ItemTemplate>
```

```
    </asp:DataList>

    </div>
    </form>
</body>
</html>
```

Listing 4.1 includes both a `FileUpload` control and a `DataList` control. When you upload a file, the file is saved to a folder named `ImageUploads`. The `DataList` control automatically displays the contents of the `ImageUploads` folder. The result is an image gallery (see Figure 4.1).

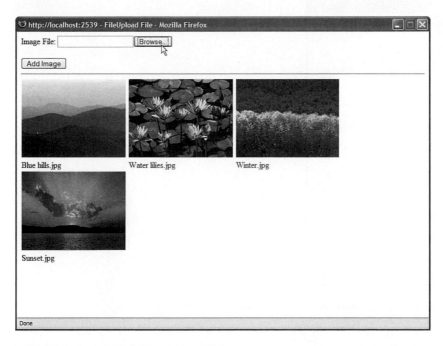

FIGURE 4.1   Displaying a photo gallery.

Notice that the page includes a method named `CheckFileType()`, which prevents users from uploading a file that does not have the `.gif`, `.jpeg`, `.jpg`, or `.png` extension. The method restricts the type of file that can be uploaded based on the file extension.

NOTE

The HTML 4.01 specifications define an `accept` attribute that you should be able to use to filter the files that can be uploaded. Unfortunately, no browser supports the `accept` attribute, so you must perform filtering on the server (or use some JavaScript to check the filename extension on the client).

To save a file to the file system, the Windows account associated with the ASP.NET page must have sufficient permissions to save the file. For Windows 2003 Servers, an ASP.NET page executes in the security context of the NETWORK SERVICE account. In the case of every other operating system, an ASP.NET page executes in the security context of the ASPNET account.

To enable the ASP.NET framework to save an uploaded file to a particular folder, you need to right-click the folder within Windows Explorer, select the Security tab, and provide either the NETWORK SERVICE or ASPNET account Write permissions for the folder (see Figure 4.2).

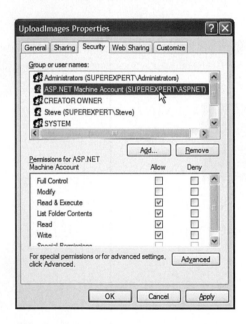

FIGURE 4.2   Adding Write permissions for the ASPNET account.

Saving Files to a Database

You also can use the FileUpload control to save files to a database table. Saving and retrieving files from a database can place more stress on your server. However, it does have certain advantages. First, you can avoid file system permissions issues. Second, saving files to a database enables you to more easily back up your information.

The page in Listing 4.2 enables you to save Microsoft Word documents to a database table (see Figure 4.3).

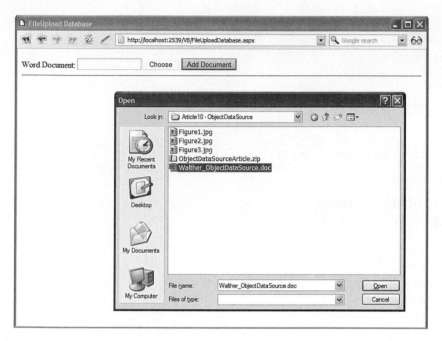

FIGURE 4.3   Uploading Microsoft Word documents.

LISTING 4.2   FileUploadDatabase.aspx

```csharp
<%@ Page Language="C#" %>
<%@ Import Namespace="System.IO" %>
<!DOCTYPE html PUBLIC "-//W3C//DTD XHTML 1.0 Transitional//EN"
"http://www.w3.org/TR/xhtml1/DTD/xhtml1-transitional.dtd">
<script runat="server">

    protected void btnAdd_Click(object sender, EventArgs e)
    {
        if (upFile.HasFile)
        {
            if (CheckFileType(upFile.FileName))
                srcFiles.Insert();
        }
    }

    bool CheckFileType(string fileName)
    {
        return Path.GetExtension(fileName).ToLower() == ".doc";
    }

</script>
<html xmlns="http://www.w3.org/1999/xhtml" >
```

LISTING 4.2   Continued

```html
<head id="Head1" runat="server">
    <style type="text/css">
        .fileList li
        {
            margin-bottom:5px;
        }
    </style>
    <title>FileUpload Database</title>
</head>
<body>
    <form id="form1" runat="server">
    <div>

    <asp:Label
        id="lblFile"
        Text="Word Document:"
        AssociatedControlID="upFile"
        Runat="server" />

    <asp:FileUpload
        id="upFile"
        Runat="server" />

    <asp:Button
        id="btnAdd"
        Text="Add Document"
        OnClick="btnAdd_Click"
        Runat="server" />

    <hr />

    <asp:Repeater
        id="rptFiles"
        DataSourceID="srcFiles"
        Runat="server">
        <HeaderTemplate>
        <ul class="fileList">
        </HeaderTemplate>
        <ItemTemplate>
        <li>
        <asp:HyperLink
            id="lnkFile"
            Text='<%#Eval("FileName")%>'
            NavigateUrl='<%#Eval("Id", "~/FileHandler.ashx?id={0}")%>'
            Runat="server" />
```

```
            </li>
        </ItemTemplate>
        <FooterTemplate>
        </ul>
        </FooterTemplate>
    </asp:Repeater>

    <asp:SqlDataSource
        id="srcFiles"
        ConnectionString="Server=.\SQLExpress;Integrated Security=True;
            AttachDbFileName=¦DataDirectory¦FilesDB.mdf;User Instance=True"
        SelectCommand="SELECT Id,FileName FROM Files"
        InsertCommand="INSERT Files (FileName,FileBytes) VALUES
        ➥(@FileName,@FileBytes)"
        Runat="server">
        <InsertParameters>
            <asp:ControlParameter Name="FileName" ControlID="upFile"
            ➥PropertyName="FileName" />
            <asp:ControlParameter Name="FileBytes" ControlID="upFile"
            ➥PropertyName="FileBytes" />
        </InsertParameters>
    </asp:SqlDataSource>

    </div>
    </form>
</body>
</html>
```

When you submit the form in Listing 4.2, the `btnAdd_Click()` method executes. This method checks the file extension to verify that the file is a Microsoft Word document. Next, the `SqlDataSource` control's `Insert()` method is called to insert the values of the `FileUpload` control's `FileName` and `FileBytes` properties into a local SQL Express database table. The SQL Express database table, named Files, looks like this:

Column Name	Data Type
Id	Int (IDENTITY)
FileName	NVarchar(50)
FileBytes	Varbinary(max)

The page also displays a list of the current Microsoft Word documents in the database. You can click any file and view the contents of the file. Exactly what happens when you click a file is browser (and browser settings) dependent. With Microsoft Internet Explorer, for example, the document opens directly in the browser.

Clicking the name of a document links you to a page named `FileHandler.ashx`. The `FileHandler.ashx` file is a generic HTTP Handler file. Chapter 25 discusses HTTP Handlers in detail. An HTTP Handler enables you to execute code when someone makes a request for a file with a certain path.

The `FileHandler.ashx` file is contained in Listing 4.3.

LISTING 4.3   `FileHandler.ashx`

```csharp
<%@ WebHandler Language="C#" Class="FileHandler" %>

using System;
using System.Web;
using System.Data;
using System.Data.SqlClient;

public class FileHandler : IHttpHandler {

    const string conString = @"Server=.\SQLExpress;Integrated Security=True;
        AttachDbFileName=¦DataDirectory¦FilesDB.mdf;User Instance=True";

    public void ProcessRequest (HttpContext context) {
        context.Response.ContentType = "application/msword";

        SqlConnection con = new SqlConnection(conString);
        SqlCommand cmd = new SqlCommand("SELECT FileBytes FROM Files WHERE
          Id=@Id", con);
        cmd.Parameters.AddWithValue("@Id", context.Request["Id"]);
        using (con)
        {
            con.Open();
            byte[] file = (byte[])cmd.ExecuteScalar();
            context.Response.BinaryWrite(file);
        }
    }

    public bool IsReusable {
        get {
            return false;
        }
    }

}
```

When the `FileHandler.aspx` page is requested, the `ProcessRequest()` method executes. This method grabs a query string item named `Id` and retrieves the matching record from the Files database table. The record contains the contents of a Microsoft Word document as a byte array. The byte array is sent to the browser with the `Response.BinaryWrite()` method.

Uploading Large Files

You must do extra work when uploading large files. You don't want to consume all your server's memory by placing the entire file in memory. When working with a large file, you need to work with the file in more manageable chunks.

First, you need to configure your application to handle large files. Two configuration settings have an effect on posting large files to the server: the `httpRuntime` `maxRequestLength` and `httpRuntime requestLengthDiskThreshold` settings.

The `maxRequestLength` setting places a limit on the largest form post that the server will accept. By default, you cannot post a form that contains more than 4MB of data—if you try, you'll get an exception. If you need to upload a file that contains more than four megabytes of data, then you need to change this setting.

The `requestLengthDiskThreshold` setting determines how a form post is buffered to the file system. In the previous version of ASP.NET (ASP.NET 1.1), uploading a large file could do horrible things to your server. The entire file was uploaded into the server memory. While a 10-megabyte video file was uploaded, for example, 10 megabytes of server memory was consumed.

The ASP.NET 3.5 Framework enables you to buffer large files onto the file system. When the size of the file passes the requestLengthDiskThreshold setting, the remainder of the file is buffered to the file system (in the Temporary ASP.NET Files folder).

By default, the ASP.NET framework is configured to buffer any post larger than 80 KB to a file buffer. If you are not happy with this setting, then you can modify the `requestLengthDiskThreshold` to configure a new threshold (The `requestLengthDiskThreshold` setting must be less than the `maxRequestLength` setting.)

The web configuration file in Listing 4.4 enables files up to 10MB to be posted. It also changes the buffering threshold to 100KB.

LISTING 4.4   Web.Config

```
<configuration>
<system.web>
  <httpRuntime
      maxRequestLength="10240"
      requestLengthDiskThreshold="100" />
</system.web>
</configuration>
```

When working with large files, you must be careful about the way that you handle the file when storing or retrieving the file from a data store. For example, when saving or retrieving a file from a database table, you should never load the entire file into memory.

The page in Listing 4.5 demonstrates how you can save a large file to a database table efficiently.

LISTING 4.5 FileUploadLarge.aspx

```
<%@ Page Language="C#" %>
<%@ Import Namespace="System.IO" %>
<%@ Import Namespace="System.Data" %>
<%@ Import Namespace="System.Data.SqlClient" %>
<!DOCTYPE html PUBLIC "-//W3C//DTD XHTML 1.0 Transitional//EN"
"http://www.w3.org/TR/xhtml1/DTD/xhtml1-transitional.dtd">
<script runat="server">

    const string conString = @"Server=.\SQLExpress;Integrated Security=True;
        AttachDbFileName=¦DataDirectory¦FilesDB.mdf;User Instance=True";


    void btnAdd_Click(Object s, EventArgs e)
    {
        if (upFile.HasFile)
        {
            if (CheckFileType(upFile.FileName))
            {
                AddFile(upFile.FileName, upFile.FileContent);
                rptFiles.DataBind();
            }
        }
    }


    bool CheckFileType(string fileName)
    {
        return Path.GetExtension(fileName).ToLower() == ".doc";
    }


    void AddFile(string fileName, Stream upload)
    {
        SqlConnection con = new SqlConnection(conString);

        SqlCommand cmd = new SqlCommand("INSERT Files (FileName) Values
          (@FileName);" +
          "SELECT @Identity = SCOPE_IDENTITY()", con);
```

```
        cmd.Parameters.AddWithValue("@FileName", fileName);
        SqlParameter idParm = cmd.Parameters.Add("@Identity", SqlDbType.Int);
        idParm.Direction = ParameterDirection.Output;

        using (con)
        {
            con.Open();
            cmd.ExecuteNonQuery();
            int newFileId = (int)idParm.Value;
            StoreFile(newFileId, upload, con);
        }
    }

    void StoreFile(int fileId, Stream upload, SqlConnection connection)
    {
        int bufferLen = 8040;
        BinaryReader br = new BinaryReader(upload);
        byte[] chunk = br.ReadBytes(bufferLen);

        SqlCommand cmd = new SqlCommand("UPDATE Files SET FileBytes=@Buffer
        ➥WHERE Id=@FileId", connection);
        cmd.Parameters.AddWithValue("@FileId", fileId);
        cmd.Parameters.Add("@Buffer", SqlDbType.VarBinary, bufferLen).Value = chunk;
        cmd.ExecuteNonQuery();


        SqlCommand cmdAppend = new SqlCommand("UPDATE Files SET FileBytes
        ➥.WRITE(@Buffer, NULL, 0) WHERE Id=@FileId", connection);
        cmdAppend.Parameters.AddWithValue("@FileId", fileId);
        cmdAppend.Parameters.Add("@Buffer", SqlDbType.VarBinary, bufferLen);
        chunk = br.ReadBytes(bufferLen);

        while (chunk.Length > 0)
        {
            cmdAppend.Parameters["@Buffer"].Value = chunk;
            cmdAppend.ExecuteNonQuery();
            chunk = br.ReadBytes(bufferLen);
        }

        br.Close();
    }

</script>
<html xmlns="http://www.w3.org/1999/xhtml" >
<head id="Head1" runat="server">
    <title>FileUpload Large</title>
```

LISTING 4.5   Continued

```
</head>
<body>
    <form id="form1" runat="server">
    <div>

    <asp:Label
        id="lblFile"
        Text="Word Document:"
        AssociatedControlID="upFile"
        Runat="server" />

    <asp:FileUpload
        id="upFile"
        Runat="server" />

    <asp:Button
        id="btnAdd"
        Text="Add Document"
        OnClick="btnAdd_Click"
        Runat="server" />

    <hr />

    <asp:Repeater
        id="rptFiles"
        DataSourceID="srcFiles"
        Runat="server">
        <HeaderTemplate>
        <ul class="fileList">
        </HeaderTemplate>
        <ItemTemplate>
        <li>
        <asp:HyperLink
            id="lnkFile"
            Text='<%#Eval("FileName")%>'
            NavigateUrl='<%#Eval("Id", "~/FileHandlerLarge.ashx?id={0}")%>'
            Runat="server" />
        </li>
        </ItemTemplate>
        <FooterTemplate>
        </ul>
        </FooterTemplate>
    </asp:Repeater>

    <asp:SqlDataSource
```

```
          id="srcFiles"
          ConnectionString="Server=.\SQLExpress;Integrated Security=True;
              AttachDbFileName=¦DataDirectory¦FilesDB.mdf;User Instance=True"
          SelectCommand="SELECT Id,FileName FROM Files"
          Runat="server" />

    </div>
    </form>
</body>
</html>
```

In Listing 4.5, the `AddFile()` method is called. This method adds a new row to the Files database table that contains the filename. Next, the `StoreFile()` method is called. This method adds the actual bytes of the uploaded file to the database. The file contents are divided into 8040-byte chunks. Notice that the SQL UPDATE statement includes a `.WRITE` clause that is used when the `FileBytes` database column is updated.

> **NOTE**
>
> Microsoft recommends that you set the buffer size to multiples of 8040 when using the `.WRITE` clause to update database data.

The page in Listing 4.5 never represents the entire uploaded file in memory. The file is yanked into memory from the file system in 8040-byte chunks and fed to SQL Server in chunks.

When you click a filename, the `FileHandlerLarge.ashx` HTTP Handler executes. This handler retrieves the selected file from the database and sends it to the browser. The handler is contained in Listing 4.6.

LISTING 4.6   FileHandlerLarge.ashx

```
<%@ WebHandler Language="C#" Class="FileHandlerLarge" %>


using System;
using System.Web;
using System.Data;
using System.Data.SqlClient;

public class FileHandlerLarge : IHttpHandler {

    const string conString = @"Server=.\SQLExpress;Integrated Security=True;
        AttachDbFileName=¦DataDirectory¦FilesDB.mdf;User Instance=True";

    public void ProcessRequest (HttpContext context) {
```

LISTING 4.6   Continued

```
        context.Response.Buffer = false;
        context.Response.ContentType = "application/msword";

        SqlConnection con = new SqlConnection(conString);
        SqlCommand cmd = new SqlCommand("SELECT FileBytes FROM Files
        ➥WHERE Id=@Id", con);
        cmd.Parameters.AddWithValue("@Id", context.Request["Id"]);
        using (con)
        {
            con.Open();
            SqlDataReader reader = cmd.ExecuteReader
            ➥(CommandBehavior.SequentialAccess);
            if (reader.Read())
            {
                int bufferSize = 8040;
                byte[] chunk = new byte[bufferSize];
                long retCount;
                long startIndex = 0;

                retCount = reader.GetBytes(0, startIndex, chunk, 0, bufferSize);


                while (retCount == bufferSize)
                {
                    context.Response.BinaryWrite(chunk);

                    startIndex += bufferSize;
                    retCount = reader.GetBytes(0, startIndex, chunk, 0, bufferSize);
                }

                byte[] actualChunk = new Byte[retCount - 1];
                Buffer.BlockCopy(chunk, 0, actualChunk, 0, (int)retCount - 1);
                context.Response.BinaryWrite(actualChunk);


            }
        }
    }

    public bool IsReusable {
        get {
            return false;
        }
    }
}
```

The HTTP Handler in Listing 4.6 uses a `SqlDataReader` to retrieve a file from the database. Notice that the `SqlDataReader` is retrieved with a `CommandBehavior.SequentialAccess` parameter. This parameter enables the `SqlDataReader` to load data as a stream. The contents of the database column are pulled into memory in 8040-byte chunks. The chunks are written to the browser with the `Response.BinaryWrite()` method.

Notice that response buffering is disabled for the handler. The `Response.Buffer` property is set to the value `False`. Because buffering is disabled, the output of the handler is not buffered in server memory before being transmitted to the browser.

> **WARNING**
>
> The method of working with large files described in this section works only with SQL Server 2005. When using earlier versions of SQL Server, you need to use the `TEXTPTR()` function instead of the `.WRITE` clause.

Displaying a Calendar

The `Calendar` control enables you to display a calendar. You can use the calendar as a date picker or you can use the calendar to display a list of upcoming events.

The page in Listing 4.7 displays a simple calendar with the `Calendar` control (see Figure 4.4).

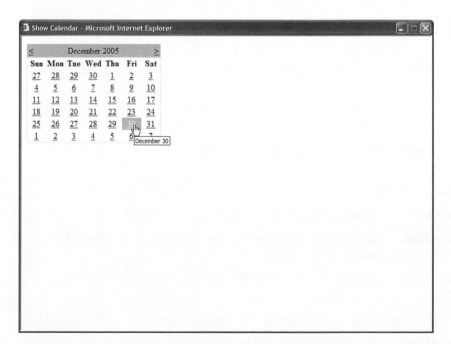

FIGURE 4.4   Displaying a calendar with the `Calendar` control.

LISTING 4.7   ShowCalendar.aspx

```
<%@ Page Language="C#" %>
<!DOCTYPE html PUBLIC "-//W3C//DTD XHTML 1.0 Transitional//EN"
"http://www.w3.org/TR/xhtml1/DTD/xhtml1-transitional.dtd">
<html xmlns="http://www.w3.org/1999/xhtml" >
<head id="Head1" runat="server">
    <title>Show Calendar</title>
</head>
<body>
    <form id="form1" runat="server">
    <div>

    <asp:Calendar
        id="Calendar1"
        Runat="server" />

    </div>
    </form>
</body>
</html>
```

The `Calendar` control supports the following properties (this is not a complete list):

▶ **DayNameFormat**—Enables you to specify the appearance of the days of the week. Possible values are `FirstLetter`, `FirstTwoLetters`, `Full`, `Short`, and `Shortest`.

▶ **NextMonthText**—Enables you to specify the text that appears for the next month link.

▶ **NextPrevFormat**—Enables you to specify the format of the next month and previous month link. Possible values are `CustomText`, `FullMonth`, and `ShortMonth`.

▶ **PrevMonthText**—Enables you to specify the text that appears for the previous month link.

▶ **SelectedDate**—Enables you to get or set the selected date.

▶ **SelectedDates**—Enables you to get or set a collection of selected dates.

▶ **SelectionMode**—Enables you to specify how dates are selected. Possible values are `Day`, `DayWeek`, `DayWeekMonth`, and `None`.

▶ **SelectMonthText**—Enables you to specify the text that appears for selecting a month.

▶ **SelectWeekText**—Enables you to specify the text that appears for selecting a week.

▶ **ShowDayHeader**—Enables you to hide or display the day names at the top of the `Calendar` control.

▶ **ShowNextPrevMonth**—Enables you to hide or display the links for the next and previous months.

▶ **ShowTitle**—Enables you to hide or display the title bar displayed at the top of the calendar.

▶ **TitleFormat**—Enables you to format the title bar. Possible values are Month and MonthYear.

▶ **TodaysDate**—Enables you to specify the current date. This property defaults to the current date on the server.

▶ **VisibleDate**—Enables you to specify the month displayed by the Calendar control. This property defaults to displaying the month that contains the date specified by TodaysDate.

The Calendar control also supports the following events:

▶ **DayRender**—Raised as each day is rendered.

▶ **SelectionChanged**—Raised when a new day, week, or month is selected.

▶ **VisibleMonthChanged**—Raised when the next or previous month link is clicked.

Notice that the SelectionMode property enables you to change the behavior of the calendar so that you can not only select days, but also select weeks or months. The page in Listing 4.8 illustrates how you can use the SelectionMode property in conjunction with the SelectedDates property to select multiple dates (see Figure 4.5).

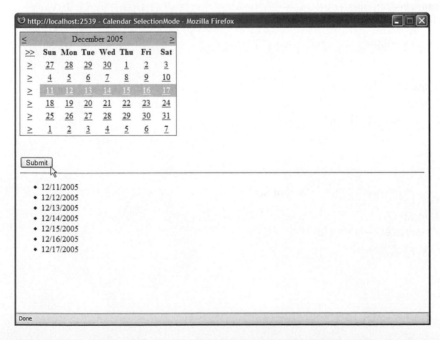

FIGURE 4.5   Selecting weeks and months with a Calendar control.

LISTING 4.8 `CalendarSelectionMode.aspx`

```
<%@ Page Language="C#" %>
<!DOCTYPE html PUBLIC "-//W3C//DTD XHTML 1.0 Transitional//EN"
"http://www.w3.org/TR/xhtml1/DTD/xhtml1-transitional.dtd">
<script runat="server">

    protected void btnSubmit_Click(object sender, EventArgs e)
    {
        bltResults.DataSource = Calendar1.SelectedDates;
        bltResults.DataBind();
    }
</script>
<html xmlns="http://www.w3.org/1999/xhtml" >
<head id="Head1" runat="server">
    <title>Calendar SelectionMode</title>
</head>
<body>
    <form id="form1" runat="server">
    <div>

    <asp:Calendar
        id="Calendar1"
        SelectionMode="DayWeekMonth"
        runat="server" />

    <br /><br />

    <asp:Button
        id="btnSubmit"
        Text="Submit"
        OnClick="btnSubmit_Click"
        Runat="server" />

    <hr />

    <asp:BulletedList
        id="bltResults"
        DataTextFormatString="{0:d}"
        Runat="server" />

    </div>
    </form>
</body>
</html>
```

When you select a date, or group of dates, from the `Calendar` control in Listing 4.8, the set of selected dates are displayed in a `BulletedList` control.

Creating a Pop-up Date Picker

You can use a `Calendar` control to create a fancy pop-up date picker if you are willing to add a little JavaScript and some Cascading Style Sheet rules to a page. The page in Listing 4.9 contains a `TextBox` and `Calendar` control (see Figure 4.6).

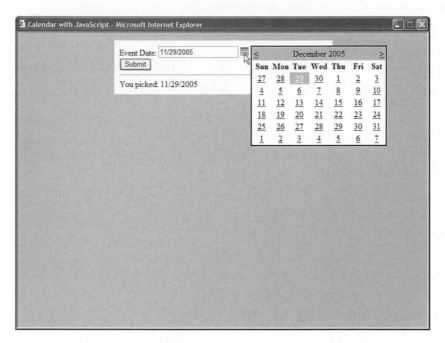

FIGURE 4.6   Displaying a pop-up calendar.

The `Calendar` control is hidden until you click the calendar image. The `#datePicker` style sheet rules sets the display property to `none`. When you click the image of the calendar, the JavaScript `displayCalendar()` function executes and sets the CSS display property to the value `block`.

When you select a date from the calendar, the page is posted back to the server and the `SelectionChanged` server-side event is raised. The `SelectionChanged` event handler updates the `TextBox` control with the selected date.

LISTING 4.9 CalendarJS.aspx

```
<%@ Page Language="C#" %>
<!DOCTYPE html PUBLIC "-//W3C//DTD XHTML 1.0 Transitional//EN"
"http://www.w3.org/TR/xhtml1/DTD/xhtml1-transitional.dtd">
<script runat="server">

    protected void calEventDate_SelectionChanged(object sender, EventArgs e)
    {
        txtEventDate.Text = calEventDate.SelectedDate.ToString("d");
    }

    protected void btnSubmit_Click(object sender, EventArgs e)
    {
        lblResult.Text = "You picked: " + txtEventDate.Text;
    }
</script>
<html xmlns="http://www.w3.org/1999/xhtml" >
<head id="Head1" runat="server">
    <script type="text/javascript">

        function displayCalendar()
        {
            var datePicker = document.getElementById('datePicker');
            datePicker.style.display = 'block';
        }

    </script>
    <style type="text/css">
        #datePicker
        {
            display:none;
            position:absolute;
            border:solid 2px black;
            background-color:white;
        }
        .content
        {
            width:400px;
            background-color:white;
            margin:auto;
            padding:10px;
        }
        html
        {
```

```
                background-color:silver;
          }
     </style>
     <title>Calendar with JavaScript</title>
</head>
<body>
     <form id="form1" runat="server">
     <div class="content">

     <asp:Label
          id="lblEventDate"
          Text="Event Date:"
          AssociatedControlID="txtEventDate"
          Runat="server" />
     <asp:TextBox
          id="txtEventDate"
          Runat="server" />
     <img src="Calendar.gif" onclick="displayCalendar()" />

     <div id="datePicker">
     <asp:Calendar
          id="calEventDate"
          OnSelectionChanged="calEventDate_SelectionChanged"
          Runat="server" />
     </div>

     <br />
     <asp:Button
          id="btnSubmit"
          Text="Submit"
          Runat="server" OnClick="btnSubmit_Click" />

     <hr />

     <asp:Label
          id="lblResult"
          Runat="server" />

     </div>
     </form>
</body>
</html>
```

Rendering a Calendar from a Database Table

You also can use the Calendar control to display events in a calendar. In this section, we build a simple schedule application that enables you to insert, update, and delete calendar entries. Each schedule entry is highlighted in a Calendar control (see Figure 4.7).

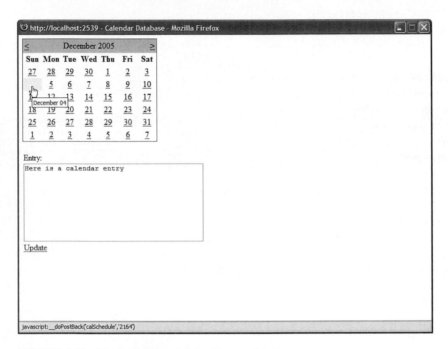

FIGURE 4.7   Displaying a calendar from a database.

The code for the schedule application is contained in Listing 4.10.

LISTING 4.10   CalendarDatabase.aspx

```csharp
<%@ Page Language="C#" ValidateRequest="false" %>
<%@ Import Namespace="System.Data" %>
<!DOCTYPE html PUBLIC "-//W3C//DTD XHTML 1.0 Transitional//EN"
"http://www.w3.org/TR/xhtml1/DTD/xhtml1-transitional.dtd">
<script runat="server">

    DataView schedule = new DataView();

    void Page_Load()
    {
        if (calSchedule.SelectedDate == DateTime.MinValue)
            calSchedule.SelectedDate = calSchedule.TodaysDate;
```

```
        }

    void Page_PreRender()
    {
        schedule = (DataView)srcCalendar.Select(DataSourceSelectArguments.Empty);
        schedule.Sort = "EntryDate";
    }

    protected void calSchedule_DayRender(object sender, DayRenderEventArgs e)
    {
        if (schedule.FindRows(e.Day.Date).Length > 0)
            e.Cell.BackColor = System.Drawing.Color.Yellow;
    }
</script>
<html xmlns="http://www.w3.org/1999/xhtml" >
<head id="Head1" runat="server">
    <title>Calendar Database</title>
</head>
<body>
    <form id="form1" runat="server">
    <div>

    <asp:Calendar
        id-"calSchedule"
        OnDayRender="calSchedule_DayRender"
        Runat="server" />

    <br />

    <asp:FormView
        id="frmSchedule"
        AllowPaging="True"
        DataKeyNames="EntryDate"
        DataSourceID="srcSchedule"
        Runat="server">
        <EmptyDataTemplate>
        <asp:LinkButton
            id="btnNew"
            Text="Add Entry"
            CommandName="New"
            Runat="server" />
        </EmptyDataTemplate>
        <ItemTemplate>
        <h1><%# Eval("EntryDate", "{0:D}") %></h1>
        <%# Eval("Entry") %>
        <br /><br />
```

4

LISTING 4.10   Continued

```
            <asp:LinkButton
                Id="btnEdit"
                Text="Edit Entry"
                CommandName="Edit"
                Runat="server" />
            <asp:LinkButton
                Id="lnkDelete"
                Text="Delete Entry"
                CommandName="Delete"
                OnClientClick="return confirm('Delete entry?');"
                Runat="server" />
        </ItemTemplate>
        <EditItemTemplate>
        <asp:Label
            id="lblEntry"
            Text="Entry:"
            AssociatedControlID="txtEntry"
            Runat="server" />
        <br />
        <asp:TextBox
            id="txtEntry"
            Text='<%#Bind("Entry") %>'
            TextMode="MultiLine"
            Columns="40"
            Rows="8"
            Runat="server" />
        <br />
        <asp:LinkButton
            id="btnUpdate"
            Text="Update"
            CommandName="Update"
            Runat="server" />
        </EditItemTemplate>
        <InsertItemTemplate>
        <asp:Label
            id="lblEntry"
            Text="Entry:"
            AssociatedControlID="txtEntry"
            Runat="server" />
        <br />
        <asp:TextBox
            id="txtEntry"
            Text='<%#Bind("Entry") %>'
            TextMode="MultiLine"
```

```
            Columns="40"
            Rows="8"
            Runat="server" />
        <br />
        <asp:Button
            id="btnInsert"
            Text="Insert"
            CommandName="Insert"
            Runat="server" />
    </InsertItemTemplate>
</asp:FormView>

<asp:SqlDataSource
    id="srcSchedule"
    ConnectionString="Server=.\SQLExpress;Integrated Security=True;
        AttachDbFileName=¦DataDirectory¦ScheduleDB.mdf;User Instance=True"
    SelectCommand="SELECT EntryDate,Entry FROM Schedule WHERE
    ➡EntryDate=@EntryDate"
    InsertCommand="INSERT Schedule (EntryDate,Entry) VALUES
    ➡(@EntryDate,@Entry)"
    UpdateCommand="UPDATE Schedule SET Entry=@Entry WHERE EntryDate=@EntryDate"
    DELETECommand="DELETE Schedule WHERE EntryDate=@EntryDate"
    Runat="server">
    <SelectParameters>
    <asp:ControlParameter
        Name="EntryDate"
        ControlID="calSchedule"
        PropertyName="SelectedDate" />
    </SelectParameters>
    <InsertParameters>
    <asp:ControlParameter
        Name="EntryDate"
        ControlID="calSchedule"
        PropertyName="SelectedDate" />
    </InsertParameters>
</asp:SqlDataSource>

<asp:SqlDataSource
    id="srcCalendar"
    ConnectionString="Server=.\SQLExpress;Integrated Security=True;
        AttachDbFileName=¦DataDirectory¦ScheduleDB.mdf;User Instance=True"
    SelectCommand="SELECT EntryDate FROM Schedule"
    Runat="server">
</asp:SqlDataSource>
```

4

LISTING 4.10   Continued

```
    </div>
    </form>
</body>
</html>
```

The page in Listing 4.10 saves and loads entries from a SQL Express database named ScheduleDB. The contents of the schedule are contained in a table named Schedule that has the following schema:

Column Name	Data Type
EntryDate	DateTime
Entry	Nvarchar(max)

The tricky part in Listing 4.10 is the code for highlighting the current entries in the calendar. In the Page_PreRender event handler, a list of all the current entries is retrieved from the database. The list is represented by a DataView object.

The DayRender event is raised when the Calendar renders each day (table cell). In the DayRender event handler in Listing 4.10, if there is an entry in the database that corresponds to the day being rendered, then the day is highlighted with a yellow background color.

Displaying Advertisements

The AdRotator control enables you to randomly display different advertisements in a page. You can store the list of advertisements in either an XML file or in a database table.

The AdRotator control supports the following properties (this is not a complete list):

▶ **AdvertisementFile**—Enables you to specify the path to an XML file that contains a list of banner advertisements.

▶ **AlternateTextField**—Enables you to specify the name of the field for displaying alternate text for the banner advertisement image. The default value is AlternateText.

▶ **DataMember**—Enables you to bind to a particular data member in the data source.

▶ **DataSource**—Enables you to specify a data source programmatically for the list of banner advertisements.

▶ **DataSourceID**—Enables you to bind to a data source declaratively.

▶ **ImageUrlField**—Enables you to specify the name of the field for the image URL for the banner advertisement. The default value for this field is ImageUrl.

▶ **KeywordFilter**—Enables you to filter advertisements by a single keyword.

▶ **NavigateUrlField**—Enables you to specify the name of the field for the advertisement link. The default value for this field is NavigateUrl.

▶ **Target**—Enables you to open a new window when a user clicks the banner advertisement.

The AdRotator control also supports the following event:

▶ **AdCreated**—Raised after the AdRotator control selects an advertisement but before the AdRotator control renders the advertisement.

Notice that the AdRotator control includes a KeywordFilter property. You can provide each banner advertisement with a keyword and then filter the advertisements displayed by the AdRotator control by using the value of the KeywordFilter property.

This property can be used in multiple ways. For example, if you are displaying more than one advertisement in the same page, then you can filter the advertisements by page regions. You can use the KeywordFilter to show the big banner advertisement on the top of the page and box ads on the side of the page.

You can also use the KeywordFilter property to filter advertisements by website section. For example, you might want to show different advertisements on your website's home page than on your website's search page.

> **NOTE**
>
> If you cache a page that contains an AdRotator control, then the AdRotator control is excluded from the cache. In other words, even if you cache a page, randomly selected banner advertisements are still displayed. The AdRotator control takes advantage of a feature of the ASP.NET Framework called post-cache substitution. You learn more about this feature in Chapter 25, "Caching Application Pages and Data."

Storing Advertisements in an XML File

You can store the list of advertisements that the AdRotator displays in an XML file by setting the AdRotator control's AdvertisementFile property. For example, the page in Listing 4.11 contains three AdRotator controls that retrieve banner advertisements from an XML file named AdList.xml (see Figure 4.8).

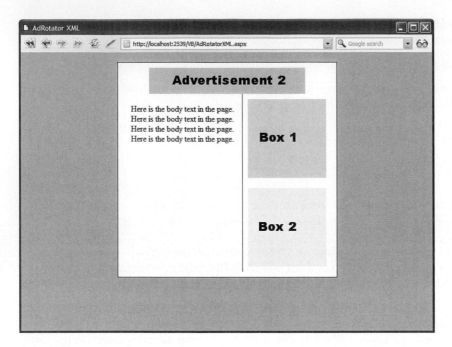

FIGURE 4.8   Displaying advertisements from an XML file.

LISTING 4.11   AdRotatorXML.aspx

```
<%@ Page Language="C#" %>
<!DOCTYPE html PUBLIC "-//W3C//DTD XHTML 1.0 Transitional//EN"
"http://www.w3.org/TR/xhtml1/DTD/xhtml1-transitional.dtd">
<html xmlns="http://www.w3.org/1999/xhtml" >
<head id="Head1" runat="server">
    <style type="text/css">
        html
        {
            background-color:silver;
        }
        .content
        {
            background-color:white;
            padding:10px;
            border:solid 1px black;
            margin:auto;
            width:400px;
            text-align:center;
        }
        .box
```

```
            {
                float:right;
                padding:10px;
                border-left:solid 1px black;
            }
            .clear
            {
                clear:both;
            }
    </style>
    <title>AdRotator XML</title>
</head>
<body>
    <form id="form1" runat="server">
    <div class="content">

    <asp:AdRotator
        id="AdRotator1"
        AdvertisementFile="~/App_Data/AdList.xml"
        KeywordFilter="banner"
        CssClass="banner"
        Runat="server" />

    <br />

    <div class="box">
        <asp:AdRotator
            id="AdRotator2"
            AdvertisementFile="~/App_Data/AdList.xml"
            KeywordFilter="box"
            Runat="server" />
        <br /><br />
        <asp:AdRotator
            id="AdRotator3"
            AdvertisementFile="~/App_Data/AdList.xml"
            KeywordFilter="box"
            Runat="server" />
    </div>


    <br />Here is the body text in the page.
    <br />Here is the body text in the page.
    <br />Here is the body text in the page.
    <br />Here is the body text in the page.
```

LISTING 4.11   Continued

```
    <br class="clear" />
    </div>
    </form>
</body>
</html>
```

The page in Listing 4.11 contains an AdRotator control that displays a banner advertisement at the top of the page. The page also contains two AdRotator controls that display box advertisements on the right of the page.

Notice that the first AdRotator has a KeyworldFilter property that has the value banner, and the remaining two AdRotator controls have KeywordFilter properties with the value box. The first AdRotator displays only banner advertisements, and the remaining two AdRotator controls display only box advertisements.

All three AdRotator controls get their list of banner advertisements from a file named AdList.xml. This file is located in the App_Data folder for security reasons. The files in the App_Data folder cannot be opened in a web browser.

NOTE

There is nothing wrong with assigning different XML files to different AdRotator controls. For example, you could create distinct BannerAd.xml and BoxAd.xml files and then you would not have to worry about the KeywordFilter property.

The file in Listing 4.12 contains the contents of the AdList.xml file.

LISTING 4.12   AdList.xml

```
<Advertisements>
  <!-- Banner Advertisements -->
  <Ad>
    <ImageUrl>~/Ads/BannerAd1.gif</ImageUrl>
    <Width>300</Width>
    <Height>50</Height>
    <NavigateUrl>http://www.AspWorkshops.com</NavigateUrl>
    <AlternateText>Banner Advertisement 1</AlternateText>
    <Impressions>50</Impressions>
    <Keyword>banner</Keyword>
  </Ad>
  <Ad>
    <ImageUrl>~/Ads/BannerAd2.gif</ImageUrl>
    <Width>300</Width>
    <Height>50</Height>
    <NavigateUrl>http://www.AspWorkshops.com</NavigateUrl>
```

```
        <AlternateText>Banner Advertisement 2</AlternateText>
        <Impressions>25</Impressions>
        <Keyword>banner</Keyword>

    <Ad>
        <ImageUrl>~/Ads/BannerAd3.gif</ImageUrl>
        <Width>300</Width>
        <Height>50</Height>
        <NavigateUrl>http://www.AspWorkshops.com</NavigateUrl>
        <AlternateText>Banner Advertisement 3</AlternateText>
        <Impressions>25</Impressions>
        <Keyword>banner</Keyword>
    </Ad>
    <!-- Box Advertisements -->
    <Ad>
        <ImageUrl>~/Ads/BoxAd1.gif</ImageUrl>
        <Width>150</Width>
        <Height>150</Height>
        <NavigateUrl>http://www.AspWorkshops.com</NavigateUrl>
        <AlternateText>Box Advertisement 1</AlternateText>
        <Impressions>50</Impressions>
        <Keyword>box</Keyword>
    </Ad>
    <Ad>
        <ImageUrl>~/Ads/BoxAd2.gif</ImageUrl>
        <Width>150</Width>
        <Height>150</Height>
        <NavigateUrl>http://www.AspWorkshops.com</NavigateUrl>
        <AlternateText>Box Advertisement 2</AlternateText>
        <Impressions>50</Impressions>
        <Keyword>box</Keyword>
    </Ad>
</Advertisements>
```

The Impressions attribute in the file in Listing 4.12 determines how often each banner advertisement is displayed. For example, the first banner advertisement is displayed 50% of the time, and the remaining two banner advertisements are displayed 25% of the time.

Storing Advertisements in a Database Table

Rather than store the list of advertisements in an XML file, you can store the list in a database table. For example, the AdRotator control contained in Listing 4.13 is bound to a SqlDataSource control. The SqlDataSource control represents the contents of a database table named AdList, which is located in a SQL Express database named AdListDB.

LISTING 4.13   `AdRotatorDatabase.aspx`

```
<%@ Page Language="C#" %>
<!DOCTYPE html PUBLIC "-//W3C//DTD XHTML 1.0 Transitional//EN"
"http://www.w3.org/TR/xhtml1/DTD/xhtml1-transitional.dtd">
<html xmlns="http://www.w3.org/1999/xhtml" >
<head id="Head1" runat="server">
    <title>AdRotator Database</title>
</head>
<body>
    <form id="form1" runat="server">
    <div>

    <asp:AdRotator
        id="AdRotator1"
        DataSourceID="srcAds"
        Runat="server" />

    <asp:SqlDataSource
        id="srcAds"
        ConnectionString="Server=.\SQLExpress;Integrated Security=True;
            AttachDbFileName=¦DataDirectory¦AdListDB.mdf;User Instance=True"
        SelectCommand="SELECT ImageUrl, Width, Height, NavigateUrl, AlternateText,
        ►Keyword, Impressions
            FROM AdList"
        Runat="server" />

    </div>
    </form>
</body>
</html>
```

To use the page in Listing 4.13, you need to create the `AdList` database table. This table has the following schema:

Column Name	Data Type
Id	Int (IDENTITY)
ImageUrl	Varchar(250)
Width	Int
Height	Int
NavigateUrl	Varchar(250)
AlternateText	NVarchar(100)

| Keyword | NVarchar(50) |
| Impressions | Int |

Notice that the columns in the AdList database table correspond to the attributes in the AdList.xml file discussed in the previous section.

Tracking Impressions and Transfers

Normally, when you are displaying advertisements, you are doing it to make money. Your advertisers will want statistics on how often their advertisements were displayed (the number of impressions) and how often their advertisements were clicked (the number of transfers).

To track the number of times that an advertisement is displayed, you need to handle the AdRotator control's AdCreated event. To track the number of times that an advertisement is clicked, you need to create a redirect handler.

WARNING

If you create an event handler for the AdCreated event and you cache the page, the content rendered by the AdRotator control will also be cached. When handling the AdCreated event, use partial page caching to cache only part of a page and not the AdRotator control itself.

The page in Listing 4.14 displays a banner advertisement with the AdRotator control. The page includes an event handler for the AdRotator control's AdCreated event.

LISTING 4.14   AdRotatorTrack.aspx

```
<%@ Page Language="C#" %>
<!DOCTYPE html PUBLIC "-//W3C//DTD XHTML 1.0 Transitional//EN"
"http://www.w3.org/TR/xhtml1/DTD/xhtml1-transitional.dtd">
<script runat="server">

    protected void AdRotator1_AdCreated(object sender, AdCreatedEventArgs e)
    {
        // Update Impressions
        srcAds.InsertParameters["AdId"].DefaultValue = e.AdProperties["Id"]
        ➥.ToString();
        srcAds.Insert();

        // Change NavigateUrl to redirect page
        e.NavigateUrl = "~/AdHandler.ashx?id=" + e.AdProperties["Id"].ToString();
    }
</script>
```

4

LISTING 4.14   Continued

```html
<html xmlns="http://www.w3.org/1999/xhtml" >
<head id="Head1" runat="server">
    <title>AdRotator Track</title>
</head>
<body>
    <form id="form1" runat="server">
    <div>

    <asp:AdRotator
        id="AdRotator1"
        DataSourceID="srcAds"
        OnAdCreated="AdRotator1_AdCreated"
        Runat="server" />


    <asp:SqlDataSource
        id="srcAds"
        ConnectionString="Server=.\SQLExpress;Integrated Security=True;
            AttachDbFileName=¦DataDirectory¦AdListDB.mdf;User Instance=True"
        SelectCommand="SELECT Id, ImageUrl, Width, Height, NavigateUrl,
        ➥AlternateText, Keyword, Impressions
            FROM AdList"
        InsertCommand="INSERT AdStats (AdId, EntryDate, Type) VALUES (@AdId,
        ➥GetDate(), 0)"
        Runat="server">
        <InsertParameters>
        <asp:Parameter Name="AdId" Type="int32" />
        </InsertParameters>
     </asp:SqlDataSource>


    </div>
    </form>
</body>
</html>
```

The AdCreated event handler does two things. First, it inserts a new record into a database table named AdStats, which records an advertisement impression. Second, the handler modifies the NavigateUrl so that the user is redirected to a handler named AdHandler.ashx.

The AdStats database table looks like this:

Column Name	Data Type
Id	Int (IDENTITY)
AdId	Int
EntryDate	DateTime
Type	Int

The Type column is used to record the type of entry. The value 0 represents an advertisement impression, and the value 1 represents an advertisement transfer.

When you click an advertisement, you link to a file named AdHandler.ashx. This file is contained in Listing 4.15.

LISTING 4.15   AdHandler.ashx

```
<%@ WebHandler Language="C#" Class="AdHandler" %>

using System;
using System.Web;
using System.Data;
using System.Data.SqlClient;

public class AdHandler : IHttpHandler {

    const string conString = @"Server=.\SQLExpress;Integrated Security=True;
        AttachDbFileName=¦DataDirectory¦AdListDB.mdf;User Instance=True";

    public void ProcessRequest (HttpContext context)
    {
        int AdId = Int32.Parse(context.Request["Id"]);

        SqlConnection con = new SqlConnection(conString);
        string navigateUrl = String.Empty;
        using (con)
        {
            con.Open();
            UpdateTransferStats(AdId, con);
            navigateUrl = GetNavigateUrl(AdId, con);
        }

        if (!String.IsNullOrEmpty(navigateUrl))
            context.Response.Redirect(navigateUrl);
    }
```

LISTING 4.15   Continued

```csharp
void UpdateTransferStats(int advertisementId, SqlConnection con)
{
    string cmdText = "INSERT AdStats (AdId, EntryDate, Type) VALUES " +
        "(@AdId, GetDate(), 1)";
    SqlCommand cmd = new SqlCommand(cmdText, con);
    cmd.Parameters.AddWithValue("@AdId", advertisementId);
    cmd.ExecuteNonQuery();
}

string GetNavigateUrl(int advertisementId, SqlConnection con)
{
    string cmdText = "SELECT NavigateUrl FROM AdList WHERE Id=@AdId";
    SqlCommand cmd = new SqlCommand(cmdText, con);
    cmd.Parameters.AddWithValue("@AdId", advertisementId);
    return cmd.ExecuteScalar().ToString();
}


public bool IsReusable
{
    get
    {
        return false;
    }
}

}
```

The handler in Listing 4.15 performs two tasks. First, it inserts a new record into the AdStats database table, recording the fact that a transfer is taking place. Next, it grabs the NavigateUrl from the AdList database table and sends the user to the advertiser's website.

The final page displays advertiser statistics from the AdStats database table (see Figure 4.9). This page is contained in Listing 4.16.

LISTING 4.16   AdRotatorStats.aspx

```aspx
<%@ Page Language="C#" %>
<!DOCTYPE html PUBLIC "-//W3C//DTD XHTML 1.0 Transitional//EN"
"http://www.w3.org/TR/xhtml1/DTD/xhtml1-transitional.dtd">
<html xmlns="http://www.w3.org/1999/xhtml" >
<head id="Head1" runat="server">
    <style type="text/css">
        .grid td,.grid th
```

```
            {
                border-bottom:solid 1px black;
                padding:5px;
            }
        </style>
        <title>AdRotator Statistics</title>
    </head>
<body>
    <form id="form1" runat="server">
    <div>

    <h1>Advertisement Statistics</h1>
    Impressions represent the number of times an advertisement has been viewed.
    Transfers represent the number of times an advertisement has been clicked.

    <h2>Impressions</h2>

    <asp:GridView
        id="grdImpressions"
        DataSourceID="srcImpressions"
        AutoGenerateColumns="false"
        GridLines="None"
        CssClass="grid"
        Runat="server">
        <Columns>
        <asp:BoundField
            DataField="AdId"
            HeaderText="Advertisement Id" />
        <asp:BoundField
            DataField="Impressions"
            HeaderText="Impressions" />
        </Columns>
    </asp:GridView>

    <asp:SqlDataSource
        id="srcImpressions"
        ConnectionString="Server=.\SQLExpress;Integrated Security=True;
            AttachDbFileName=|DataDirectory|AdListDB.mdf;User Instance=True"
        SelectCommand="SELECT AdId,Count(*) As Impressions
            FROM AdStats
            WHERE Type=0
            GROUP BY AdId
            ORDER BY Impressions DESC"
        Runat="server" />
```

LISTING 14.16   Continued

```
    <h2>Transfers</h2>

    <asp:GridView
        id="grdTransfers"
        DataSourceID="srcTransfers"
        AutoGenerateColumns="false"
        GridLines="None"
        CssClass="grid"
        Runat="server">
        <Columns>
        <asp:BoundField
            DataField="AdId"
            HeaderText="Advertisement Id" />
        <asp:BoundField
            DataField="Transfers"
            HeaderText="Transfers" />
        </Columns>
    </asp:GridView>

    <asp:SqlDataSource
        id="srcTransfers"
        ConnectionString="Server=.\SQLExpress;Integrated Security=True;
            AttachDbFileName=¦DataDirectory¦AdListDB.mdf;User Instance=True"
        SelectCommand="SELECT AdId,Count(*) As Transfers
            FROM AdStats
            WHERE Type=1
            GROUP BY AdId
            ORDER BY Transfers DESC"
        Runat="server" />

    </div>
    </form>
</body>
</html>
```

The page in Listing 4.16 contains two GridView controls bound to two SqlDataSource controls. The first GridView displays statistics on impressions, and the second GridView displays statistics on transfers.

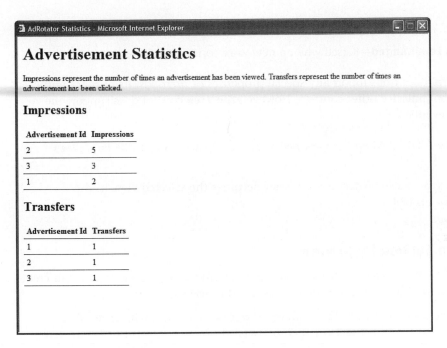

FIGURE 4.9   Displaying advertiser statistics.

Displaying Different Page Views

The MultiView control enables you to hide and display different areas of a page. This control is useful when you need to create a tabbed page. It is also useful when you need to divide a long form into multiple forms.

The MultiView control contains one or more View controls. You use the MultiView control to select a particular View control to render. (The selected View control is the Active View.) The contents of the remaining View controls are hidden. You can render only one View control at a time.

The MultiView control supports the following properties (this is not a complete list):

▸ **ActiveViewIndex**—Enables you to select the View control to render by index.

▸ **Views**—Enables you to retrieve the collection of View controls contained in the MultiView control.

The MultiView control also supports the following methods:

▸ **GetActiveView**—Enables you to retrieve the selected View control.

▸ **SetActiveView**—Enables you to select the active view.

Finally, the MultiView control supports the following event:

▶ **ActiveViewChanged**—Raised when a new View control is selected.

The View control does not support any special properties or methods. Its primary purpose is to act as a container for other controls. However, the View control does support the following two events:

▶ **Activate**—Raised when the view becomes the selected view in the MultiView control.

▶ **Deactivate**—Raised when another view becomes the selected view in the MultiView control.

Displaying a Tabbed Page View

When you use the MultiView control in conjunction with the Menu control, you can create a tabbed page view. (To make it look pretty, you need to use some CSS.)

For example, the page in Listing 4.17 contains a MultiView control with three View controls. The Menu control is used to switch between the View controls (see Figure 4.10).

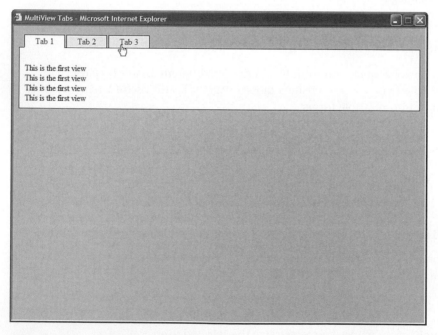

FIGURE 4.10   Displaying a tabbed page with the MultiView control.

LISTING 4.17 `MultiViewTabs.aspx`

```
<%@ Page Language="C#" %>
<!DOCTYPE html PUBLIC "-//W3C//DTD XHTML 1.0 Transitional//EN"
"http://www.w3.org/TR/xhtml1/DTD/xhtml1-transitional.dtd">
<script runat="server">

    protected void Menu1_MenuItemClick(object sender, MenuEventArgs e)
    {
        int index = Int32.Parse(e.Item.Value);
        MultiView1.ActiveViewIndex = index;
    }
</script>
<html xmlns="http://www.w3.org/1999/xhtml" >
<head id="Head1" runat="server">
    <style type="text/css">
        html
        {
            background-color:silver;
        }
        .tabs
        {
            position:relative;
            top:1px;
            left:10px;
        }
        .tab
        {
            border:solid 1px black;
            background-color:#eeeeee;
            padding:2px 10px;
        }
        .selectedTab
        {
            background-color:white;
            border-bottom:solid 1px white;
        }
        .tabContents
        {
            border:solid 1px black;
            padding:10px;
            background-color:white;
        }
    </style>
    <title>MultiView Tabs</title>
</head>
```

LISTING 4.17   Continued

```
<body>
    <form id="form1" runat="server">
    <div>

    <asp:Menu
        id="Menu1"
        Orientation="Horizontal"
        StaticMenuItemStyle-CssClass="tab"
        StaticSelectedStyle-CssClass="selectedTab"
        CssClass="tabs"
        OnMenuItemClick="Menu1_MenuItemClick"
        Runat="server">
        <Items>
        <asp:MenuItem Text="Tab 1" Value="0" Selected="true" />
        <asp:MenuItem Text="Tab 2" Value="1" />
        <asp:MenuItem Text="Tab 3" Value="2" />
        </Items>
    </asp:Menu>

    <div class="tabContents">
    <asp:MultiView
        id="MultiView1"
        ActiveViewIndex="0"
        Runat="server">
        <asp:View ID="View1" runat="server">
            <br />This is the first view
            <br />This is the first view
            <br />This is the first view
            <br />This is the first view
        </asp:View>
        <asp:View ID="View2" runat="server">
            <br />This is the second view
            <br />This is the second view
            <br />This is the second view
            <br />This is the second view
        </asp:View>
        <asp:View ID="View3" runat="server">
            <br />This is the third view
            <br />This is the third view
            <br />This is the third view
            <br />This is the third view
        </asp:View>
    </asp:MultiView>
    </div>
```

```
    </div>
    </form>
</body>
</html>
```

In Listing 4.17, the Menu control is associated with a CSS class named tabs. This class relatively positions the Menu control down one pixel to merge the bottom border of the Menu control with the top border of the <div> tag that contains the MultiView. Because the selected tab has a white bottom border, the border between the selected tab and the tab contents disappears.

Displaying a Multi-Part Form

You can use the MultiView control to divide a large form into several sub-forms. You can associate particular commands with button controls contained in a MultiView. When the button is clicked, the MultiView changes the active view.

The MultiView control recognizes the following commands:

- ▶ **NextView**—Causes the MultiView to activate the next View control.

- ▶ **PrevView**—Causes the MultiView to activate the previous View control.

- ▶ **SwitchViewByID**—Causes the MultiView to activate the view specified by the button control's CommandArgument.

- ▶ **SwitchViewByIndex**—Causes the MultiView to activate the view specified by the button control's CommandArgument.

You can use these commands with any of the button controls—Button, LinkButton, and ImageButton—by setting the button control's CommandName property and, in the case of the SwitchViewByID and SwitchViewByIndex, by setting the CommandArgument property.

The page in Listing 4.18 illustrates how you can use the NextView command to create a multiple-part form.

LISTING 4.18 MultiViewForm.aspx

```
<%@ Page Language="C#" %>
<!DOCTYPE html PUBLIC "-//W3C//DTD XHTML 1.0 Transitional//EN"
"http://www.w3.org/TR/xhtml1/DTD/xhtml1-transitional.dtd">
<script runat="server">

    protected void View3_Activate(object sender, EventArgs e)
    {
        lblFirstNameResult.Text = txtFirstName.Text;
        lblColorResult.Text = txtColor.Text;
    }
</script>
```

LISTING 4.18   Continued

```
<html xmlns="http://www.w3.org/1999/xhtml" >
<head id="Head1" runat="server">
    <title>MultiView Form</title>
</head>
<body>
    <form id="form1" runat="server">
    <div>

    <asp:MultiView
        id="MultiView1"
        ActiveViewIndex="0"
        Runat="server">
        <asp:View ID="View1" runat="server">
        <h1>Step 1</h1>
        <asp:Label
            id="lblFirstName"
            Text="Enter Your First Name:"
            AssociatedControlID="txtFirstName"
            Runat="server" />
        <br />
        <asp:TextBox
            id="txtFirstName"
            Runat="server" />

        <br /><br />

        <asp:Button
            id="btnNext"
            Text="Next"
            CommandName="NextView"
            Runat="server" />

        </asp:View>
        <asp:View ID="View2" runat="server">
        <h1>Step 2</h1>
        <asp:Label
            id="Label1"
            Text="Enter Your Favorite Color:"
            AssociatedControlID="txtColor"
            Runat="server" />
        <br />
        <asp:TextBox
            id="txtColor"
            Runat="server" />
```

```
            <br /><br />

            <asp:Button
                id="Button1"
                Text="Next"
                CommandName="NextView"
                Runat="server" />

            </asp:View>
            <asp:View ID="View3" runat="server" OnActivate="View3_Activate">
            <h1>Summary</h1>
            Your First Name:
            <asp:Label
                id="lblFirstNameResult"
                Runat="server" />
            <br /><br />
            Your Favorite Color:
            <asp:Label
                id="lblColorResult"
                Runat="server" />
            </asp:View>
        </asp:MultiView>

        </div>
        </form>
</body>
</html>
```

The first two View controls in Listing 4.18 contain a Button control. These Button controls both have a CommandName property set to the value NextView.

Displaying a Wizard

The Wizard control, like the MultiView control, can be used to divide a large form into multiple sub-forms. The Wizard control, however, supports many advanced features that are not supported by the MultiView control.

The Wizard control contains one or more WizardStep child controls. Only one WizardStep is displayed at a time.

The Wizard control supports the following properties (this is not a complete list):

▶ **ActiveStep**—Enables you to retrieve the active WizardStep control.

▶ **ActiveStepIndex**—Enables you to set or get the index of the active WizardStep control.

▶ **CancelDestinationPageUrl**—Enables you to specify the URL where the user is sent when the Cancel button is clicked.

▶ **DisplayCancelButton**—Enables you to hide or display the Cancel button.

▶ **DisplaySideBar**—Enables you to hide or display the Wizard control's sidebar. The sidebar displays a list of all the wizard steps.

▶ **FinishDestinationPageUrl**—Enables you to specify the URL where the user is sent when the Finish button is clicked.

▶ **HeaderText**—Enables you to specify the header text that appears at the top of the Wizard control.

▶ **WizardSteps**—Enables you to retrieve the WizardStep controls contained in the Wizard control.

The Wizard control also supports the following templates:

▶ **FinishNavigationTemplate**—Enables you to control the appearance of the navigation area of the finish step.

▶ **HeaderTemplate**—Enables you control the appearance of the header area of the Wizard control.

▶ **SideBarTemplate**—Enables you to control the appearance of the sidebar area of the Wizard control.

▶ **StartNavigationTemplate**—Enables you to control the appearance of the navigation area of the start step.

▶ **StepNavigationTemplate**—Enables you to control the appearance of the navigation area of steps that are not start, finish, or complete steps.

The Wizard control also supports the following methods:

▶ **GetHistory()**—Enables you to retrieve the collection of WizardStep controls that have been accessed.

▶ **GetStepType()**—Enables you to return the type of WizardStep at a particular index. Possible values are Auto, Complete, Finish, Start, and Step.

▶ **MoveTo()**—Enables you to move to a particular WizardStep.

The Wizard control also supports the following events:

▶ **ActiveStepChanged**—Raised when a new WizardStep becomes the active step.

▶ **CancelButtonClick**—Raised when the Cancel button is clicked.

▶ **FinishButtonClick**—Raised when the Finish button is clicked.

▶ **NextButtonClick**—Raised when the Next button is clicked.

▶ **PreviousButtonClick**—Raised when the Previous button is clicked.

> ► **SideBarButtonClick**—Raised when a sidebar button is clicked.

A `Wizard` control contains one or more `WizardStep` controls that represent steps in the wizard. The `WizardStep` control supports the following properties:

> ► **AllowReturn**—Enables you to prevent or allow a user to return to this step from a future step.

> ► **Name**—Enables you to return the name of the `WizardStep` control.

> ► **StepType**—Enables you to get or set the type of wizard step. Possible values are `Auto`, `Complete`, `Finish`, `Start`, and `Step`.

> ► **Title**—Enables you to get or set the title of the `WizardStep`. The title is displayed in the wizard sidebar.

> ► **Wizard**—Enables you to retrieve the `Wizard` control containing the `WizardStep`.

The `WizardStep` also supports the following two events:

> ► **Activate**—Raised when a `WizardStep` becomes active.

> ► **Deactivate**—Raised when another `WizardStep` becomes active.

The `StepType` property is the most important property. This property determines how a `WizardStep` is rendered. The default value of `StepType` is `Auto`. When `StepType` is set to the value `Auto`, the position of the `WizardStep` in the `WizardSteps` collection determines how the `WizardStep` is rendered.

You can explicitly set the `StepType` property to a particular value. If you set `StepType` to the value `Start`, then a Previous button is not rendered. If you set the `StepType` to `Step`, then both Previous and Next buttons are rendered. If you set `StepType` to the value `Finish`, then Previous and Finish buttons are rendered. Finally, when `StepType` is set to the value `Complete`, no buttons are rendered.

The page in Listing 4.19 illustrates how you can use a `Wizard` control to display a multiple part form (see Figure 4.11).

LISTING 4.19   ShowWizard.aspx

```
<%@ Page Language="C#" %>
<!DOCTYPE html PUBLIC "-//W3C//DTD XHTML 1.0 Transitional//EN"
"http://www.w3.org/TR/xhtml1/DTD/xhtml1-transitional.dtd">
<script runat="server">

    protected void Wizard1_FinishButtonClick(object sender,
    ➥WizardNavigationEventArgs e)
    {
        lblSSNResult.Text = txtSSN.Text;
        lblPhoneResult.Text = txtPhone.Text;
    }
```

LISTING 4.19   Continued

```
</script>
<html xmlns="http://www.w3.org/1999/xhtml" >
<head id="Head1" runat="server">
    <style type="text/css">
        .wizard
        {
            border:solid 1px black;
            font:14px Verdana,Sans-Serif;
            width:400px;
            height:300px;
        }
        .header
        {
            color:gray;
            font:bold 18px Verdana,Sans-Serif;
        }
        .sideBar
        {
            background-color:#eeeeee;
            padding:10px;
            width:100px;
        }
        .sideBar a
        {
            text-decoration:none;
        }
        .step
        {
            padding:10px;
        }
    </style>
    <title>Show Wizard</title>
</head>
<body>
    <form id="form1" runat="server">
    <div>

    <asp:Wizard
        id="Wizard1"
        HeaderText="Product Survey"
        OnFinishButtonClick="Wizard1_FinishButtonClick"
        CssClass="wizard"
        HeaderStyle-CssClass="header"
        SideBarStyle-CssClass="sideBar"
```

```
StepStyle-CssClass="step"
Runat="server">
<WizardSteps>
<asp:WizardStep ID="WizardStep1" Title="Introduction">
Please complete our survey so that we can improve our
products.
</asp:WizardStep>
<asp:WizardStep ID="WizardStep2" Title="Step 1">
<asp:Label
    id="lblSSN"
    Text="Social Security Number:"
    AssociatedControlID="txtSSN"
    Runat="server" />
<br />
<asp:TextBox
    id="txtSSN"
    Runat="server" />
</asp:WizardStep>
<asp:WizardStep ID="WizardStep3" Title="Step 2" StepType="Finish">
<asp:Label
    id="lblPhone"
    Text="Phone Number:"
    AssociatedControlID="txtPhone"
    Runat="server" />
<br />
<asp:TextBox
    id="txtPhone"
    Runat="server" />
</asp:WizardStep>
<asp:WizardStep ID="WizardStep4" Title="Summary" StepType="Complete">
<h1>Summary</h1>
Social Security Number:
<asp:Label
    id="lblSSNResult"
    Runat="server" />
<br /><br />
Phone Number:
<asp:Label
    id="lblPhoneResult"
    Runat="server" />
</asp:WizardStep>
</WizardSteps>
</asp:Wizard>
```

LISTING 4.19   Continued

```
      </div>
      </form>
</body>
</html>
```

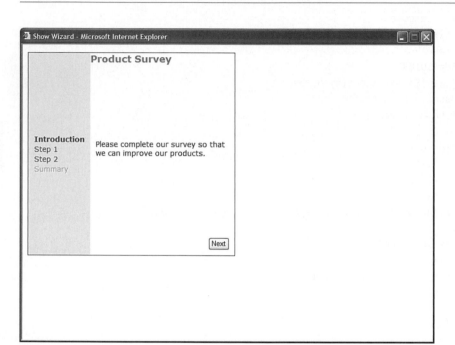

FIGURE 4.11   Displaying a wizard with the Wizard control.

The Wizard control in Listing 4.19 contains four WizardStep controls. Notice that the StepType property is explicitly set for the last two WizardStep controls. When the Finish WizardStep is rendered, a Finish button is rendered. When the Complete WizardStep is rendered, no buttons are rendered.

The Wizard control's FinishButtonClick event is handled with a method named Wizard1_FinishButtonClick(). This method updates the final WizardStep with a summary of the answers entered in the previous WizardStep controls.

Summary

This chapter tackled the rich controls. You learned how to perform file uploads with the FileUpload control. You also saw how to accept and display large file uploads by dividing the file into smaller chunks.

You also learned how to use the Calendar control to display a date picker and render a schedule of events. Using a tiny bit of JavaScript, you learned how to create a fancy pop-up date picker.

This chapter also discussed the AdRotator control. You learned how to store a list of advertisements in both an XML file and a database table. You also learned how to track advertisement impressions and transfers and build a statistics page.

You also learned how to use the MultiView control to display different views of a page. You learned how to create a tabbed page by using the MultiView control with the Menu control. You also learned how to use the MultiView to divide a large form into multiple sub-forms.

Finally, we discussed the Wizard control. You learned how to use the Wizard control to render navigation elements automatically for completing a multiple-step task.

4

PART II

Designing ASP.NET Websites

IN THIS PART

Designing Websites with Master Pages

A Master Page enables you to share the same content among multiple content pages in a website. You can use a Master Page to create a common page layout. For example, if you want all the pages in your website to share a three-column layout, you can create the layout once in a Master Page and apply the layout to multiple content pages.

You also can use Master Pages to display common content in multiple pages. For example, if you want to display a standard header and footer in each page in your website, then you can create the standard header and footer in a Master Page.

By taking advantage of Master Pages, you can make your website easier to maintain, extend, and modify. If you need to add a new page to your website that looks just like the other pages in your website, then you simply need to apply the same Master Page to the new content page. If you decide to completely modify the design of your website, you do not need to change every content page. You can modify just a single Master Page to dramatically change the appearance of all the pages in your application.

In this chapter, you learn how to create Master Pages and apply Master Pages to content pages. It describes how you can apply a Master Page to an entire application by register-ing the Master Page in the web configuration file.

It also explores different methods of modifying content in a Master Page from individual content pages. For example, you learn how to change the title displayed by a Master Page for each content page.

Finally, you learn how to load Master Pages dynamically. Loading Master Pages dynamically is useful when you need to co-brand one website with another website, or when you want to enable individual website users to customize the appearance of your website.

Creating Master Pages

You create a Master Page by creating a file that ends with the .master extension. You can locate a Master Page file any place within an application. Furthermore, you can add multiple Master Pages to the same application.

For example, Listing 5.1 contains a simple Master Page.

LISTING 5.1   SimpleMaster.master

```
<%@ Master Language="C#" %>
<!DOCTYPE html PUBLIC "-//W3C//DTD XHTML 1.1//EN"
"http://www.w3.org/TR/xhtml11/DTD/xhtml11.dtd">
<html xmlns="http://www.w3.org/1999/xhtml" >
<head id="Head1" runat="server">
    <style type="text/css">
        html
        {
            background-color:silver;
            font:14px Arial,Sans-Serif;
        }
        .content
        {
            margin:auto;
            width:700px;
            background-color:white;
            border:Solid 1px black;
        }
        .leftColumn
        {
            float:left;
            padding:5px;
            width:200px;
            border-right:Solid 1px black;
            height:700px;

        }
        .rightColumn
        {
            float:left;
            padding:5px;
        }
        .clear
```

```
            {
                clear:both;
            }
        </style>
        <title>Simple Master</title>
    </head>
    <body>
        <form id="form1" runat="server">
        <div class="content">
            <div class="leftColumn">

                <asp:contentplaceholder
                    id="ContentPlaceHolder1"
                    runat="server"/>

            </div>
            <div class="rightColumn">

                <asp:contentplaceholder
                    id="ContentPlaceHolder2"
                    runat="server"/>

            </div>
            <br class="clear" />
        </div>
        </form>
    </body>
</html>
```

Notice that the Master Page in Listing 5.1 looks very much like a normal ASP.NET page. In fact, you can place almost all the same elements in a Master Page that you could place in an ASP.NET page, including HTML, server-side scripts, and ASP.NET controls.

There are two special things about the Master Page in Listing 5.1. First, notice that the file contains a <%@ Master %> directive instead of the normal <%@ Page %> directive. Second, notice that the Master Page includes two ContentPlaceHolder controls.

When the Master Page is merged with a particular content page, the content from the content page appears in the areas marked by ContentPlaceHolder controls. You can add as many ContentPlaceHolders to a Master Page as you need.

> **WARNING**
>
> There are some things that you can't do in a Master Page that you can do in a content page. For example, you cannot cache a Master Page with the `OutputCache` directive. You also cannot apply a theme to a Master Page.

The Master Page in Listing 5.1 creates a two-column page layout. Each `ContentPlaceHolder` control is contained in a separate `<div>` tag. Cascading Style Sheet rules are used to position the two `<div>` tags into a two-column page layout (see Figure 5.1).

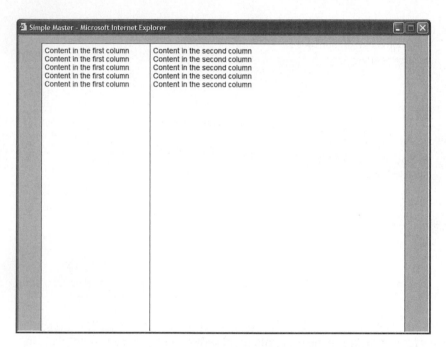

FIGURE 5.1   Creating a two-column Master Page.

> **WEB STANDARDS NOTE**
>
> The Master Page uses Cascading Style Sheets to create the page layout. You should strive to avoid using HTML tables for layout. HTML tables should be used only to display tabular information.

The content page in Listing 5.2 uses the Master Page that was just created.

LISTING 5.2 SimpleContent.aspx

```
<%@ Page Language="C#" MasterPageFile="~/SimpleMaster.master" %>

<asp:Content
    ID="Content1"
    ContentPlaceHolderID="ContentPlaceHolder1"
    Runat="Server">
    Content in the first column
    <br />Content in the first column
    <br />Content in the first column
    <br />Content in the first column
    <br />Content in the first column
</asp:Content>

<asp:Content
    ID="Content2"
    ContentPlaceHolderID="ContentPlaceHolder2"
    Runat="Server">
    Content in the second column
    <br />Content in the second column
    <br />Content in the second column
    <br />Content in the second column
    <br />Content in the second column
</asp:Content>
```

When you open the page in Listing 5.2 in a web browser, the contents of the page are merged with the Master Page.

VISUAL WEB DEVELOPER NOTE

In Visual Web Developer, you create an ASP.NET page that is associated with a particular Master Page by selecting Website, Add New Item, and selecting Web Form. Next, check the check box labeled Select Master Page. When you click Add, a dialog box appears that enables you to select a Master Page.

The Master Page is associated with the content page through the `MasterPageFile` attribute included in the `<%@ Page %>` directive. This attribute contains the virtual path to a Master Page.

Notice that the content page does not contain any of the standard opening and closing XHTML tags. All these tags are contained in the Master Page. All the content contained in the content page must be added with Content controls.

You must place all the content contained in a content page within the Content controls. If you attempt to place any content outside these controls, you get an exception.

The Content control includes a `ContentPlaceHolderID` property. This property points to the ID of a `ContentPlaceHolder` control contained in the Master Page.

Within a Content control, you can place anything that you would normally add to an ASP.NET page, including XHTML tags and ASP.NET controls.

Creating Default Content

You don't have to associate a Content control with every `ContentPlaceHolder` control contained in a Master Page. You can provide default content in a `ContentPlaceHolder` control, and the default content will appear unless it is overridden in a particular content page.

For example, the Master Page in Listing 5.3 includes an additional column, which displays a banner advertisement (see Figure 5.2). The banner advertisement is contained in a `ContentPlaceHolder` control named `contentAd`.

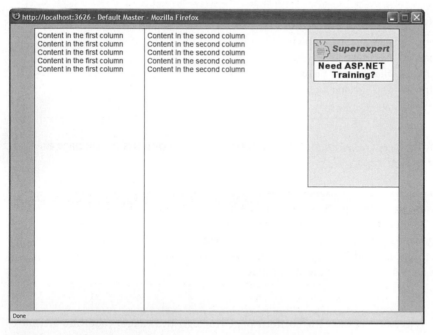

FIGURE 5.2   Displaying default content in a Master Page.

LISTING 5.3   `DefaultMaster.master`

```
<%@ Master Language="C#" %>
<!DOCTYPE html PUBLIC "-//W3C//DTD XHTML 1.1//EN"
"http://www.w3.org/TR/xhtml11/DTD/xhtml11.dtd">
```

```
<html xmlns="http://www.w3.org/1999/xhtml" >
<head id="Head1" runat="server">
    <style type="text/css">
        html
        {
            background-color:silver;
            font:14px Arial,Sans-Serif;
        }
        .content
        {
            margin:auto;
            width:700px;
            background-color:white;
            border:Solid 1px black;
        }
        .leftColumn
        {
            float:left;
            padding:5px;
            width:200px;
            border-right:Solid 1px black;
            height:700px;

        }
        .middleColumn
        {
            float:left;
            padding:5px;
        }
        .rightColumn
        {
            float:right;
            width:175px;
            height:300px;
            border-left:solid 1px black;
            border-bottom:solid 1px black;
            background-color:#eeeeee;
            text-align:center;
        }
        .ad
        {
            margin-top:20px;
        }
        .clear
        {
            clear:both;
```

5

LISTING 5.3   Continued

```
        }
    </style>
    <title>Default Master</title>
</head>
<body>
    <form id="form1" runat="server">
    <div class="content">
        <div class="leftColumn">

            <asp:contentplaceholder
                id="ContentPlaceHolder1"
                runat="server"/>

        </div>
        <div class="middleColumn">

            <asp:ContentPlaceholder
                id="ContentPlaceHolder2"
                runat="server" />

        </div>
        <div class="rightColumn">

            <asp:ContentPlaceHolder
                id="contentAd"
                Runat="server">
                <asp:Image
                    id="imgAd"
                    ImageUrl="~/BannerAd.gif"
                    CssClass="ad"
                    AlternateText="Advertisement for Superexpert ASP Workshops"
                    Runat="server" />
            </asp:ContentPlaceHolder>

        </div>
        <br class="clear" />
    </div>
    </form>
</body>
</html>
```

The content page in Listing 5.4 uses the Master Page in Listing 5.3. It does not include a Content control that corresponds to the contentAd control in the Master Page. When you open the page in a browser, the default banner advertisement is displayed.

LISTING 5.4 `DefaultContent.aspx`

```
<%@ Page Language="C#" MasterPageFile="~/DefaultMaster.master" %>


<asp:Content
    ID="Content1"
    ContentPlaceHolderID="ContentPlaceHolder1"
    Runat="Server">
    Content in the first column
    <br />Content in the first column
    <br />Content in the first column
    <br />Content in the first column
    <br />Content in the first column
</asp:Content>


<asp:Content
    ID="Content2"
    ContentPlaceHolderID="ContentPlaceHolder2"
    Runat="Server">
    Content in the second column
    <br />Content in the second column
    <br />Content in the second column
    <br />Content in the second column
    <br />Content in the second column
</asp:Content>
```

Of course, you do have the option of adding a `Content` control that overrides the default content contained in the `contentAd` control in the Master Page. For example, you might want to display different banner advertisements in different sections of your website.

> **NOTE**
>
> You can nest `ContentPlaceHolder` controls in a Master Page. If you do this, then you have the option of overriding greater or smaller areas of content in the Master Page.

Nesting Master Pages

When building a large website, you might need to create multiple levels of Master Pages. For example, you might want to create a single site-wide Master Page that applies to all the content pages in your website. In addition, you might need to create multiple section-wide Master Pages that apply to only the pages contained in a particular section.

> **NOTE**
>
> Unlike earlier versions of Visual Web Developer, Visual Web Developer 2008 supports working with nested Master Pages in Design view.

You can nest Master Pages as many levels as you need. For example, Listing 5.5 contains a Master Page named Site.master, which displays a logo image and contains a single content area. It also contains site-wide navigation links.

LISTING 5.5   Site.master

```
<%@ Master Language="C#" %>
<!DOCTYPE html PUBLIC "-//W3C//DTD XHTML 1.1//EN"
"http://www.w3.org/TR/xhtml11/DTD/xhtml11.dtd">
<html xmlns="http://www.w3.org/1999/xhtml" >
<head id="Head1" runat="server">
    <style type="text/css">
        html
        {
            background-color:DarkGreen;
            font:14px Georgia,Serif;
        }
        .content
        {
            width:700px;
            margin:auto;
            border-style:solid;
            background-color:white;
            padding:10px;
        }
        .tabstrip
        {
            padding:3px;
            border-top:solid 1px black;
            border-bottom:solid 1px black;
        }
        .tabstrip a
        {
            font:14px Arial;
            color:DarkGreen;
            text-decoration:none;
        }
        .column
        {
            float:left;
            padding:10px;
            border-right:solid 1px black;
        }
        .rightColumn
        {
```

```
            float:left;
            padding:10px;
        }
        .clear
        {
            clear:both;
        }
    </style>
    <title>Site Master</title>
</head>
<body>
    <form id="form1" runat="server">

    <div class="content">
        <asp:Image
            id="imgLogo"
            ImageUrl="~/Images/SiteLogo.gif"
            AlternateText="Website Logo"
            Runat="server" />

        <div class="tabstrip">
        <asp:HyperLink
            id="lnkProducts"
            Text="Products"
            NavigateUrl="~/Products.aspx"
            Runat="server" />
         
        <asp:HyperLink
            id="lnkServices"
            Text="Services"
            NavigateUrl="~/Services.aspx"
            Runat="server" />
        </div>
        <asp:contentplaceholder id="ContentPlaceHolder1" runat="server">
        </asp:contentplaceholder>
        <br class="clear" />
        copyright &copy; 2007 by the Company
    </div>
    </form>
</body>
</html>
```

The Master Pages in Listing 5.6 and Listing 5.7 are nested Master Pages. Notice that both Master Pages include a `MasterPageFile` attribute that points to the `Site.master` Master Page.

LISTING 5.6   `SectionProducts.master`

```
<%@ Master Language="C#" MasterPageFile="~/Site.master" %>


<asp:Content
    id="Content1"
    ContentPlaceHolderID="ContentPlaceHolder1"
    Runat="server">
    <div class="column">
        <asp:ContentPlaceHolder
            id="ContentPlaceHolder1"
            Runat="server" />
    </div>
    <div class="column">
        <asp:ContentPlaceHolder
            id="ContentPlaceHolder2"
            Runat="server" />
    </div>
    <div class="rightColumn">
        <asp:ContentPlaceHolder
            id="ContentPlaceHolder3"
            Runat="server" />
    </div>
</asp:Content>
```

LISTING 5.7   `SectionServices.master`

```
<%@ Master Language="C#" MasterPageFile="~/Site.master" %>


<asp:Content
    id="Content1"
    ContentPlaceHolderID="ContentPlaceHolder1"
    Runat="server">
    <div class="column">
        <asp:ContentPlaceHolder
            id="ContentPlaceHolder1"
            Runat="server" />
    </div>
    <div class="rightColumn">
        <asp:ContentPlaceHolder
            id="ContentPlaceHolder2"
            Runat="server" />
    </div>
</asp:Content>
```

The Master Page in Listing 5.6 creates a three-column page layout, and the Master Page in Listing 5.7 creates a two-column page layout.

The Products.aspx page in Listing 5.8 uses the SectionProducts.master Master Page. When you request the Products.aspx page, the contents of Site.master, SectionProducts.master, and Products.aspx are combined to generate the rendered output (see Figure 5.3).

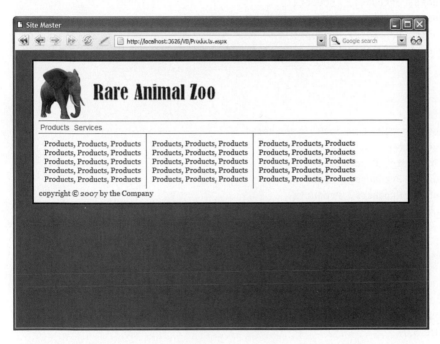

FIGURE 5.3   Nesting Master Pages to display the Products.aspx page.

LISTING 5.8   Products.aspx

```
<%@ Page Language="C#" MasterPageFile="~/SectionProducts.master" %>


<asp:Content
    ID="Content1"
    ContentPlaceHolderID="ContentPlaceHolder1"
    Runat="Server">
    Products, Products, Products
    <br />Products, Products, Products
    <br />Products, Products, Products
    <br />Products, Products, Products
    <br />Products, Products, Products
</asp:Content>
```

LISTING 5.8 Continued

```
<asp:Content
    ID="Content2"
    ContentPlaceHolderID="ContentPlaceHolder2"
    Runat="Server">
    Products, Products, Products
    <br />Products, Products, Products
    <br />Products, Products, Products
    <br />Products, Products, Products
    <br />Products, Products, Products
</asp:Content>

<asp:Content
    ID="Content3"
    ContentPlaceHolderID="ContentPlaceHolder3"
    Runat="Server">
    Products, Products, Products
    <br />Products, Products, Products
    <br />Products, Products, Products
    <br />Products, Products, Products
    <br />Products, Products, Products
</asp:Content>
```

The `Services.aspx` page in Listing 5.9 uses the `SectionService.master` Master Page. When this page is opened in a browser, the contents of `Site.master`, `SectionServices.master`, and `Services.aspx` are combined to generate the rendered output (see Figure 5.4).

LISTING 5.9 `Services.aspx`

```
<%@ Page Language="C#" MasterPageFile="~/SectionServices.master" Title="Services" %>

<asp:Content
    ID="Content1"
    ContentPlaceHolderID="ContentPlaceHolder1"
    Runat="Server">
    Services, Services, Services
    <br />Services, Services, Services
    <br />Services, Services, Services
    <br />Services, Services, Services
    <br />Services, Services, Services
</asp:Content>
<asp:Content
    ID="Content2"
    ContentPlaceHolderID="ContentPlaceHolder2"
```

```
    Runat="Server">
    Services, Services, Services, Services, Services
    <br />Services, Services, Services, Services, Services
    <br />Services, Services, Services, Services, Services
    <br />Services, Services, Services, Services, Services
    <br />Services, Services, Services, Services, Services
</asp:Content>
```

FIGURE 5.4   Nesting Master Pages to display the `Services.aspx` pages.

Using Images and Hyperlinks in Master Pages

You must be careful when using relative URLs in a Master Page. For example, you must be careful when adding images and links to a Master Page. Relative URLs are interpreted in different ways, depending on whether they are used with HTML tags or ASP.NET controls.

If you use a relative URL with an ASP.NET control, then the URL is interpreted relative to the Master Page. For example, suppose that you add the following ASP.NET Image control to a Master Page:

```
<asp:Image ImageUrl="Picture.gif" Runat="Server" />
```

The `ImageUrl` property contains a relative URL. If the Master Page is located in a folder named `MasterPages`, then the URL is interpreted like this:

```
/MasterPages/Picture.gif
```

Even if a content page is located in a completely different folder, the ImageUrl is interpreted relative to the folder that contains the Master Page and not relative to the content page.

The situation is completely different in the case of HTML elements. If an HTML element such as an <img> or <a> tag includes a relative URL, the relative URL is interpreted relative to the content page. For example, suppose you add the following <img> tag to a Master Page:

```
<img src="Picture.gif" />
```

The src attribute contains a relative URL. This URL is interpreted relative to a particular content page. For example, if you request a content page located in a folder named ContentPages, the relative URL is interpreted like this:

```
/ContentPages/Picture.gif
```

Using relative URLs with HTML elements is especially tricky because the URL keeps changing with each content page. If you request content pages from different folders, the relative URL changes. There are three ways that you can solve this problem.

First, you can replace all the HTML elements that use relative URLs with ASP.NET controls. An ASP.NET control automatically reinterprets a relative URL as relative to the Master Page.

> **NOTE**
>
> Relative URLs used by ASP.NET controls in a Master Page are automatically reinterpreted relative to the Master Page. This process of reinterpretation is called *rebasing*. Only ASP.NET control properties decorated with the UrlProperty attribute are rebased.

Second, you can avoid relative URLs and use absolute URLs. For example, if your application is named MyApp, then you can use the following <img> tag to display an image file located in the MasterPages folder:

```
<img src="/MyApp/MasterPages/Picture.gif" />
```

The disadvantage of using absolute URLs is that they make it difficult to change the location of a web application. If the name of your application changes, then the absolute URLs will no longer work and you'll end up with a bunch of broken images and links.

The final option is to use the Page.ResolveUrl() method to translate an application relative URL into an absolute URL. This approach is illustrated with the page in Listing 5.10. The Page.ResolveUrl() method is used with the <img> tag in the body of the Master Page, which displays the website logo.

LISTING 5.10 MasterPages\ImageMaster.master

```
<%@ Master Language="C#" %>
<!DOCTYPE html PUBLIC "-//W3C//DTD XHTML 1.1//EN"
"http://www.w3.org/TR/xhtml11/DTD/xhtml11.dtd">
<html xmlns="http://www.w3.org/1999/xhtml" >
<head id="Head1" runat="server">
    <title>Image Master</title>
</head>
<body>
    <form id="form1" runat="server">
    <div>

    <img src='<%=Page.ResolveUrl("~/MasterPages/Logo.gif") %>' alt="Website Logo" />

    <asp:contentplaceholder id="ContentPlaceHolder1" runat="server" />

    </div>
    </form>
</body>
</html>
```

The Master Page in Listing 5.10 is located in a folder named `MasterPages`. This folder also includes an image named `Logo.gif`. This image is displayed with the following HTML tag:

```
<img src='<%=Page.ResolveUrl("~/MasterPages/Logo.gif") %>' alt="Website Logo" />
```

The `Page.ResolveUrl()` method converts the tilde into the correct path for the current application directory.

The content page in Listing 5.11 uses the Master Page and correctly displays the website logo (see Figure 5.5).

LISTING 5.11 ImageContent.aspx

```
<%@ Page Language="C#" MasterPageFile="~/MasterPages/ImageMaster.master" %>


<asp:Content
    ID="Content1"
    ContentPlaceHolderID="ContentPlaceHolder1"
    Runat="Server">

    <h1>Content</h1>

</asp:Content>
```

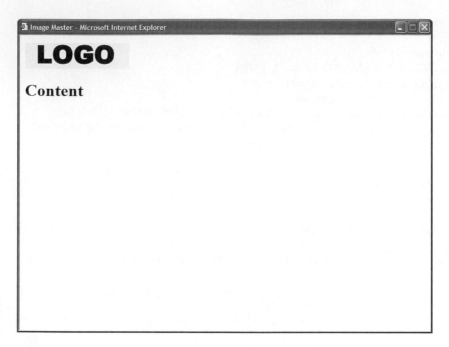

FIGURE 5.5   Displaying a Master Page relative image.

Registering Master Pages in Web Configuration

You can apply a Master Page to every content page in a particular folder or every content page in an entire application. Rather than add a `MasterPageFile` attribute to individual content pages, you can add a configuration option to the web configuration file.

For example, the web configuration file in Listing 5.12 applies the `SimpleMaster.master` Master Page to every page contained in the same folder (or subfolder) as the web configuration file.

LISTING 5.12   FolderA\Web.Config

```
<configuration>
<system.web>
  <pages masterPageFile="~/SimpleMaster.master" />
</system.web>
</configuration>
```

The Master Page is applied only to content pages. If a page does not contain any `Content` controls—it is a normal ASP.NET page—then the Master Page is ignored.

You can override the Master Page configured in the web configuration file in the case of a particular content page. In other words, a `MasterPageFile` attribute in a content page takes precedence over a Master Page specified in the web configuration file.

Modifying Master Page Content

Master Pages enable you to display the same content in multiple content pages. You'll quickly discover that you need to override the content displayed by a Master Page in the case of particular content pages.

For example, normally the Master Page contains the opening and closing HTML tags, including the <title> tag. This means that every content page will display the same title. Normally, you want each page to display a unique title.

In this section, you learn multiple techniques of modifying Master Page content from a content page.

Using the Title Attribute

If you only need to modify the title displayed in each content page, then you can take advantage of the <%@ Page %> directive's Title attribute. This attribute accepts any string value.

For example, the page in Listing 5.13 includes a Title attribute, which sets the title of the current content page to the value Content Page Title.

LISTING 5.13 TitleContent.aspx

```
<%@ Page Language="C#" MasterPageFile="~/SimpleMaster.master"
  Title="Content Page Title" %>

<asp:Content
    ID="Content1"
    ContentPlaceHolderID="ContentPlaceHolder1"
    Runat="Server">
    Content in the first column
    <br />Content in the first column
    <br />Content in the first column
    <br />Content in the first column
    <br />Content in the first column
</asp:Content>

<asp:Content
    ID="Content2"
    ContentPlaceHolderID="ContentPlaceHolder2"
    Runat="Server">
    Content in the second column
    <br />Content in the second column
    <br />Content in the second column
    <br />Content in the second column
    <br />Content in the second column
</asp:Content>
```

There is one requirement for the Title attribute to work. The HTML <head> tag in the Master Page must be a server-side Head tag. In other words, the <head> tag must include the runat="server" attribute. When you create a new Web Form or Master Page in Visual Web Developer, a server-side <head> tag is automatically created.

Using the Page Header Property

If you need to programmatically change the Title or Cascading Style Sheet rules included in a Master Page, then you can use the Page.Header property. This property returns an object that implements the IPageHeader interface. This interface has the following two properties:

▸ StyleSheet

▸ Title

For example, the content page in Listing 5.14 uses the SimpleMaster.master Master Page. It changes the Title and background color of the Master Page.

LISTING 5.14   HeaderContent.aspx

```
<%@ Page Language="C#" MasterPageFile="~/SimpleMaster.master" %>
<script runat="server">

    void Page_Load()
    {
        // Change the title
        Page.Header.Title = String.Format("Header Content ({0})", DateTime.Now);

        // Change the background color
        Style myStyle = new Style();
        myStyle.BackColor = System.Drawing.Color.Red;
        Page.Header.StyleSheet.CreateStyleRule(myStyle, null, "html");
    }

</script>
<asp:Content
    ID="Content1"
    ContentPlaceHolderID="ContentPlaceHolder1"
    Runat="Server">
    Content in the first column
    <br />Content in the first column
    <br />Content in the first column
    <br />Content in the first column
    <br />Content in the first column
</asp:Content>

<asp:Content
```

```
    ID="Content2"
    ContentPlaceHolderID="ContentPlaceHolder2"
    Runat="Server">
    Content in the second column
    <br />Content in the second column
    <br />Content in the second column
    <br />Content in the second column
    <br />Content in the second column
</asp:Content>
```

The `Page.Header` property returns the server-side <head> tag contained in the Master Page. You can cast the object returned by this property to an `HTMLHead` control. For example, the page in Listing 5.15 modifies the Master Page <meta> tags (the tags used by search engines when indexing a page).

LISTING 5.15   MetaContent.aspx

```
<%@ Page Language="C#" MasterPageFile="~/SimpleMaster.master" %>


<script runat="server">

    void Page_Load()
    {
        // Create Meta Description
        HtmlMeta metaDesc = new HtmlMeta();
        metaDesc.Name = "DESCRIPTION";
        metaDesc.Content = "A sample of using HtmlMeta controls";

        // Create Meta Keywords
        HtmlMeta metaKeywords = new HtmlMeta();
        metaKeywords.Name = "KEYWORDS";
        metaKeywords.Content = "HtmlMeta,Page.Header,ASP.NET";

        // Add Meta controls to HtmlHead
        HtmlHead head = (HtmlHead)Page.Header;
        head.Controls.Add(metaDesc);
        head.Controls.Add(metaKeywords);
    }

</script>


<asp:Content
    ID="Content1"
    ContentPlaceHolderID="ContentPlaceHolder1"
```

LISTING 5.15   Continued

```
    Runat="Server">
    Content in the first column
    <br />Content in the first column
    <br />Content in the first column
    <br />Content in the first column
    <br />Content in the first column
</asp:Content>

<asp:Content
    ID="Content2"
    ContentPlaceHolderID="ContentPlaceHolder2"
    Runat="Server">
    Content in the second column
    <br />Content in the second column
    <br />Content in the second column
    <br />Content in the second column
    <br />Content in the second column
</asp:Content>
```

Notice that the Page_Load() method in Listing 5.15 creates two HtmlMeta controls. The first control represents a Meta Description tag and the second control represents a Meta Keywords tag. Both HtmlMeta controls are added to the HtmlHead control's Controls collection.

When the page is rendered, the following tags are added to the <head> tag:

```
<meta name="DESCRIPTION" content="A sample of using HtmlMeta controls" />
<meta name="KEYWORDS" content="HtmlMeta,Page.Header,ASP.NET" />
```

WARNING

You receive a NullReference exception if you use the Page.Header property when the Master Page does not contain a server-side <head> tag.

Exposing Master Page Properties

You can expose properties and methods from a Master Page and modify the properties and methods from a particular content page. For example, the Master Page in Listing 5.16 includes a public property named BodyTitle.

LISTING 5.16   PropertyMaster.master

```
<%@ Master Language="C#" %>
<!DOCTYPE html PUBLIC "-//W3C//DTD XHTML 1.1//EN"
"http://www.w3.org/TR/xhtml11/DTD/xhtml11.dtd">
```

```
<script runat="server">

    public string BodyTitle
    {
        get { return ltlBodyTitle.Text; }
        set { ltlBodyTitle.Text = value; }
    }
</script>
<html xmlns="http://www.w3.org/1999/xhtml" >
<head id="Head1" runat="server">
    <style type="text/css">
        html
        {
            background-color:silver;
        }
        .content
        {
            margin:auto;
            width:700px;
            background-color:white;
            padding:10px;
        }
        h1
        {
            border-bottom:solid 1px blue;
        }
    </style>
    <title>Property Master</title>
</head>
<body>
    <form id="form1" runat="server">
    <div class="content">
    <h1><asp:Literal ID="ltlBodyTitle" runat="server" /></h1>
    <asp:contentplaceholder
        id="ContentPlaceHolder1"
        runat="server" />
    </div>
    </form>
</body>
</html>
```

The BodyTitle property enables you to assign a title that is rendered in a header tag in the
body of the page (see Figure 5.6).

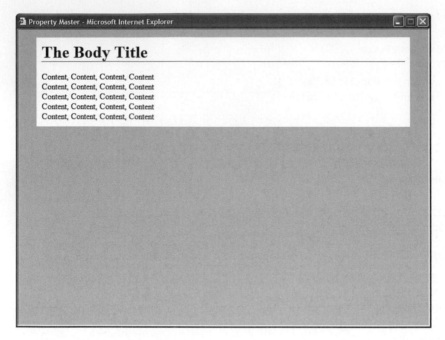

FIGURE 5.6 Displaying a body title.

Because the BodyTitle property is exposed as a public property, you can modify it from a particular content page. The page in Listing 5.17 assigns the value "The Body Title" to the BodyTitle property.

LISTING 5.17 PropertyContent.aspx

```
<%@ Page Language="C#" MasterPageFile="~/PropertyMaster.master" %>
<%@ MasterType VirtualPath="~/PropertyMaster.master" %>
<script runat="server">

    void Page_Load()
    {
        if (!Page.IsPostBack)
        {
            Master.BodyTitle = "The Body Title";
        }
    }
</script>
<asp:Content
    ID="Content1"
    ContentPlaceHolderID="ContentPlaceHolder1"
    Runat="Server">
    Content, Content, Content, Content
```

```
    <br />Content, Content, Content, Content
    <br />Content, Content, Content, Content
    <br />Content, Content, Content, Content
    <br />Content, Content, Content, Content
</asp:Content>
```

You should notice several things about the page in Listing 5.17. First, notice that you can refer to the Master Page by using the `Master` property. In the `Page_Load()` method in Listing 5.17, the `BodyTitle` property of the Master Page is assigned a value with the following line of code:

```
Master.BodyTitle = "The Body Title";
```

You should also notice that the page in Listing 5.17 includes a `<%@ MasterType %>` directive. This directive automatically casts the value of the Master property to the type of the Master Page. In other words, it casts the Master Page to the `PropertyMaster` type instead of the generic `MasterPage` type.

If you want to be able to refer to a custom property in a Master Page, such as the `BodyTitle` property, then the value of the `Master` property must be cast to the right type. The `BodyTitle` property is not a property of the generic `MasterPage` class, but it is a property of the `PropertyMaster` class.

Using `FindControl` with Master Pages

In the previous section, you learned how to modify a property of a control located in a Master Page from a content page by exposing a property from the Master Page. You have an alternative here. If you need to modify a control in a Master Page, you can use the `FindControl()` method in a content page.

For example, the Master Page in Listing 5.18 includes a Literal control named `BodyTitle`. This Master Page does not include any custom properties.

LISTING 5.18   FindMaster.master

```
<%@ Master Language="C#" %>
<!DOCTYPE html PUBLIC "-//W3C//DTD XHTML 1.1//EN"
"http://www.w3.org/TR/xhtml11/DTD/xhtml11.dtd">
<html xmlns="http://www.w3.org/1999/xhtml" >
<head id="Head1" runat="server">
    <style type="text/css">
        html
        {
            background-color:silver;
        }
        .content
        {
```

LISTING 5.18   Continued

```
            margin:auto;
            width:700px;
            background-color:white;
            padding:10px;
        }
        h1
        {
            border-bottom:solid 1px blue;
        }

    </style>
    <title>Find Master</title>
</head>
<body>
    <form id="form1" runat="server">
    <div class="content">
    <h1><asp:Literal ID="ltlBodyTitle" runat="server" /></h1>
    <asp:contentplaceholder
        id="ContentPlaceHolder1"
        runat="server" />
    </div>
    </form>
</body>
</html>
```

The content page in Listing 5.19 modifies the Text property of the Literal control located in the Master Page. The content page uses the FindControl() method to retrieve the Literal control from the Master Page.

LISTING 5.19   FindContent.aspx

```
<%@ Page Language="C#" MasterPageFile="~/FindMaster.master" %>
<script runat="server">

    void Page_Load()
    {
        if (!Page.IsPostBack)
        {
            Literal ltlBodyTitle = (Literal)Master.FindControl("ltlBodyTitle");
            ltlBodyTitle.Text = "The Body Title";
        }
    }
</script>
<asp:Content
```

```
        ID="Content1"
        ContentPlaceHolderID="ContentPlaceHolder1"
        Runat="Server">
        Content, Content, Content, Content
        <br />Content, Content, Content, Content
        <br />Content, Content, Content, Content
        <br />Content, Content, Content, Content
        <br />Content, Content, Content, Content
</asp:Content>
```

The FindControl() method enables you to search a naming container for a control with a particular ID. The method returns a reference to the control.

Loading Master Pages Dynamically

You can associate different Master Pages dynamically with a content page. This is useful in two situations.

First, you can enable the users of your website to customize the appearance of the website by loading different Master Pages. You can display a menu of Master Pages, and allow your users to pick their favorite layout.

Another situation in which loading Master Pages dynamically is useful concerns co-branding. Imagine that your company needs to make its website look like a partner website. When users link to your website from the partner website, you don't want users to know that they are traveling to a new website. You can maintain this illusion by dynamically loading different Master Pages based on a query string passed from a partner website.

A Master Page is merged with a content page very early in the page execution life-cycle. This means that you cannot dynamically load a Master Page during the Page Load event. The only event during which you can load a Master Page is during the Page PreInit event. This is the first event that is raised during the page execution life cycle.

For example, the content page in Listing 5.20 dynamically loads one of two Master Pages named Dynamic1.master and Dynamic2.master.

LISTING 5.20   DynamicContent.aspx

```
<%@ Page Language="C#" MasterPageFile="~/Dynamic1.master" %>
<script runat="server">

    protected void Page_PreInit(object sender, EventArgs e)
    {
        if (Request["master"] != null)
        {
            switch (Request["master"])
            {
```

LISTING 5.20   Continued

```
                case "Dynamic1":
                    Profile.MasterPageFile = "Dynamic1.master";
                    break;
                case "Dynamic2":
                    Profile.MasterPageFile = "Dynamic2.master";
                    break;
            }
        }

        MasterPageFile = Profile.MasterPageFile;
    }
</script>

<asp:Content
    ID="Content1"
    ContentPlaceHolderID="ContentPlaceHolder1"
    Runat="Server">

    Select a Master Page:
    <ul class="selectMaster">
        <li>
        <a href="DynamicContent.aspx?master=Dynamic1">Dynamic Master 1</a>
        </li>
        <li>
        <a href="DynamicContent.aspx?master=Dynamic2">Dynamic Master 2</a>
        </li>
    </ul>

</asp:Content>
```

The page in Listing 5.20 contains two links. Both links include a query string parameter named master, which represents the name of a Master Page. When you click the first link, the Dynamic1.master Master Page is loaded (see Figure 5.7) and when you click the second link, the Dynamic2.master Master Page is loaded (see Figure 5.8).

Notice that the page in Listing 5.20 includes a Page_PreInit() event handler. This handler grabs the value of the master query string parameter and assigns the value of this parameter to a Profile property. Next, the value of the Profile property is assigned to the page's MasterPageFile property. Assigning a value to the MasterPageFile property causes a Master Page to be dynamically loaded.

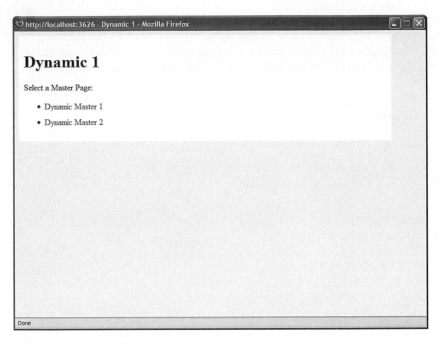

FIGURE 5.7   Displaying the Dynamic 1 Master Page.

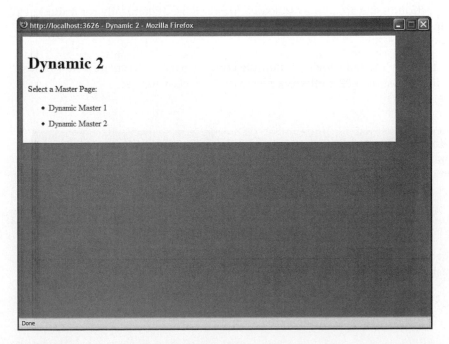

FIGURE 5.8   Displaying the Dynamic 2 Master Page.

Because the name of the Master Page is assigned to a `Profile` property, the selected Master Page loads for a user even if the user returns to the website many years in the future. The `Profile` object automatically persists the values of its properties for a user across multiple visits to a website. The `Profile` is defined in the web configuration file contained in Listing 5.21.

LISTING 5.21   Web.Config

```
<configuration>
  <system.web>
    <profile>
      <properties>
        <add
          name="MasterPageFile"
          defaultValue="Dynamic1.master" />
      </properties>
    </profile>
  </system.web>
</configuration>
```

Loading Master Pages Dynamically for Multiple Content Pages

In the previous section, you learned how to load a Master Page dynamically for a single page in a website. However, what if you need to load a Master Page dynamically for every content page in a website?

The easiest way to apply the same logic to multiple content pages is to create a new base `Page` class. The file in Listing 5.22 contains a new base `Page` class named `DynamicMasterPage`.

> **NOTE**
>
> Add the file in Listing 5.22 to your application's App_Code folder.

LISTING 5.22   DynamicMasterPage.cs

```
using System;
using System.Web.UI;
using System.Web.Profile;

public class DynamicMasterPage : Page
{
```

```
    protected override void OnPreInit(EventArgs e)
    {
        this.MasterPageFile = (string)Context.Profile["MasterPageFile"];
        base.OnPreInit(e);
    }

}
```

The class in Listing 5.22 inherits from the Page class. However, it overrides the base Page class's OnPreInit() method and adds the logic for loading a Master Page dynamically.

After you create a new base Page class, you need to register it in the web configuration file. The web configuration file in Listing 5.23 contains the necessary settings.

LISTING 5.23   Web.config

```
<configuration>
  <system.web>

    <pages pageBaseType="DynamicMasterPage" />

    <profile>
      <properties>
        <add
          name="MasterPageFile"
          defaultValue="Dynamic1.master" />
      </properties>
    </profile>
  </system.web>
</configuration>
```

After you register the DynamicMasterPage class as the base Page class, every page in your application automatically inherits from the new base class. Every page inherits the new OnPreInit() method and every page loads a Master Page dynamically.

Summary

In this chapter, you learned how to share the same content among multiple pages in an application by taking advantage of Master Pages. In the first section, you learned how to create a Master Page and apply it to multiple content pages. You also learned how to nest Master Pages and how to register a Master Page in the web configuration file.

The next section explored various techniques of modifying a Master Page from a particular content page. You learned how to use the `Title` attribute, how to use the `Page.Header` property, how to expose properties in a Master Page, and how to use the `FindControl()` method.

Finally, you learned how you can dynamically load different Master Pages and associate a particular Master Page with a particular content page at runtime. You learned how you can save a user's Master Page preference by using the `Profile` object.

CHAPTER 6

Designing Websites with Themes

An ASP.NET Theme enables you to apply a consistent style to the pages in your website. You can use a Theme to control the appearance of both the HTML elements and ASP.NET controls that appear in a page.

Themes are different than Master Pages. A Master Page enables you to share content across multiple pages in a website. A Theme, on the other hand, enables you to control the appearance of the content.

In this chapter, you learn how to create and apply ASP.NET Themes. First, you learn how to create Skins. A Skin enables you to modify the properties of an ASP.NET control that have an effect on its appearance. You learn how to create both Default and Named Skins.

Next, you learn how to format both HTML elements and ASP.NET controls by adding Cascading Style Sheets to a Theme. Cascading Style Sheets enable you to control the appearance and layout of pages in a website in a standards-compliant manner.

You also learn how you can create Global Themes, which can be used by multiple applications located on the same server. You learn how to use Global Themes with both File System and HTTP-based websites.

Finally, you learn how to load Themes and Skins dynamically at runtime. You build a page that each user of a website can customize by skinning.

Creating Themes

You create a Theme by adding a new folder to a special folder in your application named App_Themes. Each folder that you add to the App_Themes folder represents a different Theme.

If the App_Themes folder doesn't exist in your application, then you can create it. It must be located in the root of your application.

VISUAL WEB DEVELOPER NOTE

When using Visual Web Developer, you can create a new Theme folder by right-clicking the name of your project in the Solution Explorer window and selecting Add Folder, Theme Folder.

A Theme folder can contain a variety of different types of files, including images and text files. You also can organize the contents of a Theme folder by adding multiple subfolders to a Theme folder.

The most important types of files in a Theme folder are the following:

▶ Skin files

▶ Cascading Style Sheet files

In the following sections, you learn how to add both Skin files and Cascading Style Sheet files to a Theme.

WARNING

Be careful about how you name your Theme (the folder name). The contents of a Theme folder are automatically compiled in the background into a new class. So you want to be careful not to name a Theme with a class name that conflicts with an existing class name in your project.

Adding Skins to Themes

A Theme can contain one or more Skin files. A Skin enables you to modify any of the properties of an ASP.NET control that have an effect on its appearance.

For example, imagine that you decide that you want every TextBox control in your web application to appear with a yellow background color and a dotted border. If you add the file in Listing 6.1 to the Simple Theme (the App_Themes\Simple folder), then you can modify the appearance of all TextBox controls in all pages that use the Simple Theme.

LISTING 6.1   Simple\TextBox.skin

```
<asp:TextBox
    BackColor="Yellow"
    BorderStyle="Dotted"
    Runat="Server" />
```

Notice that the Skin file in Listing 6.1 is named TextBox.skin. You can name a Skin file anything you want. I recommend following a naming convention in which you name the Skin file after the name of the control that the Skin modifies.

A Theme folder can contain a single Skin file that contains Skins for hundreds of controls. Alternatively, a Theme can contain hundreds of Skin files, each of which contains a single Skin. It doesn't matter how you organize your Skins into files because everything in a Theme folder eventually gets compiled into one Theme class.

The Skin file in Listing 6.1 contains a declaration of a TextBox control. Notice that the TextBox control includes a BackColor property that is set to the value Yellow and a BorderStyle property that is set to the value Dotted.

You should notice that the TextBox control includes a Runat="Server" attribute, but it does not include an ID attribute. You must always include a Runat attribute, but you can never include the ID attribute when declaring a control in a Skin.

NOTE

You can't create a Skin that applies to the properties of a User control. However, you can Skin the controls contained inside a User control.

The Skin is applied to every page to which the Simple Theme is applied. For example, the page in Listing 6.2 uses the Simple Theme.

LISTING 6.2   ShowSkin.aspx

```
<%@ Page Language="C#" Theme="Simple" %>
<!DOCTYPE html PUBLIC "-//W3C//DTD XHTML 1.1//EN"
"http://www.w3.org/TR/xhtml11/DTD/xhtml11.dtd">
<html xmlns="http://www.w3.org/1999/xhtml" >
<head runat="server">
    <title>Show Skin</title>
</head>
<body>
    <form id="form1" runat="server">
    <div>

    <asp:TextBox
        Runat="server" />
```

LISTING 6.2   ShowSkin.aspx

```
    </div>
    </form>
</body>
</html>
```

Notice that the page in Listing 6.2 includes a `Theme` attribute in its `<%@ Page %>` directive. This attribute causes the Simple Theme to be applied to the page.

When you open the page in Listing 6.2, the Label control appears with a yellow background color and dotted border. This is the background color and border specified by the Theme (see Figure 6.1).

FIGURE 6.1   Using a TextBox Skin.

Only certain control properties are "themeable." In other words, you can create a Skin file that modifies only certain properties of a control. In general, you can use a Skin to modify properties that have an effect on a control's appearance but not its behavior. For example, you can modify the `BackColor` property of a `TextBox` control but not its `AutoPostBack` property.

> **NOTE**
>
> By default, all control properties are themeable (can be modified in a Skin file). However, certain control properties are decorated with the `Themeable(False)` attribute, which disables theming.

Creating Named Skins

In the previous section, we created something called a Default Skin. A Default Skin is applied to every instance of a control of a certain type. For example, a Default Skin is applied to every instance of a `TextBox` control.

You also have the option of creating a Named Skin. When you create a Named Skin, you can decide when you want to apply the Skin. For example, you might want required fields in a form to appear with a red border. In that case, you can create a Named Skin and apply the Skin to only particular TextBox controls.

The Skin in Listing 6.3 contains both a Default Skin and a Named Skin for a TextBox control.

LISTING 6.3   Simple2\TextBox.skin

```
<asp:TextBox
    SkinID="DashedTextBox"
    BorderStyle="Dashed"
    BorderWidth="5px"
    Runat="Server" />

<asp:TextBox
    BorderStyle="Double"
    BorderWidth="5px"
    Runat="Server" />
```

The first TextBox in Listing 6.3 is an example of a Named Skin. Notice that it includes a SkinID property. The SkinID property represents the name of the Named Skin. You use the value of this property when applying the Skin in a page.

The file in Listing 6.3 also includes a Default Skin for a TextBox control. The Default Skin does not include a SkinID property. If a TextBox control in a page is not associated with a Named Skin, then the Default Skin is applied to the TextBox.

A Theme can contain only one Default Skin for each type of control. However, a Theme can contain as many Named Skins as you please. Each Named Skin must have a unique name.

The page in Listing 6.4 contains two TextBox controls. The first TextBox control includes a SkinID attribute. This attribute causes the Named Skin to be applied to the control. The second TextBox, on the other hand, does not include a SkinID property. The Default Skin is applied to the second TextBox control.

LISTING 6.4   ShowNamedSkin.aspx

```
<%@ Page Language="C#" Theme="Simple2" %>
<!DOCTYPE html PUBLIC "-//W3C//DTD XHTML 1.1//EN"
"http://www.w3.org/TR/xhtml11/DTD/xhtml11.dtd">
<html xmlns="http://www.w3.org/1999/xhtml" >
<head runat="server">
    <title>Show Named Skin</title>
</head>
<body>
    <form id="form1" runat="server">
    <div>
```

LISTING 6.4   Continued

```
    <asp:TextBox
        id="txtFirstName"
        SkinID="DashedTextBox"
        Runat="server" />

    <br /><br />

    <asp:TextBox
        id="txtLastName"
        Runat="server" />

    </div>
    </form>
</body>
</html>
```

When you open the page in Listing 6.4, the first TextBox appears with a dashed border and the second TextBox appears with a double border (see Figure 6.2).

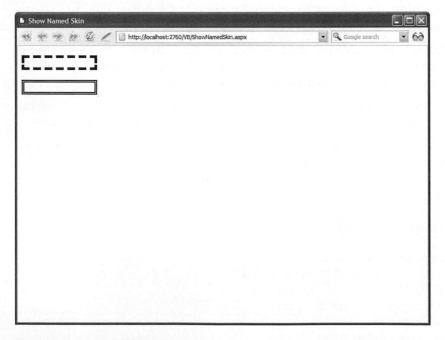

FIGURE 6.2   Using Named Skins.

Themes Versus StyleSheetThemes

When you apply a Theme to a page, the Skins in the Theme override any existing properties of the controls in the page. In other words, properties in a Skin override properties in a page.

For example, imagine that you create the Skin in Listing 6.5.

LISTING 6.5 Simple3\Label.skin

```
<asp:Label
    BackColor="Orange"
    Runat="Server" />
```

The Skin in Listing 6.5 sets the background color of all Label controls to the color Orange.

Now, image that you apply the Skin in Listing 6.5 to the ASP.NET page in Listing 6.6.

LISTING 6.6 ShowSkinTheme.aspx

```
<%@ Page Language="C#" Theme="Simple3" %>
<!DOCTYPE html PUBLIC "-//W3C//DTD XHTML 1.1//EN"
"http://www.w3.org/TR/xhtml11/DTD/xhtml11.dtd">
<html xmlns="http://www.w3.org/1999/xhtml" >
<head runat="server">
    <title>Show Skin Theme</title>
</head>
<body>
    <form id="form1" runat="server">
    <div>

    <asp:Label
        id="Label1"
        Text="What color background do I have?"
        BackColor="red"
        Runat="server" />

    </div>
    </form>
</body>
</html>
```

The page in Listing 6.6 includes a Label that has a BackColor property which is set to the value Red. However, when you open the page, the BackColor declared in the Skin overrides the BackColor declared in the page and the Label is displayed with an orange background.

The default behavior of Themes makes it very easy to modify the design of an existing website. You can override any existing control properties that have an effect on the appearance of the control.

However, there are situations in which you might want to override Skin properties. For example, you might want to display every Label in your website with an orange background color except for one Label. In that case, it would be nice if there was a way to override the `Skin` property.

You can override `Skin` properties by applying a Theme to a page with the `StyleSheetTheme` attribute instead of the `Theme` attribute. For example, the page in Listing 6.7 uses the `StyleSheetTheme` attribute to apply the Simple3 Theme to the page.

LISTING 6.7   ShowSkinStyleSheetTheme.aspx

```
<%@ Page Language="C#" StyleSheetTheme="Simple3" %>
<!DOCTYPE html PUBLIC "-//W3C//DTD XHTML 1.1//EN"
"http://www.w3.org/TR/xhtml11/DTD/xhtml11.dtd">
<html xmlns="http://www.w3.org/1999/xhtml" >
<head id="Head1" runat="server">
    <title>Show Skin Style Sheet Theme</title>
</head>
<body>
    <form id="form1" runat="server">
    <div>

    <asp:Label
        id="Label1"
        Text="What color background do I have?"
        BackColor="red"
        Runat="server" />

    </div>
    </form>
</body>
</html>
```

Notice that the `<%@Page %>` directive in Listing 6.7 includes a `StyleSheetTheme` attribute. When you open the page in Listing 6.7 in a web browser, the Label is displayed with a red background color instead of the orange background color specified by the Theme.

Disabling Themes

Every ASP.NET control includes an `EnableTheming` property. You can use the `EnableTheming` property to prevent a Skin from being applied to a particular control in a page.

For example, the page in Listing 6.8 contains two Calendar controls. The second Calendar control has its EnableTheming property set to the value False (see Figure 6.3).

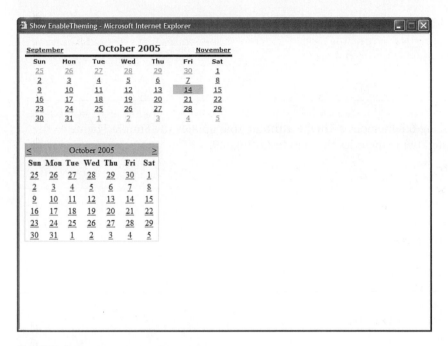

FIGURE 6.3   Disabling a Theme.

LISTING 6.8   ShowEnableTheming.aspx

```
<%@ Page Language="C#" Theme="Simple4" %>
<html xmlns="http://www.w3.org/1999/xhtml" >
<head runat="server">
    <title>Show EnableTheming</title>
</head>
<body>
    <form id="form1" runat="server">
    <div>

    <asp:Calendar
        id="Calendar1"
        Runat="server" />

    <br /><br />

    <asp:Calendar
        id="Calendar2"
```

LISTING 6.8   Continued

```
        EnableTheming="false"
        Runat="server" />


    </div>
    </form>
</body>
</html>
```

The page in Listing 6.8 includes a Theme attribute that applies the Simple Theme to the page. The Simple Theme includes the Skin in Listing 6.9.

LISTING 6.9   Simple4\Calendar.skin

```
<asp:Calendar
    BackColor="White"
    BorderColor="White"
    BorderWidth="1px"
    Font-Names="Verdana"
    Font-Size="9pt"
    ForeColor="Black"
    NextPrevFormat="FullMonth"
    Width="400px"
    Runat="Server">
    <SelectedDayStyle
        BackColor="#333399"
        ForeColor="White" />
    <OtherMonthDayStyle
        ForeColor="#999999" />
    <TodayDayStyle
        BackColor="#CCCCCC" />
    <NextPrevStyle
        Font-Bold="True"
        Font-Size="8pt"
        ForeColor="#333333"
        VerticalAlign="Bottom" />
    <DayHeaderStyle
        Font-Bold="True"
        Font-Size="8pt" />
    <TitleStyle
        BackColor="White"
        BorderColor="Black"
```

```
        BorderWidth="4px"
        Font-Bold="True"
        Font-Size="12pt"
        ForeColor="#333399" />
</asp:Calendar>
```

When you open the page in Listing 6.9 in a web browser, the Skin is applied to the first Calendar control but not the second Calendar control.

Registering Themes in the Web Configuration File

Rather than add the Theme or StyleSheetTheme attribute to each and every page to which you want to apply a Theme, you can register a Theme for all pages in your application in the web configuration file.

The Web.Config file in Listing 6.10 applies the Site Theme to every page in an application.

LISTING 6.10 Web.Config

```
<configuration>
<system.web>

  <pages theme="Site" />

</system.web>
</configuration>
```

Rather than use the theme attribute, you can use the styleSheetTheme attribute to apply a Theme to the pages in an application. If you use the styleSheetTheme attribute, you can override particular Skin properties in a page.

The web configuration file in Listing 6.11 includes the styleSheetTheme attribute.

LISTING 6.11 Web.Config

```
<configuration>
<system.web>

  <pages styleSheetTheme="Site" />

</system.web>
</configuration>
```

After you enable a Theme for an application, you can disable the Theme for a particular page by using the EnableTheming attribute with the <%@ Page %> directive. For example, the page in Listing 6.12 disables any Themes configured in the web configuration file.

LISTING 6.12   DisablePageTheme.aspx

```
<%@ Page Language="C#" EnableTheming="false" %>
<!DOCTYPE html PUBLIC "-//W3C//DTD XHTML 1.1//EN"
"http://www.w3.org/TR/xhtml11/DTD/xhtml11.dtd">
<html xmlns="http://www.w3.org/1999/xhtml" >
<head runat="server">
    <title>Disable Page Theme</title>
</head>
<body>
    <form id="form1" runat="server">
    <div>

    <asp:Label
        id="Label1"
        Text="Don't Theme Me!"
        Runat="server" />

    </div>
    </form>
</body>
</html>
```

Adding Cascading Style Sheets to Themes

As an alternative to Skins, you can use a Cascading Style Sheet file to control the appearance of both the HTML elements and ASP.NET controls contained in a page. If you add a Cascading Style Sheet file to a Theme folder, then the Cascading Style Sheet is automatically applied to every page to which the Theme is applied.

For example, the Cascading Style Sheet in Listing 6.13 contains style rules that are applied to several different HTML elements in a page.

LISTING 6.13   App_Themes\StyleTheme\SimpleStyle.css

```
html
{
    background-color:gray;
    font:14px Georgia,Serif;
}
```

```
.content
{
    margin:auto;
    width:600px;
    border:solid 1px black;
    background-color:White;
    padding:10px;
}

h1
{
    color:Gray;
    font-size:18px;
    border-bottom:solid 1px orange;
}

label
{
    font-weight:bold;
}

input
{
    background-color:Yellow;
    border:double 3px orange;
}

.button
{
    background-color:#eeeeee;
}
```

If you add the SimpleStyle.css file to a Theme named StyleTheme (a folder named
StyleTheme in the App_Themes folder), then the Cascading Style Sheet is applied automatically to the page in Listing 6.14.

LISTING 6.14 ShowSimpleCSS.aspx

```
<%@ Page Language="C#" Theme="StyleTheme" %>
<!DOCTYPE html PUBLIC "-//W3C//DTD XHTML 1.1//EN"
"http://www.w3.org/TR/xhtml11/DTD/xhtml11.dtd">
<html xmlns="http://www.w3.org/1999/xhtml" >
<head id="Head1" runat="server">
    <title>Show Simple CSS</title>
</head>
```

LISTING 6.14   Continued

```
<body>
    <form id="form1" runat="server">
    <div class="content">

    <h1>Registration Form</h1>

    <asp:Label
        id="lblFirstName"
        Text="First Name:"
        AssociatedControlID="txtFirstName"
        Runat="server" />
    <br />
    <asp:TextBox
        id="txtFirstName"
        Runat="server" />

    <br /><br />

    <asp:Label
        id="lblLastName"
        Text="Last Name:"
        AssociatedControlID="txtLastName"
        Runat="server" />
    <br />
    <asp:TextBox
        id="txtLastName"
        Runat="server" />

    <br /><br />

    <asp:Button
        id="btnSubmit"
        Text="Submit Form"
        CssClass="button"
        Runat="server" />

    </div>
    </form>
</body>
</html>
```

The Cascading Style Sheet is used to style several HTML elements in Listing 6.14 (see Figure 6.4). For example, the Style Sheet sets the background color of the page to the value Gray. It also centers the `<div>` tag containing the page content.

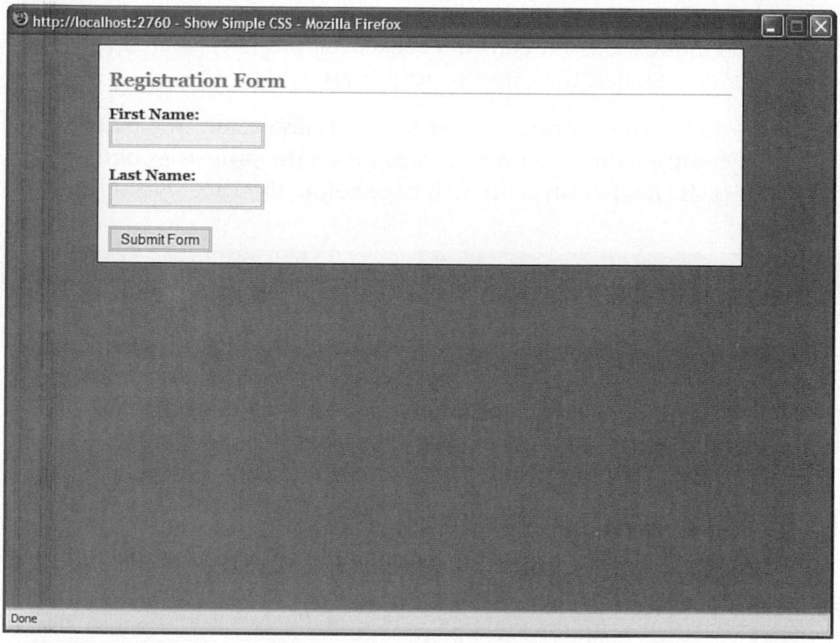

FIGURE 6.4   Styling with Cascading Style Sheets.

Because an ASP.NET control renders HTML, the Style Sheet also styles the HTML rendered by the ASP.NET Label, TextBox, and Button controls. An ASP.NET Label control renders an HTML `<label>` tag and the Style Sheet formats all `<label>` tags in bold. Both a TextBox control and a Button control render HTML `<input>` tags. The Style Sheet modifies the border and background color of the `<input>` tag.

Notice that the Button control includes a CssClass attribute. By providing a control with a CssClass attribute, you can target a particular control (or set of controls) in a Cascading Style Sheet. In this case, the background color of the `<input>` tag rendered by the Button control is set to the value #eeeeee (light gray).

I recommend that you do all your web page design by using the method discussed in this section. You should place all your page design in an external Cascading Style Sheet located in a Theme folder. In particular, you should not modify the appearance of a control by modifying its properties. Furthermore, you should avoid using Skin files.

The advantage of using Cascading Style Sheets is that they result in leaner and faster loading pages. The more content that you can place in an external Style Sheet, the less content must be loaded each time you make a page request. The contents of an external Style Sheet can be loaded and cached by a browser and applied to all pages in a web application.

If, on the other hand, you modify the appearance of a control by modifying its properties, then additional content must be rendered to the browser each time you make a page request. For example, if you modify a `Label` control's `BackColor` property, then an additional `Style` attribute is rendered when the `Label` control is rendered.

Using Skins is no different than setting control properties. Skins also result in bloated pages. For example, if you create a Skin for a `Label` control, then the properties of the Label Skin must be merged with each `Label` control on each page before the Label is rendered.

> **NOTE**
>
> In this book, you will notice that I try to avoid formatting controls by using control properties. Instead, I perform all the formatting in a Style Sheet embedded in the page (using the `<style>` tag). I would prefer to place all the control formatting in an external Style Sheet, but that would require creating a separate file for each code sample, which would make this book much longer than it already threatens to be.

Adding Multiple Cascading Style Sheets to a Theme

You can add as many Cascading Style Sheet files to a Theme folder as you need. When you add multiple Cascading Style Sheets to a Theme, all the Cascading Style Sheets are applied to a page when the Theme is applied to a page.

The order in which an external Style Sheet is linked to a page can be important. For example, style sheet rules in one Style Sheet can override style sheet rules in another Style Sheet.

When you add multiple Style Sheets to a Theme, the style sheets are linked to a page in alphabetical order (in the order of the Style Sheet file name). For example, if the Theme contains three Style Sheet files named `ThemeA.css`, `ThemeB.css`, and `ThemeC.css`, then the following three links are added to a page:

```
<link href="App_Themes/Simple/ThemeA.css" type="text/css" rel="stylesheet" />
<link href="App_Themes/Simple/ThemeB.css" type="text/css" rel="stylesheet" />
<link href="App_Themes/Simple/ThemeC.css" type="text/css" rel="stylesheet" />
```

If you want to control the order in which Style Sheets are applied to a page, then you need to follow a naming convention.

Changing Page Layouts with Cascading Style Sheets

Because you can use a Cascading Style Sheet to change the layout of a page, you can use a Theme to control page layout.

For example, the page in Listing 6.15 contains three `<div>` tags. By default, if you open the page, the contents of the `<div>` tags are stacked one on top of another (see Figure 6.5).

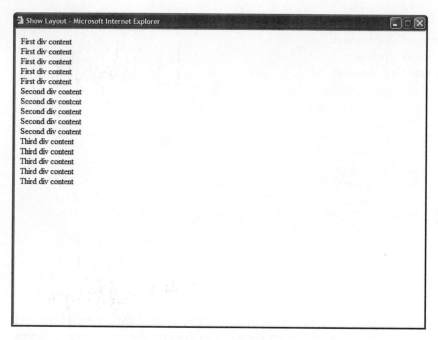

FIGURE 6.5   Page without Cascading Style Sheet.

LISTING 6.15   ShowLayout.aspx

```
<%@ Page Language="C#" %>
<!DOCTYPE html PUBLIC "-//W3C//DTD XHTML 1.1//EN"
"http://www.w3.org/TR/xhtml11/DTD/xhtml11.dtd">
<html xmlns="http://www.w3.org/1999/xhtml" >
<head runat="server">
    <title>Show Layout</title>
</head>
<body>
    <form id="form1" runat="server">

    <div id="div1">
        First div content
        <br />First div content
        <br />First div content
        <br />First div content
        <br />First div content
    </div>

    <div id="div2">
        Second div content
        <br />Second div content
```

LISTING 6.15   Continued

```
        <br />Second div content
        <br />Second div content
        <br />Second div content
    </div>

    <div id="div3">
        Third div content
        <br />Third div content
        <br />Third div content
        <br />Third div content
        <br />Third div content
    </div>

    </form>
</body>
</html>
```

If you add the Cascading Style Sheet in Listing 6.16, you can modify the layout of the <div> tags (see Figure 6.6). The Style Sheet in Listing 6.16 displays the <div> tags in three columns. (The Stylesheet floats each of the <div> tags.)

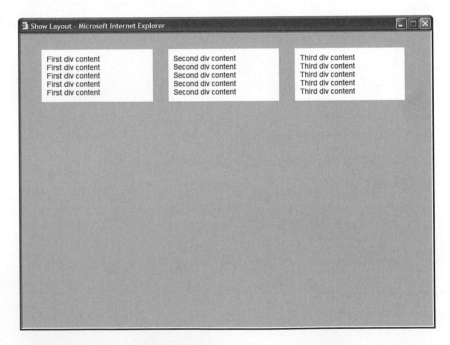

FIGURE 6.6   Using a floating layout.

LISTING 6.16   Float.css

```
html
{
    background-color:Silver;
    font:14px Arial,Sans-Serif;
}

#div1
{
    float:left;
    width:25%;
    margin:15px;
    padding:10px;
    background-color:White;
}

#div2
{
    float:left;
    width:25%;
    margin:15px;
    padding:10px;
    background-color:White;
}

#div3
{
    float:left;
    width:25%;
    margin:15px;
    padding:10px;
    background-color:White;
}
```

Alternatively, you can position the <div> tags absolutely by using the left and top style properties. The Style Sheet in Listing 6.17 reverses the order in which the three <div> tags are displayed (see Figure 6.7).

NOTE

The Cascading Style Sheets in this section work equally well with Internet Explorer 6, Firefox 1, and Opera 8.

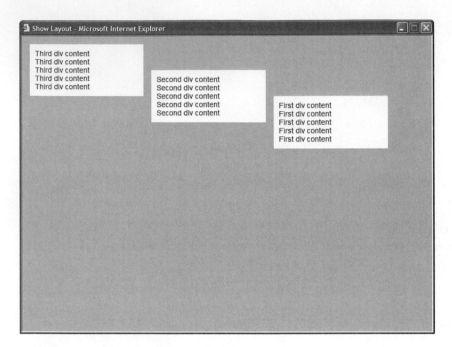

FIGURE 6.7   Using an absolute layout.

LISTING 6.17   Absolute.css

```
html
{
    background-color:Silver;
    font:14px Arial,Sans-Serif;
}

#div3
{
    position:absolute;
    left:15px;
    top:15px;
    width:200px;
    padding:10px;
    background-color:White;
}

#div2
{
    position:absolute;
    left:250px;
    top:65px;
    width:200px;
```

```
    padding:10px;
    background-color:White;
}

#div1
{
    position:absolute;
    left:485px;
    top:115px;
    width:200px;
    padding:10px;
    background-color:White;
}
```

The point of this section is to demonstrate that Cascading Style Sheets are very powerful. You can create elaborate website designs simply by creating the right Style Sheet. If you want to see some samples of some amazing website designs performed with Cascading Style Sheets, visit the CSS Zen Garden located at http://www.CSSZenGarden.com.

Creating Global Themes

You can share the same Theme among multiple web applications running on the same web server. A Global Theme can contain both Skin files and Cascading Style Sheet files. Creating a Global Theme is useful when you want to create one company-wide website design and apply it to all your company's applications.

You create a Global Theme by adding the Theme to the Themes folder located at the following path:

```
WINDOWS\Microsoft.NET\Framework\v2.0.50727\ASP.NETClientFiles\Themes
```

After you add a Theme folder to this path, you can immediately start using the Theme in any file system-based website.

If you want to use the Theme in an HTTP-based website, you need to perform an additional step. You must add the Theme folder to the following path:

```
Inetpub\wwwroot\aspnet_client\system_web\v2.0.50727\Themes
```

You can copy the Theme to this folder manually or you can use the aspnet_regiis tool to copy the Theme folder. Execute the aspnet_regiis tool from the command line like this:

```
aspnet_regiis -c
```

The aspnet_regiis tool is located in the Windows\Microsoft.NET\Framework\v2.0.50727 folder. You can open a command prompt and navigate to this folder to execute the tool.

Alternatively, if you have installed the Microsoft .NET Framework SDK, then you can execute the tool by opening the SDK Command Prompt from the Microsoft .NET Framework SDK program group.

Applying Themes Dynamically

You might want to enable each user of your website to customize the appearance of your website by selecting different Themes. Some website users might prefer a green Theme and other website users might prefer a pink Theme.

You can dynamically apply a Theme to a page by handling the Page PreInit event. This event is the first event that is raised when you request a page. You cannot apply a Theme dynamically in a later event such as the Page Load or PreRender events.

For example, the page in Listing 6.18 applies either the green Theme or the pink Theme to the page depending on which link you click in the page body (see Figure 6.8).

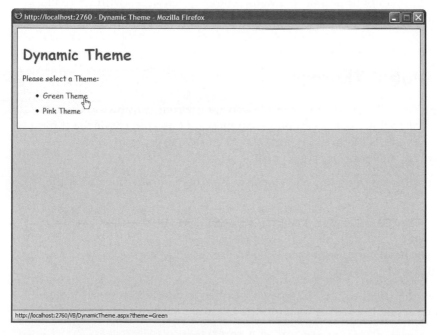

FIGURE 6.8   Selecting a Theme programmatically.

LISTING 6.18   DynamicTheme.aspx

```
<%@ Page Language="C#" %>
<!DOCTYPE html PUBLIC "-//W3C//DTD XHTML 1.1//EN"
"http://www.w3.org/TR/xhtml11/DTD/xhtml11.dtd">
<script runat="server">
```

```csharp
    protected void Page_PreInit(object sender, EventArgs e)
    {
        if (Request["theme"] != null)
        {
            switch (Request["theme"])
            {
                case "Green":
                    Profile.userTheme = "GreenTheme";
                    break;
                case "Pink":
                    Profile.userTheme = "PinkTheme";
                    break;
            }
        }
        Theme = Profile.userTheme;
    }
</script>

<html xmlns="http://www.w3.org/1999/xhtml" >
<head runat="server">
    <title>Dynamic Theme</title>
</head>
<body>
    <form id="form1" runat="server">
    <div class="content">

    <h1>Dynamic Theme</h1>

    Please select a Theme:
    <ul>
    <li>
        <a href="DynamicTheme.aspx?theme=Green">Green Theme</a>
    </li>
    <li>
        <a href="DynamicTheme.aspx?theme=Pink">Pink Theme</a>
    </li>
    </ul>

    </div>
    </form>
</body>
</html>
```

A particular Theme is applied to the page with the help of the Theme property. You can assign the name of any Theme (Theme folder) to this property in the Page PreInit event, and the Theme will be applied to the page.

Notice that the selected Theme is stored in the Profile object. When you store information in the Profile object, the information is preserved across multiple visits to the website. So, if a user selects a favorite Theme once, the Theme is applied every time the user returns to the website in the future.

The Profile is defined in the web configuration file in Listing 6.19.

LISTING 6.19   Web.Config

```
<configuration>
  <system.web>
    <profile>
      <properties>
        <add name="UserTheme" />
      </properties>
    </profile>
  </system.web>
</configuration>
```

Because the control tree has not been created when the PreInit event is raised, you can't refer to any controls in a page. Notice that hyperlinks are used in Listing 6.18 to select a Theme. You could not use a DropDownList control because the DropDownList control would not have been created.

> **NOTE**
>
> If you need to load a Theme dynamically for multiple pages in an application, then you can override the OnPreInit() method of the base Page class. This technique is discussed in the "Loading Master Pages Dynamically for Multiple Content Pages" section of Chapter 5.

Applying Skins Dynamically

You can apply skins dynamically to particular controls in a page. In the Page PreInit event, you can modify a control's SkinID property programmatically.

For example, the page in Listing 6.20 enables a user to select a favorite skin for a GridView control. The GridView control displays a list of movies (see Figure 6.9).

LISTING 6.20   ShowDynamicSkin.aspx

```
<%@ Page Language="C#" Theme="DynamicSkin" %>
<!DOCTYPE html PUBLIC "-//W3C//DTD XHTML 1.1//EN"
"http://www.w3.org/TR/xhtml11/DTD/xhtml11.dtd">
```

```
<script runat="server">

    protected void Page_PreInit(object sender, EventArgs e)
    {
        if (Request["skin"] != null)
        {
            switch (Request["skin"])
            {
                case "professional":
                    grdMovies.SkinID = "Professional";
                    break;
                case "colorful":
                    grdMovies.SkinID = "Colorful";
                    break;
            }
        }
    }
</script>
<html xmlns="http://www.w3.org/1999/xhtml" >
<head runat="server">
    <title>Show Dynamic Skin</title>
</head>
<body>
    <form id="form1" runat="server">
    <div>

    <asp:GridView
        id="grdMovies"
        DataSourceID="srcMovies"
        Runat="server" />

     <asp:SqlDataSource
        id="srcMovies"
        ConnectionString="<%$ ConnectionStrings:Movies %>"
        SelectCommand="SELECT Id,Title,Director FROM Movies"
        Runat="server" />

    <hr />

    <a href="showdynamicskin.aspx?skin-professional">Professional</a>
     ¦ 
    <a href="showdynamicskin.aspx?skin=colorful">Colorful</a>
```

9

```
    </div>
    </form>
</body>
</html>
```

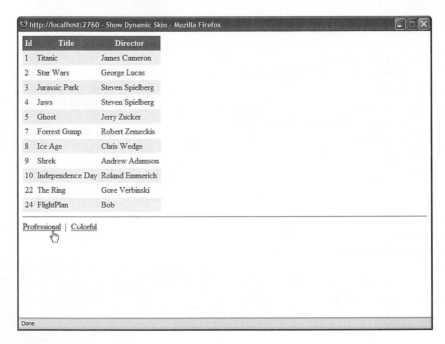

FIGURE 6.9   Applying a Skin programmatically.

A hyperlink is used to select a particular Skin. The Skin is applied to the GridView in the PreInit event when a particular value is assigned to the GridView control's SkinID property.

Of course, I don't recommend doing this. It makes more sense to use a Cascading Style Sheet and modify a control's CssClass property. This alternate approach is demonstrated by the page in Listing 6.21.

LISTING 6.21   ShowDynamicCSS.aspx

```
<%@ Page Language="C#" Theme="DynamicSkin" %>
<!DOCTYPE html PUBLIC "-//W3C//DTD XHTML 1.1//EN"
"http://www.w3.org/TR/xhtml11/DTD/xhtml11.dtd">
<script runat="server">

    protected void btnSubmit_Click(object sender, EventArgs e)
    {
        grdMovies.CssClass = ddlCssClass.SelectedItem.Text;
    }
```

```
</script>
<html xmlns="http://www.w3.org/1999/xhtml" >
<head id="Head1" runat="server">
    <title>Show Dynamic CSS</title>
</head>
<body>
    <form id="form1" runat="server">
    <div>

    <asp:GridView
        id="grdMovies"
        DataSourceID="srcMovies"
        HeaderStyle-CssClass="Header"
        AlternatingRowStyle-CssClass="Alternating"
        GridLines="none"
        Runat="server" />

     <asp:SqlDataSource
        id="srcMovies"
        ConnectionString="<%$ ConnectionStrings:Movies %>"
        SelectCommand="SELECT Id,Title,Director FROM Movies"
        Runat="server" />

    <hr />

    <asp:Label
        id="lblCssClass"
        Text="Select Style:"
        AssociatedControlID="ddlCssClass"
        Runat="server" />
    <asp:DropDownList
        id="ddlCssClass"
        Runat="server">
        <asp:ListItem Text="Professional" />
        <asp:ListItem Text="Colorful" />
    </asp:DropDownList>
    <asp:Button
        id="btnSubmit"
        Text="Select"
        Runat="server" OnClick="btnSubmit_Click" />

    </div>
    </form>
</body>
</html>
```

9

Note that in this code sample, unlike the previous one, you can use a `DropDownList` and `Button` control to change the appearance of the `GridView` control when modifying the `CssClass` property. Because you can modify the `CssClass` property during any event before the page is rendered, you can handle the `Button Click` event to modify the value of the `CssClass` property.

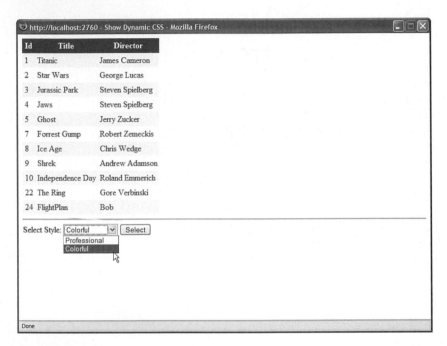

FIGURE 6.10   Modifying a `CssClass` programmatically.

Summary

In this chapter, you learned how to create a consistent look for your website by taking advantage of ASP.NET Themes. In the first section, you learned how to modify the appearance of controls in a page with Skins. You learned how to create both Default and Named Skins. You also learned how to apply a Theme by using the `Theme` attribute and `StyleSheetTheme` attribute.

Next, you learned how to add Cascading Style Sheets to Themes. I recommended that you take advantage of Cascading Style Sheets and avoid Skins whenever possible.

We also discussed how you can create Global Themes. You learned how to create a Theme that you can apply to every application executing on a web server.

Finally, you learned how to dynamically apply Themes. You learned how to use the `PreInit` event to dynamically apply either an entire Theme or a particular Skin at runtime.

CHAPTER 7

Creating Custom Controls with User Controls

A Web User control enables you to build a new control from existing controls. By taking advantage of User controls, you can easily extend the ASP.NET Framework with your own custom controls.

Imagine, for example, that you need to display the same address form in multiple pages in a web application. The address form consists of several TextBox and Validation controls for entering address information. If you want to avoid declaring all the TextBox and Validation controls in multiple pages, you can wrap these controls inside a Web User control.

Anytime you discover that you need to display the same user interface elements in multiple pages, you should consider wrapping the elements inside a User control. By taking advantage of User controls, you make your website easier to maintain and extend.

In this chapter, you learn how to build custom controls with User controls. It starts with the basics. You learn how to create a simple User control and expose properties and events from the User control.

You then examine how you can use AJAX with a User control. You learn how to modify the content displayed by a User control without posting the page that contains the User control back to the web server.

Finally, you learn how you can load User controls dynamically. You learn how to load a User control at runtime and inject the User control into a page. In the final section of this chapter, dynamically loaded User controls are used to build a multi-page wizard.

Creating User Controls

Let's start by building a simple User control that randomly displays one image from a folder of images (see Figure 7.1). The code for the User control is contained in Listing 7.1.

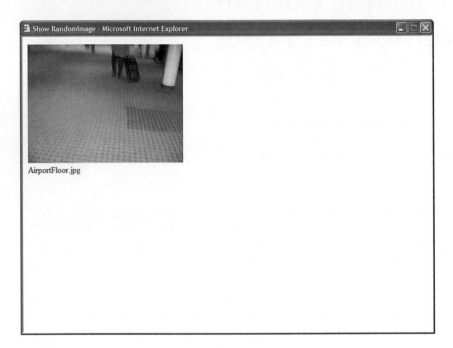

FIGURE 7.1   Displaying an image with the `RandomImage` User control.

LISTING 7.1   `RandomImage.ascx`

```csharp
<%@ Control Language="C#" ClassName="RandomImage" %>
<%@ Import Namespace="System.IO" %>

<script runat="server">

    void Page_Load()
    {
        string imageToDisplay = GetRandomImage();
        imgRandom.ImageUrl = Path.Combine("~/Images", imageToDisplay);
        lblRandom.Text = imageToDisplay;
    }

    private string GetRandomImage()
    {
        Random rnd = new Random();
```

```
        string[] images = Directory.GetFiles(MapPath("~/Images"), "*.jpg");
        string imageToDisplay = images[rnd.Next(images.Length)];
        return Path.GetFileName(imageToDisplay);
    }

</script>

<asp:Image
    id="imgRandom"
    Width="300px"
    Runat="server" />
<br />
<asp:Label
    id="lblRandom"
    Runat="server" />
```

VISUAL WEB DEVELOPER NOTE

You create a new User control in Visual Web Developer by selecting website, Add New
Item, and selecting the Web User control item.

The file in Listing 7.1 closely resembles a standard ASP.NET page. Like a standard ASP.NET
page, the User control contains a `Page_Load()` event handler. Also, the User control
contains standard controls such as the ASP.NET Image and Label controls.

User controls are closely related to ASP.NET pages. Both the `UserControl` class and the
`Page` class derive from the base `TemplateControl` class. Because they derive from the same
base class, they share many of the same methods, properties, and events.

The important difference between an ASP.NET page and a User control is that a User
control is something you can declare in an ASP.NET page. When you build a User control,
you are building a custom control.

Notice that the file in Listing 7.1 ends with the `.ascx` extension. You cannot request this
file directly from a web browser. To use the `RandomImage` User control, you must declare
the control in an ASP.NET page.

The page in Listing 7.2 contains the `RandomImage` User control. When you open the page,
a random image is displayed.

LISTING 7.2   ShowRandomImage.aspx

```
<%@ Page Language="C#" %>
<%@ Register TagPrefix="user" TagName="RandomImage" Src="~/RandomImage.ascx" %>
<!DOCTYPE html PUBLIC "-//W3C//DTD XHTML 1.1//EN"
"http://www.w3.org/TR/xhtml11/DTD/xhtml11.dtd">
<html xmlns="http://www.w3.org/1999/xhtml" >
```

LISTING 7.2   Continued

```
<head id="Head1" runat="server">
    <title>Show RandomImage</title>
</head>
<body>
    <form id="form1" runat="server">
    <div>

    <user:RandomImage
        ID="RandomImage1"
        Runat="server" />

    </div>
    </form>
</body>
</html>
```

Before you can use a web User control in a page, you must register it. The page in Listing 7.2 includes a `<%@ Register %>` directive that contains the following three attributes:

▶ **TagPrefix**—Indicates the namespace that you want to associate with the User control for the current page. You can use any string that you want.

▶ **TagName**—Indicates the name that you want to associate with the User control for the current page. You can use any string that you want.

▶ **Src**—Indicates the virtual path to the User control (the path to the `.ascx` file).

The RandomImage User control is declared in the body of the page. It looks like this:

```
<user:RandomImage ID="RandomImage1" Runat="Server" />
```

Notice that the declaration of the User control uses the TagPrefix and TagName specified in the `<%@ Register %>` directive. Furthermore, notice that you provide a User control with both an ID and a Runat attribute, just as you would for any standard ASP.NET control.

VISUAL WEB DEVELOPER NOTE

You can add a User control to a page in Visual Web Developer simply by dragging the User control from the Solution Explorer window onto the Design surface. The `<%@ Register %>` directive is automatically added to the source of the page.

Registering User Controls in the Web Configuration File

As an alternative to registering a User control in each page in which you need to use it by using the `<%@ Register %>` directive, you can register a User control once for an entire application. You can register a User control in an application's web configuration file.

For example, the web configuration file in Listing 7.3 registers the `RandomImage` control for the application.

LISTING 7.3   Web.Config

```
<configuration>
<system.web>
  <pages>
    <controls>
      <add
        tagPrefix="user"
        tagName="RandomImage"
        src="~/UserControls/RandomImage.ascx"/>
    </controls>
  </pages>
</system.web>
</configuration>
```

After you register a User control in the web configuration file, you can simply declare the User control in any page. For example, the page in Listing 7.4 contains an instance of the `RandomImage` User control, but it does not include the `<%@ Register %>` directive.

LISTING 7.4   ShowAppRegister.aspx

```
<%@ Page Language="C#" %>
<!DOCTYPE html PUBLIC "-//W3C//DTD XHTML 1.1//EN"
"http://www.w3.org/TR/xhtml11/DTD/xhtml11.dtd">
<html xmlns="http://www.w3.org/1999/xhtml" >
<head id="Head1" runat="server">
    <title>Show Application Register</title>
</head>
<body>
    <form id="form1" runat="server">
    <div>

    <user:RandomImage
        ID="RandomImage1"
        Runat="Server" />
```

LISTING 7.4   Continued

```
    </div>
    </form>
</body>
</html>
```

You need to be aware of one important limitation when registering a User control in the web configuration file. A User control cannot be located in the same folder as a page that uses it. For that reason, you should create all your User controls in a subfolder (I typically create a UserControls subfolder for each of my applications).

Exposing Properties from a User Control

The RandomImage User control always displays an image from the Images folder. It would be nice if you could specify the name of the folder that contains the images so that you could use different folder paths in different applications. You can do this by exposing a property from the RandomImage User control.

The modified RandomImage control in Listing 7.5, named PropertyRandomImage, exposes a property named ImageFolderPath.

LISTING 7.5   PropertyRandomImage.ascx

```
<%@ Control Language="C#" ClassName="PropertyRandomImage" %>
<%@ Import Namespace="System.IO" %>
<script runat="server">

    private string _imageFolderPath = "~/Images";

    public string ImageFolderPath
    {
        get { return _imageFolderPath; }
        set { _imageFolderPath = value; }
    }

    void Page_Load()
    {
        string imageToDisplay = GetRandomImage();
        imgRandom.ImageUrl = Path.Combine(_imageFolderPath, imageToDisplay);
        lblRandom.Text = imageToDisplay;
    }

    private string GetRandomImage()
    {
        Random rnd = new Random();
```

```
        string[] images = Directory.GetFiles(MapPath("~/Images"), "*.jpg");
        string imageToDisplay = images[rnd.Next(images.Length)];
        return Path.GetFileName(imageToDisplay);
    }
</script>

<asp:Image
    id="imgRandom"
    Width="300px"
    Runat="server" />
<br />
<asp:Label
    id="lblRandom"
    Runat="server" />
```

After you expose a property in a User control, you can set the property either declaratively or programmatically. The page in Listing 7.6 sets the `ImageFolderPath` property declaratively.

LISTING 7.6 ShowDeclarative.aspx

```
<%@ Page Language="C#" %>
<%@ Register TagPrefix="user" TagName="PropertyRandomImage" Src="~/PropertyRan-
domImage.ascx" %>
<!DOCTYPE html PUBLIC "-//W3C//DTD XHTML 1.1//EN"
"http://www.w3.org/TR/xhtml11/DTD/xhtml11.dtd">
<html xmlns="http://www.w3.org/1999/xhtml" >
<head id="Head1" runat="server">
    <title>Show Declarative</title>
</head>
<body>
    <form id="form1" runat="server">
    <div>

    <user:PropertyRandomImage
        ID="PropertyRandomImage1"
        ImageFolderPath="~/Images2"
        Runat="server" />

    </div>
    </form>
</body>
</html>
```

7

Notice that the `PropertyRandomImage` User control in Listing 7.6 includes an `ImageFolderPath` property. When you request the page, the random images are retrieved from the Images2 folder.

VISUAL WEB DEVELOPER NOTE

Any properties that you add to a User control appear in both Intellisense and the Property window.

The page in Listing 7.7 demonstrates how you can set the `ImageFolderPath` programmatically.

LISTING 7.7   `ShowProgrammatic.aspx`

```
<%@ Page Language="C#" %>
<%@ Register TagPrefix="user" TagName="PropertyRandomImage"
➥Src="~/PropertyRandomImage.ascx" %>
<!DOCTYPE html PUBLIC "-//W3C//DTD XHTML 1.1//EN"
"http://www.w3.org/TR/xhtml11/DTD/xhtml11.dtd">
<script runat="server">

    protected void Page_Load(object sender, EventArgs e)
    {
        PropertyRandomImage1.ImageFolderPath = "~/Images2";
    }
</script>
<html xmlns="http://www.w3.org/1999/xhtml" >
<head id="Head1" runat="server">
    <title>Show Programmatic</title>
</head>
<body>
    <form id="form1" runat="server">
    <div>

    <user:PropertyRandomImage
        ID="PropertyRandomImage1"
        Runat="server" />

    </div>
    </form>
</body>
</html>
```

The page in Listing 7.7 includes a `Page_Load()` event handler. This handler programmatically sets the `ImageFolderPath` to the value Images2.

Exposing Events from a User Control

You can expose custom events from a User control. After you expose the event, you can handle the event in the page that contains the User control.

Exposing events is useful when you need to pass information up to the containing page. Imagine, for example, that you want to create a custom tab strip with a User control. When a user clicks a tab, you want to change the content displayed in the page (see Figure 7.2).

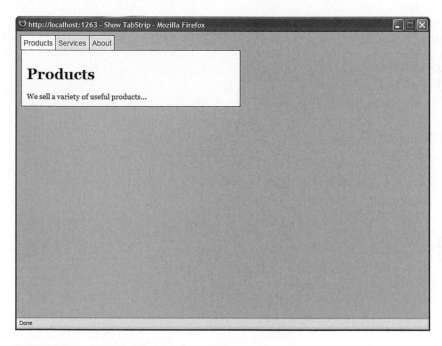

FIGURE 7.2   Displaying a tab strip with a User control.

The User control in Listing 7.8 contains the code for a simple tab strip.

LISTING 7.8   TabStrip.ascx

```
<%@ Control Language="C#" ClassName="TabStrip" %>
<%@ Import Namespace="System.Collections.Generic" %>
<script runat="server">

    public event EventHandler TabClick;

    /// <summary>
    /// The index of the selected tab
    /// </summary>
    public int SelectedIndex
```

LISTING 7.8 Continued

```
    {
        get { return dlstTabStrip.SelectedIndex; }
    }

    /// <summary>
    /// Create the tabs
    /// </summary>
    void Page_Load()
    {
        if (!Page.IsPostBack)
        {
            // Create the tabs
            List<string> tabs = new List<string>();
            tabs.Add("Products");
            tabs.Add("Services");
            tabs.Add("About");

            // Bind tabs to the DataList
            dlstTabStrip.DataSource = tabs;
            dlstTabStrip.DataBind();

            // Select first tab
            dlstTabStrip.SelectedIndex = 0;
        }
    }

    /// <summary>
    /// This method executes when a user clicks a tab
    /// </summary>
    protected void dlstTabStrip_SelectedIndexChanged(object sender, EventArgs e)
    {
        if (TabClick != null)
            TabClick(this, EventArgs.Empty);
    }
</script>

<asp:DataList
    id="dlstTabStrip"
    RepeatDirection="Horizontal"
    OnSelectedIndexChanged="dlstTabStrip_SelectedIndexChanged"
    CssClass="tabs"
    ItemStyle-CssClass="tab"
    SelectedItemStyle-CssClass="selectedTab"
    Runat="server">
    <ItemTemplate>
```

```
    <asp:LinkButton
        id="lnkTab"
        Text='<%# Container.DataItem %>'
        CommandName="Select"
        Runat="server" />
    </ItemTemplate>
</asp:DataList>
```

The tab strip is created with the help of a `DataList` control. The `DataList` control displays links for each of the items created in the `Page_Load()` event handler.

Notice that the `TabStrip` control exposes an event named `TabClick`. This event is raised in the `dlstTabStrip_SelectedIndexChanged()` event handler when a user clicks a tab.

The page in Listing 7.9 uses the `TabStrip` control to display different content depending on the tab selected.

LISTING 7.9   ShowTabStrip.aspx

```
<%@ Page Language="C#" %>
<%@ Register TagPrefix="user" TagName="TabStrip" Src="~/TabStrip.ascx" %>
<!DOCTYPE html PUBLIC "-//W3C//DTD XHTML 1.1//EN"
"http://www.w3.org/TR/xhtml11/DTD/xhtml11.dtd">
<script runat="server">

    protected void TabStrip1_TabClick(object sender, EventArgs e)
    {
        MultiView1.ActiveViewIndex = TabStrip1.SelectedIndex;
    }
</script>
<html xmlns="http://www.w3.org/1999/xhtml" >
<head id="Head1" runat="server">
    <style type="text/css">
        html
        {
            background-color:silver;
            font:14px Georgia,Serif;
        }
        .tabs a
        {
            color:blue;
            text-decoration:none;
            font:14px Arial,Sans-Serif;
        }
        .tab
        {
            background-color:#eeeeee;
```

LISTING 7.9   Continued

```
            padding:5px;
            border:Solid 1px black;
            border-bottom:none;
        }
        .selectedTab
        {
            background-color:white;
            padding:5px;
            border:Solid 1px black;
            border-bottom:none;
        }
        .views
        {
            background-color:white;
            width:400px;
            border:Solid 1px black;
            padding:10px;
        }
    </style>
    <title>Show TabStrip</title>
</head>
<body>
    <form id="form1" runat="server">
    <div>

    <user:TabStrip
        ID="TabStrip1"
        OnTabClick="TabStrip1_TabClick"
        Runat="Server" />

    <div class="views">
    <asp:MultiView
        id="MultiView1"
        ActiveViewIndex="0"
        Runat="server">
        <asp:View ID="Products" runat="server">
            <h1>Products</h1>
            We sell a variety of useful products...
        </asp:View>
        <asp:View ID="Services" runat="server">
            <h1>Services</h1>
            We offer a number of services...
        </asp:View>
        <asp:View ID="About" runat="server">
            <h1>About</h1>
```

```
            We were the first company to offer products and services...
        </asp:View>
    </asp:MultiView>
    </div>

    </div>
    </form>
</body>
</html>
```

The page in Listing 7.9 includes an event handler for the `TabStrip` control's `TabClick` event. When you click a tab, the index of the selected tab is retrieved from the tab strip, and the `View` control with the matching index is displayed.

VISUAL WEB DEVELOPER NOTE

You can add a `TabClick` event handler to the `TabStrip` control by selecting the `TabStrip` control from the top-left drop-down list and selecting the `TabClick` event from the top-right drop-down list.

NOTE

The ASP.NET Framework includes a Menu control that you can use to create both tab-strips and pop-up menus. This control is discussed in Chapter 4, "Using the Rich Controls," and Chapter 19, "Using the Navigation Controls."

Creating an `AddressForm` Control

Let's end this section by creating a generally useful Web User control. We'll build an AddressForm User control that you can reuse in multiple pages or reuse multiple times in a single page (see Figure 7.3).

The `AddressForm` User control is contained in Listing 7.10.

LISTING 7.10 `AddressForm.ascx`

```
<%@ Control Language="C#" ClassName="AddressForm" %>
<script runat="server">

    public string Title
    {
        get { return ltlTitle.Text; }
        set { ltlTitle.Text = value; }
    }


    public string Street
    {
```

LISTING 7.10   Continued

```
        get { return txtStreet.Text; }
        set { txtStreet.Text = value; }
    }

    public string City
    {
        get { return txtCity.Text; }
        set { txtCity.Text = value; }
    }

    public string State
    {
        get { return txtState.Text; }
        set { txtState.Text = value; }
    }

    public string PostalCode
    {
        get { return txtPostalCode.Text; }
        set { txtPostalCode.Text = value; }
    }

</script>

<fieldset>
<legend>
    <asp:Literal
        ID="ltlTitle"
        Text="Address Form"
        runat="server" />
</legend>

<div class="addressLabel">
<asp:Label
    ID="lblStreet"
    Text="Street:"
    AssociatedControlID="txtStreet"
    Runat="server" />
</div>
<div class="addressField">
<asp:TextBox
    ID="txtStreet"
    Runat="server" />
<asp:RequiredFieldValidator
    ID="reqStreet"
```

```
        Text="(required)"
        ControlToValidate="txtStreet"
        Runat="server" />
</div>

<br class="clear" />

<div class="addressLabel">
<asp:Label
    ID="lblCity"
    Text="City:"
    AssociatedControlID="txtCity"
    Runat="server" />
</div>
<div class="addressField">
<asp:TextBox
    ID="txtCity"
    Runat="server" />
<asp:RequiredFieldValidator
    ID="reqCity"
    Text="(required)"
    ControlToValidate="txtCity"
    Runat="server" />
</div>

<br class="clear" />

<div class="addressLabel">
<asp:Label
    ID="lblState"
    Text="State:"
    AssociatedControlID="txtState"
    Runat="server" />
</div>
<div class="addressField">
<asp:TextBox
    ID="txtState"
    Runat="server" />
<asp:RequiredFieldValidator
    ID="reqState"
    Text="(required)"
    ControlToValidate="txtState"
    Runat="server" />
</div>

<br class="clear" />
```

LISTING 7.10   Continued

```
<div class="addressLabel">
<asp:Label
    ID="lblPostalCode"
    Text="Postal Code:"
    AssociatedControlID="txtPostalCode"
    Runat="server" />
</div>
<div class="addressField">
<asp:TextBox
    ID="txtPostalCode"
    Runat="server" />
<asp:RequiredFieldValidator
    ID="RequiredFieldValidator1"
    Text="(required)"
    ControlToValidate="txtPostalCode"
    Runat="server" />
</div>

<br class="clear" />

</fieldset>
```

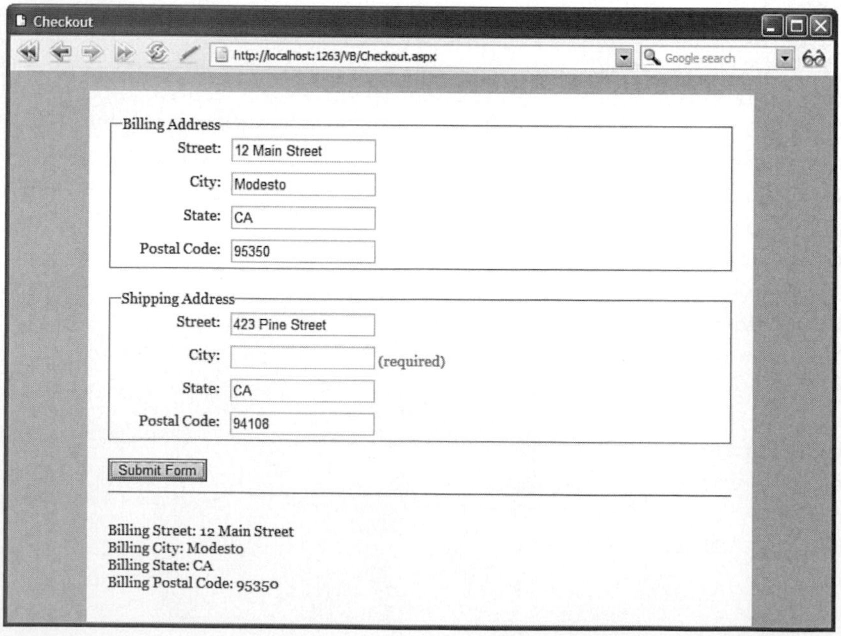

FIGURE 7.3   Displaying multiple address forms with the AddressForm User control.

The `AddressForm` control contains form controls for entering your street, city, state, and postal code. Each of these fields is validated by a `RequiredFieldValidator` control. Finally, the `AddressForm` includes a label that can be used to provide a title for the control.

The `AddressForm` exposes all of its form fields with properties. The control includes public Street, City, State, and PostalCode property, which you can read from the containing page.

The page in Listing 7.11 illustrates how you can use the `AddressForm` control in a page.

LISTING 7.11   `Checkout.aspx`

```
<%@ Page Language="C#" %>
<%@ Register TagPrefix="user" TagName="AddressForm" Src="~/AddressForm.ascx" %>
<!DOCTYPE html PUBLIC "-//W3C//DTD XHTML 1.1//EN"
"http://www.w3.org/TR/xhtml11/DTD/xhtml11.dtd">
<script runat="server">

    protected void btnSubmit_Click(object sender, EventArgs e)
    {
        // Show Billing Address Form Results
        ltlResults.Text = "<br />Billing Street: " + AddressForm1.Street;
        ltlResults.Text += "<br />Billing City: " + AddressForm1.City;
        ltlResults.Text += "<br />Billing State: " + AddressForm1.State;
        ltlResults.Text += "<br />Billing Postal Code: " + AddressForm1.PostalCode;

        ltlResults.Text += "<br /><br />";

        // Show Shipping Address Form Results
        ltlResults.Text += "<br />Shipping Street: " + AddressForm2.Street;
        ltlResults.Text += "<br />Shipping City: " + AddressForm2.City;
        ltlResults.Text += "<br />Shipping State: " + AddressForm2.State;
        ltlResults.Text += "<br />Shipping Postal Code: " + AddressForm2.PostalCode;
    }
</script>
<html xmlns="http://www.w3.org/1999/xhtml" >
<head id="Head1" runat="server">
    <style type="text/css">
        html
        {
            background-color:silver;
            font:14px Georgia,Serif;
        }
        .content
        {
```

LISTING 7.11   Continued

```
            background-color:white;
            width:600px;
            margin:auto;
            padding:20px;
        }
        .addressLabel
        {
            float:left;
            width:100px;
            padding:5px;
            text-align:right;
        }
        .addressField
        {
            float:left;
            padding:5px;
        }
        .clear
        {
            clear:both;
        }

    </style>
    <title>Checkout</title>
</head>
<body>
    <form id="form1" runat="server">
    <div class="content">

    <user:AddressForm
        id="AddressForm1"
        Title="Billing Address"
        Runat="server" />

    <br />

    <user:AddressForm
        id="AddressForm2"
        Title="Shipping Address"
        Runat="server" />

    <br />
```

```
<asp:Button
    ID="btnSubmit"
    Text="Submit Form"
    OnClick="btnSubmit_Click"
    Runat="server" />

<hr />

<asp:Literal
    id="ltlResults"
    Runat="server" />

    </div>
    </form>
</body>
</html>
```

The page in Listing 7.11 contains two instances of the `AddressForm` control: a Billing Address and Shipping Address. When you click the Button control, the address information is retrieved from the `AddressForm` controls and displayed in a Literal control. (In a real application, you would grab the data and store it in a database.)

WEB STANDARDS NOTE

The `AddressForm` User control does not use an HTML table to layout its controls. You should strive to avoid using tables except when displaying tabular information. Instead, Cascading Style Sheet rules are used to position the form elements. The page looks almost identical in Internet Explorer 6, Firefox 1.0, and Opera 8.0.

AJAX and User Controls

Ajax (Asynchronous JavaScript and XML) enables you to update content in a page without posting the page back to the server. Behind the scenes, AJAX uses the XMLHttp ActiveX component (in the case of Microsoft Internet Explorer 6.0) or the XMLHttpRequest intrinsic browser object (in the case of other browsers such as FireFox and Internet Explorer 7.0).

We explore the topic of Ajax in depth in Part IX, "ASP.NET AJAX." In this section, I want to provide you with a quick sample of using Ajax with a User control. The User control in Listing 7.12 randomly displays one of three quotations. The quotation is updated automatically every 5 seconds (see Figure 7.4).

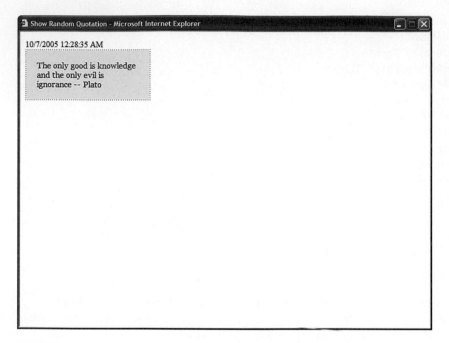

FIGURE 7.4   Using AJAX to display a random quotation.

LISTING 7.12   RandomQuotation.ascx

```csharp
<%@ Control Language="C#" ClassName="RandomQuotation" %>
<%@ Import Namespace="System.Collections.Generic" %>
<script runat="server">

    void Page_Load()
    {
        List<string> quotes = new List<string>();
        quotes.Add("All paid jobs absorb and degrade the mind -- Aristotle");
        quotes.Add("No evil can happen to a good man, either in life or after
        ➥death -- Plato");
        quotes.Add("The only good is knowledge and the only evil is ignorance
        ➥-- Plato");
        Random rnd = new Random();
        lblQuote.Text = quotes[rnd.Next(quotes.Count)];
    }
</script>

<asp:ScriptManager ID="sm1" runat="server" />
<asp:Timer ID="Timer1" Interval="5000" runat="server" />

<asp:UpdatePanel ID="up1" runat="server">
```

```
<Triggers>
    <asp:AsyncPostBackTrigger ControlID="Timer1" />
</Triggers>
<ContentTemplate>
    <div class="quote">
    <asp:Label
        id="lblQuote"
        Runat="server" />
    </div>
</ContentTemplate>
</asp:UpdatePanel>
```

A random quotation is assigned to the Label control in the `Page_Load()` method in Listing 7.12. Notice that the Label control is contained in an `UpdatePanel` control. The `UpdatePanel` is used to mark an area of the page that gets refreshed without a postback (an Ajax zone). The `UpdatePanel` control is associated with a Timer control. The Timer control causes the `UpdatePanel` to refresh its content every 5 seconds (an interval of 5,000 milliseconds).

The page in Listing 7.13 illustrates how you can use the `RandomQuotation` User control. It contains the User control and it also displays the current time.

LISTING 7.13 ShowRandomQuotation.aspx

```
<%@ Page Language="C#" %>
<%@ Register TagPrefix="user" TagName="RandomQuotation"
  Src="~/RandomQuotation.ascx" %>
<!DOCTYPE html PUBLIC "-//W3C//DTD XHTML 1.1//EN"
"http://www.w3.org/TR/xhtml11/DTD/xhtml11.dtd">
<html xmlns="http://www.w3.org/1999/xhtml" >
<head id="Head1" runat="server">
    <style type="text/css">
        .quote
        {
            width:200px;
            padding:20px;
            border:Dotted 2px orange;
            background-color:#eeeeee;
            font:16px Georgia,Serif;
        }
    </style>
    <title>Show Random Quotation</title>
</head>
<body>
    <form id="form1" runat="server">
    <div>
```

LISTING 7.13   Continued

```
    <%= DateTime.Now %>
    <br />

    <user:RandomQuotation
        id="RandomQuotation1"
        Runat="server" />

    </div>
    </form>
</body>
</html>
```

Notice that the random quotation is updated, but that the time on the page does not change. Only the area of the page that contains the random quotation is updated.

Dynamically Loading User Controls

You can dynamically load a User control at runtime and display it in a page. Imagine, for example, that you want to display different featured products randomly on the home page of your website. However, you want to display each featured product with a completely different layout. In that case, you can create a separate User control for each product and load one of the User controls randomly at runtime.

You load a User control with the `Page.LoadControl()` method. This method returns an instance of the `Control` class that you can add to a page. Typically, you add the User control to a `PlaceHolder` control that you have declared on the page.

> **NOTE**
>
> The `PlaceHolder` control was designed to do absolutely nothing. It simply acts as a placeholder on the page where you can add other controls.

For example, the page in Listing 7.14 randomly loads one of the controls from the FeaturedProducts folder and adds the control to the page.

LISTING 7.14   ShowFeaturedProduct.aspx

```
<%@ Page Language="C#" %>
<%@ Import Namespace="System.IO" %>
<!DOCTYPE html PUBLIC "-//W3C//DTD XHTML 1.1//EN"
"http://www.w3.org/TR/xhtml11/DTD/xhtml11.dtd">
<script runat="server">
```

```
    const string randomFolder = "~/FeaturedProducts";

    protected void Page_Load(object sender, EventArgs e)
    {
        string featuredProductPath = GetRandomProductPath();
        Control featuredProduct = Page.LoadControl(featuredProductPath);
        PlaceHolder1.Controls.Add(featuredProduct);
    }

    private string GetRandomProductPath()
    {
        Random rnd = new Random();
        string[] files = Directory.GetFiles(MapPath(randomFolder), "*.ascx");
        string featuredProductPath = Path.GetFileName
        ➥(files[rnd.Next(files.Length)]);
        return Path.Combine(randomFolder, featuredProductPath);
    }

</script>
<html xmlns="http://www.w3.org/1999/xhtml" >
<head id="Head1" runat="server">
    <title>Show Featured Products</title>
</head>
<body>
    <form id="form1" runat="server">
    <div>

    <asp:PlaceHolder
        id="PlaceHolder1"
        Runat="server" />

    </div>
    </form>
</body>
</html>
```

Using the Reference Directive

When you load a User control with the `Page.LoadControl()` method, the User control is returned as an instance of the `System.Web.UI.Control` class. This means that if the User control includes any custom properties, the properties aren't available when you dynamically load the User control.

If you dynamically load a User control, then you need to cast the control to the correct type before you can access any of the control's custom properties. To get a reference to a User control's type, you must use the <%@ Reference %> directive.

For example, imagine that you need to create a form that displays different questions depending on the answers that a user provides for previous questions. In that case, you can dynamically load different User controls that contain the different sets of questions.

For example, the page in Listing 7.15 contains a survey form. The first question asks you whether you are currently using ASP Classic or ASP.NET. Depending on your answer, the remainder of the form displays different questions (see Figure 7.5).

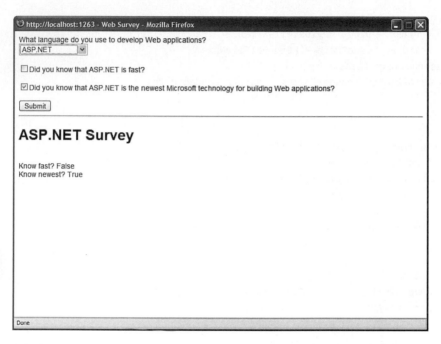

FIGURE 7.5   Displaying a survey form with dynamically loaded questions.

LISTING 7.15   WebSurvey.aspx

```
<%@ Page Language="C#" %>
<%@ Reference Control="~/ASPSurvey.ascx" %>
<%@ Reference Control="~/ASPNetSurvey.ascx" %>
<!DOCTYPE html PUBLIC "-//W3C//DTD XHTML 1.1//EN"
"http://www.w3.org/TR/xhtml11/DTD/xhtml11.dtd">
<script runat="server">

    private Control _survey = null;

    void Page_Load()
```

```
        {
            switch (ddlLanguage.SelectedIndex)
            {
                case 1:
                    _survey = Page.LoadControl("ASPSurvey.ascx");
                    break;
                case 2:
                    _survey = Page.LoadControl("ASPNetSurvey.ascx");
                    break;
            }

            if (_survey != null)
                PlaceHolder1.Controls.Add(_survey);
        }

        protected void btnSubmit_Click(object sender, EventArgs e)
        {
            switch (ddlLanguage.SelectedIndex)
            {
                case 1:
                    ASPSurvey aspResults = (ASPSurvey)_survey;
                    ltlResults.Text = "<h1>ASP Survey</h1>";
                    ltlResults.Text += "<br />Know slow? " +
                    ➥aspResults.KnowSlow.ToString();
                    ltlResults.Text += "<br />Know outdated? " +
                    ➥aspResults.KnowOutdated.ToString();
                    break;
                case 2:
                    ASPNetSurvey aspNetResults = (ASPNetSurvey)_survey;
                    ltlResults.Text = "<h1>ASP.NET Survey</h1>";
                    ltlResults.Text += "<br />Know fast? " +
                    ➥aspNetResults.KnowFast.ToString();
                    ltlResults.Text += "<br />Know newest? " +
                    ➥aspNetResults.KnowNewest.ToString();
                    break;
            }
        }
</script>
<html xmlns="http://www.w3.org/1999/xhtml" >
<head id="Head1" runat="server">
    <style type="text/css">
        html
        {
            font:14px Arial,Sans-Serif;
        }
    </style>
```

7

LISTING 7.15   Continued

```
    <title>Web Survey</title>
</head>
<body>
    <form id="form1" runat="server">
    <div>

    <asp:Label
        id="lblLanguage"
        Text="What language do you use to develop Web applications?"
        Runat="server" />
    <br />
    <asp:DropDownList
        id="ddlLanguage"
        ToolTip="Web application language (reloads form)"
        AutoPostBack="true"
        Runat="server">
        <asp:ListItem Text="Select Language" />
        <asp:ListItem Text="ASP Classic" />
        <asp:ListItem Text="ASP.NET" />
    </asp:DropDownList>

    <br /><br />

    <asp:PlaceHolder
        id="PlaceHolder1"
        Runat="server" />

    <asp:Button
        id="btnSubmit"
        Text="Submit"
        OnClick="btnSubmit_Click"
        Runat="server" />

    <hr />

    <asp:Literal
        id="ltlResults"
        Runat="server" />

    </div>
    </form>
</body>
</html>
```

WEB STANDARDS NOTE

The DropDownList control in Listing 7.15 reloads the page automatically when you select a new option. You should never reload a page without warning the user because this can be very confusing for someone who is using an assistive device such as a screen reader. In Listing 7.15, a warning is added to the ToolTip property of the DropDownList control.

Depending on the user's selection from the DropDownList control, one of two User controls is loaded in the Page_Load() event handler: the ASPSurvey.ascx or the ASPNetSurvey.ascx User control. These controls are contained in Listing 7.16 and Listing 7.17.

When you submit the survey form, the btnSubmit_Click() method executes. This method casts the User control loaded in the form to the correct type. It casts the User control to either the ASPSurvey or the ASPNetSurvey type.

Notice that the page in Listing 7.15 includes two <%@ Reference %> directives. These reference directives enable you to cast the User control to the correct type so that you can access custom properties of the control such as the KnowSlow and KnowOutdated properties.

LISTING 7.16   ASPSurvey.ascx

```
<%@ Control Language="C#" ClassName="ASPSurvey" %>
<script runat="server">

    public bool KnowSlow
    {
        get { return chkSlow.Checked; }
    }

    public bool KnowOutdated
    {
        get { return chkOutdated.Checked; }
    }

</script>

<asp:CheckBox
    id="chkSlow"
    Text="Did you know that ASP Classic is slow?"
    Runat="server" />

<br /><br />
```

LISTING 7.16   Continued

```
<asp:CheckBox
    id="chkOutdated"
    Text="Did you know that ASP Classic is outdated?"
    Runat="server" />
<br /><br />
```

LISTING 7.17   ASPNetSurvey.ascx

```
<%@ Control Language="C#" ClassName="ASPNetSurvey" %>
<script runat="server">

    public bool KnowFast
    {
        get { return chkFast.Checked; }
    }

    public bool KnowNewest
    {
        get { return chkNewest.Checked; }
    }

</script>
<asp:CheckBox
    id="chkFast"
    Text="Did you know that ASP.NET is fast?"
    Runat="server" />

<br /><br />

<asp:CheckBox
    id="chkNewest"
    Text="Did you know that ASP.NET is the newest Microsoft
        technology for building Web applications?"
    Runat="server" />
<br /><br />
```

Creating a Multi-Page Wizard

This final section discusses how you can create a multi-page wizard by dynamically loading different user controls into the same page. This is going to be a complicated sample, but it is a realistic sample of situations when you would want to load User controls dynamically (see Figure 7.6).

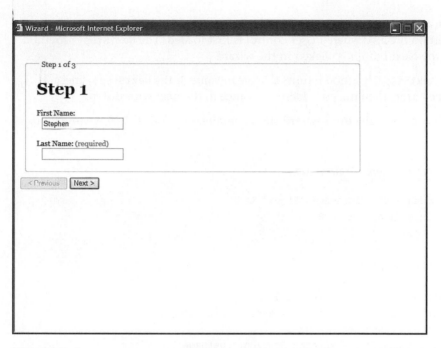

FIGURE 7.6   Displaying a wizard with a series of User controls.

Imagine that you must create a form with 200 questions in it. Displaying all 200 questions to a user in a single form would be overwhelming. Instead, it makes more sense to break the form into multiple pages. Each page of questions can be represented with a User control.

First, you need to define an interface, named the IWizardStep interface, which all the User controls will implement. An interface enables you to know, in advance, that a User control supports a particular set of properties or methods.

NOTE

You need to add the interface in Listing 7.18 to your application's App_Code folder. In Visual Web Developer, create the interface by selecting Website, Add New Item, and select Class. Visual Web Developer prompts you to create the App_Code folder.

The IWizardStep interface is contained in Listing 7.18.

LISTING 7.18   IWizardStep.cs

```
public interface IWizardStep
{
    void LoadStep();
    bool NextStep();
}
```

The interface in Listing 7.18 contains two methods: `LoadStep()` and `NextStep()`. The `LoadStep()` method is called when a User control is first loaded. The `NextStep()` method is called when the Next button is clicked in the wizard.

Notice that the `NextStep()` method returns a Boolean value. If the `NextStep()` method returns the value `False`, then the user doesn't advance to the next wizard step.

This wizard will consist of the three wizard steps contained in Listing 7.19, Listing 7.20, and Listing 7.21.

LISTING 7.19   `WizardSteps\Step1.ascx`

```
<%@ Control Language="C#" ClassName="Step1" %>
<%@ Implements Interface="IWizardStep" %>
<script runat="server">

    public void LoadStep()
    {
        if (Session["FirstName"] != null)
            txtFirstName.Text = (string)Session["FirstName"];
        if (Session["LastName"] != null)
            txtLastName.Text = (string)Session["LastName"];
    }

    public bool NextStep()
    {
        if (Page.IsValid)
        {

            Session["FirstName"] = txtFirstName.Text;
            Session["LastName"] = txtLastName.Text;
            return true;
        }
        return false;
    }
</script>
<h1>Step 1</h1>

<asp:Label
    id="lblFirstName"
    Text="First Name:"
    AssociatedControlID="txtFirstName"
    Runat="server" />
<asp:RequiredFieldValidator
    id="reqFirstName"
    Text="(required)"
```

```
        ControlToValidate="txtFirstName"
        Runat="server" />
<br />
<asp:TextBox
        id="txtFirstName"
        Runat="server" />

<br /><br />

<asp:Label
        id="lblLastName"
        Text="Last Name:"
        AssociatedControlID="txtLastName"
        Runat="server" />
<asp:RequiredFieldValidator
        id="reqLastName"
        Text="(required)"
        ControlToValidate="txtLastName"
        Runat="server" />
<br />
<asp:TextBox
        id="txtLastName"
        Runat="server" />
```

The wizard step in Listing 7.19 contains a simple form that contains Textbox controls for the user's first and last name. Both TextBox controls are validated with RequiredFieldValidator controls.

Notice that the User control in Listing 7.19 implements the IWizardStep interface. It contains an <%@ Implements %> directive at the top of the control.

The LoadStep() method assigns values to the txtFirstName and txtLastName TextBox controls from Session state. The NextStep() method grabs the values from the txtFirstName and txtLastName TextBox controls and assigns the values to Session state.

The second step of the wizard is contained in Listing 7.20.

LISTING 7.20   WizardSteps\Step2.ascx

```
<%@ Control Language="C#" ClassName="Step2" %>
<%@ Implements Interface="IWizardStep" %>
<script runat="server">

    public void LoadStep()
    {
        if (Session["FavoriteColor"] != null)
            txtFavoriteColor.Text = (string)Session["FavoriteColor"];
```

LISTING 7.20   Continued

```
    }

    public bool NextStep()
    {
        if (Page.IsValid)
        {
            Session["FavoriteColor"] = txtFavoriteColor.Text;
            return true;
        }
        return false;
    }
</script>

<h1>Step 2</h1>

<asp:Label
    id="lblFavoriteColor"
    Text="Favorite Color:"
    AssociatedControlID="txtFavoriteColor"
    Runat="server" />
<asp:RequiredFieldValidator
    id="reqFavoriteColor"
    Text="(required)"
    ControlToValidate="txtFavoriteColor"
    Runat="server" />
<br />
<asp:TextBox
    id="txtFavoriteColor"
    Runat="server" />
```

The User control in Listing 7.20 also implements the IWizardStep interface. In this step, the user enters a favorite color.

The final wizard step is contained in Listing 7.21.

LISTING 7.21   WizardSteps\Step3.ascx

```
<%@ Control Language="C#" ClassName="Step3" %>
<%@ Implements Interface="IWizardStep" %>
<script runat="server">

    public void LoadStep()
    {
        lblFirstName.Text = (string)Session["FirstName"];
```

```
        lblLastName.Text = (string)Session["LastName"];
        lblFavoriteColor.Text = (string)Session["FavoriteColor"];
    }

    public bool NextStep()
    {
        return false;
    }
</script>

<h1>Step 3</h1>

First Name:
<asp:Label
    id="lblFirstName"
    Runat="server" />
<br />
Last Name:
<asp:Label
    id="lblLastName"
    Runat="server" />
<br />
Favorite Color:
<asp:Label
    id="lblFavoriteColor"
    Runat="server" />
```

The wizard step in Listing 7.21 displays a summary of answers that the user has provided in the first two wizard steps (see Figure 7.7). Notice that it also implements the IWizardStep interface. Because this is the final wizard step, the NextStep() method always returns the value False.

The page in Listing 7.22 contains the actual wizard. This page loads each of the wizard steps.

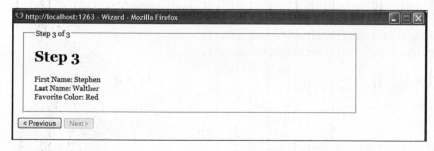

FIGURE 7.7   Displaying the wizard summary step.

LISTING 7.22   Wizard.aspx

```
<%@ Page Language="C#" %>
<%@ Import Namespace="System.Collections.Generic" %>
<!DOCTYPE html PUBLIC "-//W3C//DTD XHTML 1.1//EN"
"http://www.w3.org/TR/xhtml11/DTD/xhtml11.dtd">
<script runat="server">

    private List<String> _wizardSteps = new List<String>();
    private Control _currentStep;

    /// <summary>
    /// The current step in the Wizard
    /// </summary>
    public int StepIndex
    {
        get
        {
            if (ViewState["StepIndex"] == null)
                return 0;
            else
                return (int)ViewState["StepIndex"];
        }
        set
        {
            ViewState["StepIndex"] = value;
        }
    }

    /// <summary>
    /// Load the list of wizard steps and load
    /// current step
    /// </summary>
    void Page_Load()
    {
        _wizardSteps.Add("~/WizardSteps/Step1.ascx");
        _wizardSteps.Add("~/WizardSteps/Step2.ascx");
        _wizardSteps.Add("~/WizardSteps/Step3.ascx");

        LoadWizardStep();
    }

    /// <summary>
    /// Load the current wizard step
    /// </summary>
    private void LoadWizardStep()
```

```
{
    _currentStep = Page.LoadControl(_wizardSteps[StepIndex]);
    _currentStep.ID = "ctlWizardStep";
    plhWizardStep.Controls.Clear();
    plhWizardStep.Controls.Add(_currentStep);
    ((IWizardStep)_currentStep).LoadStep();
    ltlStep.Text = String.Format("Step {0} of {1}", StepIndex + 1,
    ➥_wizardSteps.Count);
}


/// <summary>
/// Disable the Previous and Next
/// buttons when appropriate
/// </summary>
void Page_PreRender()
{
    btnPrevious.Enabled = StepIndex > 0;
    btnNext.Enabled = StepIndex < _wizardSteps.Count - 1;
}


/// <summary>
/// Execute the step's NextStep() method
/// and move to the next step
/// </summary>
protected void btnNext_Click(object sender, EventArgs e)
{
    bool success = ((IWizardStep)_currentStep).NextStep();
    if (success)
    {
        if (StepIndex < _wizardSteps.Count - 1)
        {
            StepIndex++;
            LoadWizardStep();
        }
    }
}


/// <summary>
/// Move to the previous step
/// </summary>
protected void btnPrevious_Click(object sender, EventArgs e)
{
    if (StepIndex > 0)
    {
        StepIndex--;
        LoadWizardStep();
```

LISTING 7.22   Continued

```
        }
    }
</script>
<html xmlns="http://www.w3.org/1999/xhtml" >
<head id="Head1" runat="server">
    <style type="text/css">
        html
        {
            font:14px Georgia,Serif;
        }
        fieldset
        {
            display:block;
            width:600px;
            padding:20px;
            margin:10px;
        }
    </style>
    <title>Wizard</title>
</head>
<body>
    <form id="form1" runat="server">
    <div>

    <asp:Label
        id="lblStepNumber"
        Runat="server" />

    <fieldset>
    <legend><asp:Literal ID="ltlStep" runat="server" /></legend>
        <asp:PlaceHolder
            id="plhWizardStep"
            Runat="server" />
    </fieldset>

    <asp:Button
        id="btnPrevious"
        Text="&lt; Previous"
        CausesValidation="false"
        OnClick="btnPrevious_Click"
        Runat="server" />
```

```
<asp:Button
    id="btnNext"
    Text="Next &gt;"
    OnClick="btnNext_Click"
    Runat="server" />

</div>
</form>
</body>
</html>
```

The list of wizard steps is created in the `Page_Load()` method. The path to each wizard step User control is added to a collection of wizard steps.

The `StepIndex` property represents the index of the wizard step to display. Notice that the value of this property is stored in `ViewState` so that the value is available across multiple page requests.

The current wizard step is loaded by the `LoadWizardStep()` method. This method uses the StepIndex to grab the path to the current wizard step. Next, it uses the `Page.LoadControl()` method to actually load the wizard step User control.

After the `LoadWizardStep()` method loads the current wizard step, it calls the control's `LoadStep()` method and initializes the control.

The page also contains a Previous and Next button. When you click the Previous button, the `btnPrevious_Click()` method is called and the `StepIndex` is reduced by one. When you click the Next button, the `btnNext_Click()` method is called.

The `btnNext_Click()` method first calls the current wizard step's `NextStep()` method. If this method returns the value `True`, then one is added to the `StepIndex` property and the next wizard step is loaded. Otherwise, if the `NextStep()` method returns `false`, the next wizard step is not loaded.

Summary

In this chapter, you learned how to build custom controls by creating User controls. The first section covered the basics of User controls. You learned how to create a User control and register it both in a page and in a Web configuration file. You learned how to add custom properties and events to a User control.

The next topic was caching and User controls. You learned how to cache the rendered content of a User control in server memory. You also learned how to share the same cached content across multiple pages.

You also explored the topic of AJAX and User controls. You learned how to update content in a User control without posting the page that contains the User control back to the web server.

Finally, you learned how to add User controls dynamically to a page. You learned how to use the `<%@ Reference %>` directive to cast a User control to a particular type. You also saw a series of User controls loaded dynamically to create a multi-page wizard.

PART III

Performing Data Access

IN THIS PART

Overview of Data Access

Any web application worth writing involves data access. In this chapter, you learn how to take advantage of the rich set of controls included in the ASP.NET 3.5 Framework for working with data.

You learn how to take advantage of the DataBound controls to display data in your ASP.NET pages. You also learn how to take advantage of the DataSource controls to represent different sources of data such as databases, XML files, and business objects.

Next, you are provided with an overview of Microsoft SQL Server 2005 Express, which is the royalty-free database included with Visual Web Developer. You learn how to connect to this database and use it for all of your data access needs.

Finally, at the end of this chapter, we build a database-driven application, which illustrates how you can use many of the data controls discussed in this chapter. We build an Employee Directory application.

Using DataBound Controls

You use DataBound controls to generate your application's user interface for working with data. The DataBound controls can be used to display and edit database data, XML data, or just about any other type of data you can imagine.

There are three main types of DataBound controls: list controls, tabular DataBound controls, and hierarchical DataBound controls.

Working with List Controls

List controls are used to display simple option lists. The ASP.NET 3.5 Framework includes the following five List controls:

- ▶ **BulletedList**— Displays a bulleted list of items. Each item can be displayed as text, a link button, or a hyperlink.

- ▶ **CheckBoxList**—Displays a list of check boxes. Multiple check boxes in the list can be selected.

- ▶ **DropDownList**—Displays a drop-down list. Only one item in the drop-down list can be selected.

- ▶ **ListBox**—Displays a list box. You can configure this control so that only one item in the list can be selected or multiple items can be selected.

- ▶ **RadioButtonList**—Displays a list of radio buttons. Only one radio button can be selected.

All five controls inherit from the same base ListControl class. This means that all these controls share a core set of properties and methods. In Chapter 10, "Using List Controls," you can find detailed instructions on how to use each of the list controls.

The page in Listing 8.1 illustrates how to use all five list controls to display the same set of database records (see Figure 8.1).

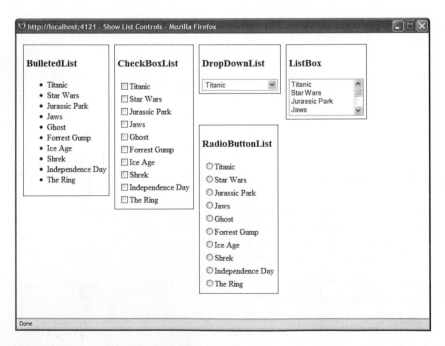

FIGURE 8.1   Using list controls.

LISTING 8.1   ShowListControls.aspx

```
<%@ Page Language="C#" %>
<!DOCTYPE html PUBLIC "-//W3C//DTD XHTML 1.1//EN"
"http://www.w3.org/TR/xhtml11/DTD/xhtml11.dtd">
<html xmlns="http://www.w3.org/1999/xhtml" >
<head id="Head1" runat="server">
    <style type="text/css">
        .floater
        {
            float:left;
            border:solid 1px black;
            padding:5px;
            margin:5px;
        }
    </style>
    <title>Show List Controls</title>
</head>
<body>
    <form id="form1" runat="server">

    <div class="floater">
    <h3>BulletedList</h3>
    <asp:BulletedList
        id="BulletedList1"
        DataSourceId="srcMovies"
        DataTextField="Title"
        Runat="server" />
    </div>

    <div class="floater">
    <h3>CheckBoxList</h3>
    <asp:CheckBoxList
        id="CheckBoxList1"
        DataSourceId="srcMovies"
        DataTextField="Title"
        Runat="server" />
    </div>

    <div class="floater">
    <h3>DropDownList</h3>
    <asp:DropDownList
        id="DropDownList1"
        DataSourceId="srcMovies"
        DataTextField="Title"
        Runat="server" />
```

8

LISTING 8.1 Continued

```
    </div>

    <div class="floater">
    <h3>ListBox</h3>
    <asp:ListBox
        id="ListBox1"
        DataSourceId="srcMovies"
        DataTextField="Title"
        Runat="server" />
    </div>

    <div class="floater">
    <h3>RadioButtonList</h3>
    <asp:RadioButtonList
        id="RadioButtonList1"
        DataSourceId="srcMovies"
        DataTextField="Title"
        Runat="server" />
    </div>

    <asp:SqlDataSource
        id="srcMovies"
        ConnectionString="Data Source=.\SQLExpress;
            AttachDbFilename=¦DataDirectory¦MyDatabase.mdf;
            Integrated Security=True;User Instance=True"
        SelectCommand="SELECT Title FROM Movies"
        Runat="server" />

    </form>
</body>
</html>
```

In Listing 8.1, each list control is bound to a `SqlDataSource` control that represents the contents of the Movies database table. For example, the `BulletedList` control is bound to the `DataSource` control like this:

```
<asp:BulletedList
    id="BulletedList1"
    DataSourceID="srcMovies"
    DataTextField="Title"
    Runat="server" />

<asp:SqlDataSource
    id="srcMovies"
```

```
ConnectionString="Data Source=.\SQLExpress;
    AttachDbFilename=¦DataDirectory¦MyDatabase.mdf;
    Integrated Security=True;User Instance=True"
SelectCommand="SELECT Title FROM Movies"
Runat="server" />
```

Notice that the `BulletedList` control includes a `DataSourceID` attribute, which points to the ID of the `SqlDataSource` control. The `DataSourceID` attribute associates a `DataBound` control with a `DataSource` control.

Working with Tabular DataBound Controls

The tabular `DataBound` controls are the main set of controls that you use when working with database data. These controls enable you to display and, in some cases, modify data retrieved from a database or other type of data source.

There are six tabular `DataBound` controls. These controls can be divided into two types: those that display multiple data items at a time and those that display a single data item at a time.

First, you can use any of the following controls to display a set of data items:

▶ **GridView**—Displays a set of data items in an HTML table. For example, you can use the `GridView` control to display all the records contained in the Movies database table. This control enables you to display, sort, page, select, and edit data.

▶ **DataList**—Displays a set of data items in an HTML table. Unlike the `GridView` control, more than one data item can be displayed in a single row.

▶ **Repeater**—Displays a set of data items using a template. Unlike the `GridView` and `DataList` controls, a `Repeater` control does not automatically render an HTML table.

▶ **ListView**—Displays a set of data items using a template. Unlike the `Repeater` control, the `ListView` control supports sorting, paging, and editing database data.

NOTE

The `ListView` control is new with the ASP.NET 3.5 Framework.

You can use either of the following two controls to display a single data item at a time:

▶ **DetailsView**—Displays a single data item in an HTML table. For example, you can use the `DetailsView` control to display a single record from the Movies database table. This control enables you to display, page, edit, and add data.

▶ **FormView**—Uses a template to display a single data item. Unlike the `DetailsView`, a `FormView` enables you to layout a form by using templates.

NOTE

What happened to the DataGrid? The DataGrid was included in the ASP.NET 1.x Framework, but it no longer appears in the Toolbox in Visual Web Developer. The DataGrid is officially deprecated. You should use the GridView control instead because the GridView is more powerful. For backward compatibility reasons, the DataGrid is included in the ASP.NET 3.5 Framework so that you can still use it in your pages.

The page in Listing 8.2 illustrates how you can use each of the tabular DataBound controls (see Figure 8.2).

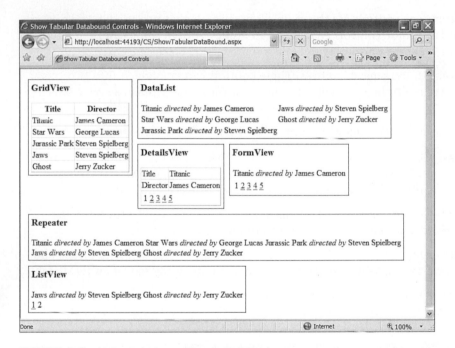

FIGURE 8.2   Using tabular DataBound controls.

LISTING 8.2   ShowTabularDataBound.aspx

```
<%@ Page Language="C#" %>
<!DOCTYPE html PUBLIC "-//W3C//DTD XHTML 1.1//EN"
"http://www.w3.org/TR/xhtml11/DTD/xhtml11.dtd">
<html xmlns="http://www.w3.org/1999/xhtml" >
<head id="Head1" runat="server">
    <style type="text/css">
        .floater
        {
            float:left;
```

```
                 border:solid 1px black;
                 padding:5px;
                 margin:5px;
            }
        </style>
        <title>Show Tabular Databound Controls</title>
    </head>
    <body>
        <form id="form1" runat="server">

        <div class="floater">
        <h3>GridView</h3>
        <asp:GridView
            id="GridView1"
            DataSourceId="srcMovies"
            Runat="server" />
        </div>




        <div class="floater">
        <h3>DataList</h3>
        <asp:DataList
            id="DataList1"
            DataSourceId="srcMovies"
            RepeatColumns="2"
            Runat="server">
            <ItemTemplate>
            <%#Eval("Title")%>
            <i>directed by</i>
            <%#Eval("Director")%>
            </ItemTemplate>
        </asp:DataList>
        </div>



        <div class="floater">
        <h3>DetailsView</h3>
        <asp:DetailsView
            id="DetailsView1"
            DataSourceId="srcMovies"
            AllowPaging="true"
            Runat="server" />
        </div>

        <div class="floater">
```

8

LISTING 8.2   Continued

```
    <h3>FormView</h3>
    <asp:FormView
        id="FormView1"
        DataSourceId="srcMovies"
        AllowPaging="true"
        Runat="server">
        <ItemTemplate>
        <%#Eval("Title")%>
        <i>directed by</i>
        <%#Eval("Director")%>
        </ItemTemplate>
    </asp:FormView>
    </div>
<br style="clear:both" />


    <div class="floater">
    <h3>Repeater</h3>
    <asp:Repeater
        id="Repeater1"
        DataSourceId="srcMovies"
        Runat="server">
        <ItemTemplate>
        <%#Eval("Title")%>
        <i>directed by</i>
        <%#Eval("Director")%>
        </ItemTemplate>
    </asp:Repeater>
    </div>

    <div class="floater">
    <h3>ListView</h3>
    <asp:ListView
        id="ListView1"
        DataSourceId="srcMovies"
        Runat="server">
        <LayoutTemplate>
        <div id="itemPlaceholder" runat="server">
        </div>
        <asp:DataPager ID="pager1" PageSize="3" runat="server">
        <Fields>
            <asp:NumericPagerField />
        </Fields>
        </asp:DataPager>
```

```
          </LayoutTemplate>
          <ItemTemplate>
          <%#Eval("Title")%>
          <i>directed by</i>
          <%#Eval("Director")%>
          </ItemTemplate>
    </asp:ListView>
    </div>

    <asp:SqlDataSource
         id="srcMovies"
         ConnectionString="Data Source=.\SQLExpress;
             AttachDbFilename=¦DataDirectory¦MyDatabase.mdf;
             Integrated Security=True;User Instance=True"
         SelectCommand="SELECT TOP 5 Title,Director FROM Movies"
         Runat="server" />

    </form>
</body>
</html>
```

For the moment, don't worry too much about formatting the controls. Each of the tabular DataBound controls supports an abundance of properties that modify the control's behavior and appearance. The GridView control gets a detailed examination in Chapter 11, "Using the GridView Control." The DetailsView and FormView controls are covered in Chapter 12, "Using the DetailsView and FormView Controls." The focus of Chapter 13 is the Repeater and DataList controls. Finally, the new ListView control is discussed in Chapter 14, "Using the ListView and DataPager Controls."

Working with Hierarchical DataBound Controls

A hierarchical DataBound control can be used to display nested data items. For example, you can use hierarchical DataBound controls to display the folder and page structure of your website, the contents of an XML file, or a set of master/detail database records.

The ASP.NET 3.5 Framework includes two hierarchical DataBound controls:

▶ **Menu**—Displays data items in a static or dynamic menu.

▶ **TreeView**—Displays data items in a tree.

The page in Listing 8.3 illustrates how you can use both the Menu and TreeView controls. Both controls are bound to an XmlDataSource control, which represents the XML file in Listing 8.4 (see Figure 8.3).

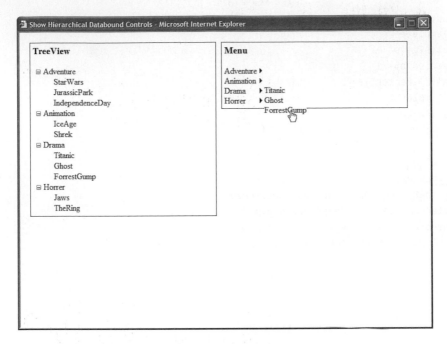

FIGURE 8.3   Using hierarchical DataBound controls.

LISTING 8.3   ShowHierarchicalDataBound.aspx

```
<%@ Page Language="C#" %>
<!DOCTYPE html PUBLIC "-//W3C//DTD XHTML 1.1//EN"
"http://www.w3.org/TR/xhtml11/DTD/xhtml11.dtd">
<html xmlns="http://www.w3.org/1999/xhtml" >
<head id="Head1" runat="server">
    <style type="text/css">
        .floater
        {
            float:left;
            width:45%;
            border:solid 1px black;
            padding:5px;
            margin:5px;
        }
    </style>
    <title>Show Hierarchical Databound Controls</title>
</head>
<body>
    <form id="form1" runat="server">

    <div class="floater">
    <h3>TreeView</h3>
```

```
        <asp:TreeView
            id="CheckBoxList1"
            DataSourceId="srcMovies"
            Runat="server" />
        </div>

        <div class="floater">
        <h3>Menu</h3>
        <asp:Menu
            id="BulletedList1"
            DataSourceId="srcMovies"
            Runat="server" />
        </div>

        <asp:XmlDataSource
            id="srcMovies"
            DataFile="~/Movies.xml"
            XPath="/movies/*"
            Runat="server" />


    </form>
</body>
</html>
```

LISTING 8.4 Movies.xml

```
<movies>
  <Adventure>
    <StarWars />
    <JurassicPark />
    <IndependenceDay />
  </Adventure>
  <Animation>
    <IceAge />
    <Shrek />
  </Animation>
  <Drama>
    <Titanic />
    <Ghost />
    <ForrestGump />
  </Drama>
  <Horrer>
    <Jaws />
    <TheRing />
  </Horrer>
</movies>
```

Again, don't worry about the appearance of the `Menu` and `TreeView` controls in the page rendered by Listing 8.3. Both controls support a rich set of options for modifying the control's appearance. We examine the properties of both of these hierarchical controls in detail in Chapter 19, "Using the Navigation Controls."

Working with Other Controls

You can bind any control in the ASP.NET Framework to the data items represented by a data source. Imagine, for example, that you want to display a photo gallery. In that case, you might want to bind a set of Image controls to a data source.

You can bind any ASP.NET control to a data item by adding the control to a template. For example, the page in Listing 8.5 automatically displays all the pictures in a folder named Photos (see Figure 8.4).

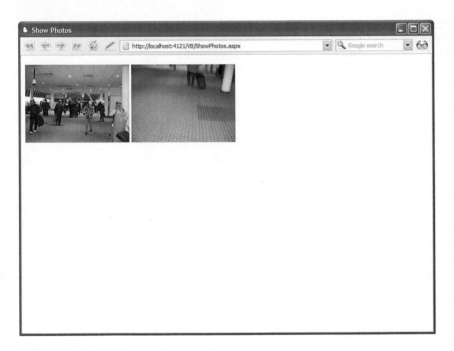

FIGURE 8.4   Binding images to a data source.

LISTING 8.5   ShowPhotos.aspx

```
<%@ Page Language="C#" %>
<%@ Import Namespace="System.IO" %>
<%@ Import Namespace="System.Collections.Generic" %>
<!DOCTYPE html PUBLIC "-//W3C//DTD XHTML 1.1//EN"
"http://www.w3.org/TR/xhtml11/DTD/xhtml11.dtd">
<script runat="server">
```

```
/// <summary>
/// Bind photos to Repeater
/// </summary>
void Page_Load()
{
    if (!Page.IsPostBack)
    {
        Repeater1.DataSource = GetPhotos();
        Repeater1.DataBind();
    }
}


/// <summary>
/// Get list of photos from Photo folder
/// </summary>
public List<String> GetPhotos()
{
    List<string> photos = new List<string>();
    string photoPath = MapPath("~/Photos");
    string[] files = Directory.GetFiles(photoPath);
    foreach (string photo in files)
        photos.Add("~/Photos/" + Path.GetFileName(photo));
    return photos;
}
</script>
<html xmlns="http://www.w3.org/1999/xhtml" >
<head id="Head1" runat="server">
    <title>Show Photos</title>
</head>
<body>
    <form id="form1" runat="server">
    <div>

    <asp:Repeater
        id="Repeater1"
        runat="server">
        <ItemTemplate>
            <asp:Image
                id="Image1"
                Width="200px"
                ImageUrl='<%# Container.DataItem %>'
                Runat="server" />
        </ItemTemplate>
    </asp:Repeater>
```

LISTING 8.5   Continued

```
    </div>
    </form>
</body>
</html>
```

Notice that the `Repeater` control contains an `ItemTemplate`, and the `ItemTemplate` contains an ASP.NET Image control. The `Image` control displays each of the photographs from the Photos folder.

Using `DataSource` Controls

You bind a `DataBound` control to a `DataSource` control. A `DataSource` control is used to represent a particular type of data.

The ASP.NET 3.5 Framework includes the following six `DataSource` controls:

▶ **`SqlDataSource`**—Represents data retrieved from a SQL relational database, including Microsoft SQL Server, Oracle, or DB2.

▶ **`LinqDataSource`**—Represents a LINQ to SQL query.

▶ **`AccessDataSource`**—Represents data retrieved from a Microsoft Access database.

▶ **`ObjectDataSource`**—Represents data retrieved from a business object.

▶ **`XmlDataSource`**—Represents data retrieved from an XML document.

▶ **`SiteMapDataSource`**—Represents data retrieved from a Site Map Provider. A Site Map Provider represents the page and folder structure of a website.

> **NOTE**
>
> The `LinqDataSource` control is new in ASP.NET 3.5. This control is discussed in detail in Chapter 18, "Data Access with LINQ to SQL."

The ASP.NET Framework contains two basic types of `DataSource` controls. The `SqlDataSource`, `AccessDataSource`, `LinqDataSource`, and `ObjectDataSource` controls all derive from the base `DataSourceControl` class. These controls can be used to represent tabular data. The `XmlDataSource` and `SiteMapDataSource` controls, on the other hand, derive from the base `HierarchicalDataSourceControl` control. These two controls can be used to represent both tabular and hierarchical data.

A `DataBound` control is associated with a particular data source control through its `DataSourceID` property. For example, the page in Listing 8.6 contains a `GridView` control bound to a `SqlDataSource` control (see Figure 8.5).

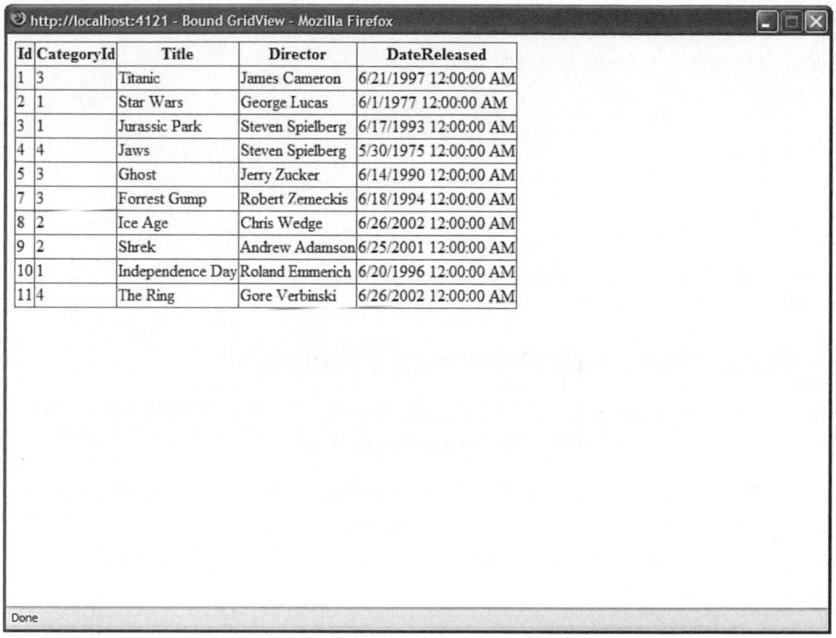

Id	CategoryId	Title	Director	DateReleased
1	3	Titanic	James Cameron	6/21/1997 12:00:00 AM
2	1	Star Wars	George Lucas	6/1/1977 12:00:00 AM
3	1	Jurassic Park	Steven Spielberg	6/17/1993 12:00:00 AM
4	4	Jaws	Steven Spielberg	5/30/1975 12:00:00 AM
5	3	Ghost	Jerry Zucker	6/14/1990 12:00:00 AM
7	3	Forrest Gump	Robert Zemeckis	6/18/1994 12:00:00 AM
8	2	Ice Age	Chris Wedge	6/26/2002 12:00:00 AM
9	2	Shrek	Andrew Adamson	6/25/2001 12:00:00 AM
10	1	Independence Day	Roland Emmerich	6/20/1996 12:00:00 AM
11	4	The Ring	Gore Verbinski	6/26/2002 12:00:00 AM

FIGURE 8.5 Using the `SqlDataSource` control.

LISTING 8.6 `BoundGridView.aspx`

```
<%@ Page Language="C#" %>
<!DOCTYPE html PUBLIC "-//W3C//DTD XHTML 1.1//EN"
"http://www.w3.org/TR/xhtml11/DTD/xhtml11.dtd">
<html xmlns="http://www.w3.org/1999/xhtml" >
<head id="Head1" runat="server">
    <title>Bound GridView</title>
</head>
<body>
    <form id="form1" runat="server">
    <div>

    <asp:GridView
        id="GridView1"
        DataSourceId="srcMovies"
        Runat="server" />

    <asp:SqlDataSource
        id="srcMovies"
        ConnectionString="Data Source=.\SQLExpress;
            AttachDbFilename=|DataDirectory|MyDatabase.mdf;
            Integrated Security=True;User Instance=True"
```

8

LISTING 8.6   Continued

```
        SelectCommand="SELECT * FROM Movies"
        Runat="server" />

    </div>
    </form>
</body>
</html>
```

Using ASP.NET Parameters with `DataSource` Controls

Many of the `DataSource` controls support ASP.NET parameters. You use ASP.NET parameters to modify the commands that a `DataSource` control executes.

Different types of `DataSource` controls use ASP.NET parameters to represent different types of things. When you use ASP.NET parameters with a `SqlDataSource` control, the ASP.NET parameters represent ADO.NET parameters. In other words, they represent parameters used with SQL statements.

When you use parameters with the `ObjectDataSource` control, the ASP.NET parameters represent method parameters. They represent parameters passed to a particular method of a business object.

The `SqlDataSource`, `AccessDataSource`, `LinqDataSource`, and `ObjectDataSource` controls all support the following types of Parameter objects:

- ▶ **Parameter**—Represents an arbitrary static value.

- ▶ **ControlParameter**—Represents the value of a `control` or page property.

- ▶ **CookieParameter**—Represents the value of a browser cookie.

- ▶ **FormParameter**—Represents the value of an HTML form field.

- ▶ **ProfileParameter**—Represents the value of a `Profile` property.

- ▶ **QueryStringParameter**—Represents the value of a query string field.

- ▶ **SessionParameter**—Represents the value of an item stored in Session state.

For example, the page in Listing 8.7 contains a `DropDownList`, `GridView`, and `SqlDataSource` control. The `DropDownList` displays a list of movie categories. When you select a new category, the `GridView` displays matching movies (see Figure 8.6).

LISTING 8.7   `ShowControlParameter.aspx`

```
<%@ Page Language="C#" %>
<!DOCTYPE html PUBLIC "-//W3C//DTD XHTML 1.1//EN"
"http://www.w3.org/TR/xhtml11/DTD/xhtml11.dtd">
<html xmlns="http://www.w3.org/1999/xhtml" >
```

```
<head id="Head1" runat="server">
    <title>Show Control Parameter</title>
</head>
<body>
    <form id="form1" runat="server">
    <div>

    <asp:DropDownList
        id="ddlMovieCategory"
        DataSourceID="srcMovieCategories"
        DataTextField="Name"
        DataValueField="Id"
        Runat="server" />

    <asp:Button
        id="btnSelect"
        Text="Select"
        ToolTip="Select Movie"
        Runat="server" />

    <hr />

    <asp:GridView
        id="grdMovies"
        DataSourceID="srcMovies"
        Runat="server" />

    <asp:SqlDataSource
        id="srcMovieCategories"
        ConnectionString="Server=.\SQLExpress;
        Trusted_Connection=True;AttachDbFileName=|DataDirectory|MyDatabase.mdf;
        User Instance=True"
        SelectCommand="SELECT Id,Name FROM MovieCategories"
        Runat="server" />


    <asp:SqlDataSource
        id="srcMovies"
        ConnectionString="Data Source=.\SQLExpress;
            AttachDbFilename=|DataDirectory|MyDatabase.mdf;
            Integrated Security=True;User Instance=True"
        SelectCommand="SELECT Title,Director FROM Movies
            WHERE CategoryId=@Id"
        Runat="server">
        <SelectParameters>
            <asp:ControlParameter
```

LISTING 8.7 Continued

```
                Name="Id"
                Type="int32"
                ControlID="ddlMovieCategory" />
        </SelectParameters>
    </asp:SqlDataSource>

    </div>
    </form>
</body>
</html>
```

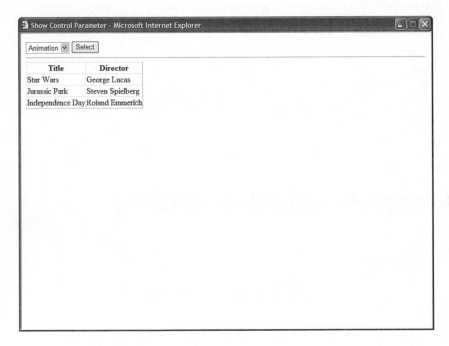

FIGURE 8.6   Using the ControlParameter object.

Notice that the SqlDataSource control includes a ControlParameter object. The ControlParameter represents the selected item in the DropDownList control. The value of the ControlParameter is used in the SqlDataSource control's SelectCommand to select movies that match the category selected in the DropDownList control.

Using Programmatic DataBinding

When you bind a DataBound control to a DataSource control, you are taking advantage of *declarative databinding*. When you use declarative databinding, the ASP.NET Framework handles all the messy details of deciding when to retrieve the data items represented by a DataSource control.

In certain situations, you'll want to handle these messy details yourself. For example, you might want to force a GridView control to refresh the data it displays after you add a new record to a database table. Or, you might want to bind a DataBound control to a data source that can't be easily represented by one of the existing DataSource controls. In these situations, you'll want to use *programmatic databinding*.

> **NOTE**
>
> The ASP.NET 1.x Framework supported only programmatic databinding. The first version of the Framework did not include any of the DataSource controls.

Every DataBound control has a DataSource property and a DataBind() method. By using this property and method, you can programmatically associate a DataBound control with a data source.

For example, the page in Listing 8.8 displays a list of all the fonts installed on your computer (see Figure 8.7).

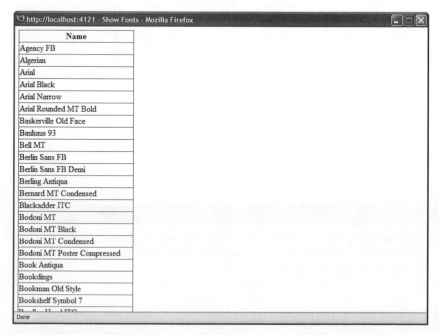

FIGURE 8.7   Programmatic databinding.

LISTING 8.8   ShowFonts.aspx

```
<%@ Page Language="C#" %>
<%@ Import Namespace="System.Drawing.Text" %>
<!DOCTYPE html PUBLIC "-//W3C//DTD XHTML 1.1//EN"
"http://www.w3.org/TR/xhtml11/DTD/xhtml11.dtd">
<script runat="server">

    void Page_Load()
    {
        if (!Page.IsPostBack)
        {
            InstalledFontCollection fonts = new InstalledFontCollection();
            GridView1.DataSource = fonts.Families;
            GridView1.DataBind();
        }
    }
</script>
<html xmlns="http://www.w3.org/1999/xhtml" >
<head id="Head1" runat="server">
    <title>Show Fonts</title>
</head>
<body>
    <form id="form1" runat="server">
    <div>

    <asp:GridView
        id="GridView1"
        Runat="server" />

    </div>
    </form>
</body>
</html>
```

NOTE

The programmatic databinding in Listing 8.8 could have been avoided by taking advantage of the ObjectDataSource control. This DataSource control is discussed in detail in Chapter 16, "Using the ObjectDataSource Control."

The list of fonts is displayed by a GridView control. The actual list of fonts is retrieved from the InstalledFontCollection class (which inhabits the System.Drawing.Text namespace). The list of fonts is assigned to the GridView control's DataSource property, and the DataBind() method is called.

In Listing 8.8, a collection of fonts has been assigned to the `DataSource` property. In general, you can assign any object that implements the `IEnumerable` interface to the `DataSource` property. For example, you can assign collections, arrays, DataSets, DataReaders, DataViews, and enumerations to the `DataSource` property.

> **NOTE**
>
> Particular `DataBound` controls support different data sources. For example, you can assign any object that implements the `IEnumerable` or `ITypedList` interface to the `DataSource` property of a `GridView` control.

When you call the `DataBind()` method, the `GridView` control actually retrieves its data from the data source. The control iterates through all of the items represented by the data source and displays each item. If you neglect to call the `DataBind()` method, the control will never display anything.

Notice that the `GridView` is bound to its data source only when the page is requested for the first time. The `Page.IsPostBack` property is used to determine whether or not the page has been posted back to the server. You don't need to rebind the `GridView` to its data source every time the page is requested because the `GridView` uses View State to remember the data items that it displays.

You can't mix declarative and programmatic databinding. If you attempt to use both the `DataSource` and `DataSourceID` properties, then you will get an exception.

On the other hand, you can call the `DataBind()` method even when you have declaratively bound a control to a `DataSource` control. When you explicitly call `DataBind()`, the `DataBound` control grabs the data items from its `DataSource` control again. Explicitly calling `DataBind()` is useful when you want to refresh the data displayed by a `DataBound` control.

Understanding Templates and DataBinding Expressions

Almost all the `DataBound` controls support templates. You can use a template to format the layout and appearance of each of the data items that a `DataBound` control displays. Within a template, you can use a DataBinding expression to display the value of a data item.

In this section, you learn about the different kinds of templates and DataBinding expressions that you can use with the `DataBound` controls.

Using Templates

Every `DataBound` control included in the ASP.NET 3.5 Framework supports templates with the sole exception of the `TreeView` control. The `Repeater`, `DataList`, `ListView`, and `FormView` controls all require you to use templates. If you don't supply a template, then these controls display nothing. The `GridView`, `DetailsView`, and `Menu` controls also support templates, but they do not require a template.

For example, when you use the `Repeater` control, you must supply an ItemTemplate. The `Repeater` control uses the ItemTemplate to format each of the records that it displays. Listing 8.9 contains a `Repeater` control that formats each of the records from the Movies database table (see Figure 8.8).

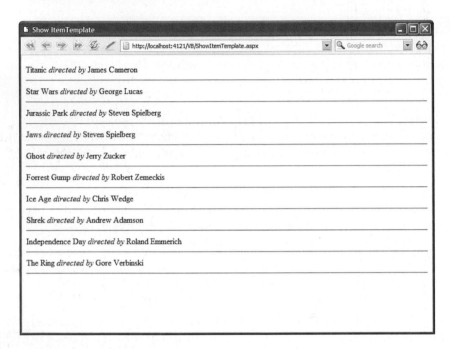

FIGURE 8.8   Using an ItemTemplate.

LISTING 8.9   ShowItemTemplate.aspx

```
<%@ Page Language="C#" %>
<!DOCTYPE html PUBLIC "-//W3C//DTD XHTML 1.1//EN"
"http://www.w3.org/TR/xhtml11/DTD/xhtml11.dtd">
<html xmlns="http://www.w3.org/1999/xhtml" >
<head id="Head1" runat="server">
    <title>Show ItemTemplate</title>
</head>
<body>
    <form id="form1" runat="server">
    <div>

    <asp:Repeater
        id="Repeater1"
        DataSourceId="srcMovies"
        Runat="server">
        <ItemTemplate>
```

```
            <%#Eval("Title")%>
            <i>directed by</i>
            <%#Eval("Director")%>
            <hr />
            </ItemTemplate>
        </asp:Repeater>


        <asp:SqlDataSource
            id="srcMovies"
            ConnectionString="Data Source=.\SQLExpress;
                AttachDbFilename=¦DataDirectory¦MyDatabase.mdf;
                Integrated Security=True;User Instance=True"
            SelectCommand="SELECT Title,Director FROM Movies"
            Runat="server" />

        </div>
        </form>
</body>
</html>
```

A template can contain HTML, DataBinding expressions, and other controls. In Listing 8.9, the template includes the following two DataBinding expressions:

```
<%# Eval("Title") %>
<%# Eval("Director") %>
```

The first DataBinding expression displays the value of the Title column and the second DataBinding expression displays the value of the Director column.

A template can contain other controls—even other DataBound controls. For example, the page in Listing 8.10 displays a list of hyperlinks (see Figure 8.9).

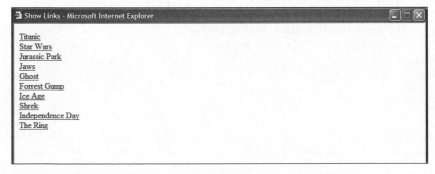

FIGURE 8.9   Displaying a list of hyperlinks.

LISTING 8.10   ShowLinks.aspx

```
<%@ Page Language="C#" %>
<!DOCTYPE html PUBLIC "-//W3C//DTD XHTML 1.1//EN"
"http://www.w3.org/TR/xhtml11/DTD/xhtml11.dtd">
<html xmlns="http://www.w3.org/1999/xhtml" >
<head id="Head1" runat="server">
    <title>Show Links</title>
</head>
<body>
    <form id="form1" runat="server">
    <div>

    <asp:Repeater
        id="Repeater1"
        DataSourceId="srcMovies"
        Runat="server">
        <ItemTemplate>

        <asp:HyperLink
            id="HyperLink1"
            Text='<%# Eval("Title") %>'
            NavigateUrl='<%# Eval("Id", "Details.aspx?id={0}") %>'
            runat="server" />
        <br />

        </ItemTemplate>
    </asp:Repeater>


    <asp:SqlDataSource
        id="srcMovies"
        ConnectionString="Data Source=.\SQLExpress;
            AttachDbFilename=|DataDirectory|MyDatabase.mdf;
            Integrated Security=True;User Instance=True"
        SelectCommand="SELECT Id, Title FROM Movies"
        Runat="server" />

    </div>
    </form>
</body>
</html>
```

In Listing 8.10, a HyperLink control is displayed for each item from the data source. The
HyperLink control displays the movie title and links to a details page for the movie.

Using DataBinding Expressions

A DataBinding expression is a special type of expression that is not evaluated until runtime. You mark a Databinding expression in a page by wrapping the expression in opening <%# and closing %> brackets.

A DataBinding expression isn't evaluated until a control's DataBinding event is raised. When you bind a `DataBound` control to a `DataSource` control declaratively, this event is raised automatically. When you bind a `DataSource` control to a data source programmatically, the DataBinding event is raised when you call the `DataBind()` method.

For example, the page in Listing 8.11 contains a `DataList` control that contains a template that includes two DataBinding expressions.

LISTING 8.11   ShowDataList.aspx

```
<%@ Page Language="C#" %>
<!DOCTYPE html PUBLIC "-//W3C//DTD XHTML 1.1//EN"
"http://www.w3.org/TR/xhtml11/DTD/xhtml11.dtd">
<html xmlns="http://www.w3.org/1999/xhtml" >
<head id="Head1" runat="server">
    <title>Show DataList</title>
</head>
<body>
    <form id="form1" runat="server">
    <div>

    <asp:DataList
        id="DataList1"
        DataSourceId="srcMovies"
        Runat="server">
        <ItemTemplate>
        <b>Movie Title:</b>
        <%#Eval("Title")%>
        <br />
        <b>Date Released:</b>
        <%#Eval("DateReleased", "{0:D}") %>
        <hr />
        </ItemTemplate>
    </asp:DataList>

    <asp:SqlDataSource
        id="srcMovies"
        ConnectionString="Data Source=.\SQLExpress;
            AttachDbFilename=|DataDirectory|MyDatabase.mdf;
            Integrated Security=True;User Instance=True"
        SelectCommand="SELECT Title,Director,DateReleased FROM Movies"
```

8

LISTING 8.11   Continued

```
        Runat="server" />

    </div>
    </form>
</body>
</html>
```

The first DataBinding expression displays the title of the movie and the second DataBinding expression displays the date the movie was released (see Figure 8.10).

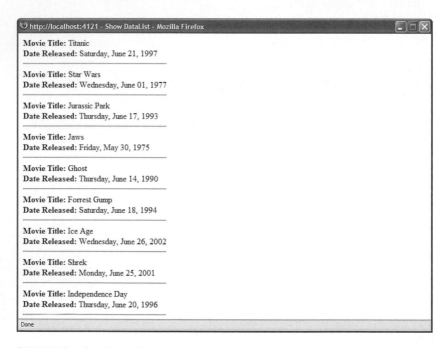

FIGURE 8.10   Using Databinding expressions.

Both DataBinding expressions call the Eval() method. The Eval() method is a protected method of the Page class. Behind the scenes, the Page.Eval() method calls the static (shared) DataBinder.Eval() method. If you want to be verbose, instead of using the Eval() method, you could use the following two expressions:

```
<%# DataBinder.Eval(Container.DataItem, "Title") %>
<%# DataBinder.Eval(Container.DataItem, "DateReleased", "{0:D}" ) %>
```

In ASP.NET version 1.x, you had to use DataBinder.Eval() when displaying data items in a template. However, Microsoft took pity on programmers after ASP.NET 2.0 and provided us with the shorter syntax.

> **NOTE**
>
> Technically, the `Eval()` method uses reflection when evaluating the data item to find a property with a certain name. You do pay a performance penalty when you use reflection.
>
> As an alternative, you can improve the performance of your DataBinding expressions by casting the data items to a particular type like this:
>
> ```
> <%# ((System.Data.DataRowView)Container.DataItem)["Title"] %>
> ```

Notice that the second DataBinding expression in Listing 8.11 includes a second parameter. The `Eval()` method, optionally, accepts a format string. You can use the format string to format values such as dates and currency amounts. In Listing 8.11, the format string is used to format the DateReleased column as a long date.

> **NOTE**
>
> Format strings use *format specifiers* such as the D format specifier when formatting strings. You can find a list of format specifiers by looking up Formatting Types in the index of the Microsoft .NET Framework SDK documentation.

You can call other methods than the `Eval()` method in a DataBinding expression. For example, the DataBinding expression in Listing 8.12 calls a method named `FormatTitle()` to format the movie titles.

LISTING 8.12 FormatMovieTitles.aspx

```
<%@ Page Language="C#" %>
<!DOCTYPE html PUBLIC "-//W3C//DTD XHTML 1.1//EN"
"http://www.w3.org/TR/xhtml11/DTD/xhtml11.dtd">
<script runat="server">

    public string FormatTitle(Object title)
    {
        return "<b>" + title.ToString().ToUpper() + "</b>";
    }

</script>
<html xmlns="http://www.w3.org/1999/xhtml" >
<head id="Head1" runat="server">
    <title>Format Movie Titles</title>
</head>
<body>
    <form id="form1" runat="server">
```

8

LISTING 8.12   Continued

```
<div>

<asp:Repeater
    id="Repeater1"
    DataSourceId="srcMovies"
    Runat="server">
    <ItemTemplate>
    <%# FormatTitle(Eval("Title")) %>
    <hr />
    </ItemTemplate>
</asp:Repeater>


<asp:SqlDataSource
    id="srcMovies"
    ConnectionString="Data Source=.\SQLExpress;
        AttachDbFilename=¦DataDirectory¦MyDatabase.mdf;
        Integrated Security=True;User Instance=True"
    SelectCommand="SELECT Title FROM Movies"
    Runat="server" />

</div>
</form>
</body>
</html>
```

The FormatTitle() method is defined in the page in Listing 8.12. This method formats
each of the titles displayed by the Repeater control by making each title bold and upper-
case (see Figure 8.11).

Using Two-Way DataBinding Expressions

The ASP.NET Framework actually supports two types of templates and two types of
DataBinding expressions. The ASP.NET Framework supports both one-way DataBinding
expressions and two-way DataBinding expressions.

Up to this point, we have used one-way DataBinding expressions exclusively. In a one-
way DataBinding expression, you use the DataBinding expression to display the value of a
data item. You use the Eval() method to display the value of a one-way DataBinding
expression.

In a two-way DataBinding expression, you not only can display the value of a data item,
you also can modify the value of a data item. You use the Bind() method when working
with a two-way DataBinding expression.

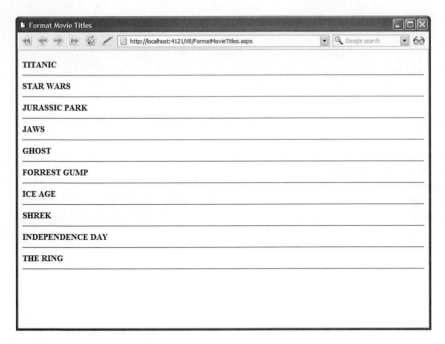

FIGURE 8.11   Formatting movie titles.

For example, the page in Listing 8.13 contains a FormView control that includes a template for editing a movie record in the Movies database table (see Figure 8.12).

FIGURE 8.12   Editing a movie.

LISTING 8.13   ShowFormView.aspx

```
<%@ Page Language="C#" %>
<!DOCTYPE html PUBLIC "-//W3C//DTD XHTML 1.1//EN"
"http://www.w3.org/TR/xhtml11/DTD/xhtml11.dtd">
<html xmlns="http://www.w3.org/1999/xhtml" >
<head id="Head1" runat="server">
    <title>Show FormView</title>
```

LISTING 8.13   Continued

```
</head>
<body>
    <form id="form1" runat="server">
    <div>

    <asp:FormView
        id="FormView1"
        DataKeyNames="Id"
        DataSourceId="srcMovies"
        DefaultMode="Edit"
        AllowPaging="true"
        Runat="server">
        <EditItemTemplate>
        <asp:Label
            id="lblTitle"
            Text="Title:"
            AssociatedControlID="txtTitle"
            Runat="server" />
        <asp:TextBox
            id="txtTitle"
            Text='<%#Bind("Title")%>'
            Runat="server" />
        <br />
        <asp:Label
            id="lblDirector"
            Text="Director:"
            AssociatedControlID="txtDirector"
            Runat="server" />
        <asp:TextBox
            id="txtDirector"
            Text='<%#Bind("Director")%>'
            Runat="server" />
        <br />
        <asp:Button
            id="btnUpdate"
            Text="Update"
            CommandName="Update"
            Runat="server" />
        </EditItemTemplate>
    </asp:FormView>

    <asp:SqlDataSource
        id="srcMovies"
        ConnectionString="Data Source=.\SQLExpress;
```

```
            AttachDbFilename=¦DataDirectory¦MyDatabase.mdf;
            Integrated Security=True;User Instance=True"
        SelectCommand="SELECT Id, Title,Director,DateReleased FROM Movies"
        UpdateCommand="UPDATE Movies SET Title=@Title,
            Director=@Director WHERE Id=@Id"
        Runat="server" />


    </div>
    </form>
</body>
</html>
```

Notice that the FormView contains an EditItemTemplate. The EditItemTemplate contains three TextBox controls. Each TextBox control has a two-way DataBinding expression assigned to its Text property.

The DataBinding expressions associate the TextBox control properties with the properties of the data item being edited. When you click the Update button, any changes you make to the Text properties are updated in the Movies database table.

NOTE

Templates that support one-way databinding implement the ITemplate interface, and templates that support two-way databinding implement the IBindableTemplate interface.

Overview of SQL Server 2005 Express

Microsoft SQL Server 2005 Express is the version of SQL Server bundled with Visual Web Developer. You can also download this database engine from the Microsoft website (http://msdn.microsoft.com/sql/2005). SQL Server Express is used for almost all the database examples in this book.

In this section, you are provided with a brief overview of the features of this database. You also learn how to connect to SQL Server Express.

Features of SQL Server Express

One of the most important features of SQL Server 2005 Express is that it is a royalty-free database engine. You can download it and use it for free in your applications. You also can distribute the database in commercial applications that you produce for others without paying royalties to Microsoft (registration at the Microsoft site is required to do this).

> **NOTE**
>
> Microsoft SQL Server 2005 Express replaces the Microsoft Desktop Engine version of SQL Server. There won't be an MSDE version of SQL Server 2005.

SQL Server 2005 Express works with the Windows Vista (all editions), Windows XP, Windows 2000, and the Windows 2003 operating systems. It requires the .NET Framework 2.0 or above to be installed on its host computer.

Microsoft SQL Server 2005 Express uses the same database engine as the full retail version of SQL Server 2005. However, because it is a free product, Microsoft has limited some of its features to encourage you to upgrade to the full version of SQL Server 2005.

First, unlike the full version of SQL Server 2005, a SQL Server Express database can be no larger than 4 gigabytes. Furthermore, SQL Server Express is limited to using 1 gigabyte of RAM. Also, SQL Server Express uses only a single processor even when used on a multi-processor server.

SQL Server Express also does not support several of the advanced features of the full version of SQL Server 2005. For example, it doesn't support Analysis Services, Notification Services, English Query, Data Transformation Services, or OLAP.

> **NOTE**
>
> The version of SQL Server Express bundled with Visual Web Developer does not include support for Full-Text Search or Reporting Services. If you need these services, you can download a version of SQL Server Express that supports Full-Text Search and Reporting Services from the Microsoft website.

However, unlike Microsoft SQL Server 2000 MSDE, SQL Server Express does not have a Workload Governor. The performance of a SQL Server Express database is never throttled. This means that you can use SQL Server Express for small websites without worrying about performance limitations.

Finally, like the full version of SQL Server 2005, SQL Server Express supports the Common Language Runtime. In other words, you can use C# or Visual Basic .NET to create stored procedures, triggers, user-defined functions, and user-defined types.

SQL Server 2005 Express Management Tools

You can use three tools to create new database objects when using SQL Server 2005 Express. You can use the Database Explorer in Visual Web Developer, you can use the Microsoft SQL Server Management Studio Express, and you can use the SQLCMD utility.

The Database Explorer included in Visual Web Developer provides you with a user-friendly interface for working with database objects (see Figure 8.13). I assume that you are using the Database Explorer in the case of the database samples in this book.

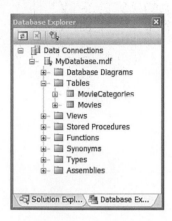

FIGURE 8.13   The Database Explorer window in Visual Web Developer.

Alternatively, you can use the Microsoft SQL Server Management Studio Express (its groovy name is XM). You can download Management Studio from the Microsoft site at http://msdn.microsoft.com/sql/2005. This tool enables you to browse database objects and execute SQL queries (see Figure 8.14).

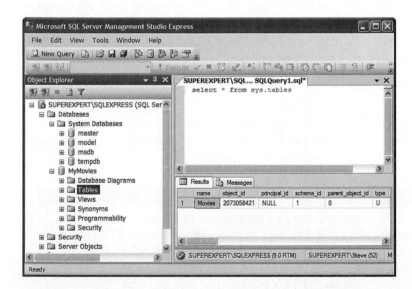

FIGURE 8.14   Using the Microsoft SQL Server Management Studio Express.

Finally, SQL Server 2005 Express includes a command-line tool named SQLCMD. You can use the SQLCMD tool to fire off SQL queries from the Command Prompt (see Figure 8.15). This alternative is the most painful, but it works.

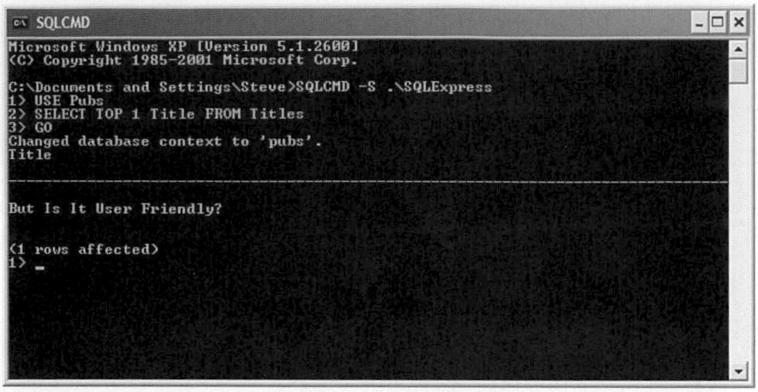

FIGURE 8.15   Executing a SQL query with SQLCMD.

You use SQLCMD by opening a command prompt and connecting to your database with the following command:

```
SQLCMD -S .\SQLExpress
```

Next, you can enter SQL statements at the command prompt. The statements are not executed until you type **GO**. You can get help using SQLCMD by typing **:HELP** after starting the tool. When you are finished using the tool, type **EXIT** to quit.

Server Databases versus Local Databases

You can create two different types of databases with SQL Server Express: Server databases and Local databases.

By default, when you install SQL Server 2005 Express, a named instance of the server is created with the name SQLExpress. You can create a new Server database by connecting to the named instance and adding a new database.

NOTE

To connect to SQL Server 2005 Express from a page served from Internet Information Server, you must add either the ASPNET account (in the case of Windows XP or Windows 2000) or the NT Authority/Network Service account (in the case of Vista or Windows 2003) to SQL Server Express.

If you own Visual Studio 2008, then you can create a new Server database directly from the Server Explorer window. Simply right-click the Data Connections node in the Server Explorer window and select the menu option Create New SQL Server Database.

Unfortunately, you can't use Visual Web Developer to create a new Server database. This option is grayed out. If you need to create a new Server database, and you don't have the full version of Visual Studio, then you need to use Microsoft SQL Server Management Studio Express as discussed in the previous section (see Figure 8.16).

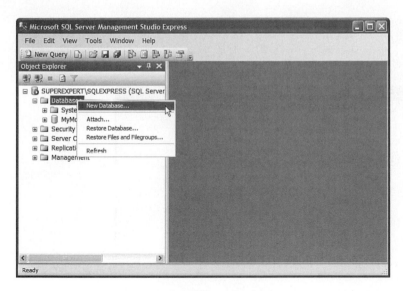

FIGURE 8.16   Creating a new Server database.

When you create a Server database, the database is attached and available to any application running on the server. You can connect to the database easily from any ASP.NET application.

For example, the following connection string enables you to connect to a Server database named MyData:

```
Data Source=.\SQLExpress;Initial Catalog=MyData;Integrated Security=True
```

> **NOTE**
>
> There are many different ways to write a connection string that does the same thing. For example, instead of the Data Source parameter, you can use the Server parameter, and instead of the Initial Catalog parameter, you can use the Database parameter. For a list of all the keywords supported when connecting to a Microsoft SQL Server database, see the `SqlConnection.ConnectionString` entry in the Microsoft .NET Framework SDK documentation.

The other option is to create a Local database instead of a Server database. When you create a Local database, you create the database in your project. The database file is added to the App_Data folder in your website.

Here are the steps for creating a Local database in Visual Web Developer:

1. Open the Add New Item dialog box by selecting the menu option website, Add New Item (see Figure 8.17).

2. Select Sql Database and provide the database with a name (for example, MyLocalData.mdf).

3. Click Add.

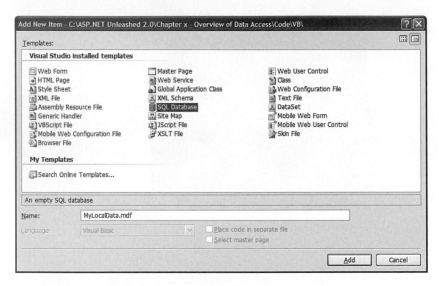

FIGURE 8.17   Creating a new Local database.

When you click Add, Visual Web Developer warns you that it needs to create the App_Data folder (if the folder doesn't already exist). The MyLocalData.mdf file will be added to this folder. Click OK to create the new folder.

You can connect to a Local database named MyLocalData.mdf by using the following connection string:

```
Data Source=.\SQLEXPRESS;AttachDbFilename=¦DataDirectory¦MyLocalData.mdf;
Integrated Security=True;User Instance=True
```

When you connect to the MyLocalData.mdf file, the database is attached automatically to Microsoft SQL Server Express.

The connection string includes an AttachDbFilename parameter. This parameter represents the physical path to a database file (.mdf file). Notice that the keyword ¦DataDirectory¦ is used in the path. The ¦DataDirectory¦ keyword represents a website's App_Data folder.

Instead of using the ¦DataDirectory¦ keyword, you could supply the entire physical path to a database file. The advantage of using the ¦DataDirectory¦ keyword is that you can move your web application easily to a new location without needing to change the connection string.

Notice that the connection string also includes a User Instance parameter. Creating a User Instance connection enables you to connect to a Local database without using an

Administrator account. Because the ASPNET account is not an Administrator account, you need to add this parameter to use Local databases from ASP.NET pages.

Including the `User Instance` parameter in a connection string causes a separate user instance of SQL Server to execute with the security context of the user. The first time a user creates a User Instance connection, copies of the system databases are copied to a user's application data folder located at the following path:

```
C:\Documents and Settings\[Username]\Local Settings\Application Data\
Microsoft\Microsoft SQL Server Data\SQLEXPRESS
```

> **NOTE**
>
> The path to the SQL Express system databases when using Microsoft Vista is
>
> ```
> C:\Users\[Username]\AppData\Local\Microsoft\Microsoft SQL Server
> Data\SQLEXPRESS
> ```

A separate set of system databases is created for each user.

> **NOTE**
>
> By default, when a page is served from Internet Information Server, the page executes in the security context of either the ASPNET or Network Service account. When a page is served from the web server included in Visual Web Developer, the page executes in the security context of the current user.

One of the primary advantages of using a Local database rather than a Server database is that a Local database can be moved easily to a new location. If you email a Local database file (the `.mdf` file stored in the App_Data folder) to a friend, your friend can start using the database immediately. The only requirement is that your friend have SQL Server Express installed on a computer.

I use Local databases for all the code samples in this book. You can simply copy the database files (the `.mdf` files) from the CD onto your local hard drive to use the sample databases.

Sample Database-Driven Web Application

The chapters that follow get into all the gritty details of the data controls. Before you get lost in the details, however, I want to provide you with a sample of a data-driven web application. I want to provide you with a "real world" application that illustrates what can be built with the data controls.

In this section, a complete Employee Directory application is built, which supports displaying, adding, editing, and deleting employee information. The sample application includes all the necessary form field validation.

One of the amazing things about the ASP.NET 3.5 Framework is how much the Framework simplifies data access. The sample application consists of a single page that contains very little code. Writing the same application with the ASP.NET 1.x Framework would require pages of code (I won't even mention how much code it would require to write the same application in ASP Classic).

Because the Employee Directory application includes all the required validation code, the page is a little too long to include in the pages of this book. However, it is included on the CD that accompanies this book. Open the page named EmployeeDirectory.aspx.

After you open the EmployeeDirectory.aspx page in your browser, you see a list of employees. This list is rendered by a GridView control (see Figure 8.18).

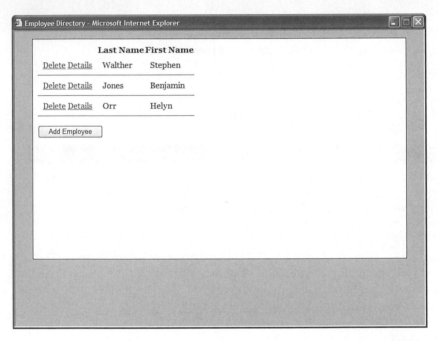

FIGURE 8.18   Displaying a list of employees with the GridView control.

Next to each employee, there is a Delete link and a Details link. If you click Delete, the selected employee is deleted from the database. Notice that a client-side confirmation dialog box appears when you click the Delete link (see Figure 8.19). This dialog box is added to each of the Delete links in the grdEmployees_RowCreated() method. This method is called automatically by the GridView control as the GridView creates each row.

If you click the Details link, a window appears that displays detailed information for the Employee (see Figure 8.20). The detailed information is rendered by a FormView control. The window that appears is created with an absolutely positioned <div> tag.

If you click Edit when viewing a employee's details, you can edit the employee record. The edit form is contained in the FormView control's EditItemTemplate. Each of the form fields is associated with a RequiredFieldValidator control.

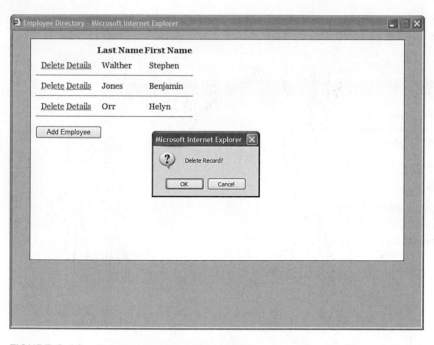

FIGURE 8.19   Deleting employee information.

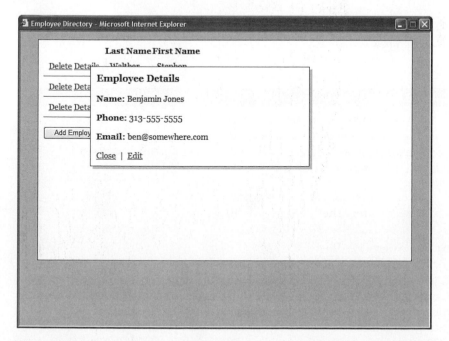

FIGURE 8.20   Displaying employee details.

Finally, you can add new employees to the directory by clicking the Add Employee button. The form that appears is also rendered by a `FormView` control (see Figure 8.21).

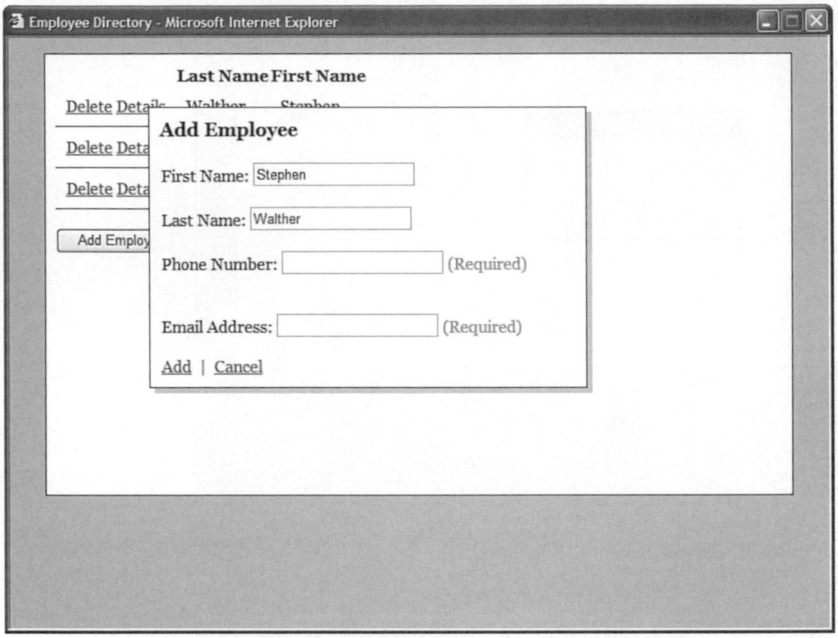

FIGURE 8.21   Adding a new employee.

WEB STANDARDS NOTE

The Employee Directory application works great in Internet Explorer 6+, FireFox 1.0+, and Opera 8.0+. The only feature of the application that breaks Web standards is the use of the Drop Shadow filter around the pop-up window. The Drop Shadow effect works only in Internet Explorer.

Summary

In this chapter, you were provided with an overview of the data controls included in the ASP.NET 3.5 Framework. You learned how to use the `DataBound` controls to render the user interface for working with data. You also were provided with an introduction to the `DataSource` controls, which can be used to represent different types of data such as database data and XML data.

You also learned about two important features of the DataBound controls. You learned how to use templates and databinding expressions. You also learned about the difference between one-way databinding and two-way databinding expressions.

Next, you were provided with an overview of SQL Server 2005 Express. You learned how to create a SQL Server Express database. You also learned how to create both Server and Local databases.

Finally, the data controls were used to build a sample application: the Employee Directory application. You learned how to use the controls to build an application that enables you to list, edit, insert, and delete database records.

CHAPTER 9

Using the SqlDataSource Control

The SqlDataSource control enables you to quickly and easily represent a SQL database in a web page. In many cases, you can take advantage of the SqlDataSource control to write a database-driven web page without writing a single line of code.

You use the SqlDataSource control to represent a connection and set of commands that can be executed against a SQL database. You can use the SqlDataSource control when working with Microsoft SQL Server, Microsoft SQL Server Express, Microsoft Access, Oracle, DB2, MySQL, or just about any other SQL relational database ever created by man.

> **NOTE**
>
> Although you can use the SqlDataSource control when working with Microsoft Access, the ASP.NET Framework does include the AccessDataSource control, which was designed specifically for Microsoft Access. Because using Microsoft Access for a website is not recommended, this book doesn't discuss the AccessDataSource control.

The SqlDataSource control is built on top of ADO.NET. Under the covers, the SqlDataSource uses ADO.NET objects such as the DataSet, DataReader, and Command objects. Because the SqlDataSource control is a control, it enables you to use these ADO.NET objects declaratively rather than programmatically.

The SqlDataSource control is a non-visual control—it doesn't render anything. You use the SqlDataSource control with other controls, such as the `GridView` or `FormView` controls, to display and edit database data. The `SqlDataSource` control can also be used to issue SQL commands against a database programmatically.

NOTE

The `SqlDataSource` control is not an appropriate control to use when building more complicated multi-tier applications. The `SqlDataSource` control forces you to mix your data access layer with your user interface layer. If you want to build a more cleanly architected multi-tier application, then you should use the `ObjectDataSource` control to represent your database data.

The ObjectDataSource is discussed in detail in Chapter 16, "Using the ObjectDataSource Control."

In this chapter, you learn how to represent connections and commands with the `SqlDataSource` control. You also learn how to use different types of parameters when executing commands. Finally, you learn how to improve the performance of your database-driven applications by taking advantage of the `SqlDataSource` control's support for caching database data.

Creating Database Connections

You can use the `SqlDataSource` control to connect to just about any SQL relational database server. In this section, you learn how to connect to Microsoft SQL Server and other databases such as Oracle. You also learn how you can store the database connection string used by the `SqlDataSource` securely in your web configuration files.

Connecting to Microsoft SQL Server

By default, the `SqlDataSource` control is configured to connect to Microsoft SQL Server version 7.0 or higher. The default provider used by the `SqlDataSource` control is the ADO.NET provider for Microsoft SQL Server.

You represent a database connection string with the `SqlDataSource` control's `ConnectionString` property. For example, the page in Listing 9.1 includes a `SqlDataSource` control that connects to a local SQL Server 2005 database (see Figure 9.1).

LISTING 9.1   ShowLocalConnection.aspx

```
<%@ Page Language="C#" %>
<!DOCTYPE html PUBLIC "-//W3C//DTD XHTML 1.1//EN"
"http://www.w3.org/TR/xhtml11/DTD/xhtml11.dtd">
<html xmlns="http://www.w3.org/1999/xhtml" >
<head id="Head1" runat="server">
    <title>Show Local Connection</title>
```

```
</head>
<body>
    <form id="form1" runat="server">
    <div>

    <asp:GridView
        id="grdMovies"
        DataSourceID="srcMovies"
        Runat="server" />

    <asp:SqlDataSource
        id="srcMovies"
        SelectCommand="SELECT * FROM Movies"
        ConnectionString="Data Source=.\SQLEXPRESS;
            AttachDbFilename=|DataDirectory|MyDatabase.mdf;
            Integrated Security=True;User Instance=True"
        Runat="server" />


    </div>
    </form>
</body>
</html>
```

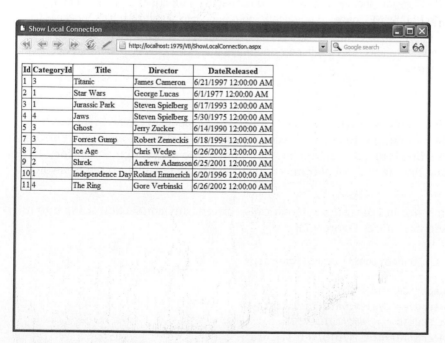

FIGURE 9.1   Displaying the Movies database table.

In Listing 9.1, the `SqlDataSource` control uses the following connection string:

```
Data Source=.\SQLEXPRESS;
AttachDbFilename=¦DataDirectory¦MyDatabase.mdf;
Integrated Security=True;User Instance=True
```

This connection string connects to an instance of SQL Server Express located on the local machine and a database file named `MyDatabase.mdf`. The connection string uses Integrated Security (a Trusted Connection) to connect to the local database.

You can use the following connection string to connect to a database located on a remote server.

```
Data Source=DataServer;Initial Catalog=Northwind;
User ID=webuser;Password=secret
```

This database connection string connects to a SQL Server database located on a remote machine named DataServer. The connection string connects to a database named Northwind.

This second connection string uses SQL Standard Security instead of Integrated Security. It contains a user ID and password that are associated with a SQL Server login.

> **WARNING**
>
> For security reasons, you should never include a connection string that contains security credentials in an ASP.NET page. Theoretically, no one should able to see the source of an ASP.NET page. However, Microsoft does not have a perfect track record. Later in this section, you learn how to store connection strings in the web configuration file (and encrypt them).

The .NET Framework includes a utility class, named the `SqlConnectionBuilder` class, that you can use when working with SQL connection strings. This class automatically converts any connection string into a canonical representation. It also exposes properties for extracting and modifying individual connection string parameters such as the Password parameters.

For example, the page in Listing 9.2 automatically converts any connection string into its canonical representation (see Figure 9.2).

LISTING 9.2   SqlConnectionStringBuilder.aspx

```
<%@ Page Language="C#" %>
<%@ Import Namespace="System.Data.SqlClient" %>
<!DOCTYPE html PUBLIC "-//W3C//DTD XHTML 1.1//EN"
"http://www.w3.org/TR/xhtml11/DTD/xhtml11.dtd">
```

```
<script runat="server">

    protected void btnConvert_Click(object sender, EventArgs e)
    {
        SqlConnectionStringBuilder builder = new
SqlConnectionStringBuilder(txtConnectionString.Text);
        lblResult.Text = builder.ConnectionString;
    }
</script>
<html xmlns="http://www.w3.org/1999/xhtml" >
<head id="Head1" runat="server">
    <title>SQL Connection String Builder</title>
</head>
<body>
    <form id="form1" runat="server">
    <div>

    <asp:TextBox
        id="txtConnectionString"
        Columns="60"
        Runat="Server" />
    <asp:Button
        id="btnConvert"
        Text="Convert"
        OnClick="btnConvert_Click"
        Runat="Server" />

    <hr />

    <asp:Label
        id="lblResult"
        Runat="server" />

    </div>
    </form>
</body>
</html>
```

After opening the page in Listing 9.2, if you enter a connection string that looks like this:

```
Server=localhost;UID=webuser;pwd=secret;database=Northwind
```

the page converts the connection string to look like this:

```
Data Source=localhost;Initial Catalog=Northwind;User ID=webuser;Password=secret
```

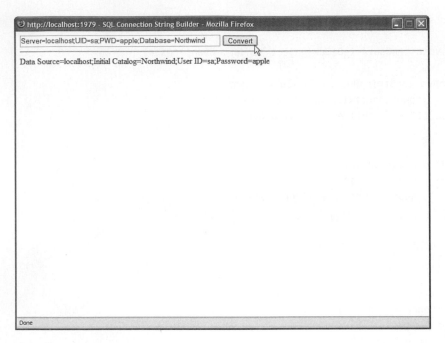

FIGURE 9.2 Converting a connection string.

Connecting to Other Databases

If you need to connect to any database server other than Microsoft SQL Server, then you need to modify the SqlDataSource control's ProviderName property.

The .NET Framework includes the following providers:

- **System.Data.OracleClient**—Use the ADO.NET provider for Oracle when connecting to an Oracle database.

- **System.Data.OleDb**—Use the OLE DB provider when connecting to a data source that supports an OLE DB provider.

- **System.Data.Odbc**—Use the ODBC provider when connecting to a data source with an ODBC driver.

> **NOTE**
>
> You can configure additional providers that you can use with the SqlDataSource control by adding new entries to the <DbProviderFactories> section of the Machine.config file.

For performance reasons, you should always use the native ADO.NET provider for a database. However, if your database does not have an ADO.NET provider, then you need to use either OLE DB or ODBC to connect to the database. Almost every database under the sun has either an OLE DB provider or an ODBC driver.

For example, the page in Listing 9.3 uses the ADO.NET Oracle provider to connect to an Oracle database.

LISTING 9.3   ConnectOracle.aspx

```
<%@ Page Language="C#" %>
<!DOCTYPE html PUBLIC "-//W3C//DTD XHTML 1.1//EN"
 "http://www.w3.org/TR/xhtml11/DTD/xhtml11.dtd">
<html xmlns="http://www.w3.org/1999/xhtml" >
<head id="Head1" runat="server">
    <title>Connect Oracle</title>
</head>
<body>
    <form id="form1" runat="server">
    <div>

    <asp:GridView
        id="grdOrders"
        DataSourceID="srcOrders"
        Runat="server" />

    <asp:SqlDataSource
        id="srcOrders"
        ProviderName="System.Data.OracleClient"
        SelectCommand="SELECT * FROM Orders"
        ConnectionString="Data Source=OracleDB;Integrated Security=yes"
        Runat="server" />

    </div>
    </form>
</body>
</html>
```

In Listing 9.3, notice that the ProviderName property is set to the value System.Data. OracleClient. The connection uses the native ADO.NET Oracle provider instead of the default provider for Microsoft SQL Server.

NOTE

To connect to an Oracle database, you need to install the Oracle client software on your web server.

> **NOTE**
>
> Oracle has produced its own native ADO.NET provider. You can download the Oracle provider at
>
> http://www.oracle.com/technology/tech/windows/odpnet/index.html.

Storing Connection Strings in the Web Configuration File

Storing connection strings in your pages is a bad idea for three reasons. First, it is not a good practice from the perspective of security. In theory, no one should ever be able to view the source code of your ASP.NET pages. In practice, however, hackers have discovered security flaws in the ASP.NET framework. To sleep better at night, you should store your connection strings in a separate file.

Also, adding a connection string to every page makes it difficult to manage a website. If you ever need to change your password, then you need to change every page that contains it. If, on the other hand, you store the connection string in one file, you can update the password by modifying the single file.

Finally, storing a connection string in a page can, potentially, hurt the performance of your application. The ADO.NET provider for SQL Server automatically uses connection pooling to improve your application's data access performance. Instead of being destroyed when they are closed, the connections are kept alive so that they can be put back into service quickly when the need arises. However, only connections that are created with the same connection strings are pooled together (an exact character-by-character match is made). Adding the same connection string to multiple pages is a recipe for defeating the benefits of connection pooling.

For these reasons, you should always place your connection strings in the web configuration file. The Web.Config file in Listing 9.4 includes a connectionStrings section.

LISTING 9.4   Web.Config

```
<configuration>
  <connectionStrings>
    <add name="Movies" connectionString="Data Source=.\SQLEXPRESS;
      AttachDbFilename=¦DataDirectory¦MyDatabase.mdf;Integrated Security=True;
User Instance=True" />
  </connectionStrings>
</configuration>
```

You can add as many connection strings to the connectionStrings section as you want. The page in Listing 9.5 includes a SqlDataSource that uses the Movies connection string.

LISTING 9.5 ShowMovies.aspx

```
<%@ Page Language="C#" %>
<!DOCTYPE html PUBLIC "-//W3C//DTD XHTML 1.1//EN"
 "http://www.w3.org/TR/xhtml11/DTD/xhtml11.dtd">
<html xmlns="http://www.w3.org/1999/xhtml" >
<head id="Head1" runat="server">
    <title>Show Movies</title>
</head>
<body>
    <form id="form1" runat="server">
    <div>

    <asp:GridView
        id="grdMovies"
        DataSourceID="srcMovies"
        Runat="server" />

    <asp:SqlDataSource
        id="srcMovies"
        SelectCommand="SELECT * FROM Movies"
        ConnectionString="<%$ ConnectionStrings:Movies %>"
        Runat="server" />

    </div>
    </form>
</body>
</html>
```

The expression <%$ ConnectionStrings:Movies %> is used to represent the connection string. This expression is not case sensitive.

Rather than add a connection string to your project's web configuration file, you can add the connection string to a web configuration file higher in the folder hierarchy. For example, you can add the connection string to the root Web.Config file and make it available to all applications running on your server. The root Web.Config file is located at the following path:

C:\WINDOWS\Microsoft.NET\Framework\v2.0.50727\CONFIG

Encrypting Connection Strings

You can encrypt the <connectionStrings> section of a web configuration file. For cxample, Listing 9.6 contains an encrypted version of the Web.Config file that was created in Listing 9.4.

LISTING 9.6   Web.Config

```
<configuration>
  <protectedData>
    <protectedDataSections>
      <add name="connectionStrings" provider="RsaProtectedConfigurationProvider"
        inheritedByChildren="false" />
    </protectedDataSections>
  </protectedData>
  <connectionStrings>
    <EncryptedData Type="http://www.w3.org/2001/04/xmlenc#Element"
      xmlns="http://www.w3.org/2001/04/xmlenc#">
      <EncryptionMethod Algorithm="http://www.w3.org/2001/04/
        xmlenc#tripledes-cbc" />
      <KeyInfo xmlns="http://www.w3.org/2000/09/xmldsig#">
        <EncryptedKey Recipient="" xmlns="http://www.w3.org/2001/04/xmlenc#">
          <EncryptionMethod Algorithm="http://www.w3.org/2001/04/xmlenc#rsa-1_5" />
          <KeyInfo xmlns="http://www.w3.org/2000/09/xmldsig#">
            <KeyName>Rsa Key</KeyName>
          </KeyInfo>
          <CipherData>

<CipherValue>MPLyXy7PoZ8E5VPk6K/azkGumO5tpeuWRzxx4PfgKeFwFccKx/8Zc7app++0
4c/dX7jA3uvNniFHTW6eKvrkLOsW2m6MxaeeLEfR9ME51Gy5jLa1KIXfTXKuJbXeZdiwrjCRdIqQpEj4fGZvr
3KkwI5HbGAqgK4Uu7IfBajdTJM=</CipherValue>

          </CipherData>
        </EncryptedKey>
      </KeyInfo>
      <CipherData>
        <CipherValue>CgnD74xMkcr7N4fgaHZNMps+e+if7dnEZ8xFw07kOBexaX+KyJvqtPuZiD2hW
        Dpqt5EOw6YM0Fs2uI5ocetbb74+d4kfHorC0bEjLEV+zcsJVGi2dZ80ll6sW+Y99osupaxOfr
        L3ld3mphMYrpcf+xafAs05s2x7H77TY01Y1goRaQ77tnkEIrQNQsHk/5eeptcE+A8scZSlaol
        FRNSSCdyO1TiKjPHF+MtI/8qzr2T6yjYM5Z+ZQ5TeiVvpg/6VD7K7dArIDmkFMTuQgdQBSJ
        UQ23dZ5V9Ja9HxqMGCea9NomBdhGC0sabDLxyPdOzGEAqOyxWKxqQM6Y0JyZKtPDg
        ==</CipherValue>
      </CipherData>
    </EncryptedData>
  </connectionStrings>
</configuration>
```

Notice that the contents of the <connectionStrings> section are no longer visible. However, an ASP.NET page can continue to read the value of the Movie database connection string by using the <%$ ConnectionStrings:Movie %> expression.

The easiest way to encrypt the <connectionStrings> section is to use the aspnet_regiis command-line tool. This tool is located in the following folder:

```
C:\WINDOWS\Microsoft.NET\Framework\v2.0.50727 \
```

Executing the following command encrypts the <connectionStrings> section of a Web.Config file located in a folder with the path c:\Websites\MyWebsite:

```
aspnet_regiis -pef connectionStrings "c:\Websites\MyWebsite"
```

The -pef option (Protect Encrypt Filepath) encrypts a particular configuration section located at a particular path.

You can decrypt a section with the -pdf option like this:

```
aspnet_regiis -pdf connectionStrings "c:\Websites\MyWebsite"
```

> **NOTE**
>
> Web configuration encryption options are discussed in more detail in Chapter 28, "Configuring Applications."

Executing Database Commands

In this section, you learn how to represent and execute SQL commands with the SqlDataSource control. In particular, you learn how to execute both inline SQL statements and external stored procedures. You also learn how to capture and gracefully handle errors that result from executing SQL commands.

Executing Inline SQL Statements

The SqlDataSource control can be used to represent four different types of SQL commands. The control supports the following four properties:

- ▶ SelectCommand

- ▶ InsertCommand

- ▶ UpdateCommand

- ▶ DeleteCommand

You can assign any SQL statement to any of these properties. For example, the page in Listing 9.7 uses all four properties to enable selecting, inserting, updating, and deleting records from the Movies database table (see Figure 9.3).

LISTING 9.7   ShowInlineCommands.aspx

```
<%@ Page Language="C#" %>
<!DOCTYPE html PUBLIC "-//W3C//DTD XHTML 1.1//EN"
  "http://www.w3.org/TR/xhtml11/DTD/xhtml11.dtd">
<html xmlns="http://www.w3.org/1999/xhtml" >
```

LISTING 9.7   Continued

```
<head id="Head1" runat="server">
    <style type="text/css">
        .detailsView
        {
            margin:0px auto;
            border:solid 4px black;
            background-color:white;
        }
        .detailsView td
        {
            padding:8px;
        }
        html
        {
            background-color:silver;
            font-family:Georgia, Serif;
        }
        a
        {
            color:blue;
            text-decoration:none;
        }
    </style>
    <title>Show Inline Commands</title>
</head>
<body>
    <form id="form1" runat="server">
    <div>

    <asp:DetailsView
        id="dtlMovies"
        DataSourceID="srcMovies"
        DataKeyNames="Id"
        AllowPaging="true"
        AutoGenerateEditButton="true"
        AutoGenerateInsertButton="true"
        AutoGenerateDeleteButton="true"
        AutoGenerateRows="false"
        CssClass="detailsView"
        PagerSettings-Mode="NumericFirstLast"
        Runat="server">
        <Fields>
        <asp:BoundField DataField="Id"
            HeaderText="Movie Id:" ReadOnly="true" InsertVisible="false" />
        <asp:BoundField DataField="Title" HeaderText="Movie Title:" />
```

```
            <asp:BoundField DataField="Director" HeaderText="Movie Director:" />
            </Fields>
    </asp:DetailsView>

    <asp:SqlDataSource
        id="srcMovies"
        SelectCommand="SELECT Id,Title,Director FROM Movies"
        InsertCommand="INSERT Movies (Title,Director,CategoryId,DateReleased)
            VALUES (@Title, @Director,0,'12/15/1966')"
        UpdateCommand="UPDATE Movies SET Title=@Title,
            Director=@Director WHERE Id=@Id"
        DeleteCommand="DELETE Movies WHERE Id=@Id"
        ConnectionString="<%$ ConnectionStrings:Movies %>"
        Runat="server" />

    </div>
    </form>
</body>
</html>
```

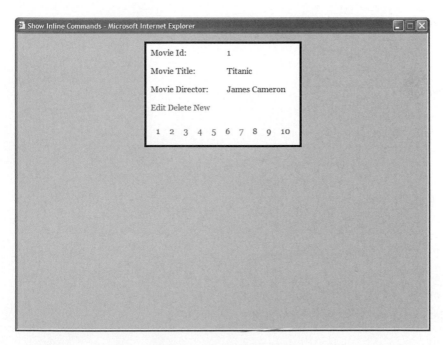

FIGURE 9.3   Executing inline SQL commands.

The page in Listing 9.7 contains a DetailsView control bound to a SqlDataSource control. You can click the Edit link to update an existing record, the New link to insert a new record, or the Delete link to delete an existing record. The DataBound control takes advantage of all four SQL commands supported by the SqlDataSource control.

Executing Stored Procedures

The SqlDataSource control can represent SQL stored procedures just as easily as it can represent inline SQL commands. You can indicate that a command represents a stored procedure by assigning the value StoredProcedure to any of the following properties:

▶ SelectCommandType

▶ InsertCommandType

▶ UpdateCommandType

▶ DeleteCommandType

You can create a new stored procedure in Visual Web Developer by opening the Database Explorer window, expanding a Data Connection, right-clicking Stored Procedures, and clicking Add New Stored Procedure (see Figure 9.4).

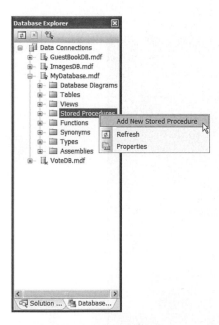

FIGURE 9.4   Creating a new stored procedure in Visual Web Developer.

The stored procedure in Listing 9.8 returns a count of the number of movies in each movie category.

LISTING 9.8   CountMoviesInCategory

```
CREATE PROCEDURE CountMoviesInCategory
AS
SELECT Name As Category, Count(*) As Count
FROM Movies
INNER JOIN MovieCategories
ON CategoryId = MovieCategories.Id
GROUP BY Name
```

The page in Listing 9.9 uses the CountMoviesInCategory stored procedure to display a report with a GridView control (see Figure 9.5).

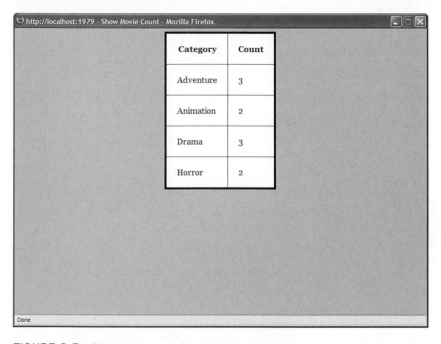

FIGURE 9.5   Showing count of movies in category.

LISTING 9.9   ShowMovieCount.aspx

```
<%@ Page Language="C#" %>
<!DOCTYPE html PUBLIC "-//W3C//DTD XHTML 1.1//EN"
 "http://www.w3.org/TR/xhtml11/DTD/xhtml11.dtd">
<html xmlns="http://www.w3.org/1999/xhtml" >
<head id="Head1" runat="server">
    <style type="text/css">
        .gridView
        {
```

LISTING 9.9   Continued

```
            margin:0px auto;
            border:solid 4px black;
            background-color:white;
        }
        .gridView td, .gridView th
        {
            padding:20px;
        }
        html
        {
            background-color:silver;
            font-family:Georgia, Serif;
        }
    </style>
    <title>Show Movie Count</title>
</head>
<body>
    <form id="form1" runat="server">
    <div>

    <asp:GridView
        id="grdMovies"
        DataSourceID="srcMovies"
        CssClass="gridView"
        Runat="server" />

    <asp:SqlDataSource
        id="srcMovies"
        SelectCommand="CountMoviesInCategory"
        SelectCommandType="StoredProcedure"
        ConnectionString="<%$ ConnectionStrings:Movies %>"
        Runat="server" />

    </div>
    </form>
</body>
</html>
```

Filtering Database Rows

The SqlDataSource control includes a FilterExpression property that enables you to filter the rows returned by the control. You can define complex Boolean filters that include parameters with this property.

For example, the page in Listing 9.10 retrieves all movies that have titles that match the string entered into the `TextBox` control (see Figure 9.6).

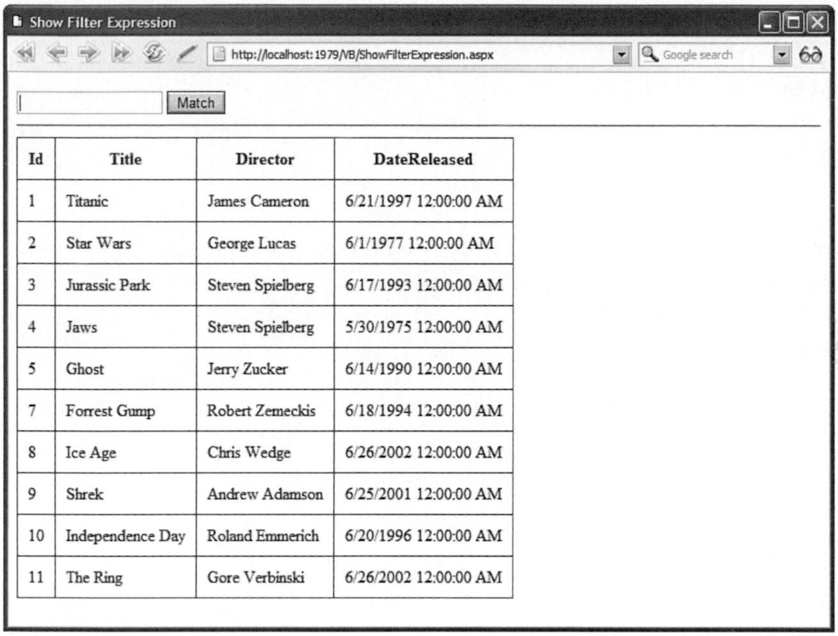

Id	Title	Director	DateReleased
1	Titanic	James Cameron	6/21/1997 12:00:00 AM
2	Star Wars	George Lucas	6/1/1977 12:00:00 AM
3	Jurassic Park	Steven Spielberg	6/17/1993 12:00:00 AM
4	Jaws	Steven Spielberg	5/30/1975 12:00:00 AM
5	Ghost	Jerry Zucker	6/14/1990 12:00:00 AM
7	Forrest Gump	Robert Zemeckis	6/18/1994 12:00:00 AM
8	Ice Age	Chris Wedge	6/26/2002 12:00:00 AM
9	Shrek	Andrew Adamson	6/25/2001 12:00:00 AM
10	Independence Day	Roland Emmerich	6/20/1996 12:00:00 AM
11	The Ring	Gore Verbinski	6/26/2002 12:00:00 AM

FIGURE 9.6 Show matching movies.

LISTING 9.10 `ShowFilterExpression.aspx`

```
<%@ Page Language="C#" %>
<!DOCTYPE html PUBLIC "-//W3C//DTD XHTML 1.1//EN"
 "http://www.w3.org/TR/xhtml11/DTD/xhtml11.dtd">
<html xmlns="http://www.w3.org/1999/xhtml" >
<head id="Head1" runat="server">
    <style type="text/css">
        td, th
        {
            padding:10px;
        }

    </style>
    <title>Show Filter Expression</title>
</head>
<body>
    <form id="form1" runat="server">
    <div>
```

LISTING 9.10   Continued

```
<asp:TextBox
    id="txtTitle"
    Runat="server" />
<asp:Button
    id="btnMatch"
    Text="Match"
    Runat="server" />
<hr />

<asp:GridView
    id="grdMovies"
    DataSourceId="srcMovies"
    Runat="server" />

<asp:SqlDataSource
    id="srcMovies"
    SelectCommand="SELECT Id,Title,Director,DateReleased
        FROM Movies"
    FilterExpression="Title LIKE '{0}%'"
    ConnectionString="<%$ ConnectionStrings:Movies %>"
    Runat="server">
    <FilterParameters>
        <asp:ControlParameter Name="Title" ControlID="txtTitle" />
    </FilterParameters>
</asp:SqlDataSource>

</div>
</form>
</body>
</html>
```

In Listing 9.10, the `FilterExpression` includes the `LIKE` operator and the ? wildcard character. The `LIKE` operator is used to perform partial matches on the movie titles.

Notice that the filter expression includes a `{0}` placeholder. The value of the `txtTitle` TextBox is plugged into this placeholder. You can use multiple parameters and multiple placeholders with the `FilterExpression` property.

NOTE

Behind the scenes, the `SqlDataSource` control uses the `DataView.RowFilter` property to filter database rows. You can find detailed documentation on proper filter syntax by looking up the `DataColumn.Expression` property in the .NET Framework SDK Documentation.

Using the `FilterExpression` property is especially useful when caching the data represented by a `SqlDataSource`. For example, you can cache the entire contents of the movies database table in memory and use the `FilterExpression` property to filter the movies displayed on a page. You can display different sets of movies depending on a user's selection from a drop-down list of movie categories.

Changing the Data Source Mode

The `SqlDataSource` control can represent the data that it retrieves in two different ways. It can represent the data using either an ADO.NET DataSct or an ADO.NET DataReader.

By default, the `SqlDataSource` represents records using the ADO.NET DataSet object. The DataSet object provides a static, memory-resident representation of data.

> **NOTE**
>
> Technically, the `SqlDataSource` control returns a `DataView` and not a `DataSet`. Because, by default, the `SqlDataSourceMode` enumeration is set to the value `DataSet`, I'll continue to refer to `DataSets` instead of `DataViews`.

Some features of the `DataBound` controls work only when the controls are bound to a `DataSet`. For example, the `GridView` control supports client-side sorting and filtering only when the control is bound to a `DataSet`.

The other option is to represent the data that a `SqlDataSource` control returns with a `DataReader` object. The advantage of using a `DataReader` is that it offers significantly better performance than the `DataSet` object. The `DataReader` represents a fast, forward-only representation of data. If you want to grab some database records and display the records in the fastest possible way, use the `DataReader` object.

For example, the page in Listing 9.11 retrieves the records from the Movies database by using a `DataReader`.

LISTING 9.11   ShowDataSourceMode.aspx

```
<%@ Page Language="C#" %>
<!DOCTYPE html PUBLIC "-//W3C//DTD XHTML 1.1//EN"
 "http://www.w3.org/TR/xhtml11/DTD/xhtml11.dtd">
<html xmlns="http://www.w3.org/1999/xhtml" >
<head id="Head1" runat="server">
    <title>Show Data Source Mode</title>
</head>
<body>
    <form id="form1" runat="server">
    <div>
```

LISTING 9.11   Continued

```
    <asp:GridView
        id="grdMovies"
        DataSourceID="srcMovies"
        Runat="server" />

    <asp:SqlDataSource
        id="srcMovies"
        DataSourceMode="DataReader"
        SelectCommand="SELECT * FROM Movies"
        ConnectionString="<%$ ConnectionStrings:Movies %>"
        Runat="server" />

    </div>
    </form>
</body>
</html>
```

Notice that the `SqlDataSource` control's `DataSourceMode` property is set to the value `DataReader`.

Handling SQL Command Execution Errors

Whenever you build a software application you need to plan for failure. Databases go down, users enter unexpected values in form fields, and networks get clogged. It is miraculous that the Internet works at all.

You can handle errors thrown by the `SqlDataSource` control by handling any or all of the following four events:

▶ **Deleted**—Happens immediately after the `SqlDataSource` executes its `delete` command.

▶ **Inserted**—Happens immediately after the `SqlDataSource` executes its `insert` command.

▶ **Selected**—Happens immediately after the `SqlDataSource` executes its `select` command.

▶ **Updated**—Happens immediately after the `SqlDataSource` executes its `delete` command.

Each of these events is passed an EventArgs parameter that includes any exceptions raised when the command was executed. For example, in the SELECT command in Listing 9.12, movies are retrieved from the DontExist database table instead of the Movies database table.

LISTING 9.12 HandleError.aspx

```
<%@ Page Language="C#" %>
<!DOCTYPE html PUBLIC "-//W3C//DTD XHTML 1.1//EN"
"http://www.w3.org/TR/xhtml11/DTD/xhtml11.dtd">

<script runat="server">
    protected void srcMovies_Selected(object sender, SqlDataSourceStatusEventArgs e)
    {
        if (e.Exception != null)
        {
            lblError.Text = e.Exception.Message;
            e.ExceptionHandled = true;
        }
    }
</script>

<html xmlns="http://www.w3.org/1999/xhtml" >
<head id="Head1" runat="server">
    <style type="text/css">
        .error
        {
            display:block;
            color:red;
            font:bold 16px Arial;
            margin:10px;
        }
    </style>
    <title>Handle Error</title>
</head>
<body>
    <form id="form1" runat="server">
    <div>

    <asp:Label
        id="lblError"
        EnableViewState="false"
        CssClass="error"
        Runat="server" />

    <asp:GridView
        id="grdMovies"
        DataSourceID="srcMovies"
        Runat="server" />

    <asp:SqlDataSource
```

LISTING 9.12   Continued

```
        id="srcMovies"
        SelectCommand="SELECT * FROM DontExist"
        ConnectionString="<%$ ConnectionStrings:Movies %>"
        OnSelected="srcMovies_Selected"
        Runat="server" />

    </div>
    </form>
</body>
</html>
```

If the page in Listing 9.12 is opened in a web browser, an exception is raised when the SqlDataSource control attempts to retrieve the rows from the DontExist database table (because it doesn't exist). In the srcMovies_Selected() method, the exception is detected and displayed in a Label control.

Notice that the ExceptionHandled property is used to suppress the exception. If you do not set ExceptionHandled to true, then the page will explode (see Figure 9.7).

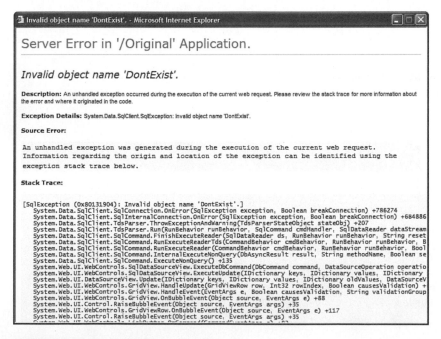

FIGURE 9.7   An unhandled exception.

As an alternative to handling exceptions at the level of the SqlDataSource control, you can handle the exception at the level of a DataBound control. The GridView, DetailsView, and FormView controls all include events that expose the Exception and ExceptionHandled properties.

For example, the page in Listing 9.13 includes a GridView that handles the exception raised when you attempt to edit the contents of the DontExist database table.

LISTING 9.13 GridViewHandleError.aspx

```
<%@ Page Language="C#" %>
<!DOCTYPE html PUBLIC "-//W3C//DTD XHTML 1.1//EN"
"http://www.w3.org/TR/xhtml11/DTD/xhtml11.dtd">
<script runat="server">

    protected void grdMovies_RowUpdated(object sender, GridViewUpdatedEventArgs e)
    {
        if (e.Exception != null)
        {
            lblError.Text = e.Exception.Message;
            e.ExceptionHandled = true;
        }
    }
</script>

<html xmlns="http://www.w3.org/1999/xhtml" >
<head id="Head1" runat="server">
    <style type="text/css">
        .error
        {
            display:block;
            color:red;
            font:bold 16px Arial;
            margin:10px;
        }
    </style>
    <title>GridView Handle Error</title>
</head>
<body>
    <form id="form1" runat="server">
    <div>

    <asp:Label
        id="lblError"
        EnableViewState="false"
        CssClass="error"
        Runat="server" />

    <asp:GridView
        id="grdMovies"
        DataKeyNames="Id"
```

LISTING 9.13   Continued

```
        AutoGenerateEditButton="true"
        DataSourceID="srcMovies"
        OnRowUpdated="grdMovies_RowUpdated"
        Runat="server" />

    <asp:SqlDataSource
        id="srcMovies"
        SelectCommand="SELECT Id,Title FROM Movies"
        UpdateCommand="UPDATE DontExist SET Title=@Title
            WHERE Id=@ID"
        ConnectionString="<%$ ConnectionStrings:Movies %>"
        Runat="server" />

    </div>
    </form>
</body>
</html>
```

After you open the page in Listing 9.13, you can click the Edit link next to any record to edit the record. If you click the Update link, an exception is raised because the update command attempts to update the DontExist database table. The exception is handled by the GridView control's RowUpdated event handler.

You can handle an exception at both the level of the SqlDataSource control and the level of a DataBound control. The SqlDataSource control's events are raised before the corresponding events are raised for the DataBound control. If you handle an exception by using the ExceptionHandled property in the SqlDataSource control's event handler, then the exception is not promoted to the DataSource control's event handler.

Canceling Command Execution

You can cancel SqlDataSource commands when some criterion is not met. For example, you might want to validate the parameters that you are using with the command before executing the command.

You can cancel a command by handling any of the following events exposed by the SqlDataSource control:

▶ **Deleting**—Happens immediately before the SqlDataSource executes its delete command.

▶ **Filtering**—Happens immediately before the SqlDataSource filters its data.

▶ **Inserting**—Happens immediately before the SqlDataSource executes its insert command.

▶ **Selecting**—Happens immediately before the SqlDataSource executes its select command.

▶ **Updating**—Happens immediately before the SqlDataSource executes its delete command.

For example, the page in Listing 9.14 contains a DetailsView control bound to a SqlDataSource control that represents the contents of the Movies database table. The DetailsView control enables you to update a particular movie record. However, if you leave one of the fields blank, then the update command is canceled (see Figure 9.8).

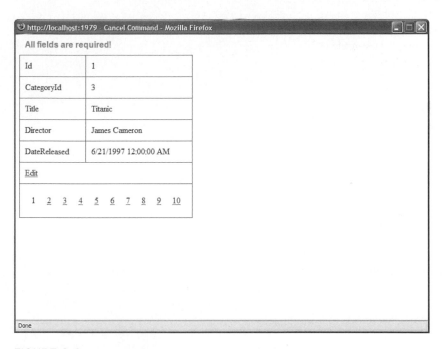

FIGURE 9.8   Canceling a command when a field is blank.

LISTING 9.14   CancelCommand.aspx

```csharp
<%@ Page Language="C#" %>
<%@ Import Namespace="System.Data.SqlClient" %>
<!DOCTYPE html PUBLIC "-//W3C//DTD XHTML 1.1//EN"
"http://www.w3.org/TR/xhtml11/DTD/xhtml11.dtd">
<script runat="server">

    /// <summary>
    /// Iterate through all parameters and check for null
    /// </summary>
    protected void srcMovies_Updating(object sender, SqlDataSourceCommandEventArgs e)
    {
```

6

LISTING 9.14   Continued

```
        foreach (SqlParameter param in e.Command.Parameters)
        if (param.Value == null)
        {
            e.Cancel = true;
            lblError.Text = "All fields are required!";
        }
    }
</script>

<html xmlns="http://www.w3.org/1999/xhtml" >
<head id="Head1" runat="server">
    <style type="text/css">
        .error
        {
            display:block;
            color:red;
            font:bold 16px Arial;
            margin:10px;
        }
        td,th
        {
            padding:10px;
        }
    </style>
    <title>Cancel Command</title>
</head>
<body>
    <form id="form1" runat="server">
    <div>

    <asp:Label
        id="lblError"
        EnableViewState="false"
        CssClass="error"
        Runat="server" />

    <asp:DetailsView
        id="dtlMovie"
        DataSourceID="srcMovies"
        DataKeyNames="Id"
        AllowPaging="true"
        AutoGenerateEditButton="true"
        Runat="server" />
```

```
<asp:SqlDataSource
    id="srcMovies"
    SelectCommand="SELECT * FROM Movies"
    UpdateCommand="UPDATE Movies SET Title=@Title,
        Director=@Director,DateReleased=@DateReleased
        WHERE Id=@id"
    ConnectionString="<%$ ConnectionStrings:Movies %>"
    Runat="server" OnUpdating="srcMovies_Updating" />

</div>
</form>
</body>
</html>
```

The page in Listing 9.14 includes a srcMovies_Updating() method. In this method, each parameter associated with the update command is compared against the value Nothing (null). If one of the parameters is null, an error message is displayed in a Label control.

Using ASP.NET Parameters with the SqlDataSource Control

You can use any of the following ASP.NET Parameter objects with the SqlDataSource control:

- ▶ **Parameter**—Represents an arbitrary static value.

- ▶ **ControlParameter**—Represents the value of a control or page property.

- ▶ **CookieParameter**—Represents the value of a browser cookie.

- ▶ **FormParameter**—Represents the value of an HTML form field.

- ▶ **ProfileParameter**—Represents the value of a Profile property.

- ▶ **QueryStringParameter**—Represents the value of a query string field.

- ▶ **SessionParameter**—Represents the value of an item stored in Session state.

The SqlDataSource control includes five collections of ASP.NET parameters: SelectParameters, InsertParameters, DeleteParameters, UpdateParameters, and FilterParameters. You can use these parameter collections to associate a particular ASP.NET parameter with a particular SqlDataSource command or filter.

In the following sections, you learn how to use each of these different types of parameter objects.

Using the ASP.NET Parameter Object

The ASP.NET parameter object has the following properties:

▶ **ConvertEmptyStringToNull**—When true, if a parameter represents an empty string then the empty string is converted to the value Nothing (null) before the associated command is executed.

▶ **DefaultValue**—When a parameter has the value Nothing (null), the DefaultValue is used for the value of the parameter.

▶ **Direction**—Indicates the direction of the parameter. Possible values are Input, InputOutput, Output, and ReturnValue.

▶ **Name**—Indicates the name of the parameter. Do not use the @ character when indicating the name of an ASP.NET parameter.

▶ **Size**—Indicates the data size of the parameter.

▶ **Type**—Indicates the .NET Framework type of the parameter. You can assign any value from the TypeCode enumeration to this property.

You can use the ASP.NET parameter object to indicate several parameter properties explicitly, such as a parameter's type, size, and default value.

For example, the page in Listing 9.15 contains a DetailsView control bound to a SqlDataSource control. You can use the page to update records in the Movies database table (see Figure 9.9).

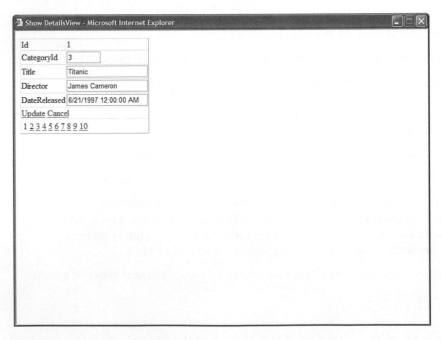

FIGURE 9.9   Updating movie records.

LISTING 9.15 `ShowDetailsView.aspx`

```
<%@ Page Language="C#" %>
<!DOCTYPE html PUBLIC "-//W3C//DTD XHTML 1.1//EN"
    "http://www.w3.org/TR/xhtml11/DTD/xhtml11.dtd">
<html xmlns="http://www.w3.org/1999/xhtml" >
<head id="Head1" runat="server">
    <title>Show DetailsView</title>
</head>
<body>
    <form id="form1" runat="server">
    <div>

    <asp:DetailsView
        id="dtlMovie"
        DataKeyNames="Id"
        DataSourceID="srcMovies"
        AutoGenerateEditButton="true"
        DefaultMode="Edit"
        AllowPaging="true"
        runat="server" />

    <asp:SqlDataSource
        id="srcMovies"
        ConnectionString="<%$ ConnectionStrings:Movies %>"
        SelectCommand="Select * FROM Movies"
        UpdateCommand="UPDATE Movies SET Title=@Title,Director=@Director,
            DateReleased=@DateReleased WHERE Id=@id"
        Runat="server" />

    </div>
    </form>
</body>
</html>
```

In Listing 9.15, no ASP.NET parameter objects are declared explicitly. The `DetailsView` control automatically creates and adds ADO.NET parameters to the `SqlDataSource` control's update command before the command is executed.

If you want to be explicit about the data types and sizes of the parameters used by a `SqlDataSource` control, then you can declare the parameters. The page in Listing 9.16 declares each of the parameters used when executing the update command.

LISTING 9.16   `ShowDetailsViewExplicit.aspx`

```
<%@ Page Language="C#" %>
<!DOCTYPE html PUBLIC "-//W3C//DTD XHTML 1.1//EN"
  "http://www.w3.org/TR/xhtml11/DTD/xhtml11.dtd">
<html xmlns="http://www.w3.org/1999/xhtml" >
<head id="Head1" runat="server">
    <title>Show DetailsView Explicit</title>
</head>
<body>
    <form id="form1" runat="server">
    <div>

    <asp:DetailsView
        id="dtlMovie"
        DataKeyNames="Id"
        DataSourceID="srcMovies"
        AutoGenerateEditButton="true"
        DefaultMode="Edit"
        AllowPaging="true"
        runat="server" />

    <asp:SqlDataSource
        id="srcMovies"
        ConnectionString="<%$ ConnectionStrings:Movies %>"
        SelectCommand="Select * FROM Movies"
        UpdateCommand="UPDATE Movies SET Title=@Title,Director=@Director,
            DateReleased=@DateReleased WHERE Id=@id"
        Runat="server">
        <UpdateParameters>
          <asp:Parameter Name="Title"
            Type="String" Size="100" DefaultValue="Untitled" />
          <asp:Parameter Name="Director"
            Type="String" Size="100" DefaultValue="Alan Smithee" />
          <asp:Parameter Name="DateReleased" Type="DateTime" />
          <asp:Parameter Name="id" Type="int32" />
        </UpdateParameters>
    </asp:SqlDataSource>
    </div>
    </form>
</body>
</html>
```

In Listing 9.16, each of the parameters used by the update command is provided with an explicit data type. For example, the `DateReleased` parameter is declared to be a

`DateTime` parameter (if you didn't assign an explicit type to this parameter, it would default to a string).

Furthermore, the `Title` and `Director` parameters are provided with default values. If you edit a movie record and do not supply a title or director, the default values are used.

> **NOTE**
>
> Another situation in which explicitly declaring `Parameter` objects is useful is when you need to explicitly order the parameters. For example, the order of parameters is important when you use the OLE DB provider with Microsoft Access.

Using the ASP.NET `ControlParameter` Object

You use the `ControlParameter` object to represent the value of a control property. You can use it to represent the value of any control contained in the same page as the `SqlDataSource` control.

The `ControlParameter` object includes all the properties of the `Parameter` object and these additional properties:

- ▶ **ControlID**—The ID of the control that the parameter represents.

- ▶ **PropertyName**—The name of the property that the parameter represents.

For example, the page in Listing 9.17 includes a `DropDownList` control and a `DetailsView` control. When you select a movie from the `DropDownList`, details for the movie are displayed in the `DetailsView` control (see Figure 9.10).

LISTING 9.17   `ShowControlParameter.aspx`

```
<%@ Page Language="C#" %>
<!DOCTYPE html PUBLIC "-//W3C//DTD XHTML 1.1//EN"
   "http://www.w3.org/TR/xhtml11/DTD/xhtml11.dtd">
<html xmlns="http://www.w3.org/1999/xhtml" >
<head id="Head1" runat="server">
    <title>Show Control Parameter</title>
</head>
<body>
    <form id="form1" runat="server">
    <div>

    <asp:DropDownList
        id="ddlMovies"
        DataSourceID="srcMovies"
        DataTextField="Title"
        DataValueField="Id"
        Runat="server" />
```

LISTING 9.17   Continued

```
<asp:Button
    id="btnSelect"
    Text="Select"
    Runat="server" />

<hr />

<asp:DetailsView
    id="dtlMovie"
    DataSourceID="srcMovieDetails"
    Runat="server" />

<asp:SqlDataSource
    id="srcMovies"
    SelectCommand="SELECT Id,Title FROM Movies"
    ConnectionString="<%$ ConnectionStrings:Movies %>"
    Runat="server" />

<asp:SqlDataSource
    id="srcMovieDetails"
    SelectCommand="SELECT * FROM Movies
        WHERE Id=@Id"
    ConnectionString="<%$ ConnectionStrings:Movies %>"
    Runat="server">
    <SelectParameters>
        <asp:ControlParameter Name="Id" ControlID="ddlMovies"
            PropertyName="SelectedValue" />
    </SelectParameters>
</asp:SqlDataSource>

</div>
</form>
</body>
</html>
```

Notice that the second SqlDataSource control in Listing 9.17 includes a ControlParameter object. The ControlParameter represents the ID of the selected movie in the DropDownList control.

When using a ControlParameter, you must always set the value of the ControlID property to point to a control on the page. On the other hand, you are not always required to set the PropertyName property. If you do not set PropertyName, the ControlParameter object automatically looks for a property that is decorated with the ControlValueProperty attribute. Because the SelectedValue property of the DropDownList control is decorated with this attribute, you do not really need to set this property in Listing 9.17.

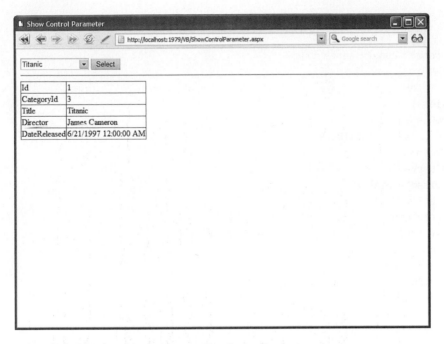

FIGURE 9.10   Show matching movies for each movie category.

Because the `Page` class derives from the `control` class, you can use the `ControlParameter` object to represent the value of a `Page` property.

For example, the page in Listing 9.18 contains a simple guestbook. When a user adds a new entry to the guestbook, the user's remote IP address is saved automatically with the guestbook entry (see Figure 9.11).

LISTING 9.18   `ShowPageControlParameter.aspx`

```
<%@ Page Language="C#" %>
<!DOCTYPE html PUBLIC "-//W3C//DTD XHTML 1.1//EN"
"http://www.w3.org/TR/xhtml11/DTD/xhtml11.dtd">
<script runat="server">

    public string IPAddress
    {
        get { return Request.UserHostAddress; }
    }

</script>
<html xmlns="http://www.w3.org/1999/xhtml" >
<head id="Head1" runat="server">
    <title>Show Page Control Parameter</title>
</head>
```

LISTING 9.18   Continued

```
<body>
    <form id="form1" runat="server">
    <div>

    <asp:FormView
        id="frmGuestBook"
        DataSourceID="srcGuestBook"
        DefaultMode="Insert"
        runat="server">
        <InsertItemTemplate>
        <asp:Label
            id="lblName"
            Text="Your Name:"
            AssociatedControlID="txtName"
            Runat="server" />
        <asp:TextBox
            id="txtName"
            Text='<%# Bind("Name") %>'
            Runat="server" />
        <br /><br />
        <asp:Label
            id="Label1"
            Text="Your Comments:"
            AssociatedControlID="txtComments"
            Runat="server" />
        <br />
        <asp:TextBox
            id="txtComments"
            Text='<%# Bind("Comments") %>'
            TextMode="MultiLine"
            Columns="60"
            Rows="4"
            Runat="server" />
        <br /><br />
        <asp:Button
            id="btnSubmit"
            Text="Submit"
            CommandName="Insert"
            Runat="server" />
        </InsertItemTemplate>
    </asp:FormView>

    <hr />
```

```
<asp:GridView
    id="grdGuestBook"
    DataSourceID="srcGuestBook"
    Runat="server" />

<asp:SqlDataSource
    id="srcGuestBook"
    SelectCommand="SELECT * FROM GuestBook ORDER BY Id DESC"
    InsertCommand="INSERT GuestBook (IPAddress,Name,Comments)
        VALUES (@IPAddress,@Name,
    ConnectionString="<%$ ConnectionStrings:GuestBook %>"
    Runat="server">
    <InsertParameters>
        <asp:ControlParameter Name="IPAddress" ControlID="__page"
            PropertyName="IPAddress" />
    </InsertParameters>
</asp:SqlDataSource>

</div>
</form>
</body>
</html>
```

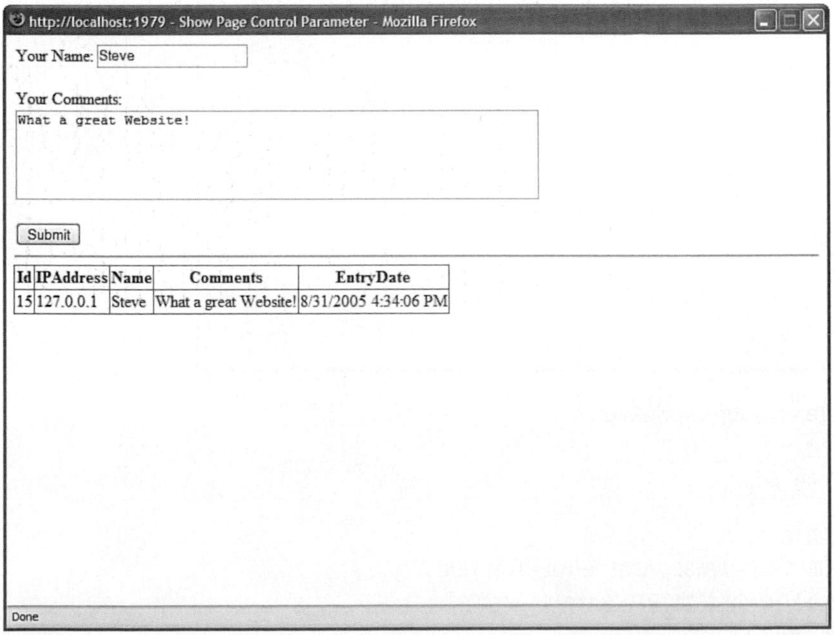

FIGURE 9.11   Saving an IP address in guest book entries.

Notice that the `ControlID` property is set to the value `__page`. This value is the automatically generated ID for the `Page` class. The `PropertyName` property has the value `IPAddress`. This property is defined in the page.

Using the ASP.NET `CookieParameter` Object

The `CookieParameter` object represents a browser-side cookie. The `CookieParameter` includes all the properties of the base `Parameter` class and the following additional property:

▶ **CookieName**—The name of the browser cookie.

The page in Listing 9.19 illustrates how you can use the `CookieParameter` object. The page contains a voting form that you can use to vote for your favorite color. A cookie is added to the user's browser to identify the user and prevent someone from cheating by voting more than once (see Figure 9.12).

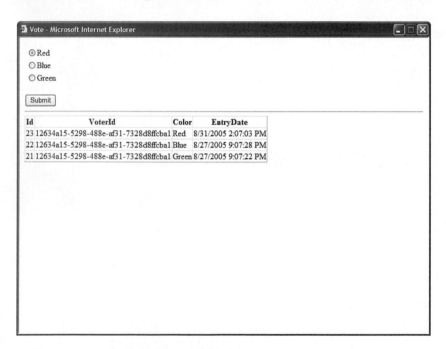

FIGURE 9.12   Vote on your favorite color.

LISTING 9.19   Vote.aspx

```
<%@ Page Language="C#" %>
<!DOCTYPE html PUBLIC "-//W3C//DTD XHTML 1.1//EN"
"http://www.w3.org/TR/xhtml11/DTD/xhtml11.dtd">
<script runat="server">

    void Page_Load()
```

```
        {
            if (Request.Cookies["VoterId"] == null)
            {
                string identifier = Guid.NewGuid().ToString();
                HttpCookie voteCookie = new HttpCookie("VoterId", identifier);
                voteCookie.Expires = DateTime.MaxValue;
                Response.AppendCookie(voteCookie);
            }
        }

</script>
<html xmlns="http://www.w3.org/1999/xhtml" >
<head id="Head1" runat="server">
    <title>Vote</title>
</head>
<body>
    <form id="form1" runat="server">
    <div>

    <asp:FormView
        id="frmVote"
        DataSourceID="srcVote"
        DefaultMode="Insert"
        Runat="server">
        <InsertItemTemplate>
        <asp:Label
            id="lblFavoriteColor"
            AssociatedControlID="rdlFavoriteColor"
            Runat="server" />
        <asp:RadioButtonList
            id="rdlFavoriteColor"
            SelectedValue='<%#Bind("Color")%>'
            Runat="server">
            <asp:ListItem Value="Red" Text="Red" Selected="True" />
            <asp:ListItem Value="Blue" Text="Blue" />
            <asp:ListItem Value="Green" Text="Green" />
        </asp:RadioButtonList>
        <br />
        <asp:Button
            id="btnSubmit"
            Text="Submit"
            CommandName="Insert"
            Runat="server" />
        </InsertItemTemplate>
    </asp:FormView>
```

6

LISTING 9.19   Continued

```
    <hr />

    <asp:GridView
        id="grdVote"
        DataSourceID="srcVote"
        Runat="server" />

    <asp:SqlDataSource
        id="srcVote"
        SelectCommand="SELECT * FROM Vote
            ORDER BY Id DESC"
        InsertCommand="INSERT Vote (VoterId,Color)
            VALUES (@VoterId,@Color)"
        ConnectionString="<%$ ConnectionStrings:Vote %>"
        Runat="server">
        <InsertParameters>
            <asp:CookieParameter Name="VoterId"
                CookieName="VoterId" />
            </InsertParameters>
    </asp:SqlDataSource>

    </div>
    </form>
</body>
</html>
```

The cookie is added in the Page_Load() method. A unique identifier (GUID) is generated to identify the user uniquely.

Using the ASP.NET FormParameter Object

The FormParameter object represents a form field submitted to the server. Typically, you never work directly with browser form fields because their functionality is encapsulated in the ASP.NET form controls.

The page in Listing 9.20 contains a client-side HTML form that enables you to enter a movie title and director. When the form is submitted to the server, the values of the form fields are saved to the Movies database table (see Figure 9.13).

LISTING 9.20   ShowFormParameter.aspx

```
<%@ Page Language="C#" %>
<!DOCTYPE html PUBLIC "-//W3C//DTD XHTML 1.1//EN"
"http://www.w3.org/TR/xhtml11/DTD/xhtml11.dtd">
<script runat="server">
```

```
    void Page_Load()
    {
        if (Request.Form["AddMovie"] != null)
            srcMovies.Insert();
    }

</script>
<html xmlns="http://www.w3.org/1999/xhtml" >
<head id="Head1" runat="server">
    <title>Show FormParameter</title>
</head>
<body>
    <form action="ShowFormParameter.aspx" method="post">

    <label for="txtTitle">Movie Title:</label>
    <br />
    <input name="txtTitle" />


    <br /><br />

    <label for="txtDirector">Movie Director:</label>
    <br />
    <input name="txtDirector" />

    <br /><br />
    <input name="AddMovie" type="submit" value="Add Movie" />

    </form>

    <form id="form1" runat="server">
    <div>

    <asp:GridView
        id="grdMovies"
        DataSourceID="srcMovies"
        Runat="server" />

    <asp:SqlDataSource
        id="srcMovies"
        SelectCommand="SELECT * FROM Movies"
        InsertCommand="INSERT Movies (Title,Director,CategoryId,DateReleased)
            VALUES (@Title,@Director,0,'12/25/1966')"
        ConnectionString="<%$ ConnectionStrings:Movies %>"
        Runat="server">
        <InsertParameters>
            <asp:FormParameter Name="Title"
```

LISTING 9.20   Continued

```
                FormField="txtTitle" DefaultValue="Untitled" />
            <asp:FormParameter Name="Director"
                FormField="txtDirector" DefaultValue="Allen Smithee" />
        </InsertParameters>
    </asp:SqlDataSource>

    </div>
    </form>
</body>
</html>
```

Notice that you check whether a form field named AddMovie exists in the `Page_Load()` method. This is the name of the submit button. If this field exists, then you know that the client-side form was submitted and the `SqlDataSource` control's `Insert()` method can be called to add the form fields to the database.

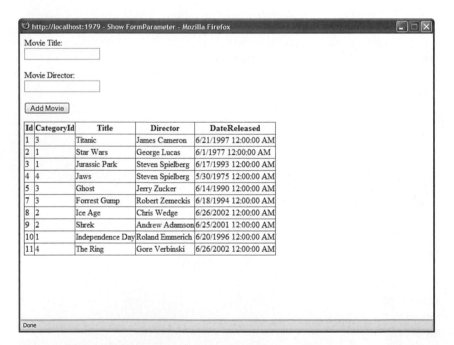

Id	CategoryId	Title	Director	DateReleased
1	3	Titanic	James Cameron	6/21/1997 12:00:00 AM
2	1	Star Wars	George Lucas	6/1/1977 12:00:00 AM
3	1	Jurassic Park	Steven Spielberg	6/17/1993 12:00:00 AM
4	4	Jaws	Steven Spielberg	5/30/1975 12:00:00 AM
5	3	Ghost	Jerry Zucker	6/14/1990 12:00:00 AM
7	3	Forrest Gump	Robert Zemeckis	6/18/1994 12:00:00 AM
8	2	Ice Age	Chris Wedge	6/26/2002 12:00:00 AM
9	2	Shrek	Andrew Adamson	6/25/2001 12:00:00 AM
10	1	Independence Day	Roland Emmerich	6/20/1996 12:00:00 AM
11	4	The Ring	Gore Verbinski	6/26/2002 12:00:00 AM

FIGURE 9.13   Using a client-side HTML form.

Using the ASP.NET `ProfileParameter` Object

The `ProfileParameter` object enables you to represent any of the properties of the `Profile` object. The `ProfileParameter` includes all the properties of the `Parameter` class and the following property:

▶ **PropertyName**—Indicates the name of the `Profile` property associated with this
  `ProfileParameter`.

For example, imagine that you are building a Guest Book application and you want to
allow users to enter their display names when adding entries to a guest book. You can
add a `DisplayName` property to the `Profile` object with the web configuration file in
Listing 9.21.

LISTING 9.21 Web.config

```
<configuration>
  <connectionStrings>
    <add name="GuestBook" connectionString="Data Source=.\SQLEXPRESS;
      AttachDbFilename=¦DataDirectory¦GuestBookDB.mdf;
Integrated Security=True;User Instance=True" />
  </connectionStrings>

  <system.web>
    <profile enabled="true">
      <properties>
        <add name="DisplayName" defaultValue="Anonymous" />
      </properties>
    </profile>
  </system.web>

</configuration>
```

> **NOTE**
>
> The `Profile` object automatically stores user specific information across visits to a
> website.
>
> The `Profile` object is discussed in detail in Chapter 24, "Maintaining Application
> State."

The web configuration file in Listing 9.21 includes the definition of a `Profile` property
named `DisplayName`. Notice that the default value of this property is `Anonymous`.

The page in Listing 9.22 uses the `ProfileParameter` object to read the value of the
`DisplayName` property automatically when new entries are added to a Guest Book.

LISTING 9.22 ShowProfileParameter.aspx

```
<%@ Page Language="C#" %>
<!DOCTYPE html PUBLIC "-//W3C//DTD XHTML 1.1//EN"
  "http://www.w3.org/TR/xhtml11/DTD/xhtml11.dtd">
```

LISTING 9.22   Continued

```
<html xmlns="http://www.w3.org/1999/xhtml" >
<head id="Head1" runat="server">
    <title>Show ProfileParameter</title>
</head>
<body>
    <form id="form1" runat="server">
    <div>

    <asp:FormView
        id="frmGuestBook"
        DataSourceID="srcGuestBook"
        DefaultMode="Insert"
        Runat="server">
        <InsertItemTemplate>
        <asp:Label
            id="lblComments"
            Text="Enter Your Comments:"
            Runat="server" />
        <br />
        <asp:TextBox
            id="txtComments"
            Text='<%# Bind("Comments") %>'
            TextMode="MultiLine"
            Columns="50"
            Rows="4"
            Runat="server" />
        <br />
        <asp:Button
            id="btnInsert"
            Text="Add Comments"
            CommandName="Insert"
            Runat="server" />
        </InsertItemTemplate>
    </asp:FormView>

    <hr />

    <asp:GridView
        id="grdGuestBook"
        DataSourceID="srcGuestBook"
        Runat="server" />

    <asp:SqlDataSource
        id="srcGuestBook"
```

```
        SelectCommand="SELECT Name,Comments,EntryDate
            FROM GuestBook ORDER BY Id DESC"
        InsertCommand="INSERT GuestBook (Name,Comments)
            VALUES (@Name,@Comments)"
        ConnectionString="<%$ ConnectionStrings:GuestBook %>"
        Runat="server">
        <InsertParameters>
            <asp:ProfileParameter Name="Name" PropertyName="DisplayName" />
        </InsertParameters>
    </asp:SqlDataSource>

    </div>
    </form>
</body>
</html>
```

Notice that the SqlDataSource control in Listing 9.22 includes a ProfileParameter object. This object represents the DisplayName profile property.

Using the QueryStringParameter Object

The QueryStringParameter object can represent any query string passed to a page. The QueryStringParameter class includes all the properties of the base Parameter class with the addition of the following property:

▶ **QueryStringField**—The name of the query string that the QueryStringParameter represents.

This type of parameter is particularly useful when you build Master/Detail pages. For example, the page in Listing 9.23 displays a list of movie titles. Each movie title links to a page that contains detailed information for the movie.

LISTING 9.23   ShowQueryStringParameterMaster.aspx

```
<%@ Page Language="C#" %>
<!DOCTYPE html PUBLIC "-//W3C//DTD XHTML 1.1//EN"
 "http://www.w3.org/TR/xhtml11/DTD/xhtml11.dtd">
<html xmlns="http://www.w3.org/1999/xhtml" >
<head id="Head1" runat="server">
    <title>Show QueryStringParameter Master</title>
</head>
<body>
    <form id="form1" runat="server">
    <div>

    <asp:GridView
        id="grdMovies"
```

LISTING 9.23   Continued

```
          DataSourceId="srcMovies"
          AutoGenerateColumns="false"
          ShowHeader="false"
          Runat="server">
          <Columns>
          <asp:HyperLinkField
              DataTextField="Title"
              DataNavigateUrlFields="Id"

DataNavigateUrlFormatString="ShowQueryStringParameterDetails.aspx?id={0}" />
          </Columns>
      </asp:GridView>

      <asp:SqlDataSource
          id="srcMovies"
          SelectCommand="SELECT * FROM Movies"
          ConnectionString="<%$ ConnectionStrings:Movies %>"
          Runat="server" />

      </div>
      </form>
</body>
</html>
```

Notice that the ID of the movie is passed to the ShowQueryStringParameterDetails.aspx page. The movie ID is passed in a query string field named id.

The page in Listing 9.24 displays detailed information for a particular movie.

LISTING 9.24   ShowQueryStringParameterDetails.aspx

```
<%@ Page Language="C#" %>
<!DOCTYPE html PUBLIC "-//W3C//DTD XHTML 1.1//EN"
  "http://www.w3.org/TR/xhtml11/DTD/xhtml11.dtd">
<html xmlns="http://www.w3.org/1999/xhtml" >
<head id="Head1" runat="server">
    <title>Show QueryStringParameter Details</title>
</head>
<body>
    <form id="form1" runat="server">
    <div>

    <asp:DetailsView
        id="dtlMovie"
        DataSourceID="srcMovie"
```

```
            Runat="server" />

    <asp:SqlDataSource
        id="srcMovie"
        SelectCommand="SELECT * FROM Movies
            WHERE Id=@Id"
        ConnectionString="<%$ ConnectionStrings:Movies %>"
        Runat="server">
        <SelectParameters>
            <asp:QueryStringParameter
                Name="Id"
                QueryStringField="Id" />
        </SelectParameters>
    </asp:SqlDataSource>

    </div>
    </form>
</body>
</html>
```

Notice that the SqlDataSource control in Listing 9.24 includes a QueryStringParameter. The QueryStringParameter is used to supply the movie ID in the SqlDataSource control's SelectCommand.

Using the SessionParameter Object

The SessionParameter object enables you to represent any item stored in Session state. It includes all the properties of the base Parameter class and the following property:

▶ **SessionField**—The name of the item stored in Session state that the SessionParameter represents.

NOTE

Session state is discussed in detail in Chapter 24, "Maintaining Application State."

The page in Listing 9.25 contains a GridView that displays a list of movies matching a movie category. The movie category is stored in Session state.

LISTING 9.25   ShowSessionParameter.aspx

```
<%@ Page Language="C#" %>
<!DOCTYPE html PUBLIC "-//W3C//DTD XHTML 1.1//EN"
"http://www.w3.org/TR/xhtml11/DTD/xhtml11.dtd">
<script runat="server">
```

LISTING 9.25 Continued

```
    void Page_Load()
    {
        Session["MovieCategoryName"] = "Animation";
    }

</script>
<html xmlns="http://www.w3.org/1999/xhtml" >
<head id="Head1" runat="server">
    <title>Show SessionParameter</title>
</head>
<body>
    <form id="form1" runat="server">
    <div>

    <asp:GridView
        id="grdMovies"
        DataSourceID="srcMovies"
        Runat="server" />

    <asp:SqlDataSource
        id="srcMovies"
        SelectCommand="SELECT Name As Category,Title,Director
            FROM Movies
            INNER JOIN MovieCategories
            ON CategoryId = MovieCategories.id
            WHERE Name=@Name"
        ConnectionString="<%$ ConnectionStrings:Movies %>"
        Runat="server">
        <SelectParameters>
        <asp:SessionParameter
            Name="Name"
            SessionField="MovieCategoryName" />
        </SelectParameters>
    </asp:SqlDataSource>

    </div>
    </form>
</body>
</html>
```

Notice that the current movie category is added to the Session object in the Page_Load() method. The SqlDataSource reads the MovieCategoryName item from Session state when it retrieves the list of movies that the GridView displays.

Programmatically Executing `SqlDataSource` Commands

You aren't required to use the `SqlDataSource` control only when working with `DataBound` controls. You can create parameters and execute the commands represented by a `SqlDataSource` control by working directly with the properties and methods of the `SqlDataSource` control in your code.

In this section, you learn how to add parameters programmatically to a `SqlDataSource` control. You also learn how to execute select, insert, update, and delete commands when using the `SqlDataSource` control.

Adding ADO.NET Parameters

Under the covers, the `SqlDataSource` control uses ADO.NET objects such as the ADO.NET `DataSet`, `DataReader`, `Parameter`, and `Command` objects to interact with a database. In particular, any ASP.NET Parameter objects that you declare when working with the `SqlDataSource` control get converted into ADO.NET `Parameter` objects.

In some cases, you will want to work directly with these ADO.NET `Parameter` objects when using the `SqlDataSource` control. For example, you might want to add additional ADO.NET parameters programmatically before executing a command.

The page in Listing 9.26 automatically adds an ADO.NET parameter that represents the current user's username to the command that the `SqlDataSource` executes.

LISTING 9.26 AddParameter.aspx

```
<%@ Page Language="C#" %>
<%@ Import Namespace="System.Data.SqlClient" %>
<!DOCTYPE html PUBLIC "-//W3C//DTD XHTML 1.1//EN"
"http://www.w3.org/TR/xhtml11/DTD/xhtml11.dtd">
<script runat="server">

    protected void srcGuestBook_Inserting(object sender,
    ➡SqlDataSourceCommandEventArgs e)
    {
        e.Command.Parameters.Add(new SqlParameter("@Name", User.Identity.Name));
    }
</script>

<html xmlns="http://www.w3.org/1999/xhtml" >
<head id="Head1" runat="server">
    <title>Show ProfileParameter</title>
</head>
<body>
```

LISTING 9.26   Continued

```
<form id="form1" runat="server">
<div>

<asp:FormView
    id="frmGuestBook"
    DataSourceID="srcGuestBook"
    DefaultMode="Insert"
    Runat="server">
    <InsertItemTemplate>
    <asp:Label
        id="lblComments"
        Text="Enter Your Comments:"
        Runat="server" />
    <br />
    <asp:TextBox
        id="txtComments"
        Text='<%# Bind("Comments") %>'
        TextMode="MultiLine"
        Columns="50"
        Rows="4"
        Runat="server" />
    <br />
    <asp:Button
        id="btnInsert"
        Text="Add Comments"
        CommandName="Insert"
        Runat="server" />
    </InsertItemTemplate>
</asp:FormView>

<hr />

<asp:GridView
    id="grdGuestBook"
    DataSourceID="srcGuestBook"
    Runat="server" />

<asp:SqlDataSource
    id="srcGuestBook"
    SelectCommand="SELECT Name,Comments,EntryDate
        FROM GuestBook ORDER BY Id DESC"
    InsertCommand="INSERT GuestBook (Name,Comments)
        VALUES (@Name,@Comments)"
    ConnectionString="<%$ ConnectionStrings:GuestBook %>"
```

```
        Runat="server" OnInserting="srcGuestBook_Inserting" />

    </div>
    </form>
</body>
</html>
```

Notice that the page in Listing 9.26 includes a srcGuestBook_Inserting() event handler. This event handler executes immediately before the SqlDataSource control executes its insert command. In the event handler, a new ADO.NET Parameter is added to the insert command, which represents the current user's username.

> **NOTE**
>
> The names of ADO.NET parameters, unlike ASP.NET parameters, always start with the character @.

Executing Insert, Update, and Delete Commands

The SqlDataSource control has methods that correspond to each of the different types of commands that it represents:

- ▶ **Delete**—Enables you to execute a SQL delete command.
- ▶ **Insert**—Enables you to execute a SQL insert command.
- ▶ **Select**—Enables you to execute a SQL select command.
- ▶ **Update**—Enables you to execute a SQL update command.

For example, the page in Listing 9.27 contains a form for adding new entries to the GuestBook database table. This form is not contained in a DataBound control such as the FormView or DetailsView controls. The form is contained in the body of the page. When you click the Add Entry button, the SqlDataSource control's Insert() method is executed.

LISTING 9.27   ExecuteInsert.aspx

```
<%@ Page Language="C#" %>
<!DOCTYPE html PUBLIC "-//W3C//DTD XHTML 1.1//EN"
"http://www.w3.org/TR/xhtml11/DTD/xhtml11.dtd">
<script runat="server">

    /// <summary>
    /// When button clicked, execute Insert command
    /// </summary>
    protected void btnAddEntry_Click(object sender, EventArgs e)
    {
        srcGuestBook.InsertParameters["Name"].DefaultValue = txtName.Text;
```

6

LISTING 9.27   Continued

```
        srcGuestBook.InsertParameters["Comments"].DefaultValue = txtComments.Text;
        srcGuestBook.Insert();
    }
</script>

<html xmlns="http://www.w3.org/1999/xhtml" >
<head id="Head1" runat="server">
    <title>Execute Insert</title>
</head>
<body>
    <form id="form1" runat="server">
    <div>

    <asp:Label
        id="lblName"
        Text="Name:"
        AssociatedControlId="txtName"
        Runat="server" />
    <br />
    <asp:TextBox
        id="txtName"
        Runat="server" />

    <br /><br />

    <asp:Label
        id="lblComments"
        Text="Comments:"
        AssociatedControlId="txtComments"
        Runat="server" />
    <br />
    <asp:TextBox
        id="txtComments"
        TextMode="MultiLine"
        Columns="50"
        Rows="2"
        Runat="server" />

    <br /><br />

    <asp:Button
        id="btnAddEntry"
        Text="Add Entry"
        Runat="server" OnClick="btnAddEntry_Click" />
```

```
    <hr />

    <asp:GridView
        id="grdGuestBook"
        DataSourceId="srcGuestBook"
        Runat="server" />

    <asp:SqlDataSource
        id="srcGuestBook"
        ConnectionString="<%$ ConnectionStrings:GuestBook %>"
        SelectCommand="SELECT Name,Comments FROM GuestBook
            ORDER BY Id DESC"
        InsertCommand="INSERT GuestBook (Name,Comments)
            VALUES (@Name,@Comments)"
        Runat="server">
        <InsertParameters>
            <asp:Parameter Name="Name" />
            <asp:Parameter Name="Comments" />
        </InsertParameters>
    </asp:SqlDataSource>

    </div>
    </form>
</body>
</html>
```

Executing Select Commands

The procedure for executing a select command is different from executing insert, update, and delete commands because a select command returns data. This section discusses how you can execute the SqlDataSource control's Select() method programmatically and represent the data that the method returns.

Remember that a SqlDataSource control can return either a DataView or DataReader depending on the value of its DataSourceMode property. The SqlDataSource control's Select() method returns an object of type IEnumerable. Both DataViews and DataReaders implement the IEnumerable interface.

To understand how you can call the Select() method programmatically, look at the following simple photo gallery application. This application enables you to upload images to a database table and display them in a page (see Figure 9.14).

First, you need to create the page that displays the images and contains the form for adding new images. The PhotoGallery.aspx page is contained in Listing 9.28.

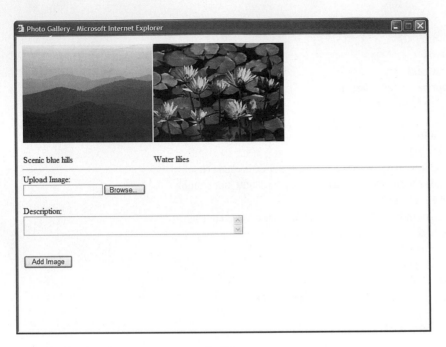

FIGURE 9.14   A photo gallery application.

LISTING 9.28   PhotoGallery.aspx

```
<%@ Page Language="C#" %>
<!DOCTYPE html PUBLIC "-//W3C//DTD XHTML 1.1//EN"
  "http://www.w3.org/TR/xhtml11/DTD/xhtml11.dtd">
<html xmlns="http://www.w3.org/1999/xhtml" >
<head id="Head1" runat="server">
    <title>Photo Gallery</title>
</head>
<body>
    <form id="form1" runat="server">
    <div>

    <asp:DataList
        id="dlstImages"
        DataSourceID="srcImages"
        RepeatColumns="3"
        Runat="server">
        <ItemTemplate>
        <asp:Image ID="Image1"
            ImageUrl='<%# String.Format("DynamicImage.ashx?id={0}", Eval("Id")) %>'
            Width="250"
            Runat="server" />
```

```
        <br />
        <%# Eval("Description") %>
</ItemTemplate>
</asp:DataList>

<hr />

<asp:FormView
    id="frmImage"
    DataSourceID="srcImages"
    DefaultMode="Insert"
    Runat="server">
    <InsertItemTemplate>
    <asp:Label
        id="lblImage"
        Text="Upload Image:"
        AssociatedControlId="upImage"
        Runat="server" />
    <br />
    <asp:FileUpload
        id="upImage"
        FileBytes='<%# Bind("Image") %>'
        Runat="server" />

    <br /><br />

    <asp:Label
        id="lblDescription"
        Text="Description:"
        AssociatedControlID="txtDescription"
        Runat="server" />
    <br />
    <asp:TextBox
        id="txtDescription"
        Text='<%# Bind("Description") %>'
        TextMode="MultiLine"
        Columns="50"
        Rows="2"
        Runat="server" />

    <br /><br />

    <asp:Button
        id="btnInsert"
        Text="Add Image"
        CommandName="Insert"
```

LISTING 9.28   Continued

```
            Runat="server" />
        </InsertItemTemplate>
    </asp:FormView>

    <asp:SqlDataSource
        id="srcImages"
        SelectCommand="SELECT ID,Description FROM Images"
        InsertCommand="INSERT Images (Image,Description)
            VALUES (@Image,@Description)"
        ConnectionString="<%$ ConnectionStrings:Images %>"
        Runat="server" />

    </div>
    </form>
</body>
</html>
```

The page in Listing 9.28 has a FormView control that contains a FileUpload control. You can use the FileUpload control to upload images from your local hard drive to the application's database table.

Also, the page contains a DataList control that is used to display the image. Notice that the Image control contained in the DataList control's ItemTemplate points to a file named DynamicImage.ashx. The DynamicImage.ashx file represents an HTTP Handler that renders a particular image. The DynamicImage.ashx handler is contained in Listing 9.29.

NOTE

HTTP handlers are discussed in detail in Chapter 27, "Working with the HTTP Runtime."

LISTING 9.29   DynamicImage.ashx

```
<%@ WebHandler Language="C#" Class="DynamicImage" %>

using System.Data;
using System.Web;
using System.Web.Configuration;
using System.Web.UI;
using System.Web.UI.WebControls;

/// <summary>
/// Displays an image corresponding to the Id passed
/// in a query string field
```

```
/// </summary>
public class DynamicImage : IHttpHandler
{

    public void ProcessRequest (HttpContext context)
    {
        // Get the Id of the image to display
        string imageId = context.Request.QueryString["Id"];

        // Use SqlDataSource to grab image bytes
        SqlDataSource src = new SqlDataSource();
        src.ConnectionString = WebConfigurationManager.ConnectionStrings
        ➥["Images"].ConnectionString;
        src.SelectCommand = "SELECT Image FROM Images WHERE Id=" + imageId;

        // Return a DataView

        DataView view = (DataView)src.Select(DataSourceSelectArguments.Empty);
        context.Response.BinaryWrite( (byte[])view[0]["Image"]);

        // Return a DataReader
        //src.DataSourceMode = SqlDataSourceMode.DataReader;
        //IDataReader reader = (IDataReader)src.Select
        ➥(DataSourceSelectArguments.Empty);
        //reader.Read();
        //context.Response.BinaryWrite((byte[])reader["Image"]);
        //reader.Close();

    }

    public bool IsReusable
    {
        get
        {
            return false;
        }
    }
}
```

In the ProcessRequest() method, an instance of the SqlDataSource control is created. The SqlDataSource control's ConnectionString and SelectCommand properties are initialized. Finally, the SqlDataSource control's Select() command is executed and the results are rendered with the Response.BinaryWrite() method.

Notice that the return value from the Select() method is cast explicitly to a DataView object. You need to cast the return value to either a DataView or IDataReader for it to work with the results of the Select() method.

In Listing 9.29, the image bytes are returned in a DataView. To illustrate how you can use the Select() method to return a DataReader, I've also included the code for returning the image with a DataReader, but I've added comments to the code so that it won't execute.

Caching Database Data with the SqlDataSource Control

The easiest way to dramatically improve the performance of a database-driven website is through caching. Retrieving data from a database is one of the slowest operations that you can perform in a web page. Retrieving data from memory, on the other hand, is lightning fast. The SqlDataSource control makes it easy to cache data in your server's memory.

Caching is discussed in detail in Chapter 25, "Caching Application Pages and Data." In that chapter, you learn about all the different caching options supported by the SqlDataSource control. However, because it is so easy to cache data with the SqlDataSource control and caching has such a dramatic impact on performance, I wanted to provide you with a quick sample of how you can use the SqlDataSource control to cache data in this chapter.

The page in Listing 9.30 displays a list of movies that are cached in memory.

LISTING 9.30   CacheSqlDataSource.aspx

```
<%@ Page Language="C#" %>
<!DOCTYPE html PUBLIC "-//W3C//DTD XHTML 1.1//EN"
"http://www.w3.org/TR/xhtml11/DTD/xhtml11.dtd">
<script runat="server">

    protected void srcMovies_Selecting(object sender,
    ➥SqlDataSourceSelectingEventArgs e)
    {
        lblMessage.Text = "Retrieving data from database";
    }
</script>
<html xmlns="http://www.w3.org/1999/xhtml" >
<head id="Head1" runat="server">
    <title>Cache SqlDataSource</title>
</head>
<body>
    <form id="form1" runat="server">
    <div>
```

```
<asp:Label
    id="lblMessage"
    EnableViewState="false"
    Runat="server" />
<br /><br />

<asp:GridView
    id="grdMovies"
    DataSourceID="srcMovies"
    Runat="server" />

<asp:SqlDataSource
    id="srcMovies"
    EnableCaching="True"
    CacheDuration="3600"
    SelectCommand="SELECT * FROM Movies"
    ConnectionString="<%$ ConnectionStrings:Movies %>"
    Runat="server" OnSelecting="srcMovies_Selecting" />

</div>
</form>
</body>
</html>
```

In Listing 9.30, two properties of the SqlDataSource control related to caching are set. First, the EnableCaching property is set to the value True. Next, the CacheDuration property is set to a value that represents 3,600 seconds (one hour). The movies are cached in memory for a maximum of one hour. If you don't supply a value for the CacheDuration property, the default value is Infinite.

> **WARNING**
>
> It is important to understand that there is no guarantee that the SqlDataSource control will cache data for the amount of time specified by its CacheDuration property. Behind the scenes, the SqlDataSource control uses the Cache object for caching. This object supports scavenging. When memory resources become low, the Cache object automatically removes items from the cache.

Notice that the page in Listing 9.30 includes a srcMovies_Selecting() event handler. This handler is called only when the movies are retrieved from the database rather than from memory. In other words, you can use this event handler to detect when the movies are dropped from the cache (see Figure 9.15).

The page in Listing 9.30 illustrates only one type of caching that you can use with the SqlDataSource control. In Chapter 25, you learn about all the advanced caching options supported by the SqlDataSource control. For example, by taking advantage of SQL cache dependencies, you can reload the cached data represented by a SqlDataSource control automatically when data in a database is changed. For more information, see the final section of Chapter 25.

Id	CategoryId	Title	Director	DateReleased
1	3	Titanic	James Cameron	6/21/1997 12:00:00 AM
2	1	Star Wars	George Lucas	6/1/1977 12:00:00 AM
3	1	Jurassic Park	Steven Spielberg	6/17/1993 12:00:00 AM
4	4	Jaws	Steven Spielberg	5/30/1975 12:00:00 AM
5	3	Ghost	Jerry Zucker	6/14/1990 12:00:00 AM
7	3	Forrest Gump	Robert Zemeckis	6/18/1994 12:00:00 AM
8	2	Ice Age	Chris Wedge	6/26/2002 12:00:00 AM
9	2	Shrek	Andrew Adamson	6/25/2001 12:00:00 AM
10	1	Independence Day	Roland Emmerich	6/20/1996 12:00:00 AM
11	4	The Ring	Gore Verbinski	6/26/2002 12:00:00 AM
21	0	King Kong	Jackson	12/25/1966 12:00:00 AM

FIGURE 9.15   Caching the data represented by a SqlDataSource control.

Summary

In this chapter, you learned how to use the SqlDataSource control to connect and execute commands against a SQL relational database. In the first section, you learned how to represent database connection strings with the SqlDataSource control. You learned how to store connection strings in the web configuration file and encrypt the connection strings.

Next, you learned how to execute both inline SQL commands and stored procedures. You also learned how to cancel commands and handle errors gracefully.

This chapter also discussed the different types of ASP.NET parameters that you can use with the SqlDataSource control. You learned how to use the Parameter, ControlParameter, CookieParameter, FormParameter, ProfileParameter, SessionParameter, and QueryStringParameter objects.

Finally, you learned how to improve the performance of your database-driven applications through caching. You learned how you can cache the data represented by a SqlDataSource control in server memory and avoid accessing the database with each page request.

CHAPTER 10

Using List Controls

The List controls enable you to display simple lists of options. For example, you can use the RadioButtonList control to display a group of radio buttons, or the BulletedList control to display a list of links.

In this chapter, you learn how to use each of the List controls included in the ASP.NET Framework. In particular, it discusses the DropDownList, RadioButtonList, ListBox, CheckBoxList, and BulletedList controls. You learn how to bind the different types of List controls to a data source such as a database table. You also learn how to work directly with the list items contained by a List control.

Finally, at the end of this chapter, you learn how to build a custom List control. We create a client-side multi-select List control that enables you to select multiple list items at a time.

Overview of the List Controls

All five of the List controls inherit from the base ListControl class. This means that all the List controls share a common set of properties and methods. In this section, you are provided with an overview of the common features of the List controls.

Declaring List Items

The List controls render a list of options. Each option is represented by an instance of the ListItem class. For example, you can use the page in Listing 10.1 to render a set of options for selecting your favorite movie (see Figure 10.1).

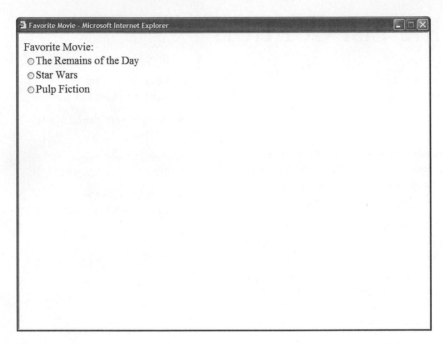

FIGURE 10.1   Displaying a list of movies.

LISTING 10.1   FavoriteMovie.aspx

```
<%@ Page Language="C#" %>
<!DOCTYPE html PUBLIC "-//W3C//DTD XHTML 1.1//EN"
"http://www.w3.org/TR/xhtml11/DTD/xhtml11.dtd">
<html xmlns="http://www.w3.org/1999/xhtml" >
<head id="Head1" runat="server">
    <title>Favorite Movie</title>
</head>
<body>
    <form id="form1" runat="server">
    <div>

    <asp:Label
        id="lblMovies"
        Text="Favorite Movie:"
        AssociatedControlID="rblMovies"
        Runat="server" />

    <asp:RadioButtonList
```

```
            id="rblMovies"
            Runat="server">
            <asp:ListItem
                Text="The Remains of the Day"
                Value="movie1" />
            <asp:ListItem
                Text="Star Wars"
                Value="movie2" />
            <asp:ListItem
                Text="Pulp Fiction"
                Value="movie3" />
        </asp:RadioButtonList>

        </div>
        </form>
</body>
</html>
```

The page in Listing 10.1 contains a `RadioButtonList` control. This control contains three `ListItem` controls that correspond to the three radio buttons. All the List controls use the `ListItem` control to represent individual list items.

The `ListItem` control supports the following five properties:

▸ **`Attributes`**—Enables you to add HTML attributes to a list item.

▸ **`Enabled`**—Enables you to disable a list item.

▸ **`Selected`**—Enables you to mark a list item as selected.

▸ **`Text`**—Enables you to specify the text displayed by the list item.

▸ **`Value`**—Enables you to specify a hidden value associated with the list item.

You use the `Text` property to indicate the text that you want the option to display, and the `Value` property to indicate a hidden value associated with the option. For example, the hidden value might represent the value of a primary key column in a database table.

The `Selected` property enables you to show a list item as selected. Selected radio buttons and check boxes appear checked. The selected option in a `DropDownList` is the default option displayed. Selected options in a `ListBox` appear highlighted. And, in the case of a `BulletedList` control, the `selected` property has no effect whatsoever.

The `Enabled` property has different effects when used with different List controls. When you set a `ListItem` control's `Enabled` property to the value `False` when using the `DropDownList` or `ListBox` controls, the list item is not rendered to the browser. When you use this property with a `CheckBoxList`, `RadioButtonList`, or `BulletedList` control, then the list item is ghosted and non-functional.

10

Binding to a Data Source

You can bind any of the List controls to a data source. The List controls support both declarative databinding and programmatic databinding.

For example, the page in Listing 10.2 contains a `DropDownList` control that is bound to the Movies database table with declarative databinding (see Figure 10.2).

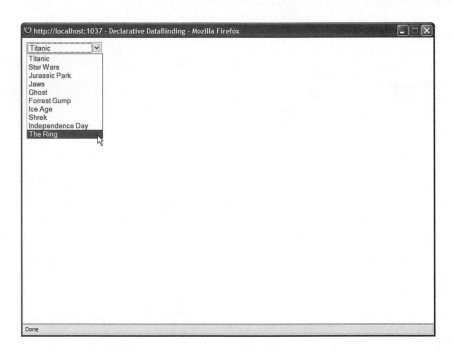

FIGURE 10.2   Displaying list items with declarative databinding.

LISTING 10.2   `DeclarativeDataBinding.aspx`

```
<%@ Page Language="C#" %>
<!DOCTYPE html PUBLIC "-//W3C//DTD XHTML 1.1//EN"
"http://www.w3.org/TR/xhtml11/DTD/xhtml11.dtd">
<html xmlns="http://www.w3.org/1999/xhtml" >
<head id="Head1" runat="server">
    <title>Declarative DataBinding</title>
</head>
<body>
    <form id="form1" runat="server">
    <div>

    <asp:DropDownList
        id="ddlMovies"
        DataSourceID="srcMovies"
```

```
        DataTextField="Title"
        DataValueField="Id"
        Runat="server" />

    <asp:SqlDataSource
        id="srcMovies"
        SelectCommand="SELECT Id, Title FROM Movies"
        ConnectionString="<%$ ConnectionStrings:Movies %>"
        Runat="server" />

    </div>
    </form>
</body>
</html>
```

Notice that the DropDownList control's DataSourceID property points to the ID of the SqlDataSource control. When you open the page in Listing 10.2, the SqlDataSource control retrieves the records from the Movies database table. The DropDownList control grabs these records from the SqlDataSource control and creates a ListItem control for each data item.

You also should notice that the DropDownList control has both its DataTextField and DataValueField properties set. When the DropDownList control creates each of its list items, it uses the values of the DataTextField and DataValueField properties to set the Text and Value properties of each list item.

As an alternative to declarative databinding, you can programmatically bind any of the List controls to a data source. For example, the page in Listing 10.3 binds a ListBox control to a collection which represents a shopping cart (see Figure 10.3).

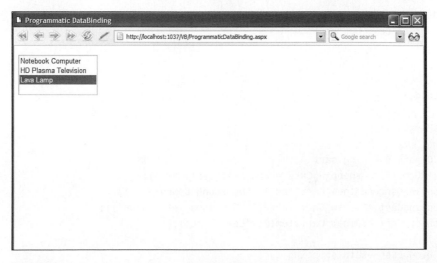

FIGURE 10.3   Show list items with programmatic binding.

LISTING 10.3   ProgrammaticDataBinding.aspx

```
<%@ Page Language="C#" %>
<%@ Import Namespace="System.Collections.Generic" %>
<!DOCTYPE html PUBLIC "-//W3C//DTD XHTML 1.1//EN"
"http://www.w3.org/TR/xhtml11/DTD/xhtml11.dtd">
<script runat="server">

    /// <summary>
    /// Represents an item in the
    /// shopping cart
    /// </summary>
    public class CartItem
    {
        private int _id;
        public string _description;

        public int Id
        {
            get { return _id; }
        }

        public string Description
        {
            get { return _description; }
        }

        public CartItem(int id, string description)
        {
            _id = id;
            _description = description;
        }
    }

    void Page_Load()
    {
        if (!IsPostBack)
        {
            // Create shopping cart
            List<CartItem> shoppingCart = new List<CartItem>();
            shoppingCart.Add(new CartItem(1, "Notebook Computer"));
            shoppingCart.Add(new CartItem(2, "HD Plasma Television"));
            shoppingCart.Add(new CartItem(3, "Lava Lamp"));

            // Bind ListBox to shopping cart
```

```
            lstShoppingCart.DataSource = shoppingCart;
            lstShoppingCart.DataBind();
        }
    }
</script>

<html xmlns="http://www.w3.org/1999/xhtml" >
<head id="Head1" runat="server">
    <title>Programmatic DataBinding</title>
</head>
<body>
    <form id="form1" runat="server">
    <div>

    <asp:ListBox
        id="lstShoppingCart"
        DataTextField="Description"
        DataValueField="Id"
        Runat="server" />

    </div>
    </form>
</body>
</html>
```

In Listing 10.3, the ListBox is bound to the collection in the Page_Load() method. Notice that the DataTextField and DataValueField properties of the ListBox control represent properties of the CartItem class.

NOTE

A List control's DataTextField and DataValueField properties can refer to any public property of a class, but you cannot bind a List control to a public field.

Determining the Selected List Item

Displaying options with the List controls is all very nice, but at some point you need to be able to determine which option a user has selected. The List controls support three properties that you can use to determine the selected list item:

▶ **SelectedIndex**—Gets or sets the index of the selected list item.

▶ **SelectedItem**—Gets the first selected list item.

▶ **SelectedValue**—Gets or sets the value of the first selected list item.

For example, the page in Listing 10.4 enables you to select an item from the DropDownList control and display the value of the selected item's Text property (see Figure 10.4).

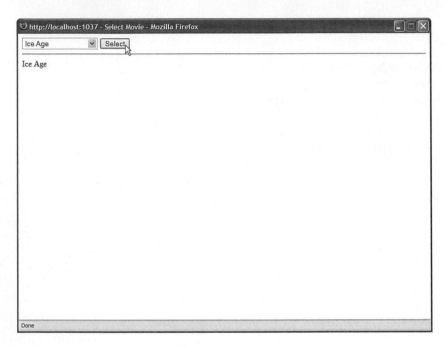

FIGURE 10.4 Selecting an item from a DropDownList control.

LISTING 10.4 SelectMovie.aspx

```
<%@ Page Language="C#" %>
<!DOCTYPE html PUBLIC "-//W3C//DTD XHTML 1.1//EN"
"http://www.w3.org/TR/xhtml11/DTD/xhtml11.dtd">
<script runat="server">

    protected void btnSelect_Click(object sender, EventArgs e)
    {
        lblSelectedMovie.Text = ddlMovies.SelectedItem.Text;
    }
</script>
<html xmlns="http://www.w3.org/1999/xhtml" >
<head id="Head1" runat="server">
    <title>Select Movie</title>
</head>
<body>
    <form id="form1" runat="server">
    <div>
```

```
<asp:DropDownList
    id="ddlMovies"
    DataSourceID="srcMovies"
    DataTextField="Title"
    DataValueField="Id"
    Runat="server" />

<asp:Button
    id="btnSelect"
    Text="Select"
    OnClick="btnSelect_Click"
    Runat="server" />

<hr />

<asp:Label
    id="lblSelectedMovie"
    Runat="server" />

<asp:SqlDataSource
    id="srcMovies"
    SelectCommand="SELECT Id, Title FROM Movies"
    ConnectionString="<%$ ConnectionStrings:Movies %>"
    Runat="server" />

</div>
</form>
</body>
</html>
```

The SelectedItem property is used to retrieve the selected ListItem control from the DropDownList control. The value of the selected item's Text property is displayed in the Label control.

You can use these properties when you want to associate a List control with another DataBound control. For example, the page in Listing 10.5 contains a DropDownList control that displays a list of movie categories and a GridView control that displays a list of movies that match the selected category (see Figure 10.5).

LISTING 10.5   ShowMoviesByCategory.aspx

```
<%@ Page Language="C#" %>
<!DOCTYPE html PUBLIC "-//W3C//DTD XHTML 1.1//EN"
"http://www.w3.org/TR/xhtml11/DTD/xhtml11.dtd">
<html xmlns="http://www.w3.org/1999/xhtml" >
<head id="Head1" runat="server">
```

LISTING 10.5   Continued

```
    <style type="text/css">
        .gridView
        {
            margin-top:20px;
        }
        .gridView td, .gridView th
        {
            padding:10px;
        }
    </style>
    <title>Show Movies by Category</title>
</head>
<body>
    <form id="form1" runat="server">
    <div>

    <asp:DropDownList
        id="ddlMovieCategory"
        DataSourceID="srcMovieCategories"
        DataTextField="Name"
        DataValueField="Id"
        Runat="server" />

    <asp:Button
        id="btnSelect"
        Text="Select"
        Runat="server" />

    <asp:GridView
        id="grdMovies"
        DataSourceID="srcMovies"
        CssClass="gridView"
        Runat="server" />

    <asp:SqlDataSource
        id="srcMovieCategories"
        SelectCommand="SELECT Id, Name FROM MovieCategories"
        ConnectionString="<%$ ConnectionStrings:Movies %>"
        Runat="server" />

    <asp:SqlDataSource
        id="srcMovies"
        SelectCommand="SELECT Title,Director FROM Movies
            WHERE CategoryId=@Id"
```

```
        ConnectionString="<%$ ConnectionStrings:Movies %>"
        Runat="server">
        <SelectParameters>
        <asp:ControlParameter
            Name="Id"
            ControlID="ddlMovieCategory"
            PropertyName="SelectedValue" />
        </SelectParameters>
    </asp:SqlDataSource>

    </div>
    </form>
</body>
</html>
```

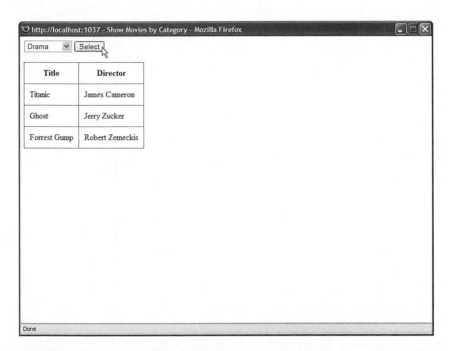

FIGURE 10.5   Master/Details form with a list control.

The DropDownList control is bound to the srcMovieCategories SqlDataSource control, and the GridView control is bound to the srcMovies SqlDataSource control. The srcMovies SqlDataSource control includes a ControlParameter, which represents the SelectedValue property of the DropDownList control. When you select a movie category from the DropDownList control, the selected value changes and the GridView control displays a list of matching movies.

10

Appending Data Items

You can mix the list items that you declare in a List control and the list items that are added to the control when it is bound to a data source. This is useful when you want to display a default selection.

For example, imagine that you are creating a form in which you want to require a user to pick an item from a List control. In this situation, you should add a default item to the List control so you can detect whether a user has actually picked an item.

You can mix declarative list items with databound list items by assigning the value True to the AppendDataBoundItems property. The page in Listing 10.6 illustrates how you can add a default list item to a List control (see Figure 10.6).

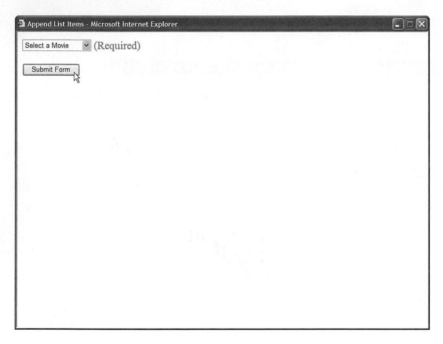

FIGURE 10.6   Displaying a default list item.

LISTING 10.6   AppendListItems.aspx

```
<%@ Page Language="C#" %>
<!DOCTYPE html PUBLIC "-//W3C//DTD XHTML 1.1//EN"
"http://www.w3.org/TR/xhtml11/DTD/xhtml11.dtd">
<html xmlns="http://www.w3.org/1999/xhtml" >
<head id="Head1" runat="server">
    <title>Append List Items</title>
</head>
```

```
<body>
    <form id="form1" runat="server">
    <div>

    <asp:DropDownList
        id="ddlMovies"
        DataSourceID="srcMovies"
        DataTextField="Title"
        DataValueField="Id"
        AppendDataBoundItems="True"
        Runat="server">
        <asp:ListItem
            Text="Select a Movie"
            Value="" />
    </asp:DropDownList>

    <asp:RequiredFieldValidator
        id="valMovies"
        Text="(Required)"
        ControlToValidate="ddlMovies"
        Runat="server" />

    <br /><br />

    <asp:Button
        id="btnSubmit"
        Text="Submit Form"
        Runat="server" />

    <asp:SqlDataSource
        id="srcMovies"
        SelectCommand="SELECT Id, Title FROM Movies"
        ConnectionString="<%$ ConnectionStrings:Movies %>"
        Runat="server" />

    </div>
    </form>
</body>
</html>
```

The page in Listing 10.6 includes both a DropDownList control and a
RequiredFieldValidator control. The DropDownList control includes a list item that
displays the text "Select a Movie." The Value property of this list item is set to the empty
string. If you attempt to submit the form without selecting a list item other than the
default list item, then the RequiredFieldValidator displays an error message.

Notice that the `DropDownList` control includes an `AppendDataBoundItems` property that is set to the value `True`. If you neglect to set this property, then the databound list items overwrite any declarative list items.

Enabling Automatic PostBacks

All the List controls, except for the `BulletedList` control, support a property named the `AutoPostBack` property. When this property is assigned the value `True`, the form containing the List control is automatically posted back to the server whenever a new selection is made.

For example, the page in Listing 10.7 contains a `DropDownList` control that has its `AutoPostBack` property enabled. When you select a new item from the `DropDownList` control, the page is automatically posted back to the server and the Label control displays the selected item.

LISTING 10.7   `AutoPostBackListControl.aspx`

```
<%@ Page Language="C#" %>
<!DOCTYPE html PUBLIC "-//W3C//DTD XHTML 1.1//EN"
"http://www.w3.org/TR/xhtml11/DTD/xhtml11.dtd">
<script runat="server">

    protected void ddlMovies_SelectedIndexChanged(object sender, EventArgs e)
    {
        lblSelectedMovie.Text = ddlMovies.SelectedItem.Text;
    }
</script>
<html xmlns="http://www.w3.org/1999/xhtml" >
<head id="Head1" runat="server">
    <title>AutoPostBack List Control</title>
</head>
<body>
    <form id="form1" runat="server">
    <div>

    <asp:DropDownList
        id="ddlMovies"
        DataSourceID="srcMovies"
        DataTextField="Title"
        DataValueField="Id"
        AutoPostBack="true"
        OnSelectedIndexChanged="ddlMovies_SelectedIndexChanged"
        Runat="server" />

    <br /><br />
```

```
    <asp:Label
        id="lblSelectedMovie"
        Runat="server" />

    <asp:SqlDataSource
        id="srcMovies"
        SelectCommand="SELECT Id, Title FROM Movies"
        ConnectionString="<%$ ConnectionStrings:Movies %>"
        Runat="server" />

    </div>
    </form>
</body>
</html>
```

When you enable the `AutoPostBack` property, a JavaScript `onchange()` event handler is added to the List control. The `onchange` event is supported by all recent browsers including Firefox 1.0 and Opera 8.0.

Notice that the `DropDownList` control has a `SelectedIndexChanged` event handler named `ddlMovies_SelectedIndexChanged()`. The `SelectedIndexChanged` event is raised whenever you make a new selection in the List control (independent of the `AutoPostBack` property). The `ddlMovies_SelectedIndexChanged()` method displays the selected list item in a Label control.

WEB STANDARDS NOTE

You should avoid using the `AutoPostBack` property because it creates accessibility problems for persons with disabilities. If you can't use a mouse, and you are interacting with a website through the keyboard, having a page post back to the server whenever you make a selection change is a very frustrating experience.

Using the Items Collection

All the list items rendered by a List control are contained in the List control's list item collection. This collection is exposed by the `Items` property.

You can work directly with the list items in this collection. For example, you can add or remove particular list items or you can change the order of the list items.

The page in Listing 10.8 contains two `ListBox` controls and two button controls. When you click the Add button, a list item is moved from the first `ListBox` to the second `ListBox` control. When you click Remove, the list item is moved back to the original List control (see Figure 10.7).

10

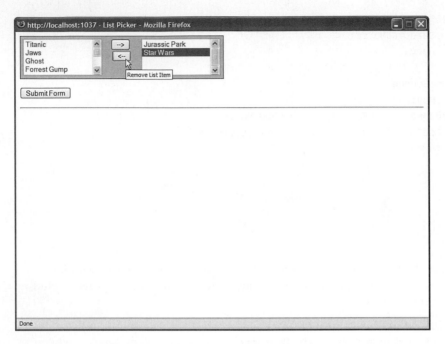

FIGURE 10.7   Using the `ListPicker` to select list items.

LISTING 10.8   ListPicker.aspx

```
<%@ Page Language="C#" %>
<!DOCTYPE html PUBLIC "-//W3C//DTD XHTML 1.1//EN"
"http://www.w3.org/TR/xhtml11/DTD/xhtml11.dtd">
<script runat="server">

    /// <summary>
    /// Move item from All Movies to Favorite Movies
    /// </summary>
    protected void btnAdd_Click(object sender, EventArgs e)
    {
        ListItem item = lstAllMovies.SelectedItem;
        if (item != null)
        {
            lstAllMovies.Items.Remove(item);
            lstFavoriteMovies.ClearSelection();
            lstFavoriteMovies.Items.Add(item);
        }
    }


    /// <summary>
    /// Move item from Favorite Movies to All Movies
```

```
    /// </summary>
    protected void btnRemove_Click(object sender, EventArgs e)
    {
        ListItem item = lstFavoriteMovies.SelectedItem;
        if (item != null)
        {
            lstFavoriteMovies.Items.Remove(item);
            lstAllMovies.ClearSelection();
            lstAllMovies.Items.Add(item);
        }
    }


    /// <summary>
    /// When the form is submitted,
    /// show the contents of the
    /// Favorite Movies ListBox
    /// </summary>
    protected void btnSubmit_Click(object sender, EventArgs e)
    {
        foreach (ListItem item in lstFavoriteMovies.Items)
            lblResults.Text += "<li>" + item.Text;
    }
</script>
<html xmlns="http://www.w3.org/1999/xhtml" >
<head id="Head1" runat="server">
    <style type="text/css">
        .listPicker
        {
            border:solid 1px black;
            padding:5px;
            width:380px;
            background-color:silver;
        }
        .listPicker select
        {
            width:100%;
        }
    </style>
    <title>List Picker</title>
</head>
<body>
    <form id="form1" runat="server">


    <div class="listPicker">
    <div style="float:left;width:40%">
```

10

LISTING 10.8   Continued

```
<asp:ListBox
    id="lstAllMovies"
    DataSourceID="srcMovies"
    DataTextField="Title"
    DataValueField="Id"
    Runat="server" />
</div>
<div style="float:left;width:20%;text-align:center">
<asp:Button
    id="btnAdd"
    Text="—&gt;"
    ToolTip="Add List Item"
    Runat="server" OnClick="btnAdd_Click" />
<br />
<asp:Button
    id="btnRemove"
    Text="&lt;—"
    ToolTip="Remove List Item"
    Runat="server" OnClick="btnRemove_Click" />
</div>
<div style="float:left;width:40%">
<asp:ListBox
    id="lstFavoriteMovies"
    Runat="server" />
</div>
<br style="clear:both" />
</div>

<p>
<asp:Button
    id="btnSubmit"
    Text="Submit Form"
    Runat="server" OnClick="btnSubmit_Click" />
</p>

<hr />

<asp:Label
    id="lblResults"
    EnableViewState="false"
    Runat="server" />
```

```
<asp:SqlDataSource
    id="srcMovies"
    SelectCommand="SELECT Id, Title FROM Movies"
    ConnectionString="<%$ ConnectionStrings:Movies %>"
    Runat="server" />

    </form>
</body>
</html>
```

The first ListBox in Listing 10.8 is bound to the Movies database table. You can use the ListBox controls to pick your favorite movies by moving movie titles from the first ListBox to the second ListBox.

When you click the Add button, the btnAdd_Click() method executes. This method grabs the selected item from the All Movies ListBox and adds it to the Favorite Movies ListBox. The Remove button does exactly the opposite.

Notice that both the btnAdd_Click() and btnRemove_Click() methods call the ClearSelection() method of the ListBox class. This method iterates through all the list items and sets the Selected property for each list item to the value False. If multiple list items are selected, an exception is thrown.

> **NOTE**
>
> One problem with the page discussed in this section is that the page must be posted back to the server each time you move an item from the first ListBox to the second ListBox. At the end of this chapter, you learn how to create a MultiSelectList control, which uses a client-side script to get around this limitation.

Working with the DropDownList Control

The DropDownList control enables you to display a list of options while requiring a minimum of screen real estate. A user can select only one option at a time when using this control.

The page in Listing 10.9 illustrates how you can use the DropDownList control to display all the movie titles from the Movies database table (see Figure 10.8).

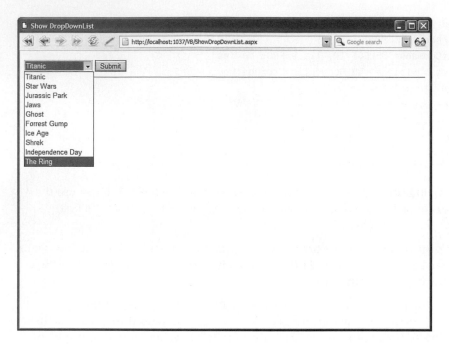

FIGURE 10.8   Displaying list items with the `DropDownList` control.

LISTING 10.9   ShowDropDownList.aspx

```
<%@ Page Language="C#" %>
<!DOCTYPE html PUBLIC "-//W3C//DTD XHTML 1.1//EN"
"http://www.w3.org/TR/xhtml11/DTD/xhtml11.dtd">
<script runat="server">

    protected void btnSubmit_Click(object sender, EventArgs e)
    {
        lblMovie.Text = ddlMovies.SelectedItem.Text;
    }
</script>
<html xmlns="http://www.w3.org/1999/xhtml" >
<head id="Head1" runat="server">
    <title>Show DropDownList</title>
</head>
<body>
    <form id="form1" runat="server">
    <div>

    <asp:DropDownList
        id="ddlMovies"
        DataSourceID="srcMovies"
```

```
            DataTextField="Title"
            DataValueField="Id"
            Runat="server" />

        <asp:Button
            id="btnSubmit"
            Text="Submit"
            OnClick="btnSubmit_Click"
            Runat="server" />

        <hr />

        <asp:Label
            id="lblMovie"
            Runat="server" />

        <asp:SqlDataSource
            id="srcMovies"
            SelectCommand="SELECT Id, Title FROM Movies"
            ConnectionString="<%$ ConnectionStrings:Movies %>"
            Runat="server" />

    </div>
    </form>
</body>
</html>
```

The `DropDownList` control renders an HTML `<select>` tag. One problem with the HTML `<select>` tag is that it has an infinite z index. In other words, you can't place other objects, such as an absolutely positioned `<div>` tag, in front of a `DropDownList` control in a page.

One way to get around this problem is to use a third-party control such as the `EasyListBox` control (available at http://www.EasyListBox.com). This control works fine when other objects are layered over it. It also supports several advanced features such as multiple columns and images in list items.

Working with the `RadioButtonList` Control

The `RadioButtonList` control, like the `DropDownList` control, enables a user to select only one list item at a time. The `RadioButttonList` control displays a list of radio buttons that can be arranged either horizontally or vertically.

The page in Listing 10.10 illustrates how you can use the `RadioButtonList` control to display a list of movie titles (see Figure 10.9).

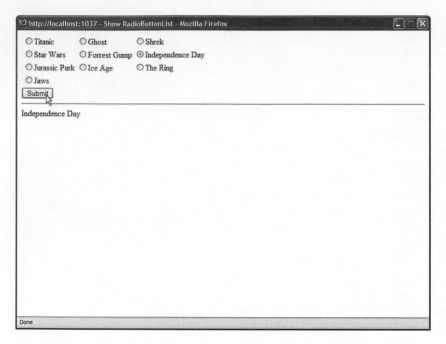

FIGURE 10.9   Displaying list items with the `RadioButtonList` control.

LISTING 10.10   ShowRadioButtonList.aspx

```
<%@ Page Language="C#" %>
<!DOCTYPE html PUBLIC "-//W3C//DTD XHTML 1.1//EN"
"http://www.w3.org/TR/xhtml11/DTD/xhtml11.dtd">
<script runat="server">

    protected void btnSubmit_Click(object sender, EventArgs e)
    {
        lblMovie.Text = rblMovies.SelectedItem.Text;
    }
</script>
<html xmlns="http://www.w3.org/1999/xhtml" >
<head id="Head1" runat="server">
    <title>Show RadioButtonList</title>
</head>
<body>
    <form id="form1" runat="server">
    <div>
```

```
<asp:RadioButtonList
    id="rblMovies"
    DataSourceID="srcMovies"
    DataTextField="Title"
    DataValueField="Id"
    RepeatColumns="3"
    Runat="server" />

<asp:Button
    id="btnSubmit"
    Text="Submit"
    Runat="server" OnClick="btnSubmit_Click" />

<hr />

<asp:Label
    id="lblMovie"
    Runat="server" />

<asp:SqlDataSource
    id="srcMovies"
    SelectCommand="SELECT Id, Title FROM Movies"
    ConnectionString="<%$ ConnectionStrings:Movies %>"
    Runat="server" />

    </div>
    </form>
</body>
</html>
```

In Listing 10.10, the radio buttons are rendered in a three-column layout. The RadioButtonList control includes three properties that have an effect on its layout:

▶ **RepeatColumns**—The number of columns of radio buttons to display.

▶ **RepeatDirection**—The direction that the radio buttons are repeated. Possible values are Horizontal and Vertical.

▶ **RepeatLayout**—Determines whether the radio buttons are displayed in an HTML table. Possible values are Table and Flow.

By default, the radio buttons rendered by the RadioButtonList control are rendered in an HTML table. If you set the RepeatLayout property to the value Flow, then the radio buttons are not rendered in a table. Even when the RadioButtonList renders its items in Flow layout mode, you can specify multiple columns.

10

Working with the `ListBox` Control

The `ListBox` control is similar to the `DropDownList` control with two important differences. First, the `ListBox` control requires more screen real estate because it always displays a certain number of list items. Furthermore, unlike the `DropDownList` control, the `ListBox` control enables a user to select multiple items.

The page in Listing 10.11 illustrates how you can enable a user to select a single item from a `ListBox` control (see Figure 10.10).

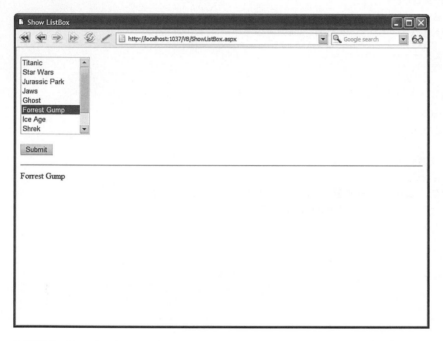

FIGURE 10.10   Displaying list items with the `ListBox` control.

LISTING 10.11   ShowListBox.aspx

```
<%@ Page Language="C#" %>
<!DOCTYPE html PUBLIC "-//W3C//DTD XHTML 1.1//EN"
"http://www.w3.org/TR/xhtml11/DTD/xhtml11.dtd">
<script runat="server">

    protected void btnSubmit_Click(object sender, EventArgs e)
    {
        lblMovie.Text = lstMovies.SelectedItem.Text;
    }
</script>
<html xmlns="http://www.w3.org/1999/xhtml" >
```

```
<head id="Head1" runat="server">
    <title>Show ListBox</title>
</head>
<body>
    <form id="form1" runat="server">
    <div>

    <asp:ListBox
        id="lstMovies"
        DataSourceID="srcMovies"
        DataTextField="Title"
        DataValueField="Id"
        Rows="8"
        Runat="server" />

    <p>
    <asp:Button
        id="btnSubmit"
        Text="Submit"
        OnClick="btnSubmit_Click"
        Runat="server" />
    </p>

    <hr />

    <asp:Label
        id="lblMovie"
        Runat="server" />

    <asp:SqlDataSource
        id="srcMovies"
        SelectCommand="SELECT Id, Title FROM Movies"
        ConnectionString="<%$ ConnectionStrings:Movies %>"
        Runat="server" />

    </div>
    </form>
</body>
</html>
```

Notice that the ListBox control in Listing 10.11 includes a Rows property. The Rows property determines the number of list items that the ListBox displays.

You can also configure the ListBox control to enable a user to select multiple items. This is illustrated in the page in Listing 10.12 (see Figure 10.11).

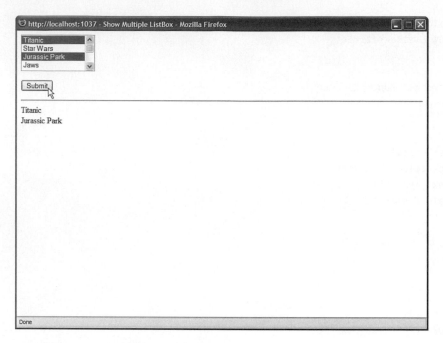

FIGURE 10.11   Selecting multiple list items.

LISTING 10.12   ShowMultipleListBox.aspx

```
<%@ Page Language="C#" %>
<!DOCTYPE html PUBLIC "-//W3C//DTD XHTML 1.1//EN"
"http://www.w3.org/TR/xhtml11/DTD/xhtml11.dtd">
<script runat="server">

    protected void btnSubmit_Click(object sender, EventArgs e)
    {
        foreach (ListItem item in lstMovies.Items)
            if (item.Selected)
                lblMovie.Text += "<li>" + item.Text;
    }
</script>
<html xmlns="http://www.w3.org/1999/xhtml" >
<head id="Head1" runat="server">
    <title>Show Multiple ListBox</title>
</head>
<body>
    <form id="form1" runat="server">
    <div>

    <asp:ListBox
```

```
        id="lstMovies"
        DataSourceID="srcMovies"
        DataTextField="Title"
        DataValueField="Id"
        SelectionMode="Multiple"
        Runat="server" />

    <p>
    <asp:Button
        id="btnSubmit"
        Text="Submit"
        OnClick="btnSubmit_Click"
        Runat="server" />
    </p>

    <hr />

    <asp:Label
        id="lblMovie"
        EnableViewState="false"
        Runat="server" />

    <asp:SqlDataSource
        id="srcMovies"
        SelectCommand="SELECT Id, Title FROM Movies"
        ConnectionString="<%$ ConnectionStrings:Movies %>"
        Runat="server" />

    </div>
    </form>
</body>
</html>
```

Notice that the `ListBox` in Listing 10.12 includes a `SelectionMode` property that is set to the value `Multiple`. A user can select multiple items from the `ListBox` by using the Ctrl or Shift key when clicking more than one list item.

WARNING

Most users don't understand how to select multiple items from a `ListBox` control. If you want to enable users to pick multiple items, a better approach is to use either the `CheckBoxList` control (discussed in the next section) or the `MultiSelectList` control (discussed in the final section of this chapter).

When you click the Submit button in Listing 10.12, all the selected list items are displayed in a Label control. The SelectedItem, SelectedIndex, and SelectedValue properties return only the first list item selected. When multiple items are selected, you need to iterate through the Items collection of the ListBox control to detect the selected items.

Working with the **CheckBoxList** Control

The CheckBoxList control renders a list of check boxes. The check boxes can be rendered horizontally or vertically. Unlike the other List controls, a user always can select multiple items when using a CheckBoxList control.

For example, the page in Listing 10.13 contains a CheckBoxList control that renders its list items in two columns (see Figure 10.12).

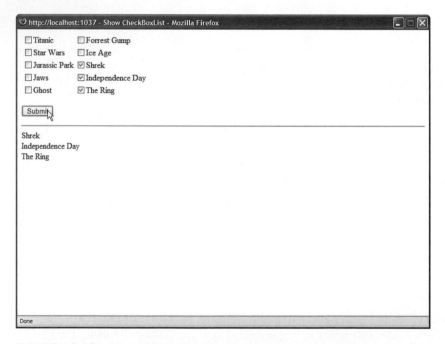

FIGURE 10.12   Displaying list items with the CheckBoxList control.

LISTING 10.13   ShowCheckBoxList.aspx

```
<%@ Page Language="C#" %>
<!DOCTYPE html PUBLIC "-//W3C//DTD XHTML 1.1//EN"
"http://www.w3.org/TR/xhtml11/DTD/xhtml11.dtd">
<script runat="server">
```

```
    protected void btnSubmit_Click(object sender, EventArgs e)
    {
        foreach (ListItem item in cblMovies.Items)
            if (item.Selected)
                lblMovie.Text += "<li>" + item.Text;
    }
</script>
<html xmlns="http://www.w3.org/1999/xhtml" >
<head id="Head1" runat="server">
    <title>Show CheckBoxList</title>
</head>
<body>
    <form id="form1" runat="server">
    <div>

    <asp:CheckBoxList
        id="cblMovies"
        DataSourceID="srcMovies"
        DataTextField="Title"
        DataValueField="Id"
        RepeatColumns="2"
        Runat="server" />

    <p>
    <asp:Button
        id="btnSubmit"
        Text="Submit"
        OnClick="btnSubmit_Click"
        Runat="server" />
    </p>

    <hr />

    <asp:Label
        id="lblMovie"
        EnableViewState="false"
        Runat="server" />

    <asp:SqlDataSource
        id="srcMovies"
        SelectCommand="SELECT Id, Title FROM Movies"
        ConnectionString="<%$ ConnectionStrings:Movies %>"
        Runat="server" />
```

10

LISTING 10.13   Continued

```
    </div>
    </form>
</body>
</html>
```

When you click the Submit button, the values of the Text property of any selected check boxes are displayed in a Label control. The selected check boxes are retrieved from the CheckBoxList control's Items property.

The CheckBoxList control includes three properties that affect its layout:

▶ **RepeatColumns**—The number of columns of check boxes to display.

▶ **RepeatDirection**—The direction in which the check boxes are rendered. Possible values are Horizontal and Vertical.

▶ **RepeatLayout**—Determines whether the check boxes are displayed in an HTML table. Possible values are Table and Flow.

Normally, a CheckBoxList control renders its list items in an HTML table. When the RepeatLayout property is set to the value Flow, the items are not rendered in a table.

Working with the `BulletedList` Control

The BulletedList control renders either an unordered (bulleted) or ordered (numbered) list. Each list item can be rendered as plain text, a LinkButton control, or a link to another web page.

For example, the page in Listing 10.14 uses the BulletedList control to render an unordered list of movies (see Figure 10.13).

LISTING 10.14   ShowBulletedList.aspx

```
<%@ Page Language="C#" %>
<!DOCTYPE html PUBLIC "-//W3C//DTD XHTML 1.1//EN"
"http://www.w3.org/TR/xhtml11/DTD/xhtml11.dtd">
<html xmlns="http://www.w3.org/1999/xhtml" >
<head id="Head1" runat="server">
    <title>Show BulletedList</title>
</head>
<body>
    <form id="form1" runat="server">
    <div>
```

```
<asp:BulletedList
    id="blMovies"
    DataSourceID="srcMovies"
    DataTextField="Title"
    Runat="server" />

<asp:SqlDataSource
    id="srcMovies"
    SelectCommand="SELECT Title FROM Movies"
    ConnectionString="<%$ ConnectionStrings:Movies %>"
    Runat="server" />

</div>
</form>
</body>
</html>
```

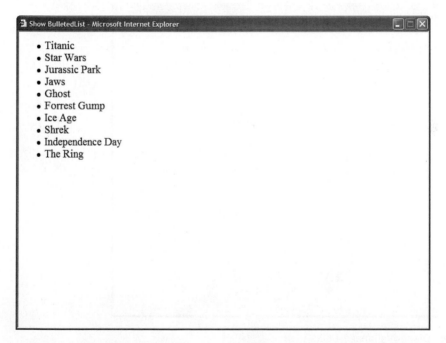

FIGURE 10.13   Displaying a list items with the BulletedList control.

You can control the appearance of the bullets that appear for each list item with the BulletStyle property. This property accepts the following values:

▶ Circle

▶ CustomImage

- ▶ Disc

- ▶ LowerAlpha

- ▶ LowerRoman

- ▶ NotSet

- ▶ Numbered

- ▶ Square

- ▶ UpperAlpha

- ▶ UpperRoman

You can set BulletStyle to Numbered to display a numbered list. If you set this property
to the value CustomImage and assign an image path to the BulletImageUrl property,
then you can associate an image with each list item. For example, the page in Listing
10.15 displays an image named Bullet.gif with each list item (see Figure 10.14).

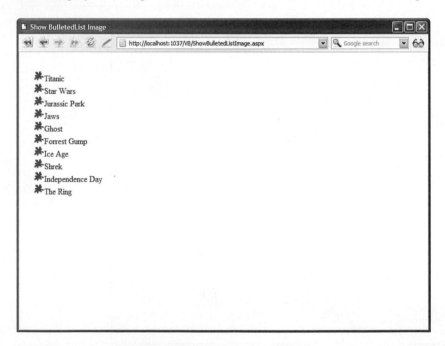

FIGURE 10.14   Displaying image bullets.

LISTING 10.15   ShowBulletedListImage.aspx

```
<%@ Page Language="C#" %>
<!DOCTYPE html PUBLIC "-//W3C//DTD XHTML 1.1//EN"
"http://www.w3.org/TR/xhtml11/DTD/xhtml11.dtd">
<html xmlns="http://www.w3.org/1999/xhtml" >
<head id="Head1" runat="server">
```

```
        <title>Show BulletedList Image</title>
</head>
<body>
    <form id="form1" runat="server">
    <div>

    <asp:BulletedList
        id="blMovies"
        DataSourceID="srcMovies"
        DataTextField="Title"
        BulletStyle="CustomImage"
        BulletImageUrl="~/Images/Bullet.gif"
        Runat="server" />

    <asp:SqlDataSource
        id="srcMovies"
        SelectCommand="SELECT Title FROM Movies"
        ConnectionString="<%$ ConnectionStrings:Movies %>"
        Runat="server" />

    </div>
    </form>
</body>
</html>
```

You can modify the appearance of each list item by modifying the value of the `DisplayMode` property. This property accepts one of the following values from the `BulletedListDisplayMode` enumeration:

▶ **HyperLink**—Each list item is rendered as a link to another page.

▶ **LinkButton**—Each list item is rendered by a LinkButton control.

▶ **Text**—Each list item is rendered as plain text.

For example, the page in Listing 10.16 displays a list of links to other websites (see Figure 10.15).

LISTING 10.16   `ShowBulletedListHyperLinks.aspx`

```
<%@ Page Language="C#" %>
<!DOCTYPE html PUBLIC "-//W3C//DTD XHTML 1.1//EN"
"http://www.w3.org/TR/xhtml11/DTD/xhtml11.dtd">
<html xmlns="http://www.w3.org/1999/xhtml" >
<head id="Head1" runat="server">
    <title>Show BulletedList HyperLinks</title>
</head>
```

10

LISTING 10.16   Continued

```
<body>
    <form id="form1" runat="server">

    <asp:BulletedList
        id="blWebsites"
        DisplayMode="HyperLink"
        Target="_blank"
        Runat="server">
        <asp:ListItem
            Text="Yahoo"
            Value="http://www.Yahoo.com" />
        <asp:ListItem
            Text="Google"
            Value="http://www.Google.com" />
        <asp:ListItem
            Text="Deja"
            Value="http://www.Deja.com" />
    </asp:BulletedList>

    </form>
</body>
</html>
```

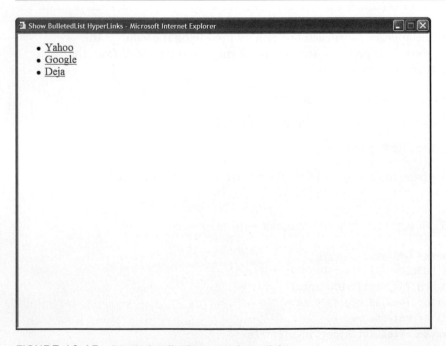

FIGURE 10.15   Displaying list items as hyperlinks.

Each list item has both its Text and Value properties set. The Text property contains the text that is displayed for the list item, and the Value property contains the URL for the other website. Notice that the Target property is set to the value blank. When you click one of the hyperlinks, the page is opened in a new window.

> **WARNING**
>
> The BulletedList control is different from the other List controls because it does not support the SelectedIndex, SelectedItem, and SelectedValue properties.

Creating a Custom List Control

All the List controls inherit from the base ListControl class. If you are not happy with the existing List controls, there is nothing to prevent you from building your own.

In this section, we create a custom List control named the MultiSelectList control. This control renders two list boxes and an Add and Remove button. You can click the buttons to move items between the two list boxes (see Figure 10.16).

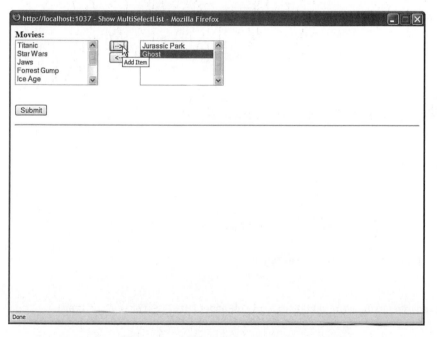

FIGURE 10.16   Using the MultiSelectList control.

The custom control uses client-side JavaScript to move the items between the two list boxes. Using JavaScript enables you to avoid posting the page back to the server each time a list item is moved. The client-side JavaScript is standards compliant so it will work with Internet Explorer 6.0, FireFox 1.0, and Opera 8.0.

The code for the custom `MultiSelectList` is contained in Listing 10.17.

LISTING 10.17 MultiSelectList.cs

```
using System;
using System.Data;
using System.Configuration;
using System.Web;
using System.Web.Security;
using System.Web.UI;
using System.Web.UI.WebControls;
using System.Web.UI.WebControls.WebParts;
using System.Web.UI.HtmlControls;

namespace MyControls
{
    /// <summary>
    /// Enables you to select mulitple list items
    /// from two list boxes
    /// </summary>
    [ValidationProperty("SelectedItem")]
    public class MultiSelectList : ListControl, IPostBackDataHandler
    {
        private int _rows = 5;
        private Unit _UnSelectedWidth = Unit.Parse("300px");
        private Unit _SelectedWidth = Unit.Parse("300px");


        /// <summary>
        /// This control is contained in a div
        /// tag
        /// </summary>
        protected override HtmlTextWriterTag TagKey
        {
            get { return HtmlTextWriterTag.Div; }
        }

        protected override void AddAttributesToRender(HtmlTextWriter writer)
        {
            writer.AddStyleAttribute("position", "relative");
            base.AddAttributesToRender(writer);
        }

        /// <summary>
        /// The number of rows of list items to display
        /// </summary>
```

```csharp
public int Rows
{
    get { return _rows; }
    set { _rows = value; }
}


/// <summary>
/// Name passed to client-side script
/// </summary>
private string BaseName
{
    get { return ClientID + ClientIDSeparator; }
}

/// <summary>
/// Name of unselected items list box
/// </summary>
private string UnselectedListName
{
    get { return BaseName + "unselected"; }
}

/// <summary>
/// Name of selected items list box
/// </summary>
private string SelectedListName
{
    get { return BaseName + "selected"; }
}

/// <summary>
/// Name of hidden input field
/// </summary>
private string HiddenName
{
    get { return BaseName + "hidden"; }
}

/// <summary>
/// Register client scripts
/// </summary>
protected override void OnPreRender(EventArgs e)
{
    Page.RegisterRequiresPostBack(this);
```

10

LISTING 10.17   Continued

```
      // Register hidden field
      Page.ClientScript.RegisterHiddenField(HiddenName, String.Empty);

      // Register Include File
      if (!Page.ClientScript.IsClientScriptIncludeRegistered
      ➥("MultiSelectList"))
          Page.ClientScript.RegisterClientScriptInclude("MultiSelectList",
          ➥Page.ResolveUrl("~/ClientScripts/MultiSelectList.js"));

      // Register submit script
      string submitScript = String.Format("multiSelectList_submit('{0}')",
      ➥BaseName);
      Page.ClientScript.RegisterOnSubmitStatement(this.GetType(),
      ➥this.ClientID, submitScript);

      base.OnPreRender(e);
  }

  /// <summary>
  /// Render list boxes and buttons
  /// </summary>
  protected override void RenderContents(HtmlTextWriter writer)
  {

      // Render Unselected
      RenderUnselected(writer);

      // Render Buttons
      RenderButtons(writer);

      // Render Selected
      RenderSelected(writer);

      // Render clear break
      writer.AddStyleAttribute("clear", "both");
      writer.RenderBeginTag(HtmlTextWriterTag.Br);
      writer.RenderEndTag();
  }

  /// <summary>
  /// Render the buttons
  /// </summary>
  private void RenderButtons(HtmlTextWriter writer)
  {
```

```
    writer.AddStyleAttribute("float", "left");
    writer.AddStyleAttribute(HtmlTextWriterStyle.Padding, "10px");
    writer.AddStyleAttribute(HtmlTextWriterStyle.TextAlign, "center");
    writer.RenderBeginTag(HtmlTextWriterTag.Div);

    string addScript = String.Format("return multiSelectList_add('{0}');",
    ➥BaseName);
    writer.AddAttribute(HtmlTextWriterAttribute.Onclick, addScript);
    writer.AddAttribute(HtmlTextWriterAttribute.Title, "Add Item");
    writer.RenderBeginTag(HtmlTextWriterTag.Button);
    writer.Write("—&gt;");
    writer.RenderEndTag();
    writer.WriteBreak();
    string removeScript = String.Format("return multiSelectList_remove
    ➥('{0}');", BaseName);
    writer.AddAttribute(HtmlTextWriterAttribute.Onclick, removeScript);
    writer.AddAttribute(HtmlTextWriterAttribute.Title, "Remove Item");
    writer.RenderBeginTag(HtmlTextWriterTag.Button);
    writer.Write("&lt;—");
    writer.RenderEndTag();

    writer.RenderEndTag();
}

/// <summary>
/// Render unselected list box
/// </summary>
private void RenderUnselected(HtmlTextWriter writer)
{
    writer.AddStyleAttribute("float", "left");
    writer.AddAttribute(HtmlTextWriterAttribute.Size, _rows.ToString());
    writer.AddStyleAttribute(HtmlTextWriterStyle.Width,
    ➥_UnSelectedWidth.ToString());
    writer.AddAttribute(HtmlTextWriterAttribute.Id, UnselectedListName);
    writer.AddAttribute(HtmlTextWriterAttribute.Name, UnselectedListName);
    writer.AddAttribute(HtmlTextWriterAttribute.Multiple, "true");
    writer.RenderBeginTag(HtmlTextWriterTag.Select);
    foreach (ListItem item in Items)
        if (!item.Selected)
            RenderListItem(writer, item);
    writer.RenderEndTag();
}

/// <summary>
/// Render selected list items
/// </summary>
```

10

LISTING 10.17   Continued

```
    private void RenderSelected(HtmlTextWriter writer)
    {
        writer.AddStyleAttribute("float", "left");
        writer.AddAttribute(HtmlTextWriterAttribute.Size, _rows.ToString());
        writer.AddStyleAttribute(HtmlTextWriterStyle.Width,
        ➥_SelectedWidth.ToString());
        writer.AddAttribute(HtmlTextWriterAttribute.Id, SelectedListName);
        writer.AddAttribute(HtmlTextWriterAttribute.Name, SelectedListName);
        writer.AddAttribute(HtmlTextWriterAttribute.Multiple, "true");
        writer.RenderBeginTag(HtmlTextWriterTag.Select);
        foreach (ListItem item in Items)
            if (item.Selected)
                RenderListItem(writer, item);
        writer.RenderEndTag();
    }


    /// <summary>
    /// Render a list item
    /// </summary>
    private void RenderListItem(HtmlTextWriter writer, ListItem item)
    {
        writer.AddAttribute(HtmlTextWriterAttribute.Value, item.Value);
        writer.RenderBeginTag(HtmlTextWriterTag.Option);
        writer.Write(item.Text);
        writer.RenderEndTag();
    }


    /// <summary>
    /// Process postback data
    /// </summary>
    public bool LoadPostData(string postDataKey, System.Collections.
    ➥Specialized.NameValueCollection postCollection)
    {
        EnsureDataBound();
        ClearSelection();

        string values = postCollection[HiddenName];
        if (values != String.Empty)
        {
            string[] splitValues = values.Split(',');
            foreach (string value in splitValues)
            {
                Items.FindByValue(value).Selected = true;
            }
        }
```

```
            return false;
        }


        /// <summary>
        /// Required by the IPostBackDataHandler interface
        /// </summary>
        public void RaisePostDataChangedEvent()
        {
        }
    }
}
```

Notice that the TagKey property of the base ListControl class is overridden. The elements of the control are contained in an HTML <div> tag.

The MultiSelectList renders its user interface in the RenderContents() method. This method renders the two list boxes and button controls. Each unselected list item is rendered in the first list box and each selected item is rendered in the second list box.

Furthermore, the MultiSelectList control implements the IPostBackDataHandler interface. When a user posts a page that contains the MultiSelectList control to the server, each item that the user selected is retrieved and the Items collection of the List control is updated.

The control takes advantage of a client-side JavaScript library contained in a file named MultiSelectList.js. This JavaScript library is registered in the control's OnPreRender() method. The MultiSelectList.js library is contained in Listing 10.18.

LISTING 10.18 MultiSelectList.js

```
function multiSelectList_add(baseName)
{
    var unselectedList = document.getElementById(baseName + 'unselected');
    var selectedList = document.getElementById(baseName + 'selected');

    // Copy selected items
    var selectedItems = Array.clone(unselectedList.options);

    for (var i=0;i < selectedItems.length;i++)
    {
        if (selectedItems[i].selected)
        {
            var item = unselectedList.removeChild(selectedItems[i]);
            selectedList.appendChild(item);
        }
    }
}
    // Prevent post
```

10

LISTING 10.18   Continued

```
        return false;
}

function multiSelectList_remove(baseName)
{
    var unselectedList = document.getElementById(baseName + 'unselected');
    var selectedList = document.getElementById(baseName + 'selected');

    // Copy unselected items
    var selectedItems = Array.clone(selectedList.options);

    for (var i=0;i < selectedItems.length;i++)
    {
        if (selectedItems[i].selected)
        {
            var item = selectedList.removeChild(selectedItems[i]);
            unselectedList.appendChild(item);
        }
    }
    // Prevent post
    return false;
}

// This function executes when the page
// is submitted. It stuffs all of the
// selected items into a hidden field
function multiSelectList_submit(baseName)
{

    var hidden = document.getElementById(baseName + 'hidden');
    var selectedList = document.getElementById(baseName + 'selected');
    var values = new Array();
    for (var i=0;i<selectedList.options.length;i++)
        values.push(selectedList.options[i].value);
    hidden.value = values.join(',');
}

Array.clone = function(arrItems)
{
  var results = [];
  for (var i=0;i < arrItems.length; i++)
    results.push(arrItems[i]);
  return results;
};
```

Listing 10.18 contains three JavaScript functions. The first two functions simply move list items from one list box to the other list box. The `multiSelectList_submit()` function is called immediately before a page containing the `MultiSelectList` control is posted to the server. This control records each of the selected list items (the items in the second list box) to a hidden form field.

The page in Listing 10.19 illustrates how you can use the `MultiSelectList` control.

LISTING 10.19 ShowMultiSelectList.aspx

```
<%@ Page Language="C#" %>
<%@ Register TagPrefix="custom" Namespace="MyControls" %>
<!DOCTYPE html PUBLIC "-//W3C//DTD XHTML 1.1//EN"
"http://www.w3.org/TR/xhtml11/DTD/xhtml11.dtd">
<script runat="server">

    protected void btnSubmit_Click(object sender, EventArgs e)
    {
        foreach (ListItem item in MultiSelectList1.Items)
            if (item.Selected)
                lblSelected.Text += String.Format("<li>{0}
                ➥({1})",item.Text,item.Value);
    }
</script>
<html xmlns="http://www.w3.org/1999/xhtml" >
<head id="Head1" runat="server">
    <title>Show MultiSelectList</title>
</head>
<body>
    <form id="form1" runat="server">
    <div>

    <b>Movies:</b>
    <asp:RequiredFieldValidator
        id="val"
        ControlToValidate="MultiSelectList1"
        Text="Required"
        Runat="server" />

    <custom:MultiSelectList
        id="MultiSelectList1"
        DataSourceID="srcMovies"
        DataTextField="Title"
        DataValueField="Id"
        Runat="server" />
```

10

LISTING 10.19   Continued

```
    <asp:SqlDataSource
        id="srcMovies"
        SelectCommand="SELECT Id, Title FROM Movies"
        ConnectionString="<%$ ConnectionStrings:Movies %>"
        Runat="server" />

    <p>
    <asp:Button
        id="btnSubmit"
        Text="Submit"
        Runat="server" OnClick="btnSubmit_Click" />
    </p>

    <hr />

    <asp:Label
        id="lblSelected"
        EnableViewState="false"
        Runat="server" />

    </div>
    </form>
</body>
</html>
```

In the page in Listing 10.19, the MultiSelectList control is bound to a SqlDataSource control, which represents the contents of the Movies database table. You can select movie titles in the MultiSelectList control by moving movie titles from one list box to the second list box. When you click the Submit button, the selected movies are displayed in a Label control.

Summary

In this chapter, you learned how to use List controls to display simple option lists. You saw the DropDownList, RadioButtonList, ListBox, CheckBoxList, and BulletedList controls.

You also saw the common features of the List controls. You learned how to append data items to a List control and automatically post a form containing a List control back to the server.

Finally, you worked through the creation of a custom List control, which involved deriving a new control from the base ListControl class. The custom List control takes advantage of client-side JavaScript to enable users to select multiple list items without requiring a page to be posted back to the server when each item is selected.

CHAPTER 11

Using the GridView Control

The GridView control is the workhorse of the ASP.NET Framework. It is one of the most feature-rich and complicated of all the ASP.NET controls. The GridView control enables you to display, select, sort, page, and edit data items such as database records.

NOTE

The GridView control supersedes the DataGrid control included in the ASP.NET 1.x Framework. The DataGrid control is still included in ASP.NET 3.5 for backward compatibility, but you should use the GridView instead because it is a more powerful control.

In this chapter, you learn everything you ever wanted to know about the GridView control. You learn how to use all the basic features of the GridView control. For example, you learn how to use this control to display, select, sort, page, and edit database records. You also learn how to use AJAX with the GridView control when sorting and paging records.

You also get the chance to tackle several advanced topics. For example, you learn how to highlight certain rows in a GridView depending on the data the row represents. You also learn how to display column summaries.

Finally, you learn how to extend the GridView control by building custom GridView fields. At the end of this chapter, we build a LongTextField, a DeleteButtonField, and a ValidatedField.

GridView Control Fundamentals

In this section, you learn how to take advantage of all the basic features of the GridView control. In particular, you learn how to display, select, sort, page, and edit database data with a GridView control. We also discuss GridView formatting options.

Displaying Data

The GridView renders its data items in an HTML table. Each data item is rendered in a distinct HTML table row. For example, the page in Listing 11.1 demonstrates how you can use the GridView to display the contents of the Movies database table (see Figure 11.1).

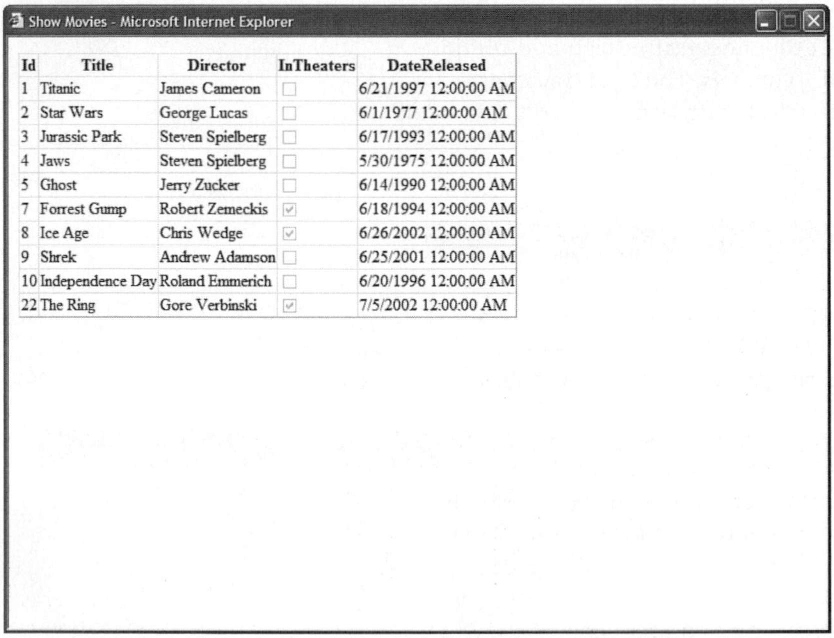

Id	Title	Director	InTheaters	DateReleased
1	Titanic	James Cameron	☐	6/21/1997 12:00:00 AM
2	Star Wars	George Lucas	☐	6/1/1977 12:00:00 AM
3	Jurassic Park	Steven Spielberg	☐	6/17/1993 12:00:00 AM
4	Jaws	Steven Spielberg	☐	5/30/1975 12:00:00 AM
5	Ghost	Jerry Zucker	☐	6/14/1990 12:00:00 AM
7	Forrest Gump	Robert Zemeckis	☑	6/18/1994 12:00:00 AM
8	Ice Age	Chris Wedge	☑	6/26/2002 12:00:00 AM
9	Shrek	Andrew Adamson	☐	6/25/2001 12:00:00 AM
10	Independence Day	Roland Emmerich	☐	6/20/1996 12:00:00 AM
22	The Ring	Gore Verbinski	☑	7/5/2002 12:00:00 AM

FIGURE 11.1   Displaying data with the GridView control.

LISTING 11.1   ShowMovies.aspx

```
<%@ Page Language="C#" %>
<!DOCTYPE html PUBLIC "-//W3C//DTD XHTML 1.1//EN"
  "http://www.w3.org/TR/xhtml11/DTD/xhtml11.dtd">
<html xmlns="http://www.w3.org/1999/xhtml" >
<head id="Head1" runat="server">
    <title>Show Movies</title>
</head>
<body>
    <form id="form1" runat="server">
    <div>
```

```
    <asp:GridView
        id="grdMovies"
        DataSourceID="srcMovies"
        Runat="server" />

    <asp:SqlDataSource
        id="srcMovies"
        ConnectionString="<%$ ConnectionStrings:Movies %>"
        SelectCommand="SELECT Id,Title,Director,InTheaters,DateReleased
            FROM Movies"
        Runat="server" />

    </div>
    </form>
</body>
</html>
```

In Listing 11.1, the GridView control is bound to a SqlDataSource control, which represents the Movies database table. The GridView is associated with its data source through its DataSourceID property.

Notice that the GridView control automatically renders a check box for any Boolean fields. In the case of Listing 11.1, the GridView renders a check box for the InTheaters database column. For all other types of fields, the GridView simply renders the contents of the field.

WEB STANDARDS NOTE

The GridView control was designed to meet XHTML and accessibility guidelines. For example, the control uses the <th> tag to render its headers. Furthermore, each header tag includes a scope="col" attribute.

VISUAL WEB DEVELOPER NOTE

You can add a GridView and SqlDataSource control to a page quickly by dragging a database table from the Database Explorer window onto a page in Design view. When you drag a database table onto the page, a SqlDataSource is automatically created, which retrieves all the rows and all the columns from a database table.

The GridView control also supports programmatic databinding. In Listing 11.2, the GridView control is used to display a list of shopping list items represented by a Generic List collection.

LISTING 11.2   ShowShoppingList.aspx

```
<%@ Page Language="C#" %>
<%@ Import Namespace="System.Collections.Generic" %>
```

LISTING 11.2   Continued

```
<!DOCTYPE html PUBLIC "-//W3C//DTD XHTML 1.1//EN"
"http://www.w3.org/TR/xhtml11/DTD/xhtml11.dtd">
<script runat="server">

    void Page_Load()
    {
        // Build shopping list
        List<string> shoppingList = new List<string>();
        shoppingList.Add("Bread");
        shoppingList.Add("Milk");
        shoppingList.Add("Beer");
        shoppingList.Add("Waffles");

        // Bind to GridView
        grdShoppingList.DataSource = shoppingList;
        grdShoppingList.DataBind();
    }

</script>
<html xmlns="http://www.w3.org/1999/xhtml" >
<head id="Head1" runat="server">
    <title>Show Shopping List</title>
</head>
<body>
    <form id="form1" runat="server">
    <div>

    <asp:GridView
        id="grdShoppingList"
        Runat="server" />

    </div>
    </form>
</body>
</html>
```

Notice that the GridView is bound to the shopping list in the Page_Load() method. Its DataSource property points to the List collection, and its DataBind() method is called to load the items from the List collection and display them.

Selecting Data

You can enable a user to select a particular row in a GridView control. This is useful when you want to build single-page Master/Details forms. For example, the page in Listing 11.3

contains two GridView controls. The first GridView displays a list of movie categories. When you select a category, the second GridView displays a list of matching movies (see Figure 11.2).

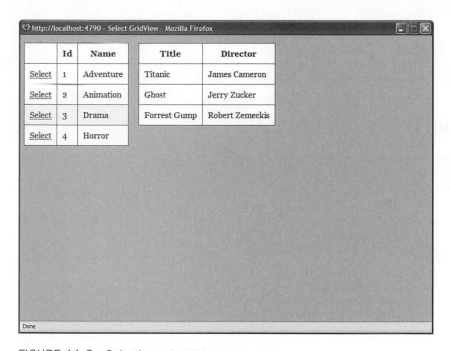

FIGURE 11.2   Selecting a GridView row.

LISTING 11.3   SelectGridView.aspx

```
<%@ Page Language="C#" %>
<!DOCTYPE html PUBLIC "-//W3C//DTD XHTML 1.1//EN"
    "http://www.w3.org/TR/xhtml11/DTD/xhtml11.dtd">
<html xmlns="http://www.w3.org/1999/xhtml" >
<head id="Head1" runat="server">
    <style type="text/css">
        html
        {
            background-color:silver;
            font-family:Georgia, Serif;
        }
        .gridView
        {
            float:left;
            margin-right:20px;
            background-color:white;
        }
```

LISTING 11.3   Continued

```
        .gridView td, .gridView th
        {
            padding:10px;
        }
        .selectedRow
        {
            background-color:yellow;
        }
    </style>
    <title>Select GridView</title>
</head>
<body>
    <form id="form1" runat="server">
    <div>

    <asp:GridView
        id="grdMovieCategories"
        DataKeyNames="Id"
        DataSourceID="srcMovieCategories"
        AutoGenerateSelectButton="true"
        SelectedRowStyle-CssClass="selectedRow"
        CssClass="gridView"
        Runat="server" />

    <asp:GridView
        id="grdMovies"
        DataSourceID="srcMovies"
        CssClass="gridView"
        Runat="server" />

    <asp:SqlDataSource
        id="srcMovieCategories"
        ConnectionString="<%$ ConnectionStrings:Movies %>"
        SelectCommand="SELECT Id, Name FROM MovieCategories"
        Runat="server" />

    <asp:SqlDataSource
        id="srcMovies"
        ConnectionString="<%$ ConnectionStrings:Movies %>"
        SelectCommand="SELECT Title,Director FROM Movies
            WHERE CategoryId=@CategoryId"
        Runat="server">
        <SelectParameters>
        <asp:ControlParameter
```

```
            Name="CategoryId"
            ControlID="grdMovieCategories"
            PropertyName="SelectedValue" />
        </SelectParameters>
    </asp:SqlDataSource>

    </div>
    </form>
</body>
</html>
```

Notice that the first GridView has its AutoGenerateSelectButton property enabled. When this property has the value True, a Select link is displayed next to each row.

You can determine which row is selected in a GridView control by using any of the following methods:

▶ **SelectedDataKey()**—Returns the DataKey object associated with the selected row (useful when there are multiple data keys).

▶ **SelectedIndex()**—Returns the (zero-based) index of the selected row.

▶ **SelectedValue()**—Returns the data key associated with the selected row.

▶ **SelectedRow()**—Returns the actual row (GridViewRow object) associated with the selected row.

In most cases, you use the SelectedValue() method to determine the value associated with a particular row. The SelectedValue() method returns the data key associated with a row. The following section discusses data keys.

NOTE

If you want to customize the appearance of the Select link, then you can use a CommandField control instead of using the AutoGenerateSelectButton property. The CommandField control is discussed later in this chapter in the section entitled "Using Fields with the GridView Control."

Using Data Keys

You associate a value with each row in a GridView by providing a value for the GridView control's DataKeyNames property. You can assign the name of a single database column to this property or you can assign a comma-separated list of column names to this property.

For example, the Employees database table uses two columns—the employee first and last name—as a primary key. The page in Listing 11.4 displays employee details when you select a particular employee (see Figure 11.3).

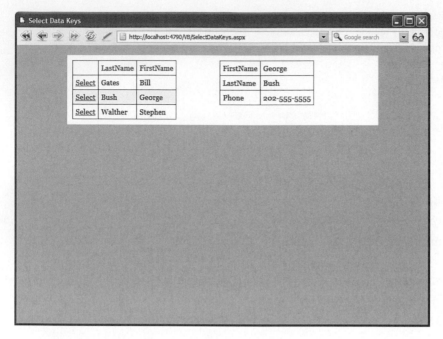

FIGURE 11.3   Displaying employee details.

LISTING 11.4   SelectDataKeys.aspx

```
<%@ Page Language="C#" %>
<!DOCTYPE html PUBLIC "-//W3C//DTD XHTML 1.1//EN"
    "http://www.w3.org/TR/xhtml11/DTD/xhtml11.dtd">
<html xmlns="http://www.w3.org/1999/xhtml" >
<head id="Head1" runat="server">
    <style type="text/css">
        html
        {
            background-color:silver;
        }
        .content
        {
            width:600px;
            margin:auto;
            background-color:white;
        }
        .column
        {
            float:left;
            padding:10px;
            width:265px;
        }
```

```
            .column td,.column th
            {
                padding:5px;
                font:14px Georgia, Serif
            }
            .selectedRow
            {
                background-color:yellow;
            }
    </style>
    <title>Select Data Keys</title>
</head>
<body>
    <form id="form1" runat="server">
    <div class="content">
    <div class="column">

    <asp:GridView
        id="grdEmployees"
        DataSourceID="srcEmployees"
        DataKeyNames="LastName,FirstName"
        AutoGenerateSelectButton="true"
        SelectedRowStyle-CssClass="selectedRow"
        Runat="server" />

    </div>
    <div class="column">

    <asp:DetailsView
        id="dtlEmployees"
        DataSourceID="srcEmployeeDetails"
        Runat="server" />

    </div>

    <br style="clear:both" />
    </div>

    <asp:SqlDataSource
        id="srcEmployees"
        ConnectionString="<%$ ConnectionStrings:Employees %>"
        SelectCommand="SELECT LastName,FirstName
            FROM Employees"
        Runat="server" />

    <asp:SqlDataSource
```

LISTING 11.4   Continued

```
        id="srcEmployeeDetails"
        ConnectionString="<%$ ConnectionStrings:Employees %>"
        SelectCommand="SELECT * FROM Employees
            WHERE FirstName=@FirstName AND LastName=@LastName"
        Runat="server">
        <SelectParameters>
        <asp:ControlParameter
            Name="FirstName"
            ControlID="grdEmployees"
            PropertyName='SelectedDataKey("FirstName")' />
        <asp:ControlParameter
            Name="LastName"
            ControlID="grdEmployees"
            PropertyName='SelectedDataKey("LastName")' />
        </SelectParameters>
    </asp:SqlDataSource>

    </form>
</body>
</html>
```

In Listing 11.4, notice that the `SelectedDataKey()` method is used to retrieve the primary key of the selected employee. The `SelectedDataKey()` method is used in both of the `ControlParameters` contained in the second `SqlDataSource` control. If you use `SelectedValue()` instead of `SelectedDataKey()`, then you can return only the value of the first data key and not both values.

A `GridView` stores data keys in a collection called the `DataKeys` collection. This collection is exposed by the `GridView` control's `DataKeys` property. You can retrieve the data key associated with any row by using a statement that looks like this:

```
Object key = GridView1.DataKeys[6].Value;
```

This statement returns the value of the data key associated with the seventh row in the `GridView` (remember that the rows collection is zero based).

If you have assigned multiple data keys to each row, then you can use a statement that looks like this:

```
Object key = GridView1.DataKeys[6].Values["LastName"];
```

This statement retrieves the value of the `LastName` key for the seventh row in the `GridView`.

Sorting Data

You can sort the rows rendered by a `GridView` control by enabling the `AllowSorting` property. For example, the page in Listing 11.5 illustrates how you can sort the contents of the Movies database table.

LISTING 11.5 SortGrid.aspx

```
<%@ Page Language="C#" %>
<!DOCTYPE html PUBLIC "-//W3C//DTD XHTML 1.1//EN"
    "http://www.w3.org/TR/xhtml11/DTD/xhtml11.dtd">
<html xmlns="http://www.w3.org/1999/xhtml" >
<head id="Head1" runat="server">
    <title>Sort Grid</title>
</head>
<body>
    <form id="form1" runat="server">
    <div>

    <asp:GridView
        id="grdMovies"
        DataSourceID="srcMovies"
        AllowSorting="true"
        Runat="server" />

    <asp:SqlDataSource
        id="srcMovies"
        ConnectionString="<%$ ConnectionStrings:Movies %>"
        SelectCommand="SELECT Id,Title,DateReleased FROM Movies"
        Runat="server" />

    </div>
    </form>
</body>
</html>
```

When `AllowSorting` has the value `True`, column headers are rendered as links. When you click a column header, you can sort the rows contained in the `GridView` in the order of the selected column.

> **NOTE**
>
> When using explicitly specified fields with a `GridView`, such as `BoundFields`, you need to specify values for the fields's `SortExpression` properties. Otherwise, nothing happens when you click a header.

Notice that the `GridView` supports ascending and descending sorts. In other words, if you click a column header more than once, the rows toggle between being sorted in ascending and descending order.

Sorting with AJAX   By default, whenever you click a column header to sort the rows contained in a `GridView`, the page containing the `GridView` is posted back to the server.

When sorting records with the `GridView` control, you can avoid posting the entire page back to the server by taking advantage of Ajax (Asynchronous JavaScript and XML).

We get into the messy details of Ajax in Part IX, "ASP.NET AJAX," of this book. In this section, I want to provide you with a quick code sample that demonstrates how to use Ajax with the GridView control. The page in Listing 11.6 illustrates how you can take advantage of AJAX when sorting records.

LISTING 11.6   AjaxSorting.aspx

```
<%@ Page Language="C#" %>
<!DOCTYPE html PUBLIC "-//W3C//DTD XHTML 1.1//EN"
"http://www.w3.org/TR/xhtml11/DTD/xhtml11.dtd">
<html xmlns="http://www.w3.org/1999/xhtml" >
<head id="Head1" runat="server">
    <title>AJAX Sorting</title>
</head>
<body>
    <form id="form1" runat="server">
    <div>

    <asp:ScriptManager ID="sm1" runat="server" />

    <%= DateTime.Now.ToString("T") %>

    <asp:UpdatePanel ID="up1" runat="server">
    <ContentTemplate>
    <asp:GridView
        id="grdMovies"
        DataSourceID="srcMovies"
        AllowSorting="true"
        Runat="server" />
    </ContentTemplate>
    </asp:UpdatePanel>

    <asp:SqlDataSource
        id="srcMovies"
        ConnectionString="<%$ ConnectionStrings:Movies %>"
        SelectCommand="SELECT Id,Title,DateReleased FROM Movies"
        Runat="server" />

    </div>
    </form>
</body>
</html>
```

The `GridView` in Listing 11.6 is contained in an `UpdatePanel` control. When you sort the `GridView`, only the region of the page contained in the `UpdatePanel` is updated.

The current time is displayed at the top of the page. Notice that the time is not updated when you sort the records in the `GridView`. The entire page is not posted back to the server; only the content of the `UpdatePanel` control is updated.

> **NOTE**
>
> An alternative method for Ajax sorting with the GridView control is to enable the GridView control's EnableSortingAndPagingCallbacks property. I don't suggest that you use this method because it limits the types of fields that you can add to the GridView. For example, if you enable EnableSortingAndPagingCallbacks, then you can't use TemplateFields with a GridView. The UpdatePanel control is not subject to these same limitations.

Customizing the Sorting Interface   You can customize the appearance of the sort links by handling the `GridView` control's `RowDataBound` event. This event is raised for each row rendered by the `GridView` after the `GridView` is bound to its data source.

For example, the page in Listing 11.7 displays an image that represents whether a column is sorted in ascending or descending order (see Figure 11.4).

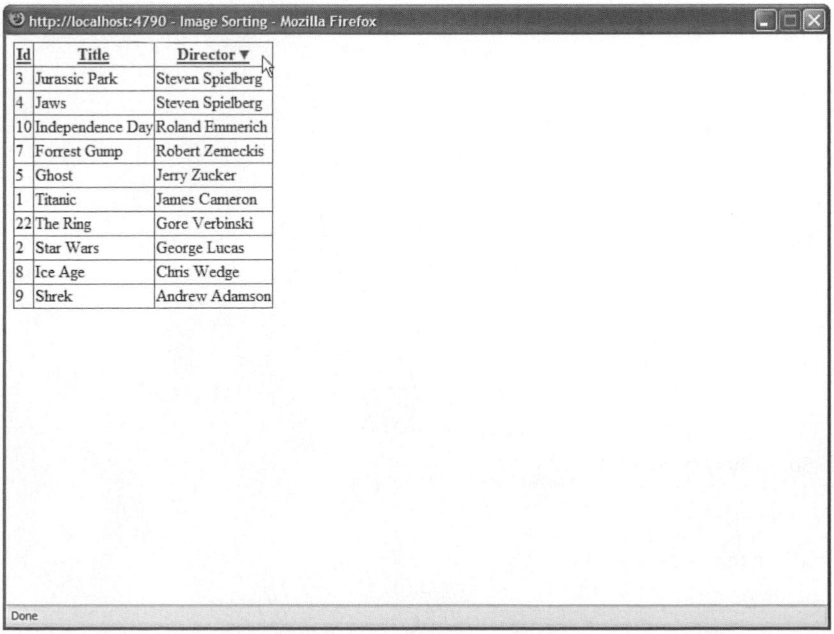

FIGURE 11.4   Displaying an image when sorting.

LISTING 11.7   ImageSorting.aspx

```
<%@ Page Language="C#" %>
<!DOCTYPE html PUBLIC "-//W3C//DTD XHTML 1.1//EN"
"http://www.w3.org/TR/xhtml11/DTD/xhtml11.dtd">
<script runat="server">

    protected void grdMovies_RowDataBound(object sender, GridViewRowEventArgs e)
    {
        if (e.Row.RowType == DataControlRowType.Header)
        {
            foreach (TableCell cell in e.Row.Cells)
            {
                LinkButton sortLink = (LinkButton)cell.Controls[0];
                if (sortLink.Text == grdMovies.SortExpression)
                {
                    if (grdMovies.SortDirection == SortDirection.Ascending)
                        sortLink.Text += " <img src='asc.gif' title=
                          'Sort ascending' />";
                    else
                        sortLink.Text += " <img src='desc.gif' title=
                          'Sort descending' />";

                }
            }
        }
    }
</script>
<html xmlns="http://www.w3.org/1999/xhtml" >
<head id="Head1" runat="server">
    <style type="text/css">
        img
        {
            border:0px;
        }
    </style>
    <title>Image Sorting</title>
</head>
<body>
    <form id="form1" runat="server">
    <div>

    <asp:GridView
        id="grdMovies"
        DataSourceID="srcMovies"
```

```
            AllowSorting="true"
            Runat="server" OnRowDataBound="grdMovies_RowDataBound" />

        <asp:SqlDataSource
            id="srcMovies"
            ConnectionString="<%$ ConnectionStrings:Movies %>"
            SelectCommand="SELECT Id,Title,Director FROM Movies"
            Runat="server" />

        </div>
        </form>
</body>
</html>
```

In Listing 11.7, the image is added to the header row in the grdMovies_RowDataBound()
method. The current row's RowType property is checked to verify that the row is a header
row. Next, an HTML <img> tag is added to the LinkButton that matches the column that is
currently selected for sorting.

If you need to completely customize the appearance of the sorting user interface, then you
can call the GridView control's Sort() method programmatically. This approach is illustrated in the page in Listing 11.8 (see Figure 11.5).

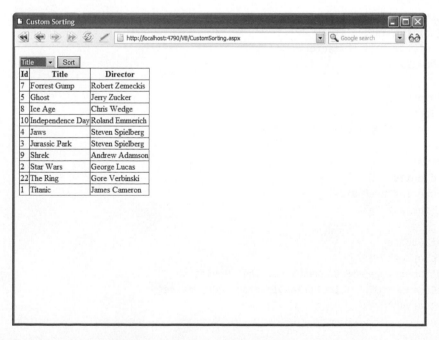

FIGURE 11.5   Displaying a custom sorting interface.

LISTING 11.8 CustomSorting.aspx

```
<%@ Page Language="C#" %>
<!DOCTYPE html PUBLIC "-//W3C//DTD XHTML 1.1//EN"
"http://www.w3.org/TR/xhtml11/DTD/xhtml11.dtd">
<script runat="server">

    protected void btnSort_Click(object sender, EventArgs e)
    {
        grdMovies.Sort(ddlSort.Text, SortDirection.Ascending);
    }
</script>
<html xmlns="http://www.w3.org/1999/xhtml" >
<head id="Head1" runat="server">
    <title>Custom Sorting</title>
</head>
<body>
    <form id="form1" runat="server">
    <div>

    <asp:DropDownList
        id="ddlSort"
        Runat="server">
        <asp:ListItem Text="Id" />
        <asp:ListItem Text="Title" />
        <asp:ListItem Text="Director" />
    </asp:DropDownList>
    <asp:Button
        id="btnSort"
        Text="Sort"
        Runat="server" OnClick="btnSort_Click" />

    <asp:GridView
        id="grdMovies"
        DataSourceID="srcMovies"
        Runat="server" />

    <asp:SqlDataSource
        id="srcMovies"
        ConnectionString="<%$ ConnectionStrings:Movies %>"
        SelectCommand="SELECT Id,Title,Director FROM Movies"
        Runat="server" />

    </div>
```

```
    </form>
</body>
</html>
```

The page in Listing 11.8 includes a `DropDownList` control, which you can use to sort the contents of the `GridView`. When a list item is selected from the `DropDownList` control and the Sort button is clicked, the `btnSort_Click()` method executes. This method calls the `Sort()` method of the `GridView` control to sort the contents of the `GridView`.

Paging Through Data

When working with a large number of database rows, it is useful to be able to display the rows in different pages. You can enable paging with the `GridView` control by enabling its `AllowPaging` property.

For example, the page in Listing 11.9 enables you to page through the records in the Movies database table (see Figure 11.6).

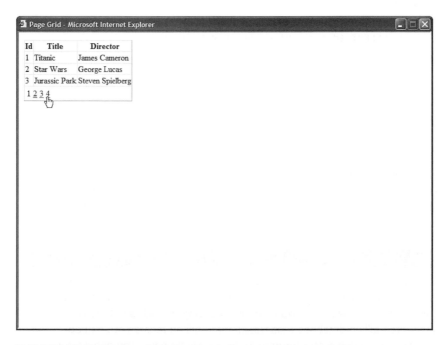

FIGURE 11.6   Paging through records in a `GridView` control.

LISTING 11.9   `PageGrid.aspx`

```
<%@ Page Language="C#" %>
<!DOCTYPE html PUBLIC "-//W3C//DTD XHTML 1.1//EN"
    "http://www.w3.org/TR/xhtml11/DTD/xhtml11.dtd">
<html xmlns="http://www.w3.org/1999/xhtml" >
```

Notice that the page in Listing 11.10 includes an UpdatePanel control. Since the GridView is contained in the UpdatePanel, the page containing the GridView is not posted back to the server when you page through the GridView.

The page in Listing 11.10 displays the current time at the top of the page. When you page through the records rendered by the GridView control, notice that the time does not change. Only the contents of the GridView control are modified.

Customizing the Paging Interface   By default, when paging is enabled, the GridView renders a list of page numbers at the bottom of the grid. You can modify the user interface for paging through records by modifying the GridView control's PagerSettings property. For example, the page in Listing 11.11 contains a GridView that renders First, Previous, Next, and Last links at both the top and bottom of the GridView (see Figure 11.7).

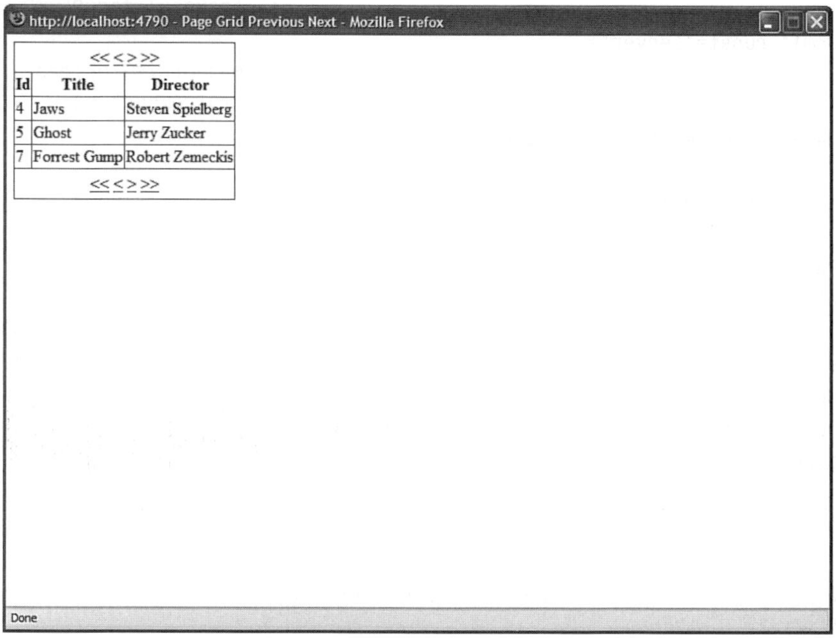

FIGURE 11.7   Modifying pager settings.

LISTING 11.11   PageGridPreviousNext.aspx

```
<%@ Page Language="C#" %>
<!DOCTYPE html PUBLIC "-//W3C//DTD XHTML 1.1//EN"
    "http://www.w3.org/TR/xhtml11/DTD/xhtml11.dtd">
<html xmlns="http://www.w3.org/1999/xhtml" >
<head id="Head1" runat="server">
    <title>Page Grid Previous Next</title>
</head>
<body>
```

```
<form id="form1" runat="server">
<div>

<asp:GridView
    id="grdMovies"
    DataSourceID="srcMovies"
    AllowPaging="true"
    PageSize="3"
    PagerSettings-Mode="NextPreviousFirstLast"
    PagerSettings-Position="TopAndBottom"
    PagerStyle-HorizontalAlign="Center"
    Runat="server" />

<asp:SqlDataSource
    id="srcMovies"
    ConnectionString="<%$ ConnectionStrings:Movies %>"
    SelectCommand="SELECT Id,Title,Director FROM Movies"
    Runat="server" />

</div>
</form>
</body>
</html>
```

The `PagerSettings` class supports the following properties:

- **`FirstPageImageUrl`**—Enables you to display an image for the first page link.

- **`FirstPageText`**—Enables you to specify the text for the first page link.

- **`LastPageImageUrl`**—Enables you to display an image for the last page link.

- **`LastPageText`**—Enables you to specify the text for the last page link.

- **`Mode`**—Enables you to select a display mode for the pager user interface. Possible values are `NextPrevious`, `NextPreviousFirstLast`, `Numeric`, and `NumericFirstLast`.

- **`NextPageImageUrl`**—Enables you to display an image for the next page link.

- **`NextPageText`**—Enables you to specify the text for the next page link.

- **`PageButtonCount`**—Enables you to specify the number of page number links to display.

- **`Position`**—Enables you to specify the position of the paging user interface. Possible values are `Bottom`, `Top`, and `TopAndBottom`.

- **`PreviousPageImageUrl`**—Enables you to display an image for the previous page link.

- **`PreviousPageText`**—Enables you to specify the text for the previous page link.

- **`Visible`**—Enables you to hide the paging user interface.

The PageButtonCount requires more explanation. Imagine that you are displaying the contents of a database table that contains 3 billion records and you are displaying two records per page. In that case, you would need to render an overwhelming number of page numbers. The PageButtonCount property enables you to limit the number of page numbers displayed at once. When PageButtonCount has a value less than the number of page numbers, the GridView renders ellipsis, which enables a user to move between ranges of page numbers.

The GridView control includes a PagerTemplate, which enables you to completely customize the appearance of the paging user interface. For example, the page in Listing 11.12 uses a Menu control in a PagerTemplate to display a list of page numbers. The PagerTemplate also includes two LinkButton controls, which represent a Previous and Next link (see Figure 11.8).

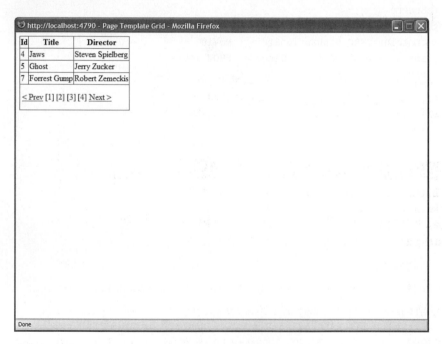

FIGURE 11.8   Using a template for the paging interface.

LISTING 11.12   PageTemplateGrid.aspx

```
<%@ Page Language="C#" %>
<!DOCTYPE html PUBLIC "-//W3C//DTD XHTML 1.1//EN"
"http://www.w3.org/TR/xhtml11/DTD/xhtml11.dtd">

<script runat="server">

    protected void grdMovies_DataBound(object sender, EventArgs e)
```

```
    {
        Menu menuPager = (Menu)grdMovies.BottomPagerRow.FindControl("menuPager");
        for (int i = 0; i < grdMovies.PageCount; i++)
        {
            MenuItem item = new MenuItem();
            item.Text = String.Format("",i + 1);
            item.Value = i.ToString();
            if (grdMovies.PageIndex == i)
                item.Selected = true;
            menuPager.Items.Add(item);
        }
    }

    protected void menuPager_MenuItemClick(object sender, MenuEventArgs e)
    {
        grdMovies.PageIndex = Int32.Parse(e.Item.Value);
    }
</script>

<html xmlns="http://www.w3.org/1999/xhtml" >
<head id="Head1" runat="server">
    <style type="text/css">
        .menu td
        {
            padding:5px 0px;
        }
        .selectedPage a
        {
            font-weight:bold;
            color:red;
        }
    </style>
    <title>Page Template Grid</title>
</head>
<body>
    <form id="form1" runat="server">
    <div>

    <asp:GridView
        id="grdMovies"
        DataSourceID="srcMovies"
        AllowPaging="true"
        PageSize="3"
        Runat="server" OnDataBound="grdMovies_DataBound">
        <PagerTemplate>
        <table>
```

LISTING 11.12   Continued

```
        <tr><td>
        <asp:LinkButton
            id="lnkPrevious"
            Text="&lt; Prev"
            CommandName="Page"
            CommandArgument="Prev"
            ToolTip="Previous Page"
            Runat="server" />
        </td><td>
        <asp:Menu
            id="menuPager"
            Orientation="Horizontal"
            OnMenuItemClick="menuPager_MenuItemClick"
            StaticSelectedStyle-CssClass="selectedPage"
            CssClass="menu"
            Runat="server" />
        </td><td>
        <asp:LinkButton
            id="lnkNext"
            Text="Next &gt;"
            CommandName="Page"
            CommandArgument="Next"
            ToolTip="Next Page"
            Runat="server" />
        </td></tr>
        </table>
        </PagerTemplate>
    </asp:GridView>

    <asp:SqlDataSource
        id="srcMovies"
        ConnectionString="<%$ ConnectionStrings:Movies %>"
        SelectCommand="SELECT Id,Title,Director FROM Movies"
        Runat="server" />

    </div>
    </form>
</body>
</html>
```

The GridView in Listing 11.12 includes a PagerTemplate that contains a Menu control.
When the GridView is bound to its data source, the grdMovies_DataBound() method
executes and creates menu items that correspond to each page in the GridView. When you
click a menu item, the page index of the GridView is updated.

To customize the PagerTemplate, you can add button controls to the template such as the Button, ImageButton, or LinkButton controls. Set the CommandName property of the button control to the value Page and the CommandArgument property to one of the following values:

- ▶ **Next**—Causes the GridView to display the next page of data items.

- ▶ **Prev**—Causes the GridView to display the previous page of data items.

- ▶ **First**—Causes the GridView to display the first page of data items.

- ▶ **Last**—Causes the GridView to display the last page of data items.

- ▶ **Integer Value**—Causes the GridView to display a particular page of data items.

Editing Data

The GridView control also enables you to edit database data. The amazing thing is that you can use the GridView to edit the contents of a database table row without writing a single line of code.

The page in Listing 11.13 illustrates how you can update and delete records in the Movies database table by using the GridView control (see Figure 11.9).

FIGURE 11.9   Editing records with the GridView.

LISTING 11.13   EditGrid.aspx

```
<%@ Page Language="C#" MaintainScrollPositionOnPostback="true" %>
<!DOCTYPE html PUBLIC "-//W3C//DTD XHTML 1.1//EN"
  "http://www.w3.org/TR/xhtml11/DTD/xhtml11.dtd">
```

LISTING 11.13   Continued

```
<html xmlns="http://www.w3.org/1999/xhtml" >
<head id="Head1" runat="server">
    <title>Edit GridView</title>
</head>
<body>
    <form id="form1" runat="server">
    <div>

    <asp:GridView
        id="grdMovies"
        DataSourceID="srcMovies"
        DataKeyNames="Id"
        AutoGenerateEditButton="true"
        AutoGenerateDeleteButton="true"
        Runat="server" />

    <asp:SqlDataSource
        id="srcMovies"
        ConnectionString="<%$ ConnectionStrings:Movies %>"
        SelectCommand="SELECT Id,Title,Director FROM Movies"
        UpdateCommand="UPDATE Movies SET Title=@Title, Director=@Director
            WHERE Id=@Id"
        DeleteCommand="DELETE Movies WHERE Id=@Id"
        Runat="server" />

    </div>
    </form>
</body>
</html>
```

In Listing 11.13, notice that the GridView control has both its AutoGenerateEditButton
and AutoGenerateDeleteButton properties enabled. When these properties are enabled,
Edit and Delete links are automatically rendered next to each row in the GridView.

> **NOTE**
>
> You can take advantage of the `<%@ Page %>` directive's MaintainScrollPosition-
> OnPostback attribute to scroll a page back automatically to the same position
> whenever the page is posted back to the server. For example, if you add this attribute
> and click an Edit link rendered by a GridView, the page automatically scrolls to the
> record being edited. This attribute works with Internet Explorer 6+, Firefox 1+, and
> Opera 8+.

When you click an Edit link, you can edit a particular database row. The GridView automatically renders a check box for any Boolean columns and a text field for any other type of column.

> **NOTE**
>
> The GridView control does not support inserting new records into a database table. If you need to insert new records, use the ListView, DetailsView, or FormView control.

Furthermore, notice that the GridView control includes a DataKeyNames property. When editing and deleting rows with the GridView, you need to assign the name of the primary key field from the database table being modified to this property. In Listing 11.13, the Movies ID column is assigned to the DataKeyNames property.

Finally, notice that the SqlDataSource control associated with the GridView control includes a SelectCommand, UpdateCommand, and DeleteCommand property. These properties contain the SQL statements that are executed when you display, insert, and delete records with the GridView control.

The SQL statements contained in both the UpdateCommand and DeleteCommand include parameters. For example, the UpdateCommand looks like this:

```
UPDATE Movies SET Title=@Title, Director=@Director
WHERE Id=@Id
```

The @Title and @Director parameters represent the new values for these columns that a user enters when updating a record with the GridView control. The @Id parameter represents the primary key column from the database table.

Handling Concurrency Issues   The GridView control can track both the original and modified value of each database column. The GridView control tracks the original and updated values of a column so that you can handle concurrency conflicts. Imagine that you are building a massive order entry system. Your company has hundreds of employees modifying orders with a page that contains a GridView control. If two employees open the same customer record at the same time, then one employee might overwrite changes made by the other employee.

You can prevent this type of concurrency conflict by using the page in Listing 11.14.

LISTING 11.14   Concurrency.aspx

```
<%@ Page Language="C#" %>
<!DOCTYPE html PUBLIC "-//W3C//DTD XHTML 1.1//EN"
"http://www.w3.org/TR/xhtml11/DTD/xhtml11.dtd">

<script runat="server">

    protected void srcMovies_Updated(object sender, SqlDataSourceStatusEventArgs e)
```

LISTING 11.14   Continued

```
        {
            if (e.AffectedRows == 0)
                lblMessage.Text = "Could not update record";
        }
</script>

<html xmlns="http://www.w3.org/1999/xhtml" >
<head id="Head1" runat="server">
    <title>Concurrency</title>
</head>
<body>
    <form id="form1" runat="server">
    <div>

    <asp:Label ID="lblMessage" EnableViewState="false" runat="server" />

    <asp:GridView
        id="grdMovies"
        DataSourceID="srcMovies"
        DataKeyNames="Id"
        AutoGenerateEditButton="true"
        Runat="server" />

    <asp:SqlDataSource
        id="srcMovies"
        ConflictDetection="CompareAllValues"
        OldValuesParameterFormatString="original_{0}"
        ConnectionString="<%$ ConnectionStrings:Movies %>"
        SelectCommand="SELECT Id,Title,Director FROM Movies"
        UpdateCommand="UPDATE Movies SET Title=@Title, Director=@Director
            WHERE Id=@original_Id AND Title=@original_Title AND
            ➥Director=@original_Director"
        Runat="server" OnUpdated="srcMovies_Updated" />

    </div>
    </form>
</body>
</html>
```

In Listing 11.14, the SqlDataSource control includes both a ConflictDetection and OldValuesParameterFormatString property. These two properties cause the SqlDataSource control to track both the original and modified versions of each column.

The ConflictDetection property can have one of the following two values:

- ▶ CompareAllValues

- ▶ OverwriteChanges

By default, the ConflictDetection property has the value OverwriteChanges, which causes the SqlDataSource control to overwrite the previous value of a column with its new value. When ConflictDetection is set to the value CompareAllValues, the SqlDataSource tracks both the original and modified version of each column.

The OldValuesParameterFormatString property is used to provide a distinguishing name for the original value of a column. For example, the value of the SqlDataSource control's UpdateCommand looks like this:

```
UPDATE Movies SET Title=@Title, Director=@Director
WHERE Id=@original_Id AND Title=@original_Title
AND Director=@original_Director
```

The @original_Id, @original_Title, and @original_Director parameters represent the original values of these columns. If the value of the Title or Director columns has changed in the underlying database, then the record is not updated. In other words, if someone else beats you to the record change, then your modifications are ignored.

Notice that the page in Listing 11.14 includes an Updated event handler for the SqlDataSource control. If there is a concurrency conflict, no records will be affected by the update. The event handler displays an error message when the e.AffectedRows property has the value 0.

Displaying Empty Data

The GridView includes two properties that enable you to display content when no results are returned from the GridView control's data source. You can use either the EmptyDataText property or the EmptyDataTemplate property to handle empty data.

For example, the page in Listing 11.15 contains a movie search form. If you enter a search string that does not match the start of any movie title, then the contents of the EmptyDataText property are displayed (see Figure 11.10).

LISTING 11.15 ShowEmptyDataText.aspx

```
<%@ Page Language="C#" %>
<!DOCTYPE html PUBLIC "-//W3C//DTD XHTML 1.1//EN"
"http://www.w3.org/TR/xhtml11/DTD/xhtml11.dtd">
<script runat="server">

    protected void btnSubmit_Click(object sender, EventArgs e)
    {
        grdMovies.Visible = true;
    }
</script>
```

LISTING 11.15   Continued

```
<html xmlns="http://www.w3.org/1999/xhtml" >
<head id="Head1" runat="server">
    <title>Show Empty Data Text</title>
</head>
<body>
    <form id="form1" runat="server">
    <div>

    <asp:TextBox
        id="txtTitle"
        Runat="server" />
    <asp:Button
        id="btnSubmit"
        Text="Search"
        OnClick="btnSubmit_Click"
        Runat="server" />
    <hr />

    <asp:GridView
        id="grdMovies"
        DataSourceID="srcMovies"
        EmptyDataText="<img src='sad.gif'/> No Matching Movies!"
        Visible="false"
        Runat="server" />

    <asp:SqlDataSource
        id="srcMovies"
        ConnectionString="<%$ ConnectionStrings:Movies %>"
        SelectCommand="SELECT Title,Director FROM Movies
            WHERE Title LIKE @Title+'%'"
        Runat="server">
        <SelectParameters>
        <asp:ControlParameter
            Name="Title"
            ControlID="txtTitle"
            PropertyName="Text" />
        </SelectParameters>
    </asp:SqlDataSource>

    </div>
    </form>
</body>
</html>
```

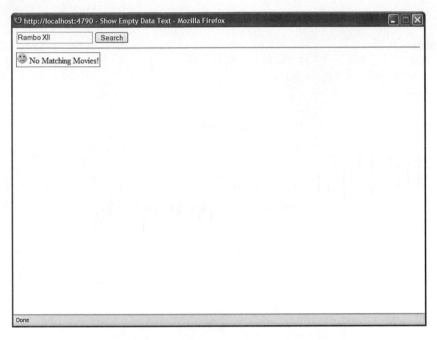

FIGURE 11.10   Displaying a message when no records match.

If you use the search form in Listing 11.15 to search for a movie that doesn't exist, then an icon of a frowning face and the text No Matching Movies! is displayed.

Notice that the initial value of the GridView control's Visible property is set to False. The GridView is displayed only after you click the button. If you did not add this additional logic, then the EmptyDataText message would be displayed when the page is first opened.

As an alternative to using the EmptyDataText property, you can use an EmptyDataTemplate to display content when a data source does not return any results. For example, the page in Listing 11.16 prompts you to enter a new movie when no matching movies are found (see Figure 11.11).

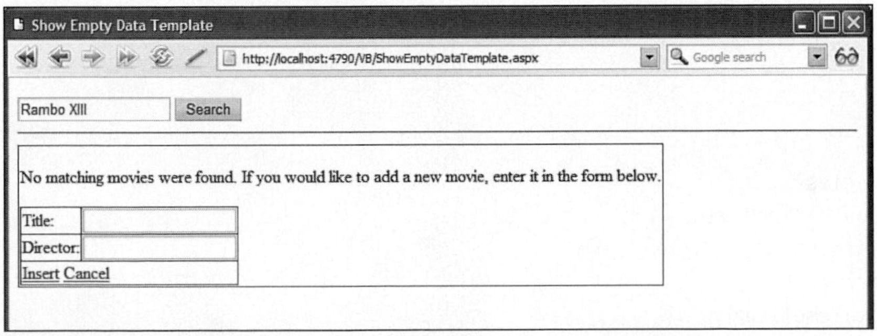

FIGURE 11.11   Displaying a template when no records match.

LISTING 11.16   ShowEmptyDataTemplate.aspx

```
<%@ Page Language="C#" %>
<!DOCTYPE html PUBLIC "-//W3C//DTD XHTML 1.1//EN"
"http://www.w3.org/TR/xhtml11/DTD/xhtml11.dtd">
<script runat="server">

    protected void btnSubmit_Click(object sender, EventArgs e)
    {
        grdMovies.Visible = true;
    }

    protected void dtlMovie_ItemInserted(object sender,
    ➥DetailsViewInsertedEventArgs e)
    {
        txtTitle.Text = (string)e.Values["Title"];
        grdMovies.DataBind();
    }
</script>

<html xmlns="http://www.w3.org/1999/xhtml" >
<head id="Head1" runat="server">
    <title>Show Empty Data Template</title>
</head>
<body>
    <form id="form1" runat="server">
    <div>

    <asp:TextBox
        id="txtTitle"
        Runat="server" />
    <asp:Button
        id="btnSubmit"
        Text="Search"
        OnClick="btnSubmit_Click"
        Runat="server" />
    <hr />

    <asp:GridView
        id="grdMovies"
        DataSourceID="srcMovies"
        Visible="false"
        Runat="server">
        <EmptyDataTemplate>
```

```
        <p>
        No matching movies were found. If you would like
        to add a new movie, enter it in the form below.
        </p>
        <asp:DetailsView
            id="dtlMovie"
            DataSourceID="srcMovies"
            DefaultMode="Insert"
            AutoGenerateInsertButton="true"
            AutoGenerateRows="false"
            Runat="server" OnItemInserted="dtlMovie_ItemInserted">
            <Fields>
            <asp:BoundField
                HeaderText="Title:"
                DataField="Title" />
            <asp:BoundField
                HeaderText="Director:"
                DataField="Director" />
            </Fields>
        </asp:DetailsView>

        </EmptyDataTemplate>
    </asp:GridView>

    <asp:SqlDataSource
        id="srcMovies"
        ConnectionString="<%$ ConnectionStrings:Movies %>"
        SelectCommand="SELECT Title,Director FROM Movies
            WHERE Title LIKE @Title+'%'"
        InsertCommand="INSERT Movies (Title, Director)
            VALUES (@Title, @Director)"
        Runat="server">
        <SelectParameters>
        <asp:ControlParameter
            Name="Title"
            ControlID="txtTitle"
            PropertyName="Text" />
        </SelectParameters>
    </asp:SqlDataSource>

    </div>
    </form>
</body>
</html>
```

The `EmptyDataTemplate` in Listing 11.16 contains some text and a `DetailsView` control that you can use to insert a new movie into the Movies database table. You can add any HTML content or ASP.NET controls to an `EmptyDataTemplate` that you need.

Formatting the `GridView` Control

The `GridView` control includes a rich set of formatting properties that you can use to modify its appearance. I recommend that you don't use most of these properties because using these properties results in bloated pages. Instead, I recommend that you use Cascading Style Sheets to format the `GridView` control.

The `GridView` control includes a `CssClass` property. The control also exposes several `Style` objects that include the `CssClass` property:

▶ **AlternatingRowStyle**—Enables you to format every other row.

▶ **FooterStyle**—Enables you to format the footer row.

▶ **HeaderStyle**—Enables you to format the header row.

▶ **PagerStyle**—Enables you to format the pager row.

▶ **RowStyle**—Enables you to format each row.

▶ **SelectedRowStyle**—Enables you to format the selected row.

For example, the page in Listing 11.17 contains a `GridView` that is formatted with Cascading Style Sheet rules (see Figure 11.12).

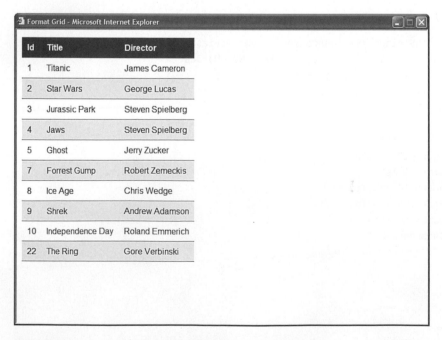

FIGURE 11.12   A `GridView` control formatted with CSS.

LISTING 11.17 FormatGrid.aspx

```
<%@ Page Language="C#" %>
<!DOCTYPE html PUBLIC "-//W3C//DTD XHTML 1.1//EN"
    "http://www.w3.org/TR/xhtml11/DTD/xhtml11.dtd">
<html xmlns="http://www.w3.org/1999/xhtml" >
<head id="Head1" runat="server">
    <style type="text/css">
        .grid
        {
            font:16px Arial, Sans-Serif;
        }
        .grid td, .grid th
        {
            padding:10px;
        }
        .header
        {
            text-align:left;
            color:white;
            background-color:blue;
        }
        .row td
        {
            border-bottom:solid 1px blue;
        }
        .alternating
        {
            background-color:#eeeeee;
        }
        .alternating td
        {
            border-bottom:solid 1px blue;
        }
    </style>
    <title>Format Grid</title>
</head>
<body>
    <form id="form1" runat="server">
    <div>

    <asp:GridView
        id="grdMovies"
        DataSourceID="srcMovies"
        GridLines="None"
        CssClass="grid"
```

LISTING 11.17   Continued

```
        HeaderStyle-CssClass="header"
        RowStyle-CssClass="row"
        AlternatingRowStyle-CssClass="alternating"
        Runat="server" />

    <asp:SqlDataSource
        id="srcMovies"
        ConnectionString="<%$ ConnectionStrings:Movies %>"
        SelectCommand="SELECT Id,Title,Director FROM Movies"
        Runat="server" />

    </div>
    </form>
</body>
</html>
```

In Listing 11.17, the column header text is left aligned. Also notice that banding is added to the table rendered by the GridView. Alternating rows are rendered with a gray background.

The GridView control has a few formatting properties that you might need to use even when formatting a GridView with Cascading Style Sheets. For example, in Listing 11.17, the GridLines property was assigned the value None to suppress the default rendering of borders around each table cell. Here is a list of these properties.

▸ **GridLines**—Renders borders around table cells. Possible values are Both, Vertical, Horizontal, and None.

▸ **ShowFooter**—When True, renders a footer row at the bottom of the GridView.

▸ **ShowHeader**—When True, renders a header row at the top of the GridView.

Using ViewState with the GridView Control

By default, the GridView control stores the values of all the columns contained in all the rows that it renders in ViewState. In other words, all the rows that the GridView retrieves from its data source are stuffed in a hidden form field.

The advantage of using ViewState is that the GridView does not need to query the database for the same set of records every time a page containing the GridView is displayed. The records are retrieved from the database only when the page first loads.

The disadvantage of using ViewState is that it means that a lot of information might need to be pushed over the wire to a user's browser. All ViewState information is stored in a hidden form field. When a large number of rows are displayed, this hidden form field can become enormous. When ViewState becomes too large, it can significantly impact a page's performance.

You can disable ViewState by assigning the value False to the GridView control's EnableViewState property. Even if you disable ViewState, you can still display, sort, page, and edit database records with the GridView control. (The GridView uses ControlState to track vital state information.) When displaying a large number of records, you should turn ViewState off.

You can view the amount of ViewState that a GridView is using by enabling tracing for the page that contains the GridView. Add the Trace="True" attribute to the Page directive like this:

```
<%@ Page Trace="true" %>
```

When tracing is enabled, a Control Tree section is appended to the end of a page when the page is rendered in a browser. The Control Tree section displays the ViewState size used by each control contained in the page.

Using Fields with the GridView Control

In all the sample code in the previous section, the GridView control was used to render automatically an HTML table that contains a list of data items. However, there is a problem with allowing the GridView to render its columns automatically. The result does not look very professional.

For example, the column headers are simply the names of the underlying database columns. Displaying the column name EntryDate as a column header seems, well, a little cheesy. We really need to be able to specify custom column headers.

Another problem with enabling the GridView to render its columns automatically is that you give up any control over column formatting. For example, the BoxOfficeTotals column is displayed as a decimal amount without any currency formatting. The EntryDate column always displays in short-date and long-time format.

Furthermore, it would be nice to be able to display the values of certain columns as images, drop-down lists, or hyperlinks. If you use the automatically generated columns, then you are stuck with the user interface you are given.

The solution to all these problems is to specify explicitly the fields that a GridView displays. The GridView control supports the following types of fields:

- ▶ **BoundField**—Enables you to display the value of a data item as text.
- ▶ **CheckBoxField**—Enables you to display the value of a data item as a check box.
- ▶ **CommandField**—Enables you to display links for editing, deleting, and selecting rows.
- ▶ **ButtonField**—Enables you to display the value of a data item as a button (image button, link button, or push button).
- ▶ **HyperLinkField**—Enables you to display the value of a data item as a link.

▸ **ImageField**—Enables you to display the value of a data item as an image.

▸ **TemplateField**—Enables you to customize the appearance of a data item.

The following sections examine how you can take advantage of each of these different types of fields.

NOTE

You can create custom fields that work with the `GridView` control. This option is explored in the final section of this chapter.

Using BoundFields

A `BoundField` always displays the value of a data item as text when a row is in normal display mode. When a row is selected for editing, a `BoundField` displays the value of a data item in a single line text field.

The most important three properties of the `BoundField` class are the `DataField`, `DataFormatString`, and `HeaderText` properties. The page in Listing 11.18 illustrates how to use these properties when displaying a list of movies (see Figure 11.13).

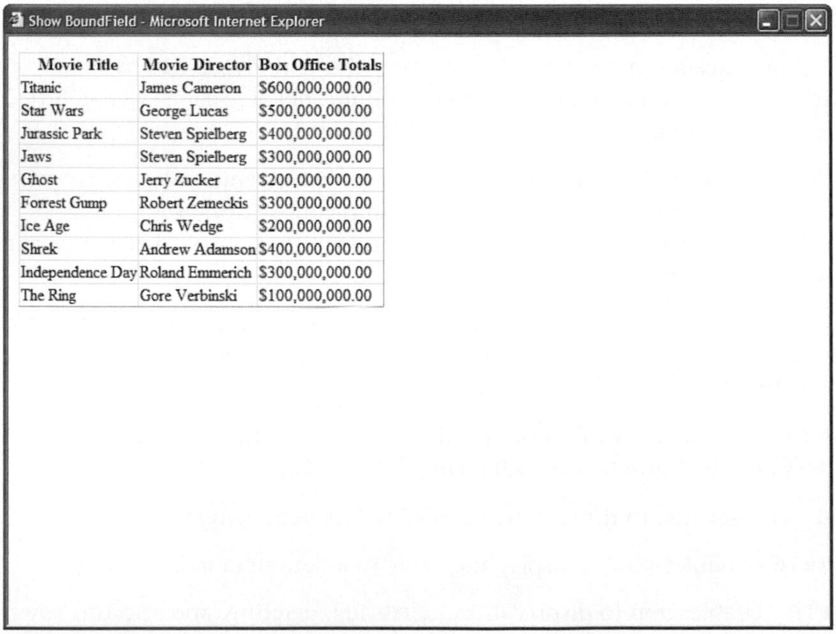

Movie Title	Movie Director	Box Office Totals
Titanic	James Cameron	$600,000,000.00
Star Wars	George Lucas	$500,000,000.00
Jurassic Park	Steven Spielberg	$400,000,000.00
Jaws	Steven Spielberg	$300,000,000.00
Ghost	Jerry Zucker	$200,000,000.00
Forrest Gump	Robert Zemeckis	$300,000,000.00
Ice Age	Chris Wedge	$200,000,000.00
Shrek	Andrew Adamson	$400,000,000.00
Independence Day	Roland Emmerich	$300,000,000.00
The Ring	Gore Verbinski	$100,000,000.00

FIGURE 11.13   Using `BoundFields` with the `GridView` control.

LISTING 11.18   ShowBoundField.aspx

```
<%@ Page Language="C#" %>
<!DOCTYPE html PUBLIC "-//W3C//DTD XHTML 1.1//EN"
    "http://www.w3.org/TR/xhtml11/DTD/xhtml11.dtd">
<html xmlns="http://www.w3.org/1999/xhtml" >
<head id="Head1" runat="server">
    <title>Show BoundField</title>
</head>
<body>
    <form id="form1" runat="server">
    <div>

    <asp:GridView
        id="grdMovies"
        DataSourceID="srcMovies"
        AutoGenerateColumns="false"
        Runat="server">
        <Columns>
        <asp:BoundField
            DataField="Title"
            HeaderText="Movie Title" />
        <asp:BoundField
            DataField="Director"
            HeaderText="Movie Director" />
        <asp:BoundField
            DataField="BoxOfficeTotals"
            DataFormatString="{0:c}"
            HtmlEncode="false"
            HeaderText="Box Office Totals" />
        </Columns>
    </asp:GridView>

    <asp:SqlDataSource
        id="srcMovies"
        ConnectionString="<%$ ConnectionStrings:Movies %>"
        SelectCommand="SELECT * FROM Movies"
        Runat="server" />

    </div>
    </form>
</body>
</html>
```

Notice that the `GridView` control includes an `AutoGenerateColumns` property that is assigned the value `False`. If you don't disable automatically generated columns, then both columns represented by the `BoundFields` and all the columns from the data source are displayed redundantly.

In Listing 11.18, `BoundFields` are used to display the Title, Director, and BoxOfficeTotals columns. The `DataField` property is used to represent the column that a `BoundField` displays. The `HeaderText` property determines the column header.

The `BoundField` used to display the BoxOfficeTotals column includes a `DataFormatString` property. This format string formats the values of the BoxOfficeTotals column as a currency amount.

NOTE

For more information about string formatting, see the Formatting Types topic in the Microsoft .NET Framework documentation.

A `BoundField` supports several other useful properties:

▶ **AccessibleHeaderText**—Enables you to add an HTML abbr attribute to the column header.

▶ **ApplyFormatInEditMode**—Enables you to apply the `DataFormatString` to the field when the row is in edit display mode.

▶ **ConvertEmptyStringToNull**—Enables you to convert an empty string " " into the value `Nothing` (null) when editing a column.

▶ **DataField**—Enables you to specify the name of the field that the `BoundField` displays.

▶ **DataFormatString**—Enables you to use a format string to format a data item.

▶ **FooterStyle**—Enables you to format the column footer.

▶ **FooterText**—Enables you to display text in the column footer.

▶ **HeaderImageUrl**—Enables you to display an image in the column header.

▶ **HeaderStyle**—Enables you to format the column header.

▶ **HeaderText**—Enables you to display text in the column header.

▶ **HtmlEncode**—Enables you to HTML-encode the value of a data item, which enables you to avoid script injection attacks.

▶ **InsertVisible**—Enables you to not display a column when inserting a new record (does not apply to the `GridView` control).

▶ **ItemStyle**—Enables you to format a data item.

▶ **NullDisplayText**—Enables you to specify text that is displayed when a data item has the value `Nothing` (null).

▶ **ReadOnly**—Enables you to prevent the data item from being edited in edit mode.

▶ **ShowHeader**—Enables you to display the column header.

▶ **SortExpression**—Enables you to associate a sort expression with the column.

▶ **Visible**—Enables you to hide a column.

Using CheckBoxFields

A CheckBoxField, as you can probably guess, displays a check box. When a row is not in edit mode, the check box is displayed but it is disabled.

The page in Listing 11.19 illustrates how you can use a CheckBoxField (see Figure 11.14).

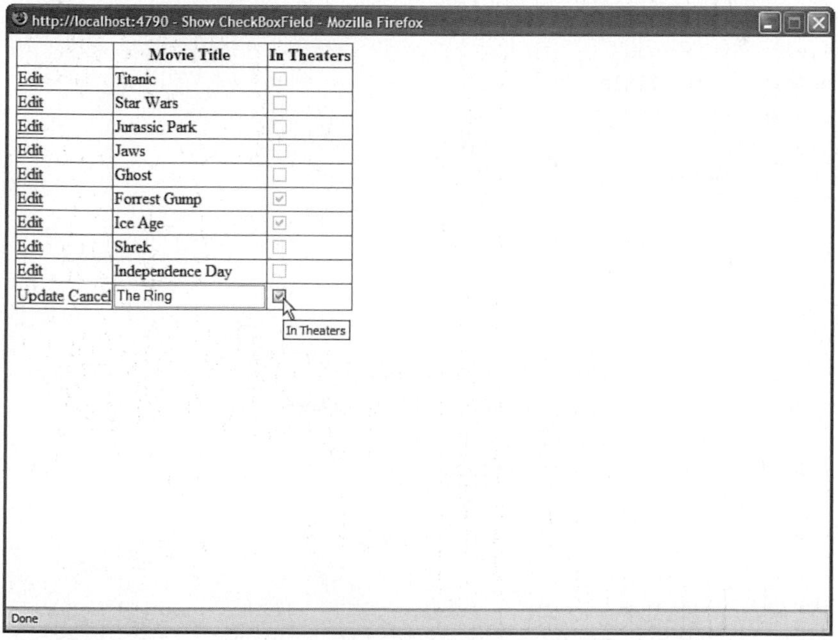

FIGURE 11.14   Using the CheckBoxField with the GridView control.

LISTING 11.19   ShowCheckBoxField.aspx

```
<%@ Page Language="C#" %>
<!DOCTYPE html PUBLIC "-//W3C//DTD XHTML 1.1//EN"
    "http://www.w3.org/TR/xhtml11/DTD/xhtml11.dtd">
<html xmlns="http://www.w3.org/1999/xhtml" >
<head id="Head1" runat="server">
    <title>Show CheckBoxField</title>
```

LISTING 11.19   Continued

```
</head>
<body>
    <form id="form1" runat="server">
    <div>

    <asp:GridView
        id="grdMovies"
        DataSourceID="srcMovies"
        DataKeyNames="Id"
        AutoGenerateColumns="false"
        AutoGenerateEditButton="true"
        Runat="server">
        <Columns>
        <asp:BoundField
            DataField="Title"
            HeaderText="Movie Title" />
        <asp:CheckBoxField
            DataField="InTheaters"
            HeaderText="In Theaters" />
        </Columns>
    </asp:GridView>

    <asp:SqlDataSource
        id="srcMovies"
        ConnectionString="<%$ ConnectionStrings:Movies %>"
        SelectCommand="SELECT Id,Title,InTheaters FROM Movies"
        UpdateCommand="UPDATE Movies SET
            Title=@Title, InTheaters=@InTheaters
            WHERE Id=@Id"
        Runat="server" />

    </div>
    </form>
</body>
</html>
```

The CheckBoxField inherits from the BoundField class, so it includes all the properties of the BoundField class. It also supports the following property:

▶ **Text**—Displays text next to each check box.

Using `CommandFields`

You can use a `CommandField` to customize the appearance of the Edit, Delete, Update, Cancel, and Select buttons displayed by the `GridView` control. For example, the page in Listing 11.20 uses icons for the standard edit buttons (see Figure 11.15).

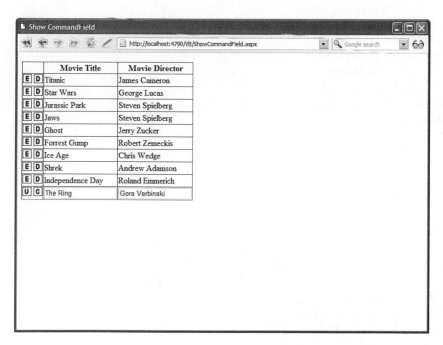

FIGURE 11.15   Using a `CommandField` with the `GridView` control.

LISTING 11.20   `ShowCommandField.aspx`

```
<%@ Page Language="C#" %>
<!DOCTYPE html PUBLIC "-//W3C//DTD XHTML 1.1//EN"
  "http://www.w3.org/TR/xhtml11/DTD/xhtml11.dtd">
<html xmlns="http://www.w3.org/1999/xhtml" >
<head id="Head1" runat="server">
    <title>Show CommandField</title>
</head>
<body>
    <form id="form1" runat="server">
    <div>

    <asp:GridView
        id="grdMovies"
```

LISTING 11.20   Continued

```
        DataSourceID="srcMovies"
        DataKeyNames="Id"
        AutoGenerateColumns="false"
        Runat="server">
        <Columns>
        <asp:CommandField
            ButtonType="Image"
            ShowEditButton="true"
            EditText="Edit Movie"
            EditImageUrl="Edit.gif"
            UpdateText="Update Movie"
            UpdateImageUrl="Update.gif"
            ShowCancelButton="true"
            CancelText="Cancel Edit"
            CancelImageUrl="Cancel.gif"
            ShowDeleteButton="true"
            DeleteText="Delete Movie"
            DeleteImageUrl="Delete.gif" />
        <asp:BoundField
            DataField="Title"
            HeaderText="Movie Title" />
        <asp:BoundField
            DataField="Director"
            HeaderText="Movie Director" />
        </Columns>
    </asp:GridView>

    <asp:SqlDataSource
        id="srcMovies"
        ConnectionString="<%$ ConnectionStrings:Movies %>"
        SelectCommand="SELECT Id,Title,Director FROM Movies"
        UpdateCommand="UPDATE Movies SET
            Title=@Title, Director=@Director
            WHERE Id=@Id"
        DeleteCommand="DELETE Movies
            WHERE Id=@Id"
        Runat="server" />

    </div>
    </form>
</body>
</html>
```

Notice that you do not enable the `AutoGenerateEditButton` or `AutoGenerateDeleteButton` properties when using a `CommandField`. Instead, you use the `CommandField` to set up the standard editing buttons explicitly.

The `CommandField` supports the following properties:

▶ **ButtonType** —Enables you to specify the type of button displayed by the `CommandField`. Possible values are `Button`, `Image`, and `Link`.

▶ **CancelImageUrl**—Enables you to specify an image to display for the Cancel button.

▶ **CancelText**—Enables you to specify the text to display for the Cancel button.

▶ **CausesValidation**—Enables you to disable validation when an Edit button is clicked.

▶ **DeleteImageUrl**—Enables you to specify an image to display for the Delete button.

▶ **DeleteText**—Enables you to specify the text to display for the Delete button.

▶ **EditImageUrl**—Enables you to specify an image to display for the Edit button.

▶ **EditText**—Enables you to specify the text to display for the Edit button.

▶ **InsertImageUrl**—Enables you to specify an image to display for the Insert button.

▶ **InsertText**—Enables you to specify the text to display for the Insert button.

▶ **NewImageUrl**—Enables you to specify an image to display for the New button (does not apply to `GridView`).

▶ **NewText**—Enables you to specify the text to display for the New button.

▶ **SelectImageUrl**—Enables you to specify the image to display for the Select button.

▶ **SelectText**—Enables you to specify the text to display for the Select button.

▶ **ShowCancelButton**—Enables you to display the Cancel button.

▶ **ShowDeleteButton**—Enables you to display the Delete button.

▶ **ShowEditButton**—Enables you to display the Edit button.

▶ **ShowInsertButton**—Enables you to display the Insert button (does not apply to `GridView`).

▶ **ShowSelectButton**—Enables you to display the Select button.

▶ **UpdateImageUrl**—Enables you to specify the image to display for the Update button.

▶ **UpdateText**—Enables you to specify the text to display for the Update button.

▶ **ValidationGroup**—Enables you to associate the edit buttons with a validation group.

Using **ButtonFields**

You use a ButtonField to display a button in a GridView. You can use a ButtonField to represent a custom command or one of the standard edit commands.

For example, the GridView in Listing 11.21 contains two ButtonFields that a user can click to change the display order of the movie category records (see Figure 11.16).

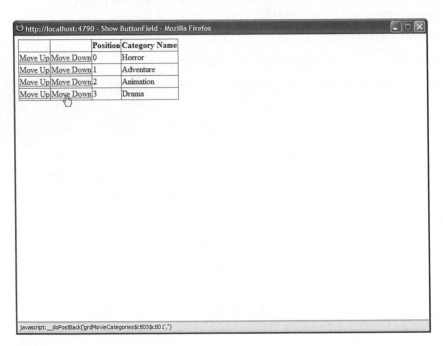

FIGURE 11.16   Using ButtonFields with the GridView control.

LISTING 11.21   ShowButtonField.aspx

```
<%@ Page Language="C#" %>
<!DOCTYPE html PUBLIC "-//W3C//DTD XHTML 1.1//EN"
"http://www.w3.org/TR/xhtml11/DTD/xhtml11.dtd">
<script runat="server">

    protected void grdMovieCategories_RowCommand(object sender,
    ➥GridViewCommandEventArgs e)
    {
        int index = Int32.Parse((string)e.CommandArgument);
        int id = (int)grdMovieCategories.DataKeys[index].Values["Id"];
        int position = (int)grdMovieCategories.DataKeys[index].Values["Position"];
        switch (e.CommandName)
        {
            case "Up":
```

```
                        position—;
                        break;
                case "Down":
                        position++;
                        break;
        }
        srcMovieCategories.UpdateParameters["Id"].DefaultValue = id.ToString();
        srcMovieCategories.UpdateParameters["Position"].DefaultValue =
        ➥position.ToString();
        srcMovieCategories.Update();
    }
</script>
<html xmlns="http://www.w3.org/1999/xhtml" >
<head id="Head1" runat="server">
    <title>Show ButtonField</title>
</head>
<body>
    <form id="form1" runat="server">
    <div>

    <asp:GridView
        id="grdMovieCategories"
        DataSourceID="srcMovieCategories"
        DataKeyNames="Id,Position"
        AutoGenerateColumns="false"
        OnRowCommand="grdMovieCategories_RowCommand"
        Runat="server">
        <Columns>
        <asp:ButtonField
            Text="Move Up"
            CommandName="Up" />
        <asp:ButtonField
            Text="Move Down"
            CommandName="Down" />
        <asp:BoundField
            DataField="Position"
            HeaderText="Position" />
        <asp:BoundField
            DataField="Name"
            HeaderText="Category Name" />
        </Columns>
    </asp:GridView>

    <asp:SqlDataSource
        id="srcMovieCategories"
        ConnectionString="<%$ ConnectionStrings:Movies %>"
```

LISTING 11.21   Continued

```
        SelectCommand="SELECT Id, Name, Position FROM MovieCategories
            ORDER BY Position"
        UpdateCommand="UPDATE MovieCategories SET
            Position=@Position WHERE Id=@Id"
        Runat="server">
        <UpdateParameters>
        <asp:Parameter
            Name="Id" />
        <asp:Parameter
            Name="Position" />
        </UpdateParameters>
    </asp:SqlDataSource>

    </div>
    </form>
</body>
</html>
```

When you click either the Move Up or Move Down buttons in the page in Listing 11.21, the GridView control's RowCommand event is raised. This event is handled by the grdMovieCategories_RowCommand() method.

The grdMovieCategories_RowCommand() retrieves the index of the row containing the button that was clicked. The row index is grabbed from the GridViewCommandEventArgs's CommandArgument property passed as the second parameter to the event handler.

The grdMovieCategories_RowCommand() method updates the position of a record by setting the SqlDataSource control's Update parameters and calling the SqlDataSource control's Update() method.

A ButtonField supports the following properties:

▶ **ButtonType**—Enables you to specify the type of button displayed by the CommandField. Possible values are Button, Image, and Link.

▶ **CausesValidation**—Enables you to disable validation when the button is clicked.

▶ **CommandName**—Enables you to associate a standard edit command with the ButtonField. Possible values include Delete, Edit, Update, and Cancel.

▶ **DataTextField**—Enables you to use a data column to specify the button text.

▶ **DataTextFormatString**—Enables you to format the button text.

▶ **Text**—Enables you to specify the button text.

▶ **ValidationGroup**—Enables you to associate the button with a validation group.

Notice that you can use `CommandName` to associate a `ButtonField` with one of the standard edit commands. For example, you can create a Delete button by assigning the value `Delete` to the `CommandName` property.

Using `HyperLinkFields`

You use a `HyperLinkField` to create a link to another page. A `HyperLinkField` is particularly useful when you need to build two page Master/Detail forms.

For example, the page in Listing 11.22 displays a list of movie categories, and the page in Listing 11.23 displays a list of movies that match the selected category.

LISTING 11.22   Master.aspx

```
<%@ Page Language="C#" %>
<html xmlns="http://www.w3.org/1999/xhtml" >
<head id="Head1" runat="server">
    <title>Master</title>
</head>
<body>
    <form id="form1" runat="server">
    <div>

    <asp:GridView
        id="grdMovieCategories"
        DataSourceID="srcMovieCategories"
        AutoGenerateColumns="false"
        Runat="server">
        <Columns>
        <asp:HyperLinkField
            HeaderText="Movie Categories"
            DataTextField="Name"
            DataNavigateUrlFields="Id"
            DataNavigateUrlFormatString="Details.aspx?id={0}" />
        </Columns>
    </asp:GridView>

    <asp:SqlDataSource
        id="srcMovieCategories"
        ConnectionString="<%$ ConnectionStrings:Movies %>"
        SelectCommand="SELECT Id, Name FROM MovieCategories"
        Runat="server" />

    </div>
    </form>
</body>
</html>
```

LISTING 11.23   `Details.aspx`

```
<%@ Page Language="C#" %>
<!DOCTYPE html PUBLIC "-//W3C//DTD XHTML 1.1//EN"
  "http://www.w3.org/TR/xhtml11/DTD/xhtml11.dtd">
<html xmlns="http://www.w3.org/1999/xhtml" >
<head id="Head1" runat="server">
    <title>Details</title>
</head>
<body>
    <form id="form1" runat="server">
    <div>

    <asp:GridView
        id="grdMovies"
        DataSourceID="srcMovies"
        Runat="server" />

    <asp:SqlDataSource
        id="srcMovies"
        ConnectionString="<%$ ConnectionStrings:Movies %>"
        SelectCommand="SELECT Title,Director FROM Movies
            WHERE CategoryId=@CategoryId"
        Runat="server">
        <SelectParameters>
        <asp:QueryStringParameter
            Name="CategoryId"
            QueryStringField="id" />
        </SelectParameters>
    </asp:SqlDataSource>

    </div>
    </form>
</body>
</html>
```

The page in Listing 11.22 includes a GridView control that contains a HyperLinkField. The HyperLinkField creates a link to the Details.aspx page and passes the movie category ID as a query string parameter.

The HyperLinkField looks like this:

```
<asp:HyperLinkField
    HeaderText="Movie Categories"
    DataTextField="Name"
```

```
DataNavigateUrlFields="Id"
DataNavigateUrlFormatString="Details.aspx?id={0}" />
```

The DataNavigateUrlFields property represents the fields used with the
DataNavigateFormatString. The DataNavigateFormatString plugs the value of the ID
column from the DataNavigateUrlFields into the {0} placeholder.

> **NOTE**
>
> The DataNavigateUrlFields property accepts a comma-separated list of column
> names. You can use multiple placeholders in the DataNavigateUrlFormatString.

When you link to the page in Listing 11.23, the list of matching movies is displayed.
Notice that the SqlDataSource control includes a QueryStringParameter that represents
the movie category ID query string parameter.

You also can use HyperLinkFields when working with frames. For example, the page in
Listing 11.24 employs a GridView to display a list of movies. The page also includes an
iframe (inline frame), which displays details for a particular movie. The iframe displays
the page contained in Listing 11.25 (see Figure 11.17).

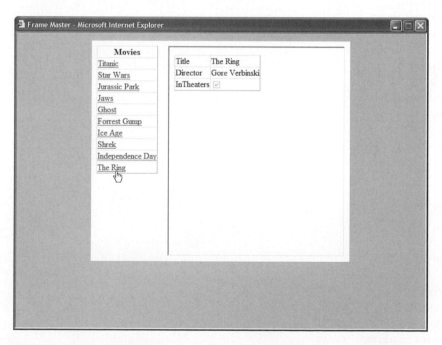

FIGURE 11.17   Displaying a single-page Master/Detail form.

LISTING 11.24   FrameMaster.aspx

```
<%@ Page Language="C#" %>
<!DOCTYPE html PUBLIC "-//W3C//DTD XHTML 1.0 Transitional//EN"
    "http://www.w3.org/TR/xhtml1/DTD/xhtml1-transitional.dtd">
<html xmlns="http://www.w3.org/1999/xhtml" >
<head id="Head1" runat="server">
    <style type="text/css">
        html
        {
            background-color:silver;
        }
        .content
        {
            width:500px;
            margin:auto;
            background-color:white;
        }
        .column
        {
            padding:10px;
            float:left;
        }
        #FrameDetails
        {
            width:100%;
            height:400px;
        }
    </style>
    <title>Frame Master</title>
</head>
<body>
    <form id="form1" runat="server">
    <div class="content">

    <div class="column">

    <asp:GridView
        id="grdMovies"
        DataSourceID="srcMovies"
        AutoGenerateColumns="false"
        Runat="server">
        <Columns>
        <asp:HyperLinkField
            HeaderText="Movies"
            DataTextField="Title"
```

11

```
                DataNavigateUrlFields="Id"
                DataNavigateUrlFormatString="FrameDetails.aspx?id={0}"
                Target="FrameDetails" />
        </Columns>
    </asp:GridView>

    <asp:SqlDataSource
        id="srcMovies"
        ConnectionString="<%$ ConnectionStrings:Movies %>"
        SelectCommand="SELECT * FROM Movies"
        Runat="server" />

    </div>
    <div class="column">

    <iframe name="FrameDetails" id="FrameDetails"></iframe>

    </div>

    <br style="clear:both" />
    </div>
    </form>
</body>
</html>
```

LISTING 11.25   FrameDetails.aspx

```
<%@ Page Language="C#" %>
<!DOCTYPE html PUBLIC "-//W3C//DTD XHTML 1.0 Transitional//EN"
    "http://www.w3.org/TR/xhtml1/DTD/xhtml1-transitional.dtd">
<html xmlns="http://www.w3.org/1999/xhtml" >
<head id="Head1" runat="server">
    <title>Frame Details</title>
</head>
<body>
    <form id="form1" runat="server">
    <div>

    <asp:DetailsView
        id="dtlMovie"
        DataSourceID="srcMovieDetails"
        Runat="server" />

    <asp:SqlDataSource
        id="srcMovieDetails"
```

LISTING 11.25   Continued

```
    ConnectionString="<%$ ConnectionStrings:Movies %>"
    SelectCommand="SELECT Title, Director, InTheaters
        FROM Movies WHERE Id=@MovieId"
    Runat="server">
    <SelectParameters>
    <asp:QueryStringParameter
        Name="MovieId"
        QueryStringField="id" />
    </SelectParameters>
</asp:SqlDataSource>

</div>
</form>
</body>
</html>
```

Notice that the HyperLinkField contained in Listing 11.24 includes a Target property. The Target property contains the name of the iframe. When you click a movie link, the FrameDetails.aspx page opens in the named iframe.

The HyperLinkField supports the following properties:

▶ **DataNavigateUrlFields**—Represents the field or fields from the data source to use with the DataNavigateUrlFormatString.

▶ **DataNavigateUrlFormatString**—Represents a format string that can be used to create the hyperlink.

▶ **DataTextField**—Represents a field from the data source to use for the hyperlink label.

▶ **DataTextFormatString**—Represents a format string that can be used to format the hyperlink label.

▶ **NavigateUrl**—Represents a fixed link to another page.

▶ **Target**—Represents the target of a link. Possible values include blank, parent, self, and top. You can also supply the name of a frame or iframe.

▶ **Text**—Represents fixed text to display as the label for the hyperlink.

Using ImageFields

You use an ImageField to display an image stored on the server's hard drive. You can't use an ImageField to display images stored in a database table.

The page in Listing 11.26 illustrates how you can use the ImageField when creating a simple photo gallery (see Figure 11.18).

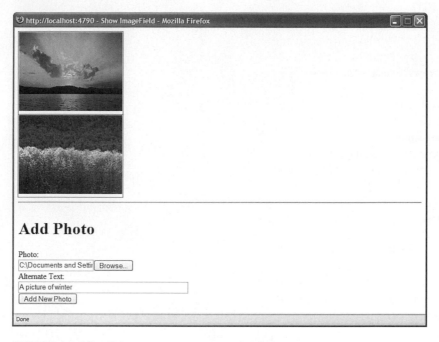

FIGURE 11.18   Using an `ImageField` with the `GridView` control.

LISTING 11.26   `ShowImageField.aspx`

```
<%@ Page Language="C#" %>
<!DOCTYPE html PUBLIC "-//W3C//DTD XHTML 1.1//EN"
"http://www.w3.org/TR/xhtml11/DTD/xhtml11.dtd">
<script runat="server">

    protected void frmPhoto_ItemInserting(object sender, FormViewInsertEventArgs e)
    {
        // Get the FileUpload control
        FileUpload upPhoto = (FileUpload)frmPhoto.FindControl("upPhoto");
        srcImages.InsertParameters["FileName"].DefaultValue = upPhoto.FileName;

        string savePath = MapPath("~/Photos/" + upPhoto.FileName);
        // Save contents to file system
        upPhoto.SaveAs(savePath);
    }
</script>

<html xmlns="http://www.w3.org/1999/xhtml" >
<head id="Head1" runat="server">
    <title>Show ImageField</title>
```

LISTING 11.26   Continued

```
</head>
<body>
    <form id="form1" runat="server">
    <div>

    <asp:GridView
        id="grdImages"
        DataSourceID="srcImages"
        AutoGenerateColumns="false"
        ShowHeader="false"
        Runat="server">
        <Columns>
        <asp:ImageField
            DataImageUrlField="FileName"
            DataImageUrlFormatString="~/Photos/{0}"
            DataAlternateTextField="AltText"
            ControlStyle-Width="200px" />
        </Columns>
    </asp:GridView>

    <asp:SqlDataSource
        id="srcImages"
        ConnectionString="<%$ ConnectionStrings:Photos %>"
        SelectCommand="SELECT FileName, AltText FROM Photos"
        InsertCommand="INSERT Photos (FileName, AltText)
            VALUES (@FileName, @AltText)"
        Runat="server">
        <InsertParameters>
            <asp:Parameter Name="FileName" />
        </InsertParameters>
    </asp:SqlDataSource>

    <hr />
    <asp:FormView
        id="frmPhoto"
        DefaultMode="Insert"
        DataSourceID="srcImages"
        OnItemInserting="frmPhoto_ItemInserting"
        Runat="server">
        <InsertItemTemplate>
        <h1>Add Photo</h1>
        <asp:Label
            id="lblPhoto"
```

```
                Text="Photo:"
                AssociatedControlID="upPhoto"
                Runat="server" />
        <br />
        <asp:FileUpload
            id="upPhoto"
            Runat="server" />
        <br />
        <asp:Label
            id="lblAltText"
            Text="Alternate Text:"
            AssociatedControlID="txtAltText"
            Runat="server" />
        <br />
        <asp:TextBox
            id="txtAltText"
            Text='<%# Bind("AltText") %>'
            Columns="50"
            Runat="server" />
        <br />
        <asp:Button
            id="btnInsert"
            Text="Add New Photo"
            CommandName="Insert"
            Runat="server" />
        </InsertItemTemplate>
    </asp:FormView>

    </div>
    </form>
</body>
</html>
```

The `GridView` in Listing 11.26 contains an `ImageField` that looks like this:

```
<asp:ImageField
    DataImageUrlField="FileName"
    DataImageUrlFormatString="~/Photos/{0}"
    DataAlternateTextField="AltText"
    ControlStyle-Width="200px" />
```

The `DataImageUrlField` property contains the name of a field from the data source that represents the path to an image on the server hard drive. The `DataImageUrlFormatString` enables you to format this path. Finally, the `DataAlternateTextField` enables you to specify the value of the `alt` attribute used by the `<img>` tag.

WEB STANDARDS NOTE

Always supply an `alt` attribute for your `<img>` tags so that blind users of your web application can interpret an image's meaning. In the case of purely decorative images, create an empty `alt` attribute (`alt=""`).

An `ImageField` supports the following properties:

- **`AlternateText`**—Enables you to specify fixed alternate text.

- **`DataAlternateTextField`**—Enables you to specify a field that represents the alternate text.

- **`DataAlternateTextFormatString`**—Enables you to format the alternate text.

- **`DataImageUrlField`**—Enables you to specify a field that represents the image path.

- **`DataImageUrlFormatString`**—Enables you to format the image path.

- **`NullImageUrl`**—Enables you to specify an alternate image when the `DataImageUrlField` is `Nothing` (null).

Using `TemplateFields`

A `TemplateField` enables you to add any content to a `GridView` column that you need. A `TemplateField` can contain HTML, `DataBinding` expressions, or ASP.NET controls.

`TemplateFields` are particularly useful when you are using a `GridView` to edit database records. You can use a `TemplateField` to customize the user interface and add validation to the fields being edited.

For example, the page in Listing 11.27 contains a `GridView` that enables you to edit the records contained in the Movies database table. `TemplateFields` are used to render the user interface for editing the movie title and category columns (see Figure 11.19).

LISTING 11.27   ShowTemplateField.aspx

```
<%@ Page Language="C#" %>
<!DOCTYPE html PUBLIC "-//W3C//DTD XHTML 1.1//EN"
  "http://www.w3.org/TR/xhtml11/DTD/xhtml11.dtd">
<html xmlns="http://www.w3.org/1999/xhtml" >
<head id="Head1" runat="server">
    <title>Show TemplateField</title>
</head>
<body>
    <form id="form1" runat="server">
    <div>

    <asp:GridView
        id="grdMovies"
```

```
    DataSourceID="srcMovies"
    DataKeyNames="Id"
    AutoGenerateColumns="false"
    AutoGenerateEditButton="true"
    Runat="server">
    <Columns>
    <asp:TemplateField HeaderText="Title">
        <ItemTemplate>
        <%# Eval("Title") %>
        </ItemTemplate>
        <EditItemTemplate>
        <asp:TextBox
            id="txtTitle"
            Text='<%# Bind("Title") %>'
            Runat="server" />
        <asp:RequiredFieldValidator
            id="valTitle"
            ControlToValidate="txtTitle"
            Text="(required)"
            Runat="server" />
        </EditItemTemplate>
    </asp:TemplateField>
    <asp:TemplateField HeaderText="Category">
        <ItemTemplate>
        <%# Eval("Name") %>
        </ItemTemplate>
        <EditItemTemplate>
        <asp:DropDownList
            id="ddlCategory"
            DataSourceID="srcMovieCategories"
            DataTextField="Name"
            DataValueField="Id"
            SelectedValue='<%# Bind("CategoryId") %>'
            Runat="server" />
        </EditItemTemplate>
    </asp:TemplateField>
    </Columns>
</asp:GridView>

<asp:SqlDataSource
    id="srcMovies"
    ConnectionString='<%$ ConnectionStrings:Movies %>'
    SelectCommand="SELECT Movies.Id, Title, CategoryId, Name
        FROM Movies JOIN MovieCategories
        ON MovieCategories.Id = Movies.CategoryId"
    UpdateCommand="UPDATE Movies SET Title=@Title, CategoryId=@CategoryId
```

LISTING 11.27   Continued

```
                WHERE Id=@Id"
        Runat="server" />

    <asp:SqlDataSource
        id="srcMovieCategories"
        ConnectionString='<%$ ConnectionStrings:Movies %>'
        SelectCommand="SELECT Id, Name FROM MovieCategories"
        Runat="server" />

    </div>
    </form>
</body>
</html>
```

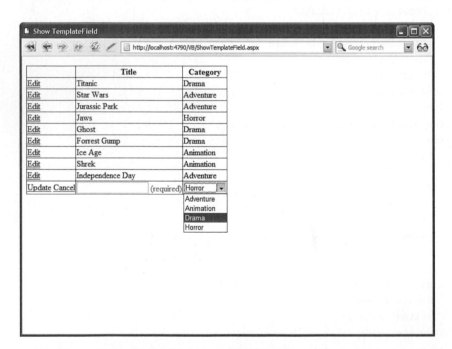

FIGURE 11.19   Using TemplateFields with the GridView control.

The GridView in Listing 11.27 contains two TemplateFields. The first TemplateField enables you to display and edit the value of the Title column. The contents of the ItemTemplate are displayed when a row *is not* selected for editing. The contents of the EditItemTemplate are displayed when the row *is* selected for editing.

The EditItemTemplate for the Title column includes a RequiredFieldValidator control. This RequiredFieldValidator control prevents a user from updating a record without entering a value for the Title column.

The second `TemplateField` displays the value of the movie category column. The `EditItemTemplate` contains a `DropDownList` control, which enables you to change the movie category associated with the record being edited.

A `TemplateField` supports the following six types of templates:

- ▶ **AlternatingItemTemplate**—The contents of this template are displayed for every other row rendered by the `GridView`.

- ▶ **EditItemTemplate**—The contents of this template are displayed when a row is selected for editing.

- ▶ **FooterTemplate**—The contents of this template are displayed in the column footer.

- ▶ **HeaderTemplate**—The contents of this template are displayed in the column header.

- ▶ **InsertItemTemplate**—The contents of this template are displayed when a new data item is inserted (does not apply to the `GridView` control).

- ▶ **ItemTemplate**—The contents of this template are displayed for every row rendered by the `GridView`.

Working with `GridView` Control Events

The `GridView` control includes a rich set of events that you can handle to customize the control's behavior and appearance. These events can be divided into three groups.

First, the `GridView` control supports the following set of events that are raised when the control displays its rows:

- ▶ **DataBinding**—Raised immediately before the `GridView` is bound to its data source.

- ▶ **DataBound**—Raised immediately after a `GridView` is bound to its data source.

- ▶ **RowCreated**—Raised when each row in the `GridView` is created.

- ▶ **RowDataBound**—Raised when each row in the `GridView` is bound to data.

Second, the `GridView` control includes the following set of events that are raised when you are editing records:

- ▶ **RowCommand**—Raised when an event is raised by a control contained in the `GridView`.

- ▶ **RowUpdating**—Raised immediately before a `GridView` updates a record.

- ▶ **RowUpdated**—Raised immediately after a `GridView` updates a record.

- ▶ **RowDeleting**—Raised immediately before a `GridView` deletes a record.

- ▶ **RowDeleted**—Raised immediately after a `GridView` deletes a record.

- ▶ **RowCancelingEdit**—Raised when you cancel updating a record.

Finally, the `GridView` control supports the following events related to sorting, selecting, and paging:

- **`PageIndexChanging`**—Raised immediately before the current page is changed.
- **`PageIndexChanged`**—Raised immediately after the current page is changed.
- **`Sorting`**—Raised immediately before sorting.
- **`Sorted`**—Raised immediately after sorting.
- **`SelectedIndexChanging`**—Raised immediately before a row is selected.
- **`SelectedIndexChanged`**—Raised immediately after a row is selected.

In this section, you learn how to handle the `RowDataBound` event (my favorite event included with the `GridView` control) to create `GridView` special effects. You learn how to handle the `RowDataBound` event to highlight particular rows, show column summaries, and create nested Master/Detail forms.

Highlighting `GridView` Rows

Imagine that you want to highlight particular rows in a `GridView`. For example, when displaying a table of sales totals, you might want to highlight the rows in which the sales are greater than a certain amount.

You can modify the appearance of individual rows in a `GridView` control by handling the `RowDataBound` event. For example, the page in Listing 11.28 displays every movie that has a box office total greater than $300,000.00 with a yellow background color (see Figure 11.20).

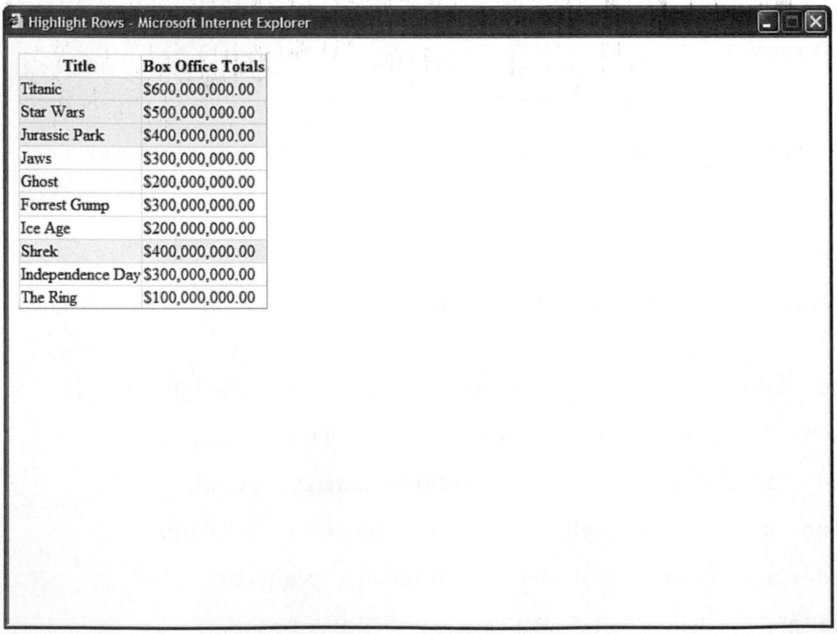

Title	Box Office Totals
Titanic	$600,000,000.00
Star Wars	$500,000,000.00
Jurassic Park	$400,000,000.00
Jaws	$300,000,000.00
Ghost	$200,000,000.00
Forrest Gump	$300,000,000.00
Ice Age	$200,000,000.00
Shrek	$400,000,000.00
Independence Day	$300,000,000.00
The Ring	$100,000,000.00

FIGURE 11.20 Highlighting rows in the `GridView` control.

LISTING 11.28 HighlightRows.aspx

```csharp
<%@ Page Language="C#" %>
<!DOCTYPE html PUBLIC "-//W3C//DTD XHTML 1.1//EN"
"http://www.w3.org/TR/xhtml11/DTD/xhtml11.dtd">
<script runat="server">

    protected void grdMovies_RowDataBound(object sender, GridViewRowEventArgs e)
    {
        if (e.Row.RowType == DataControlRowType.DataRow)
        {
            decimal boxOfficeTotals = (decimal)DataBinder.Eval(e.Row.DataItem,
            ➥"BoxOfficeTotals");
            if (boxOfficeTotals > 300000000)
                e.Row.BackColor = System.Drawing.Color.Yellow;
        }
    }
</script>
<html xmlns="http://www.w3.org/1999/xhtml" >
<head id="Head1" runat="server">
    <title>Highlight Rows</title>
</head>
<body>
    <form id="form1" runat="server">
    <div>

    <asp:GridView
        id="grdMovies"
        DataSourceID="srcMovies"
        OnRowDataBound="grdMovies_RowDataBound"
        AutoGenerateColumns="false"
        Runat="server">
        <Columns>
        <asp:BoundField
            DataField="Title"
            HeaderText="Title" />
        <asp:BoundField
            DataField="BoxOfficeTotals"
            DataFormatString="{0:c}"
            HtmlEncode="false"
            HeaderText="Box Office Totals" />
        </Columns>
    </asp:GridView>

    <asp:SqlDataSource
        id="srcMovies"
```

LISTING 11.28 Continued

```
        ConnectionString="<%$ ConnectionStrings:Movies %>"
        SelectCommand="SELECT * FROM Movies"
        Runat="server" />

    </div>
    </form>
</body>
</html>
```

In Listing 11.28, the grdMovies_RowDataBound() method is executed when the GridView renders each of its rows (including its header and footer). The second parameter passed to this event handler is an instance of the GridViewRowEventArgs class. This class exposes a GridViewRow object that represents the row being bound.

The GridViewRow object supports several useful properties (this is not a complete list):

▶ **Cells**—Represents the collection of table row cells associated with the row being bound.

▶ **DataItem**—Represents the data item associated with the row being bound.

▶ **DataItemIndex**—Represents the index of the data item in its DataSet associated with the row being bound.

▶ **RowIndex**—Represents the index of the row being bound.

▶ **RowState**—Represents the state of the row being bound. Possible values are Alternate, Normal, Selected, and Edit. Because these values can be combined (for example, the RowState can be Alternate Edit), use a bitwise comparison with RowState.

▶ **RowType**—Represents the type of row being bound. Possible values are DataRow, Footer, Header, NullRow, Pager, and Separator.

In Listing 11.28, the RowType property is used to verify that the row is a DataRow (not a header row or some other type of row). The DataItem property is used to retrieve the database record associated with the row. Notice that the DataBinder.Eval() method is used to retrieve the value of the BoxOfficeColumn.

Displaying Column Summaries

Imagine that you want to display a column total at the bottom of a column. In that case, you can handle the GridView RowDataBound event to sum the values in a column and display the summary in the column footer.

For example, the page in Listing 11.29 contains a GridView control that displays a summary column representing the total box office sales of all movies (see Figure 11.21).

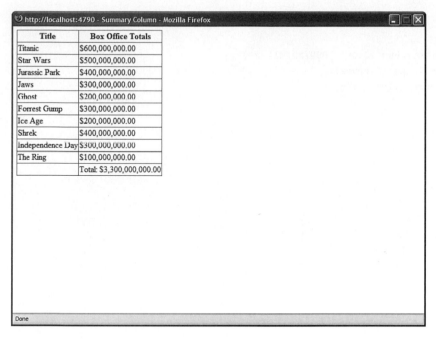

FIGURE 11.21   Displaying a column summary.

LISTING 11.29   SummaryColumn.aspx

```
<%@ Page Language="C#" %>
<!DOCTYPE html PUBLIC "-//W3C//DTD XHTML 1.1//EN"
"http://www.w3.org/TR/xhtml11/DTD/xhtml11.dtd">
<script runat="server">

    private decimal _boxOfficeTotalsTotal = 0;

    protected void grdMovies_RowDataBound(object sender, GridViewRowEventArgs e)
    {
        if (e.Row.RowType == DataControlRowType.DataRow)
        {
            decimal boxOfficeTotals = (decimal)DataBinder.Eval(e.Row.DataItem,
            ➥"BoxOfficeTotals");
            _boxOfficeTotalsTotal += boxOfficeTotals;
        }
        if (e.Row.RowType == DataControlRowType.Footer)
        {
            Label lblSummary = (Label)e.Row.FindControl("lblSummary");
            lblSummary.Text = String.Format("Total: {0:c}", _boxOfficeTotalsTotal);
        }
    }
```

LISTING 11.29   Continued

```
</script>
<html xmlns="http://www.w3.org/1999/xhtml" >
<head id="Head1" runat="server">
    <title>Summary Column</title>
</head>
<body>
    <form id="form1" runat="server">
    <div>

    <asp:GridView
        id="grdMovies"
        DataSourceID="srcMovies"
        OnRowDataBound="grdMovies_RowDataBound"
        AutoGenerateColumns="false"
        ShowFooter="true"
        Runat="server">
        <Columns>
        <asp:BoundField
            DataField="Title"
            HeaderText="Title" />
        <asp:TemplateField HeaderText="Box Office Totals">
        <ItemTemplate>
            <%# Eval("BoxOfficeTotals", "{0:c}") %>
        </ItemTemplate>
        <FooterTemplate>
            <asp:Label
                id="lblSummary"
                Runat="server" />
        </FooterTemplate>
        </asp:TemplateField>
        </Columns>
    </asp:GridView>

    <asp:SqlDataSource
        id="srcMovies"
        ConnectionString="<%$ ConnectionStrings:Movies %>"
        SelectCommand="SELECT * FROM Movies"
        Runat="server" />

    </div>
    </form>
</body>
</html>
```

Notice that the `GridView` control uses a `TemplateField` to represent the BoxOfficeTotals column. The `TemplateField` includes a `<FooterTemplate>` that contains a `Label` control. The `grdMovies_RowDataBound()` method displays the total of the box office totals in this Label control.

Displaying Nested Master/Details Forms

You also can handle the `RowDataBound` event to create nested Master/Details forms. The page in Listing 11.30 displays a list of movie categories and displays a list of matching movies under each category (see Figure 11.22).

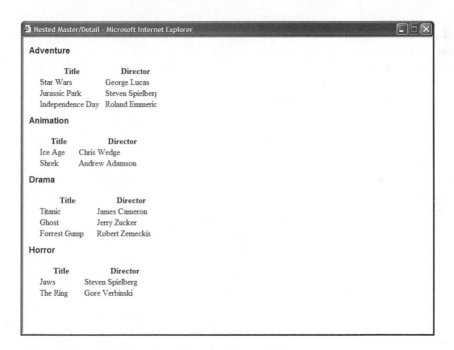

FIGURE 11.22   Displaying a nested Master/Detail form.

LISTING 11.30   NestedMasterDetail.aspx

```
<%@ Page Language="C#" %>
<!DOCTYPE html PUBLIC "-//W3C//DTD XHTML 1.1//EN"
"http://www.w3.org/TR/xhtml11/DTD/xhtml11.dtd">
<script runat="server">

    protected void grdMovieCategories_RowDataBound(object sender,
    ➥GridViewRowEventArgs e)
    {
```

LISTING 11.30   Continued

```
        if (e.Row.RowType == DataControlRowType.DataRow)
        {
            int categoryId = (int)DataBinder.Eval(e.Row.DataItem,"Id");
            SqlDataSource srcMovies = (SqlDataSource)e.Row.FindControl("srcMovies");
            srcMovies.SelectParameters["CategoryId"].DefaultValue =
            ➥categoryId.ToString();
        }
    }

</script>
<html xmlns="http://www.w3.org/1999/xhtml" >
<head id="Head1" runat="server">
    <style type="text/css">
        .categories h1
        {
            font:bold 16px Arial, Sans-Serif;
        }
        .movies
        {
            margin-left:20px;
            margin-bottom:10px;
            width:100%;
        }
    </style>
    <title>Nested Master/Detail</title>
</head>
<body>
    <form id="form1" runat="server">
    <div>

    <asp:GridView
        id="grdMovies"
        DataSourceID="srcMovieCategories"
        OnRowDataBound="grdMovieCategories_RowDataBound"
        AutoGenerateColumns="false"
        CssClass="categories"
        ShowHeader="false"
        GridLines="none"
        Runat="server">
        <Columns>
        <asp:TemplateField>
```

```
            <ItemTemplate>
                <h1><%# Eval("Name") %></h1>
                <asp:GridView
                    id="grdMovies"
                    DataSourceId="srcMovies"
                    CssClass="movies"
                    GridLines="none"
                    Runat="server" />

                <asp:SqlDataSource
                    id="srcMovies"
                    ConnectionString="<%$ ConnectionStrings:Movies %>"
                    SelectCommand="SELECT Title,Director FROM Movies
                        WHERE CategoryId=@CategoryId"
                    Runat="server">
                    <SelectParameters>
                        <asp:Parameter Name="CategoryId" />
                    </SelectParameters>
                </asp:SqlDataSource>
            </ItemTemplate>
            </asp:TemplateField>
            </Columns>
    </asp:GridView>

    <asp:SqlDataSource
        id="srcMovieCategories"
        ConnectionString="<%$ ConnectionStrings:Movies %>"
        SelectCommand="SELECT Id,Name FROM MovieCategories"
        Runat="server" />



    </div>
    </form>
</body>
</html>
```

The grdMovieCategories_RowDataBound() method handles the RowDataBound event. This event handler grabs the movie category ID from the current row's DataItem property. Next, it retrieves the SqlDataSource control contained in the grdMovieCategories TemplateField. Finally, it assigns the movie category ID to a parameter contained in the SqlDataSource control's SelectParameters collection.

NOTE

Notice that you must use the `FindControl()` method to get the `SqlDataSource` control from the `TemplateField`. The templates in a `TemplateField` each create their own naming containers to prevent naming collisions. The `FindControl()` method enables you to search a naming container for a control with a matching ID.

Extending the `GridView` Control

Like any other control in the ASP.NET framework, if you don't like any aspect of the `GridView` control, you always have the option of extending the control. In this section, you learn how to extend the `GridView` control with custom fields.

To create a custom field, you can inherit a new class from any of the existing fields or any of the following base classes:

- ▶ **DataControlField**—The base class for all fields.

- ▶ **ButtonFieldBase**—The base class for all button fields, such as the `ButtonField` and `CommandField`.

In this section, you learn how to create a long text field, a delete button field, and a validated field.

Creating a `LongTextField`

None of the existing `GridView` fields do a good job of handling large amounts of text. You can fix this problem by creating a custom field, named the `LongTextField`, which you can use to display the value of text columns regardless of the length of the text.

In normal display mode, the `LongTextField` displays the text in a scrolling <div> tag. In edit display mode, the text appears in a multi-line `TextBox` control (see Figure 11.23).

To create a custom field, a new class must be inherited from the base `BoundField` control. The custom `LongTextField` is contained in Listing 11.31.

LISTING 11.31   LongTextField.cs

```
using System;
using System.Web.UI;
using System.Web.UI.WebControls;
using System.Web.UI.HtmlControls;

namespace myControls
{
    /// <summary>
    /// Enables you to display a long text field
    /// </summary>
    public class LongTextField : BoundField
```

```csharp
{
    private Unit _width = new Unit("250px");
    private Unit _height = new Unit("60px");

    /// <summary>
    /// The Width of the field
    /// </summary>
    public Unit Width
    {
        get { return _width; }
        set { _width = value; }
    }

    /// <summary>
    /// The Height of the field
    /// </summary>
    public Unit Height
    {
        get { return _height; }
        set { _height = value; }
    }

    /// <summary>
    /// Builds the contents of the field
    /// </summary>
    protected override void InitializeDataCell(DataControlFieldCell cell,
    ➥DataControlRowState rowState)
    {
        // If not editing, show in scrolling div
        if ((rowState & DataControlRowState.Edit) == 0)
        {
            HtmlGenericControl div = new HtmlGenericControl("div");
            div.Attributes["class"] = "longTextField";
            div.Style[HtmlTextWriterStyle.Width] = _width.ToString();
            div.Style[HtmlTextWriterStyle.Height] = _height.ToString();
            div.Style[HtmlTextWriterStyle.Overflow] = "auto";

            div.DataBinding += new EventHandler(div_DataBinding);

            cell.Controls.Add(div);
        }
        else
        {
            TextBox txtEdit = new TextBox();
            txtEdit.TextMode = TextBoxMode.MultiLine;
            txtEdit.Width = _width;
```

LISTING 11.31   Continued

```csharp
            txtEdit.Height = _height;

            txtEdit.DataBinding += new EventHandler(txtEdit_DataBinding);

            cell.Controls.Add(txtEdit);
        }
    }

    /// <summary>
    /// Called when databound in display mode
    /// </summary>
    void div_DataBinding(object s, EventArgs e)
    {
        HtmlGenericControl div = (HtmlGenericControl)s;

        // Get the field value
        Object value = this.GetValue(div.NamingContainer);

        // Assign the formatted value
        div.InnerText = this.FormatDataValue(value, this.HtmlEncode);
    }

    /// <summary>
    /// Called when databound in edit mode
    /// </summary>
    void txtEdit_DataBinding(object s, EventArgs e)
    {
        TextBox txtEdit = (TextBox)s;

        // Get the field value
        Object value = this.GetValue(txtEdit.NamingContainer);

        // Assign the formatted value
        txtEdit.Text = this.FormatDataValue(value, this.HtmlEncode);
    }

    }
}
```

In Listing 11.31, the `InitializeDataCell()` method is overridden. This method is responsible for creating all the controls that the custom field contains.

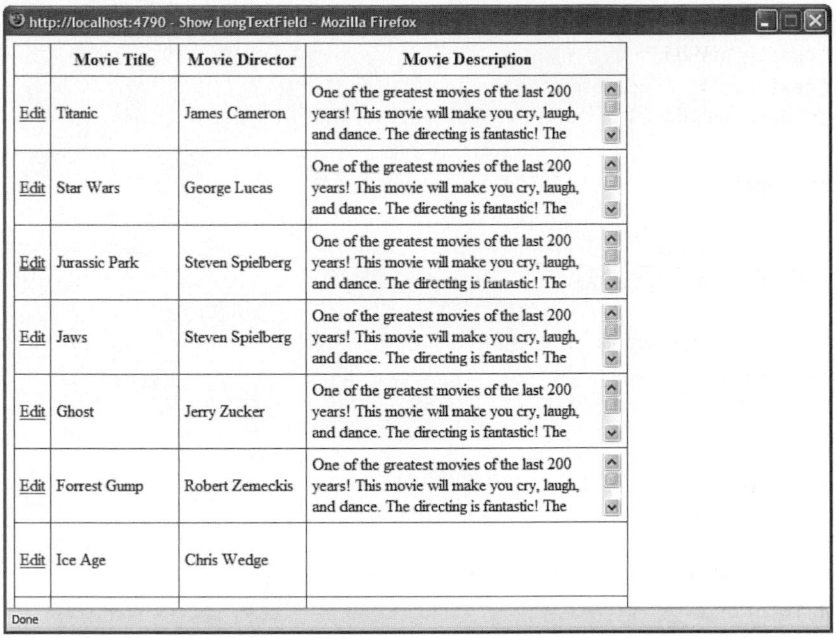

FIGURE 11.23   Displaying a long text field.

First, a check is made to determine whether the field is being rendered when the row is selected for editing. Notice that a bitwise comparison must be performed with the rowState parameter because the rowState parameter can contain combinations of the values Alternate, Normal, Selected, and Edit (for example, the RowState can be both Alternate and Edit).

When the row is not in edit mode, a <div> tag is created to contain the text. An HtmlGenericControl represents the <div> tag. When the GridView is bound to its data source, the <div> tags get the value of its innerText property from the div_DataBinding() method.

When the row is selected for editing, a multi-line TextBox control is created. When the GridView is bound to its data source, the TextBox control's Text property gets its value from the txtEdit_DataBinding() method.

You can experiment with the LongTextField with the page in Listing 11.32. This page uses the LongTextField to display the value of the Movie Description column.

LISTING 11.32   ShowLongTextField.aspx

```
<%@ Page Language="C#" %>
<%@ Register TagPrefix="custom" Namespace="myControls" %>
<!DOCTYPE html PUBLIC "-//W3C//DTD XHTML 1.1//EN"
    "http://www.w3.org/TR/xhtml11/DTD/xhtml11.dtd">
<html xmlns="http://www.w3.org/1999/xhtml" >
```

LISTING 11.32   Continued

```
<head id="Head1" runat="server">
    <style type="text/css">
        .grid td, .grid th
        {
            padding:5px;
        }
    </style>
    <title>Show LongTextField</title>
</head>
<body>
    <form id="form1" runat="server">
    <div>

    <asp:GridView
        id="grdMovies"
        CssClass="grid"
        DataSourceID="srcMovies"
        DataKeyNames="Id"
        AutoGenerateColumns="false"
        AutoGenerateEditButton="true"
        Runat="server">
        <Columns>
        <asp:BoundField
            DataField="Title"
            HeaderText="Movie Title" />
        <asp:BoundField
            DataField="Director"
            HeaderText="Movie Director" />
        <custom:LongTextField
            DataField="Description"
            Width="300px"
            Height="60px"
            HeaderText="Movie Description" />
        </Columns>
    </asp:GridView>

    <asp:SqlDataSource
        id="srcMovies"
        ConnectionString="<%$ ConnectionStrings:Movies %>"
        SelectCommand="SELECT Id, Title, Director, Description
            FROM Movies"
        UpdateCommand="UPDATE Movies SET
            Title=@Title,Director=@Director,Description=
            WHERE Id=@Id"
```

```
        Runat="server" />

    </div>
    </form>
</body>
</html>
```

Creating a `DeleteButtonField`

I don't like the Delete button rendered by the `GridView` control's `CommandField`. The problem is that it does not provide you with any warning before you delete a record. In this section, we fix this problem by creating a Delete button that displays a client-side confirmation dialog box (see Figure 11.24).

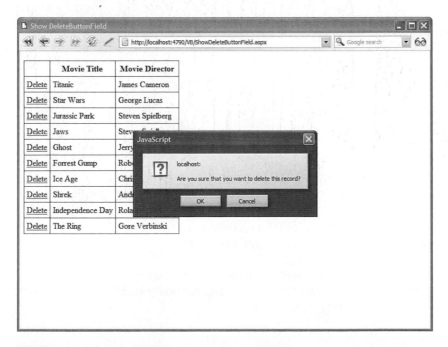

FIGURE 11.24   Displaying a confirmation dialog box.

The `DeleteButtonField` inherits from the `ButtonField` class. The code for the custom field is contained in Listing 11.33.

LISTING 11.33   DeleteButtonField.cs

```csharp
using System;
using System.Web.UI.WebControls;

namespace myControls
{
    /// <summary>
    /// Displays a confirmation before deleting a record
    /// </summary>
    public class DeleteButtonField : ButtonField
    {
        private string _confirmText = "Delete this record?";

        public string ConfirmText
        {
            get { return _confirmText; }
            set { _confirmText = value; }
        }

        public DeleteButtonField()
        {
            this.CommandName = "Delete";
            this.Text = "Delete";
        }

        public override void InitializeCell(DataControlFieldCell cell,
        ➥DataControlCellType cellType, DataControlRowState rowState, int rowIndex)
        {
            base.InitializeCell(cell, cellType, rowState, rowIndex);
            if (cellType == DataControlCellType.DataCell)
            {
                WebControl button = (WebControl)cell.Controls[0];
                button.Attributes["onclick"] = String.Format("return
                ➥confirm('{0}');", _confirmText);
            }
        }
    }
}
```

Most of the work in Listing 11.33 is handled by the base ButtonField class. The InitializeCell() method is overridden so that the button can be grabbed. The button is added to the cell by the base ButtonField's InitializeCell() method.

To create the confirmation dialog box, an `onclick` attribute is added to the button. If the JavaScript confirm statement returns `false`, then the button click is canceled.

You can test the `DeleteButtonField` with the page in Listing 11.34. This page enables you to delete records from the Movies database table.

LISTING 11.34 ShowDeleteButtonField.aspx

```
<%@ Page Language="C#" %>
<%@ Register TagPrefix="custom" Namespace="myControls" %>
<!DOCTYPE html PUBLIC "-//W3C//DTD XHTML 1.1//EN"
  "http://www.w3.org/TR/xhtml11/DTD/xhtml11.dtd">
<html xmlns="http://www.w3.org/1999/xhtml" >
<head id="Head1" runat="server">
    <style type="text/css">
        .grid td, .grid th
        {
            padding:5px;
        }
    </style>
    <title>Show DeleteButtonField</title>
</head>
<body>
    <form id="form1" runat="server">
    <div>

    <asp:GridView
        id="grdMovies"
        CssClass="grid"
        DataSourceID="srcMovies"
        DataKeyNames="Id"
        AutoGenerateColumns="false"
        Runat="server">
        <Columns>
        <custom:DeleteButtonField
            ConfirmText="Are you sure that you want to delete this record?" />
        <asp:BoundField
            DataField="Title"
            HeaderText="Movie Title" />
        <asp:BoundField
            DataField="Director"
            HeaderText="Movie Director" />
        </Columns>
    </asp:GridView>

    <asp:SqlDataSource
```

LISTING 11.34   Continued

```
        id="srcMovies"
        ConnectionString="<%$ ConnectionStrings:Movies %>"
        SelectCommand="SELECT Id, Title, Director FROM Movies"
        DeleteCommand="DELETE Movies WHERE Id=@Id"
        Runat="server" />

    </div>
    </form>
</body>
</html>
```

Creating a `ValidatedField`

In this final section, we create a `ValidatedField` custom field. This field automatically validates the data that a user enters into a `GridView` when editing a record. The `ValidatedField` uses a `RequiredFieldValidator` to check whether a user has entered a value, and a `CompareValidator` to check whether the value is the correct data type (see Figure 11.25).

The `ValidatedField` is a composite field. The field contains three child controls—`TextBox`, `RequiredFieldValidator`, and `CompareValidator`—wrapped up in a container control.

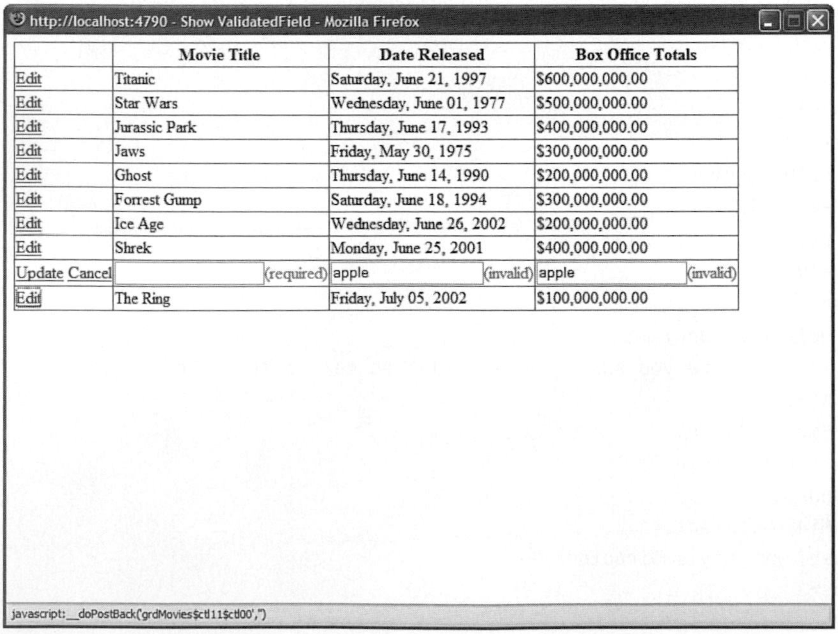

FIGURE 11.25   Using the `ValidatedField` to edit a record.

The code for the `ValidatedField` is too long to include in this chapter. The entire source code (in both C# and VB.NET) is included on the CD that accompanies this book.

The source code for the `ValidatedField` contains two classes. It contains the `ValidatedField` class and the `EditContainer` class.

The `ValidatedField` class derives from the `BoundField` class and overrides the `InitializeDataCell()` method. When a row is not selected for editing, the field simply displays the value of the data item associated with it. When a row is selected for editing, the field creates a new `EditContainer` control.

The `EditContainer` control contains a `TextBox`, `RequiredFieldValidator`, and `CompareValidator`. Notice that the `EditContainer` implements the `INamingContainer` interface. Implementing this interface prevents naming collisions when more than one instance of the `ValidatedField` is used in a `GridView` row.

The `ValidatedField` is used in the page in Listing 11.35. This page contains a `GridView` control that you can use to edit the Movies database table. The `GridView` control includes three `ValidatedFields`: one for the Title, DateReleased, and BoxOfficeTotals columns.

If you edit a column, and attempt to submit the column without entering a value, then a validation error is displayed. Furthermore, if you attempt to enter a value that is not a date for the `DateReleased` column or a value that is not a currency amount for the `BoxOfficeTotals` column, then a validation error is displayed.

LISTING 11.35   ShowValidatedField.aspx

```
<%@ Page Language="C#" %>
<%@ Register TagPrefix="custom" Namespace="myControls" %>
<!DOCTYPE html PUBLIC "-//W3C//DTD XHTML 1.1//EN"
    "http://www.w3.org/TR/xhtml11/DTD/xhtml11.dtd">
<html xmlns="http://www.w3.org/1999/xhtml" >
<head id="Head1" runat="server">
    <title>Show ValidatedField</title>
</head>
<body>
    <form id="form1" runat="server">
    <div>

    <asp:GridView
        id="grdMovies"
        DataKeyNames="Id"
        DataSourceID="srcMovies"
        AutoGenerateEditButton="true"
        AutoGenerateColumns="false"
        Runat="server">
        <Columns>
        <custom:ValidatedField
```

LISTING 11.35   Continued

```
            DataField="Title"
            HeaderText="Movie Title" />
        <custom:ValidatedField
            DataField="DateReleased"
            DataFormatString="{0:D}"
            HtmlEncode="false"
            ValidationDataType="Date"
            HeaderText="Date Released" />
        <custom:ValidatedField
            DataField="BoxOfficeTotals"
            DataFormatString="{0:c}"
            HtmlEncode="false"
            ValidationDataType="Currency"
            HeaderText="Box Office Totals" />
        </Columns>
    </asp:GridView>

    <asp:SqlDataSource
        id="srcMovies"
        ConnectionString="<%$ ConnectionStrings:Movies %>"
        SelectCommand="SELECT * FROM Movies"
        UpdateCommand="UPDATE Movies SET Title=@Title,
            DateReleased=@DateReleased, BoxOfficeTotals=@BoxOfficeTotals
            WHERE Id=@Id"
        Runat="server" />

    </div>
    </form>
</body>
</html>
```

Summary

In this chapter, you learned how to use the GridView control to display, select, sort, page, and edit database records. You also learn how to customize the appearance of the columns rendered by a column by using different types of fields. In particular, you learned how to use BoundFields, CheckboxFields, CommandFields, ImageFields, TemplateFields, ButtonFields, and HyperLinkFields.

Next, you learned how to handle the `RowDataBound` event to create `GridView` special effects. For example, you learned how to add column summaries to a `GridView`.

Finally, you learned how to extend the `GridView` control with custom fields. We created custom fields, which enable you to display large text fields, display a confirmation dialog box before a record is deleted, and display validation error messages when editing a record.

11

Using the DetailsView and FormView Controls

The DetailsView and FormView controls, the subject of this chapter, enable you to work with a single data item at a time. Both controls enable you to display, edit, insert, and delete data items such as database records. Furthermore, both controls enable you to page forward and backward through a set of data items.

The difference between the two controls concerns the user interface that the controls render. The DetailsView control always renders each field in a separate HTML table row. The FormView control, on the other hand, uses a template that enables you to completely customize the user interface rendered by the control.

Using the DetailsView Control

In this section, you learn how to use the DetailsView control when working with database records. In particular, you learn how to display, page, edit, insert, and delete database records with the DetailsView. You also learn how to format the appearance of the DetailsView control.

Displaying Data with the DetailsView Control

A DetailsView control renders an HTML table that displays the contents of a single database record. The DetailsView supports both declarative and programmatic databinding.

For example, the page in Listing 12.1 displays a record from the Movies database table, using declarative databinding (see Figure 12.1).

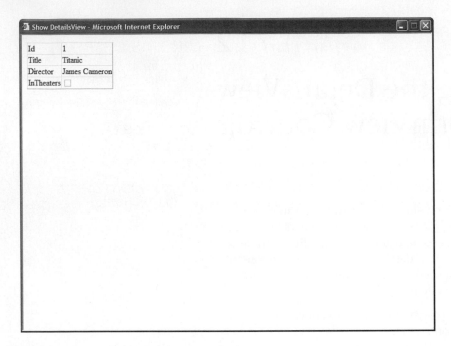

FIGURE 12.1   Displaying a movie record.

LISTING 12.1   ShowDetailsView.aspx

```
<%@ Page Language="C#" %>
<!DOCTYPE html PUBLIC "-//W3C//DTD XHTML 1.1//EN"
    "http://www.w3.org/TR/xhtml11/DTD/xhtml11.dtd">
<html xmlns="http://www.w3.org/1999/xhtml" >
<head id="Head1" runat="server">
    <title>Show DetailsView</title>
</head>
<body>
    <form id="form1" runat="server">
    <div>

    <asp:DetailsView
        id="dtlMovies"
        DataSourceID="srcMovies"
        Runat="server" />

    <asp:SqlDataSource
        id="srcMovies"
        ConnectionString="<%$ ConnectionStrings:Movies %>"
        SelectCommand="SELECT Id,Title,Director,InTheaters FROM Movies
            WHERE Id=1"
        Runat="server" />
```

```
        </div>
    </form>
</body>
</html>
```

In Listing 12.1, the SQL Select statement associated with the `SqlDataSource` control retrieves the first movie from the Movies database table. The `DetailsView` control is bound to the `SqlDataSource` control through its `DataSourceID` property.

You also can bind a `DetailsView` control programmatically to a data source. The page in Listing 12.2 contains a `DetailsView` that is bound to a collection of employees.

LISTING 12.2 ShowEmployee.aspx

```
<%@ Page Language="C#" %>
<%@ Import Namespace="System.Collections.Generic" %>
<!DOCTYPE html PUBLIC "-//W3C//DTD XHTML 1.1//EN"
"http://www.w3.org/TR/xhtml11/DTD/xhtml11.dtd">
<script runat="server">

    /// <summary>
    /// Represents an employee
    /// </summary>
    public class Employee
    {
        public string _firstName;
        public string _lastName;
        public bool _retired;

        public string FirstName
        {
            get { return _firstName; }
        }

        public string LastName
        {
            get { return _lastName; }
        }

        public bool Retired
        {
            get { return _retired; }
        }

        public Employee(string firstName, string lastName, bool retired)
```

LISTING 12.2   Continued

```
        {
            _firstName = firstName;
            _lastName = lastName;
            _retired = retired;
        }
    }

    /// <summary>
    /// Load employees into DetailsView
    /// </summary>
    void Page_Load()
    {
        // Create employees collection with one employee
        Employee newEmployee = new Employee("Steve", "Walther", false);
        List<Employee> employees = new List<Employee>();
        employees.Add(newEmployee);

        // Bind employees to DetailsView
        dtlMovies.DataSource = employees;
        dtlMovies.DataBind();
    }

</script>
<html xmlns="http://www.w3.org/1999/xhtml" >
<head id="Head1" runat="server">
    <title>Show Employee</title>
</head>
<body>
    <form id="form1" runat="server">
    <div>

    <asp:DetailsView
        id="dtlMovies"
        Runat="server" />

    </div>
    </form>
</body>
</html>
```

In Listing 12.2, an Employee class is defined, which contains properties for the employee first name, last name, and retirement status. In the Page_Load() method, a new employee is created and added to a generic collection. This collection is bound to the DetailsView control.

Using Fields with the `DetailsView` Control

If you need more control over the appearance of the `DetailsView`, including the particular order in which columns are displayed, then you can use fields with the `DetailsView` control. The `DetailsView` control supports exactly the same fields as the `GridView` control:

- ▶ **`BoundField`**—Enables you to display the value of a data item as text.

- ▶ **`CheckBoxField`**—Enables you to display the value of a data item as a check box.

- ▶ **`CommandField`**—Enables you to display links for editing, deleting, and selecting rows.

- ▶ **`ButtonField`**—Enables you to display the value of a data item as a button (image button, link button, or push button).

- ▶ **`HyperLinkField`**—Enables you to display the value of a data item as a link.

- ▶ **`ImageField`**—Enables you to display the value of a data item as an image.

- ▶ **`TemplateField`**—Enables you to customize the appearance of a data item.

NOTE

Another option is to create custom fields for the `DetailsView` control. You can create custom fields that work with the `DetailsView` control in exactly the same way as you create custom fields that work with the `GridView` control. Custom fields for the `GridView` control are discussed in the final section of Chapter 11, "Using the GridView Control."

The page in Listing 12.3 contains a `DetailsView` control that contains three `BoundFields`. The `BoundFields` display the values of the Title, Director, and BoxOfficeTotals database columns (see Figure 12.2).

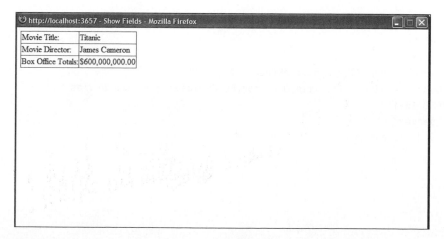

FIGURE 12.2   Using `BoundFields` with the `DetailsView` control.

LISTING 12.3   ShowFields.aspx

```
<%@ Page Language="C#" %>
<!DOCTYPE html PUBLIC "-//W3C//DTD XHTML 1.1//EN"
   "http://www.w3.org/TR/xhtml11/DTD/xhtml11.dtd">
<html xmlns="http://www.w3.org/1999/xhtml" >
<head id="Head1" runat="server">
    <title>Show Fields</title>
</head>
<body>
    <form id="form1" runat="server">
    <div>

    <asp:DetailsView
        id="dtlMovies"
        DataSourceID="srcMovies"
        AutoGenerateRows="false"
        Runat="server">
        <Fields>
        <asp:BoundField
            DataField="Title"
            HeaderText="Movie Title:" />
        <asp:BoundField
            DataField="Director"
            HeaderText="Movie Director:" />
        <asp:BoundField
            DataField="BoxOfficeTotals"
            DataFormatString="{0:c}"
            HeaderText="Box Office Totals:" />
        </Fields>
    </asp:DetailsView>

    <asp:SqlDataSource
        id="srcMovies"
        ConnectionString="<%$ ConnectionStrings:Movies %>"
        SelectCommand="SELECT Id,Title,Director,BoxOfficeTotals FROM Movies
            WHERE Id=1"
        Runat="server" />

    </div>
    </form>
</body>
</html>
```

Notice that the `DetailsView` control has an `AutoGenerateRows` property that has the value `False`. When you specify fields for a `DetailsView` control, you'll want to include this property so that the fields do not appear more than once.

Each of the `BoundFields` in Listing 12.3 includes a `HeaderText` attribute that is used to specify the label for the field. In addition, the `BoundField` associated with the BoxOfficeTotals column includes a `DataFormatString` property that is used to format the value of the column as a currency amount.

Displaying Empty Data with the `DetailsView` Control

The `DetailsView` control includes two properties that you can use to display a message when no results are returned from its data source. You can use the `EmptyDataText` property to display an HTML string, or the `EmptyDataTemplate` property to display more complicated content.

For example, the `SqlDataSource` in Listing 12.4 does not return a record because no record in the Movies database table has an ID of -1.

LISTING 12.4   ShowEmptyDataText.aspx

```
<%@ Page Language="C#" %>
<!DOCTYPE html PUBLIC "-//W3C//DTD XHTML 1.1//EN"
  "http://www.w3.org/TR/xhtml11/DTD/xhtml11.dtd">
<html xmlns="http://www.w3.org/1999/xhtml" >
<head id="Head1" runat="server">
    <title>Show Empty Data Text</title>
</head>
<body>
    <form id="form1" runat="server">
    <div>

    <asp:DetailsView
        id="dtlMovies"
        DataSourceID="srcMovies"
        EmptyDataText="<b>No Matching Record!</b>"
        Runat="server" />

    <asp:SqlDataSource
        id="srcMovies"
        ConnectionString="<%$ ConnectionStrings:Movies %>"
        SelectCommand="SELECT Id,Title,Director,InTheaters FROM Movies
            WHERE Id=-1"
        Runat="server" />
```

LISTING 12.4   Continued

```
    </div>
    </form>
</body>
</html>
```

When you open the page in Listing 12.4, the contents of the `EmptyDataText` property are displayed.

If you need to display more complicated content when no results are returned, such as ASP.NET controls, then you can specify an `EmptyDataTemplate`. The page in Listing 12.5 illustrates how you can use the `EmptyDataTemplate` to display complicated HTML content (see Figure 12.3).

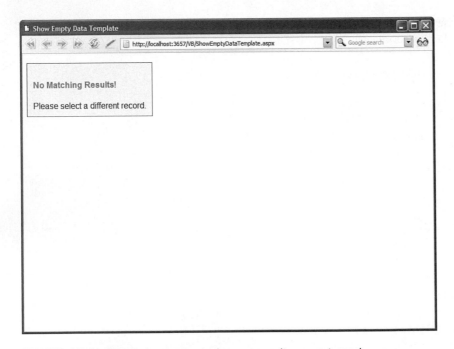

FIGURE 12.3   Displaying content when no results are returned.

LISTING 12.5   ShowEmptyDataTemplate.aspx

```
<%@ Page Language="C#" %>
<!DOCTYPE html PUBLIC "-//W3C//DTD XHTML 1.1//EN"
"http://www.w3.org/TR/xhtml11/DTD/xhtml11.dtd">
<html xmlns="http://www.w3.org/1999/xhtml" >
<head id="Head1" runat="server">
```

```
        <style type="text/css">
            .noMatch
            {
                background-color:#ffff66;
                padding:10px;
                font-family:Arial,Sans-Serif;
            }
            .noMatch h1
            {
                color:red;
                font-size:16px;
                font-weight:bold;
            }
        </style>
        <title>Show Empty Data Template</title>
    </head>
<body>
    <form id="form1" runat="server">
    <div>

    <asp:DetailsView
        id="dtlMovies"
        DataSourceID="srcMovies"
        Runat="server">
        <EmptyDataTemplate>
        <div class="noMatch">
            <h1>No Matching Results!</h1>
            Please select a different record.
        </div>
        </EmptyDataTemplate>
    </asp:DetailsView>

    <asp:SqlDataSource
        id="srcMovies"
        ConnectionString="<%$ ConnectionStrings:Movies %>"
        SelectCommand="SELECT Id,Title,Director,InTheaters FROM Movies
            WHERE Id=-1"
        Runat="server" />

    </div>
    </form>
</body>
</html>
```

Paging Through Data with the `DetailsView` Control

You can use the `DetailsView` to page through a set of database records by enabling the `DetailsView` control's `AllowPaging` property. The page in Listing 12.6 illustrates how you can page through the records in the Movies database table (see Figure 12.4).

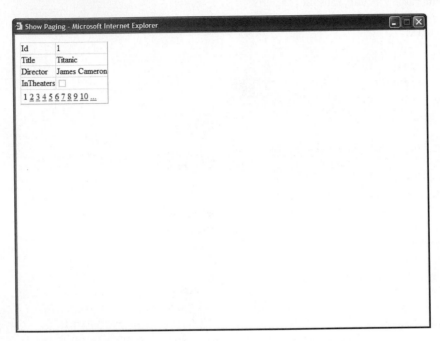

FIGURE 12.4   Paging through records with the `DetailsView` control.

LISTING 12.6   ShowPaging.aspx

```
<%@ Page Language="C#" %>
<!DOCTYPE html PUBLIC "-//W3C//DTD XHTML 1.1//EN"
    "http://www.w3.org/TR/xhtml11/DTD/xhtml11.dtd">
<html xmlns="http://www.w3.org/1999/xhtml" >
<head id="Head1" runat="server">
    <title>Show Paging</title>
</head>
<body>
    <form id="form1" runat="server">
    <div>

    <asp:DetailsView
        id="dtlMovies"
        DataSourceID="srcMovies"
        AllowPaging="true"
```

```
        Runat="server" />

    <asp:SqlDataSource
        id="srcMovies"
        ConnectionString="<%$ ConnectionStrings:Movies %>"
        SelectCommand="SELECT Id,Title,Director,InTheaters FROM Movies"
        Runat="server" />

    </div>
    </form>
</body>
</html>
```

WARNING

In this section, you learn how to take advantage of user interface paging when paging through records with the DetailsView control. Although user interface paging is convenient, it is not efficient. When working with large sets of records, you should use data source paging. This option is described in Chapter 16, "Using the ObjectDataSource Control."

Paging with AJAX   By default, when you page through records with the DetailsView control, the page is posted back to the server each and every time you click a page number. As an alternative, you can take advantage of AJAX to page through records. When you take advantage of AJAX, only the DetailsView control and not the entire page is updated when you navigate to a new page of records.

NOTE

Ajax (Asynchronous JavaScript and XML) enables you to retrieve content from a web server without reloading the page. Ajax works with all modern browsers including Microsoft Internet Explorer 6.0, Firefox 1.0, and Opera 8.0.

The page in Listing 12.7 illustrates how you can use AJAX with the DetailsView control.

LISTING 12.7   ShowAJAX.aspx

```
<%@ Page Language="C#" %>
<!DOCTYPE html PUBLIC "-//W3C//DTD XHTML 1.1//EN"
"http://www.w3.org/TR/xhtml11/DTD/xhtml11.dtd">
<html xmlns="http://www.w3.org/1999/xhtml" >
<head id="Head1" runat="server">
    <title>Show Paging</title>
```

LISTING 12.7   Continued

```
</head>
<body>
    <form id="form1" runat="server">
    <div>

    <asp:ScriptManager id="sm1" runat="server" />

    <%= DateTime.Now %>

    <asp:UpdatePanel id="up1" runat="Server">
    <ContentTemplate>

    <asp:DetailsView
        id="dtlMovies"
        DataSourceID="srcMovies"
        AllowPaging="true"
        Runat="server" />

    </ContentTemplate>
    </asp:UpdatePanel>

    <asp:SqlDataSource
        id="srcMovies"
        ConnectionString="<%$ ConnectionStrings:Movies %>"
        SelectCommand="SELECT Id,Title,Director,InTheaters FROM Movies"
        Runat="server" />

    </div>
    </form>
</body>
</html>
```

Notice that the DetailsView control in Listing 12.7 is contained inside of an UpdatePanel control. When you page through the records displayed by the DetailsView control, only the content inside the UpdatePanel is updated.

Furthermore, notice that the page in Listing 12.7 displays the current time. The time is not updated when you navigate to a new page of records. The time is not updated because the entire page is not updated. When you navigate to a new page, only the contents of the DetailsView are updated.

> **NOTE**
>
> The DetailsView control has an EnablePagingCallbacks property that also enables Ajax. This is a holdover property from the ASP.NET 2.0 Framework. The UpdatePanel is a more flexible method of doing Ajax.

Customizing the Paging Interface   You can customize the appearance of the paging interface by modifying the PagerSettings property. For example, the DetailsView control in Listing 12.8 displays first, previous, next, and last links instead of page numbers (see Figure 12.5).

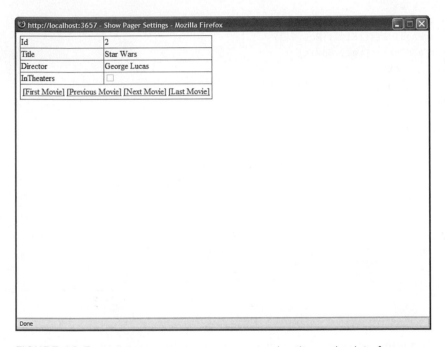

FIGURE 12.5   Using PagerSettings to customize the paging interface.

LISTING 12.8   ShowPagerSettings.aspx

```
<%@ Page Language="C#" %>
<!DOCTYPE html PUBLIC "-//W3C//DTD XHTML 1.1//EN"
  "http://www.w3.org/TR/xhtml11/DTD/xhtml11.dtd">
<html xmlns="http://www.w3.org/1999/xhtml" >
<head id="Head1" runat="server">
    <title>Show Pager Settings</title>
</head>
```

LISTING 12.8   Continued

```
<body>
    <form id="form1" runat="server">
    <div>

    <asp:DetailsView
        id="dtlMovies"
        DataSourceID="srcMovies"
        AllowPaging="true"
        Runat="server">
        <PagerSettings
            Mode="NextPreviousFirstLast"
            FirstPageText="[First Movie]"
            LastPageText="[Last Movie]"
            NextPageText="[Next Movie]"
            PreviousPageText="[Previous Movie]" />
    </asp:DetailsView>

    <asp:SqlDataSource
        id="srcMovies"
        ConnectionString="<%$ ConnectionStrings:Movies %>"
        SelectCommand="SELECT Id,Title,Director,InTheaters FROM Movies"
        Runat="server" />

    </div>
    </form>
</body>
</html>
```

The PagerSettings class supports the following properties:

▶ **FirstPageImageUrl**—Enables you to display an image for the first page link.

▶ **FirstPageText**—Enables you to specify the text for the first page link.

▶ **LastPageImageUrl**—Enables you to display an image for the last page link.

▶ **LastPageText**—Enables you to specify the text for the last page link.

▶ **Mode**—Enables you to select a display mode for the pager user interface. Possible values are NextPrevious, NextPreviousFirstLast, Numeric, and NumericFirstLast.

▶ **NextPageImageUrl**—Enables you to specify the text for the next page link.

▶ **NextPageText**—Enables you to specify the text for the next page link.

▶ **PageButtonCount**—Enables you to specify the number of page number links to display.

▶ **Position**—Enables you to specify the position of the paging user interface. Possible values are Bottom, Top, and TopAndBottom.

▶ **PreviousPageImageUrl**—Enables you to display an image for the previous page link.

▶ **PreviousPageText**—Enables you to specify the text for the previous page link.

▶ **Visible**—Enables you to hide the paging user interface.

If you need to customize the paging interface completely, then you can use a template. For example, the page in Listing 12.9 displays a list of page numbers in a drop-down list control (see Figure 12.6).

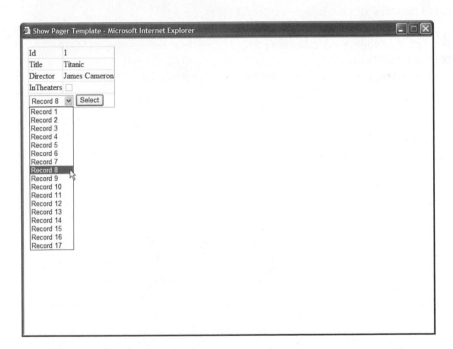

FIGURE 12.6   Using a PagerTemplate to customize the paging interface.

LISTING 12.9   ShowPagerTemplate.aspx

```
<%@ Page Language="C#" %>
<!DOCTYPE html PUBLIC "-//W3C//DTD XHTML 1.1//EN"
"http://www.w3.org/TR/xhtml11/DTD/xhtml11.dtd">
<script runat="server">

    protected void dtlMovies_DataBound(object sender, EventArgs e)
    {
        DropDownList ddlPager = (DropDownList)dtlMovies.BottomPagerRow.Cells[0].
        ➡FindControl("ddlPager");
```

LISTING 12.9   Continued

```
                for (int i = 0; i < dtlMovies.PageCount; i++)
                {
                    ListItem item = new ListItem( String.Format("Record {0}",i+1),
                    ➥i.ToString());
                    if (dtlMovies.PageIndex == i)
                        item.Selected = true;
                    ddlPager.Items.Add(item);
                }
        }

        protected void btnPage_Click(object sender, EventArgs e)
        {
            DropDownList ddlPager = (DropDownList)dtlMovies.BottomPagerRow.Cells[0].
            ➥FindControl("ddlPager");
            dtlMovies.PageIndex = Int32.Parse(ddlPager.SelectedValue);
        }
</script>
<html xmlns="http://www.w3.org/1999/xhtml" >
<head id="Head1" runat="server">
    <title>Show Pager Template</title>
</head>
<body>
    <form id="form1" runat="server">
    <div>

    <asp:DetailsView
        id="dtlMovies"
        DataSourceID="srcMovies"
        AllowPaging="true"
        OnDataBound="dtlMovies_DataBound"
        Runat="server">
        <PagerTemplate>
            <asp:DropDownList
                id="ddlPager"
                Runat="server" />
            <asp:Button
                id="btnPage"
                Text="Select"
                Runat="server" OnClick="btnPage_Click" />
        </PagerTemplate>
    </asp:DetailsView>

    <asp:SqlDataSource
        id="srcMovies"
```

```
            ConnectionString="<%$ ConnectionStrings:Movies %>"
            SelectCommand="SELECT Id,Title,Director,InTheaters FROM Movies"
            Runat="server" />

    </div>
    </form>
</body>
</html>
```

After you open the page in Listing 12.9, you can select a record from the DropDownList control and navigate to the record by clicking the Button control.

Updating Data with the DetailsView Control

You can use the DetailsView control to update existing database records. In order to update an existing record, assign the value True to the DetailsView control's AutoGenerateEditButton property as illustrated in Listing 12.10 (see Figure 12.7).

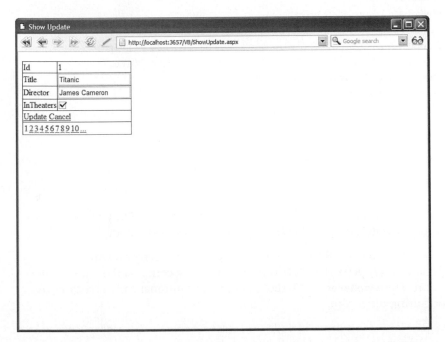

FIGURE 12.7   Editing a record with the DetailsView control.

LISTING 12.10   ShowUpdate.aspx

```
<%@ Page Language="C#" %>
<!DOCTYPE html PUBLIC "-//W3C//DTD XHTML 1.1//EN"
    "http://www.w3.org/TR/xhtml11/DTD/xhtml11.dtd">
```

LISTING 12.10   Continued

```
<html xmlns="http://www.w3.org/1999/xhtml" >
<head id="Head1" runat="server">
    <title>Show Update</title>
</head>
<body>
    <form id="form1" runat="server">
    <div>

    <asp:DetailsView
        id="dtlMovies"
        DataKeyNames="Id"
        AutoGenerateEditButton="true"
        AllowPaging="true"
        DataSourceID="srcMovies"
        Runat="server" />

    <asp:SqlDataSource
        id="srcMovies"
        ConnectionString="<%$ ConnectionStrings:Movies %>"
        SelectCommand="SELECT Id,Title,Director,InTheaters FROM Movies"
        UpdateCommand="UPDATE Movies SET Title=@Title,Director=@Director,
            InTheaters=@InTheaters WHERE Id=@Id"
        Runat="server" />

    </div>
    </form>
</body>
</html>
```

When you open the page in Listing 12.10, the record appears in Read Only mode. You can click the Edit button to switch the DetailsView into Edit mode and update the record.

Notice that the DetailsView control includes a DataKeyNames property and an AutoGenerateEditButton property. The DataKeyNames property contains the name of the primary key column. The AutoGenerateEditButton property automatically generates the user interface for editing the record.

Notice that the SqlDataSource control includes an UpdateCommand. The UpdateCommand updates the Title, Director, and InTheaters database columns.

If you want the DetailsView control to initially appear in Edit mode, then you can set the DetailsView control's DefaultMode property to the value Edit. For example, the page in Listing 12.11 contains a Master/Detail form. If you select any of the records in the GridView, you can edit the record with the DetailsView control (see Figure 12.8).

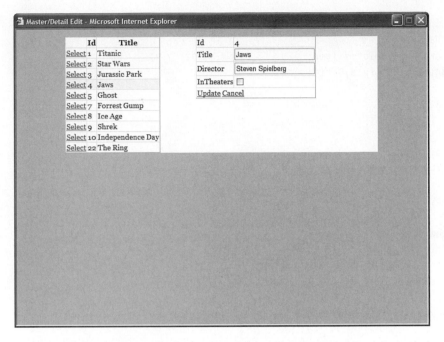

FIGURE 12.8   Displaying a Master/Detail form with the DetailsView control.

LISTING 12.11   MasterDetailEdit.aspx

```
<%@ Page Language="C#" %>
<!DOCTYPE html PUBLIC "-//W3C//DTD XHTML 1.1//EN"
"http://www.w3.org/TR/xhtml11/DTD/xhtml11.dtd">
<script runat="server">

    void Page_Load()
    {
        if (!Page.IsPostBack)
            grdMovies.SelectedIndex = 0;
    }

    protected void dtlMovies_ItemUpdated(object sender, DetailsViewUpdatedEventArgs e)
    {
        grdMovies.DataBind();
    }
</script>
<html xmlns="http://www.w3.org/1999/xhtml" >
<head id="Head1" runat="server">
    <style type="text/css">
        html
```

12

LISTING 12.11   Continued

```
        {
            background-color:silver;
            font:14px Georgia,Serif;
        }
        .content
        {
            margin:auto;
            width:600px;
            background-color:white;
        }
        .column
        {
            float:left;
            width:250px;
        }
        .selectedRow
        {
            background-color:yellow;
        }
    </style>
    <title>Master/Detail Edit</title>
</head>
<body>
    <form id="form1" runat="server">
    <div class="content">

    <div class="column">
    <asp:GridView
        id="grdMovies"
        DataSourceID="srcMovies"
        DataKeyNames="Id"
        AutoGenerateSelectButton="true"
        SelectedRowStyle-CssClass="selectedRow"
        Runat="server" />
    </div>

    <div class="column">
    <asp:DetailsView
        id="dtlMovies"
        DefaultMode="Edit"
        AutoGenerateEditButton="true"
        AllowPaging="true"
        DataSourceID="srcMovieDetails"
```

```
            DataKeyNames="Id"
            Runat="server" OnItemUpdated="dtlMovies_ItemUpdated" />

        <asp:SqlDataSource
            id="srcMovies"
            ConnectionString="<%$ ConnectionStrings:Movies %>"
            SelectCommand="SELECT Id,Title FROM Movies"
            Runat="server" />
    </div>

    <asp:SqlDataSource
        id="srcMovieDetails"
        ConnectionString="<%$ ConnectionStrings:Movies %>"
        SelectCommand="SELECT Id,Title,Director,InTheaters FROM
            Movies WHERE Id=@MovieId"
        UpdateCommand="UPDATE Movies SET Title=@Title,Director=@Director,
            InTheaters=@InTheaters WHERE Id=@Id"
        Runat="server">
        <SelectParameters>
            <asp:ControlParameter Name="MovieId" ControlID="grdMovies" />
        </SelectParameters>
    </asp:SqlDataSource>

    </div>
    </form>
</body>
</html>
```

Notice that the DetailsView control includes a DefaultMode property that is set to the value Edit. When you select a record, the record is displayed by the DetailsView in Edit mode by default.

Using Templates When Editing   By default, you don't get any validation when editing records with the DetailsView control. In other words, there is nothing to prevent you from attempting to submit a null value to a database column that does not accept null values. If you need to perform validation, then you need to use templates with the DetailsView control.

The page in Listing 12.12 uses TemplateFields for the Title and BoxOfficeTotals columns. Both TemplateFields contain a RequiredFieldValidator. The BoxOfficeTotals column also includes a CompareValidator to check whether the value entered is a currency value (see Figure 12.9).

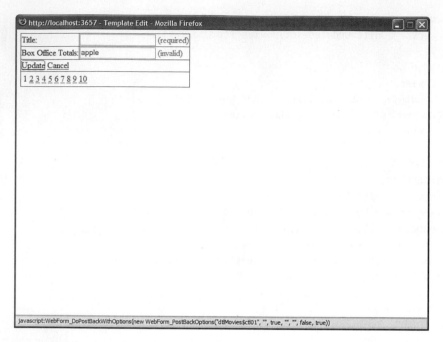

FIGURE 12.9   Using a template when editing with the DetailsView control.

LISTING 12.12   TemplateEdit.aspx

```
<%@ Page Language="C#" %>
<!DOCTYPE html PUBLIC "-//W3C//DTD XHTML 1.1//EN"
  "http://www.w3.org/TR/xhtml11/DTD/xhtml11.dtd">
<html xmlns="http://www.w3.org/1999/xhtml" >
<head id="Head1" runat="server">
    <title>Template Edit</title>
</head>
<body>
    <form id="form1" runat="server">
    <div>

    <asp:DetailsView
        id="dtlMovies"
        AutoGenerateRows="false"
        AutoGenerateEditButton="true"
        AllowPaging="true"
        DefaultMode="Edit"
        DataSourceID="srcMovies"
        DataKeyNames="Id"
        Runat="server">
        <Fields>
```

```
    <asp:TemplateField HeaderText="Title:">
    <EditItemTemplate>
    <asp:TextBox
        id="txtTitle"
        Text='<%# Bind("Title") %>'
        runat="server" />
    <asp:RequiredFieldValidator
        id="reqTitle"
        ControlToValidate="txtTitle"
        Text="(required)"
        Display="Dynamic"
        Runat="server" />
    </EditItemTemplate>
    </asp:TemplateField>
    <asp:TemplateField HeaderText="Box Office Totals:">
    <EditItemTemplate>
    <asp:TextBox
        id="txtBoxOfficeTotals"
        Text='<%# Bind("BoxOfficeTotals", "{0:f}") %>'
        runat="server" />
    <asp:RequiredFieldValidator
        id="reqBoxOfficeTotals"
        ControlToValidate="txtBoxOfficeTotals"
        Text="(required)"
        Display="Dynamic"
        Runat="server" />
    <asp:CompareValidator
        id="cmpBoxOfficeTotals"
        ControlToValidate="txtBoxOfficeTotals"
        Text="(invalid)"
        Display="Dynamic"
        Operator="DataTypeCheck"
        Type="currency"
        Runat="server" />
    </EditItemTemplate>
    </asp:TemplateField>
    </Fields>
</asp:DetailsView>

<asp:SqlDataSource
    id="srcMovies"
    ConnectionString="<%$ ConnectionStrings:Movies %>"
    SelectCommand="SELECT Id,Title,BoxOfficeTotals FROM Movies"
    UpdateCommand="UPDATE Movies SET Title=@Title,
        BoxOfficeTotals=@BoxOfficeTotals WHERE Id=@Id"
    Runat="server" />
```

LISTING 12.12   Continued

```
    </div>
    </form>
</body>
</html>
```

If you attempt to edit a record, and you do not provide a value for the Title or BoxOfficeTotals columns, then a validation error is displayed. Also, if you enter anything other than a currency amount for the BoxOfficeTotals column, a validation error message is displayed.

Handling Concurrency Issues   What happens when two users edit the same record at the same time? By default, the last user to update the database record wins. In other words, one user can overwrite changes made by another user.

Imagine that Sally opens a page to edit a database record. After opening the page, Sally leaves for her two-week vacation in Las Vegas. While Sally is vacationing, Jim edits the same record and submits his changes. When Sally returns from vacation, she submits her changes. Any modifications that Jim makes are overwritten by Sally's changes.

If you need to prevent this scenario, then you can take advantage of optimistic concurrency. The SqlDataSource control's ConflictDetection property supports the following two values:

▶ CompareAllValues

▶ OverwriteChanges

By default, the ConflictDetection property has the value OverwriteChanges. If you set this property to the value CompareAllValues, then the SqlDataSource tracks both the original and modified versions of each column.

For example, the page in Listing 12.13 doesn't allow a user to update a record when the original record has been modified after the user has opened the page.

LISTING 12.13   Concurrency.aspx

```
<%@ Page Language="C#" %>
<!DOCTYPE html PUBLIC "-//W3C//DTD XHTML 1.1//EN"
"http://www.w3.org/TR/xhtml11/DTD/xhtml11.dtd">

<script runat="server">

    protected void srcMovies_Updated(object sender, SqlDataSourceStatusEventArgs e)
    {
        if (e.AffectedRows == 0)
```

```
                            lblMessage.Text = "Could not update record";
        }
    </script>

    <html xmlns="http://www.w3.org/1999/xhtml" >
    <head id="Head1" runat="server">
        <title>Concurrency</title>
    </head>
    <body>
        <form id="form1" runat="server">
        <div>

        <asp:Label ID="lblMessage" EnableViewState="false" runat="server" />

        <asp:DetailsView
            id="dtlMovies"
            DataKeyNames="Id"
            AutoGenerateEditButton="true"
            AllowPaging="true"
            DataSourceID="srcMovies"
            Runat="server" />

        <asp:SqlDataSource
            id="srcMovies"
            ConnectionString="<%$ ConnectionStrings:Movies %>"
            SelectCommand="SELECT Id,Title,Director,InTheaters FROM Movies"
            UpdateCommand="UPDATE Movies
                SET Title=@Title,Director=@Director,InTheaters=
                WHERE Title=@original_Title
                AND Director=@original_Director
                AND InTheaters=@InTheaters
                AND Id=@original_Id"
            ConflictDetection="CompareAllValues"
            OldValuesParameterFormatString="original_{0}"
            Runat="server" OnUpdated="srcMovies_Updated" />

        </div>
        </form>
    </body>
    </html>
```

Notice the contents of the UpdateCommand in Listing 12.13. The current values are
compared against the original values for each database column when updating a record.
If the current and original values don't match, then the record is not updated.

LISTING 12.15   Continued

```
                    font:14px Arial,Sans-Serif;
            }
            td,th
            {
                padding:10px;
            }
            #divDisplay
            {
                border:solid 1px black;
                width:400px;
                padding:15px;
                background-color:#eeeeee;
            }
            #divInsert
            {
                display:none;
                border:solid 1px black;
                width:400px;
                position:absolute;
                top:30px;
                left:100px;
                padding:10px;
                background-color:white;
            }

        </style>
        <script type="text/javascript">
            function showInsert()
            {
                var divInsert = document.getElementById('divInsert');
                divInsert.style.display = 'block';
            }
        </script>
        <title>Show Insert Mode</title>
    </head>
<body>
    <form id="form1" runat="server">
    <div id="divDisplay">
    <asp:GridView
        id="grdMovies"
        DataSourceID="srcMovies"
        Runat="server" />
    <br />
    <a href="JavaScript:showInsert();">Insert Movie</a>
    </div>
```

```
    <div id="divInsert">
    <h1>Insert Movie</h1>
    <asp:DetailsView
        id="dtlMovies"
        DataSourceID="srcMovies"
        AutoGenerateInsertButton="true"
        AutoGenerateRows="false"
        DefaultMode="Insert"
        Runat="server">
        <Fields>
        <asp:BoundField
            DataField="Title"
            HeaderText="Title:" />
        <asp:BoundField
            DataField="Director"
            HeaderText="Director:" />
        <asp:CheckBoxField
            DataField="InTheaters"
            HeaderText="In Theaters:" />
        </Fields>
    </asp:DetailsView>
    </div>

    <asp:SqlDataSource
        id="srcMovies"
        ConnectionString="<%$ ConnectionStrings:Movies %>"
        SelectCommand="SELECT Title,Director,InTheaters FROM Movies"
        InsertCommand="INSERT Movies (Title,Director,InTheaters)
            VALUES (@Title,@Director,
        Runat="server" />

    </form>
</body>
</html>
```

The page in Listing 12.15 contains both a GridView and DetailsView control. The DetailsView control is hidden until you click the Insert Movie link. This link executes a JavaScript function named ShowInsert(), which displays the DetailsView control.

Deleting Data with the `DetailsView` Control

You can delete records with the `DetailsView` control by enabling its `AutoGenerateDeleteButton` property. The page in Listing 12.16 enables you to both insert and delete records in the Movies database table.

LISTING 12.16   ShowDelete.aspx

```
<%@ Page Language="C#" %>
<!DOCTYPE html PUBLIC "-//W3C//DTD XHTML 1.1//EN"
    "http://www.w3.org/TR/xhtml11/DTD/xhtml11.dtd">
<html xmlns="http://www.w3.org/1999/xhtml" >
<head id="Head1" runat="server">
    <title>Show Delete</title>
</head>
<body>
    <form id="form1" runat="server">
    <div>

    <asp:DetailsView
        id="dtlMovies"
        AllowPaging="true"
        DataSourceID="srcMovies"
        DataKeyNames="Id"
        AutoGenerateInsertButton="true"
        AutoGenerateDeleteButton="true"
        AutoGenerateRows="false"
        Runat="server">
        <Fields>
        <asp:BoundField
            DataField="Id"
            HeaderText="ID:"
            InsertVisible="false" />
        <asp:BoundField
            DataField="Title"
            HeaderText="Title:" />
        <asp:BoundField
            DataField="Director"
            HeaderText="Director:" />
        <asp:CheckBoxField
            DataField="InTheaters"
            HeaderText="In Theaters:" />
        </Fields>
    </asp:DetailsView>

    <asp:SqlDataSource
```

```
            id="srcMovies"
            ConnectionString="<%$ ConnectionStrings:Movies %>"
            SelectCommand="SELECT Id,Title,Director,InTheaters FROM Movies"
            InsertCommand="INSERT Movies (Title,Director,InTheaters)
                VALUES (@Title,@Director,
            DeleteCommand="DELETE Movies WHERE id=@Id"
            Runat="server" />

    </div>
    </form>
</body>
</html>
```

When deleting records, you need to supply a value for the DetailsView control's DataKeyNames property. Notice that a parameter named @Id is used to represent the value of the ID column in the DeleteCommand property.

Working with DetailsView Control Events

The DetailsView control supports the following events:

▶ **DataBinding**—Raised immediately before the DetailsView control is bound to its data source.

▶ **DataBound**—Raised immediately after the DetailsView control is bound to its data source.

▶ **ItemCommand**—Raised when any control contained in the DetailsView raises an event (for example, when you click a button rendered by a ButtonField).

▶ **ItemCreated**—Raised when a DetailsView renders a data item.

▶ **ItemDeleting**—Raised immediately before a data item is deleted.

▶ **ItemDeleted**—Raised immediately after a data item is deleted.

▶ **ItemInserting**—Raised immediately before a data item is inserted.

▶ **ItemInserted**—Raised immediately after a data item is inserted.

▶ **ItemUpdating**—Raised immediately before a data item is updated.

▶ **ItemUpdated**—Raised immediately after a data item is updated.

▶ **ModeChanging**—Raised immediately before the DetailsView control's mode is changed.

▶ **ModeChanged**—Raised immediately after the DetailsView control's mode is changed.

▶ **PageIndexChanging**—Raised immediately before the current page is changed.

▶ **PageIndexChanged**—Raised immediately after the current page is changed.

Notice that several of these events reflect similar events exposed by the DataSource controls. For example, the SqlDataSource control includes Inserting and Inserted events, which mirror the DetailsView control's ItemInserting and ItemInserted events.

The page in Listing 12.17 demonstrates how to use the ItemInserted event to handle any errors which might be raised when inserting a new record into a database table (see Figure 12.11).

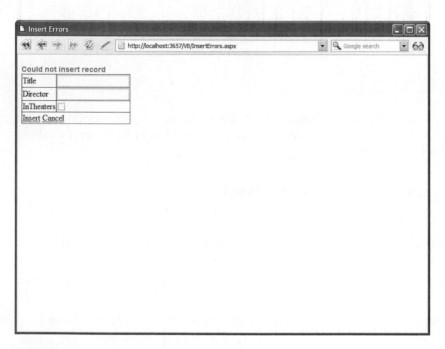

FIGURE 12.11   Handling database insert errors.

LISTING 12.17   InsertErrors.aspx

```csharp
<%@ Page Language="C#" %>
<!DOCTYPE html PUBLIC "-//W3C//DTD XHTML 1.1//EN"
"http://www.w3.org/TR/xhtml11/DTD/xhtml11.dtd">
<script runat="server">

    protected void dtlMovies_ItemInserted(object sender,
    ➥DetailsViewInsertedEventArgs e)
    {
        if (e.Exception != null)
        {
            e.ExceptionHandled = true;
            e.KeepInInsertMode = true;
            lblError.Visible = true;
        }
```

12

```
        }
</script>
<html xmlns="http://www.w3.org/1999/xhtml" >
<head id="Head1" runat="server">
    <style type="text/css">
        .error
        {
            color:red;
            font:bold 14px Arial,Sans-Serif;
        }
    </style>
    <title>Insert Errors</title>
</head>
<body>
    <form id="form1" runat="server">
    <div>

    <asp:Label
        id="lblError"
        Text="Could not insert record"
        Visible="false"
        EnableViewState="false"
        CssClass="error"
        Runat="server" />

    <asp:DetailsView
        id="dtlMovies"
        AllowPaging="true"
        DataSourceID="srcMovies"
        AutoGenerateInsertButton="true"
        OnItemInserted="dtlMovies_ItemInserted"
        Runat="server" />

    <asp:SqlDataSource
        id="srcMovies"
        ConnectionString="<%$ ConnectionStrings:Movies %>"
        SelectCommand="SELECT Title,Director,InTheaters FROM Movies"
        InsertCommand="INSERT Movies (Title,Director,InTheaters)
            VALUES (@Title,@Director,
        Runat="server" />

    </div>
    </form>
</body>
</html>
```

If you attempt to insert a record without providing values for the Title or Director column, then the error message contained in the Label control is displayed.

When you insert a record, the `DetailsView` control raises the `ItemInserted` event. The second parameter passed to the event handler for this method contains a property that exposes any exceptions raised when inserting the record. In Listing 12.17, if there is an exception, then the exception is suppressed with the `ExceptionHandled` property. Furthermore, the `KeepInInsertMode` property prevents the `DetailsView` from automatically switching out of Insert mode.

Formatting the `DetailsView` Control

The `DetailsView` control includes an abundance of properties for formatting the control. I recommend that you format the `DetailsView` control by taking advantage of Cascading Style Sheets. All the following properties expose a Style object that includes a `CssClass` property:

- ▶ **CssClass**—Enables you to associate a style sheet class with the `DetailsView` control.

- ▶ **AlternatingRowStyle**—Represents every other row rendered by the `DetailsView` control.

- ▶ **CommandRowStyle**—Represents the row that contains the edit buttons.

- ▶ **EditRowStyle**—Represents rows when the `DetailsView` control is in Edit mode.

- ▶ **EmptyDataRowStyle**—Represents the row displayed when the data source does not return any data items.

- ▶ **FieldHeaderStyle**—Represents the cell displayed for the field labels.

- ▶ **FooterStyle**—Represents the footer row.

- ▶ **HeaderStyle**—Represents the header row.

- ▶ **InsertRowStyle**—Represents rows when the `DetailsView` control is in Insert mode.

- ▶ **PagerStyle**—Represents the row or rows that display the paging user interface.

- ▶ **RowStyle**—Represents the rows displayed by the `DetailsView` control.

Furthermore, you can take advantage of the following properties when formatting a `DetailsView` control:

- ▶ **GridLines**—Enables you to specify the appearance of the rules that appear around the cells of the table rendered by a `DetailsView` control. Possible values are None, Horizontal, Vertical, and Both.

- ▶ **HeaderText**—Enables you to specify text that appears in the header of the `DetailsView` control.

- ▶ **FooterText**—Enables you to specify text that appears in the footer of the `DetailsView` control.

The page in Listing 12.18 uses several of these properties to format a `DetailsView` control (see Figure 12.12).

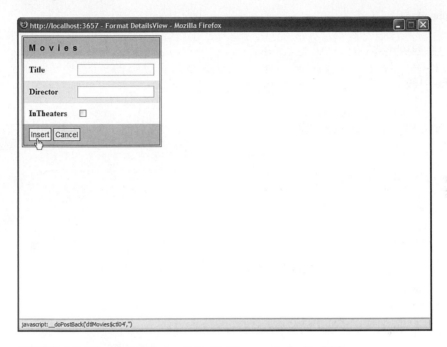

FIGURE 12.12   Formatting a `DetailsView` control with CSS.

LISTING 12.18   FormatDetailsView.aspx

```
<%@ Page Language="C#" %>
<!DOCTYPE html PUBLIC "-//W3C//DTD XHTML 1.1//EN"
  "http://www.w3.org/TR/xhtml11/DTD/xhtml11.dtd">
<html xmlns="http://www.w3.org/1999/xhtml" >
<head id="Head1" runat="server">
    <style type="text/css">
        .movies td,.movies th
        {
            padding:10px;
        }
        .movies
        {
            border:double 4px black;
        }
        .header
        {
            letter-spacing:8px;
            font:bold 16px Arial,Sans-Serif;
            background-color:silver;
```

LISTING 12.18   Continued

```
        }
        .fieldHeader
        {
            font-weight:bold;
        }
        .alternating
        {
            background-color:#eeeeee;
        }
        .command
        {
            background-color:silver;
        }
        .command a
        {
            color:black;
            background-color:#eeeeee;
            font:14px Arials,Sans-Serif;
            text-decoration:none;
            padding:3px;
            border:solid 1px black;
        }
        .command a:hover
        {
            background-color:yellow;
        }
        .pager td
        {
            padding:2px;
        }
    </style>
    <title>Format DetailsView</title>
</head>
<body>
    <form id="form1" runat="server">
    <div>

    <asp:DetailsView
        id="dtlMovies"
        DataSourceID="srcMovies"
        AutoGenerateInsertButton="true"
        AllowPaging="true"
        GridLines="None"
        HeaderText="Movies"
```

```
        CssClass="movies"
        HeaderStyle-CssClass="header"
        FieldHeaderStyle-CssClass="fieldHeader"
        AlternatingRowStyle-CssClass="alternating"
        CommandRowStyle-CssClass="command"
        PagerStyle-CssClass="pager"
        Runat="server" />

    <asp:SqlDataSource
        id="srcMovies"
        ConnectionString="<%$ ConnectionStrings:Movies %>"
        SelectCommand="SELECT Title,Director,InTheaters FROM Movies"
        InsertCommand="INSERT Movies (Title,Director,InTheaters)
            VALUES (@Title,@Director,
        Runat="server" />

    </div>
    </form>
</body>
</html>
```

Using the `FormView` Control

You can use the `FormView` control to do anything that you can do with the `DetailsView` control. Just as you can with the `DetailsView` control, you can use the `FormView` control to display, page, edit, insert, and delete database records. However, unlike the `DetailsView` control, the `FormView` control is entirely template driven.

I end up using the `FormView` control much more than the `DetailsView` control. The `FormView` control provides you with more control over the layout of a form. Furthermore, adding validation controls to a `FormView` is easier than adding validation controls to a `DetailsView` control.

> **WEB STANDARDS NOTE**
>
> Unfortunately, from a web standards perspective, the `FormView` control does, in fact, render an HTML table. It creates an HTML table that contains a single cell.

Displaying Data with the `FormView` Control

You can display a database record with the `FormView` control by using an `ItemTemplate`. For example, the page in Listing 12.19 displays a record from the Movies database table (see Figure 12.13).

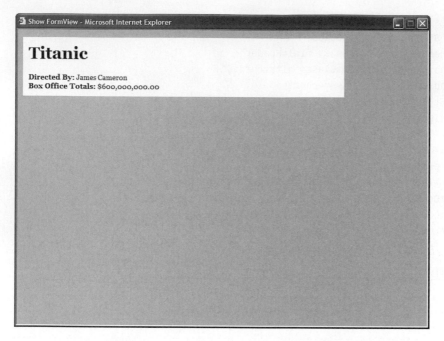

FIGURE 12.13   Displaying a database record with the FormView control.

LISTING 12.19   ShowFormView.aspx

```
<%@ Page Language="C#" %>
<!DOCTYPE html PUBLIC "-//W3C//DTD XHTML 1.1//EN"
  "http://www.w3.org/TR/xhtml11/DTD/xhtml11.dtd">
<html xmlns="http://www.w3.org/1999/xhtml" >
<head id="Head1" runat="server">
    <style type="text/css">
    html
    {
        background-color:silver;
    }
    #content
    {
        margins:auto;
        width:600px;
        padding:10px;
        background-color:white;
        font:14px Georgia,Serif;
    }
    </style>
    <title>Show FormView</title>
</head>
```

```
<body>
    <form id="form1" runat="server">
    <div id="content">

    <asp:FormView
        id="frmMovies"
        DataSourceID="srcMovies"
        Runat="server">
        <ItemTemplate>
        <h1><%# Eval("Title") %></h1>
        <b>Directed By:</b>
        <%# Eval("Director") %>
        <br />
        <b>Box Office Totals:</b>
        <%#Eval("BoxOfficeTotals", "{0:c}") %>
        </ItemTemplate>
    </asp:FormView>

    <asp:SqlDataSource
        id="srcMovies"
        ConnectionString="<%$ ConnectionStrings:Movies %>"
        SelectCommand="SELECT Id,Title,Director,BoxOfficeTotals FROM Movies
            WHERE Id=1"
        Runat="server" />

    </div>
    </form>
</body>
</html>
```

Notice that the FormView control's DataSourceID property points to the SqlDataSource control. The SqlDataSource control retrieves the first record from the Movies database table.

The ItemTemplate contains databinding expressions that display the values of the Title, Director, and BoxOfficeTotals columns. The Eval() method retrieves the values of these columns. The databinding expression for the BoxOfficeTotals column formats the value of the column as a currency amount.

Paging Through Data with the FormView Control

You can enable users to navigate through a set of data items by enabling paging. You can allow the FormView control to automatically render the paging interface or you can use a PagerTemplate to customize the paging interface.

The page in Listing 12.20 automatically renders an additional row that contains buttons for navigating between data items.

LISTING 12.20   ShowFormViewPaging.aspx

```
<%@ Page Language="C#" %>
<!DOCTYPE html PUBLIC "-//W3C//DTD XHTML 1.1//EN"
   "http://www.w3.org/TR/xhtml11/DTD/xhtml11.dtd">
<html xmlns="http://www.w3.org/1999/xhtml" >
<head id="Head1" runat="server">
    <style type="text/css">
    html
    {
        background-color:silver;
    }
    #content
    {
        margins:auto;
        width:600px;
        padding:10px;
        background-color:white;
        font:14px Georgia,Serif;
    }
    a
    {
        color:blue;
    }
    </style>
    <title>Show FormView Paging</title>
</head>
<body>
    <form id="form1" runat="server">
    <div id="content">

    <asp:FormView
        id="frmMovies"
        DataSourceID="srcMovies"
        AllowPaging="true"
        Runat="server">
        <ItemTemplate>
        <h1><%# Eval("Title") %></h1>
        <b>Directed By:</b>
        <%# Eval("Director") %>
        <br />
        <b>Box Office Totals:</b>
        <%#Eval("BoxOfficeTotals", "{0:c}") %>
        </ItemTemplate>
    </asp:FormView>
```

```
        <asp:SqlDataSource
            id="srcMovies"
            ConnectionString="<%$ ConnectionStrings:Movies %>"
            SelectCommand="SELECT Id,Title,Director,BoxOfficeTotals FROM Movies"
            Runat="server" />

        </div>
        </form>
</body>
</html>
```

Notice that the FormView in Listing 12.20 includes an AllowPaging property that is assigned the value True. Adding this property generates the paging interface automatically.

> **NOTE**
>
> You can enable Ajax paging for a FormView control in exactly the same way you enable Ajax paging for a GridView or DetailsView control. If you wrap the FormView control in an UpdatePanel, then you can page through the records in the FormView without performing a noticeable postback to the server.

> **WARNING**
>
> This section describes user interface paging. User interface paging is not an efficient method to use when paging through large record sets because all the data must be loaded into memory. In Chapter 16, "Using the ObjectDataSource Control," you learn how to implement data source paging.

You can customize the appearance of the automatically rendered paging interface with the PagerSettings property, which exposes the PagerSettings class. The PagerSettings class supports the following properties:

- ▶ **FirstPageImageUrl**—Enables you to display an image for the first page link.
- ▶ **FirstPageText**—Enables you to specify the text for the first page link.
- ▶ **LastPageImageUrl**—Enables you to display an image for the last page link.
- ▶ **LastPageText**—Enables you to specify the text for the last page link.
- ▶ **Mode**—Enables you to select a display mode for the pager user interface. Possible values are NextPrevious, NextPreviousFirstLast, Numeric, and NumericFirstLast.
- ▶ **NextPageImageUrl**—Enables you to specify the text for the next page link.
- ▶ **NextPageText**—Enables you to specify the text for the next page link.
- ▶ **PageButtonCount**—Enables you to specify the number of page number links to display.

- ▶ **Position**—Enables you to specify the position of the paging user interface. Possible values are Bottom, Top, and TopAndBottom.

- ▶ **PreviousPageImageUrl**—Enables you to display an image for the previous page link.

- ▶ **PreviousPageText**—Enables you to specify the text for the previous page link.

- ▶ **Visible**—Enables you to hide the paging user interface.

If you need to customize the appearance of the paging interface completely, then you can create a PagerTemplate. The page in Listing 12.21 uses the PagerTemplate to create a custom paging interface. The PagerTemplate displays the current page number. It also contains buttons for navigating to the previous and next page (see Figure 12.14).

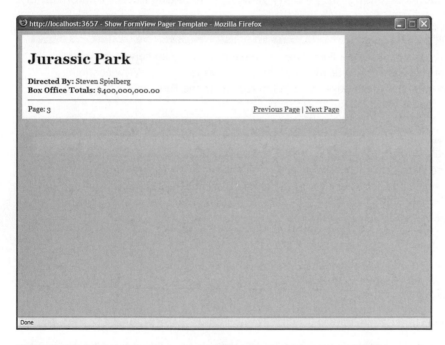

FIGURE 12.14   Using a PagerTemplate with the FormView control.

LISTING 12.21   ShowFormViewPagerTemplate.aspx

```
<%@ Page Language="C#" %>
<!DOCTYPE html PUBLIC "-//W3C//DTD XHTML 1.1//EN"
    "http://www.w3.org/TR/xhtml11/DTD/xhtml11.dtd">
<html xmlns="http://www.w3.org/1999/xhtml" >
<head id="Head1" runat="server">
    <style type="text/css">
    html
```

```
        {
            background-color:silver;
        }
        #content
        {
            margins:auto;
            width:600px;
            padding:10px;
            background-color:white;
            font:14px Georgia,Serif;
        }
        .frmMovies
        {
            width:100%;
        }
        </style>
        <title>Show FormView Pager Template</title>
</head>
<body>
    <form id="form1" runat="server">
    <div id="content">

    <asp:FormView
        id="frmMovies"
        DataSourceID="srcMovies"
        AllowPaging="true"
        CssClass="frmMovies"
        Runat="server">
        <ItemTemplate>
        <h1><%# Eval("Title") %></h1>
        <b>Directed By:</b>
        <%# Eval("Director") %>
        <br />
        <b>Box Office Totals:</b>
        <%#Eval("BoxOfficeTotals", "{0:c}") %>
        </ItemTemplate>
        <PagerTemplate>
        <hr />
        <div style="float:left">
        Page: <%# frmMovies.PageIndex + 1 %>
        </div>

        <div style="float:right;white-space:nowrap">
        <asp:LinkButton
            id="lnkPrevious"
            Text="Previous Page"
```

LISTING 12.21 Continued

```
                CommandName="Page"
                CommandArgument="Prev"
                Runat="server" />

            <asp:LinkButton
                id="lnkNext"
                Text="Next Page"
                CommandName="Page"
                CommandArgument="Next"
                Runat="server" />
            </div>
            </PagerTemplate>
    </asp:FormView>

    <asp:SqlDataSource
        id="srcMovies"
        ConnectionString="<%$ ConnectionStrings:Movies %>"
        SelectCommand="SELECT Id,Title,Director,BoxOfficeTotals FROM Movies"
        Runat="server" />

    </div>
    </form>
</body>
</html>
```

Notice that each button contained in the PagerTemplate has both a CommandName and CommandArgument property. The CommandName is set to the value Page. The CommandArgument specifies a particular type of paging operation.

You can use the following values for the CommandArgument property:

- ▶ **First**—Navigates to the first page.
- ▶ **Last**—Navigates to the last page.
- ▶ **Prev**—Navigates to the previous page.
- ▶ **Next**—Navigates to the next page.
- ▶ *number*—Navigates to a particular page number.

Editing Data with the FormView Control

You can edit a database record with the FormView control. For example, you can use the page in Listing 12.22 to edit any of the records in the Movies database table (see Figure 12.15).

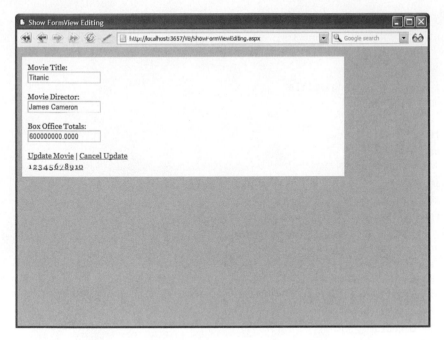

FIGURE 12.15   Editing a record with the FormView control.

LISTING 12.22   ShowFormViewEditing.aspx

```
<%@ Page Language="C#" %>
<!DOCTYPE html PUBLIC "-//W3C//DTD XHTML 1.1//EN"
  "http://www.w3.org/TR/xhtml11/DTD/xhtml11.dtd">
<html xmlns="http://www.w3.org/1999/xhtml" >
<head id="Head1" runat="server">
    <style type="text/css">
    html
    {
        background-color:silver;
    }
    #content
    {
        margins:auto;
        width:600px;
        padding:10px;
        background-color:white;
        font:14px Georgia,Serif;
    }
    a
    {
```

LISTING 12.22   Continued

```
        color:blue;
    }
    </style>
    <title>Show FormView Editing</title>
</head>
<body>
    <form id="form1" runat="server">
    <div id="content">

    <asp:FormView
        id="frmMovies"
        DataSourceID="srcMovies"
        DataKeyNames="Id"
        AllowPaging="true"
        Runat="server">
        <ItemTemplate>
        <h1><%# Eval("Title") %></h1>
        <b>Directed By:</b>
        <%# Eval("Director") %>
        <br />
        <b>Box Office Totals:</b>
        <%#Eval("BoxOfficeTotals", "{0:c}") %>
        <hr />
        <asp:LinkButton
            id="lnkEdit"
            Text="Edit Movie"
            CommandName="Edit"
            Runat="server" />
        </ItemTemplate>
        <EditItemTemplate>
        <asp:Label
            id="lblTitle"
            Text="Movie Title:"
            AssociatedControlID="txtTitle"
            Runat="server" />
        <br />
        <asp:TextBox
            id="txtTitle"
            Text='<%# Bind("Title") %>'
            Runat="server" />
        <br /><br />
        <asp:Label
            id="lblDirector"
            Text="Movie Director:"
            AssociatedControlID="txtDirector"
```

```
                Runat="server" />
        <br />
        <asp:TextBox
            id="txtDirector"
            Text='<%# Bind("Director") %>'
            Runat="server" />
        <br /><br />
        <asp:Label
            id="lblBoxOfficeTotals"
            Text="Box Office Totals:"
            AssociatedControlID="txtBoxOfficeTotals"
            Runat="server" />
        <br />
        <asp:TextBox
            id="txtBoxOfficeTotals"
            Text='<%# Bind("BoxOfficeTotals") %>'
            Runat="server" />
        <br /><br />
        <asp:LinkButton
            id="lnkUpdate"
            Text="Update Movie"
            CommandName="Update"
            Runat="server" />
        |
        <asp:LinkButton
            id="lnkCancel"
            Text="Cancel Update"
            CommandName="Cancel"
            Runat="server" />
        </EditItemTemplate>
    </asp:FormView>

    <asp:SqlDataSource
        id="srcMovies"
        ConnectionString="<%$ ConnectionStrings:Movies %>"
        SelectCommand="SELECT Id,Title,Director,BoxOfficeTotals
            FROM Movies"
        UpdateCommand="UPDATE Movies SET Title=@Title,
            Director=@Director,BoxOfficeTotals=@BoxOfficeTotals
            WHERE Id=@Id"
        Runat="server" />

    </div>
    </form>
</body>
</html>
```

You should notice several things about the `FormView` control in Listing 12.22. First, notice that the `FormView` control includes a `DataKeyNames` property that contains the name of the primary key from the data source. You need to specify a primary key when editing records.

Next, notice that the `FormView` control's `ItemTemplate` includes a `LinkButton` that looks like this:

```
<asp:LinkButton
  id="lnkEdit"
  Text="Edit Movie"
  CommandName="Edit"
  Runat="server" />
```

This `LinkButton` includes a `CommandName` property with the value `Edit`. Clicking the link switches the `FormView` control into Edit mode. You could use any other control here that supports the `CommandName` property such as a `Button` or `ImageButton` control.

Next, notice that the `FormView` control includes an `EditItemTemplate`. This template contains the form for editing the record. Each form field uses a two-way databinding expression. For example, the form field for editing the movie title looks like this:

```
<asp:TextBox
  id="txtTitle"
  Text='<%# Bind("Title") %>'
  Runat="server" />
```

The `Bind("Title")` method binds the Title column to the `Text` property of the `TextBox` control.

Finally, notice that the `EditItemTemplate` includes both a `LinkButton` for updating the database record and a `LinkButton` for canceling the update. The `LinkButton` for updating the record looks like this:

```
<asp:LinkButton
    id="lnkUpdate"
    Text="Update Movie"
    CommandName="Update"
    Runat="server" />
```

This `LinkButton` includes a `CommandName` property, which has the value `Update`. When you click this `LinkButton`, the SQL statement represented by the `SqlDataSource` control's `UpdateCommand` is executed.

NOTE

If you want the `FormView` control to be in Edit mode by default, then you can assign the value `Edit` to the `FormView` control's `DefaultMode` property.

Inserting Data with the `FormView` Control

You can use the `FormView` control to insert new records into a database table. For example, the page in Listing 12.23 enables you to insert a new movie record into the Movies database table.

LISTING 12.23 `ShowFormViewInserting.aspx`

```
<%@ Page Language="C#" %>
<!DOCTYPE html PUBLIC "-//W3C//DTD XHTML 1.1//EN"
  "http://www.w3.org/TR/xhtml11/DTD/xhtml11.dtd">
<html xmlns="http://www.w3.org/1999/xhtml" >
<head id="Head1" runat="server">
    <style type="text/css">
    html
    {
        background-color:silver;
    }
    #content
    {
        margins:auto;
        width:600px;
        padding:10px;
        background-color:white;
        font:14px Georgia,Serif;
    }
    a
    {
        color:blue;
    }
    </style>
    <title>Show FormView Inserting</title>
</head>
<body>
    <form id="form1" runat="server">
    <div id="content">

    <asp:FormView
        id="frmMovies"
        DataSourceID="srcMovies"
        AllowPaging="true"
        Runat="server">
        <ItemTemplate>
        <h1><%# Eval("Title") %></h1>
        <b>Directed By:</b>
        <%# Eval("Director") %>
```

LISTING 12.23   Continued

```
<br />
<b>In Theaters:</b>
<%#Eval("InTheaters") %>
<hr />
<asp:LinkButton
    id="lnkNew"
    Text="New Movie"
    CommandName="New"
    Runat="server" />
</ItemTemplate>
<InsertItemTemplate>
<asp:Label
    id="lblTitle"
    Text="Movie Title:"
    AssociatedControlID="txtTitle"
    Runat="server" />
<br />
<asp:TextBox
    id="txtTitle"
    Text='<%# Bind("Title") %>'
    Runat="server" />
<br /><br />
<asp:Label
    id="lblDirector"
    Text="Movie Director:"
    AssociatedControlID="txtDirector"
    Runat="server" />
<br />
<asp:TextBox
    id="txtDirector"
    Text='<%# Bind("Director") %>'
    Runat="server" />
<br /><br />
<asp:CheckBox
    id="chkInTheaters"
    Text="In Theaters"
    Checked='<%# Bind("InTheaters") %>'
    Runat="server" />
<br /><br />
<asp:LinkButton
    id="lnkInsert"
    Text="Insert Movie"
    CommandName="Insert"
    Runat="server" />
```

```
        <asp:LinkButton
            id="lnkCancel"
            Text="Cancel Insert"
            CommandName="Cancel"
            Runat="server" />
        </InsertItemTemplate>
    </asp:FormView>

    <asp:SqlDataSource
        id="srcMovies"
        ConnectionString="<%$ ConnectionStrings:Movies %>"
        SelectCommand="SELECT Id,Title,Director,InTheaters
            FROM Movies"
        InsertCommand="INSERT Movies (Title,Director,InTheaters)
            VALUES (@Title,@Director,
        Runat="server" />

    </div>
    </form>
</body>
</html>
```

You should notice several things about the page in Listing 12.23. First, notice that the ItemTemplate includes a LinkButton control that looks like this:

```
<asp:LinkButton
    id="lnkNew"
    Text="New Movie"
    CommandName="New"
    Runat="server" />
```

When you click this LinkButton control, the FormView switches into Insert mode and displays the contents of the InsertTemplate. Notice that the CommandName property has the value New.

The FormView control includes an InsertItemTemplate that contains the form for inserting a new movie record. Each form field uses a two-way databinding expression. For example, the InTheaters CheckBox looks like this:

```
<asp:CheckBox
    id="chkInTheaters"
    Text="In Theaters"
    Checked='<%# Bind("InTheaters") %>'
    Runat="server" />
```

The Bind("InTheaters") method binds the value of the CheckBox control's Checked property to the InTheaters database column.

The InsertItemTemplate contains a LinkButton for inserting the record and a LinkButton for canceling the insert operation. The LinkButton for inserting a record looks like this:

```
<asp:LinkButton
  id="lnkInsert"
  Text="Insert Movie"
  CommandName="Insert"
  Runat="server" />
```

Notice that this LinkButton control includes a CommandName property that has the value Insert. When you click the LinkButton, the SQL command represented by the SqlDataSource control's InsertCommand is executed.

> **NOTE**
>
> You can place the FormView control into Insert mode by default by assigning the value Insert to the control's DefaultMode property.

Deleting Data with the FormView Control

You can use the FormView control to delete database records. For example, the page in Listing 12.24 enables you to delete records from the Movies database table (see Figure 12.16).

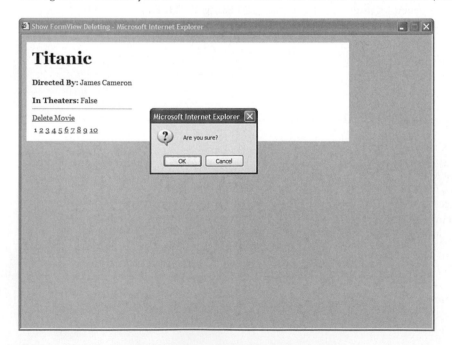

FIGURE 12.16   Deleting a record with the FormView control.

LISTING 12.24 ShowFormViewDeleting.aspx

```
<%@ Page Language="C#" %>
<!DOCTYPE html PUBLIC "-//W3C//DTD XHTML 1.1//EN"
    "http://www.w3.org/TR/xhtml11/DTD/xhtml11.dtd">
<html xmlns="http://www.w3.org/1999/xhtml" >
<head id="Head1" runat="server">
    <style type="text/css">
    html
    {
        background-color:silver;
    }
    #content
    {
        margins:auto;
        width:600px;
        padding:10px;
        background-color:white;
        font:14px Georgia,Serif;
    }
    a
    {
        color:blue;
    }
    </style>
    <title>Show FormView Deleting</title>
</head>
<body>
    <form id="form1" runat="server">
    <div id="content">

    <asp:FormView
        id="frmMovies"
        DataSourceID="srcMovies"
        DataKeyNames="Id"
        AllowPaging="true"
        Runat="server">
        <ItemTemplate>
        <h1><%# Eval("Title") %></h1>
        <b>Directed By:</b>
        <%# Eval("Director") %>
        <br />
        <b>In Theaters:</b>
        <%#Eval("InTheaters") %>
        <hr />
        <asp:LinkButton
```

LISTING 12.24   Continued

```
                id="lnkDelete"
                Text="Delete Movie"
                CommandName="Delete"
                OnClientClick="return confirm('Are you sure?');"
                Runat="server" />
        </ItemTemplate>
    </asp:FormView>

    <asp:SqlDataSource
        id="srcMovies"
        ConnectionString="<%$ ConnectionStrings:Movies %>"
        SelectCommand="SELECT Id,Title,Director,InTheaters
            FROM Movies"
        DeleteCommand="DELETE Movies WHERE Id=@Id"
        Runat="server" />

    </div>
    </form>
</body>
</html>
```

Notice that the FormView control includes a DataKeyNames property, which contains the name of the primary key column from the data source. When deleting records with the FormView control, you need to indicate the primary key column.

Furthermore, notice that the ItemTemplate includes a LinkButton for deleting a record. The LinkButton looks like this:

```
<asp:LinkButton
  id="lnkDelete"
  Text="Delete Movie"
  CommandName="Delete"
  OnClientClick="return confirm('Are you sure?');"
  Runat="server" />
```

This LinkButton includes a CommandName property that has the value Delete. When you click the LinkButton, the SQL command represented by the SqlDataSource control's DeleteCommand property is executed.

Notice, also, that the LinkButton includes an OnClientClick property that calls the JavaScript confirm() method to display a confirmation dialog box. This extra script prevents users from accidentally deleting database records.

Summary

In this chapter, you learned how to work with individual database records by using the `DetailsView` and `FormView` controls. You learned how to use both controls to display, page, edit, insert, and delete database records. You also learned how to format the appearance of both controls.

For example, the page in Listing 13.2 contains a Repeater control that renders a JavaScript array. The Repeater control is programmatically databound to the list of files in the Photos directory.

LISTING 13.2   ShowRepeaterPhotos.aspx

```
<%@ Page Language="C#" %>
<%@ Import Namespace="System.IO" %>
<!DOCTYPE html PUBLIC "-//W3C//DTD XHTML 1.1//EN"
"http://www.w3.org/TR/xhtml11/DTD/xhtml11.dtd">
<script runat="server">

    void Page_Load()
    {
        if (!Page.IsPostBack)
        {
            DirectoryInfo dir = new DirectoryInfo(MapPath("~/Photos"));
            rptPhotos.DataSource = dir.GetFiles("*.jpg");
            rptPhotos.DataBind();
        }
    }
</script>
<html xmlns="http://www.w3.org/1999/xhtml" >
<head id="Head1" runat="server">
    <style type="text/css">
        .photo
        {
            width:400px;
            background-color:white;
            filter:progid:DXImageTransform.Microsoft.Fade(duration=2);
        }
    </style>
    <script type="text/javascript">
    var photos = new Array();
    window.setInterval(showImage, 5000);

    function showImage()
    {
        if (photos.length > 0)
        {
            var index = Math.floor(Math.random() * photos.length);
            var image = document.getElementById('imgPhoto');
            image.src = photos[index];
            if (image.filters)
            {
                image.filters[0].Apply();
```

```
                image.filters[0].Play();
            }
        }
    }
    </script>
    <title>Show Repeater Photos</title>
</head>
<body>
    <form id="form1" runat="server">
    <div>


    <img id="imgPhoto" alt="" class="photo" />
    <script type="text/javascript">
    <asp:Repeater
        id="rptPhotos"
        Runat="server">
        <ItemTemplate>
        <%# Eval("Name", "photos.push('Photos/{0}')") %>
        </ItemTemplate>
    </asp:Repeater>
    showImage();
    </script>


    </div>
    </form>
</body>
</html>
```

The page in Listing 13.2 randomly displays a different photo every five seconds. A random image is selected from the JavaScript array and displayed by the JavaScript showImage() function. An Internet Explorer transition filter is used to create a fade-in effect.

WEB STANDARDS NOTE

The transition filter is an Internet Explorer–only extension to Cascading Style Sheets. The page still works with Opera 8 and Firefox 1, but you don't get the fade-in effect.

Using Templates with the Repeater Control

The Repeater control supports five different types of templates:

▶ **ItemTemplate**—Formats each item from the data source.

▶ **AlternatingItemTemplate**—Formats every other item from the data source.

▶ **SeparatorTemplate**—Formats between each item from the data source.

▶ **HeaderTemplate**—Formats before all items from the data source.

▶ **FooterTemplate**—Formats after all items from the data source.

You are required to use only an ItemTemplate; the other types of templates can be used at your own discretion. The order in which you declare the templates in the Repeater control does not matter.

You can use the SeparatorTemplate to create a banding effect (as in old-time computer paper). In other words, you can use the SeparatorTemplate to display alternating rows with a different background color. This approach is illustrated by the page in Listing 13.3 (see Figure 13.2).

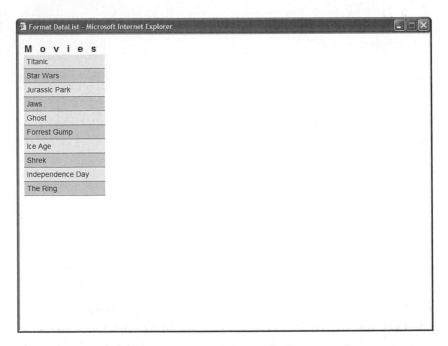

FIGURE 13.2   Displaying an HTML table with the Repeater control.

LISTING 13.3   ShowRepeaterTable.aspx

```
<%@ Page Language="C#" %>
<!DOCTYPE html PUBLIC "-//W3C//DTD XHTML 1.1//EN"
    "http://www.w3.org/TR/xhtml11/DTD/xhtml11.dtd">
<html xmlns="http://www.w3.org/1999/xhtml" >
<head id="Head1" runat="server">
    <style type="text/css">
    html
    {
        background-color:silver;
    }
```

```
    .content
    {
        width:600px;
        border:solid 1px black;
        background-color:white;
    }
    .movies
    {
        border-collapse:collapse;
    }
    .movies th,.movies td
    {
        padding:10px;
        border-bottom:1px solid black;
    }
    .alternating
    {
        background-color:#eeeeee;
    }
    </style>
    <title>Show Repeater Table</title>
</head>
<body>
    <form id="form1" runat="server">
    <div class="content">

    <asp:Repeater
        id="rptMovies"
        DataSourceID="srcMovies"
        Runat="server">
        <HeaderTemplate>
        <table class="movies">
        <tr>
            <th>Movie Title</th>
            <th>Movie Director</th>
            <th>Box Office Totals</th>
        </tr>
        </HeaderTemplate>
        <ItemTemplate>
        <tr>
            <td><%#Eval("Title") %></td>
            <td><%#Eval("Director") %></td>
            <td><%#Eval("BoxOfficeTotals","{0:c}") %></td>
        </tr>
        </ItemTemplate>
        <AlternatingItemTemplate>
```

13

LISTING 13.3   Continued

```
        <tr class="alternating">
            <td><%#Eval("Title") %></td>
            <td><%#Eval("Director") %></td>
            <td><%#Eval("BoxOfficeTotals","{0:c}") %></td>
        </tr>
        </AlternatingItemTemplate>
        <FooterTemplate>
        </table>
        </FooterTemplate>
    </asp:Repeater>

    <asp:SqlDataSource
        id="srcMovies"
        ConnectionString="<%$ ConnectionStrings:Movies %>"
        SelectCommand="SELECT Title,Director,BoxOfficeTotals
            FROM Movies"
        Runat="server" />

    </div>
    </form>
</body>
</html>
```

The Repeater control in Listing 13.3 renders an HTML table in which every other row appears with a gray background color. Notice that this Repeater control uses four out of five of the templates supported by the Repeater: the ItemTemplate, AlternatingItemTemplate, HeaderTemplate, and FooterTemplate.

Notice that the AlternatingItemTemplate contains almost exactly the same content as the ItemTemplate. The only difference is that the <tr> tag includes a class attribute that changes its background color.

The SeparatorTemplate is used to add content between each data item from the data source. For example, the page in Listing 13.4 uses a SeparatorItemTemplate to create a tab strip with the Repeater control (see Figure 13.3).

LISTING 13.4   ShowSeparatorTemplate.aspx

```
<%@ Page Language="C#" %>
<!DOCTYPE html PUBLIC "-//W3C//DTD XHTML 1.1//EN"
    "http://www.w3.org/TR/xhtml11/DTD/xhtml11.dtd">
<html xmlns="http://www.w3.org/1999/xhtml" >
<head id="Head1" runat="server">
```

```
    <style type="text/css">
    html
    {
        background-color:silver;
    }
    .content
    {
        width:600px;
        height:400px;
        padding:10px;
        border:solid 1px black;
        background-color:white;
    }
    a
    {
        color:blue;
    }
    </style>
    <title>Show SeparatorTemplate</title>
</head>
<body>
    <form id="form1" runat="server">
    <div class="content">

    <asp:Repeater
        id="rptMovieCategories"
        DataSourceID="srcMovieCategories"
        Runat="server">
        <ItemTemplate>
        <asp:HyperLink
            id="lnkMenu"
            Text='<%#Eval("Name")%>'
            NavigateUrl='<%#Eval("Id","ShowSeparatorTemplate.aspx?id={0}")%>'
            Runat="server" />
        </ItemTemplate>
        <SeparatorTemplate>
         | 
        </SeparatorTemplate>
    </asp:Repeater>

    <asp:Repeater
        id="rptMovies"
        DataSourceID="srcMovies"
```

13

LISTING 13.4   Continued

```
            Runat="server">
            <HeaderTemplate>
            <ul>
            </HeaderTemplate>
            <ItemTemplate>
            <li><%#Eval("Title")%></li>
            </ItemTemplate>
            <FooterTemplate>
            </ul>
            </FooterTemplate>
        </asp:Repeater>

        <asp:SqlDataSource
            id="srcMovieCategories"
            ConnectionString="<%$ ConnectionStrings:Movies %>"
            SelectCommand="SELECT Id, Name
                FROM MovieCategories"
            Runat="server" />

        <asp:SqlDataSource
            id="srcMovies"
            ConnectionString="<%$ ConnectionStrings:Movies %>"
            SelectCommand="SELECT Title FROM Movies
                WHERE CategoryId=@CategoryId"
            Runat="server">
            <SelectParameters>
            <asp:QueryStringParameter
                Name="CategoryId"
                QueryStringField="Id" />
            </SelectParameters>
        </asp:SqlDataSource>

    </div>
    </form>
</body>
</html>
```

The page in Listing 13.4 contains two Repeater controls. The first Repeater control displays a tab strip of movie categories. The second Repeater control displays a bulleted list of matching movies.

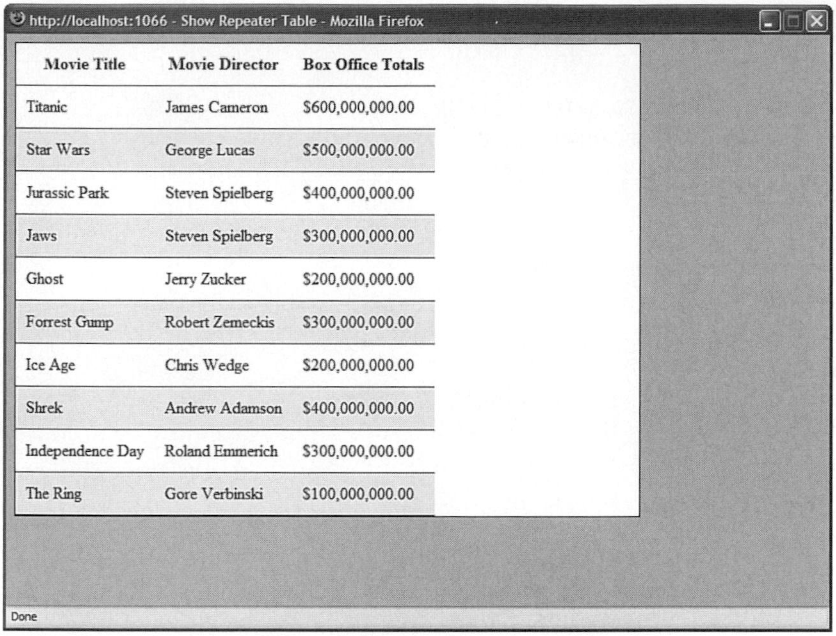

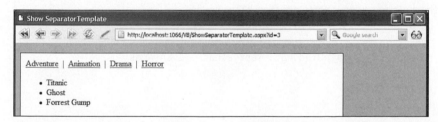

FIGURE 13.3   Displaying a tab strip with the Repeater control.

Handling Repeater Control Events

The Repeater control supports the following events:

- ▶ **DataBinding**—Raised when the Repeater control is bound to its data source.

- ▶ **ItemCommand**—Raised when a control contained in the Repeater control raises an event.

- ▶ **ItemCreated**—Raised when each Repeater item is created.

- ▶ **ItemDataBound**—Raised when each Repeater item is bound.

The page in Listing 13.5 illustrates how you can use the DataBinding, ItemCommand, and ItemDataBound events. This page uses a Repeater control to update, delete, and insert database records (see Figure 13.4).

FIGURE 13.4   Editing database records with the Repeater control.

LISTING 13.5   EditRepeater.aspx

```csharp
<%@ Page Language="C#" %>
<!DOCTYPE html PUBLIC "-//W3C//DTD XHTML 1.1//EN"
"http://www.w3.org/TR/xhtml11/DTD/xhtml11.dtd">

<script runat="server">

    // The name of the primary key column
    string DataKeyName = "Id";


    /// <summary>
    /// Stores the primary keys in ViewState
    /// </summary>
    Hashtable Keys
    {
        get
        {
            if (ViewState["Keys"] == null)
                ViewState["Keys"] = new Hashtable();
            return (Hashtable)ViewState["Keys"];
        }
    }


    /// <summary>
    /// Build the primary key collection
    /// </summary>
    protected void rptMovies_ItemDataBound(object sender, RepeaterItemEventArgs e)
    {
        if (e.Item.ItemType == ListItemType.Item || e.Item.ItemType ==
          ListItemType.AlternatingItem)
        {
            Keys.Add(e.Item.ItemIndex, DataBinder.Eval(e.Item.DataItem, "Id"));
        }
    }


    /// <summary>
    /// Clear the primary keys when Repeater is rebound
    /// to its data source
    /// </summary>
    protected void rptMovies_DataBinding(object sender, EventArgs e)
    {
        Keys.Clear();
    }
```

```csharp
/// <summary>
/// When you click the Update,Insert, or Delete
/// button, this method executes
/// </summary>
protected void rptMovies_ItemCommand(object source, RepeaterCommandEventArgs e)
{
    switch (e.CommandName)
    {
        case "Update":
            UpdateMovie(e);
            break;
        case "Insert":
            InsertMovie(e);
            break;
        case "Delete":
            DeleteMovie(e);
            break;
    }
}


/// <summary>
/// Update a movie record
/// </summary>
void UpdateMovie(RepeaterCommandEventArgs e)
{
    // Get the form fields
    TextBox txtTitle = (TextBox)e.Item.FindControl("txtTitle");
    TextBox txtDirector = (TextBox)e.Item.FindControl("txtDirector");
    CheckBox chkInTheaters = (CheckBox)e.Item.FindControl("chkInTheaters");

    // Set the DataSource parameters
    srcMovies.UpdateParameters["Id"].DefaultValue =
      Keys[e.Item.ItemIndex].ToString();
    srcMovies.UpdateParameters["Title"].DefaultValue = txtTitle.Text;
    srcMovies.UpdateParameters["Director"].DefaultValue = txtDirector.Text;
    srcMovies.UpdateParameters["InTheaters"].DefaultValue =
      chkInTheaters.Checked.ToString();

    // Fire the UpdateCommand
    srcMovies.Update();
}


/// <summary>
/// Insert a movie record
/// </summary>
```

LISTING 13.5   Continued

```
    void InsertMovie(RepeaterCommandEventArgs e)
    {
        // Get the form fields
        TextBox txtTitle = (TextBox)e.Item.FindControl("txtTitle");
        TextBox txtDirector = (TextBox)e.Item.FindControl("txtDirector");
        CheckBox chkInTheaters = (CheckBox)e.Item.FindControl("chkInTheaters");

        // Set the DataSource parameters
        srcMovies.InsertParameters["Title"].DefaultValue = txtTitle.Text;
        srcMovies.InsertParameters["Director"].DefaultValue = txtDirector.Text;
        srcMovies.InsertParameters["InTheaters"].DefaultValue =
          chkInTheaters.Checked.ToString();

        // Fire the InsertCommand
        srcMovies.Insert();
    }


    /// <summary>
    /// Delete a movie record
    /// </summary>
    void DeleteMovie(RepeaterCommandEventArgs e)
    {
        // Set the DataSource parameters
        srcMovies.DeleteParameters["Id"].DefaultValue =
          Keys[e.Item.ItemIndex].ToString();

        // Fire the DeleteCommand
        srcMovies.Delete();


    }

</script>
<html xmlns="http://www.w3.org/1999/xhtml" >
<head id="Head1" runat="server">
    <style type="text/css">
    html
    {
        background-color:silver;
    }
    .content
    {
        width:600px;
        height:400px;
        padding:10px;
```

```
        border:solid 1px black;
        background-color:white;
    }
    .movies td
    {
        text-align:center;
    }
    a
    {
        color:blue;
    }
    </style>
    <title>Edit Repeater</title>
</head>
<body>
    <form id="form1" runat="server">
    <div class="content">

    <asp:Repeater
        id="rptMovies"
        DataSourceID="srcMovies"
        Runat="server" OnItemCommand="rptMovies_ItemCommand" OnItemDataBound=
          "rptMovies_ItemDataBound" OnDataBinding="rptMovies_DataBinding">
        <HeaderTemplate>
        <table class="movies">
        <tr>
            <th>Title</th>
            <th>Director</th>
            <th>In Theaters</th>
        </tr>
        </HeaderTemplate>
        <ItemTemplate>
        <tr>
            <td>
            <asp:TextBox
                id="txtTitle"
                Text='<%#Eval("Title")%>'
                Runat="server" />
            </td>
            <td>
            <asp:TextBox
                id="txtDirector"
                Text='<%#Eval("Director")%>'
                Runat="server" />
            </td>
            <td>
```

LISTING 13.5   Continued

```
            <asp:CheckBox
                id="chkInTheaters"
                Checked='<%#Eval("InTheaters")%>'
                Runat="server" />
        </td>
        <td>
        <asp:LinkButton
            id="lnkUpdate"
            CommandName="Update"
            Text="Update"
            Runat="server" />
         | 
        <asp:LinkButton
            id="lnkDelete"
            CommandName="Delete"
            Text="Delete"
            OnClientClick="return confirm('Are you sure?');"
            Runat="server" />
        </td>
    </tr>
    </ItemTemplate>
    <FooterTemplate>
    <tr>
        <td>
        <asp:TextBox
            id="txtTitle"
            Runat="server" />
        </td>
        <td>
        <asp:TextBox
            id="txtDirector"
            Runat="server" />
        </td>
        <td>
        <asp:CheckBox
            id="chkInTheaters"
            Runat="server" />
        </td>
        <td>
        <asp:LinkButton
            id="lnkInsert"
            CommandName="Insert"
            Text="Insert"
```

```
                    Runat="server" />
            </td>
        </tr>
        </table>
        </FooterTemplate>
    </asp:Repeater>

    <asp:SqlDataSource
        id="srcMovies"
        ConnectionString="<%$ ConnectionStrings:Movies %>"
        SelectCommand="SELECT Id,Title,Director,InTheaters
            FROM Movies"
        UpdateCommand="UPDATE Movies SET Title=@Title,
            Director=@Director,InTheaters=@InTheaters
            WHERE Id=@Id"
        InsertCommand="INSERT Movies (Title,Director,InTheaters)
            VALUES (@Title,@Director,
        DeleteCommand="DELETE Movies WHERE Id=@Id"
        Runat="server">
        <UpdateParameters>
            <asp:Parameter Name="Id" />
            <asp:Parameter Name="Title" />
            <asp:Parameter Name="Director" />
            <asp:Parameter Name="InTheaters" />
        </UpdateParameters>
        <InsertParameters>
            <asp:Parameter Name="Title" />
            <asp:Parameter Name="Director" />
            <asp:Parameter Name="InTheaters" />
        </InsertParameters>
        <DeleteParameters>
            <asp:Parameter Name="Id" />
        </DeleteParameters>
    </asp:SqlDataSource>

    </div>
    </form>
</body>
</html>
```

In Listing 13.5, the `ItemDataBound` event handler builds a collection of primary keys from the data source. The collection of primary keys is stored in ViewState so that they will be available after a postback to the server.

The DataBinding event handler clears the primary key collection when the Repeater is rebound to its data source (after a record is updated or deleted). If you don't clear the collection, then you get duplicates of the primary keys and an exception is raised.

The ItemCommand event handler takes care of processing the button click events. When you click an Insert, Update, or Delete button, the event bubbles up and raises the ItemCommand event. The ItemCommand event handler grabs the values from the form fields and calls the Insert(), Update(), or Delete() methods of the SqlDataSource control.

Using the DataList Control

The DataList control, like the Repeater control, is template driven. Unlike the Repeater control, by default, the DataList renders an HTML table. Because the DataList uses a particular layout to render its content, you are provided with more formatting options when using the DataList control.

In this section, you learn how to use the DataList control to display data. You also learn how to render database records in both single-column and multi-column HTML tables. We also explore how you can edit data with the DataList control.

Displaying Data with the DataList Control

To display data with the DataList control, you must supply the control with an ItemTemplate. The contents of the ItemTemplate are rendered for each data item from the data source.

For example, the page in Listing 13.6 uses a DataList to display the contents of the Movies database table. The ItemTemplate displays the values of the Title, Director, and BoxOfficeTotals columns (see Figure 13.5).

LISTING 13.6   ShowDataList.aspx

```
<%@ Page Language="C#" %>
<!DOCTYPE html PUBLIC "-//W3C//DTD XHTML 1.1//EN"
    "http://www.w3.org/TR/xhtml11/DTD/xhtml11.dtd">
<html xmlns="http://www.w3.org/1999/xhtml" >
<head id="Head1" runat="server">
    <title>Show DataList</title>
</head>
<body>
    <form id="form1" runat="server">
    <div>

    <asp:DataList
        id="dlstMovies"
        DataSourceID="srcMovies"
        Runat="server">
```

```
        <ItemTemplate>
        <h1><%#Eval("Title")%></h1>
        Directed by:
        <%#Eval("Director") %>
        <br />
        Box Office Totals:
        <%#Eval("BoxOfficeTotals","{0:c}") %>
        </ItemTemplate>
    </asp:DataList>

    <asp:SqlDataSource
        id="srcMovies"
        ConnectionString="<%$ ConnectionStrings:Movies %>"
        SelectCommand="SELECT Title,Director,BoxOfficeTotals
            FROM Movies"
        Runat="server" />

    </div>
    </form>
</body>
</html>
```

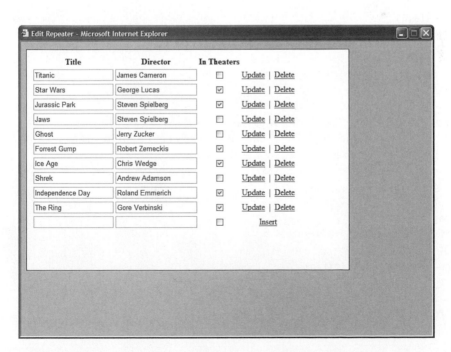

FIGURE 13.5   Displaying database records with the DataList control.

The DataList in Listing 13.6 renders an HTML table. Each data item is rendered into a separate table cell (<td> tag). The rendered output of the DataList control in Listing 13.6 looks like this:

```
<table id="dlstMovies" cellspacing="0" border="0"
  style="border-collapse:collapse;">
<tr>
  <td>
  <h1>Titanic</h1>
  Directed by:
  James Cameron
  <br />
  Box Office Totals:
  $600,000,000.00
  </td>
</tr>
<tr>
  <td>
  <h1>Star Wars</h1>
  Directed by:
  George Lucas
  <br />
  Box Office Totals:
  $500,000,000.00
  </td>
</tr>
...
</table>
```

The default behavior of the DataList control is to render an HTML table. However, you can override this default behavior and display the contents of each data item in a separate HTML <span> tag. This approach is illustrated in Listing 13.7.

LISTING 13.7   ShowFlowDataList.aspx

```
<%@ Page Language="C#" %>
<html xmlns="http://www.w3.org/1999/xhtml" >
<head id="Head1" runat="server">
    <title>Show Flow DataList</title>
</head>
<body>
    <form id="form1" runat="server">
    <div>

    <asp:DataList
        id="dlstMovies"
```

```
        DataSourceID="srcMovies"
        RepeatLayout="Flow"
        Runat="server">
        <ItemTemplate>
        <%#Eval("Title")%>
        </ItemTemplate>
    </asp:DataList>

    <asp:SqlDataSource
        id="srcMovies"
        ConnectionString="<%$ ConnectionStrings:Movies %>"
        SelectCommand="SELECT Title FROM Movies"
        Runat="server" />

    </div>
    </form>
</body>
</html>
```

Notice that the DataList control in Listing 13.7 includes a RepeatLayout property that has the value Flow. Each movie title is rendered in a <span> tag followed by a line-break tag (<br>).

The RepeatLayout property accepts one of the following two values:

- ▶ **Table**—Data Items are rendered in HTML table cells.
- ▶ **Flow**—Data Items are rendered in HTML <span> tags.

Displaying Data in Multiple Columns

You can render the contents of a DataList control into a multi-column table in which each data item occupies a separate table cell. Two properties modify the layout of the HTML table rendered by the DataList control:

- ▶ **RepeatColumns**—The number of columns to display.
- ▶ **RepeatDirection**—The direction to render the cells. Possible values are Horizontal and Vertical.

For example, the page in Listing 13.8 displays the contents of the Movies database table in a three-column layout (see Figure 13.6).

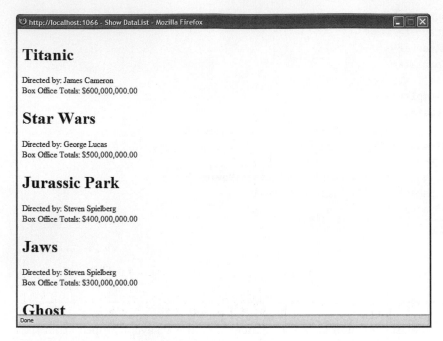

FIGURE 13.6   Displaying a multi-column DataList.

LISTING 13.8   MultiColumnDataList.aspx

```
<%@ Page Language="C#" %>
<html xmlns="http://www.w3.org/1999/xhtml" >
<head id="Head1" runat="server">
    <title>MultiColumn DataList</title>
</head>
<body>
    <form id="form1" runat="server">
    <div>

    <asp:DataList
        id="dlstMovies"
        DataSourceID="srcMovies"
        RepeatColumns="3"
        GridLines="Both"
        Runat="server">
        <ItemTemplate>
        <h1><%#Eval("Title")%></h1>
        Directed by:
        <%#Eval("Director") %>
        <br />
```

```
        Box Office Totals:
        <%#Eval("BoxOfficeTotals","{0:c}") %>
        </ItemTemplate>
    </asp:DataList>

    <asp:SqlDataSource
        id="srcMovies"
        ConnectionString="<%$ ConnectionStrings:Movies %>"
        SelectCommand="SELECT Title,Director,BoxOfficeTotals
            FROM Movies"
        Runat="server" />

    </div>
    </form>
</body>
</html>
```

Notice that the DataList control in Listing 13.8 includes a `RepeatColumns` property that has the value 3.

If you set the `RepeatDirection` property to the value `Horizontal` and do not assign a value to the `RepeatColumns` property, then the DataList renders its data items horizontally without end.

NOTE

You can display data items in multiple columns when the DataList is in Flow layout mode. In that case, <br> tags are used to create the row breaks.

Using Templates with the DataList Control

The DataList control supports all the same templates as the Repeater control:

- ▶ **ItemTemplate**—Formats each item from the data source.

- ▶ **AlternatingItemTemplate**—Formats every other item from the data source.

- ▶ **SeparatorTemplate**—Formats between each item from the data source.

- ▶ **HeaderTemplate**—Formats before all items from the data source.

- ▶ **FooterTemplate**—Formats after all items from the data source

In addition, the DataList supports the following templates:

- ▶ **EditItemTemplate**—Displayed when a row is selected for editing.

- ▶ **SelectedItemTemplate**—Displayed when a row is selected.

The DataList control in Listing 13.9 includes both a HeaderTemplate and a FooterTemplate. The HeaderTemplate contains the caption for the table. The FooterTemplate contains a Label control that displays the total for all the preceding rows (see Figure 13.7).

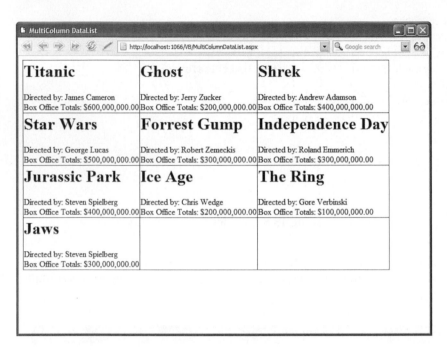

FIGURE 13.7   Displaying a HeaderTemplate and FooterTemplate.

LISTING 13.9   ShowDataListTemplates.aspx

```csharp
<%@ Page Language="C#" %>
<!DOCTYPE html PUBLIC "-//W3C//DTD XHTML 1.1//EN"
"http://www.w3.org/TR/xhtml11/DTD/xhtml11.dtd">
<script runat="server">

    decimal totals;

    protected void dlstMovies_ItemDataBound(object sender, DataListItemEventArgs e)
    {
        if (e.Item.DataItem != null)
            totals += (decimal)DataBinder.Eval(e.Item.DataItem, "BoxOfficeTotals");
        if (e.Item.ItemType == ListItemType.Footer)
        {
            Label lblTotal = (Label)e.Item.FindControl("lblTotal");
            lblTotal.Text = totals.ToString("c");
        }
```

```
        }
    </script>
    <html xmlns="http://www.w3.org/1999/xhtml" >
    <head id="Head1" runat="server">
        <style type="text/css">
        .movies td
        {
            padding:10px;
            text-align:right;
        }
        </style>
        <title>Show DataList Templates</title>
    </head>
    <body>
        <form id="form1" runat="server">
        <div>

        <asp:DataList
            id="dlstMovies"
            DataSourceID="srcMovies"
            GridLines="Horizontal"
            UseAccessibleHeader="true"
            OnItemDataBound="dlstMovies_ItemDataBound"
            CssClass="movies"
            Runat="server" >
            <HeaderTemplate>
            Movie Box Office Totals
            </HeaderTemplate>
            <ItemTemplate>
            <%#Eval("Title")%>:
            <%#Eval("BoxOfficeTotals","{0:c}") %>
            </ItemTemplate>
            <FooterTemplate>
            <b>Total:</b>
            <asp:Label
                id="lblTotal"
                Runat="server" />
            </FooterTemplate>
        </asp:DataList>

        <asp:SqlDataSource
            id="srcMovies"
            ConnectionString="<%$ ConnectionStrings:Movies %>"
            SelectCommand="SELECT Title,BoxOfficeTotals
                FROM Movies"
            Runat="server" />
```

LISTING 13.9   Continued

```
        </div>
    </form>
</body>
</html>
```

The total displayed in the FooterTemplate is calculated by the ItemDataBound event handler. The Label control is extracted by the FindControl() method and the total is assigned to the control's Text property.

Selecting Data with the DataList Control

You can use a DataList control as a menu by taking advantage of the control's SelectedValue property. For example, the page in Listing 13.10 enables you to pick a movie category and display a list of matching movies (see Figure 13.8).

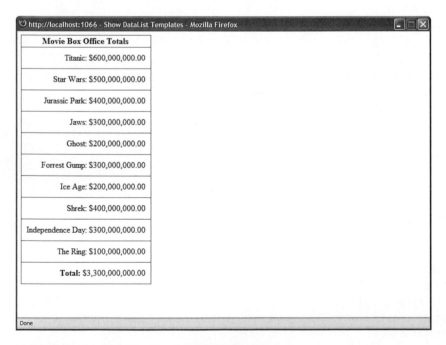

FIGURE 13.8   Selecting a row in the DataList.

LISTING 13.10   SelectDataList.aspx

```
<%@ Page Language="C#" %>
<!DOCTYPE html PUBLIC "-//W3C//DTD XHTML 1.1//EN"
    "http://www.w3.org/TR/xhtml11/DTD/xhtml11.dtd">
```

```html
<html xmlns="http://www.w3.org/1999/xhtml" >
<head id="Head1" runat="server">
    <style type="text/css">
    html
    {
        background-color:orange;
    }
    .content
    {
        margin:auto;
        width:600px;
        background-color:white;
    }
    .column
    {
        float:left;
        width:250px;
        padding:20px;
    }
    .movies td
    {
        padding:10px;
    }
    a
    {
        padding:10px;
        color:red;
    }
    a:hover
    {
        background-color:Gold;
    }
    </style>
    <title>Select DataList</title>
</head>
<body>
    <form id="form1" runat="server">
    <div class="content">

    <div class="column">
    <asp:DataList
        id="dlstMovieCategories"
        DataSourceID="srcMovieCategories"
        DataKeyField="Id"
        GridLines="Both"
```

LISTING 13.10   Continued

```
        CssClass="movies"
        Runat="server">
        <ItemTemplate>
        <asp:LinkButton
            id="lnkMovie"
            Text='<%#Eval("Name") %>'
            CommandName="Select"
            Runat="server" />
        </ItemTemplate>
    </asp:DataList>
    </div>

    <div class="column">
    <asp:DataList
        id="dlstMovieDetails"
        DataSourceID="srcMovieDetails"
        Runat="server">
        <ItemTemplate>
        <h1><%#Eval("Title")%></h1>
        Directed by:
        <%#Eval("Director") %>
        <br />
        Box Office Totals:
        <%#Eval("BoxOfficeTotals","{0:c}") %>
        </ItemTemplate>
    </asp:DataList>
    </div>
    <br style="clear:both" />
    </div>

    <asp:SqlDataSource
        id="srcMovieCategories"
        ConnectionString="<%$ ConnectionStrings:Movies %>"
        SelectCommand="SELECT Id, Name FROM MovieCategories"
        Runat="server" />

    <asp:SqlDataSource
        id="srcMovieDetails"
        ConnectionString="<%$ ConnectionStrings:Movies %>"
        SelectCommand="SELECT Title,Director,BoxOfficeTotals
            FROM Movies WHERE CategoryId=@CategoryId"
        Runat="server">
        <SelectParameters>
```

```
        <asp:ControlParameter
            Name="CategoryId"
            ControlID="dlstMovieCategories"
            PropertyName="SelectedValue" />
        </SelectParameters>
    </asp:SqlDataSource>
    </form>
</body>
</html>
```

The page in Listing 13.10 contains two DataList controls. The first control displays a menu of movie categories and the second DataList control displays a list of matching movies.

Notice that the first DataList in Listing 13.10 includes a DataKeyField property. The DataKeyField property accepts the name of a primary key column from the data source. When this property is set, the DataList control's DataKeys collection is populated with the primary keys from the data source when the control is bound to its data source.

The first DataList contains a LinkButton inside its ItemTemplate, which looks like this:

```
<asp:LinkButton
  id="lnkMovie"
  Text='<%#Eval("Name") %>'
  CommandName="Select"
  Runat="server" />
```

Because the LinkButton control's CommandName property has the value Select, clicking the button changes the value of the DataList control's SelectedValue property. The DataList control's SelectedValue property is used by the second SqlDataSource control to return movies that match the selected category.

> **NOTE**
>
> Unlike the GridView, DetailsView, ListView, and FormView controls, you cannot assign the names of multiple primary key columns to the DataKeyField property.

Editing Data with the DataList Control

You can use the DataList control to edit database records. However, editing with the DataList control requires more coding than editing with other DataBound controls such as the GridView, FormView, or DetailsView controls.

The page in Listing 13.11 illustrates how you can edit and delete database records with the DataList control (see Figure 13.9).

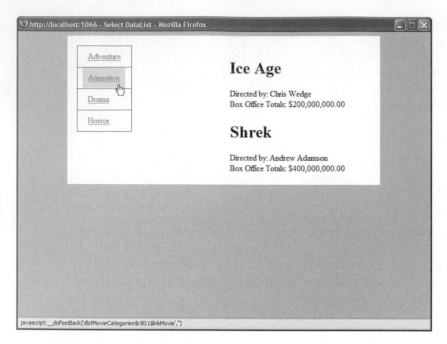

FIGURE 13.9   Editing database records with the DataList control.

LISTING 13.11   EditDataList.aspx

```
<%@ Page Language="C#" MaintainScrollPositionOnPostback="true" %>
<!DOCTYPE html PUBLIC "-//W3C//DTD XHTML 1.1//EN"
"http://www.w3.org/TR/xhtml11/DTD/xhtml11.dtd">
<script runat="server">

    protected void dlstMovies_EditCommand(object source, DataListCommandEventArgs e)
    {
        dlstMovies.EditItemIndex = e.Item.ItemIndex;
        dlstMovies.DataBind();
    }

    protected void dlstMovies_UpdateCommand(object source, DataListCommandEventArgs e)
    {
        // Get form fields
        TextBox txtTitle = (TextBox)e.Item.FindControl("txtTitle");
        TextBox txtDirector = (TextBox)e.Item.FindControl("txtDirector");
        CheckBox chkInTheaters = (CheckBox)e.Item.FindControl("chkInTheaters");

        // Assign parameters
```

```
        srcMovies.UpdateParameters["Id"].DefaultValue =
          dlstMovies.DataKeys[e.Item.ItemIndex].ToString();
        srcMovies.UpdateParameters["Title"].DefaultValue = txtTitle.Text;
        srcMovies.UpdateParameters["Director"].DefaultValue = txtDirector.Text;
        srcMovies.UpdateParameters["InTheaters"].DefaultValue =
          chkInTheaters.Checked.ToString();

        // Call SqlDataSource Update
        srcMovies.Update();

        // Take out of Edit mode
        dlstMovies.EditItemIndex = -1;
    }


    protected void dlstMovies_DeleteCommand(object source, DataListCommandEventArgs e)
    {
        // Assign parameters
        srcMovies.DeleteParameters["Id"].DefaultValue =
          dlstMovies.DataKeys[e.Item.ItemIndex].ToString();

        // Call SqlDataSource Delete
        srcMovies.Delete();
    }


    protected void dlstMovies_CancelCommand(object source, DataListCommandEventArgs e)
    {
        dlstMovies.EditItemIndex = -1;
        dlstMovies.DataBind();
    }
</script>
<html xmlns="http://www.w3.org/1999/xhtml">
<head id="Head1" runat="server">
    <style type="text/css">
    html
    {
        background-color:silver;
    }
    .movies
    {
        background-color:white;
    }
    .movies td,.movies th
    {
        padding:10px;
        border:solid 1px black;
```

13

LISTING 13.11   Continued

```
        }
        .edit
        {
            background-color:yellow;
        }
        a
        {
            color:blue;
        }
        </style>
        <title>Edit DataList</title>
</head>
<body>
    <form id="form1" runat="server">
    <div>

    <asp:DataList
        id="dlstMovies"
        DataSourceID="srcMovies"
        DataKeyField="Id"
        GridLines="None"
        OnEditCommand="dlstMovies_EditCommand"
        OnCancelCommand="dlstMovies_CancelCommand"
        OnUpdateCommand="dlstMovies_UpdateCommand"
        OnDeleteCommand="dlstMovies_DeleteCommand"
        CssClass="movies"
        EditItemStyle-CssClass="edit"
        Runat="server">
        <ItemTemplate>
        <h1><%#Eval("Title")%></h1>
        Directed by:
        <%#Eval("Director") %>
        <br />
        In Theaters:
        <%#Eval("InTheaters") %>
        <br /><br />
        <asp:LinkButton
            id="lnkEdit"
            CommandName="Edit"
            Text="Edit"
            Runat="server" />
         ¦ 
        <asp:LinkButton
            id="lnkDelete"
```

```
            CommandName="Delete"
            Text="Delete"
            OnClientClick="return confirm('Are you sure?');"
            Runat="server" />
    </ItemTemplate>
    <EditItemTemplate>
    <asp:Label
        id="lblTitle"
        Text="Title:"
        AssociatedControlID="txtTitle"
        Runat="server" />
    <br />
    <asp:TextBox
        id="txtTitle"
        Text='<%#Eval("Title")%>'
        Runat="server" />
    <br /><br />
    <asp:Label
        id="lblDirector"
        Text="Director:"
        AssociatedControlID="txtDirector"
        Runat="server" />
    <br />
    <asp:TextBox
        id="txtDirector"
        Text='<%#Eval("Director")%>'
        Runat="server" />
    <br /><br />
    <asp:CheckBox
        id="chkInTheaters"
        Text="In Theaters"
        Checked='<%#Eval("InTheaters")%>'
        Runat="server" />
    <br /><br />
    <asp:LinkButton
        id="lnkUpdate"
        CommandName="Update"
        Text="Update"
        Runat="server" />
     | 
    <asp:LinkButton
        id="lnkCancel"
        CommandName="Cancel"
        Text="Cancel"
        Runat="server" />
    </EditItemTemplate>
```

LISTING 13.11 Continued

```
    </asp:DataList>

    <asp:SqlDataSource
        id="srcMovies"
        ConnectionString="<%$ ConnectionStrings:Movies %>"
        SelectCommand="SELECT Id,Title,Director,InTheaters
            FROM Movies"
        UpdateCommand="UPDATE Movies SET Title=@Title,
            Director=@Director,InTheaters=@InTheaters
            WHERE Id=@Id"
        DeleteCommand="DELETE Movies WHERE Id=@Id"
        Runat="server">
        <UpdateParameters>
            <asp:Parameter Name="Id" />
            <asp:Parameter Name="Title" />
            <asp:Parameter Name="Director" />
            <asp:Parameter Name="InTheaters" />
        </UpdateParameters>
        <DeleteParameters>
            <asp:Parameter Name="Id" />
        </DeleteParameters>
    </asp:SqlDataSource>

    </div>
    </form>
</body>
</html>
```

The ItemTemplate contained in the DataList in Listing 13.11 includes an Edit LinkButton and a Delete LinkButton. When you click the Edit LinkButton, the DataList raises its EditCommand event and the dlstMovies_Edit() method is executed. Clicking the Delete LinkButton raises the DeleteCommand event and the dlstMovies_Delete() method is executed.

The dlstMovies_Edit() method sets the EditItemIndex property of the DataList control. The EditItemTemplate is displayed for the item in the DataList that matches the EditItemIndex.

The EditItemTemplate includes form fields for editing a movie record and an Update and Cancel LinkButton. These LinkButtons raise the UpdateCommand and CancelCommand events, and execute the corresponding event handlers.

NOTE

Notice that the <%@ Page %> directive includes a MaintainScrollPositionOnPostback attribute. This attribute causes a page to scroll to the same position whenever you post the page back to the server. For example, when you click the Edit link next to a row in the DataList, the page scrolls to the Edit link that you clicked. This attribute works with Internet Explorer 6+, FireFox 1+, and Opera 8+.

Formatting the DataList Control

The DataList control includes a rich set of properties that you can use to format the HTML rendered by the control. If you want to associate Cascading Style Sheet rules with different elements of the DataList, then you can take advantage of any of the following properties:

- ▶ **CssClass**—Enables you to associate a CSS class with the DataList.

- ▶ **AlternatingItemStyle**—Enables you to format every other row of the DataList.

- ▶ **EditItemStyle**—Enables you to format the DataList row selected for editing.

- ▶ **FooterStyle**—Enables you to format the footer row of the DataList.

- ▶ **HeaderStyle**—Enables you to format the header row of the DataList.

- ▶ **ItemStyle**—Enables you to format each row displayed by the DataList.

- ▶ **SelectedItemStyle**—Enables you to format the selected row in the DataList.

- ▶ **SeparatorStyle**—Enables you to format the row separator displayed by the DataList.

When formatting the DataList, you also need to work with the following properties:

- ▶ **GridLines**—Enables you to add rules around the cells in the DataList. Possible values are None, Horizontal, Vertical, and Both.

- ▶ **ShowFooter**—Enables you to show or hide the footer row.

- ▶ **ShowHeader**—Enables you to show or hide the header row.

- ▶ **UseAccessibleHeader**—Enables you to render HTML <th> tags instead of <td> tags for the cells in the header row.

WEB STANDARDS NOTE

To make a page that contains a DataList more accessible to persons with disabilities, you should always include a HeaderTemplate and enable the UserAccessibleHeader property.

The page in Listing 13.12 illustrates how you can take advantage of several of these formatting properties (see Figure 13.10).

FIGURE 13.10   Formatting a DataList.

LISTING 13.12   FormatDataList.aspx

```
<%@ Page Language="C#" %>
<!DOCTYPE html PUBLIC "-//W3C//DTD XHTML 1.1//EN"
    "http://www.w3.org/TR/xhtml11/DTD/xhtml11.dtd">
<html xmlns="http://www.w3.org/1999/xhtml" >
<head id="Head1" runat="server">
    <style type="text/css">
    html
    {
        background-color:#Silver;
    }
    .movies
    {
        font:14px Arial,Sans-Serif;
    }
    .header
    {
        font-size:18px;
```

```
            letter-spacing:15px;
        }
        .item
        {
            padding:5px;
            background-color:#eeeeee;
            border-bottom:Solid 1px blue;
        }
        .alternating
        {
            padding:5px;
            background-color:LightBlue;
            border-bottom:Solid 1px blue;
        }
        </style>
        <title>Format DataList</title>
</head>
<body>
    <form id="form1" runat="server">
    <div>

    <asp:DataList
        id="dlstMovies"
        DataSourceID="srcMovies"
        UseAccessibleHeader="true"
        CssClass="movies"
        HeaderStyle-CssClass="header"
        ItemStyle-CssClass="item"
        AlternatingItemStyle-CssClass="alternating"
        Runat="server">
        <HeaderTemplate>
        Movies
        </HeaderTemplate>
        <ItemTemplate>
        <%#Eval("Title")%>
        </ItemTemplate>
    </asp:DataList>

    <asp:SqlDataSource
        id="srcMovies"
        ConnectionString="<%$ ConnectionStrings:Movies %>"
        SelectCommand="SELECT Title FROM Movies"
        Runat="server" />
```

LISTING 13.12   Continued

```
    </div>
    </form>
</body>
</html>
```

Summary

In this chapter, you learned how to use the Repeater control and the DataList controls to display a set of database records. First, you learned how to use the Repeater control to display and edit database records. For example, you learned how to use the Repeater control to enable users to edit, delete, and insert database records.

In the second half of this chapter, you learned how to work with the DataList control. You learned how to render both single and multi-column tables with the DataList control. You also learned how to selected rows with the DataList control. Finally, you learned how to edit records using the DataList control.

CHAPTER 14

Using the ListView and DataPager Controls

In this chapter, we examine the two new databound controls introduced with the .NET Framework 3.5: the ListView and the DataPager controls. The ListView control is an extremely flexible control. You can use it in many of the same situations in which you would have used the GridView, DataList, FormView, or Repeater control in the past.

The DataPager control works with the ListView control. It enables you to add support for paging to a ListView control.

Using the ListView Control

You can think of the ListView control as a super-flexible GridView control. Like a GridView control, the ListView control can be used to display, edit, delete, select, page through, and sort database data. However, unlike the GridView, the ListView control is entirely template driven. Furthermore, unlike the GridView control, you can use the ListView control to insert new data into a database.

You also can think of the ListView control as a replacement for the DataList control. Like a DataList control, the ListView control can be used to display database records in multiple columns. For example, you can use the ListView control to render a photo gallery.

Finally, you can think of the ListView control as a super-fancy Repeater control. Like a Repeater control, the ListView control is entirely template driven. However, unlike a Repeater control, the ListView control can be used to edit, page through, and sort database data.

The `ListView` control supports the following templates:

▶ **LayoutTemplate**—Used to specify the containing element for the contents of the `ListView`.

▶ **ItemTemplate**—Used to format each item rendered by the `ListView`.

▶ **ItemSeparatorTemplate**—Used to display content between each item rendered by the `ListView`.

▶ **GroupTemplate**—Used to specify the containing element for a group of items rendered by the `ListView`.

▶ **GroupSeparatorTemplate**—Used to display content between each group of items rendered by the `ListView`.

▶ **EmptyItemTemplate**—Used to render content for the remaining items in a `GroupTemplate`.

▶ **EmptyDataTemplate**—Used to specify content that is displayed when no items are returned from the `ListView` control's data source.

▶ **SelectedItemTemplate**—Used to specify the content displayed for the selected item in the `ListView`.

▶ **AlternatingItemTemplate**—Used to render different content for alternating items in a `ListView`.

▶ **EditItemTemplate**—Used to render content for editing an item in a `ListView`.

▶ **InsertItemTemplate**—Used to render content for inserting a new item in a `ListView`.

You learn how to use these various types of templates in the following sections.

Using the LayoutTemplate and ItemTemplate

Let's start with a simple scenario in which you might want to use the `ListView` control. Suppose that you have a set of database records that you want to display in a set of HTML <div> tags. The page in Listing 14.1 illustrates how you can use the LayoutTemplate and ItemTemplate templates to display the records from the Movie database table.

LISTING 14.1   SimpleListView.aspx

```
<%@ Page Language="C#" %>
<!DOCTYPE html PUBLIC "-//W3C//DTD XHTML 1.0 Transitional//EN"
 "http://www.w3.org/TR/xhtml1/DTD/xhtml1-transitional.dtd">
<html xmlns="http://www.w3.org/1999/xhtml">
<head id="Head1" runat="server">
    <title>Simple ListView</title>
</head>
<body>
    <form id="form1" runat="server">
```

```
<asp:ListView
    ID="lstMovies"
    DataSourceId="srcMovies"
    runat="server">
    <LayoutTemplate>
        <div style="border:dashed 1px black">
            <asp:Placeholder
                id="itemPlaceholder"
                runat="server" />
        </div>
    </LayoutTemplate>
    <ItemTemplate>
        <div style="border:solid 1px black">
        <%# Eval("Title") %>
        </div>
    </ItemTemplate>
    <AlternatingItemTemplate>
        <div style="border:solid 1px black;background-color:Silver">
        <%# Eval("Title") %>
        </div>
    </AlternatingItemTemplate>
    <EmptyDataTemplate>
        No records found
    </EmptyDataTemplate>
</asp:ListView>

<asp:SqlDataSource
    id="srcMovies"
    SelectCommand="SELECT Id, Title, Director FROM Movie"
    ConnectionString='<%$ ConnectionStrings:con %>'
    Runat="server" />

    </form>
</body>
</html>
```

The ListView control in Listing 14.1 contains five templates. First, the LayoutTemplate is used to create a single containing `<div>` tag for all the items rendered by the ListView. The content contained in the LayoutTemplate is rendered once and only once. In the page in Listing 14.1, the LayoutTemplate is used to display a `<div>` tag with a dashed border (see Figure 14.1).

The `<div>` tag contains a Placeholder control with an Id of itemPlaceholder. This control is never rendered to the browser. The Placeholder control gets replaced with the contents of the ItemTemplate.

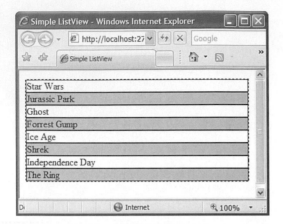

FIGURE 14.1   Displaying database records with a ListView control.

NOTE

Technically, you are not required to use a Placeholder control with a ListView control. Instead of using a ListView control, you can use any server-side control with an Id of itemPlaceholder. However, since the control gets replaced, it makes sense to stick with using the Placeholder control.

The ItemTemplate is used to render each of the items from the data source (or every other item when an AlternatingItemTemplate is present). In Listing 14.1, the ItemTemplate is used to render a <div> tag with a solid border. A data-binding expression is used with the <div> tag to display the value of the database Title column.

The AlternatingItemTemplate is optional. If it is present, then every other item displayed by the ListView control is rendered with the AlternatingItemTemplate. In Listing 14.1, the AlternatingItemTemplate is used to give alternating items a silver background color.

Finally, the EmptyDataTemplate is used to display content when no results are retrieved from the data source. In Listing 14.1, the EmptyDataTemplate is used to display the text "No records found" when no items are returned from the data source.

You can use the ListView control to render any HTML elements you can imagine. You can use the ListView control to render bulleted lists, an HTML table, a blog tag cloud, or even the elements of a JavaScript array. For example, the page in Listing 14.2 uses a ListView control to render an HTML table.

LISTING 14.2   TableListView.aspx

```
<%@ Page Language="C#" %>
<!DOCTYPE html PUBLIC "-//W3C//DTD XHTML 1.0 Transitional//EN"
 "http://www.w3.org/TR/xhtml1/DTD/xhtml1-transitional.dtd">
<html xmlns="http://www.w3.org/1999/xhtml">
```

```
<head id="Head1" runat="server">
    <title>Table ListView</title>
</head>
<body>
    <form id="form1" runat="server">
    <div>

        <asp:ListView
            ID="lstMovies"
            DataSourceId="srcMovies"
            runat="server">
            <LayoutTemplate>
                <table>
                <thead>
                    <tr>
                        <th>Title</th>
                        <th>Director</th>
                    </tr>
                </thead>
                <tbody>
                    <asp:Placeholder
                        id="itemPlaceholder"
                        runat="server" />
                </tbody>
                </table>
            </LayoutTemplate>
            <ItemTemplate>
                <tr>
                    <td><%# Eval("Title") %></td>
                    <td><%# Eval("Director") %></td>
                </tr>
            </ItemTemplate>
            <EmptyDataTemplate>
                No records found
            </EmptyDataTemplate>
        </asp:ListView>

        <asp:SqlDataSource
            id="srcMovies"
            SelectCommand="SELECT Id, Title, Director FROM Movie"
            ConnectionString='<%$ ConnectionStrings:con %>'
            Runat="server" />
    </div>
    </form>
</body>
</html>
```

14

Notice that the `itemPlaceholder` element in Listing 14.2 is replaced with `<tr>` elements. The `<tr>` elements are rendered by the ItemTemplate (see Figure 14.2).

FIGURE 14.2   Displaying a table with a `ListView` control.

Using the GroupTemplate

You can use the ListView control's GroupTemplate to group multiple items together. Grouping items is useful when you want to display items in multiple columns. For example, you might want to display a photo gallery in which three pictures are displayed per row.

The page in Listing 14.3 displays a set of photographs within a series of HTML `<div>` tags. A maximum of three photographs are displayed in each `<div>` tag (see Figure 14.3).

LISTING 14.3   PhotoGallery.aspx

```
<%@ Page Language="C#" %>
<%@ Import Namespace="System.Collections.Generic" %>
<!DOCTYPE html PUBLIC "-//W3C//DTD XHTML 1.0 Transitional//EN"
 "http://www.w3.org/TR/xhtml1/DTD/xhtml1-transitional.dtd">
<script runat="server">

    void Page_Load()
    {
        List<string> photos = new List<string>();
        photos.Add( "~/Images/Ascent.jpg" );
        photos.Add( "~/Images/Autumn.jpg" );
        photos.Add( "~/Images/Azul.jpg" );
        photos.Add( "~/Images/Home.jpg" );
        photos.Add( "~/Images/Peace.jpg" );
```

```
            photos.Add( "~/Images/Stonehenge.jpg" );
            photos.Add( "~/Images/Tulips.jpg" );

            lstPhotos.DataSource = photos;
            lstPhotos.DataBind();
        }
    </script>
    <html xmlns="http://www.w3.org/1999/xhtml">
    <head runat="server">
        <title>Photo Gallery</title>
    </head>
    <body>
        <form id="form1" runat="server">
        <div>

        <asp:ListView
            ID="lstPhotos"
            GroupItemCount="3"
            runat="server">
            <LayoutTemplate>
                <asp:Placeholder
                    id="groupPlaceholder"
                    runat="server" />
            </LayoutTemplate>
            <GroupTemplate>
                <div>
                <asp:Placeholder
                    id="itemPlaceholder"
                    runat="server" />
                </div>
            </GroupTemplate>
            <ItemTemplate>
                <asp:Image
                    id="imgPhoto"
                    ImageUrl='<%# Container.DataItem %>'
                    Width="200px"
                    Runat="server" />
            </ItemTemplate>
        </asp:ListView>

        </div>
        </form>
    </body>
    </html>
```

FIGURE 14.3   Displaying a photo gallery with a ListView control.

In Listing 14.3, the photographs are represented with a List collection. The List is bound to the ListView programmatically in the Page_Load() method.

Notice that the ListView includes a LayoutTemplate, GroupTemplate, and ItemTemplate. In previous listings, the LayoutTemplate included an element with an ID of itemPlaceholder. In this listing, the LayoutTemplate includes an element with an ID of groupPlaceholder. The groupPlaceholder is replaced with the containers of the GroupTemplate.

The GroupTemplate includes the itemPlaceholder element. The itemPlaceholder is replaced with the contents of the ItemTemplate.

Notice that the ListView control includes a GroupItemCount attribute. This property determines the number of items displayed in a GroupTemplate before a new GroupTemplate is created.

NOTE

The ListView control also supports an EmptyItemTemplate that can be used to render content for the leftover items in a GroupTemplate. For example, if you set the GroupItemCount property to 3 and there are four items, then the contents of the EmptyItemTemplate are displayed for the final two items.

Selecting a Row

You can set up the ListView control so you can use it to select items. This is useful when you want to create a master/detail form.

For example, the page in Listing 14.4 contains two ListView controls. The first ListView works like a tab strip. It enables you to select a movie category. The second ListView displays a numbered list of matching movies.

LISTING 14.4   MasterDetail.aspx

```
<%@ Page Language="C#" %>
<!DOCTYPE html PUBLIC "-//W3C//DTD XHTML 1.0 Transitional//EN"
 "http://www.w3.org/TR/xhtml1/DTD/xhtml1-transitional.dtd">
<html xmlns="http://www.w3.org/1999/xhtml">
<head runat="server">
    <title>Master/Detail</title>
    <style type="text/css">

        .categoryContainer div
        {
            width: 100px;
            font-size:small;
            border: 1px solid black;
            float:left;
            padding:3px;
            margin:3px;
        }

        .categoryContainer a
        {
            text-decoration:none;
        }

        .categoryContainer div:hover
        {
            background-color:#eeeeee;
        }

        #selected
        {
            background-color:silver;
        }

    </style>
</head>
<body>
```

LISTING 14.4   Continued

```
<form id="form1" runat="server">
<div>

    <asp:ListView
        ID="lstMovieCategories"
        DataSourceId="srcMovieCategory"
        DataKeyNames="Id"
        runat="server">
        <LayoutTemplate>
            <div class="categoryContainer">
            <asp:PlaceHolder
                id="itemPlaceholder"
                Runat="server" />
            </div>
        </LayoutTemplate>
        <ItemTemplate>
            <div>
            <asp:LinkButton
                id="lnkSelect"
                Text='<%# Eval("Name") %>'
                CommandName="Select"
                Runat="server" />
            </div>
        </ItemTemplate>
        <SelectedItemTemplate>
            <div id="selected">
            <%# Eval("Name") %>
            </div>
        </SelectedItemTemplate>
    </asp:ListView>

    <br style="clear:both" /><br />

    <asp:ListView
        ID="lstMovies"
        DataSourceId="srcMovies"
        runat="server">
        <LayoutTemplate>
            <ol>
            <asp:PlaceHolder
                id="itemPlaceholder"
                runat="server" />
            </ol>
        </LayoutTemplate>
```

```
            <ItemTemplate>
                <li><%# Eval("Title") %></li>
            </ItemTemplate>
        </asp:ListView>

        <asp:SqlDataSource
            id="srcMovieCategory"
            SelectCommand="SELECT Id, Name FROM MovieCategory"
            ConnectionString='<%$ ConnectionStrings:con %>'
            Runat="server" />

        <asp:SqlDataSource
            id="srcMovies"
            SelectCommand="SELECT Title FROM Movie
                WHERE CategoryId=@CategoryId"
            ConnectionString='<%$ ConnectionStrings:con %>'
            Runat="server">
            <SelectParameters>
                <asp:ControlParameter
                    Name="CategoryId"
                    ControlID="lstMovieCategories" />
            </SelectParameters>
        </asp:SqlDataSource>
    </div>
    </form>
</body>
</html>
```

The first ListView control in Listing 14.4 is used to render something resembling a tab strip (see Figure 14.4). Notice that this ListView control has its DataKeyNames property set. Setting the DataKeyNames property causes the ListView control to build a hidden collection of primary key values when the ListView is bound to its data source. Each item in the ListView is associated with an ID value.

Furthermore, notice that the ListView control includes a SelectedItemTemplate. The contents of this template are rendered for the selected item in the ListView. You select an item by clicking one of the links rendered by the ListView control's ItemTemplate. The links are rendered with a LinkButton control. Notice that the CommandName property of the LinkButton has the value Select. This magic command name causes the ListView to change the selected item.

The second ListView control uses the first ListView control as the source value for a select parameter. When you select a new item in the first ListView control, the second ListView control displays matching movies.

FIGURE 14.4   Displaying a master/detail form with a ListView control.

Sorting Database Data

You can sort the items in a ListView control by adding one or more button controls to the ListView that have a CommandName property set to the value Sort and a CommandArgument property set to the name of a property to sort by. For example, the page in Listing 14.5 contains a ListView that renders an HTML table. You can click the column headers to sort the table by a particular column (see Figure 14.5).

LISTING 14.5   SortListView.aspx

```
<%@ Page Language="C#" %>
<!DOCTYPE html PUBLIC "-//W3C//DTD XHTML 1.0 Transitional//EN"
 "http://www.w3.org/TR/xhtml1/DTD/xhtml1-transitional.dtd">
<html xmlns="http://www.w3.org/1999/xhtml">
<head id="Head1" runat="server">
    <title>Sort ListView</title>
</head>
<body>
    <form id="form1" runat="server">
    <div>

        <asp:ListView
            ID="lstMovies"
            DataSourceId="srcMovies"
            runat="server">
```

```
    <LayoutTemplate>
        <table>
        <thead>
            <tr>
                <th>
                <asp:LinkButton
                    id="lnkTitle"
                    Text="Title"
                    CommandName="Sort"
                    CommandArgument="Title"
                    Runat="server" />
                </th>
                <th>
                <asp:LinkButton
                    id="LinkButton1"
                    Text="Director"
                    CommandName="Sort"
                    CommandArgument="Director"
                    Runat="server" />
                </th>
            </tr>
        </thead>
        <tbody>
        <asp:Placeholder
            id="itemPlaceholder"
            runat="server" />
        </tbody>
        </table>
    </LayoutTemplate>
    <ItemTemplate>
        <tr>
            <td><%# Eval("Title") %></td>
            <td><%# Eval("Director") %></td>
        </tr>
    </ItemTemplate>
    <EmptyDataTemplate>
        No records found
    </EmptyDataTemplate>
</asp:ListView>

<asp:SqlDataSource
    id="srcMovies"
    SelectCommand="SELECT Id, Title, Director FROM Movie"
    ConnectionString='<%$ ConnectionStrings:con %>'
    Runat="server" />
```

14

LISTING 14.5   Continued

```
        </div>
        </form>
</body>
</html>
```

The two LinkButtons used for sorting the items in the ListView are contained in the LayoutTemplate. Both LinkButtons have a CommandName property set to the value Sort. The first LinkButton sorts by the Title property and the second LinkButton sorts by the Director property.

FIGURE 14.5   Sorting data with the ListView control.

Editing Database Data

You can use the ListView control to update, delete, and insert items. The page in Listing 14.6 illustrates how you can use the ListView to modify or delete the records in the Movie database table (see Figure 14.6).

LISTING 14.6   EditListView.aspx

```
<%@ Page Language="C#" %>

<!DOCTYPE html PUBLIC "-//W3C//DTD XHTML 1.0 Transitional//EN"
 "http://www.w3.org/TR/xhtml1/DTD/xhtml1-transitional.dtd">
```

```
<style type="text/css">

    .movie
    {
       border: solid 1px black;
       padding:5px;
       margin:3px;
    }

    .edit
    {
        background-color:lightyellow;
    }

</style>

<html xmlns="http://www.w3.org/1999/xhtml">
<head runat="server">
    <title>Edit ListView</title>
</head>
<body>
    <form id="form1" runat="server">
    <div>

        <asp:ListView
            ID="lstMovies"
            DataSourceId="srcMovies"
            DataKeyNames="Id"
            runat="server">
            <LayoutTemplate>
                <asp:Placeholder
                    id="itemPlaceholder"
                    runat="server" />
            </LayoutTemplate>
            <ItemTemplate>
                <div class="movie">
                <strong><%# Eval("Title") %></strong>
                <br />
                <em>Directed by <%# Eval("Director") %></em>
                <br />
                <asp:LinkButton
                    id="lnkEdit"
                    Text="{Edit}"
                    CommandName="Edit"
                    Runat="server" />
                <asp:LinkButton
```

LISTING 14.6   Continued

```
                id="lnkDelete"
                Text="{Delete}"
                CommandName="Delete"
                OnClientClick="return confirm('Delete this movie?')"
                Runat="server" />
        </div>
    </ItemTemplate>
    <EditItemTemplate>
        <div class="movie edit">
        <asp:Label
            id="lblTitle"
            Text="Title:"
            AssociatedControlID="txtTitle"
            Runat="server" />
        <br />
        <asp:TextBox
            id="txtTitle"
            Text='<%# Bind("Title") %>'
            Runat="server" />

        <br /><br />

        <asp:Label
            id="lblDirector"
            Text="Director:"
            AssociatedControlID="txtDirector"
            Runat="server" />
        <br />
        <asp:TextBox
            id="txtDirector"
            Text='<%# Bind("Director") %>'
            Runat="server" />

        <br /><br />
        <asp:LinkButton
            id="lnkUpdate"
            Text="Save"
            CommandName="Update"
            Runat="server" />
    <asp:LinkButton
            id="lnkCancel"
            Text="Cancel"
            CommandName="Cancel"
            Runat="server" />
```

```
            </div>
        </EditItemTemplate>
    </asp:ListView>

    <asp:SqlDataSource
        id="srcMovies"
        SelectCommand="SELECT Id, Title, Director FROM Movie"
        UpdateCommand="Update Movie SET Title=@Title, Director=@Director
            WHERE Id=@Id"
        DeleteCommand="Delete Movie WHERE Id=@Id"
        ConnectionString='<%$ ConnectionStrings:con %>'
        Runat="server" />

    </div>
    </form>
</body>
</html>
```

FIGURE 14.6   Editing database data with the ListView control.

The ListView control in Listing 14.6 has an ItemTemplate that contains two LinkButtons. The first LinkButton has a CommandName property set to the value Edit and the second LinkButton has a CommandName property set to the value Delete. When you click the first LinkButton, the ListView control's EditItemTemplate is displayed. When you click the second LinkButton, the current database record is deleted (after you confirm that you really want to delete the movie record).

The EditItemTemplate contains a form for editing a movie record. The form contains two TextBox controls that have two-way data-binding expressions assigned to their Text properties. The form also contains two LinkButton controls. The first LinkButton control has a CommandName of Update. When you click this button, the database is updated with the form changes and the EditItemTemplate switches back to the normal ItemTemplate. If you click the Cancel button, the EditItemTemplate switches to an ItemTemplate without updating the database.

When editing with a ListView, you need to assign the primary key column names to the ListView control's DataKeyNames property. The ListView control uses this to determine which database record to update.

Notice that all the ListView editing is driven by the following magic command names: Edit, Delete, Update, and Cancel. By setting button control CommandName properties to these magic command names, you can control how the ListView edits items.

You also can use the ListView control to insert new records into a database table. The ListView control supports an InsertItemTemplate. The page in Listing 14.7 illustrates how you can use the InsertItemTemplate to create a simple customer feedback form (see Figure 14.7).

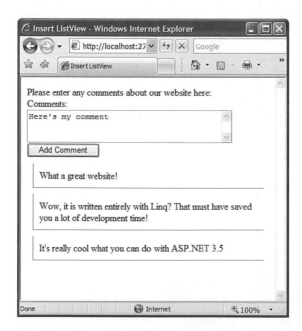

FIGURE 14.7　Inserting new records with the ListView control.

LISTING 14.7　InsertListView.aspx

```
<%@ Page Language="C#" %>
<!DOCTYPE html PUBLIC "-//W3C//DTD XHTML 1.0 Transitional//EN"
 "http://www.w3.org/TR/xhtml1/DTD/xhtml1-transitional.dtd">
```

```
<html xmlns="http://www.w3.org/1999/xhtml">
<head id="Head1" runat="server">
    <title>Insert ListView</title>
    <style type="text/css">

    .comment
    {
        margin:10px;
        padding: 10px;
        border-left:solid 1px gray;
        border-bottom:solid 1px gray;
    }

    </style>
</head>
<body>
    <form id="form1" runat="server">
    <div>

        <asp:ListView
            ID="lstFeedback"
            DataSourceId="srcFeedback"
            InsertItemPosition="FirstItem"
            runat="server">
            <LayoutTemplate>
                <asp:Placeholder
                    id="itemPlaceholder"
                    runat="server" />
            </LayoutTemplate>
            <ItemTemplate>
                <div class="comment">
                <%# Eval("Comment") %>
                </div>
            </ItemTemplate>
            <InsertItemTemplate>
                <div>
                Please enter any comments
                about our website here:
                <br />
                <asp:Label
                    id="lblComments"
                    Text="Comments:"
                    AssociatedControlID="txtComment"
                    Runat="server" />
                <br />
                <asp:TextBox
```

14

LISTING 14.7   Continued

```
                id="txtComment"
                Text='<%# Bind("Comment") %>'
                TextMode="MultiLine"
                Columns="40"
                Rows="3"
                Runat="server" />
            <br />
            <asp:Button
                id="lnkInsert"
                Text="Add Comment"
                CommandName="Insert"
                Runat="server" />
            </div>
        </InsertItemTemplate>
    </asp:ListView>

    <asp:SqlDataSource
        id="srcFeedback"
        SelectCommand="SELECT Id, Comment FROM Feedback"
        InsertCommand="INSERT Feedback (Comment) VALUES (@Comment)"
        ConnectionString='<%$ ConnectionStrings:con %>'
        Runat="server" />

    </div>
    </form>
</body>
</html>
```

The InsertItemTemplate appears only when you set the ListView control's InsertItemPosition property. You can set this property to the value FirstItem, LastItem, or None. In Listing 14.7, it's set to the value FirstItem so that the insert form appears above all the current items.

The InsertItemTemplate contains a single TextBox control that has its Text property set to a data-binding expression. The template also contains a Button control that has a CommandName property set to the value Insert. When you click the button, the new item is inserted into the database.

Using the DataPager Control

The DataPager control displays a user interface for navigating through multiple pages of items. The DataPager control works with any control that supports the

IPageableItemContainer interface. Unfortunately, there is currently only a single control that supports this interface: the ListView control. So this means that you can only use the DataPager with the ListView control.

The DataPager control includes the following properties:

- ▶ **PageSize**—Gets or sets the number of items to display at a time.

- ▶ **PagedControlId**—Gets or sets the control to page (the control must implement IPageableItemContainer).

- ▶ **Fields**—Gets the fields contained by the DataPager.

- ▶ **StartRowIndex**—Gets the index of the first item to show.

- ▶ **MaximumRows**—Gets the maximum number of rows to retrieve from the data source.

- ▶ **TotalRowCount**—Gets the total number of items available from the data source.

You set the PageSize to control the number of items to display per page. The PagerControlId property is optional. If you place the DataPager within the ListView control's LayoutTemplate, you don't need to set the PagerControlId property. If, on the other hand, you place the DataPager outside of the ListView control, you need to set the PagerControlId property to the ID of the ListView.

If you add a DataPager to a page and do nothing else, the DataPager won't render anything. To display a user interface for the DataPager, you need to add one or more fields to the DataPager. The DataPager control supports the following fields:

- ▶ **NextPreviousPagerField**—Used to display Next, Previous, First, and Last links.

- ▶ **NumericPagerField**—Used to display Next, Previous, and page numbers links.

- ▶ **TemplatePagerField**—Used to create a custom user interface for paging.

The page in Listing 14.8 demonstrates how you can use the DataPager control to page through movies displayed by a ListView control (see Figure 14.8).

FIGURE 14.8   Using a DataPager control with the ListView control.

LISTING 14.8 DataPagerListView.aspx

```
<%@ Page Language="C#" %>
<!DOCTYPE html PUBLIC "-//W3C//DTD XHTML 1.0 Transitional//EN"
 "http://www.w3.org/TR/xhtml1/DTD/xhtml1-transitional.dtd">
<html xmlns="http://www.w3.org/1999/xhtml">
<head id="Head1" runat="server">
    <title>DataPager ListView</title>
</head>
<body>
    <form id="form1" runat="server">
    <div>

        <asp:ListView
            ID="lstMovies"
            DataSourceId="srcMovies"
            runat="server">
            <LayoutTemplate>
                <ol>
                <asp:PlaceHolder
                    id="itemPlaceholder"
                    runat="server" />
                </ol>
                <asp:DataPager
                    id="pg"
                    PageSize="2"
                    Runat="server">
                    <Fields>
                        <asp:NextPreviousPagerField
                            ShowFirstPageButton="true"
                            ShowPreviousPageButton="true"
                            ShowNextPageButton="false"
                            ShowLastPageButton="false" />
                        <asp:NumericPagerField />
                        <asp:NextPreviousPagerField
                            ShowFirstPageButton="false"
                            ShowPreviousPageButton="false"
                            ShowNextPageButton="true"
                            ShowLastPageButton="true" />
                    </Fields>
                </asp:DataPager>

            </LayoutTemplate>
            <ItemTemplate>
                <li>
                <%# Eval("Title") %>
```

```
            </li>
        </ItemTemplate>
    </asp:ListView>

    <asp:SqlDataSource
        id="srcMovies"
        SelectCommand="SELECT Id, Title, Director FROM Movie"
        ConnectionString='<%$ ConnectionStrings:con %>'
        Runat="server" />

    </div>
    </form>
</body>
</html>
```

The DataPager contains three fields: NextPreviousPagerField, NumericPagerField, and NextPreviousPagerField. Notice that the DataPager contains two NextPreviousPagerFields. The first one is used to display the First and Previous links, and the second one is used to display the Next and Last links.

Creating a Custom User Interface for Paging

If you need total and complete control over the paging user interface, you can use the TemplatePagerField to customize the appearance of the DataPager. The page in Listing 14.9 illustrates how you can use the TemplatePagerField.

LISTING 14.9   DataPagerTemplate.aspx

```
<%@ Page Language="C#" %>
<!DOCTYPE html PUBLIC "-//W3C//DTD XHTML 1.0 Transitional//EN"
 "http://www.w3.org/TR/xhtml1/DTD/xhtml1-transitional.dtd">
<script runat="server">

    protected void pg_PagerCommand(object sender, DataPagerCommandEventArgs e)
    {
        e.NewMaximumRows = e.Item.Pager.MaximumRows;
        switch (e.CommandName)
        {
            case "Previous":
                if (e.Item.Pager.StartRowIndex > 0)
                    e.NewStartRowIndex = e.Item.Pager.StartRowIndex - 2;
                break;

            case "Next":
                e.NewStartRowIndex = e.Item.Pager.StartRowIndex + 2;
                break;
```

LISTING 14.9   Continued

```
        }
    }

</script>
<html xmlns="http://www.w3.org/1999/xhtml">
<head id="Head1" runat="server">
    <title>DataPager Template</title>
</head>
<body>
    <form id="form1" runat="server">
    <div>

        <asp:ListView
            ID="lstMovies"
            DataSourceId="srcMovies"
            runat="server">
            <LayoutTemplate>
                <ul>
                <asp:Placeholder
                    id="itemPlaceholder"
                    runat="server" />
                </ul>
                <asp:DataPager
                    id="pg"
                    PageSize="2"
                    Runat="server">
                    <Fields>
                        <asp:TemplatePagerField
                            OnPagerCommand="pg_PagerCommand">
                            <PagerTemplate>
                            <asp:LinkButton
                                id="lnkPrevious"
                                Text="Previous"
                                CommandName="Previous"
                                Runat="server" />
                            <asp:LinkButton
                                id="lnkNext"
                                Text="Next"
                                CommandName="Next"
                                Runat="server" />
                            </PagerTemplate>
                        </asp:TemplatePagerField>
```

```
                    </Fields>
                </asp:DataPager>

            </LayoutTemplate>
            <ItemTemplate>
                <li>
                <%# Eval("Title") %>
                </li>
            </ItemTemplate>
        </asp:ListView>

        <asp:SqlDataSource
            id="srcMovies"
            SelectCommand="SELECT Id, Title, Director FROM Movie"
            ConnectionString='<%$ ConnectionStrings:con %>'
            Runat="server" />

    </div>
    </form>
</body>
</html>
```

The TemplatePagerField in Listing 14.9 contains two LinkButton controls (see Figure 14.9). The first LinkButton has a CommandName set to the value Previous, and the second LinkButton control has a CommandName set to the value Next.

The page also contains an event handler for the TemplatePagerField's PagerCommand event. The actual work of paging is done within this event handler. The second argument passed to the event handler is an instance of the DataPagerCommandEventArgs class. You change the current page by assigning new values to this object's NewStartRowIndex and NewMaximumRows properties.

FIGURE 14.9   Creating a custom paging user interface.

Data Source Paging with the `DataPager` Control

You can take advantage of the `DataPager` control when performing data source paging. The page in Listing 14.10 contains a ListView control bound to a `LinqDataSource` control. Because, the `LinqDataSource` control has its `AutoPage` property set to the value `true`, it performs paging on the database server.

> **NOTE**
>
> The LinqDataSource control and LINQ to SQL are discussed in Chapter 18. LINQ to SQL is the preferred method of data access in .NET Framework 3.5.

LISTING 14.10   DataPagerDataSource.aspx

```
<%@ Page Language="C#" Trace="true" %>
<!DOCTYPE html PUBLIC "-//W3C//DTD XHTML 1.0 Transitional//EN"
"http://www.w3.org/TR/xhtml1/DTD/xhtml1-transitional.dtd">
<html xmlns="http://www.w3.org/1999/xhtml">
<head runat="server">
    <title>DataPager DataSource Paging</title>
</head>
<body>
    <form id="form1" runat="server">
    <div>


    <asp:ListView
        ID="lstMovies"
        DataSourceId="srcMovies"
        runat="server">
        <LayoutTemplate>
            <ol>
            <asp:PlaceHolder
                id="itemPlaceholder"
                runat="server" />
            </ol>
            <asp:DataPager
                id="pg"
                PageSize="2"
                Runat="server">
                <Fields>
                    <asp:NumericPagerField />
                </Fields>
            </asp:DataPager>

        </LayoutTemplate>
```

```
            <ItemTemplate>
                <li>
                <%# Eval("Title") %>
                </li>
            </ItemTemplate>
        </asp:ListView>


        <asp:LinqDataSource
            id="srcMovies"
            ContextTypeName="MyDatabaseDataContext"
            TableName="Movies"
            AutoPage="true"
            Runat="server" />

        </div>
        </form>
</body>
</html>
```

So that you can verify that the paging is happening through the database, I've set the DataContext to log to ASP.NET trace. If you look at the Trace Information section at the bottom of the page, you can see the actual SQL commands executed by the LinqDataSource control (see Figure 14.10).

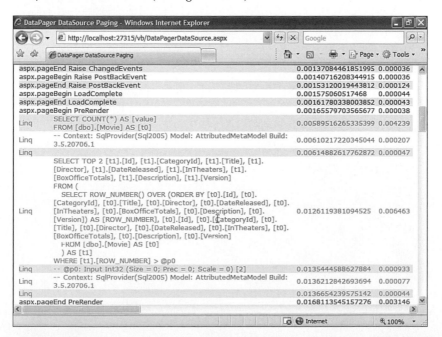

FIGURE 14.10   Performing data source paging with the DataPager control.

Summary

I'm a huge fan of the new `ListView` and `DataPager` controls. I'm constantly running into layout limitations when using the `GridView` control. Because the `ListView` is entirely template driven, it is not subject to these same limitations.

In this chapter, you learned how to use the `ListView` control to display, sort, edit, and insert data. You also learned how to take advantage of the `DataPager` control to add paging to the `ListView` control. You learned how to create a custom pager template and how to perform data source paging.

PART IV

Building Components

IN THIS PART

Building Components

Components enable you to reuse application logic across multiple pages or even across multiple applications. For example, you can write a method named `GetProducts()` once and use the method in all the pages in your website. By taking advantage of components, you can make your applications easier to maintain and extend.

For simple applications, there is no reason to take advantage of components. However, as soon as your application contains more than a few pages, you'll discover that you are repeating the same work over and over again. Whenever you discover that you need to write the same method more than once, you should immediately rip the method out of your page and add the method to a component.

CLASSIC ASP NOTE

In classic ASP, programmers often used massive and difficult to maintain #INCLUDE files to create libraries of reusable subroutines and functions. In ASP.NET, you use components to build these libraries.

In this chapter, you learn how to build components in the .NET Framework. First, you are provided with an overview of writing components: You learn how to create simple components and use them in the pages in your application. In particular, you learn how to define component methods, properties, and constructors. You also learn how to take advantage of overloading, inheritance, and interfaces.

Next, you learn how to build component libraries that can be shared across multiple applications. Different methods of compiling a set of components into assemblies are examined. You also learn how you can add a component library to the Global Assembly Cache.

Finally, architectural issues involved in using components are discussed. The final section of this chapter shows you how to build a simple three-tiered application that is divided into distinct User Interface, Business Logic, and Data Access layers.

NOTE

Let's clarify the terminology. In this book, I use the word *component* as a synonym for the word *class*. Furthermore, by the word *object*, I mean an instance of a class.

I am ignoring a special meaning for the word *component* in the .NET Framework. Technically, a component is a class that implements the System.ComponentModel. IComponent interface. I am ignoring this special meaning of the word *component* in favor of the common language use of the word.

Building Basic Components

Let's start by building a super simple component. The HelloWorld component is contained in Listing 15.1.

LISTING 15.1   HelloWorld.cs

```
public class HelloWorld
{
    public string SayMessage()
    {
        return "Hello World!";
    }
}
```

VISUAL WEB DEVELOPER NOTE

When using Visual Web Developer, you create a component by selecting the menu option Website, Add New Item, and then selecting the Class item (see Figure 15.1). The first time you add a component to a project, Visual Web Developer prompts you to create a new folder named App_Code. You want your new component to be added to this folder.

The HelloWorld component consists of a single method named SayMessage() which returns the string Hello World!.

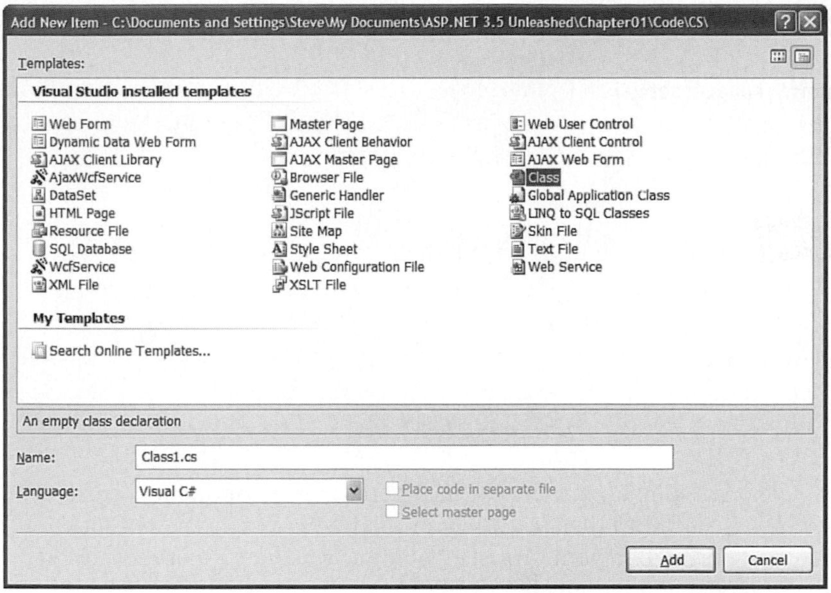

FIGURE 15.1   Creating a new component with Visual Web Developer.

Make sure that you save the `HelloWorld.cs` file to your application's App_Code folder. If you don't save the component to this folder, then you won't be able to use the component in your pages.

Next, you need to create a page that uses the new component. This page is contained in Listing 15.2.

LISTING 15.2   ShowHelloWorld.aspx

```
<%@ Page Language="C#" %>
<!DOCTYPE html PUBLIC "-//W3C//DTD XHTML 1.1//EN"
"http://www.w3.org/TR/xhtml11/DTD/xhtml11.dtd">
<script runat="server">

    void Page_Load()
    {
        HelloWorld objHelloWorld = new HelloWorld();
        lblMessage.Text = objHelloWorld.SayMessage();
    }

</script>
<html xmlns="http://www.w3.org/1999/xhtml" >
<head id="Head1" runat="server">
    <title>Show Hello World</title>
</head>
```

LISTING 15.2   Continued

```
<body>
    <form id="form1" runat="server">
    <div>

    <asp:Label
        id="lblMessage"
        Runat="server" />

    </div>
    </form>
</body>
</html>
```

In the `Page_Load()` event handler, an instance of the `HelloWorld` component is created. Next, the result returned by a call to the `SayMessage()` method is assigned to a `Label` control. When you open the page in your browser, you'll see the message `Hello World!`.

Notice how simple this process of creating the component is. You don't need to perform any special registration and you don't need to compile anything explicitly. Everything just works magically.

Components and Dynamic Compilation

You are not required to explicitly compile (build) the component because the ASP.NET Framework automatically compiles the component for you. Any component that you add to the App_Code folder is compiled dynamically in the same way as an ASP.NET page. If you add a new component to the App_Code folder and request any page from your website, the contents of the App_Code folder are compiled into a new assembly and saved to the Temporary ASP.NET Files folder, located at the following path:

```
C:\WINDOWS\Microsoft.NET\Framework\v2.0.50727\
Temporary ASP.NET Files\[application name]
```

Whenever you modify the component, the existing assembly in the Temporary ASP.NET Files folder is deleted. The App_Code folder is compiled again when you make a new page request.

> **NOTE**
>
> An assembly is the dll file (or dll files) in which components are stored.

You can add as many subfolders to the App_Code folder as you need to organize your components. The ASP.NET Framework finds your component no matter how deeply you nest the component in a subfolder.

One significant drawback of this process of dynamic compilation is that any errors in any component contained in the App_Code folder prevent any pages from executing. Even if a page does not use a particular component, any syntax errors in the component raise an exception when you request the page.

> **TIP**
>
> If a component contains an error, and you want to temporarily hide the component from the ASP.NET Framework, change the file extension to an extension that the ASP.NET Framework does not recognize, such as `HelloWorld.cs.exclude`. Visual Web Developer uses this method to hide a component when you right-click a component and select the menu option Exclude From Project.

Mixing Different Language Components in the App_Code Folder

You don't have to do anything special, just as long as all the components in the App_Code folder are written in the same language. For example, if you use Visual Basic .NET to create all your components, then the ASP.NET Framework automatically infers the language of your components and everything just works.

However, if you mix components written in more than one language in the App_Code folder—for example, Visual Basic .NET, and C#—then you must perform some extra steps.

First, you need to place components written in different languages in different subfolders. You can name the subfolders anything you want. The point is to not mix different language components in the same folder.

Furthermore, you need to modify your web configuration file to recognize the different subfolders. For example, if you create two subfolders in the App_Code folder named VBCode and CSCode, then you can use the web configuration file in Listing 15.3 to use components written in both VB.NET and C#.

LISTING 15.3 Web.Config

```
<configuration>
  <system.web>
    <compilation>
    <codeSubDirectories>
      <add directoryName="VBCode" />
      <add directoryName="CSCode" />
    </codeSubDirectories>
    </compilation>
  </system.web>
</configuration>
```

When the contents of the App_Code folder are compiled, two assemblies are created: one that corresponds to the VBCode folder and one that corresponds to the CSCode folder.

Notice that you don't need to indicate the language used for each folder—the ASP.NET Framework infers the language for you.

There is nothing wrong with mixing components written in different languages in the same ASP.NET page. After a component is compiled, the .NET Framework treats VB.NET and C# components in the same way.

Declaring Methods

The simple `HelloWorld` component in Listing 15.1 contains a single method named `SayMessage()`, which returns a string value. When writing components with Visual Basic .NET, you create methods by creating either a subroutine or a function. Use a subroutine when a method does not return a value, and use a function when a method does return a value.

The `SayMessage()` method in Listing 15.1 is an instance method. In other words, you must create a new instance of the `HelloWorld` class before you can call the `SayMessage()`, method like this:

```
HelloWorld objHelloWorld = new HelloWorld();
lblMessage.Text = objHelloWorld.SayMessage();
```

In the first line, a new instance of the `HelloWorld` component is created. The `SayMessage()` method is called from this instance. For this reason, the `SayMessage()` method is an instance method.

As an alternative to creating an instance method, you can create a static method. The advantage of a static method is that you do not need to create an instance of a component before calling it. For example, the `SayMessage()` method in the modified `HelloWorld` component in Listing 15.4 is a static method.

NOTE

Static methods are called *shared methods* in Visual Basic .NET.

LISTING 15.4   `StaticHelloWorld.cs`

```
public class StaticHelloWorld
{
    public static string SayMessage()
    {
        return "Hello World!";
    }
}
```

The StaticHelloWorld component defined in Listing 15.3 is exactly the same as the HelloWorld component created in Listing 15.1 with one change: The SayMessage() method includes a static modifier.

The page in Listing 15.5 uses the StaticHelloWorld component to display the Hello World! message.

LISTING 15.5   ShowStaticHelloWorld.aspx

```
<%@ Page Language="C#" %>
<!DOCTYPE html PUBLIC "-//W3C//DTD XHTML 1.1//EN"
"http://www.w3.org/TR/xhtml11/DTD/xhtml11.dtd">
<script runat="server">

    void Page_Load()
    {
        lblMessage.Text = StaticHelloWorld.SayMessage();
    }

</script>
<html xmlns="http://www.w3.org/1999/xhtml" >
<head id="Head1" runat="server">
    <title>Show Shared Hello World</title>
</head>
<body>
    <form id="form1" runat="server">
    <div>

    <asp:Label
        id="lblMessage"
        Runat="server" />

    </div>
    </form>
</body>
</html>
```

Notice that the page in Listing 15.5 does not create an instance of the StaticHelloWorld component. The SayMessage() method is called directly from the StaticHelloWorld class.

The advantage of using static methods is that they save you typing. You don't have to go through the pain of instantiating a component before calling the method. Many classes in the .NET Framework include static methods. For example, the String.Format()

method, the `Int32.Parse()` method, and the `DateTime.DaysInMonth()` method are all static methods.

There is nothing wrong with mixing both static and instance methods in the same component. For example, you might want to create a `Product` component that has a static `GetProducts()` method and an instance `SaveProduct()` method.

The one significant limitation of using a static method is that a static method cannot refer to an instance field or property. In other words, static methods must be stateless.

Declaring Fields and Properties

You can define a property for a component in two ways: the lazy way and the virtuous way.

The lazy way to create a property is to create a public field. If you declare any field with the Public access modifier, then the field can be accessed from outside the component.

For example, the component in Listing 15.6 contains a public field named `Message`.

LISTING 15.6   FieldHelloWorld.cs

```csharp
public class FieldHelloWorld
{
    public string Message;
    public string SayMessage()
    {
        return Message;
    }
}
```

The `Message` field is declared near the top of the `FieldHelloWorld` class definition. Notice that the Message field is returned by the `SayMessage()` method.

The page in Listing 15.7 uses the `FieldHelloWorld` component to display a message.

LISTING 15.7   ShowFieldHelloWorld.aspx

```
<%@ Page Language="C#" %>
<!DOCTYPE html PUBLIC "-//W3C//DTD XHTML 1.1//EN"
"http://www.w3.org/TR/xhtml11/DTD/xhtml11.dtd">
<script runat="server">

    void Page_Load()
    {
        FieldHelloWorld objFieldHelloWorld = new FieldHelloWorld();
```

```
            objFieldHelloWorld.Message = "Good Day!";
            lblMessage.Text = objFieldHelloWorld.SayMessage();
        }

</script>
<html xmlns="http://www.w3.org/1999/xhtml" >
<head id="Head1" runat="server">
    <title>Show Field Hello World</title>
</head>
<body>
    <form id="form1" runat="server">
    <div>

    <asp:Label
        id="lblMessage"
        Runat="server" />

    </div>
    </form>
</body>
</html>
```

15

In the `Page_Load()` event handler in Listing 15.7, an instance of the `FieldHelloWorld` class is created, a value is assigned to the `Message` field, and the `SayMessage()` method is called.

There are a couple of serious disadvantages to creating properties by creating public fields. First, the .NET Framework recognizes properties as separate entities. Several methods in the .NET Framework recognize properties but not fields.

For example, you can refer to component properties and not fields when using the `Eval()` method in a databinding expression. If you want to bind a collection of `Product` objects to a `GridView` control, then you should expose the properties of the Product component as true properties and not as fields.

The other disadvantage of fields is that they do not provide you with a chance to validate the value being assigned to the field. For example, imagine that a property represents a database column and the column accepts no more than five characters. In that case, you should check whether the value being assigned to the property is less than five characters.

The component in Listing 15.8 uses a property instead of a field. (It does things the virtuous way.)

LISTING 15.8   PropertyHelloWorld.cs

```csharp
using System;

public class PropertyHelloWorld
{
    private string _message;

    public string Message
    {
        get
        {
            return _message;
        }
        set
        {
            if (value.Length > 5)
                throw new Exception("Message too long!");
            _message = value;
        }
    }

    public string SayMessage()
    {
        return _message;
    }
}
```

Notice that the component in Listing 15.8 contains a property named Message and a private backing field named _message. The Message property contains both a getter (get) and a setter (set). The getter is called when you read the value of the Message property, and the setter is called when you assign a value to the Message property.

The getter simply returns the value of the private _message field. The setter assigns a value to the private _message field. The setter throws an exception if the length of the value being assigned to the _message field exceeds five characters.

NOTE

In Listing 15.8, the private field is named _message. The underscore character (_) has no programmatic significance. By convention, private members of a class are named with a leading underscore, but there is nothing wrong with following some other convention.

> **NOTE**
>
> The version of C# included with the .NET Framework 3.5 supports a new feature named *automatic properties*. Automatic properties provide you with a shorthand syntax for creating a property with a backing field. To learn more about automatic properties, see Chapter 18, "Data Access with LINQ to SQL."

The page in Listing 15.9 uses the `PropertyHelloWorld` component.

LISTING 15.9   ShowPropertyHelloWorld.aspx

```
<%@ Page Language="C#" %>
<!DOCTYPE html PUBLIC "-//W3C//DTD XHTML 1.1//EN"
"http://www.w3.org/TR/xhtml11/DTD/xhtml11.dtd">
<script runat="server">
    void Page_Load()
    {
        PropertyHelloWorld objPropertyHelloWorld = new PropertyHelloWorld();
        objPropertyHelloWorld.Message = "Hello World!";
        lblMessage.Text = objPropertyHelloWorld.SayMessage();
    }
</script>
<html xmlns="http://www.w3.org/1999/xhtml" >
<head id="Head1" runat="server">
    <title>Show Property Hello World</title>
</head>
<body>
    <form id="form1" runat="server">
    <div>

    <asp:Label
        id="lblMessage"
        Runat="server" />

    </div>
    </form>
</body>
</html>
```

If you open the page in Listing 15.9 in your web browser, you will get a big, fat error message (see Figure 15.2). Because a string longer than five characters is assigned to the Message property in the `Page_Load()` method, the Message property raises an exception.

15

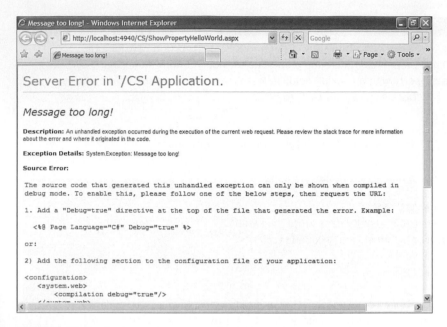

FIGURE 15.2   Assigning more than five characters.

You can also create read-only properties when the situation warrants it. For example, the component in Listing 15.10 returns the current server time. It would not make sense to assign a value to this property, so the property is declared as read-only.

LISTING 15.10   ServerTime.cs

```
using System;

public class ServerTime
{
    public string CurrentTime
    {
        get
        {
            return DateTime.Now.ToString();
        }
    }
}
```

NOTE

You can create static fields and properties in the same way as you create shared methods, by using the `static` keyword. Any value you assign to a static field or property is shared among all instances of a component.

I recommend that you avoid using static fields and properties when building ASP.NET applications. Using static fields and properties raise nasty concurrency issues in a multithreaded environment such as ASP.NET. If you insist on creating a static field or property, make it read-only.

Declaring Constructors

A constructor is a special class method that is called automatically when you create a new instance of a class. Typically, you use the constructor to initialize private fields contained in the class.

When creating a constructor in C#, you create a method with the same name as the class name. For example, the class in Listing 15.11 displays a random quotation (see Figure 15.3). The collection of random quotations is created in the component's constructor.

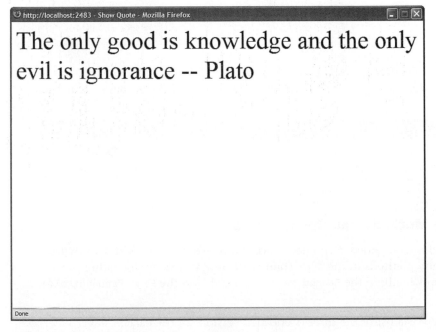

FIGURE 15.3   Displaying a random quotation.

LISTING 15.11 `Quote.cs`

```
using System;
using System.Collections.Generic;

public class Quote
{
    private List<string> _quotes = new List<string>();

    public string GetQuote()
    {
        Random rnd = new Random();
        return _quotes[rnd.Next(_quotes.Count)];
    }

    public Quote()
    {
        _quotes.Add("All paid jobs absorb and degrade the mind — Aristotle");
        _quotes.Add("No evil can happen to a good man, either in life or after
            death — Plato");
        _quotes.Add("The only good is knowledge and the only evil is ignorance —
            Plato");
    }
}
```

Notice that the collection named _quotes is declared in the body of the class. That way, you can refer to the _quotes field in both the constructor and the `GetQuote()` method.

> **NOTE**
>
> You can create static constructors by using the `static` keyword when declaring a constructor. A static constructor is called once before any instance constructors.

Overloading Methods and Constructors

When a method is overloaded, a component contains two methods with exactly the same name. Many methods in the .NET Framework are overloaded, including the `String.Replace()` method, the `Random.Next()` method, and the `Page.FindControl()` method.

For example, here is a list of the three overloaded versions of the `Random.Next()` method:

▶ **Next()**—Returns a random number between 0 and 2,147,483,647.

▶ **Next(upperbound)**—Returns a number between 0 and the upper bound.

▶ **Next(lowerbound, upperbound)**—Returns a number between the lower bound and the upper bound.

Because all three methods do the same thing—they all return a random number—it makes sense to overload the `Next()` method. The methods differ only in their *signatures*. A method signature consists of the order and type of parameters that a method accepts. For example, you can't overload two methods that have exactly the same set of parameters (even if the names of the parameters differ).

Overloading is useful when you want to associate related methods. Overloading is also useful when you want to provide default values for parameters. For example, the `StoreProduct` component in Listing 15.12 contains three overloaded versions of its `SaveProduct()` method.

LISTING 15.12 `StoreProduct.cs`

```
using System;

public class StoreProduct
{
    public void SaveProduct(string name)
    {
        SaveProduct(name, 0, String.Empty);
    }

    public void SaveProduct(string name, decimal price)
    {
        SaveProduct(name, price, String.Empty);
    }

    public void SaveProduct(string name, decimal price, string description)
    {
        // Save name, price, description to database
    }
}
```

You can call any of the three `SaveProduct()` methods in Listing 15.12 to save a new product. You can supply the new product with a name, a name and a price, or a name and a price and a description.

VISUAL WEB DEVELOPER NOTE

When typing an overloaded method in Source view, the Intellisense pops up with all the different sets of parameters that you can use with the overloaded method. See Figure 15.4.

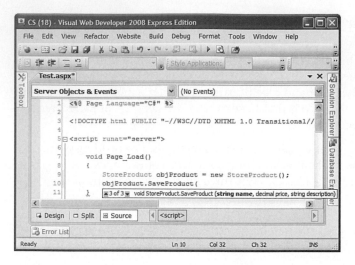

FIGURE 15.4   Typing an overloaded method in Visual Web Developer.

Because a constructor is just a special method, you also can use overloading when declaring constructors for a class. For example, the ProductConstructor class in Listing 15.13 contains three overloaded constructors that can be used to initialize the Product class.

LISTING 15.13   ProductConstructor.cs

```
using System;

public class ProductConstructor
{
    public ProductConstructor(string name)
        : this(name, 0, String.Empty) { }

    public ProductConstructor(string name, decimal price)
        : this(name, price, String.Empty) { }

    public ProductConstructor(string name, decimal price, string description)
    {
        // Use name, price, and description
    }
}
```

When you instantiate the component in Listing 15.13, you can instantiate it in any of the following ways:

```
ProductConstructor objProduct = new ProductConstructor("Milk");
```

```
ProductConstructor objProduct = new ProductConstructor("Milk", 2.99d);

ProductConstructor objProduct = new ProductConstructor("Milk", 2.99d, "While Milk");
```

Declaring Namespaces

A namespace enables you to group logically related classes. You are not required to provide a class with a namespace. To this point, all the components you have seen created have been members of the global namespace. However, several advantages result from grouping components into namespaces.

First, namespaces prevent naming collisions. If two companies produce a component with the same name, then namespaces provide you with a method of distinguishing the components.

Second, namespaces make it easier to understand the purpose of a class. If you group all your data access components into a DataAccess namespace and all your business logic components in a BusinessLogic namespace, then you can immediately understand the function of a particular class.

In an ASP.NET page, you import a namespace like this:

```
<%@ Import Namespace="System.Collections" %>
```

In a C# component, on the hand, you import a namespace like this:

```
using System.Collections;
```

You can create your own custom namespaces and group your components into namespaces by using the namespace statement. For example, the component in Listing 15.14 is contained in the AspUnleashed.SampleCode namespace.

LISTING 15.14 Namespaced.cs

```
namespace AspNetUnleashed.SampleCode
{
    public class Namespaced
    {
        public string SaySomething()
        {
            return "Something";
        }
    }
}
```

15

The file in Listing 15.14 uses the `Namespace` statement to group the `Namespaced` component into the `AspUnleashed.SampleCode` namespace. Components in different files can share the same namespace, and different components in the same file can occupy different namespaces.

The periods in a namespace name have no special significance. The periods are used to break up the words in the namespace, but you could use another character, such as an underscore character, instead.

Microsoft recommends a certain naming convention when creating namespaces:

```
CompanyName.TechnologyName[.Feature][.Design]
```

So, if your company is named Acme Consulting and you are building a data access component, you might add your component to the following namespace:

```
AcmeConsulting.DataAccess
```

Of course this is simply a naming convention. No serious harm will come to you if you ignore it.

Creating Partial Classes

You can define a single component that spans multiple files by taking advantage of a feature of the .NET Framework called *partial classes*.

For example, the files in Listings 15.15 and 15.16 contain two halves of the same component.

LISTING 15.15   FirstHalf.cs

```
public partial class Tweedle
{
    private string _message = @"THEY were standing under a tree,
        each with an arm round the other's neck, and Alice knew
        which was which in a moment, because one of them had
        ""DUM"" embroidered on his collar, and the other ""DEE"".";
}
```

LISTING 15.16   SecondHalf.cs

```
public partial class Tweedle
{
    public string GetMessage()
    {
        return _message;
    }
}
```

Notice that the `private _message` field is defined in the first file, but this private field is used in the `GetMessage()` method in the second file. When the `GetMessage()` method is called, it returns the value of the private field from the other class.

Both files define a class with the same name. The class declaration includes the keyword `Partial`. The `Partial` keyword marks the classes as partial classes.

> **NOTE**
>
> Partial classes are the basis for code-behind pages in the ASP.NET Framework. The code-behind file and the presentation page are two partial classes that get compiled into the same class.

Inheritance and Abstract Classes

When one class inherits from a second class, the inherited class automatically includes all the nonprivate methods and properties of its parent class. In other words, what's true of the parent is true of the child, but not the other way around.

Inheritance is used throughout the .NET Framework. For example, every ASP.NET page inherits from the base `System.Web.UI.Page` class. The only reason that you can use properties such as the `IsPostback` property in an ASP.NET page is that the page derives from the base `Page` class.

All classes in the .NET Framework derive from the base `System.Object` class. The `Object` class is the great-grandmother of every other class. This means that any methods or properties of the `Object` class, such as the `ToString()` method, are shared by all classes in the Framework.

You can take advantage of inheritance when building your own components. You indicate that one class inherits from a second class when you declare a class.

For example, the file in Listing 15.17 includes three components: a `BaseProduct` class, a `ComputerProduct` class, and a `TelevisionProduct` class.

LISTING 15.17   Inheritance.cs

```
public class BaseProduct
{
    private decimal _price;

    public decimal Price
    {
        get { return _price; }
        set { _price = value; }
    }
}
```

LISTING 15.17   Continued

```
}

public class ComputerProduct : BaseProduct
{
    private string _processor;

    public string Processor
    {
        get { return _processor; }
        set { _processor = value; }
    }

}

public class TelevisionProduct : BaseProduct
{
    private bool _isHDTV;

    public bool IsHDTV
    {
        get { return _isHDTV; }
        set { _isHDTV = value; }
    }

}
```

Notice that both the ComputerProduct and TelevisionProduct components inherit from the BaseProduct component. Because the BaseProduct class includes a Price property, both inherited components automatically inherit this property.

When inheriting one class from another, you also can override methods and properties of the base class. Overriding a method or property is useful when you want to modify the behavior of an existing class.

To override a property or method of a base class, the property or method must be marked with the C# virtual or abstract keyword or the Visual Basic .NET Overridable or MustOverride keyword. Only methods or properties marked with the virtual or abstract keyword can be overridden.

For example, the file in Listing 15.18 contains two components: a ProductBase class and a OnSaleProduct class. The second class inherits from the first class and overrides its Price property. The Price property of the OnSaleProduct component divides the price by half.

LISTING 15.18   OnSaleProduct.cs

```csharp
public class ProductBase
{
    private decimal _price;

    public virtual decimal Price
    {
        get { return _price; }
        set { _price = value; }
    }
}

public class OnSaleProduct : ProductBase
{
    override public decimal Price
    {
        get { return base.Price / 2; }
        set { base.Price = value; }
    }
}
```

Notice that the base keyword (MyBase in Visual Basic) is used in Listing 15.18 to refer to the base class (the ProductBase class).

Finally, you can use the abstract keyword when declaring a class to mark the class as class that requires inheritance. You cannot instantiate an abstract class. To use an abstract class, you must derive a new class from the abstract class and instantiate the derived class.

Abstract classes are the foundation for the ASP.NET Provider Model. Personalization, Membership, Roles, Session State, and Site Maps all use the Provider model.

For example, the MembershipProvider class is the base class for all Membership Providers. The SqlMembershipProvider and ActiveDirectoryMembershipProvider classes both derive from the base MembershipProvider class.

> **NOTE**
>
> Chapter 23, "Using ASP.NET Membership," discusses the MembershipProvider classes in detail. The MembershipProvider is responsible for saving and loading membership information such as application usernames and passwords.

The base MembershipProvider class is an abstract class. You cannot use this class directly in your code. Instead, you must use one of its derived classes. However, the base MembershipProvider class provides a common set of methods and properties that all MembershipProvider-derived classes inherit.

The base `MembershipProvider` class includes a number of methods and properties marked as `abstract`. A derived `MembershipProvider` class is required to override these properties and methods.

The file in Listing 15.19 contains two components. The first component, the `BaseEmployee` component, is an abstract class that contains an abstract property named `Salary`. The second component, the `SalesEmployee`, inherits the `BaseEmployee` component and overrides the `Salary` property.

LISTING 15.19   Employees.cs

```
public abstract class BaseEmployee
{
    public abstract decimal Salary
    {
        get;
    }

    public string Company
    {
        get { return "Acme Software"; }
    }
}

public class SalesEmployee : BaseEmployee
{
    public override decimal Salary
    {
        get { return 67000.23m; }
    }
}
```

Declaring Interfaces

An interface is a list of properties and methods that a class must implement. If a class implements an interface, then you know that the class includes all the properties and methods contained in the interface.

For example, the file in Listing 15.20 contains an interface named `IProduct` and two components named `MusicProduct` and `BookProduct`.

LISTING 15.20   Products.cs

```
public interface IProduct
{
    decimal Price
```

```csharp
    {
        get;
    }

    void SaveProduct();
}

public class MusicProduct : IProduct
{
    public decimal Price
    {
        get { return 12.99m; }
    }

    public void SaveProduct()
    {
        // Save Music Product
    }
}

public class BookProduct : IProduct
{
    public decimal Price
    {
        get { return 23.99m; }
    }

    public void SaveProduct()
    {
        // Save Book Product
    }
}
```

Both components in Listing 15.17 are declared as implementing the IProduct interface. (The colon can mean implements or inherits.) Notice, furthermore, that both components include the SaveProduct() method and the Price property. Both components are required to have this method and property since they are declared as implementing the IProduct interface.

Interfaces are similar to abstract classes with two important differences. First, a component can inherit from only one class. On the other hand, a component can implement many different interfaces.

Second, an abstract class can contain application logic. You can add methods to an absract class that all derived classes inherit and can use. An interface, on the other hand, cannot contain any logic. An interface is nothing more than a list of methods and properties.

Using Access Modifiers

C# supports the following access modifiers, which you can use when declaring a class, method, or property:

▶ **Public**—A public class, method, or property has no access restrictions.

▶ **Protected**—A protected method or property can be accessed only within the class itself or a derived class.

▶ **Internal**—An internal class, method, or property can be accessed only by a component within the same assembly (dll file). Because ASP.NET pages are compiled into different assemblies than the contents of the App_Code folder, you cannot access an internal member of a class outside of the App_Code folder.

▶ **Private**—A private class, method, or property can be accessed only within the class itself.

Visual Basic .NET supports the following access modifiers (also called *access levels*), which you can use when declaring a class, method, or property:

▶ **Public**—A Public class, method, or property has no access restrictions.

▶ **Protected**—A Protected method or property can be accessed only within the class itself or a derived class.

▶ **Friend**—A Friend class, method, or property can be accessed only by a component within the same assembly (dll file). Because ASP.NET pages are compiled into different assemblies than the contents of the App_Code folder, you cannot access a Friend member of a class outside of the App_Code folder.

▶ **Protected Friend**—A Protected Friend method or property can be accessed within the class itself or a derived class, or any other class located in the same assembly.

▶ **Private**—A Private class, method, or property can be accessed only within the class itself.

Using access modifiers is useful when you are developing a component library that might be used by other members of your development team (or you in the future). For example, you should mark all methods that you don't want to expose from your component as private.

Intellisense and Components

Visual Web Developer automatically pops up with Intellisense when you type the names of classes, properties, or methods in Source view. You can add comments that appear in Intellisense to your custom components to make it easier for other developers to use your components.

If you add XML comments to a component, then the contents of the XML comments appear automatically in Intellisense. For example, the component in Listing 15.21

includes XML comments for its class definition, property definitions, and method definition (see Figure 15.5).

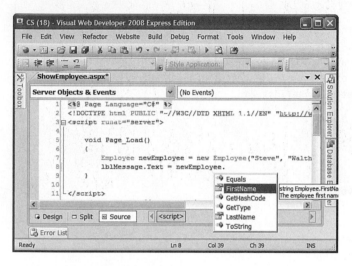

FIGURE 15.5   Adding comments to a component.

LISTING 15.21   Employee.cs

```
/// <summary>
/// Represents an employee of Acme.com
/// </summary>
public class Employee
{
    private string _firstName;
    private string _lastName;

    /// <summary>
    /// The employee first name
    /// </summary>
    public string FirstName
    {
        get { return _firstName; }
    }

    /// <summary>
    /// The employee last name
    /// </summary>
    public string LastName
    {
        get { return _lastName; }
```

LISTING 15.21   Continued

```csharp
    }

    /// <summary>
    /// Returns an employee from the database
    /// </summary>
    /// <param name="id">The unique employee identifier</param>
    /// <returns>An instance of the Employee class</returns>
    public static Employee getEmployee(int id)
    {
        return null;
    }

    /// <summary>
    /// Initializes an employee
    /// </summary>
    /// <param name="firstName">First Name</param>
    /// <param name="lastName">Last Name</param>
    public Employee(string firstName, string lastName)
    {
        _firstName = firstName;
        _lastName = lastName;
    }

}
```

NOTE

You can generate an XML documentation file—a file that contains all the XML comments—for the components contained in a folder by using the /doc switch with the C# or Visual Basic command-line compiler. The command-line compiler is discussed in the second part of this chapter, "Building Component Libraries."

Using ASP.NET Intrinsics in a Component

When you add code to an ASP.NET page, you are adding code to an instance of the Page class. The Page class exposes several ASP.NET intrinsic objects such as the Request, Response, Cache, Session, and Trace objects.

If you want to use these objects within a component, then you need to do a little more work. Realize that when you create a component, you are not creating an ASP.NET component. In this chapter, we are creating .NET components, and a .NET component can be used by any type of .NET application, including a Console application or Windows Forms application.

To use the ASP.NET instrinsics in a component, you need to get a reference to the current HtppContext. The HttpContext object is the one object that is available behind the scenes through the entire page processing lifecycle. You can access the HttpContext object from any user control, custom control, or component contained in a page.

To get a reference to the current HttpContext object, you can use the static (shared) Current property included in the HttpContext class. For example, the component in Listing 15.22 uses the HttpContext object to use both the Session and Trace objects.

LISTING 15.22 Preferences.cs

```
using System.Web;

public class Preferences
{
    public static string FavoriteColor
    {
        get
        {
            HttpContext context = HttpContext.Current;
            context.Trace.Warn("Getting FavoriteColor");
            if (context.Session["FavoriteColor"] == null)
                return "Blue";
            else
                return (string)context.Session["FavoriteColor"];
        }
        set
        {
            HttpContext context = HttpContext.Current;
            context.Trace.Warn("Setting FavoriteColor");
            context.Session["FavoriteColor"] = value;
        }
    }
}
```

15

The `Preferences` component contains a single property named `FavoriteColor`. The value of this property is stored in `Session` state. Anytime this property is modified, the `Trace` object writes a warning.

You can use the `Preferences` component in the page contained in Listing 15.23.

LISTING 15.23   ShowPreferences.aspx

```
<%@ Page Language="C#" trace="true" %>
<!DOCTYPE html PUBLIC "-//W3C//DTD XHTML 1.1//EN"
"http://www.w3.org/TR/xhtml11/DTD/xhtml11.dtd">
<script runat="server">

    void Page_PreRender()
    {
        body1.Style["background-color"] = Preferences.FavoriteColor;
    }

    protected void btnSelect_Click(object sender, EventArgs e)
    {
        Preferences.FavoriteColor = ddlFavoriteColor.SelectedItem.Text;
    }
</script>

<html xmlns="http://www.w3.org/1999/xhtml" >
<head id="Head1" runat="server">
    <style type="text/css">
        .content
        {
            width:80%;
            padding:20px;
            background-color:white;
        }
    </style>
    <title>Show Preferences</title>
</head>
<body id="body1" runat="server">
    <form id="form1" runat="server">
    <div class="content">

    <h1>Show Preferences</h1>

    <asp:DropDownList
        id="ddlFavoriteColor"
        Runat="server">
```

```
                <asp:ListItem Text="Blue" />
                <asp:ListItem Text="Red" />
                <asp:ListItem Text="Green" />
        </asp:DropDownList>
        <asp:Button
            id="btnSelect"
            Text="Select"
            Runat="server" OnClick="btnSelect_Click" />



        </div>
        </form>
</body>
</html>
```

After you open the page in Listing 15.23, you can select your favorite color from the
DropDownList control. Your favorite color is stored in the Preferences object
(see Figure 15.6).

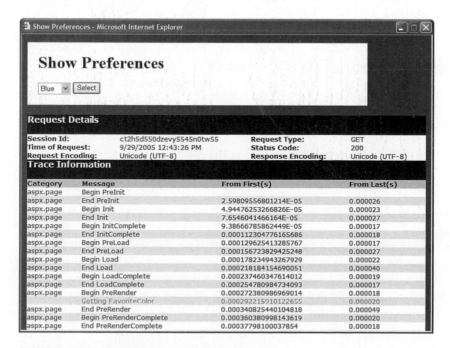

FIGURE 15.6   Selecting a favorite color.

Building Component Libraries

One of the advertised benefits of using components is code reuse. You write a method once, and then you never need to write the same method ever again.

One problem with the components that have been created to this point is that they have all been application specific. In other words, you cannot reuse the components across multiple websites without copying all the source code from one App_Code folder to another.

If you want to share components among multiple websites, then you can no longer take advantage of dynamic compilation. To share components, you need to compile the components explicitly in a separate assembly.

Compiling Component Libraries

You can use a number of methods to compile a set of components into an assembly:

- ▶ Use the command-line compiler.
- ▶ Use C# or Visual Basic Express.
- ▶ Use the full version of Visual Studio 2008.

These options are explored in turn.

Using the C# Command-Line Compiler   You can use the C# or Visual Basic command-line compiler to compile a source code file, or set of source code files, into an assembly. The C# compiler is located at the following path:

```
C:\WINDOWS\Microsoft.NET\Framework\v2.0.50727\csc.exe
```

The Visual Basic command-line compiler is located at the following path:

```
C:\WINDOWS\Microsoft.NET\Framework\v2.0.50727\vbc.exe
```

> **NOTE**
>
> If you have installed the .NET Framework SDK, then you can open the SDK Command Prompt from the Microsoft .NET Framework SDK program group. When the command prompt opens, the paths to the C# and Visual Basic .NET compiler are added to the environment automatically.

You can use the `csc.exe` tool to compile any C# source file like this:

```
csc /t:library SomeFile.cs
```

The /t (target) option causes the compiler to create a component library and not a Console or Windows application. When you execute this command, a new file named SomeFile.dll is created, which is the compiled assembly.

As an alternative to compiling a single file, you can compile all the source code files in a folder (and every subfolder) like this:

```
csc /t:library /recurse:*.cs /out:MyLibrary.dll
```

The /recurse option causes the compiler to compile the contents of all the subfolders. The /out option provides a name for the resulting assembly.

Using Visual C# Express   You can download a trial edition of Visual C# Express from the MSDN website (http://msdn.microsoft.com). Visual C# Express enables you to build Windows applications, Console applications, and class libraries.

To create a class library that you can use with an ASP.NET application, you create a Class Library project in Visual C# Express (see Figure 15.7). When you build the project, a new assembly is created.

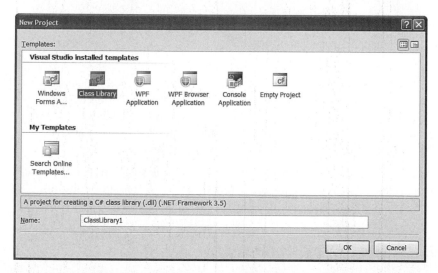

FIGURE 15.7   Creating a Class Library in C# Express.

If you need to use ASP.NET classes in your class library, such as the HttpContext class, then you need to add a reference to the System.Web.dll assembly to your Class Library project. Select the menu option Project, Add Reference and add the System.Web.dll from beneath the .NET tab (see Figure 15.8).

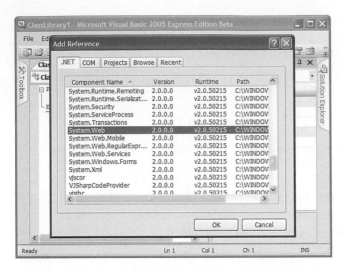

FIGURE 15.8   Adding a reference to `System.Web.dll`.

NOTE

If you are a VB.NET developer, then you can download Visual Basic Express from the MSDN Website (http://msdn.microsoft.com).

Using Visual Studio 2008   The easiest way to create a class library that you can share among multiple ASP.NET applications is to use the full version of Visual Studio 2008 instead of Visual Web Developer. Visual Studio 2008 was designed to enable you to easily build enterprise applications. Building class libraries is one of the features you get in Visual Studio 2008 that you don't get in Visual Web Developer Express.

Visual Studio 2008 enables you to add multiple projects to a single solution. For example, you can add both an ASP.NET project and a Class Library project to the same solution. When you update the Class Library project, the ASP.NET project is updated automatically (see Figure 15.9).

Adding a Reference to a Class Library

Now that you understand how you can create a class library in a separate assembly, you need to know how you can use this class library in another project. In other words, how do you use the components contained in an assembly within an ASP.NET page?

There are two ways to make an assembly available to an ASP.NET application. You can add the assembly to the application's /Bin folder or you can add the assembly to the Global Assembly Cache.

Adding an Assembly to the Bin Folder   In general, the best way to use an assembly in an ASP.NET application is to add the assembly to the application's root Bin folder. There is nothing magical about this folder. The ASP.NET Framework automatically checks this

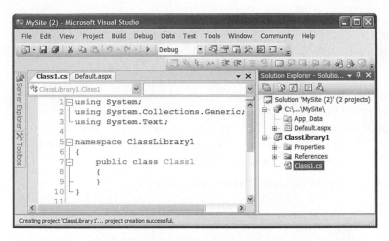

FIGURE 15.9   A solution that contains multiple projects.

folder for any assemblies. If the folder contains an assembly, the assembly is referenced automatically by the ASP.NET application when it is compiled dynamically.

If you are using Visual Web Developer, then you can select the menu option Website, Add Reference to add a new assembly to your application's Bin folder (see Figure 15.10). Alternatively, you can simply copy an assembly into this folder. (If the folder doesn't exist, just create it.)

FIGURE 15.10   Adding an assembly reference with Visual Web Developer.

When you add an assembly to an ASP.NET application's Bin folder, the assembly is scoped to the application. This means that you can add different versions of the same assembly to different applications without worrying about any conflicts.

Furthermore, if you add an assembly to the Bin folder, then you can take advantage of XCopy deployment. In other words, if you need to move your website to a new server, then you can simply copy all the files in your website from one server to another. As long as you copy your Bin folder, the assembly is available at the new location.

Adding an Assembly to the Global Assembly Cache   All the assemblies that make up the .NET Framework class library are contained in the Global Assembly Cache. For example, the Random class is located in the System.dll assembly, and the System.dll assembly is contained in the Global Assembly Cache. Any assembly located in the Global Assembly Cache can be referenced by any application running on a server.

The Global Assembly Cache's physical location is at the following path:

```
C:\WINDOWS\assembly
```

Before you can add an assembly to the Global Assembly Cache, you must add a strong name to the assembly. A strong name is similar to a GUID. You use a strong name to provide your assembly with a universally unique identifier.

> **NOTE**
>
> Technically, a strong name consists of the name, version number, and culture of the assembly. A strong name also includes the public key from a public/private key pair. Finally, a strong name includes a hash of the assembly's contents so that you know whether the assembly has been modified.

You can generate a strong name by using the sn.exe command-line tool like this:

```
sn.exe -k KeyPair.snk
```

Executing this command creates a new file named KeyPair.snk, which includes a new random public/private key pair.

> **WARNING**
>
> Protect your key file. You should not reveal the private key to anyone.

You can compile an assembly that includes a strong name by executing the Visual Basic .NET command-line compiler like this:

```
csc /t:library /keyfile:KeyPair.snk /recurse:*.cs /out:MyLibrary.dll
```

The resulting assembly is strongly named with the public key from the KeyPair.snk file. The /keyfile option associates the key file with the assembly. In this case, the name of the resulting assembly is MyLibrary.dll.

An alternative method of associating a strong name with an assembly is to use the <Assembly: AssemblyKeyFile> attribute. You can add this attribute to any of the source files that get compiled into the assembly. For example, you can drop the file in

Listing 15.24 into the folder that you are compiling and it associates the public key from the KeyPair.snk file with the compiled assembly.

LISTING 15.24 AssemblyInfo.cs

```
using System.Reflection;


[assembly:AssemblyKeyFile("KeyPair.snk")]
[assembly:AssemblyVersion("0.0.0.0")]
```

The file in Listing 15.24 actually includes two attributes. The first attribute associates the KeyPair.snk public key with the assembly. The second attribute associates a version number with the assembly. The version number consists of four sets of numbers: the major version, minor version, build number, and revision number.

After you add the file in Listing 15.24 to a folder that contains the source code for your components, use the following command to compile the folder:

```
csc /t:library /recurse:*.cs /out:MyLibrary.dll
```

After you associate a strong name with an assembly, you can use the GacUtil.exe command-line tool to add the assembly to the Global Assembly Cache. Executing the following statement from a command prompt adds the MyLibrary.dll assembly to the Global Assembly Cache:

```
GacUtil.exe /i MyLibrary.dll
```

You can verify that the MyLibrary.dll assembly has been added successfully to the Global Assembly Cache by opening your Global Assembly Cache folder located at the following path:

```
C:\WINDOWS\assembly
```

You should see the MyLibrary.dll assembly listed in the Assembly Name column (see Figure 15.11). Note the Version and the PublicKeyToken columns. You need to know the values of these columns to use the assembly in an application.

After you install an assembly in the Global Assembly Cache, you can use the assembly in your ASP.NET Pages and App_Code components by adding a reference to the assembly in your web configuration file. The web configuration file in Listing 15.25 adds the MyLibrary.dll assembly to your application.

LISTING 15.25 Web.Config

```
<configuration>
  <system.web>
    <compilation>
      <assemblies>
```

15

LISTING 15.25   Continued

```
      <add assembly="MyLibrary,Version=0.0.0.0,Culture=neutral,
         PublicKeyToken=250c66fc9dd31989"/>
    </assemblies>
  </compilation>
 </system.web>
</configuration>
```

The web configuration file in Listing 15.25 adds the MyLibrary assembly. Notice that you must supply the Version, Culture, and PublicKeyToken associated with the assembly. You need to substitute the correct values for these properties in Listing 15.25 before you use the file with an assembly that you have compiled. (Remember that you can get these values by opening the c:\WINDOWS\assembly folder.)

> **NOTE**
>
> When using Visual C# Express or Visual Studio 2008, you can create a strong name automatically and associate the strong name with an assembly. Right-click the name of your project in the Solution Explorer window and select Properties. Next, select the Signing tab.

In general, you should avoid adding your assemblies to the Global Assembly Cache because using the Global Assembly Cache defeats XCopy deployment. Using the Global Assembly Cache makes it more difficult to back up an application. It also makes it more difficult to move an application from one server to another.

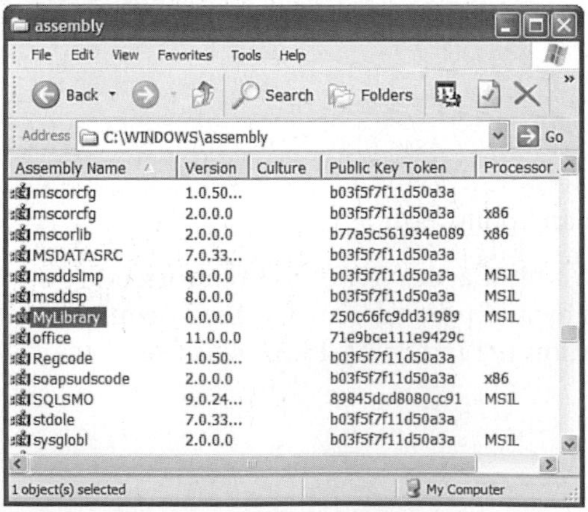

FIGURE 15.11   Viewing the Global Assembly Cache.

Architectural Considerations

If you embark on a large ASP.NET project, you'll quickly discover that you spend more time writing code for components than writing code for your pages. This is not a bad thing. Placing as much of your application logic as possible in components makes it easier to maintain and extend your application.

However, the process of organizing the components itself can become time consuming. In other words, you start to run into architectural issues concerning the best way to design your web application.

The topic of architecture, like the topics of politics and religion, should not be discussed in polite company. People have passionate opinions about architecture, and discussions on this topic quickly devolve into people throwing things. Be aware that any and all statements about proper architecture are controversial.

With these disclaimers out of the way, in this section I provide you with an overview of one of the most common architectures for ASP.NET applications. In this section, you learn how to build a three-tiered ASP.NET application.

Building Multi-Tier Applications

One very common architecture for an application follows an n-tier design model. When using an n-tier architecture, you encapsulate your application logic into separate layers.

In particular, it is recommended that an application should be divided into the following three application layers:

- ▶ User Interface layer.
- ▶ Business Logic layer.
- ▶ Data Access layer.

The idea is that the User Interface layer should contain nothing but user interface elements such as HTML and ASP.NET controls. The User Interface layer should not contain any business logic or data access code.

The Business Logic layer contains all your business rules and validation code. It manages all data access for the User Interface layer.

Finally, the Data Access layer contains all the code for interacting with a database. For example, all the code for interacting with Microsoft SQL Server should be encapsulated in this layer.

The advantage of encapsulating your application logic into different layers is that it makes it easier to modify your application without requiring you to rewrite your entire application. Changes in one layer can be completely isolated from the other layers.

For example, imagine that (one fine day) your company decides to switch from using Microsoft SQL Server to using Oracle as their database server. If you have been careful to create an isolated Data Access layer, then you would need to rewrite only your Data Access layer. It might be a major project, but you would not need to start from scratch.

Or imagine that your company decides to create a Silverlight version of an existing ASP.NET application. Again, if you have been careful to isolate your User Interface layer from your Business Logic layer, then you can extend your application to support a Silverlight interface without rewriting your entire application. The Siverlight application can use your existing Business Logic and Data Access layers.

> **NOTE**
>
> I spend my working life training companies on implementing ASP.NET applications. Typically, a company is migrating a web application written in some other language such as Java or ASP Classic to the ASP.NET Framework. It always breaks my heart to see how much code is wasted in these transitions (thousands of man hours of work lost). If you are careful in the way that you design your ASP.NET application now, you can avoid this sorry fate in the future.

I realize that this is all very abstract, so let's examine a particular sample. We'll create a simple product management system that enables you to select, insert, update, and delete products. However, we'll do it the right way by dividing the application into distinct User Interface, Business Logic, and Data Access layers.

Creating the User Interface Layer

The User Interface layer is contained in Listing 15.26. Notice that the User Interface layer consists of a single ASP.NET page. This page contains no code whatsoever.

LISTING 15.26   Products.aspx

```
<%@ Page Language="C#" %>
<!DOCTYPE html PUBLIC "-//W3C//DTD XHTML 1.1//EN"
  "http://www.w3.org/TR/xhtml11/DTD/xhtml11.dtd">
<html xmlns="http://www.w3.org/1999/xhtml" >
<head id="Head1" runat="server">
    <style type="text/css">
    html
    {
        background-color:silver;
    }
    .content
    {
        padding:10px;
        background-color:white;
```

```
        }
        .products
        {
            margin-bottom:20px;
        }
        .products td,.products th
        {
            padding:5px;
            border-bottom:solid 1px blue;
        }
        a
        {
            color:blue;
        }
        </style>
        <title>Products</title>
</head>
<body>
        <form id="form1" runat="server">
        <div class="content">

        <asp:GridView
            id="grdProducts"
            DataSourceID="srcProducts"
            DataKeyNames="Id"
            AutoGenerateEditButton="true"
            AutoGenerateDeleteButton="true"
            AutoGenerateColumns="false"
            CssClass="products"
            GridLines="none"
            Runat="server">
            <Columns>
            <asp:BoundField
                DataField="Id"
                ReadOnly="true"
                HeaderText="Id" />
            <asp:BoundField
                DataField="Name"
                HeaderText="Name" />
            <asp:BoundField
                DataField="Price"
                DataFormatString="{0:c}"
                HeaderText="Price" />
            <asp:BoundField
                DataField="Description"
                HeaderText="Description" />
```

15

LISTING 15.26   Continued

```
            </Columns>
        </asp:GridView>

        <fieldset>
        <legend>Add Product</legend>
        <asp:DetailsView
            id="dtlProduct"
            DataSourceID="srcProducts"
            DefaultMode="Insert"
            AutoGenerateInsertButton="true"
            AutoGenerateRows="false"
            Runat="server">
            <Fields>
            <asp:BoundField
                DataField="Name"
                HeaderText="Name:" />
            <asp:BoundField
                DataField="Price"
                HeaderText="Price:"/>
            <asp:BoundField
                DataField="Description"
                HeaderText="Description:" />
            </Fields>
        </asp:DetailsView>
        </fieldset>


        <asp:ObjectDataSource
            id="srcProducts"
            TypeName="AcmeStore.BusinessLogicLayer.Product"
            SelectMethod="SelectAll"
            UpdateMethod="Update"
            InsertMethod="Insert"
            DeleteMethod="Delete"
            Runat="server" />

    </div>
    </form>
</body>
</html>
```

The page in Listing 15.26 contains a GridView, DetailsView, and ObjectDataSource
control. The GridView control enables you to view, update, and delete the products

contained in the Products database table (see Figure 15.12). The `DetailsView` enables you to add new products to the database. Both controls use the `ObjectDataSource` as their data source.

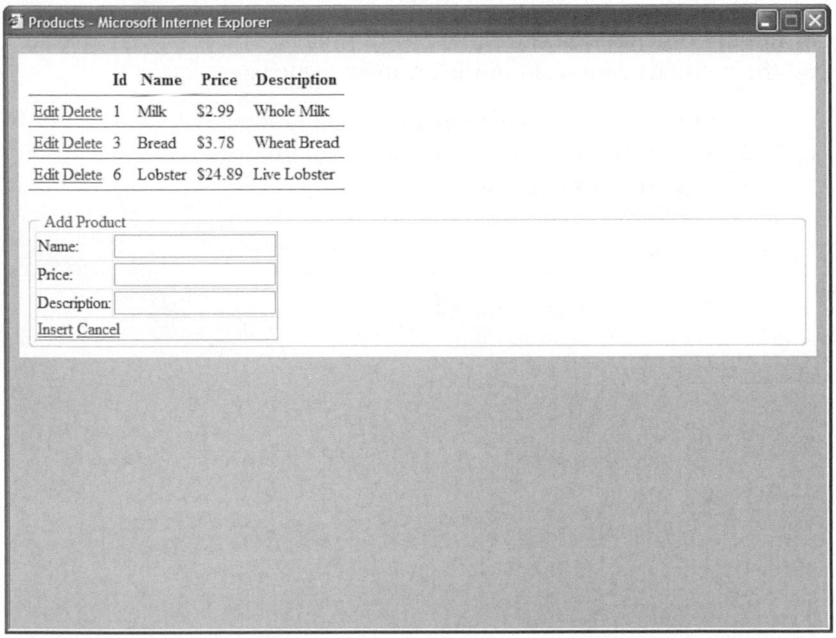

FIGURE 15.12   The `Products.aspx` page.

NOTE

The next chapter is entirely devoted to the `ObjectDataSource` control.

The page in Listing 15.26 does not interact with a database directly. Instead, the `ObjectDataSource` control is used to bind the `GridView` and `DetailsView` controls to a component named `AcmeStore.BusinessLogicLayer.Product`. The `Product` component is contained in the Business Logic layer.

NOTE

The page in Listing 15.26 does not contain any validation controls. I omitted adding validation controls for reasons of space. In a real application, you would want to toss some `RequiredFieldValidator` and `CompareValidator` controls into the page.

Creating the Business Logic Layer

The ASP.NET pages in your application should contain a minimum amount of code. All your application logic should be pushed into separate components contained in either the Business Logic or Data Access layers.

Your ASP.NET pages should not communicate directly with the Data Access layer. Instead, the pages should call the methods contained in the Business Logic layer.

The Business Logic layer consists of a single component named Product, which is contained in Listing 15.27. (A real-world application might contain dozens or even hundreds of components in its Business Logic layer.)

LISTING 15.27   BLL/Product.cs

```
using System;
using System.Collections.Generic;
using AcmeStore.DataAccessLayer;

namespace AcmeStore.BusinessLogicLayer
{
    /// <summary>
    /// Represents a store product and all the methods
    /// for selecting, inserting, and updating a product
    /// </summary>
    public class Product
    {
        private int _id = 0;
        private string _name = String.Empty;
        private decimal _price = 0;
        private string _description = String.Empty;

        /// <summary>
        /// Product Unique Identifier
        /// </summary>
        public int Id
        {
            get { return _id; }
        }

        /// <summary>
        /// Product Name
        /// </summary>
        public string Name
        {
            get { return _name; }
        }
```

```csharp
/// <summary>
/// Product Price
/// </summary>
public decimal Price
{
    get { return _price; }
}


/// <summary>
/// Product Description
/// </summary>
public string Description
{
    get { return _description; }
}


/// <summary>
/// Retrieves all products
/// </summary>
/// <returns></returns>
public static List<Product> SelectAll()
{
    SqlDataAccessLayer dataAccessLayer = new SqlDataAccessLayer();
    return dataAccessLayer.ProductSelectAll();
}


/// <summary>
/// Updates a particular product
/// </summary>
/// <param name="id">Product Id</param>
/// <param name="name">Product Name</param>
/// <param name="price">Product Price</param>
/// <param name="description">Product Description</param>
public static void Update(int id, string name, decimal price, string
➥description)
{
    if (id < 1)
        throw new ArgumentException("Product Id must be greater than 0",
        ➥"id");

    Product productToUpdate = new Product(id, name, price, description);
    productToUpdate.Save();
}


/// <summary>
/// Inserts a new product
```

15

LISTING 15.27   Continued

```
    /// </summary>
    /// <param name="name">Product Name</param>
    /// <param name="price">Product Price</param>
    /// <param name="description">Product Description</param>
    public static void Insert(string name, decimal price, string description)
    {
        Product newProduct = new Product(name, price, description);
        newProduct.Save();
    }

    /// <summary>
    /// Deletes an existing product
    /// </summary>
    /// <param name="id">Product Id</param>
    public static void Delete(int id)
    {
        if (id < 1)
            throw new ArgumentException("Product Id must be greater than 0",
            ➥"id");

        SqlDataAccessLayer dataAccessLayer = new SqlDataAccessLayer();
        dataAccessLayer.ProductDelete(id);
    }

    /// <summary>
    /// Validates product information before saving product
    /// properties to the database
    /// </summary>
    private void Save()
    {
        if (String.IsNullOrEmpty(_name))
            throw new ArgumentException("Product Name not supplied", "name");
        if (_name.Length > 50)
            throw new ArgumentException("Product Name must be less than 50
            ➥characters", "name");
        if (String.IsNullOrEmpty(_description))
            throw new ArgumentException("Product Description not supplied",
            ➥"description");

        SqlDataAccessLayer dataAccessLayer = new SqlDataAccessLayer();
        if (_id > 0)
            dataAccessLayer.ProductUpdate(this);
        else
```

```
                dataAccessLayer.ProductInsert(this);
        }

        /// <summary>
        /// Initializes Product
        /// </summary>
        /// <param name="name">Product Name</param>
        /// <param name="price">Product Price</param>
        /// <param name="description">Product Description</param>
        public Product(string name, decimal price, string description)
            : this(0, name, price, description) { }


        /// <summary>
        /// Initializes Product
        /// </summary>
        /// <param name="id">Product Id</param>
        /// <param name="name">Product Name</param>
        /// <param name="price">Product Price</param>
        /// <param name="description">Product Description</param>
        public Product(int id, string name, decimal price, string description)
        {
            _id = id;
            _name = name;
            _price = price;
            _description = description;
        }


    }
}
```

The Product component contains four public methods named SelectAll(), Update(), Insert(), and Delete(). All four of these methods use the SqlDataAccessLayer component to interact with the Products database table. The SqlDataAccessLayer is contained in the Data Access layer.

For example, the SelectAll() method returns a collection of Product objects. This collection is retrieved from the SqlDataAccessLayer component.

The Insert(), Update(), and Delete() methods validate their parameters before passing the parameters to the Data Access layer. For example, when you call the Insert() method, the length of the Name parameter is checked to verify that it is less than 50 characters.

Notice that the Business Logic layer does not contain any data access logic. All this logic is contained in the Data Access layer.

Creating the Data Access Layer

The Data Access layer contains all the specialized code for interacting with a database. The Data Access layer consists of the single component in Listing 15.28. (A real-world application might contain dozens or even hundreds of components in its Data Access layer.)

LISTING 15.28   DAL\SqlDataAccessLayer.cs

```
using System;
using System.Data;
using System.Data.SqlClient;
using System.Web.Configuration;
using System.Collections.Generic;
using AcmeStore.BusinessLogicLayer;

namespace AcmeStore.DataAccessLayer
{
    /// <summary>
    /// Data Access Layer for interacting with Microsoft
    /// SQL Server 2005
    /// </summary>
    public class SqlDataAccessLayer
    {
        private static readonly string _connectionString = string.Empty;

        /// <summary>
        /// Selects all products from the database
        /// </summary>
        public List<Product> ProductSelectAll()
        {
            // Create Product collection
            List<Product> colProducts = new List<Product>();

            // Create connection
            SqlConnection con = new SqlConnection(_connectionString);

            // Create command
            SqlCommand cmd = new SqlCommand();
            cmd.Connection = con;
            cmd.CommandText = "SELECT Id,Name,Price,Description FROM Products";

            // Execute command
            using (con)
            {
                con.Open();
                SqlDataReader reader = cmd.ExecuteReader();
```

```csharp
            while (reader.Read())
            {
                colProducts.Add(new Product(
                    (int)reader["Id"],
                    (string)reader["Name"],
                    (decimal)reader["Price"],
                    (string)reader["Description"]));
            }
        }
        return colProducts;
    }


    /// <summary>
    /// Inserts a new product into the database
    /// </summary>
    /// <param name="newProduct">Product</param>
    public void ProductInsert(Product newProduct)
    {
        // Create connection
        SqlConnection con = new SqlConnection(_connectionString);

        // Create command
        SqlCommand cmd = new SqlCommand();
        cmd.Connection = con;
        cmd.CommandText = "INSERT Products (Name,Price,Description) VALUES
    ➥(@Name,@Price,

        // Add parameters
        cmd.Parameters.AddWithValue("@Name", newProduct.Name);
        cmd.Parameters.AddWithValue("@Price", newProduct.Price);
        cmd.Parameters.AddWithValue("@Description", newProduct.Description);

        // Execute command
        using (con)
        {
            con.Open();
            cmd.ExecuteNonQuery();

        }
    }


    /// <summary>
    /// Updates an existing product into the database
    /// </summary>
    /// <param name="productToUpdate">Product</param>
    public void ProductUpdate(Product productToUpdate)
```

15

LISTING 15.28   Continued

```
{
    // Create connection
    SqlConnection con = new SqlConnection(_connectionString);

    // Create command
    SqlCommand cmd = new SqlCommand();
    cmd.Connection = con;
    cmd.CommandText = "UPDATE Products SET
    ➥Name=@Name,Price=@Price,Description=
    // Add parameters
    cmd.Parameters.AddWithValue("@Name", productToUpdate.Name);
    cmd.Parameters.AddWithValue("@Price", productToUpdate.Price);
    cmd.Parameters.AddWithValue("@Description", productToUpdate.Description);
    cmd.Parameters.AddWithValue("@Id", productToUpdate.Id);

    // Execute command
    using (con)
    {
        con.Open();
        cmd.ExecuteNonQuery();

    }
}

/// <summary>
/// Deletes an existing product in the database
/// </summary>
/// <param name="id">Product Id</param>
public void ProductDelete(int Id)
{
    // Create connection
    SqlConnection con = new SqlConnection(_connectionString);

    // Create command
    SqlCommand cmd = new SqlCommand();
    cmd.Connection = con;
    cmd.CommandText = "DELETE Products WHERE Id=@Id";

    // Add parameters
    cmd.Parameters.AddWithValue("@Id", Id);

    // Execute command
    using (con)
    {
```

```
            con.Open();
            cmd.ExecuteNonQuery();

        }
    }

    /// <summary>
    /// Initialize the data access layer by
    /// loading the database connection string from
    /// the Web.Config file
    /// </summary>
    static SqlDataAccessLayer()
    {
        _connectionString = WebConfigurationManager.ConnectionStrings["Store"].
        ➥ConnectionString;
        if (string.IsNullOrEmpty(_connectionString))
            throw new Exception("No connection string configured in Web.Config
            ➥file");
    }
  }
}
```

The `SqlDataAccessLayer` component in Listing 15.28 grabs the database connection string that it uses when communicating with Microsoft SQL Server in its constructor. The connection string is assigned to a private field so that it can be used by all the component's methods.

The `SqlDataAccessLayer` component has four public methods: `ProductSelectAll()`, `ProductInsert()`, `ProductUpdate()`, and `ProductDelete()`. These methods use the ADO.NET classes from the `System.Data.SqlClient` namespace to communicate with Microsoft SQL Server.

NOTE

We discuss ADO.NET in Chapter 17, "Building Data Access Components with ADO.NET."

NOTE

In this section, the Data Access layer was built using ADO.NET. It could just have as easily been built using LINQ to SQL. We discuss LINQ to SQL in Chapter 18.

Notice that the `SqlDataAccessLayer` component is not completely isolated from the components in the Business Logic Layer. The `ProductSelectAll()` method builds a collection of `Product` objects, which the method returns to the Business Logic layer. You should strive to isolate each layer as much as possible. However, in some cases, you cannot completely avoid mixing objects from different layers.

Summary

In this chapter, you learned how to build components in the .NET Framework. In the first part, you were given an overview of component building. You learned how to take advantage of dynamic compilation by using the App_Code folder. You also learned how to create component properties, methods, and constructors. You also examined several advanced topics related to components such as overloading, inheritance, MustInherit classes, and interfaces.

In the second half of this chapter, you learned how to build component libraries. You saw different methods for compiling a set of components into an assembly. You also examined how you can add components to both an application's Bin folder and the Global Assembly Cache.

Finally, you had a chance to consider architectural issues related to building applications with components. You learned how to build a three-tiered application, divided into isolated User Interface, Business Logic, and Data Access layers.

CHAPTER 16

Using the ObjectDataSource Control

The ObjectDataSource control enables you to bind DataBound controls such as the GridView, DetailsView, and FormView controls to a component. You can use the ObjectDataSource control to easily build multi-tier applications with the ASP.NET Framework. Unlike the SqlDataSource control, which mixes data access logic in the User Interface Layer, the ObjectDataSource control enables you to cleanly separate your User Interface Layer from your Business Logic and Data Access Layers.

In this chapter, you learn how to use the ObjectDataSource control to represent different types of objects. For example, you learn how to use the ObjectDataSource control with components that represent database data. You also learn how to use the ObjectDataSource control to represent different types of method parameters.

In the course of this chapter, we tackle a number of advanced topics. For example, you learn how to page, sort, and filter database records represented by the ObjectDataSource control. You learn how to page and sort through large database tables efficiently.

In the final section of this chapter, you learn how to extend the ObjectDataSource control to represent specialized data sources. You also learn how to extend the ObjectDataSource control with custom parameters.

Representing Objects with the ObjectDataSource Control

The ObjectDataSource control includes five main properties:

- ▶ **TypeName**—The name of the type of object that the ObjectDataSource control represents.

- ▶ **SelectMethod**—The name of a method that the ObjectDataSource calls when selecting data.

- ▶ **UpdateMethod**—The name of a method that the ObjectDataSource calls when updating data.

- ▶ **InsertMethod**—The name of a method that the ObjectDataSource calls when inserting data.

- ▶ **DeleteMethod**—The name of a method that the ObjectDataSource calls when deleting data.

An ObjectDataSource control can represent any type of object in the .NET Framework. This section discusses several types of objects you might want to represent. For example, you learn how to use the ObjectDataSource control with components that represent collections, ADO.NET DataReaders, DataSets, LINQ to SQL queries, and web services.

> **NOTE**
>
> You can use the ObjectDataSource control to represent any object (any class that derives from the System.Object class). If the object does not support the IEnumerable interface, the ObjectDataSource control automatically wraps the object in a new object that supports the IEnumerable interface. You can even represent an ASP.NET ListBox control with an ObjectDataSource (not that a ListBox has any interesting methods).

Binding to a Component

Let's start with a really simple component. The component in Listing 16.1 is named MovieCollection. It contains one method named GetMovies(), which returns a collection of movie titles.

LISTING 16.1   MovieCollection.cs

```
using System;
using System.Web.Configuration;
using System.Collections.Generic;
```

```csharp
public class MovieCollection
{
    public List<string> GetMovies()
    {
        List<string> movies = new List<string>();
        movies.Add("Star Wars");
        movies.Add("Independence Day");
        movies.Add("War of the Worlds");
        return movies;
    }

}
```

You can use the page in Listing 16.2 to display the list of movies returned by the GetMovies() method in a GridView control. The page contains an ObjectDataSource control that represents the MovieCollection component.

LISTING 16.2   ShowMovieCollection.aspx

```aspx
<%@ Page Language="C#" %>
<!DOCTYPE html PUBLIC "-//W3C//DTD XHTML 1.1//EN"
    "http://www.w3.org/TR/xhtml11/DTD/xhtml11.dtd">
<html xmlns="http://www.w3.org/1999/xhtml" >
<head id="Head1" runat="server">
    <title>Show Movie Collection</title>
</head>
<body>
    <form id="form1" runat="server">
    <div>

    <asp:GridView
        id="grdMovies"
        DataSourceID="srcMovies"
        Runat="server" />

    <asp:ObjectDataSource
        id="srcMovies"
        TypeName="MovieCollection"
        SelectMethod="GetMovies"
        Runat="server" />

    </div>
    </form>
</body>
</html>
```

In Listing 16.2, the ObjectDataSource control includes two properties named TypeName and SelectMethod. The TypeName property contains the name of the component that you want to represent with the ObjectDataSource control. The SelectMethod property represents the method of the component that you want to call when selecting data.

Notice that the GridView control is bound to the ObjectDataSource control through its DataSourceID property. When you open the page in Listing 16.2, the list of movies is retrieved from the MovieCollection component and displayed in the GridView.

The MovieCollection component contains instance methods. The ObjectDataSource automatically creates a new instance of the MovieCollection component before calling its GetMovies() method. It automatically destroys the object after it is finished using the object.

You also can use the ObjectDataSource control to call shared (static) methods. In that case, the ObjectDataSource doesn't need to instantiate a component before calling the method.

Binding to a DataReader

Typically, you use the ObjectDataSource control to represent database data. The .NET Framework provides you with multiple ways of representing data. This section discusses how you can use an ObjectDataSource to represent a DataReader.

> **NOTE**
>
> The different ADO.NET objects are compared and contrasted in the next chapter, "Building Data Access Components with ADO.NET."

The ADO.NET DataReader object provides you with a fast, read-only representation of database data. If you need to retrieve database records in the fastest possible way, then you should use a DataReader object.

For example, the component in Listing 16.3, the MovieDataReader component, returns all the movies from the Movies database table by using the SqlDataReader object. Notice that the component imports the System.Data.SqlClient namespace to use this Microsoft SQL Server–specific ADO.NET object.

LISTING 16.3   MovieDataReader.cs

```
using System;
using System.Data;
using System.Data.SqlClient;
using System.Web.Configuration;

public class MovieDataReader
{
```

```
    private readonly string _conString;

    public SqlDataReader GetMovies()
    {
        // Create Connection
        SqlConnection con = new SqlConnection(_conString);

        // Create Command
        SqlCommand cmd = new SqlCommand();
        cmd.Connection = con;
        cmd.CommandText = "SELECT Id,Title,Director FROM Movies";

        // Return DataReader
        con.Open();
        return cmd.ExecuteReader(CommandBehavior.CloseConnection);
    }

    public MovieDataReader()
    {
        _conString = WebConfigurationManager.ConnectionStrings["Movies"].
        ➥ConnectionString;
    }
}
```

16

The component in Listing 16.3 actually uses three ADO.NET objects: the Connection, Command, and DataReader object. The SqlCommand object uses the SqlConnection object to connect to the database. The records are returned from the SqlCommand object and represented by the SqlDataReader object.

Notice that the WebConfigurationManager class is used to retrieve the database connection string from the web configuration file. To use this class, you need to import the System.Web.Confiugration namespace (and have a reference to the System.Web.dll assembly).

The ObjectDataSource control in Listing 16.4 represents the MovieDataReader object. It binds the movies to a GridView control.

LISTING 16.4   ShowMovieDataReader.aspx

```
<%@ Page Language="C#" %>
<!DOCTYPE html PUBLIC "-//W3C//DTD XHTML 1.1//EN"
  "http://www.w3.org/TR/xhtml11/DTD/xhtml11.dtd">
<html xmlns="http://www.w3.org/1999/xhtml" >
<head id="Head1" runat="server">
    <title>Show Movie DataReader</title>
</head>
```

LISTING 16.4   Continued

```
<body>
    <form id="form1" runat="server">
    <div>

    <asp:GridView
        id="grdMovies"
        DataSourceID="srcMovies"
        Runat="server" />

    <asp:ObjectDataSource
        id="srcMovies"
        TypeName="MovieDataReader"
        SelectMethod="GetMovies"
        Runat="server" />

    </div>
    </form>
</body>
</html>
```

Binding to a DataSet

You also can use the ObjectDataSource when you need to represent an ADO.NET DataSet. Using a DataSet is slower than using a DataReader. However, you can perform advanced operations, such as filtering and sorting, on data represented with a DataSet.

The component in Listing 16.5 returns all the records from the Movies database table. However, it uses a DataSet instead of a DataReader object.

LISTING 16.5   MovieDataSet.cs

```
using System;
using System.Data;
using System.Data.SqlClient;
using System.Web.Configuration;

public class MovieDataSet
{
    private readonly string _conString;

    public DataSet GetMovies()
    {
        // Create DataAdapter
```

```
        string commandText = "SELECT Id,Title,Director FROM Movies";
        SqlDataAdapter dad = new SqlDataAdapter(commandText, _conString);

        // Return DataSet
        DataSet dstMovies = new DataSet();
        using (dad)
        {
            dad.Fill(dstMovies);
        }
        return dstMovies;
    }


    public MovieDataSet()
    {
        _conString = WebConfigurationManager.ConnectionStrings["Movies"].
        ➥ConnectionString;
    }
}
```

The component in Listing 16.5 uses two ADO.NET objects: a DataAdapter and a DataSet. The SqlDataAdapter is used to represent the SQL select command, and it populates the DataSet with the results of executing the command. Notice that the WebConfigurationManager class is used to read the database connection string from the web configuration file.

The page in Listing 16.6 binds the list of movies to a DropDownList control.

LISTING 16.6   ShowMovieDataSet.aspx

```
<%@ Page Language="C#" %>
<!DOCTYPE html PUBLIC "-//W3C//DTD XHTML 1.1//EN"
  "http://www.w3.org/TR/xhtml11/DTD/xhtml11.dtd">
<html xmlns="http://www.w3.org/1999/xhtml" >
<head id="Head1" runat="server">
    <title>Show Movie DataSet</title>
</head>
<body>
    <form id="form1" runat="server">
    <div>

    <asp:GridView
        id="grdMovies"
        DataSourceID="srcMovies"
        Runat="server" />
```

LISTING 16.6   Continued

```
<asp:ObjectDataSource
    id="srcMovies"
    TypeName="MovieDataReader"
    SelectMethod="GetMovies"
    Runat="server" />


    </div>
    </form>
</body>
</html>
```

Binding to a LINQ to SQL Query

LINQ to SQL is the preferred method of data access in the .NET Framework 3.5. The expectation is that you will use LINQ to SQL instead of ADO.NET to interact with a database. Chapter 18, "Data Access with LINQ to SQL," is devoted to the topic of LINQ.

Let's do a quick sample of binding an ObjectDataSource to a component that represents a LINQ to SQL query. The component that contains the LINQ query is contained in Listing 16.7.

LISTING 16.7   Employee.cs

```
using System.Collections.Generic;
using System.Linq;
using System.Data.Linq;

public partial class Employee
{
    public static IEnumerable<Employee> Select()
    {
        EmployeesDataContext db = new EmployeesDataContext();
        return db.Employees.OrderBy( e=>e.LastName );
    }
}
```

Before you can use the component in Listing 16.7, you first must create the EmployeesDataContext. The easiest way to create the DataContext is to select the menu option Website, Add New Item and select the LINQ to SQL Classes template. Name the LINQ to SQL Classes **Employees**.

After the Object Relational Designer appears, drag the Employees database table onto the Designer surface from the Database Explorer window. At this point, the EmployeesDataContext will be ready.

The page in Listing 16.8 contains an ObjectDataSource that represents the Employee class.

LISTING 16.8   ShowLINQ.aspx

```
<%@ Page Language="C#" %>
<!DOCTYPE html PUBLIC "-//W3C//DTD XHTML 1.0 Transitional//EN"
"http://www.w3.org/TR/xhtml1/DTD/xhtml1-transitional.dtd">
<html xmlns="http://www.w3.org/1999/xhtml">
<head runat="server">
    <title>Show LINQ</title>
</head>
<body>
    <form id="form1" runat="server">
    <div>

    <asp:GridView
        id="grdEmployees"
        DataSourceID="srcEmployees"
        runat="server" />

    <asp:ObjectDataSource
        id="srcEmployees"
        TypeName="Employee"
        SelectMethod="Select"
        Runat="server" />

    </div>
    </form>
</body>
</html>
```

Binding to a Web Service

Web services enable you to share information across the Internet. When you communicate with a remote web service, you use a local proxy class to represent the web service located on the remote machine. You can use the ObjectDataSource to represent this proxy class.

For example, the file in Listing 16.9 contains a simple web service that returns the current server time. You can create this file in Visual Web Developer by selecting the menu option Web Site, Add New Item, and selecting the Web Service item.

LISTING 16.9   TimeService.asmx

```csharp
<%@ WebService Language="C#" Class="TimeService" %>
using System;
using System.Web;
using System.Web.Services;
using System.Web.Services.Protocols;

[WebService(Namespace = "http://tempuri.org/")]
[WebServiceBinding(ConformsTo = WsiProfiles.BasicProfile1_1)]
public class TimeService   : System.Web.Services.WebService {

    [WebMethod]
    public DateTime GetServerTime() {
        return DateTime.Now;
    }

}
```

After you create the web service in Listing 16.9, you can communicate with the service from anywhere in the world (or the galaxy, or the universe). Just as long as a computer is connected to the Internet, the computer can call the GetServerTime() method.

Before you can call the web service, you need to create a web service proxy class. If you are using Visual Web Developer, select the menu option Web Site, Add Web Reference and enter the URL of the TimeService.asmx file (You can click the Web services in this solution link to list all the web services in your current project.) Change the name of the web reference to LocalServices and click Add Reference (see Figure 16.1).

NOTE

If you are not using Visual Web Developer, you can create a web service proxy class from the command line by using the Wsdl.exe (Web Services Description Language) tool.

When you click Add Reference, a new folder is added to your project named App_WebReferences. The App_WebReferences folder contains a subfolder named LocalServices. Finally, your web configuration file is updated to include the URL to the TimeService web service.

Now that we have a consumable web service, we can represent the Web service using the ObjectDataSource control. The page in Listing 16.10 displays the server time using a FormView control bound to an ObjectDataSource control (see Figure 16.2).

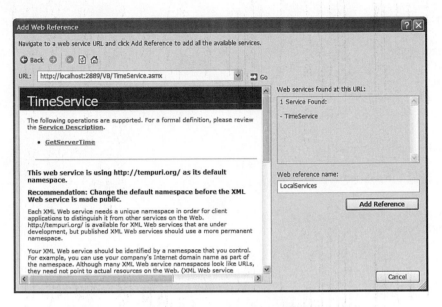

FIGURE 16.1   Adding a Web Reference in Visual Web Developer.

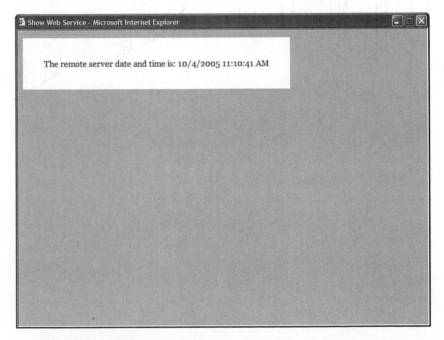

FIGURE 16.2   Retrieving the time from a web service.

LISTING 16.10   ShowWebService.aspx

```csharp
<%@ Page Language="C#" %>
<html xmlns="http://www.w3.org/1999/xhtml" >
<head id="Head1" runat="server">
    <style type="text/css">
        html
        {
            background-color:silver;
        }
        .serverTime
        {
            background-color:white;
            font:16px Georgia,Serif;
        }
        .serverTime td
        {
            padding:40px;
        }
    </style>
    <title>Show Web Service</title>
</head>
<body>
    <form id="form1" runat="server">
    <div>

    <asp:FormView
        id="frmServerTime"
        DataSourceID="srcServerTime"
        CssClass="serverTime"
        Runat="server">
        <ItemTemplate>
        The remote server date and time is: <%# Container.DataItem %>
        </ItemTemplate>
    </asp:FormView>

    <asp:ObjectDataSource
        id="srcServerTime"
        TypeName="LocalServices.TimeService"
        SelectMethod="GetServerTime"
        Runat="server" />

    </div>
    </form>
</body>
</html>
```

Notice that the `ObjectDataSource` control's `TypeName` property contains both the name-space and name of the web service proxy class (the web reference). In other words, it contains the fully qualified name of the proxy class. The `SelectMethod` property contains the name of the web method represented by the proxy class.

> **NOTE**
>
> If you open the `ShowWebService.aspx` page from the CD that accompanies this book, you receive an error. Before the page will work correctly, you need to update the web configuration file with the correct path to the web service on your computer.

Using Parameters with the `ObjectDataSource` Control

You can use parameters when calling a method with the `ObjectDataSource` control. The `ObjectDataSource` control includes five parameter collections:

- ▶ **SelectParameters**—Collection of parameters passed to the method represented by the `SelectMethod` property.

- ▶ **InsertParameters**—Collection of parameters passed to the method represented by the `InsertMethod` property.

- ▶ **UpdateParameters**—Collection of parameters passed to the method represented by the `UpdateMethod` property.

- ▶ **DeleteParameters**—Collection of parameters passed to the method represented by the `DeleteParameters` property.

- ▶ **FilterParameters**—Collection of parameters used by the `FilterExpression` property.

DataBound controls—such as the `GridView`, `DetailsView`, and `FormView` controls—can build the necessary parameter collections for you automatically.

For example, the component in Listing 16.11 enables you select movies and update a particular movie in the Movies database table. The `UpdateMovie()` method has four parameters: `id`, `title`, `director`, and `dateReleased`.

LISTING 16.11 Movies.cs

```
using System;
using System.Data;
using System.Data.SqlClient;
using System.Web.Configuration;

public class Movies
{
```

16

LISTING 16.11   Continued

```
private readonly string _conString;

public void UpdateMovie(int id, string title, string director, DateTime
➥dateReleased)
{
    // Create Command
    SqlConnection con = new SqlConnection(_conString);
    SqlCommand cmd = new SqlCommand();
    cmd.Connection = con;
    cmd.CommandText = "UPDATE Movies SET
    ➥Title=@Title,Director=@Director,DateReleased=
    // Add parameters
    cmd.Parameters.AddWithValue("@Title", title);
    cmd.Parameters.AddWithValue("@Director", director);
    cmd.Parameters.AddWithValue("@DateReleased", dateReleased);
    cmd.Parameters.AddWithValue("@Id", id);

    // Execute command
    using (con)
    {
        con.Open();
        cmd.ExecuteNonQuery();
    }
}

public SqlDataReader GetMovies()
{
    // Create Connection
    SqlConnection con = new SqlConnection(_conString);

    // Create Command
    SqlCommand cmd = new SqlCommand();
    cmd.Connection = con;
    cmd.CommandText = "SELECT Id,Title,Director,DateReleased FROM Movies";

    // Return DataReader
    con.Open();
    return cmd.ExecuteReader(CommandBehavior.CloseConnection);
}

public Movies()
{
```

```
    _conString = WebConfigurationManager.ConnectionStrings["Movies"].
    ➥ConnectionString;
    }
}
```

The page in Listing 16.12 contains a GridView and ObjectDataSource control. Notice that the ObjectDataSource control includes an UpdateMethod property that points to the UpdateMovie() method.

LISTING 16.12   ShowMovies.aspx

```
<%@ Page Language="C#" %>
<!DOCTYPE html PUBLIC "-//W3C//DTD XHTML 1.1//EN"
"http://www.w3.org/TR/xhtml11/DTD/xhtml11.dtd">
<html xmlns="http://www.w3.org/1999/xhtml" >
<head id="Head1" runat="server">
    <title>Show Movies</title>
</head>
<body>
    <form id="form1" runat="server">
    <div>

    <asp:GridView
        id="grdMovies"
        DataSourceID="srcMovies"
        DataKeyNames="Id"
        AutoGenerateEditButton="true"
        Runat="server" />

    <asp:ObjectDataSource
        id="srcMovies"
        TypeName="Movies"
        SelectMethod="GetMovies"
        UpdateMethod="UpdateMovie"
        Runat="server"/>

    </div>
    </form>
</body>
</html>
```

In Listing 16.12, the GridView automatically adds the update parameters to the ObjectDataSource control's UpdateParameters collection. As an alternative, you can declare the parameters used by the ObjectDataSource control explicitly. For example, the page in Listing 16.13 declares all the parameters passed to the UpdateMovie() method.

LISTING 16.13   ExplicitShowMovies.aspx

```
<%@ Page Language="C#" %>
<!DOCTYPE html PUBLIC "-//W3C//DTD XHTML 1.1//EN"
"http://www.w3.org/TR/xhtml11/DTD/xhtml11.dtd">
<html xmlns="http://www.w3.org/1999/xhtml" >
<head id="Head1" runat="server">
    <title>Show Movies</title>
</head>
<body>
    <form id="form1" runat="server">
    <div>

    <asp:GridView
        id="grdMovies"
        DataSourceID="srcMovies"
        DataKeyNames="Id"
        AutoGenerateEditButton="true"
        Runat="server" />

    <asp:ObjectDataSource
        id="srcMovies"
        TypeName="Movies"
        SelectMethod="GetMovies"
        UpdateMethod="UpdateMovie"
        Runat="server">
        <UpdateParameters>
        <asp:Parameter Name="title" />
        <asp:Parameter Name="director" />
        <asp:Parameter Name="dateReleased" Type="DateTime" />
        <asp:Parameter Name="id" Type="Int32" />
        </UpdateParameters>
    </asp:ObjectDataSource>

    </div>
    </form>
</body>
</html>
```

The ObjectDataSource uses reflection to match its parameters against the parameters of the method that it calls. The order of the parameters does not matter and the case of the parameters does not matter. However, the one thing that does matter is the names of the parameters.

You specify the type of a parameter with the Type property, which represents a member of the TypeCode enumeration. The TypeCode enumeration represents an enumeration of common .NET Framework data types such as Int32, Decimal, and DateTime. If the enumeration does not include a data type that you need, then you can use the TypeCode.Object member from the enumeration.

Using Different Parameter Types

You can use all the same types of parameters with the ObjectDataSource control that you can use with the SqlDataSource control:

▶ **Parameter**—Represents an arbitrary static value.

▶ **ControlParameter**—Represents the value of a control or page property.

▶ **CookieParameter**—Represents the value of a browser cookie.

▶ **FormParameter**—Represents the value of an HTML form field.

▶ **ProfileParameter**—Represents the value of a Profile property.

▶ **QueryStringParameter**—Represents the value of a query string field.

▶ **SessionParameter**—Represents the value of an item stored in Session state.

For example, the page in Listing 16.14 contains a DropDownList control and a GridView control, which enables you to view movies that match a selected category (see Figure 16.3).

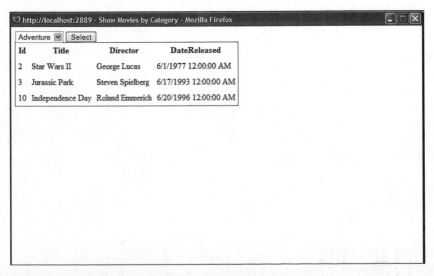

FIGURE 16.3   Displaying movies by category.

LISTING 16.14   ShowMoviesByCategory.aspx

```
<%@ Page Language="C#" %>
<!DOCTYPE html PUBLIC "-//W3C//DTD XHTML 1.1//EN"
"http://www.w3.org/TR/xhtml11/DTD/xhtml11.dtd">
<html xmlns="http://www.w3.org/1999/xhtml" >
<head id="Head1" runat="server">
    <style type="text/css">
    .movies
    {
        border:Solid 1px black;
    }
    .movies td,.movies th
    {
        padding:5px;
    }
    </style>
    <title>Show Movies by Category</title>
</head>
<body>
    <form id="form1" runat="server">
    <div>

    <asp:DropDownList
        id="ddlMovieCategory"
        DataSourceID="srcMovieCategories"
        DataTextField="Name"
        DataValueField="Id"
        ToolTip="Movie Category"
        Runat="server" />
    <asp:Button
        id="btnSelect"
        Text="Select"
        Runat="server" />

    <asp:GridView
        id="grdMovies"
        DataSourceID="srcMovies"
        CssClass="movies"
        GridLines="None"
        Runat="server" />

    <asp:ObjectDataSource
        id="srcMovieCategories"
        TypeName="MovieCategories"
```

```
        SelectMethod="GetCategories"
        Runat="server" />

    <asp:ObjectDataSource
        id="srcMovies"
        TypeName="MovieCategories"
        SelectMethod="GetMovies"
        Runat="server">
        <SelectParameters>
        <asp:ControlParameter
            Name="CategoryId"
            ControlID="ddlMovieCategory" />
        </SelectParameters>
    </asp:ObjectDataSource>

    </div>
    </form>
</body>
</html>
```

The ObjectDataSource control in Listing 16.14 is bound to the component contained in
Listing 16.15. Notice that the ObjectDataSource control includes a SelectParameters
collection. The SelectParameters collection contains a ControlParameter, which represents the current value of the ddlMovieCategory DropDownList control.

LISTING 16.15   MovieCategories.cs

```
using System;
using System.Data;
using System.Data.SqlClient;
using System.Web.Configuration;

public class MovieCategories
{
    private readonly string _conString;

    public SqlDataReader GetMovies(int categoryId)
    {
        // Create Connection
        SqlConnection con = new SqlConnection(_conString);

        // Create Command
        SqlCommand cmd = new SqlCommand();
        cmd.Connection = con;
```

16

LISTING 16.15   Continued

```
        cmd.CommandText = "SELECT Id,Title,Director,DateReleased "
            + " FROM Movies WHERE CategoryId=@CategoryId";

        // Add parameters
        cmd.Parameters.AddWithValue("@CategoryId", categoryId);

        // Return DataReader
        con.Open();
        return cmd.ExecuteReader(CommandBehavior.CloseConnection);
    }

    public SqlDataReader GetCategories()
    {
        // Create Connection
        SqlConnection con = new SqlConnection(_conString);

        // Create Command
        SqlCommand cmd = new SqlCommand();
        cmd.Connection = con;
        cmd.CommandText = "SELECT Id,Name FROM MovieCategories";

        // Return DataReader
        con.Open();
        return cmd.ExecuteReader(CommandBehavior.CloseConnection);
    }

    public MovieCategories()
    {
        _conString = WebConfigurationManager.ConnectionStrings["Movies"].
        ➥ConnectionString;
    }
}
```

Passing Objects as Parameters

Passing long lists of parameters to methods can make it difficult to maintain an application. If the list of parameters changes, you need to update every method that accepts the list of parameters.

Rather than pass a list of parameters to a method, you can pass a particular object. For example, you can pass a CompanyEmployee object to a method used to update an employee, rather than a list of parameters that represent employee properties.

If you specify a value for an ObjectDataSource control's DataObjectTypeName property, then you can pass an object rather than a list of parameters to the methods that an ObjectDataSource represents. In that case, the ObjectDataSource parameters represent properties of the object.

For example, the EmployeeData component in Listing 16.16 contains an InsertEmployee() method for creating a new employee. This method is passed an instance of the CompanyEmployee object that represents a particular employee. The CompanyEmployee class also is included in Listing 16.16.

LISTING 16.16   EmployeeData.cs

```
using System;
using System.Data;
using System.Data.SqlClient;
using System.Collections.Generic;
using System.Web.Configuration;

public class EmployeeData
{
    string _connectionString;

    public void UpdateEmployee(CompanyEmployee employeeToUpdate)
    {
        // Initialize ADO.NET objects
        SqlConnection con = new SqlConnection(_connectionString);
        SqlCommand cmd = new SqlCommand();
        cmd.CommandText = "UPDATE Employees SET FirstName=@FirstName," +
            "LastName=@LastName,Phone=@Phone WHERE Id=@Id";
        cmd.Connection = con;

        // Create parameters
        cmd.Parameters.AddWithValue("@Id", employeeToUpdate.Id);
        cmd.Parameters.AddWithValue("@FirstName", employeeToUpdate.FirstName);
        cmd.Parameters.AddWithValue("@LastName", employeeToUpdate.LastName);
        cmd.Parameters.AddWithValue("@Phone", employeeToUpdate.Phone);

        // Execute command
        using (con)
        {
            con.Open();
            cmd.ExecuteNonQuery();
        }
    }
```

LISTING 16.16   Continued

```
public List<CompanyEmployee> GetEmployees()
{
    List<CompanyEmployee> employees = new List<CompanyEmployee>();

    SqlConnection con = new SqlConnection(_connectionString);
    SqlCommand cmd = new SqlCommand();
    cmd.CommandText = "SELECT Id,FirstName,LastName,Phone FROM Employees";
    cmd.Connection = con;
    using (con)
    {
        con.Open();
        SqlDataReader reader = cmd.ExecuteReader();
        while (reader.Read())
        {
            CompanyEmployee newEmployee = new CompanyEmployee();
            newEmployee.Id = (int)reader["Id"];
            newEmployee.FirstName = (string)reader["FirstName"];
            newEmployee.LastName = (string)reader["LastName"];
            newEmployee.Phone = (string)reader["Phone"];
            employees.Add(newEmployee);
        }
    }
    return employees;
}

public EmployeeData()
{
    _connectionString = WebConfigurationManager.ConnectionStrings["Employees"].
    ➥ConnectionString;
}
}

public class CompanyEmployee
{
    private int _id;
    private string _firstName;
    private string _lastName;
    private string _phone;

    public int Id
    {
        get { return _id; }
        set { _id = value; }
    }
```

```csharp
    public string FirstName
    {
        get { return _firstName; }
        set { _firstName = value; }
    }

    public string LastName
    {
        get { return _lastName; }
        set { _lastName = value; }
    }

    public string Phone
    {
        get { return _phone; }
        set { _phone = value; }
    }
}
```

The page in Listing 16.17 contains a DetailsView control and an ObjectDataSource control. The DetailsView control enables you to update existing employees in the Employees database table.

LISTING 16.17   UpdateEmployees.aspx

```aspx
<%@ Page Language="C#" %>
<!DOCTYPE html PUBLIC "-//W3C//DTD XHTML 1.1//EN"
"http://www.w3.org/TR/xhtml11/DTD/xhtml11.dtd">
<html xmlns="http://www.w3.org/1999/xhtml" >
<head id="Head1" runat="server">
    <title>Update Employees</title>
</head>
<body>
    <form id="form1" runat="server">
    <div>

    <asp:DetailsView ID="DetailsView1"
        DataSourceID="srcEmployees"
        DataKeyNames="Id"
        AutoGenerateRows="True"
        AutoGenerateEditButton="True"
        AllowPaging="true"
        Runat="server" />
```

16

LISTING 16.17   Continued

```
    <asp:ObjectDataSource
        id="srcEmployees"
        TypeName="EmployeeData"
        DataObjectTypeName="CompanyEmployee"
        SelectMethod="GetEmployees"
        UpdateMethod="UpdateEmployee"
        Runat="server" />

    </div>
    </form>
</body>
</html>
```

Notice that the ObjectDataSource control includes a DataObjectTypeName property. This property contains the name of an object that is used with the UpdateEmployee() method. When the UpdateEmployee() method is called, an instance of the CompanyEmployee component is created and passed to the method.

> **NOTE**
>
> The DataObjectTypeName property has an effect on only the methods represented by the InsertMethod, UpdateMethod, and DeleteMethod properties. It does not have an effect on the method represented by the SelectMethod property.

There is one important limitation when using the DataObjectTypeName property. The object represented by this property must have a parameterless constructor. For example, you could not use the following CompanyEmployee class with the DataObjectTypeName property:

```
public class CompanyEmployee
{
    private string _firstName;

    public string FirstName
    {
        get
        {
            return _firstName;
        }
    }

    public void CompanyEmployee(string firstName)
    {
```

```
        _firstName = firstName;
    }
}
```

The problem with this class is that it initializes its FirstName property in its constructor. Its constructor requires a firstName parameter. Instead, you need to use a class that looks like this:

```
public class CompanyEmployee
{
    private string _firstName;

    public string FirstName
    {
        get
        {
            return _firstName;
        }
        set
        {
            _firstName = value;
        }
    }
}
```

This class has a parameterless constructor. The FirstName property is a read/write property.

If you really have the need, you can get around this limitation by handling the Inserting, Updating, or Deleting event. When you handle one of these events, you can pass any object that you need to a method. These events are discussed later in this chapter in the section entitled "Handling ObjectDataSource Events."

Paging, Sorting, and Filtering Data with the ObjectDataSource Control

The ObjectDataSource control provides you with two options for paging and sorting database data. You can take advantage of either user interface or data source paging and sorting. The first option is easy to configure, and the second option has much better performance. In this section, you learn how to take advantage of both options.

You also learn how to take advantage of the ObjectDataSource control's support for filtering. When you combine filtering with caching, you can improve the performance of your data-driven web pages dramatically.

User Interface Paging

Imagine that you want to use a GridView control to display the results of a database query in multiple pages. The easiest way to do this is to take advantage of user interface paging.

For example, the page in Listing 16.18 uses a GridView and ObjectDataSource control to display the records from the Movies database table in multiple pages (see Figure 16.4).

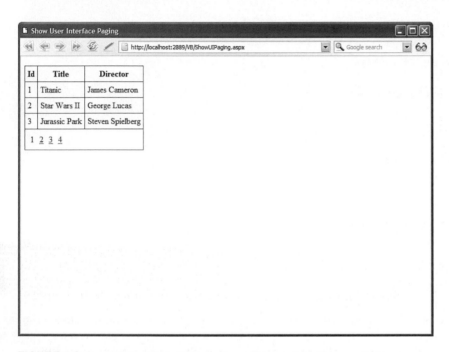

FIGURE 16.4   Displaying multiple pages with user interface paging.

LISTING 16.18   ShowUIPaging.aspx

```
<%@ Page Language="C#" %>
<!DOCTYPE html PUBLIC "-//W3C//DTD XHTML 1.1//EN"
"http://www.w3.org/TR/xhtml11/DTD/xhtml11.dtd">
<html xmlns="http://www.w3.org/1999/xhtml" >
<head id="Head1" runat="server">
    <style type="text/css">
        .movies td,.movies th
        {
            padding:5px;
        }
    </style>
    <title>Show User Interface Paging</title>
```

```
</head>
<body>
    <form id="form1" runat="server">
    <div>

    <asp:GridView
        id="grdMovies"
        DataSourceID="srcMovies"
        AllowPaging="true"
        PageSize="3"
        CssClass="movies"
        Runat="server" />

    <asp:ObjectDataSource
        id="srcMovies"
        TypeName="MovieUIPaging"
        SelectMethod="GetMoviesDataSet"
        Runat="server" />

    </div>
    </form>
</body>
</html>
```

The `GridView` control in Listing 16.18 includes an `AllowPaging` property that is set to the value `True`. Setting this property enables user interface paging.

The `ObjectDataSource` control in Listing 16.18 represents the `MovieUIPaging` component in Listing 16.19. This component includes a `GetMoviesDataSet()` method that returns an ADO.NET `DataSet` object.

To take advantage of user interface paging, you must bind the `GridView` control to the right type of data source. The right type of data source includes a collection, a `DataSet`, a `DataTable`, and a `DataView`. The right type of data source does not include, for example, a `DataReader`.

LISTING 16.19 MovieUIPaging.cs

```
using System;
using System.Data;
using System.Data.SqlClient;
using System.Web.Configuration;

public class MovieUIPaging
{
```

LISTING 16.19   Continued

```
    private readonly string _conString;

    public DataSet GetMoviesDataSet()
    {
        // Create DataAdapter
        string commandText = "SELECT Id,Title,Director FROM Movies";
        SqlDataAdapter dad = new SqlDataAdapter(commandText, _conString);

        // Return DataSet
        DataSet dstMovies = new DataSet();
        using (dad)
        {
            dad.Fill(dstMovies);
        }
        return dstMovies;
    }

    public MovieUIPaging()
    {
        _conString = WebConfigurationManager.ConnectionStrings["Movies"].
        ➥ConnectionString;
    }
}
```

User interface paging is convenient because you can enable it by setting a single property. However, there is a significant drawback to this type of paging. When user interface paging is enabled, all the movie records must be loaded into server memory. If the Movies database table contains 3 billion records, and you are displaying 3 records a page, then all 3 billion records must be loaded to display the 3 records. This places an incredible burden on both the web server and database server. In the next section, you learn how to use data source paging, which enables you to work efficiently with large sets of records.

Data Source Paging

Data source paging enables you to write custom logic for retrieving pages of database records. You can perform the paging in the component, a stored procedure, or a LINQ to SQL query.

If you want the best performance, then you should write your paging logic in either a stored procedure or a LINQ query. We'll examine both approaches in this section.

The page in Listing 16.20 contains an ObjectDataSource control with data source paging enabled.

> **NOTE**
>
> Chapter 18 is devoted to the topic of LINQ.

LISTING 16.20 ShowDSPaging.aspx

```
<%@ Page Language="C#" %>
<!DOCTYPE html PUBLIC "-//W3C//DTD XHTML 1.1//EN"
    "http://www.w3.org/TR/xhtml11/DTD/xhtml11.dtd">
<html xmlns="http://www.w3.org/1999/xhtml" >
<head id="Head1" runat="server">
    <style type="text/css">
        .movies td,.movies th
        {
            padding:5px;
        }
    </style>
    <title>Show Data Source Paging</title>
</head>
<body>
    <form id="form1" runat="server">
    <div>

    <asp:GridView
        id="grdMovies"
        DataSourceID="srcMovies"
        AllowPaging="true"
        PageSize="3"
        CssClass="movies"
        Runat="server" />

    <asp:ObjectDataSource
        id="srcMovies"
        TypeName="MoviesDSPaging"
        SelectMethod="GetMovies"
        SelectCountMethod="GetMovieCount"
        EnablePaging="True"
        Runat="server" />

    </div>
    </form>
</body>
</html>
```

16

Notice that the `ObjectDataSource` control includes an `EnablePaging` property that has the value `True`. The `ObjectDataSource` also includes a `SelectCountMethod` property that represents the name of a method that retrieves a record count from the data source.

Notice, furthermore, that the `GridView` control includes both an `AllowPaging` and `PageSize` property. Even when using data source paging, you need to enable the `AllowPaging` property for the `GridView` so that the `GridView` can render its paging user interface.

When an `ObjectDataSource` control has its `EnablePaging` property set to the value `True`, the `ObjectDataSource` passes additional parameters when calling the method represented by its `SelectMethod` property. The two additional parameters are named `StartRowIndex` and `MaximumRows`.

Now that we have the page setup for data source paging, we need to create the component. Let's start by using a LINQ to SQL query. This approach is the easiest and recommended way. The component in Listing 16.21 uses LINQ to SQL queries to implement both the `GetMovies()` and `GetMovieCount()` methods.

LISTING 16.21   MoviesLINQPaging.cs

```csharp
using System;
using System.Collections.Generic;
using System.Linq;
using System.Data.Linq;
using System.Web;

public class MoviesDSPaging
{
    public static IEnumerable<Movie> GetMovies(int startRowIndex, int maximumRows)
    {
        MyDatabaseDataContext db = new MyDatabaseDataContext();
        return db.Movies.Skip(startRowIndex).Take(maximumRows);
    }

    public static int GetMovieCount()
    {
        HttpContext context = HttpContext.Current;
        if (context.Cache["MovieCount"] == null)
            context.Cache["MovieCount"] = GetMovieCountFromDB();
        return (int)context.Cache["MovieCount"];
    }

    private static int GetMovieCountFromDB()
    {
```

```
        MyDatabaseDataContext db = new MyDatabaseDataContext();
        return db.Movies.Count();
    }
}
```

Before you can use the component in Listing 16.21, you need to create a DataContext named `MyDatabaseDataContext`. You can create this DataContext by selecting the menu option Website, Add New Item, and adding a new LINQ to SQL Classes item to your website. Name the new LINQ to SQL Classes item `MyDatabase.dbml`. Next, after the Object Relational Designer opens, drag the Movies database table from the Database Explorer window onto the Designer surface.

NOTE

Unfortunately, when you drag the Movies database table onto the Object Relational Designer surface, the Designer creates a new entity named Movy. The Designer is attempting to singularize the word and it fails badly. You must rename the entity to `Movie` in the Properties window. (I hope this Visual Web Developer grammar bug will be fixed by the time you read this).

You are not required to use LINQ to SQL when you want to implement data source paging. As an alternative to LINQ to SQL, you can perform your paging logic within a SQL stored procedure. The component in Listing 16.22 contains ADO.NET code instead of LINQ to SQL queries.

LISTING 16.22 MoviesSQLPaging.cs

```
using System;
using System.Web;
using System.Data;
using System.Data.SqlClient;
using System.Web.Configuration;

public class MoviesDSPaging
{
    private static readonly string _conString;

    public static SqlDataReader GetMovies(int startRowIndex, int maximumRows)
    {
        // Initialize connection
        SqlConnection con = new SqlConnection(_conString);

        // Initialize command
        SqlCommand cmd = new SqlCommand();
```

LISTING 16.22   Continued

```csharp
        cmd.Connection = con;
        cmd.CommandText = "GetPagedMovies";
        cmd.CommandType = CommandType.StoredProcedure;

        // Add ADO.NET parameters
        cmd.Parameters.AddWithValue("@StartRowIndex", startRowIndex);
        cmd.Parameters.AddWithValue("@MaximumRows", maximumRows);

        // Execute command
        con.Open();
        return cmd.ExecuteReader(CommandBehavior.CloseConnection);
    }

    public static int GetMovieCount()
    {
        HttpContext context = HttpContext.Current;
        if (context.Cache["MovieCount"] == null)
            context.Cache["MovieCount"] = GetMovieCountFromDB();
        return (int)context.Cache["MovieCount"];
    }

    private static int GetMovieCountFromDB()
    {
        int result = 0;

        // Initialize connection
        SqlConnection con = new SqlConnection(_conString);

        // Initialize command
        SqlCommand cmd = new SqlCommand();
        cmd.Connection = con;
        cmd.CommandText = "SELECT Count(*) FROM Movies";

        // Execute command
        using (con)
        {
            con.Open();
            result = (int)cmd.ExecuteScalar();
        }
        return result;
    }
```

```
    static MoviesDSPaging()
    {
        _conString = WebConfigurationManager.ConnectionStrings["Movies"].Connection-
String;
    }

}
```

To improve performance, the `GetMovieCount()` method attempts to retrieve the total count of movie records from the server cache. If the record count cannot be retrieved from the cache, the count is retrieved from the database.

The `GetMovies()` method calls a stored procedure named `GetPagedMovies` to retrieve a particular page of movies. The `StartRowIndex` and `MaximumRows` parameters are passed to the stored procedure. The `GetPagedMovies` stored procedure is contained in Listing 16.23.

LISTING 16.23   GetPagedMovies.sql

```
CREATE PROCEDURE dbo.GetPagedMovies
(
    @StartRowIndex INT,
    @MaximumRows INT
)
AS

-- Create a temp table to store the select results
CREATE TABLE #PageIndex
(
    IndexId INT IDENTITY (1, 1) NOT NULL,
    RecordId INT
)

-- INSERT into the temp table
INSERT INTO #PageIndex (RecordId)
SELECT Id FROM Movies

-- Get a page of movies
SELECT
    Id,
    Title,
    Director,
    DateReleased
FROM
    Movies
    INNER JOIN #PageIndex WITH (nolock)
    ON Movies.Id = #PageIndex.RecordId
```

16

LISTING 16.23 Continued

```
WHERE
    #PageIndex.IndexID > @startRowIndex
    AND #PageIndex.IndexID < (@startRowIndex + @maximumRows + 1)
ORDER BY
    #PageIndex.IndexID
```

The GetPagedMovies stored procedure returns a particular page of database records. The stored procedure creates a temporary table named #PageIndex that contains two columns: an identity column and a column that contains the primary key values from the Movies database table. The temporary table fills in any holes in the primary key column that might result from deleting records.

Next, the stored procedure retrieves a certain range of records from the #PageIndex table and joins the results with the Movies database table. The end result is that only a single page of database records is returned.

When you open the page in Listing 16.20, the GridView displays its paging interface, which you can use to navigate between different pages of records (see Figure 16.5).

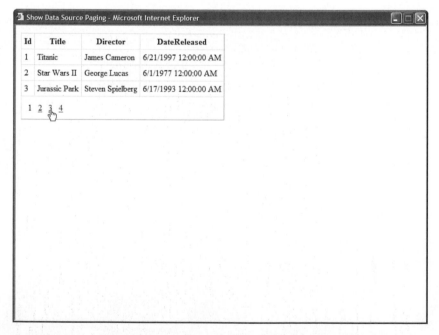

FIGURE 16.5 Displaying multiple pages with data source paging.

> **NOTE**
>
> The paging mechanism described in this section is based on the mechanism used by the Microsoft ASP.NET forums at http://www.asp.net/forums and the XBOX forums at http://www.xbox.com. Both of these websites handle an incredible number of message posts every day. The forums software was written with ASP.NET, and it is available from TelligentSystems (www.telligentsystems.com) as part of their Community Server product.

If temporary tables make you anxious, you have an alternative when working with Microsoft SQL Server 2005. You can take advantage of the new ROW_NUMBER() function to select a range of rows. The ROW_NUMBER() function automatically calculates the sequential number of a row within a resultset.

The modified stored procedure in Listing 16.24 does the same thing as the stored procedure in Listing 16.23. However, the modified stored procedure avoids any temporary tables.

LISTING 16.24 GetPagedMovies2005.sql

```
CREATE PROCEDURE dbo.GetPagedMovies2005
(
    @StartRowIndex INT,
    @MaximumRows INT
)
AS

WITH OrderedMovies AS
(
SELECT
    Id,
    ROW_NUMBER() OVER (ORDER BY Id) AS RowNumber
FROM Movies
)

SELECT
    OrderedMovies.RowNumber,
    Movies.Id,
    Movies.Title,
    Movies.Director
FROM
    OrderedMovies
    JOIN Movies
    ON OrderedMovies.Id = Movies.Id
WHERE
    RowNumber BETWEEN (@StartRowIndex + 1) AND (@startRowIndex + @maximumRows + 1)
```

16

User Interface Sorting

If you need to sort the records displayed by the GridView control, then the easiest type of sorting to enable is user interface sorting. When you take advantage of user interface sorting, the records are sorted in the server's memory.

For example, the page in Listing 16.25 contains a GridView that has its AllowSorting property set to the value True. The GridView is bound to an ObjectDataSource that represents the Employees database table (see Figure 16.6).

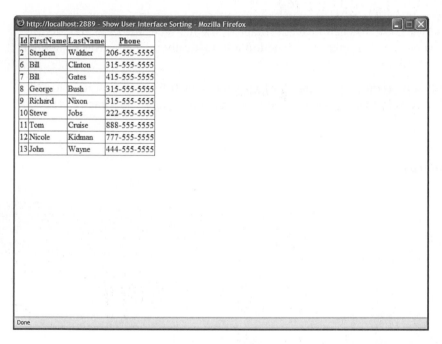

FIGURE 16.6   Sorting records with user interface sorting.

LISTING 16.25   ShowUISorting.aspx

```
<%@ Page Language="C#" %>
<!DOCTYPE html PUBLIC "-//W3C//DTD XHTML 1.1//EN"
"http://www.w3.org/TR/xhtml11/DTD/xhtml11.dtd">
<html xmlns="http://www.w3.org/1999/xhtml" >
<head id="Head1" runat="server">
    <title>Show User Interface Sorting</title>
</head>
<body>
    <form id="form1" runat="server">
    <div>

    <asp:GridView
```

```
        id="grdEmployees"
        DataSourceID="srcEmployees"
        AllowSorting="True"
        Runat="server" />

    <asp:ObjectDataSource
        id="srcEmployees"
        TypeName="EmployeesUISorting"
        SelectMethod="GetEmployees"
        Runat="server" />

    </div>
    </form>
</body>
</html>
```

The `ObjectDataSource` control in Listing 16.25 is bound to the component in Listing 16.26. Notice that the `GetEmployees()` method returns an ADO.NET `DataSet` object. When taking advantage of user interface sorting, the `ObjectDataSource` control must represent the right type of data source. The right type of data source includes a `DataSet`, a `DataTable`, and a `DataView`.

LISTING 16.26   EmployeesUISorting.cs

```csharp
using System;
using System.Data;
using System.Data.SqlClient;
using System.Web.Configuration;

public class EmployeesUISorting
{
    private static readonly string _conString;

    public static DataSet GetEmployees()
    {
        // Initialize ADO.NET objects
        string selectText = "SELECT Id,FirstName,LastName,Phone FROM Employees";
        SqlDataAdapter dad = new SqlDataAdapter(selectText, _conString);
        DataSet dstEmployees = new DataSet();

        // Fill the DataSet
        using (dad)
        {
            dad.Fill(dstEmployees);
        }
```

16

LISTING 16.26   Continued

```
        return dstEmployees;
    }


    static EmployeesUISorting()
    {
        _conString = WebConfigurationManager.ConnectionStrings["Employees"].
        ➥ConnectionString;
    }


}
```

User interface sorting is convenient. You can enable this type of sorting by setting a single property of the GridView control. Unfortunately, just as with user interface paging, some serious performance drawbacks result from user interface sorting. All the records from the underlying database must be loaded and sorted in memory. This is a particular problem when you want to enable both sorting and paging at the same time. In the next section, you learn how to implement data source sorting, which avoids this performance issue.

Data Source Sorting

Imagine that you are working with a database table that contains 3 billion records and you want to enable users to both sort the records contained in this table and page through the records contained in this table. In that case, you'll want to implement both data source sorting and paging.

The page in Listing 16.27 contains a GridView and ObjectDataSource control. The GridView has both its AllowSorting and AllowPaging properties enabled (see Figure 16.7).

LISTING 16.27   ShowDSSorting.aspx

```
<%@ Page Language="C#" %>
<!DOCTYPE html PUBLIC "-//W3C//DTD XHTML 1.1//EN"
 "http://www.w3.org/TR/xhtml11/DTD/xhtml11.dtd">
<html xmlns="http://www.w3.org/1999/xhtml" >
<head id="Head1" runat="server">
    <style type="text/css">
    .employees td,.employees th
    {
        font:16px Georgia,Serif;
        padding:5px;
    }
    a
    {
        color:blue;
    }
```

```
        </style>
        <title>Show Data Source Sorting</title>
</head>
<body>
    <form id="form1" runat="server">
    <div>

    <asp:GridView
        id="grdEmployees"
        DataSourceID="srcEmployees"
        AllowSorting="true"
        AllowPaging="true"
        PageSize="3"
        CssClass="employees"
        Runat="server" />

    <asp:ObjectDataSource
        id="srcEmployees"
        TypeName="EmployeesDSSorting"
        SelectMethod="GetEmployees"
        SelectCountMethod="GetEmployeeCount"
        EnablePaging="true"
        SortParameterName="sortExpression"
        Runat="server" />

    </div>
    </form>
</body>
</html>
```

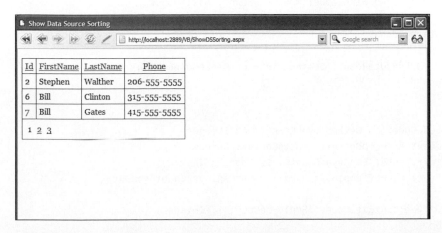

FIGURE 16.7   Paging and sorting database records.

The ObjectDataSource control in Listing 16.27 represents the EmployeesDSSorting component in Listing 16.28. Notice that the ObjectDataSource control includes a SortParameterName property. When this property is present, the ObjectDataSource control uses data source sorting instead of user interface sorting.

LISTING 16.28   EmployeesDSSorting.cs

```
Imports System
Imports System.Data
Imports System.Data.SqlClient
Imports System.Web.Configuration


Public Class EmployeesDSSorting

    Private Shared ReadOnly _conString As String

    Public Shared Function GetEmployees(ByVal sortExpression As String, ByVal
    ➥startRowIndex As Integer, ByVal maximumRows As Integer) As SqlDataReader
        ' Initialize connection
        Dim con As New SqlConnection(_conString)

        ' Initialize command
        Dim cmd As New SqlCommand()
        cmd.Connection = con
        cmd.CommandText = "GetSortedEmployees"
        cmd.CommandType = CommandType.StoredProcedure

        ' Create parameters
        cmd.Parameters.AddWithValue("@SortExpression", sortExpression)
        cmd.Parameters.AddWithValue("@StartRowIndex", startRowIndex)
        cmd.Parameters.AddWithValue("@MaximumRows", maximumRows)

        ' Execute command
        con.Open()
        Return cmd.ExecuteReader(CommandBehavior.CloseConnection)
    End Function


    Public Shared Function GetEmployeeCount() As Integer
        Dim context As HttpContext = HttpContext.Current
        If context.Cache("EmployeeCount") Is Nothing Then
            context.Cache("EmployeeCount") = GetEmployeeCountFromDB()
        End If
        Return CType(context.Cache("EmployeeCount"), Integer)
    End Function
```

```vb
Private Shared Function GetEmployeeCountFromDB() As Integer
    Dim result As Integer = 0

    ' Initialize connection
    Dim con As SqlConnection = New SqlConnection(_conString)

    ' Initialize command
    Dim cmd As SqlCommand = New SqlCommand()
    cmd.Connection = con
    cmd.CommandText = "SELECT Count(*) FROM Employees"

    ' Execute command
    Using con
        con.Open()
        result = CType(cmd.ExecuteScalar(), Integer)
    End Using
    Return result
End Function



Shared Sub New()
    _conString = WebConfigurationManager.ConnectionStrings("Employees").
    ➥ConnectionString
End Sub

End Class
```

The `GetEmployees()` method in the component in Listing 16.28 calls a stored procedure to sort and page records. The stored procedure, named `GetSortedEmployees`, returns a sorted page of records from the Employees database table. This stored procedure is contained in Listing 16.29.

LISTING 16.29 GetSortedEmployees.sql

```sql
CREATE PROCEDURE GetSortedEmployees
(
    @SortExpression NVarChar(100),
    @StartRowIndex INT,
    @MaximumRows INT
)
AS

-- Create a temp table to store the select results
```

LISTING 16.29   Continued

```
CREATE TABLE #PageIndex
(
    IndexId INT IDENTITY (1, 1) NOT NULL,
    RecordId INT
)

-- INSERT into the temp table
INSERT INTO #PageIndex (RecordId)
SELECT Id FROM Employees
ORDER BY
CASE WHEN @SortExpression='Id' THEN Id END ASC,
CASE WHEN @SortExpression='Id DESC' THEN Id END DESC,
CASE WHEN @SortExpression='FirstName' THEN FirstName END ASC,
CASE WHEN @SortExpression='FirstName DESC' THEN FirstName END DESC,
CASE WHEN @SortExpression='LastName' THEN LastName END ASC,
CASE WHEN @SortExpression='LastName DESC' THEN LastName END DESC,
CASE WHEN @SortExpression='Phone' THEN Phone END ASC,
CASE WHEN @SortExpression='Phone DESC' THEN Phone END DESC

-- Get a page of records
SELECT
    Id,
    FirstName,
    LastName,
    Phone
FROM
    Employees
    INNER JOIN #PageIndex WITH (nolock)
    ON Employees.Id = #PageIndex.RecordId
WHERE
    #PageIndex.IndexID > @StartRowIndex
    AND #PageIndex.IndexID < (@StartRowIndex + @MaximumRows + 1)
ORDER BY
    #PageIndex.IndexID
```

Notice that the stored procedure in Listing 16.29 uses SQL CASE functions to sort the records before they are added to the temporary table. Unfortunately, you can't use a parameter with an ORDER BY clause, so the sort columns must be hard-coded in the CASE functions. Next, a page of records is selected from the temporary table.

> **NOTE**
>
> As an alternative to the data source sorting method described in this section, you can use LINQ to SQL. For more information on LINQ to SQL, see Chapter 18.

Filtering Data

You can supply the ObjectDataSource control with a filter expression. The filter expression is applied to the data returned by the control's select method. A filter is particularly useful when used in combination with caching. You can load all the data into the cache and then apply different filters to the cached data.

> **NOTE**
>
> You learn how to cache data with the ObjectDataSource control in Chapter 25, "Caching Application Pages and Data."

For example, the page in Listing 16.30 contains a DropDownList and GridView control. The DropDownList displays a list of movie categories, and the GridView displays matching movies (see Figure 16.8).

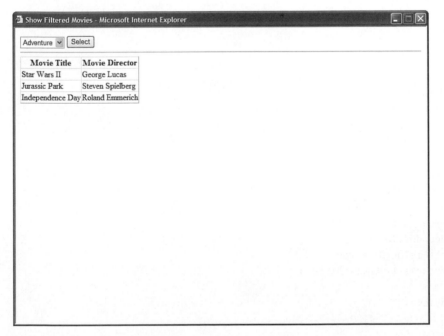

FIGURE 16.8   Filtering movies with the ObjectDataSource control.

LISTING 16.30 ShowFilteredMovies.aspx

```
<%@ Page Language="C#" %>
<!DOCTYPE html PUBLIC "-//W3C//DTD XHTML 1.1//EN"
    "http://www.w3.org/TR/xhtml11/DTD/xhtml11.dtd">
<html xmlns="http://www.w3.org/1999/xhtml" >
<head id="Head1" runat="server">
    <title>Show Filtered Movies</title>
</head>
<body>
    <form id="form1" runat="server">
    <div>

    <asp:DropDownList
        id="ddlMovieCategory"
        DataSourceID="srcMovieCategories"
        DataTextField="Name"
        DataValueField="Id"
        Runat="server" />
    <asp:Button
        id="btnSelect"
        Text="Select"
        Runat="server" />

    <hr />

    <asp:GridView
        id="grdMovies"
        DataSourceID="srcMovies"
        AutoGenerateColumns="false"
        Runat="server">
        <Columns>
        <asp:BoundField
            DataField="Title"
            HeaderText="Movie Title" />
        <asp:BoundField
            DataField="Director"
            HeaderText="Movie Director" />
        </Columns>
    </asp:GridView>

    <asp:ObjectDataSource
        id="srcMovieCategories"
        TypeName="FilterMovies"
        SelectMethod="GetMovieCategories"
```

```
        EnableCaching="true"
        CacheDuration="Infinite"
        Runat="server" />

    <asp:ObjectDataSource
        id="srcMovies"
        TypeName="FilterMovies"
        SelectMethod="GetMovies"
        EnableCaching="true"
        CacheDuration="Infinite"
        FilterExpression="CategoryID={0}"
        Runat="server">
        <FilterParameters>
        <asp:ControlParameter
            Name="Category"
            ControlID="ddlMovieCategory" />
        </FilterParameters>
    </asp:ObjectDataSource>


    </div>
    </form>
</body>
</html>
```

Both ObjectDataSource controls in Listing 16.30 have caching enabled. Furthermore, the second ObjectDataSource control includes a FilterExpression property that filters the cached data, using the selected movie category from the DropDownList control.

Both ObjectDataSource controls represent the component in Listing 16.31.

LISTING 16.31   FilterMovies.cs

```
using System;
using System.Web;
using System.Data;
using System.Data.SqlClient;
using System.Web.Configuration;

public class FilterMovies
{
    private readonly string _conString;

    public DataSet GetMovies()
    {
```

LISTING 16.31   Continued

```
    // Initialize connection
    SqlConnection con = new SqlConnection(_conString);

    // Initialize DataAdapter
    string commandText = "SELECT Title,Director,CategoryId FROM Movies";
    SqlDataAdapter dad = new SqlDataAdapter(commandText, con);

    // Return DataSet
    DataSet dstMovies = new DataSet();
    using (con)
    {
        dad.Fill(dstMovies);
    }
    return dstMovies;
}

public DataSet GetMovieCategories()
{
    // Initialize connection
    SqlConnection con = new SqlConnection(_conString);

    // Initialize DataAdapter
    string commandText = "SELECT Id,Name FROM MovieCategories";
    SqlDataAdapter dad = new SqlDataAdapter(commandText, con);

    // Return DataSet
    DataSet dstCategories = new DataSet();
    using (con)
    {
        dad.Fill(dstCategories);
    }
    return dstCategories;
}

public FilterMovies()
{
    _conString = WebConfigurationManager.ConnectionStrings["Movies"].
    ➥ConnectionString;
}
}
```

The `ObjectDataSource` enables you to filter data only when the data is represented by a `DataSet`, `DataTable`, or `DataView` object. This means that if you use filtering, the data must be returned as one of these objects.

NOTE

Behind the scenes, the `ObjectDataSource` control uses the `DataView.RowFilter` property to filter database rows. You can find detailed documentation on proper filter syntax by looking up the `DataColumn.Expression` property in the .NET Framework SDK Documentation.

Handling `ObjectDataSource` Control Events

The `ObjectDataSource` control supports the following events:

▶ **Deleting**—Occurs immediately before the method represented by the `DeleteMethod` property is called.

▶ **Deleted**—Occurs immediately after the method represented by the `DeleteMethod` property is called.

▶ **Inserting**—Occurs immediately before the method represented by the `InsertMethod` property is called.

▶ **Inserted**—Occurs immediately after the method represented by the `InsertMethod` property is called.

▶ **Selecting**—Occurs immediately before the method represented by the `SelectMethod` property is called.

▶ **Selected**—Occurs immediately after the method represented by the `InsertMethod` property is called.

▶ **Updating**—Occurs immediately before the method represented by the `InsertMethod` property is called.

▶ **Updated**—Occurs immediately after the method represented by the `InsertMethod` property is called.

▶ **Filtering**—Occurs immediately before the filter expression is evaluated.

▶ **ObjectCreating**—Occurs immediately before the object represented by the `ObjectDataSource` control is created.

▶ **ObjectCreated**—Occurs immediately after the object represented by the `ObjectDataSource` control is created.

▶ **ObjectDisposing**—Occurs before the object represented by the `ObjectDataSource` control is destroyed.

16

Notice that most of these events come in pairs. One event happens immediately before a method is called, and one event happens immediately after a method is called.

You can handle these events to modify the parameters and objects represented by an ObjectDataSource control. You can also handle these events to handle any errors that might result from calling methods with the ObjectDataSource control.

Adding and Modifying Parameters

You can handle the Selecting, Inserting, Updating, and Deleting events to modify the parameters that are passed to the methods called by the ObjectDataSource control. There are several situations in which you might want to do this.

First, if you are working with an existing component, you might need to change the names of the parameters passed to the component. For example, instead of passing a parameter named id to an update method, you might want to rename the parameter to movieId.

Second, you might want to pass additional parameters to the method being called. For example, you might need to pass the current username, the current IP address, or the current date and time as a parameter to a method.

For example, imagine that you want to create a guestbook and automatically associate the IP address of the user making an entry with each entry in the guestbook. The page in Listing 16.32 illustrates how you can do this with the help of a FormView control and an ObjectDataSource control (see Figure 16.9).

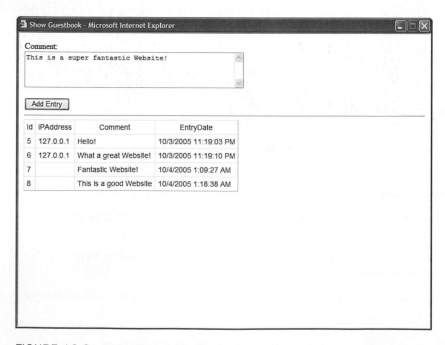

FIGURE 16.9   Displaying a guestbook.

LISTING 16.32 `ShowGuestbook.aspx`

```
<%@ Page Language="C#" %>
<!DOCTYPE html PUBLIC "-//W3C//DTD XHTML 1.1//EN"
"http://www.w3.org/TR/xhtml11/DTD/xhtml11.dtd">
<script runat="server">

    protected void srcGuestbook_Inserting(object sender, ObjectDataSourceMethodE-
ventArgs e)
    {
        e.InputParameters.Add("IPAddress", Request.UserHostAddress);
    }
</script>
<html xmlns="http://www.w3.org/1999/xhtml">
<head id="Head1" runat="server">
    <style type="text/css">
        .guestbook td,.guestbook th
        {
            padding:5px;
            font:14px Arial,Sans-Serif;
        }
    </style>
    <title>Show Guestbook</title>
</head>
<body>
    <form id="form1" runat="server">
    <div>

    <asp:FormView
        id="frmGuestbook"
        DataSourceID="srcGuestbook"
        DefaultMode="Insert"
        Runat="server">
        <InsertItemTemplate>
        <asp:Label
            ID="lblComment"
            Text="Comment:"
            AssociatedControlID="txtComment"
            Runat="server" />
        <br />
        <asp:TextBox
            id="txtComment"
            Text='<%# Bind("comment") %>'
            TextMode="MultiLine"
            Columns="50"
```

16

LISTING 16.32   Continued

```
            Rows="4"
            Runat="server" />
        <br />
        <asp:Button
            id="btnInsert"
            Text="Add Entry"
            CommandName="Insert"
            Runat="server" />
    </InsertItemTemplate>
</asp:FormView>

<hr />

<asp:GridView
    id="grdGuestbook"
    DataSourceID="srcGuestbook"
    CssClass="guestbook"
    Runat="server" />

<asp:ObjectDataSource
    id="srcGuestbook"
    TypeName="Guestbook"
    SelectMethod="GetEntries"
    InsertMethod="AddEntry"
    OnInserting="srcGuestbook_Inserting"
    Runat="server" />

</div>
</form>
</body>
</html>
```

The page in Listing 16.32 includes an `Inserting` event handler. When the `insert` method is called, the IP address of the current user is added to the parameters collection.

The `ObjectDataSource` control in Listing 16.32 is bound to the `Guestbook` component in Listing 16.33.

LISTING 16.33   Guestbook.cs

```
using System;
using System.Data;
using System.Data.SqlClient;
using System.Web.Configuration;
```

```csharp
public class Guestbook
{
    private string _conString;

    public SqlDataReader GetEntries()
    {
        // Initialize connection
        SqlConnection con = new SqlConnection(_conString);

        // Initialize command
        SqlCommand cmd = new SqlCommand();
        cmd.Connection = con;
        cmd.CommandText = "SELECT Id,IPAddress,Comment,EntryDate FROM Guestbook";

        // Execute command
        con.Open();
        return cmd.ExecuteReader(CommandBehavior.CloseConnection);
    }

    public void AddEntry(string IPAddress, string comment)
    {
        // Initialize connection
        SqlConnection con = new SqlConnection(_conString);

        // Initialize command
        SqlCommand cmd = new SqlCommand();
        cmd.Connection = con;
        cmd.CommandText = "INSERT Guestbook (IPAddress,Comment)" +
            " VALUES (@IPAddress, @Comment)";

        // Add ADO.NET parameters
        cmd.Parameters.AddWithValue("@IPAddress", IPAddress);
        cmd.Parameters.AddWithValue("@Comment", comment);

        // Execute command
        using (con)
        {
            con.Open();
            cmd.ExecuteNonQuery();
        }
    }

    public Guestbook()
    {
```

16

LISTING 16.33   Continued

```
    _conString = WebConfigurationManager.ConnectionStrings["Guestbook"].
    ➥ConnectionString;
    }

}
```

Realize that you can manipulate the parameters collection in any way that you need. You can change the names, types, or values of any of the parameters.

Handling Method Errors

You can handle the Selected, Inserted, Updated, or Deleted events in order to handle any errors that might result from calling a method. For example, the page in Listing 16.34 handles the Inserting event to capture any errors raised when the method represented by the ObjectDataSource control's InsertMethod property is called.

LISTING 16.34   HandleErrors.aspx

```
<%@ Page Language="C#" %>
<!DOCTYPE html PUBLIC "-//W3C//DTD XHTML 1.1//EN"
"http://www.w3.org/TR/xhtml11/DTD/xhtml11.dtd">
<script runat="server">

    protected void srcMovies_Inserted(object sender,
    ➥ObjectDataSourceStatusEventArgs e)
    {
        if (e.Exception != null)
        {
            e.ExceptionHandled = true;
            lblError.Text = "Could not insert movie";
        }
    }
</script>

<html xmlns="http://www.w3.org/1999/xhtml" >
<head id="Head1" runat="server">
    <style type="text/css">
        html
        {
            background-color:silver;
        }
        .insertForm
        {
```

```
                background-color:white;
            }
            .insertForm td,.insertForm th
            {
                padding:10px;
            }
            .error
            {
                color:red;
                font:bold 14px Arial,Sans-Serif;
            }
        </style>
        <title>Handle Errors</title>
    </head>
    <body>
        <form id="form1" runat="server">
        <div>

        <asp:Label
            id="lblError"
            EnableViewState="false"
            CssClass="error"
            Runat="server" />

        <h1>Insert Movie</h1>
        <asp:DetailsView
            id="dtlMovies"
            DataSourceID="srcMovies"
            DefaultMode="Insert"
            AutoGenerateInsertButton="true"
            AutoGenerateRows="false"
            CssClass="insertForm"
            GridLines="None"
            Runat="server">
            <Fields>
            <asp:BoundField
                DataField="Title"
                HeaderText="Title:"/>
            <asp:BoundField
                DataField="Director"
                HeaderText="Director:" />
            </Fields>
        </asp:DetailsView>
```

LISTING 16.34   Continued

```
<asp:ObjectDataSource
    id="srcMovies"
    TypeName="InsertMovie"
    InsertMethod="Insert"
    Runat="server" OnInserted="srcMovies_Inserted" />

    </div>
    </form>
</body>
</html>
```

In Listing 16.34, the Inserted event handler checks for an exception. If an exception exists, then the exception is handled and an error message is displayed (see Figure 16.10).

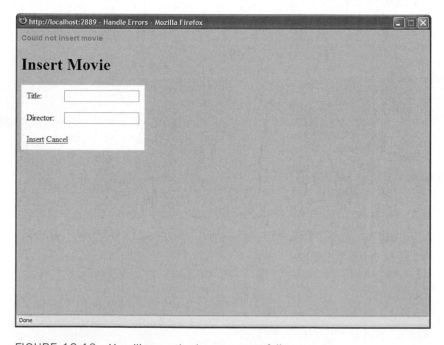

FIGURE 16.10   Handling method errors gracefully.

The page in Listing 16.34 is bound to the component in Listing 16.35.

LISTING 16.35   InsertMovie.cs

```
using System;
using System.Web;
using System.Data;
```

```csharp
using System.Data.SqlClient;
using System.Web.Configuration;

public class InsertMovie
{
    private static readonly string _conString;

    public static SqlDataReader GetMovies()
    {
        // Initialize connection
        SqlConnection con = new SqlConnection(_conString);

        // Initialize command
        SqlCommand cmd = new SqlCommand();
        cmd.Connection = con;
        cmd.CommandText = "SELECT Id,Title,Director FROM Movies";

        // Execute command
        con.Open();
        return cmd.ExecuteReader(CommandBehavior.CloseConnection);
    }

    public static void Insert(string title, string director)
    {
        // Initialize connection
        SqlConnection con = new SqlConnection(_conString);

        // Initialize command
        SqlCommand cmd = new SqlCommand();
        cmd.Connection = con;
        cmd.CommandText = "INSERT Movies (Title,Director)" +
            " VALUES (@Title,@Director)";

        // Add ADO.NET parameters
        cmd.Parameters.AddWithValue("@Title", title);
        cmd.Parameters.AddWithValue("@Director", director);

        // Execute command
        using (con)
        {
            con.Open();
            cmd.ExecuteNonQuery();
        }
    }
}
```

16

LISTING 16.35   Continued

```
static InsertMovie()
{
    _conString = WebConfigurationManager.ConnectionStrings["Movies"].
    ➥ConnectionString;
}
}
```

You can create an exception by entering a new movie record and not supplying a value for one of the fields. For example, the Title column in the Movies database table does not accept null values.

> **NOTE**
>
> Instead of handling errors at the level of the DataSource control, you can handle errors at the level of the DataBound control. For example, the DetailsView control supports an ItemInserted event.

Handling the `ObjectCreating` Event

By default, the ObjectDataSource control can represent only components that have a constructor that does not require any parameters. If you are forced to use a component that does require parameters for its constructor, then you can handle the ObjectDataSource control's ObjectCreating event.

For example, the component in Listing 16.36 must be initialized with a movie category parameter. The component returns only movies in the specified category.

LISTING 16.36   MoviesByCategory.cs

```
using System;
using System.Web;
using System.Data;
using System.Data.SqlClient;
using System.Web.Configuration;

public class MoviesByCategory
{
    private readonly string _conString;
    private readonly string _movieCategory;

    public SqlDataReader GetMovies()
    {
```

```
        // Initialize connection
        SqlConnection con = new SqlConnection(_conString);

        // Initialize command
        SqlCommand cmd = new SqlCommand();
        cmd.Connection = con;
        cmd.CommandText = "SELECT Title,Director,DateReleased FROM Movies"
            + " JOIN MovieCategories ON Movies.CategoryId=MovieCategories.Id"
            + " WHERE MovieCategories.Name=@CategoryName";

        // Create ADO.NET parameters
        cmd.Parameters.AddWithValue("@CategoryName", _movieCategory);

        // Execute command
        con.Open();
        return cmd.ExecuteReader(CommandBehavior.CloseConnection);
    }

    public MoviesByCategory(string movieCategory)
    {
        _movieCategory = movieCategory;
        _conString = WebConfigurationManager.ConnectionStrings["Movies"].
        ➥ConnectionString;
    }
}
```

The page in Listing 16.37 contains an ObjectDataSource control that represents the MoviesByCategory component. The page includes a handler for the ObjectCreating event so that it can assign an initialized instance of the MoviesByCategory component to the ObjectDataSource control.

LISTING 16.37   ShowAdventureMovies.aspx

```
<%@ Page Language="C#" %>
<!DOCTYPE html PUBLIC "-//W3C//DTD XHTML 1.1//EN"
"http://www.w3.org/TR/xhtml11/DTD/xhtml11.dtd">
<script runat="server">

    protected void srcMovies_ObjectCreating(object sender,
    ➥ObjectDataSourceEventArgs e)
    {
        MoviesByCategory movies = new MoviesByCategory("Adventure");
        e.ObjectInstance = movies;
    }
```

16

LISTING 16.37   Continued

```
</script>
<html xmlns="http://www.w3.org/1999/xhtml" >
<head id="Head1" runat="server">
    <title>Adventure Movies</title>
</head>
<body>
    <form id="form1" runat="server">
    <div>

    <h1>Adventure Movies</h1>

    <asp:GridView
        id="grdMovies"
        DataSourceID="srcMovies"
        Runat="server" />

    <asp:ObjectDataSource
        id="srcMovies"
        TypeName="MoviesByCategory"
        SelectMethod="GetMovies"
        OnObjectCreating="srcMovies_ObjectCreating"
        Runat="server" />

    </div>
    </form>
</body>
</html>
```

Notice that even though the MoviesByCategory component is initialized in the
ObjectCreating event handler, you still must assign the name of the component to the
ObjectDataSource control's TypeName property. The ObjectDataSource control needs to
know what type of object it is representing when it calls its methods.

> **NOTE**
>
> The ObjectCreating event is not raised when a shared method is called.

Concurrency and the `ObjectDataSource` Control

Imagine that two users open the same page for editing the records in the movies database table at the same time. By default, if the first user submits changes before the second user, then the first user's changes are overwritten. In other words, the last user to submit changes wins.

This default behavior of the `ObjectDataSource` control can be problematic in an environment in which a lot of users are working with the same set of data. You can modify this default behavior by modifying the `ObjectDataSource` control's `ConflictDetection` property. This property accepts the following two values:

- ▶ **`CompareAllValues`**—Causes the `ObjectDataSource` control to track both the original and new values of its parameters.

- ▶ **`OverwriteChanges`**—Causes the `ObjectDataSource` to overwrite the original values of its parameters with new values (the default value).

When you set the `ConflictDetection` property to the value `CompareAllValues`, you should add an `OldValuesParameterFormatString` property to the `ObjectDataSource` control. You use this property to indicate how the original values the database columns should be named.

The page in Listing 16.38 contains a `GridView` and `ObjectDataSource` control, which you can use to edit the movies in the Movies database table. The `ObjectDataSource` control includes a `ConflictDetection` property with the value `CompareAllValues` and an `OldValuesParameterFormatString` property with the value `original_{0}`.

LISTING 16.38 ShowConflictDetection.aspx

```
<%@ Page Language="C#" %>
<!DOCTYPE html PUBLIC "-//W3C//DTD XHTML 1.1//EN"
"http://www.w3.org/TR/xhtml11/DTD/xhtml11.dtd">
<script runat="server">

    protected void srcMovies_Updated(object sender,
    ➡ObjectDataSourceStatusEventArgs e)
    {
        if (e.Exception != null)
        {
            e.ExceptionHandled = true;
            lblError.Text = "Could not update record";
        }
    }
</script>
<html xmlns="http://www.w3.org/1999/xhtml" >
<head id="Head1" runat="server">
    <style type="text/css">
```

16

LISTING 16.38   Continued

```
        .error
        {
            color:red;
            font:bold 16px Arial,Sans-Serif;
        }
        a
        {
            color:blue;
        }
    </style>
    <title>Show Conflict Detection</title>
</head>
<body>
    <form id="form1" runat="server">
    <div>

    <asp:Label
        id="lblError"
        EnableViewState="false"
        CssClass="error"
        Runat="server" />

    <asp:GridView
        id="grdMovies"
        DataSourceID="srcMovies"
        DataKeyNames="Id"
        AutoGenerateEditButton="true"
        Runat="server" />

    <asp:ObjectDataSource
        id="srcMovies"
        ConflictDetection="CompareAllValues"
        OldValuesParameterFormatString="original_{0}"
        TypeName="ConflictedMovies"
        SelectMethod="GetMovies"
        UpdateMethod="UpdateMovie"
        OnUpdated="srcMovies_Updated"
        Runat="server" />

    </div>
    </form>
</body>
</html>
```

The `ObjectDataSource` control in Listing 16.38 is bound to the component in Listing 16.39.

LISTING 16.39 `ConflictedMovies.cs`

```
using System;
using System.Data;
using System.Data.SqlClient;
using System.Web.Configuration;

public class ConflictedMovies
{
    private static readonly string _conString;

    public static SqlDataReader GetMovies()
    {
        // Initialize connection
        SqlConnection con = new SqlConnection(_conString);

        // Initialize command
        SqlCommand cmd = new SqlCommand();
        cmd.Connection = con;
        cmd.CommandText = "SELECT Id,Title,Director FROM Movies";

        // Execute command
        con.Open();
        return cmd.ExecuteReader(CommandBehavior.CloseConnection);
    }

    public static void UpdateMovie(string title, string director, string
    ➥original_title, string original_director, int original_id)
    {
        // Initialize connection
        SqlConnection con = new SqlConnection(_conString);

        // Initialize command
        SqlCommand cmd = new SqlCommand();
        cmd.Connection = con;
        cmd.CommandText = "UPDATE Movies SET Title=@Title,Director=@Director"
            + " WHERE Id=@original_Id AND Title=@original_Title AND
            ➥Director=@original_Director";

        // Create parameters
        cmd.Parameters.AddWithValue("@Title", title);
        cmd.Parameters.AddWithValue("@Director", director);
```

16

LISTING 16.39   Continued

```
        cmd.Parameters.AddWithValue("@original_Id", original_id);
        cmd.Parameters.AddWithValue("@original_Title", original_title);
        cmd.Parameters.AddWithValue("@original_Director", original_director);

        using (con)
        {
            con.Open();
            int rowsAffected = cmd.ExecuteNonQuery();
            if (rowsAffected == 0)
                throw new Exception("Could not update movie record");
        }
    }

    static ConflictedMovies()
    {
        _conString = WebConfigurationManager.ConnectionStrings["Movies"].
        ➥ConnectionString;
    }
}
```

The component in Listing 16.39 includes an UpdateMovie() method. Notice that this method accepts five parameters: the original_title, title, original_director, director, and original_id parameters.

The UpdateMovie() method raises an exception when the original parameter values don't match the current values in the Movies database table. Notice that the command executed by the Command object looks like this:

```
UPDATE Movies SET Title=@Title, Director=@Director
WHERE Id=@original_id AND Title=@original_Title AND Director=@original_Director
```

This statement updates a row in the database only when the current values from the row match the original values selected from the row. If the original and current values don't match, no records are affected and the UpdateMovie() method raises an exception.

Extending the ObjectDataSource Control

In this final section, we examine two methods of extending the ObjectDataSource control. You learn how to create a custom data source control by deriving a new control from the ObjectDataSource control. You also learn how to create custom parameters that can be used with the ObjectDataSource (and other DataSource controls).

Creating a Custom `ObjectDataSource` Control

If you discover that you are declaring an `ObjectDataSource` control with the same properties on multiple pages, then it makes sense to derive a new control from the `ObjectDataSource` control that has these properties by default. That way, you can simply declare the derived control in a page.

For example, if you are displaying a list of movies in multiple pages in your website, then it would make sense to create a specialized `MovieDataSource` control.

The control in Listing 16.40, named the `MovieDataSource` control, derives from the base `ObjectDataSource` control class. The `MovieDataSource` control represents the `MoviesComponent`, which is also contained in Listing 16.40.

LISTING 16.40   MovieDataSource.cs

```
using System;
using System.Data;
using System.Data.SqlClient;
using System.Web.Configuration;
using System.Web.UI.WebControls;

namespace AspNetUnleashed.Samples
{
    public class MovieDataSource : ObjectDataSource
    {
        public MovieDataSource()
        {
            this.TypeName = "AspNetUnleashed.Samples.MoviesComponent";
            this.SelectMethod = "GetMovies";
        }
    }

    public class MoviesComponent
    {
        private readonly string _conString;

        public SqlDataReader GetMovies()
        {
            // Initialize connection
            SqlConnection con = new SqlConnection(_conString);

            // Initialize command
            SqlCommand cmd = new SqlCommand();
            cmd.Connection = con;
            cmd.CommandText = "SELECT Title,Director,DateReleased FROM Movies";
```

16

LISTING 16.40   Continued

```
        // Execute command
        con.Open();
        return cmd.ExecuteReader(CommandBehavior.CloseConnection);
    }

    public MoviesComponent()
    {
        _conString = WebConfigurationManager.ConnectionStrings["Movies"].
        ➥ConnectionString;
    }
  }
}
```

The MovieDataSource control initializes the base ObjectDataSource control's TypeName and
SelectMethod properties in its constructor. The TypeName is assigned the fully qualified
name of the MoviesComponent.

The page in Listing 16.41 illustrates how you can use the MovieDataSource control in a
page (see Figure 16.11).

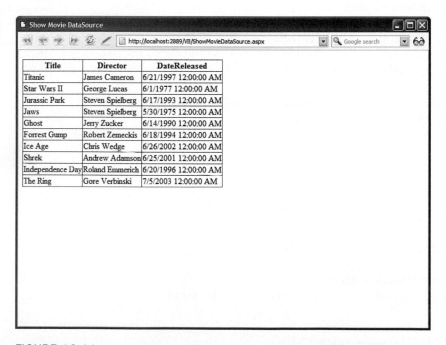

FIGURE 16.11   Using the MovieDataSource control to display movies.

LISTING 16.41   ShowMovieDataSource.aspx

```
<%@ Page Language="C#" %>
<%@ Register TagPrefix="custom" Namespace="AspNetUnleashed.Samples" %>
<!DOCTYPE html PUBLIC "-//W3C//DTD XHTML 1.1//EN"
    "http://www.w3.org/TR/xhtml11/DTD/xhtml11.dtd">
<html xmlns="http://www.w3.org/1999/xhtml" >
<head id="Head1" runat="server">
    <title>Show Movie DataSource</title>
</head>
<body>
    <form id="form1" runat="server">
    <div>

    <asp:GridView
        id="grdMovies"
        DataSourceID="srcMovies"
        Runat="server" />

    <custom:MovieDataSource
        id="srcMovies"
        Runat="server" />

    </div>
    </form>
</body>
</html>
```

Notice that the custom control must be registered with a `<%@ Register %>` directive at the top of Listing 16.41. After you register the control, you can simply declare the `MovieDataSource` control in the page to represent the contents of the Movies database table.

> **NOTE**
>
> As an alternative to registering the `MovieDataSource` control in a page, you can register the control for an entire application in the web configuration file within the `<pages>` element.

Creating Custom Parameter Objects

The standard DataSource Parameter objects included in the ASP.NET Framework enable you to represent objects such as query string values, items from Session state, and values of control properties. If none of the standard Parameter objects satisfy your requirements, you always have the option of creating a custom Parameter object.

16

You create a custom Parameter object by deriving a new class from the base `Parameter` class. In this section, we create two custom parameters. The first is a `UsernameParameter` that automatically represents the current username. Next is a `PagePropertyParameter` that represents the current value of a property contained in the page.

Creating a Username Parameter   The `UsernameParameter` class is contained in Listing 16.42. Notice that the class in Listing 16.42 derives from the Parameter class and overrides the `Evaluate()` method of the base class. The `Evaluate()` method determines what the parameter represents.

LISTING 16.42   UsernameParameter.cs

```
using System;
using System.Web;
using System.Web.UI;
using System.Web.UI.WebControls;

namespace MyControls
{
    public class UsernameParameter : Parameter
    {
        protected override object Evaluate(HttpContext context, Control control)
        {
            if (context != null)
                return context.User.Identity.Name;
            else
                return null;
        }
    }
}
```

The `UsernameParameter` returns the current username. The parameter retrieves this information from the current `HttpContext` passed to the `Evaluate()` method. The `UsernameParameter` is used in the page in Listing 16.43.

LISTING 16.43   ShowUsernameParameter.aspx

```
<%@ Page Language="C#" %>
<%@ Register TagPrefix="custom" Namespace="MyControls" %>
<!DOCTYPE html PUBLIC "-//W3C//DTD XHTML 1.1//EN"
    "http://www.w3.org/TR/xhtml11/DTD/xhtml11.dtd">
<html xmlns="http://www.w3.org/1999/xhtml" >
<head id="Head1" runat="server">
    <style type="text/css">
        .guestbook td,.guestbook th
```

```
                {
                    padding:5px;
                    font:14px Arial,Sans-Serif;
                }
        </style>
        <title>Show Username Parameter</title>
</head>
<body>
        <form id="form1" runat="server">
        <div>
        <asp:FormView
            id="frmGuestbook"
            DataSourceID="srcGuestbook"
            DefaultMode="Insert"
            Runat="server">
            <InsertItemTemplate>
            <asp:Label
                ID="lblComment"
                Text="Comment:"
                AssociatedControlID="txtComment"
                Runat="server" />
            <br />
            <asp:TextBox
                id="txtComment"
                Text='<%# Bind("comment") %>'
                TextMode="MultiLine"
                Columns="50"
                Rows="4"
                Runat="server" />
            <br />
            <asp:Button
                id="btnInsert"
                Text="Add Entry"
                CommandName="Insert"
                Runat="server" />
            </InsertItemTemplate>
        </asp:FormView>

        <hr />

        <asp:GridView
            id="grdGuestbook"
            DataSourceID="srcGuestbook"
            CssClass="guestbook"
            Runat="server" />
```

16

LISTING 16.43   Continued

```
<asp:ObjectDataSource
    id="srcGuestbook"
    TypeName="GuestbookComponent"
    SelectMethod="GetEntries"
    InsertMethod="AddEntry"
    Runat="server">
    <InsertParameters>
        <custom:UsernameParameter name="username" />
    </InsertParameters>
</asp:ObjectDataSource>

</div>
</form>
</body>
</html>
```

The UsernameParameter is declared in the ObjectDataSource control's InsertParameters collection. When you add a new entry to the guestbook, your username is added automatically (see Figure 16.12).

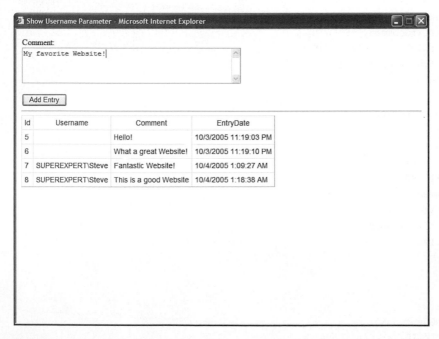

FIGURE 16.12   Inserting records with the UsernameParameter.

Creating a Page Property Parameter   The PagePropertyParameter enables you to represent an arbitrary property of the current page. The property being represented can return whatever type of value you want. The code for the PagePropertyParameter is contained in Listing 16.44.

LISTING 16.44   PagePropertyParameter.cs

```
using System;
using System.Web;
using System.Web.UI;
using System.Web.UI.WebControls;

namespace MyControls
{
    public class PagePropertyParameter : Parameter
    {
        private string _propertyName;

        protected override object Evaluate(HttpContext context, Control control)
        {
            return DataBinder.Eval(control.Page, PropertyName);
        }

        public string PropertyName
        {
            get { return _propertyName; }
            set { _propertyName = value; }
        }


    }
}
```

The component in Listing 16.44 overrides the Evaluate method of the base Parameter class. The DataBinder.Eval() method is used to return the value of a property of the current page.

The page in Listing 16.45 uses the PagePropertyParameter to represent a property of the page named CurrentUsername. This property returns the current username.

LISTING 16.45   ShowPagePropertyParameter.aspx

```
<%@ Page Language="C#" %>
<%@ Register TagPrefix="custom" Namespace="MyControls" %>
<!DOCTYPE html PUBLIC "-//W3C//DTD XHTML 1.1//EN"
  "http://www.w3.org/TR/xhtml11/DTD/xhtml11.dtd">
<script runat="server">
```

LISTING 16.45   Continued

```
    Public ReadOnly Property CurrentUsername() As String
        Get
            Return User.Identity.Name
        End Get
    End Property

</script>
<html xmlns="http://www.w3.org/1999/xhtml">
<head id="Head1" runat="server">
    <style type="text/css">
        .guestbook td,.guestbook th
        {
            padding:5px;
            font:14px Arial,Sans-Serif;
        }
    </style>
    <title>Show Page Property Parameter</title>
</head>
<body>
    <form id="form1" runat="server">
    <div>

    <asp:FormView
        id="frmGuestbook"
        DataSourceID="srcGuestbook"
        DefaultMode="Insert"
        Runat="server">
        <InsertItemTemplate>
        <asp:Label
            ID="lblComment"
            Text="Comment:"
            AssociatedControlID="txtComment"
            Runat="server" />
        <br />
        <asp:TextBox
            id="txtComment"
            Text='<%# Bind("comment") %>'
            TextMode="MultiLine"
            Columns="50"
            Rows="4"
            Runat="server" />
        <br />
        <asp:Button
            id="btnInsert"
```

```
        Text="Add Entry"
        CommandName="Insert"
        Runat="server" />
    </InsertItemTemplate>
</asp:FormView>

<hr />

<asp:GridView
    id="grdGuestbook"
    DataSourceID="srcGuestbook"
    CssClass="guestbook"
    Runat="server" />

<asp:ObjectDataSource
    id="srcGuestbook"
    TypeName="GuestbookComponent"
    SelectMethod="GetEntries"
    InsertMethod="AddEntry"
    Runat="server">
    <InsertParameters>
    <custom:PagePropertyParameter
        Name="Username"
        PropertyName="CurrentUsername" />
    </InsertParameters>
</asp:ObjectDataSource>

</div>
</form>
</body>
</html>
```

In Listing 16.45, the PagePropertyParameter is used to represent the current username. Because the PagePropertyParameter can represent any page property, the parameter could represent any type of value.

Summary

In this chapter, you learned how to use the ObjectDataSource control to represent different types of objects. In the first section, you were provided with sample code that demonstrated how you can use the ObjectDataSource control to represent a collection, a DataReader, and a DataSet, a LINQ to SQL query, and a web service.

We also discussed how you can use the `ObjectDataSource` control to page, sort, and filter data. You learned how to implement both user interface paging and data source paging, which enables you to efficiently work with very large sets of records.

Next, we examined how you can handle `ObjectDataSource` control events. You learned how to add and modify the parameters represented by the `ObjectDataSource` control. You also learned how to gracefully handle errors raised when executing an `ObjectDataSource` control method.

Finally, we discussed two methods of extending the `ObjectDataSource` control. You learned how to derive a new control from the base `ObjectDataSource` control to represent specialized data sources such as a Product data source. We also discussed how you can create custom `Parameter` objects that can be used with the `ObjectDataSource` control.

CHAPTER 17

Building Data Access Components with ADO.NET

In the previous chapter, you learned how to use the ObjectDataSource control to bind data controls—such as the GridView or DetailsView controls—to a data access component. In this chapter, we shift focus from the ObjectDataSource control to the topic of building data access components.

This chapter provides you with an overview of ADO.NET, which is the main set of classes included in the .NET Framework for working with database data. For example, under the covers, the SqlDataSource control uses ADO.NET classes to retrieve data from a SQL Server database.

The classes in the ADO.NET framework support two models of data access: a connected and disconnected model. In the first part of this chapter, you learn how to take advantage of the connected model of data access. You learn how to use the ADO.NET Connection, Command, and DataReader classes to retrieve and modify database data.

In the next part of this chapter, you learn how to take advantage of the disconnected model of data access represented by the ADO.NET DataAdapter, DataTable, DataView, and DataSet classes. You can use these classes to build an in-memory representation of database data.

Finally, at the end of this chapter, we explore two advanced topics. You learn how to take advantage of two important new features included in ADO.NET 2.0. First, you learn how to improve the performance of your database access code by executing asynchronous database commands. You learn how to build asynchronous ASP.NET pages that execute asynchronous ADO.NET commands.

You also learn how to build Microsoft SQL Server database objects, such as stored procedures and user-defined types, by using the .NET Framework. For example, you learn how to write a Microsoft SQL Server stored procedure, using the C# programming language.

> **NOTE**
>
> If you don't want to get your hands dirty touching any actual SQL or ADO.NET code, then skip this chapter and start reading the next chapter, "Data Access with LINQ to SQL." LINQ to SQL enables you to access the database without writing any ADO.NET or SQL code.

Connected Data Access

The ADO.NET Framework encompasses a huge number of classes. However, at its heart, it really consists of the following three classes:

- ▶ **Connection**—Enables you to represent a connection to a data source.

- ▶ **Command**—Enables you to execute a command against a data source.

- ▶ **DataReader**—Enables you to represent data retrieved from a data source.

Most of the other classes in the ADO.NET Framework are built from these three classes. These three classes provide you with the fundamental methods of working with database data. They enable you to connect to a database, execute commands against a database, and represent the data returned from a database.

Now that you understand the importance of these three classes, it's safe to tell you that they don't really exist. ADO.NET uses the Provider model. You use different sets of ADO.NET classes for communicating with different data sources.

For example, there is no such thing as the Connection class. Instead, there is the SqlConnection class, the OracleConnection class, the OleDbConnection class, and the ODBCConnection class. You use different Connection classes to connect to different data sources.

The different implementations of the Connection, Command, and DataReader classes are grouped into the following namespaces:

- ▶ **System.Data.SqlClient**—Contains ADO.NET classes for connecting to Microsoft SQL Server version 7.0 or higher.

- ▶ **System.Data.OleDb**—Contains ADO.NET classes for connecting to a data source with an OLEDB provider.

- ▶ **System.Data.Odbc**—Contains ADO.NET classes for connecting to a data source with an ODBC driver.

- ▶ **System.Data.OracleClient**—Contains ADO.NET classes for connecting to an Oracle database (requires Oracle 8i Release 3/8.1.7 Client or later).

▶ **System.Data.SqlServerCe**—Contains ADO.NET classes for connecting to SQL Server Mobile.

If you are connecting to Microsoft SQL Server 7.0 or higher, you should always use the classes from the SqlClient namespace. These classes provide the best performance because they connect directly to SQL Server at the level of the Tabular Data Stream (the low-level protocol that Microsoft SQL Server uses to communicate with applications).

Of course, there are other databases in the world than Microsoft SQL Server. If you are communicating with an Oracle database, you should use the classes from the OracleClient namespace. If you are communicating with another type of database, you need to use the classes from either the OleDb or Odbc namespaces. Just about every database ever created has either an OLEDB provider or an ODBC driver.

Because ADO.NET follows the Provider model, all implementations of the Connection, Command, and DataReader classes inherit from a set of base classes. Here is a list of these base classes:

▶ **DbConnection**—The base class for all Connection classes.

▶ **DbCommand**—The base class for all Command classes.

▶ **DbDataReader**—The base class for all DataReader classes.

These base classes are contained in the System.Data.Common namespace.

All the sample code in this chapter assumes that you are working with Microsoft SQL Server. Therefore, all the sample code uses the classes from the SqlClient namespace. However, because ADO.NET uses the Provider model, the methods that you would use to work with another database are very similar to the methods described in this chapter.

NOTE

Before you can use the classes from the SqlClient namespaces in your components and pages, you need to import the System.Data.SqlClient namespace.

Before we examine the Connection, Command, and DataReader classes in detail, let's look at how you can build a simple data access component with these classes. The component in Listing 17.1, named Movie1, includes a method named GetAll() that returns every record from the Movies database table.

LISTING 17.1 App_Code\Movie1.cs

```
using System;
using System.Data;
using System.Data.SqlClient;
using System.Web.Configuration;
using System.Collections.Generic;
```

17

LISTING 17.1   Continued

```
public class Movie1
{
    private static readonly string _connectionString;

    private string _title;
    private string _director;

    public string Title
    {
        get { return _title; }
        set { _title = value; }
    }

    public string Director
    {
        get { return _director; }
        set { _director = value; }
    }

    public List<Movie1> GetAll()
    {
        List<Movie1> results = new List<Movie1>();
        SqlConnection con = new SqlConnection(_connectionString);
        SqlCommand cmd = new SqlCommand("SELECT Title,Director FROM Movies", con);
        using (con)
        {
            con.Open();
            SqlDataReader reader = cmd.ExecuteReader();
            while (reader.Read())
            {
                Movie1 newMovie = new Movie1();
                newMovie.Title = (string)reader["Title"];
                newMovie.Director = (string)reader["Director"];
                results.Add(newMovie);
            }
        }
        return results;
    }

    static Movie1()
    {
        _connectionString = WebConfigurationManager.ConnectionStrings["Movies"].
        ➥ConnectionString;
    }
}
```

In Listing 17.1, a `SqlConnection` object is used to represent a connection to a Microsoft SQL Server database. A `SqlCommand` object is used to represent a SQL `SELECT` command. The results of executing the command are represented with a `SqlDataReader`.

Each row returned by the `SELECT` command is retrieved by a call to the `SqlDataReader.Read()` method from within a `While` loop. When the last row is retrieved from the `SELECT` command, the `SqlDataReader.Read()` method returns `False` and the `While` loop ends.

Each row retrieved from the database is added to a List collection. An instance of the `Movie1` class is used to represent each record.

The page in Listing 17.2 uses a `GridView` and `ObjectDataSource` control to display the records returned by the `Movie1` data access component (see Figure 17.1).

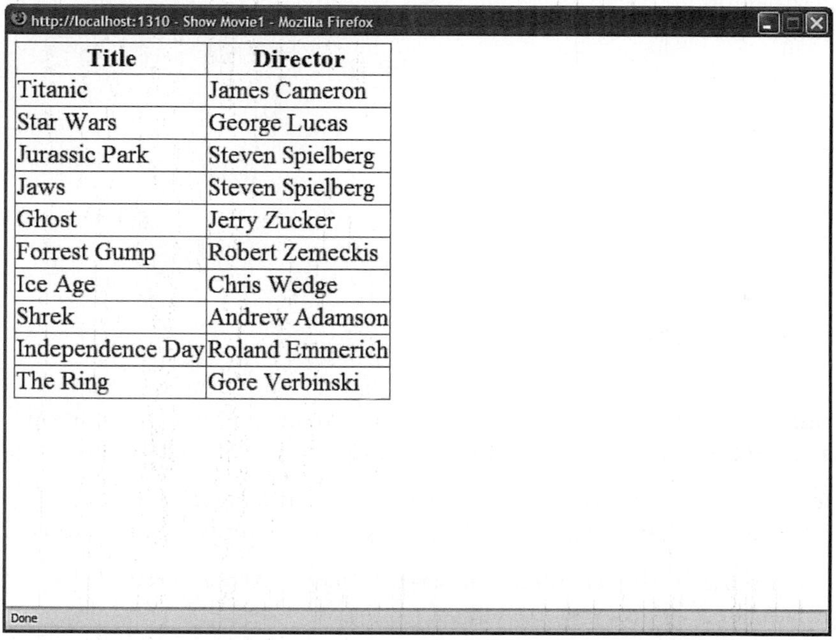
http://localhost:1310 - Show Movie1 - Mozilla Firefox
Title
Director
Titanic
James Cameron
Star Wars
George Lucas
Jurassic Park
Steven Spielberg
Jaws
Steven Spielberg
Ghost
Jerry Zucker
Forrest Gump
Robert Zemeckis
Ice Age
Chris Wedge
Shrek
Andrew Adamson
Independence Day
Roland Emmerich
The Ring
Gore Verbinski
Done

FIGURE 17.1 Displaying movie records.

LISTING 17.2 `ShowMovie1.aspx`

```
<%@ Page Language="C#" %>
<!DOCTYPE html PUBLIC "-//W3C//DTD XHTML 1.0 Transitional//EN"
"http://www.w3.org/TR/xhtml1/DTD/xhtml1-transitional.dtd">
<html xmlns="http://www.w3.org/1999/xhtml" >
<head id="Head1" runat="server">
    <title>Show Movie1</title>
</head>
```

LISTING 17.2   Continued

```
<body>
    <form id="form1" runat="server">
    <div>

    <asp:GridView
        id="grdMovies"
        DataSourceID="srcMovies"
        Runat="server" />

    <asp:ObjectDataSource
        id="srcMovies"
        TypeName="Movie1"
        SelectMethod="GetAll"
        Runat="server" />

    </div>
    </form>
</body>
</html>
```

Using the Connection Object

The Connection object represents a connection to a data source. When you instantiate a Connection, you pass a connection string to the constructor, which contains information about the location and security credentials required for connecting to the data source.

For example, the following statement creates a SqlConnection that represents a connection to a Microsoft SQL Server database named Pubs that is located on the local machine:

```
SqlConnection con = new SqlConnection("Data Source=localhost;Integrated
Security=True;Initial Catalog=Pubs");
```

For legacy reasons, there are a number of ways to write a connection string that does exactly the same thing. For example, the keywords Data Source, Server, Address, Addr, and Network Address are all synonyms. You can use any of these keywords to specify the location of the database server.

> **NOTE**
>
> You can use the SqlConnectionStringBuilder class to convert any connection string into canonical syntax. For example, this class replaces the keyword Server with the keyword Data Source in a connection string.

Before you execute any commands against the data source, you first must open the connection. After you finish executing commands, you should close the connection as quickly as possible.

A database connection is a valuable resource. Strive to open database connections as late as possible and close database connections as early as possible. Furthermore, always include error handling code to make sure that a database connection gets closed even when there is an exception.

For example, you can take advantage of the Using statement to force a connection to close even when an exception is raised, like this:

```
SqlConnection con = new SqlConnection("Data Source=localhost;Integrated
Security=True;Initial Catalog=Pubs");
SqlCommand cmd = new SqlCommand("INSERT Titles (Title) VALUES ('Some Title')", con);
using (con)
{
  con.Open();
  cmd.ExecuteNonQuery();
}
```

The using statement forces the connection to close, regardless of whether there is an error when a command is executed against the database. The using statement also disposes of the Connection object. (If you need to reuse the Connection, then you need to reinitialize it.)

Alternatively, you can use a try...catch statement to force a connection to close like this:

```
SqlConnection con = new SqlConnection("Data Source=localhost;Integrated
Security=True;Initial Catalog=Pubs");
SqlCommand cmd = new SqlCommand("INSERT Titles (Title) VALUES ('Some Title')", con);
try
{
  con.Open();
  cmd.ExecuteNonQuery();
}
finally
{
  con.Close();
}
```

The finally clause in this try...catch statement forces the database connection to close both when there are no errors and when there are errors.

Retrieving Provider Statistics   When you use the SqlConnection object, you can retrieve statistics about the database commands executed with the connection. For example, you can retrieve statistics on total execution time.

The GetAll() method exposed by the component in Listing 17.3 includes a parameter named executionTime. After the database command executes, the value of executionTime is retrieved from the Connection statistics.

LISTING 17.3   App_Code\Movie2.cs

```
using System;
using System.Data;
using System.Data.SqlClient;
using System.Web.Configuration;
using System.Collections;
using System.Collections.Generic;

public class Movie2
{
    private static readonly string _connectionString;

    private string _title;
    private string _director;

    public string Title
    {
        get { return _title; }
        set { _title = value; }
    }

    public string Director
    {
        get { return _director; }
        set { _director = value; }
    }

    public List<Movie2> GetAll(out long executionTime)
    {
        List<Movie2> results = new List<Movie2>();
        SqlConnection con = new SqlConnection(_connectionString);
        SqlCommand cmd = new SqlCommand("WAITFOR DELAY '0:0:03';SELECT Title,
        ➥Director FROM Movies", con);
        con.StatisticsEnabled = true;
        using (con)
        {
            con.Open();
            SqlDataReader reader = cmd.ExecuteReader();
            while (reader.Read())
            {
```

```
                Movie2 newMovie = new Movie2();
                newMovie.Title = (string)reader["Title"];
                newMovie.Director = (string)reader["Director"];
                results.Add(newMovie);
            }
        }
        IDictionary stats = con.RetrieveStatistics();
        executionTime = (long)stats["ExecutionTime"];
        return results;
    }

    static Movie2()
    {
        _connectionString = WebConfigurationManager.ConnectionStrings["Movies"].
        ➥ConnectionString;
    }
}
```

In Listing 17.3, the SqlConnection.StatisticsEnabled property is set to the value True.
You must enable statistics before you can gather statistics. After the command executes, a
dictionary of statistics is retrieved with the SqlConnection.RetrieveStatistics()
method. Finally, you retrieve the executionTime by looking up the ExecutionTime key in
the dictionary.

NOTE

In Listing 17.3, the SQL WAITFOR statement is used to pause the execution of
the SELECT command for 3 seconds so that a more interesting execution time is
retrieved from the ExecutionTime statistic. Because the SELECT command is such
a simple command, if you don't add a delay, you often receive an execution time of 0
milliseconds.

17

The page in Listing 17.4 illustrates how you can use this component to display both the
results of a database query and the database query execution time (see Figure 17.2).

LISTING 17.4   ShowMovie2.aspx

```
<%@ Page Language="C#" %>
<!DOCTYPE html PUBLIC "-//W3C//DTD XHTML 1.0 Transitional//EN"
"http://www.w3.org/TR/xhtml1/DTD/xhtml1-transitional.dtd">

<script runat="server">
```

LISTING 17.4 Continued

```
    protected void srcMovies_Selected(object sender,
    ➥ObjectDataSourceStatusEventArgs e)
    {
        lblExecutionTime.Text = e.OutputParameters["executionTime"].ToString();
    }
</script>

<html xmlns="http://www.w3.org/1999/xhtml" >
<head id="Head1" runat="server">
    <title>Show Movie2</title>
</head>
<body>
    <form id="form1" runat="server">
    <div>

    <asp:GridView
        id="grdMovies"
        DataSourceID="srcMovies"
        Runat="server" />

    <asp:ObjectDataSource
        id="srcMovies"
        TypeName="Movie2"
        SelectMethod="GetAll"
        Runat="server" OnSelected="srcMovies_Selected">
        <SelectParameters>
        <asp:Parameter Name="executionTime" Type="Int64" Direction="Output" />
        </SelectParameters>
    </asp:ObjectDataSource>

    <br />

    Execution time was
    <asp:Label
        id="lblExecutionTime"
        Runat="server" />
    milliseconds

    </div>
    </form>
</body>
</html>
```

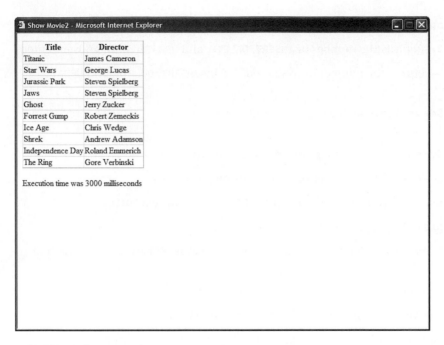

FIGURE 17.2   Displaying execution time statistics.

The `SqlConnection` object supports the following properties and methods related to gathering statistics:

▶ **StatisticsEnabled**—Enables you to turn on statistics gathering.

▶ **RetrieveStatistics()**—Enables you to retrieve statistics represented with an `IDictionary` collection.

▶ **ResetStatistics()**—Resets all statistics to 0.

You can call the `RetrieveStatistics()` method multiple times on the same `SqlConnection`. Each time you call the method, you get another snapshot of the `Connection` statistics.

Here's a list of the statistics that you can gather:

▶ **BuffersReceived**—Returns the number of TDS packets received.

▶ **BuffersSent**—Returns the number of TDS packets sent.

▶ **BytesReceived**—Returns the number of bytes received.

▶ **BytesSent**—Returns the number of bytes sent.

▶ **ConnectionTime**—Returns the total amount of time that the connection has been opened.

▶ **CursorsOpen**—Returns the number of cursors opened.

▶ **ExecutionTime**—Returns the connection execution time in milliseconds.

▶ **IduCount**—Returns the number of INSERT, DELETE, and UPDATE commands executed.

▶ **IduRows**—Returns the number of rows modified by INSERT, DELETE, and UPDATE commands.

▶ **NetworkServerTime**—Returns the amount of time spent waiting for a reply from the database server.

▶ **PreparedExecs**—Returns the number of prepared commands executed.

▶ **Prepares**—Returns the number of statements prepared.

▶ **SelectCount**—Returns the number of SELECT commands executed.

▶ **SelectRows**—Returns the number of rows selected.

▶ **ServerRoundtrips**—Returns the number of commands sent to the database that received a reply.

▶ **SumResultSets**—Returns the number of resultsets retrieved.

▶ **Transactions**—Returns the number of user transactions created.

▶ **UnpreparedExecs**—Returns the number of unprepared commands executed.

The page in Listing 17.5 displays the values of all these statistics in a GridView control (see Figure 17.3).

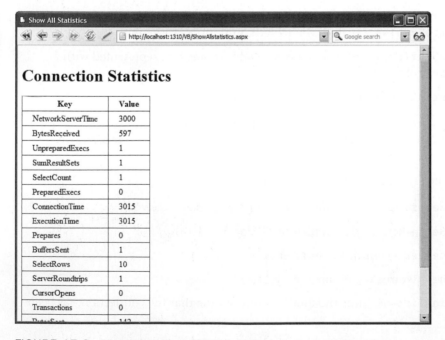

FIGURE 17.3   Displaying all provider statistics.

LISTING 17.5   ShowAllStatistics.aspx

```csharp
<%@ Page Language="C#" %>
<%@ Import Namespace="System.Data.SqlClient" %>
<%@ Import Namespace="System.Web.Configuration" %>
<!DOCTYPE html PUBLIC "-//W3C//DTD XHTML 1.0 Transitional//EN"
"http://www.w3.org/TR/xhtml1/DTD/xhtml1-transitional.dtd">
<script runat="server">

    void Page_Load()
    {
        string connectionString = WebConfigurationManager.
        ➥ConnectionStrings["Movies"].ConnectionString;
        SqlConnection con = new SqlConnection(connectionString);
        SqlCommand cmd = new SqlCommand("WAITFOR DELAY '0:0:03';SELECT Title,
        ➥Director FROM Movies", con);
        con.StatisticsEnabled = true;
        using (con)
        {
            con.Open();
            SqlDataReader reader = cmd.ExecuteReader();
        }
        grdStats.DataSource = con.RetrieveStatistics();
        grdStats.DataBind();
    }

</script>
<html xmlns="http://www.w3.org/1999/xhtml" >
<head id="Head1" runat="server">
    <style type="text/css">
        td,th
        {
            padding:4px 20px;
        }
    </style>
    <title>Show All Statistics</title>
</head>
<body>
    <form id="form1" runat="server">
    <div>

    <h1>Connection Statistics</h1>

    <asp:GridView
        id="grdStats"
        AutoGenerateColumns="false"
```

LISTING 17.5   Continued

```
        Runat="server">
        <Columns>
        <asp:BoundField DataField="Key" HeaderText="Key" />
        <asp:BoundField DataField="Value" HeaderText="Value" />
        </Columns>
    </asp:GridView>

    </div>
    </form>
</body>
</html>
```

Improving Performance with Connection Pooling   Database connections are precious resources. If you want your ASP.NET application to scale to handle the demands of thousands of users, then you need to do everything in your power to prevent database connections from being wasted.

Opening a database connection is a slow operation. Rather than open a new database connection each time you need to connect to a database, you can create a pool of connections that can be reused for multiple database queries.

When connection pooling is enabled, closing a connection does not really close the connection to the database server. Instead, closing the connection releases the database connection back into the pool. That way, the next time a database query is performed, a new connection to the database does not need to be opened.

When you use the SqlConnection object, connection pooling is enabled by default. By default, the ADO.NET framework keeps a maximum of 100 connections open in a connection pool.

You need to be warned about two things in regard to connection pooling. First, when taking advantage of connection pooling, it is still very important to close your connections by calling the SqlConnection.Close() method. If you don't close a connection, the connection is not returned to the pool. It might take a very long time for an unclosed connection to be reclaimed by ADO.NET.

Second, different connection pools are created for different connection strings. In particular, a different connection pool is created for each unique combination of connection string, process, application domain, and Windows identity.

An exact character-by-character match is performed on the connection string. For this reason, you should always store your connection strings in the web configuration file. Don't hardcode connection strings inside your components. If there is a slight variation between two connection strings, then separate connection pools are created, which defeats the performance gains that you get from connection pooling.

The `SqlConnection` object supports two methods for clearing connection pools programmatically:

▶ **ClearAllPools**—Enables you to clear all database connections from all connection pools.

▶ **ClearPool**—Enables you to clear all database connections associated with a particular `SqlConnection` object.

These methods are useful when you are working with a cluster of database servers. For example, if you take a database server down, you can programmatically clear the connection pool to the database server that no longer exists.

You can control how connections are pooled by using the following attributes in a connection string:

▶ **Connection Timeout**—Enables you to specify the maximum lifetime of a connection in seconds. (The default value is 0, which indicates that connections are immortal.)

▶ **Connection Reset**—Enables you to reset connections automatically when retrieved from the connection pool (default value is `True`).

▶ **Enlist**—Enables you to enlist a connection in the current transaction context (default value is `True`).

▶ **Load Balance Timeout**—Same as `Connection Timeout`.

▶ **Max Pool Size**—Enables you to specify the maximum number of connections kept in the connection pool (default value is `100`).

▶ **Min Pool Size**—Enables you to specify the minimum number of connections kept in the connection pool (default value is `0`).

▶ **Pooling**—Enables you to turn on or off connection pooling (default value is `True`).

The page in Listing 17.6 displays a list of all the current user connections to a database in a `GridView` (see Figure 17.4). Notice that the connection string used when connecting to the database creates a minimum connection pool size of 10 connections. (You'll have to refresh the page at least once to see the 10 connections.)

LISTING 17.6 ShowUserConnections.aspx

```
<%@ Page Language="C#" %>
<%@ Import Namespace="System.Data.SqlClient" %>
<%@ Import Namespace="System.Web.Configuration" %>
<!DOCTYPE html PUBLIC "-//W3C//DTD XHTML 1.0 Transitional//EN"
"http://www.w3.org/TR/xhtml1/DTD/xhtml1-transitional.dtd">
<script runat="server">
```

17

LISTING 17.6 Continued

```
    void Page_Load()
    {
        string connectionString = @"Min Pool Size=10;Data Source=.\SQLExpress;
        ➥Integrated Security=True;AttachDbFileName=¦DataDirectory¦MyDatabase.mdf;
        ➥User Instance=True";
        SqlConnection con = new SqlConnection(connectionString);
        SqlCommand cmd = new SqlCommand("SELECT * FROM master..sysprocesses WHERE
        ➥hostname<>''", con);
        using (con)
        {
            con.Open();
            grdStats.DataSource = cmd.ExecuteReader();
            grdStats.DataBind();
        }
    }
</script>
<html xmlns="http://www.w3.org/1999/xhtml" >
<head id="Head1" runat="server">
    <style type="text/css">
        td,th
        {
            padding:2px;
        }
    </style>
    <title>Show User Connections</title>
</head>
<body>
    <form id="form1" runat="server">
    <div>

    <h1>User Connections</h1>

    <asp:GridView
        id="grdStats"
        Runat="server" />

    </div>
    </form>
</body>
</html>
```

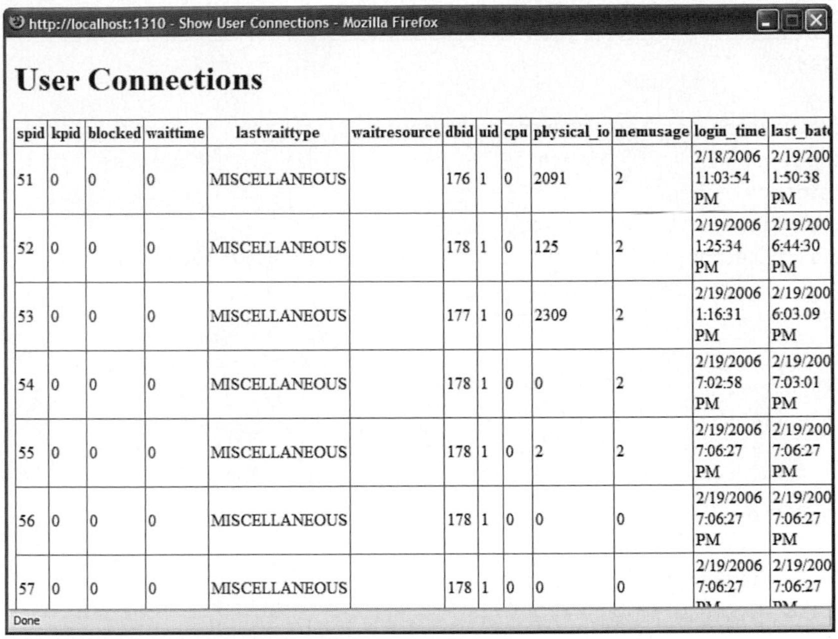

spid	kpid	blocked	waittime	lastwaittype	waitresource	dbid	uid	cpu	physical_io	memusage	login_time	last_bat
51	0	0	0	MISCELLANEOUS		176	1	0	2091	2	2/18/2006 11:03:54 PM	2/19/200 1:50:38 PM
52	0	0	0	MISCELLANEOUS		178	1	0	125	2	2/19/2006 1:25:34 PM	2/19/200 6:44:30 PM
53	0	0	0	MISCELLANEOUS		177	1	0	2309	2	2/19/2006 1:16:31 PM	2/19/200 6:03.09 PM
54	0	0	0	MISCELLANEOUS		178	1	0	0	2	2/19/2006 7:02:58 PM	2/19/200 7:03:01 PM
55	0	0	0	MISCELLANEOUS		178	1	0	2	2	2/19/2006 7:06:27 PM	2/19/200 7:06:27 PM
56	0	0	0	MISCELLANEOUS		178	1	0	0	0	2/19/2006 7:06:27 PM	2/19/200 7:06:27 PM
57	0	0	0	MISCELLANEOUS		178	1	0	0	0	2/19/2006 7:06:27	2/19/200 7:06:27

FIGURE 17.4 Displaying user database connections.

Using the `Command` Object

The `Command` object represents a command that can be executed against a data source. In this section, you learn how to use the `SqlCommand` object to execute different types of database commands against Microsoft SQL Server.

17

Executing a Command You can use the `SqlCommand.ExecuteNonQuery()` method to execute a SQL command that does not return a set of rows. You can use this method when executing `SQL UPDATE`, `DELETE`, and `INSERT` commands. You can also use this method when executing more specialized commands, such as a `CREATE TABLE` or `DROP DATABASE` command.

For example, the component in Listing 17.7 includes `Update()` and `Delete()` methods that update and delete movie records.

LISTING 17.7 `App_Code\Movie3.cs`

```
using System;
using System.Data;
using System.Data.SqlClient;
using System.Web.Configuration;
using System.Collections.Generic;
```

LISTING 17.7   Continued

```
public class Movie3
{
    private static readonly string _connectionString;

    private int _id;
    private string _title;
    private string _director;

    public int Id
    {
        get { return _id; }
        set { _id = value; }
    }

    public string Title
    {
        get { return _title; }
        set { _title = value; }
    }

    public string Director
    {
        get { return _director; }
        set { _director = value; }
    }

    public void Update(int id, string title, string director)
    {
        SqlConnection con = new SqlConnection(_connectionString);
        SqlCommand cmd = new SqlCommand("UPDATE MOVIES SET
        ➡Title=@Title,Director=@Director WHERE Id=@Id", con);
        cmd.Parameters.AddWithValue("@Title", title);
        cmd.Parameters.AddWithValue("@Director", director);
        cmd.Parameters.AddWithValue("@Id", id);
        using (con)
        {
            con.Open();
            cmd.ExecuteNonQuery();
        }
    }

    public void Delete(int id)
    {
```

```
            SqlConnection con = new SqlConnection(_connectionString);
            SqlCommand cmd = new SqlCommand("DELETE MOVIES WHERE Id=@Id", con);
            cmd.Parameters.AddWithValue("@Id", id);
            using (con)
            {
                con.Open();
                cmd.ExecuteNonQuery();
            }
        }

        public List<Movie3> GetAll()
        {
            List<Movie3> results = new List<Movie3>();
            SqlConnection con = new SqlConnection(_connectionString);
            SqlCommand cmd = new SqlCommand("SELECT Id,Title,Director FROM Movies", con);
            using (con)
            {
                con.Open();
                SqlDataReader reader = cmd.ExecuteReader();
                while (reader.Read())
                {
                    Movie3 newMovie = new Movie3();
                    newMovie.Id = (int)reader["Id"];
                    newMovie.Title = (string)reader["Title"];
                    newMovie.Director = (string)reader["Director"];
                    results.Add(newMovie);
                }
            }
            return results;
        }

        static Movie3()
        {
            _connectionString = WebConfigurationManager.ConnectionStrings["Movies"].
            ➥ConnectionString;
        }
}
```

The page in Listing 17.8 contains a GridView that binds to the data access component in Listing 17.7. The GridView enables you to display, update, and delete database records (see Figure 17.5).

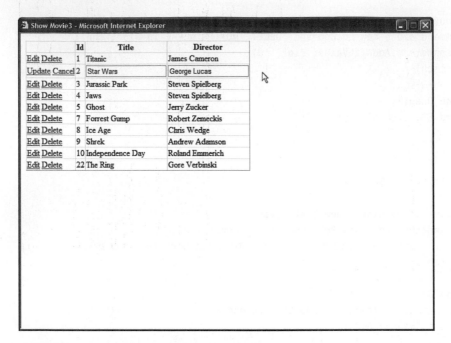

FIGURE 17.5   Updating and deleting database records.

LISTING 17.8   ShowMovie3.aspx

```
<%@ Page Language="C#" %>
<!DOCTYPE html PUBLIC "-//W3C//DTD XHTML 1.0 Transitional//EN"
"http://www.w3.org/TR/xhtml1/DTD/xhtml1-transitional.dtd">
<html xmlns="http://www.w3.org/1999/xhtml" >
<head id="Head1" runat="server">
    <title>Show Movie3</title>
</head>
<body>
    <form id="form1" runat="server">
    <div>

    <asp:GridView
        id="grdMovies"
        DataSourceID="srcMovies"
        DataKeyNames="Id"
        AutoGenerateEditButton="true"
        AutoGenerateDeleteButton="true"
        Runat="server" />
```

```
<asp:ObjectDataSource
    id="srcMovies"
    TypeName="Movie3"
    SelectMethod="GetAll"
    UpdateMethod="Update"
    DeleteMethod="Delete"
    Runat="server" />

</div>
</form>
</body>
</html>
```

Executing a Command with Parameters   Most database commands that you execute include parameters. For example, when updating a database record, you need to supply parameters that represent the new values of the database record columns.

WARNING

Never build command parameters through string concatenation because concatenating strings is an open invitation for SQL injection attacks. If a user enters the proper sequence of characters in a form field, and a SQL command is built through concatenation, then a user can execute an arbitrary SQL command.

Always explicitly create parameters by creating instances of the SqlParameter object. When a SQL command is executed with explicit parameters, the parameters are passed individually to a SQL Server stored procedure named sp_executesql.

You represent a parameter with the SqlParameter object. You can create a new SqlParameter in multiple ways. The easiest way is to call the SqlCommand.AddWithValue() method like this:

```
SqlCommand cmd = new SqlCommand("INSERT Titles (Title) VALUES (@Title)", con);
cmd.Parameters.AddWithValue("@Title", "ASP.NET 3.5 Unleashed");
```

The first statement creates a SqlCommand object that represents a SQL INSERT command. Notice that the command includes a parameter named @Title.

The second statement adds a SqlParameter to the SqlCommand object's Parameters collection. The AddWithValue() method enables you to add a parameter with a certain name and value. In this case, the method is used to supply the value for the @Title parameter.

17

When you execute the SqlCommmand, the following command is sent to Microsoft SQL Server:

```
exec sp_executesql N'INSERT Titles (Title) VALUES (@Title)',N'@Title nvarchar(17)',
@Title = N'ASP.NET Unleashed'
```

The `SqlCommand` object calls the `sp_executesql` stored procedure when it executes a command. In this case, it passes the type, size, and value of the `@Title` parameter to the `sp_executesql` stored procedure.

When you use `AddWithValue()`, the `SqlCommand` object infers the type and size of the parameter for you. The method assumes that string values are SQL NVarChar values, integer values are SQL Int values, decimal values are SQL decimal values, and so on.

As an alternative to using the `AddWithValue()` method, you can create a `SqlParameter` explicitly and add the `SqlParameter` to a `SqlCommand` object's Parameters collection. The advantage of creating a parameter explicitly is that you can specify parameter properties explicitly, such as its name, type, size, precision, scale, and direction.

For example, the following code creates a parameter named `@Title` with a particular data type, size, and value:

```
SqlCommand cmd = new SqlCommand("INSERT Titles (Title) VALUES (@Title)", con);
SqlParameter paramTitle = new SqlParameter();
paramTitle.ParameterName = "@Title";
paramTitle.SqlDbType = SqlDbType.NVarChar;
paramTitle.Size = 50;
paramTitle.Value = "ASP.NET 3.5 Unleashed";
cmd.Parameters.Add(paramTitle);
```

If this seems like a lot of code to do something simple, then you can use one of the overloads of the `Add()` method to create a new `SqlParameter` like this:

```
SqlCommand cmd = new SqlCommand("INSERT Test (Title) VALUES (@Title)", con);
cmd.Parameters.Add("@Title", SqlDbType.NVarChar,50).Value = "ASP.NET 3.5
Unleashed";
```

In general, in this book and in the code that I write, I use the `AddWithValue()` method to create parameters.

I like the `AddWithValue()` method because it involves the least typing.

Executing a Command That Represents a Stored Procedure   You can use a `SqlCommand` object to represent a Microsoft SQL Server stored procedure. For example, you can use the following two statements to create a `SqlCommand` object that represents a stored procedure named GetTitles:

```
SqlCommand cmd = new SqlCommand("GetTitles", con);
cmd.CommandType = CommandType.StoredProcedure;
```

When you execute this `SqlCommand`, the `GetTitles` stored procedure is executed.

When you create `SqlParameters` for a `SqlCommand` that represents a stored procedure, the `SqlParameters` represent stored procedure parameters. The modified `Movie` component in Listing 17.9 uses stored procedures to retrieve and update movie records.

LISTING 17.9   App_Code\Movie4.cs

```
using System;
using System.Data;
using System.Data.SqlClient;
using System.Web.Configuration;
using System.Collections.Generic;

public class Movie4
{
    private static readonly string _connectionString;

    private int _id;
    private string _title;
    private string _director;

    public int Id
    {
        get { return _id; }
        set { _id = value; }
    }

    public string Title
    {
        get { return _title; }
        set { _title = value; }
    }

    public string Director
    {
        get { return _director; }
        set { _director = value; }
    }

    public void Update(int id, string title, string director)
    {
        SqlConnection con = new SqlConnection(_connectionString);
        SqlCommand cmd = new SqlCommand("MovieUpdate", con);
        cmd.CommandType = CommandType.StoredProcedure;
        cmd.Parameters.AddWithValue("@Id", id);
```

LISTING 17.9   Continued

```
        cmd.Parameters.AddWithValue("@Title", title);
        cmd.Parameters.AddWithValue("@Director", director);
        using (con)
        {
            con.Open();
            cmd.ExecuteNonQuery();
        }
    }

    public List<Movie4> GetAll()
    {
        List<Movie4> results = new List<Movie4>();
        SqlConnection con = new SqlConnection(_connectionString);
        SqlCommand cmd = new SqlCommand("MovieSelect", con);
        cmd.CommandType = CommandType.StoredProcedure;
        using (con)
        {
            con.Open();
            SqlDataReader reader = cmd.ExecuteReader();
            while (reader.Read())
            {
                Movie4 newMovie = new Movie4();
                newMovie.Id = (int)reader["Id"];
                newMovie.Title = (string)reader["Title"];
                newMovie.Director = (string)reader["Director"];
                results.Add(newMovie);
            }
        }
        return results;
    }

    static Movie4()
    {
        _connectionString = WebConfigurationManager.ConnectionStrings
        ➥["Movies"].ConnectionString;
    }
}
```

The component in Listing 17.9 uses the MovieSelect and MovieUpdate stored procedures contained in Listing 17.10.

LISTING 17.10   MovieStoredProcedures.sql

```sql
CREATE PROCEDURE dbo.MovieSelect
AS
SELECT Id, Title, Director FROM Movies

CREATE PROCEDURE dbo.MovieUpdate
(
    @Id int,
    @Title NVarchar(100),
    @Director NVarchar(100)
)
AS
UPDATE Movies SET
    Title = @Title,
    Director = @Director
WHERE Id = @Id
```

The ASP.NET page in Listing 17.11 contains a GridView that is bound to the modified Movie component. This GridView enables you to display and update movie records.

LISTING 17.11   ShowMovie4.aspx

```aspx
<%@ Page Language="C#" %>
<!DOCTYPE html PUBLIC "-//W3C//DTD XHTML 1.0 Transitional//EN"
"http://www.w3.org/TR/xhtml1/DTD/xhtml1-transitional.dtd">
<html xmlns="http://www.w3.org/1999/xhtml" >
<head id="Head1" runat="server">
    <title>Show Movie4</title>
</head>
<body>
    <form id="form1" runat="server">
    <div>

    <asp:GridView
        id="grdMovies"
        DataSourceID="srcMovies"
        DataKeyNames="Id"
        AutoGenerateEditButton="true"
        Runat="server" />

    <asp:ObjectDataSource
        id="srcMovies"
        TypeName="Movie4"
        SelectMethod="GetAll"
```

17

LISTING 17.11   Continued

```
        UpdateMethod="Update"
        Runat="server" />

    </div>
    </form>
</body>
</html>
```

You can use a `SqlParameter` to represent not only stored procedure input parameters, but also to represent stored procedure return values and output parameters. If you need to return an integer value from a stored procedure, then you can create a `SqlParameter` that represents a return value. For example, the stored procedure in Listing 17.12 returns the number of rows in the Movies database table.

LISTING 17.12   GetMovieCount.sql

```
CREATE PROCEDURE dbo.GetMovieCount
AS
 RETURN (SELECT COUNT(*) FROM Movies)
```

The page in Listing 17.13 displays the return value from the `GetMovieCount` stored procedure with a `Label` control (see Figure 17.6).

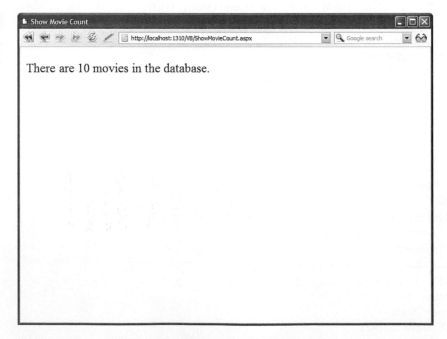

FIGURE 17.6   Displaying a stored procedure return value.

LISTING 17.13   ShowMovieCount.aspx

```
<%@ Page Language="C#" %>
<%@ Import Namespace="System.Data" %>
<%@ Import Namespace="System.Data.SqlClient" %>
<%@ Import Namespace="System.Web.Configuration" %>
<!DOCTYPE html PUBLIC "-//W3C//DTD XHTML 1.0 Transitional//EN"
"http://www.w3.org/TR/xhtml1/DTD/xhtml1-transitional.dtd">
<script runat="server">

    void Page_Load()
    {
        lblMovieCount.Text = GetMovieCount().ToString();
    }

    private int GetMovieCount()
    {
        int result = 0;
        string connectionString = WebConfigurationManager.
        ➥ConnectionStrings["Movies"].ConnectionString;
        SqlConnection con = new SqlConnection(connectionString);
        SqlCommand cmd = new SqlCommand("GetMovieCount", con);
        cmd.CommandType = CommandType.StoredProcedure;
        cmd.Parameters.Add("@ReturnVal", SqlDbType.Int).Direction =
        ➥ParameterDirection.ReturnValue;
        using (con)
        {
            con.Open();
            cmd.ExecuteNonQuery();
            result = (int)cmd.Parameters["@ReturnVal"].Value;
        }
        return result;
    }
</script>
<html xmlns="http://www.w3.org/1999/xhtml" >
<head id="Head1" runat="server">
    <title>Show Movie Count</title>
</head>
<body>
    <form id="form1" runat="server">
    <div>

    There are
    <asp:Label
        id="lblMovieCount"
        Runat="server" />
```

17

LISTING 17.13   Continued

```
    movies in the database.

    </div>
    </form>
</body>
</html>
```

In Listing 17.13, a SqlParameter is created that has the name ReturnVal. The name of the SqlParameter is not important. However, notice that the SqlParameter.Direction property is set to the value ReturnValue. After the SqlCommand is executed, the return value can be retrieved by reading the value of this parameter.

A stored procedure has only one return value, and it must be an integer value. If you need to return more than one value, or values of a different data type than an integer, then you need to use stored procedure output parameters.

For example, the stored procedure in Listing 17.14 returns movie titles and box office totals. Notice that the stored procedure includes an output parameter named @SumBoxOfficeTotals. This output parameter represents a sum of all box office totals.

LISTING 17.14   GetBoxOfficeTotals.sql

```
CREATE PROCEDURE dbo.GetBoxOfficeTotals
(
  @SumBoxOfficeTotals Money OUTPUT
)
AS
-- Assign Sum Box Office Totals
SELECT @SumBoxOfficeTotals = SUM(BoxOfficeTotals) FROM Movies

-- Return all rows
SELECT Title, BoxOfficeTotals FROM Movies
```

The data access component in Listing 17.15 contains a method named GetBoxOffice() that calls the GetBoxOfficeTotals stored procedure. The method adds an output parameter to the SqlCommand object.

LISTING 17.15   App_Code\Movie5.cs

```
using System;
using System.Data;
using System.Data.SqlClient;
using System.Web.Configuration;
using System.Collections.Generic;
```

```csharp
public class Movie5
{
    private static readonly string _connectionString;

    private string _title;
    private decimal _boxOfficeTotals;

    public string Title
    {
        get { return _title; }
        set { _title = value; }
    }

    public decimal BoxOfficeTotals
    {
        get { return _boxOfficeTotals; }
        set { _boxOfficeTotals = value; }
    }

    public List<Movie5> GetBoxOffice(out decimal SumBoxOfficeTotals)
    {
        List<Movie5> results = new List<Movie5>();
        SqlConnection con = new SqlConnection(_connectionString);
        SqlCommand cmd = new SqlCommand("GetBoxOfficeTotals", con);
        cmd.CommandType = CommandType.StoredProcedure;
        cmd.Parameters.Add("@SumBoxOfficeTotals", SqlDbType.Money).Direction =
        ➥ParameterDirection.Output;
        using (con)
        {
            con.Open();
            SqlDataReader reader = cmd.ExecuteReader();

            while (reader.Read())
            {
                Movie5 newMovie = new Movie5();
                newMovie.Title = (string)reader["Title"];
                newMovie.BoxOfficeTotals = (decimal)reader["BoxOfficeTotals"];
                results.Add(newMovie);
            }
            reader.Close();
            SumBoxOfficeTotals = (decimal)cmd.Parameters["@SumBoxOfficeTotals"].
            ➥Value;

        }
        return results;
    }
```

LISTING 17.5   Continued

```
    static Movie5()
    {
        _connectionString = WebConfigurationManager.ConnectionStrings
        ➥["Movies"].ConnectionString;
    }
}
```

In Listing 17.15, notice that the SqlDataReader is explicitly closed before the output parameter is read. If you do not close the SqlDataReader first, then attempting to read the
value of the output parameter raises an exception.

Finally, the page in Listing 17.16 displays the movie box office totals in a GridView. In
addition, it displays the value of the output parameter in a Label control (see Figure 17.7).

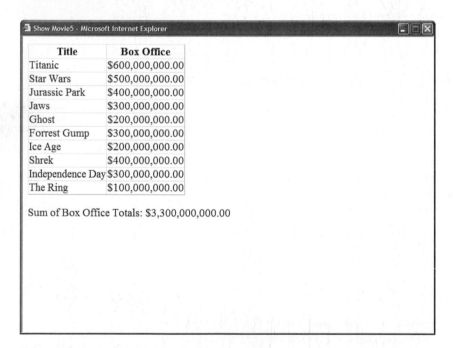

Title	Box Office
Titanic	$600,000,000.00
Star Wars	$500,000,000.00
Jurassic Park	$400,000,000.00
Jaws	$300,000,000.00
Ghost	$200,000,000.00
Forrest Gump	$300,000,000.00
Ice Age	$200,000,000.00
Shrek	$400,000,000.00
Independence Day	$300,000,000.00
The Ring	$100,000,000.00

Sum of Box Office Totals: $3,300,000,000.00

FIGURE 17.7   Displaying an output parameter.

LISTING 17.16   ShowMovie5.aspx

```
<%@ Page Language="C#" %>
<!DOCTYPE html PUBLIC "-//W3C//DTD XHTML 1.0 Transitional//EN"
"http://www.w3.org/TR/xhtml1/DTD/xhtml1-transitional.dtd">
<script runat="server">
```

```
    protected void srcMovies_Selected(object sender,
    ➥ObjectDataSourceStatusEventArgs e)
    {
        decimal sum = (decimal)e.OutputParameters["SumBoxOfficeTotals"];
        lblSum.Text = sum.ToString("c");
    }
</script>
<html xmlns="http://www.w3.org/1999/xhtml" >
<head id="Head1" runat="server">
    <title>Show Movie5</title>
</head>
<body>
    <form id="form1" runat="server">
    <div>

    <asp:GridView
        id="grdMovies"
        DataSourceID="srcMovies"
        AutoGenerateColumns="false"
        Runat="server">
        <Columns>
        <asp:BoundField DataField="Title" HeaderText="Title" />
        <asp:BoundField
            DataField="BoxOfficeTotals"
            HeaderText="Box Office"
            HtmlEncode="false"
            DataFormatString="{0:c}" />
        </Columns>
    </asp:GridView>
    <br />
    Sum of Box Office Totals:
    <asp:Label
        id="lblSum"
        Runat="server" />

    <asp:ObjectDataSource
        id="srcMovies"
        TypeName="Movie5"
        SelectMethod="GetBoxOffice"
        Runat="server" OnSelected="srcMovies_Selected">
        <SelectParameters>
        <asp:Parameter
            Name="SumBoxOfficeTotals"
            Type="Decimal"
            Direction="Output" />
        </SelectParameters>
```

17

LISTING 17.16   Continued

```
    </asp:ObjectDataSource>

    </div>
    </form>
</body>
</html>
```

Returning a Single Value   If you need to return a single value from a database query, you can use the `SqlCommand.ExecuteScalar()` method. This method always returns the value of the first column from the first row of a resultset. Even when a query returns hundreds of columns and billions of rows, everything is ignored except for the value of the first column from the first row.

For example, the page in Listing 17.17 contains a lookup form. If you enter the title of a movie, the movie's total box office returns are displayed in a `Label` control (see Figure 17.8).

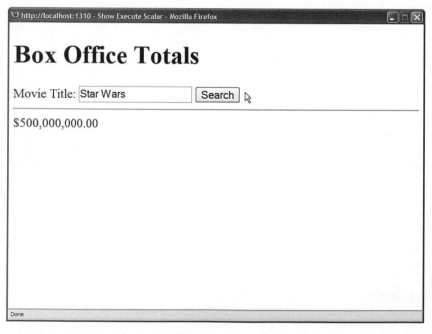

FIGURE 17.8   Retrieving a value with `ExecuteScalar()`.

LISTING 17.17   ShowExecuteScalar.aspx

```
<%@ Page Language="C#" %>
<%@ Import Namespace="System.Data" %>
<%@ Import Namespace="System.Data.SqlClient" %>
<%@ Import Namespace="System.Web.Configuration" %>
```

```
<!DOCTYPE html PUBLIC "-//W3C//DTD XHTML 1.0 Transitional//EN"
"http://www.w3.org/TR/xhtml1/DTD/xhtml1-transitional.dtd">
<script runat="server">

    protected void btnSearch_Click(object sender, EventArgs e)
    {
        string connectionString = WebConfigurationManager.
        ➥ConnectionStrings["Movies"].ConnectionString;
        SqlConnection con = new SqlConnection(connectionString);
        SqlCommand cmd = new SqlCommand("SELECT BoxOfficeTotals FROM Movies WHERE
        ➥Title=@Title", con);
        cmd.Parameters.AddWithValue("@Title", txtTitle.Text);
        using (con)
        {
            con.Open();
            Object result = cmd.ExecuteScalar();
            if (result != null)
                lblResult.Text = String.Format("{0:c}", result);
            else
                lblResult.Text = "No match!";
        }

    }
</script>
<html xmlns="http://www.w3.org/1999/xhtml" >
<head id="Head1" runat="server">
    <title>Show Execute Scalar</title>
</head>
<body>
    <form id="form1" runat="server">
    <div>

    <h1>Box Office Totals</h1>

    <asp:Label
        id="lblTitle"
        Text="Movie Title:"
        AssociatedControlID="txtTitle"
        Runat="server" />

    <asp:TextBox
        id="txtTitle"
        Runat="server" />

    <asp:Button
        id="btnSearch"
```

17

LISTING 17.17   Continued

```
            Text="Search"
            OnClick="btnSearch_Click"
            Runat="server" />

    <hr />

    <asp:Label
        id="lblResult"
        Runat="server" />

    </div>
    </form>
</body>
</html>
```

The `ExecuteScalar()` method returns a value of type `Object`. This means that you must cast the value returned from `ExecuteScalar()` to a particular type before you do anything with the value. In Listing 17.17, after verifying that a value is returned, the value is cast to a decimal.

Notice that you have a choice here. Rather than use the `ExecuteScalar()` method, you can use an output parameter. You can use either method to return a single value from a database. There is no real difference in performance between using the `ExecuteScalar()` method with a stored procedure or using an output parameter. The approach you take is largely a matter of preference.

NOTE

For performance comparisons between `ExecuteScalar` and output parameters, see Priya Dhawan's article at the Microsoft MSDN website (msdn.Microsoft.com), entitled "Performance Comparison: Data Access Techniques."

Returning a Resultset   If you need to return multiple rows of data with a `SqlCommand` object, then you can call the `SqlCommand.ExecuteReader()` method. This method returns a `SqlDataReader` that you can use to fetch each row of records from the database.

For example, the data access component in Listing 17.18 contains a method named `GetAll()` that returns all the movies from the Movies database table. After the `ExecuteReader()` method is called, each row is retrieved from the `SqlDataReader` and dumped into a generic List collection.

LISTING 17.18   App_Code\Movie6.cs

```csharp
using System;
using System.Data;
using System.Data.SqlClient;
using System.Web.Configuration;
using System.Collections.Generic;

public class Movie6
{
    private static readonly string _connectionString;

    private string _title;
    private string _director;

    public string Title
    {
        get { return _title; }
        set { _title = value; }
    }

    public string Director
    {
        get { return _director; }
        set { _director = value; }
    }

    public List<Movie6> GetAll()
    {
        List<Movie6> results = new List<Movie6>();
        SqlConnection con = new SqlConnection(_connectionString);
        SqlCommand cmd = new SqlCommand("SELECT Title,Director FROM Movies", con);
        using (con)
        {
            con.Open();
            SqlDataReader reader = cmd.ExecuteReader();
            while (reader.Read())
            {
                Movie6 newMovie = new Movie6();
                newMovie.Title = (string)reader["Title"];
                newMovie.Director = (string)reader["Director"];
                results.Add(newMovie);
            }
        }
        return results;
    }
```

17

LISTING 17.18 Continued

```
    static Movie6()
    {
        _connectionString = WebConfigurationManager.ConnectionStrings["Movies"].
        ➥ConnectionString;
    }
}
```

The page in Listing 17.19 contains a `GridView` bound to an `ObjectDataSource` that represents the component in Listing 17.18 (see Figure 17.9).

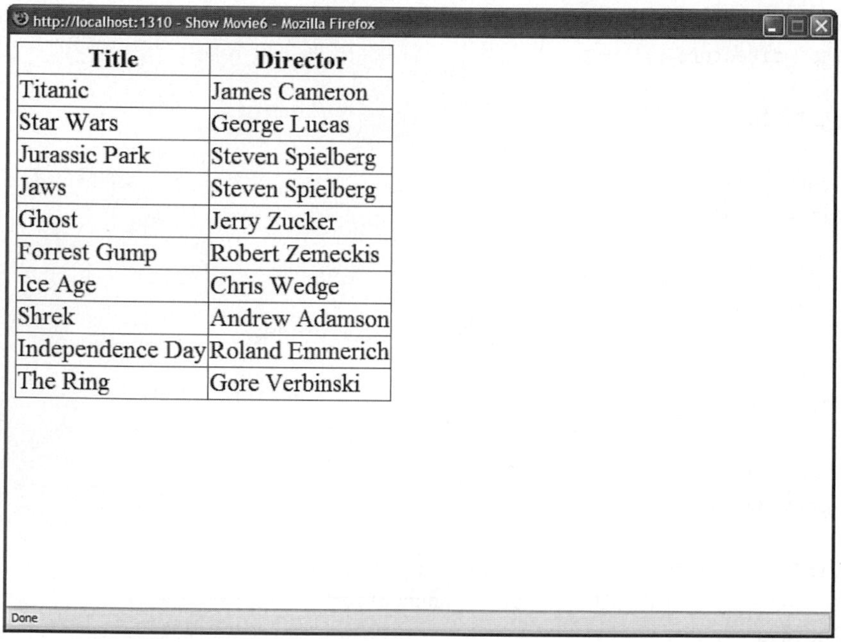
http://localhost:1310 - Show Movie6 - Mozilla Firefox
Title
Director
Titanic
James Cameron
Star Wars
George Lucas
Jurassic Park
Steven Spielberg
Jaws
Steven Spielberg
Ghost
Jerry Zucker
Forrest Gump
Robert Zemeckis
Ice Age
Chris Wedge
Shrek
Andrew Adamson
Independence Day
Roland Emmerich
The Ring
Gore Verbinski
Done

FIGURE 17.9 Returning a resultset.

LISTING 17.19 ShowMovie6.aspx

```
<%@ Page Language="C#" %>
<!DOCTYPE html PUBLIC "-//W3C//DTD XHTML 1.0 Transitional//EN"
  "http://www.w3.org/TR/xhtml1/DTD/xhtml1-transitional.dtd">
<html xmlns="http://www.w3.org/1999/xhtml" >
<head id="Head1" runat="server">
    <title>Show Movie6</title>
</head>
<body>
    <form id="form1" runat="server">
    <div>
```

```
        <asp:GridView
            id="grdMovies"
            DataSourceID="srcMovies"
            Runat="server" />

        <asp:ObjectDataSource
            id="srcMovies"
            TypeName="Movie6"
            SelectMethod="GetAll"
            Runat="server" />

    </div>
    </form>
</body>
</html>
```

The component in Listing 17.18 copies all the records from the `SqlDataReader` to a collection before returning the results of the query.

If you want to skip the copying step, and not add the records to a collection, then you can pass a `CommandBehavior.CloseConnection` parameter to the `ExecuteReader()` method. This parameter causes the database connection associated with the `SqlDataReader` to close automatically after all the records have been fetched from the `SqlDataReader`.

The component in Listing 17.20 illustrates how you can use `CommandBehavior.CloseConnection` with the `ExecuteReader()` method.

LISTING 17.20 App_Code\Movie7.cs

```
using System;
using System.Data;
using System.Data.SqlClient;
using System.Web.Configuration;
using System.Collections.Generic;

public class Movie7
{
    private static readonly string _connectionString;

    public SqlDataReader GetAll()
    {
        SqlConnection con = new SqlConnection(_connectionString);
        SqlCommand cmd = new SqlCommand("SELECT Title,Director FROM Movies", con);
        con.Open();
        return cmd.ExecuteReader(CommandBehavior.CloseConnection);
    }
```

LISTING 17.20   Continued

```
    static Movie7()
    {
        _connectionString = WebConfigurationManager.ConnectionStrings["Movies"].
        ➥ConnectionString;
    }
}
```

The page in Listing 17.21 displays the records returned from the component in Listing 17.20 in a GridView.

LISTING 17.21   ShowMovie7.aspx

```
<%@ Page Language="C#" %>
<!DOCTYPE html PUBLIC "-//W3C//DTD XHTML 1.0 Transitional//EN"
  "http://www.w3.org/TR/xhtml1/DTD/xhtml1-transitional.dtd">
<html xmlns="http://www.w3.org/1999/xhtml" >
<head id="Head1" runat="server">
    <title>Show Movie7</title>
</head>
<body>
    <form id="form1" runat="server">
    <div>

    <asp:GridView
        id="grdMovies"
        DataSourceID="srcMovies"
        Runat="server" />

    <asp:ObjectDataSource
        id="srcMovies"
        TypeName="Movie7"
        SelectMethod="GetAll"
        Runat="server" />

    </div>
    </form>
</body>
</html>
```

The CommandBehavior.CloseConnection parameter enables you to return a SqlDataReader from a method. When all the records are read from the SqlDataReader, the CommandBehavior.CloseConnection parameter causes the SqlConnection object associated with the SqlDataReader to close automatically.

The big disadvantage of using the CommandBehavior.CloseConnection parameter is that it prevents you from adding any exception handling code. You can't use a Using statement or Try...Catch statement with the SqlConnection created in the component in Listing 17.19. A Using statement or Try...Catch statement would force the SqlConnection to close before the SqlDataReader is returned from the method.

Using the DataReader Object

The DataReader object represents the results of a database query. You get a DataReader by calling a Command object's ExecuteReader() method.

You can verify whether a DataReader represents any rows by checking the HasRows property or calling the Read() method. The Read() method returns true when the DataReader can advance to a new row. (Calling this method also advances you to the next row.)

The DataReader represents a single row of data at a time. To get the next row of data, you need to call the Read() method. When you get to the last row, the Read() method returns False.

There are multiple ways to refer to the columns returned by a DataReader. For example, imagine that you are using a SqlDataReader named reader to represent the following query:

```
SELECT Title, Director FROM Movies
```

If you want to retrieve the value of the Title column for the current row represented by a DataReader, then you can use any of the following methods:

```
string title = (string)reader["Title"];
```

```
string title = (string)reader[0];
```

```
string title = reader.GetString(0);
```

```
SqlString title = reader.GetSqlString(0);
```

The first method returns the Title column by name. The value of the Title column is returned as an Object. Therefore, you must cast the value to a string before you can assign the value to a string variable.

The second method returns the Title column by position. It also returns the value of the Title column as an Object, so you must cast the value before using it.

The third method returns the Title column by position. However, it retrieves the value as a String value. You don't need to cast the value in this case.

Finally, the last method returns the Title column by position. However, it returns the value as a SqlString rather than a normal String. A SqlString represents the value using the specialized data types defined in the System.Data.SqlTypes namespace.

NOTE

SqlTypes is a new feature of ADO.NET 2.0. There is a SqlType that corresponds to each of the types supported by Microsoft SQL Server 2005. For example, there is a SqlDecimal, SqlBinary, and SqlXml type.

There are tradeoffs between the different methods of returning a column value. Retrieving a column by its position rather than its name is faster. However, this technique also makes your code more brittle. If the order of your columns changes in your query, your code no longer works.

Returning Multiple Resultsets   A single database query can return multiple resultsets. For example, the following query returns the contents of both the MovieCategories and Movies tables as separate resultsets:

```
SELECT * FROM MoviesCategories;SELECT * FROM Movies
```

Notice that a semicolon is used to separate the two queries.

Executing multiple queries in one shot can result in better performance. When you execute multiple queries with a single command, you don't tie up multiple database connections.

The component in Listing 17.22 illustrates how you can retrieve multiple resultsets with a single query when using a SqlDataReader. The GetMovieData() method returns two collections: a collection representing MovieCategories and a collection representing Movies.

LISTING 17.22   App_Code\DataLayer1.cs

```csharp
using System;
using System.Data;
using System.Data.SqlClient;
using System.Web.Configuration;
using System.Collections.Generic;

public class DataLayer1
{
    private static readonly string _connectionString;

    public class MovieCategory
    {
        private int _id;
        private string _name;
```

```csharp
    public int Id
    {
        get { return _id; }
        set { _id = value; }
    }

    public string Name
    {
        get { return _name; }
        set { _name = value; }
    }
}

public class Movie
{
    private string _title;
    private int _categoryId;

    public string Title
    {
        get { return _title; }
        set { _title = value; }
    }

    public int CategoryId
    {
        get { return _categoryId; }
        set { _categoryId = value; }
    }
}

public static void GetMovieData(List<DataLayer1.MovieCategory> movieCategories,
➥List<DataLayer1.Movie> movies)
{
    string commandText = "SELECT Id,Name FROM MovieCategories;SELECT Title,
    ➥CategoryId FROM Movies";
    SqlConnection con = new SqlConnection(_connectionString);
    SqlCommand cmd = new SqlCommand(commandText, con);
    using (con)
    {
        // Execute command
        con.Open();
        SqlDataReader reader = cmd.ExecuteReader();
```

LISTING 17.22   Continued

```
            // Create movie categories
            while (reader.Read())
            {
                DataLayer1.MovieCategory newCategory = new DataLayer1.
                ➥MovieCategory();
                newCategory.Id = (int)reader["Id"];
                newCategory.Name = (string)reader["Name"];
                movieCategories.Add(newCategory);
            }

            // Move to next result set
            reader.NextResult();

            // Create movies
            while (reader.Read())
            {
                DataLayer1.Movie newMovie = new DataLayer1.Movie();
                newMovie.Title = (string)reader["Title"];
                newMovie.CategoryId = (int)reader["CategoryID"];
                movies.Add(newMovie);
            }
        }
    }

    static DataLayer1()
    {
        _connectionString = WebConfigurationManager.ConnectionStrings["Movies"].
        ➥ConnectionString;
    }
}
```

The `SqlDataReader.NextResult()` method is called to advance to the next resultset. This method returns either `True` or `False` depending on whether a next resultset exists. In Listing 17.22, it is assumed that there is both a movies category and movies resultset.

The page in Listing 17.23 displays the contents of the two database tables in two `GridView` controls (see Figure 17.10).

LISTING 17.23   ShowDataLayer1.aspx

```
<%@ Page Language="C#" %>
<%@ Import Namespace="System.Collections.Generic" %>
<!DOCTYPE html PUBLIC "-//W3C//DTD XHTML 1.0 Transitional//EN"
"http://www.w3.org/TR/xhtml1/DTD/xhtml1-transitional.dtd">
```

```
<script runat="server">

    void Page_Load()
    {
        // Get database data
        List<DataLayer1.MovieCategory> categories = new List<DataLayer1.
        ➥MovieCategory>();
        List<DataLayer1.Movie> movies = new List<DataLayer1.Movie>();
        DataLayer1.GetMovieData(categories, movies);

        // Bind the data
        grdCategories.DataSource = categories;
        grdCategories.DataBind();
        grdMovies.DataSource = movies;
        grdMovies.DataBind();
    }
</script>
<html xmlns="http://www.w3.org/1999/xhtml" >
<head id="Head1" runat="server">
    <title>Show DataLayer1</title>
</head>
<body>
    <form id="form1" runat="server">
    <div>

    <h1>Movie Categories</h1>
    <asp:GridView
        id="grdCategories"
        Runat="server" />

    <h1>Movies</h1>
    <asp:GridView
        id="grdMovies"
        Runat="server" />

    </div>
    </form>
</body>
</html>
```

17

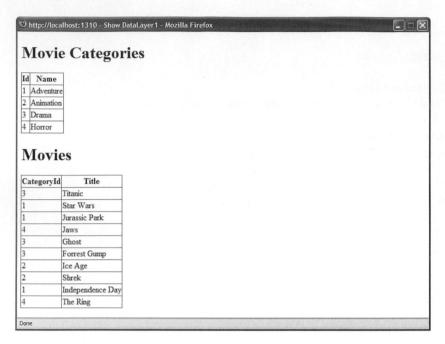

FIGURE 17.10   Displaying two resultsets.

Working with Multiple Active Resultsets   ADO.NET 2.0 includes a new feature named
Multiple Active Results Sets (MARS). In the previous version of ADO.NET, a database
connection could represent only a single resultset at a time. If you take advantage of
MARS, you can represent multiple resultsets with a single database connection.

Using MARS is valuable in scenarios in which you need to iterate through a resultset and
perform an additional database operation for each record in the resultset.

MARS is disabled by default. To enable MARS, you must include a
`MultipleActiveResultSets=True` attribute in a connection string.

For example, the page in Listing 17.24 programmatically builds the nodes in a `TreeView`
control. The page displays a list of movie categories and, beneath each movie category, it
displays a list of matching movies (see Figure 17.11).

LISTING 17.24   ShowMARS.aspx

```
<%@ Page Language="C#" %>
<%@ Import Namespace="System.Data" %>
<%@ Import Namespace="System.Data.SqlClient" %>
<!DOCTYPE html PUBLIC "-//W3C//DTD XHTML 1.0 Transitional//EN"
"http://www.w3.org/TR/xhtml1/DTD/xhtml1-transitional.dtd">
<script runat="server">

    void Page_Load()
```

```
{
    if (!Page.IsPostBack)
        BuildTree();
}

void BuildTree()
{
    // Create MARS connection
    string connectionString = @"MultipleActiveResultSets=True;"
        + @"Data Source=.\SQLExpress;Integrated Security=True;"
        + @"AttachDBFileName=¦DataDirectory¦MyDatabase.mdf;User Instance=True";
    SqlConnection con = new SqlConnection(connectionString);

    // Create Movie Categories command
    string cmdCategoriesText = "SELECT Id,Name FROM MovieCategories";
    SqlCommand cmdCategories = new SqlCommand(cmdCategoriesText, con);

    // Create Movie command
    string cmdMoviesText = "SELECT Title FROM Movies "
        + "WHERE CategoryId=@CategoryID";
    SqlCommand cmdMovies = new SqlCommand(cmdMoviesText, con);
    cmdMovies.Parameters.Add("@CategoryId", SqlDbType.Int);

    using (con)
    {
        con.Open();

        // Iterate through categories
        SqlDataReader categories = cmdCategories.ExecuteReader();
        while (categories.Read())
        {
            // Add category node
            int id = categories.GetInt32(0);
            string name = categories.GetString(1);
            TreeNode catNode = new TreeNode(name);
            TreeView1.Nodes.Add(catNode);

            // Iterate through matching movies
            cmdMovies.Parameters["@CategoryId"].Value = id;
            SqlDataReader movies = cmdMovies.ExecuteReader();
            while (movies.Read())
            {
                // Add movie node
                string title = movies.GetString(0);
                TreeNode movieNode = new TreeNode(title);
                catNode.ChildNodes.Add(movieNode);
```

17

LISTING 17.24   Continued

```
                }
                movies.Close();
            }
        }
    }
</script>
<html xmlns="http://www.w3.org/1999/xhtml" >
<head id="Head1" runat="server">
    <title>Show MARS</title>
</head>
<body>
    <form id="form1" runat="server">
    <div>

    <asp:TreeView
        id="TreeView1"
        Runat="server" />

    </div>
    </form>
</body>
</html>
```

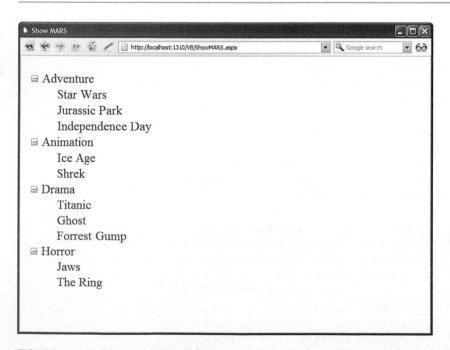

FIGURE 17.11   Fetching database records with MARS enabled.

Notice that the `MultipleActiveResultSets` attribute is included in the connection string used to open the database connection. If MARS were not enabled, then you would not be able to loop through the interior `SqlDataReader` that represents the matching movies while the containing `SqlDataReader` that represents the movie categories is open.

Disconnected Data Access

The ADO.NET Framework supports two models of data access. In the first part of this chapter, you saw how you can use the `SqlConnection`, `SqlCommand`, and `SqlDataReader` objects to connect to a database and retrieve data. When you read data from a database by using a `SqlDataReader` object, an open connection must be maintained between your application and the database.

In this section, we examine the second model of data access supported by ADO.NET: the disconnected model. When you use the objects discussed in this section, you do not need to keep a connection to the database open.

This section discusses four new ADO.NET objects:

▶ **DataAdapter**—Enables you to transfer data from the physical database to the in-memory database and back again.

▶ **DataTable**—Represents an in-memory database table.

▶ **DataView**—Represents an in-memory database view.

▶ **DataSet**—Represents an in-memory database.

The ADO.NET objects discussed in this section are built on top of the ADO.NET objects discussed in the previous section. For example, behind the scenes, the `DataAdapter` uses a `DataReader` to retrieve data from a database.

The advantage of using the objects discussed in this section is that they provide you with more functionality. For example, you can filter and sort the rows represented by a `DataView`. Furthermore, you can use the `DataTable` object to track changes made to records and accept or reject the changes.

The big disadvantage of using the objects discussed in this section is that they tend to be slower and more resource intensive. Retrieving 500 records with a `DataReader` is much faster than retrieving 500 records with a `DataAdapter`.

> **NOTE**
>
> For detailed performance comparisons between the `DataReader` and `DataAdapter`, see Priya Dhawan's article at the Microsoft MSDN website (msdn.Microsoft.com), entitled "Performance Comparison: Data Access Techniques."

Therefore, unless you need to use any of the specialized functionality supported by these objects, my recommendation is that you stick with the objects discussed in the first part

17

of this chapter when accessing a database. In other words, DataReaders are good and DataAdapters are bad.

Using the DataAdapter Object

The DataAdapter acts as the bridge between an in-memory database table and a physical database table. You use the DataAdapter to retrieve data from a database and populate a DataTable. You also use a DataAdapter to push changes that you have made to a DataTable back to the physical database.

The component in Listing 17.25 illustrates how you can use a SqlDataAdapter to populate a DataTable.

LISTING 17.25   App_Code\Movie8.cs

```
using System;
using System.Data;
using System.Data.SqlClient;
using System.Web.Configuration;
using System.Collections.Generic;

public class Movie8
{
    private static readonly string _connectionString;

    public DataTable GetAll()
    {
        // Initialize the DataAdapter
        SqlDataAdapter dad = new SqlDataAdapter("SELECT Title,Director FROM
        ➥Movies", _connectionString);

        // Create a DataTable
        DataTable dtblMovies = new DataTable();

        // Populate the DataTable
        dad.Fill(dtblMovies);

        // Return results
        return dtblMovies;
    }

    static Movie8()
    {
        _connectionString = WebConfigurationManager.ConnectionStrings["Movies"].
        ➥ConnectionString;
    }
}
```

The page in Listing 17.26 contains a `GridView` that is bound to an `ObjectDataSource` that represents the component in Listing 17.25 (see Figure 17.12).

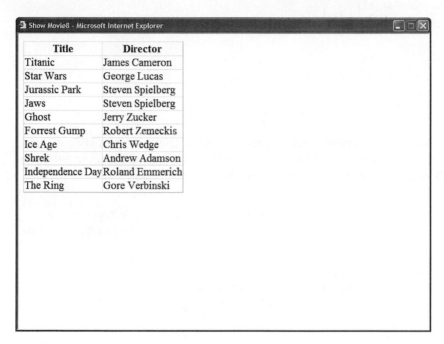

Title	Director
Titanic	James Cameron
Star Wars	George Lucas
Jurassic Park	Steven Spielberg
Jaws	Steven Spielberg
Ghost	Jerry Zucker
Forrest Gump	Robert Zemeckis
Ice Age	Chris Wedge
Shrek	Andrew Adamson
Independence Day	Roland Emmerich
The Ring	Gore Verbinski

FIGURE 17.12   Displaying data with a `DataAdapter`.

LISTING 17.26   ShowMovie8.aspx

```
<%@ Page Language="C#" %>
<!DOCTYPE html PUBLIC "-//W3C//DTD XHTML 1.0 Transitional//EN"
  "http://www.w3.org/TR/xhtml1/DTD/xhtml1-transitional.dtd">
<html xmlns="http://www.w3.org/1999/xhtml" >
<head id="Head1" runat="server">
    <title>Show Movie8</title>
</head>
<body>
    <form id="form1" runat="server">
    <div>

    <asp:GridView
        id="grdMovies"
        DataSourceID="srcMovies"
        Runat="server" />

    <asp:ObjectDataSource
        id="srcMovies"
```

17

LISTING 17.26   Continued

```
        TypeName="Movie8"
        SelectMethod="GetAll"
        Runat="server" />

    </div>
    </form>
</body>
</html>
```

Notice that a `SqlConnection` is never explicitly created in the component in Listing 17.25. When you call the `SqlDataAdapter` object's `Fill()` method, the `SqlDataAdapter` automatically creates and opens a connection. After the data is fetched from the database, the `Fill()` method automatically closes the connection.

You don't need to wrap the call to the `Fill()` method within a `Using` or `Try...Catch` statement. Internally, the `SqlDataAdapter` uses a `Try...Catch` statement to ensure that its connection gets closed.

Opening and closing a database connection is a slow operation. If you know that you will need to perform another database operation after using the `SqlDataAdapter`, then you should explicitly create a `SqlConnection` and open it like this:

```
SqlConnection con = new SqlConnection(...connection string...);
SqlDataAdapter dad = new SqlDataAdapter("SELECT Title,Director FROM Movies", con);
using (con)
{
  con.Open();
  dad.Fill(dtblMovies);
  ... Perform other database operations with connection ...
}
```

If a `SqlConnection` is already open when you call the `Fill()` method, the `Fill()` method doesn't close it. In other words, the `Fill()` method maintains the state of the connection.

Performing Batch Updates   You can think of a `SqlDataAdapter` as a collection of four `SqlCommand` objects:

▶ **SelectCommand**—Represents a `SqlCommand` used for selecting data from a database.

▶ **UpdateCommand**—Represents a `SqlCommand` used for updating data in a database.

▶ **InsertCommand**—Represents a `SqlCommand` used for inserting data into a database.

▶ **DeleteCommand**—Represents a `SqlCommand` used for deleting data from a database.

You can use a `DataAdapter` not only when retrieving data from a database. You can also use a `DataAdapter` when updating, inserting, and deleting data from a database.

If you call a `SqlDataAdapter` object's `Update()` method and pass the method a `DataTable`, then the `SqlDataAdapter` calls its `UpdateCommand`, `InsertCommand`, and `DeleteCommand` to make changes to the database.

You can assign a `SqlCommand` object to each of the four properties of the `SqlDataAdapter`. Alternatively, you can use the `SqlCommandBuilder` object to create the `UpdateCommand`, `InsertCommand`, and `DeleteCommand`. The `SqlCommandBuilder` class takes a `SqlDataAdapter` that has a `SELECT` command and generates the other three commands automatically.

For example, the page in Listing 17.27 displays all the records from the Movies database table in a spreadsheet created with a `Repeater` control (see Figure 17.13). If you make changes to the data and click the Update button, then the Movies database table is updated with the changes.

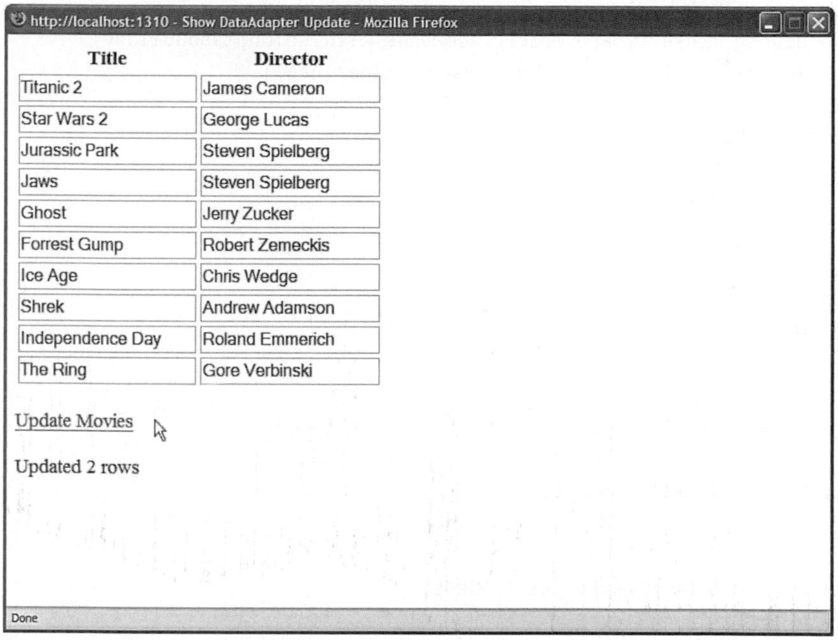

FIGURE 17.13   Batch updating database records.

LISTING 17.27   `ShowDataAdapterUpdate.aspx`

```
<%@ Page Language="C#" %>
<%@ Import Namespace="System.Data" %>
<%@ Import Namespace="System.Data.SqlClient" %>
<%@ Import Namespace="System.Web.Configuration" %>
<!DOCTYPE html PUBLIC "-//W3C//DTD XHTML 1.0 Transitional//EN"
"http://www.w3.org/TR/xhtml1/DTD/xhtml1-transitional.dtd">
<script runat="server">
```

LISTING 16.27   Continued

```csharp
private SqlDataAdapter dad;
private DataTable dtblMovies;

void Page_Load()
{
    // Create connection
    string connectionString = WebConfigurationManager.
    ➥ConnectionStrings["Movies"].ConnectionString;
    SqlConnection con = new SqlConnection(connectionString);

    // Create Select command
    dad = new SqlDataAdapter("SELECT Id,Title,Director FROM Movies", con);

    // Create Update, Insert, and Delete commands with SqlCommandBuilder
    SqlCommandBuilder builder = new SqlCommandBuilder(dad);

    // Add data to DataTable
    dtblMovies = new DataTable();
    dad.Fill(dtblMovies);

    // Bind data to Repeater
    rptMovies.DataSource = dtblMovies;
    rptMovies.DataBind();
}

protected void lnkUpdate_Click(object sender, EventArgs e)
{
    // Update DataTable with changes
    for (int i=0; i < rptMovies.Items.Count;i++)
    {
        RepeaterItem item = rptMovies.Items[i];
        TextBox txtTitle = (TextBox)item.FindControl("txtTitle");
        TextBox txtDirector = (TextBox)item.FindControl("txtDirector");
        if (dtblMovies.Rows[i]["Title"] != txtTitle.Text)
            dtblMovies.Rows[i]["Title"] = txtTitle.Text;
        if (dtblMovies.Rows[i]["Director"] != txtDirector.Text)
            dtblMovies.Rows[i]["Director"] = txtDirector.Text;
    }

    // Set batch size to maximum size
    dad.UpdateBatchSize = 0;

    // Perform update
    int numUpdated = dad.Update(dtblMovies);
```

```
            lblResults.Text = String.Format("Updated {0} rows", numUpdated);
    }
</script>
<html xmlns="http://www.w3.org/1999/xhtml" >
<head id="Head1" runat="server">
    <title>Show DataAdapter Update</title>
</head>
<body>
    <form id="form1" runat="server">
    <div>

    <asp:Repeater
        id="rptMovies"
        EnableViewState="false"
        Runat="server">
        <HeaderTemplate>
        <table>
        <tr>
            <th>Title</th><th>Director</th>
        </tr>
        </HeaderTemplate>
        <ItemTemplate>
        <tr>
        <td>
        <asp:TextBox
            id="txtTitle"
            Text='<%#Eval("Title")%>'
            Runat="server" />
        </td>
        <td>
        <asp:TextBox
            id="txtDirector"
            Text='<%#Eval("Director")%>'
            Runat="server" />
        </td>
        </tr>
        </ItemTemplate>
        <FooterTemplate>
        </table>
        </FooterTemplate>
    </asp:Repeater>
    <br />

    <asp:LinkButton
        id="lnkUpdate"
        Text="Update Movies"
```

17

LISTING 17.27   Continued

```
        Runat="server" OnClick="lnkUpdate_Click" />

    <br /><br />

    <asp:Label
        id="lblResults"
        EnableViewState="false"
        Runat="server" />

    </div>
    </form>
</body>
</html>
```

The `SqlDataAdapter` in Listing 17.27 performs a batch update. When a `SqlDataAdapter` object's `UpdateBatchSize` property is set to the value 0, the `SqlDataAdapter` performs all its updates in a single batch. If you want to perform updates in smaller batches, then you can set the `UpdateBatchSize` to a particular size.

NOTE

Performing batch updates is a new feature of ADO.NET 2.0.

Using the `DataTable` Object

The `DataTable` object represents an in-memory database table. You can add rows to a DataTable with a `SqlDataAdapter`, with a `SqlDataReader`, with an XML file, or programmatically.

For example, the page in Listing 17.28 builds a new `DataTable` programmatically. The contents of the `DataTable` are then displayed in a `GridView` control (see Figure 17.14).

LISTING 17.28   ShowDataTableProgram.aspx

```
<%@ Page Language="C#" %>
<%@ Import Namespace="System.Data" %>
<!DOCTYPE html PUBLIC "-//W3C//DTD XHTML 1.0 Transitional//EN"
"http://www.w3.org/TR/xhtml1/DTD/xhtml1-transitional.dtd">
<script runat="server">

    void Page_Load()
    {
        // Create the DataTable columns
        DataTable newDataTable = new DataTable();
```

```
        newDataTable.Columns.Add("Id", typeof(int));
        newDataTable.Columns.Add("ProductName", typeof(string));
        newDataTable.Columns.Add("ProductPrice", typeof(decimal));

        // Mark the Id column as an autoincrement column
        newDataTable.Columns["Id"].AutoIncrement = true;

        // Add some data rows
        for (int i = 1; i < 11; i++)
        {
            DataRow newRow = newDataTable.NewRow();
            newRow["ProductName"] = "Product " + i.ToString();
            newRow["ProductPrice"] = 12.34m;
            newDataTable.Rows.Add(newRow);
        }

        // Bind DataTable to GridView
        grdProducts.DataSource = newDataTable;
        grdProducts.DataBind();
    }
</script>
<html xmlns="http://www.w3.org/1999/xhtml" >
<head id="Head1" runat="server">
    <title>Show DataTable Programmatically</title>
</head>
<body>
    <form id="form1" runat="server">
    <div>

    <h1>Products</h1>

    <asp:GridView
        id="grdProducts"
        Runat="server" />

    </div>
    </form>
</body>
</html>
```

In Listing 17.28, a DataTable with the following three columns is created: Id,
ProductName, and ProductPrice. The data type of each column is specified with a .NET
Framework type. For example, the ProductPrice column is created as a decimal column.
Alternatively, you could create each column with a SqlType. For example, you could use
System.Data.SqlTypes.SqlDecimal for the type of the ProductPrice column.

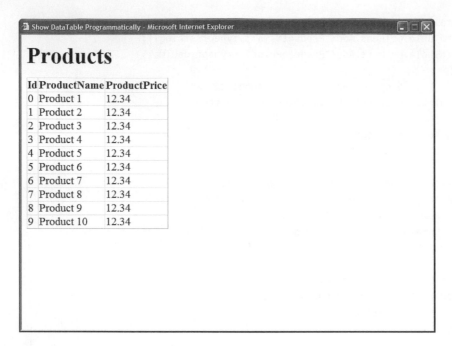

FIGURE 17.14   Displaying a DataTable that was built programmatically.

Notice that the Id column is created as an auto-increment column. When you add new rows to the DataTable, the column increments its value automatically.

Selecting DataRows   You can retrieve particular rows from a DataTable by using the DataTable object's Select() method. The Select() method accepts a filter parameter. You can use just about anything that you would use in a SQL WHERE clause with the filter parameter.

When you retrieve an array of rows with the Select() method, you can also specify a sort order for the rows. When specifying a sort order, you can use any expression that you would use with a SQL ORDER BY clause.

For example, the page in Listing 17.29 caches a DataTable in memory with the ASP.NET Cache object. The page contains a TextBox control. When you enter a partial movie title into the TextBox control, a list of matching movies is displayed in a GridView control. The rows are sorted in order of the movie title (see Figure 17.15).

LISTING 17.29   ShowDataTableSelect.aspx

```
<%@ Page Language="C#" %>
<%@ Import Namespace="System.Data" %>
<%@ Import Namespace="System.Data.SqlClient" %>
<%@ Import Namespace="System.Web.Configuration" %>
<!DOCTYPE html PUBLIC "-//W3C//DTD XHTML 1.0 Transitional//EN"
```

```
"http://www.w3.org/TR/xhtml1/DTD/xhtml1-transitional.dtd">
<script runat="server">

    protected void btnSearch_Click(object sender, EventArgs e)
    {
        // Get movies DataTable from Cache
        DataTable dtblMovies = (DataTable)Cache["MoviesToFilter"];
        if (dtblMovies == null)
        {
            dtblMovies = GetMoviesFromDB();
            Cache["MoviesToFilter"] = dtblMovies;
        }

        // Select matching rows
        string filter = String.Format("Title LIKE '{0}*'", txtTitle.Text);
        DataRow[] rows = dtblMovies.Select(filter, "Title");

        // Bind to GridView
        grdMovies.DataSource = rows;
        grdMovies.DataBind();
    }

    private DataTable GetMoviesFromDB()
    {
        string connectionString = WebConfigurationManager.
        ➥ConnectionStrings["Movies"].ConnectionString;
        SqlDataAdapter dad = new SqlDataAdapter("SELECT Title, Director FROM
        ➥Movies", connectionString);
        DataTable dtblMovies = new DataTable();
        dad.Fill(dtblMovies);
        return dtblMovies;

    }
</script>
<html xmlns="http://www.w3.org/1999/xhtml" >
<head id="Head1" runat="server">
    <style type="text/css">
        th, td
        {
            padding:5px;
        }
    </style>
    <title>Show DataTable Select</title>
</head>
<body>
    <form id="form1" runat="server">
```

17

LISTING 17.29   Continued

```
<div>

<asp:TextBox
    id="txtTitle"
    Tooltip="Search"
    Runat="server" />
<asp:Button
    id="btnSearch"
    Text="Search"
    Runat="server" OnClick="btnSearch_Click" />


<hr />

<asp:GridView
    id="grdMovies"
    AutoGenerateColumns="false"
    Runat="server">
    <Columns>
    <asp:TemplateField HeaderText="Title">
    <ItemTemplate>
        <%# ((DataRow)Container.DataItem)["Title"] %>
    </ItemTemplate>
    </asp:TemplateField>
    <asp:TemplateField HeaderText="Director">
    <ItemTemplate>
        <%# ((DataRow)Container.DataItem)["Director"] %>
    </ItemTemplate>
    </asp:TemplateField>
    </Columns>
    </asp:GridView>

    </div>
    </form>
</body>
</html>
```

The DataTable Select() method returns an array of DataRow objects. Notice that there is nothing wrong with binding an array of DataRow objects to a GridView control. However, you must explicitly cast each data item to a DataRow and read within a GridView TemplateField.

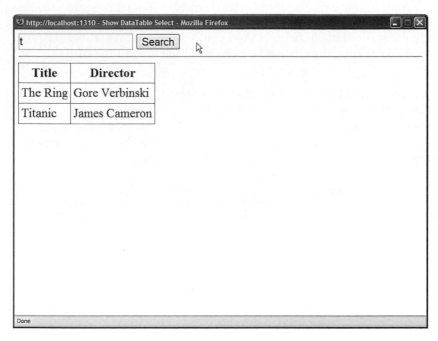

FIGURE 17.15   Selecting matching rows from a cached `DataTable`.

DataRow States and DataRow Versions   When you modify the rows in a `DataTable`, the `DataTable` keeps track of the changes that you make. A `DataTable` maintains both the original and modified version of each row.

Each row in a `DataTable` has a particular `RowState` that has one of the following values:

- **Unchanged**—The row has not been changed.
- **Added**—The row has been added.
- **Modified**—The row has been modified.
- **Deleted**—The row has been deleted.
- **Detached**—The row has been created but not added to the `DataTable`.

Each row in a `DataTable` can have more than one version. Each version is represented by one of the following values of the `DataRowVersion` enumeration:

- **Current**—The current version of the row.
- **Default**—The default version of the row.
- **Original**—The original version of the row.
- **Proposed**—The version of a row that exists during editing.

17

You can use the DataTable.AcceptChanges() method to copy the current versions of all the rows to the original versions of all the rows. And you can use the DataTable.RejectChanges() method to copy the original versions of all the rows to the current versions of all the rows.

For example, the component in Listing 17.30 includes an AcceptChanges() and RejectChanges() method. The component maintains a DataTable in Session state. If you update a row in the DataTable, the row is updated in memory. If the RejectChanges() method is called, any changes made to the DataTable are rejected. If the AcceptChanges() method is called, the database is updated and all changes are accepted.

LISTING 17.30   App_Code\Movie9.cs

```
using System;
using System.Data;
using System.Data.SqlClient;
using System.Web;
using System.Web.Configuration;

public class Movie9
{
    private SqlDataAdapter dad = new SqlDataAdapter();

    public DataTable GetAll()
    {
        return (DataTable)HttpContext.Current.Session["MoviesToEdit"];
    }

    public void Update(int id, string title, string director)
    {
        DataTable movies = (DataTable)HttpContext.Current.Session["MoviestoEdit"];
        DataRow rowToEdit = movies.Rows.Find(id);
        rowToEdit["title"] = title;
        rowToEdit["director"] = director;
    }

    public void RejectChanges()
    {
        DataTable movies = (DataTable)HttpContext.Current.Session["MoviestoEdit"];
        movies.RejectChanges();
    }

    public void AcceptChanges()
    {
        DataTable movies = (DataTable)HttpContext.Current.Session["MoviestoEdit"];
        dad.Update(movies);
        movies.AcceptChanges();
```

```
    }

    public Movie9()
    {
        // Create Data Adapter
        string connectionString = WebConfigurationManager.ConnectionStrings
        ➥["Movies"].ConnectionString;
        dad = new SqlDataAdapter("SELECT Id,Title,Director FROM Movies",
        ➥connectionString);
        SqlCommandBuilder builder = new SqlCommandBuilder(dad);
        dad.UpdateBatchSize = 0;

        HttpContext context = HttpContext.Current;
        if (context.Session["MoviesToEdit"] == null)
        {
            // Add data to DataTable
            DataTable dtblMovies = new DataTable();
            dad.Fill(dtblMovies);
            dtblMovies.PrimaryKey = new DataColumn[] { dtblMovies.Columns["Id"] };
            context.Session["MoviesToEdit"] = dtblMovies;
        }
    }
}
```

The page in Listing 17.31 contains a `GridView` that is bound to the component in Listing 17.30. The `GridView` includes a column that indicates whether each row has been changed. The column displays the value of the corresponding `DataRow` object's `RowState` property (see Figure 17.16).

LISTING 17.31   ShowMovie9.aspx

```
<%@ Page Language="C#" %>
<%@ Import Namespace="System.Data" %>
<!DOCTYPE html PUBLIC "-//W3C//DTD XHTML 1.0 Transitional//EN"
"http://www.w3.org/TR/xhtml1/DTD/xhtml1-transitional.dtd">
<script runat="server">

    protected void btnReject_Click(object sender, EventArgs e)
    {
        Movie9 movie = new Movie9();
        movie.RejectChanges();
        grdMovies.DataBind();
    }

    protected void btnAccept_Click(object sender, EventArgs e)
    {
```

17

LISTING 17.31   Continued

```
            Movie9 movie = new Movie9();
            movie.AcceptChanges();
            grdMovies.DataBind();
        }
</script>
<html xmlns="http://www.w3.org/1999/xhtml" >
<head id="Head1" runat="server">
    <title>Show Movie9</title>
</head>
<body>
    <form id="form1" runat="server">
    <div>

    <h1>Edit Movies</h1>

    <asp:GridView
        id="grdMovies"
        DataSourceID="srcMovies"
        DataKeyNames="Id"
        AutoGenerateEditButton="true"
        Runat="server">
        <Columns>
        <asp:TemplateField>
        <ItemTemplate>
        <%# ((DataRowView)Container.DataItem).Row.RowState %>
        </ItemTemplate>
        </asp:TemplateField>
        </Columns>
    </asp:GridView>

    <br />

    <asp:Button
        id="btnReject"
        Text="Reject Changes"
        OnClick="btnReject_Click"
        Runat="server" />

    <asp:Button
        id="btnAccept"
        Text="Accept Changes"
        OnClick="btnAccept_Click"
        Runat="server" />
```

```
    <asp:ObjectDataSource
        id="srcMovies"
        TypeName="Movie9"
        SelectMethod="GetAll"
        UpdateMethod="Update"
        Runat="server" />

    </div>
    </form>
</body>
</html>
```

If you click the Accept Changes button, all the changes made to the rows in the GridView are sent to the database. If you click the Reject Changes button, all the rows revert to their original values.

FIGURE 17.16   Tracking data row changes.

Using the DataView Object

The DataView object represents an in-memory database view. You can use a DataView object to create a sortable, filterable view of a DataTable.

The DataView object supports three important properties:

▶ **Sort**—Enables you to sort the rows represented by the DataView.

▶ **RowFilter**—Enables you to filter the rows represented by the DataView.

- **RowStateFilter**—Enables you to filter the rows represented by the DataView according to the row state (for example, OriginalRows, CurrentRows, Unchanged).

The easiest way to create a new DataView is to use the DefaultView property exposed by the DataTable class like this:

```
Dim dataView1 As DataView = dataTable1.DefaultView;
```

The DefaultView property returns an unsorted, unfiltered view of the data contained in a DataTable.

You also can directly instantiate a new DataView object by passing a DataTable, filter, sort order, and DataViewRowState filter to the DataView object's constructor, like this:

```
DataView dataView1 = new DataView(dataTable1,
    "BoxOfficeTotals > 100000",
    "Title ASC",
    DataViewRowState.CurrentRows);
```

This statement creates a new DataView from a DataTable that represents the Movies database table. The rows are filtered to include only the movies that have a box office total greater than 100,000 dollars. Also, the rows are sorted by the movie title in ascending order. Finally, all the current rows are represented from the DataTable (as opposed, for instance, to rows that have been deleted).

The page in Listing 17.30 illustrates one way that you can use a DataView. In Listing 17.32, a DataView is cached in Session state. You can sort the cached DataView by clicking on the header links rendered by the GridView control (see Figure 17.17).

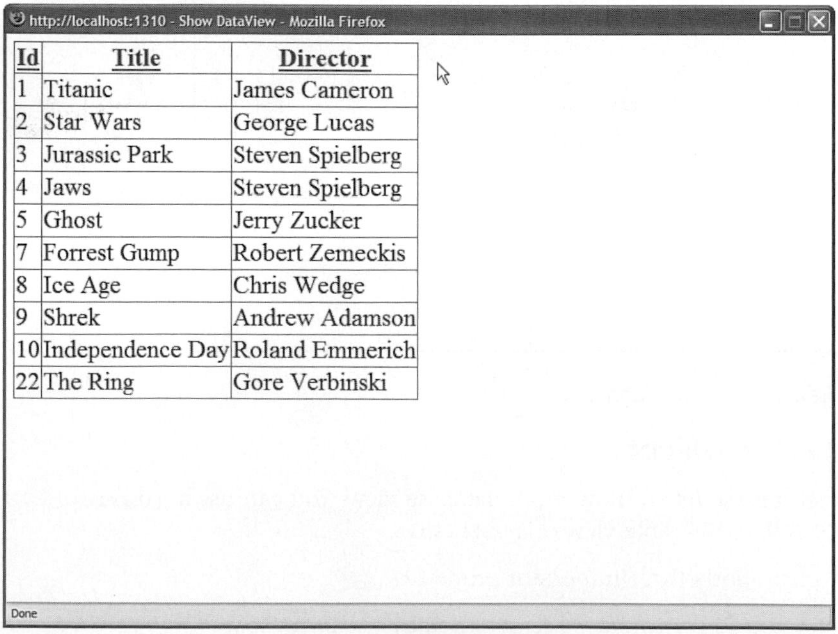

Id	Title	Director
1	Titanic	James Cameron
2	Star Wars	George Lucas
3	Jurassic Park	Steven Spielberg
4	Jaws	Steven Spielberg
5	Ghost	Jerry Zucker
7	Forrest Gump	Robert Zemeckis
8	Ice Age	Chris Wedge
9	Shrek	Andrew Adamson
10	Independence Day	Roland Emmerich
22	The Ring	Gore Verbinski

FIGURE 17.17 Sorting a cached DataView.

LISTING 17.32 ShowDataView.aspx

```
<%@ Page Language="C#" %>
<%@ Import Namespace="System.Data" %>
<%@ Import Namespace="System.Data.SqlClient" %>
<%@ Import Namespace="System.Web.Configuration" %>
<!DOCTYPE html PUBLIC "-//W3C//DTD XHTML 1.0 Transitional//EN"
"http://www.w3.org/TR/xhtml1/DTD/xhtml1-transitional.dtd">
<script runat="server">

    void Page_Load()
    {
        if (Session["MoviesToSort"] == null)
        {
            string connectionString = WebConfigurationManager.
            ➥ConnectionStrings["Movies"].ConnectionString;
            SqlDataAdapter dad = new SqlDataAdapter("SELECT Id,Title,Director FROM
            ➥Movies", connectionString);
            DataTable dtblMovies = new DataTable();
            dad.Fill(dtblMovies);
            Session["MoviesToSort"] = dtblMovies.DefaultView;
        }

        if (!Page.IsPostBack)
            BindMovies();
    }

    void BindMovies()
    {
        grdMovies.DataSource = Session["MoviesToSort"];
        grdMovies.DataBind();
    }

    protected void grdMovies_Sorting(object sender, GridViewSortEventArgs e)
    {
        DataView dvwMovies = (DataView)Session["MoviesToSort"];
        dvwMovies.Sort = e.SortExpression;
        BindMovies();
    }
</script>

<html xmlns="http://www.w3.org/1999/xhtml" >
<head id="Head1" runat="server">
    <title>Show DataView</title>
</head>
<body>
```

17

LISTING 17.32   Continued

```
    <form id="form1" runat="server">
    <div>

    <asp:GridView
        id="grdMovies"
        AllowSorting="true"
        OnSorting="grdMovies_Sorting"
        Runat="server" />

    </div>
    </form>
</body>
</html>
```

Using the DataSet Object

The DataSet object represents an in-memory database. A single DataSet can contain one or many DataTable objects. You can define parent/child relationships between the DataTable objects contained in a DataSet.

For example, the page in Listing 17.33 contains a TreeView control. The TreeView displays a list of movie categories and, beneath each movie category, a list of matching movies (see Figure 17.18).

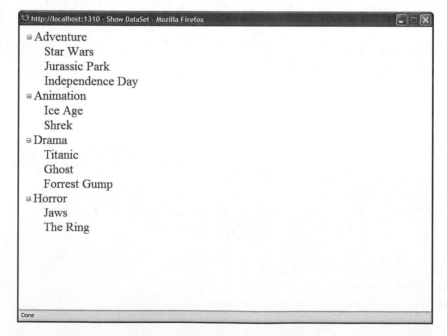

FIGURE 17.18   Building a TreeView from a DataSet.

LISTING 17.33   ShowDataSet.aspx

```csharp
<%@ Page Language="C#" %>
<%@ Import Namespace="System.Data" %>
<%@ Import Namespace="System.Data.SqlClient" %>
<%@ Import Namespace="System.Web.Configuration" %>
<!DOCTYPE html PUBLIC "-//W3C//DTD XHTML 1.0 Transitional//EN"
"http://www.w3.org/TR/xhtml1/DTD/xhtml1-transitional.dtd">
<script runat="server">

    void Page_Load()
    {
        if (!Page.IsPostBack)
            BuildTree();
    }

    void BuildTree()
    {
        // Create Connection
        string connectionString = WebConfigurationManager.
        ➥ConnectionStrings["Movies"].ConnectionString;
        SqlConnection con = new SqlConnection(connectionString);

        // Create Movie Categories DataAdapter
        SqlDataAdapter dadCategories = new SqlDataAdapter("SELECT Id,Name FROM
        ➥MovieCategories", con);

        // Create Movies DataAdapter
        SqlDataAdapter dadMovies = new SqlDataAdapter("SELECT Title,CategoryId FROM
        ➥Movies", con);

        // Add the DataTables to the DataSet
        DataSet dstMovies = new DataSet();
        using (con)
        {
            con.Open();
            dadCategories.Fill(dstMovies, "Categories");
            dadMovies.Fill(dstMovies, "Movies");
        }

        // Add a DataRelation
        dstMovies.Relations.Add("Children",
        ➥dstMovies.Tables["Categories"].Columns["Id"],
        ➥dstMovies.Tables["Movies"].Columns["CategoryId"]);

        // Add the Movie Category nodes
```

17

LISTING 17.33   Continued

```
        foreach (DataRow categoryRow in dstMovies.Tables["Categories"].Rows)
        {
            string name = (string)categoryRow["Name"];
            TreeNode catNode = new TreeNode(name);
            TreeView1.Nodes.Add(catNode);

            // Get matching movies
            DataRow[] movieRows = categoryRow.GetChildRows("Children");
            foreach (DataRow movieRow in movieRows)
            {
                string title = (string)movieRow["Title"];
                TreeNode movieNode = new TreeNode(title);
                catNode.ChildNodes.Add(movieNode);
            }
        }
    }
</script>
<html xmlns="http://www.w3.org/1999/xhtml" >
<head id="Head1" runat="server">
    <title>Show DataSet</title>
</head>
<body>
    <form id="form1" runat="server">
    <div>

    <asp:TreeView
        id="TreeView1"
        Runat="server" />

    </div>
    </form>
</body>
</html>
```

The TreeView is built programmatically. In the BuildTree() method, a DataSet is created that contains two DataTable objects. The first DataTable represents the MovieCategories database table and the second DataTable represents the Movies database table. A parent/child relationship is created between the two DataTable objects with the help of a DataRelation.

The DataRelation is used to get the movies that match each movie category. The DataRow.GetChildRows() method is called to retrieve the movies that match a particular movie category.

Executing Asynchronous Database Commands

ADO.NET 2.0 supports asynchronous database commands. Normally, when you execute a database command, the thread that is executing the command must wait until the command is finished before executing any additional code. In other words, normally, when you execute a database command, the thread is blocked.

When you take advantage of asynchronous commands, on the other hand, the database command is executed on another thread so that the current thread can continue performing other work. For example, you can use the current thread to execute yet another database command.

There are two reasons that you might want to use asynchronous database commands when building an ASP.NET page. First, executing multiple database commands simultaneously can significantly improve your application's performance. This is especially true when the database commands are executed against different database servers.

Second, the ASP.NET Framework uses a limited thread pool to service page requests. When the ASP.NET Framework receives a request for a page, it assigns a thread to handle the request. If the ASP.NET Framework runs out of threads, the request is queued until a thread becomes available. If too many threads are queued, then the framework rejects the page request with a 503—Server Too Busy response code.

If you execute a database command asynchronously, then the current thread is released back into the thread pool so that it can be used to service another page request. While the asynchronous database command is executing, the ASP.NET Framework can devote its attention to handling other page requests. When the asynchronous command completes, the framework reassigns a thread to the original request and the page finishes executing.

17

> **NOTE**
>
> You can configure the ASP.NET thread pool with the `httpRuntime` element in the web configuration file. You can modify the `appRequestQueueLimit`, `minFreeThreads`, and `minLocalRequestFreeThreads` attributes to control how many requests the ASP.NET Framework queues before giving up and sending an error.

There are two parts to this task undertaken in this section. A data access component that supports asynchronous ADO.NET methods must be created, as well as an ASP.NET page that executes asynchronously.

Using Asynchronous ADO.NET Methods

ADO.NET 2.0 introduces asynchronous versions of several of its methods. These methods come in pairs: a `Begin` and `End` method. For example, the `SqlCommand` object supports the following asynchronous methods:

▶ BeginExecuteNonQuery()

▶ EndExecuteNonQuery()

▶ BeginExecuteReader()

▶ EndExecuteReader()

▶ BeginExecuteXmlReader()

▶ EndExecuteXmlReader()

The idea is that when you execute the Begin method, the asynchronous task is started on a separate thread. When the method finishes executing, you can use the End method to get the results.

To use these asynchronous methods, you must use a special attribute in your connection string: the Asynchronous Processing=true attribute.

The data access component in Listing 17.34 contains a BeginGetMovies() and EndGetMovies() method that fetches movies from the Movies database table asynchronously. These methods use the ADO.NET BeginExecuteReader() and EndExecuteReader() to fetch a DataReader asynchronously.

LISTING 17.34   App_Code\AsyncDataLayer.cs

```
using System;
using System.Data;
using System.Data.SqlClient;
using System.Web.Configuration;
using System.Collections.Generic;

public class AsyncDataLayer
{
    private static readonly string _connectionString;
    private SqlCommand _cmdMovies;

    public IAsyncResult BeginGetMovies(AsyncCallback callback, Object state)
    {
        SqlConnection con = new SqlConnection(_connectionString);
        _cmdMovies = new SqlCommand("WAITFOR DELAY '0:0:01';SELECT Title,Director
        ➥FROM Movies", con);
        con.Open();
        return _cmdMovies.BeginExecuteReader(callback, state,
        ➥CommandBehavior.CloseConnection);
    }

    public List<AsyncDataLayer.Movie> EndGetMovies(IAsyncResult result)
    {
```

```
        List<AsyncDataLayer.Movie> results = new List<AsyncDataLayer.Movie>();
        SqlDataReader reader = _cmdMovies.EndExecuteReader(result);
        while (reader.Read())
        {
            AsyncDataLayer.Movie newMovie = new AsyncDataLayer.Movie();
            newMovie.Title = (string)reader["Title"];
            newMovie.Director = (string)reader["Director"];
            results.Add(newMovie);
        }
        return results;
    }

    static AsyncDataLayer()
    {
        _connectionString = WebConfigurationManager.ConnectionStrings["Movies"].
        ➥ConnectionString
            + ";Asynchronous Processing=true";
    }

    public class Movie
    {
        private string _title;
        private string _director;

        public string Title
        {
            get { return _title; }
            set { _title = value; }
        }

        public string Director
        {
            get { return _director; }
            set { _director = value; }
        }
    }
}
```

Using Asynchronous ASP.NET Pages

When you take advantage of asynchronous ADO.NET methods, you must also enable asynchronous ASP.NET page execution. You enable an asynchronous ASP.NET page by adding the following two attributes to a page directive:

```
<%@ Page Async="true" AsyncTimeout="8" %>
```

The first attribute enables asynchronous page execution. The second attribute specifies a timeout value in seconds. The timeout value specifies the amount of time that the page gives a set of asynchronous tasks to complete before the page continues execution.

After you enable asynchronous page execution, you must set up the asychronous tasks and register the tasks with the page. You represent each asynchronous task with an instance of the `PageAsyncTask` object. You register an asynchronous task for a page by calling the `Page.RegisterAsyncTask()` method.

For example, the page in Listing 17.35 displays the records from the Movies database table in a `GridView` control. The database records are retrieved asynchronously from the `AsyncDataLayer` component created in the previous section.

LISTING 17.35   `ShowPageAsyncTask.aspx`

```
<%@ Page Language="C#" Async="true" AsyncTimeout="1" Trace="true" %>
<%@ Import Namespace="System.Threading" %>
<!DOCTYPE html PUBLIC "-//W3C//DTD XHTML 1.0 Transitional//EN"
"http://www.w3.org/TR/xhtml1/DTD/xhtml1-transitional.dtd">
<script runat="server">

    private AsyncDataLayer dataLayer = new AsyncDataLayer();

    void Page_Load()
    {
        // Setup asynchronous data execution
        PageAsyncTask task = new PageAsyncTask(BeginGetData, EndGetData,
        ➥TimeoutData, null, true);
        Page.RegisterAsyncTask(task);

        // Fire off asynchronous tasks
        Page.ExecuteRegisteredAsyncTasks();
    }

    IAsyncResult BeginGetData(object sender, EventArgs e, AsyncCallback callback,
    ➥object state)
    {
        // Show Page Thread ID
        Trace.Warn("BeginGetData: " + Thread.CurrentThread.GetHashCode());

        // Execute asynchronous command
        return dataLayer.BeginGetMovies(callback, state);
    }

    void EndGetData(IAsyncResult ar)
    {
        // Show Page Thread ID
```

```
            Trace.Warn("EndGetDate: " + Thread.CurrentThread.GetHashCode());

            // Bind results
            grdMovies.DataSource = dataLayer.EndGetMovies(ar);
            grdMovies.DataBind();
        }

        void TimeoutData(IAsyncResult ar)
        {
            // Display error message
            lblError.Text = "Could not retrieve data!";
        }
    </script>
    <html xmlns="http://www.w3.org/1999/xhtml" >
    <head id="Head1" runat="server">
        <title>Show Page AsyncTask</title>
    </head>
    <body>
        <form id="form1" runat="server">
        <div>

        <asp:Label
            id="lblError"
            Runat="server" />

        <asp:GridView
            id="grdMovies"
            Runat="server" />

        </div>
        </form>
    </body>
    </html>
```

The page in Listing 17.35 creates an instance of the `PageAsyncTask` object that represents the asynchronous task. Next, the `PageAsyncTask` object is registered for the page with the `Page.RegisterAsyncTask()` method. Finally, a call to the `Page.ExecuteRegisteredAsyncTasks()` method executes the task. (If you don't call this method, any asynchronous tasks registered for the page are executed during the `PreRender` event automatically.)

The constructor for the `PageAsyncTask` object accepts the following parameters:

- **beginHandler**—The method that executes when the asynchronous task begins.

- **endHandler**—The method that executes when the asynchronous task ends.

▶ **timoutHandler**—The method that executes when the asynchronous task runs out of time according to the Page directive's AsyncTimeout attribute.

▶ **state**—An arbitrary object that represents state information.

▶ **executeInParallel**—A Boolean value that indicates whether multiple asynchronous tasks should execute at the same time or execute in sequence.

You can create multiple PageAsyncTask objects and register them for the same page. When you call the ExecuteRegisteredAsyncTasks() method, all the registered tasks are executed.

If an asynchronous task does not complete within the time alloted by the AsyncTimeout attribute, then the timoutHandler method executes. For example, the page in Listing 17.35 gives the asychronous tasks 5 seconds to execute. If the database SELECT command does not return a record within the 5 seconds, then the TimeoutData() method executes.

It is important to understand that the asynchronous task continues to execute even when the task executes longer than the interval of time specified by the AsyncTimeout attribute. The AsyncTimeout attribute specifies the amount of time that a page is willing to wait before continuing execution. An asynchronous task is not canceled if takes too long.

The page in Listing 17.35 has tracing enabled, and it is sprinkled liberally with calls to Trace.Warn() so that you can see when different events happen. The Trace.Warn() statements writes out the ID of the current Page thread. The Page thread ID can change between the BeginGetData() and EndGetData() methods (see Figure 17.19).

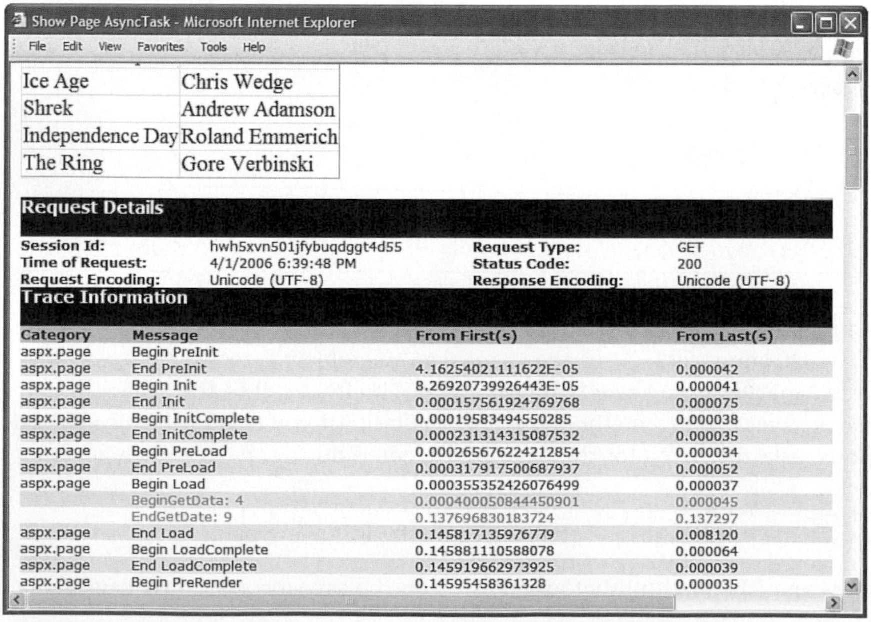

FIGURE 17.19   Trace information for a page executed asynchronously.

You can force the asynchronous task in Listing 17.35 to time out by adding a delay to the database command executed by the AsyncDataLayer.BeginGetMovies() method. For example, the following SELECT statement waits 15 seconds before returning results:

```
WAITFOR DELAY '0:0:15';SELECT Title,Director FROM Movies
```

If you use this modified SELECT statement, then the asynchronous task times out and the TimeoutData() method executes. The TimeoutData() method simply displays a message in a Label control.

NOTE

As an alternative to using the Page.RegisterAsyncTask() method to register an asynchronous task, you can use the Page.AddOnPreRenderCompleteAsync() method. However, this latter method does not provide you with as many options.

Building Database Objects with the .NET Framework

Microsoft SQL Server 2005 (including Microsoft SQL Server Express) supports building database objects with the .NET Framework. For example, you can create user-defined types, stored procedures, user-defined functions, and triggers written with the Visual Basic .NET or C# programming language.

The SQL language is optimized for retrieving database records. However, it is a crazy language that doesn't look like any other computer language on earth. Doing basic string parsing with SQL, for example, is a painful experience. Doing complex logic in a stored procedure is next to impossible (although many people do it).

When you work in the .NET Framework, on the other hand, you have access to thousands of classes. You can perform complex string matching and manipulation by using the Regular expression classes. You can implement business logic, no matter how complex.

By taking advantage of the .NET Framework when writing database objects, you no longer have to struggle with the SQL language when implementing your business logic. In this section, you learn how to build both user-defined types and stored procedures by using the .NET Framework.

Enabling CLR Integration

By default, support for building database objects with the .NET Framework is disabled. You must enable CLR integration by executing the following SQL Server command:

```
sp_configure 'clr enabled', 1
RECONFIGURE
```

17

When using SQL Express, you can execute these two commands by right-clicking a database in the Database Explorer window and selecting the New Query menu option. Enter the following string:

```
sp_configure 'clr enabled', 1; RECONFIGURE
```

Select Query Designer, Execute SQL to execute the commands (see Figure 17.20). You'll receive warnings that the query can't be parsed, which you can safely ignore.

FIGURE 17.20   Executing a database query in Visual Web Developer.

Creating User-Defined Types with the .NET Framework

You can create a new user-defined type by creating either a .NET class or .NET structure. After you create a user-defined type, you can use it in exactly the same way as the built-in SQL types such as the Int, NVarChar, or Decimal types. For example, you can create a new type and use the type to define a column in a database table.

To create a user-defined type with the .NET Framework, you must complete each of the following steps:

1. Create an assembly that contains the new type.
2. Register the assembly with SQL Server.
3. Create a type based on the assembly.

We'll go through each of these steps and walk through the process of creating a new user-defined type. We'll create a new user-defined type named DBMovie. The DBMovie type represents information about a particular movie. The type includes properties for the Title, Director, and BoxOfficeTotals for the movie.

After we create the `DBMovie` type, we can use the new type to define a column in a database table. Next, we write ADO.NET code that inserts and retrieves `DBMovie` objects from the database.

Creating the User-Defined Type Assembly   You can create a new user-defined type by creating either a class or a structure. We create the DBMovie type by creating a new .NET class.

When creating a class that will be used as a user-defined type, you must meet certain requirements:

▶ The class must be decorated with a `SqlUserDefinedType` attribute.

▶ The class must be able to equal `NULL`.

▶ The class must be serializable to/from a byte array.

▶ The class must be serializable to/from a string.

If you plan to use a class as a user-defined type, then you must add the `SqlUserDefinedType` attribute to the class. This attribute supports the following properties:

▶ **Format**—Enables you to specify how a user-defined type is serialized in SQL Server. Possible values are `Native` and `UserDefined`.

▶ **IsByteOrdered**—Enables you to cause the user-defined type to be ordered in the same way as its byte representation.

▶ **IsFixedLength**—Enables you to specify that all instances of this type have the same length.

▶ **MaxByteSize**—Enables you to specify the maximum size of the user-defined type in bytes.

▶ **Name**—Enables you to specify a name for the user-defined type.

▶ **ValidationMethodName**—Enables you to specify the name of a method that is called to verify whether a user-defined type is valid (useful when retrieving a user-defined type from an untrusted source).

The most important of these properties is the `Format` property. You use this property to specify how the user-defined type is serialized. The easiest option is to pick `Native`. In that case, SQL Server handles all the serialization issues, and you don't need to perform any additional work.

Unfortunately, you can take advantage of native serialization only for simple classes. If your class exposes a nonvalue type property such as a `String`, then you can't use native serialization.

Because the `DBMovie` class includes a `Title` and `Director` property, it's necessary to use `UserDefined` serialization. This means that it's also necessary to implement the `IBinarySerialize` interface to specify how the class gets serialized.

The `DBMovie` class is contained in Listing 17.36.

17

LISTING 17.36 DBMovie.cs

```csharp
using System;
using System.Text;
using Microsoft.SqlServer.Server;
using System.Data.SqlTypes;
using System.Runtime.InteropServices;
using System.IO;

[SqlUserDefinedType(Format.UserDefined, MaxByteSize = 512, IsByteOrdered = true)]
public class DBMovie : INullable, IBinarySerialize
{
    private bool _isNull;
    private string _title;
    private string _director;
    private decimal _boxOfficeTotals;

    public bool IsNull
    {
        get { return _isNull; }
    }

    public static DBMovie Null
    {
        get
        {
            DBMovie movie = new DBMovie();
            movie._isNull = true;
            return movie;
        }
    }

    public string Title
    {
        get { return _title; }
        set { _title = value; }
    }


    public string Director
    {
        get { return _director; }
        set { _director = value; }
    }

    [SqlFacet(Precision = 38, Scale = 2)]
```

```
public decimal BoxOfficeTotals
{
    get { return _boxOfficeTotals; }
    set { _boxOfficeTotals = value; }
}


[SqlMethod(OnNullCall = false)]
public static DBMovie Parse(SqlString s)
{
    if (s.IsNull)
        return Null;

    DBMovie movie = new DBMovie();
    string[] parts = s.Value.Split(new char[] { ',' });
    movie.Title = parts[0];
    movie.Director = parts[1];
    movie.BoxOfficeTotals = decimal.Parse(parts[2]);
    return movie;
}

public override string ToString()
{
    if (this.IsNull)
        return "NULL";

    StringBuilder builder = new StringBuilder();
    builder.Append(_title);
    builder.Append(",");
    builder.Append(_director);
    builder.Append(",");
    builder.Append(_boxOfficeTotals.ToString());
    return builder.ToString();
}

public void Write(BinaryWriter w)
{
    w.Write(_title);
    w.Write(_director);
    w.Write(_boxOfficeTotals);
}

public void Read(BinaryReader r)
{
    _title = r.ReadString();
    _director = r.ReadString();
```

17

LISTING 17.36   Continued

```
        _boxOfficeTotals = r.ReadDecimal();
    }

    public DBMovie()
    {
    }
}
```

The class in Listing 17.36 exposes three properties: the movie `Title`, `Director`, and `BoxOfficeTotals` properties. Notice that the `BoxOfficeTotals` property is decorated with a `SqlFacet` attribute that indicates the precision and scale of the property value. You must include this attribute if you want to perform SQL queries that use comparison operators with this property.

The class in Listing 17.36 also includes both an `IsNull` and `Null` property. SQL Server uses a three-valued logic (`True,False,Null`). All SQL Server types must be nullable.

The `DBMovie` class also includes both a `Parse()` and a `ToString()` method. These methods are required for converting the `DBMovie` class back and forth to a string representation.

Finally, the `DBMovie` class includes both a `Write()` and `Read()` method. These methods are required by the `IBinarySerialize` interface. The `Write()` method serializes the class. The `Read()` method deserializes the class. These methods must be implemented because the class uses `UserDefined` serialization.

You need to compile the `DBMovie` class into a separate assembly (`.dll` file). After you create (and debug) the class, move the class from your App_Code folder to another folder in your application, such as the root folder. Next, open the SDK Command prompt and execute the following command:

```
csc /t:library DBMovie.cs
```

This command uses the Visual Basic command-line compiler to compile the `DBMovie` class into an assembly.

Registering the User-Defined Type Assembly with SQL Server   After you create the assembly that contains your user-defined type, you must register the assembly in SQL Server. You can register the `DBMovie` assembly by executing the following command:

```
CREATE ASSEMBLY DBMovie
FROM 'C:\DBMovie.dll'
```

You need to provide the right path for the `DBMovie.dll` file on your hard drive. After you complete this step, the assembly is added to Microsoft SQL Server. When using Visual Web Developer, you can see the assembly by expanding the Assemblies folder in the Database

Explorer window. Alternatively, you can view a list of all the assemblies installed on SQL Server by executing the following query:

```
SELECT * FROM sys.assemblies
```

You can drop any assembly by executing the DROP Assembly command. For example, the following command removes the DBMovie assembly from SQL Server:

```
DROP Assembly DBMovie
```

Creating the User-Defined Type   After you have loaded the DBMovie assembly, you can create a new user-defined type from the assembly. Execute the following command:

```
CREATE TYPE dbo.DBMovie EXTERNAL NAME DBMovie.DBMovie
```

If you need to delete the type, you can execute the following command:

```
DROP TYPE DBMovie
```

After you have added the type, you can use it just like any other SQL Server native type. For example, you can create a new database table with the following command:

```
CREATE TABLE DBMovies(Id INT IDENTITY, Movie DBMovie)
```

You can insert a new record into this table with the following command:

```
INSERT DBMovies (Movie)
VALUES ('Star Wars,George Lucas,12.34')
```

Finally, you can perform queries against the table with queries like the following:

```
SELECT Id, Movie FROM DBMovies WHERE Movie.BoxOfficeTotals > 13.23
SELECT MAX(Movie.BoxOfficeTotals) FROM DBMovies
SELECT Movie FROM DBMovies WHERE Movie.Director LIKE 'g%'
```

I find the fact that you can execute queries like this truly amazing.

Building a Data Access Layer with a User-Defined Type

In this final section, let's actually do something with our new user-defined type. We'll create a new data access component that uses the DBMovie class and an ASP.NET page that interfaces with the component.

Before we can do anything with the DBMovie type, we need to add a reference to the DBMovie.dll assembly to our application. In Visual Web Developer, select the menu option Website, Add Reference, and browse to the DBMovie.dll. Alternatively, you can create an application root Bin folder and copy the DBMovie.dll into the Bin folder.

17

Our new data access component is contained in Listing 17.37.

LISTING 17.37   App_Code\DBDataLayer.cs

```csharp
using System;
using System.Data;
using System.Data.SqlClient;
using System.Web.Configuration;
using System.Collections.Generic;

public class DBDataLayer
{
    private static readonly string _connectionString;

    public List<DBMovie> GetAll()
    {
        List<DBMovie> results = new List<DBMovie>();
        SqlConnection con = new SqlConnection(_connectionString);
        SqlCommand cmd = new SqlCommand("SELECT Movie FROM DBMovies", con);
        using (con)
        {
            con.Open();
            SqlDataReader reader = cmd.ExecuteReader();
            while (reader.Read())
            {
                DBMovie newMovie = (DBMovie)reader["Movie"];
                results.Add(newMovie);
            }
        }
        return results;
    }

    public void Insert(DBMovie movieToAdd)
    {
        SqlConnection con = new SqlConnection(_connectionString);
        SqlCommand cmd = new SqlCommand("INSERT DBMovies (Movie) VALUES
➥(@Movie)", con);
        cmd.Parameters.Add("@Movie", SqlDbType.Udt);
        cmd.Parameters["@Movie"].UdtTypeName = "DBMovie";
        cmd.Parameters["@Movie"].Value = movieToAdd;
        using (con)
        {
            con.Open();
            cmd.ExecuteNonQuery();
        }
    }
}
```

```
    static DBDataLayer()
    {
        _connectionString = WebConfigurationManager.ConnectionStrings["Movies"].
        ➥ConnectionString;
    }
}
```

The component in Listing 17.37 contains two methods: `GetAll()` and `Insert()`. The `GetAll()` method retrieves all the `Movie` objects from the DBMovies database table. Notice that you can cast the object represented by the `DataReader` directly to a `DBMovie`.

The `Insert()` method adds a new `DBMovie` to the DBMovies database table. The method creates a normal ADO.NET `Command` object. However, notice that a special parameter is added to the command that represents the `DBMovie` object.

When you create a parameter that represents a user-defined type, you must specify a `UdtTypeName` property that represents the name of the user-defined type. In Listing 17.37, the value `DBMovie` is assigned to the `UdtTypeName` property. When the command executes, a new `DBMovie` object is added to the DBMovies database table.

The page in Listing 17.38 contains a `GridView`, `DetailsView`, and `ObjectDataSource` control. The `GridView` displays all the movies from the DBMovies database table. The `DetailsView` control enables you to insert a new `DBMovie` into the database (see Figure 17.21).

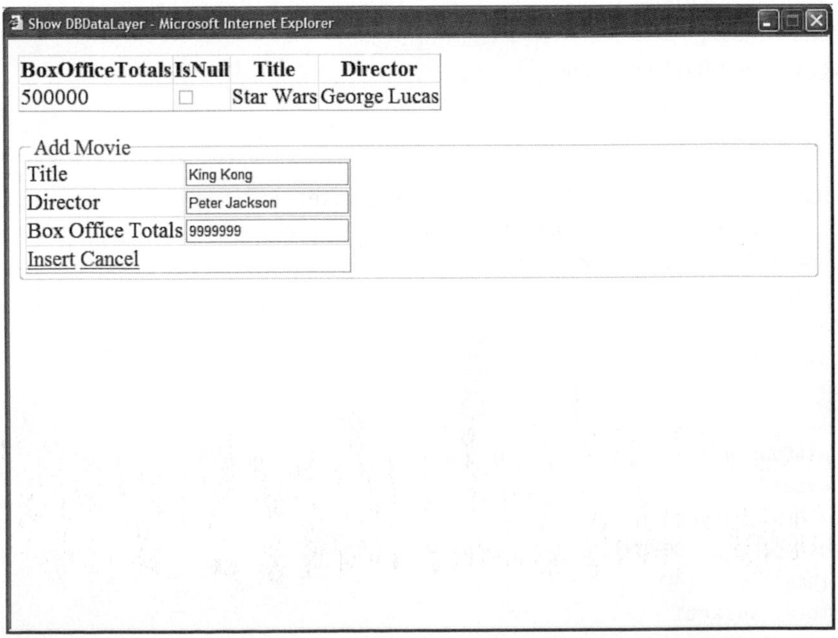

FIGURE 17.21   Displaying and inserting `DBMovie` objects.

LISTING 17.38   ShowDBDataLayer.aspx

```
<%@ Page Language="C#" %>
<!DOCTYPE html PUBLIC "-//W3C//DTD XHTML 1.0 Transitional//EN"
  "http://www.w3.org/TR/xhtml1/DTD/xhtml1-transitional.dtd">
<html xmlns="http://www.w3.org/1999/xhtml" >
<head id="Head1" runat="server">
    <title>Show DBDataLayer</title>
</head>
<body>
    <form id="form1" runat="server">
    <div>

    <asp:GridView
        id="grdMovies"
        DataSourceID="srcMovies"
        Runat="server" />


    <br />


    <fieldset>
    <legend>Add Movie</legend>
    <asp:DetailsView
        id="dtlMovie"
        DataSourceID="srcMovies"
        DefaultMode="Insert"
        AutoGenerateInsertButton="true"
        AutoGenerateRows="false"
        Runat="server">
        <Fields>
        <asp:BoundField DataField="Title" HeaderText="Title" />
        <asp:BoundField DataField="Director" HeaderText="Director" />
        <asp:BoundField DataField="BoxOfficeTotals"
            HeaderText="Box Office Totals" />
        </Fields>
    </asp:DetailsView>
    </fieldset>


    <asp:ObjectDataSource
        id="srcMovies"
        TypeName="DBDataLayer"
        DataObjectTypeName="DBMovie"
        SelectMethod="GetAll"
        InsertMethod="Insert"
        Runat="server" />
```

```
    </div>
    </form>
</body>
</html>
```

Creating Stored Procedures with the .NET Framework

You can use the .NET Framework to build a SQL stored procedure by mapping a stored procedure to a method defined in a class. You must complete the following steps:

1. Create an assembly that contains the stored procedure method.

2. Register the assembly with SQL Server.

3. Create a stored procedure based on the assembly.

In this section, we create two stored procedures with the .NET Framework. The first stored procedure, named GetRandomRow(), randomly returns a single row from a database table. The second stored procedure, GetRandomRows(), randomly returns a set of rows from a database table.

Creating the Stored Procedure Assembly

Creating a stored procedure with the .NET Framework is easy. All you need to do is decorate a method with the SqlProcedure attribute.

The method used for the stored procedure must satisfy two requirements. The method must be a shared (static) method. Furthermore, the method must be implemented either as a subroutine or as a function that returns an integer value.

Within your method, you can take advantage of the SqlPipe class to send results back to your application. The SqlPipe class supports the following methods:

- **Send()**—Enables you to send a DataReader, single-row resultset, or string.

- **ExecuteAndSend()**—Enables you to execute a SqlCommand and send the results.

- **SendResultsStart()**—Enables you to initiate the sending of a resultset.

- **SendResultsRow()**—Enables you to send a single row of a resultset.

- **SendResultsEnd()**—Enables you to end the sending of a resultset.

Within the method used for creating the stored procedure, you can use ADO.NET objects such as the SqlCommand, SqlDataReader, and SqlDataAdapter objects in the normal way. However, rather than connect to the database by using a normal connection string, you can create something called a *context connection*. A context connection enables you to connect to the same database server as the stored procedure without authenticating.

Here's how you can initialize a SqlConnection to use a context connection:

```
SqlConnection con = new SqlConnection("context connection=true");
```

17

Notice that you don't specify credentials or the location of the database in the connection string. Remember that the method actually executes within SQL Server. Therefore, you don't need to connect to SQL Server in the normal way.

The class in Listing 17.39 contains two methods named GetRandomRow() and GetRandomRows(). Both methods use a SqlDataAdapter to fill a DataTable with the contents of the Movies database table. The GetRandomRow() method grabs a single row from the DataTable and sends it back to the client. The GetRandomRows() method sends multiple rows back to the client.

LISTING 17.39   RandomRows.cs

```
using System;
using System.Data;
using System.Data.SqlClient;
using Microsoft.SqlServer.Server;

public class RandomRows
{
    [SqlProcedure]
    public static void GetRandomRow()
    {
        // Dump all records from Movies into a DataTable
        SqlDataAdapter dad = new SqlDataAdapter("SELECT Id,Title FROM Movies",
        ➥"context connection=true");
        DataTable dtblMovies = new DataTable();
        dad.Fill(dtblMovies);

        // Grab a random row
        Random rnd = new Random();
        DataRow ranRow = dtblMovies.Rows[rnd.Next(dtblMovies.Rows.Count)];

        // Build a SqlDataRecord that represents the row
        SqlDataRecord result = new SqlDataRecord(new SqlMetaData("Id",
        ➥SqlDbType.Int), new SqlMetaData("Title", SqlDbType.NVarChar, 100));
        result.SetSqlInt32(0, (int)ranRow["Id"]);
        result.SetSqlString(1, (string)ranRow["Title"]);

        // Send result
        SqlContext.Pipe.Send(result);
    }

    [SqlProcedure]
    public static void GetRandomRows(int rowsToReturn)
    {
        // Dump all records from Movies into a DataTable
```

```
    SqlDataAdapter dad = new SqlDataAdapter("SELECT Id,Title FROM Movies",
    ➥"context connection=true");
    DataTable dtblMovies = new DataTable();
    dad.Fill(dtblMovies);

    // Send start record
    SqlDataRecord result = new SqlDataRecord(new SqlMetaData("Id",
    ➥SqlDbType.Int), new SqlMetaData("Title", SqlDbType.NVarChar, 100));
    SqlContext.Pipe.SendResultsStart(result);

    Random rnd = new Random();
    for (int i = 0; i < rowsToReturn; i++)
    {
        // Grab a random row
        DataRow ranRow = dtblMovies.Rows[rnd.Next(dtblMovies.Rows.Count)];

        // Set the record
        result.SetSqlInt32(0, (int)ranRow["Id"]);
        result.SetSqlString(1, (string)ranRow["Title"]);

        // Send record
        SqlContext.Pipe.SendResultsRow(result);
    }

    // Send end record
    SqlContext.Pipe.SendResultsEnd();
  }

}
```

17

You need to compile the RandomRows class into a separate assembly (.dll file). After you create (and debug) the class, move the class from your App_Code folder to another folder in your application, such as the root folder. Next, open the SDK Command prompt and execute the following command:

```
csc /t:library RandomRows.cs
```

This command uses the Visual Basic command-line compiler to compile the RandomRows class into an assembly.

Registering the Stored Procedure Assembly with SQL Server   After you compile the RandomRows assembly, you are ready to deploy the assembly to SQL Server. You can load the assembly into SQL Server by executing the following command:

```
CREATE ASSEMBLY RandomRows
FROM 'C:\RandomRows.dll'
```

You need to supply the proper path to the `RandomRows.dll` assembly on your hard drive.

If you need to remove the assembly, you can execute the following command:

```
DROP Assembly RandomRows
```

Creating the Stored Procedures   Now that the assembly is loaded, you can create two stored procedures that correspond to the two methods defined in the assembly. Execute the following two SQL commands:

```
CREATE PROCEDURE GetRandomRow AS
EXTERNAL NAME RandomRows.RandomRows.GetRandomRow

CREATE PROCEDURE GetRandomRows(@rowsToReturn Int) AS
EXTERNAL NAME RandomRows.RandomRows.GetRandomRows
```

After you execute these two commands, you'll have two new stored procedures named `GetRandomRow` and `GetRandomRows`. You can treat these stored procedures just like normal stored procedures. For example, executing the following command displays three random movies from the Movies database:

```
GetRandomRows 3
```

If you need to delete these stored procedures, you can execute the following two commands:

```
DROP PROCEDURE GetRandomRow
DROP PROCEDURE GetRandomRows
```

Executing a .NET Stored Procedure from an ASP.NET Page   After the two stored procedures have been created, you can use the stored procedures with an ASP.NET page. For example, the component in Listing 17.40 contains two methods that call the two stored procedures.

LISTING 17.40   App_Code\RandomDataLayer.cs

```csharp
using System;
using System.Data;
using System.Data.SqlClient;
using System.Web.Configuration;
using System.Collections.Generic;

public class RandomDataLayer
{
    private static readonly string _connectionString;

    public List<String> GetRandomMovies()
    {
```

```
            List<String> results = new List<String>();
            SqlConnection con = new SqlConnection(_connectionString);
            SqlCommand cmd = new SqlCommand("GetRandomRows", con);
            cmd.CommandType = CommandType.StoredProcedure;
            cmd.Parameters.AddWithValue("@rowsToReturn", 5);
            using (con)
            {
                con.Open();
                SqlDataReader reader = cmd.ExecuteReader();
                while (reader.Read())
                    results.Add((string)reader["Title"]);
            }
            return results;
        }


        public static string GetRandomMovie()
        {
            string result = String.Empty;
            SqlConnection con = new SqlConnection(_connectionString);
            SqlCommand cmd = new SqlCommand("GetRandomRow", con);
            cmd.CommandType = CommandType.StoredProcedure;
            using (con)
            {
                con.Open();
                SqlDataReader reader = cmd.ExecuteReader();
                if (reader.Read())
                    result = (string)reader["Title"];
            }
            return result;
        }

        static RandomDataLayer()
        {
            _connectionString = WebConfigurationManager.ConnectionStrings["Movies"].
            ➥ConnectionString;
        }

}
```

17

In Listing 17.40, the `GetRandomRow` and `GetRandomRows` stored procedures are executed with the help of `SqlCommand` objects.

The page in Listing 17.41 contains a `GridView` and `ObjectDataSource` control. The `ObjectDataSource` control represents the `RandomDataLayer` component. When you request the page, a single random movie title is displayed in a Label control. Furthermore, a list of five random movie titles is displayed in the GridView control (see Figure 17.22).

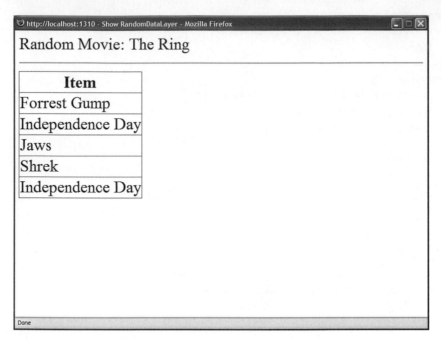

FIGURE 17.22   Calling a .NET stored procedure from an ASP.NET page.

LISTING 17.41   ShowRandomDataLayer.aspx

```
<%@ Page Language="C#" %>
<!DOCTYPE html PUBLIC "-//W3C//DTD XHTML 1.0 Transitional//EN"
"http://www.w3.org/TR/xhtml1/DTD/xhtml1-transitional.dtd">
<script runat="server">

    void Page_Load()
    {
        lblRandomMovie.Text = RandomDataLayer.GetRandomMovie();
    }
</script>
<html xmlns="http://www.w3.org/1999/xhtml" >
<head id="Head1" runat="server">
    <title>Show RandomDataLayer</title>
</head>
<body>
    <form id="form1" runat="server">
    <div>
```

```
    Random Movie:
    <asp:Label
        id="lblRandomMovie"
        Runat="server" />

    <hr />

    <asp:GridView
        id="grdMovies"
        DataSourceID="srcMovies"
        Runat="server" />
    <asp:ObjectDataSource
        id="srcMovies"
        TypeName="RandomDataLayer"
        SelectMethod="GetRandomMovies"
        Runat="server" />
    </div>
    </form>
</body>
</html>
```

Summary

This chapter provided you with an overview of ADO.NET. It described how you can use ADO.NET to represent database data with both a connected and disconnected model of data access.

In the first part of this chapter, you learned how to use the Connection, Command, and DataReader objects to connect to a database, execute commands, and represent the results of a database query. You learned how to retrieve provider statistics such as command execution times. You also learned how to represent stored procedures with the Command object. Finally, you learned how to work with multiple active resultsets (MARS).

In the second part of this chapter, you learned how to work with the DataAdapter, DataTable, DataView, and DataSet objects. You learned how you can perform batch updates with the DataAdapter object. You also learned how to use the DataTable object to represent and edit database rows.

Next, you learned how to improve the data access performance of your ASP.NET pages by executing asynchronous database commands within asynchronous ASP.NET pages.

Finally, you got a chance to tackle the advanced topic of building database objects with the .NET Framework. You learned how you can use the .NET Framework to build both user-defined types and stored procedures. For example, you learned how to insert and select a custom class from a database table by creating a user-defined type with the .NET Framework.

17

Data Access with LINQ to SQL

Of all the new features introduced in .NET Framework 3.5, LINQ to SQL is the most significant one. Indeed, it might represent the biggest change in the way applications interact with databases since the introduction of SQL.

A vast chasm separates the way developers work with transient application data and the way developers work with persistent database data. In our applications, we work with objects and properties (created with either C# or VB.NET). In most databases, on the other hand, we work with tables and columns.

This is true in spite of the fact that our applications and our databases are used to represent the very same data. For example, you might have both a class and a database table named Product that represents a list of products you sell through your website. However, the languages we use to interact with these entities are very different. The C# and VB.NET languages are very different from the SQL language. Larger companies typically have different developers who specialize in C# or VB.NET, on the one hand, or SQL, on the other hand.

A huge amount of developer time is spent performing brain-dead, tedious translations between the object and relational universes. I cringe when I think of the number of hours I've spent declaring classes that contain a one-to-one mapping between properties and database columns. This is time I could have devoted to going to the park with my children, seeing a movie, walking my dog, and so on.

LINQ to SQL promises to finally allow us to put SQL to a well-deserved death. Or more accurately, it promises to make SQL a subterranean language that we never need to interact with again (SQL is plumbing, and I am not a plumber). This is a good thing. Death to SQL!

This is a hard chapter. LINQ to SQL is not easy to understand because it relies on several mind-bending, new features introduced into C#, VB.NET, and the .NET Framework. So please have patience. Take a deep breath. I promise you everything will make sense in the end.

This chapter is divided into four parts. In the first part, I discuss the new features introduced in C#, VB.NET, and .NET Framework 3.5 to support LINQ. Next, you learn how to represent database tables with LINQ to SQL entities. In the following part, I explain how to perform standard SQL commands—such as SELECT, INSERT, UPDATE, and DELETE commands—with LINQ to SQL. In the final part of this chapter, I demonstrate how you can create a custom entity base class (and integrate form validation into your LINQ entities).

> **NOTE**
>
> The sample application included in the last chapter of this book uses LINQ for all database access.

New C# and VB.NET Language Features

To get LINQ to SQL to work, Microsoft had to introduce several new language features to both C# and VB.NET. Many of these features make C# and VB.NET behave more like a dynamic language (think JavaScript). Although the primary motivation for introducing these new features was to support LINQ, the new features are also interesting in their own right.

> **NOTE**
>
> To use these new language features, you'll need to make sure your website is targeting .NET Framework 3.5. Ensure that you have a web.config file in your project. Next, select the menu option Website, Start Options and then select the Build tab. For Target Framework, select .NET Framework 3.5. Performing these steps will modify your web.config file so that it references the necessary assemblies and uses the right version of the C# or VB.NET compiler.

Understanding Automatic Properties

The first of these new language features we will explore is called *automatic properties*. Unfortunately, this feature is supported only by C# and not VB.NET.

Automatic properties provide you with a shorthand method for defining a new property. For example, Listing 18.1 contains a class named Product that contains Id, Description, and Price properties.

LISTING 18.1   LanguageChanges\App_Code\AutomaticProperties.cs

```csharp
public class AutomaticProperties
{
    // Automatic Properties

    public int Id { get; set; }

    public string Description { get; set; }


    // Normal Property

    private decimal _Price;

    public decimal Price
    {
        get { return _Price; }
        set { _Price = value; }
    }
}
```

Notice that the first two properties, Id and Description, unlike the last property, Price, do not include Getters or Setters. The C# compiler creates the Getters and Setters—and the secret, private, backing fields—for you automatically.

You can't add any logic to the Getters and Setters for an automatic property. You also can't create read-only automatic properties.

Why are automatic properties relevant to LINQ to SQL? When working with LINQ to SQL, you often use classes to represent nothing more than the list of columns you want to retrieve from the database (the shape of the data) like the select list in a SQL query. In those cases, you just want to do the minimum amount of work possible to create a list of properties, and automatic properties allow you to do this.

NOTE

You can quickly add an automatic property to a class or page when using Visual Web Developer/Visual Studio by typing **prop** and hitting the Tab key twice.

Understanding Initializers

You can use initializers to reduce the amount of work it takes to create a new instance of a class. For example, assume that you have a class that looks like Listing 18.2 (in C#) or like Listing 18.3 (in VB.NET).

18

LISTING 18.2   LanguageChanges\App_Code\Product.cs

```csharp
public class Product
{
    public int Id { get; set; }

    public string Name { get; set; }

    public decimal Price { get; set; }
}
```

LISTING 18.3   LanguageChanges\App_Code\Product.vb

```vbnet
Public Class Product

    Private _Id As Integer

    Public Property Id() As Integer
        Get
            Return _Id
        End Get
        Set(ByVal value As Integer)
            _Id = value
        End Set
    End Property

    Private _Name As String

    Public Property Name() As String
        Get
            Return _Name
        End Get
        Set(ByVal value As String)
            _Name = value
        End Set
    End Property

    Private _Price As Decimal

    Public Property Price() As Decimal
        Get
            Return _Price
        End Get
        Set(ByVal value As Decimal)
```

```
            _Price = value
        End Set
    End Property

End Class
```

The Product class has three public properties (declared by taking advantage of automatic properties in the case of C#—sorry VB.NET).

Now, let's say you want to create an instance of the Product class. Here's how you would do it in .NET Framework 2.0 (with C#):

```
Product product1 = new Product();
product1.Id = 1;
product1.Name = "Laptop Computer";
product1.Price = 800.00m;
```

And here is how you would do it in .NET Framework 2 (with VB.NET):

```
Dim product1 As New Product()
product1.Id = 1
product1.Name = "Laptop Computer"
product1.Price = 800.0
```

Notice that it takes four lines of code to initialize this trivial little Product class. That's too much work. By taking advantage of initializers, you can do everything in a single line of code. Here's how you use initializers in C#:

```
Product product2 = new Product {Id=1, Name="Laptop Computer", Price=800.00m};
```

Here's how you use initializers in VB.NET:

```
Dim product2 As New Product() With {.Id = 1, .Name = "Laptop Computer",
  .Price = 800.0}
```

Now, clearly, you could do something very similar by declaring a constructor on the Product class that accepts Id, Name, and Price parameters. However, then your class would become more bloated with code because you would need to assign the constructor parameter values to the class properties. Initializers are useful because, by taking advantage of this feature, you can declare agile little classes and initialize these svelte classes with a minimum of code.

Understanding Type Inference

Here's a new feature that makes C# and VB.NET look much more like a dynamic language such as JavaScript: local variable type inference. When you take advantage of type inference, you allow the C# or VB.NET compiler to determine the type of a variable at compile time.

Here's an example of how you use type inference with C#:

```
var message = "Hello World!";
```

And here is how you would use type inference with VB.NET:

```
Dim message = "Hello World!"
```

Notice that the message variable is declared without specifying a type. The C# and VB.NET compilers can infer the type of the variable (it's a `String`) from the value you use to initialize the variable.

No performance impact results from using type inference (the variable is not late bound). The compiler does all the work of figuring out the data type at compile time.

Notice that a new keyword has been introduced into C# to support type inference: the `var` keyword. You declare a variable as type `var` when you want the compiler to figure out the variable's data type all by itself.

You can take advantage of type inference only when you provide a local variable with an initial value. For example, this won't work (C#):

```
var message;
message = "Hello World!";
```

The C# compiler will refuse to compile this code because the message variable is not initialized when it is declared.

The following code will work in VB.NET (but it won't do what you want):

```
Dim message
message = "Hello World!"
```

In this case, VB.NET will treat the message variable as type `Object`. At runtime, it will cast the value of the variable to a string when you assign the string to the variable. This is not good from a performance perspective.

> **NOTE**
>
> VB.NET 9.0 includes a new option called Option Infer. Option Infer must be enabled in order for the implicit typing feature to work. You can enable it for a particular class file by adding the line `Option Infer On` at the very top of a code file.

The relevance of type inference to LINQ to SQL will be apparent after you read the next section. In many circumstances when using LINQ to SQL, you won't actually know the name of the type of a variable, so you have to let the compiler infer the type.

Understanding Anonymous Types

Anonymous types is another idea that might be familiar to you from dynamic languages. Anonymous types are useful when you need a transient, fleeting type and you don't want to do the work to create a class.

Here's an example of creating an anonymous type in C#:

```
var customer = new {FirstName = "Stephen", LastName = "Walther"};
```

Here's how you would create the same anonymous type in VB.NET:

```
Dim customer = New With {.FirstName = "Stephen", .LastName = "Walther"}
```

Notice that the customer variable is used without specifying a type (this looks very much like JavaScript or VBScript). However, it is important to understand that customer does have a type, you just don't know its name: It's anonymous.

In a single line of code, we've managed to both create a new class and initialize its properties. The terseness brings tears to my eyes.

Anonymous types are useful when working with LINQ to SQL because you'll discover that you'll often need to create new types on the fly. For example, you might want to return a class that represents a limited set of database columns when performing a particular query. You'll need to create a transient class that represents the columns.

Understanding Generics

Yes, I realize that generics are not new to .NET 3.5. However, they are such an important aspect of LINQ to SQL that it is worth using a little space to review this feature.

> **NOTE**
>
> To use generics, you need to import the `System.Collections.Generic` namespace.

I most often use generics by taking advantage of generic collections. For example, if you want to represent a list of strings, you can declare a list of strings like this (in C#):

```
List<string> stuffToBuy = new List<string>();
stuffToBuy.Add("socks");
stuffToBuy.Add("beer");
stuffToBuy.Add("cigars");
```

Here's how you would declare the list of strings in VB.NET:

```
Dim stuffToBuy As New List(Of String)
stuffToBuy.Add("socks")
stuffToBuy.Add("beer")
```

```
stuffToBuy.Add("cigars")
```

And, by taking advantage of collection initializers, you can now declare a strongly typed list of strings in a single line like this (in C#):

```
List<string> stuffToBuy2 = new List<string> {"socks", "beer", "cigars"};
```

> **NOTE**
>
> Unfortunately, VB.NET does not support collection intializers or array initializers.

The List class is an example of a generic because you specify the type of object that the class will contain when you declare the List class. In C#, you specify the type in between the alligator mouths (< >), and in VB.NET you use the 0f keyword. In the preceding examples, we created a List class that contains strings. Alternatively, we could have created a List class that contains integers or a custom type such as products or customers represented by a Product or Customer class.

A generic collection like a List is superior to a nongeneric collection like an ArrayList because a generic is strongly typed. An ArrayList stores everything as an object. A generic stores everything as a particular type. When you pull an item out of an ArrayList, you must cast it to a particular type before you use it. An item pulled from a generic, on the other hand, does not need to be cast to a type.

Generics are not limited solely to collections. You can create generic methods, generic classes, and generic interfaces.

For example, when working with ADO.NET classes, I like to convert my data readers into strongly typed List collections. The method GetListFromCommand(), shown in Listing 18.4, takes a command object, executes it, and generates a typed List automatically.

LISTING 18.4   LanguageChanges\App_Code\GenericMethods.cs

```
using System;
using System.Collections.Generic;
using System.Data.SqlClient;

public class GenericMethods
{
    public static List<T> GetListFromCommand<T>(SqlCommand command)
    where T: ICreatable, new()
    {
        List<T> results = new List<T>();
        using (command.Connection)
        {
            command.Connection.Open();
            SqlDataReader reader = command.ExecuteReader();
```

```
            while (reader.Read())
            {
                T newThing = new T();
                newThing.Create(reader);
                results.Add( newThing );
            }
        }
        return results;
    }
}


public interface ICreatable
{
    void Create(SqlDataReader reader);
}
```

Notice that the `GetListFromCommand()` method in Listing 18.4 accepts a SqlCommand object and returns a generic `List<T>`. The generic type is constrained by the where clause. The generic constraint restricts the types that can be used for T to types that implement the `ICreatable` interface and types that can be instantiated with new.

The `ICreatable` interface is also defined in Listing 18.4. The interface requires a class to implement a single method named `Create()`.

Now that we have created a generic method for converting data readers into strongly typed lists, we can use it with any class that implements the `ICreatable` interface, such as the `Movie` class in Listing 18.5.

LISTING 18.5   Movie.cs

```
using System;
using System.Data.SqlClient;

public class Movie : ICreatable
{
    public int Id { get; set; }

    public string Title { get; set; }

    public void Create(SqlDataReader reader)
    {
        Id = (int)reader["Id"];
        Title = (string)reader["Title"];
    }

}
```

You can call the generic `GetListFromCommand()` method with the `Movie` type like this (the page named ShowGenericMethods.aspx on the CD uses this code):

```
string conString = WebConfigurationManager.ConnectionStrings["con"].ConnectionString;
SqlConnection con = new SqlConnection(conString);
SqlCommand cmd = new SqlCommand("SELECT Id, Title FROM Movie", con);
List<Movie> movies = GenericMethods.GetListFromCommand<Movie>(cmd);
```

The beautiful thing about generics here is that you don't have to write the same code to convert a data reader to a generic List for each type. You write the `GetListFromCommand()` method as a generic method once, and you can use the method with any type that meets the generic constraints in the future.

The right way to think of generics is to think of a code template. You can use generics to define a certain pattern of code into which you can plug a particular type.

Understanding Lambda Expressions

Lambda expressions, another new language feature introduced with .NET Framework 3.5, provide you with an extremely terse way of defining methods.

Imagine, for example, that you want to programmatically wire up a `Click` event handler to a button control. Listing 18.6 is an example of one way of doing this.

LISTING 18.6   LanguageChanges\NormalMethod.aspx

```
<%@ Page Language="C#" %>
<!DOCTYPE html PUBLIC "-//W3C//DTD XHTML 1.0 Transitional//EN"
"http://www.w3.org/TR/xhtml1/DTD/xhtml1-transitional.dtd">
<script runat="server">

    void Page_Init()
    {
        btn.Click += new EventHandler(btn_Click);
    }

    void btn_Click(object sender, EventArgs e)
    {
        lblResult.Text = DateTime.Now.ToString();
    }
</script>

<html xmlns="http://www.w3.org/1999/xhtml">
<head runat="server">
    <title>Normal Method</title>
</head>
<body>
    <form id="form1" runat="server">
```

```
    <div>

    <asp:Button
        id="btn"
        Text="Go!"
        Runat="server" />

    <asp:Label
        id="lblResult"
        Runat="server" />

    </div>
    </form>
</body>
</html>
```

In Listing 18.6, the `Page_Init()` method associates the Button `Click` event with the `btn_Click()` method. When you click the button, the `btn_Click()` method executes and displays the current date and time. Nothing special here.

In .NET Framework 2.0, the notion of anonymous methods for C# was introduced. The advantage of an anonymous method is that you can declare it inline. For example, Listing 18.7 does the same thing as the previous page, except for the fact that it uses an anonymous method to handle the Button `Click` event.

LISTING 18.7   LanguageChanges\AnonymousMethod.aspx

```
<%@ Page Language="C#" %>
<!DOCTYPE html PUBLIC "-//W3C//DTD XHTML 1.0 Transitional//EN"
 "http://www.w3.org/TR/xhtml1/DTD/xhtml1-transitional.dtd">
<script runat="server">

    void Page_Init()
    {
        btn.Click += delegate(object sender, EventArgs e)
                        {
                            lblResult.Text = DateTime.Now.ToString();
                        };
    }

</script>

<html xmlns="http://www.w3.org/1999/xhtml">
<head id="Head1" runat="server">
    <title>Anonymous Method</title>
</head>
```

LISTING 18.7   Continued

```
<body>
    <form id="form1" runat="server">
    <div>

    <asp:Button
        id="btn"
        Text="Go!"
        Runat="server" />

    <asp:Label
        id="lblResult"
        Runat="server" />

    </div>
    </form>
</body>
</html>
```

In Listing 18.7, the `Click` event is handled with a function declared within the `Page_Init()` method.

> **NOTE**
>
> Anonymous methods are not supported by VB.NET, but VB.NET does support lambda expressions—so don't stop reading if you use VB.NET.

Lambda expressions take the notion of the anonymous method one step further. Lambda expressions reduce the amount of syntax required to define a method to its semantic minimum. Listing 18.8 does the same thing as the previous two listings, except for the fact that the page uses a lambda expression.

LISTING 18.8   LanguageChanges\LambdaExpression.aspx

```
<%@ Page Language="C#" %>
<!DOCTYPE html PUBLIC "-//W3C//DTD XHTML 1.0 Transitional//EN"
 "http://www.w3.org/TR/xhtml1/DTD/xhtml1-transitional.dtd">
<script runat="server">

    void Page_Init()
    {
        btn.Click += (sender, e) => lblResult.Text = DateTime.Now.ToString();
    }
```

```
</script>

<html xmlns="http://www.w3.org/1999/xhtml">
<head id="Head1" runat="server">
    <title>Lambda Expressions</title>
</head>
<body>
    <form id="form1" runat="server">
    <div>

    <asp:Button
        id="btn"
        Text="Go!"
        Runat="server" />

    <asp:Label
        id="lblResult"
        Runat="server" />

    </div>
    </form>
</body>
</html>
```

The lambda expression in Listing 18.8 is the one that looks like this:

```
(sender, e) => lblResult.Text = DateTime.Now.ToString();
```

This is just a terse way of writing a method. A lambda expression uses the => operator (the "goes into" operator) to separate a list of method parameters from the method body. The compiler (usually) can infer the data types of the parameters. However, if you want, you can be explicit about the parameter types, like this:

```
(object sender, EventArgs e) => lblResult.Text = DateTime.Now.ToString();
```

It is also worth mentioning that the parentheses around the parameters are optional when there is a single parameter. So, a lambda expression can be very terse.

Visual Basic also supports lambda expressions, but in a more limited way. A lambda expression in Visual Basic cannot contain statements, it can only contain expressions.

Here's the syntax in VB for creating a lambda expression:

```
Dim AddNumbers = Function(x, y) x + y
Response.Write(AddNumbers(5, 6))
```

18

The first statement creates a variable named AddNumbers that represents a lambda expression. The VB syntax Function(x,y) x + y is equivalent to the C# syntax (x,y) => x + y. Next, the lambda function is called with two arguments.

Understanding Extension Methods

The idea behind extension methods should also be familiar to anyone who has worked with JavaScript (think prototype).

By taking advantage of extension methods, you can add new methods to existing classes. For example, you can make up any method you want and add the method to the String class.

I'm constantly HTML-encoding strings because I am paranoid about JavaScript injection attacks. In .NET Framework 2.0, you HTML-encode a string by calling the Server.HtmlEncode() static method, like this:

```
string evilString = "<script>alert('boom!')<" + "/script>";
ltlMessage.Text = Server.HtmlEncode(evilString);
```

In this statement, the static HtmlEncode() method is called on the Server class. Wouldn't it be nice if we could just call HtmlEncode() on a string directly like this:

```
string evilString = "<script>alert('boom!')<" + "/script>";
ltlMessage.Text = evilString.HtmlEncode();
```

Using extension methods, we can do exactly that. We can add any methods to a class that we feel like. You create an extension method by creating a static class and declaring a static method that has a special first parameter. Listing 18.9 demonstrates how you create an extension method to add the HtmlEncode() method to the String class.

LISTING 18.9   LanguageChanges\MyExtensions.vb

```
public static class MyExtensions
{
    public static string HtmlEncode(this string str)
    {
        return System.Web.HttpUtility.HtmlEncode(str);
    }
}
```

Notice that the one and only parameter for the HtmlEncode() method is preceded by the keyword this. The parameter indicates the type that the extension method applies to.

Creating extension methods in VB.NET is very similar to creating extension methods in C#. Listing 18.10 contains the same `HtmlEncode()` method as the previous listing.

LISTING 18.10   LanguageChanges\MyExtensions.cs

```
Imports System.Runtime.CompilerServices


Public Module MyExtensions


    <Extension()> _
    Public Function HtmlEncode(ByVal str As String) As String
        Return System.Web.HttpUtility.HtmlEncode(str)
    End Function


End Module
```

When working with VB.NET, you must declare an extension method in a module. Furthermore, you mark the extension methods with the `System.Runtime.CompilerServices.Extension` attribute.

Understanding LINQ

Finally, we get to the topic of LINQ—the last topic we need to examine before we can dive into the true subject of this chapter: LINQ to SQL.

LINQ stands for Language Integrated Query. LINQ consists of a set of new language features added to both the C# and VB.NET languages that enable you to perform queries. LINQ enables you to use SQL query–like syntax within C# or VB.NET.

Here's a simple example of a LINQ query:

```
var words = new List<string> {"zephyr", "apple", "azure"};


var results = from w in words
  where w.Contains("z")
  select w;
```

The first statement creates a generic List of three strings named "words." The second statement is the LINQ query.

The LINQ query resembles a backward SQL statement. It retrieves all the words from the List that contain the letter *z*. After you execute the query, the results variable will contain the following list of two words:

```
zephyr
azure
```

You can perform a standard LINQ query against any object that implements the
IEnumerable<T> interface. An object that implements this interface is called a *sequence*.
Notable examples of sequences are both the generic List class and the standard Array
class (so anything you can dump into an array, you can query with LINQ).

The C# language supports the following clauses that you can use in a query:

- ▶ **from**—Enables you to specify the data source and a variable for iterating over the
  data source (a range variable).

- ▶ **where**—Enables you to filter the results of a query.

- ▶ **select**—Enables you to specify the items included in the results of the query.

- ▶ **group**—Enables you to group related values by a common key.

- ▶ **into**—Enables you to store the results of a group or join into a temporary variable.

- ▶ **orderby**—Enables you to order query results in ascending or descending order.

- ▶ **join**—Enables you to join two data sources using a common key.

- ▶ **let**—Enables you to create a temporary variable to represent subquery results.

Building a LINQ query is like building a backward SQL query. You start by specifying a
from clause that indicates where you want to get your data. Next, optionally, you specify a
where clause that filters your data. Finally, you specify a select clause that gives shape to
your data (determines the objects and properties you want to return).

Under the covers, standard LINQ queries are translated into method calls on the
System.Linq.Enumerable class. The Enumerable class contains extension methods that are
applied to any class that implements the IEnumerable<T> interface.

So, the query

```
var results = from w in words
  where w.Contains("z")
  select w;
```

is translated into this query by the C# compiler:

```
var results = words.Where( w => w.Contains("z") ).Select( w => w );
```

The first query uses *query syntax* and the second query uses *method syntax*. The two queries
are otherwise identical.

Notice that the query using method syntax accepts lambda expressions for its Where() and
Select() methods. The lambda expression used with the Where() method filters the
results so that only words that contain the letter *z* are returned. The Select() method
indicates the object and property to return. If we had passed the lambda expression

`w => w.Length` to the `Select()` method, the query would return the length of each word instead of the word itself.

The choice of whether to use query or method syntax when building LINQ queries is purely a matter of preference. Query syntax uses language-specific syntax (C# or VB.NET). Method syntax is language independent.

I find that I use method syntax more than query syntax because query syntax is a subset of method syntax. In other words, you can do more with method syntax. That said, in some cases, writing a query in method syntax is just too verbose. For example, writing left outer joins with LINQ to SQL is much easier using query syntax than method syntax.

At the end of the day, the choice of whether to use method or query syntax doesn't really matter because all the query syntax statements get translated by the compiler into method syntax. In the case of standard LINQ, those method calls are calls on methods of the `Enumerable` class.

Lookup the `System.Linq.Enumerable` class in the SDK documentation to view the full list of methods that the `Enumerable` class supports. Here is a list of some of the more interesting and useful methods:

- **Aggregate()**—Enables you to apply a function to every item in a sequence.

- **Average()**—Returns the average value of every item in a sequence.

- **Count()**—Returns the count of items from a sequence.

- **Distinct()**—Returns distinct items from a sequence.

- **Max()**—Returns the maximum value from a sequence.

- **Min()**—Returns the minimum value from a sequence.

- **Select()**—Returns certain items or properties from a sequence.

- **Single()**—Returns a single value from a sequence.

- **Skip()**—Enables you to skip a certain number of items in a sequence and return the remaining elements.

- **Take()**—Enables you to return a certain number of elements from a sequence.

- **Where()**—Enables you to filter the elements in a sequence.

In this section, we've been discussing standard LINQ (also called LINQ to Objects). LINQ uses the provider model. There are many different implementations of LINQ, including LINQ to SQL, LINQ to XML, LINQ over DataSets, and LINQ to Entities. There are also third-party implementations of LINQ, including LINQ to NHibernate and LINQ to SharePoint. Each of these different flavors of LINQ can be used to query different types of data sources, such as XML files, SharePoint lists, and so on.

18

In this chapter, we are interested in LINQ to SQL because this is the Microsoft version of LINQ designed exclusively for working with database data. So LINQ to SQL is the subject to which we turn now.

Creating LINQ to SQL Entities

LINQ to SQL enables you to perform LINQ queries against database data. Currently, you can use LINQ to SQL with Microsoft SQL Server 2000 or Microsoft SQL Server 2005 (including the SQL Server Express editions). Other databases—such as Oracle, DB2, and Access databases—might be supported in the future, but they are not right now.

> **NOTE**
>
> To use LINQ to SQL, you need to add a reference to the System.Data.Linq.dll assembly. Select the menu option Website, Add Reference and, beneath the .NET tab, select System.Data.Linq.dll. Performing this action will add a new assembly reference to the `<assemblies>` section of your web.config file. If you use the Object Rational Designer, this reference is added automatically.

In this section, you learn how to create LINQ to SQL entities. An *entity* is a C# or VB.NET class that represents a database table (or view). You can use a set of standard custom attributes to map classes and properties to tables and columns. You learn how to create entities both by hand and by using the Object Rational Designer.

Building Entities by Hand

Before you can start performing queries using LINQ to SQL, you need to create one or more entity classes that represent the data you are querying. In this section, you learn how to code these classes by hand.

Imagine that you have the following database table named Movie that you want to perform queries against:

Movie

Column Name	Data Type	Is Identity?
Id	Int	TRUE
Title	NVarchar(100)	FALSE
Director	NVarchar	FALSE
DateReleased	DateTime	FALSE
BoxOfficeTotals	Money	FALSE

You can use the class in Listing 18.11 to represent this table.

LISTING 18.11   Entities\App_Code\Movie.cs

```
using System;
using System.Data.Linq.Mapping;

[Table]
public class Movie
{
    [Column(IsPrimaryKey=true, IsDbGenerated=true)]
    public int Id { get; set; }

    [Column]
    public string Title { get; set; }

    [Column]
    public string Director { get; set; }

    [Column]
    public DateTime DateReleased { get; set; }

    [Column]
    public decimal BoxOfficeTotals { get; set; }
}
```

The class in Listing 18.11 contains a property that corresponds to each column in the Movie database table. Notice that each property is decorated with a custom attribute named Column. This attribute marks the property as one that represents a database column.

NOTE

The Column and Table attribute classes live in the System.Data.Linq.Mapping namespace.

Furthermore, notice that the class itself is decorated with a Table attribute. This attribute marks the class as representing a database table.

The Column attribute supports the following properties:

▶ **AutoSync**—Indicates whether the value of the property is synchronized with the value of the database column automatically. Possible values are OnInsert, Always, and None.

▶ **CanBeNull**—Indicates whether the property can represent a null value.

▶ **DbType**—Indicates the database column data type.

▶ **Expression**—Indicates the expression used by a computed database column.

18

▶ **IsDbGenerated**—Indicates that the value of the property is generated in the database (for example, an identity column).

▶ **IsDiscriminator**—Indicates whether the property holds the discriminator value for an inheritance hierarchy.

▶ **IsPrimaryKey**—Indicates whether the property represents a primary key column.

▶ **IsVersion**—Indicates whether the property represents a column that represents a row version (for example, a timestamp column).

▶ **Name**—Indicates the name of the database column that corresponds to the property.

▶ **Storage**—Indicates a field where the value of the property is stored.

▶ **UpdateCheck**—Indicates whether the property participates in optimistic concurrency comparisons.

The Table attribute supports the following single property:

▶ **Name**—Indicates the name of the database table that corresponds to the class.

Some comments about these attributes are needed. First, you don't need to specify a Name property when your property or class name corresponds to your database column or table name. If, on the other hand, your database table were named Movies and your class were named Movie, you would need to supply the Name property for the Table attribute to map the correct table to the class.

Second, you always want to specify the primary key column by using the IsPrimaryKey property. For example, if you don't specify a primary key column, you can't do updates against your database using LINQ.

Finally, even though we didn't do this in our Movie class, you almost always want to include a timestamp column in your database table and indicate the timestamp column by using the IsVersion property. If you don't do this, LINQ to SQL will check whether the values of all the properties match the values of all the columns before performing an update command to prevent concurrency conflicts. If you specify a version property, LINQ to SQL can check the value of this single property against the database rather than all the columns.

Now that we've created an entity, we can start performing queries against the database using LINQ to SQL. For example, the page in Listing 18.12 contains a form that enables you to search for movies by a particular director.

LISTING 18.12   Entities\SearchMovies.aspx

```
<%@ Page Language="C#" %>
<%@ Import Namespace="System.Web.Configuration" %>
<%@ Import Namespace="System.Linq" %>
<%@ Import Namespace="System.Data.Linq" %>
<!DOCTYPE html PUBLIC "-//W3C//DTD XHTML 1.0 Transitional//EN"
  "http://www.w3.org/TR/xhtml1/DTD/xhtml1-transitional.dtd">
```

```
<script runat="server">

    protected void btnSearch_Click(object sender, EventArgs e)
    {
        string conString = WebConfigurationManager.ConnectionStrings["con"]
        ➥.ConnectionString;
        DataContext db = new DataContext(conString);
        var tMovie = db.GetTable<Movie>();

        grdMovies.DataSource = tMovie.Where( m =>
          m.Director.Contains(txtDirector.Text) );
        grdMovies.DataBind();
    }
</script>
<html xmlns="http://www.w3.org/1999/xhtml">
<head runat="server">
    <title>SearchMovies.aspx</title>
</head>
<body>
    <form id="form1" runat="server">
    <div>

    <asp:Label
        id="lblDirector"
        Text="Director:"
        AssociatedControlID="txtDirector"
        Runat="server" />
    <asp:TextBox
        id="txtDirector"
        Runat="server" />
    <asp:Button
        id="btnSearch"
        Text="Search"
        OnClick="btnSearch_Click"
        Runat="Server" />

    <br /><br />

    <asp:GridView
        id="grdMovies"
        Runat="server" />

    </div>
    </form>
</body>
</html>
```

18

When you click the Search button, the btnSearch_Click() method executes the LINQ to SQL query.

First, a DataContext is created by passing a database connection string to the class's constructor. The DataContext is responsible for tracking all the LINQ to SQL entities and representing the database connection.

Next, a variable named tMovie is instantiated that represents a particular database table from the DataContext. Because we pass the Movie entity to the GetTable<T>() method, the method returns a Table<T> object that represents the Movie database table. The Table<T> object implements the IQueryable interface and can, therefore, be queried with a LINQ to SQL query.

Finally, the following LINQ to SQL query is executed:

```
tMovie.Where( m => m.Director.Contains(txtDirector.Text)
```

The lambda expression m => m.Director.Contains(txtDirector.Text) passed to the Where() method returns every movie record from the database in which the Director column contains the text entered into the TextBox control.

Notice that we had to import two namespaces to use the LINQ to SQL query: System.Linq and System.Data.Linq.

> **NOTE**
>
> To keep things simple, I use the LINQ to SQL query directly within the ASP.NET page in Listing 18.12. In real life, to avoid mixing user interface and data access layers, I would perform the LINQ to SQL query in a separate class and use an ObjectDataSource to represent the class.

Building Entities with the Object Relational Designer

As an alternative to building entities by hand, you can use the Object Relational Designer. You can simply drag database tables from the Database Explorer (Server Explorer) onto the Designer. The Designer generates the entity classes with the correct attributes automatically.

Follow these steps to use the Object Relational Designer:

1. Select the menu option Website, Add New Item to open the Add New Item dialog box.
2. Select the LINQ to SQL Classes template, give it the name MyDatabase, and click the Add button.
3. When prompted to create the LINQ to SQL classes in the App_Code folder, click the Yes button.
4. After the Object Relational Designer opens, drag one or more database tables from the Database Explorer/Server Explorer window onto the Designer surface.

You can view the code that the Designer generates by expanding the MyDatabase.dbml node in the App_Code folder and double-clicking the MyDatabase.designer.cs file.

The Designer generates a strongly typed DataContext class named `MyDatabaseContext`. Each database table that you drag onto the Designer surface gets exposed by the DataContext class as a strongly typed property.

The Designer, furthermore, generates a distinct class for each database table you drag onto the Designer. For example, after you drag the Movie table onto the Designer, a new class named `Movie` is created in the MyDatabase.designer.cs file.

> **NOTE**
>
> The Object Relational Designer attempts to pluralize table names automatically when you add them to the Designer. So, when you drag the Movie table onto the Designer, the Designer generates a DataContext property named `Movies`. Most of the time, but not all of the time, it gets the pluralization right. You can turn off this feature by selecting the menu option Tools, Options and selecting the Database Tools, O/R Designer tab.

The page in Listing 18.13 demonstrates how you can use the `MyDatabaseContext` class when performing a LINQ to SQL query (after dragging the Movie database table onto the Object Relational Designer).

LISTING 18.13   Entities\ListMoviesByBoxOffice.aspx

```
<%@ Page Language="C#" %>
<%@ Import Namespace="System.Linq" %>
<%@ Import Namespace="System.Data.Linq" %>
<!DOCTYPE html PUBLIC "-//W3C//DTD XHTML 1.0 Transitional//EN"
 "http://www.w3.org/TR/xhtml1/DTD/xhtml1-transitional.dtd">
<script runat="server">

    void Page_Load()
    {
        MyDatabaseDataContext db = new MyDatabaseDataContext();
        grd.DataSource = db.Movies.OrderBy(m => m.BoxOfficeTotals);
        grd.DataBind();
    }

</script>
<html xmlns="http://www.w3.org/1999/xhtml">
<head runat="server">
    <title>List Movies by Box Office</title>
</head>
```

LISTING 18.13   Continued

```
<body>
    <form id="form1" runat="server">
    <div>

    <asp:GridView
        id="grd"
        runat="server" />

    </div>
    </form>
</body>
</html>
```

The page in Listing 18.13 displays a list of all movies in order of the movie's box office totals.

The Object Relational Designer creates partial classes for each table you drag onto the Designer surface. This means that you extend the functionality of each entity by creating a new partial class. For example, the class in Listing 18.14 extends the Movie class that the Object Relational Designer generates.

LISTING 18.14   Entities\App_Code\Movie.cs

```
using System;
using System.Collections.Generic;
using System.Linq;
using System.Data.Linq;

public partial class Movie
{
    public static IEnumerable<Movie> Select()
    {
        MyDatabaseDataContext db = new MyDatabaseDataContext();
        return db.Movies;
    }

    public static IEnumerable<Movie> SelectByBoxOfficeTotals()
    {
        return Select().OrderBy( m => m.BoxOfficeTotals);
    }
}
```

The Movie class in Listing 18.14 is declared as a partial class. It extends the partial class in the MyDatabase.designer.cs file by adding both a Select() method and a SelectByBoxOfficeTotals() method.

> **NOTE**
>
> Notice that the `SelectByBoxOfficeTotals()` method calls the `Select()` method. It is important to understand that this does not cause two SQL `SELECT` commands to be executed against the database. Until the GridView control starts iterating through the results of the LINQ to SQL query, you are just building an expression.

The page in Listing 18.15 demonstrates how you represent the `Movie` class with an ObjectDataSource control.

LISTING 18.15   Entities\PartialMovie.aspx

```
<%@ Page Language="C#" %>
<!DOCTYPE html PUBLIC "-//W3C//DTD XHTML 1.0 Transitional//EN"
 "http://www.w3.org/TR/xhtml1/DTD/xhtml1-transitional.dtd">
<html xmlns="http://www.w3.org/1999/xhtml">
<head runat="server">
    <title>Partial Movie</title>
</head>
<body>
    <form id="form1" runat="server">
    <div>

    <asp:GridView
        id="grdMovies"
        DataSourceID="srcMovies"
        Runat="server" />

    <asp:ObjectDataSource
        id="srcMovies"
        TypeName="Movie"
        SelectMethod="SelectByBoxOfficeTotals"
        runat="server" />

    </div>
    </form>
</body>
</html>
```

Notice that there is no code in the page in Listing 18.15. All the code is where it should be, in the data access layer implemented by the `Movie` class.

> **NOTE**
>
> If you don't want to use the Object Relational Designer, you can still generate your entity classes automatically from your database by using the SqlMetal.exe command-line tool. This tool is installed in the C:\WINDOWS\Microsoft.NET\Framework\v3.5 folder when you install .NET Framework 3.5.

Building Entity Associations

One entity can be associated with another entity. For example, a `MovieCategory` entity might be associated with one or more `Movie` entities.

If you have defined foreign key relationships between your database tables, these relationships are preserved when you drag your tables onto the Object Relational Designer. The Object Relational Designer will generate entity associations based on the foreign key relationships automatically.

For example, the `MovieCategory` entity is related to the `Movie` entity through the `Movie` entity's `CategoryId` property. As long as you have defined a foreign key relationship between `Movie.CategoryId` and `MovieCategory.Id`, you can use a query like this following:

```
MyDatabaseDataContext db = new MyDatabaseDataContext();
var category = db.MovieCategories.Single( c => c.Name == "Drama" );
var query = category.Movies;
```

The second statement grabs the Drama movie category. The third statement returns all movies associated with the Drama movie category. In this case, we've followed a one-to-many relationship and got a list of movies that match a movie category.

You can also go the opposite direction and retrieve the one and only movie category that matches a particular movie:

```
string categoryName = db.Movies.Single(m=>m.Id==1).MovieCategory.Name;
```

This query retrieves the name of the movie category associated with the movie that has an ID of 1.

> **NOTE**
>
> Under the covers, the Object Relational Designer creates the entity relationships by adding association attributes to entity properties. The Object Relational Designer also adds some tricky synchronization logic to keep the properties of associated entities synchronized.
>
> Although I wish that I could code all my entities by hand, adding all the logic necessary to get the entity associations to work correctly is too much work. For that reason, I use the Object Relational Designer.

Using the LinqDataSource Control

I want to briefly describe the LinqDataSource control. You can use this control to represent
LINQ queries. For example, the page in Listing 18.16 contains a simple search form for
searching movies by director. The page uses a LinqDataSource to represent the LINQ query.

LISTING 18.16   Entities\ShowLinqDataSource.aspx

```
<%@ Page Language="C#" %>
<!DOCTYPE html PUBLIC "-//W3C//DTD XHTML 1.0 Transitional//EN"
 "http://www.w3.org/TR/xhtml1/DTD/xhtml1-transitional.dtd">
<html xmlns="http://www.w3.org/1999/xhtml">
<head runat="server">
    <title>Show LinqDataSource</title>
</head>
<body>
    <form id="form1" runat="server">
    <div>

    <asp:Label
        id="lblSearch"
        AssociatedControlID="txtSearch"
        Text="Search:"
        Runat="server" />
    <asp:TextBox
        id="txtSearch"
        Runat="server" />
    <asp:Button
        id="btnSearch"
        Text="Search"
        Runat="server" />

    <br /><br />

    <asp:GridView
        id="grd"
        DataSourceID="LinqDataSource1"
        Runat="server" />

        <asp:LinqDataSource
            ID="LinqDataSource1"
            ContextTypeName="MyDatabaseDataContext"
            TableName="Movies"
            Where="Director == @Director"
            OrderBy="DateReleased"
            Select="new (Title, Director)"
```

LISTING 18.16   Continued

```
            runat="server">
            <whereparameters>
                <asp:controlparameter
                    Name="Director"
                    ControlID="txtSearch"
                    PropertyName="Text"
                    Type="String" />
            </whereparameters>
        </asp:LinqDataSource>


    </div>
    </form>
</body>
</html>
```

The LinqDataSource in Listing 18.16 represents the following LINQ query:

```
var query = db.Movies
    .Where(m => m.Director == txtSearch.Text)
    .OrderBy(m => m.DateReleased)
    .Select(m => new {m.Title, m.Director});
```

You also can use the LinqDataSource to generate Update, Insert, and Delete LINQ queries automatically. Simply set the EnableInsert, EnableUpdate, or EnableDelete property to the value True. For example, the page in Listing 18.17 contains a DetailsView control and a GridView control that you can use to insert, edit, and delete movie records. The inserting, editing, and deleting is performed by the LinqDataSource control.

LISTING 18.17   Entities\EditLinqDataSource.aspx

```
<%@ Page Language="C#" %>
<!DOCTYPE html PUBLIC "-//W3C//DTD XHTML 1.0 Transitional//EN"
 "http://www.w3.org/TR/xhtml1/DTD/xhtml1-transitional.dtd">
<script runat="server">

    protected void frmMovie_ItemInserted
    (
      object sender,
      DetailsViewInsertedEventArgs e
    )
    {
        grdMovies.DataBind();
    }
</script>
```

```html
<html xmlns="http://www.w3.org/1999/xhtml">
<head runat="server">
    <title>Edit LinqDataSource</title>
</head>
<body>
    <form id="form1" runat="server">
    <div>

    <asp:DetailsView
        id="frmMovie"
        DataSourceID="srcMovies"
        DefaultMode="Insert"
        AutoGenerateRows="false"
        AutoGenerateInsertButton="true"
        Runat="server" OnItemInserted="frmMovie_ItemInserted">
        <Fields>
        <asp:BoundField DataField="Title" HeaderText="Title" />
        <asp:BoundField DataField="Director" HeaderText="Director" />
        <asp:BoundField DataField="DateReleased" HeaderText="Date Released" />
        </Fields>
    </asp:DetailsView>

    <br /><br />

    <asp:GridView
        id="grdMovies"
        DataKeyNames="Id"
        DataSourceID="srcMovies"
        AllowPaging="true"
        PageSize="5"
        AutoGenerateEditButton="true"
        AutoGenerateDeleteButton="true"
        Runat="server" />

    <asp:LinqDataSource
        id="srcMovies"
        ContextTypeName="MyDatabaseDataContext"
        TableName="Movies"
        OrderBy="Id descending"
        EnableInsert="true"
        EnableUpdate="true"
        EnableDelete="true"
        AutoPage="true"
        Runat="server" />

    </div>
```

18

LISTING 18.17   Continued

```
    </form>
</body>
</html>
```

One other thing that you should notice about the LinqDataSource control in Listing 18.17: the LinqDataSource control has an AutoPage attribute set to the value True. When this property has the value True, the LinqDataSource performs data source paging automatically.

I don't use the LinqDataSource control in production applications. Instead, I wrap up all my LINQ queries in a separate class and I use the ObjectDataSource control to represent the class. The LinqDataSource control is similar to the SqlDataSource control in that both controls are great for prototyping and doing demos, but they are not appropriate controls to use in production applications.

Performing Standard Database Commands with LINQ to SQL

In this section, you learn how to use LINQ to SQL as a replacement for working directly with SQL. We'll start by discussing how LINQ to SQL queries differ from standard LINQ queries. Next, we'll examine how you can perform standard database queries and commands using LINQ to SQL such as Select, Update, Insert, and Delete commands. We'll also discuss how you can create dynamic queries with LINQ. Finally, we'll investigate the very important topic of how you can debug LINQ to SQL queries.

LINQ to Objects versus LINQ to SQL

You can use standard LINQ (LINQ to Objects) with any object that implements the IEnumerable<T> interface. You can use LINQ to SQL, on the other hand, with any object that implements the IQueryable<T> interface. Standard LINQ is implemented with the extension methods exposed by the System.Linq.Enumerable class. LINQ to SQL, on the other hand, uses the extension methods exposed by the System.Linq.Queryable class. Why the difference?

When you build a query using standard LINQ, the query executes immediately. When you build a query using LINQ to SQL, on the hand, the query does not execute until you start enumerating the results. In other words, the query doesn't execute until you use a foreach loop to walk through the query results.

Consider the following valid LINQ to SQL query:

```
var query = tMovie.Where(m => m.Director == "Steven Spielberg")
                .OrderBy( m => m.BoxOfficeTotals )
                .Select( m => m.Title );
```

This query returns a list of movies directed by Steven Spielberg in order of the movie box office totals.

You want LINQ to SQL to execute this query against the database in the most efficient way possible. In particular, you don't want LINQ to SQL to execute each method independently; you want LINQ to SQL to execute one smart database query.

When executing this query, it would be very bad if LINQ to SQL (1) grabbed all of the Movie records that were directed by Steven Spielberg, and (2) sorted the records, and then (3) discarded all of the columns except the Title column. You want LINQ to SQL to perform one smart database query that looks like this:

```
SELECT [t0].[Title] FROM [Movie] AS [t0] WHERE [t0].[Director] = @p0
ORDER BY [t0].[BoxOfficeTotals]
```

This SQL query is the exact query that LINQ to SQL performs. LINQ to SQL defers execution of a query until you start iterating through the results of the query. When you build a query, you are in reality building a representation of the query. Technically, you are building an expression tree. That way, LINQ to SQL can translate the query into one efficient SQL statement when it comes time to actually execute it.

To summarize, when you build a query using standard LINQ, the query executes as you build it. When you build a query using LINQ to SQL, you are building a representation of a query that doesn't actually execute until you start iterating through the query's results.

NOTE

When people first start using LINQ, they always worry about how they can build the equivalent of dynamic SQL commands. Later in this section, you learn how create dynamic LINQ to SQL queries by dynamically building expression trees.

Selecting with LINQ to SQL

If you want to perform a simple, unordered `select`, you can use the following query (assuming that you have an entity named `Movie` that represents the Movie database table):

```
MyDatabaseDataContext db = new MyDatabaseDataContext();
var query = db.Movies;
```

Notice that no LINQ extension methods are used in this query. All the items are retrieved from the Movies table.

If you prefer, you can use query syntax instead of method syntax, like this:

```
MyDatabaseDataContext db = new MyDatabaseDataContext();
var query = from m in db.Movies select m;
```

Selecting Particular Columns   If you want to select only particular columns, and not all the columns, from a database table, you can create an anonymous type on the fly, like this:

```
MyDatabaseDataContext db = new MyDatabaseDataContext();
var query = db.Movies.Select( m => new {m.Id, m.Title} );
```

The expression new {m.Id, m.Title} creates an anonymous type that has two properties: Id and Title. Notice that the names of the properties of the anonymous type are inferred. If you want to be more explicit, or if you want to change the names of the anonymous type's properties, you can construct your query like this:

```
MyDatabaseDataContext db = new MyDatabaseDataContext();
var query = db.Movies.Select( m => new {Id = m.Id, MovieTitle = m.Title} );
```

Selecting Particular Rows   If you want to select only particular rows from a database table and not all the rows, you can take advantage of the Where() method. The following LINQ to SQL query retrieves all the movies directed by George Lucas with box office totals greater than $100,000 dollars:

```
MyDatabaseDataContext db = new MyDatabaseDataContext();
var query = db.Movies
  .Where( m => m.Director == "George Lucas" && m.BoxOfficeTotals > 100000.00m)
  .Select( m => new {m.Title, m.Director, m.BoxOfficeTotals});
```

Remember to always call the Where() method before the Select() method. You need to filter your data with Where() before you shape it with Select().

Selecting Rows in a Particular Order   You can use the following methods to control the order in which rows are returned from a LINQ to SQL query:

▶ **OrderBy()**—Returns query results in a particular ascending order.

▶ **OrderByDescending()**—Returns query results in a particular descending order.

▶ **ThenBy()**—Returns query results using in an additional ascending order.

▶ **ThenByDescending()**—Returns query results using an additional descending order.

The OrderBy() and OrderBy() methods return an IOrderedQueryable<T> collection instead of the normal IQueryable<T> collection type. If you want to perform additional sorting, you need to call either the ThenBy() or ThenByDescending() method.

The following query returns movies in order of release date and then in order of box office totals:

```
MyDatabaseDataContext db = new MyDatabaseDataContext();
var query = db.Movies.OrderBy(m=>m.DateReleased).ThenBy(m=>m.BoxOfficeTotals);
```

Executing this LINQ to SQL query executes the following SQL query:

```
SELECT
  [t0].[Id],
  [t0].[CategoryId],
  [t0].[Title],
  [t0].[Director],
  [t0].[DateReleased],
  [t0].[InTheaters],
  [t0].[BoxOfficeTotals],
  [t0].[Description]
FROM [dbo].[Movie] AS [t0]
ORDER BY [t0].[DateReleased], [t0].[BoxOfficeTotals]
```

Selecting a Single Row If you want to select a single row from the database, you can use one of the following two query methods:

▶ **Single()**—Selects a single record.

▶ **SingleOrDefault()**—Selects a single record or a default instance.

The first method assumes there is at least one element to be returned (if not, you get an exception). The second method returns null (for a reference type) when no matching element is found.

Here's a sample query that retrieves the one and only record where the movie Id has the value 1:

```
MyDatabaseDataContext db = new MyDatabaseDataContext();
Movie result = db.Movies.SingleOrDefault(m => m.Id == 1);
if (result != null)
  Response.Write(result.Title);
```

This query returns a single object of type Movie. If there is no movie record that matches the query, result is null and the value of the Movie Title property is not written.

NOTE

When you execute a query that returns a single result, there is no deferred query execution. The LINQ query is translated into a SQL command and executed immediately.

Performing a LIKE Select You can perform the equivalent of a LIKE Select with LINQ to SQL in several ways. First, you can use String methods such as Length, Substring, Contains, StartsWith, EndsWith, IndexOf, Insert, Remove, Replace, Trim, ToLower,

18

ToUpper, LastIndexOf, PadRight, and PadLeft with LINQ to SQL queries. For example, the following query returns all movies that start with the letter *t*:

```
MyDatabaseDataContext db = new MyDatabaseDataContext();
var query = db.Movies.Where(m=>m.Title.StartsWith("t"));
```

Behind the scenes, this query is translated into a SQL query that uses the LIKE operator:

```
SELECT [t0].[Id], [t0].[CategoryId], [t0].[Title], [t0].[Director],
[t0].[DateReleased], [t0].[InTheaters], [t0].[BoxOfficeTotals], [t0].[Description]
FROM [dbo].[Movie] AS [t0]
WHERE [t0].[Title] LIKE @p0
```

An alternative, more flexible way to make LIKE queries is to use the System.Data.Linq.SqlClient.SqlMethods.Like() method:

```
MyDatabaseDataContext db = new MyDatabaseDataContext();
var query = db.Movies.Where(m=>SqlMethods.Like(m.Title, "t%"));
```

Using the SqlMethods.Like() method is more flexible than using the standard String methods because you can add as many wildcards to the match pattern as you need.

> **NOTE**
>
> The SqlMethods class also contains a number of useful methods for expressing the SQL DateDiff() function in a LINQ to SQL Query.

Paging Through Records   Doing database paging right when working with ADO.NET is difficult. The SQL language is not designed to make it easy to retrieve a range of records. Doing database paging using LINQ to SQL queries, on the other hand, is trivial.

You can take advantage of the following two query methods to perform database paging:

- ▶ **Skip()**—Enables you to skip a certain number of records.
- ▶ **Take()**—Enables you to take a certain number of records.

For example, the class in Listing 18.18 contains a method named SelectedPaged() that gets a particular page of movie records from the Movie database table.

LISTING 18.18   Standard\App_Code\Movie.cs

```
using System;
using System.Collections.Generic;
using System.Linq;
using System.Data.Linq;
```

```
public partial class Movie
{
    public static IEnumerable<Movie> Select()
    {
        MyDatabaseDataContext db = new MyDatabaseDataContext();
        return db.Movies;
    }

    public static IEnumerable< Movie> SelectPaged
    (
      int startRowIndex,
      int maximumRows
    )
    {
        return Select().Skip(startRowIndex).Take(maximumRows);
    }

    public static int SelectCount()
    {
        return Select().Count();
    }
}
```

I'm assuming, in the case of Listing 18.18, that you have already created a Movie entity by using the Object Relational Designer. The Movie class in Listing 18.18 is a partial class that extends the existing Movie class generated by the Designer.

The ASP.NET page in Listing 18.19 illustrates how you can use the Movie class with the ObjectDataSource control to page through movie records.

LISTING 18.19   Standard\ShowPagedMovies.aspx

```
<%@ Page Language="C#" %>
<!DOCTYPE html PUBLIC "-//W3C//DTD XHTML 1.0 Transitional//EN"
 "http://www.w3.org/TR/xhtml1/DTD/xhtml1-transitional.dtd">
<html xmlns="http://www.w3.org/1999/xhtml">
<head runat="server">
    <title>Show Paged Movies</title>
</head>
<body>
    <form id="form1" runat="server">
    <div>

    <asp:GridView
        id="grdMovies"
        DataSourceID="srcMovies"
```

18

LISTING 18.19   Continued

```
            AllowPaging="true"
            PageSize="5"
            Runat="server" />

        <asp:ObjectDataSource
            id="srcMovies"
            TypeName="Movie"
            SelectMethod="SelectPaged"
            SelectCountMethod="SelectCount"
            EnablePaging="true"
            Runat="server" />

    </div>
    </form>
</body>
</html>
```

Joining Records from Different Tables   You can perform joins when selecting entities just like you can when joining database tables. For example, imagine that you want to join the Movie and MovieCategory tables on the CategoryId key. Assuming that you have both a Movie and MovieCategory entity, you can use the following query:

```
MyDatabaseDataContext db = new MyDatabaseDataContext();
var query = db.MovieCategories
    .Join(db.Movies, c=>c.Id, m=>m.CategoryId, (c,m)=>new {c.Id,c.Name,m.Title});
```

This LINQ query gets translated into the following SQL command:

```
SELECT [t0].[Id], [t0].[Name], [t1].[Title]
FROM [dbo].[MovieCategory] AS [t0]
INNER JOIN [dbo].[Movie] AS [t1] ON [t0].[Id] = [t1].[CategoryId]
```

This query performs an inner join. If you want to perform an outer join, the syntax is a little more complicated. Here's how you do a left outer join using query syntax:

```
MyDatabaseDataContext db = new MyDatabaseDataContext();
var query = from c in db.MovieCategories
            join m in db.Movies
            on c.Id equals m.CategoryId into cm
            from m in cm.DefaultIfEmpty()
            select new { c.Id, c.Name, m.Title };
```

This LINQ query gets translated into the following SQL SELECT:

```
SELECT [t0].[Id], [t0].[Name], [t1].[Title] AS [value]
FROM [dbo].[MovieCategory] AS [t0]
LEFT OUTER JOIN [dbo].[Movie] AS [t1] ON [t0].[Id] = [t1].[CategoryId]
```

As an alternative to using joins, consider taking advantage of the associations between entities. Remember that the following type of query is perfectly valid:

```
MyDatabaseDataContext db = new MyDatabaseDataContext();
var category = db.MovieCategories.Single( c => c.Name == "Drama" );
var query = category.Movies;
```

Caching Records   Getting caching to work with LINQ to SQL is a little tricky. Remember that a LINQ to SQL query represents a query expression and not the actual query results. The SQL command is not executed, and the results are not retrieved until you start iterating through the query results.

For example, imagine that you declare the following ObjectDataSource control in a page and that this ObjectDataSource control represents a class that returns a LINQ to SQL query:

```
<asp:ObjectDataSource
    id="srcMovies"
    TypeName="Movie"
    SelectMethod="Select"
    EnableCaching="true"
    CacheDuration="9999"
    Runat="server" />
```

This ObjectDataSource has been set up to cache its results. Notice that its EnableCaching and CacheDuration properties are set.

However, what gets cached here is the query expression and not that actual query results. The SQL select statement that corresponds to the LINQ to SQL query will execute each and every time the page is requested.

To get caching to work, we need to force the query results and not the query into the cache. The Movie class in Listing 18.20 contains a SelectCached() method that successfully caches database data with a LINQ to SQL query.

LISTING 18.20   Standard\App_Code\Movie.cs

```
using System;
using System.Web;
using System.Collections.Generic;
using System.Linq;
using System.Data.Linq;
```

18

LISTING 18.20   Continued

```
public partial class Movie
{
    public static IEnumerable<Movie> Select()
    {
        MyDatabaseDataContext db = new MyDatabaseDataContext();
        return db.Movies;
    }

    public static IEnumerable<Movie> SelectCached()
    {
        HttpContext context = HttpContext.Current;
        List<Movie> movies = (List<Movie>)context.Cache["Movies"];
        if (movies == null)
        {
            movies = Select().ToList();
            context.Cache["Movies"] = movies;
            context.Trace.Warn("Retrieving movies from database");
        }
        return movies;
    }
}
```

The `SelectCached()` method attempts to retrieve movie records from the cache. If the records can't be retrieved from the cache, the movies are retrieved from the database. The vast majority of the time, the movies are retrieved from the cache.

The trick here is to use the `ToList()` method to convert the `IEnumerable<Movie>` into a `List<Movie>`. When the `List<Movie>` is created, the SQL query associated with the LINQ to SQL query is executed and the actual data is returned.

You can use the class in Listing 18.20 with the ASP.NET page in Listing 18.21.

LISTING 18.21   Standard\ShowCachedMovies.aspx

```
<%@ Page Language="C#" Trace="true" %>
<!DOCTYPE html PUBLIC "-//W3C//DTD XHTML 1.0 Transitional//EN"
 "http://www.w3.org/TR/xhtml1/DTD/xhtml1-transitional.dtd">
<html xmlns="http://www.w3.org/1999/xhtml">
<head runat="server">
    <title>Show Cached Movies</title>
</head>
<body>
    <form id="form1" runat="server">
    <div>
```

```
<asp:GridView
    id="grdMovies"
    DataSourceID="srcMovies"
    Runat="server" />

<asp:ObjectDataSource
    id="srcMovies"
    TypeName="Movie"
    SelectMethod="SelectCached"
    Runat="server" />

</div>
</form>
</body>
</html>
```

Notice that the ObjectDataSource in Listing 18.21 does not have caching enabled. All the caching happens in the data access layer (the Movie class).

Inserting with LINQ to SQL

There are two steps to adding and inserting a new record with LINQ to SQL. First, you need to use the InsertOnSubmit() method to add an entity to an existing table. Next, you call SubmitChanges() on the DataContext to execute the SQL INSERT statement against the database.

The class in Listing 18.22 illustrates how you can write a method to add a new record into the Movie database table.

LISTING 18.22   Standard\App_Code\Movie.cs

```
using System;
using System.Web;
using System.Collections.Generic;
using System.Linq;
using System.Data.Linq;

public partial class Movie
{
    public static int Insert(Movie movieToInsert)
    {
        MyDatabaseDataContext db = new MyDatabaseDataContext();
        db.Movies.InsertOnSubmit( movieToInsert );
        db.SubmitChanges();
        return movieToInsert.Id;
    }
```

LISTING 18.22   Continued

```
public static IEnumerable<Movie> Select()
{
    MyDatabaseDataContext db = new MyDatabaseDataContext();
    return db.Movies.OrderByDescending(m=>m.Id);
}

}
```

The Movie class includes an Insert() method that inserts a new movie into the database. Notice that the Insert() method returns an integer that represents the identity value of the new record. As soon as SubmitChanges() is called, the Id property is updated with the new identity value from the database.

> **NOTE**
>
> I'm assuming in this section that you have used the Object Relational Designer to create entities for the Movie and MovieCategories database tables.

The page in Listing 18.23 contains a FormView control and a GridView control. You can use the FormView to insert new movie records into the database. The FormView control is bound to an ObjectDataSource control that represents the Movie class.

LISTING 18.23   Standard\InsertMovie.aspx

```
<%@ Page Language="C#" Trace="true" %>
<!DOCTYPE html PUBLIC "-//W3C//DTD XHTML 1.0 Transitional//EN"
 "http://www.w3.org/TR/xhtml1/DTD/xhtml1-transitional.dtd">
<html xmlns="http://www.w3.org/1999/xhtml">
<head runat="server">
    <title>Insert Movie</title>
</head>
<body>
    <form id="form1" runat="server">
    <div>

    <asp:FormView
        id="frmMovie"
        DataSourceID="srcMovies"
        DefaultMode="Insert"
        Runat="Server">
        <InsertItemTemplate>
            <asp:Label
                id="lblTitle"
```

```
        Text="Title:"
        AssociatedControlID="txtTitle"
        Runat="server" />
<br />
<asp:TextBox
        id="txtTitle"
        Text='<%# Bind("Title") %>'
        Runat="server" />


<br /><br />


<asp:Label
        id="lblCategory"
        Text="Category:"
        AssociatedControlID="ddlCategory"
        Runat="server" />
<br />
<asp:DropDownList
        id="ddlCategory"
        DataSourceId="srcMovieCategories"
        SelectedValue='<%# Bind("CategoryId") %>'
        DataTextField="Name"
        DataValueField="Id"
        Runat="server" />
<asp:ObjectDataSource
        id="srcMovieCategories"
        TypeName="MovieCategory"
        SelectMethod="Select"
        Runat="Server" />
<br /><br / >


<asp:Label
        id="lblDirector"
        Text="Director:"
        AssociatedControlID="txtDirector"
        Runat="server" />
<br />
<asp:TextBox
        id="txtDirector"
        Text='<%# Bind("Director") %>'
        Runat="server" />


<br /><br />


<asp:Label
        id="lblDescription"
```

18

LISTING 18.23   Continued

```
                    Text="Description:"
                    AssociatedControlID="txtDescription"
                    Runat="server" />
                <br />
                <asp:TextBox
                    id="txtDescription"
                    Text='<%# Bind("Description") %>'
                    TextMode="MultiLine"
                    Columns="60"
                    Rows="3"
                    Runat="server" />

                <br /><br />

                <asp:Label
                    id="lblDateReleased"
                    Text="Date Released:"
                    AssociatedControlID="txtDateReleased"
                    Runat="server" />
                <br />
                <asp:TextBox
                    id="txtDateReleased"
                    Text='<%# Bind("DateReleased") %>'
                    Runat="server" />

                <br /><br />

                <asp:Button
                    id="btnInsert"
                    Text="Insert"
                    CommandName="Insert"
                    Runat="server" />

        </InsertItemTemplate>
    </asp:FormView>

    <hr />

    <asp:GridView
        id="grdMovies"
        DataSourceID="srcMovies"
        Runat="server" />

    <asp:ObjectDataSource
        id="srcMovies"
```

```
         TypeName="Movie"
         DataObjectTypeName="Movie"
         SelectMethod="Select"
         InsertMethod="Insert"
         Runat="server" />

    </div>
    </form>
</body>
</html>
```

Notice that the `ObjectDataSource` control in Listing 18.23 includes a `DataObjectTypeName` attribute that is set to the value `Movie`. The `ObjectDataSource` instantiates a new `Movie` object automatically when calling the `Movie.Insert()` method.

Updating with LINQ to SQL

You can update a LINQ to SQL entity and the underlying database table by modifying the entity's properties and calling the DataContext's `SubmitChanges()` method, like this:

```
MyDatabaseDataContext db = new MyDatabaseDataContext();
Movie movieToUpdate = db.Movies.Single(m=>m.Id==1);
movieToUpdate.Title = "King Kong II";
movieToUpdate.Director = "George Lucas";
db.SubmitChanges();
```

This code first grabs the movie that has an `Id` value of 1. Next, the movie `Title` and `Director` properties are modified. Finally, these changes are submitted to the database by calling the `SubmitChanges()` method.

This code works, but it is not the best code to use when building an ASP.NET page. Typically, when performing an update in ASP.NET, you already have information about the entity in view state. You don't want or need to grab the entity from the database in order to modify it.

For example, if you are using a FormView control to update the database, the FormView control will do a select automatically and store the entity information in view state. You don't want to grab the entity information a second time after the user clicks the Insert button.

Instead, what you really want to do is reattach the entity back into the DataContext from view state. You already have the entity; you just want to make the DataContext aware of the entity again.

You can use the `Attach()` method to attach an entity back into a data context. There are three overloads of the `Attach()` method:

▶ **Attach(Object)**—Enables you to attach an unmodified entity to the data context.

▶ **Attach(Object, Boolean)**—Enables you to attach a modified entity to the data context. The second parameter represents whether or not the entity has been modified. To use this overload, the entity must have a version/timestamp property.

▶ **Attach(Object, Object)**—Enables you to attach a modified entity to the data context. The first parameter represents the modified entity. The second parameter represents the original entity.

If you retain the original entity in view state, then you can use the third overload of the Attach() method to update an entity. This approach is illustrated in the class in Listing 18.24.

LISTING 18.24   Standard\App_Code\Movie.cs

```
using System;
using System.Web;
using System.Collections.Generic;
using System.Linq;
using System.Data.Linq;

public partial class Movie
{
    public static void Update(Movie oldMovie, Movie newMovie)
    {
        MyDatabaseDataContext db = new MyDatabaseDataContext();
        db.Movies.Attach(newMovie,oldMovie);
        db.SubmitChanges();
    }

    public static IEnumerable<Movie> Select()
    {
        MyDatabaseDataContext db = new MyDatabaseDataContext();
        return db.Movies;
    }
}
```

The Update() method in Listing 18.24 receives both the original and new version of the Movie entity. The Attach() method is called with both the new version and old version of the Movie object. Passing both versions of the Movie object to the Attach() method causes the method to attach the old version of the object and then modify the old version of the object to match the new version of the object. Finally, SubmitChanges() is called to perform the SQL UPDATE command against the database.

LISTING 18.25   Standard\UpdateMovie.aspx

```
<%@ Page Language="C#" Trace="true" %>
<!DOCTYPE html PUBLIC "-//W3C//DTD XHTML 1.0 Transitional//EN"
 "http://www.w3.org/TR/xhtml1/DTD/xhtml1-transitional.dtd">
<html xmlns="http://www.w3.org/1999/xhtml">
<head runat="server">
    <title>Update Movie</title>
</head>
<body>
    <form id="form1" runat="server">
    <div>

    <asp:GridView
        id="grdMovies"
        DataSourceID="srcMovies"
        DataKeyNames="Id"
        AutoGenerateEditButton="true"
        Runat="server" />

    <asp:ObjectDataSource
        id="srcMovies"
        TypeName="Movie"
        DataObjectTypeName="Movie"
        SelectMethod="Select"
        UpdateMethod="Update"
        ConflictDetection="CompareAllValues"
        OldValuesParameterFormatString="oldMovie"
        Runat="server" />

    </div>
    </form>
</body>
</html>
```

Notice that the ObjectDataSource control has both its ConflictDetection and
OldValuesParameterFormatString attributes set. The ConflictDetection attribute is set to
the value CompareAllValues. This value causes the ObjectDataSource to store the original
movie property values in view state. The OldValuesParameterFormatString attribute
determines the name of the parameter that represents the old Movie entity.

When you update a movie by using the page in Listing 18.25, the following SQL
command is sent to the database:

```
UPDATE [dbo].[Movie]
SET [Title] = @p7
```

18

```
WHERE ([Id] = @p0) AND ([CategoryId] = @p1)
AND ([Title] = @p2) AND ([Director] = @p3)
AND ([DateReleased] = @p4) AND (NOT ([InTheaters] = 1))
AND ([BoxOfficeTotals] = @p5) AND ([Description] = @p6)
```

Notice that LINQ to SQL compares all the new column values against the old column values. This is done to prevent concurrency conflicts. If someone else makes a change to a record before you have a chance to submit your changes, the record won't be updated with your changes. However, all of this comparing of column values seems wasteful and silly.

If you don't want LINQ to SQL to compare all the column values when it does an update, you need to add a version property to your entity. The easiest way to do this is to add a timestamp column to the database table that corresponds to the entity (and re-create the entity in the Object Relational Designer so that it has the new timestamp column property). So, our modified Movie table looks like this:

Movie

Column Name	Data Type	Is Identity?
Id	Int	TRUE
Title	NVarchar(100)	FALSE
Director	NVarchar	FALSE
DateReleased	DateTime	FALSE
BoxOfficeTotals	Money	FALSE
Version	TimeStamp	FALSE

You'll also need to ensure that the Version property gets saved into view state. You can do this by adding the Version property to a DataBound control's DataKeyNames property. This approach is illustrated by the page in Listing 18.26.

LISTING 18.26   Standard\UpdateMovieVersion.aspx

```
<%@ Page Language="C#" Trace="true" %>
<!DOCTYPE html PUBLIC "-//W3C//DTD XHTML 1.0 Transitional//EN"
 "http://www.w3.org/TR/xhtml1/DTD/xhtml1-transitional.dtd">
<html xmlns="http://www.w3.org/1999/xhtml">
<head id="Head1" runat="server">
    <title>Update Movie Version</title>
</head>
<body>
    <form id="form1" runat="server">
    <div>

    <asp:GridView
```

```
        id="grdMovies"
        DataSourceID="srcMovies"
        DataKeyNames="Id,Version"
        AutoGenerateEditButton="true"
        Runat="server" />

    <asp:ObjectDataSource
        id="srcMovies"
        TypeName="Movie"
        DataObjectTypeName="Movie"
        SelectMethod="Select"
        UpdateMethod="Update"
        ConflictDetection="CompareAllValues"
        OldValuesParameterFormatString="oldMovie"
        Runat="server" />

    </div>
    </form>
</body>
</html>
```

Notice that both the Id and Version properties are assigned to the GridView control's DataKeyNames attribute.

After you make these changes, the update SQL command looks like this:

```
UPDATE [dbo].[Movie]
SET [Title] = @p2
WHERE ([Id] = @p0) AND ([Version] = @p1)
```

Deleting with LINQ to SQL

You can delete an entity with LINQ to SQL by using code like the following:

```
MyDatabaseDataContext db = new MyDatabaseDataContext();
Movie movieToDelete = db.Movies.Single(m=>m.Id==1);
db.Movies.DeleteOnSubmit( movieToDelete );
db.SubmitChanges();
```

This code starts by retrieving the record with an Id of 1 from the Movie database table. Next, the Movie entity is removed from the Movies collection by calling the DeleteOnSubmit() method. Finally, this change is submitted to the database and the following SQL command executes:

```
DELETE FROM [dbo].[Movie]
WHERE ([Id] = @p0) AND ([Version] = @p1)
```

NOTE

I'm assuming in this section that you have added a Version property to your Movie database table. If not, see the previous section, because you should add a Version property when deleting for the same reasons you should add a Version property when updating.

It seems weird and silly to retrieve a record from the database just so that you can delete it. And, in fact, that is weird and silly. What you really want to do is reattach the Movie entity so that you can delete it. Thus, you can avoid making two calls to the database.

The modified Movie class in Listing 18.27 includes a Delete() method that removes a movie without retrieving it first.

LISTING 18.27   Standard\App_Code\Movie.cs

```csharp
using System;
using System.Web;
using System.Collections.Generic;
using System.Linq;
using System.Data.Linq;

public partial class Movie
{
    public static void Delete(Movie movieToDelete)
    {
        MyDatabaseDataContext db = new MyDatabaseDataContext();
        db.Movies.Attach(movieToDelete);
        db.Movies.DeleteOnSubmit(movieToDelete);
        db.SubmitChanges();
    }

    public static IEnumerable<Movie> Select()
    {
        MyDatabaseDataContext db = new MyDatabaseDataContext();
        return db.Movies;
    }
}
```

You can use the class in Listing 18.27 with the ASP.NET page in Listing 18.28.

LISTING 18.28   Standard\DeleteMovie.aspx

```
<%@ Page Language="C#" Trace="true" %>
<!DOCTYPE html PUBLIC "-//W3C//DTD XHTML 1.0 Transitional//EN"
 "http://www.w3.org/TR/xhtml1/DTD/xhtml1-transitional.dtd">
<html xmlns="http://www.w3.org/1999/xhtml">
<head id="Head1" runat="server">
    <title>Delete Movie</title>
</head>
<body>
    <form id="form1" runat="server">
    <div>

    <asp:GridView
        id="grdMovies"
        DataSourceID="srcMovies"
        DataKeyNames="Id,Version"
        AutoGenerateDeleteButton="true"
        Runat="server" />

    <asp:ObjectDataSource
        id="srcMovies"
        TypeName="Movie"
        DataObjectTypeName="Movie"
        SelectMethod="Select"
        DeleteMethod="Delete"
        ConflictDetection="CompareAllValues"
        OldValuesParameterFormatString="oldMovie"
        Runat="server" />

    </div>
    </form>
</body>
</html>
```

The `ObjectDataSource` control in Listing 18.28 has both its `ConflictDetection` and `OldValuesParameterFormatString` attributes set. The `ObjectDataSource` remembers a `Movie` entity across postbacks. It passes the original `Movie` entity to the `Delete()` method so that the entity can be reattached and deleted.

Dynamic Queries

One concern that everyone has when they start working with LINQ to SQL is the problem of representing dynamic queries. When you create a query by using ADO.NET and SQL, you can dynamically modify the SQL query simply by modifying the string that represents the SQL command. When working with LINQ to SQL, on the other hand, you can't do this because you are not working with strings.

In this section, we explore two methods of executing dynamic queries. You learn how to pass normal SQL commands while using LINQ to SQL. You also learn how to dynamically build LINQ to SQL query expressions.

Executing Dynamic SQL Statements   If you simply want to execute a SQL statement or query, and you don't want to use ADO.NET directly, you can take advantage of the DataContext `ExecuteCommand()` and `ExecuteQuery()` methods. The `ExecuteCommand()` method executes a SQL command against a database. The `ExecuteQuery()` method executes a SQL query against a database and returns the results as entities.

The following code illustrates how to use both of these methods:

```
MyDatabaseDataContext db = new MyDatabaseDataContext();
db.ExecuteCommand("INSERT Movie (Title,Director,CategoryId)
  ➥VALUES (@p0,@p1,
var query = db.ExecuteQuery(typeof(Movie), "SELECT * FROM Movie
  ➥WHERE CategoryId=@p0", new object[]{2});
```

Here, the `ExecuteCommand()` method is used to insert a new record into the Movie database table. The `ExecuteQuery()` method is used to grab all the records from the Movie table where the CategoryId column has the value 2.

Notice that you indicate parameters by using parameter names like @p0, @p1, @p2, and so on. You do not use named parameters like you would in the case of an ADO.NET command. Parameters are identified by their ordinal position.

Building Query Expressions Dynamically   Resorting to executing SQL statements against the database feels like a type of cheating. The whole point of LINQ to SQL is to get away from working with SQL directly. What we really want to do is build LINQ to SQL queries dynamically in the same way we can build a SQL command dynamically.

You can build LINQ to SQL query expressions dynamically by taking advantage of the `System.Linq.Expressions.Expression` class. This class contains all the methods for building query expressions dynamically. Here is a (very partial) list of methods supported by this class:

- ▶ **Add()**—Creates an expression that represents addition.

- ▶ **And()**—Creates an expression that represents a logical AND.

- ▶ **Condition()**—Creates an expression that represents a condition.

- ▶ **Constant()**—Creates an expression that represents a constant value.

- ▶ **Convert()**—Creates an expression that represents a conversion from one type to another.

- ▶ **Divide()**—Creates an expression that represents division.

- ▶ **Equal()**—Creates an expression that represents whether two expressions are equal.

- ▶ **Field()**—Creates an expression that represents a field.

- ▶ **Lambda()**—Creates a lambda expression.

- ▶ **Multiply()**—Creates an expression that represents multiplication.

- ▶ **Or()**—Creates an expression that represents a logical OR.

- ▶ **Parameter()**—Creates an expression that represents a function parameter.

- ▶ **Property()**—Creates an expression that represents accessing a property.

- ▶ **PropertyOrField()**—Creates an expression that represents accessing a property or field.

- ▶ **Subtract()**—Creates an expression that represents subtraction.

Again, this is not a complete list of methods supported by the Expression class. However, it should give you some idea of how you can go about building expressions.

Let's discuss a real-world situation in which you need dynamic LINQ to SQL expressions: sorting. If you want to enable sorting when using a GridView control with LINQ to SQL, you have a choice. You can create a switch (SELECT CASE) block to sort by every possible column that a user can click or you can create a dynamic LINQ to SQL expression.

The class in Listing 18.29 contains a method called GetDynamicSort() that returns a dynamic lambda expression that can be used with either the OrderBy() or OrderByDescending() method.

LISTING 18.29   Standard\App_Code\Movie.cs

```
using System;
using System.Web;
using System.Collections.Generic;
using System.Linq;
using System.Linq.Expressions;
using System.Data.Linq;
using System.Reflection;

public partial class Movie
{
    public static IEnumerable<Movie> Select(string orderBy)
    {
        string orderByColumn = "Id";
        string orderByDirection = "asc";
        if (!String.IsNullOrEmpty(orderBy))
            ParseOrderBy(orderBy, ref orderByColumn, ref orderByDirection);
```

18

LISTING 18.29   Continued

```
        MyDatabaseDataContext db = new MyDatabaseDataContext();
        if (orderByDirection == "asc")
            return db.Movies.OrderBy(GetDynamicSort(orderByColumn));
        else
            return db.Movies.OrderByDescending(GetDynamicSort(orderByColumn));
    }



    public static void ParseOrderBy
    (
      string orderBy,
      ref string orderByColumn,
      ref string orderByDirection
    )
    {
        string[] orderByParts = orderBy.Split(' ');
        orderByColumn = orderByParts[0];
        if (orderByParts.Length > 1)
            orderByDirection = orderByParts[1].ToLower();
    }



    private static Expression<Func<Movie, string>> GetDynamicSort
    (
        string orderByColumn
    )
    {

        // Create expression to represent Movie parameter into lambda expression
        ParameterExpression pMovie = Expression.Parameter(typeof(Movie), "m");

        // Create expression to access value of order by column
        PropertyInfo propInfo = typeof(Movie).GetProperty(orderByColumn);
        MemberExpression m = Expression.MakeMemberAccess(pMovie, propInfo);

        // Box it
        UnaryExpression b = Expression.TypeAs(m, typeof(object));

        // Convert to string
        MethodInfo convertMethod = typeof(Convert).GetMethod("ToString",
            new Type[] { typeof(object) });
        MethodCallExpression c = Expression.Call(null, convertMethod, b);

        // Return lambda
```

```
        return Expression.Lambda<Func<Movie, string>>(c, pMovie);
    }
}
```

The GetDynamicSort() method builds a lambda expression dynamically. It creates an expression that looks like this:

```
m => Convert.ToString(m.Id As Object)
```

When the LINQ to SQL query gets translated to SQL, the following SQL command is executed:

```
SELECT [t0].[Id], [t0].[CategoryId], [t0].[Title],
[t0].[Director], [t0].[DateReleased], [t0].[InTheaters],
[t0].[BoxOfficeTotals], [t0].[Description], [t0].[Version]
FROM [dbo].[Movie] AS [t0]
ORDER BY CONVERT(NVarChar(MAX),[t0].[Title])
```

You can use the class in Listing 18.29 with the ASP.NET page in Listing 18.30. When you click a header column in the GridView, the GridView is sorted by the column.

LISTING 18.30   Standard\ShowDynamicSort.aspx

```
<%@ Page Language="C#" trace="true" %>
<!DOCTYPE html PUBLIC "-//W3C//DTD XHTML 1.0 Transitional//EN"
 "http://www.w3.org/TR/xhtml1/DTD/xhtml1-transitional.dtd">
<html xmlns="http://www.w3.org/1999/xhtml">
<head runat="server">
    <title>Show Dynamic Sort</title>
</head>
<body>
    <form id="form1" runat="server">
    <div>

    <asp:GridView
        id="grdMovies"
        DataSourceId="srcMovies"
        AllowSorting="true"
        Runat="server" />

    <asp:ObjectDataSource
        id="srcMovies"
        TypeName="Movie"
        SelectMethod="Select"
        SortParameterName="orderBy"
        Runat="server" />
```

LISTING 18.30   Continued

```
    </div>
    </form>
</body>
</html>
```

Notice that the `GridView` control has its `AllowSorting` attribute set to the value `true` and the `ObjectDataSource` control has its `SortParameterName` attribute set to the value `orderBy`. The page is set up to enable data source paging.

> **NOTE**
>
> The `GetDynamicSort()` method described in this section does a sort after converting the values of a column to strings. For non-string data types such as dates and integers, doing string sorts produces the wrong results. For example, after sorting, the id column is ordered as 10, 2, 22, 29, 3, 30, 31, and so on.
>
> In the final part of this chapter, you learn how to create a custom entity base class. This class implements a more sophisticated version of a dynamic sort that sorts different column types correctly.

Debugging LINQ to SQL

For the sake of performance, you had better know what is going on beneath the covers when you execute LINQ to SQL queries. In particular, it is very useful to know how your LINQ to SQL queries get translated into SQL and when your LINQ to SQL queries execute. In this section, I describe three methods of debugging LINQ to SQL.

Using the LINQ to SQL Debug Visualizer   The LINQ to SQL Debug Visualizer is a really useful tool for viewing how a LINQ to SQL query gets translated into SQL. The LINQ to SQL Debug Visualizer is not included with the .NET 3.5 Framework. You need to download it from the following address:

`http://www.scottgu.com/blogposts/linqquery/SqlServerQueryVisualizer.zip`

After you download the LINQ to SQL Visualizer, you can use it like other Visualizers in Visual Web Developer and Visual Studio. If you set a breakpoint after a LINQ to SQL query and hover your mouse over the query, you can click the magnifying glass to see the full SQL command into which the query gets translated (see Figure 18.1). You also have the option of executing the SQL query directly from the Visualizer.

Logging LINQ to SQL Queries   My favorite method of debugging LINQ to SQL queries is to log all the DataContext output to ASP.NET trace. That way, I can see all the LINQ to SQL queries that execute at the bottom of each of my ASP.NET pages (see Figure 18.2).

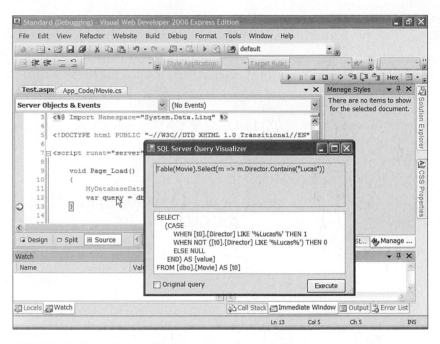

FIGURE 18.1   Using the LINQ to SQL Debug Visualizer.

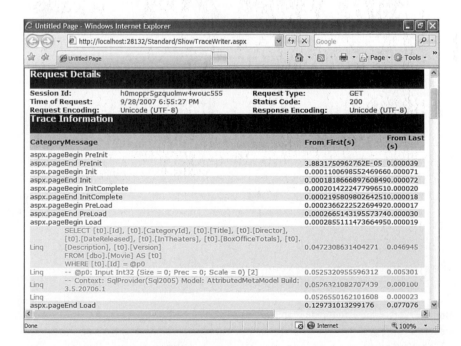

FIGURE 18.2   Logging LINQ to Trace.

The DataContext class includes a Log property. You can assign a TextWriter to the Log property, and DataContext will write to this TextWriter whenever it executes a query.

Unfortunately, the .NET Framework does not include a TextWriter that writes to ASP.NET Trace. Fortunately, it is not that difficult to write one, and I've included the code for a Trace TextWriter in Listing 18.31.

LISTING 18.31   Standard\TraceWriter.cs

```
using System;
using System.Text;
using System.Web;
using System.IO;
using System.Globalization;

public class TraceWriter : TextWriter
{
    public override void Write(string value)
    {
        HttpContext.Current.Trace.Warn(value);
    }

    public override void Write(char[] buffer, int index, int count)
    {
        HttpContext.Current.Trace.Warn("Linq", new string(buffer, index, count));
    }

    public override Encoding Encoding
    {
        get { return Encoding.Unicode; }
    }

    public TraceWriter()
        : base(CultureInfo.CurrentCulture)
    {
    }
}
```

After you drop the class in Listing 18.31 in your App_Code folder, you can set the DataContext class to write to the TraceWriter like this:

```
MyDatabaseDataContext db = new MyDatabaseDataContext();
db.Log = new TraceWriter();
grd.DataSource = db.Movies.Where(m=>m.Id==2);
grd.DataBind();
```

After you set up the TraceWriter, you can enable Trace (by adding the `Trace="true"` attribute to the `<%@ Page %>` directive) on any page that uses a LINQ query and view the output.

Using the `GetCommand` Method   Finally, you can use the `DataContext.GetCommand()` method to get the ADO.NET command object that executes when a LINQ to SQL query executes. After you grab the command object, you can examine its parameters or its command text.

The following code assigns the command text of a command associated with a LINQ to SQL query to a Label control:

```
MyDatabaseDataContext db = new MyDatabaseDataContext();
var query = db.Movies.Where(m=>m.Id==2);

lblQuery.Text = db.GetCommand(query).CommandText;
```

The following `SELECT` command is displayed in the Label control:

```
SELECT [t0].[Id], [t0].[CategoryId], [t0].[Title], [t0].[Director],
[t0].[DateReleased], [t0].[InTheaters], [t0].[BoxOfficeTotals],
[t0].[Description],
[t0].[Version] FROM [dbo].[Movie] AS [t0] WHERE [t0].[Id] = @p0
```

Creating a Custom LINQ Entity Base Class

18

In this final part of this chapter, we will build a custom LINQ to SQL base class. Our base class will contain standard methods for selecting records, inserting records, updating records, and deleting records. It will also support paging and caching. Finally, our base class will contain methods for performing validation.

The files for the custom classes can be found on the CD that accompanies this book in the folder EntityBaseClasses. This folder contains the following files:

▶ **EntityBase**—A custom base class for LINQ to SQL entities.

▶ **EntityDataSource**—A custom data source control derived from the ObjectDataSource control for representing LINQ to SQL entities.

▶ **EntityValidator**—A custom validation control.

▶ **EntityCallOutValidator**—A custom validation control that displays a call-out validation error message.

▶ **ValidationError**—A class that represents a validation error.

▶ **ValidationErrorCollection**—A collection of validation errors.

▶ **ValidationException**—An exception thrown when there is a validation error.

▶ **TraceWriter**—A class for logging LINQ to SQL queries to ASP.NET trace.

The motivation for writing these classes was to make standard database operations easier when using LINQ to SQL. I discovered that I was writing the exact same queries and commands over and over again whenever I created a new entity. Writing a standard base class made my life easier because it freed me from writing the same repetitive code.

Using the Entity Base Class

Follow these steps to use the custom entity base classes:

1. Create a new website.
2. Add an App_Code folder to your website and copy the EntityBaseClasses folder to the App_Code folder.
3. Create one or more LINQ to SQL entities with the help of the Object Relational Designer.
4. Add a connection string named con to your database in the web.config file.
5. Create a separate partial class for each LINQ to SQL entity and derive the class from the `EntityBase` class.
6. Create an empty `Validate()` method for each entity class.

For example, imagine that you have used the Object Relational Designer to create an entity named `Movie`. You created the `Movie` entity by dragging the Movie database table from the Database Explorer (Server Explorer) window onto the Object Relational Designer surface. At this point, you are ready to inherit your new `Movie` entity from the `EntityBase` class.

Listing 18.32 contains the file that you add to your website to create a `Movie` entity that inherits from the `EntityBase` class.

LISTING 18.32   ShowEntityBase\App_Code\Movie.cs

```
using System;


public partial class Movie : EntityBase<Movie>
{
    protected override void Validate()
    {
    }
}
```

Now that you have derived the `Movie` entity from `EntityBase`, the `Movie` class inherits methods for selecting, inserting, updating, and deleting records.

Performing Standard Data-Access Operations with the EntityBase Class

Any entity that you inherit from the EntityBase class inherits the following methods automatically:

- ▶ **`Select()`**—Selects all entities.

- ▶ **`Select(string orderBy)`**—Selects all entities in a certain order.

- ▶ **`SelectCached()`**—Selects all entities from the cache.

- ▶ **`SelectCached(string orderBy)`**—Selects all entities from the cache in a certain order.

- ▶ **`Select(int startRowIndex, int maximumRows)`**—Selects a page of entities.

- ▶ **`Select(int startRowIndex, int maximumRows, orderBy)`**—Selects a page of entities in a certain order.

- ▶ **`SelectCount()`**—Returns a count of entities.

- ▶ **`SelectCount(string orderBy)`**—Returns a count of entities.

- ▶ **`SelectCountCached()`**—Returns a count of entities from the cache.

- ▶ **`Get(int? Id)`**—Gets a single entity using the entity's identity value.

- ▶ **`Save(T oldEntity, T newEntity)`**—Either performs an insert or update depending on whether the identity value is 0.

- ▶ **`Insert(T entityToInsert)`**—Inserts a new entity.

- ▶ **`Update(T oldEntity, T newEntity)`**—Updates an existing entity.

- ▶ **`Delete(T entityToDelete)`**—Deletes an entity.

Notice that two of these methods—`Get()` and `Save()`—require that the database table an entity represents include an identity column. The other methods do not make this assumption.

The page in Listing 18.33 illustrates how you can use these methods.

LISTING 18.33   ShowEntityBase\SelectPagedSortedMovies.aspx

```
<%@ Page Language="C#" Trace="true" %>
<!DOCTYPE html PUBLIC "-//W3C//DTD XHTML 1.0 Transitional//EN"
 "http://www.w3.org/TR/xhtml1/DTD/xhtml1-transitional.dtd">
<html xmlns="http://www.w3.org/1999/xhtml">
<head id="Head1" runat="server">
```

18

LISTING 18.33   Continued

```
    <title>Select Paged Sorted Movies</title>
</head>
<body>
    <form id="form1" runat="server">
    <div>

    <asp:GridView
        id="grdMovies"
        DataSourceId="srcMovies"
        AllowPaging="true"
        AllowSorting="true"
        Runat="server" />

    <asp:ObjectDataSource
        id="srcMovies"
        TypeName="Movie"
        SelectMethod="Select"
        EnablePaging="true"
        SelectCountMethod="SelectCountCached"
        SortParameterName="orderBy"
        Runat="Server" />

    </div>
    </form>
</body>
</html>
```

The page in Listing 18.33 contains a GridView bound to an ObjectDataSource control. The ObjectDataSource control represents the Movie entity. The ObjectDataSource is configured to support data source paging and sorting. You get both the Select() and SelectCountCached() methods for free from the EntityBase class.

The EntityBaseClasses folder also contains a control named EntityDataSource. The EntityDataSource control can be used instead of the normal ObjectDataSource. The EntityDataSource control inherits from the ObjectDataSource control and provides default values for several ObjectDataSource control properties.

For example, you could swap the ObjectDataSource control in Listing 18.33 with the following EntityDataSource control:

```
    <custom:EntityDataSource
        id="srcMovies"
        TypeName="Movie"
        EnablePaging="true"
```

```
                SortParameterName="orderBy"
                Runat="Server" />
```

Why use the EntityDataSource control? Less typing. I don't want to program all day; I want to see a movie.

Performing Validation with the `EntityBase` Class

One complaint I've always had about the ASP.NET Framework is that validation happens at the wrong place. When building ASP.NET pages, you write the vast majority of your validation code in the user interface layer instead of your business logic layer where your validation code properly belongs.

Performing validation in your user interface layer is bad for two main reasons. First, it means that if you switch user interfaces for your application, you must rewrite all your validation logic. For example, you might want to create a cool Silverlight interface for your application. In that case, you have to write all your validation logic again from scratch. Validation logic should be user interface independent.

Also, placing your validation logic in your user interface layer means that you have to rewrite the exact same validation logic on each page that you use an entity. This is an extraordinary timewaster. I want to write my validation logic for an entity once and use the same logic everywhere.

The `EntityBase` class includes a `Validate()` method that you can use to incorporate validation logic into your entities (and thus, your business logic layer). Listing 18.34 illustrates how you can write the `Movie` class so that it validates the `Title`, `Director`, and `DateReleased` properties.

LISTING 18.34   ShowEntityBase\App_Code\Movie.cs

```csharp
using System;

public partial class Movie : EntityBase<Movie>
{
    protected override void Validate()
    {
        // Title is required
        if (!ValidationUtility.SatisfiesRequired(Title))
            ValidationErrors.Add("Title", "Required");
        // Director is required
        if (!ValidationUtility.SatisfiesRequired(Director))
            ValidationErrors.Add("Director", "Required");
        // DateReleased is required
        if (DateReleased == DateTime.MinValue)
            ValidationErrors.Add("DateReleased", "Required");
        // DateReleased can't be more than 10 years ago
```

18

LISTING 18.34   Continued

```
        if ((DateTime.Now.Year - DateReleased.Year) > 10)
            ValidationErrors.AddIfNotAlready("DateReleased", "Movie too old");
    }
}
```

The Validate() method validates the properties of the Movie entity. The method takes advantage of the ValidationUtility class. The ValidationUtility class contains a set of methods to make it easier to perform standard types of validation:

▶ **SatisfiesRequired()**—Enables you to check whether an expression has a value.

▶ **SatisfiesType()**—Enables you to validate against a regular expression defined in the Web.config file.

▶ **SatisfiesExpression()**—Enables you to validate against a regular expression.

▶ **IsInRole()**—Enables you to check whether the current user is in a particular role.

▶ **IsUserName()**—Enables you to check whether the current user has a particular username.

▶ **ShowValidationErrors()**—Displays validation errors on a page.

The ASP.NET page in Listing 18.35 demonstrates how you take advantage of entity validation when inserting new movie records into the database (see Figure 18.3).

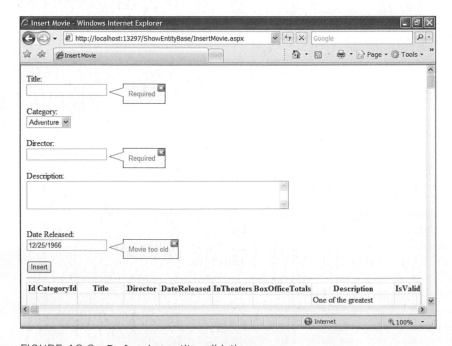

FIGURE 18.3   Performing entity validation.

LISTING 18.35   ShowEntityBase\InsertMovie.aspx

```
<%@ Page Language="C#" Trace="true" %>
<%@ Register TagPrefix="custom" Namespace="Superexpert.Controls" %>
<!DOCTYPE html PUBLIC "-//W3C//DTD XHTML 1.0 Transitional//EN"
 "http://www.w3.org/TR/xhtml1/DTD/xhtml1-transitional.dtd">
<script runat="server">

    protected void frmMovie_ItemInserted
    (
      object sender,
      FormViewInsertedEventArgs e
    )
    {
        if (e.Exception != null)
        {
            e.ExceptionHandled = true;
            e.KeepInInsertMode = true;
            ValidationUtility.ShowValidationErrors(this, e.Exception);
        }
    }

</script>
<html xmlns="http://www.w3.org/1999/xhtml">
<head id="Head1" runat="server">
    <title>Insert Movie</title>
</head>
<body>
    <form id="form1" runat="server">
    <div>

    <asp:FormView
        id="frmMovie"
        DataSourceID="srcMovies"
        DefaultMode="Insert"
        OnItemInserted="frmMovie_ItemInserted"
        Runat="Server">
        <InsertItemTemplate>
            <asp:Label
                id="lblTitle"
                Text="Title:"
                AssociatedControlID="txtTitle"
                Runat="server" />
            <br />
            <asp:TextBox
                id="txtTitle"
```

LISTING 18.35   Continued

```
                    Text='<%# Bind("Title") %>'
                    Runat="server" />
            <custom:EntityCallOutValidator
                    id="valTitle"
                    PropertyName="Title"
                    Runat="Server" />
            <br /><br />

            <asp:Label
                    id="lblCategory"
                    Text="Category:"
                    AssociatedControlID="ddlCategory"
                    Runat="server" />
            <br />
            <asp:DropDownList
                    id="ddlCategory"
                    DataSourceId="srcMovieCategories"
                    SelectedValue='<%# Bind("CategoryId") %>'
                    DataTextField="Name"
                    DataValueField="Id"
                    Runat="server" />
            <asp:ObjectDataSource
                    id="srcMovieCategories"
                    TypeName="MovieCategory"
                    SelectMethod="Select"
                    Runat="Server" />
            <br /><br / >

            <asp:Label
                    id="lblDirector"
                    Text="Director:"
                    AssociatedControlID="txtDirector"
                    Runat="server" />
            <br />
            <asp:TextBox
                    id="txtDirector"
                    Text='<%# Bind("Director") %>'
                    Runat="server" />
            <custom:EntityCallOutValidator
                    id="valDirector"
                    PropertyName="Director"
                    Runat="Server" />

            <br /><br />
```

```
                  <asp:Label
                      id="lblDescription"
                      Text="Description:"
                      AssociatedControlID="txtDescription"
                      Runat="server" />
                  <br />
                  <asp:TextBox
                      id="txtDescription"
                      Text='<%# Bind("Description") %>'
                      TextMode="MultiLine"
                      Columns="60"
                      Rows="3"
                      Runat="server" />

                  <br /><br />

                  <asp:Label
                      id="lblDateReleased"
                      Text="Date Released:"
                      AssociatedControlID="txtDateReleased"
                      Runat="server" />
                  <br />
                  <asp:TextBox
                      id="txtDateReleased"
                      Text='<%# Bind("DateReleased") %>'
                      Runat="server" />
                  <custom:EntityCallOutValidator
                      id="valDateReleased"
                      PropertyName="DateReleased"
                      ControlToValidate="txtDateReleased"
                      TypeName="date"
                      Runat="Server" />
                  <br /><br />

                  <asp:Button
                      id="btnInsert"
                      Text="Insert"
                      CommandName="Insert"
                      Runat="server" />

         </InsertItemTemplate>
     </asp:FormView>

<hr />

<asp:GridView
```

LISTING 18.35   Continued

```
        id="grdMovies"
        DataSourceID="srcMovies"
        Runat="server" />

    <custom:EntityDataSource
        id="srcMovies"
        TypeName="Movie"
        Runat="server" />

    </div>
    </form>
</body>
</html>
```

You should notice several things about the page in Listing 18.35. First, the page includes a method for handling the FormView control's ItemInserted event. This handler checks for an exception. If Movie.Validate() creates one or more validation errors, the Movie entity will throw a ValidationException when inserting or updating automatically.

If there is an exception, the exception is passed to the ValidationUtility. ShowValidationErrors() method. The ShowValidationErrors() method finds the EntityCallOutValidator that corresponds to each validation error and displays the correct error message.

The Validate() method executes only if a Movie entity can be created. If someone enters the wrong type of value into a field, the ObjectDataSource can't even create the entity and the Validate() method never executes. Notice that the EntityCallOutValidator associated with the DateReleased property includes ControlToValidate and TypeName properties. This validation control checks whether the value entered into the DateReleased TextBox is a valid date even before the Movie entity is created.

NOTE

The sample application contained in the last chapter of this book uses the approach to validation described in this section.

Summary

You read the whole chapter? I'm impressed. We covered a lot of material over the course of this chapter. In the first part, we discussed all the new additions to the C# and VB.NET languages included with Microsoft .NET Framework 3.5. For example, we discussed anonymous types, extension methods, and lambda expressions.

Next, we discussed LINQ to SQL entities. You learned how to build entities that represent your database objects both by hand and by using the Object Relational Designer. We also briefly examined the LinqDataSource control.

In the following part of this chapter, we discussed how you can perform basic database operations with LINQ to SQL. For example, you learned how to select records, page through records, and cache records. You also learned how to insert, update, and delete database records with LINQ to SQL.

In the final part of this chapter, you learned how to build a custom LINQ to SQL base class. You learned how to use this class to support selecting, inserting, deleting, and updating entities without writing any code. You also learned how to add validation logic to your entities.

18

PART V

Site Navigation

IN THIS PART

Using the Navigation Controls

In this chapter, you learn how to use the `SiteMapPath`, `Menu`, and `TreeView` controls. All three of these controls can be used to enable users to navigate your website. Furthermore, the `Menu` and `TreeView` controls can be used independently of website navigation. You can bind these two controls to other data sources such as XML documents or database data.

This chapter explores different methods of binding the `Menu` and `TreeView` controls to different data sources and shows you how to format the rendered output of both of these controls. You also learn how to take advantage of AJAX when working with the `TreeView` control.

In the final section of this chapter, we build a `SqlHierarchicalDataSource` control, which enables you to bind controls such as the `TreeView` and `Menu` controls to hierarchical database data.

Understanding Site Maps

Before you learn about the navigation controls, you first need to understand Site Maps. All three navigation controls use Site Maps to retrieve navigation information. A Site Map enables you to represent the navigational relationships between the pages in an application, independent of the actual physical relationship between pages as stored in the file system.

Site Maps use the provider model. In the next chapter, you learn how to create custom Site Map providers to store Site Maps in custom data stores such as database tables. The examples in this chapter take advantage of the default XML Site Map provider, which enables you to store a Site Map in an XML file.

By default, the navigation controls assume the existence of an XML file named Web.sitemap, which is located in the root of your application.

For example, Listing 19.1 contains a simple Site Map.

LISTING 19.1   Web.sitemap

```
<siteMap xmlns="http://schemas.microsoft.com/AspNet/SiteMap-File-1.0" >

<siteMapNode
  url="~/Default.aspx"
  title="Home"
  description="The home page of the Website">

  <!-- Product Nodes -->
  <siteMapNode
    title="Products"
    description="Website products">
    <siteMapNode
      url="~/Products/FirstProduct.aspx"
      title="First Product"
      description="The first product" />
    <siteMapNode
      url="~/Products/SecondProduct.aspx"
      title="Second Product"
      description="The second product" />
  </siteMapNode>

  <!-- Services Nodes -->
  <siteMapNode
    title="Services"
    description="Website services">
    <siteMapNode
      url="~/Service/FirstService.aspx"
      title="First Service"
      description="The first service" />
    <siteMapNode
      url="~/Products/SecondService.aspx"
      title="Second Service"
      description="The second service" />
  </siteMapNode>
```

```
    </siteMapNode>

  </siteMapNode>

</siteMap>
```

A Site Map file contains `<siteMapNode>` elements. There can be only one top-level node. In the case of Listing 19.1, the top-level node represents the website's homepage.

A `<siteMapNode>` supports three main attributes:

- ▸ **title**—A brief title that you want to associate with a node.

- ▸ **description**—A longer description that you want to associate with a node.

- ▸ **url**—A URL that points to a page or other resource.

Notice that the `url` attribute is not required. Both the Products and Services nodes do not include a `url` attribute because these nodes do not represent pages to which you can navigate.

Each `<siteMapNode>` can contain any number of child nodes. In Listing 19.1, both the Products and Services nodes include two child nodes.

The Site Map in Listing 19.1 represents a website that has the following folder and page structure:

```
Default.aspx
Products
  FirstProduct.aspx
  SecondProduct.aspx
Services
  FirstService.aspx
  SecondService.aspx
```

The navigational structure of a website as represented by a Site Map is not required to have any relationship to the navigational structure of a website as stored in the file system. You can create any relationship between the nodes in a Site Map that you want.

19

Using the `SiteMapPath` Control

The `SiteMapPath` control enables you to navigate easily to any parent page of the current page. It displays the standard bread crumb trail that you see on many popular websites (see Figure 19.1).

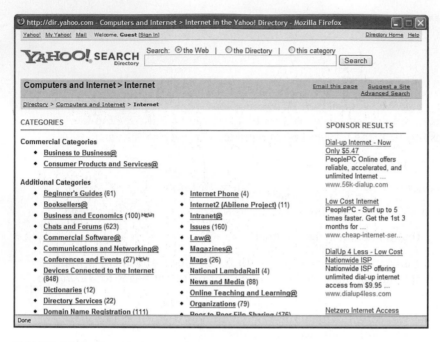

FIGURE 19.1   Bread crumb trail at Yahoo.com.

You can use the `SiteMapPath` control simply by declaring the control in a page. The control automatically uses the `Web.sitemap` file located in the root of your application. For example, the page in Listing 19.2 includes the `SiteMapPath` control (see Figure 19.2).

LISTING 19.2   UsingSiteMapPath/DisplaySiteMapPath.aspx

```
<%@ Page Language="C#" %>
<!DOCTYPE html PUBLIC "-//W3C//DTD XHTML 1.1//EN"
 "http://www.w3.org/TR/xhtml11/DTD/xhtml11.dtd">
<html xmlns="http://www.w3.org/1999/xhtml" >
<head id="Head1" runat="server">
    <title>Display SiteMapPath</title>
</head>
<body>
    <form id="form1" runat="server">
    <div>

    <asp:SiteMapPath
        id="SiteMapPath1"
        Runat="server" />

    <hr />
```

```
      <h1>Displaying a SiteMapPath Control</h1>

      </div>
      </form>
</body>
</html>
```

FIGURE 19.2   Displaying the SiteMapPath control.

Notice that you can click the Home link rendered by the SiteMapPath control to navigate to the website's home page.

The SiteMapPath uses both the title and description attributes from the <siteMapNode> elements contained in the Web.sitemap file. The title attribute is used for the node (link) text, and the description attribute is used for the node tool tip.

NOTE

Typically, you do not add a SiteMapPath control to individual pages in your website. If you add a SiteMapPath control to a Master Page, then you can display the SiteMapPath control automatically on every page. To learn more about Master Pages, see Chapter 5, "Designing Websites with Master Pages."

19

The SiteMapPath control supports the following properties:

▶ **ParentLevelsDisplay**—Enables you to limit the number of parent nodes displayed. By default, a SiteMapPath control displays all the parent nodes.

▶ **PathDirection**—Enables you to reverse the order of the links displayed by the SiteMapPath control. Possible values are RootToCurrent (the default) or CurrentToRoot.

▶ **PathSeparator**—Enables you to specify the character used to separate the nodes displayed by the SiteMapPath control. The default value is >.

▶ **RenderCurrentNodeAsLink**—Enables you to render the SiteMapPath node that represents the current page as a link. By default, the current node is not rendered as a link.

▶ **ShowToolTips**—Enables you to disable the display of tool tips.

▶ **SiteMapProvider**—Enables you to specify the name of an alternate Site Map provider to use with the SiteMapPath control.

▶ **SkipLinkText**—Enables you to specify more specific text for skipping the links displayed by the SiteMapPath control. The default value for this property is Skip Navigation Links.

WEB STANDARDS NOTE

All the navigation controls automatically render a skip navigation link to meet accessibility requirements. The skip navigation link is read by a screen reader, but it is not displayed in a normal browser.

If you are interacting with a web page through a screen reader, you don't want to hear the list of navigation links each and every time you open a page. (It is the equivalent of listening to a phone menu every time you open a page.) The skip navigation link enables users of screen readers to skip the repetitive reading of links.

Formatting the SiteMapPath Control

You can use either styles or templates to format the SiteMapPath control.

The control supports the following Style objects:

▶ **CurrentNodeStyle**—Formats the SiteMapPath node that represents the current page.

▶ **NodeStyle**—Formats every node rendered by the SiteMapPath control.

▶ **PathSeparatorStyle**—Formats the text displayed between each SiteMapPath node.

▶ **RootNodeStyle**—Formats the root (first) node rendered by the SiteMapPath control.

For example, the page in Listing 19.3 takes advantage of all four Style properties to modify the default appearance of the SiteMapPath control (see Figure 19.3).

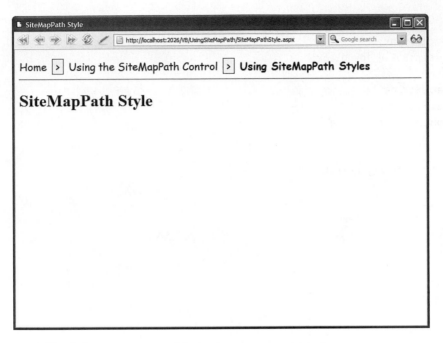

FIGURE 19.3   Using styles with the SiteMapPath control.

LISTING 19.3   UsingSiteMapPath/SiteMapPathStyle.aspx

```
<%@ Page Language="C#" %>
<!DOCTYPE html PUBLIC "-//W3C//DTD XHTML 1.1//EN"
    "http://www.w3.org/TR/xhtml11/DTD/xhtml11.dtd">
<html xmlns="http://www.w3.org/1999/xhtml" >
<head id="Head1" runat="server">
    <style type="text/css">
        .siteMapPath
        {
            font:20px Comic Sans MS,Serif;
        }
        .currentNodeStyle
        {
            font-weight:bold;
        }
        .nodeStyle
        {
            text-decoration:none;
        }
        .pathSeparatorStyle
        {
            background-color:yellow;
```

LISTING 19.3   Continued

```
            margin:10px;
            border:Solid 1px black;
        }
        .rootNodeStyle
        {
            text-decoration:none;
        }
    </style>
    <title>SiteMapPath Style</title>
</head>
<body>
    <form id="form1" runat="server">
    <div>

    <asp:SiteMapPath
        id="SiteMapPath1"
        CssClass="siteMapPath"
        CurrentNodeStyle-CssClass="currentNodeStyle"
        NodeStyle-CssClass="nodeStyle"
        PathSeparatorStyle-CssClass="pathSeparatorStyle"
        RootNodeStyle-CssClass="rootNodeStyle"
        Runat="server" />
    <hr />

    <h1>SiteMapPath Style</h1>

    </div>
    </form>
</body>
</html>
```

Furthermore, you can use templates with the SiteMapPath control to format the appearance of the control (and change its behavior). The SiteMapPath control supports the following templates:

▶ **CurrentNodeTemplate**—Template for the SiteMapPath node that represents the current page.

▶ **NodeTemplate**—Template for each SiteMapPath node that is not the current or root node.

▶ **PathSeparatorTemplate**—Template for the text displayed between each SiteMapPath node.

▶ **RootNodeTemplate**—Template for the root (first) node rendered by the SiteMapPath control.

For example, the SiteMapPath control in Listing 19.4 includes a NodeTemplate. The NodeTemplate includes a HyperLink control that displays the current SiteMapPath node. The template also displays a count of the child nodes of the current node (see Figure 19.4).

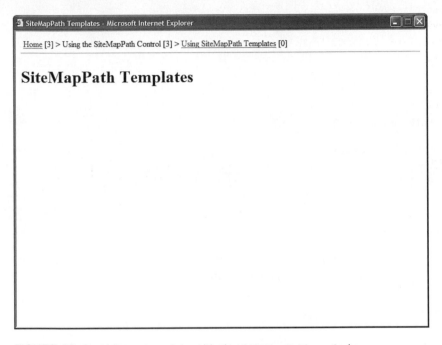

FIGURE 19.4   Using a template with the SiteMapPath control.

LISTING 19.4   UsingSiteMapPath/SiteMapPathTemplates.aspx

```
<%@ Page Language="C#" %>
<!DOCTYPE html PUBLIC "-//W3C//DTD XHTML 1.1//EN"
  "http://www.w3.org/TR/xhtml11/DTD/xhtml11.dtd">
<html xmlns="http://www.w3.org/1999/xhtml" >
<head id="Head1" runat="server">
    <title>SiteMapPath Templates</title>
</head>
<body>
    <form id="form1" runat="server">
    <div>

    <asp:SiteMapPath
        id="SiteMapPath1"
        Runat="server">
        <NodeTemplate>
        <asp:HyperLink
            id="lnkPage"
            Text='<%# Eval("Title") %>'
```

19

LISTING 19.4   Continued

```
            NavigateUrl='<%# Eval("Url") %>'
            ToolTip='<%# Eval("Description") %>'
            Runat="server" />
        [<%# Eval("ChildNodes.Count") %>]
        </NodeTemplate>
    </asp:SiteMapPath>

    <hr />

    <h1>SiteMapPath Templates</h1>


    </div>
    </form>
</body>
</html>
```

Within a template, the data item represents a `SiteMapNode`. Therefore, you can refer to any of the properties of the `SiteMapNode` class in a databinding expression.

Using the `Menu` Control

The `Menu` control enables you to create two types of menus. You can use the `Menu` control to create the left-column menu that appears in many websites. In other words, you can use the `Menu` control to display a vertical list of links.

You also can use the `Menu` control to create a menu that more closely resembles the drop-down menus that appear in traditional desktop applications. In this case, the `Menu` control renders a horizontal list of links.

Unlike the `SiteMapPath` control, the `Menu` control can represent other types of data than Site Map data. Technically, you can bind a `Menu` control to any data source that implements the `IHierarchicalDataSource` or `IHierarchicalEnumerable` interface.

In this section, you learn how to create different types of menus with the `Menu` control. First, you learn how to add menu items declaratively to a `Menu` control. Next, we discuss how the `Menu` control can be used with the `MultiView` control to display a tabbed page.

You also examine how you can bind the `Menu` control to different types of data sources. You learn how to use the `Menu` control with Site Map data, XML data, and database data.

Declaratively Adding Menu Items

You can display a menu with the `Menu` control by adding one or more `MenuItem` objects to its `Items` property. For example, the page in Listing 19.5 uses a `Menu` control to create a simple vertical menu (see Figure 19.5).

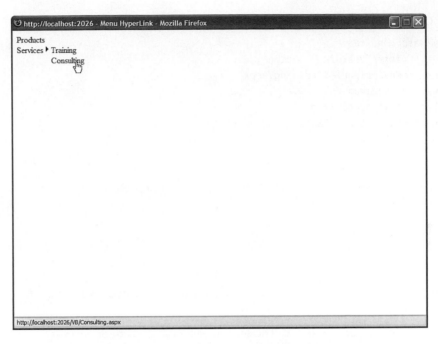

FIGURE 19.5   Displaying a menu with the Menu control.

LISTING 19.5   MenuHyperLink.aspx

```
<%@ Page Language="C#" %>
<!DOCTYPE html PUBLIC "-//W3C//DTD XHTML 1.1//EN"
 "http://www.w3.org/TR/xhtml11/DTD/xhtml11.dtd">
<html xmlns="http://www.w3.org/1999/xhtml" >
<head id="Head1" runat="server">
    <title>Menu HyperLink</title>
</head>
<body>
    <form id="form1" runat="server">
    <div>

    <asp:Menu
        id="Menu1"
        Runat="server">
        <Items>
            <asp:MenuItem
                Text="Products"
                NavigateUrl="Products.aspx" />
            <asp:MenuItem
                Text="Services"
                NavigateUrl="Services.aspx">
```

19

LISTING 19.5   Continued

```
                <asp:MenuItem
                    Text="Training"
                    NavigateUrl="Training.aspx" />
                <asp:MenuItem
                    Text="Consulting"
                    NavigateUrl="Consulting.aspx" />
            </asp:MenuItem>
        </Items>
    </asp:Menu>

    </div>
    </form>
</body>
</html>
```

The Menu in Listing 19.5 is created from MenuItem objects. Each menu item in Listing 19.5 contains a link to another page.

Notice that MenuItem objects can be nested. The second MenuItem object—Services—includes two child MenuItem objects. When you hover your mouse over a parent menu item, the child menu items are displayed.

Each MenuItem in Listing 19.5 includes a Text and NavigateUrl property. Rather than use a MenuItem to link to a new page, you also can use a MenuItem to link back to the same page. In other words, each MenuItem can act like a Linkbutton control instead of a HyperLink control.

For example, each MenuItem object in Listing 19.6 includes a Text and Value property. When you click a menu item, the same page is reloaded and the value of the selected menu item is displayed (see Figure 19.6).

LISTING 19.6   MenuLinkButton.aspx

```
<%@ Page Language="C#" %>
<!DOCTYPE html PUBLIC "-//W3C//DTD XHTML 1.1//EN"
"http://www.w3.org/TR/xhtml11/DTD/xhtml11.dtd">
<script runat="server">

    protected void Menu1_MenuItemClick(object sender, MenuEventArgs e)
    {
        lblMessage.Text = "You selected " + Menu1.SelectedValue;
    }
</script>
<html xmlns="http://www.w3.org/1999/xhtml" >
<head id="Head1" runat="server">
```

```
        <title>Menu LinkButton</title>
</head>
<body>
    <form id="form1" runat="server">
    <div>

    <asp:Menu
        id="Menu1"
        OnMenuItemClick="Menu1_MenuItemClick"
        Runat="server">
        <Items>
            <asp:MenuItem
                Text="Products Page"
                Value="Products" />
            <asp:MenuItem
                Text="Services Page"
                Value="Services">
                <asp:MenuItem
                    Text="Training Page"
                    Value="Training" />
                <asp:MenuItem
                    Text="Consulting Page"
                    Value="Consulting" />
            </asp:MenuItem>
        </Items>
    </asp:Menu>

    <hr />

    <asp:Label
        id="lblMessage"
        EnableViewState="false"
        Runat="server" />

    </div>
    </form>
</body>
</html>
```

Notice that the page includes a MenuItemClick event handler. When you click a
MenuItem (and the MenuItem does not have a NavigateUrl property), the MenuItemClick
event is raised.

In Listing 19.6, the MenuItemClick handler displays the value of the selected MenuItem in a
Label control.

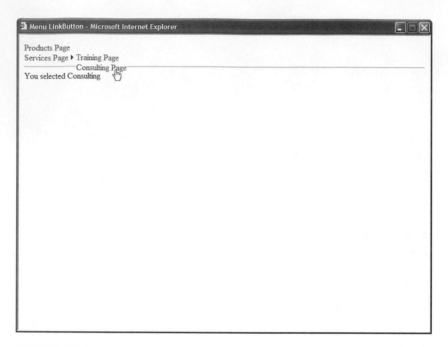

FIGURE 19.6   Selecting menu items.

Using the `Menu` Control with the `MultiView` Control

When the `Menu` control is used with the `MultiView` control, you can create tabbed pages. You use the `Menu` control to display the tabs and the `MultiView` control to display the content that corresponds to the selected tab.

For example, the page in Listing 19.7 displays three tabs (see Figure 19.7).

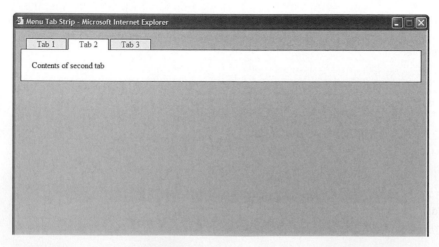

FIGURE 19.7   Displaying a tabbed page.

LISTING 19.7   MenuTabStrip.aspx

```csharp
<%@ Page Language="C#" %>
<!DOCTYPE html PUBLIC "-//W3C//DTD XHTML 1.1//EN"
"http://www.w3.org/TR/xhtml11/DTD/xhtml11.dtd">
<script runat="server">

    protected void menuTabs_MenuItemClick(object sender, MenuEventArgs e)
    {
        multiTabs.ActiveViewIndex = Int32.Parse(menuTabs.SelectedValue);
    }
</script>
<html xmlns="http://www.w3.org/1999/xhtml" >
<head id="Head1" runat="server">
    <style type="text/css">
        html
        {
            background-color:silver;
        }
        .menuTabs
        {
            position:relative;
            top:1px;
            left:10px;
        }
        .tab
        {
            border:Solid 1px black;
            border-bottom:none;
            padding:0px 10px;
            background-color:#eeeeee;
        }
        .selectedTab
        {
            border:Solid 1px black;
            border-bottom:Solid 1px white;
            padding:0px 10px;
            background-color:white;
        }
        .tabBody
        {
            border:Solid 1px black;
            padding:20px;
            background-color:white;
        }
    </style>
```

19

LISTING 19.7   Continued

```
    <title>Menu Tab Strip</title>
</head>
<body>
    <form id="form1" runat="server">
    <div>

    <asp:Menu
        id="menuTabs"
        CssClass="menuTabs"
        StaticMenuItemStyle-CssClass="tab"
        StaticSelectedStyle-CssClass="selectedTab"
        Orientation="Horizontal"
        OnMenuItemClick="menuTabs_MenuItemClick"
        Runat="server">
        <Items>
        <asp:MenuItem
            Text="Tab 1"
            Value="0"
            Selected="true" />
        <asp:MenuItem
            Text="Tab 2"
            Value="1"/>
        <asp:MenuItem
            Text="Tab 3"
            Value="2" />

        </Items>
    </asp:Menu>


    <div class="tabBody">
    <asp:MultiView
        id="multiTabs"
        ActiveViewIndex="0"
        Runat="server">
        <asp:View ID="view1" runat="server">

        Contents of first tab

        </asp:View>
        <asp:View ID="view2" runat="server">

        Contents of second tab
```

```
        </asp:View>
        <asp:View ID="view3" runat="server">

        Contents of third tab

        </asp:View>
    </asp:MultiView>
    </div>

    </div>
    </form>
</body>
</html>
```

After you open the page in Listing 19.7 and click a tab, the MenuItemClick event is raised. The MenuItemClick event handler changes the ActiveViewIndex property of the MultiView control to display the content of the selected tab.

WEB STANDARDS NOTE

The Menu control in Listing 19.7 is pushed down one pixel and pushed right 10 pixels to hide the border between the selected tab and the contents of the tab. (The Menu control has a relative position.) Notice that the style rule for the selected tab includes a white bottom border. This trick works in Internet Explorer 6, Firefox 1, and Opera 8.

Binding to a Site Map

Like the SiteMapPath control, you can use the Menu control with a Site Map. Users can click menu items to navigate to particular pages in your website.

Unlike the SiteMapPath control, however, the Menu control does not automatically bind to a Site Map. You must explicitly bind the Menu control to a SiteMapDataSource control to display nodes from a Site Map.

For example, the page in Listing 19.8 contains a menu that contains links to all the pages in a website (see Figure 19.8).

LISTING 19.8 UsingMenu/MenuSiteMap.aspx

```
<%@ Page Language="C#" %>
<!DOCTYPE html PUBLIC "-//W3C//DTD XHTML 1.1//EN"
    "http://www.w3.org/TR/xhtml11/DTD/xhtml11.dtd">
<html xmlns="http://www.w3.org/1999/xhtml" >
<head id="Head1" runat="server">
    <title>Menu SiteMap</title>
</head>
```

LISTING 19.8   Continued

```
<body>
    <form id="form1" runat="server">
    <div>

    <asp:Menu
        id="Menu1"
        DataSourceID="srcSiteMap"
        Runat="server" />

    <asp:SiteMapDataSource
        id="srcSiteMap"
        Runat="server" />

    </div>
    </form>
</body>
</html>
```

When you initially open the page in Listing 19.8, the only menu item that appears is the link to the Home page. If you hover your mouse over this link, links to additional pages are displayed.

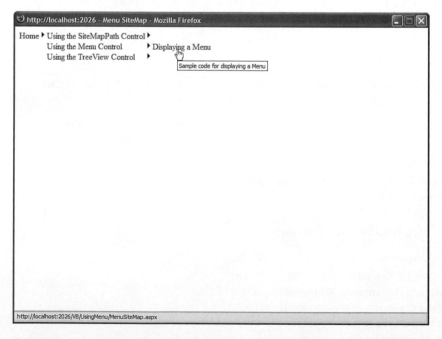

FIGURE 19.8   Displaying a Site Map with a Menu control.

Normally, you do not want the Home link to be displayed in a navigation menu. Instead, you want to display the second level of menu items. You can use the ShowStartingNode property of the SiteMapDataSource control to hide the topmost node in a Site Map.

For example, the page in Listing 19.9 uses a Menu control that renders a standard left-column navigational menu (see Figure 19.9).

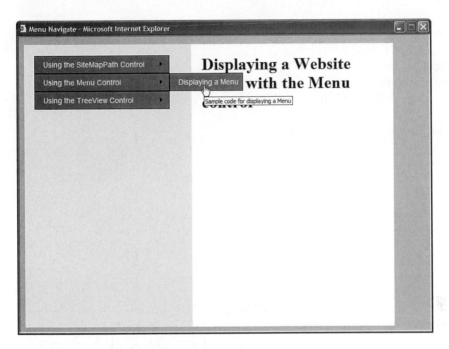

FIGURE 19.9   Displaying a navigation menu.

LISTING 19.9   UsingMenu/MenuNavigate.aspx

```
<%@ Page Language="C#" %>
<!DOCTYPE html PUBLIC "-//W3C//DTD XHTML 1.1//EN"
    "http://www.w3.org/TR/xhtml11/DTD/xhtml11.dtd">
<html xmlns="http://www.w3.org/1999/xhtml" >
<head id="Head1" runat="server">
    <style type="text/css">
        html
        {
            background-color:silver;
        }
        .navigation
        {
            float:left;
            width:280px;
```

LISTING 19.9   Continued

```
                height:500px;
                padding:20px;
                background-color:#eeeeee;
        }
        .content
        {
                float:left;
                width:550px;
                height:500px;
                padding:20px;
                background-color:white;
        }
        .menuItem
        {
                border:Outset 1px black;
                background-color:Gray;
                font:14px Arial;
                color:White;
                padding:8px;
        }
    </style>
    <title>Menu Navigate</title>
</head>
<body>
    <form id="form1" runat="server">


    <div class="navigation">

    <asp:Menu
        id="Menu1"
        DataSourceID="srcSiteMap"
        StaticMenuItemStyle-CssClass="menuItem"
        DynamicMenuItemStyle-CssClass="menuItem"
        Runat="server" />

    <asp:SiteMapDataSource
        id="srcSiteMap"
        ShowStartingNode="false"
        Runat="server" />

    </div>

    <div class="content">
```

```
    <h1>Displaying a Website menu with the Menu control</h1>

    </div>


    </form>
</body>
</html>
```

When you open the page in Listing 19.9, the second-level nodes from the Site Map are initially displayed. Furthermore, the Menu control is styled to appear more like a traditional website navigation menu.

Binding to an XML File

As an alternative to binding a Menu control to a SiteMapDataSource control, you can bind the control to an XML document by using the XmlDataSource control. For example, suppose that you have the XML file in Listing 19.10.

LISTING 19.10   Menu.xml

```
<menu>
  <appetizer>
    <soup />
    <cheese />
  </appetizer>
  <entree>
    <duck />
    <chicken />
  </entree>
  <dessert>
    <cake />
    <pie />
  </dessert>
</menu>
```

The page in Listing 19.11 displays the contents of Listing 19.10 by using an XmlDataSource control to represent the XML document.

LISTING 19.11   MenuXML.aspx

```
<%@ Page Language="C#" %>
<!DOCTYPE html PUBLIC "-//W3C//DTD XHTML 1.1//EN"
    "http://www.w3.org/TR/xhtml11/DTD/xhtml11.dtd">
<html xmlns="http://www.w3.org/1999/xhtml" >
```

19

LISTING 19.11   Continued

```
<head id="Head1" runat="server">
    <title>Menu XML</title>
</head>
<body>
    <form id="form1" runat="server">
    <div>

    <asp:Menu
        id="Menu1"
        DataSourceID="srcMenu"
        Runat="server" />

    <asp:XmlDataSource
        id="srcMenu"
        DataFile="Menu.xml"
        Runat="server" />

    </div>
    </form>
</body>
</html>
```

When using the XmlDataSource control, you can use the XPath property to supply an xpath query that restricts the nodes returned by the XmlDataSource. You also can use either the Transform or TransformFile property to apply an XSLT Style Sheet to the XML document and transform the nodes returned by the XmlDataSource.

The XML file in Listing 19.10 is very simple. The nodes do not contain any attributes. When you bind the Menu control to the XML file, the ToString() method is called on each XML file node.

You also can bind the Menu control to more complex XML documents. For example, the item nodes in the XML document in Listing 19.12 include two attributes: text and price.

LISTING 19.12   MenuComplex.xml

```
<menu>
  <category text="appetizer">
    <item text="soup" price="12.56" />
    <item text="cheese" price="17.23" />
  </category>
  <category text="entree">
    <item text="duck" price="89.21" />
    <item text="chicken" price="34.56" />
  </category>
```

```
    <category text="dessert">
      <item text="cake" price="23.43" />
      <item text="pie" price="115.46" />
    </category>
</menu>
```

When you bind to the XML document in Listing 19.12, you must specify one or more menu item bindings. The menu item bindings specify the relationship between node attributes and the menu items displayed by the Menu control.

The Menu control in Listing 19.13 includes MenuItemBinding subtags (see Figure 19.10).

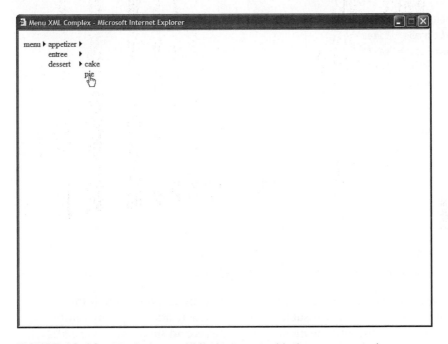

FIGURE 19.10   Displaying an XML document with the Menu control.

LISTING 19.13   MenuXMLComplex.aspx

```
<%@ Page Language="C#" %>
<!DOCTYPE html PUBLIC "-//W3C//DTD XHTML 1.1//EN"
    "http://www.w3.org/TR/xhtml11/DTD/xhtml11.dtd">
<html xmlns="http://www.w3.org/1999/xhtml" >
<head id="Head1" runat="server">
    <title>Menu XML Complex</title>
</head>
<body>
```

LISTING 19.13   Continued

```
<form id="form1" runat="server">
<div>

<asp:Menu
    id="Menu1"
    DataSourceID="srcMenu"
    Runat="server">
    <DataBindings>
    <asp:MenuItemBinding
        DataMember="category"
        TextField="text" />
    <asp:MenuItemBinding
        DataMember="item"
        TextField="text"
        ValueField="price" />
    </DataBindings>
</asp:Menu>

<asp:XmlDataSource
    id="srcMenu"
    DataFile="MenuComplex.xml"
    Runat="server" />

</div>
</form>
</body>
</html>
```

Notice that the Menu control includes a `<DataBindings>` element. This element includes two MenuItemBinding subtags. The first subtag represents the relationship between the category nodes in the XML file and the menu items. The second subtag represents the relationship between the item nodes in the XML file and the menu items.

Binding to Database Data

You can't bind a Menu control directly to database data. Neither the SqlDataSource nor ObjectDataSource controls implement the IHierachicalDataSource interface. Therefore, if you want to represent database data with the Menu control, then you need to perform some more work.

One option is to create your own SqlHierarchicalDataSource control. You can do this either by deriving from the base HierarchicalDataSourceControl class or implementing the IHierachicalDataSource interface. You'll see this approach in the final section of this chapter, when a custom SqlHierarchicalDataSource control is built.

A second option is to build the menu items programmatically in the Menu control. This is the approach that is followed here.

Imagine that you want to represent the contents of the following database table with a Menu control:

CategoryId	ParentId	Name
1	null	Beverages
2	null	Fruit
3	1	Milk
4	1	Juice
5	4	Apple Juice
6	4	Orange Juice
7	2	Apples
8	2	Pears

This database table represents product categories. The categories are nested with the help of the ParentId column. For example, the Orange Juice category is nested below the Juice category, and the Juice category is nested below the Beverages category.

The page in Listing 19.14 illustrates how you can display this database table with a Menu control (see Figure 19.11).

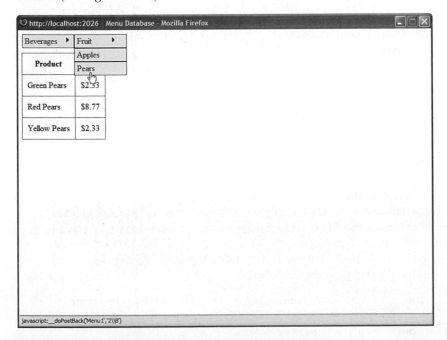

FIGURE 19.11   Displaying database data with the Menu control.

LISTING 19.14   `MenuDatabase.aspx`

```csharp
<%@ Page Language="C#" %>
<%@ Import Namespace="System.Web.Configuration" %>
<%@ Import Namespace="System.Data" %>
<%@ Import Namespace="System.Data.SqlClient" %>
<!DOCTYPE html PUBLIC "-//W3C//DTD XHTML 1.1//EN"
"http://www.w3.org/TR/xhtml11/DTD/xhtml11.dtd">
<script runat="server">


    /// <summary>
    /// Only populate the menu when the page first loads
    /// </summary>
    void Page_Load()
    {
        if (!Page.IsPostBack)
            PopulateMenu();
    }


    /// <summary>
    /// Get the data from the database and create the top-level
    /// menu items
    /// </summary>
    private void PopulateMenu()
    {
        DataTable menuData = GetMenuData();
        AddTopMenuItems(menuData);
    }


    /// <summary>
    /// Use a DataAdapter and DataTable to grab the database data
    /// </summary>
    /// <returns></returns>
    private DataTable GetMenuData()
    {
        // Get Categories table
        string selectCommand = "SELECT CategoryId,ParentId,Name FROM Categories";
        string conString = WebConfigurationManager.ConnectionStrings["Categories"].
        ➥ConnectionString;
        SqlDataAdapter dad = new SqlDataAdapter(selectCommand, conString);
        DataTable dtblCategories = new DataTable();
        dad.Fill(dtblCategories);
        return dtblCategories;
    }
```

```csharp
    /// <summary>
    /// Filter the data to get only the rows that have a
    /// null ParentID (these are the top-level menu items)
    /// </summary>
    private void AddTopMenuItems(DataTable menuData)
    {
        DataView view = new DataView(menuData);
        view.RowFilter = "ParentID IS NULL";
        foreach (DataRowView row in view)
        {
            MenuItem newMenuItem = new MenuItem(row["Name"].ToString(),
            ➥row["CategoryId"].ToString());
            Menu1.Items.Add(newMenuItem);
            AddChildMenuItems(menuData, newMenuItem);
        }

    }


    /// <summary>
    /// Recursively add child menu items by filtering by ParentID
    /// </summary>
    private void AddChildMenuItems(DataTable menuData, MenuItem parentMenuItem)
    {
        DataView view = new DataView(menuData);
        view.RowFilter = "ParentID=" + parentMenuItem.Value;
        foreach (DataRowView row in view)
        {
            MenuItem newMenuItem = new MenuItem(row["Name"].ToString(),
            ➥row["CategoryId"].ToString());
            parentMenuItem.ChildItems.Add(newMenuItem);
            AddChildMenuItems(menuData, newMenuItem);
        }
    }

</script>
<html xmlns="http://www.w3.org/1999/xhtml" >
<head id="Head1" runat="server">
    <style type="text/css">
        .menuItem
        {
            border:Solid 1px black;
            width:100px;
            padding:2px;
            background-color:#eeeeee;
        }
        .menuItem a
```

19

LISTING 19.4   Continued

```
        {
            color:blue;
        }
        .grid
        {
            margin-top:10px;
        }

        .grid td, .grid th
        {
            padding:10px;
        }
    </style>
    <title>Menu Database</title>
</head>
<body>
    <form id="form1" runat="server">
    <div>

    <asp:Menu
        id="Menu1"
        Orientation="horizontal"
        StaticMenuItemStyle-CssClass="menuItem"
        DynamicMenuItemStyle-CssClass="menuItem"
        Runat="server" />

    <asp:GridView
        id="grdProducts"
        DataSourceID="srcProducts"
        CssClass="grid"
        AutoGenerateColumns="false"
        Runat="server">
        <Columns>
        <asp:BoundField
            DataField="ProductName"
            HeaderText="Product" />
        <asp:BoundField
            DataField="Price"
            HeaderText="Price"
            DataFormatString="{0:c}" />
        </Columns>
    </asp:GridView>

    <asp:SqlDataSource
```

```
        id="srcProducts"
        ConnectionString="<%$ ConnectionStrings:Categories %>"
        SelectCommand="SELECT ProductName,Price FROM Products
            WHERE CategoryId=@CategoryId"
        Runat="server">
        <SelectParameters>
        <asp:ControlParameter
            Name="CategoryId"
            ControlID="Menu1" />
        </SelectParameters>
    </asp:SqlDataSource>


    </div>
    </form>
</body>
</html>
```

The menu items are added to the Menu control in the PopulateMenu() method. This method first grabs a DataTable that contains the contents of the Categories database table. Next, it creates a menu item for each row that does not have a parent row (each row where the ParentId column has the value null).

The child menu items for each menu item are added recursively. The ParentId column is used to filter the contents of the Categories DataTable.

The page in Listing 19.14 also includes a GridView control that displays a list of products that match the category selected in the menu. The GridView is bound to a SqlDataSource control, which includes a ControlParameter that filters the products based on the selected menu item.

Formatting the Menu Control

The Menu control supports an abundance of properties that can be used to format the appearance of the control. Many of these properties have an effect on static menu items, and many of these properties have an effect on dynamic menu items. Static menu items are menu items that always appear. Dynamic menu items are menu items that appear only when you hover your mouse over another menu item.

First, the Menu control supports the following general properties related to formatting:

► **DisappearAfter**—Enables you to specify the amount of time, in milliseconds, that a dynamic menu item is displayed after a user moves the mouse away from the menu item.

► **DynamicBottomSeparatorImageUrl**—Enables you to specify the URL to an image that appears under each dynamic menu item.

19

- ▶ **DynamicEnableDefaultPopOutImage**—Enables you to disable the image (triangle) that indicates that a dynamic menu item has child menu items.

- ▶ **DynamicHorizontalOffset**—Enables you to specify the number of pixels that a dynamic menu item is shifted relative to its parent menu item.

- ▶ **DynamicItemFormatString**—Enables you to format the text displayed in a dynamic menu item.

- ▶ **DynamicPopOutImageTextFormatString**—Enables you to format the alt text displayed for the popout image.

- ▶ **DynamicPopOutImageUrl**—Enables you to specify the URL for the dynamic popout image. (By default, a triangle is displayed.)

- ▶ **DynamicTopSeparatorImageUrl**—Enables you to specify the URL to an image that appears above each dynamic menu item.

- ▶ **DynamicVerticalOffset**—Enables you to specify the number of pixels that a dynamic menu item is shifted relative to its parent menu item.

- ▶ **ItemWrap**—Enables you to specify whether the text in menu items should wrap.

- ▶ **MaximumDynamicDisplayLevels**—Enables you to specify the maximum number of levels of dynamic menu items to display.

- ▶ **Orientation**—Enables you to display a menu horizontally or vertically. (The default value is Vertical.)

- ▶ **ScollDownImageUrl**—Enables you to specify the URL to an image that is displayed and that enables you to scroll down through menu items.

- ▶ **ScrollDownText**—Enables you to specify alt text for the ScrollDown image.

- ▶ **ScrollUpImageUrl**—Enables you to specify the URL to an image that is displayed and that enables you to scroll up through menu items.

- ▶ **ScrollUpText**—Enables you to specify alt text for the ScrollUp image.

- ▶ **SkipLinkText**—Enables you to modify the text displayed by the skip link. (The skip link enables blind users to skip past the contents of a menu.)

- ▶ **StaticBottomSeparatorImageUrl**—Enables you to specify the URL to an image that appears below each static menu item.

- ▶ **StaticDisplayLevels**—Enables you to specify the number of static levels of menu items to display.

- ▶ **StaticEnableDefaultPopOutImage**—Enables you to disable the default popout image that indicates that a menu item has child menu items.

- ▶ **StaticItemFormatString**—Enables you to format the text displayed in each static menu item.

- ▶ **StaticImagePopOutFormatString**—Enables you to specify the alt text displayed by the popout image.

- ▶ **StaticPopOutImageUrl**—Enables you to specify the URL for the popout image.

- ▶ **StaticSubMenuIndent**—Enables you to specify the number of pixels that a static menu item is indented relative to its parent menu item.

- ▶ **StaticTopSeparatorImageUrl**—Enables you to specify the URL to an image that appears above each static menu item.

- ▶ **Target**—Enables you to specify the window in which a new page opens when you click a menu item.

This list includes several interesting properties. For example, notice that you can specify images for scrolling up and down through a list of menu items. These images appear when you constrain the height of either the static or dynamic menu.

The Menu control also exposes several Style objects. You can use these Style objects as hooks to which you can attach Cascading Style Sheet classes:

- ▶ **DynamicHoverStyle**—Style applied to a dynamic menu item when you hover your mouse over it.

- ▶ **DynamicMenuItemStyle**—Style applied to each dynamic menu item.

- ▶ **DynamicMenuStyle**—Style applied to the container tag for the dynamic menu.

- ▶ **DynamicSelectedStyle**—Style applied to the selected dynamic menu item.

- ▶ **StaticHoverStyle**—Style applied to a static menu item when you hover your mouse over it.

- ▶ **StaticMenuItemStyle**—Style applied to each static menu item.

- ▶ **StaticMenuStyle**—Style applied to the container tag for the static menu.

- ▶ **StaticSelectedStyle**—Style applied to the selected static menu item.

Furthermore, you can apply styles to menu items based on their level in the menu. For example, you might want the font size to get progressively smaller depending on how deeply nested a menu item is within a menu. You can use three properties of the Menu control to format menu items, depending on their level:

- ▶ **LevelMenuItemStyles**—Contains a collection of MenuItemStyle controls, which correspond to different menu levels.

- ▶ **LevelSelectedStyles**—Contains a collection of MenuItemStyle controls, which correspond to different menu levels of selected menu items.

- ▶ **LevelSubMenuStyles**—Contains a collection of MenuItemStyle controls, which correspond to different menu levels of static menu items.

For example, the page in Listing 19.15 illustrates how you can apply different formatting to menu items that appear at different menu levels (see Figure 19.12).

19

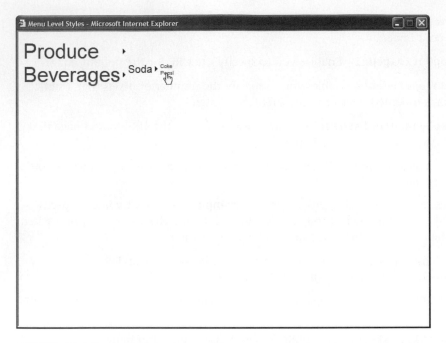

FIGURE 19.12   Applying styles to different menu levels.

LISTING 19.15   MenuLevelStyles.aspx

```
<%@ Page Language="C#" %>
<!DOCTYPE html PUBLIC "-//W3C//DTD XHTML 1.1//EN"
  "http://www.w3.org/TR/xhtml11/DTD/xhtml11.dtd">
<html xmlns="http://www.w3.org/1999/xhtml" >
<head id="Head1" runat="server">
    <style type="text/css">
        .menuLevel1
        {
            font:40px Arial,Sans-Serif;
        }
        .menuLevel2
        {
            font:20px Arial,Sans-Serif;
        }
        .menuLevel3
        {
            font:10px Arial,Sans-Serif;
        }
    </style>
    <title>Menu Level Styles</title>
```

```
    </head>
<body>
    <form id="form1" runat="server">
    <div>

    <asp:Menu
        id="Menu1"
        Runat="server">
        <LevelMenuItemStyles>
            <asp:MenuItemStyle CssClass="menuLevel1" />
            <asp:MenuItemStyle CssClass="menuLevel2" />
            <asp:MenuItemStyle CssClass="menuLevel3" />
        </LevelMenuItemStyles>
        <Items>
        <asp:MenuItem Text="Produce">
            <asp:MenuItem Text="Apples" />
            <asp:MenuItem Text="Oranges" />
        </asp:MenuItem>
        <asp:MenuItem Text="Beverages">
            <asp:MenuItem Text="Soda">
                <asp:MenuItem Text="Coke" />
                <asp:MenuItem Text="Pepsi" />
            </asp:MenuItem>
        </asp:MenuItem>
        </Items>
    </asp:Menu>

    </div>
    </form>
</body>
</html>
```

The MenuItemStyle controls are applied to the menu level that corresponds to their order of declaration. The first MenuItemStyle is applied to the first menu level, the second MenuItemStyle is applied to the second menu level, and so on.

Finally, the MenuItem class itself includes several useful formatting properties:

▶ **ImageUrl**—Enables you to specify the URL for an image that is displayed next to a menu item.

▶ **PopOutImageUrl**—Enables you to specify the URL for an image that is displayed when a menu item contains child menu items.

▶ **SeparatorImageUrl**—Enables you to specify the URL for an image that appears below a menu item.

19

▶ **Selectable**—Enables you to prevent users from selecting (clicking) a menu item.

▶ **Selected**—Enables you to specify whether a menu item is selected.

▶ **Target**—Enables you to specify the name of the window that opens when you click a menu item.

For example, the page in Listing 19.16 displays a menu that resembles a traditional desktop application menu (see Figure 19.13).

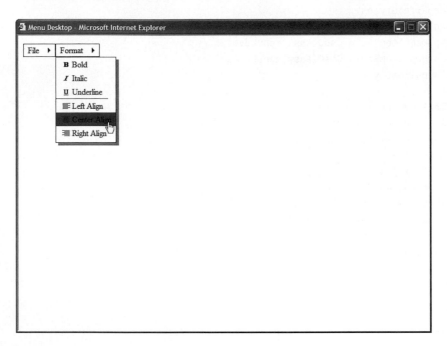

FIGURE 19.13   Displaying a desktop application menu.

LISTING 19.16   MenuDesktop.aspx

```
<%@ Page Language="C#" %>
<!DOCTYPE html PUBLIC "-//W3C//DTD XHTML 1.1//EN"
    "http://www.w3.org/TR/xhtml11/DTD/xhtml11.dtd">
<html xmlns="http://www.w3.org/1999/xhtml" >
<head id="Head1" runat="server">
    <style type="text/css">
        .staticMenuItem
        {
            color:black;
            border:solid 1px black;
            padding:2px 4px;
        }
```

```
        .menuHover
        {
            color:white;
            background-color:blue;
        }
        .dynamicMenuItem
        {
            color:black;
            padding:2px 4px;
        }
        .dynamicMenu
        {
            border:Solid 1px black;
            filter:progid:DXImageTransform.Microsoft.dropshadow(OffX=5, OffY=5,
            ➥Color='gray', Positive='true')"
        }
    </style>
    <title>Menu Desktop</title>
</head>
<body>
    <form id="form1" runat="server">
    <div>

    <asp:Menu
        id="Menu1"
        Orientation="Horizontal"
        StaticMenuItemStyle-CssClass="staticMenuItem"
        StaticHoverStyle-CssClass="menuHover"
        DynamicHoverStyle-CssClass="menuHover"
        DynamicMenuItemStyle-CssClass="dynamicMenuItem"
        DynamicMenuStyle-CssClass="dynamicMenu"
        Runat="server">
        <Items>
        <asp:MenuItem
            Text="File"
            Selectable="false">
            <asp:MenuItem
                Text="Save" />
            <asp:MenuItem
                Text="Open" />
        </asp:MenuItem>
        <asp:MenuItem
            Text="Format"
            Selectable="false">
            <asp:MenuItem
                Text="Bold"
```

19

LISTING 19.16   Continued

```
                    ImageUrl="Images/Bold.gif" />
                <asp:MenuItem
                    Text="Italic"
                    ImageUrl="Images/Italic.gif" />
                <asp:MenuItem
                    Text="Underline"
                    ImageUrl="Images/Underline.gif"
                    SeparatorImageUrl="Images/Divider.gif" />
                <asp:MenuItem
                    Text="Left Align"
                    ImageUrl="Images/JustifyLeft.gif" />
                <asp:MenuItem
                    Text="Center Align"
                    ImageUrl="Images/JustifyCenter.gif" />
                <asp:MenuItem
                    Text="Right Align"
                    ImageUrl="Images/JustifyRight.gif" />
            </asp:MenuItem>
            </Items>
    </asp:Menu>

    </div>
    </form>
</body>
</html>
```

Using Templates with the Menu Control

The Menu control supports templates. You can use templates to completely customize the appearance of the Menu control.

The Menu control supports the following two templates:

▶ **DynamicItemTemplate**—Template applied to dynamic menu items.

▶ **StaticItemTemplate**—Template applied to static menu items.

The page in Listing 19.17 uses both templates to display menu items. The templates display a count of child items for each menu item (see Figure 19.14).

LISTING 19.17   MenuTemplates.aspx

```
<%@ Page Language="C#" %>
<!DOCTYPE html PUBLIC "-//W3C//DTD XHTML 1.1//EN"
"http://www.w3.org/TR/xhtml11/DTD/xhtml11.dtd">
```

```
<script runat="server">

    protected void Menu1_MenuItemClick(object sender, MenuEventArgs e)
    {
        lblMessage.Text = Menu1.SelectedValue;
    }
</script>
<html xmlns="http://www.w3.org/1999/xhtml" >
<head id="Head1" runat="server">
    <style type="text/css">
        .menuItem
        {
            color:black;
            border:Solid 1px Gray;
            background-color:#c9c9c9;
            padding:2px 5px;
        }
    </style>
    <title>Menu Templates</title>
</head>
<body>
    <form id="form1" runat="server">
    <div>

    <asp:Menu
        id="Menu1"
        OnMenuItemClick="Menu1_MenuItemClick"
        Orientation="Horizontal"
        StaticMenuItemStyle-CssClass="menuItem"
        DynamicMenuItemStyle-CssClass="menuItem"
        Runat="server">
        <StaticItemTemplate>
        <%# Eval("Text") %>
        (<%# Eval("ChildItems.Count") %>)
        </StaticItemTemplate>
        <DynamicItemTemplate>
        <%# Eval("Text") %>
        (<%# Eval("ChildItems.Count") %>)
        </DynamicItemTemplate>
        <Items>
        <asp:MenuItem Text="Produce">
            <asp:MenuItem Text="Apples" />
            <asp:MenuItem Text="Oranges" />
        </asp:MenuItem>
        <asp:MenuItem Text="Beverages">
            <asp:MenuItem Text="Soda">
```

LISTING 19.17   Continued

```
                    <asp:MenuItem Text="Coke" />
                    <asp:MenuItem Text="Pepsi" />
                </asp:MenuItem>
            </asp:MenuItem>
            </Items>
        </asp:Menu>

        <hr />

        <asp:Label
            id="lblMessage"
            EnableViewState="false"
            Runat="server" />

        </div>
        </form>
</body>
</html>
```

Notice that you do not need to create LinkButton controls in the templates. The content of the template is wrapped in a link automatically when it is appropriate.

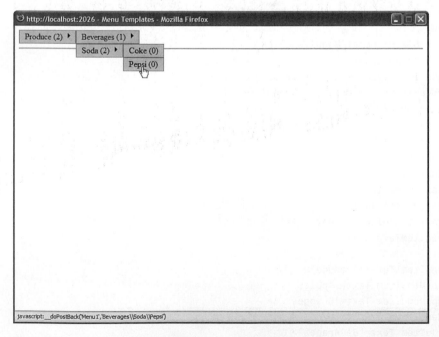

FIGURE 19.14   Using templates with the Menu control.

Using the `TreeView` Control

The `TreeView` control is very similar to the `Menu` control. Like the `Menu` control, you can use the `TreeView` control to display hierarchical data. The `TreeView` control binds to any data source that implements the `IHierarchicalDataSource` or `IHierarchicalEnumerable` interface.

In this section, you learn how to add items declaratively to the `TreeView` control. You also learn how to bind a `TreeView` control to hierarchical data sources such as the `SiteMapDataSource` and `XmlDataSource` controls.

You also see how you can use the `TreeView` control with database data. A `TreeView` is built programmatically from database data.

Finally, you learn how you can use AJAX with the `TreeView` control to display large sets of data efficiently. By taking advantage of AJAX, you can update a `TreeView` without posting a page back to the server.

Declaratively Adding Tree Nodes

A `TreeView` control is made up of `TreeNode` objects. You can build a `TreeView` control by declaring `TreeNode` objects in the `TreeView` control's Items collection.

For example, Listing 19.18 contains a `TreeView` which renders a nested set of links to pages (see Figure 19.15).

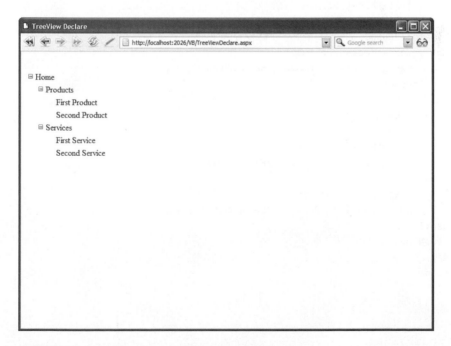

FIGURE 19.15   Displaying a `TreeView` control.

19

LISTING 19.18   TreeViewDeclare.aspx

```
<%@ Page Language="C#" %>
<!DOCTYPE html PUBLIC "-//W3C//DTD XHTML 1.1//EN"
    "http://www.w3.org/TR/xhtml11/DTD/xhtml11.dtd">
<html xmlns="http://www.w3.org/1999/xhtml" >
<head id="Head1" runat="server">
    <title>TreeView Declare</title>
</head>
<body>
    <form id="form1" runat="server">
    <div>

    <asp:TreeView
        id="TreeView1"
        Runat="server">
        <Nodes>
        <asp:TreeNode
            Text="Home"
            NavigateUrl="~/Default.aspx">
            <asp:TreeNode
                Text="Products">
                <asp:TreeNode
                    Text="First Product"
                    NavigateUrl="~/Products/FirstProduct.aspx" />
                <asp:TreeNode
                    Text="Second Product"
                    NavigateUrl="~/Products/SecondProduct.aspx" />
            </asp:TreeNode>
            <asp:TreeNode
                Text="Services">
                <asp:TreeNode
                    Text="First Service"
                    NavigateUrl="~/Services/FirstService.aspx" />
                <asp:TreeNode
                    Text="Second Service"
                    NavigateUrl="~/Services/SecondService.aspx" />
            </asp:TreeNode>
        </asp:TreeNode>
        </Nodes>
    </asp:TreeView>


    </div>
    </form>
</body>
</html>
```

Some of the `TreeNodes` in Listing 19.18 include a `Text` property, and some of the `TreeNodes` include both a `Text` and `NavigateUrl` property. You can click the `TreeNodes` that include a `NavigateUrl` property to link to a new page.

You also can associate a `Value` property with a `TreeNode`. This is useful when you want to post back to the same page. For example, the page in Listing 19.19 enables you to display the value of the selected `TreeNode` in a Label control (see Figure 19.16).

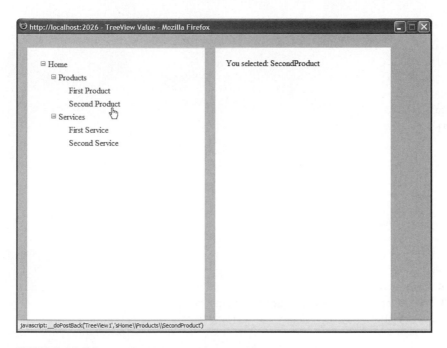

FIGURE 19.16   Selecting a `TreeView` node.

LISTING 19.19   `TreeViewValue.aspx`

```
<%@ Page Language="C#" %>
<!DOCTYPE html PUBLIC "-//W3C//DTD XHTML 1.1//EN"
"http://www.w3.org/TR/xhtml11/DTD/xhtml11.dtd">

<script runat="server">

    protected void TreeView1_SelectedNodeChanged(object sender, EventArgs e)
    {
        lblMessage.Text = TreeView1.SelectedValue;
    }
</script>
<html xmlns="http://www.w3.org/1999/xhtml" >
```

LISTING 19.19   Continued

```
<head id="Head1" runat="server">
    <style type="text/css">
        html
        {
            background-color:silver;
        }
        .content
        {
            float:left;
            width:350px;
            height:500px;
            padding:20px;
            margin:10px;
            background-color:white;
        }
    </style>
    <title>TreeView Value</title>
</head>
<body>
    <form id="form1" runat="server">

    <div class="content">
    <asp:TreeView
        id="TreeView1"
        OnSelectedNodeChanged="TreeView1_SelectedNodeChanged"
        Runat="server" >
        <Nodes>
        <asp:TreeNode
            Text="Home"
            Value="Home">
            <asp:TreeNode
                Text="Products">
                <asp:TreeNode
                    Text="First Product"
                    Value="FirstProduct" />
                <asp:TreeNode
                    Text="Second Product"
                    Value="SecondProduct" />
            </asp:TreeNode>
            <asp:TreeNode
                Text="Services">
                <asp:TreeNode
```

```
                    Text="First Service"
                    Value="FirstService" />
                <asp:TreeNode
                    Text="Second Service"
                    Value="SecondService" />
            </asp:TreeNode>
        </asp:TreeNode>
        </Nodes>
    </asp:TreeView>
    </div>

    <div class="content">
    You selected:
    <asp:Label
        id="lblMessage"
        EnableViewState="false"
        Runat="server" />
    </div>

    </form>
</body>
</html>
```

Notice that the page in Listing 19.19 includes a SelectedNodeChanged event handler. When you select a new node, the SelectedNodeChanged event handler displays the value of the selected TreeNode in a Label control.

Displaying Check Boxes with the TreeView Control

You can display check boxes next to each node in a TreeView control by assigning a value to the ShowCheckBoxes property. This property accepts the following values:

- ▶ All

- ▶ Leaf

- ▶ None

- ▶ Parent

- ▶ Root

You can use a bitwise combination of these values when specifying the nodes to display with check boxes.

The page in Listing 19.20 illustrates the ShowCheckBoxes property (see Figure 19.17).

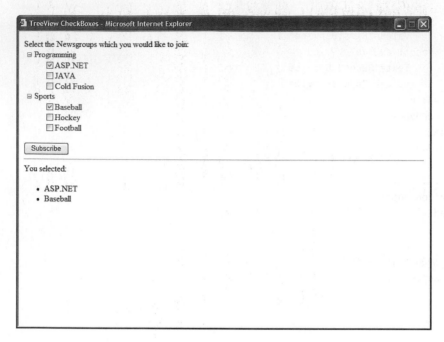

FIGURE 19.17   Displaying TreeView check boxes.

LISTING 19.20   TreeViewCheckBoxes.aspx

```
<%@ Page Language="C#" %>
<!DOCTYPE html PUBLIC "-//W3C//DTD XHTML 1.1//EN"
"http://www.w3.org/TR/xhtml11/DTD/xhtml11.dtd">
<script runat="server">

    protected void btnSubscribe_Click(object sender, EventArgs e)
    {
        foreach (TreeNode node in TreeView1.CheckedNodes)
            bltSubscribed.Items.Add(node.Text);
    }
</script>
<html xmlns="http://www.w3.org/1999/xhtml" >
<head id="Head1" runat="server">
    <title>TreeView CheckBoxes</title>
</head>
<body>
    <form id="form1" runat="server">
    <div>

    Select the Newsgroups which you
```

would like to join:

```
<br />

<asp:TreeView
    id="TreeView1"
    ShowCheckBoxes="Leaf"
    Runat="server">
    <Nodes>
    <asp:TreeNode
        Text="Programming">
        <asp:TreeNode Text="ASP.NET" />
        <asp:TreeNode Text="JAVA" />
        <asp:TreeNode Text="Cold Fusion" />
    </asp:TreeNode>
    <asp:TreeNode
        Text="Sports">
        <asp:TreeNode Text="Baseball" />
        <asp:TreeNode Text="Hockey" />
        <asp:TreeNode Text="Football" />
    </asp:TreeNode>
    </Nodes>
</asp:TreeView>

<br />

<asp:Button
    id="btnSubscribe"
    Text="Subscribe"
    OnClick="btnSubscribe_Click"
    Runat="server" />

<hr />

You selected:

<asp:BulletedList
    id="bltSubscribed"
    EnableViewState="false"
    Runat="server" />

</div>
</form>
</body>
</html>
```

19

The page in Listing 19.20 displays nested newsgroups. You can subscribe to the newsgroups by clicking the Subscribe button.

When you click the Subscribe button, the CheckedNodes property is used to return a list of all of the checked TreeNodes. This list is displayed in a BulletedList control.

Binding to a Site Map

You can use a TreeView control as a navigation element in your pages by binding the TreeView to a Site Map. The page in Listing 19.21 demonstrates how you can bind a TreeView to a SiteMapDataSource control (see Figure 19.18).

FIGURE 19.18   Displaying a Site Map with a TreeView control.

LISTING 19.21   UsingTreeView/TreeViewSiteMap.aspx

```
<%@ Page Language="C#" %>
<!DOCTYPE html PUBLIC "-//W3C//DTD XHTML 1.1//EN"
 "http://www.w3.org/TR/xhtml11/DTD/xhtml11.dtd">
<html xmlns="http://www.w3.org/1999/xhtml" >
<head id="Head1" runat="server">
    <title>TreeView Site Map</title>
</head>
<body>
    <form id="form1" runat="server">
```

```
        <div>

        <asp:TreeView
            id="TreeView1"
            DataSourceID="srcSiteMap"
            Runat="server" />

        <asp:SiteMapDataSource
            id="srcSiteMap"
            Runat="server" />

        </div>
        </form>
</body>
</html>
```

When you open the page in Listing 19.21, all the nodes from the Site Map are displayed automatically in the TreeView control. By default, the SiteMapDataSource uses the XmlSiteMapProvider, which represents a file named Web.sitemap located at the root of an application.

> **NOTE**
>
> You can add a TreeView and SiteMapDataSource control to a Master Page to show the TreeView in multiple pages. To learn more about Master Pages, see Chapter 5.

Binding to an XML File

Because an XmlDataSource control returns hierarchical data, you can bind a TreeView directly to an XmlDataSource. For example, imagine that you need to display the XML document contained in Listing 19.22.

LISTING 19.22 Movies.xml

```
<movies>
  <action>
    <StarWars />
    <IndependenceDay />
  </action>
  <horror>
    <Jaws />
    <NightmareBeforeChristmas />
  </horror>
</movies>
```

The page in Listing 19.23 illustrates how you can display the contents of this XML document with a `TreeView` control.

LISTING 19.23   TreeViewXml.aspx

```
<%@ Page Language="C#" %>
<!DOCTYPE html PUBLIC "-//W3C//DTD XHTML 1.1//EN"
 "http://www.w3.org/TR/xhtml11/DTD/xhtml11.dtd">
<html xmlns="http://www.w3.org/1999/xhtml" >
<head id="Head1" runat="server">
    <title>TreeView XML</title>
</head>
<body>
    <form id="form1" runat="server">
    <div>

    <asp:TreeView
        id="TreeView1"
        DataSourceID="srcMovies"
        Runat="server" />

     <asp:XmlDataSource
        id="srcMovies"
        DataFile="~/Movies.xml"
        Runat="server" />

    </div>
    </form>
</body>
</html>
```

The `Movies.xml` document in Listing 19.22 is extremely simple. The elements do not include any attributes. You can display more complicated XML documents with the `TreeView` control by declaring one or more `TreeNodeBinding` elements.

For example, the nodes in the XML document in Listing 19.24 include `id` and `text` attributes.

LISTING 19.24   MoviesComplex.xml

```
<movies>
  <category id="category1" text="Action">
    <movie id="movie1" text="Star Wars" />
    <movie id="movie2" text="Independence Day" />
  </category>
  <category id="category2" text="Horror">
```

```
    <movie id="movie3" text="Jaws" />
    <movie id="movie4" text="Nightmare Before Christmas" />
  </category>
</movies>
```

The page in Listing 19.25 displays the contents of the XML document in Listing 19.24.

LISTING 19.25   TreeViewXMLComplex.aspx

```
<%@ Page Language="C#" %>
<!DOCTYPE html PUBLIC "-//W3C//DTD XHTML 1.1//EN"
  "http://www.w3.org/TR/xhtml11/DTD/xhtml11.dtd">
<html xmlns="http://www.w3.org/1999/xhtml" >
<head id="Head1" runat="server">
    <title>TreeView XML Complex</title>
</head>
<body>
    <form id="form1" runat="server">
    <div>

    <asp:TreeView
        id="TreeView1"
        DataSourceID="srcMovies"
        Runat="server">
        <DataBindings>
        <asp:TreeNodeBinding
            DataMember="category"
            TextField="text"
            ValueField="id" />
        <asp:TreeNodeBinding
            DataMember="movie"
            TextField="text"
            ValueField="id" />
        </DataBindings>
    </asp:TreeView>

    <asp:XmlDataSource
        id="srcMovies"
        DataFile="~/MoviesComplex.xml"
        Runat="server" />

    </div>
    </form>
</body>
</html>
```

19

The TreeView in Listing 19.25 includes a DataBindings subtag. This tag includes two TreeNodeBinding elements. The first TreeNodeBinding specifies the relationship between <category> nodes in the XML document and TreeView nodes. The second TreeNodeBinding specifies the relationship between <movie> nodes and TreeView nodes.

Binding to Database Data

You cannot bind a TreeView control directly to a SqlDataSource or ObjectDataSource control because neither of these two controls expose hierarchical data. If you want to display database data with the TreeView control then you have a choice: create a custom SqlHierarchicalDataSource control or programmatically bind the TreeView to the database data.

The hard option is to build a SQL hierarchical DataSource control. You can do this by deriving a new control from the base HierarchicalDataSourceControl class or by implementing the IHierarchicalDataSource interface. We explore this option in the final section of this chapter.

The second option is to build the TreeView control programmatically from a set of database records. This is the approach that we will follow in this section.

Imagine that you have a database table that looks like this:

MessageId	ParentId	Subject
1	null	How do you use the Menu control?
2	null	What is the TreeView control?
3	1	RE:How do you use the Menu control?
4	1	RE:How do you use the Menu control?
5	2	RE:What is the TreeView control?
6	5	RE:RE:What is the TreeView control?

This database table represents a discussion forum. The relationship between the messages is determined by the ParentId column. The messages that have a null ParentID represent the threads, and the other messages represent replies to the threads.

The page in Listing 19.26 uses a TreeView control to display the contents of the Discuss database table (see Figure 19.19).

LISTING 19.26   TreeViewDatabase.aspx

```
<%@ Page Language="C#" %>
<%@ Import Namespace="System.Web.Configuration" %>
<%@ Import Namespace="System.Data" %>
<%@ Import Namespace="System.Data.SqlClient" %>
<!DOCTYPE html PUBLIC "-//W3C//DTD XHTML 1.1//EN"
"http://www.w3.org/TR/xhtml11/DTD/xhtml11.dtd">
```

```
<script runat="server">

    /// <summary>
    /// Only populate the TreeView when the page first loads
    /// </summary>
    void Page_Load()
    {
        if (!Page.IsPostBack)
            PopulateTreeView();
    }


    /// <summary>
    /// Get the data from the database and create the top-level
    /// TreeView items
    /// </summary>
    private void PopulateTreeView()
    {
        DataTable treeViewData = GetTreeViewData();
        AddTopTreeViewNodes(treeViewData);
    }


    /// <summary>
    /// Use a DataAdapter and DataTable to grab the database data
    /// </summary>
    /// <returns></returns>
    private DataTable GetTreeViewData()
    {
        // Get Discuss table
        string selectCommand = "SELECT MessageId,ParentId,Subject FROM Discuss";
        string conString = WebConfigurationManager.ConnectionStrings["Discuss"].
        ➥ConnectionString;
        SqlDataAdapter dad = new SqlDataAdapter(selectCommand, conString);
        DataTable dtblDiscuss = new DataTable();
        dad.Fill(dtblDiscuss);
        return dtblDiscuss;
    }


    /// <summary>
    /// Filter the data to get only the rows that have a
    /// null ParentID (these are the top-level TreeView items)
    /// </summary>
    private void AddTopTreeViewNodes(DataTable treeViewData)
    {
        DataView view = new DataView(treeViewData);
        view.RowFilter = "ParentID IS NULL";
        foreach (DataRowView row in view)
```

LISTING 19.26   Continued

```
        {
            TreeNode newNode = new TreeNode(row["Subject"].ToString(),
            ➥row["MessageId"].ToString());
            TreeView1.Nodes.Add(newNode);
            AddChildTreeViewNodes(treeViewData, newNode);
        }

    }

    /// <summary>
    /// Recursively add child TreeView items by filtering by ParentID
    /// </summary>
    private void AddChildTreeViewNodes(DataTable treeViewData, TreeNode
    ➥parentTreeViewNode)
    {
        DataView view = new DataView(treeViewData);
        view.RowFilter = "ParentID=" + parentTreeViewNode.Value;
        foreach (DataRowView row in view)
        {
            TreeNode newNode = new TreeNode(row["Subject"].ToString(),
            ➥row["MessageId"].ToString());
            parentTreeViewNode.ChildNodes.Add(newNode);
            AddChildTreeViewNodes(treeViewData, newNode);
        }
    }

</script>
<html xmlns="http://www.w3.org/1999/xhtml" >
<head id="Head1" runat="server">
    <style type="text/css">
    </style>
    <title>TreeView Database</title>
</head>
<body>
    <form id="form1" runat="server">
    <div>

    <asp:TreeView
        id="TreeView1"
        Runat="server" />

    </div>
    </form>
</body>
</html>
```

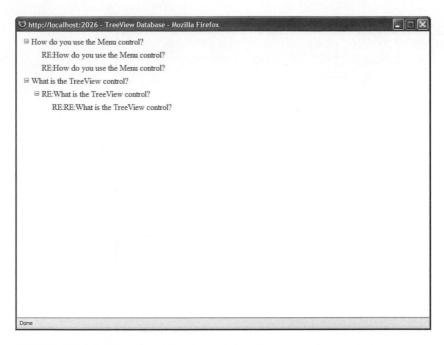

FIGURE 19.19   Displaying database data with a `TreeView` control.

The page in Listing 19.26 filters the contents of the Discuss database table by its ParentID column. First, the top-level nodes are added to the `TreeView`. Next, the child nodes are recursively added to the `TreeView` with the help of the `AddChildTreeViewNodes()` method.

Using Populate On Demand and AJAX

You can use the `TreeView` control even when working with a large set of data. For example, the Microsoft MSDN website (msdn.Microsoft.com) has links to thousands of articles. This website uses a tree view to display the nested links to the articles.

Because thousands of articles are hosted at the MSDN website, not all the tree nodes are downloaded to the browser when you open a page. Instead, additional nodes are downloaded to your browser only when you expand a particular node.

You can use a feature named Populate On Demand with the `TreeView` control. When you enable the `PopulateOnDemand` property for a Tree node, child nodes are not added to the parent node until the parent node is expanded.

For example, the page in Listing 19.27 contains an infinitely expanding `TreeView`. Each time you expand a Tree node, five new child nodes are displayed. Each time you expand a child node, five more child nodes are displayed, and so on (see Figure 19.20).

19

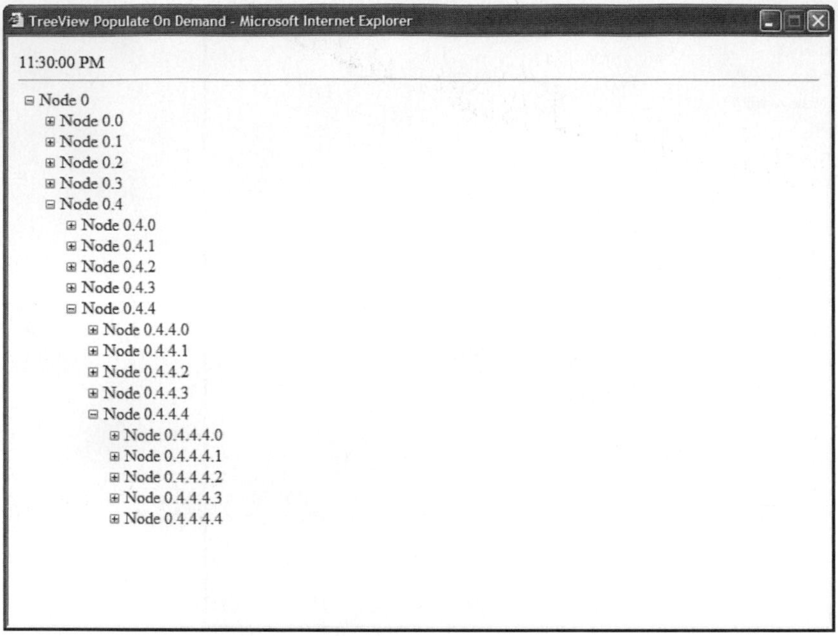

FIGURE 19.20   An infinitely expanding `TreeView` control.

LISTING 19.27   TreeViewPopulateOnDemand.aspx

```
<%@ Page Language="C#" %>
<!DOCTYPE html PUBLIC "-//W3C//DTD XHTML 1.1//EN"
"http://www.w3.org/TR/xhtml11/DTD/xhtml11.dtd">
<script runat="server">

        void TreeView1_TreeNodePopulate(object s, TreeNodeEventArgs e)
        {
            for (int i=0;i<5;i++)
            {
                TreeNode newNode = new TreeNode();
                newNode.Text = String.Format("{0}.{1}", e.Node.Text, i);
                newNode.PopulateOnDemand = true;
                e.Node.ChildNodes.Add(newNode);
            }
        }

</script>
<html xmlns="http://www.w3.org/1999/xhtml" >
<head id="Head1" runat="server">
    <title>TreeView Populate On Demand</title>
</head>
```

```
<body>
    <form id="form1" runat="server">
    <div>

    <%=DateTime.Now.ToString("T") %>

    <hr />

    <asp:TreeView
        ID="TreeView1"
        ExpandDepth="0"
        OnTreeNodePopulate="TreeView1_TreeNodePopulate"
        Runat="server">
        <Nodes>
        <asp:TreeNode
            PopulateOnDemand="true"
            Text="Node 0" />
        </Nodes>
    </asp:TreeView>

    </div>
    </form>
</body>
</html>
```

The `TreeView` in Listing 19.27 includes a single statically declared `TreeNode`. Notice that this `TreeNode` includes a `PopulateOnDemand` property that is set to the value `True`.

Additionally, the `TreeView` control itself includes a `TreeNodePopulate` event handler. When you expand a `TreeNode` that has its `PopulateOnDemand` property enabled, the `TreeNodePopulate` event handler executes. In the case of Listing 19.27, the event handler adds five new `TreeNodes` to the `TreeNode` that was expanded.

When you use the Populate On Demand feature with a modern browser (Internet Explorer 6, Firefox 1, Opera 8), the page containing the `TreeView` is not posted back to the server when you expand a `TreeNode`. Instead, the browser uses AJAX (Asynchronous JavaScript and XML) to communicate with the web server. The additional `TreeNodes` are retrieved from the server, without performing a postback.

The page in Listing 19.27 displays the current time when you open the page. Notice that the time is not updated when you expand a particular `TreeNode`. The time is not updated because the only content in the page that is updated when you expand a node is the `TreeView` content. AJAX can have a dramatic impact on performance because it does not require the entire page to be re-rendered each time you expand a `TreeNode`.

19

> **NOTE**
>
> If, for some reason, you don't want to use AJAX with Populate On Demand, you can assign the value `False` to the `TreeView` control's `PopulateNodesFromClient` property.

The page in Listing 19.28 contains a more realistic sample of using Populate On Demand and AJAX. This page uses a `TreeView` control to display the contents of the Discuss database table (see Figure 19.21).

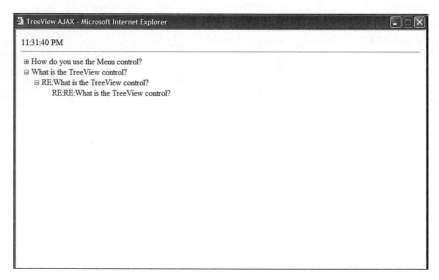

FIGURE 19.21   Displaying database data with AJAX.

LISTING 19.28   TreeViewAJAX.aspx

```csharp
<%@ Page Language="C#" %>
<%@ Import Namespace="System.Web.Configuration" %>
<%@ Import Namespace="System.Data" %>
<%@ Import Namespace="System.Data.SqlClient" %>
<!DOCTYPE html PUBLIC "-//W3C//DTD XHTML 1.1//EN"
"http://www.w3.org/TR/xhtml11/DTD/xhtml11.dtd">
<script runat="server">

    /// <summary>
    /// Only populate the TreeView when the page first loads
    /// </summary>
    void Page_Load()
    {
        if (!Page.IsPostBack)
            PopulateTopNodes();
    }
```

```csharp
/// <summary>
/// Get the top level nodes (nodes with a null ParentId)
/// </summary>
private void PopulateTopNodes()
{
    string selectCommand = "SELECT MessageId,ParentId,Subject FROM Discuss
    ➥WHERE ParentId IS NULL";
    string conString = WebConfigurationManager.ConnectionStrings["Discuss"].
    ➥ConnectionString;
    SqlDataAdapter dad = new SqlDataAdapter(selectCommand, conString);
    DataTable dtblMessages = new DataTable();
    dad.Fill(dtblMessages);

    foreach (DataRow row in dtblMessages.Rows)
    {
        TreeNode newNode = new TreeNode(row["Subject"].ToString(),
        ➥row["MessageId"].ToString());
        newNode.PopulateOnDemand = true;
        TreeView1.Nodes.Add(newNode);
    }
}


/// <summary>
/// Get the child nodes of the expanded node
/// </summary>
protected void TreeView1_TreeNodePopulate(object sender, TreeNodeEventArgs e)
{
    string selectCommand = "SELECT MessageId,ParentId,Subject FROM Discuss
    ➥WHERE ParentId=@ParentId";
    string conString = WebConfigurationManager.ConnectionStrings["Discuss"].
    ➥ConnectionString;
    SqlDataAdapter dad = new SqlDataAdapter(selectCommand, conString);
    dad.SelectCommand.Parameters.AddWithValue("@ParentId", e.Node.Value);
    DataTable dtblMessages = new DataTable();
    dad.Fill(dtblMessages);

    foreach (DataRow row in dtblMessages.Rows)
    {
        TreeNode newNode = new TreeNode(row["Subject"].ToString(),
        ➥row["MessageId"].ToString());
        newNode.PopulateOnDemand = true;
        e.Node.ChildNodes.Add(newNode);
```

19

LISTING 19.28   Continued

```
            }
        }

</script>
<html xmlns="http://www.w3.org/1999/xhtml" >
<head id="Head1" runat="server">
    <style type="text/css">
    </style>
    <title>TreeView AJAX</title>
</head>
<body>
    <form id="form1" runat="server">
    <div>

    <%= DateTime.Now.ToString("T") %>

    <hr />

    <asp:TreeView
        id="TreeView1"
        ExpandDepth="0"
        OnTreeNodePopulate="TreeView1_TreeNodePopulate"
        Runat="server" />

    </div>
    </form>
</body>
</html>
```

When the page in Listing 19.28 first opens, only the first-level message subjects are displayed. These messages are retrieved by the PopulateTopNodes() method.

When you expand a thread, the matching replies are retrieved for the thread. These replies are retrieved in the TreeView1_TreeNodePopulate() event handler.

The TreeView in Listing 19.28 performs well even when working with a large set of data. At any time, only the child messages of a message are retrieved from the database. At no time are all the messages retrieved from the database.

When the page is used with a modern browser, AJAX is used to retrieve the messages from the web server. The page does not need to be posted back to the web server when you expand a particular message thread.

Formatting the `TreeView` Control

The `TreeView` control supports an abundance of properties that have an effect on how the `TreeView` is formatted.

Here are some of the more useful properties of a `TreeView` control, which modify its appearance (this is not a complete list):

- ▶ **`CollapseImageToolTip`**—Enables you to specify the title attribute for the collapse image.

- ▶ **`CollapseImageUrl`**—Enables you to specify a URL to an image for the collapse image.

- ▶ **`ExpandDepth`**—Enables you to specify the number of `TreeNode` levels to display initially.

- ▶ **`ExpandImageToolTip`**—Enables you to specify the title attribute for the expand image.

- ▶ **`ExpandImageUrl`**—Enables you to specify the URL to an image for the expand image.

- ▶ **`ImageSet`**—Enables you to specify a set of images to use with the `TreeView` control.

- ▶ **`LineImagesFolder`**—Enables you to specify a folder that contains line images.

- ▶ **`MaxDataBindDepth`**—Enables you to specify the maximum levels of `TreeView` levels to display when binding to a data source.

- ▶ **`NodeIndent`**—Enables you to specify the number of pixels to indent a child Tree node.

- ▶ **`NodeWrap`**—Enables you to specify whether text is wrapped in a Tree node.

- ▶ **`NoExpandImageUrl`**—Enables you to specify the URL to an image for the `NoExpand` image (typically, an invisible spacer image).

- ▶ **`ShowCheckBoxes`**—Enables you to display check boxes next to each Tree node. Possible values are `All`, `Leaf`, `None`, `Parent`, and `Root`.

- ▶ **`ShowExpandCollapse`**—Enables you to disable the expand and collapse icons that appear next to each expandable node.

- ▶ **`ShowLines`**—Enables you to show connecting lines between Tree nodes.

- ▶ **`SkipLinkText`**—Enables you to specify the text used for skipping the contents of the `TreeView` control. (The Skip Link contains hidden text that is accessible only to users of assistive devices.)

- ▶ **`Target`**—Enables you to specify the name of the window that opens when you navigate to a URL with the `TreeView` control.

19

The two most interesting properties in this list are the ImageSet and the ShowLines properties. You can set the ImageSet property to any of the following values to modify the images displayed by the TreeView control:

▶ Arrows

▶ BulletedList

▶ BulletedList2

▶ BulletedList3

▶ BulletedList4

▶ Contacts

▶ Custom

▶ Events

▶ Faq

▶ Inbox

▶ Msdn

▶ News

▶ Simple

▶ Simple2

▶ WindowsHelp

▶ XPFileExplorer

The ShowLines property causes connecting line images to be rendered between TreeView nodes. Displaying lines between Tree nodes can make it easier to visually discern the nested relationships between nodes. If you want to create custom lines, you can specify a value for the LinesImagesFolder property.

VISUAL WEB DEVELOPER NOTE

Visual Web Developer includes a TreeView Line Image Generator that enables you to create custom connecting lines. You can open this tool in Design view by selecting the TreeView control and opening the Tasks dialog box and selecting Customize Line Images.

The page in Listing 19.29 illustrates how to use both the ImageSet and ShowLines properties (see Figure 19.22).

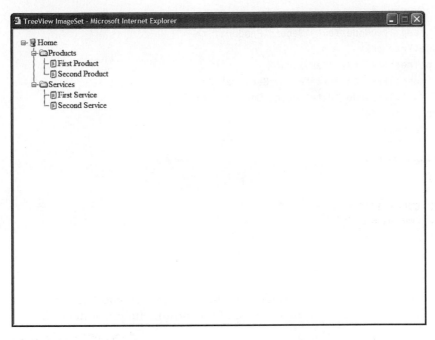

FIGURE 19.22   Formatting a TreeView with an image set and lines.

LISTING 19.29   TreeViewImageSet.aspx

```
<%@ Page Language="C#" %>
<!DOCTYPE html PUBLIC "-//W3C//DTD XHTML 1.1//EN"
   "http://www.w3.org/TR/xhtml11/DTD/xhtml11.dtd">
<html xmlns="http://www.w3.org/1999/xhtml" >
<head id="Head1" runat="server">
    <title>TreeView ImageSet</title>
</head>
<body>
    <form id="form1" runat="server">
    <div>

    <asp:TreeView
        id="TreeView1"
        ImageSet="XPFileExplorer"
        ShowLines="true"
        Runat="server">
        <Nodes>
        <asp:TreeNode
            Text="Home">
            <asp:TreeNode Text="Products">
                <asp:TreeNode Text="First Product" />
```

LISTING 19.29   Continued

```
                    <asp:TreeNode Text="Second Product" />
                </asp:TreeNode>
                <asp:TreeNode Text="Services">
                    <asp:TreeNode Text="First Service" />
                    <asp:TreeNode Text="Second Service" />
                </asp:TreeNode>
            </asp:TreeNode>
            </Nodes>
        </asp:TreeView>



        </div>
        </form>
</body>
</html>
```

The TreeNode object itself also supports several properties that have an effect on the appearance of its containing TreeView. Here is a list of the most useful properties of the TreeNode object:

▶ **Checked**—Enables you to check the check box that appears next to the Tree node.

▶ **Expanded**—Enables you to initially expand a node.

▶ **ImageToolTip**—Enables you to associate alt text with a Tree node image.

▶ **ImageUrl**—Enables you to specify an image that appears next to a Tree node.

▶ **NavigateUrl**—Enables you to specify the URL to which the current Tree node links.

▶ **SelectAction**—Enables you to specify the action that occurs when you click a Tree node. Possible values are Expand, None, Select, or SelectExpand.

▶ **Selected**—Enables you to specify whether the current Tree node is selected.

▶ **ShowCheckBox**—Enables you to display a check box for the current Tree node.

▶ **Target**—Enables you to specify the name of the window that opens when you navigate to a URL.

▶ **ToolTip**—Enables you to specify a title attribute for the current Tree node.

You can style the TreeView control by attaching Cascading Style Sheet classes to the Style object exposed by the TreeView control. The TreeView control supports the following Style objects:

▶ **HoverNodeStyle**—Style applied to a Tree node when you hover your mouse over a node.

▶ **LeafNodeStyle**—Style applied to leaf Tree nodes (tree nodes without child nodes).

▶ **NodeStyle**—Style applied to Tree nodes by default.

▶ **ParentNodeStyle**—Style applied to parent nodes (tree nodes with child nodes).

▶ **RootNodeStyle**—Style applied to root nodes (tree nodes with no parent nodes).

▶ **SelectedNodeStyle**—Style applied to the selected node.

For example, the page in Listing 19.30 uses several of these Style objects to format a `TreeView` control (see Figure 19.23).

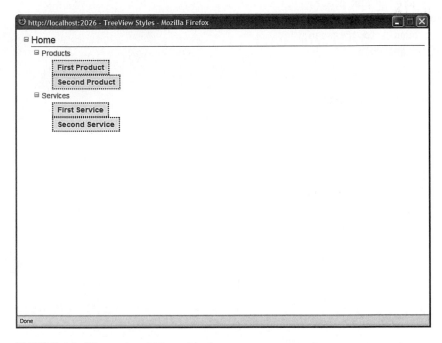

FIGURE 19.23   Using Styles with the `TreeView` control.

LISTING 19.30   `TreeViewStyles.aspx`

```
<%@ Page Language="C#" %>
<!DOCTYPE html PUBLIC "-//W3C//DTD XHTML 1.1//EN"
 "http://www.w3.org/TR/xhtml11/DTD/xhtml11.dtd">
<html xmlns="http://www.w3.org/1999/xhtml" >
<head id="Head1" runat="server">
    <style type="text/css">
        .treeNode
        {
            color:blue;
            font:14px Arial, Sans-Serif;
        }
        .rootNode
```

19

LISTING 19.30   Continued

```
        {
            font-size:18px;
            width:100%;
            border-bottom:Solid 1px black;
        }
        .leafNode
        {
            border:Dotted 2px black;
            padding:4px;
            background-color:#eeeeee;
            font-weight:bold;
        }
    </style>
    <title>TreeView Styles</title>
</head>
<body>
    <form id="form1" runat="server">
    <div>

    <asp:TreeView
        id="TreeView1"
        NodeStyle-CssClass="treeNode"
        RootNodeStyle-CssClass="rootNode"
        LeafNodeStyle-CssClass="leafNode"
        Runat="server">
        <Nodes>
        <asp:TreeNode
            Text="Home">
            <asp:TreeNode Text="Products">
                <asp:TreeNode Text="First Product" />
                <asp:TreeNode Text="Second Product" />
            </asp:TreeNode>
            <asp:TreeNode Text="Services">
                <asp:TreeNode Text="First Service" />
                <asp:TreeNode Text="Second Service" />
            </asp:TreeNode>
        </asp:TreeNode>
        </Nodes>
    </asp:TreeView>

    </div>
    </form>
</body>
</html>
```

Furthermore, you can apply styles to particular Tree node levels by taking advantage of the TreeView control's LevelStyles property. The page in Listing 19.31 uses the LevelStyles property to format first level nodes differently than second level nodes and third level nodes (see Figure 19.24).

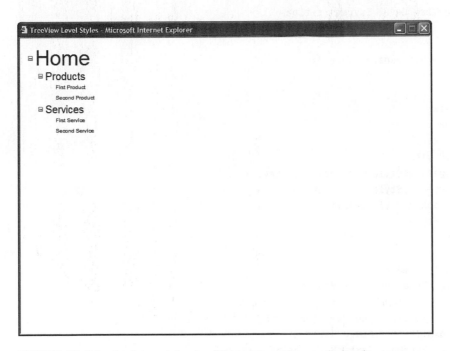

FIGURE 19.24   Applying styles to different TreeView node levels.

LISTING 19.31   TreeViewLevelStyles.aspx

```
<%@ Page Language="C#" %>
<!DOCTYPE html PUBLIC "-//W3C//DTD XHTML 1.1//EN"
  "http://www.w3.org/TR/xhtml11/DTD/xhtml11.dtd">
<html xmlns="http://www.w3.org/1999/xhtml" >
<head id="Head1" runat="server">
    <style type="text/css">
        .nodeLevel1
        {
            font:40px Arial,Sans-Serif;
        }
        .nodeLevel2
        {
            font:20px Arial,Sans-Serif;
        }
        .nodeLevel3
        {
```

LISTING 19.31 Continued

```
            font:10px Arial,Sans-Serif;
        }
    </style>
    <title>TreeView Level Styles</title>
</head>
<body>
    <form id="form1" runat="server">
    <div>

    <asp:TreeView
        id="TreeView1"
        Runat="server">
        <LevelStyles>
        <asp:TreeNodeStyle CssClass="nodeLevel1" />
        <asp:TreeNodeStyle CssClass="nodeLevel2" />
        <asp:TreeNodeStyle CssClass="nodeLevel3" />
        </LevelStyles>
        <Nodes>
        <asp:TreeNode
            Text="Home">
            <asp:TreeNode Text="Products">
                <asp:TreeNode Text="First Product" />
                <asp:TreeNode Text="Second Product" />
            </asp:TreeNode>
            <asp:TreeNode Text="Services">
                <asp:TreeNode Text="First Service" />
                <asp:TreeNode Text="Second Service" />
            </asp:TreeNode>
        </asp:TreeNode>
        </Nodes>
    </asp:TreeView>

    </div>
    </form>
</body>
</html>
```

Building a SQL Hierarchical Data Source Control

In this final section of this chapter, we build a `SqlHierarchicalDataSource` control. This custom control enables you to declaratively and (thus) easily bind controls such as the `Menu` and `TreeView` controls to data retrieved from a database.

NOTE

The code samples in this section can be found in the `SqlHierarchicalDataSourceVB` and `SqlHierarchicalDataSourceCS` applications on the CD.

The page in Listing 19.32 illustrates how you can use the `SqlHierarchicalDataSource` control to bind a `Menu` control to a database table that contains nested categories.

LISTING 19.32   ShowMenu.aspx

```
<%@ Page Language="C#" %>
<%@ Register TagPrefix="custom" Namespace="AspNetUnleashed" %>
<!DOCTYPE html PUBLIC "-//W3C//DTD XHTML 1.1//EN"
"http://www.w3.org/TR/xhtml11/DTD/xhtml11.dtd">
<script runat="server">

    protected void Menu1_MenuItemClick(object sender, MenuEventArgs e)
    {
        lblSelected.Text = Menu1.SelectedValue;
    }
</script>
<html xmlns="http://www.w3.org/1999/xhtml" >
<head id="Head1" runat="server">
    <style type="text/css">
        .menu
        {
            border:solid 1px black;
            padding:4px;
        }
    </style>
    <title>Show Menu</title>
</head>
<body>
    <form id="form1" runat="server">
    <div>

    <asp:Menu
        id="Menu1"
        DataSourceId="srcCategories"
        OnMenuItemClick="Menu1_MenuItemClick"
        Orientation="Horizontal"
        DynamicMenuStyle-CssClass="menu"
        Runat="server">
        <DataBindings>
            <asp:MenuItemBinding TextField="Name" ValueField="Name" />
```

19

LISTING 19.32   Continued

```
            </DataBindings>
        </asp:Menu>

        <custom:SqlHierarchicalDataSource
            id="srcCategories"
            ConnectionString='<%$ ConnectionStrings:Categories %>'
            DataKeyName="CategoryId"
            DataParentKeyName="ParentId"
            SelectCommand="SELECT CategoryId, ParentId, Name FROM Categories"
            Runat="server" />

        <hr />

        <asp:Label
            id="lblSelected"
            Runat="server" />

        </div>
        </form>
</body>
</html>
```

When you open the page in Listing 19.32, all the rows from the Categories table are displayed in the Menu control.

Notice that the SqlHierarchicalDataSource control includes two properties: DataKeyName and DataParentKeyName. The DataKeyName property represents the name of a database column that contains a unique value for each database table row. The DataParentKeyName column represents the name of a database column that relates each row to its parent row.

Furthermore, notice that the Menu control includes a MenuItemBinding, which associates the database Name column with the Menu item Text property, and the Name column with the Menu item Value property.

You also can use the SqlHierarchicalDataSource control when working with the TreeView control. The page in Listing 19.33 displays all the rows from the Discuss database table in a TreeView control.

LISTING 19.33   ShowTreeView.aspx

```
<%@ Page Language="C#" %>
<%@ Register TagPrefix="custom" Namespace="AspNetUnleashed" %>
<!DOCTYPE html PUBLIC "-//W3C//DTD XHTML 1.1//EN"
"http://www.w3.org/TR/xhtml11/DTD/xhtml11.dtd">
<script runat="server">
```

```
        protected void TreeView1_SelectedNodeChanged(object sender, EventArgs e)
        {
            lblSelected.Text = TreeView1.SelectedValue;
        }
</script>
<html xmlns="http://www.w3.org/1999/xhtml" >
<head id="Head1" runat="server">
    <title>Show TreeView</title>
</head>
<body>
    <form id="form1" runat="server">
    <div>

    <asp:TreeView
        id="TreeView1"
        DataSourceID="srcDiscuss"
        OnSelectedNodeChanged="TreeView1_SelectedNodeChanged"
        ImageSet="News"
        Runat="server">
        <DataBindings>
            <asp:TreeNodeBinding
                TextField="Subject"
                ValueField="MessageId" />
        </DataBindings>
    </asp:TreeView>

    <custom:SqlHierarchicalDataSource
        id="srcDiscuss"
        ConnectionString='<%$ ConnectionStrings:Discuss %>'
        DataKeyName="MessageId"
        DataParentKeyName="ParentId"
        SelectCommand="SELECT MessageId,ParentId,Subject FROM Discuss"
        Runat="server" />

    <hr />

    You selected message number:
    <asp:Label
        id="lblSelected"
        Runat="server" />

    </div>
    </form>
</body>
</html>
```

When you open the page in Listing 19.33, the contents of the Discuss database table are displayed in the `TreeView` control.

All the code for the `SqlHierarchicalDataSource` control is included on the CD that accompanies this book. The control is composed out of five separate classes:

- ▶ **SqlHierarchicalDataSource**—This class represents the actual control. It inherits from the base `SqlDataSource` control and implements the `IHierarchicalDataSource` interface.

- ▶ **SqlHierarchicalDataSourceView**—This class represents the hierarchical data returned by the control. It inherits from the base `HierarchicalDataSourceView` class.

- ▶ **SqlHierarchicalEnumerable**—This class represents a collection of `SqlNodes`.

- ▶ **SqlNode**—This class represents a particular database row from the data source. It includes methods for retrieving child and parent rows.

- ▶ **SqlNodePropertyDescriptor**—This class inherits from the base `PropertyDescriptor` class. It converts the database columns represented by a `SqlNode` into class properties so that you can bind to the columns using `TreeView` and `Menu` control DataBindings.

> **NOTE**
>
> The Microsoft .NET Framework SDK Documentation includes a sample of a `FileSystemDataSource` control that implements the `IHierarchicalDataSource` interface. Look up the `IHearchicalDataSource` topic in the documentation index.

Summary

In this chapter, you learned how to use the `SiteMapPath`, `Menu`, and `TreeView` controls. First, you learned how to use the `SiteMapPath` control to display a bread crumb trail. You learned how to format the `SiteMapPath` control with styles and templates.

Next, you explored the `Menu` control. You learned how to create both vertical and horizontal menus. You also learned how you can bind a `Menu` control to different data sources such as Site Maps, XML documents, and database data.

The `TreeView` control was also discussed. You learned how to display check boxes with a `TreeView` control. You also learned how to bind a `TreeView` control to different data sources such as Site Maps, XML documents, and database data. You also learned how to display a large set of Tree nodes efficiently by using AJAX and the `TreeView` control.

Finally, we created a custom `SqlHierarchicalDataSource` control that enables you to easily bind controls such as the `Menu` and `TreeView` controls to hierarchical database data.

Using Site Maps

This chapter jumps into the details of Site Maps. First, you learn how to use the `SiteMapDataSource` control to represent a Site Map on a page. For example, you learn how to use the `SiteMapDataSource` control to display a list of all the pages contained in a folder.

Next, you explore the `SiteMap` and `SiteMapNode` classes. You learn how to create new Site Map nodes dynamically. You also learn how to programmatically retrieve Site Map nodes and display the properties of a node in a page.

This chapter also examines several advanced features of Site Maps. For example, you learn how to show different Site Maps to different users depending on their roles. You also learn how you can extend Site Maps with custom attributes.

You also learn how to create custom Site Map providers. The first custom Site Map provider—the AutoSiteMapProvider—automatically builds a Site Map based on the folder and page structure of your website. The second custom Site Map provider—the SqlSiteMapProvider—enables you to store a Site Map in a Microsoft SQL Server database table.

Finally, you learn how to generate Google SiteMaps from ASP.NET Site Maps automatically. You can use a Google SiteMap to improve the way that your website is indexed by the Google search engine.

Using the `SiteMapDataSource` Control

The `SiteMapDataSource` control enables you to represent a Site Map declaratively in a page. You can bind navigation controls such as the `TreeView` and `Menu` controls to a `SiteMapDataSource` control. You also can bind other controls such as the `GridView` or `DropDownList` control to a `SiteMapDataSource` control.

Imagine, for example, that your website contains the `Web.sitemap` file in Listing 20.1. Because the default `SiteMapProvider` is the `XmlSiteMapProvider`, the `SiteMapDataSource` control automatically represents the contents of this XML file.

NOTE

The code samples in this section are located in the `SiteMaps` application on the CD that accompanies this book.

LISTING 20.1   `Web.sitemap`

```
<siteMap xmlns="http://schemas.microsoft.com/AspNet/SiteMap-File-1.0" >
<siteMapNode
  url="Default.aspx"
  title="Home"
  description="The Home Page">
  <siteMapNode
    url="Products/Default.aspx"
    title="Our Products"
    description="Products that we offer">
    <siteMapNode
      url="Products/FirstProduct.aspx"
      title="First Product"
      description="The description of the First Product" />
    <siteMapNode
      url="Products/SecondProduct.aspx"
      title="Second Product"
      description="The description of the Second Product" />
  </siteMapNode>
  <siteMapNode
    url="Services/Default.aspx"
    title="Our Services"
    description="Services that we offer">
    <siteMapNode
      url="Services/FirstService.aspx"
      title="First Service"
      description="The description of the First Service"
      metaDescription="The first service" />
    <siteMapNode
```

```
        url="Services/SecondService.aspx"
        title="Second Service"
        description="The description of the Second Service" />
    </siteMapNode>
  </siteMapNode>
</siteMap>
```

The Site Map file in Listing 20.1 represents a website with the following folder and page structure:

```
Default.aspx
Products
    FirstProduct.aspx
    SecondProduct.aspx
Services
    FirstService.aspx
    SecondService.aspx
```

The page in Listing 20.2 illustrates how you can represent a Site Map by binding a TreeView control to the SiteMapDataSource control.

LISTING 20.2   Default.aspx

```
<%@ Page Language="C#" %>
<!DOCTYPE html PUBLIC "-//W3C//DTD XHTML 1.1//EN"
"http://www.w3.org/TR/xhtml11/DTD/xhtml11.dtd">
<html xmlns="http://www.w3.org/1999/xhtml" >
<head id="Head1" runat="server">
    <title>Home</title>
</head>
<body>
    <form id="form1" runat="server">
    <div>

    <asp:SiteMapPath
        id="SiteMapPath1"
        Runat="server" />

    <hr />

    <asp:TreeView
        id="TreeView1"
        DataSourceID="srcSiteMap"
        Runat="server" />

    <asp:SiteMapDataSource
```

20

LISTING 20.2   Continued

```
            id="srcSiteMap"
            Runat="server" />

    </div>
    </form>
</body>
</html>
```

When you open the page in Listing 20.2, all the elements from the `Web.sitemap` file are displayed in the `TreeView` control with the help of the `SiteMapDataSource` control (see Figure 20.1).

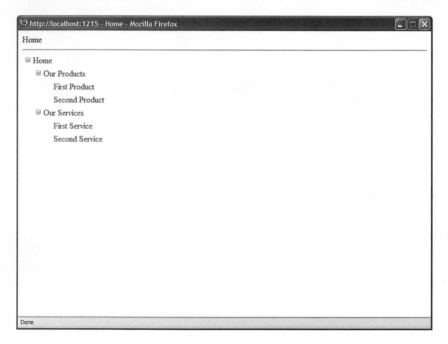

FIGURE 20.1   Displaying a Site Map with a `TreeView` control.

Setting `SiteMapDataSource` Properties

The `SiteMapDataSource` control includes several valuable properties that you can set to modify the nodes that the control returns:

▶ **ShowStartingNode**—Enables you to hide the starting node.

▶ **StartFromCurrentNode**—Enables you to return all nodes starting from the current node.

▶ **StartingNodeOffset**—Enables you to specify a positive or negative offset from the current node.

▶ **StartingNodeUrl**—Enables you to return all nodes, starting at a node associated with a specified URL.

The most useful of these properties is the ShowStartingNode property. Normally, when you display a list of nodes with a Menu or TreeView control, you do not want to display the starting node (the link to the home page). The page in Listing 20.3 illustrates how you can bind a Menu control to a SiteMapDataSource that has the value False assigned to its ShowStartingNode property.

LISTING 20.3 Services/Default.aspx

```
<%@ Page Language="C#" %>
<!DOCTYPE html PUBLIC "-//W3C//DTD XHTML 1.1//EN"
"http://www.w3.org/TR/xhtml11/DTD/xhtml11.dtd">
<html xmlns="http://www.w3.org/1999/xhtml" >
<head id="Head1" runat="server">
    <style type="text/css">
        .menuItem
        {
            border:solid 1px black;
            background-color:#eeeeee;
            padding:4px;
            margin:1px 0px;
        }
    </style>
    <title>Our Services</title>
</head>
<body>
    <form id="form1" runat="server">
    <div>

    <asp:SiteMapPath
        id="SiteMapPath1"
        Runat="server" />

    <hr />

    <asp:Menu
        id="Menu1"
        DataSourceID="srcSiteMap"
        StaticMenuItemStyle-CssClass="menuItem"
        DynamicMenuItemStyle-CssClass="menuItem"
        Runat="server" />
```

20

LISTING 20.3   Continued

```
    <asp:SiteMapDataSource
        id="srcSiteMap"
        ShowStartingNode="false"
        Runat="server" />

    </div>
    </form>
</body>
</html>
```

When you open the page in Listing 20.3, only the second-level nodes and descendent nodes are displayed (see Figure 20.2).

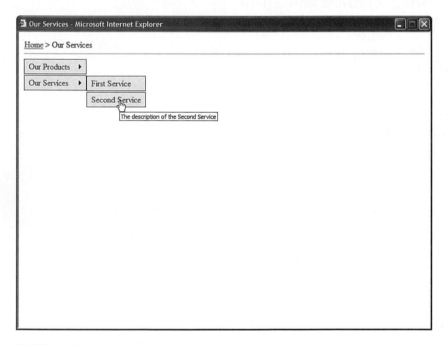

FIGURE 20.2   Hiding the starting node.

The StartFromCurrentNode property is useful when you want to display a list of all nodes below the current node. For example, the page in Listing 20.4 is the Default.aspx page contained in the Products folder. It displays a list of all the product pages contained in the folder.

LISTING 20.4   Products/Default.aspx

```
<%@ Page Language="C#" %>
<!DOCTYPE html PUBLIC "-//W3C//DTD XHTML 1.1//EN"
"http://www.w3.org/TR/xhtml11/DTD/xhtml11.dtd">
<html xmlns="http://www.w3.org/1999/xhtml" >
<head id="Head1" runat="server">
    <style type="text/css">
        html
        {
            font:16px Georgia,Serif;
        }
        .productList li
        {
            margin:5px;
        }
    </style>
    <title>Our Products</title>
</head>
<body>
    <form id="form1" runat="server">
    <div>

    <h1>Products</h1>

    <asp:BulletedList
        id="bltProducts"
        DisplayMode="HyperLink"
        DataTextField="Title"
        DataValueField="Url"
        DataSourceID="srcSiteMap"
        CssClass="productList"
        Runat="server" />

    <asp:SiteMapDataSource
        id="srcSiteMap"
        ShowStartingNode="false"
        StartFromCurrentNode="true"
        Runat="server" />

    </div>
    </form>
</body>
</html>
```

The page in Listing 20.4 contains a BulletedList control bound to a SiteMapDataSource control. Because the SiteMapDataSource control has its StartFromCurrentNode property set to the value True and its ShowStartingNode property set to the value False, all immediate child nodes of the current node are displayed (see Figure 20.3).

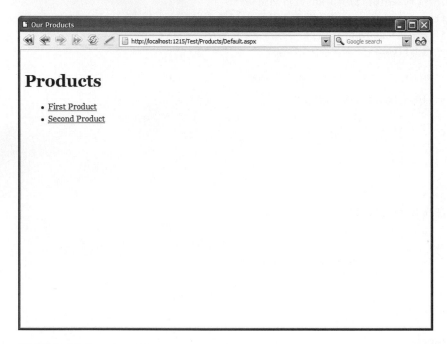

FIGURE 20.3   Displaying the contents of a folder.

Using the `SiteMap` Class

Under the covers, the `SiteMapDataSource` control represents the contents of the `SiteMap` class. The `SiteMap` class represents an application's Site Map regardless of whether the Site Map is stored in an XML file, a database, or some other data source. The class is a memory-resident representation of Site Map data.

All the properties exposed by the `SiteMap` class are shared (static) properties:

> ▶ **CurrentNode**—Enables you to retrieve the `SiteMapNode` that corresponds to the current page.

> ▶ **Enabled**—Enables you to determine whether the Site Map is enabled.

> ▶ **Provider**—Enables you to retrieve the default `SiteMapProvider`.

> ▶ **Providers**—Enables you to retrieve all the configured `SiteMapProviders`.

> ▶ **RootNode**—Enables you to retrieve the root `SiteMapNode`.

The CurrentNode and RootNode properties return a SiteMapNode object. Because a Site Map can contain only one root node, and the root node contains all the other nodes as children, the RootNode property enables you to iterate through all the nodes in a Site Map.

The Provider property returns the default SiteMapProvider. You can use this property to access all the properties and methods of the SiteMapProvider class, such as the FindSiteMapNode() and GetParentNode() methods.

The SiteMap class also supports a single event:

▶ **SiteMapResolve**—Raised when the current node is accessed.

You can handle this event to modify the node returned when the current node is retrieved. For example, the Global.asax file in Listing 20.5 automatically adds a new node when the current page does not include a node in the Site Map.

LISTING 20.5   Global.asax

```
<%@ Application Language="C#" %>
<%@ Import Namespace="System.IO" %>
<script runat="server">

    void Application_Start(Object sender, EventArgs e)
    {
        SiteMap.SiteMapResolve += new SiteMapResolveEventHandler
        ➥(SiteMap_SiteMapResolve);
    }

    SiteMapNode SiteMap_SiteMapResolve(object sender, SiteMapResolveEventArgs e)
    {
        if (SiteMap.CurrentNode == null)
        {
            string url = e.Context.Request.Path;
            string title = Path.GetFileNameWithoutExtension(url);
            SiteMapNode newNode = new SiteMapNode(e.Provider, url, url, title);
            newNode.ParentNode = SiteMap.RootNode;
            return newNode;
        }
        return SiteMap.CurrentNode;
    }
</script>
```

20

The Application_Start() event handler in Listing 20.5 executes only once when the application first starts. The handler adds a SiteMapResolve event handler to the SiteMap class.

Whenever any control retrieves the current node, the SiteMap_SiteMapResolve() method executes. If there is no node that corresponds to a page, then the method creates a new node and returns it.

The `About.aspx` page in Listing 20.6 is not included in the `Web.sitemap` file. However, this page includes a `SiteMapPath` control. The `SiteMapPath` control works correctly because the `About.aspx` page is dynamically added to the Site Map when you access the page (see Figure 20.4).

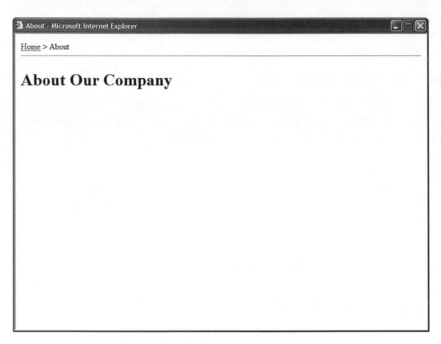

FIGURE 20.4   Adding nodes to a Site Map dynamically.

LISTING 20.6   About.aspx

```
<%@ Page Language="C#" %>
<!DOCTYPE html PUBLIC "-//W3C//DTD XHTML 1.1//EN"
"http://www.w3.org/TR/xhtml11/DTD/xhtml11.dtd">
<html xmlns="http://www.w3.org/1999/xhtml" >
<head id="Head1" runat="server">
    <title>About</title>
</head>
<body>
    <form id="form1" runat="server">
    <div>

    <asp:SiteMapPath
        id="SiteMapPath1"
        Runat="server" />

    <hr />
```

```
    <h1>About Our Company</h1>

    </div>
    </form>
</body>
</html>
```

Using the `SiteMapNode` Class

All pages and folders in a Site Map are represented by instances of the `SiteMapNode` class. The `SiteMapNode` class contains the following properties:

- **`ChildNodes`**—Returns the child nodes of the current node.

- **`Description`**—Returns the description of the current node.

- **`HasChildNodes`**—Returns `True` when the current node has child nodes.

- **`Item`**—Returns a custom attribute (or resource string).

- **`Key`**—Returns a unique identifier for the current node.

- **`NextSibling`**—Returns the next sibling of the current node.

- **`ParentNode`**—Returns the parent node of the current node.

- **`PreviousSibling`**—Returns the previous sibling of the current node.

- **`Provider`**—Returns the `SiteMapProvider` associated with the current node.

- **`ReadOnly`**—Returns true when a node is read-only.

- **`ResourceKey`**—Returns the resource key associated with the current node (enables localization).

- **`Roles`**—Returns the user roles associated with the current node.

- **`RootNode`**—Returns the Site Map root node.

- **`Title`**—Returns the title associated with the current node.

- **`Url`**—Returns the URL associated with the current node.

The `SiteMapNode` class also supports the following methods:

- **`Clone()`**—Returns a clone of the current node.

- **`GetAllNodes()`**—Returns all descendent nodes of the current node.

- **`GetDataSourceView()`**—Returns a `SiteMapDataSourceView` object.

- **`GetHierarchicalDataSourceView()`**—Returns a `SiteMapHierarchicalDataSourceView`.

20

▶ **IsAccessibleToUser()**—Returns True when the current user has permissions to view the current node.

▶ **IsDescendantOf()**—Returns True when the current node is a descendant of a particular node.

By taking advantage of the SiteMap and SiteMapNode classes, you can work directly with Site Maps in a page. For example, imagine that you want to display the value of the SiteMapNode title attribute in both the browser's title bar and in the body of the page. Listing 20.7 demonstrates how you can retrieve the value of the Title property associated with the current page programmatically.

LISTING 20.7   Products/FirstProduct.aspx

```
<%@ Page Language="C#" %>
<!DOCTYPE html PUBLIC "-//W3C//DTD XHTML 1.1//EN"
"http://www.w3.org/TR/xhtml11/DTD/xhtml11.dtd">
<script runat="server">
    void Page_Load()
    {
        if (!Page.IsPostBack)
        {
            SiteMapNode currentNode = SiteMap.CurrentNode;
            this.Title = currentNode.Title;
            ltlBodyTitle.Text = currentNode.Title;
            lblDescription.Text = currentNode.Description;
        }
    }

</script>
<html xmlns="http://www.w3.org/1999/xhtml" >
<head id="Head1" runat="server">
    <title>First Product</title>
</head>
<body>
    <form id="form1" runat="server">
    <div>

    <h1><asp:Literal ID="ltlBodyTitle" runat="server" /></h1>

    <asp:Label
        id="lblDescription"
        Runat="server" />
```

```
    </div>
    </form>
</body>
</html>
```

When you open the page in Listing 20.7, the Page_Load() event handler grabs the current SiteMapNode and modifies the Page Title property. The handler also assigns the value of the Title property to a Literal control contained in the body of the page. Finally, the value of the SiteMapNode's Description property is assigned to a Label control (see Figure 20.5).

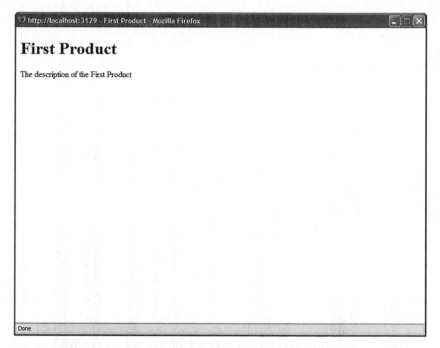

FIGURE 20.5   Retrieving Site Map node properties.

> **NOTE**
>
> It would make sense to place the code in Listing 20.7 in a Master Page. To learn more about Master Pages, see Chapter 5, "Designing Websites with Master Pages."

20

Advanced Site Map Configuration

This section explores several advanced features of Site Maps. For example, you learn how to display different SiteMap nodes, depending on the roles associated with the current user. You also learn how to create multiple Site Maps for a single application. Finally, you learn how you can extend Site Maps with custom attributes.

Using Security Trimming

You might want to display different navigation links to different users, depending on their roles. For example, if a user is a member of the Administrators role, you might want to display links to pages for administrating the website. However, you might want to hide these links from other users.

To display different links to different users depending on their roles, you must enable a feature of Site Maps named Security Trimming. This feature is disabled by default. The web configuration file in Listing 20.8 enables Security Trimming.

LISTING 20.8   Web.Config

```
<configuration>
  <system.web>

    <authentication mode="Windows" />
    <roleManager enabled="true" />

    <siteMap defaultProvider="MySiteMapProvider">
      <providers>
        <add
          name="MySiteMapProvider"
          type="System.Web.XmlSiteMapProvider"
          securityTrimmingEnabled="true"
          siteMapFile="Web.sitemap" />

      </providers>
    </siteMap>

  </system.web>
</configuration>
```

Notice that the configuration file in Listing 20.8 includes a `<siteMap>` element that configures a new `SiteMapProvider` named `MySiteMapProvider`. The new provider enables Security Trimming with its `securityTrimmingEnabled` property.

After you enable Security Trimming, any pages a user is not allowed to view are automatically hidden. For example, imagine that your website includes a folder named Admin that contains the web configuration file in Listing 20.9.

LISTING 20.9   Web.Config

```
<configuration xmlns="http://schemas.microsoft.com/.NetConfiguration/v2.0">
<system.web>

  <authorization>
    <allow users="WebAdmin" />
```

```
    <deny users="*" />
  </authorization>

</system.web>
</configuration>
```

The configuration file in Listing 20.9 prevents anyone who is not a member of the WebAdmin role from viewing pages in the same folder (and below) as the configuration file. Even if the Web.sitemap file includes nodes that represent pages in the Admin folder, the links don't appear for anyone except members of the WebAdmin role.

Another option is to explicitly associate roles with nodes in a Site Map. This is useful in two situations. First, if your website contains links to another website, then you can hide or display these links based on the user role. Second, if you explicitly associate roles with pages, then you hide page links even when a user has permission to view a page.

The Web.sitemap file in Listing 20.10 contains links to the Microsoft, Google, and Yahoo websites. A different set of roles is associated with each link.

LISTING 20.10   Web.sitemap

```
<siteMap xmlns="http://schemas.microsoft.com/AspNet/SiteMap-File-1.0" >
  <siteMapNode
    title="External Links"
    description="Links to external Websites"
    roles="RoleA,RoleB,RoleC">
    <siteMapNode
      title="Google"
      url="http://www.Google.com"
      description="The Google Website"
      roles="RoleA" />
    <siteMapNode
      title="Microsoft"
      url="http://www.Microsoft.com"
      description="The Microsoft Website"
      roles="RoleB" />
    <siteMapNode
      title="Yahoo"
      url="http://www.Yahoo.com"
      description="The Yahoo Website"
      roles="RoleC" />
  </siteMapNode>
</siteMap>
```

20

The page in Listing 20.11 enables you to add yourself and remove yourself from different roles. Notice that different links appear in the TreeView control, depending on which roles you select.

LISTING 20.11   ShowSecurityTrimming.aspx

```
<%@ Page Language="C#" %>
<!DOCTYPE html PUBLIC "-//W3C//DTD XHTML 1.1//EN"
"http://www.w3.org/TR/xhtml11/DTD/xhtml11.dtd">
<script runat="server">

    void Page_Load()
    {
        if (!Page.IsPostBack)
        {
            foreach (ListItem item in cblSelectRoles.Items)
                if (!Roles.RoleExists(item.Text))
                {
                    Roles.CreateRole(item.Text);
                    Roles.AddUserToRole(User.Identity.Name, item.Text);
                }
        }
    }

    protected void btnSelect_Click(object sender, EventArgs e)
    {
        foreach (ListItem item in cblSelectRoles.Items)
        {
            if (item.Selected)
            {
                if (!User.IsInRole(item.Text))
                    Roles.AddUserToRole(User.Identity.Name, item.Text);
            }
            else
            {
                if (User.IsInRole(item.Text))
                    Roles.RemoveUserFromRole(User.Identity.Name, item.Text);
            }
        }
        Response.Redirect(Request.Path);
    }

    void Page_PreRender()
    {
        foreach (ListItem item in cblSelectRoles.Items)
            item.Selected = User.IsInRole(item.Text);
```

```
        }
</script>
<html xmlns="http://www.w3.org/1999/xhtml" >
<head id="Head1" runat="server">
    <style type="text/css">
        html
        {
            background-color:silver;
        }
        .column
        {
            float:left;
            width:300px;
            border:Solid 1px black;
            background-color:white;
            padding:10px;
        }
    </style>
    <title>Show Security Trimming</title>
</head>
<body>
    <form id="form1" runat="server">

    <div class="column">

    <asp:Label
        id="lblSelectRoles"
        Text="Select Roles:"
        AssociatedControlID="cblSelectRoles"
        Runat="server" />

    <br />

    <asp:CheckBoxList
        id="cblSelectRoles"
        Runat="server">
        <asp:ListItem Text="RoleA" />
        <asp:ListItem Text="RoleB" />
        <asp:ListItem Text="RoleC" />
    </asp:CheckBoxList>

    <asp:Button
        id="btnSelect"
        Text="Select"
        OnClick="btnSelect_Click"
        Runat="server" />
```

LISTING 20.11   Continued

```
    </div>

    <div class="column">

    <asp:TreeView
        id="TreeView1"
        DataSourceID="srcSiteMap"
        Runat="server" />

    <asp:SiteMapDataSource
        id="srcSiteMap"
        Runat="server" />

    </div>

    </form>
</body>
</html>
```

When you first open the page in Listing 20.11, the `Page_Load()` handler creates three roles—RoleA, RoleB, and RoleC—and adds the current user to each role.

The `CheckBoxList` control in the body of the page enables you to select the roles that you want to join. Notice that different links to external websites appear, depending on which roles you select (see Figure 20.6).

Merging Multiple Site Maps

To make it easier to manage a large application, you can store Site Maps in more than one location and merge the Site Maps at runtime. For example, if you are using the default `SiteMapProvider`—the `XmlSiteMapProvider`—then you can create multiple sitemap files that describe the navigation structure of different sections of your website.

For example, the `Web.sitemap` file in Listing 20.12 includes a node that points to another sitemap file.

LISTING 20.12   Web.sitemap

```
<siteMap xmlns="http://schemas.microsoft.com/AspNet/SiteMap-File-1.0" >
<siteMapNode
  url="Default.aspx"
  title="Home"
  description="The Home Page">
  <siteMapNode
    url="Products/Default.aspx"
```

```
        title="Our Products"
        description="Products that we offer">
        <siteMapNode
          url="Products/FirstProduct.aspx"
          title="First Product"
          description="The description of the First Product" />
        <siteMapNode
          url="Products/SecondProduct.aspx"
          title="Second Product"
          description="The description of the Second Product" />
    </siteMapNode>
    <siteMapNode
      url="Services"
      title="Our Services"
      description="Services that we offer">
        <siteMapNode
          url="Services/FirstService.aspx"
          title="First Service"
          description="The description of the First Service"
          metaDescription="The first service" />
        <siteMapNode
          url="Services/SecondService.aspx"
          title="Second Service"
          description="The description of the Second Service" />
    </siteMapNode>
    <siteMapNode
      siteMapFile="Employees/Employees.sitemap" />
</siteMapNode>
</siteMap>
```

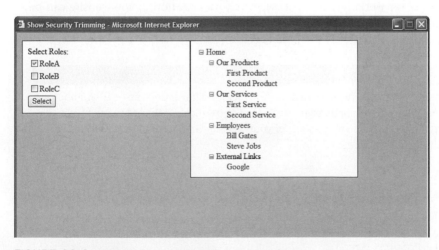

FIGURE 20.6   Hiding Site Map nodes by user role.

The sitemap in Listing 20.12 includes the following node:

```
<siteMapNode siteMapFile="Employees/Employees.sitemap" />
```

This node includes a `siteMapFile` attribute that points to a sitemap located in the Employees subdirectory of the current application. The contents of the `Employees.sitemap` are automatically merged with the default `Web.sitemap`.

The `Employees.sitemap` is contained in Listing 20.13.

LISTING 20.13   Employees/Employees.sitemap

```
<siteMap xmlns="http://schemas.microsoft.com/AspNet/SiteMap-File-1.0" >
  <siteMapNode
    url="Employees/Default.aspx"
    title="Employees"
    description="Contains descriptions of employees">
    <siteMapNode
      url="Employees/BillGates.aspx"
      title="Bill Gates"
      description="Bill Gates Page" />
    <siteMapNode
      url="Employees/SteveJobs.aspx"
      title="Steve Jobs"
      description="Steve Jobs Page" />
  </siteMapNode>
</siteMap>
```

Notice that there is nothing special about the sitemap in Listing 20.13. It contains a description of the two pages in the Employees subdirectory.

This is a great feature for working with large websites. Each section of the website can be managed by a different developer. When the website is accessed by a user, the contents of the different sitemaps are seamlessly stitched together.

> **NOTE**
>
> You also can associate different `SiteMapProviders` with different nodes in a sitemap file by taking advantage of the `provider` attribute. For example, a Site Map might be stored in a database table for one section of your website and stored in an XML file for another section of your website.

Creating Custom Site Map Attributes

You can extend a Site Map with your own custom attributes. You can use a custom attribute to represent any type of information that you want. For example, imagine that you want to associate <meta> Description tags with each page in your web application to make it easier for search engines to index your website. In that case, you can add a metaDescription attribute to the nodes in a Web.sitemap file.

The Web.sitemap file in Listing 20.14 includes metaDescription attributes for the two Services pages.

LISTING 20.14   Web.sitemap

```
<siteMap xmlns="http://schemas.microsoft.com/AspNet/SiteMap-File-1.0" >
  <siteMapNode
    url="Default.aspx"
    title="Home"
    description="The Home Page">
    <siteMapNode
      url="Products/Default.aspx"
      title="Our Products"
      description="Products that we offer">
      <siteMapNode
        url="Products/FirstProduct.aspx"
        title="First Product"
        description="The description of the First Product" />
      <siteMapNode
        url="Products/SecondProduct.aspx"
        title="Second Product"
        description="The description of the Second Product" />
    </siteMapNode>
    <siteMapNode
      url="Services/Default.aspx"
      title="Our Services"
      description="Services that we offer">
      <siteMapNode
        url="Services/FirstService.aspx"
        title="First Service"
        description="The description of the First Service"
        metaDescription="The first service" />
      <siteMapNode
        url="Services/SecondService.aspx"
        title="Second Service"
        description="The description of the Second Service"
        metaDescription="The second service"  />
    </siteMapNode>
  </siteMapNode>
</siteMap>
```

20

VISUAL WEB DEVELOPER NOTE

Visual Web Developer displays blue squiggles (warning messages) under any custom attributes in a SiteMap file. You can safely ignore these warnings.

Any custom attributes that you add to a Site Map are exposed by instances of the `SiteMapNode` class. For example, the page in Listing 20.15 retrieves the value of the `metaDescription` attribute from the current node and displays the value in an actual `<meta>` tag.

LISTING 20.15   Services/FirstService.aspx

```
<%@ Page Language="C#" %>
<!DOCTYPE html PUBLIC "-//W3C//DTD XHTML 1.1//EN"
"http://www.w3.org/TR/xhtml11/DTD/xhtml11.dtd">
<script runat="server">

    void Page_Load()
    {
        HtmlMeta meta = new HtmlMeta();
        meta.Name = "Description";
        meta.Content = SiteMap.CurrentNode["metaDescription"];
        head1.Controls.Add(meta);
    }
</script>
<html xmlns="http://www.w3.org/1999/xhtml" >
<head id="head1" runat="server">
    <title>First Service</title>
</head>
<body>
    <form id="form1" runat="server">
    <div>

    <h1>The First Service</h1>

    </div>
    </form>
</body>
</html>
```

After you open the page in Listing 20.15 in a web browser, you can select View, Source to see the `<meta>` tag added to the source of the page (see Figure 20.7).

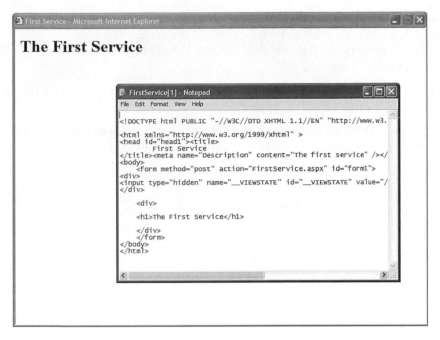

FIGURE 20.7   Extending a Site Map with a <meta> tag.

It is important to emphasize that you can do anything you want with custom SiteMapNode attributes. You can represent page titles, section titles, product icons, or anything else with a custom attribute.

Creating Custom Site Map Providers

Site Maps use the provider model. This means that you can easily modify or extend the way Site Maps work by creating your own Site Map provider.

In this section, we create two custom Site Map providers. First, we create the AutoSiteMapProvider. This provider automatically builds a Site Map based on the file and folder structure of a website.

Next, we create a SqlSiteMapProvider. This provider enables you to store a Site Map in a Microsoft SQL Server database table instead of an XML file.

Creating the AutoSiteMapProvider

All Site Map providers inherit from the base SiteMapProvider class. If you want to create your own Site Map provider, then you can override the methods of this base class.

20

However, in most cases it makes more sense to derive a custom Site Map provider from the base `StaticSiteMapProvider` class. This is the base class for the default Site Map provider—the `XmlSiteMapProvider`—and this class includes default implementations of many of the `SiteMapProvider` methods.

This `AutoSiteMapProvider` derives from the `StaticSiteMapProvider` class. It overrides two methods of the base class: `GetRootNodeCore()` and `BuildSiteMap()`.

The `GetRootNodeCore()` method returns the root node of the Site Map. The `BuildSiteMap()` method is the method that is actually responsible for building the Site Map.

The AutoSiteMapProvider is contained in Listing 20.16.

LISTING 20.16   App_Code/AutoSiteMapProvider.cs

```
using System;
using System.Collections.Generic;
using System.IO;
using System.Web;
using System.Web.Caching;

namespace AspNetUnleashed
{
    public class AutoSiteMapProvider : StaticSiteMapProvider
    {
        private SiteMapNode _rootNode;
        private static List<string> _excluded = new List<string>();
        private List<string> _dependencies = new List<string>();

        /// <summary>
        /// These folder and pages won't be added
        /// to the Site Map
        /// </summary>
        static AutoSiteMapProvider()
        {
            _excluded.Add("app_code");
            _excluded.Add("app_data");
            _excluded.Add("app_themes");
            _excluded.Add("bin");
        }

        /// <summary>
        /// Return the root node of the Site Map
        /// </summary>
        protected override SiteMapNode GetRootNodeCore()
        {
            return BuildSiteMap();
```

```csharp
}

/// <summary>
/// Where all of the work of building the Site Map happens
/// </summary>
public override SiteMapNode BuildSiteMap()
{
    // Only allow the Site Map to be created by a single thread
    lock (this)
    {
        // Attempt to get Root Node from Cache
        HttpContext context = HttpContext.Current;
        _rootNode = (SiteMapNode)context.Cache["RootNode"];
        if (_rootNode == null)
        {
            // Clear current Site Map
            Clear();

            // Create root node
            string folderUrl = HttpRuntime.AppDomainAppVirtualPath;
            string defaultUrl = folderUrl + "/Default.aspx";
            _rootNode = new SiteMapNode(this, folderUrl, defaultUrl, "Home");
            AddNode(_rootNode);

            // Create child nodes
            AddChildNodes(_rootNode);
            _dependencies.Add(HttpRuntime.AppDomainAppPath);

            // Add root node to cache with file dependencies
            CacheDependency fileDependency = new CacheDependency
            ➥(_dependencies.ToArray());
            context.Cache.Insert("RootNode", _rootNode, fileDependency);
        }
        return _rootNode;
    }
}

/// <summary>
/// Add child folders and pages to the Site Map
/// </summary>
private void AddChildNodes(SiteMapNode parentNode)
{

    AddChildFolders(parentNode);
    AddChildPages(parentNode);
}
```

LISTING 20.16   Continued

```
/// <summary>
/// Add child folders to the Site Map
/// </summary>
/// <param name="parentNode"></param>
private void AddChildFolders(SiteMapNode parentNode)
{
    HttpContext context = HttpContext.Current;
    string parentFolderPath = context.Server.MapPath(parentNode.Key);
    DirectoryInfo folderInfo = new DirectoryInfo(parentFolderPath);

    // Get sub folders
    DirectoryInfo[] folders = folderInfo.GetDirectories();
    foreach (DirectoryInfo folder in folders)
    {
        if (!_excluded.Contains(folder.Name.ToLower()))
        {
            string folderUrl = parentNode.Key + "/" + folder.Name;
            SiteMapNode folderNode = new SiteMapNode(this, folderUrl, null,
            ➥GetName(folder.Name));
            AddNode(folderNode, parentNode);
            AddChildNodes(folderNode);
            _dependencies.Add(folder.FullName);
        }
    }
}

/// <summary>
/// Add child pages to the Site Map
/// </summary>
private void AddChildPages(SiteMapNode parentNode)
{
    HttpContext context = HttpContext.Current;
    string parentFolderPath = context.Server.MapPath(parentNode.Key);
    DirectoryInfo folderInfo = new DirectoryInfo(parentFolderPath);

    FileInfo[] pages = folderInfo.GetFiles("*.aspx");
    foreach (FileInfo page in pages)
    {
        if (!_excluded.Contains(page.Name.ToLower()))
        {
            string pageUrl = parentNode.Key + "/" + page.Name;
            if (String.Compare(pageUrl, _rootNode.Url, true) !=0)
            {
```

```
                    SiteMapNode pageNode = new SiteMapNode(this, pageUrl,
                    ➥pageUrl, GetName(page.Name));
                    AddNode(pageNode, parentNode);
                }
            }
        }
    }

    /// <summary>
    /// Fix the name of the page or folder
    /// by removing the extension and replacing
    /// underscores with spaces
    /// </summary>
    private string GetName(string name)
    {
        name = Path.GetFileNameWithoutExtension(name);
        return name.Replace("_", " ");
    }
  }
}
```

Almost all of the work in Listing 20.16 happens in the `BuildSiteMap()` method. This method recursively iterates through all the folders and pages in the current web application creating `SiteMapNodes`. When the method completes its work, a Site Map that reflects the folder and page structure of the website is created.

You should notice two special aspects of the code in Listing 20.16. First, file dependencies are created for each folder. If you add a new folder or page to your website, the `BuildSiteMap()` method is automatically called the next time you request a page.

Second, notice that the constructor for the `AutoSiteMapProvider` class creates a list of excluded files. For example, this list includes the `App_Code` and Bin folders. You do not want these files to appear in a Site Map. If there are other special files that you want to hide, then you need to add the filenames to the list of excluded files in the constructor.

After you create the `AutoSiteMapProvider` class, you need to configure your application to use the custom Site Map provider. You can use the configuration file in Listing 20.17 to enable the `AutoSiteMapProvider`.

LISTING 20.17 Web.Config

```
<configuration xmlns="http://schemas.microsoft.com/.NetConfiguration/v2.0">
    <system.web>

        <siteMap defaultProvider="MyAutoSiteMapProvider">
          <providers>
            <add
```

20

LISTING 20.17   Continued

```
            name="MyAutoSiteMapProvider"
            type="AspNetUnleashed.AutoSiteMapProvider" />
      </providers>
    </siteMap>


  </system.web>
</configuration>
```

The configuration file in Listing 20.17 configures the AutoSiteMapProvider as the application's default provider.

You can try out the AutoSiteMapProvider by requesting the Default.aspx page from the AutoSiteMapProviderApp Web application contained on the CD that accompanies this book. This application does not include a Web.sitemap file. The Site Map is automatically generated from the structure of the website.

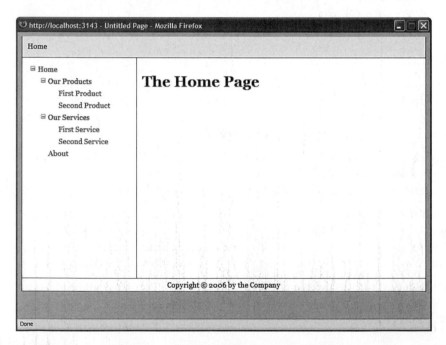

FIGURE 20.8   Displaying an automatically generated Site Map.

Creating the SqlSiteMapProvider

For certain applications it makes more sense to store a Site Map in a database table than an XML file. In this section, you can see the creation of the SqlSiteMapProvider, which stores a Site Map in a Microsoft SQL Server database.

To use the `SqlSiteMapProvider` class, you must create a SQL database table named SiteMap. Furthermore, the SiteMap database table must look like this:

Id	ParentId	Url	Title	Description
1	null	Default.aspx	Home	The Home Page
2	1		Products	Products
3	2	Products/FirstProduct.aspx	First Product	The First Product
4	2	Products/SecondProduct.aspx	Second Product	The Second Product
6	1		Services	Services
7	6	Services/FirstService.aspx	First Service	The First Service

Each row in the SiteMap table represents a particular Site Map node. The relationship between the nodes is represented by the ParentId column. The row that represents the root node has a ParentId column with the value null. Every other row is either a child of the root node or the child of some other node.

The code for the `SqlSiteMapProvider` is contained in Listing 20.18.

LISTING 20.18   App_Code\SqlSiteMapProvider.cs

```
using System;
using System.Collections.Specialized;
using System.Web.Configuration;
using System.Data;
using System.Data.SqlClient;
using System.Web;
using System.Web.Caching;

namespace AspNetUnleashed
{
    /// <summary>
    /// Summary description for SqlSiteMapProvider
    /// </summary>
    public class SqlSiteMapProvider : StaticSiteMapProvider
    {
        private bool _isInitialized = false;
        private string _connectionString;
        private SiteMapNode _rootNode;

        public override void Initialize(string name, NameValueCollection attributes)
        {
            if (_isInitialized)
```

LISTING 20.18   Continued

```
            return;

        base.Initialize(name, attributes);

        string connectionStringName = attributes["connectionStringName"];
        if (String.IsNullOrEmpty(connectionStringName))
            throw new Exception("You must provide a connectionStringName
            ➥attribute");

        _connectionString = WebConfigurationManager.ConnectionStrings
        ➥[connectionStringName].ConnectionString;
        if (String.IsNullOrEmpty(_connectionString))
            throw new Exception("Could not find connection string " +
            ➥connectionStringName);

        _isInitialized = true;
    }

    protected override SiteMapNode GetRootNodeCore()
    {
        return BuildSiteMap();
    }

    public override SiteMapNode BuildSiteMap()
    {
        // Only allow the Site Map to be created by a single thread
        lock (this)
        {
            // Attempt to get Root Node from Cache
            HttpContext context = HttpContext.Current;
            _rootNode = (SiteMapNode)context.Cache["RootNode"];

            if (_rootNode == null)
            {
                HttpContext.Current.Trace.Warn("Loading from database");

                // Clear current Site Map
                Clear();

                // Load the database data
                DataTable tblSiteMap = GetSiteMapFromDB();

                // Get the root node
                _rootNode = GetRootNode(tblSiteMap);
```

```
            AddNode(_rootNode);

            // Build the child nodes
            BuildSiteMapRecurse(tblSiteMap, _rootNode);

            // Add root node to cache with database dependency
            SqlCacheDependency sqlDepend = new SqlCacheDependency
            ➥("SiteMapDB", "SiteMap");
            context.Cache.Insert("RootNode", _rootNode, sqlDepend);
        }
        return _rootNode;
    }
}


private DataTable GetSiteMapFromDB()
{
    string selectCommand = "SELECT Id,ParentId,Url,Title,Description FROM
    ➥SiteMap";
    SqlDataAdapter dad = new SqlDataAdapter(selectCommand,
    ➥_connectionString);
    DataTable tblSiteMap = new DataTable();
    dad.Fill(tblSiteMap);
    return tblSiteMap;
}


private SiteMapNode GetRootNode(DataTable siteMapTable)
{
    DataRow[] results = siteMapTable.Select("ParentId IS NULL");
    if (results.Length == 0)
        throw new Exception("No root node in database");
    DataRow rootRow = results[0];
    return new SiteMapNode(this, rootRow["Id"].ToString(),
    ➥rootRow["url"].ToString(), rootRow["title"].ToString(),
    ➥rootRow["description"].ToString());
}

private void BuildSiteMapRecurse(DataTable siteMapTable, SiteMapNode
➥parentNode)
{
    DataRow[] results = siteMapTable.Select("ParentId=" + parentNode.Key);
    foreach (DataRow row in results)
    {
```

20

LISTING 20.18   Continued

```
                        SiteMapNode node = new SiteMapNode(this, row["Id"].ToString(),
                        ➥row["url"].ToString(), row["title"].ToString(),
                        ➥row["description"].ToString());
                        AddNode(node, parentNode);
                        BuildSiteMapRecurse(siteMapTable, node);
                }
        }


        }
}
```

Like the custom Site Map provider created in the previous section, the `SqlSiteMapProvider` derives from the base `StaticSiteMapProvider` class. The `SqlSiteMapProvider` class overrides three methods of the base class: `Initialize()`, `GetRootNodeCore()`, and `BuildSiteMap()`.

The `Initialize()` method retrieves a database connection string from the web configuration file. If a database connection string cannot be retrieved, then the method throws a big, fat exception.

Almost all the work happens in the `BuildSiteMap()` method. This method loads the contents of the SiteMap database table into an ADO.NET DataTable. Next, it recursively builds the Site Map nodes from the DataTable.

There is one special aspect of the code in Listing 20.18. It uses a SQL cache dependency to automatically rebuild the Site Map when the contents of the SiteMap database table are changed.

To enable SQL cache dependencies for a database, you must configure the database with either the `enableNotifications` tool or the `aspnet_regsql` tool. Use the `enableNotifications` tool when enabling SQL cache dependencies for a SQL Express database table, and use the `aspnet_regsql` tool when enabling SQL cache dependencies for the full version of Microsoft SQL Server.

> **NOTE**
>
> To learn more about configuring SQL cache dependencies, see Chapter 25, "Caching Application Pages and Data."

To enable SQL cache dependencies for a SQL Express database named SiteMapDB that contains a table named SiteMap, browse to the folder that contains the SiteMapDB.mdf file and execute the following command from a Command Prompt:

```
enableNotifications "SiteMapDB.mdf" "SiteMap"
```

You can configure your website to use the `SqlSiteMapProvider` class with the Web configuration file in Listing 20.19.

LISTING 20.19   Web.Config

```
<configuration>
  <connectionStrings>
    <add
      name="conSiteMap"
      connectionString="Data Source=.\SQLExpress;Integrated
 Security=True;AttachDbFileName=¦DataDirectory¦SiteMapDB.mdf;User Instance=True"/>
  </connectionStrings>

    <system.web>
      <siteMap defaultProvider="myProvider">
        <providers>
          <add
            name="myProvider"
            type="AspNetUnleashed.SqlSiteMapProvider"
            connectionStringName="conSiteMap" />

        </providers>
      </siteMap>

      <caching>
      <sqlCacheDependency enabled = "true" pollTime = "5000" >
        <databases>
          <add name="SiteMapDB"
                connectionStringName="conSiteMap"
          />
        </databases>
      </sqlCacheDependency>
      </caching>

    </system.web>
</configuration>
```

The configuration file in Listing 20.19 accomplishes several tasks. First, it configures the `SqlSiteMapProvider` as the default Site Map provider. Notice that the provider includes a `connectionStringName` attribute that points to the connection string for the local SQL Express database named SiteMapDB.

The configuration file also enables SQL cache dependency polling. The application is configured to poll the SiteMapDB database for changes every 5 seconds. In other words, if you make a change to the SiteMap database table, the Site Map is updated to reflect the change within 5 seconds.

You can try out the `SqlSiteMapProvider` by opening the `Default.aspx` page included in the `SqlSiteMapProviderApp` web application on the CD that accompanies this book. If you modify the SiteMap database table, the changes are automatically reflected in the Site Map (see Figure 20.9).

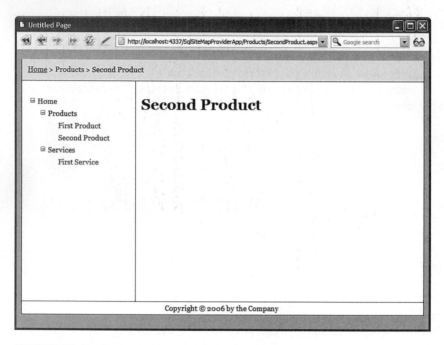

FIGURE 20.9   Displaying a Site Map from a Microsoft SQL database.

Generating a Google SiteMap File

Google provides a free service, named Google SiteMaps, that you can use to monitor and improve the way that Google indexes the pages on your website. For example, you can use Google SiteMaps to discover which Google search queries have returned pages from your website and the ranking of your pages in Google search results. You also can use Google SiteMaps to view any problems that the Google crawler encounters when indexing your site.

You can sign up for Google SiteMaps by visiting the following URL:

`http://www.google.com/webmasters/sitemaps`

To use Google SiteMaps, you must provide Google with the URL of a Google SiteMap file hosted on your website. The Google SiteMap file is an XML file that contains a list of URLs you want Google to index.

The Google SiteMap XML file has the following format:

```
<urlset xmlns="http://www.google.com/schemas/sitemap/0.84">
  <url>
    <loc>http://www.example.com/</loc>
    <lastmod>2005-01-01</lastmod>
  </url>
  <url>
    <loc>http://www.example.com/sample.html/</loc>
    <lastmod>2006-03-11</lastmod>
  </url>
</urlset>
```

The Google SiteMap file contains a simple list of `<url>` elements that contain `<loc>` elements representing the location of the URL and `<lastmod>` elements representing the last modified date of the URL.

> **NOTE**
>
> The Google SiteMap file also can contain `<changefreq>` and `<priority>` elements. The `<changefreq>` element indicates how frequently a URL changes, and the `<priority>` element represents the priority of a URL relative to other URLs in your site. These elements are optional and are ignored here.

You can generate a Google SiteMap file automatically from an ASP.NET SiteMap. The HTTP Handler in Listing 20.20 generates a Google SiteMap that conforms to Google's requirements for a valid SiteMap file.

LISTING 20.20   PublicSiteMap.ashx

```csharp
<%@ WebHandler Language="C#" Class="PublicSiteMap" %>
using System;
using System.Web;
using System.Xml;
using System.Text;
using System.IO;

public class PublicSiteMap : IHttpHandler {

    private XmlWriter _xmlWriter;

    public void ProcessRequest (HttpContext context) {
        context.Response.ContentType = "text/xml";

        XmlWriterSettings settings = new XmlWriterSettings();
```

LISTING 20.20   Continued

```
        settings.Encoding = Encoding.UTF8;
        settings.Indent = true;
        _xmlWriter = XmlWriter.Create(context.Response.OutputStream,settings);
        _xmlWriter.WriteStartDocument();
        _xmlWriter.WriteStartElement("urlset","http://www.google.com/
        ➥schemas/sitemap/0.84");

        // Add root node
        AddUrl(SiteMap.RootNode);

        // Add all other nodes
        SiteMapNodeCollection nodes = SiteMap.RootNode.GetAllNodes();
        foreach (SiteMapNode node in nodes)
            AddUrl(node);

        _xmlWriter.WriteEndElement();
        _xmlWriter.WriteEndDocument();
        _xmlWriter.Flush();
    }

    private void AddUrl(SiteMapNode node)
    {
        // Skip empty Urls
        if (String.IsNullOrEmpty(node.Url))
            return;
        // Skip remote nodes
        if (node.Url.StartsWith("http", true, null))
            return;
        // Open url tag
        _xmlWriter.WriteStartElement("url");
        // Write location
        _xmlWriter.WriteStartElement("loc");
        _xmlWriter.WriteString(GetFullUrl(node.Url));
        _xmlWriter.WriteEndElement();
        // Write last modified
        _xmlWriter.WriteStartElement("lastmod");
        _xmlWriter.WriteString(GetLastModified(node.Url));
        _xmlWriter.WriteEndElement();
        // Close url tag
        _xmlWriter.WriteEndElement();
    }
```

```
    private string GetFullUrl(string url)
    {
        HttpContext context = HttpContext.Current;
        string server = context.Request.Url.GetComponents(UriComponents.
        ➥SchemeAndServer,UriFormat.UriEscaped);
        return Combine(server, url);
    }

    private string Combine(string baseUrl, string url)
    {
        baseUrl = baseUrl.TrimEnd(new char[] {'/'});
        url = url.TrimStart(new char[] { '/' });
        return baseUrl + "/" + url;
    }

    private string GetLastModified(string url)
    {
        HttpContext context = HttpContext.Current;
        string physicalPath = context.Server.MapPath(url);
        return File.GetLastWriteTimeUtc(physicalPath).ToString("s") + "Z";
    }

    public bool IsReusable {
        get {
            return true;
        }
    }
}
```

The HTTP Handler in Listing 20.20 generates an XML file by iterating through each of the nodes in an ASP.NET Site Map. The XML file is created with the help of the `XmlWriter` class. This class is used to generate each of the XML tags.

NOTE

You can think of an HTTP Handler is a lightweight ASP.NET page. You learn about HTTP Handlers in Chapter 27, "Working with the HTTP Runtime."

20

The file in Listing 20.21 contains the XML file returned by the `PublicSiteMap.ashx` handler when the Handler is called from the sample application contained on the CD that accompanies this book. (The file has been abridged for reasons of space.)

LISTING 20.21   PublicSiteMap.ashx Results

```
<urlset xmlns="http://www.google.com/schemas/sitemap/0.84">
  <url>
    <loc>http://localhost:2905/SiteMaps/Default.aspx</loc>
    <lastmod>2005-10-30T03:13:58Z</lastmod>
  </url>
  <url>
    <loc>http://localhost:2905/SiteMaps/Products/Default.aspx</loc>
    <lastmod>2005-10-28T21:48:04Z</lastmod>
  </url>
  <url>
    <loc>http://localhost:2905/SiteMaps/Services</loc>
    <lastmod>2005-10-30T04:31:57Z</lastmod>
  </url>
  <url>
    <loc>http://localhost:2905/SiteMaps/Employees/Default.aspx</loc>
    <lastmod>1601-01-01T00:00:00Z</lastmod>
  </url>
  <url>
    <loc>http://localhost:2905/SiteMaps/Products/FirstProduct.aspx</loc>
    <lastmod>2005-10-30T03:43:52Z</lastmod>
  </url>
</urlset>
```

When you sign up at the Google SiteMaps website, submit the URL of the PublicSiteMap.ashx file when you are asked to enter your SiteMap URL. The Google service retrieves your SiteMap from the handler automatically.

Summary

In this chapter, you learned how to work with Site Maps. The first section discussed the SiteMapDataSource control. You learned how to declaratively represent different sets of nodes in a Site Map with this control.

Next, the SiteMap and SiteMapNode classes were examined. You learned how to create new Site Map nodes dynamically by handling the SiteMapResolve event. You also learned how to programmatically retrieve the current Site Map node in a page.

The next section discussed several advanced features of Site Maps. You learned how to display different Site Map nodes to different users depending on their roles. You also learned how to merge SiteMap files located in different subfolders. Finally, you learned how to extend Site Maps with custom attributes.

We also built two custom Site Map providers. We created an `AutoSiteMapProvider` that automatically builds a Site Map that reflects the folder and page structure of a website. We also created a `SqlSiteMapProvider` that stores a Site Map in a Microsoft SQL Server database table.

Finally, you learned how to use ASP.NET Site Maps with Google SiteMaps. In the final section of this chapter, you learned how to create a custom HTTP Handler that converts an ASP.NET Site Map into a Google SiteMap so that you can improve the way that Google indexes your website's pages.

20

CHAPTER 21

Advanced Navigation

Websites tend to be organic—they grow and change over time. This can create problems when other applications link to your application. You need some way of modifying your website without breaking all the existing links to it.

In this chapter, you learn how to remap URLs. In other words, you learn how to serve a different page than the page a user requests. In the first section of the chapter, you learn how to remap URLs in the web configuration file.

Next, you learn how to remap URLs by creating a custom HTTP module. Using a module is useful when you need to support wildcard matches and other types of pattern matching when remapping a URL.

Finally, you learn how to use the VirtualPathProvider class to remap URLs. You learn how you can store all your website pages in a database. In the last section of this chapter, a simple Content Management System (CMS) is built with the VirtualPathProvider class.

Remapping URLs

The simplest way to remap a URL is to specify the remapping in your application's web configuration file. For example, the web configuration file in Listing 21.1 remaps the Home.aspx page to the Default.aspx page.

LISTING 21.1 Web.Config

```
<configuration>
<system.web>
  <urlMappings>
```

LISTING 22.1   Continued

```
    <add
      url="~/Home.aspx"
      mappedUrl="~/Default.aspx"/>
  </urlMappings>
</system.web>
</configuration>
```

The configuration file in Listing 21.1 contains a `<urlMappings>` element. This element can contain one or more elements that remap a page from a URL to a mapped Url.

CD NOTE

The code samples in this section can be found in the `UrlMappingsApp` application on the CD that accompanies this book.

The `mappedUrl` attribute can contain query strings. However, it cannot contain wildcards. You can use the `<urlMappings>` element only when performing simple page-to-page mappings.

After you add the web configuration file in Listing 21.1 to your application, any requests for the `Home.aspx` page are modified automatically to requests for the `Default.aspx` page. It doesn't matter whether the `Home.aspx` page actually exists. If the `Home.aspx` page does exist, you can never open the page.

NOTE

The tilde character (~) has a special meaning when used with a path. It represents the current application root. A forward slash (/) at the start of a URL, on the other hand, represents the website root.

You can use the tilde only with properties of ASP.NET controls. For example, you can use it with the ASP.NET Image control's `ImageUrl` property, but you cannot use it with the HTML `<img>` src attribute.

In code, you can use the tilde character with a path by using the `Page.ResolveUrl()` method. This method automatically expands the tilde to the application root.

When working with remapped URLs, you often need to determine the original URL that a user requested. For example, you might want to display a message that tells users to update their bookmarks (favorites) to point to the new URL.

You can use the following to determine the current URL:

▶ **Request.RawUrl**—Returns the original URL (before being remapped).

▶ **Request.Path**—Returns the current URL (after being remapped).

► **Request.AppRelativeCurrentExecutionFilePath**—Returns the application relative URL (after being remapped).

The last property automatically replaces the name of the web application with a tilde (~) character.

For example, the `Default.aspx` page in Listing 21.2 illustrates all three properties.

LISTING 21.2   Default.aspx

```
<%@ Page Language="C#" %>
<!DOCTYPE html PUBLIC "-//W3C//DTD XHTML 1.1//EN"
"http://www.w3.org/TR/xhtml11/DTD/xhtml11.dtd">
<script runat="server">

    void Page_Load()
    {
        if (String.Compare(Request.Path, Request.RawUrl, true) != 0)
            lblMessage.Text = "The URL to this page has changed, " +
                "please update your bookmarks.";
    }

</script>
<html xmlns="http://www.w3.org/1999/xhtml" >
<head runat="server">
    <style type="text/css">
        html
        {
            font:14px Georgia,Serif;
        }
        .message
        {
            border:Dotted 2px red;
            background-color:yellow;
        }
    </style>
    <title>Default Page</title>
</head>
<body>
    <form id="form1" runat="server">
    <div>

    <h1>The Default Page</h1>

    <p>
    <asp:Label
        id="lblMessage"
```

LISTING 21.2   Continued

```
        CssClass="message"
        Runat="server" />
    </p>

    The original request was for:
    <blockquote>
        <%=Request.RawUrl%>
    </blockquote>
    which got remapped to:
    <blockquote>
        <%= Request.Path %>
    </blockquote>
    and the application relative version is:
    <blockquote>
        <%= Request.AppRelativeCurrentExecutionFilePath %>
    </blockquote>

    </div>
    </form>
</body>
</html>
```

If you request the Home.aspx page, the request is remapped to the Default.aspx page by the web configuration file in Listing 21.1. The Page_Load() event handler displays a message asking users to update their bookmarks when the RawUrl does not match the path (see Figure 21.1).

Each property displayed in the body of the page displays a different value:

```
Request.RawUrl = /UrlMappingsApp/Home.aspx
Request.Path = /UrlMappingsApp/Default.aspx
Request.AppRelativeCurrentExecutionFilePath = ~/Default.aspx
```

Creating a Custom UrlRemapper Module

The <urlMappings> configuration element discussed in the previous section performs a very simple task. It remaps one page to another. However, you'll quickly discover that you need to perform more complex remappings.

For example, imagine that you have a database that contains a table of product categories and a table of products. You want your website's users to request a URL that contains a product category and be able to see matching products. For example, if someone requests the /Products/Soda.aspx page, you want to display all the products in the Soda category. If someone requests the /Products/Milk.aspx page, you want to display all the products in the Milk category.

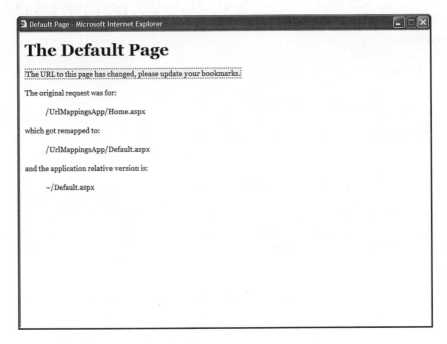

FIGURE 21.1   Remapping the Home page.

In that case, you need to use a wildcard when matching URLs. When someone requests any path that matches the pattern /Products/*, you want to redirect the user to a page where you can display matching products for the category specified in the path.

In this section, we create a custom HTTP module that remaps one URL to another. The module supports regular expression matching. Therefore it supports wildcard matches.

CD NOTE

The code samples in this section are located in the UrlRemapperApp application on the CD that accompanies this book.

The code for the custom module—named UrlRemapper—is contained in Listing 21.3.

LISTING 21.3   UrlRemapper.cs

```
using System;
using System.Web;
using System.Xml;
using System.Web.Caching;
using System.Text.RegularExpressions;
```

LISTING 21.3   Continued

```
namespace AspNetUnleashed
{
    public class UrlRemapper : IHttpModule
    {
        public void Init(HttpApplication app)
        {
            app.BeginRequest += new EventHandler(app_BeginRequest);
        }

        public void app_BeginRequest(Object s, EventArgs e)
        {
            // Get HTTP Context
            HttpApplication app = (HttpApplication)s;
            HttpContext context = app.Context;

            // Get current URL
            string currentUrl = context.Request.AppRelativeCurrentExecutionFilePath;

            // Get URL Mappings
            XmlDocument urlMappings = GetUrlMappings(context);

            // Compare current URL against each URL from mappings file
            XmlNodeList nodes = urlMappings.SelectNodes("//add");
            foreach (XmlNode node in nodes)
            {
                string url = node.Attributes["url"].Value;
                string mappedUrl = node.Attributes["mappedUrl"].Value;
                if (Regex.Match(currentUrl, url, RegexOptions.IgnoreCase).Success)
                    context.RewritePath(mappedUrl);
            }
        }

        private XmlDocument GetUrlMappings(HttpContext context)
        {
            XmlDocument urlMappings = (XmlDocument)context.Cache["UrlMappings"];
            if (urlMappings == null)
            {
                urlMappings = new XmlDocument();
                string path = context.Server.MapPath("~/UrlMappings.config");
                urlMappings.Load(path);
                CacheDependency fileDepend = new CacheDependency(path);
                context.Cache.Insert("UrlMappings", urlMappings, fileDepend);
```

```
        }
        return urlMappings;
    }

    public void Dispose() { }

    }
}
```

Notice that the class in Listing 21.3 implements the `IHttpModule` interface. An HTTP module is a special class that executes whenever you make a page request. HTTP Modules are discussed in detail in Chapter 27, "Working with the HTTP Runtime."

The module in Listing 21.3 includes an `Init()` method. This method adds an event handler for the Application `BeginRequest` event. The `BeginRequest` event is the first event that is raised when you request a page.

The `BeginRequest` handler gets a list of URL remappings from an XML file named `UrlMappings.config`. The contents of this XML file are cached in memory until the `UrlMappings.config` file is changed on the hard drive.

Next, the module iterates through each remapping from the XML file and performs a regular expression match against the current URL. If the match is successful, then the `Context.RewritePath()` method is used to change the current path to the remapped path.

Before you can use the module in Listing 21.3 in an application, you must first register the module in your application's web configuration file. The web configuration file in Listing 21.4 contains an `<httpModules>` element that includes the `UrlRemapper` module.

LISTING 21.4   Web.Config

```
<configuration xmlns="http://schemas.microsoft.com/.NetConfiguration/v2.0">
<system.web>

  <httpModules>
    <add
      name="UrlRemapper"
      type="AspNetUnleashed.UrlRemapper" />
  </httpModules>

</system.web>
</configuration>
```

A sample `UrlMappings.config` file is contained in Listing 21.5.

LISTING 21.5   `UrlMappings.config`

```
<urlMappings>
  <add
    url="~/Home.aspx"
    mappedUrl="~/Default.aspx" />
  <add
    url="/Products/.*"
    mappedUrl="~/Products/Default.aspx" />
</urlMappings>
```

The XML file in Listing 21.5 contains two remappings. First, it remaps any request for the `Home.aspx` page to the `Default.aspx` page. Second, it remaps any request for any page in the Products directory to the `Default.aspx` page located in the Products folder.

The second mapping uses a regular expression to match the incoming URL. The `.*` expression matches any sequence of characters.

The `Default.aspx` page in the Products folder is contained in Listing 21.6.

LISTING 21.6   `Products/Default.aspx`

```
<%@ Page Language="C#" %>
<%@ Import Namespace="System.IO" %>
<!DOCTYPE html PUBLIC "-//W3C//DTD XHTML 1.1//EN"
"http://www.w3.org/TR/xhtml11/DTD/xhtml11.dtd">
<script runat="server">

    void Page_Load()
    {
        if (!Page.IsPostBack)
        {
            string category = Path.GetFileNameWithoutExtension(Request.RawUrl);
            ltlCategory.Text = category;
            srcProducts.SelectParameters["Category"].DefaultValue = category;
        }
    }
</script>
<html xmlns="http://www.w3.org/1999/xhtml" >
<head id="Head1" runat="server">
    <style type="text/css">
        .grid td,.grid th
        {
            padding:4px;
            border-bottom:solid 1px black;
        }
    </style>
    <title>Products</title>
```

21

```
    </head>
    <body>
        <form id="form1" runat="server">
        <div>

        <h1>
        <asp:Literal
            ID="ltlCategory"
            runat="server" />
        </h1>

        <asp:GridView
            id="grdProducts"
            DataSourceID="srcProducts"
            CssClass="grid"
            GridLines="None"
            AutoGenerateColumns="false"
            Runat="server">
            <Columns>
            <asp:BoundField
                HeaderText="Product Name"
                DataField="Name" />
            <asp:BoundField
                HeaderText="Price"
                DataField="Price"
                DataFormatString="{0:c}" />
            </Columns>
        </asp:GridView>


        <asp:SqlDataSource
            id="srcProducts"
            ConnectionString="<%$ ConnectionStrings:Products %>"
            SelectCommand="SELECT Products.* FROM Products
                JOIN Categories ON Products.CategoryId=Categories.Id
                WHERE Categories.Name=@Category"
            Runat="server">
            <SelectParameters>
            <asp:Parameter Name="Category" />
            </SelectParameters>
        </asp:SqlDataSource>


        </div>
        </form>
    </body>
    </html>
```

The Page_Load() event handler in Listing 21.6 grabs the path of the original request, using the Request.RawUrl property. Next, it extracts the filename from the path, using the System.IO.Path.GetFileNameWithoutExtension() method. Finally, it assigns the name of the page (the category name) to a Label and SqlDataSource control. Products that match the category are displayed in a GridView control.

For example, if you request the /Products/Soda.aspx page, then all the products in the Soda category are displayed (see Figure 21.2). If you request the /Products/Milk.aspx page, then all products in the Milk category are displayed.

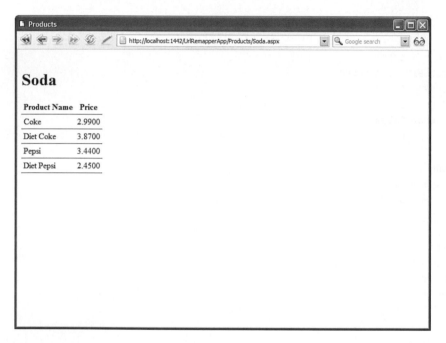

FIGURE 21.2   Displaying matching products.

Using the VirtualPathProvider Class

The VirtualPathProvider class enables you to abstract the pages in a web application from the file system. In other words, it enables you to store your ASP.NET pages any way you please.

For example, you can use the VirtualPathProvider class to store all the pages in your application in a database. This would be an appropriate choice when you need to build a CMS. If you store pages in a database, then users can update the pages easily in an application through an HTML form interface and save the changes to the database.

In this section, you learn how to store the pages in an ASP.NET application in a Microsoft SQL Server 2005 Express database. But first, it's a good idea to examine the classes related to the VirtualPathProvider class in more detail.

Limitations of the `VirtualPathProvider` Class

Unfortunately, you can't use the VirtualPathProvider with every type of file. In particular, the following types of files must always be located on the file system:

▶ Global.asax file

▶ Web.Config files

▶ App_Data folder

▶ App_Code folder

▶ App_GlobalResources folder

▶ App_LocalResource folders

▶ Bin folder

Every other type of file is fair game. This includes ASP.NET pages, User Controls, Themes, and Master Pages.

Understanding the `VirtualPathProvider` Class

The VirtualPathProvider class is a MustInherit (abstract) class. It contains the following methods, which you can override:

▶ **CombineVirtualPaths()**—Returns a combined path from two paths.

▶ **DirectoryExists()**—Returns true when a directory exists.

▶ **FileExists()**—Returns true when a file exists.

▶ **GetCacheDependency()**—Returns a cache dependency object that indicates when a file has been changed.

▶ **GetCacheKey()**—Returns the key used by the cache dependency.

▶ **GetDirectory()**—Returns a VirtualDirectory.

- ► **GetFile()**—Returns a VirtualFile.

- ► **GetFileHash()**—Returns a hash of the files used by the cache dependency.

- ► **OpenFile()**—Returns the contents of a file.

Typically, you override the FileExists() and GetFile() methods to retrieve a file from your data store. If you want to represent directories, then you also need to override the DirectoryExists() and GetDirectory() methods.

Notice that several of these methods are related to caching. VirtualPathProvider needs to know when a file has been modified so that it can retrieve the new version of the file and compile it. By default, the ASP.NET Framework uses a file dependency to determine when a file has been modified on the hard drive. However, in this situation a SqlCacheDependency is used because the files will be stored in a database.

VirtualPathProvider also includes a very useful property:

- ► **Previous**—Returns the previously registered VirtualPathProvider.

The Previous property enables you to use the default VirtualPathProvider. For example, if you want to store some files in the file system and other files in the database, then you can use the Previous property to avoid rewriting all of the logic for working with files in the file system.

The GetFile() method returns an instance of the VirtualFile class. When using the VirtualPathProvider, you must create a new class that inherits from the VirtualFile class. This class contains the following properties:

- ► **IsDirectory**—Always returns False.

- ► **Name**—Returns the name of the file.

- ► **VirtualPath**—Returns the virtual path of the file.

The VirtualFile class also contains the following method:

- ► **Open()**—Returns the contents of the file.

Typically, when creating a class that inherits from the VirtualFile class, you override the Open() method. For example, we'll override this method to get the contents of a file from a database table in the code sample built in this section.

The GetDirectory() method returns an instance of the VirtualDirectory class. This class contains the following properties:

- ► **Children**—Returns all the files and directories that are children of the current directory.

- ► **Directories**—Returns all the directories that are children of the current directory.

- ► **Files**—Returns all the files that are children of the current directory.

- ► **IsDirectory**—Always returns True.

▶ **Name**—Returns the name of the directory.

▶ **VirtualPath**—Returns the virtual path of the directory.

There is another class in the ASP.NET Framework that you'll want to use when working with the VirtualPathProvider class. The VirtualPathUtility class contains several useful methods for working with virtual paths:

▶ **AppendTrailingSlash()**—Returns a path with at most one forward slash appended to the end of the path.

▶ **Combine()**—Returns the combination of two virtual paths.

▶ **GetDirectory()**—Returns the directory portion of a path.

▶ **GetExtension()**—Returns the file extension of a path.

▶ **GetFileName()**—Returns the file name from a path.

▶ **IsAbsolute()**—Returns True when a path starts with a forward slash.

▶ **IsAppRelative()**—Returns True when a path starts with a tilde (~).

▶ **MakeRelative()**—Returns a relative path from an application-relative path.

▶ **RemoveTrailingSlash()**—Removes trailing slash from the end of a path.

▶ **ToAbsolute()**—Returns a path that starts with a forward slash.

▶ **ToAppRelative()**—Returns a path that starts with a tilde (~).

By taking advantage of the VirtualPathUtility class, you can avoid doing a lot of tedious string parsing on paths.

Registering a VirtualPathProvider Class

Before you can use an instance of the VirtualPathProvider class, you must register it for your application. You can register a VirtualPathProvider instance with the HostingEnvironment.RegisterVirtualPathProvider() method.

You need to register VirtualPathProvider when an application first initializes. You can do this by creating a shared method named AppInitialize() and adding the method to any class contained in the App_Code folder. The AppInitialize() method is automatically called by the ASP.NET Framework when an application starts.

For example, the following AppInitialize method registers a VirtualPathProvider named MyVirtualPathProvider:

```
public static void AppInitialize()
{
  MyVirtualPathProvider myProvider = new MyVirtualPathProvider();
  HostingEnvironment.RegisterVirtualPathProvider(myProvider);
}
```

In our `VirtualPathProvider` application, we'll include the `AppInitialize()` method in the `VirtualPathProvider` class itself.

Storing a Website in Microsoft SQL Server

In this section, we'll create a `VirtualPathProvider` that stores files and directories in two Microsoft SQL Server database tables named `VirtualFiles` and `VirtualDirectories`. The VirtualFiles table looks like this:

Path	Name	Content
~/	Test.aspx	The time is now `<%= DateTime.Now.ToString() %>`
~/Products/	FirstProduct.aspx	The first product
~/Products/	SecondProduct.aspx	The second product

The Path column represents the directory that contains the file. The Name column contains the name of the file. Finally, the Content column contains the actual file content.

Notice that the file can contain scripts. The `Test.aspx` page displays the current date and time. You can place anything that you would place in a normal ASP.NET page, including ASP.NET controls, in the Content column.

The `VirtualDirectories` table looks like this:

Path	ParentPath
~/	NULL
~/Products	~/

The Path column represents the entire directory path. The ParentPath column represents the entire directory path of the directory that contains the directory.

The `VirtualPathProvider` class in Listing 21.7—named `SqlVirtualPathProvider`—uses both database tables.

LISTING 21.7   SqlVirtualPathProvider.cs

```
using System;
using System.Web;
using System.Web.Caching;
using System.Collections;
using System.Collections.Generic;
using System.Web.Hosting;

namespace AspNetUnleashed
{
```

```
public class SqlVirtualPathProvider : VirtualPathProvider
{
    /// <summary>
    /// Register VirtualPathProvider for the application
    /// </summary>
    public static void AppInitialize()
    {
        SqlVirtualPathProvider sqlProvider = new SqlVirtualPathProvider();
        HostingEnvironment.RegisterVirtualPathProvider(sqlProvider);
    }

    public SqlVirtualPathProvider() : base() { }

    /// <summary>
    /// Returns true when the file is a virtual file
    /// instead of a normal filesystem file
    /// </summary>
    private bool IsVirtualFile(string virtualPath)
    {
        String appVirtualPath = VirtualPathUtility.ToAppRelative(virtualPath);
        return !appVirtualPath.StartsWith("~/admin/",
        ➥StringComparison.InvariantCultureIgnoreCase);
    }

    /// <summary>
    /// Returns true when a file exists
    /// </summary>
    public override bool FileExists(string virtualPath)
    {
        if (IsVirtualFile(virtualPath))
            return VirtualFiles.FileExists(virtualPath);
        else
            return Previous.FileExists(virtualPath);
    }

    /// <summary>
    /// Gets a SqlVirtualFile which corresponds
    /// to a file with a certain path
    /// </summary>
    public override VirtualFile GetFile(string virtualPath)
    {
        if (IsVirtualFile(virtualPath))
            return new SqlVirtualFile(virtualPath);
        else
            return Previous.GetFile(virtualPath);
    }
```

LISTING 21.7   Continued

```
        /// <summary>
        /// Returns true when a directory exists
        /// </summary>
        public override bool DirectoryExists(string virtualPath)
        {
            if (IsVirtualFile(virtualPath))
                return VirtualFiles.DirectoryExists(virtualPath);
            else
                return Previous.DirectoryExists(virtualPath);
        }


        /// <summary>
        /// Returns a SqlVirtualDirectory which corresponds
        /// to a virtual path
        /// </summary>
        public override VirtualDirectory GetDirectory(string virtualPath)
        {
            if (IsVirtualFile(virtualPath))
                return new SqlVirtualDirectory(virtualPath);
            else
                return Previous.GetDirectory(virtualPath);
        }


        /// <summary>
        /// Gets the SqlCacheDependency object for the VirtualFilesDB
        /// database
        /// </summary>
        public override CacheDependency GetCacheDependency(string virtualPath,
        ➥IEnumerable virtualPathDependencies, DateTime utcStart)
        {
            if (IsVirtualFile(virtualPath))
                return new SqlCacheDependency("VirtualFiles", "VirtualFiles");
            else
                return Previous.GetCacheDependency(virtualPath,
                    ➥virtualPathDependencies, utcStart);
        }

    }
}
```

The class in Listing 21.7 overrides the FileExists(), GetFile(), DirectoryExists(), and GetDirectory() methods of the base VirtualPathProvider class.

The class also includes a private method named IsVirtualFile(). This method returns the value True when a file is not contained in the Admin folder. The Admin directory contains a normal file system file. You'll notice that each method, such as the `FileExists()` method, checks the `IsVirtualFile()` method. If the method returns `False`, the `Previous` property is used to pass the handling of the file to the file system.

The `SqlVirtualPathProvider` class also overrides the `GetCacheDependency()` method. This method returns a `SqlCacheDependency`. The SQL cache dependency is configured with the Web configuration file in Listing 21.8.

LISTING 21.8   Web.Config

```
<configuration xmlns="http://schemas.microsoft.com/.NetConfiguration/v2.0">
  <connectionStrings>
    <add
      name="VirtualFiles"
      connectionString="Data Source=.\SQLExpress;Integrated
  Security=True;AttachDbFileName=¦DataDirectory¦VirtualFilesDB.mdf;
  User Instance=True"/>
  </connectionStrings>
    <system.web>
      <caching>
        <sqlCacheDependency enabled="true">
          <databases>
            <add
              name="VirtualFiles"
              connectionStringName="VirtualFiles"
              pollTime="5000"/>
          </databases>
        </sqlCacheDependency>
      </caching>
    </system.web>
</configuration>
```

To use the SQL cache dependency, you must configure the SQL database to support the cache dependency. You can enable SQL cache dependencies for the VirtualFilesDB database and the two database tables contained in the database by executing the following two commands from a Command Prompt after navigating to the application's App_Data folder:

```
enableNotifications "VirtualFilesDB.mdf", "VirtualDirectories"
enableNotifications "VirtualFilesDB.mdf", "VirtualFiles"
```

> **NOTE**
>
> SQL cache dependencies are discussed in detail in Chapter 25, "Caching Application Pages and Data."

The `GetFile()` method in the `SqlVirtualPathProvider` class returns an instance of the `SqlVirtualFile` class. This class is contained in Listing 21.9.

LISTING 21.9   SqlVirtualFile.cs

```
using System;
using System.Data;
using System.Data.SqlClient;
using System.Web.Hosting;
using System.IO;
using System.Web;

namespace AspNetUnleashed
{
    /// <summary>
    /// Summary description for SqlVirtualFile
    /// </summary>
    public class SqlVirtualFile : VirtualFile
    {

        public SqlVirtualFile(string virtualPath)
            : base(virtualPath){}

        public override Stream Open()
        {
            // Get content from database
            string content = VirtualFiles.FileContentSelect(this.VirtualPath);

            // return results as stream
            MemoryStream mem = new MemoryStream();
            StreamWriter writer = new StreamWriter(mem);
            writer.Write(content);
            writer.Flush();
            mem.Seek(0, SeekOrigin.Begin);
            return mem;
        }

        public string Content
        {
            get
            {
                return VirtualFiles.FileContentSelect(this.VirtualPath);
            }
        }
    }
}
```

The SqlVirtualFile class overrides the Open() method of the base VirtualFile class. The Open() method grabs the contents of the file from the Content column of the VirtualFiles database table.

The GetDirectory() method returns an instance of the SqlVirtualDirectory class.

The SqlVirtualDirectory class overrides three properties of the base VirtualDirectory class: the Children, Directories, and Files properties. These properties return files and subfolders from the VirtualFiles and VirtualDirectories database tables.

The VirtualPathProvider classes use the VirtualFiles class to interact with the SQL database. The VirtualFiles class acts as the data access layer. The code for the VirtualFiles class is too long to contain in the body of this book. However, the complete source is included on the CD that accompanies this book.

The CD that accompanies this book includes an application named SqlVirtualPathProviderApp, which contains all the files discussed in this section. The application also includes an Admin folder with a Default.aspx page which enables you to add, edit, and delete virtual directories and files (see Figures 21.3 and 21.4). You can use this page to build an entire application that is stored in the database.

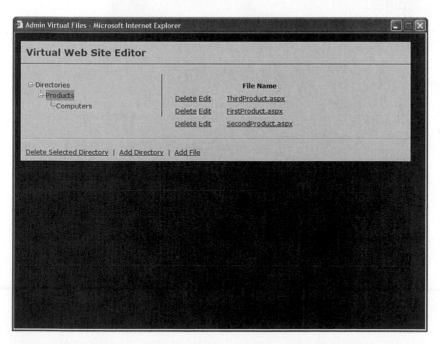

FIGURE 21.3   Listing virtual files in the virtual Products directory.

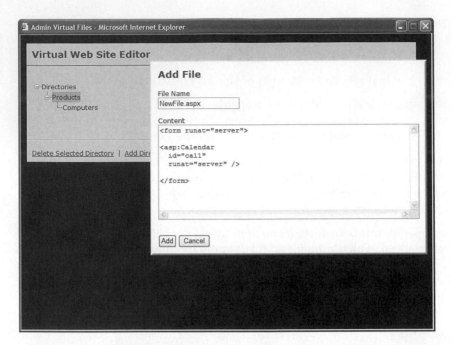

FIGURE 21.4   Adding a new virtual file.

Summary

This chapter explored several advanced topics related to website navigation. In the first two sections, you learned how to map URLs from one path to another. In the first section, you learned how to configure remappings in the Web configuration file. In the second section, you learned how to build a custom HTTP module, which enables you to use wildcard matches when remapping a URL.

In the final section of this chapter, you learned how to abstract pages in your application from the file system by using the VirtualPathProvider class. You saw the creation of an application that enables you to store application files in a Microsoft SQL Server database table.

PART VI
Security

IN THIS PART

Using the Login Controls

You can use the ASP.NET Login controls to easily build a user registration system for your website. You can use the Login controls to display user registration forms, login forms, change password forms, and password reminder forms.

By default, the Login controls use ASP.NET Membership to authenticate users, create new users, and change user properties. When you use the Login controls, you are not required to write any code when performing these tasks.

> **NOTE**
>
> ASP.NET Membership is discussed in detail in the following chapter.

In the first part of this chapter, you are provided with an overview of the Login controls. You learn how to password-protect a section of your website and enable users to register and log in to your website.

In the remainder of this chapter, you learn how to use each of the following Login controls in detail:

▶ **Login**—Enables you to display a user login form.

▶ **CreateUserWizard**—Enables you to display a user registration form.

▶ **LoginStatus**—Enables you to display either a log in or log out link, depending on a user's authentication status.

▶ **LoginName**—Enables you to display the current user's registered username.

▶ **ChangePassword**—Enables you to display a form that allows users to change their passwords.

▶ **PasswordRecovery**—Enables you to display a form that allows a user to receive an email containing his or her password.

▶ **LoginView**—Enables you to display different content to different users depending on the user's authentication status or role.

Overview of the Login Controls

You won't have any fun using the Login controls unless you have confidential information to protect. Therefore, let's start by creating a page that needs password protection.

Create a new folder in your application named SecretFiles and add the page in Listing 22.1 to the SecretFiles folder.

LISTING 22.1   SecretFiles\Secret.aspx

```
<%@ Page Language="C#" %>
<!DOCTYPE html PUBLIC "-//W3C//DTD XHTML 1.0 Transitional//EN"
  "http://www.w3.org/TR/xhtml1/DTD/xhtml1-transitional.dtd">
<html xmlns="http://www.w3.org/1999/xhtml" >
<head id="Head1" runat="server">
    <title>Secret</title>
</head>
<body>
    <form id="form1" runat="server">
    <div>

    <h1>This Page is Secret!</h1>

    </div>
    </form>
</body>
</html>
```

There is nothing special about the page in Listing 22.1. It just displays the message This Page is Secret!.

To password-protect the Secret.aspx page, you need to make two configuration changes to your application: You need to configure both authentication and authorization.

First, you need to enable the proper type of authentication for your application. By default, Windows authentication is enabled. To use the Login controls, you need enable

Forms authentication by adding the web configuration file in Listing 22.2 to the root of your application.

LISTING 22.2 `Web.Config`

```
<configuration>
  <system.web>
    <authentication mode="Forms" />
  </system.web>
</configuration>
```

The web configuration file in Listing 22.2 contains an authentication element that includes a mode attribute. The mode attribute has the value Forms.

NOTE

Authentication and authorization is discussed in more detail in Chapter 23, "Using ASP.NET Membership."

By default, all users have access to all pages in an application. If you want to restrict access to the pages in a folder, then you need to configure authorization for the folder.

If you add the web configuration file in Listing 22.3 to the SecretFiles folder, then anonymous users are prevented from accessing any pages in the folder.

LISTING 22.3 `SecretFiles\Web.Config`

```
<configuration>
  <system.web>
    <authorization>
      <deny users="?"/>
    </authorization>
  </system.web>
</configuration>
```

The web configuration file in Listing 22.3 contains an authorization element. This element contains a list of authorization rules for the folder. The single authorization rule in Listing 22.3 prevents anonymous users from accessing pages in the folder. (The ? represents anonymous users.)

VISUAL WEB DEVELOPER NOTE

If you prefer, you can use the Web Site Administration Tool to configure authentication and authorization. This tool provides you with a form interface for performing these configuration changes. When using Visual Web Developer, you can open the Web Site Administration Tool by selecting the menu option Website, ASP.NET Configuration.

22

If you attempt to request the Secret.aspx page after adding the web configuration file in Listing 22.3, then you are redirected to a page named Login.aspx automatically. Therefore, the next page that we need to create is the Login.aspx page. (By default, this page must be located in the root of your application.)

The Login.aspx page in Listing 22.4 contains a Login control. The Login control automatically generates a login form (see Figure 22.1).

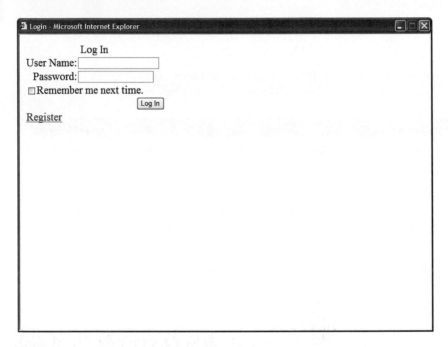

FIGURE 22.1   Displaying a Login form.

LISTING 22.4   Login.aspx

```
<%@ Page Language="C#" %>
<!DOCTYPE html PUBLIC "-//W3C//DTD XHTML 1.0 Transitional//EN"
  "http://www.w3.org/TR/xhtml1/DTD/xhtml1-transitional.dtd">
<html xmlns="http://www.w3.org/1999/xhtml" >
<head id="Head1" runat="server">
    <title>Login</title>
</head>
<body>
    <form id="form1" runat="server">
    <div>
```

```
    <asp:Login
        id="Login1"
        CreateUserText="Register"
        CreateUserUrl="~/Register.aspx"
        Runat="server" />

    </div>
    </form>
</body>
</html>
```

Notice that the `Login` control includes a `CreateUserText` and `CreateUserUrl` property. Adding these properties to the `Login` control causes the control to display a link to a page that enables a new user to register for your application. The `Login` control in Listing 22.4 links to a page named `Register.aspx`. This page is contained in Listing 22.5.

LISTING 22.5   `Register.aspx`

```
<%@ Page Language="C#" %>
<!DOCTYPE html PUBLIC "-//W3C//DTD XHTML 1.0 Transitional//EN"
   "http://www.w3.org/TR/xhtml1/DTD/xhtml1-transitional.dtd">
<html xmlns="http://www.w3.org/1999/xhtml" >
<head id="Head1" runat="server">
    <title>Register</title>
</head>
<body>
    <form id="form1" runat="server">
    <div>

    <asp:CreateUserWizard
        id="CreateUserWizard1"
        ContinueDestinationPageUrl="~/SecretFiles/Secret.aspx"
        Runat="server" />

    </div>
    </form>
</body>
</html>
```

The `Register.aspx` page contains a `CreateUserWizard` control. This control automatically generates a user registration form (see Figure 22.2). After you submit the form, a new user is created, and you are redirected back to the `Secret.aspx` page.

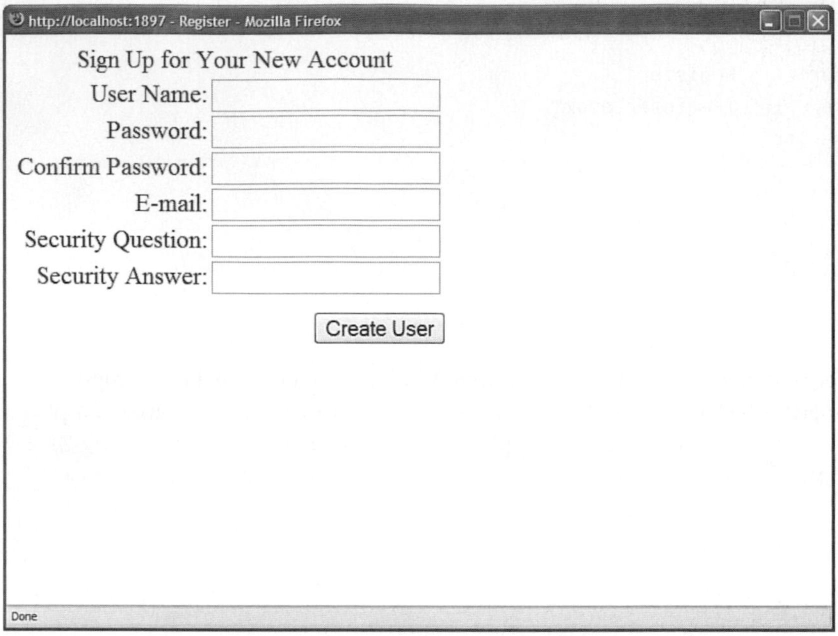

FIGURE 22.2   Displaying a registration form.

WARNING

The default ASP.NET Membership provider requires you to create a password that contains at least seven characters, and at least one of the characters must be nonalphanumeric (not a letter and not a number). So, secret_ is a valid password, but not secret9. In the next chapter, you learn how to change these default passwords requirements.

That's all there is to it. Notice that we have created a complete user registration system without writing a single line of code. All the messy details of storing usernames and passwords are taken care of by the ASP.NET Framework in the background.

Using the `Login` Control

The `Login` control renders a standard user login form. By default, the `Login` control uses ASP.NET Membership to authenticate users. However, as you'll see in a moment, you can customize how the `Login` control authenticates users.

The `Login` control supports a large number of properties that enable you to customize the appearance and behavior of the control (too many properties to list here). The page in Listing 22.6 illustrates how you can modify several of the `Login` control's properties to customize the form rendered by the control (see Figure 22.3).

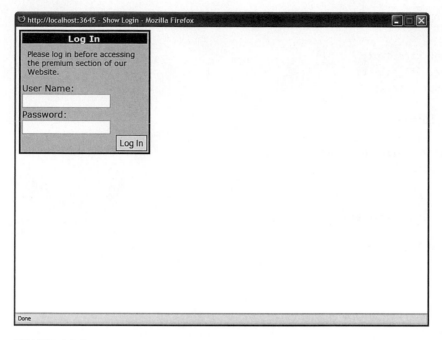

FIGURE 22.3   Customizing the Login form.

LISTING 22.6   ShowLogin.aspx

```
<%@ Page Language="C#" %>
<!DOCTYPE html PUBLIC "-//W3C//DTD XHTML 1.0 Transitional//EN"
   "http://www.w3.org/TR/xhtml1/DTD/xhtml1-transitional.dtd">
<html xmlns="http://www.w3.org/1999/xhtml" >
<head id="Head1" runat="server">
    <style type="text/css">
        .login
        {
            width:250px;
            font:14px Verdana,Sans-Serif;
            background-color:lightblue;
            border:solid 3px black;
            padding:4px;
        }
        .login_title
        {
            background-color:darkblue;
            color:white;
            font-weight:bold;
        }
        .login_instructions
```

LISTING 22.6   Continued

```
        {
            font-size:12px;
            text-align:left;
            padding:10px;
        }
        .login_button
        {
            border:solid 1px black;
            padding:3px;
        }
    </style>
    <title>Show Login</title>
</head>
<body>
    <form id="form1" runat="server">
    <div>

    <asp:Login
        id="Login1"
        InstructionText="Please log in before
            accessing the premium section of our Website."
        TitleText="Log In"
        TextLayout="TextOnTop"
        LoginButtonText="Log In"
        DisplayRememberMe="false"
        CssClass="login"
        TitleTextStyle-CssClass="login_title"
        InstructionTextStyle-CssClass="login_instructions"
        LoginButtonStyle-CssClass="login_button"
        Runat="server" />

    </div>
    </form>
</body>
</html>
```

The page in Listing 22.6 uses Cascading Style Sheets to change the appearance of the login form rendered by the Login control. By taking advantage of Cascading Style Sheets, you can customize the appearance of the Login control in any way that you can imagine.

> **NOTE**
>
> For the complete list of properties supported by the Login control, see the Microsoft .NET Framework SDK documentation.

Automatically Redirecting a User to the Referring Page

If you request a page that you are not authorized to view, then the ASP.NET Framework automatically redirects you to the Login.aspx page. After you log in successfully, you are redirected back to the original page that you requested.

When you are redirected to the Login.aspx page, a query string parameter named ReturnUrl is automatically added to the page request. This query string parameter contains the path of the page that you originally requested. The Login control uses the ReturnUrl parameter when redirecting you back to the original page.

You need to be aware of two special circumstances. First, if you request the Login.aspx page directly, then a ReturnUrl parameter is not passed to the Login.aspx page. In that case, after you successfully log in, you are redirected to the Default.aspx page.

Second, if you add the Login control to a page other than the Login.aspx page, then the ReturnUrl query string parameter is ignored. In this case, you need to set the Login control's DestinationPageUrl property. When you successfully log in, you are redirected to the URL represented by this property. If you don't supply a value for the DestinationPageUrl property, the same page is reloaded.

Automatically Hiding the Login Control from Authenticated Users

Some websites display a login form at the top of every page. That way, registered users can log in at any time to view additional content. The easiest way to add a Login control to all the pages in an application is to take advantage of Master Pages. If you add a Login control to a Master Page, then the Login control is included in every content page that uses the Master Page.

You can change the layout of the Login control by modifying the Login control's Orientation property. If you set this property to the value Horizontal, then the Username and Password text boxes are rendered in the same row.

If you include a Login control in all your pages, you should also modify the Login control's VisibleWhenLoggedIn property. If you set this property to the value False, then the Login control is not displayed when a user has already authenticated.

For example, the Master Page in Listing 22.7 contains a Login control that has both its Orientation and VisibleWhenLoggedIn properties set.

LISTING 22.7   LoginMaster.master

```
<%@ Master Language="C#" %>
<!DOCTYPE html PUBLIC "-//W3C//DTD XHTML 1.0 Transitional//EN"
  "http://www.w3.org/TR/xhtml1/DTD/xhtml1-transitional.dtd">
<html xmlns="http://www.w3.org/1999/xhtml" >
<head id="Head1" runat="server">
    <style type="text/css">
```

LISTING 22.7   Continued

```
        html
        {
            background-color:silver;
        }
        .content
        {
            margin:auto;
            width:650px;
            border:solid 1px black;
            background-color:white;
            padding:10px;
        }
        .login
        {
            font:10px Arial,Sans-Serif;
            margin-left:auto;
        }
        .login input
        {
            font:10px Arial,Sans-Serif;
        }
    </style>
    <title>My Website</title>
</head>
<body>
    <form id="form1" runat="server">
    <div class="content">
    <asp:Login
        id="Login1"
        Orientation="Horizontal"
        VisibleWhenLoggedIn="false"
        DisplayRememberMe="false"
        TitleText=""
        CssClass="login"
        Runat="server" />
        <hr />
        <asp:contentplaceholder
            id="ContentPlaceHolder1"
            runat="server">
        </asp:contentplaceholder>
    </div>
    </form>
</body>
</html>
```

The content page in Listing 22.8 uses the Master Page in Listing 22.7 (see Figure 22.4). When you open the page in a browser, the Login control is hidden after you successfully log in to the application.

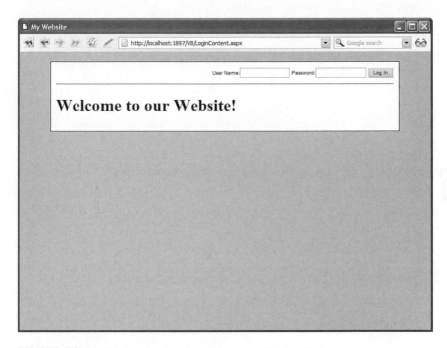

FIGURE 22.4   Adding the Login control to a Master Page.

LISTING 22.8   LoginContent.aspx

```
<%@ Page Language="C#" MasterPageFile="~/LoginMaster.master" %>
<asp:Content
    ID="Content1"
    ContentPlaceHolderID="ContentPlaceHolder1"
    Runat="Server">

    <h1>Welcome to our Website!</h1>

</asp:Content>
```

Using a Template with the Login Control

If you need to completely customize the appearance of the Login control, then you can use a template. The Login control includes a LayoutTemplate property that enables you to customize the layout of the controls rendered by the Login control.

When you create a Layout template, you can add controls to the template that have the following IDs:

▶ UserName

▶ Password

▶ RememberMe

▶ FailureText

You also need to add a Button control that includes a CommandName property with the value Login.

The page in Listing 22.9 illustrates how you can use a LayoutTemplate to customize the appearance of the Login control (see Figure 22.5).

FIGURE 22.5   Using a template with the Login control.

LISTING 22.9   LoginTemplate.aspx

```
<%@ Page Language="C#" %>
<!DOCTYPE html PUBLIC "-//W3C//DTD XHTML 1.0 Transitional//EN"
   "http://www.w3.org/TR/xhtml1/DTD/xhtml1-transitional.dtd">
<html xmlns="http://www.w3.org/1999/xhtml" >
<head id="Head1" runat="server">
    <style type="text/css">
        .loginError
        {
            color:red;
            font:bold 14px Arial,Sans-Serif;
        }
    </style>
    <title>Login Template</title>
</head>
<body>
    <form id="form1" runat="server">
    <div>

    <asp:Login
        id="Login1"
        Runat="server">
        <LayoutTemplate>
        <asp:Label
            id="FailureText"
            EnableViewState="false"
            CssClass="loginError"
            Runat="server" />

        <br />
        <asp:Label
            id="lblUserName"
            AssociatedControlID="UserName"
            Text="User Name:"
            Runat="server" />
        <br />
        <asp:TextBox
            id="UserName"
            Runat="server" />

        <br /><br />
        <asp:Label
            id="lblPassword"
            AssociatedControlID="Password"
            Text="Password:"
```

LISTING 22.9   Continued

```
            Runat="server" />
        <br />
        <asp:TextBox
            id="Password"
            TextMode="Password"
            Runat="server" />

        <br /><br />
        <asp:Button
            id="btnLogin"
            Text="Login"
            CommandName="Login"
            Runat="server" />
        </LayoutTemplate>
    </asp:Login>

    </div>
    </form>
</body>
</html>
```

WEB STANDARDS NOTE

The Login control renders an HTML table for layout even when you use a
LayoutTemplate.

Performing Custom Authentication with the Login Control

By default, the Login control uses ASP.NET Membership to authenticate a username and
password. If you need to change this default behavior, then you can handle the Login
control's Authenticate event.

Imagine, for example, that you are building a simple application and you want to store a
list of usernames and passwords in the web configuration file. The web configuration file
in Listing 22.10 contains the credentials for two users named Bill and Ted.

LISTING 22.10   Web.Config

```
<configuration>
  <system.web>
    <authentication mode="Forms">
      <forms>
        <credentials passwordFormat="Clear">
```

```
                <user name="Bill" password="secret" />
                <user name="Ted" password="secret" />
            </credentials>
          </forms>
        </authentication>
      </system.web>
</configuration>
```

The page in Listing 22.11 contains a Login control that authenticates users against the list of usernames and passwords stored in the web configuration file.

LISTING 22.11   LoginCustom.aspx

```
<%@ Page Language="C#" %>
<!DOCTYPE html PUBLIC "-//W3C//DTD XHTML 1.0 Transitional//EN"
"http://www.w3.org/TR/xhtml1/DTD/xhtml1-transitional.dtd">
<script runat="server">
    protected void Login1_Authenticate(object sender, AuthenticateEventArgs e)
    {
        string userName = Login1.UserName;
        string password = Login1.Password;
        e.Authenticated = FormsAuthentication.Authenticate(userName, password);
    }
</script>
<html xmlns="http://www.w3.org/1999/xhtml" >
<head id="Head1" runat="server">
    <title>Login Custom</title>
</head>
<body>
    <form id="form1" runat="server">
    <div>

    <asp:Login
        id="Login1"
        OnAuthenticate="Login1_Authenticate"
        Runat="server" />

    </div>
    </form>
</body>
</html>
```

Notice that the page in Listing 22.11 includes a method that handles the Login control's Authenticate event. The second parameter passed to the Authenticate event handler is an instance of the `AuthenticateEventArgs` class. This class includes the following property:

▶ Authenticated

If you assign the value `True` to this property, then the `Login` control authenticates the user.

In Listing 22.11, the `FormsAuthentication.Authenticate()` method is called to check for a username and password in the web configuration file that matches the username and password entered into the login form. The value returned from this method is assigned to the `AuthenticateEventArgs.Authenticated` property.

Using the `CreateUserWizard` Control

The `CreateUserWizard` control renders a user registration form. If a user successfully submits the form, then a new user is added to your website. In the background, the `CreateUserWizard` control uses ASP.NET membership to create the new user.

The `CreateUserWizard` control supports a large number of properties (too many to list here) that enables you to modify the appearance and behavior of the control. For example, the page in Listing 22.12 uses several of the `CreateUserWizard` properties to customize the appearance of the form rendered by the control.

LISTING 22.12   ShowCreateUserWizard.aspx

```
<%@ Page Language="C#" %>
<!DOCTYPE html PUBLIC "-//W3C//DTD XHTML 1.0 Transitional//EN"
  "http://www.w3.org/TR/xhtml1/DTD/xhtml1-transitional.dtd">
<html xmlns="http://www.w3.org/1999/xhtml" >
<head id="Head1" runat="server">
    <style type="text/css">
        .createUser
        {
            width:350px;
            font:14px Verdana,Sans-Serif;
            background-color:lightblue;
            border:solid 3px black;
            padding:4px;
        }
        .createUser_title
        {
            background-color:darkblue;
            color:white;
            font-weight:bold;
```

```
        }
        .createUser_instructions
        {
            font-size:12px;
            text-align:left;
            padding:10px;
        }
        .createUser_button
        {
            border:solid 1px black;
            padding:3px;
        }
    </style>
    <title>Show CreateUserWizard</title>
</head>
<body>
    <form id="form1" runat="server">
    <div>

    <asp:CreateUserWizard
        id="CreateUserWizard1"
        ContinueDestinationPageUrl="~/Default.aspx"
        InstructionText="Please complete the following form
            to register at this Website."
        CompleteSuccessText="Your new account has been
            created. Thank you for registering."
        CssClass="createUser"
        TitleTextStyle-CssClass="createUser_title"
        InstructionTextStyle-CssClass="createUser_instructions"
        CreateUserButtonStyle-CssClass="createUser_button"
        ContinueButtonStyle-CssClass="createUser_button"
        Runat="server" />


    </div>
    </form>
</body>
</html>
```

The CreateUserWizard control in Listing 22.12 is formatted with Cascading Style Sheets (see Figure 22.6). Notice that the control's ContinueDestinationPageUrl property is set to the value "~/Default.aspx". After you successfully register, you are redirected to the Default.aspx page.

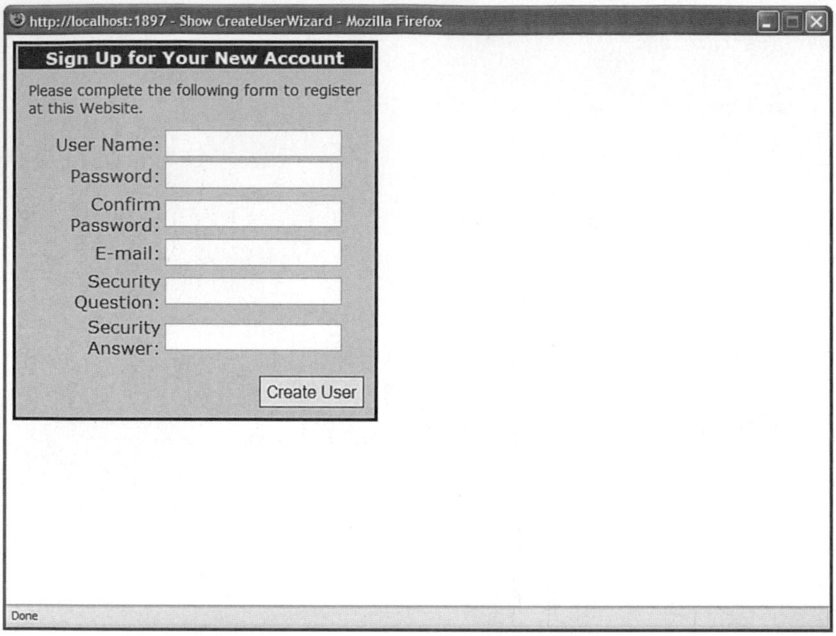

FIGURE 22.6   Formatting the `CreateUserWizard` control.

> **NOTE**
>
> For the complete list of properties supported by the `CreateUserWizard` control, see the Microsoft .NET Framework SDK documentation.

Configuring Create User Form Fields

By default, the `CreateUserWizard` control displays the following form fields:

▶ Username

▶ Password

▶ Confirm Password

▶ Email

▶ Security Question

▶ Security Answer

These are the default form fields. The last three fields are optional.

If you don't want to require a user to enter either an email address or a security question and answer, then you need to modify the configuration of the default membership provider. The web configuration file in Listing 22.13 makes both an email address and security question and answer optional.

LISTING 22.13 Web.Config

```
<configuration>
  <system.web>

    <authentication mode="Forms" />

    <membership defaultProvider="MyMembership">
      <providers>
        <add
          name="MyMembership"
          type="System.Web.Security.SqlMembershipProvider"
          connectionStringName="LocalSqlServer"
          requiresQuestionAndAnswer="false"
          requiresUniqueEmail="false" />
      </providers>
    </membership>

  </system.web>
</configuration>
```

If you add the web configuration file in Listing 22.13 to your application, then the CreateUserWizard control does not render fields for a security question and answer. However, the CreateUserWizard control still renders an email field. If you don't want the email form field to be rendered, then you must perform an additional step. You must set the CreateUserWizard control's RequireEmail property to the value False.

If you add the page in Listing 22.14 to an application that contains the web configuration file in Listing 22.13, then the email, security question, and security answer form fields are not displayed (see Figure 22.7).

LISTING 22.14 CreateUserWizardShort.aspx

```
<%@ Page Language="C#" %>
<!DOCTYPE html PUBLIC "-//W3C//DTD XHTML 1.0 Transitional//EN"
  "http://www.w3.org/TR/xhtml1/DTD/xhtml1-transitional.dtd">
<html xmlns="http://www.w3.org/1999/xhtml" >
<head id="Head1" runat="server">
    <title>CreateUserWizard Short</title>
</head>
<body>
    <form id="form1" runat="server">
    <div>

    <asp:CreateUserWizard
        id="CreateUserWizard1"
```

LISTING 22.14   Continued

```
        RequireEmail="false"
        Runat="server" />


    </div>
    </form>
</body>
</html>
```

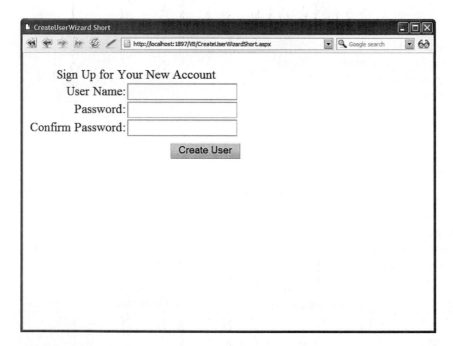

FIGURE 22.7   An abbreviated registration form.

WARNING

Don't set the CreateUserWizard control's RequireEmail property to the value False when the membership provider's requiresUniqueEmail property is set to the value True. In other words, don't require an email address when you haven't provided a user with a method for entering an email address.

Sending a Create User Email Message

You can set up the CreateUserWizard control so that it automatically sends an email when a new user registers. For example, you can send an email that contains the new user's registered username and password to that user's email account.

> **WARNING**
>
> Sending an unencrypted email across the Internet with a user's password is dangerous. However, it also is a very common practice to include a password in a registration confirmation email.

The page in Listing 22.15 includes a `MailDefinition` property that specifies the properties of the email that is sent to a user after the user successfully registers.

LISTING 22.15   `CreateUserWizardEmail.aspx`

```
<%@ Page Language="C#" %>
<!DOCTYPE html PUBLIC "-//W3C//DTD XHTML 1.0 Transitional//EN"
  "http://www.w3.org/TR/xhtml1/DTD/xhtml1-transitional.dtd">
<html xmlns="http://www.w3.org/1999/xhtml" >
<head id="Head1" runat="server">
    <title>CreateUserWizard Email</title>
</head>
<body>
    <form id="form1" runat="server">
    <div>

    <asp:CreateUserWizard
        id="CreateUserWizard1"
        Runat="server">
        <MailDefinition
            BodyFileName="Register.txt"
            Subject="Registration Confirmation"
            From="Admin@YourSite.com" />
    </asp:CreateUserWizard>

    </div>
    </form>
</body>
</html>
```

The `MailDefinition` class supports the following properties:

▶ **`BodyFileName`**—Enables you to specify the path to the email message.

▶ **`CC`**—Enables you to send a carbon copy of the email message.

▶ **`EmbeddedObjects`**—Enables you to embed objects, such as images, in the email message.

▶ **From**—Enables you to specify the FROM email address.

▶ **IsBodyHtml**—Enables you to send an HTML email message.

▶ **Priority**—Enables you to specify the priority of the email message. Possible values are High, Low, and Normal.

▶ **Subject**—Enables you to specify the subject of the email message.

The MailDefinition associated with the CreateUserWizard control in Listing 22.15 sends the contents of the text file in Listing 22.16.

LISTING 22.16 Register.txt

```
Thank you for registering!


Here is your new username and password:

  username: <% UserName %>
  password: <% Password %>
```

Notice that the email message in Listing 22.16 includes two special expressions: <% UserName %> and <% Password %>. When the email is sent, the user's registered username and password are substituted for these expressions (see Figure 22.8).

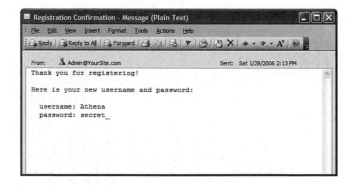

FIGURE 22.8   Receiving a registration email.

NOTE

You can send a user's password in an email message even when password is encrypted or hashed by the Membership provider.

The MailDefinition class uses the email server configured by the smtp element in the web configuration file. For example, the web configuration file in Listing 22.17 illustrates how you can configure the `MailDefinition` class to use the local SMTP server included with Internet Information Services. (You can enable the local SMTP Server by opening Internet Information Services from the Administrative Tools folder.)

LISTING 22.17 Web.Config

```
<configuration>
  <system.net>
    <mailSettings>
      <smtp deliveryMethod="PickupDirectoryFromIis"/>
    </mailSettings>
  </system.net>
  <system.web>
    <authentication mode="Forms" />
  </system.web>
</configuration>
```

If you need to connect to a mail server located on another machine, you can use the web configuration file in Listing 22.18. In Listing 22.18, the `smtp` element includes a network element that specifies a mail host, username, and password.

LISTING 22.18 Web.Config

```
<configuration>
  <system.net>
    <mailSettings>
      <smtp>
        <network
            host="mail.YourServer.com"
            userName="admin"
            password="secret" />
      </smtp>
    </mailSettings>
  </system.net>
  <system.web>
    <authentication mode="Forms" />
  </system.web>
</configuration>
```

> **NOTE**
>
> If you need to customize the email message sent by the `CreateUserWizard` control, then you can handle the `CreateUserWizard` control's `SendingMail` event. See the `CreateUserWizardCodeConfirmation.aspx` page in the next section.

Automatically Redirecting a User to the Referring Page

When you successfully log in from the Login.aspx page, you automatically are redirected back to the original page you requested. The CreateUserWizard control, on the other hand, does not redirect you back anywhere. If you want the CreateUserWizard control to work in the same way as the Login control, you need to write some code.

The Login control in Listing 22.19 includes a link to a user registration page named CreateUserWizardReturn.aspx. In the Page_Load() event handler, the value of the ReturnUrl query string parameter is added to the link to the registration page.

LISTING 22.19   LoginReturn.aspx

```
<%@ Page Language="C#" %>
<!DOCTYPE html PUBLIC "-//W3C//DTD XHTML 1.0 Transitional//EN"
"http://www.w3.org/TR/xhtml1/DTD/xhtml1-transitional.dtd">
<script runat="server">

    protected void Page_Load(object sender, EventArgs e)
    {
        if (!Page.IsPostBack)
        {
            string dest = Request.QueryString["ReturnUrl"];
            Login1.CreateUserUrl = "~/CreateUserWizardReturn.aspx?ReturnUrl=" +
Server.UrlEncode(dest);
        }
    }
</script>
<html xmlns="http://www.w3.org/1999/xhtml" >
<head id="Head1" runat="server">
    <title>Login Return</title>
</head>
<body>
    <form id="form1" runat="server">
    <div>

    <asp:Login
        id="Login1"
        CreateUserText="Register"
        CreateUserUrl="~/CreateUserWizardReturn.aspx"
        Runat="server" />

    </div>
    </form>
</body>
</html>
```

Before you use the page in Listing 22.19, you need to rename the page to `Login.aspx`. If a user requests a page that the user is not authorized to access, then the user is automatically redirected to the `Login.aspx` page. The `ReturnUrl` parameter is automatically added to the request for `Login.aspx`.

The page in Listing 22.20 contains a `CreateUserWizard` control. This page also contains a `Page_Load()` event handler. The value of the `ReturnUrl` query string parameter is used to redirect the user back to the originally requested page.

LISTING 22.20   CreateUserWizardReturn.aspx

```
<%@ Page Language="C#" %>
<!DOCTYPE html PUBLIC "-//W3C//DTD XHTML 1.0 Transitional//EN"
"http://www.w3.org/TR/xhtml1/DTD/xhtml1-transitional.dtd">
<script runat="server">

    void Page_Load()
    {
        if (!Page.IsPostBack)
        {
            string dest = "~/Default.aspx";
            if (!String.IsNullOrEmpty(Request.QueryString["ReturnURL"]))
                dest = Request.QueryString["ReturnURL"];
            CreateUserWizard1.ContinueDestinationPageUrl = dest;
        }
    }
</script>
<html xmlns="http://www.w3.org/1999/xhtml" >
<head id="Head1" runat="server">
    <title>CreateUserWizard Return</title>
</head>
<body>
    <form id="form1" runat="server">
    <div>

    <asp:CreateUserWizard
        id="CreateUserWizard1"
        Runat="server" />

    </div>
    </form>
</body>
</html>
```

Automatically Generating a Password

Some websites require you to complete multiple steps when registering. For example, you must complete the following steps when registering for a new account at eBay:

1. Complete the registration form.
2. Receive an email with a confirmation code.
3. Enter the confirmation code into a form.

This method of registration enables you to verify a user's email address. If someone enters an invalid email address, then the confirmation code is never received.

If you need to implement this registration scenario, then you need to know about the following three properties of the CreateUserWizard control:

▸ **AutoGeneratePassword**—Enables the CreateUserWizard control to generate a new password automatically.

▸ **DisableCreatedUser**—Enables you to disable the new user account created by the CreateUserWizard control.

▸ **LoginCreatedUser**—Enables you to prevent a new user from being logged in automatically.

You can send two types of confirmation email messages. First, you can generate a new password automatically and send the password to the user. In that case, you'll want to enable the AutoGeneratePassword property and disable the LoginCreatedUser properties.

Alternatively, you can allow a new user to enter her own password and send a distinct confirmation code in the confirmation email message. In that case, you'll want to enable the DisableCreatedUser property and disable the LoginCreatedUser property. Let's examine each of these scenarios in turn.

The page in Listing 22.21 contains a CreateUserWizard control that does not render a password form field. The control has its AutoGeneratePassword property enabled and its LoginCreatedUser property disabled. After you complete the form rendered by the CreateUserWizard control, you can click the Continue button to open the Login.aspx page.

LISTING 22.21   CreateUserWizardPasswordConfirmation.aspx

```
<%@ Page Language="C#" %>
<!DOCTYPE html PUBLIC "-//W3C//DTD XHTML 1.0 Transitional//EN"
  "http://www.w3.org/TR/xhtml1/DTD/xhtml1-transitional.dtd">
<html xmlns="http://www.w3.org/1999/xhtml" >
<head id="Head1" runat="server">
    <title>CreateUserWizard Password Confirmation</title>
</head>
<body>
```

```
    <form id="form1" runat="server">
    <div>

    <asp:CreateUserWizard
        id="CreateUserWizard1"
        CompleteSuccessText="A confirmation email
            containing your new password has been
            sent to your email address."
        AutoGeneratePassword="true"
        LoginCreatedUser="false"
        ContinueDestinationPageUrl="~/Login.aspx"
        Runat="server">
        <MailDefinition
            From="Admin@YourSite.com"
            BodyFileName="PasswordConfirmation.htm"
            IsBodyHtml="true"
            Subject="Registration Confirmation" />
    </asp:CreateUserWizard>

    </div>
    </form>
</body>
</html>
```

WARNING

Don't set the membership provider's passwordStrengthRegularExpression attribute when enabling the CreateUserWizard control's AutoGeneratePassword property.

The CreateUserWizard control in Listing 22.21 sends the email message contained in Listing 22.22.

LISTING 22.22   PasswordConfirmation.htm

```
<!DOCTYPE html PUBLIC "-//W3C//DTD XHTML 1.0 Transitional//EN"
  "http://www.w3.org/TR/xhtml1/DTD/xhtml1-transitional.dtd">
<html xmlns="http://www.w3.org/1999/xhtml" >
<head>
    <title>Password Confirmation</title>
</head>
<body>
```

LISTING 22.22   Continued

```
    Your new password is <% Password %>.

</body>
</html>
```

The email message in Listing 22.22 includes the automatically generated password. When the new user receives the automatically generated password in her inbox, she can enter the password in the Login.aspx page.

In the second scenario, the user gets to choose his password. However, the user's account is disabled until he enters his confirmation code.

The CreateUserWizard control in Listing 22.23 has its DisableCreateUser property enabled and its LoginCreatedUser property disabled.

LISTING 22.23   CreateUserWizardCodeConfirmation.aspx

```
<%@ Page Language="C#" %>
<!DOCTYPE html PUBLIC "-//W3C//DTD XHTML 1.0 Transitional//EN"
"http://www.w3.org/TR/xhtml1/DTD/xhtml1-transitional.dtd">
<script runat="server">

    protected void CreateUserWizard1_SendingMail(object sender,
    ➥MailMessageEventArgs e)
    {
        MembershipUser user = Membership.GetUser(CreateUserWizard1.UserName);
        string code = user.ProviderUserKey.ToString();
        e.Message.Body = e.Message.Body.Replace("<%ConfirmationCode%>", code);
    }
</script>
<html xmlns="http://www.w3.org/1999/xhtml" >
<head id="Head1" runat="server">
    <title>CreateUserWizard Code Confirmation</title>
</head>
<body>
    <form id="form1" runat="server">
    <div>

    <asp:CreateUserWizard
        id="CreateUserWizard1"
        CompleteSuccessText="A confirmation email
```

```
                containing your new password has been
                sent to your email address."
            DisableCreatedUser="true"
            ContinueDestinationPageUrl="~/ConfirmCode.aspx"
            OnSendingMail="CreateUserWizard1_SendingMail"
            Runat="server">
            <MailDefinition
                From="Admin@YourSite.com"
                BodyFileName="CodeConfirmation.htm"
                IsBodyHtml="true"
                Subject="Registration Confirmation" />
        </asp:CreateUserWizard>

        </div>
        </form>
</body>
</html>
```

Notice that the page in Listing 22.23 includes a SendingMail event handler. The confirmation code is the unique key assigned to the new user by the membership provider (a GUID). The confirmation code is substituted into the email message before the message is sent. The email message is contained in Listing 22.24.

LISTING 22.24   CodeConfirmation.htm

```
<!DOCTYPE html PUBLIC "-//W3C//DTD XHTML 1.0 Transitional//EN"
  "http://www.w3.org/TR/xhtml1/DTD/xhtml1-transitional.dtd">
<html xmlns="http://www.w3.org/1999/xhtml" >
<head>
    <title>Code Confirmation</title>
</head>
<body>

<%UserName%>,
your confirmation code is <%ConfirmationCode%>

</body>
</html>
```

After you complete the form rendered by the CreateUserWizard control, you can click the Continue button to open the ConfirmCode.aspx page (see Figure 22.9).

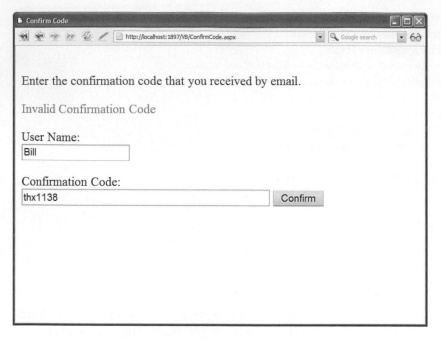

FIGURE 22.9   Entering a confirmation code.

LISTING 22.25   ConfirmCode.aspx

```
<%@ Page Language="C#" %>
<!DOCTYPE html PUBLIC "-//W3C//DTD XHTML 1.0 Transitional//EN"
"http://www.w3.org/TR/xhtml1/DTD/xhtml1-transitional.dtd">
<script runat="server">

    protected void btnConfirm_Click(object sender, EventArgs e)
    {
        MembershipUser user = Membership.GetUser(txtUserName.Text);
        if (user == null)
        {
            lblError.Text = "Invalid User Name";
        }
        else
        {
            string providerCode = user.ProviderUserKey.ToString();
            string userCode = txtConfirmationCode.Text.Trim();
            if (providerCode != userCode)
            {
                lblError.Text = "Invalid Confirmation Code";
            }
            else
```

```
            {
                user.IsApproved = true;
                Membership.UpdateUser(user);
                Response.Redirect("~/SecretFiles/Secret.aspx");
            }
        }
    }
</script>
<html xmlns="http://www.w3.org/1999/xhtml" >
<head id="Head1" runat="server">
    <title>Confirm Code</title>
</head>
<body>
    <form id="form1" runat="server">
    <div>

    <p>
    Enter the confirmation code that you received by email.
    </p>

    <asp:Label
        id="lblError"
        EnableViewState="false"
        ForeColor="Red"
        Runat="server" />

    <br /><br />
    <asp:Label
        id="lblUserName"
        Text="User Name:"
        AssociatedControlID="txtUserName"
        Runat="server" />
    <br />
    <asp:TextBox
        id="txtUserName"
        Runat="server" />

    <br /><br />
    <asp:Label
        id="lblConfirmationCode"
        Text="Confirmation Code:"
        AssociatedControlID="txtConfirmationCode"
        Runat="server" />
    <br />
    <asp:TextBox
        id="txtConfirmationCode"
```

LISTING 22.25   Continued

```
        Columns="50"
        Runat="server" />
    <asp:Button
        id="btnConfirm"
        Text="Confirm"
        OnClick="btnConfirm_Click"
        Runat="server" />

    </div>
    </form>
</body>
</html>
```

If the user enters the correct username and confirmation code, then his account is enabled. The MembershipUser.IsApproved property is assigned the value True and the updated user information is saved with the Membership.UpdateUser() method.

Using Templates with the CreateUserWizard Control

If you need to customize the appearance of the form rendered by the CreateUserWizard control, then you can create templates for the CreateUserWizardStep and the CompleteWizardStep. For example, the page in Listing 22.26 displays a drop-down list to display options for the security question (see Figure 22.10).

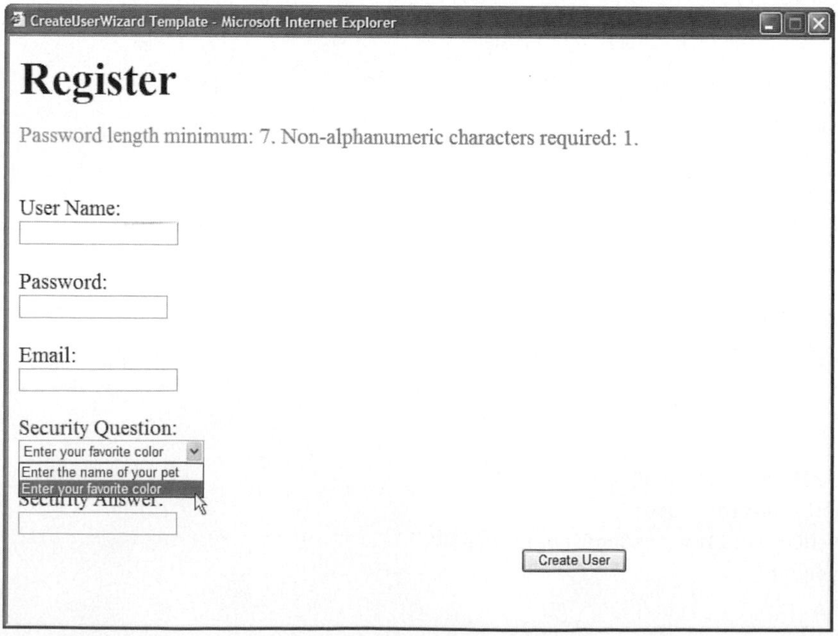

FIGURE 22.10   Customizing the CreateUserWizard control with templates.

LISTING 22.26 CreateUserWizardTemplate.aspx

```
<%@ Page Language="C#" %>
<!DOCTYPE html PUBLIC "-//W3C//DTD XHTML 1.0 Transitional//EN"
  "http://www.w3.org/TR/xhtml1/DTD/xhtml1-transitional.dtd">
<html xmlns="http://www.w3.org/1999/xhtml" >
<head id="Head1" runat="server">
    <title>CreateUserWizard Template</title>
</head>
<body>
    <form id="form1" runat="server">
    <div>

    <asp:CreateUserWizard
        id="CreateUserWizard1"
        Runat="server">
        <WizardSteps>
        <asp:CreateUserWizardStep>
        <ContentTemplate>
        <h1>Register</h1>

        <asp:Label
            id="ErrorMessage"
            ForeColor="Red"
            Runat="server" />

        <br /><br />
        <asp:Label
            id="lblUserName"
            Text="User Name:"
            AssociatedControlID="UserName"
            Runat="server" />
        <br />
        <asp:TextBox
            id="UserName"
            Runat="server" />

        <br /><br />
        <asp:Label
            id="lblPassword"
            Text="Password:"
            AssociatedControlID="Password"
            Runat="server" />
        <br />
        <asp:TextBox
            id="Password"
```

LISTING 22.26   Continued

```
        TextMode="Password"
        Runat="server" />

    <br /><br />
    <asp:Label
        id="lblEmail"
        Text="Email:"
        AssociatedControlID="Email"
        Runat="server" />
    <br />
    <asp:TextBox
        id="Email"
        Runat="server" />

    <br /><br />
    <asp:Label
        id="lblQuestion"
        Text="Security Question:"
        AssociatedControlID="Question"
        Runat="server" />
    <br />
    <asp:DropDownList
        id="Question"
        Runat="server">
        <asp:ListItem
            Text="Enter the name of your pet"
            Value="Pet Name" />
        <asp:ListItem
            Text="Enter your favorite color"
            Value="Favorite Color" />
    </asp:DropDownList>

    <br /><br />
    <asp:Label
        id="lblAnswer"
        Text="Security Answer:"
        AssociatedControlID="Answer"
        Runat="server" />
    <br />
    <asp:TextBox
        id="Answer"
        Runat="server" />
    </ContentTemplate>
    </asp:CreateUserWizardStep>
```

```
        <asp:CompleteWizardStep>
        <ContentTemplate>
            Your account was successfully created.
        </ContentTemplate>
        </asp:CompleteWizardStep>
        </WizardSteps>
    </asp:CreateUserWizard>

    </div>
    </form>
</body>
</html>
```

In the `CreateUserWizardStep`, you can add controls with the following IDs:

▶ `UserName`

▶ `Password`

▶ `Email`

▶ `ConfirmPassword`

▶ `Question`

▶ `Answer`

▶ `ErrorMessage`

Of course, you can add any other controls that you need. For example, you can request additional information when a new user registers and store the information in a separate database table (see the next section).

In the `CreateUserWizardStep`, you also can add `Button` controls that contain `CommandName` properties with the following values:

▶ `CreateUser`

▶ `Cancel`

Adding Steps to the `CreateUserWizard` Control

The `CreateUserWizard` control inherits from the base `Wizard` control. That means that you can use all the properties supported by the `Wizard` control when using the `CreateUserWizard` control. In particular, you can extend the `CreateUserWizard` control with additional wizard steps.

For example, imagine that you want to require new users to enter their first and last names. The page in Listing 22.27 contains an additional `WizardStep` that includes both first and last name form fields.

LISTING 22.27   CreateUserWizardExtra.aspx

```
<%@ Page Language="C#" %>
<%@ Import Namespace="System.Data.SqlClient" %>
<%@ Import Namespace="System.Web.Configuration" %>
<!DOCTYPE html PUBLIC "-//W3C//DTD XHTML 1.0 Transitional//EN"
"http://www.w3.org/TR/xhtml1/DTD/xhtml1-transitional.dtd">

<script runat="server">

    protected void CreateUserWizard1_CreatedUser(object sender, EventArgs e)
    {

CreateUserProfile(CreateUserWizard1.UserName,txtFirstName.Text,txtLastName.Text);
    }

    private void CreateUserProfile(string userName, string firstName,
    ➥string lastName)
    {
        string conString = WebConfigurationManager.ConnectionStrings
        ➥["UserProfiles"].ConnectionString;
        SqlConnection con = new SqlConnection(conString);
        SqlCommand cmd = new SqlCommand("INSERT UserProfiles
        ➥(UserName,FirstName,LastName) VALUES (@UserName,@FirstName,
        cmd.Parameters.AddWithValue("@UserName", userName);
        cmd.Parameters.AddWithValue("@FirstName", firstName);
        cmd.Parameters.AddWithValue("@LastName", lastName);
        using (con)
        {
            con.Open();
            cmd.ExecuteNonQuery();
        }
    }

</script>

<html xmlns="http://www.w3.org/1999/xhtml" >
<head id="Head1" runat="server">
    <title>CreateUserWizard Extra</title>
</head>
<body>
    <form id="form1" runat="server">
    <div>

    <asp:CreateUserWizard
        id="CreateUserWizard1"
```

```
        Runat="server" OnCreatedUser="CreateUserWizard1_CreatedUser">
        <WizardSteps>
        <asp:WizardStep>
            <asp:Label
                id="lblFirstName"
                Text="First Name:"
                AssociatedControlID="txtFirstName"
                Runat="server" />
            <br />
            <asp:TextBox
                id="txtFirstName"
                Runat="server" />

            <br /><br />
            <asp:Label
                id="lblLastName"
                Text="Last Name:"
                AssociatedControlID="txtLastName"
                Runat="server" />
            <br />
            <asp:TextBox
                id="txtLastName"
                Runat="server" />
        </asp:WizardStep>
        <asp:CreateUserWizardStep />
        </WizardSteps>
    </asp:CreateUserWizard>

    </div>
    </form>
</body>
</html>
```

The page in Listing 22.27 includes a `CreatedUser` event handler that executes after the new user is created. This handler adds the new user's first and last name to a database named `UserProfilesDB`.

Using the `LoginStatus` Control

The `LoginStatus` control displays either a Login link or a Logout link, depending on your authentication status. When you click the Login link, you are transferred to the `Login.aspx` page. When you click the Logout link, you are logged out of the website.

The page in Listing 22.28 contains a `LoginStatus` control (see Figure 22.11).

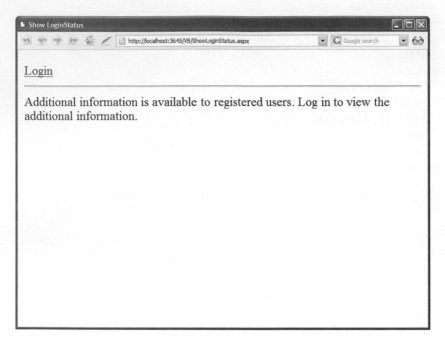

FIGURE 22.11   Displaying a Login link with the LoginStatus control.

LISTING 22.28   ShowLoginStatus.aspx

```
<%@ Page Language="C#" %>
<!DOCTYPE html PUBLIC "-//W3C//DTD XHTML 1.0 Transitional//EN"
  "http://www.w3.org/TR/xhtml1/DTD/xhtml1-transitional.dtd">
<html xmlns="http://www.w3.org/1999/xhtml" >
<head id="Head1" runat="server">
    <title>Show LoginStatus</title>
</head>
<body>
    <form id="form1" runat="server">
    <div>

    <asp:LoginStatus
        id="LoginStatus1"
        Runat="server" />

    <hr />

    Additional information is available to registered users. Log in to view
    the additional information.
```

```
        </div>
        </form>
</body>
</html>
```

After you open the page in Listing 22.28, if you click the Login link, you are redirected to the Login page. If you enter a valid username and password, you are redirected back to the ShowLoginStatus.aspx page.

The LoginStatus control supports the following properties:

- ▶ **LoginImageUrl**—Enables you to specify an image for the Login link.

- ▶ **LoginText**—Enables you to specify the text for the Login link.

- ▶ **LogoutAction**—Enables you to control what happens when the Logout link is clicked. Possible values are Redirect, RedirectToLoginPage, and Refresh.

- ▶ **LogoutImageUrl**—Enables you to specify an image for the Logout link.

- ▶ **LogoutPageUrl**—Enables you to specify a page to which the user is redirected when the user logs out. This property is ignored unless the LogoutAction property is set to the value Redirect.

- ▶ **LogoutText**—Enables you to specify the text for the Logout link.

The LoginStatus control also supports the following two events:

- ▶ **LoggingOut**—Raised before the user is logged out.

- ▶ **LoggedOut**—Raised after the user is logged out.

Using the LoginName Control

The LoginName control displays the current user's registered username. If the current user is not authenticated, the LoginName control renders nothing.

The page in Listing 22.29 contains both a LoginName and LoginStatus control.

LISTING 22.29   ShowLoginName.aspx

```
<%@ Page Language="C#" %>
<!DOCTYPE html PUBLIC "-//W3C//DTD XHTML 1.0 Transitional//EN"
  "http://www.w3.org/TR/xhtml1/DTD/xhtml1-transitional.dtd">
<html xmlns="http://www.w3.org/1999/xhtml" >
<head id="Head1" runat="server">
    <title>Show LoginName</title>
</head>
<body>
    <form id="form1" runat="server">
```

LISTING 22.29   Continued

```
    <div>

    <asp:LoginName
        id="LoginName1"
        FormatString="{0} /"
        Runat="server" />

    <asp:LoginStatus
        id="LoginStatus1"
        Runat="server" />

    <hr />

    Additional information is available to registered users. Log in to view
    the additional information.

    </div>
    </form>
</body>
</html>
```

When you first open the page in Listing 22.29, the LoginName control displays nothing. However, if you login by clicking the Login link, then the LoginName control displays your username (see Figure 22.12).

The LoginName control supports the following property:

▶ **FormatString**—Enables you to format the user name when the user name is rendered

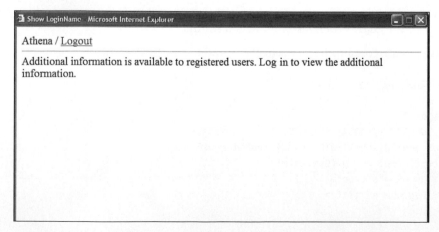

FIGURE 22.12   Displaying the current username with the LoginName control.

Using the `ChangePassword` Control

The `ChangePassword` control enables a user (or administrator) to change a user password.
The page in Listing 22.30 illustrates how you can use this control.

LISTING 22.30   ShowChangePassword.aspx

```
<%@ Page Language="C#" %>
<!DOCTYPE html PUBLIC "-//W3C//DTD XHTML 1.0 Transitional//EN"
 "http://www.w3.org/TR/xhtml1/DTD/xhtml1-transitional.dtd">
<html xmlns="http://www.w3.org/1999/xhtml" >
<head id="Head1" runat="server">
    <style type="text/css">
        .changePassword
        {
            font:14px Verdana,Sans-Serif;
            background-color:lightblue;
            border:solid 3px black;
            padding:4px;
        }
        .changePassword_title
        {
            background-color:darkblue;
            color:white;
            font-weight:bold;
        }
        .changePassword_instructions
        {
            font-size:12px;
            text-align:left;
            padding:10px;
        }
        .changePassword_button
        {
            border:solid 1px black;
            padding:3px;
        }
    </style>
    <title>Show ChangePassword</title>
</head>
<body>
    <form id="form1" runat="server">
    <div>

    <asp:LoginName ID="LoginName1" runat="server" />
```

LISTING 22.30   Continued

```
<asp:ChangePassword
    id="ChangePassword1"
    InstructionText="Complete this form to create
        a new password."
    DisplayUserName="true"
    ContinueDestinationPageUrl="~/Default.aspx"
    CancelDestinationPageUrl="~/Default.aspx"
    CssClass="changePassword"
    TitleTextStyle-CssClass="changePassword_title"
    InstructionTextStyle-CssClass="changePassword_instructions"
    ChangePasswordButtonStyle-CssClass="changePassword_button"
    CancelButtonStyle-CssClass="changePassword_button"
    ContinueButtonStyle-CssClass="changePassword_button"
    Runat="server" />

    </div>
    </form>
</body>
</html>
```

The form in Listing 22.30 includes form fields for entering your username, old password, and new password (see Figure 22.13). After you submit the form, your old password is changed to the new password.

Notice that the ChangePassword control in Listing 22.30 includes a DisplayUserName property. When this property is enabled, the username form field is rendered. You don't need to include the DisplayUserName property when you place the page within a password-protected section of your web application. In that case, the ChangePassword control uses the name of the current user automatically.

Sending a Change Password Email

After the user changes his password, you can use the ChangePassword control to automatically send an email message that contains the new password. The page in Listing 22.31 contains a ChangePassword control that automatically sends an email.

NOTE

You can send a user's password in an email message even when password is encrypted or hashed by the membership provider.

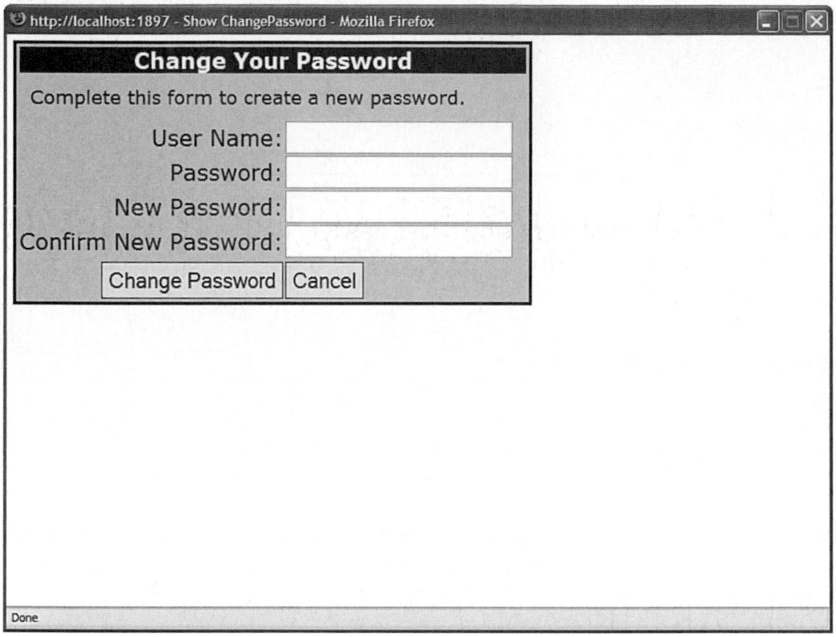

FIGURE 22.13   Changing your password with the `ChangePassword` control.

LISTING 22.31   ChangePasswordEmail.aspx

```csharp
<%@ Page Language="C#" %>
<!DOCTYPE html PUBLIC "-//W3C//DTD XHTML 1.0 Transitional//EN"
    "http://www.w3.org/TR/xhtml1/DTD/xhtml1-transitional.dtd">
<html xmlns="http://www.w3.org/1999/xhtml" >
<head id="Head1" runat="server">
    <title>ChangePassword Email</title>
</head>
<body>
    <form id="form1" runat="server">
    <div>

    <asp:ChangePassword
        id="ChangePassword1"
        DisplayUserName="true"
        Runat="server">
        <MailDefinition
            From="Admin@YourSite.com"
            BodyFileName="ChangePassword.txt"
            Subject="Your New Password" />
    </asp:ChangePassword>
```

LISTING 22.31   Continued

```
    </div>
    </form>
</body>
</html>
```

Notice that the `ChangePassword` control in Listing 22.31 includes a `MailDefinition` property that defines the email sent by the control. The `ChangePassword` control emails the message contained in Listing 22.32.

LISTING 22.32   ChangePassword.txt

```
<%UserName%>,
your new password is <%Password%>.
```

The email message in Listing 22.32 includes two special expressions: `<% UserName %>` and `<% Password %>`. When the email is sent, the user's existing username and new password are substituted for these expressions.

> **NOTE**
>
> The `MailDefinition` class uses the email server configured by the `smtp` element in the web configuration file. For more information on configuring the `smtp` element, see the earlier section of this chapter, "Sending a Create User Email Message."

Using Templates with the `ChangePassword` Control

If you need to completely modify the appearance of the `ChangePassword` control, then you can use templates to format the control. The `ChangePassword` control supports both a `ChangePasswordTemplate` and a `SuccessTemplate`.

The page in Listing 22.33 illustrates how you can use both the templates supported by the `ChangePassword` control (see Figure 22.14).

LISTING 22.33   ChangePasswordTemplate.aspx

```
<%@ Page Language="C#" %>
<!DOCTYPE html PUBLIC "-//W3C//DTD XHTML 1.0 Transitional//EN"
  "http://www.w3.org/TR/xhtml1/DTD/xhtml1-transitional.dtd">
<html xmlns="http://www.w3.org/1999/xhtml" >
<head id="Head1" runat="server">
    <title>ChangePassword Template</title>
</head>
<body>
    <form id="form1" runat="server">
```

```
<div>

<asp:ChangePassword
    id="ChangePassword1"
    DisplayUserName="true"
    Runat="server">
    <ChangePasswordTemplate>
        <h1>Change Password</h1>
        <asp:Label
            id="FailureText"
            EnableViewState="false"
            ForeColor="Red"
            Runat="server" />
        <br />
        <asp:Label
            id="lblUserName"
            Text="User Name:"
            AssociatedControlID="UserName"
            Runat="server" />
        <br />
        <asp:TextBox
            id="UserName"
            Runat="server" />
        <br /><br />
        <asp:Label
            id="lblCurrentPassword"
            Text="Current Password:"
            AssociatedControlID="CurrentPassword"
            Runat="server" />
        <br />
        <asp:TextBox
            id="CurrentPassword"
            TextMode="Password"
            Runat="server" />
        <br /><br />
        <asp:Label
            id="lblNewPassword"
            Text="New Password:"
            AssociatedControlID="NewPassword"
            Runat="server" />
        <br />
        <asp:TextBox
            id="NewPassword"
            TextMode="Password"
            Runat="server" />
        <br /><br />
```

LISTING 22.33   Continued

```
            <asp:Button
                id="btnChangePassword"
                Text="Change Password"
                CommandName="ChangePassword"
                Runat="server" />
        </ChangePasswordTemplate>
        <SuccessTemplate>
            Your password has been changed!
        </SuccessTemplate>
    </asp:ChangePassword>

    </div>
    </form>
</body>
</html>
```

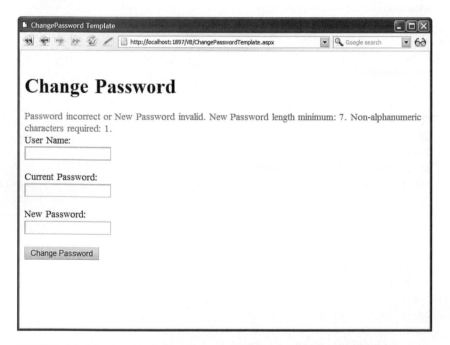

FIGURE 22.14   Customizing the ChangePassword control with templates.

You can use controls with the following IDs in the ChangePasswordTemplate template:

▶ UserName

▶ CurrentPassword

▶ ConfirmPassword

▶ NewPassword

▶ FailureText

You also can add Button controls with the following values for the CommandName property:

▶ ChangePassword

▶ Cancel

▶ Continue

Using the PasswordRecovery Control

If a user forgets her password, then she can use the PasswordRecovery control to email herself her password. The PasswordRecovery control either sends the user's original password or resets the password and sends the new password.

The page in Listing 22.34 contains a PasswordRecovery control.

LISTING 22.34 ShowPasswordRecovery.aspx

```
<%@ Page Language="C#" %>
<!DOCTYPE html PUBLIC "-//W3C//DTD XHTML 1.0 Transitional//EN"
  "http://www.w3.org/TR/xhtml1/DTD/xhtml1-transitional.dtd">
<html xmlns="http://www.w3.org/1999/xhtml" >
<head id="Head1" runat="server">
    <style type="text/css">
        .passwordRecovery
        {
            font:14px Verdana,Sans-Serif;
            background-color:lightblue;
            border:solid 3px black;
            padding:4px;
        }
        .passwordRecovery_title
        {
            background-color:darkblue;
            color:white;
            font-weight:bold;
        }
        .passwordRecovery_instructions
        {
```

LISTING 23.34   Continued

```
            font-size:12px;
            text-align:left;
            padding:10px;
        }
        .passwordRecovery_button
        {
            border:solid 1px black;
            padding:3px;
        }
    </style>
    <title>Show PasswordRecovery</title>
</head>
<body>
    <form id="form1" runat="server">
    <div>

    <asp:PasswordRecovery
        id="PasswordRecovery1"
        CssClass="passwordRecovery"
        TitleTextStyle-CssClass="passwordRecovery_title"
        InstructionTextStyle-CssClass="passwordRecovery_instructions"
        SubmitButtonStyle-CssClass="passwordRecovery_button"
        Runat="server">
        <MailDefinition
            From="Admin@YourSite.com"
            Subject="Password Reminder" />
    </asp:PasswordRecovery>

    </div>
    </form>
</body>
</html>
```

After you open the page in Listing 22.34 in your web browser, you are first asked to enter your username (see Figure 22.15). Next, you are asked to enter the answer to the security question that you entered when registering. Finally, a password is emailed to your registered email account.

> **NOTE**
>
> Before you use the PasswordRecovery control, you must specify your mail server settings in your application's web configuration file. See the earlier section in this chapter, "Sending a Create User Email Message."

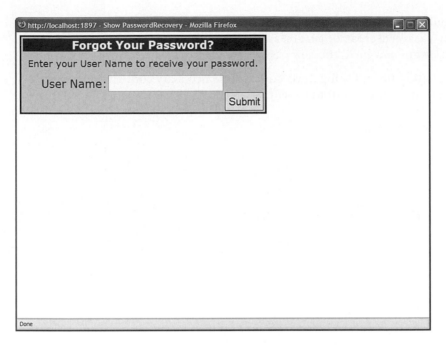

FIGURE 22.15   Retrieving a lost password with the `PasswordRecovery` control.

By default, the `PasswordRecovery` control first resets your password before sending you the password. In the next section, you learn how to send a user's original password.

Sending the Original Password

By default, the `PasswordRecovery` control does not send a user's original password. If you don't want the `PasswordRecovery` control to reset a user's password before sending it, then you must change the configuration of the membership provider. Three configuration settings matter: `passwordFormat`, `enablePasswordRetrieval`, and `enablePasswordReset`.

By default, the `passwordFormat` attribute has the value `Hashed`. When passwords are hashed, the `PasswordRecovery` control cannot send a user's original password. This limitation makes sense because when passwords are hashed, the actual passwords are never stored anywhere. If you want to send a user his original password, then you need to set the `passwordFormat` attribute to either the value `Clear` or `Encrypted`.

By default, the `enablePasswordRetrieval` attribute has the value `False`. Therefore, if you want to send a user his original password, you must enable this property in the web configuration file.

Finally, by default, the enablePasswordReset attribute has the value True. Regardless of the value of the passwordFormat or enablePasswordRetrieval attributes, you can always reset a user's password and email the new password to the user.

The web configuration file in Listing 22.35 contains the necessary configuration settings to enable a user's original password to be sent.

LISTING 22.35   Web.Config

```
<configuration>
  <system.web>
    <authentication mode="Forms" />

    <membership defaultProvider="MyMembership">
      <providers>
        <add
          name="MyMembership"
          type="System.Web.Security.SqlMembershipProvider"
          connectionStringName="LocalSqlServer"
          passwordFormat="Clear"
          enablePasswordRetrieval="true"
          />
      </providers>
    </membership>

  </system.web>
</configuration>
```

The configuration file in Listing 22.35 causes passwords to be stored in plain text rather than hashed. Furthermore, password retrieval is enabled.

Requiring a Security Question and Answer

When you use the CreateUserWizard control to register, you are required to select a security question and answer. The PasswordRecovery control displays a form that contains the security question. If you cannot enter the correct security answer, then your password is not sent.

If you do not want to require users to answer a security question before receiving their passwords, then you can modify the configuration of the membership provider. The web configuration file in Listing 22.36 assigns the value false to the requiresQuestionAndAnswer attribute.

LISTING 22.36   Web.Config

```
<configuration>
  <system.web>
    <authentication mode="Forms" />

    <membership defaultProvider="MyMembership">
      <providers>
        <add
          name="MyMembership"
          type="System.Web.Security.SqlMembershipProvider"
          connectionStringName="LocalSqlServer"
          requiresQuestionAndAnswer="false"
          />
      </providers>
    </membership>

  </system.web>
</configuration>
```

Using Templates with the PasswordRecovery Control

If you need to completely customize the appearance of the PasswordRecovery control, you can use templates. The PasswordRecovery control supports the following three types of templates:

▶ UserNameTemplate

▶ QuestionTemplate

▶ SuccessTemplate

The page in Listing 22.37 illustrates how you can use all three of these templates.

LISTING 22.37   PasswordRecoveryTemplate.aspx

```
<%@ Page Language="C#" %>
<!DOCTYPE html PUBLIC "-//W3C//DTD XHTML 1.0 Transitional//EN"
  "http://www.w3.org/TR/xhtml1/DTD/xhtml1-transitional.dtd">
<html xmlns="http://www.w3.org/1999/xhtml" >
<head id="Head1" runat="server">
    <style type="text/css">
        html
        {
```

LISTING 23.37 Continued

```
            font:12px Arial,Sans-Serif;
        }
        h1
        {
            font:bold 16px Arial,Sans-Serif;
            color:DarkGray;
        }
    </style>
    <title>PasswordRecovery Template</title>
</head>
<body>
    <form id="form1" runat="server">
    <div>

    <asp:PasswordRecovery
        id="PasswordRecovery1"
        Runat="server">
        <MailDefinition
            From="Admin@YourSite.com"
            Subject="Password Reminder"
            BodyFileName="PasswordRecovery.txt" />
        <UserNameTemplate>
        <h1>User Name</h1>
        <asp:Label
            id="FailureText"
            EnableViewState="false"
            ForeColor="Red"
            Runat="server" />
        <br />
        <asp:Label
            id="lblUserName"
            Text="Enter your user name:"
            AssociatedControlID="UserName"
            Runat="server" />
        <br />
        <asp:TextBox
            id="UserName"
            Runat="server" />
        <br />
        <asp:Button
            id="btnSubmit"
            Text="Next"
            CommandName="Submit"
            Runat="server" />
```

```
                    </UserNameTemplate>
                    <QuestionTemplate>
                    <h1>Security Question</h1>
                    <asp:Label
                        id="FailureText"
                        EnableViewState="false"
                        ForeColor="Red"
                        Runat="server" />
                    <br />
                    <asp:Label
                        id="Question"
                        Text="Enter your user name:"
                        AssociatedControlID="Answer"
                        Runat="server" />
                    <br />
                    <asp:TextBox
                        id="Answer"
                        Runat="server" />
                    <br />
                    <asp:Button
                        id="btnSubmit"
                        Text="Next"
                        CommandName="Submit"
                        Runat="server" />
                    </QuestionTemplate>
                    <SuccessTemplate>
                    <h1>Success</h1>
                    An email has been sent to your registered
                    email account that contains your user name
                    and password.
                    </SuccessTemplate>
                </asp:PasswordRecovery>

        </div>
        </form>
</body>
</html>
```

The UserNameTemplate must contain a control with an ID of UserName. You also can include a control with an ID of FailureText when you want to display error messages. This template also must contain a Button control with a CommandName that has the value Submit.

The QuestionTemplate must contain a control with an ID of Question and a control with an ID of Answer. Optionally, you can include a FailureText control when you want to display error messages. It also must have a `Button` control with a `CommandName` that has the value `Submit`.

The `SuccessTemplate`, on the other hand, does not require any special controls.

Notice that the `PasswordRecovery` control in Listing 22.37 includes a `MailDefinition` property that references a custom email message. The message is contained in Listing 22.38.

LISTING 22.38   `PasswordRecovery.txt`

```
Here's your login information:


  user name: <%UserName%>
   password: <%Password%>
```

The email message in Listing 22.38 contains substitution expressions for both the username and password.

Using the `LoginView` Control

The `LoginView` control enables you to display different content to different users depending on their authentication status. For example, the page in Listing 22.39 displays different content for authenticated users and anonymous users (see Figure 22.16).

LISTING 22.39   `ShowLoginView.aspx`

```
<%@ Page Language="C#" %>
<!DOCTYPE html PUBLIC "-//W3C//DTD XHTML 1.0 Transitional//EN"
   "http://www.w3.org/TR/xhtml1/DTD/xhtml1-transitional.dtd">
<html xmlns="http://www.w3.org/1999/xhtml" >
<head id="Head1" runat="server">
    <title>Show LoginView</title>
</head>
<body>
    <form id="form1" runat="server">
    <div>

    <asp:LoginStatus
        id="LoginStatus"
        Runat="server" />
    <hr />

    <asp:LoginView
        id="LoginView1"
```

```
        Runat="server">
        <AnonymousTemplate>
        This content is displayed to anonymous users.
        </AnonymousTemplate>
        <LoggedInTemplate>
        This content is displayed to authenticated users.
        </LoggedInTemplate>
    </asp:LoginView>

    </div>
    </form>
</body>
</html>
```

The LoginView control in Listing 22.39 contains two templates: an AnonymousTemplate and a LoggedInTemplate. Only one of the two templates is displayed at a time.

The page also includes a LoginStatus control. You can use this control to log in and log out quickly.

NOTE

You can use the LoginView control with Windows authentication as well as Forms authentication.

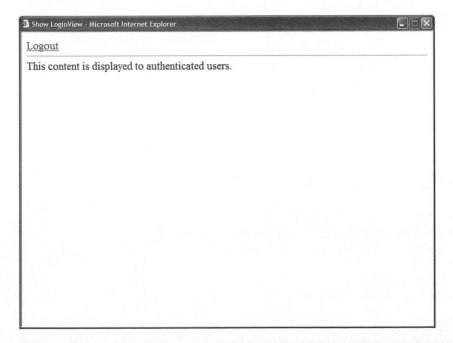

FIGURE 22.16   Displaying content to authenticated users with the LoginView control.

Using Roles with the `LoginView` Control

You also can use the `LoginView` control to display different content to users who belong to different roles. The page in Listing 22.40 contains a `LoginView` that contains two `RoleGroup` controls. The first `RoleGroup` contains content that is displayed to members of the Administrator role. The second `RoleGroup` contains content that is displayed to members of the Manager and Worker roles.

LISTING 22.40   `LoginViewRoles.aspx`

```
<%@ Page Language="C#" %>
<!DOCTYPE html PUBLIC "-//W3C//DTD XHTML 1.0 Transitional//EN"
"http://www.w3.org/TR/xhtml1/DTD/xhtml1-transitional.dtd">
<script runat="server">

    protected void Page_Load(object sender, EventArgs e)
    {
        MembershipCreateStatus status;
        // Create Bill

Membership.CreateUser("Bill","secret_","bill@somewhere.com","dog","rover",true,
➥out status);
        // Create Ted
        Membership.CreateUser("Ted", "secret_", "ted@somewhere.com", "dog",
        ➥"rover", true,out status);
        // Create Fred
        Membership.CreateUser("Fred", "secret_", "fred@somewhere.com", "dog",
        ➥"rover", true, out status);
        // Create Administrator Role
        if (!Roles.RoleExists("Administrator"))
        {
            Roles.CreateRole("Administrator");
            Roles.AddUserToRole("Bill", "Administrator");
        }
        // Create Manager Role
        if (!Roles.RoleExists("Manager"))
        {
            Roles.CreateRole("Manager");
            Roles.AddUserToRole("Bill", "Manager");
            Roles.AddUserToRole("Ted", "Manager");
        }
        // Create Worker Role
        if (!Roles.RoleExists("Worker"))
        {
            Roles.CreateRole("Worker");
            Roles.AddUserToRole("Fred", "Worker");
```

```
        }
    }
</script>
<html xmlns="http://www.w3.org/1999/xhtml" >
<head id="Head1" runat="server">
    <title>LoginView Roles</title>
</head>
<body>
    <form id="form1" runat="server">
    <div>

    <asp:LoginStatus
        id="LoginStatus"
        Runat="server" />
    <hr />

    <asp:LoginView
        id="LoginView1"
        Runat="server">
        <RoleGroups>
        <asp:RoleGroup Roles="Administrator">
        <ContentTemplate>
        This content is displayed to Administrators.
        </ContentTemplate>
        </asp:RoleGroup>
        <asp:RoleGroup Roles="Manager,Worker">
        <ContentTemplate>
        This content is displayed to Managers
        and Workers.
        </ContentTemplate>
        </asp:RoleGroup>
        </RoleGroups>
    </asp:LoginView>

    </div>
    </form>
</body>
</html>
```

The Page_Load() handler in Listing 22.40 creates three users named Bill, Ted, and Fred. Bill is added to both the Administrator and Manager roles, Ted is added to the Manager role, and Fred is added to the Worker role.

The content of only one RoleGroup is displayed by the LoginView control at a time. If a user matches more than one RoleGroup, then the content of the first RoleGroup matched is displayed and the other RoleGroups are ignored.

Before you can use the page in Listing 22.40, you must enable roles in the web configuration file. The file in Listing 22.41 contains the necessary `roleManager` element.

LISTING 22.41   Web.Config

```
<configuration>
  <system.web>

    <authentication mode="Forms" />

    <roleManager enabled="true" />

  </system.web>
</configuration>
```

Summary

This chapter was devoted to the ASP.NET `Login` controls. In the first section, you were provided with an overview of the `Login` controls. You learned how to create both a Login and Registration page.

Next, we examined each of the `Login` controls one by one. You learned how to use the `Login` control to authenticate users and the `CreateUserWizard` control to register new users. You also learned how to send an email to new users automatically.

We also examined the `LoginStatus` and `LoginView` controls. You learned how to display either a Login or Logout link with the `LoginStatus` control. You learned how to display the current user's name with the `LoginName` control.

You also learned how to change passwords and send password reminders by using the `ChangePassword` and `PasswordRecovery` controls. You learned how to customize both of these controls by using templates.

Finally, you learned how to use the `LoginView` control to display different content to different users, depending on their authentication status. We also discussed how you can use roles with the `LoginView` control.

CHAPTER 23

Using ASP.NET Membership

In the previous chapter, you learned how to use the Login controls to create an entire user registration system. This chapter looks under the covers and examines the security frameworks on which the Login controls are built.

The ASP.NET Framework includes four frameworks related to security:

▶ **ASP.NET Authentication**—Enables you to identify users.

▶ **ASP.NET Authorization**—Enables you to authorize users to request particular resources.

▶ **ASP.NET Membership**—Enables you to represent users and modify their properties.

▶ **Role Manager**—Enables you to represent user roles and modify their properties.

In this chapter, you learn how to configure authentication, authorization, ASP.NET Membership, and the Role Manager. You learn how to enable Forms authentication and configure advanced Forms authentication features such as cookieless authentication and cross-application authentication.

You learn how to configure authorization to control access to resources. We explore several advanced features of authorization. For example, you learn how to password-protect images and ASP classic pages.

You also learn how to configure different Membership providers, create custom Membership providers, and work with the properties and methods of the Membership class.

For example, you learn how to build a custom XmlMembershipProvider that stores membership information in an XML file.

Finally, we examine the Role Manager. You learn how to create user roles and add and remove users from a particular role. You also learn how to configure the different Role providers included in the ASP.NET Framework.

Configuring Authentication

Authentication refers to the process of identifying who you are. The ASP.NET Framework supports three types of authentication:

▶ Windows Authentication

▶ .NET Passport Authentication

▶ Forms Authentication

A particular application can have only one type of authentication enabled. You can't, for example, enable both Windows and Forms authentication at the same time.

Windows authentication is enabled by default. When Windows authentication is enabled, users are identified by their Microsoft Windows account names. Roles correspond to Microsoft Windows groups.

Windows authentication delegates the responsibility of identifying users to Internet Information Server. Internet Information Server can be configured to use Basic, Integrated Windows, or Digest authentication.

.NET Passport authentication is the same type of authentication used at Microsoft websites such as MSN and Hotmail. If you want to enable users to log in to your application by using their existing Hotmail usernames and passwords, then you can enable .NET Passport authentication.

NOTE

You must download and install the Microsoft .NET Passport SDK, register with Microsoft, and pay Microsoft a fee before you can use .NET Passport authentication. For more information, see the MSDN website (msdn.microsoft.com).

The final type of authentication is Forms authentication. When Forms authentication is enabled, users are typically identified by a cookie (but see the next section). When a user is authenticated, an encrypted cookie is added to the user's browser. As the user moves from page to page, the user is identified by the cookie.

When Forms authentication is enabled, user and role information is stored in a custom data store. You can store user information anywhere that you want. For example, you can store usernames and passwords in a database, an XML file, or even a plain text file.

In ASP.NET 1.x, after enabling Forms authentication, you had to write all the code for storing and retrieving user information. When building an ASP.NET 3.5 application, on the other hand, you can let ASP.NET Membership do all this work for you. ASP.NET Membership can handle all the details of storing and retrieving user and role information.

You enable a particular type of authentication for an application in an application's root web configuration file. The file in Listing 23.1 enables Forms authentication.

LISTING 23.1 Web.Config

```
<configuration>
    <system.web>

      <authentication mode="Forms" />

    </system.web>
</configuration>
```

In Listing 23.1, the authentication element's mode attribute is set to the value Forms. The possible values for the mode attribute are None, Windows, Forms, and Passport.

> **NOTE**
>
> Windows, Forms, and Passport authentication are implemented with HTTP Modules. If you need to implement a custom authentication scheme, then you can create a custom HTTP Module. For more information on HTTP Module, see Chapter 27, "Working with the HTTP Runtime."

> **VISUAL WEB DEVELOPER NOTE**
>
> If you prefer, you can enable a particular type of authentication by using the Web Site Administration Tool. This tool provides you with a form interface for modifying the web configuration file. You can open the Web Site Administration Tool by selecting the menu option Website, ASP.NET Configuration.

Configuring Forms Authentication

Several configuration options are specific to Forms authentication:

▶ **cookieless**—Enables you to use Forms authentication even when a browser does not support cookies. Possible values are UseCookies, UseUri, AutoDetect, and UseDeviceProfile. The default value is UseDeviceProfile.

▶ **defaultUrl**—Enables you to specify the page to which a user is redirected after being authenticated. The default value is Default.aspx.

▶ **domain**—Enables you to specify the domain associated with the authentication cookie. The default value is an empty string.

▶ **enableCrossAppRedirects**—Enables you to authenticate users across applications by passing an authentication ticket in a query string. The default value is `false`.

▶ **loginUrl**—Enables you to specify the path to the Login page. The default value is `Login.aspx`.

▶ **name**—Enables you to specify the name of the authentication cookie. The default value is `.ASPXAUTH`.

▶ **path**—Enables you to specify the path associated with the authentication cookie. The default value is `/`.

▶ **protection**—Enables you to specify how the authentication cookie is encrypted. Possible values are `All`, `Encryption`, `None`, and `Validation`. The default value is `All`.

▶ **requiresSSL**—Enables you to require a SSL (Secure Sockets Layer) connection when transmitting the authentication cookie. The default value is `false`.

▶ **slidingExpiration**—Enables you to prevent the authentication cookie from expiring as long as a user continues to make requests within an interval of time. Possible values are `True` and `False`. The default value is `True`.

▶ **timeout**—Enables you to specify the amount of time in minutes before the authentication cookie expires. The default value is `30`.

Several of these configuration settings are related to the authentication cookie. For example, you can use the web configuration file in Listing 23.2 to change the name of the authentication cookie.

LISTING 23.2 Web.Config

```
<configuration>

  <system.web>
    <authentication mode="Forms">
      <forms name="MyApp" />
    </authentication>

  </system.web>
</configuration>
```

Several of these options require additional explanation. In the following sections, you learn how to enable cookieless authentication, modify the cookie expiration policy, and enable authentication across applications.

Using Cookieless Forms Authentication

Normally, Forms authentication uses a cookie to identify a user. However, Forms authentication also supports a feature named cookieless authentication. When cookieless authentication is enabled, a user can be identified without a browser cookie.

By taking advantage of cookieless authentication, you can use Forms Authentication and ASP.NET Membership to authenticate users even when someone is using a browser that does not support cookies or a browser with cookies disabled.

When cookieless authentication is enabled, a user can be identified by a unique token added to a page's URL. If a user uses relative URLs to link from one page to another, then the token is passed from page to page automatically and the user can be identified across multiple page requests.

When you request a page that requires authentication and cookieless authentication is enabled, the URL in the browser address bar looks like this:

```
http://localhost:2500/Original/(F(WfAnevWxFyuN4SpenRclAEh_lY6OKWVllOKdQkRk
tOqV7cfcrgUJ2NKxNhH9dTA7fgzZ-cZwyr4ojyU6EnarC-bbf8g4sl6m4k5kk6Nmcsg1))
/SecretFiles/Secret2.aspx
```

That long, ugly code in the URL is the user's encoded authentication ticket.

You configure cookieless authentication by assigning a value to the cookieless attribute of the forms element in the web configuration file. The cookieless attribute accepts any of the following four values:

- **UseCookies**—Always use an authentication cookie.

- **UseUri**—Never use an authentication cookie.

- **AutoDetect**—Automatically detect when to use an authentication cookie.

- **UseDeviceProfile**—Use the device profile to determine when to use an authentication cookie.

The default value is UseDeviceProfile. By default, the ASP.NET Framework issues a cookie only when a particular type of device supports cookies. The ASP.NET Framework maintains a database of device capabilities in a set of files contained in the following folder:

```
\WINDOWS\Microsoft.NET\Framework\v2.0.50727\CONFIG\Browsers
```

By default, the ASP.NET Framework never uses cookieless authentication with a browser such as Microsoft Internet Explorer. According to the device profile for Internet Explorer, Internet Explorer supports cookies, so cookieless authentication is not used. The Framework doesn't use cookieless authentication even when cookies are disabled in a browser.

If you want the ASP.NET Framework to automatically detect whether a browser supports cookies, then you need to set the cookieless attribute to the value AutoDetect. When AutoDetect is enabled, the ASP.NET Framework checks whether a browser sends an HTTP COOKIE header. If the COOKIE header is present, then an authentication cookie is assigned to the browser. Otherwise, the ASP.NET Framework uses cookieless authentication.

The web configuration file in Listing 23.3 enables AutoDetect.

LISTING 23.3 `Web.Config`

```
<configuration>
    <system.web>
      <authentication mode="Forms">
        <forms cookieless="AutoDetect"/>
      </authentication>
    </system.web>
</configuration>
```

Using Sliding Expiration with Forms Authentication

By default, Forms authentication uses a sliding expiration policy. As long as a user lets no more than 30 minutes pass without requesting a page, the user continues to be authenticated. However, if the user does not request a page for 30 minutes, then the user is logged out automatically.

If you have strict security requirements, you can use an absolute expiration policy rather than a sliding expiration policy. In other words, you can force a user to log in again after a particular interval of time.

The web configuration file in Listing 23.4 forces a user to log in again every minute.

LISTING 23.4 `Web.Config`

```
<configuration>
    <system.web>
      <authentication mode="Forms">
        <forms slidingExpiration="false" timeout="1" />
      </authentication>
    </system.web>
</configuration>
```

Using Forms Authentication Across Applications

By default, Forms authentication is application relative. In other words, if you log in to one application, you aren't logged in to any other application—even when the other application is located on the same web server.

This creates problems in two situations. First, you don't want to require the employees of your company to log in multiple times as they move between different applications hosted by your company. An employee should be able to log in once and use any application provided by your company automatically.

Second, if you are hosting a web farm, you don't want to force a user to log in whenever a request is served by a different web server. From the perspective of a user, a web farm should seem just like a single server.

By default, the Forms authentication cookie is encrypted and signed. Furthermore, by default, each application generates a unique decryption and validation key. Therefore, by default, you can't share the same authentication cookie across applications.

You specify encryption and validation options with the machineKey element in the web configuration file. Here are the default settings for this element:

```
<machineKey
  decryption="Auto"
  validation="SHA1"
  decryptionKey="AutoGenerate,IsolateApps"
  validationKey="AutoGenerate,IsolateApps" />
```

The decryption attribute specifies the algorithm used to encrypt and decrypt the forms authentication cookie. Possible values are Auto, AES (the government standard encryption algorithm), and 3DES (Triple DES). By default, the decryption attribute is set to Auto, which causes the ASP.NET Framework to select the encryption algorithm based on the capabilities of the web server.

The validation attribute specifies the hash or encryption algorithm used when an authentication cookie is signed. Possible values are AES, MD5, SHA1, and TripleDES.

The decryptionKey attribute represents the key used to encrypt and decrypt the authentication cookie. The validationKey represents the key used when the authentication cookie is signed. By default, both attributes are set to the value AutoGenerate, which causes the ASP.NET Framework to generate a random key and store it in the LSA (your web server's Local Security Authority).

Notice that both the decryptionKey and validationKey attributes include an IsolateApps modifier. When the IsolateApps modifier is present, a unique key is created for each application on the same web server.

If you want to share the same authentication cookie across every application hosted on the same web server, then you can override the default machineKey element in the machine root web configuration file and remove the IsolateApps attribute from both the decryptionKey and validationKey attributes. You can add the following machineKey element anywhere within the system.web section in the web configuration file:

```
<machineKey
  decryption="Auto"
  validation="SHA1"
  decryptionKey="AutoGenerate"
  validationKey="AutoGenerate" />
```

The root web configuration file is located at the following path:

```
C:\WINDOWS\Microsoft.NET\Framework\v2.0.50727\CONFIG\Web.Config
```

On the other hand, if you need to share the same authentication cookie across separate web servers, then you need to specify the decryptionKey and validationKey manually.

You cannot allow the ASP.NET Framework to generate these keys automatically because you need to share the keys across the different web servers.

For example, the following machineKey element contains explicit decryption and validation keys:

```
<machineKey
  decryption="AES"
  validation="SHA1"
  decryptionKey="306C1FA852AB3B0115150DD8BA30821CDFD125538A0C606DACA53DBB3C3E0AD2"
    validationKey="61A8E04A146AFFAB81B6AD19654F99EA7370807F18F5002725DAB98B8EF
    D19C711337E26948E26D1D174B159973EA0BE8CC9CAA6AAF513BF84E44B2247792265" />
```

When using AES, you need to set the decryption key to a random sequence of 64 hex characters. When using SHA1, you need to set the decryption key to a random sequence of 128 hex characters. You can use the page in Listing 23.5 to generate these random character sequences for you (see Figure 23.1).

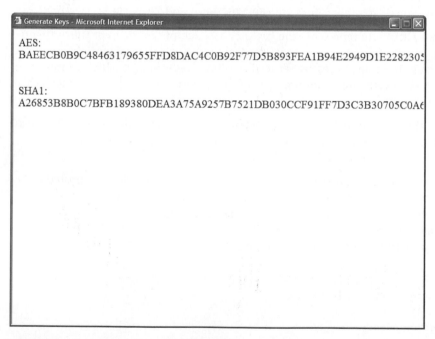

FIGURE 23.1   Generating cryptographically strong keys.

LISTING 23.5   GenerateKeys.aspx

```
<%@ Page Language="C#" %>
<%@ Import Namespace="System.Security.Cryptography" %>
```

```
<!DOCTYPE html PUBLIC "-//W3C//DTD XHTML 1.0 Transitional//EN"
"http://www.w3.org/TR/xhtml1/DTD/xhtml1-transitional.dtd">

<script runat="server">

    void Page_Load()
    {
        lblAES.Text = GetSequence(64);
        lblSHA1.Text = GetSequence(128);
    }

    private string GetSequence(int length)
    {
        byte[] buffer = new byte[length/2];
        RNGCryptoServiceProvider provider = new RNGCryptoServiceProvider();
        provider.GetBytes(buffer);
        StringBuilder builder = new StringBuilder(length);
        for (int i = 0; i < buffer.Length; i++)
            builder.Append(string.Format("{0:X2}", buffer[i]));
        return builder.ToString();
    }
</script>
<html xmlns="http://www.w3.org/1999/xhtml" >
<head id="Head1" runat="server">
    <title>Generate Keys</title>
</head>
<body>
    <form id="form1" runat="server">
    <div>

    AES:
    <asp:Label
        id="lblAES"
        Runat="server" />
    <br /><br />
    SHA1:
    <asp:Label
        id="lblSHA1"
        Runat="server" />

    </div>
    </form>
</body>
</html>
```

23

The page in Listing 23.5 uses the `RNGCryptoServiceProvider` to generate the random sequence of characters. The `GetBytes()` method returns a cryptographically strong sequence of random values.

> **NOTE**
>
> The `GenerateKeys.aspx` page is based on a code sample from an article entitled "How To: Configure MachineKey in ASP.NET 2.0," located at the Microsoft MSDN website (msdn.microsoft.com).

You can add a `machineKey` element with explicit keys to either the machine root web configuration file or to particular application web configuration files. If you don't want to share the same keys across all the applications on a web server, then you should add the `machineKey` element only to the applications that you need to share.

Using Forms Authentication Across Domains

In the previous section, you learned how to share the same authentication cookie across applications located on the same server or a different server. But how do you share the same authentication cookie across domains?

A browser cookie is always domain relative. For example, the Amazon website cannot read cookies set by the Barnes and Noble website, which is a good thing. However, you might discover that you need to share authentication information across websites with different domains.

You can work around this problem by passing an authentication ticket in a query string parameter rather than in a cookie. There is nothing to prevent you from passing query strings between domains.

To enable this scenario, you must configure your applications to accept authentication tickets passed in a query string. The web configuration file in Listing 23.6 includes an `enableCrossAppRedirects` attribute that enables sharing authentication tickets across domains.

LISTING 23.6   Web.config

```
<configuration>
  <system.web>
    <authentication mode="Forms">
      <forms enableCrossAppRedirects="true" />
    </authentication>

    <machineKey
      decryption="AES"
      validation="SHA1"
      decryptionKey="306C1FA852AB3B0115150DD8BA30821CDFD125538A0C606
      ➥DACA53DBB3C3E0AD2"
```

```
validationKey="61A8E04A146AFFAB81B6AD19654F99EA7370807F18F5002725DAB98B
➥8EFD19C711337E26948E26D1D174B159973EA0BE8CC9CAA6AAF513BF84E44B2247792265" />
```

```
  </system.web>
</configuration>
```

If you add the web configuration file in Listing 23.6 to two applications located in different domains, the two applications can share the same authentication ticket.

WARNING

Make sure that you change the validation and encryption keys in Listing 23.6. You can use the `GenerateKeys.aspx` page discussed in the previous section to generate new random keys.

When you link or redirect from one application to another, you must pass the authentication ticket in a query string parameter. The page in Listing 23.7 adds the necessary query string parameter to a hyperlink.

LISTING 23.7   QueryStringAuthenticate.aspx

```
<%@ Page Language="C#" %>
<!DOCTYPE html PUBLIC "-//W3C//DTD XHTML 1.0 Transitional//EN"
"http://www.w3.org/TR/xhtml1/DTD/xhtml1-transitional.dtd">
<script runat="server">

    void Page_Load()
    {
        string cookieName = FormsAuthentication.FormsCookieName;
        string cookieValue = FormsAuthentication.GetAuthCookie(User.Identity.Name,
        ➥false).Value;
        lnkOtherDomain.NavigateUrl += String.Format("?{0}={1}", cookieName,
        ➥cookieValue);
    }
</script>
<html xmlns="http://www.w3.org/1999/xhtml" >
<head id="Head1" runat="server">
    <title>Query String Authenticate</title>
</head>
<body>
    <form id="form1" runat="server">
    <div>

    <asp:HyperLink
```

LISTING 23.7   Continued

```
        id="lnkOtherDomain"
        Text="Link to Other Domain"
        NavigateUrl="http://www.OtherDomain.com/Secret.aspx"
        Runat="server" />


    </div>
    </form>
</body>
</html>
</html>
```

Using the FormsAuthentication Class

The main application programming interface for interacting with Forms authentication is the FormsAuthentication class. This class supports the following properties:

▶ **CookieDomain**—Returns the domain associated with the authentication cookie.

▶ **CookieMode**—Returns the cookieless authentication mode. Possible values are AutoDetect, UseCookies, UseDeviceProfile, and UseUri.

▶ **CookiesSupported**—Returns true when a browser supports cookies and Forms authentication is configured to use cookies.

▶ **DefaultUrl**—Returns the URL of the page to which a user is redirected after being authenticated.

▶ **EnableCrossAppRedirects**—Returns true when an authentication ticket can be removed from a query string.

▶ **FormsCookieName**—Returns the name of the authentication cookie.

▶ **FormsCookiePath**—Returns the path associated with the authentication cookie.

▶ **LoginUrl**—Returns the URL of the page to which a user is redirected when being authenticated.

▶ **RequireSSL**—Returns True when the authentication cookie must be transmitted with SSL (the Secure Sockets Layer).

▶ **SlidingExpiration**—Returns True when the authentication cookie uses a sliding expiration policy.

These properties return the configuration settings for Forms authentication from the web configuration file.

The FormsAuthentication class supports the following methods:

▶ **Authenticate**—Enables you to validate a username and password against a list of usernames and passwords stored in the web configuration file.

▶ **Decrypt**—Enables you to decrypt an authentication cookie.

▶ **GetAuthCookie**—Enables you to retrieve an authentication cookie.

▶ **GetRedirectUrl**—Enables you to retrieve the path to the original page that caused the redirect to the Login page.

▶ **HashPasswordForStoringInConfigFile**—Enables you to hash a password so that it can be stored in the web configuration file.

▶ **RedirectFromLoginPage**—Enables you to redirect a user back to the original page requested before the user was redirected to the Login page.

▶ **RedirectToLoginPage**—Enables you to redirect the user to the Login page.

▶ **RenewTicketIfOld**—Enables you to update the expiration time of an authentication cookie.

▶ **SetAuthCookie**—Enables you to create and issue an authentication cookie.

▶ **SignOut**—Enables you to remove an authentication cookie and log out a user.

You can use the methods and properties of the FormsAuthentication class to build a user registration and authentication system without using ASP.NET Membership. For example, the web configuration file in Listing 23.8 contains a list of usernames and passwords.

LISTING 23.8   Web.Config

```
<configuration>
  <system.web>

    <authentication mode="Forms">
      <forms>
        <credentials passwordFormat="Clear">
          <user name="Bill" password="secret" />
          <user name="Jane" password="secret" />
          <user name="Fred" password="secret" />
        </credentials>
      </forms>
    </authentication>

  </system.web>
</configuration>
```

The web configuration file in Listing 23.8 contains a forms element that contains a credentials element. The credentials element includes a list of usernames and passwords.

Notice that the credentials element includes a passwordFormat attribute that is set to the value Clear. If you prefer, rather than store passwords in clear text, you can store password hash values. That way, anyone working on the web server can't see everyone else's passwords. The other two possible values for the passwordFormat attribute are MD5 and SHA1.

NOTE

If you need to hash a password so that you can store it in the web configuration file, you can use the (appropriately named) FormsAuthentication. HashPasswordForStoringInConfigFile() method. This method accepts a clear text password and the name of a hash algorithm, and it returns a hashed version of the password.

The Login page in Listing 23.9 contains a User Name and a Password text box (see Figure 23.2).

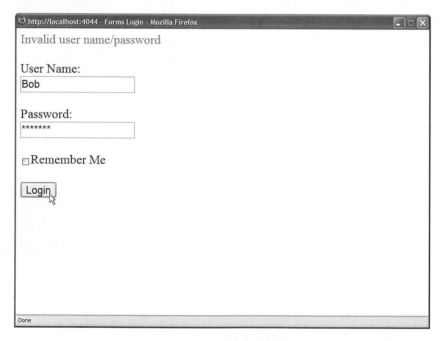

FIGURE 23.2   Authenticating against web configuration credentials.

LISTING 23.9   FormsLogin.aspx

```
<%@ Page Language="C#" %>
<!DOCTYPE html PUBLIC "-//W3C//DTD XHTML 1.0 Transitional//EN"
"http://www.w3.org/TR/xhtml1/DTD/xhtml1-transitional.dtd">
<script runat="server">
```

```
        protected void btnLogin_Click(object sender, EventArgs e)
        {
            if (FormsAuthentication.Authenticate(txtUserName.Text,txtPassword.Text))
                FormsAuthentication.RedirectFromLoginPage(txtUserName.Text,
                ➥chkRememberMe.Checked);
            else
                lblError.Text = "Invalid user name/password";
        }
</script>
<html xmlns="http://www.w3.org/1999/xhtml" >
<head id="Head1" runat="server">
    <title>Forms Login</title>
</head>
<body>
    <form id="form1" runat="server">
    <div>

    <asp:Label
        id="lblError"
        EnableViewState="false"
        ForeColor="Red"
        Runat="server" />

    <br /><br />
    <asp:Label
        id="lblUserName"
        Text="User Name:"
        AssociatedControlID="txtUserName"
        Runat="server" />
    <br />
    <asp:TextBox
        id="txtUserName"
        Runat="server" />
    <br /><br />
    <asp:Label
        id="lblPassword"
        Text="Password:"
        AssociatedControlID="txtPassword"
        Runat="server" />
    <br />
    <asp:TextBox
        id="txtPassword"
        TextMode="Password"
        Runat="server" />
    <br /><br />
    <asp:CheckBox
```

LISTING 23.9   Continued

```
        id="chkRememberMe"
        Text="Remember Me"
        Runat="server" />
    <br /><br />
    <asp:Button
        id="btnLogin"
        Text="Login"
        OnClick="btnLogin_Click"
        Runat="server" />

    </div>
    </form>
</body>
</html>
```

When you click the Login button, the btnLogin_Click() handler executes, and the
FormsAuthentication.Authenticate() method is used to check whether the username
and password entered into the TextBox controls match a username and password in the
web configuration file. If the user successfully authenticates, the FormsAuthentication.
RedirectFromLoginPage() method is called.

The RedirectFromLoginPage() method does two things. The method adds an authentication cookie to the user's browser. The method also redirects the user back to whatever page
the user originally requested. If the user requests the Login page directly, then the user is
redirected to the Default.aspx page.

The second parameter passed to the RedirectFromLoginPage() method indicates whether
you want to create a session or persistent cookie. If you create a persistent cookie, then a
user does not need to log in when the user returns to the website in the future.

Using the User Class

You can use the Page.User or the HttpContext.User property to retrieve information
about the current user. The Page.User property exposes a Principal object that supports
the following method:

▶ **IsInRole**—Enables you to check whether a user is a member of a particular role.

For example, when Windows authentication is enabled, you can use the IsInRole()
method to check whether a user is a member of a particular Microsoft Windows group
such as the BUILTIN\Administrators group:

```
if (User.IsInRole("BUILTIN\Administrators"))
{
```

```
    // Do some Administrator only operation
}
```

> **NOTE**
>
> If the Role Manager is enabled, then you must configure the Role Manager to use the
> `WindowsTokenRoleProvider` before you can use the `User.IsInRole()` method with
> Windows groups.

The `Principal` object also includes an `Identity` property that enables you to get information about the current user's identity. The `Identity` object supports the following three properties:

- **AuthenticationType**—Enables you to determine how the user was authenticated. Examples of possible values are `Forms`, `Basic`, and `NTLM`.

- **IsAuthenticated**—Enables you to determine whether a user is authenticated.

- **Name**—Enables you to retrieve the user's name.

If you want to get the name of the current user, then you can use logic that looks like this:

```
Dim name As String = User.Identity.Name
```

If a user is not authenticated, the `User.Identity.Name` property returns an empty string.

Configuring Authorization

Authorization refers to the process of identifying the resources that you are allowed to access. You control authorization by adding an authorization element to a web configuration file.

Authorization works the same way regardless of the type of authentication that is enabled. In other words, you configure authorization in the same way when using Forms, Windows, and .NET Passport authentication.

Typically, you place all the pages that you want to password-protect in a separate folder. If you add a web configuration file to the folder, then the settings in the web configuration file apply to all pages in the folder and all subfolders.

For example, if you add the web configuration file in Listing 23.10 to a folder, then unauthenticated users are blocked from accessing pages in the folder.

LISTING 23.10   SecretFiles\Web.Config

```
<configuration>
    <system.web>

        <authorization>
```

LISTING 23.10   Continued

```
        <deny users="?"/>
    </authorization>

    </system.web>
</configuration>
```

If you add the file in Listing 23.10 to a folder, then unauthenticated users cannot access any pages in the folder. When Forms authentication is enabled, unauthenticated users are automatically redirected to the Login page.

The web configuration file in Listing 23.9 contains an authorization element that contains a single authorization rule. The configuration file denies access to anonymous users. The ? symbol represents anonymous (unauthenticated) users.

You can use the following two special symbols with the users attribute:

▶ ?—Represents unauthenticated users.

▶ *—Represents all users (unauthenticated or authenticated).

You also can assign a particular username, or comma-delimited list of usernames, to the deny element. For example, the authorization element in Listing 23.11 allows access for a user named Jane, but denies access to anyone else (even authenticated users).

LISTING 23.11   SecretFiles\Web.Config

```
<configuration>
    <system.web>

        <authorization>
            <allow users="Jane" />
            <deny users="*" />
        </authorization>

    </system.web>
</configuration>
```

The order of the authorization rules is important. The ASP.NET Framework uses a first-match algorithm. If you switched the allow and deny rules in Listing 23.11, then no one, not event Jane, would be allowed to access the pages in the folder.

> **NOTE**
>
> You can prevent anonymous users from accessing any page in an application by adding an authorization element to the application root web configuration file. In that case, anonymous users are still allowed to access the Login page. (Otherwise, no one would ever be able to log in when using Forms authentication.)

VISUAL WEB DEVELOPER NOTE

If you prefer, you can configure authorization rules by using the Web Site Administration Tool. This tool provides you with a form interface for configuring authorization rules for different folders. You can open the Web Site Administration Tool by selecting the menu option Website, ASP.NET Configuration.

Authorizing by Role

When creating authorization rules, you can authorize by user role. For example, the web configuration file in Listing 23.12 prevents access to any pages in a folder by anyone except members of the Administrators role.

LISTING 23.12   SecretFiles\Web.Config

```
<configuration>
    <system.web>

      <authorization>
        <allow roles="Administrator"/>
        <deny users="*"/>

      </authorization>

    </system.web>
</configuration>
```

When Forms authentication is enabled, the role refers to a custom role. In the final section of this chapter, "Using the Role Manager," you learn how to configure and create custom roles. When Windows authentication is enabled, the role refers to a Microsoft Windows group.

Authorizing Files by Location

By default, authorization rules are applied to all pages in a folder and all subfolders. However, you also have the option of using the location element with the authorization element. The location element enables you to apply a set of authorization rules to a folder or page at a particular path.

For example, imagine that you want to password-protect one, and only one, page in a folder. In that case, you can use the location element to specify the path of the single page. The web configuration file in Listing 23.13 password-protects a page named Secret.aspx.

LISTING 23.13 Web.Config

```
<configuration>

  <system.web>
    <authentication mode="Forms" />
  </system.web>

  <location path="Secret.aspx">
    <system.web>
      <authorization>
        <deny users="?"/>
      </authorization>
    </system.web>
  </location>

</configuration>
```

You also can use the location element to apply configuration settings to a particular subfolder. For example, the web configuration file in Listing 23.14 password-protects a folder named SecretFiles.

LISTING 23.14 Web.Config

```
<configuration>

  <system.web>
    <authentication mode="Forms" />
  </system.web>

  <location path="SecretFiles">
    <system.web>
      <authorization>
        <deny users="?"/>
      </authorization>
    </system.web>
  </location>

</configuration>
```

Using Authorization with Images and Other File Types

Authorization rules are applied only to files mapped into the ASP.NET Framework. The Visual Web Developer web server maps all file types to the ASP.NET Framework. Internet Information Server, on the other hand, maps only particular file types to the ASP.NET Framework.

If you are using Internet Information Server, and you add an image to a password-protected folder, then users aren't blocked from requesting the image. By default, authorization rules apply only to ASP.NET file types such as ASP.NET pages. Files such as images, Microsoft Word documents, and classic ASP pages are ignored by the ASP.NET Framework.

If you need to password-protect a particular type of static file, such as an image or Microsoft Word document, then you need to map the file's extension to the ASP.NET ISAPI extension.

For example, follow these steps to enable authorization for .gif image files:

1. Open Internet Information Services by selecting Start, Control Panel, Administrative Tools, Internet Information Services.

2. Open the property sheet for a particular website or virtual directory.

3. Open the Application Configuration dialog box by selecting the Directory tab and clicking the Configuration button.

4. Select the Mappings tab (see Figure 23.3).

5. Click the Add button to open the Add/Edit Application Extension Mapping dialog box.

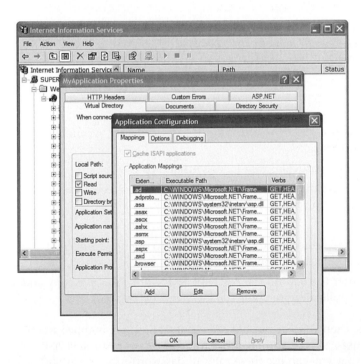

FIGURE 23.3   The Mappings tab in Internet Information Services (Windows XP).

6. In the Executable field, enter the path to the ASP.NET ISAPI DLL. (You can copy and paste this path from the Application Mapping for the `.aspx` extension.)

7. In the Extension field, enter `.gif`.

After you complete these steps, requests for `.gif` images are passed to the ASP.NET Framework. You can then use authentication and authorization rules with `.gif` images.

You can complete the same sequence of steps to password-protect other static file types, such as Microsoft Word documents, Excel spreadsheets, or video files.

Using Authorization with ASP Classic Pages

You can mix ASP.NET pages and ASP classic pages in the same application. However, normally ASP.NET pages and ASP classic pages live in parallel but separate universes. In particular, ASP.NET authentication and authorization is not applied to ASP classic pages.

If you are using Internet Information Server 6 (available with Windows Server 2003), then you can map ASP classic pages into the ASP.NET Framework. In that case, you can apply ASP.NET authorization rules to ASP classic pages.

Internet Information Server 6 supports a feature named *wildcard application mappings*. You can use a wildcard mapping to intercept requests for ASP classic pages and process the requests with the ASP.NET Framework. The ASP.NET Framework can then pass the request back to be executed by ASP classic.

To enable wildcard mapping for ASP.NET, follow these steps:

1. Open Internet Information Services by selecting Start, Control Panel, Administrative Tools, Internet Information Services.

2. Open the property sheet for a particular website or virtual directory.

3. Open the Application Configuration dialog box by selecting the Directory tab and clicking the Configuration button.

4. Select the Mappings tab.

5. Click the Insert button at the bottom of the Mappings tab to open the Add/Edit Application Extension Mapping dialog box (see Figure 23.4).

6. In the Executable field, enter the path to the ASP.NET ISAPI DLL. (You can copy and paste this path from the Application Mapping for the `.aspx` extension.)

After you complete these steps, then all files, not only ASP classic files, are mapped to the ASP.NET Framework. You can use ASP.NET authorization rules to password-protect ASP classic pages in the same way that you can use these rules to password-protect ASP.NET pages. The authorization rules also work with image files, Microsoft Word documents, and any other type of file.

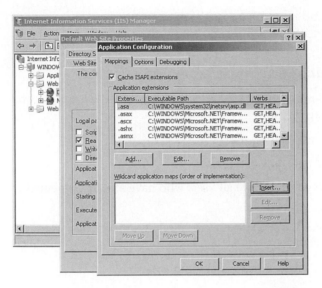

FIGURE 23.4   Enabling wildcard mappings in Internet Information Services (Windows Server 2003).

Using ASP.NET Membership

ASP.NET Membership enables you to create new users, delete users, and edit user properties. It's the framework that is used behind the scenes by the Login controls.

ASP.NET Membership picks up where Forms authentication leaves off. Forms authentication provides you with a way of identifying users. ASP.NET Membership is responsible for representing the user information.

ASP.NET Membership uses the provider model. The ASP.NET Framework includes two Membership providers:

- **SqlMembershipProvider**—Stores user information in a Microsoft SQL Server database.

- **ActiveDirectoryMembershipProvider**—Stores user information in the Active Directory or an Active Directory Application Mode server.

In this section, you learn how to use the ASP.NET Membership application programming interface. You learn how to use the Membership class to modify membership information programmatically.

You also learn how to configure both the SqlMembershipProvider and the ActiveDirectoryMembershipProvider. For example, you learn how to modify the requirements for a valid membership password.

Finally, we build a custom Membership provider. It is an `XmlMembershipProvider` that stores membership information in an XML file.

Using the Membership Application Programming Interface

The main application programming interface for ASP.NET Membership is the `Membership` class. This class supports the following methods:

- ▶ **CreateUser**—Enables you to create a new user.
- ▶ **DeleteUser**—Enables you to delete an existing user.
- ▶ **FindUsersByEmail**—Enables you to retrieve all users who have a particular email address.
- ▶ **FindUsersByName**—Enables you to retrieve all users who have a particular username.
- ▶ **GeneratePassword**—Enables you to generate a random password.
- ▶ **GetAllUsers**—Enables you to retrieve all users.
- ▶ **GetNumberOfUsersOnline**—Enables you to retrieve a count of all users online.
- ▶ **GetUser**—Enables you to retrieve a user by username.
- ▶ **GetUserNameByEmail**—Enables you to retrieve the username for a user with a particular email address.
- ▶ **UpdateUser**—Enables you to update a user.
- ▶ **ValidateUser**—Enables you to validate a username and password.

This class also supports the following event:

- ▶ **ValidatingPassword**—Raised when a user password is validated. You can handle this event to implement a custom validation algorithm.

You can use the methods of the `Membership` class to administer the users of your website. For example, the page in Listing 23.15 displays a list of every registered user (see Figure 23.5).

LISTING 23.15   ListUsers.aspx

```
<%@ Page Language="C#" %>
<!DOCTYPE html PUBLIC "-//W3C//DTD XHTML 1.0 Transitional//EN"
  "http://www.w3.org/TR/xhtml1/DTD/xhtml1-transitional.dtd">
<html xmlns="http://www.w3.org/1999/xhtml" >
<head id="Head1" runat="server">
    <title>List Users</title>
</head>
<body>
```

```
    <form id="form1" runat="server">
    <div>

    <asp:GridView
        id="grdUsers"
        DataSourceID="srcUsers"
        Runat="server" />

    <asp:ObjectDataSource
        id="srcUsers"
        TypeName="System.Web.Security.Membership"
        SelectMethod="GetAllUsers"
        Runat="server" />

    </div>
    </form>
</body>
</html>
```

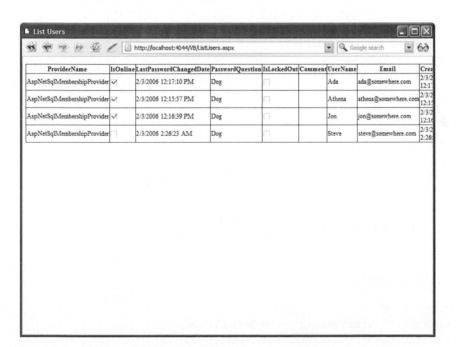

FIGURE 23.5   Displaying registered users.

In Listing 23.15, an ObjectDataSource control is used to represent the Membership class. The GetAllUsers() method is called to get the list of users.

23

You also can use the methods of the Membership class to create custom Login controls. For example, notice that you can retrieve the number of users currently online by calling the GetNumberOfUsersOnline() method. The custom control in Listing 23.16 displays the value returned by this method.

> **NOTE**
>
> Chapter 29, "Building Custom Controls," discusses custom control building.

LISTING 23.16   UsersOnline.cs

```csharp
using System;
using System.Web.Security;
using System.Web.UI;
using System.Web.UI.WebControls;

namespace myControls
{
    /// <summary>
    /// Displays Number of Users Online
    /// </summary>
    public class UsersOnline : WebControl
    {
        protected override void RenderContents(HtmlTextWriter writer)
        {
            writer.Write(Membership.GetNumberOfUsersOnline());
        }
    }
}
```

The page in Listing 23.17 uses the UsersOnline control to display the number of users currently online (see Figure 23.6).

LISTING 23.17   ShowUsersOnline.aspx

```aspx
<%@ Page Language="C#" %>
<%@ Register TagPrefix="custom" Namespace="myControls" %>
<!DOCTYPE html PUBLIC "-//W3C//DTD XHTML 1.0 Transitional//EN"
  "http://www.w3.org/TR/xhtml1/DTD/xhtml1-transitional.dtd">
<html xmlns="http://www.w3.org/1999/xhtml" >
<head id="Head1" runat="server">
    <title>Show UsersOnline</title>
</head>
<body>
```

```
    <form id="form1" runat="server">
    <div>

    How many people are online?
    <br />
    <custom:UsersOnline
        id="UsersOnline1"
        Runat="server" />

    </div>
    </form>
</body>
</html>
```

> **NOTE**
>
> A user is considered online if his username was used in a call to the `ValidateUser()`, `UpdateUser()`, or `GetUser()` method in the last 15 minutes. You can modify the default time interval of 15 minutes by modifying the `userIsOnlineTimeWindow` attribute of the membership element in the web configuration file.

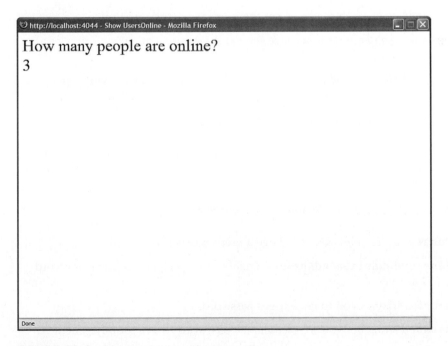

FIGURE 23.6   Display number of users online.

Several of the methods of the Membership class return one or more MembershipUser objects. The MembershipUser object is used to represent a particular website member. This class supports the following properties:

▶ **Comment**—Enables you to associate a comment with the user.

▶ **CreationDate**—Enables you to get the date when the user was created.

▶ **Email**—Enables you to get or set the user's email address.

▶ **IsApproved**—Enables you to get or set whether the user is approved and her account is active.

▶ **IsLockedOut**—Enables you to get the user's lockout status.

▶ **IsOnline**—Enables you to determine whether the user is online.

▶ **LastActivityDate**—Enables you to get or set the date of the user's last activity. This date is updated automatically with a call to CreateUser(), ValidateUser(), or GetUser().

▶ **LastLockoutDate**—Enables you to get the date that the user was last locked out.

▶ **LastLoginDate**—Enables you to get the date that the user last logged in.

▶ **LastPasswordChangedDate**—Enables you to get the date that the user last changed her password.

▶ **PasswordQuestion**—Enables you to get the user's password question.

▶ **ProviderName**—Enables you to retrieve the name of the Membership provider associated with this user.

▶ **ProviderUserKey**—Enables you to retrieve a unique key associated with the user. In the case of the SqlMembershipProvider, this is the value of a GUID column.

▶ **UserName**—Enables you to get the name of the user.

Notice that the MembershipUser class does not contain a property for the user's password or password answer. This is intentional. If you need to change a user's password, then you need to call a method.

The MembershipUser class supports the following methods:

▶ **ChangePassword**—Enables you to change a user's password.

▶ **ChangePasswordQuestionAndAnswer**—Enables you to change a user's password question and answer.

▶ **GetPassword**—Enables you to get a user's password.

▶ **ResetPassword**—Enables you to reset a user's password to a randomly generated password.

▶ **UnlockUser**—Enables you to unlock a user account that has been locked out.

Encrypting and Hashing User Passwords

Both of the default Membership providers included in the ASP.NET Framework enable you to store user passwords in three ways:

▶ **Clear**—Passwords are stored in clear text.

▶ **Encrypted**—Passwords are encrypted before they are stored.

▶ **Hashed**—Passwords are not stored. Only the hash values of passwords are stored. (This is the default value.)

You configure how passwords are stored by setting the `passwordFormat` attribute in the web configuration file. For example, the web configuration file in Listing 23.18 configures the `SqlMembershipProvider` to store passwords in plain text.

LISTING 23.18   Web.Config

```
<configuration>
    <system.web>
      <authentication mode="Forms" />

      <membership defaultProvider="MyProvider">
        <providers>
          <add
            name="MyProvider"
            type="System.Web.Security.SqlMembershipProvider"
            passwordFormat="Clear"
            connectionStringName="LocalSqlServer"/>
        </providers>

      </membership>
    </system.web>
</configuration>
```

The default value of the `passwordFormat` attribute is `Hashed`. By default, actual passwords are not stored anywhere. A hash value is generated for a password and the hash value is stored.

NOTE

A hash algorithm generates a unique value for each input. The distinctive thing about a hash algorithm is that it works in only one direction. You can easily generate a hash value from any value. However, you cannot easily determine the original value from a hash value.

The advantage of storing hash values is that even if your website is compromised by a hacker, the hacker cannot steal anyone's passwords. The disadvantage of using hash values is that you also cannot retrieve user passwords. For example, you cannot use the PasswordRecovery control to email a user his original password.

Instead of hashing passwords, you can encrypt the passwords. The disadvantage of encrypting passwords is that it is more processor intensive than hashing passwords. The advantage of encrypting passwords is that you can retrieve user passwords.

The web configuration file in Listing 23.19 configures the SqlMembershipProvider to encrypt passwords. Notice that the web configuration file includes a machineKey element. You must supply an explicit decryptionKey when encrypting passwords.

NOTE

For more information on the machineKey element, see the "Using Forms Authentication Across Applications" section, earlier in this chapter.

LISTING 23.19 Web.Config

```
<configuration>
  <system.web>
    <authentication mode="Forms" />

    <membership defaultProvider="MyProvider">
      <providers>
        <add
          name="MyProvider"
          type="System.Web.Security.SqlMembershipProvider"
          passwordFormat="Encrypted"
          connectionStringName="LocalSqlServer"/>
      </providers>
    </membership>

    <machineKey
        decryption="AES"
        decryptionKey="306C1FA852AB3B0115150DD8BA30821CDFD125538A0C606
        ➥DACA53DBB3C3E0AD2" />


  </system.web>
</configuration>
```

> **WARNING**
>
> Make sure that you change the value of the decryptionKey attribute before using the web configuration file in Listing 23.19. You can generate a new decryptionKey with the GenerateKeys.aspx page described in the "Using Forms Authentication Across Applications" section, earlier in this chapter.

Modifying User Password Requirements

By default, passwords are required to contain at least seven characters and one non-alphanumeric character (a character that is not a letter or a number such as *,_, or !). You can set three Membership provider attributes that determine password policy:

- ▶ **minRequiredPasswordLength**—The minimum required password length (the default value is 7).

- ▶ **minRequiredNonalphanumericCharacters**—The minimum number of non-alphanumeric characters (the default value is 1).

- ▶ **passwordStrengthRegularExpression**—The regular expression pattern that a valid password must match (the default value is an empty string).

The minRequiredNonAlphanumericCharacters attribute confuses everyone. Website users are not familiar with the requirement that they must enter a nonalphanumeric character. The web configuration file in Listing 23.20 illustrates how you can disable this requirement when using the SqlMembershipProvider.

LISTING 23.20   Web.Config

```
<configuration>
  <system.web>
    <authentication mode="Forms" />

    <membership defaultProvider="MyProvider">
      <providers>
        <add
          name="MyProvider"
          type="System.Web.Security.SqlMembershipProvider"
          minRequiredNonalphanumericCharacters="0"
          connectionStringName="LocalSqlServer"/>
      </providers>
    </membership>

  </system.web>
</configuration>
```

23

Locking Out Bad Users

By default, if you enter a bad password more than five times within 10 minutes, your account is automatically locked out. In other words, it is disabled.

Also, if you enter the wrong answer for the password answer more than five times in a 10-minute interval, your account is locked out. You get five attempts at your password and five attempts at your password answer. (These two things are tracked independently.)

Two configuration settings control when an account gets locked out:

▶ **maxInvalidPasswordAttempts**—The maximum number of bad passwords or bad password answers that you are allowed to enter (default value is 5).

▶ **passwordAttemptWindow**—The time interval in minutes in which entering bad passwords or bad password answers results in being locked out.

For example, the web configuration file in Listing 23.21 modifies the default settings to enable you to enter a maximum of three bad passwords or bad password answers in one hour.

LISTING 23.21   Web.Config

```
<configuration>
  <system.web>
    <authentication mode="Forms" />

    <membership defaultProvider="MyProvider">
      <providers>
        <add
          name="MyProvider"
          type="System.Web.Security.SqlMembershipProvider"
          maxInvalidPasswordAttempts="3"
          passwordAttemptWindow="60"
          connectionStringName="LocalSqlServer"/>
      </providers>
    </membership>

  </system.web>
</configuration>
```

After a user has been locked out, you must call the MembershipUser.UnlockUser() method to re-enable the user account. The page in Listing 23.22 enables you to enter a username and remove a lock (see Figure 23.7).

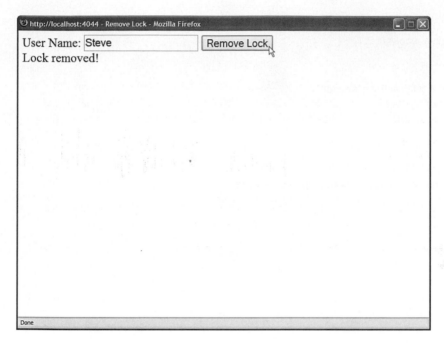

FIGURE 23.7   Removing a user lock.

LISTING 23.22   RemoveLock.aspx

```
<%@ Page Language="C#" %>
<!DOCTYPE html PUBLIC "-//W3C//DTD XHTML 1.0 Transitional//EN"
"http://www.w3.org/TR/xhtml1/DTD/xhtml1-transitional.dtd">
<script runat="server">

    protected void btnRemove_Click(object sender, EventArgs e)
    {
        MembershipUser userToUnlock = Membership.GetUser(txtUserName.Text);
        if (userToUnlock == null)
        {
            lblMessage.Text = "User not found!";
        }
        else
        {
            userToUnlock.UnlockUser();
            lblMessage.Text = "Lock removed!";
        }
    }
</script>
<html xmlns="http://www.w3.org/1999/xhtml" >
<head runat="server">
```

LISTING 23.22   Continued

```
    <title>Remove Lock</title>
</head>
<body>
    <form id="form1" runat="server">
    <div>

    <asp:Label
        id="lblUserName"
        Text="User Name:"
        AssociatedControlID="txtUserName"
        Runat="server" />
    <asp:TextBox
        id="txtUserName"
        Runat="server" />
    <asp:Button
        id="btnRemove"
        Text="Remove Lock"
        Runat="server" OnClick="btnRemove_Click" />
    <br />
    <asp:Label
        id="lblMessage"
        EnableViewState="false"
        Runat="server" />
    </div>
    </form>
</body>
</html>
```

Configuring the SQLMembershipProvider

The SqlMembershipProvider is the default Membership provider. Unless otherwise configured, it stores membership information in the local ASPNETDB.mdf Microsoft SQL Server
Express database located in your application's App_Data folder. This database is created for
you automatically the first time that you use Membership.

If you want to store membership information in some other Microsoft SQL Server database, then you need to perform the following two tasks:

▶ Add the necessary database objects to the Microsoft SQL Server database.

▶ Configure your application to use the new database.

To complete the first task, you can use the aspnet_regiis command-line tool. This tool is
located in the following folder:

```
\WINDOWS\Microsoft.NET\Framework\v2.0.50727
```

> **NOTE**
>
> If you open the SDK Command Prompt, then you don't need to navigate to the Microsoft.NET folder before using the aspnet_regsql tool.

If you execute the aspnet_regsql tool without supplying any parameters, then the ASP.NET SQL Server Setup Wizard appears (see Figure 23.8). You can use this wizard to select a database and install the Membership objects automatically.

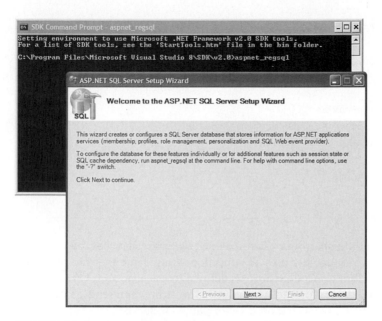

FIGURE 23.8   Using the ASP.NET SQL Setup Wizard.

If you prefer, rather than use the aspnet_reqsql tool, you can execute the following two SQL batch files to install Membership:

```
\WINDOWS\Microsoft.NET\Framework\v2.0.50727\InstallCommon.sql
\WINDOWS\Microsoft.NET\Framework\v2.0.50727\InstallMembership.sql
```

If you don't want to install the .NET Framework on your database server, then you can execute these SQL batch files.

After you have configured your database to support ASP.NET Membership, you must configure your application to connect to your database when using Membership. The web configuration file in Listing 23.23 connects to a database named MyDatabase located on a server named MyServer.

LISTING 23.23   Web.Config

```
<configuration>
  <connectionStrings>
    <add name="MyConnection" connectionString="Data Source=MyServer;IntegratedSecu-
rity=True;Initial Catalog=MyDatabase"/>
  </connectionStrings>

  <system.web>
    <authentication mode="Forms" />

    <membership defaultProvider="MyMembershipProvider" >
      <providers>
        <add
          name="MyMembershipProvider"
          type="System.Web.Security.SqlMembershipProvider"
          connectionStringName="MyConnection" />
      </providers>
    </membership>
  </system.web>
</configuration>
```

In Listing 23.23, a new default Membership provider named MyMembershipProvider is configured. The new Membership provider uses a connection string name that has the value MyConnection. The MyConnection connection string is defined in the connectionStrings element near the top of the configuration file. This connection string represents a connection to a database named MyDatabase located on a server named MyServer.

Configuring the ActiveDirectoryMembershipProvider

The other Membership provider included in the ASP.NET Framework is the ActiveDirectoryMembershipProvider. You can use this provider to store user information in Active Directory or ADAM (Active Directory Application Mode).

ADAM is a lightweight version of Active Directory. You can download ADAM from the Microsoft website (www.microsoft.com/adam). ADAM is compatible with both Microsoft Windows Server 2003 and Microsoft Windows XP Professional (Service Pack 1).

If you want to use ASP.NET Membership with ADAM, then you need to complete the following two steps:

1. Create an ADAM instance and create the required classes.
2. Configure your application to use the ActiveDirectoryMembershipProvider and connect to the ADAM instance.

The following sections examine each of these steps in turn.

Configuring ADAM   First, you need to set up a new instance of ADAM. After downloading and installing ADAM, follow these steps:

1. Launch the Active Directory Application Mode Setup Wizard by selecting Create an ADAM Instance from the ADAM program group (see Figure 23.9).

FIGURE 23.9   Creating a new ADAM instance.

2. In the Setup Options step, select the option to create a unique instance.
3. In the Instance Name step, enter the name **WebUsersInstance**.
4. In the Ports step, use the default LDAP and SSL port numbers (389 and 636).
5. In the Application Directory Partition step, create a new directory application partition named O=WebUsersDirectory.
6. In the File Locations step, use the default data file locations.
7. In the Service Account Selection step, select Network Service Account.
8. In the ADAM Administrators step, select Currently Logged on User for the administrator account.
9. In the Importing LDIF Files step, select MS-AZMan.ldf, MS-InetOrgPerson.ldf, MS-User.ldf, MS-UserProxy.ldf.

After you have completed the preceding steps, a new ADAM instance named WebUsersInstance is created. The next step is to configure an ADAM administrator account. Follow these steps:

WARNING

If you are using Windows XP, and you don't have an SSL certificate installed, then you need to perform an additional configuration step. Otherwise, you'll receive an error when you attempt to reset a user password.

By default, you are not allowed to perform password operations over a non-secured connection to an ADAM instance. You can disable this requirement by using the dsmgmt.exe tool included with ADAM. Open the ADAM Tools Command Prompt and type the following series of commands:

1. Type **dsmgmt**.
2. Type **ds behavior**.
3. Type **connections**.
4. Type **connect to server localhost:389**.
5. Type **quit**.
6. Type **allow passwd op on unsecured connection**.
7. Type **quit**.

If you don't use an SSL connection, then passwords are transmitted in plain text. Don't do this in the case of a production application.

1. Open the ADAM ADSI Edit application from the ADAM program group (see Figure 23.10).

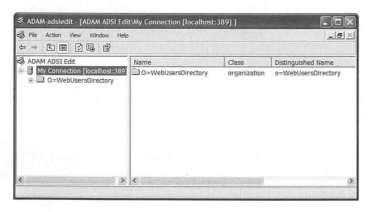

FIGURE 23.10   Using ADAM ADSI Edit.

2. Open the Connection Settings dialog box by selecting the menu option Action, Connect To.

3. In the Connection Settings dialog box, select the option to connect to a node by using a distinguished name and enter the name **O=WebUsersDirectory**. Click OK.

4. Expand the new connection and select the **O=WebUsersDirectory node**.

5. Select the menu option Action, New, Object.

6. In the Create Object dialog box, select the organizationalUnit class and name the new class WebUsers.

7. Select the OU=WebUsers node and select the menu option Action, New, Object.

8. In the Create Object dialog box, select the user class and name the new class `ADAMAdministrator`.

9. Select `CN=ADAMAdministrator` and select the menu option Action, Reset Password and enter the password **secret_**.

10. Select the `CN=Roles` node and double-click the `CN-Administrators` node.

11. Double-click the `Member` attribute and add the distinguished name for the `ADAMAdministrator` ADAM account (`CN=ADAMAdministrator, OU=WebUsers,O=WebUsersDirectory`).

After you complete this series of steps, an `ADAMAdministrator` account is configured. You need to use this account when connecting to the ADAM instance from the `ActiveDirectoryMembershipProvider`.

Configuring the `ActiveDirectoryMembershipProvider`   The next step is to configure your application to use the `ActiveDirectoryMembership` provider. You can use the web configuration file in Listing 23.24.

LISTING 23.24   Web.Config

```
<configuration>

  <connectionStrings>
    <add
      name="ADAMConnection"
      connectionString="LDAP://localhost:389/OU=WebUsers,O=WebUsersDirectory"/>
  </connectionStrings>

  <system.web>
    <authentication mode="Forms" />

    <membership defaultProvider="MyMembershipProvider">
      <providers>
        <add
          name="MyMembershipProvider"
          type="System.Web.Security.ActiveDirectoryMembershipProvider"
          connectionStringName="ADAMConnection"
          connectionProtection="None"
          connectionUsername="CN=ADAMAdministrator,OU=WebUsers,O=WebUsersDirectory"
          connectionPassword="secret_"
          enableSearchMethods="true" />

      </providers>
    </membership>
  </system.web>
</configuration>
```

The web configuration file in Listing 23.24 configures a new default Membership provider named `MyMembershipProvider`. This provider is an instance of the `ActiveDirectoryMembershipProvider`.

Several of the attributes used with the `ActiveDirectoryMembershipProvider` require additional explanation. The `connectionStringName` attribute points to the connection string defined in the `connectionStrings` section. This connection string connects to a local ADAM instance that listens on port 389.

Notice that the `connectionProtection` attribute is set to the value `None`. If you don't modify this attribute, then you are required to use an SSL connection. If you do use an SSL connection, you need to change the port used in the connection string (typically port 636).

The `connectionUsername` and `connectionPassword` attributes use the `ADAMAdministrator` account that you configured in the previous section. When you don't use an SSL connection, you must provide both a `connectionUsername` and `connectionPassword` attribute.

Finally, notice that the provider declaration includes an `enableSearchMethods` attribute. If you want to be able to configure users by using the Web Site Administration Tool, then you must include this attribute.

The `ActiveDirectoryMembershipProvider` class supports several attributes specific to working with Active Directory:

▶ **connectionStringName**—Enables you to specify the name of the connection to the Active Directory Server in the `connectionStrings` section.

▶ **connectionUsername**—Enables you to specify the Active Directory account used to connect to Active Directory.

▶ **connectionPassword**—Enables you to specify the Active Directory password used to connect to Active Directory.

▶ **connectionProtection**—Enables you to specify whether or not the connection is encrypted. Possible values are `None` and `Secure`.

▶ **enableSearchMethods**—Enables the `ActiveDirectoryMembershipProvider` class to use additional methods. You must enable this attribute when using the Web Site Administration Tool.

▶ **attributeMapPasswordQuestion**—Enables you to map the Membership security question to an Active Directory attribute.

▶ **attributeMapPasswordAnswer**—Enables you to map the Membership security answer to an Active Directory attribute.

▶ **attributeMapFailedPasswordAnswerCount**—Enables you to map the Membership `MaxInvalidPasswordAttempts` property to an Active Directory attribute.

▶ **attributeMapFailedPasswordAnswerTime**—Enables you to map the Membership `PasswordAttemptWindow` property to an Active Directory attribute.

▶ **attributeMapFailedPasswordAnswerLockoutTime**—Enables you to map the Membership PasswordAnswerAttemptLockoutDuration property to an Active Directory attribute.

After you finish these configuration steps, you can use the ActiveDirectoryMembershipProvider in precisely the same way that you can use the SqlMembershipProvider. When you use the Login control, users are validated against Active Directory. When you use the CreateUserWizard control, new users are created in Active Directory.

Creating a Custom Membership Provider

Because ASP.NET Membership uses the provider model, you can easily extend ASP.NET membership by creating a custom Membership provider. There are two main situations in which you might need to create a custom Membership provider.

First, imagine that you have an existing ASP.NET 1.x or ASP classic application. You are currently storing membership information in your own custom set of database tables. Furthermore, your table schemas don't easily map to the table schemas used by the SqlMembershipProvider.

In this situation, it makes sense to create a custom Membership provider that reflects your existing database schema. If you create a custom Membership provider, you can use your existing database tables with ASP.NET Membership.

Second, imagine that you need to store membership information in a data store other than Microsoft SQL Server or Active Directory. For example, your organization might be committed to Oracle or DB2. In that case, you need to create a custom Membership provider to work with the custom data store.

In this section, we create a simple custom Membership provider: an XmlMembershipProvider that stores membership information in an XML file.

Unfortunately, the code for the XmlMembershipProvider is too long to place here. The code is included on the CD that accompanies this book in a file named XmlMembershipProvider.cs, located in the App_Code folder.

The XmlMembershipProvider class inherits from the abstract MembershipProvider class. This class has over 25 properties and methods that you are required to implement.

For example, you are required to implement the ValidateUser() method. The Login control calls this method when it validates a username and password.

You also are required to implement the CreateUser() method. This method is called by the CreateUserWizard control when a new user is created.

The web configuration file used to set up the XmlMembershipProvider is contained in Listing 23.25.

LISTING 23.25   Web.Config

```
<configuration>
    <system.web>

      <authentication mode="Forms" />

      <membership defaultProvider="MyMembershipProvider">
        <providers>
          <add
            name="MyMembershipProvider"
            type="AspNetUnleashed.XmlMembershipProvider"
            dataFile="~/App_Data/Membership.xml"
            requiresQuestionAndAnswer="false"
            enablePasswordRetrieval="true"
            enablePasswordReset="true"
            passwordFormat="Clear" />
        </providers>
      </membership>

    </system.web>
</configuration>
```

Notice that the XmlMembershipProvider supports a number of attributes. For example, it supports a passwordFormat attribute that enables you to specify whether passwords are stored as hash values or as plain text. (It does not support encrypted passwords.)

The XmlMembershipProvider stores membership information in an XML file named Membership.xml, located in the App_Data folder. If you want, you can add users to the file by hand. Alternatively, you can use the CreateUserWizard control or the Web Site Administration Tool to create new users.

A sample of the Membership.xml file is contained in Listing 23.26.

LISTING 23.26   App_Data\Membership.xml

```
<credentials>
  <user name="Steve" password="secret" email="steve@somewhere.com" />
  <user name="Andrew" password="secret" email="andrew@somewhere.com" />
</credentials>
```

The sample code folder on the CD includes a Register.aspx, Login.aspx, and ChangePassword.aspx page. You can use these pages to try out different features of the XmlMembershipProvider.

> **WARNING**
>
> Dynamic XPath queries are open to XPath Injection Attacks in the same way that dynamic SQL queries are open to SQL Injection Attacks. When writing the `XmlMembershipProvider` class, I avoided using methods such as `SelectSingleNode()` method to avoid XPath Injection Attack issues, even though using this method would result in leaner and faster code. Sometimes, it is better to be safe than fast.

Using the Role Manager

Instead of configuring authorization for particular users, you can group users into roles and assign authorization rules to the roles. For example, you might want to password-protect a section of your website so that only members of the Administrators role can access the pages in that section.

Like ASP.NET Membership, the Role Manager is built on the existing ASP.NET authentication framework. You configure role authorization rules by adding an authorization element to one or more web configuration files.

Furthermore, like ASP.NET Membership, the Role Manager uses the provider model. You can customize where role information is stored by configuring a particular Role provider.

The ASP.NET Framework includes three role providers:

- ▶ **SqlRoleProvider**—Enables you to store role information in a Microsoft SQL Server database.

- ▶ **WindowsTokenRoleProvider**—Enables you to use Microsoft Windows groups to represent role information.

- ▶ **AuthorizationStoreRoleProvider**—Enables you to use Authorization Manager to store role information in an XML file, Active Directory, or Activity Directory Application Mode (ADAM).

In the following sections, you learn how to configure each of these Role providers. You also learn how to manage role information programmatically by working with the Roles application programming interface.

Configuring the SqlRoleProvider

The SqlRoleProvider is the default role provider. You can use the SqlRoleProvider to store role information in a Microsoft SQL Server database. The SqlRoleProvider enables you to create custom roles. You can make up any roles that you need.

You can use the SqlRoleProvider with either Forms authentication or Windows authentication. When Forms authentication is enabled, you can use ASP.NET Membership to represent users and assign the users to particular roles. When Windows authentication is enabled, you assign particular Windows user accounts to custom roles. I assume, in this section, that you are using Forms authentication.

The web configuration file in Listing 23.27 enables the SqlRoleProvider.

LISTING 23.27   Web.Config

```
<configuration>
    <system.web>
        <roleManager enabled="true" />
        <authentication mode="Forms" />
    </system.web>
</configuration>
```

The Role Manager is disabled by default. The configuration file in Listing 23.27 simply
enables the Role Manager. Notice that the configuration file also enables Forms authentication.

If you don't want to type the file in Listing 23.27, you can let the Web Site Administration
Tool create the file for you. Open the Web Site Administration Tool in Visual Web
Developer by selecting the menu option Website, ASP.NET Configuration. Next, click the
Security tab and click the Enable roles link (see Figure 23.11).

After you enable the Role Manager, you need to create some roles. You can create roles in
two ways. You can use the Web Site Administration Tool or you can create the roles
programmatically.

Open the Web Site Administration Tool and click the Create or Manage Roles link located
under the Security tab. At this point, you can start creating roles. I'll assume that you have
created a role named Managers.

After you create a set of roles, you need to assign users to the roles. Again, you can do this
by using the Web Site Administration Tool or you can assign users to roles programmatically.

If you have not created any users for your application, create a user now by clicking the
Create User link under the Security tab. Notice that you can assign a user to one or more
roles when you create the user (see Figure 23.12). You can click the Create or Manage
Roles link to assign roles to users at a later date.

After you finish creating your roles and assigning users to the roles, you can use the roles
in the authentication section of a web configuration file. For example, imagine that your
website includes a folder named SecretFiles and you want only members of the Managers
role to be able to access the pages in that folder. The web configuration file in Listing 23.28
blocks access to anyone except members of the Managers role to the SecretFiles folder.

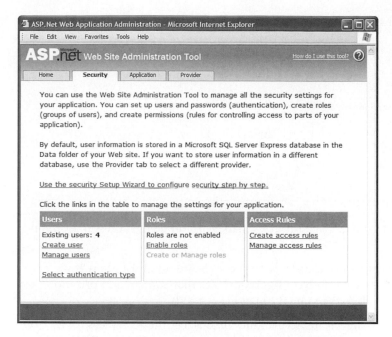

FIGURE 23.11   Enabling Roles with the Web Site Administration Tool.

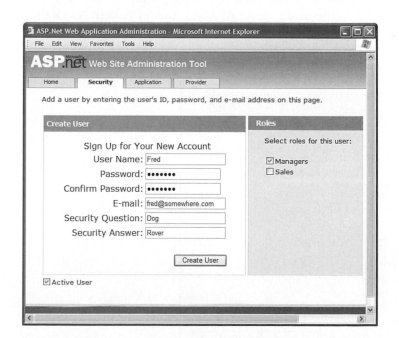

FIGURE 23.12   Assigning a new user to a role.

LISTING 23.28   Web.Config

```
<configuration>
    <system.web>

      <authorization>
        <allow roles="Managers"/>
        <deny users="*"/>
      </authorization>

    </system.web>
</configuration>
```

The configuration file in Listing 23.28 authorizes Managers and denies access to everyone else.

If you prefer, you can manage authorization with the Web Site Administration Tool. Behind the scenes, this tool creates web configuration files that contain authorization elements (in other words, it does the same thing as we just did).

Under the Security tab, click the Create Access Rules link. Select the SecretFiles folder from the tree view, select the Managers role, and select Allow (see Figure 23.13). Click the OK button to create the rule. Next, create a second access rule to deny access to users not in the Managers role. Select the SecretFiles folder, select All Users, and select Deny. Click the OK button to add the new rule.

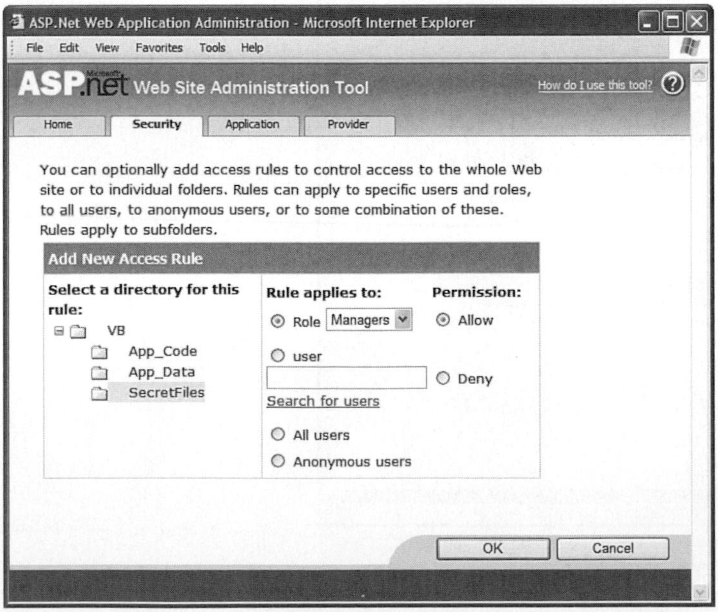

FIGURE 23.13   Creating authorization rules.

Using a Different Database with the SqlRoleProvider   By default, the SqlRoleProvider uses the same Microsoft SQL Server Express database as ASP.NET Membership: the AspNetDB.mdf database. This database is created for you automatically in your application's root App_Data folder.

If you want to store role information in another Microsoft SQL Server database, then you must perform the following two configuration steps:

1. Configure the database so that it contains the necessary database objects.

2. Configure your application to use the new database.

Before you can store role information in a database, you need to add the necessary tables and stored procedures to the database. The easiest way to add these objects is to use the aspnet_regsql command-line tool. This tool is located in the following folder:

```
C:\WINDOWS\Microsoft.NET\Framework\v2.0.50727
```

NOTE

You don't need to navigate to the Microsoft.NET folder when you open the SDK Command Prompt.

If you execute aspnet_regsql without any parameters, then the ASP.NET SQL Server Setup Wizard opens (see Figure 23.14). You can use this wizard to connect to a database and add the necessary database objects automatically.

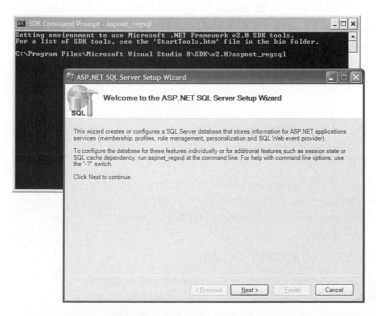

FIGURE 23.14   Using the SQL Server Setup Wizard.

Alternatively, you can set up a database by executing the following two SQL batch files.

▶ `InstallCommon.sql`

▶ `InstallRoles.sql`

These batch files are located in the same folder as the `aspnet_regsql` tool.

After you set up your database, you need to configure a new `SqlRoleProvider` that includes the proper connection string for your database. The web configuration file in Listing 23.29 configures a new provider named `MyRoleProvider` that connects to a database named MyDatabase located on a server named MyServer.

LISTING 23.29 Web.Config

```
<configuration>
  <connectionStrings>
    <add
      name="MyConnection"
      connectionString="Data Source=MyServer;Integrated Security=True;Initial Cata-
log=MyDatabase"/>
  </connectionStrings>

  <system.web>
      <authentication mode="Forms" />

      <roleManager enabled="true" defaultProvider="MyRoleProvider">
        <providers>
          <add
            name="MyRoleProvider"
            type="System.Web.Security.SqlRoleProvider"
            connectionStringName="MyConnection"/>
        </providers>
      </roleManager>

  </system.web>
</configuration>
```

The configuration file in Listing 23.29 creates a new default `RoleManager` named `MyRoleProvider`. Notice that the `MyRoleProvider` provider includes a `connectionStringName` attribute that points to the `MyConnection` connection.

Configuring the `WindowsTokenRoleProvider`

When you use the `WindowsTokenRoleProvider`, roles correspond to Microsoft Windows groups. You must enable Windows authentication when using the `WindowsTokenRoleProvider`. You cannot use Forms authentication or ASP.NET Membership with the `WindowsTokenRoleProvider`.

The configuration file in Listing 23.30 configures the WindowsTokenRoleProvider as the default provider.

LISTING 23.30   Web.Config

```
<configuration>
    <system.web>
        <authentication mode="Windows" />

        <roleManager enabled="true" defaultProvider="MyRoleProvider">
            <providers>
                <add
                    name="MyRoleProvider"
                    type="System.Web.Security.WindowsTokenRoleProvider" />
            </providers>
        </roleManager>

    </system.web>
</configuration>
```

The page in Listing 23.31 contains a LoginView control. The LoginView control displays different content to the members of the Windows Administrators group than it displays to everyone else (see Figure 23.15).

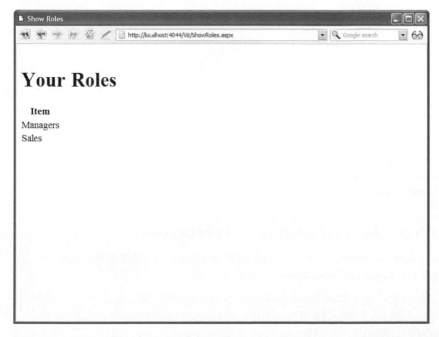

FIGURE 23.15   Displaying different content to members of the Windows Administrators group.

LISTING 23.31   `ShowWindowsRoles.aspx`

```
<%@ Page Language="C#" %>
<!DOCTYPE html PUBLIC "-//W3C//DTD XHTML 1.0 Transitional//EN"
   "http://www.w3.org/TR/xhtml1/DTD/xhtml1-transitional.dtd">
<html xmlns="http://www.w3.org/1999/xhtml" >
<head id="Head1" runat="server">
    <title>Show Windows Roles</title>
</head>
<body>
    <form id="form1" runat="server">
    <div>

    <asp:LoginView
        id="LoginView1"
        Runat="server">
        <RoleGroups>
        <asp:RoleGroup Roles="BUILTIN\Administrators">
            <ContentTemplate>
            <h1>Welcome Administrator!</h1>
            </ContentTemplate>
        </asp:RoleGroup>
        </RoleGroups>
        <LoggedInTemplate>
            <h1>Welcome Average User!</h1>
        </LoggedInTemplate>
    </asp:LoginView>

    </div>
    </form>
</body>
</html>
```

If you request the page in Listing 23.31 after enabling the `WindowsTokenRoleProvider`, then you see the content displayed by the `LoginView` control only when you are a member of the Windows Administrators group.

Configuring the `AuthorizationStoreRoleProvider`

Authorization Manager (AzMan) is a component of Windows Server 2003. You can use AzMan to define roles, tasks, and operations.

AzMan supports more features than the authorization framework included in the ASP.NET Framework. For example, AzMan supports role inheritance, which enables you to easily define new roles based on existing roles.

> **NOTE**
>
> You can use AzMan with Windows XP Professional. However, you must install it first. You need to download the Windows Server 2003 Administrative Tools Pack from the Microsoft MSDN website (msdn.microsoft.com).

AzMan can store role information in three different ways. You can create an authorization store by using an XML file, by using Active Directory, or by using Active Directory Application Mode (ADAM).

Before you use AzMan with the ASP.NET Framework, you need to create an authorization store. Role information is stored in an XML file local to the application. Follow these steps:

1. Launch AzMan by executing the command AzMan.msc from a command prompt (see Figure 23.16).

FIGURE 23.16   Using AzMan.

2. Switch AzMan into Developer mode by selecting the menu option Action, Options and selecting Developer mode.

3. Open the New Authorization Store dialog box by selecting the menu option Action, New Authorization Store.

4. Select the XML file option and enter the path to your application's App_Data folder for the Store Name field. For example:

```
c:\Websites\MyWebsite\App_Data\WebRoles.xml
```

5. Create a new AzMan application by right-clicking the name of your authorization store and selecting New Application. Enter the name WebRoles for your application (you can leave the other fields blank).

After you complete these steps, a new XML file is added to your application. This XML file contains the authorization store.

Next, you need to configure the ASP.NET Role Manager to use the authorization store. The web configuration file in Listing 23.32 uses the `WebRoles.xml` authorization store.

LISTING 23.32   Web.Config

```
<configuration>
  <connectionStrings>
    <add
      name="AZConnection"
      connectionString="msxml://~/App_Data/WebRoles.xml"/>
  </connectionStrings>

  <system.web>
    <authentication mode="Windows" />

    <roleManager enabled="true" defaultProvider="MyRoleProvider">
      <providers>
        <add
          name="MyRoleProvider"
          type="System.Web.Security.AuthorizationStoreRoleProvider"
          connectionStringName="AZConnection"
          applicationName="WebRoles"
          />
      </providers>
    </roleManager>

  </system.web>
</configuration>
```

You should notice a couple of things about the configuration file in Listing 23.32. First, notice that the connection string uses the prefix msxml: to indicate that the connection string represents a connection to an XML file.

Second, notice that the AuthorizationStoreRoleProvider includes an applicationName attribute. This attribute must contain the name of the AzMan application that you created in the preceding steps.

After you complete these configuration steps, you can use the AzMan just as you do the default `SqlMembershipProvider`. You can define new roles by using either the Web Site Administration Tool or the Authorization Manager interface (see Figure 23.17).

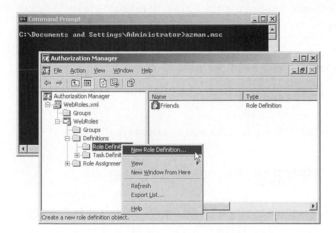

FIGURE 23.17   Creating a new role definition with Authorization Manager.

Caching Roles in a Browser Cookie

To improve your application's performance, you can cache user roles in a browser cookie. That way, the Role Manager does not have to perform a query against the Role provider each and every time a user visits a page.

Caching roles in cookies is disabled by default. You can enable this feature with the web configuration file in Listing 23.33.

LISTING 23.33   Web.Config

```
<configuration>
    <system.web>
      <roleManager
        enabled="true"
        cacheRolesInCookie="true"
        createPersistentCookie="true" />
    </system.web>
</configuration>
```

The web configuration in Listing 23.33 enables role caching. Furthermore, it causes the roles to be cached in a persistent cookie rather than a session cookie.

> **WARNING**
>
> When you cache roles in a cookie, there is the potential that a user's cached roles can become out of sync with a user's actual roles. If you update a user's roles on the server, they don't get updated on the browser. You can call the `Roles.DeleteCookie()` method to delete the cached cookies.

You can set a number of attributes that are related to the roles cookie:

- ▶ **cacheRolesInCookie**—Enables you to cache user roles in a browser cookie (the default value is `false`).

- ▶ **cookieName**—Enables you to specify the name for the roles cookie (the default value is `.ASPXROLES`).

- ▶ **cookiePath**—Enables you to specify the path associated with the cookie (the default value is `/`).

- ▶ **cookieProtection**—Enables you to encrypt and validate the roles cookie. Possible values are `All`, `Encryption`, `None`, and `Validation` (the default value is `All`).

- ▶ **cookieRequireSSL**—Enables you to require that the roles cookie be transmitted over a Secure Sockets Layer connection (the default value is `false`).

- ▶ **cookieSlidingExpiration**—Enables you to prevent a cookie from expiring just as long as a user continues to request pages (the default value is `true`).

- ▶ **cookieTimeout**—Enables you to specify the amount of time in minutes before a cookie times out (the default value is `30`).

- ▶ **createPersistentCookie**—Enables you to create a persistent rather than a session cookie (the default value is `false`).

- ▶ **domain**—Enables you to specify the domain associated with the cookie (the default value is an empty string).

- ▶ **maxCachedResults**—Enables you to specify the maximum number of roles that are cached in a cookie (the default is 25).

Using the Roles Application Programming Interface

The `Roles` class exposes the main application programming interface for manipulating roles. If you need to create roles programmatically, delete roles, or assign users to roles, then you use the methods of the `Roles` class.

The `Roles` class includes the following methods:

- ▶ **AddUsersToRole**—Enables you to add an array of users to a role.

- ▶ **AddUsersToRoles**—Enables you to add an array of users to an array of roles.

- ▶ **AddUserToRole**—Enables you to add a user to a role.

- ▶ **AddUserToRoles**—Enables you to add a user to an array of roles.

- ▶ **CreateRole**—Enables you to create a new role.

- ▶ **DeleteCookie**—Enables you to delete the roles cookie.

- ▶ **DeleteRole**—Enables you to delete a particular role.

- ▶ **FindUsersInRole**—Enables you to return a list of users in a role that has a particular username.

- ▶ **GetAllRoles**—Enables you to retrieve a list of all roles.

- ▶ **GetRolesForUser**—Enables you to get a list of all roles to which a user belongs.

- ▶ **GetUsersInRole**—Enables you to get a list of users in a particular role.

- ▶ **IsUserInRole**—Enables you to determine whether a particular user is a member of a particular role.

- ▶ **RemoveUserFromRole**—Enables you to remove a particular user from a particular role.

- ▶ **RemoveUserFromRoles**—Enables you to remove a particular user from an array of roles.

- ▶ **RemoveUsersFromRole**—Enables you to remove an array of users from a particular role.

- ▶ **RemoveUsersFromRoles**—Enables you to remove an array of users from an array of roles.

- ▶ **RoleExists**—Enables you to determine whether a particular role exists.

The page in Listing 23.34 illustrates how you can use the methods of the Roles class. The Page_Load() method creates two roles named Sales and Managers (if they don't already exist). Next, it assigns the current user to both roles. The body of the page contains a GridView that displays all the roles to which the current user belongs (see Figure 23.18).

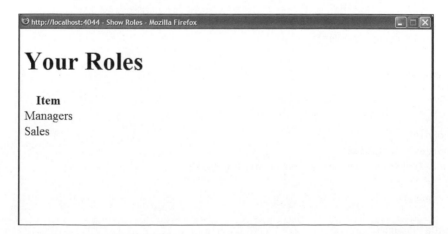

FIGURE 23.18   Displaying a user's roles.

LISTING 23.34   ShowRoles.aspx

```
<%@ Page Language="C#" %>
<!DOCTYPE html PUBLIC "-//W3C//DTD XHTML 1.0 Transitional//EN"
"http://www.w3.org/TR/xhtml1/DTD/xhtml1-transitional.dtd">
<script runat="server">
    void Page_Load()
    {
        // If user is not authenticated, redirect to Login page
        if (!Request.IsAuthenticated)
        {
            FormsAuthentication.RedirectToLoginPage();
            Response.End();
        }
        // Create two roles
        if (!Roles.RoleExists("Managers"))
            Roles.CreateRole("Managers");
        if (!Roles.RoleExists("Sales"))
            Roles.CreateRole("Sales");


        // Add current user to both roles
        if (!Roles.IsUserInRole("Managers"))
            Roles.AddUserToRole(User.Identity.Name, "Managers");
        if (!Roles.IsUserInRole("Sales"))
            Roles.AddUserToRole(User.Identity.Name, "Sales");
    }
</script>
<html xmlns="http://www.w3.org/1999/xhtml" >
<head id="Head1" runat="server">
    <title>Show Roles</title>
</head>
<body>
    <form id="form1" runat="server">
    <div>

    <h1>Your Roles</h1>

    <asp:GridView
        id="grdRoles"
        DataSourceID="srcRoles"
        EmptyDataText="You are not a member of any roles"
        GridLines="none"
        Runat="server" />

    <asp:ObjectDataSource
        id="srcRoles"
```

```
        TypeName="System.Web.Security.Roles"
        SelectMethod="GetRolesForUser"
        Runat="server" />

    </div>
    </form>
</body>
</html>
```

Summary

In this chapter, you learned about the four security frameworks included in the ASP.NET Framework. In the first part of the chapter, you learned how to authenticate users by enabling both Forms and Windows authentication. You learned how to take advantage of several advanced features of authentication such as cookieless authentication and cross-application authentication.

You also learn how to authorize users to access particular resources. You not only learned how to control access to ASP.NET pages, but how you can control access to image files and ASP classic pages.

Next, you learned how to use ASP.NET Membership to represent user information. You learned how to use the Membership class to create users, delete users, and modify user properties programmatically. You also explored the two Membership providers included with the ASP.NET Framework: the SqlMembershipProvider and the ActiveDirectoryMembershipProvider. Finally, we created a custom MembershipProvider: the XmlMembershipProvider.

The final section of this chapter was devoted to the Role Manager. You learned how to configure the three Role providers included in the ASP.NET Framework: the SqlRoleProvider, WindowsTokenRoleProvider, and the AuthorizationStoreRoleProvider. You also learned how to take advantage of the Roles class to create roles, delete roles, and assign users to roles programmatically.

PART VII

Building ASP.NET
Applications

IN THIS PART

Maintaining Application State

Developers who are new to programming for the web always have difficulty understanding the problem of maintaining state. The HTTP protocol, the fundamental protocol of the World Wide Web, is a stateless protocol. What this means is that from a web server's perspective, every request is from a new user. The HTTP protocol does not provide you with any method of determining whether any two requests are made by the same person.

However, maintaining state is important in just about any web application. The paradigmatic example is a shopping cart. If you want to associate a shopping cart with a user over multiple page requests, then you need some method of maintaining state.

This chapter looks at three methods included in the ASP.NET 3.5 Framework for associating data with a particular user over multiple page requests. In the first section, you learn how to create and manipulate browser cookies. A browser cookie enables you to associate a little bit of text with each website user.

Next, you learn how to take advantage of Session state. Session state enables you to associate an arbitrary object with any user. For example, you can store a shipping cart object in Session state.

You learn how take advantage of cookieless Session state so that you can use Session state even when a browser has cookies disabled. You also learn how to make Session state more robust by enabling out-of-process Session state.

Finally, we examine a new feature introduced with the ASP.NET 2.0 framework: the Profile object. The Profile object provides you with a method of creating a strongly typed and persistent form of session state.

You learn different methods of defining a profile. You also learn how to use the `Profile` object from within a component. Finally, you learn how to implement a custom `Profile` provider.

Using Browser Cookies

Cookies were introduced into the world with the first version of the Netscape browser. The developers at Netscape invented cookies to solve a problem that plagued the Internet at the time. There was no way to make money because there was no way to create a shopping cart.

NOTE

You can read Netscape's original cookie specification at http://home.netscape.com/ newsref/std/cookie_spec.html.

Here's how cookies work. When a web server creates a cookie, an additional HTTP header is sent to the browser when a page is served to the browser. The HTTP header looks like this:

```
Set-Cookie: message=Hello
```

This `Set-Cookie` header causes the browser to create a cookie named `message` that has the value `Hello`.

After a cookie has been created on a browser, whenever the browser requests a page from the same application in the future, the browser sends a header that looks like this:

```
Cookie: message=Hello
```

The `Cookie` header contains all the cookies that have been set by the web server. The cookies are sent back to the web server each time a request is made from the browser.

Notice that a cookie is nothing more than a little bit of text. You can store only string values when using a cookie.

You actually can create two types of cookies: session cookies and persistent cookies. A session cookie exists only in memory. If a user closes the web browser, the session cookie disappears forever.

A persistent cookie, on the other hand, can last for months or even years. When you create a persistent cookie, the cookie is stored permanently by the user's browser on the user's computer. Internet Explorer, for example, stores cookies in a set of text files contained in the following folder:

```
\Documents and Settings\[user]\Cookies
```

The Mozilla Firefox browser, on the other hand, stores cookies in the following file:

```
\Documents and Settings\[user]\Application Data\Mozilla\Firefox\Profiles\[random
  folder name]\Cookies.txt
```

Because different browsers store cookies in different locations, cookies are browser-relative. If you request a page that creates a cookie when using Internet Explorer, the cookie doesn't exist when you open Firefox or Opera.

Furthermore, notice that both Internet Explorer and Firefox store cookies in clear text. You should never store sensitive information—such as social security numbers or credit card numbers—in a cookie.

> **NOTE**
>
> Where does the name *cookie* come from? According to the original Netscape cookie specification, the term cookie was selected "for no compelling reason." However, the name most likely derives from the UNIX world in which a "magic cookie" is an opaque token passed between programs.

Cookie Security Restrictions

Cookies raise security concerns. When you create a persistent cookie, you are modifying a file on a visitor's computer. There are people who sit around all day dreaming up evil things that they can do to your computer. To prevent cookies from doing horrible things to people's computers, browsers enforce a number of security restrictions on cookies.

First, all cookies are domain-relative. If the Amazon website sets a cookie, then the Barnes and Noble website cannot read the cookie. When a browser creates a cookie, the browser records the domain associated with the cookie and doesn't send the cookie to another domain.

> **NOTE**
>
> An image contained in a web page might be served from another domain than the web page itself. Therefore, when the browser makes a request for the image, a cookie can be set from the other domain. Companies, such as DoubleClick, that display and track advertisements on multiple websites take advantage of this loophole to track advertisement statistics across multiple websites. This type of cookie is called a third-party cookie.

The other important restriction that browsers place on cookies is a restriction on size. A single domain cannot store more than 4096 bytes. This size restriction encompasses the size of both the cookie names and the cookie values.

Finally, most browsers restrict the number of cookies that can be set by a single domain to no more than 20 cookies (but not Internet Explorer). If you attempt to set more than 20 cookies, the oldest cookies are automatically deleted.

Because of all the security concerns related to cookies, all modern browsers provide users with the option of disabling cookies. This means that unless you are building an intranet application and you control every user's browser, you should attempt to not rely on cookies. Strive to use cookies only when storing noncrucial information.

That said, many parts of the ASP.NET Framework rely on cookies. For example, Web Parts, Forms Authentication, `Session` state, and anonymous Profiles all depend on cookies by default. If you are depending on one of these features anyway, then there is no reason not to use cookies.

Furthermore, many websites rely on cookies. There are many sections of the Yahoo! and MSDN websites that you cannot visit without having cookies enabled. In other words, requiring visitors to have cookies enabled to use your website is not an entirely unreasonable requirement.

Creating Cookies

You create a new cookie by adding a cookie to the `Response.Cookies` collection. The `Response.Cookies` collection contains all the cookies sent from the web server to the web browser.

For example, the page in Listing 24.1 enables you to create a new cookie named `Message`. The page contains a form that enables you to enter the value of the `Message` cookie (see Figure 24.1).

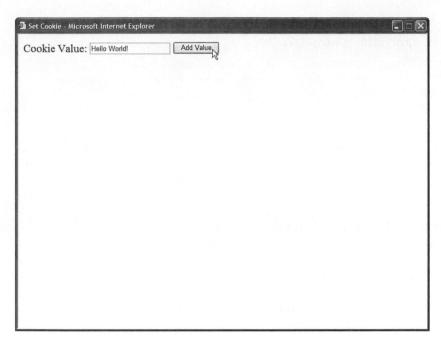

FIGURE 24.1   Creating a new cookie.

LISTING 24.1   SetCookie.aspx

```
<%@ Page Language="C#" %>
<!DOCTYPE html PUBLIC "-//W3C//DTD XHTML 1.0 Transitional//EN"
"http://www.w3.org/TR/xhtml1/DTD/xhtml1-transitional.dtd">
<script runat="server">

    protected void btnAdd_Click(object sender, EventArgs e)
    {
        Response.Cookies["message"].Value = txtCookieValue.Text;
    }
</script>
<html xmlns="http://www.w3.org/1999/xhtml" >
<head id="Head1" runat="server">
    <title>Set Cookie</title>
</head>
<body>
    <form id="form1" runat="server">
    <div>

    <asp:Label
        id="lblCookieValue"
        Text="Cookie Value:"
```

24

LISTING 24.1   Continued

```
            AssociatedControlID="txtCookieValue"
            Runat="server" />
        <asp:TextBox
            id="txtCookieValue"
            Runat="server" />
        <asp:Button
            id="btnAdd"
            Text="Add Value"
            OnClick="btnAdd_Click"
            Runat="server" />

    </div>
    </form>
</body>
</html>
```

Be warned that cookie names are case sensitive. Setting a cookie named message is different from setting a cookie named Message.

If you want to modify the value of the cookie created by the page in Listing 24.1, then you can open the page and enter a new value for the message cookie. When the web server sends its response to the browser, the modified value of the cookie is set on the browser.

The page in Listing 24.1 creates a session cookie. The cookie disappears when you close your web browser. If you want to create a persistent cookie, then you need to specify an expiration date for the cookie.

The page in Listing 24.2 creates a persistent cookie.

LISTING 24.2   SetPersistentCookie.aspx

```
<%@ Page Language="C#" %>
<!DOCTYPE html PUBLIC "-//W3C//DTD XHTML 1.0 Transitional//EN"
"http://www.w3.org/TR/xhtml1/DTD/xhtml1-transitional.dtd">
<script runat="server">

    void Page_Load()
    {
        // Get current value of cookie
        int counter = 0;
        if (Request.Cookies["counter"] != null)
            counter = Int32.Parse(Request.Cookies["counter"].Value);

        // Increment counter
        counter++;
```

```
        // Add persistent cookie to browser
        Response.Cookies["counter"].Value = counter.ToString();
        Response.Cookies["counter"].Expires = DateTime.Now.AddYears(2);

        // Display value of counter cookie
        lblCounter.Text = counter.ToString();
    }
</script>
<html xmlns="http://www.w3.org/1999/xhtml" >
<head id="Head1" runat="server">
    <title>Set Persistent Cookie</title>
</head>
<body>
    <form id="form1" runat="server">
    <div>

    You have visited this page
    <asp:Label
        id="lblCounter"
        Runat="server" />
    times!

    </div>
    </form>
</body>
</html>
```

The page in Listing 24.2 tracks the number of times that you have requested the page. A persistent cookie named counter is used to track page requests. Notice that the counter cookie's Expires property is set to two years in the future. When you set a particular expiration date for a cookie, the cookie is stored as a persistent cookie.

Reading Cookies

You use the Response.Cookies collection to create and modify cookies. You use the Request.Cookies collection to retrieve a cookie's value.

For example, the page in Listing 24.3 retrieves the message cookie's value.

LISTING 24.3 GetCookie.aspx

```
<%@ Page Language="C#" %>
<!DOCTYPE html PUBLIC "-//W3C//DTD XHTML 1.0 Transitional//EN"
"http://www.w3.org/TR/xhtml1/DTD/xhtml1-transitional.dtd">
<script runat="server">
```

LISTING 24.3   Continued

```csharp
    void Page_Load()
    {
        if (Request.Cookies["message"] != null)
            lblCookieValue.Text = Request.Cookies["message"].Value;
    }

</script>
<html xmlns="http://www.w3.org/1999/xhtml" >
<head id="Head1" runat="server">
    <title>Get Cookie</title>
</head>
<body>
    <form id="form1" runat="server">
    <div>

    The value of the message cookie is:
    <asp:Label
        id="lblCookieValue"
        Runat="server" />

    </div>
    </form>
</body>
</html>
```

In Listing 24.3, the `IsNothing()` function is used to check whether the cookie exists before reading its value. If you don't include this check, you might get a null reference exception. Also, don't forget that cookie names are case-sensitive.

The page in Listing 24.4 lists all cookies contained in the `Request.Cookies` collection (see Figure 24.2).

LISTING 24.4   GetAllCookies.aspx

```csharp
<%@ Page Language="C#" %>
<!DOCTYPE html PUBLIC "-//W3C//DTD XHTML 1.0 Transitional//EN"
"http://www.w3.org/TR/xhtml1/DTD/xhtml1-transitional.dtd">
<script runat="server">

    void Page_Load()
    {

        ArrayList colCookies = new ArrayList();
        for (int i = 0; i < Request.Cookies.Count; i++)
            colCookies.Add(Request.Cookies[i]);
```

```
        grdCookies.DataSource = colCookies;
        grdCookies.DataBind();
    }
</script>
<html xmlns="http://www.w3.org/1999/xhtml" >
<head id="Head1" runat="server">
    <title>Get All Cookies</title>
</head>
<body>
    <form id="form1" runat="server">
    <div>

    <asp:GridView
        id="grdCookies"
        Runat="server"/>

    </div>
    </form>
</body>
</html>
```

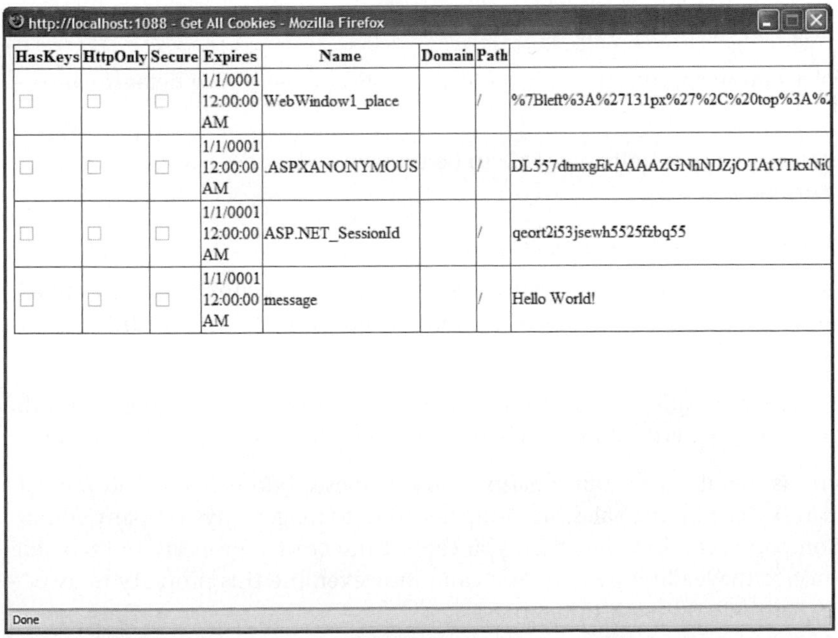

HasKeys	HttpOnly	Secure	Expires	Name	Domain	Path	
☐	☐	☐	1/1/0001 12:00:00 AM	WebWindow1_place		/	%7Bleft%3A%27131px%27%2C%20top%3A%2
☐	☐	☐	1/1/0001 12:00:00 AM	.ASPXANONYMOUS		/	DL557dtmxgEkAAAAZGNhNDZjOTAtYTkxNi(
☐	☐	☐	1/1/0001 12:00:00 AM	ASP.NET_SessionId		/	qeort2i53jsewh5525fzbq55
☐	☐	☐	1/1/0001 12:00:00 AM	message		/	Hello World!

FIGURE 24.2   Displaying a list of all cookies.

Notice that the only meaningful information that you get back from iterating through the `Request.Cookies` collection is the `HasKeys`, `Name`, and `Value` properties. The other columns show incorrect information. For example, the `Expires` column always displays a minimal date. Browsers don't communicate these additional properties with page requests, so you can't retrieve these property values.

When using the `Request.Cookies` collection, it is important to understand that a `For...Each` loop returns different values than a `For...Next` loop. If you iterate through the `Request.Cookies` collection with a `For...Each` loop, you get the cookie names. If you iterate through the collection with a `For...Next` loop, then you get instances of the `HttpCookie` class (described in the next section).

Setting Cookie Properties

Cookies are represented with the `HttpCookie` class. When you create or read a cookie, you can use any of the properties of this class:

- **Domain**—Enables you to specify the domain associated with the cookie. The default value is the current domain.

- **Expires**—Enables you to create a persistent cookie by specifying an expiration date.

- **HasKeys**—Enables you to determine whether a cookie is a multivalued cookie. (See the section "Working with Multivalued Cookies" later in this chapter.)

- **HttpOnly**—Enables you to prevent a cookie from being accessed by JavaScript.

- **Name**—Enables you to specify a name for a cookie.

- **Path**—Enables you to specify the path associated with a cookie. The default value is /.

- **Secure**—Enables you to require a cookie to be transmitted across a Secure Sockets Layer (SSL) connection.

- **Value**—Enables you to get or set a cookie value.

- **Values**—Enables you to get or set a particular value when working with a multivalued cookie (see the section "Working with Multivalued Cookies" later in this chapter).

A couple of these properties require additional explanation. For example, you might find the `Domain` property confusing because you can't change the domain associated with a cookie.

The `Domain` property is useful when your organization includes subdomains. If you want to set a cookie that can be read by the Sales.MyCompany.com, Managers.MyCompany.com, and Support.MyCompany.com domains, then you can set the `Domain` property to the value .MyCompany.com (notice the leading period). You can't, however, use this property to associate a cookie with an entirely different domain.

The HttpOnly property enables you to specify whether a cookie can be accessed from JavaScript code. This property works only with Internet Explorer 6 (Service Pack 1) and above. The property was introduced to help prevent cross-site scripting attacks.

The Path property enables you to scope cookies to a particular path. For example, if you are hosting multiple applications in the same domain, and you do not want the applications to share the same cookies, then you can use the Path property to prevent one application from reading another application's cookies.

The Path property sounds really useful. Unfortunately, you should never use it. Internet Explorer performs a case-sensitive match against the path. If a user uses a different case when typing the path to a page into the address bar, then the cookie isn't sent. In other words, the following two paths don't match:

```
http://localhost/original/GetAllCookies.aspx
```

```
http://localhost/ORIGINAL/GetAllCookies.aspx
```

Deleting Cookies

The method for deleting cookies is not intuitive. To delete an existing cookie, you must set its expiration date to a date in the past.

The page in Listing 24.5 illustrates how you can delete a single cookie. The page contains a form field for the cookie name. When you submit the form, the cookie with the specified name is deleted.

LISTING 24.5   DeleteCookie.aspx

```
<%@ Page Language="C#" %>
<!DOCTYPE html PUBLIC "-//W3C//DTD XHTML 1.0 Transitional//EN"
"http://www.w3.org/TR/xhtml1/DTD/xhtml1-transitional.dtd">
<script runat="server">

    protected void btnDelete_Click(object sender, EventArgs e)
    {
        Response.Cookies[txtCookieName.Text].Expires = DateTime.Now.AddDays(-1);
    }
</script>
<html xmlns="http://www.w3.org/1999/xhtml" >
<head id="Head1" runat="server">
    <title>Delete Cookie</title>
</head>
<body>
    <form id="form1" runat="server">
    <div>
```

LISTING 24.5   Continued

```
    <asp:Label
        id="lblCookieName"
        Text="Cookie Name:"
        AssociatedControlID="txtCookieName"
        Runat="server" />
    <asp:TextBox
        id="txtCookieName"
        Runat="server" />
    <asp:Button
        id="btnDelete"
        Text="Delete Cookie"
        OnClick="btnDelete_Click"
        Runat="server" />

    </div>
    </form>
</body>
</html>
```

The particular date that you specify when deleting a cookie doesn't really matter as long as it is in the past. In Listing 24.5, the expiration date is set to 1 day ago.

The page in Listing 24.6 deletes all cookies sent from the browser to the current domain (and path).

LISTING 24.6   DeleteAllCookies.aspx

```
<%@ Page Language="C#" %>
<!DOCTYPE html PUBLIC "-//W3C//DTD XHTML 1.0 Transitional//EN"
"http://www.w3.org/TR/xhtml1/DTD/xhtml1-transitional.dtd">
<script runat="server">

    void Page_Load()
    {
        string[] cookies = Request.Cookies.AllKeys;
        foreach (string cookie in cookies)
        {
            BulletedList1.Items.Add("Deleting " + cookie);
            Response.Cookies[cookie].Expires = DateTime.Now.AddDays(-1);
        }
    }
</script>
<html xmlns="http://www.w3.org/1999/xhtml" >
<head id="Head1" runat="server">
```

```
            <title>Delete All Cookies</title>
    </head>
    <body>
        <form id="form1" runat="server">
        <div>

        <h1>Delete All Cookies</h1>

        <asp:BulletedList
            id="BulletedList1"
            EnableViewState="false"
            Runat="server" />

        </div>
        </form>
    </body>
</html>
```

The page in Listing 24.6 loops through all the cookie names from the `Request.Cookies` collection and deletes each cookie.

Working with Multivalued Cookies

According to the cookie specifications, browsers should not store more than 20 cookies from a single domain. You can work around this limitation by creating multivalued cookies.

A multivalued cookie is a single cookie that contains subkeys. You can create as many subkeys as you need.

For example, the page in Listing 24.7 creates a multivalued cookie named `preferences`. The `preferences` cookie is used to store a first name, last name, and favorite color (see Figure 24.3).

LISTING 24.7   SetCookieValues.aspx

```
<%@ Page Language="C#" %>
<!DOCTYPE html PUBLIC "-//W3C//DTD XHTML 1.0 Transitional//EN"
"http://www.w3.org/TR/xhtml1/DTD/xhtml1-transitional.dtd">
<script runat="server">

    void btnSubmit_Click(Object s, EventArgs e)
    {
        Response.Cookies["preferences"]["firstName"] = txtFirstName.Text;
        Response.Cookies["preferences"]["lastName"] = txtLastName.Text;
```

LISTING 24.7   Continued

```
        Response.Cookies["preferences"]["favoriteColor"] = txtFavoriteColor.Text;
        Response.Cookies["preferences"].Expires = DateTime.MaxValue;
    }
</script>
<html xmlns="http://www.w3.org/1999/xhtml" >
<head id="Head1" runat="server">
    <title>Set Cookie Values</title>
</head>
<body>
    <form id="form1" runat="server">
    <div>

    <asp:Label
        id="lblFirstName"
        Text="First Name:"
        AssociatedControlID="txtFirstName"
        Runat="server" />
    <br />
    <asp:TextBox
        id="txtFirstName"
        Runat="server" />
    <br /><br />
    <asp:Label
        id="lblLastName"
        Text="Last Name:"
        AssociatedControlID="txtFirstName"
        Runat="server" />
    <br />
    <asp:TextBox
        id="txtLastName"
        Runat="server" />
    <br /><br />
    <asp:Label
        id="lblFavoriteColor"
        Text="Favorite Color:"
        AssociatedControlID="txtFavoriteColor"
        Runat="server" />
    <br />
    <asp:TextBox
        id="txtFavoriteColor"
        Runat="server" />
    <br /><br />
    <asp:Button
        id="btnSubmit"
```

```
        Text="Submit"
        OnClick="btnSubmit_Click"
        Runat="server" />


    </div>
    </form>
</body>
</html>
```

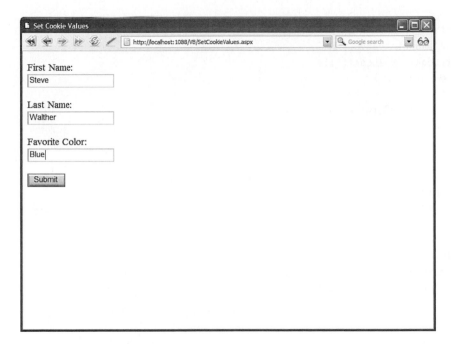

FIGURE 24.3   Creating a multi-valued cookie.

When you submit the page in Listing 24.7, the following HTTP header is sent to the browser:

```
Set-Cookie: preferences=firstName=Steve&lastName=Walther&favoriteColor=green;
expires=Fri, 31-Dec-9999 23:59:59 GMT; path=/
```

The page in Listing 24.8 reads the values from the preferences cookie.

LISTING 24.8   GetCookieValues.aspx

```
<%@ Page Language="C#" %>
<!DOCTYPE html PUBLIC "-//W3C//DTD XHTML 1.0 Transitional//EN"
"http://www.w3.org/TR/xhtml1/DTD/xhtml1-transitional.dtd">
<script runat="server">
```

LISTING 24.8   Continued

```csharp
    void Page_Load()
    {
        if (Request.Cookies["preferences"] != null)
        {
            lblFirstName.Text = Request.Cookies["preferences"]["firstName"];
            lblLastName.Text = Request.Cookies["preferences"]["lastName"];
            lblFavoriteColor.Text = Request.Cookies["preferences"]["favoriteColor"];
        }
    }
</script>
<html xmlns="http://www.w3.org/1999/xhtml" >
<head id="Head1" runat="server">
    <title>Get Cookie Values</title>
</head>
<body>
    <form id="form1" runat="server">
    <div>

    First Name:
    <asp:Label
        id="lblFirstName"
        Runat="server" />
    <br />
    Last Name:
    <asp:Label
        id="lblLastName"
        Runat="server" />
    <br />
    Favorite Color:
    <asp:Label
        id="lblFavoriteColor"
        Runat="server" />

    </div>
    </form>
</body>
</html>
```

You can use the HttpCookie.HasKeys property to detect whether a cookie is a normal cookie or a multivalued cookie.

Using Session State

You can't really use a cookie to store a shopping cart. A cookie is just too small and too simple. To enable you to work around the limitations of cookies, the ASP.NET Framework supports a feature called Session state.

Like cookies, items stored in Session state are scoped to a particular user. You can use Session state to store user preferences or other user-specific data across multiple page requests.

Unlike cookies, Session state has no size limitations. If you had a compelling need, you could store gigabytes of data in Session state.

Furthermore, unlike cookies, Session state can represent more complex objects than simple strings of text. You can store any object in Session state. For example, you can store a DataSet or a custom shopping cart object in Session state.

You add items to Session state by using the Session object. For example, the page in Listing 24.9 adds a new item named message to Session state that has the value Hello World!.

LISTING 24.9   SessionSet.aspx

```csharp
<%@ Page Language="C#" %>
<!DOCTYPE html PUBLIC "-//W3C//DTD XHTML 1.0 Transitional//EN"
"http://www.w3.org/TR/xhtml1/DTD/xhtml1-transitional.dtd">
<script runat="server">

    void Page_Load()
    {
        Session["message"] = "Hello World!";
    }
</script>
<html xmlns="http://www.w3.org/1999/xhtml" >
<head id="Head1" runat="server">
    <title>Session Set</title>
</head>
<body>
    <form id="form1" runat="server">
    <div>

    <h1>Session item added!</h1>

    </div>
    </form>
</body>
</html>
```

In the Page_Load() event handler in Listing 24.9, a new item is added to the Session object. Notice that you can use the Session object just as you would use a Hashtable collection.

The page in Listing 24.10 illustrates how you can retrieve the value of an item that you have stored in Session state.

LISTING 24.10   SessionGet.aspx

```
<%@ Page Language="C#" %>
<!DOCTYPE html PUBLIC "-//W3C//DTD XHTML 1.0 Transitional//EN"
"http://www.w3.org/TR/xhtml1/DTD/xhtml1-transitional.dtd">
<script runat="server">

    void Page_Load()
    {
        lblMessage.Text = Session["message"].ToString();
    }
</script>
<html xmlns="http://www.w3.org/1999/xhtml" >
<head id="Head1" runat="server">
    <title>Session Get</title>
</head>
<body>
    <form id="form1" runat="server">
    <div>

    <asp:Label
        id="lblMessage"
        Runat="server" />

    </div>
    </form>
</body>
</html>
```

When you use Session state, a session cookie named ASP.NET_SessionId is added to your browser automatically. This cookie contains a unique identifier. It is used to track you as you move from page to page.

When you add items to the Session object, the items are stored on the web server and not the web browser. The ASP.NET_SessionId cookie is used to associate the correct data with the correct user.

By default, if cookies are disabled, `Session` state does not work. You don't receive an error, but items that you add to Session state aren't available when you attempt to retrieve them in later page requests. (You learn how to enable cookieless `Session` state later in this section.)

WARNING

Be careful not to abuse `Session` state by overusing it. A separate copy of each item added to `Session` state is created for each user who requests the page. If you place a `DataSet` with 400 records into `Session` state in a page, and 500 users request the page, then you'll have 500 copies of that `DataSet` in memory.

By default, the ASP.NET Framework assumes that a user has left the website when the user has not requested a page for more than 20 minutes. At that point, any data stored in `Session` state for the user is discarded.

Storing Database Data in `Session` State

You can use `Session` state to create a user-relative cache. For example, you can load data for a user and enable the user to sort or filter the data.

The page in Listing 24.11 loads a `DataView` into `Session` state. The user can sort the contents of the `DataView` by using a `GridView` control (see Figure 24.4).

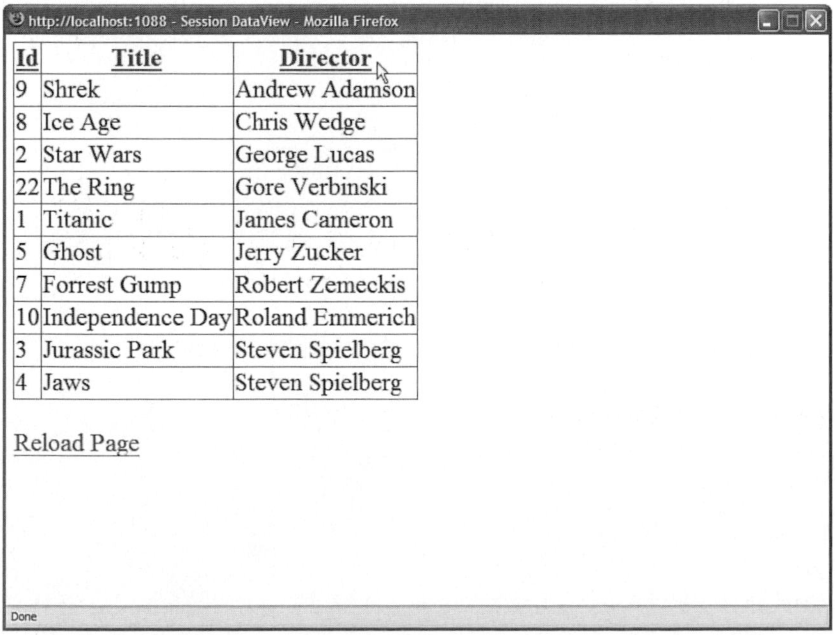
http://localhost:1088 - Session DataView - Mozilla Firefox
Id
Title
Director
9 Shrek Andrew Adamson
8 Ice Age Chris Wedge
2 Star Wars George Lucas
22 The Ring Gore Verbinski
1 Titanic James Cameron
5 Ghost Jerry Zucker
7 Forrest Gump Robert Zemeckis
10 Independence Day Roland Emmerich
3 Jurassic Park Steven Spielberg
4 Jaws Steven Spielberg
Reload Page
Done

FIGURE 24.4 Sorting a `DataView` stored in `Session` state.

LISTING 24.11 SessionDataView.aspx

```
<%@ Page Language="C#" %>
<%@ Import Namespace="System.Data" %>
<%@ Import Namespace="System.Data.SqlClient" %>
<%@ Import Namespace="System.Web.Configuration" %>
<!DOCTYPE html PUBLIC "-//W3C//DTD XHTML 1.0 Transitional//EN"
"http://www.w3.org/TR/xhtml1/DTD/xhtml1-transitional.dtd">
<script runat="server">

    DataView dvMovies;

    /// <summary>
    /// Load the Movies
    /// </summary>
    void Page_Load()
    {
        dvMovies = (DataView)Session["Movies"];
        if (dvMovies == null)
        {
            string conString = WebConfigurationManager.ConnectionStrings["Movies"].
            ➥ConnectionString;
            SqlDataAdapter dad = new SqlDataAdapter("SELECT Id,Title,Director FROM
            ➥Movies", conString);
            DataTable dtblMovies = new DataTable();
            dad.Fill(dtblMovies);
            dvMovies = new DataView(dtblMovies);
            Session["Movies"] = dvMovies;
        }
    }

    /// <summary>
    /// Sort the Movies
    /// </summary>
    protected void grdMovies_Sorting(object sender, GridViewSortEventArgs e)
    {
        dvMovies.Sort = e.SortExpression;
    }

    /// <summary>
    /// Render the Movies
    /// </summary>
    void Page_PreRender()
    {
```

```
            grdMovies.DataSource = dvMovies;
            grdMovies.DataBind();
        }
</script>
<html xmlns="http://www.w3.org/1999/xhtml" >
<head id="Head1" runat="server">
    <title>Session DataView</title>
</hcad>
<body>
    <form id="form1" runat="server">
    <div>

    <asp:GridView
        id="grdMovies"
        AllowSorting="true"
        EnableViewState="false"
        OnSorting="grdMovies_Sorting"
        Runat="server" />
    <br />
    <asp:LinkButton
        id="lnkReload"
        Text="Reload Page"
        Runat="server" />

    </div>
    </form>
</body>
</html>
```

In Listing 24.11, a `DataView` object is stored in `Session` state. When you sort the `GridView` control, the `DataView` is sorted.

The page in Listing 24.11 includes a link that enables you to reload the page. Notice that the sort order of the records displayed by the `GridView` is remembered across page requests. The sort order is remembered even if you navigate to another page before returning to the page.

Using the Session Object

The main application programming interface for working with `Session` state is the `HttpSessionState` class. This object is exposed by the `Page.Session`, `Context.Session`, `UserControl.Session`, `WebService.Session`, and `Application.Session` properties. This means that you can access `Session` state from just about anywhere.

This HttpSessionState class supports the following properties (this is not a complete list):

- **CookieMode**—Enables you to specify whether cookieless sessions are enabled. Possible values are AutoDetect, UseCookies, UseDeviceProfile, and UseUri.

- **Count**—Enables you to retrieve the number of items in Session state.

- **IsCookieless**—Enables you to determine whether cookieless sessions are enabled.

- **IsNewSession**—Enables you to determine whether a new user session was created with the current request.

- **IsReadOnly**—Enables you to determine whether the Session state is read-only.

- **Keys**—Enables you to retrieve a list of item names stored in Session state.

- **Mode**—Enables you to determine the current Session state store provider. Possible values are Custom, InProc, Off, SqlServer, and StateServer.

- **SessionID**—Enables you to retrieve the unique session identifier.

- **Timeout**—Enables you to specify the amount of time in minutes before the web server assumes that the user has left and discards the session. The maximum value is 525,600 (1 year).

The HttpSessionState object also supports the following methods:

- **Abandon**—Enables you to end a user session.

- **Clear**—Enables you to clear all items from Session state.

- **Remove**—Enables you to remove a particular item from Session state.

The Abandon() method enables you to end a user session programmatically. For example, you might want to end a user session automatically when a user logs out from your application to clear away all of a user's session state information.

Handling Session Events

There are two events related to Session state that you can handle in the Global.asax file: the Session Start and Session End events.

The Session Start event is raised whenever a new user session begins. You can handle this event to load user information from the database. For example, you can handle the Session Start event to load the user's shopping cart.

The Session End event is raised when a session ends. A session comes to an end when it times out because of user inactivity or when it is explicitly ended with the Session.Abandon() method. You can handle the Session End event, for example, when you want to automatically save the user's shopping cart to a database table.

The `Global.asax` file in Listing 24.12 demonstrates how you can handle both the `Session Start` and `End` events.

LISTING 24.12   `Global.asax`

```
<%@ Application Language="C#" %>
<script runat="server">
    void Application_Start(object sender, EventArgs e)
    {
        Application["SessionCount"] = 0;
    }

    void Session_Start(object sender, EventArgs e)
    {
        Application.Lock();
        int count = (int)Application["SessionCount"];
        Application["SessionCount"] = count + 1;
        Application.UnLock();
    }

    void Session_End(object sender, EventArgs e)
    {
        Application.Lock();
        int count = (int)Application["SessionCount"];
        Application["SessionCount"] = count - 1;
        Application.UnLock();
    }
</script>
```

In Listing 24.12, the `Global.asax` file is used to track the number of active sessions. Whenever a new session begins, the `Session Start` event is raised and the `SessionCount` variable is incremented by one. When a session ends, the `Session End` event is raised and the `SessionCount` variable is decremented by one.

The `SessionCount` variable is stored in the `Application` state, which contains items that are shared among all users of a web application. Notice that the `Application` object is locked before it is modified. You must lock and unlock the `Application` object because multiple users could potentially access the same item in `Application` state at the same time.

> **NOTE**
>
> Application state is little used in ASP.NET applications. In most cases, you should use the `Cache` object instead of `Application` state because the `Cache` object is designed to manage memory automatically.

The page in Listing 24.13 displays the number of active sessions with a Label control (see Figure 24.5).

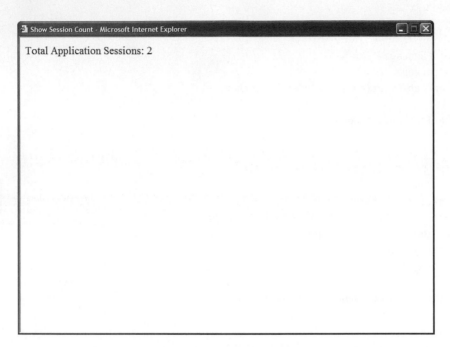

FIGURE 24.5   Displaying a count of user sessions.

LISTING 24.13   ShowSessionCount.aspx

```
<%@ Page Language="C#" %>
<!DOCTYPE html PUBLIC "-//W3C//DTD XHTML 1.0 Transitional//EN"
"http://www.w3.org/TR/xhtml1/DTD/xhtml1-transitional.dtd">
<script runat="server">

    void Page_Load()
    {
        lblSessionCount.Text = Application["SessionCount"].ToString();
    }
</script>
<html xmlns="http://www.w3.org/1999/xhtml" >
<head id="Head1" runat="server">
    <title>Show Session Count</title>
</head>
<body>
    <form id="form1" runat="server">
    <div>
```

```
   Total Application Sessions:
   <asp:Label
       id="lblSessionCount"
       Runat="server" />


   </div>
   </form>
</body>
</html>
```

> **WARNING**
>
> The Session End event is not raised by all session store providers. The event is raised by the InProc session store provider (the default provider), but it is not raised by the StateServer or SQLServer state providers.

Controlling When a Session Times Out

By default, the ASP.NET Framework assumes that a user has left an application after 20 minutes have passed without the user requesting a page. In some situations, you'll want to modify the default timeout value.

For example, imagine that you are creating a college admissions website and the website includes a form that enables an applicant to enter a long essay. In that situation, you would not want the user session to timeout after 20 minutes. Please, give the poor college applicants at least 1 hour to write their essays.

The disadvantage of increasing the Session timeout is that more memory is consumed by your application. The longer the Session timeout, the more server memory is potentially consumed.

You can specify the Session timeout in the web configuration file or you can set the Session timeout programmatically. For example, the web configuration file in Listing 24.14 changes the Session timeout value to 60 (1 hour).

LISTING 24.14   Web.Config

```
<configuration>
<system.web>

  <sessionState timeout="60" />

</system.web>
</configuration>
```

You can modify the Session timeout value programmatically with the Timeout property of the Session object. For example, the following statement changes the timeout value from the default of 20 minutes to 60 minutes.

```
Session.Timeout = 60;
```

After you execute this statement, the timeout value is modified for the remainder of the user session. This is true even when the user visits other pages.

Using Cookieless Session State

By default, Session state depends on cookies. The ASP.NET Framework uses the ASP.NET_SessionId cookie to identity a user across page requests so that the correct data can be associated with the correct user. If a user disables cookies in the browser, then Session state doesn't work.

If you want Session state to work even when cookies are disabled, then you can take advantage of cookieless sessions. When cookieless sessions are enabled, a user's session ID is added to the page URL.

Here's a sample of what a page URL looks like when cookieless sessions are enabled:

```
http://localhost:4945/Original/(S(5pnh11553sszre45oevthxnn))/SomePage.aspx
```

The strange-looking code in this URL is the current user's Session ID. It is the same value as the one you get from the Session.SessionID property.

You enable cookieless sessions by modifying the sessionState element in the web configuration file. The sessionState element includes a cookieless attribute that accepts the following values:

▶ **AutoDetect**—The Session ID is stored in a cookie when a browser has cookies enabled. Otherwise, the cookie is added to the URL.

▶ **UseCookies**—The Session ID is always stored in a cookie (the default value).

▶ **UseDeviceProfile**—The Session ID is stored in a cookie when a browser supports cookies. Otherwise, the cookie is added to the URL.

▶ **UseUri**—The Session ID is always added to the URL.

When you set cookieless to the value UseDeviceProfile, the ASP.NET Framework determines whether the browser supports cookies by looking up the browser's capabilities from a set of files contained in the following folder:

```
C:\WINDOWS\Microsoft.NET\Framework\v2.0.50727\CONFIG\Browsers
```

If, according to these files, a browser supports cookies, then the ASP.NET Framework uses a cookie to store the Session ID. The Framework attempts to add a cookie even when a user has disabled cookies in the browser.

When cookieless is set to the value AutoDetect, the framework checks for the existence of the HTTP Cookie header. If the Cookie header is detected, then the framework stores the

Session ID in a cookie. Otherwise, the framework falls back to storing the Session ID in the page URL.

The web configuration file in Listing 24.15 enables cookieless sessions by assigning the value `AutoDetect` to the `cookieless` attribute.

LISTING 24.15   Web.Config

```
<configuration>
<system.web>

  <sessionState
    cookieless="AutoDetect"
    regenerateExpiredSessionId="true" />

</system.web>
</configuration>
```

> **NOTE**
>
> The easiest way to test cookieless sessions is to use the Mozilla Firefox browser because this browser enables you to disable cookies easily. Select the menu option Tools, Options. Select the Privacy tab and uncheck Allow Sites to Set Cookies.

Notice that the configuration file in Listing 24.16 also includes a `regenerateExpiredSessionId` attribute. When you enable cookieless session state, you should also enable this attribute because it can help prevent users from inadvertently sharing session state.

For example, imagine that someone posts a link in a discussion forum to an ASP.NET website that has cookieless sessions enabled. The link includes the Session ID. If someone follows the link after the original session has timed out, then a new Session is started automatically. However, if multiple people follow the link at the same time, then all the people will share the same Session ID and, therefore, they will share the same `Session` state, which is a major security problem.

On the other hand, when `regenerateExpiredSessionId` is enabled and a session times out, the Session ID in the URL is regenerated when a person requests the page. A redirect back to the same page is performed to change the Session ID in the URL. If a link is posted in a discussion forum, or sent to multiple users in an email, then each user who follows the link is assigned a new Session ID.

When you enable cookieless sessions, you need to be careful to use relative URLs when linking between pages in your application. If you don't use a relative URL, then the Session ID cannot be added to the URL automatically.

For example, when linking to another page in your website, use a URL that looks like this (a relative URL):

`/SomeFolder/SomePage.aspx`

Do not use a URL that looks like this (an absolute URL):

`http://SomeSite.com/SomeFolder/SomePage.aspx`

If, for some reason, you really need to use an absolute URL, you can add the Session ID to the URL by using the `Response.ApplyAppPathModifier()` method. This method takes an absolute URL and returns the URL with a Session ID embedded in it.

Configuring a Session State Store

By default, `Session` state is stored in memory in the same process as the ASP.NET process. There are two significant disadvantages to storing `Session` state in the ASP.NET process.

First, in-process `Session` state is fragile. If your application restarts, then all `Session` state is lost. A number of different events can cause an application restart. For example, modifying the web configuration file or errors in your application both can cause an application restart.

Second, in-process `Session` state is not scalable. When `Session` state is stored in-process, it is stored on a particular web server. In other words, you can't use in-process `Session` state with a web farm.

If you need to implement a more robust version of `Session` state, then the ASP.NET Framework supplies you with a number of options. You can configure the ASP.NET Framework to store `Session` state in an alternate location by modifying the `Session` state mode.

You can set the `Session` state mode to any of the following values:

- ▶ **Off**—Disables `Session` state.

- ▶ **InProc**—Stores `Session` state in the same process as the ASP.NET process.

- ▶ **StateServer**—Stores `Session` state in a Windows NT process, which is distinct from the ASP.NET process.

- ▶ **SQLServer**—Stores `Session` state in a SQL Server database.

- ▶ **Custom**—Stores `Session` state in a custom location.

By default, the `Session` state mode is set to the value `InProc`. This is done for performance reasons. In-process `Session` state results in the best performance. However, it sacrifices robustness and scalability.

When you set the `Session` state mode to either `StateServer` or `SQLServer`, you get robustness and scalability at the price of performance. Storing `Session` state out-of-process results in worse performance because `Session` state information must be passed back and forth over your network.

Finally, you can create a custom `Session` state store provider by inheriting a new class from the `SessionStateStoreProviderBase` class. In that case, you can store `Session` state any place that you want. For example, you can create a Session state store provider that stores Session state in an Oracle or FoxPro database.

Configuring State Server Session State   When you enable State Server Session state, Session state information is stored in a separate Windows NT Service. The Windows NT Service can be located on the same server as your web server, or it can be located on another server in your network.

If you store Session state in the memory of a separate Windows NT Service, then Session state information survives even when your ASP.NET application doesn't. For example, if your ASP.NET application crashes, then your Session state information is not lost because it is stored in a separate process.

Furthermore, you can create a web farm when you store state information by using a Windows NT Service. You can designate one server in your network as your state server. All the web servers in your web farm can use the central state server to store Session state.

You must complete the following two steps to use State Server Session state:

▶ Start the ASP.NET State Service.

▶ Configure your application to use the ASP.NET State Service.

You can start the ASP.NET State Service by opening the Services applet located at Start, Control Panel, Administrative Tools (see Figure 24.6). After you open the Services applet, double-click the ASP.NET State Service and click Start to run the service. You also should change the Startup type of the service to the value Automatic so that the service starts automatically every time that you reboot your machine.

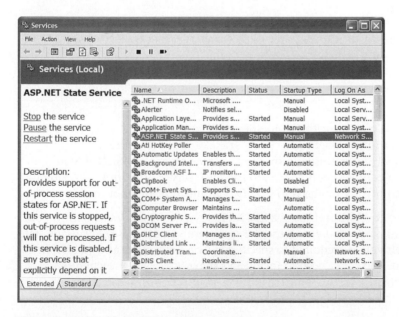

FIGURE 24.6   Starting the ASP.NET State service.

If you want to run the ASP.NET State Service on a separate server on your network, then you must edit a Registry setting on the server that hosts the ASP.NET State Service. By default, the ASP.NET State Service does not accept remote connections. To allow remote connections, execute RegEdit from a command prompt and set the following Registry key to the value 1:

```
HKEY_LOCAL_MACHINE\SYSTEM\CurrentControlSet\Services\aspnet_state\Parameters\
  AllowRemoteConnection
```

After you start the ASP.NET State Service, you need to configure your ASP.NET application to use it. The web configuration file in Listing 24.16 enables State Server Session State.

LISTING 24.16   Web.Config

```
<configuration>
    <system.web>

      <sessionState
        mode="StateServer"
        stateConnectionString="tcpip=localhost:42424"
        stateNetworkTimeout="10" />

      <machineKey
        decryption="AES"
        validation="SHA1"
        decryptionKey="306C1FA852AB3B0115150DD8BA30821CDFD125538A0C606D
          ACA53DBB3C3E0AD2"
        validationKey="61A8E04A146AFFAB81B6AD19654F99EA7370807F18F5002725DAB98B8EFD
          19C711337E26948E26D1D174B159973EA0BE8CC9CAA6AAF513BF84E44B2247792265" />

    </system.web>
</configuration>
```

The web configuration file in Listing 24.16 modifies three attributes of the sessionState element. First, the mode attribute is set to the value StateServer. Next, the stateConnectionString attribute is used to specify the location of the ASP.NET State Server. In Listing 24.16, a connection is created to the local server on port 42424. Finally, the stateNetworkTimeout attribute is used to specify a connection timeout in seconds.

Notice that the web configuration in Listing 24.17 includes a machineKey element. If you are setting up a web farm, and you need to use the same State Server to store Session state for multiple servers, then you are required to specify explicit encryption and validation keys. On the other hand, you don't need to include a machineKey element when the ASP.NET State Server is hosted on the same machine as your ASP.NET application.

NOTE

You can configure the ASP.NET State Server to use a different port by modifying the following Registry value:

```
HKEY_LOCAL_MACHINE\SYSTEM\CurrentControlSet\Services\aspnet_state\
Parameters\Port
```

You need to stop and restart the ASP.NET State Service with the Services applet after making this modification.

WARNING

Don't use the web configuration file in Listing 24.17 without modifying the values of both the decryptionKey and validationKey attributes. Those values must be secret. You can use the GenerateKeys.aspx page discussed in the previous chapter (Chapter 23, "Using ASP.NET Membership") to generate new values for these attributes.

24

After you complete these configuration steps, Session state information is stored in the ASP.NET State Server automatically. You don't need to modify any of your application code when you switch to out-of-process Session state.

Configuring SQL Server Session State

If you want to store Session state in the most reliable way possible, then you can store Session state in a Microsoft SQL Server database. Because you can set up failover SQL Server clusters, Session state stored in SQL Server should be able to survive just anything, including a major nuclear war.

You must complete the following two steps to enable SQL Server Session state:

▶ Configure your database to support SQL Server Session state.

▶ Configure your application to use SQL Server Session state.

You can use the aspnet_regsql tool to add the necessary tables and stored procedures to your database to support SQL Server Session state. The aspnet_regsql tool is located in the following path:

```
C:\WINDOWS\Microsoft.NET\Framework\v2.0.50727\aspnet_regsql.exe
```

NOTE

If you open the SDK Command Prompt, you don't need to navigate to the Microsoft.NET folder to use the aspnet_regsql tool.

Executing the following command enables SQL Server Session state for a database server named YourServer.

```
aspnet_regsql -C "Data Source=YourServer;Integrated Security=True" -ssadd
```

When you execute this command, a new database is created on your database server named ASPState. The ASPState database contains all the stored procedures used by Session state. However, by default, Session state information is stored in the TempDB database. When your database server restarts, the TempDB database is cleared automatically.

If you want to use SQL Server Session state with a failover cluster of SQL Servers, then you can't store Session state in the TempDB database. Also, if you want Session state to survive database restarts, then you can't store the state information in the TempDB database.

If you execute the following command, then Session state is stored in the ASPState database instead of the TempDB database:

```
aspnet_regsql -C "Data Source=YourServer;Integrated Security=True" -ssadd -sstype p
```

Notice that this command includes a -sstype p switch. The p stands for persistent. Session state that is stored in the ASPState database is called persistent Session state because it survives database server restarts.

Finally, you can store Session state in a custom database. The following command stores Session state in a database named MySessionDB:

```
aspnet_regsql -C "Data Source=YourServer;Integrated Security=True" -ssadd -sstype c
-d MySessionDB
```

Executing this command creates a new database named MySessionDB that contains both the tables and stored procedures for storing Session state. Notice that the -sstype switch has the value c for custom. The command also includes a -d switch that enables you to specify the name of the new database.

If you want to remove the Session state tables and stored procedures from a server, then you can execute the following command:

```
aspnet_regsql -C "Data Source=YourServer;Integrated Security=True" -ssremove
```

Executing this command removes the ASPState database. It does not remove a custom Session state database. You must remove a custom database manually.

After you configure your database server to support Session state, you must configure your ASP.NET application to connect to your database. You can use the web configuration file in Listing 24.17 to connect to a database named YourServer.

LISTING 24.17 Web.Config

```
<configuration>
    <system.web>

        <sessionState
          mode="SQLServer"
          sqlConnectionString="Data Source=YourServer;Integrated Security=True"
          sqlCommandTimeout="30" />
```

```
<machineKey
  decryption="AES"
  validation="SHA1"
  decryptionKey="306C1FA852AB3B0115150DD8BA30821CDFD125538A0C606D
➥ACA53DBB3C3E0AD2"
  validationKey="61A8E04A146AFFAB81B6AD19654F99EA7370807F18F5002725DAB98B8EF
➥D19C711337E26948E26D1D174B159973EA0BE8CC9CAA6AAF513BF84E44B2247792265" />

  </system.web>
</configuration>
```

The sessionState element includes three attributes. The mode attribute is set to the value
SQLServer to enable SQL Server Session state. The second attribute, sqlConnectionString,
contains the connection string to the Session state database. Finally, the sqlCommandTimeout
specifies the maximum amount of time in seconds before a command that retrieves or stores
Session state times out.

Notice that the configuration file in Listing 24.18 includes a machineKey element. If your
Session state database is located on a different machine than your ASP.NET application,
then you are required to include a machineKey element that contains explicit encryption
and validation keys.

> **WARNING**
>
> Don't use the web configuration file in Listing 24.17 without modifying the values of
> both the decryptionKey and validationKey attributes. Those values must be secret.
> You can use the GenerateKeys.aspx page discussed in the previous chapter (Chapter
> 23) to generate new values for these attributes.

If you select the option to store Session state in a custom database when executing the
aspnet_regsql tool, then you need to specify the name of the custom database in your
configuration file. You can use the web configuration file in Listing 24.18.

LISTING 24.18 Web.config

```
<configuration>
   <system.web>

   <sessionState
      mode="SQLServer"
      sqlConnectionString="Data Source=YourServer;
Integrated Security=True;database=MySessionDB"
      sqlCommandTimeout="30"
      allowCustomSqlDatabase="true"/>
```

24

LISTING 24.18   Continued

```
    <machineKey
      decryption="AES"
      validation="SHA1"
      decryptionKey="306C1FA852AB3B0115150DD8BA30821CDFD125538A0C606D
      ➥ACA53DBB3C3E0AD2"
      validationKey="61A8E04A146AFFAB81B6AD19654F99EA7370807F18F5002725DAB98B8EFD
      ➥19C711337E26948E26D1D174B159973EA0BE8CC9CAA6AAF513BF84E44B2247792265" />


    </system.web>
</configuration>
```

The `sessionState` element in the configuration file in Listing 24.18 includes an `allowCustomSqlDatabase` attribute. Furthermore, the `sqlConnectionString` attribute contains the name of the custom database.

Enabling SQL Server session state has no effect on how you write your application code. You can initially build your application using in-process `Session` state and, when you have the need, you can switch to SQL Server `Session` state.

Using Profiles

The ASP.NET Framework provides you with an alternative to using cookies or `Session` state to store user information: the `Profile` object. The `Profile` object provides you with a strongly typed, persistent form of session state.

You create a `Profile` by defining a list of `Profile` properties in your application root web configuration file. The ASP.NET Framework dynamically compiles a class that contains these properties in the background.

For example, the web configuration file in Listing 24.19 defines a `Profile` that contains three properties: `firstName`, `lastName`, and `numberOfVisits`.

LISTING 24.19   Web.Config

```
<configuration>
<system.web>

  <profile>
    <properties>
      <add name="firstName" />
      <add name="lastName" />
      <add name="numberOfVisits" type="Int32" defaultValue="0" />
    </properties>
```

```
    </profile>

</system.web>
</configuration>
```

When you define a `Profile` property, you can use any of the following attributes:

- **name**—Enables you to specify the name of the property.

- **type**—Enables you to specify the type of the property. The type can be any custom type, including a custom component that you define in the `App_Code` folder. (The default type is string.)

- **defaultValue**—Enables you to specify a default value for the property.

- **readOnly**—Enables you to create a read-only property. (The default value is `false`.)

- **serializeAs**—Enables you to specify how a property is persisted into a static representation. Possible values are `Binary`, `ProviderSpecific`, `String`, and `Xml`. (The default value is `ProviderSpecific`.)

- **allowAnonymous**—Enables you to allow anonymous users to read and set the property. (The default value is false.)

- **provider**—Enables you to associate the property with a particular Profile provider.

- **customProviderData**—Enables you to pass custom data to a Profile provider.

After you define a `Profile` in the web configuration file, you can use the `Profile` object to modify the `Profile` properties. For example, the page in Listing 24.20 enables you to modify the `firstName` and `lastName` properties with a form. Furthermore, the page automatically updates the `numberOfVisits` property each time the page is requested (see Figure 24.7).

LISTING 24.20   ShowProfile.aspx

```
<%@ Page Language="C#" %>
<!DOCTYPE html PUBLIC "-//W3C//DTD XHTML 1.0 Transitional//EN"
"http://www.w3.org/TR/xhtml1/DTD/xhtml1-transitional.dtd">
<script runat="server">

    void Page_PreRender()
    {
        lblFirstname.Text = Profile.firstName;
        lblLastName.Text = Profile.lastName;

        Profile.numberOfVisits++;
        lblNumberOfVisits.Text = Profile.numberOfVisits.ToString();
    }
```

LISTING 24.20   Continued

```
    protected void btnUpdate_Click(object sender, EventArgs e)
    {
        Profile.firstName = txtNewFirstName.Text;
        Profile.lastName = txtNewLastName.Text;
    }
</script>
<html xmlns="http://www.w3.org/1999/xhtml" >
<head id="Head1" runat="server">
    <title>Show Profile</title>
</head>
<body>
    <form id="form1" runat="server">
    <div>

    First Name:
    <asp:Label
        id="lblFirstname"
        Runat="server" />
    <br /><br />
    Last Name:
    <asp:Label
        id="lblLastName"
        Runat="server" />
    <br /><br />
    Number of Visits:
    <asp:Label
        id="lblNumberOfVisits"
        Runat="server" />

    <hr />

    <asp:Label
        id="lblNewFirstName"
        Text="New First Name:"
        AssociatedControlID="txtNewFirstName"
        Runat="server" />
    <asp:TextBox
        id="txtNewFirstName"
        Runat="server" />
    <br /><br />
    <asp:Label
        id="lblNewLastName"
        Text="New Last Name:"
```

```
            AssociatedControlID="txtNewLastName"
            Runat="server" />
        <asp:TextBox
            id="txtNewLastName"
            Runat="server" />
        <br /><br />
        <asp:Button
            id="btnUpdate"
            Text="Update Profile"
            OnClick="btnUpdate_Click"
            Runat="server" />

    </div>
    </form>
</body>
</html>
```

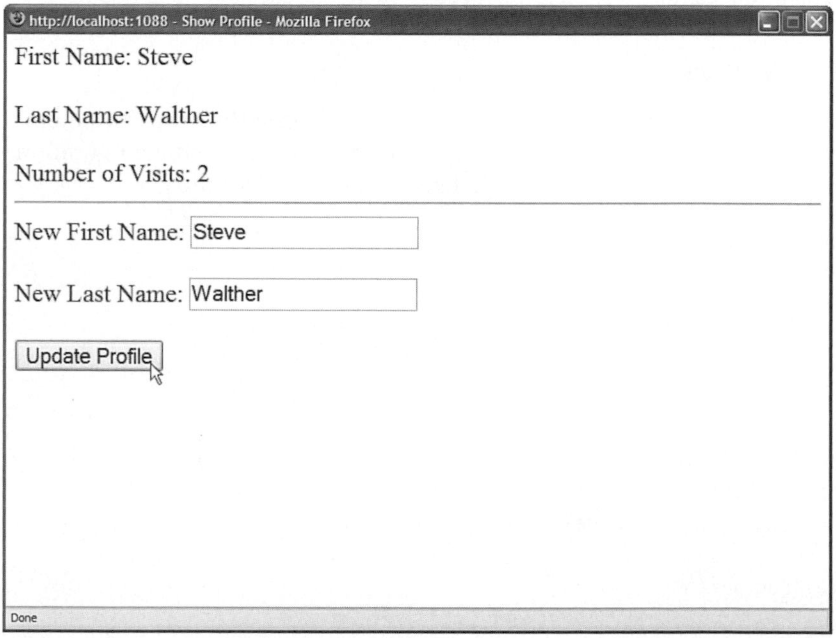

FIGURE 24.7   Displaying Profile information.

Notice that Profile properties are exposed as strongly typed properties. The numberOfVisits property, for example, is exposed as an integer property because you defined it as an integer property.

It is important to understand that `Profile` properties are persistent. If you set a `Profile` property for a user, and that user does not return to your website for 500 years, the property retains its value. Unlike `Session` state, when you assign a value to a `Profile` property, the value does not evaporate after a user leaves your website.

The `Profile` object uses the Provider model. The default `Profile` provider is the `SqlProfileProvider`. By default, this provider stores the `Profile` data in a Microsoft SQL Server 2005 Express database named `ASPNETDB.mdf`, located in your application's App_Code folder. If the database does not exist, it is created automatically the first time that you use the `Profile` object.

By default, you cannot store `Profile` information for an anonymous user. The ASP.NET Framework uses your authenticated identity to associate `Profile` information with you. You can use the `Profile` object with any of the standard types of authentication supported by the ASP.NET Framework, including both Forms and Windows authentication. (Windows authentication is enabled by default.)

> **NOTE**
>
> Later in this section, you learn how to store `Profile` information for anonymous users.

Creating Profile Groups

If you need to define a lot of `Profile` properties, then you can make the properties more manageable by organizing the properties into groups. For example, the web configuration file in Listing 24.21 defines two groups named Preferences and ContactInfo.

LISTING 24.21   Web.Config

```
<configuration>
<system.web>

  <profile>
    <properties>
      <group name="Preferences">
        <add name="BackColor" defaultValue="lightblue"/>
        <add name="Font" defaultValue="Arial"/>
      </group>
      <group name="ContactInfo">
        <add name="Email" defaultValue="Your Email"/>
        <add name="Phone" defaultValue="Your Phone"/>
      </group>
    </properties>
  </profile>

</system.web>
</configuration>
```

The page in Listing 24.22 illustrates how you can set and read properties in different groups.

LISTING 24.22   ShowProfileGroups.aspx

```
<%@ Page Language="C#" %>
<%@ Import Namespace="System.Drawing" %>
<!DOCTYPE html PUBLIC "-//W3C//DTD XHTML 1.0 Transitional//EN"
"http://www.w3.org/TR/xhtml1/DTD/xhtml1-transitional.dtd">
<script runat="server">

    void Page_Load()
    {
        // Display Contact Info
        lblEmail.Text = Profile.ContactInfo.Email;
        lblPhone.Text = Profile.ContactInfo.Phone;

        // Apply Preferences
        Style pageStyle = new Style();
        pageStyle.BackColor = ColorTranslator.FromHtml(Profile.Preferences.
        ➥BackColor);
        pageStyle.Font.Name = Profile.Preferences.Font;
        Header.StyleSheet.CreateStyleRule(pageStyle, null, "html");
    }
</script>
<html xmlns="http://www.w3.org/1999/xhtml" >
<head id="Head1" runat="server">
    <title>Untitled Page</title>
</head>
<body>
    <form id="form1" runat="server">
    <div>

    Email:
    <asp:Label
        id="lblEmail"
        Runat="server" />
    <br /><br />
    Phone:
    <asp:Label
        id="lblPhone"
        Runat="server" />
```

24

LISTING 24.22   Continued

```
    </div>
    </form>
</body>
</html>
```

Supporting Anonymous Users

By default, anonymous users cannot modify `Profile` properties. The problem is that the ASP.NET Framework has no method of associating `Profile` data with a particular user unless the user is authenticated.

If you want to enable anonymous users to modify `Profile` properties, you must enable a feature of the ASP.NET Framework called Anonymous Identification. When Anonymous Identification is enabled, a unique identifier (a GUID) is assigned to anonymous users and stored in a persistent browser cookie.

> **NOTE**
>
> You can enable cookieless anonymous identifiers. Cookieless anonymous identifiers work just like cookieless sessions: The anonymous identifier is added to the page URL instead of a cookie. You enable cookieless anonymous identifiers by setting the cookie-less attribute of the `anonymousIdentification` element in the web configuration file to the value `UseURI` or `AutoDetect`.

Furthermore, you must mark all `Profile` properties that you want anonymous users to be able to modify with the `allowAnonymous` attribute. For example, the web configuration file in Listing 24.23 enables Anonymous Identification and defines a `Profile` property that can be modified by anonymous users.

LISTING 24.23   Web.Config

```
<configuration>
<system.web>

  <authentication mode="Forms" />

  <anonymousIdentification enabled="true" />

  <profile>
    <properties>
      <add
        name="numberOfVisits"
        type="Int32"
```

```
        defaultValue="0"
        allowAnonymous="true" />
    </properties>
  </profile>

</system.web>
</configuration>
```

The numberOfVisits property defined in Listing 24.23 includes the allowAnonymous attribute. Notice that the web configuration file also enables Forms authentication. When Forms authentication is enabled, and you don't log in, then you are an anonymous user.

The page in Listing 24.24 illustrates how you modify a Profile property when Anonymous Identification is enabled.

LISTING 24.24   ShowAnonymousIdentification.aspx

```
<%@ Page Language="C#" %>
<!DOCTYPE html PUBLIC "-//W3C//DTD XHTML 1.0 Transitional//EN"
"http://www.w3.org/TR/xhtml1/DTD/xhtml1-transitional.dtd">
<script runat="server">

    void Page_PreRender()
    {
        lblUserName.Text = Profile.UserName;
        lblIsAnonymous.Text = Profile.IsAnonymous.ToString();
        Profile.numberOfVisits++;
        lblNumberOfVisits.Text = Profile.numberOfVisits.ToString();
    }

    protected void btnLogin_Click(object sender, EventArgs e)
    {
        FormsAuthentication.SetAuthCookie("Bob", false);
        Response.Redirect(Request.Path);
    }

    protected void btnLogout_Click(object sender, EventArgs e)
    {
        FormsAuthentication.SignOut();
        Response.Redirect(Request.Path);
    }
</script>
<html xmlns="http://www.w3.org/1999/xhtml" >
<head id="Head1" runat="server">
    <title>Show Anonymous Identification</title>
```

LISTING 24.24   Continued

```
</head>
<body>
    <form id="form1" runat="server">
    <div>

    User Name:
    <asp:Label
        id="lblUserName"
        Runat="server" />
    <br />
    Is Anonymous:
    <asp:Label
        id="lblIsAnonymous"
        Runat="server" />
    <br />
    Number Of Visits:
    <asp:Label
        id="lblNumberOfVisits"
        Runat="server" />

    <hr />
    <asp:Button
        id="btnReload"
        Text="Reload"
        Runat="server" />

    <asp:Button
        id="btnLogin"
        Text="Login"
        OnClick="btnLogin_Click"
        Runat="server" />

    <asp:Button
        id="btnLogout"
        Text="Logout"
        OnClick="btnLogout_Click"
        Runat="server" />

    </div>
    </form>
</body>
</html>
```

Each time that you request the page in Listing 24.24, the numberOfVisits Profile property is incremented and displayed. The page includes three buttons: Reload, Login, and Logout (see Figure 24.8).

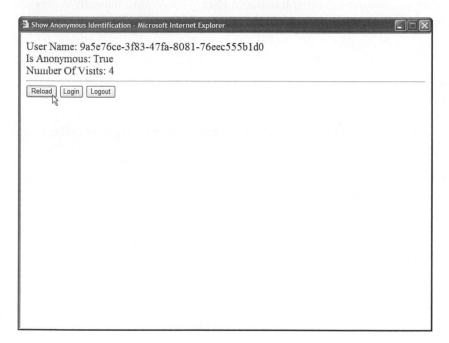

User Name: 9a5e76ce-3f83-47fa-8081-76eec555b1d0
Is Anonymous: True
Number Of Visits: 4

[Reload] [Login] [Logout]

FIGURE 24.8   Creating an anonymous profile.

The page also displays the value of the Profile.UserName property. This property represents either the current username or the anonymous identifier. The value of the numberOfVisits Profile property is tied to the value of the Profile.UserName property.

You can click the Reload button to quickly reload the page and increment the value of the numberOfVisits property.

If you click the Login button, then the Profile.UserName property changes to the value Bob. The numberOfVisits property is reset.

If you click the Logout button, then the Profile.UserName property switches back to your anonymous identifier. The numberOfVisits property reverts to its previous value.

Migrating Anonymous Profiles

In the previous section, you saw that all profile information is lost when a user transitions from anonymous to authenticated. For example, if you store a shopping cart in the Profile object and a user logs in, then all the shopping cart items are lost.

You can preserve the value of Profile properties when a user transitions from anonymous to authenticated by handling the MigrateAnonymous event in the Global.asax file. This event is raised when an anonymous user that has a profile logs in.

For example, the MigrateAnonymous event handler in Listing 24.25 automatically copies the values of all anonymous Profile properties to the user's current authenticated profile.

LISTING 24.25   Global.asax

```
<%@ Application Language="C#" %>
<script runat="server">

    public void Profile_OnMigrateAnonymous(object sender, ProfileMigrateEventArgs
    ➥args)
    {
        // Get anonymous profile
        ProfileCommon anonProfile = Profile.GetProfile(args.AnonymousID);

        // Copy anonymous properties to authenticated
        foreach (SettingsProperty prop in ProfileBase.Properties)
            Profile[prop.Name] = anonProfile[prop.Name];

        // Kill the anonymous profile
        ProfileManager.DeleteProfile(args.AnonymousID);
        AnonymousIdentificationModule.ClearAnonymousIdentifier();
    }

</script>
```

The anonymous Profile associated with the user is retrieved when the user's anonymous identifier is passed to the Profile.GetProfile() method. Next, each Profile property is copied from the anonymous Profile to the current Profile. Finally, the anonymous Profile is deleted and the anonymous identifier is destroyed. (If you don't destroy the anonymous identifier, then the MigrateAnonymous event continues to be raised with each page request after the user authenticates.)

Inheriting a Profile from a Custom Class

Instead of defining a list of Profile properties in the web configuration file, you can define Profile properties in a separate class. For example, the class in Listing 24.26 contains two properties named FirstName and LastName.

LISTING 24.26 App_Code\SiteProfile.cs

```csharp
using System;
using System.Web.Profile;

public class SiteProfile : ProfileBase
{
    private string _firstName = "Your First Name";
    private string _lastName = "Your Last Name";

    [SettingsAllowAnonymous(true)]
    public string FirstName
    {
        get { return _firstName; }
        set { _firstName = value; }
    }

    [SettingsAllowAnonymous(true)]
    public string LastName
    {
        get { return _lastName; }
        set { _lastName = value; }
    }
}
```

Notice that the class in Listing 24.26 inherits from the BaseProfile class.

After you declare a class, you can use it to define a profile by inheriting the Profile object from the class in the web configuration file. The web configuration file in Listing 24.27 uses the inherits attribute to inherit the Profile from the SiteProfile class.

LISTING 24.27 Web.Config

```xml
<configuration>
<system.web>

  <anonymousIdentification enabled="true" />

  <profile inherits="SiteProfile" />

</system.web>
</configuration>
```

After you inherit a Profile in the web configuration file, you can use the Profile in the normal way. You can set or read any of the properties that you defined in the SiteProfile class by accessing the properties through the Profile object.

NOTE

The CD that accompanies this book includes a page named `ShowSiteProfile.aspx`, which displays the `Profile` properties defined in Listing 24.27.

NOTE

If you inherit `Profile` properties from a class and define `Profile` properties in the web configuration file, then the two sets of `Profile` properties are merged.

When you define `Profile` properties in a class, you can decorate the properties with the following attributes:

▶ **SettingsAllowAnonymous**—Enables you to allow anonymous users to read and set the property.

▶ **ProfileProvider**—Enables you to associate the property with a particular `Profile` provider.

▶ **CustomProviderData**—Enables you to pass custom data to a `Profile` provider.

For example, both properties declared in the `SiteProfile` class in Listing 24.28 include the `SettingsAllowAnonymous` attribute, which allows anonymous users to read and modify the properties.

Creating Complex Profile Properties

To this point, we've used the `Profile` properties to represent simple types such as strings and integers. You can use `Profile` properties to represent more complex types such as a custom `ShoppingCart` class.

For example, the class in Listing 24.28 represents a simple shopping cart.

LISTING 24.28   App_Code\ShoppingCart.cs

```
using System;
using System.Collections.Generic;
using System.Web.Profile;

namespace AspNetUnleashed
{
    public class ShoppingCart
    {
        private List<CartItem> _items = new List<CartItem>();

        public List<CartItem> Items
        {
```

```
            get { return _items; }
        }
    }

    public class CartItem
    {
        private string _name;
        private decimal _price;
        private string _description;

        public string Name
        {
            get { return _name; }
            set { _name = value; }
        }

        public decimal Price
        {
            get { return _price; }
            set { _price = value; }
        }

        public string Description
        {
            get { return _description; }
            set { _description = value; }
        }

        public CartItem() { }

        public CartItem(string name, decimal price, string description)
        {
            _name = name;
            _price = price;
            _description = description;
        }
    }
}
```

The file in Listing 24.28 actually contains two classes: the ShoppingCart class and the CartItem class. The ShoppingCart class exposes a collection of CartItem objects.

The web configuration file in Listing 24.29 defines a Profile property named ShoppingCart that represents the ShoppingCart class. The type attribute is set to the fully qualified name of the ShoppingCart class.

LISTING 24.29   Web.Config

```
<configuration>
<system.web>

  <profile>
    <properties>
      <add name="ShoppingCart" type="AspNetUnleashed.ShoppingCart" />
    </properties>
  </profile>

</system.web>
</configuration>
```

Finally, the page in Listing 24.30 uses the Profile.ShoppingCart property. The contents of the ShoppingCart are bound and displayed in a GridView control. The page also contains a form that enables you to add new items to the ShoppingCart (see Figure 24.9).

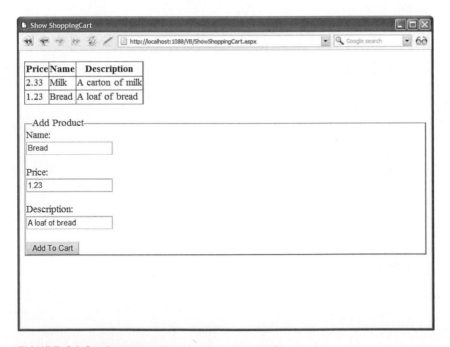

FIGURE 24.9   Storing a shopping cart in a profile.

LISTING 24.30   ShowShoppingCart.aspx

```
<%@ Page Language="C#" %>
<%@ Import Namespace="AspNetUnleashed" %>
```

```
<!DOCTYPE html PUBLIC "-//W3C//DTD XHTML 1.0 Transitional//EN"
"http://www.w3.org/TR/xhtml1/DTD/xhtml1-transitional.dtd">
<script runat="server">

    void Page_PreRender()
    {
        grdShoppingCart.DataSource = Profile.ShoppingCart.Items;
        grdShoppingCart.DataBind();
    }

    protected void btnAdd_Click(object sender, EventArgs e)
    {
        CartItem newItem = new CartItem(txtName.Text, decimal.Parse(txtPrice.Text),
        ➥txtDescription.Text);
        Profile.ShoppingCart.Items.Add(newItem);
    }
</script>
<html xmlns="http://www.w3.org/1999/xhtml" >
<head id="Head1" runat="server">
    <title>Show ShoppingCart</title>
</head>
<body>
    <form id="form1" runat="server">
    <div>

    <asp:GridView
        id="grdShoppingCart"
        EmptyDataText="There are no items in your shopping cart"
        Runat="server" />

    <br />

    <fieldset>
    <legend>Add Product</legend>
    <asp:Label
        id="lblName"
        Text="Name:"
        AssociatedControlID="txtName"
        Runat="server" />
    <br />
    <asp:TextBox
        id="txtName"
        Runat="server" />
    <br /><br />
    <asp:Label
        id="lblPrice"
```

24

LISTING 24.30   Continued

```
            Text="Price:"
            AssociatedControlID="txtPrice"
            Runat="server" />
        <br />
        <asp:TextBox
            id="txtPrice"
            Runat="server" />
        <br /><br />
        <asp:Label
            id="lblDescription"
            Text="Description:"
            AssociatedControlID="txtDescription"
            Runat="server" />
        <br />
        <asp:TextBox
            id="txtDescription"
            Runat="server" />
        <br /><br />
        <asp:Button
            id="btnAdd"
            Text="Add To Cart"
            Runat="server" OnClick="btnAdd_Click" />
        </fieldset>

    </div>
    </form>
</body>
</html>
```

If you want to take control over how complex properties are stored, you can modify the
value of the serializeAs attribute associated with a Profile property. The serializeAs
attribute accepts the following four values:

▶ Binary

▶ ProviderSpecific

▶ String

▶ Xml

The default value, when using the SqlProfileProvider, is ProviderSpecific. In other
words, the SqlProfileProvider decides on the best method for storing properties. In
general, simple types are serialized as strings and complex types are serialized with the
XML Serializer.

One disadvantage of the XML Serializer is that it produces a more bloated representation of a property than the Binary Serializer. For example, the results of serializing the ShoppingCart class with the XML Serializer are contained in Listing 24.31.

LISTING 24.31   Serialized Shopping Cart

```
<ShoppingCart xmlns:xsi=http://www.w3.org/2001/XMLSchema-instance
 xmlns:xsd="http://www.w3.org/2001/XMLSchema">
  <Items>
    <CartItem>
      <Name>First Product</Name>
      <Price>2.99</Price>
      <Description>The First Product</Description>
    </CartItem>
    <CartItem>
      <Name>Second Product</Name>
      <Price>2.99</Price>
      <Description>The Second Product</Description>
    </CartItem>
  </Items>
</ShoppingCart>
```

If you want to serialize a Profile property with the Binary Serializer (and save some database space), then you need to do two things. First, you need to indicate in the web configuration file that the Profile property should be serialized with the Binary Serializer. Furthermore, you need to mark the class that the Profile property represents as serializable.

The modified ShoppingClass (named BinaryShoppingCart) in Listing 24.32 includes a Serializable attribute. Notice that both the BinaryShoppingCart and BinaryCartItem classes are decorated with the Serializable attribute.

LISTING 24.32   App_Code\BinaryShoppingCart.cs

```
using System;
using System.Collections.Generic;
using System.Web.Profile;

namespace AspNetUnleashed
{
    [Serializable]
    public class BinaryShoppingCart
    {
        private List<BinaryCartItem> _items = new List<BinaryCartItem>();

        public List<BinaryCartItem> Items
```

LISTING 24.32   Continued

```
        {
            get { return _items; }
        }
    }

[Serializable]
public class BinaryCartItem
{
    private string _name;
    private decimal _price;
    private string _description;

    public string Name
    {
        get { return _name; }
        set { _name = value; }
    }

    public decimal Price
    {
        get { return _price; }
        set { _price = value; }
    }

    public string Description
    {
        get { return _description; }
        set { _description = value; }
    }

    public BinaryCartItem() { }

    public BinaryCartItem(string name, decimal price, string description)
    {
        _name = name;
        _price = price;
        _description = description;
    }
    }
}
```

The Profile in the web configuration file in Listing 24.33 includes a property that represents the BinaryShoppingCart class. Notice that the property includes a serializeAs attribute that has the value `Binary`. If you don't include this attribute, the `BinaryShoppingCart` will be serialized as XML.

LISTING 24.33   Web.Config

```
<configuration>
<system.web>

  <profile>
    <properties>
      <add
        name="ShoppingCart"
        type="AspNetUnleashed.BinaryShoppingCart"
        serializeAs="Binary" />
    </properties>
  </profile>

</system.web>
</configuration>
```

> **NOTE**
>
> The CD that accompanies this book includes a page named `ShowBinaryShoppingCart.aspx` that displays the `BinaryShoppingCart`.

Saving Profiles Automatically

A profile is loaded from its profile provider the first time that a property from the profile is accessed. For example, if you use a `Profile` property in a `Page_Load()` handler, then the profile is loaded during the Page Load event. If you use a `Profile` property in a `Page_PreRender()` handler, then the `Profile` is loaded during the page `PreRender` event.

If a `Profile` property is modified, then the `Profile` is saved automatically at the end of page execution. The ASP.NET Framework can detect automatically when certain types of properties are changed but not others. In general, the ASP.NET Framework can detect changes made to simple types but not to complex types.

For example, if you access a property that exposes a simple type such as a string, integer, or Datetime, then the ASP.NET Framework can detect when the property has been changed. In that case, the framework sets the `Profile.IsDirty` property to the value `true`. At the end of page execution, if a profile is marked as dirty, then the profile is saved automatically.

The ASP.NET Framework cannot detect when a `Profile` property that represents a complex type has been modified. For example, if your profile includes a property that represents a custom `ShoppingCart` class, then the ASP.NET Framework has no way of determining when the contents of the `ShoppingCart` class have been changed.

LISTING 24.38   Continued

```
public class ProfileComponent
{
    public static string GetFirstNameFromProfile()
    {
        ProfileCommon profile = (ProfileCommon)HttpContext.Current.Profile;
        return profile.firstName;
    }
}
```

WARNING

To avoid conflicts with other code samples in this chapter, the component in Listing 24.38 is named `ProfileComponent.cs_listing38` on the CD that accompanies this book. You'll need to rename the file to `ProfileComponent.cs` before you use the component.

Finally, the page in Listing 24.39 illustrates how you can call the `ProfileComponent` from within an ASP.NET page to retrieve and display the `firstName` attribute.

LISTING 24.39   ShowProfileComponent.aspx

```
<%@ Page Language="C#" %>
<!DOCTYPE html PUBLIC "-//W3C//DTD XHTML 1.0 Transitional//EN"
"http://www.w3.org/TR/xhtml1/DTD/xhtml1-transitional.dtd">
<script runat="server">

    void Page_Load()
    {
        lblFirstName.Text = ProfileComponent.GetFirstNameFromProfile();
    }

</script>
<html xmlns="http://www.w3.org/1999/xhtml" >
<head id="Head1" runat="server">
    <title>Show Profile Component</title>
</head>
<body>
    <form id="form1" runat="server">
    <div>

    First Name:
    <asp:Label
        id="lblFirstName"
```

```
        Runat="server" />

    </div>
    </form>
</body>
</html>
</html>
```

Using the Profile Manager

Unlike Session state, profile data does not evaporate when a user leaves your application. Over time, as more users visit your application, the amount of data stored by the Profile object can become huge. If you allow anonymous profiles, the situation becomes even worse.

The ASP.NET Framework includes a class named the ProfileManager class that enables you to delete old profiles. This class supports the following methods:

- ▶ **DeleteInactiveProfiles**—Enables you to delete profiles that have not been used since a specified date.

- ▶ **DeleteProfile**—Enables you to delete a profile associated with a specified username.

- ▶ **DeleteProfiles**—Enables you to delete profiles that match an array of usernames or collection of ProfileInfo objects.

- ▶ **FindInactiveProfilesByUserName**—Enables you to retrieve all profiles associated with a specified username that have been inactive since a specified date.

- ▶ **FindProfilesByUserName**—Enables you to retrieve all profiles associated with a specified user.

- ▶ **GetAllInactiveProfiles**—Enables you to retrieve all profiles that have been inactive since a specified date.

- ▶ **GetAllProfiles**—Enables you to retrieve every profile.

- ▶ **GetNumberOfInactiveProfiles**—Enables you to retrieve a count of profiles that have been inactive since a specified date.

- ▶ **GetNumberOfProfiles**—Enables you to retrieve a count of the total number of profiles.

You can use the ProfileManager class from within a console application and execute the DeleteInactiveProfiles() method on a periodic basis to delete inactive profiles. Alternatively, you can create an administrative page in your web application that enables you to manage profile data.

The page in Listing 24.40 illustrates how you can use the ProfileManager class to remove inactive profiles (see Figure 24.10).

24

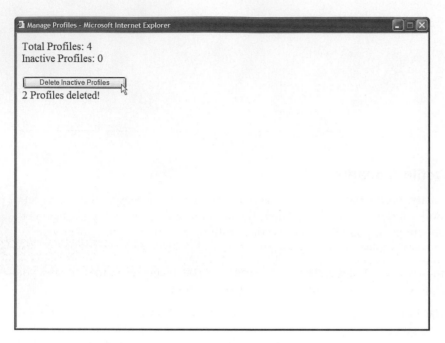

FIGURE 24.10   Deleting inactive profiles.

LISTING 24.40   ManageProfiles.aspx

```
<%@ Page Language="C#" %>
<!DOCTYPE html PUBLIC "-//W3C//DTD XHTML 1.0 Transitional//EN"
"http://www.w3.org/TR/xhtml1/DTD/xhtml1-transitional.dtd">
<script runat="server">

    DateTime inactiveDate = DateTime.Now.AddMonths(-3);

    void Page_PreRender()
    {
        lblProfiles.Text = ProfileManager.GetNumberOfProfiles
        ➥(ProfileAuthenticationOption.All).ToString();
        lblInactiveProfiles.Text = ProfileManager.GetNumberOfInactiveProfiles
        ➥(ProfileAuthenticationOption.All, inactiveDate).ToString();
    }

    protected void btnDelete_Click(object sender, EventArgs e)
    {
        int results = ProfileManager.DeleteInactiveProfiles
        ➥(ProfileAuthenticationOption.All, inactiveDate);
        lblResults.Text = String.Format("{0} Profiles deleted!", results);
```

```
        }
</script>
<html xmlns="http://www.w3.org/1999/xhtml" >
<head id="Head1" runat="server">
    <title>Manage Profiles</title>
</head>
<body>
    <form id="form1" runat="server">
    <div>

    Total Profiles:
    <asp:Label
        id="lblProfiles"
        Runat="server" />
    <br />
    Inactive Profiles:
    <asp:Label
        id="lblInactiveProfiles"
        Runat="server" />
    <br /><br />

    <asp:Button
        id="btnDelete"
        Text="Delete Inactive Profiles"
        Runat="server" OnClick="btnDelete_Click" />
    <br />
    <asp:Label
        id="lblResults"
        EnableViewState="false"
        Runat="server" />

    </div>
    </form>
</body>
</html>
```

The page in Listing 24.40 displays the total number of profiles and the total number of
inactive profiles. An inactive profile is a profile that has not been accessed for more than
three months. The page also includes a Delete Inactive Profiles button that enables you to
remove the old profiles.

Configuring the Profile Provider

By default, profile data is stored in a Microsoft SQL Server Express database named
ASPNETDB.mdf, located in your application's root App_Data folder. If you want to store

profile data in another database in your network, then you need to perform the following two tasks:

1. Add the necessary database objects required by the profile object to the database.

2. Configure your application to connect to the database.

You can add the necessary database tables and stored procedures required by the Profile object to a database by executing the aspnet_regsql command-line tool. The aspnet_regsql tool is located at the following path:

```
C:\WINDOWS\Microsoft.NET\Framework\v2.0.50727\aspnet_regsql.exe
```

> **NOTE**
>
> If you open the SDK Command Prompt, then you do not need to navigate to the Microsoft.NET directory to execute the aspnet_regsql tool.

If you execute this tool without supplying any parameters, then the ASP.NET SQL Server Setup Wizard launches. This wizard guides you through the process of connecting to a database and adding the necessary database objects.

As an alternative to using the aspnet_regsql tool, you can install the necessary database objects by executing the following two SQL batch files:

```
C:\WINDOWS\Microsoft.NET\Framework\v2.0.50727\InstallCommon.sql
C:\WINDOWS\Microsoft.NET\Framework\v2.0.50727\InstallProfile.sql
```

After you have set up your database, you need to configure the default profile provider to connect to the database. The web configuration file in Listing 24.41 connects to a database named MyDatabase on a server named MyServer.

LISTING 24.41   Web.Config

```
<configuration>
  <connectionStrings>
    <add
      name="conProfile"
      connectionString="Data Source=MyServer;
Integrated Security=true;database=MyDatabase"/>
  </connectionStrings>
  <system.web>

    <profile defaultProvider="MyProfileProvider">
      <properties>
        <add name="firstName" />
        <add name="lastName" />
      </properties>
```

```
      <providers>
        <add
          name="MyProfileProvider"
          type="System.Web.Profile.SqlProfileProvider"
          connectionStringName="conProfile"/>
      </providers>
    </profile>

  </system.web>
</configuration>
```

After you complete these configuration steps, all profile data is stored in a custom database.

Creating a Custom Profile Provider

The Profile object uses the Provider Model. The ASP.NET Framework includes a single profile provider, the SqlProfileProvider, that stores profile data in a Microsoft SQL Server database. In this section, you learn how to build a custom profile provider.

One problem with the default SqlProfileProvider is that it serializes an entire profile into a single blob and stores the blob in a database table column. This means that you can't execute SQL queries against the properties in a profile. In other words, the default SqlProfileProvider makes it extremely difficult to generate reports off the properties stored in a profile.

In this section, we create a new profile provider that is modestly named the BetterProfileProvider. The BetterProfileProvider stores each Profile property in a separate database column.

Unfortunately, the code for the BetterProfileProvider is too long to place in this book. However, the entire source code is included on the CD that accompanies this book.

The BetterProfileProvider inherits from the base ProfileProvider class. The two most important methods that must be overridden in the base ProfileProvider class are the GetPropertyValues() and SetPropertyValues() methods. These methods are responsible for loading and saving a profile for a particular user.

Imagine that you want to use the BetterProfileProvider to represent a profile that contains the following three properties: FirstName, LastName, and NumberOfVisits. Before you can use the BetterProfileProvider, you must create a database table that contains three columns that correspond to these Profile properties. In addition, the database table must contain an int column named ProfileID.

You can create the necessary database table with the following SQL command:

```
CREATE TABLE ProfileData
{
  ProfileID Int,
  FirstName NVarChar(50),
```

```
  LastName NVarChar(50),
  NumberOfVisits Int
}
```

Next, you need to create a database table named Profiles. This table is used to describe the properties of each profile. You can create the Profiles table with the following SQL command:

```
CREATE TABLE Profiles
(
  UniqueID IDENTITY NOT NULL PRIMARY KEY,
  UserName NVarchar(255) NOT NULL,
  ApplicationName NVarchar(255) NOT NULL,
  IsAnonymous BIT,
  LastActivityDate DateTime,
  LastUpdatedDate DateTime,
)
```

After you create these two database tables, you are ready to use the BetterProfileProvider. The web configuration file in Listing 24.42 configures the BetterProfileProvider as the default profile provider.

LISTING 24.42   Web.Config

```
<configuration>
  <connectionStrings>
    <add
      name="conProfile"
      connectionString="Data Source=.\SQLExpress;
Integrated Security=true;AttachDBFileName=¦DataDirectory¦ProfilesDB.mdf;User
Instance=true" />
  </connectionStrings>
  <system.web>

    <profile defaultProvider="MyProfileProvider">
      <properties>
        <add name="FirstName" />
        <add name="LastName" />
        <add name="NumberOfVisits" type="Int32" />
      </properties>
      <providers>
        <add
          name="MyProfileProvider"
          type="AspNetUnleashed.BetterProfileProvider"
          connectionStringName="conProfile"
          profileTableName="ProfileData" />
      </providers>
    </profile>
```

```
    </system.web>
</configuration>
```

Notice that the BetterProfileProvider is configured with both a connectionStringName and profileTableName attribute. The connectionStringName points to the database that contains the two database tables that were created earlier. The profileTableName property contains the name of the table that contains the profile data. (This attribute defaults to the value ProfileData, so it really isn't necessary here.)

After you configure the BetterProfileProvider, you can use it in a similar manner to the default SqlProfileProvider. For example, the page in Listing 24.43 displays the values of the FirstName, LastName, and NumberOfVisits profile properties and enables you to modify the FirstName and LastName properties.

24

WARNING

The BetterProfileProvider has several important limitations. It does not support serialization, so you cannot use it with complex types such as a custom shopping cart class. It also does not support default values for Profile properties.

LISTING 24.43   ShowBetterProfileProvider.aspx

```csharp
<%@ Page Language="C#" %>
<!DOCTYPE html PUBLIC "-//W3C//DTD XHTML 1.0 Transitional//EN"
"http://www.w3.org/TR/xhtml1/DTD/xhtml1-transitional.dtd">
<script runat="server">

    void Page_PreRender()
    {
        Profile.NumberOfVisits++;
        lblNumberOfVisits.Text = Profile.NumberOfVisits.ToString();

        lblFirstName.Text = Profile.FirstName;
        lblLastName.Text = Profile.LastName;
    }

    protected void btnUpdate_Click(object sender, EventArgs e)
    {
        Profile.FirstName = txtNewFirstName.Text;
        Profile.LastName = txtNewLastName.Text;
    }
</script>
<html xmlns="http://www.w3.org/1999/xhtml" >
```

LISTING 24.43   Continued

```
<head id="Head1" runat="server">
    <title>Show BetterProfileProvider</title>
</head>
<body>
    <form id="form1" runat="server">
    <div>

    Number of Visits:
    <asp:Label
        id="lblNumberOfVisits"
        Runat="server" />
    <br />
    First Name:
    <asp:Label
        id="lblFirstName"
        Runat="server" />
    <br />
    Last Name:
    <asp:Label
        id="lblLastName"
        Runat="server" />

    <hr />

    <asp:Label
        id="lblNewFirstName"
        Text="First Name:"
        AssociatedControlID="txtNewFirstName"
        Runat="server" />
    <asp:TextBox
        id="txtNewFirstName"
        Runat="server" />
    <br />
    <asp:Label
        id="lblNewLastname"
        Text="Last Name:"
        AssociatedControlID="txtNewLastName"
        Runat="server" />
    <asp:TextBox
        id="txtNewLastName"
        Runat="server" />
    <br />
    <asp:Button
        id="btnUpdate"
```

```
            Text="Update"
            OnClick="btnUpdate_Click"
            Runat="server" />

    </div>
    </form>
</body>
</html>
```

The main advantage of the `BetterProfileProvider` is that you can perform SQL queries against the data stored in the ProfileData table. For example, the page in Listing 24.44 displays the contents of the ProfileData table in a `GridView` control (see Figure 24.11). You can't do this when using the default `SqlProfileProvider` because the `SqlProfileProvider` stores profile data in a blob.

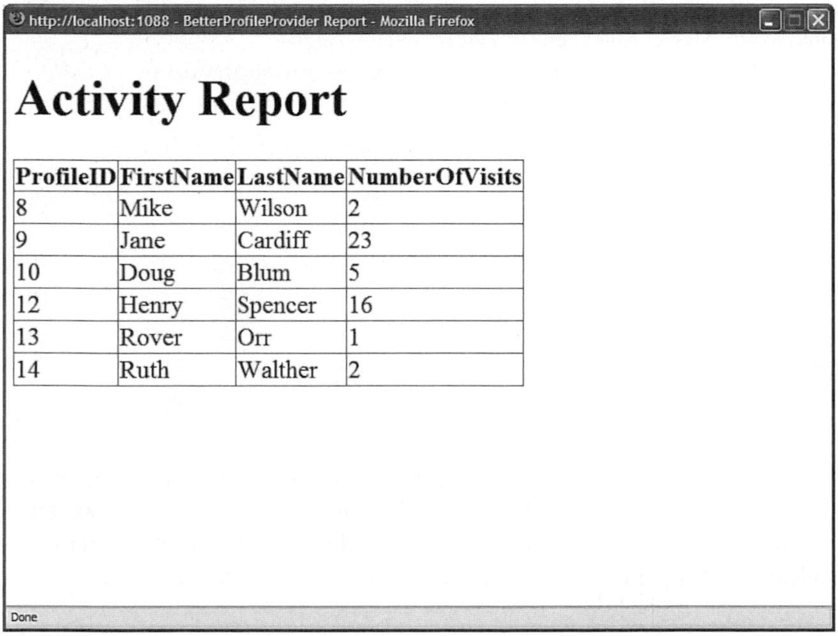
http://localhost:1088 - BetterProfileProvider Report - Mozilla Firefox

Activity Report

ProfileID	FirstName	LastName	NumberOfVisits
8	Mike	Wilson	2
9	Jane	Cardiff	23
10	Doug	Blum	5
12	Henry	Spencer	16
13	Rover	Orr	1
14	Ruth	Walther	2

Done

FIGURE 24.11 Displaying a profile report.

LISTING 24.44 `BetterProfileProviderReport.aspx`

```
<%@ Page Language="C#" %>
<!DOCTYPE html PUBLIC "-//W3C//DTD XHTML 1.0 Transitional//EN"
"http://www.w3.org/TR/xhtml1/DTD/xhtml1-transitional.dtd">
<html xmlns="http://www.w3.org/1999/xhtml" >
<head id="Head1" runat="server">
```

LISTING 22.44   Continued

```
    <title>BetterProfileProvider Report</title>
</head>
<body>
    <form id="form1" runat="server">
    <div>

    <h1>Activity Report</h1>

    <asp:GridView
        id="grdProfiles"
        DataSourceID="srcProfiles"
        Runat="server" />

    <asp:SqlDataSource
        id="srcProfiles"
        ConnectionString="<%$ ConnectionStrings:conProfile %>"
        SelectCommand="SELECT ProfileID,FirstName,LastName,NumberOfVisits
            FROM ProfileData"
        Runat="server" />

    </div>
    </form>
</body>
</html>
```

Summary

In this chapter, you learned how to maintain state in your ASP.NET applications. In the first section, you learned how to create, modify, and delete browser cookies. You learned how you can take advantage of cookies when you need to add a small amount of data to a browser. You also learned how to preserve precious cookie space by creating multi-valued cookies.

Next, we examined the topic of Session state. You learned how to take advantage of Session state to store larger amounts of data than can be stored in a cookie. You also learned how to configure cookieless Session state so that Session state works even when a browser has cookies disabled. We also discussed how to make Session state more robust by storing Session state data in a Windows NT Service or a Microsoft SQL Server database table.

Finally, you learned how to use the Profile object to create a typed and persistent form of Session state. You learned how to enable anonymous profiles. In the final section of this chapter, we built a custom Profile provider that enables you to store Profile properties in separate database table columns.

CHAPTER 25

Caching Application Pages and Data

If someone put a gun to my head and told me that I had 5 minutes to improve the performance of a website, then I would immediately think of caching. By taking advantage of caching, you can dramatically improve the performance of your web applications.

The slowest operation that you can perform in an ASP.NET page is database access. Opening a database connection and retrieving data is a slow operation. The best way to improve the performance of your data access code is not to access the database at all.

By taking advantage of caching, you can cache your database records in memory. Retrieving data from a database is dog slow. Retrieving data from the cache, on the other hand, is lightning fast.

In this chapter, you learn about the different caching mechanisms supported by the ASP.NET Framework. The ASP.NET Framework provides you with an (almost) overwhelming number of caching options. I attempt to clarify all these caching options over the course of this chapter.

In the final section of this chapter, you learn how to use SQL Cache Dependencies. A SQL Cache Dependency enables you to reload cached data automatically when data changes in a database table. You learn how to use both polling and push SQL Cache Dependencies.

Overview of Caching

The ASP.NET 3.5 Framework supports the following types of caching:

▶ Page Output Caching

▶ Partial Page Caching

▶ DataSource Caching

▶ Data Caching

Page Output Caching enables you to cache the entire rendered contents of a page in memory (everything that you see when you select View Source in your web browser). The next time that any user requests the same page, the page is retrieved from the cache.

Page Output Caching caches an entire page. In some situations, this might create problems. For example, if you want to display different banner advertisements randomly in a page, and you cache the entire page, then the same banner advertisement is displayed with each page request.

NOTE

The AdRotator control included in the ASP.NET Framework takes advantage of a feature called post-cache substitution to randomly display different advertisements even when a page is cached. Post-cache substitution is described later in this chapter.

Partial Page Caching enables you to get around this problem by enabling you to cache only particular regions of a page. By taking advantage of Partial Page Caching, you can apply different caching policies to different areas of a page.

You use DataSource Caching with the different ASP.NET DataSource controls such as the SqlDataSource and ObjectDataSource controls. When you enable caching with a DataSource control, the DataSource control caches the data that it represents.

Finally, Data Caching is the fundamental caching mechanism. Behind the scenes, all the other types of caching use Data Caching. You can use Data Caching to cache arbitrary objects in memory. For example, you can use Data Caching to cache a DataSet across multiple pages in a web application.

In the following sections, you learn how to use each of these different types of caching in detail.

NOTE

Caching LINQ to SQL queries raises special issues, which are addressed in Chapter 18, "Data Access with LINQ to SQL."

NOTE

When configuring and debugging caching, having a tool that enables you to monitor the HTTP traffic between web server and browser is extremely helpful. You can download the free Fiddler tool, which enables you to view the raw request and response HTTP traffic, from www.FiddlerTool.com.

Using Page Output Caching

You enable Page Output Caching by adding an `<%@ OutputCache %>` directive to a page. For example, the page in Listing 25.1 caches its contents for 15 seconds.

LISTING 25.1 `CachePageOutput.aspx`

```
<%@ Page Language="C#" %>
<%@ OutputCache Duration="15" VaryByParam="none" %>
<!DOCTYPE html PUBLIC "-//W3C//DTD XHTML 1.0 Transitional//EN"
"http://www.w3.org/TR/xhtml1/DTD/xhtml1-transitional.dtd">
<script runat="server">

    void Page_Load()
    {
        lblTime.Text = DateTime.Now.ToString("T");
    }

</script>
<html xmlns="http://www.w3.org/1999/xhtml" >
<head id="Head1" runat="server">
    <title>Cache Page Output</title>
</head>
<body>
    <form id="form1" runat="server">
    <div>

    <asp:Label
        id="lblTime"
        Runat="server" />

    </div>
    </form>
</body>
</html>
```

The page in Listing 25.1 displays the current server time in a `Label` control. The page also includes an `<%@ OutputCache %>` directive. If you refresh the page multiple times, you will notice that the time is not updated until at least 15 seconds have passed.

When you cache a page, the contents of the page are not regenerated each time you request the page. The .NET class that corresponds to the page is not executed with each page request. The rendered contents of the page are cached for every user that requests the page.

The page is cached in multiple locations. By default, the page is cached on the browser, any proxy servers, and on the web server.

25

In Listing 25.1, the page is cached for 15 seconds. You can assign a much larger number to the duration attribute. For example, if you assign the value 86400 to the duration parameter, then the page is cached for a day.

> **NOTE**
>
> There is no guarantee that a page will be cached for the amount of time that you specify. When server memory resources become low, items are automatically evicted from the cache.

Varying the Output Cache by Parameter

Imagine that you need to create a separate master and details page. The master page displays a list of movies. When you click a movie title, the details page displays detailed information on the movie selected.

When you create a master/details page, you typically pass a query string parameter between the master and details page to indicate the particular movie to display in the details page. If you cache the output of the details page, however, then everyone will see the first movie selected.

You can get around this problem by using the VaryByParam attribute. The VaryByParam attribute causes a new instance of a page to be cached when a different parameter is passed to the page. (The parameter can be either a query string parameter or a form parameter.)

For example, the page in Listing 25.2 contains a master page that displays a list of movie titles as links.

LISTING 25.2   Master.aspx

```
<%@ Page Language="C#" %>
<!DOCTYPE html PUBLIC "-//W3C//DTD XHTML 1.0 Transitional//EN"
 "http://www.w3.org/TR/xhtml1/DTD/xhtml1-transitional.dtd">
<html xmlns="http://www.w3.org/1999/xhtml" >
<head id="Head1" runat="server">
    <title>Master</title>
</head>
<body>
    <form id="form1" runat="server">
    <div>

    <asp:GridView
        id="grdMovies"
        DataSourceID="srcMovies"
        AutoGenerateColumns="false"
        ShowHeader="false"
        GridLines="none"
        Runat="server">
```

```
        <Columns>
        <asp:HyperLinkField
            DataTextField="Title"
            DataNavigateUrlFields="Id"
            DataNavigateUrlFormatString="~/Details.aspx?id={0}" />
        </Columns>
    </asp:GridView>

    <asp:SqlDataSource
        id="srcMovies"
        ConnectionString="<%$ ConnectionStrings:Movies %>"
        SelectCommand="SELECT Id,Title FROM Movies"
        Runat="server" />

    </div>
    </form>
</body>
</html>
```

If you hover your mouse over the links displayed in Listing 25.2, you can see the query string parameter passed by each link in the browser status bar (see Figure 25.1). For example, the first movie link includes a query string parameter with the value 1, the second link includes a query string parameter with the value 2, and so on. When you click a movie link, this query string parameter is passed to the details page in Listing 25.3.

LISTING 25.3   Details.aspx

```
<%@ Page Language="C#" %>
<%@ OutputCache Duration="3600" VaryByParam="id" %>
<!DOCTYPE html PUBLIC "-//W3C//DTD XHTML 1.0 Transitional//EN"
  "http://www.w3.org/TR/xhtml1/DTD/xhtml1-transitional.dtd">
<html xmlns="http://www.w3.org/1999/xhtml" >
<head id="Head1" runat="server">
    <title>Details</title>
</head>
<body>
    <form id="form1" runat="server">
    <div>

    <%= DateTime.Now.ToString("T") %>

    <hr />

    <asp:DetailsView
        id="dtlMovie"
```

LISTING 25.3   Continued

```
        DataSourceID="srcMovies"
        Runat="server" />

    <asp:SqlDataSource
        id="srcMovies"
        ConnectionString="<%$ ConnectionStrings:Movies %>"
        SelectCommand="SELECT * FROM Movies
            WHERE Id=@Id"
        Runat="server">
        <SelectParameters>
            <asp:QueryStringParameter
                Name="Id"
                Type="int32"
                QueryStringField="Id" />
        </SelectParameters>
    </asp:SqlDataSource>

    </div>
    </form>
</body>
</html>
```

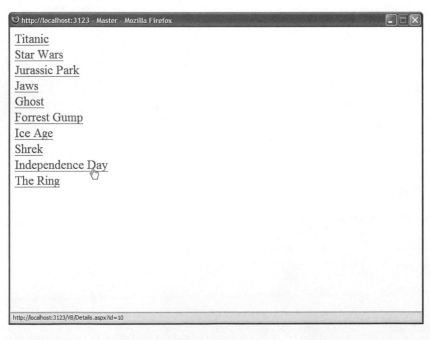

FIGURE 25.1   Displaying the Master page.

The page in Listing 25.3 uses a `DetailsView` to display detailed information on the movie selected from the master page (see Figure 25.2). The `DetailsView` is bound to a `SqlDataSource` control that includes a `QueryStringParameter` `SELECT` parameter that represents the `id` query string parameter.

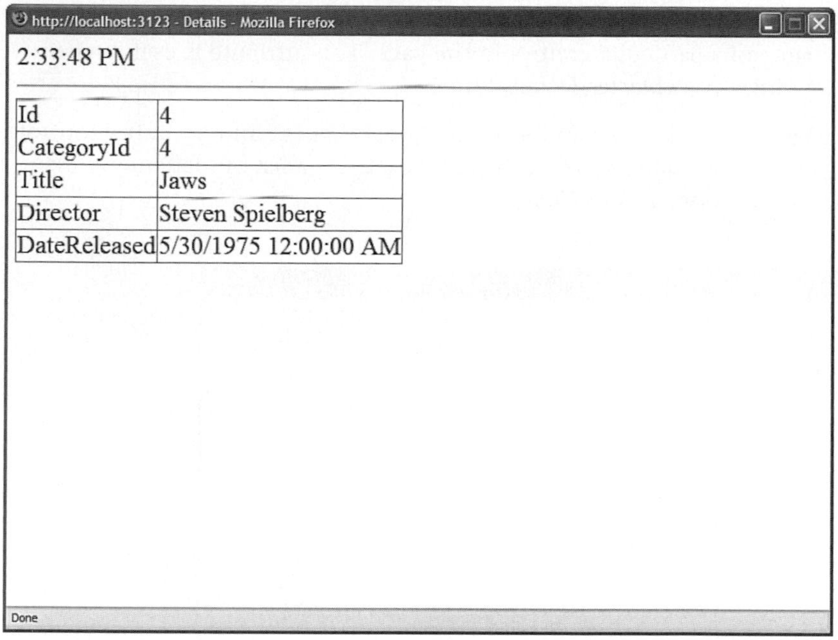

FIGURE 25.2   Displaying the Details page.

Notice that the `Details.aspx` page includes an `<%@ OutputCache %>` directive. The `VaryByParam` attribute in the `<%@ OutputCache %>` directive has the value `id`. If you request the `Details.aspx` page with a different value for the `id` query string parameter, then a different cached version of the page is created.

It is important to understand that using `VaryByParam` results in more caching and not less caching. Each time a different `id` parameter is passed to the `Details.aspx` page, another version of the same page is cached in memory.

The `Details.aspx` page displays the current time. Notice that the time does not change when you request the `Details.aspx` page with the same query string parameter.

You can assign two special values to the `VaryByParam` attribute:

▶ **none**—Causes any query string or form parameters to be ignored. Only one version of the page is cached.

▶ *****—Causes a new cached version of the page to be created whenever there is a change in any query string or form parameter passed to the page.

You also can assign a semicolon-delimited list of parameters to the `VaryByParam` attribute when you want to create different cached versions of a page, depending on the values of more than one parameter.

Varying the Output Cache by Control

The `VaryByControl` attribute enables you to generate different cached versions of a page depending on the value of a particular control in the page. This attribute is useful when you need to create a single-page Master/Details form.

For example, the page in Listing 25.4 contains both a `DropDownList` and `GridView` control. When you select a new movie category from the `DropDownList`, a list of matching movies is displayed in the `GridView` (see Figure 25.3).

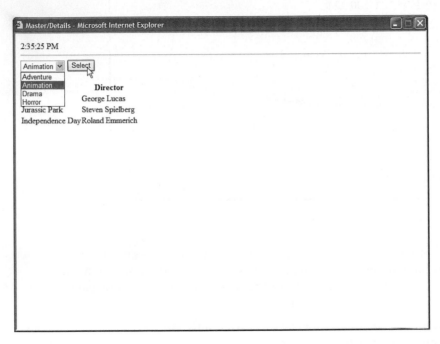

FIGURE 25.3   Displaying a single-page Master/Details form.

LISTING 25.4   `MasterDetails.aspx`

```
<%@ Page Language="C#" %>
<%@ OutputCache Duration="3600" VaryByControl="dropCategories" %>
<!DOCTYPE html PUBLIC "-//W3C//DTD XHTML 1.0 Transitional//EN"
  "http://www.w3.org/TR/xhtml1/DTD/xhtml1-transitional.dtd">
<html xmlns="http://www.w3.org/1999/xhtml" >
<head id="Head1" runat="server">
    <title>Master/Details</title>
```

```
</head>
<body>
    <form id="form1" runat="server">
    <div>

    <%= DateTime.Now.ToString("T") %>
    <hr />

    <asp:DropDownList
        id="dropCategories"
        DataSourceID="srcCategories"
        DataTextField="Name"
        DataValueField="Id"
        Runat="server" />
    <asp:Button
        id="btnSelect"
        Text="Select"
        Runat="server" />

    <br /><br />

    <asp:GridView
        id="grdMovies"
        DataSourceID="srcMovies"
        GridLines="none"
        Runat="server" />

    <asp:SqlDataSource
        id="srcCategories"
        ConnectionString="<%$ ConnectionStrings:Movies %>"
        SelectCommand="SELECT Id,Name FROM MovieCategories"
        Runat="server" />

    <asp:SqlDataSource
        id="srcMovies"
        ConnectionString="<%$ ConnectionStrings:Movies %>"
        SelectCommand="SELECT Title,Director FROM Movies
            WHERE CategoryId=@CategoryId"
        Runat="server">
        <SelectParameters>
        <asp:ControlParameter
            Name="CategoryId"
            ControlID="dropCategories" />
        </SelectParameters>
    </asp:SqlDataSource>
```

LISTING 25.4   Continued

```
    </div>
    </form>
</body>
</html>
```

The page in Listing 25.4 contains an `<%@ OutputCache %>` directive. This directive includes a `VaryByControl` parameter. The ID of the `DropDownList` control is assigned to this parameter.

If you neglected to add the `VaryByControl` attribute, then the same list of movies would be displayed in the `GridView` regardless of which movie category is selected. The `VaryByControl` attribute causes different cached versions of the page to be created whenever the `DropDownList` represents a different value.

Varying the Output Cache by Header

Another option is to use the `VaryByHeader` attribute to create different cached versions of a page when the value of a particular browser header changes. Several standard browser headers are transmitted with each page request, including

- **Accept-Language**—Represents a prioritized list of languages that represent the preferred human language of the user making the request.

- **User-Agent**—Represents the type of device making the request.

- **Cookie**—Represents the browser cookies created in the current domain.

For example, the page in Listing 25.5 includes an `<%@ OutputCache %>` directive that has a `VaryByHeader` attribute with the value `User-Agent`. When you request the page with different browsers, different versions of the page are cached.

LISTING 25.5   VaryByHeader.aspx

```
<%@ Page Language="C#" %>
<%@ OutputCache Duration="3600" VaryByParam="none" VaryByHeader="User-Agent" %>
<!DOCTYPE html PUBLIC "-//W3C//DTD XHTML 1.0 Transitional//EN"
   "http://www.w3.org/TR/xhtml1/DTD/xhtml1-transitional.dtd">
<html xmlns="http://www.w3.org/1999/xhtml" >
<head id="Head1" runat="server">
    <title>Vary By Header</title>
</head>
<body>
    <form id="form1" runat="server">
    <div>

    <%= DateTime.Now.ToString("T") %>
```

```
    <hr />

    <%= Request.UserAgent %>

    </div>
    </form>
</body>
</html>
```

I don't recommend using the `VaryByHeader` attribute with the `User-Agent` header. The problem with this attribute is that it is too fine-grained. If there is any variation in the `User-Agent` header, then a different cached version of a page is generated.

Consider the `User-Agent` header sent by the Internet Explorer browser installed on my computer. It looks like this:

```
Mozilla/4.0 (compatible; MSIE 6.0; Windows NT 5.1; SV1; .NET CLR 1.1.4322;
.NET CLR 2.0.50727)
```

This header includes the major and minor version of the browser, the platform (Windows XP), a string indicating that Service Pack 2 has been installed (SV1), and the versions of the .NET framework installed on my machine. If someone else requests the same page with a slight difference in the `User-Agent` header, then a different cached version of the page is generated. In other words, the web server must do more work rather than less, which defeats the point of caching.

Instead of using the `VaryByHeader` attribute, I recommend that you use the `VaryByCustom` attribute described in the next two sections.

Varying the Output Cache by Browser

A better way to create different cached versions of a page that depend on the type of browser being used to request the page is to use the `VaryByCustom` attribute. This attribute accepts the special value `browser`. When `VaryByCustom` has the value `browser`, only two attributes of the browser are considered important: the type of browser and its major version.

For example, a page request from Internet Explorer results in a different cached version of the page than does one from Firefox. A page request from Internet Explorer 5 rather than Internet Explorer 6.5 also results in a different cached version. Any other variations in the `User-Agent` header are ignored.

The page in Listing 25.6 illustrates how you can use the `VaryByCustom` attribute with the value browser. The page displays the current time and the value of the `User-Agent` header. If you request the page with Internet Explorer and request the page with Firefox, different cached versions of the page are created.

25

LISTING 25.6 VaryByBrowser.aspx

```
<%@ Page Language="C#" %>
<%@ OutputCache Duration="3600" VaryByParam="none" VaryByCustom="browser" %>
<!DOCTYPE html PUBLIC "-//W3C//DTD XHTML 1.0 Transitional//EN"
    "http://www.w3.org/TR/xhtml1/DTD/xhtml1-transitional.dtd">
<html xmlns="http://www.w3.org/1999/xhtml" >
<head id="Head1" runat="server">
    <title>Vary By Browser</title>
</head>
<body>
    <form id="form1" runat="server">
    <div>

    <%= DateTime.Now.ToString("T") %>

    <hr />

    <%= Request.UserAgent %>

    </div>
    </form>
</body>
</html>
```

Varying the Output Cache by a Custom Function

The VaryByCustom attribute is named the VaryByCustom attribute for a reason. You can specify a custom function that determines when a different cached version of a page is generated.

You can use any criteria that you please with the custom function. You can create different cached versions of a page depending on the browser minor version, the browser DOM support, the time of day, or even the weather.

You create the custom function in the Global.asax file by overriding the GetVaryByCustomString() method. For example, the Global.asax file in Listing 25.7 illustrates how you can override the GetVaryByCustomString() method to create different cached versions of a page depending on a particular feature of a browser. If the VaryByCustom attribute in a page has the value css, then the function returns a string representing whether the current browser supports Cascading Style Sheets.

LISTING 25.7 Global.asax

```
<%@ Application Language="C#" %>
<script runat="server">
```

```
public override string GetVaryByCustomString(HttpContext context, string custom)
{
    if (String.Compare(custom, "css") == 0)
    {
        return Request.Browser.SupportsCss.ToString();
    }
    return base.GetVaryByCustomString(context, custom);
}
```

```
</script>
```

The page in Listing 25.8 displays one of two `Panel` controls. The first `Panel` contains text formatted with a Cascading Style Sheet style, and the second `Panel` contains text formatted with (outdated) HTML. Depending on whether a browser supports CSS, either the first or second `Panel` is displayed.

LISTING 25.8   VaryByCustom.aspx

```
<%@ Page Language="C#" %>
<%@ OutputCache Duration="3600" VaryByParam="none" VaryByCustom="css" %>
<!DOCTYPE html PUBLIC "-//W3C//DTD XHTML 1.0 Transitional//EN"
"http://www.w3.org/TR/xhtml1/DTD/xhtml1-transitional.dtd">
<script runat="server">

    void Page_Load()
    {
        if (Request.Browser.SupportsCss)
            pnlCss.Visible = true;
        else
            pnlNotCss.Visible = true;
    }
</script>
<html xmlns="http://www.w3.org/1999/xhtml" >
<head id="Head1" runat="server">
    <title>Vary By Custom</title>
</head>
<body>
    <form id="form1" runat="server">
    <div>

    <asp:Panel
        id="pnlCss"
        Visible="false"
        Runat="server">
        <span style="font-weight:bold">Hello!</span>
```

LISTING 25.8   Continued

```
    </asp:Panel>

    <asp:Panel
        id="pnlNotCss"
        Visible="false"
        Runat="server">
        <b>Hello!</b>
    </asp:Panel>

    </div>
    </form>
</body>
</html>
```

> **NOTE**
>
> You can detect browser capabilities by using the HttpBrowserCapabilities class
> exposed by the Request.Browser property. This class includes dozens of properties
> that enable you to detect the features of the browser being used to request a page.

The page contains an <%@ OutputCache %> directive with a VaryByCustom attribute set to the value css. Two different cached versions of the same page are generated: one version for CSS browsers and another version for non-CSS browsers.

Specifying the Cache Location

You can use the Location attribute of the <%@ OutputCache %> directive to specify where a page is cached. This attribute accepts the following values:

- ▶ **Any**—The page is cached on the browser, proxy servers, and web server (the default value).

- ▶ **Client**—The page is cached only on the browser.

- ▶ **Downstream**—The page is cached on the browser and any proxy servers but not the web server.

- ▶ **None**—The page is not cached.

- ▶ **Server**—The page is cached on the web server but not the browser or any proxy servers.

- ▶ **ServerAndClient**—The page is cached on the browser and web server, but not on any proxy servers.

By default, when you use Page Output Caching, a page is cached in three locations: web server, any proxy servers, and browser. There are situations in which you might need to modify this default behavior. For example, if you are caching private information, then you don't want to cache the information on the web server or any proxy servers.

> **NOTE**
>
> When Windows authentication is enabled in the web configuration file (the default), the `Cache-Control` header is automatically set to the value `private`, and the setting of the `Location` attribute is ignored.

For example, the page in Listing 25.9 caches a page only on the browser and not on any proxy servers or the web server. The page displays a random number (see Figure 25.4).

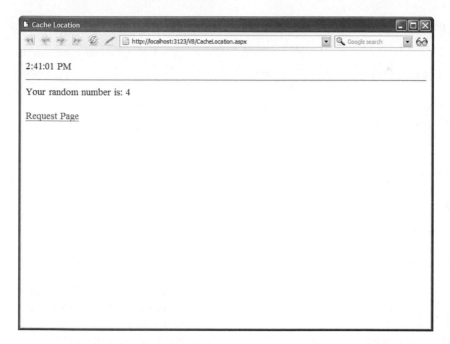

FIGURE 25.4   Caching a page on the browser.

LISTING 25.9   `CacheLocation.aspx`

```
<%@ Page Language="C#" %>
<%@ OutputCache Duration="3600" VaryByParam="none" Location="Client" %>
<!DOCTYPE html PUBLIC "-//W3C//DTD XHTML 1.0 Transitional//EN"
"http://www.w3.org/TR/xhtml1/DTD/xhtml1-transitional.dtd">
<script runat="server">

    void Page_Load()
    {
```

25

LISTING 25.9   Continued

```
            Random rnd = new Random();
            lblRandom.Text = rnd.Next(10).ToString();
    }
</script>
<html xmlns="http://www.w3.org/1999/xhtml" >
<head id="Head1" runat="server">
    <title>Cache Location</title>
</head>
<body>
    <form id="form1" runat="server">
    <div>

    <%= DateTime.Now.ToString("T") %>
    <hr />

    Your random number is:
    <asp:Label
        id="lblRandom"
        Runat="server" />

    <br /><br />
    <a href="CacheLocation.aspx">Request Page</a>

    </div>
    </form>
</body>
</html>
```

If you click the link located at the bottom of the page in Listing 25.9 and request the same page, then the page is retrieved from the browser cache and the same random number is displayed. If you reload the page in your web browser by clicking your browser's Reload button, then the page is reloaded from the web server and a new random number is displayed. The page is cached only in your local browser cache and nowhere else.

> **NOTE**
>
> Behind the scenes, the ASP.NET Framework uses the Cache-Control HTTP header to specify where a page is cached. This header is defined in RFC 2616, "Hypertext Transfer Protocol—HTTP/1.1."

Creating a Page Output Cache File Dependency

You can create a dependency between a cached page and a file (or set of files) on your hard drive. When the file is modified, the cached page is automatically dropped and regenerated with the next page request.

For example, the page in Listing 25.10 displays the contents of an XML file in a GridView. The page is cached until the XML file is modified (see Figure 25.5).

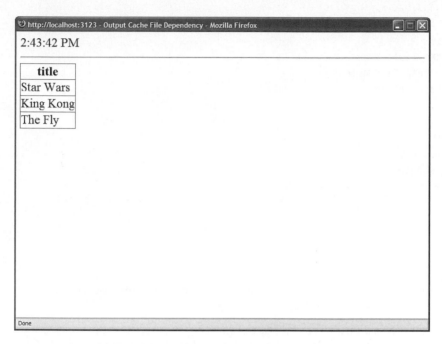

FIGURE 25.5   Caching a page with a file dependency.

LISTING 25.10   OutputCacheFileDependency.aspx

```
<%@ Page Language="C#" %>
<%@ OutputCache Duration="9999" VaryByParam="none" %>
<!DOCTYPE html PUBLIC "-//W3C//DTD XHTML 1.0 Transitional//EN"
"http://www.w3.org/TR/xhtml1/DTD/xhtml1-transitional.dtd">
<script runat="server">

    void Page_Load()
    {
        Response.AddFileDependency(MapPath("Movies.xml"));
    }
</script>
<html xmlns="http://www.w3.org/1999/xhtml" >
<head id="Head1" runat="server">
    <title>Output Cache File Dependency</title>
</head>
<body>
    <form id="form1" runat="server">
    <div>
```

LISTING 25.10   Continued

```
    <%= DateTime.Now.ToString("T") %>
    <hr />

    <asp:GridView
        id="grdMovies"
        DataSourceID="srcMovies"
        Runat="server" />

    <asp:XmlDataSource
        id="srcMovies"
        DataFile="Movies.xml"
        Runat="server" />

    </div>
    </form>
</body>
</html>
```

The page in Listing 25.10 displays the current time. Notice that the time does not change until you modify the `Movies.xml` XML file.

The page in Listing 25.10 uses the `Response.AddFileDependency()` method to create a dependency between the cached page and a single file on disk. If you need to create a dependency on multiple files, then you can use the `AddFileDependencies()` method instead.

Expiring the Page Output Cache Programmatically

You can remove a page from the cache programmatically by using the `Response.RemoveOutputCacheItem()` method. For example, imagine that you are caching a page that displays a list of products. Furthermore, imagine that your website includes a separate page for adding a new product. In that case, you'll want to remove the first page programmatically from the cache when the list of products is updated.

The page in Listing 25.11 uses a GridView control to display a list of movies. The page is cached for 1 hour with an `<%@ OutputCache %>` directive.

LISTING 25.11   MovieList.aspx

```
<%@ Page Language="C#" %>
<%@ OutputCache Duration="3600" VaryByParam="none" %>
<!DOCTYPE html PUBLIC "-//W3C//DTD XHTML 1.0 Transitional//EN"
    "http://www.w3.org/TR/xhtml1/DTD/xhtml1-transitional.dtd">
<html xmlns="http://www.w3.org/1999/xhtml" >
<head id="Head1" runat="server">
```

```
        <title>Movie List</title>
</head>
<body>
        <form id="form1" runat="server">
        <div>

        <%= DateTime.Now.ToString("T") %>
        <hr />

        <asp:GridView
            id="grdMovies"
            DataSourceID="srcMovies"
            Runat="server" />

        <asp:SqlDataSource
            id="srcMovies"
            ConnectionString="<%$ ConnectionStrings:Movies %>"
            SelectCommand="SELECT Title, Director FROM Movies"
            Runat="server" />

        <br /><br />
        <a href="AddMovie.aspx">Add Movie</a>

        </div>
        </form>
</body>
</html>
```

The page in Listing 25.12 contains a `DetailsView` control that enables you to add a new movie. When you insert a new movie into the database, the `Response.RemoveOutputCacheItem()` method is called to remove the `MovieList.aspx` page from the cache. Because this method accepts only a "virtual absolute" path, the `Page.ResolveUrl()` method is used to convert the tilde into the application root path.

LISTING 25.12 AddMovie.aspx

```
<%@ Page Language="C#" %>
<!DOCTYPE html PUBLIC "-//W3C//DTD XHTML 1.0 Transitional//EN"
"http://www.w3.org/TR/xhtml1/DTD/xhtml1-transitional.dtd">
<script runat="server">

    protected void dtlMovie_ItemInserted(object sender,
    ➥DetailsViewInsertedEventArgs e)
    {
        HttpResponse.RemoveOutputCacheItem(Page.ResolveUrl("~/MovieList.aspx"));
```

LISTING 25.12   Continued

```
            Response.Redirect("~/MovieList.aspx");
    }
</script>
<html xmlns="http://www.w3.org/1999/xhtml" >
<head id="Head1" runat="server">
    <title>Add Movie</title>
</head>
<body>
    <form id="form1" runat="server">
    <div>

    <h1>Add Movie</h1>

    <asp:DetailsView
        id="dtlMovie"
        DefaultMode="Insert"
        DataSourceID="srcMovies"
        AutoGenerateRows="false"
        AutoGenerateInsertButton="true"
        Runat="server" OnItemInserted="dtlMovie_ItemInserted">
        <Fields>
        <asp:BoundField
            DataField="Title"
            HeaderText="Title:" />
        <asp:BoundField
            DataField="Director"
            HeaderText="Director:" />
        </Fields>
    </asp:DetailsView>

    <asp:SqlDataSource
        id="srcMovies"
        ConnectionString="<%$ ConnectionStrings:Movies %>"
        InsertCommand="INSERT Movies (Title, Director)
            VALUES (@Title, @Director)"
        Runat="server" />

    </div>
    </form>
</body>
</html>
```

The Response.RemoveOutputCacheItem() method enables you to remove only one page from the cache at a time. If you need to remove multiple pages, then you can create something called a *key dependency*. A key dependency enables you to create a dependency between one item in the cache and another item. When the second item is removed from the cache, the first item is removed automatically.

For example, the page in Listing 25.13 also displays a list of movies. However, the page is cached with a dependency on an item in the cache named Movies.

LISTING 25.13   MovieListKeyDependency.aspx

```
<%@ Page Language="C#" %>
<%@ OutputCache Duration="3600" VaryByParam="none" %>
<!DOCTYPE html PUBLIC "-//W3C//DTD XHTML 1.0 Transitional//EN"
"http://www.w3.org/TR/xhtml1/DTD/xhtml1-transitional.dtd">
<script runat="server">

    protected void Page_Load(object sender, EventArgs e)
    {
        Cache.Insert("Movies", DateTime.Now);
        Response.AddCacheItemDependency("Movies");
    }
</script>
<html xmlns="http://www.w3.org/1999/xhtml" >
<head id="Head1" runat="server">
    <title>Movie List Key Dependency</title>
</head>
<body>
    <form id="form1" runat="server">
    <div>

    <%= DateTime.Now.ToString("T") %>
    <hr />

    <asp:GridView
        id="grdMovies"
        DataSourceID="srcMovies"
        Runat="server" />

    <asp:SqlDataSource
        id="srcMovies"
        ConnectionString="<%$ ConnectionStrings:Movies %>"
        SelectCommand="SELECT Title, Director FROM Movies"
        Runat="server" />

  <br /><br />
  <a href="AddMovieKeyDependency.aspx">Add Movie</a>
```

25

LISTING 25.13   Continued

```
        </div>
        </form>
</body>
</html>
```

The page in Listing 25.14 enables you to add a new movie to the Movies database table. When the new movie is inserted, the Movies item is removed and any pages that are dependent on the Movies item are dropped from the cache automatically.

LISTING 25.14   AddMovieKeyDependency.aspx

```
<%@ Page Language="C#" %>
<!DOCTYPE html PUBLIC "-//W3C//DTD XHTML 1.0 Transitional//EN"
"http://www.w3.org/TR/xhtml1/DTD/xhtml1-transitional.dtd">
<script runat="server">

    protected void dtlMovie_ItemInserted(object sender,
    ➥DetailsViewInsertedEventArgs e)
    {
        Cache.Remove("Movies");
        Response.Redirect("~/MovieListKeyDependency.aspx");
    }
</script>
<html xmlns="http://www.w3.org/1999/xhtml" >
<head id="Head1" runat="server">
    <title>Add Movie Key Dependency</title>
</head>
<body>
    <form id="form1" runat="server">
    <div>

    <h1>Add Movie</h1>

    <asp:DetailsView
        id="dtlMovie"
        DefaultMode="Insert"
        DataSourceID="srcMovies"
        AutoGenerateRows="false"
        AutoGenerateInsertButton="true"
        Runat="server" OnItemInserted="dtlMovie_ItemInserted">
        <Fields>
        <asp:BoundField
            DataField="Title"
            HeaderText="Title:" />
```

```
        <asp:BoundField
            DataField="Director"
            HeaderText="Director:" />
        </Fields>
    </asp:DetailsView>

    <asp:SqlDataSource
        id="srcMovies"
        ConnectionString="<%$ ConnectionStrings:Movies %>"
        InsertCommand="INSERT Movies (Title, Director)
            VALUES (@Title, @Director)"
        Runat="server" />

    </div>
    </form>
</body>
</html>
```

Manipulating the Page Output Cache Programmatically

If you need more control over how the ASP.NET Framework caches pages, then you can work directly with the `HttpCachePolicy` class. This class is exposed by the `Response.Cache` property.

The `HttpCachePolicy` class includes properties and methods that enable you to perform programmatically all the tasks that you can perform with the `<%@ OutputCache %>` directive. You also can use the methods of this class to manipulate the HTTP cache headers that are sent to proxy servers and browsers.

This class supports the following properties:

- **VaryByHeaders**—Gets the list of headers that are used to vary cache output.

- **VaryByParams**—Gets the list of query string and form parameters that are used to vary cache output.

The `HttpCachePolicy` class also supports the following methods:

- **AddValidationCallback**—Enables you to create a method that is called automatically before a page is retrieved from the cache.

- **AppendCacheExtension**—Enables you to add custom text to the `Cache-Control` HTTP header.

- **SetAllowResponseInBrowserHistory**—Enables you to prevent a page from appearing in the browser history cache.

- **SetCacheability**—Enables you to set the `Cache-Control` header and the server cache.

▶ **SetETag**—Enables you to set the ETag HTTP header.

▶ **SetETagFromFileDependencies**—Enables you to set the ETag HTTP header from the time stamps of all files on which the page is dependent.

▶ **SetExpires**—Enables you to set the Expires HTTP header.

▶ **SetLastModified**—Enables you to set the Last-Modified HTTP header.

▶ **SetLastModifiedFromFileDependencies**—Enables you to set the Last-Modified HTTP header from the time stamps of all files on which the page is dependent.

▶ **SetMaxAge**—Enables you to set the Cache-Control:max-age HTTP header.

▶ **SetNoServerCaching**—Enables you to disable web server caching.

▶ **SetNoStore**—Enables you to send a Cache-Control:no-store HTTP header.

▶ **SetNoTransform**—Enables you to send a Cache-Control:no-transform HTTP header.

▶ **SetOmitVaryStar**—Enables you to not send the vary:* HTTP header.

▶ **SetProxyMaxAge**—Enables you to set the Cache-Control:s-maxage HTTP header.

▶ **SetRevalidation**—Enables you to set the Cache-Control HTTP header to either must-revalidation or proxy-revalidate.

▶ **SetSlidingExpiration**—Enables you to set a sliding expiration policy.

▶ **SetValidUntilExpires**—Enables you to prevent a page from expiring from the web server cache when a browser sends a Cache-Control header.

▶ **SetVaryByCustom**—Enables you to set the string passed to the GetVaryByCustomString() method in the Global.asax file.

For example, the page in Listing 25.15 programmatically places a page in the output cache. The page is cached on the browser, proxy servers, and web server for 15 seconds.

LISTING 25.15 ProgramOutputCache.aspx

```
<%@ Page Language="C#" %>
<!DOCTYPE html PUBLIC "-//W3C//DTD XHTML 1.0 Transitional//EN"
"http://www.w3.org/TR/xhtml1/DTD/xhtml1-transitional.dtd">
<script runat="server">

    void Page_Load()
    {
        Response.Cache.SetCacheability(HttpCacheability.Public);
        Response.Cache.SetExpires(DateTime.Now.AddSeconds(15));
        Response.Cache.SetMaxAge(TimeSpan.FromSeconds(15));
        Response.Cache.SetValidUntilExpires(true);
        Response.Cache.SetLastModified(DateTime.Now);
        Response.Cache.SetOmitVaryStar(true);
```

```
        }
</script>
<html xmlns="http://www.w3.org/1999/xhtml" >
<head id="Head1" runat="server">
    <title>Program OutputCache</title>
</head>
<body>
    <form id="form1" runat="server">
    <div>

    <%- DateTime.Now.ToString("T") %>

    <br /><br />
    <a href="ProgramOutputCache.aspx">Request this Page</a>

    </div>
    </form>
</body>
</html>
```

Clearly, it is more difficult to enable Page Output Caching programmatically than declaratively. You need to call many methods to cache a page in the same way as you can with a single <%@ OutputCache %> directive. However, programmatically manipulating the cache provides you with fine-grained control over the HTTP headers sent to proxy servers and browsers.

Creating Page Output Cache Profiles

Instead of configuring Page Output Caching for each page in an application, you can configure Page Output Caching in a web configuration file and apply the settings to multiple pages. You can create something called a Cache Profile. Creating Cache Profiles makes your website easier to manage.

For example, the web configuration file in Listing 25.16 contains the definition for a Cache Profile named Cache1Hour that caches a page for one hour.

LISTING 25.16   Web.Config

```
<configuration>
  <system.web>
    <caching>
      <outputCacheSettings>
        <outputCacheProfiles>
          <add name="Cache1Hour" duration="3600" varyByParam="none" />
        </outputCacheProfiles>
      </outputCacheSettings>
```

LISTING 25.16   Continued

```
    </caching>
  </system.web>
</configuration>
```

The page in Listing 25.17 uses the Cache1Hour profile. This profile is set with the <%@ OutputCache %> directive's CacheProfile attribute.

LISTING 25.17   OutputCacheProfile.aspx

```
<%@ Page Language="C#" %>
<%@ OutputCache CacheProfile="Cache1Hour" %>
<!DOCTYPE html PUBLIC "-//W3C//DTD XHTML 1.0 Transitional//EN"
  "http://www.w3.org/TR/xhtml1/DTD/xhtml1-transitional.dtd">
<html xmlns="http://www.w3.org/1999/xhtml" >
<head id="Head1" runat="server">
    <title>Output Cache Profile</title>
</head>
<body>
    <form id="form1" runat="server">
    <div>

    <%= DateTime.Now.ToString("T") %>

    </div>
    </form>
</body>
</html>
```

You can set the same caching properties in a Cache Profile as you can set in an individual page's <%@ OutputCache %> directive. For example, you can set varyByParam, varyByControl, varyByHeader, and even varyByCustom attributes in a Cache Profile.

Using Partial Page Caching

In the previous section of this chapter, you learned how to cache the entire output of a page. In this section, you learn how to take advantage of Partial Page Caching to cache particular regions of a page.

Partial Page Caching makes sense when a page contains both dynamic and static content. For example, you might want to cache a set of database records displayed in a page, but not cache a random list of news items displayed in the same page.

In this section, you learn about two methods for enabling Partial Page Caching. You can use post-cache substitution to cache an entire page except for a particular region. You can use User Controls to cache particular regions in a page, but not the entire page.

Using Post-Cache Substitution

In some cases, you might want to cache an entire page except for one small area. For example, you might want to display the current username dynamically at the top of a page but cache the remainder of a page. In these cases, you can take advantage of a feature of the ASP.NET Framework called *post-cache substitution*.

Post-cache substitution is used internally by the AdRotator control. Even when you use Page Output Caching to cache a page that contains an AdRotator control, the content rendered by the AdRotator control is not cached.

You can use post-cache substitution either declaratively or programmatically. If you want to use post-cache substitution declaratively, then you can use the ASP.NET Substitution control. For example, the page in Listing 25.18 uses the Substitution control to display the current time on a page that has been output cached (see Figure 25.6).

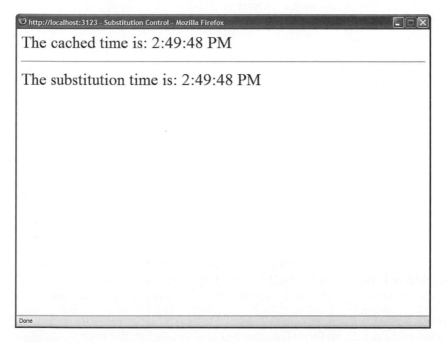

FIGURE 25.6   Using the Substitution control.

LISTING 25.18   SubstitutionControl.aspx

```
<%@ Page Language="C#" %>
<%@ OutputCache Duration="15" VaryByParam="none" %>
```

LISTING 25.18   Continued

```
<!DOCTYPE html PUBLIC "-//W3C//DTD XHTML 1.0 Transitional//EN"
"http://www.w3.org/TR/xhtml1/DTD/xhtml1-transitional.dtd">
<script runat="server">

    public static string GetTime(HttpContext context)
    {
        return DateTime.Now.ToString("T");
    }
</script>
<html xmlns="http://www.w3.org/1999/xhtml" >
<head id="Head1" runat="server">
    <title>Substitution Control</title>
</head>
<body>
    <form id="form1" runat="server">
    <div>

    The cached time is: <%= DateTime.Now.ToString("T") %>
    <hr />
    The substitution time is:
    <asp:Substitution
        id="Substitution1"
        MethodName="GetTime"
        Runat="server" />

    </div>
    </form>
</body>
</html>
```

In Listing 25.18, the time is displayed twice. The time displayed in the body of the page is output cached. The time displayed by the Substitution control is not cached.

The Substitution control has one important property: MethodName. The MethodName property accepts the name of a method defined in the page. The method must be a shared (static) method because an instance of the class is not created when the page is output cached.

Alternatively, you can use post-cache substitution programmatically by using the Response.WriteSubstitution() method. This method is illustrated in the page in Listing 25.19.

LISTING 25.19   ShowWriteSubstitution.aspx

```
<%@ Page Language="C#" %>
<%@ OutputCache Duration="15" VaryByParam="none" %>
```

```
<!DOCTYPE html PUBLIC "-//W3C//DTD XHTML 1.0 Transitional//EN"
"http://www.w3.org/TR/xhtml1/DTD/xhtml1-transitional.dtd">
<script runat="server">

    public static string GetTime(HttpContext context)
    {
        return DateTime.Now.ToString("T");
    }
</script>
<html xmlns="http://www.w3.org/1999/xhtml" >
<head id="Head1" runat="server">
    <title>Show WriteSubstitution</title>
</head>
<body>
    <form id="form1" runat="server">
    <div>

    The cached time is: <%= DateTime.Now.ToString("T") %>
    <hr />
    The substitution time is:
    <% Response.WriteSubstitution(GetTime); %>

    </div>
    </form>
</body>
</html>
```

There are two advantages to using the WriteSubstitution() method. First, the method referenced by the WriteSubstitution() method does not have to be a method of the current class. The method can be either an instance or shared method on any class.

The second advantage of the WriteSubstitution() method is that you can use it within a custom control to perform post-cache substitutions. For example, the NewsRotator control in Listing 25.20 uses the WriteSubstitution() method when displaying a random news item. If you use this control in a page that has been output cached, the NewsRotator control continues to display news items randomly.

LISTING 25.20 NewsRotator.cs

```
using System;
using System.Data;
using System.Web;
using System.Web.UI;
using System.Web.UI.WebControls;
using System.Collections.Generic;
```

LISTING 25.20   Continued

```
namespace myControls
{
    public class NewsRotator : WebControl
    {

        public static string GetNews(HttpContext context)
        {
            List<String> news = new List<string>();
            news.Add("Martians attack!");
            news.Add("Moon collides with earth!");
            news.Add("Life on Jupiter!");

            Random rnd = new Random();
            return news[rnd.Next(news.Count)];
        }

        protected override void RenderContents(HtmlTextWriter writer)
        {
            Context.Response.WriteSubstitution(GetNews);
        }

    }
}
```

> **NOTE**
>
> Building custom controls is discussed in detail in Chapter 29, "Building Custom Controls."

The CD that accompanies this book includes a page named ShowNewsRotator.aspx. If you open this page, all the content of the page is cached except for the random news item displayed by the NewsRotator control (see Figure 25.7).

When you use post-cache substitution (declaratively or programmatically) then caching no longer happens beyond the web server. Using post-cache substitution causes a Cache-Control:no-cache HTTP header to be included in the HTTP response, which disables caching on proxy servers and browsers. This limitation is understandable because the substitution content must be generated dynamically with each page request.

Caching with a User Control

Using post-cache substitution is appropriate only when working with a string of text or HTML. If you need to perform more complex partial page caching, then you should take advantage of User Controls.

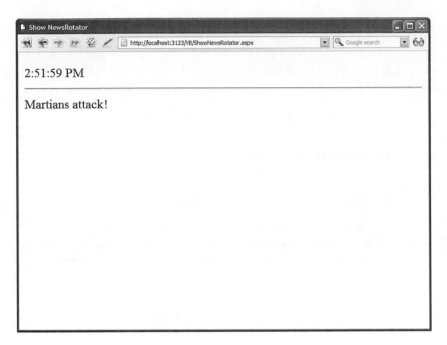

FIGURE 25.7   Displaying dynamic news items in a cached page.

You can cache the rendered contents of a User Control in memory in the same way as you can cache an ASP.NET page. When you add an `<%@ OutputCache %>` directive to a User Control, the rendered output of the User Control is cached.

> **NOTE**
>
> When you cache a User Control, the content is cached on the web server and not on any proxy servers or web browsers. When a web browser or proxy server caches a page, it always caches an entire page.

For example, the Movies User Control in Listing 25.21 displays all the rows from the Movies database table. Furthermore, it includes an `OutputCache` directive, which causes the contents of the User Control to be cached in memory for a maximum of 10 minutes (600 seconds).

LISTING 25.21   Movies.ascx

```
<%@ Control Language="C#" ClassName="Movies" %>
<%@ OutputCache Duration="600" VaryByParam="none" %>

User Control Time:
<%= DateTime.Now.ToString("T") %>
```

LISTING 25.21   Continued

```
<asp:GridView
    id="grdMovies"
    DataSourceID="srcMovies"
    Runat="server" />

<asp:SqlDataSource
    id="srcMovies"
    ConnectionString="<%$ ConnectionStrings:Movies %>"
    SelectCommand="SELECT Title,Director FROM Movies"
    Runat="server" />
```

The User Control in Listing 25.21 displays the records from the Movies database table with a GridView control. It also displays the current time. Because the control includes an OutputCache directive, the entire rendered output of the control is cached in memory.

The page in Listing 25.22 includes the Movies User Control in the body of the page. It also displays the current time at the top of the page. When you refresh the page, the time displayed by the Movies control changes, but not the time displayed in the body of the page (see Figure 25.8).

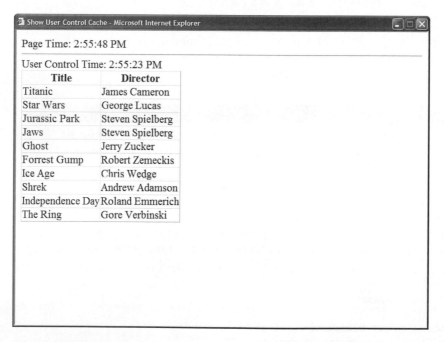

FIGURE 25.8   Caching the output of a User Control.

LISTING 25.22   ShowUserControlCache.aspx

```
<%@ Page Language="C#" %>
<%@ Register TagPrefix="user" TagName="Movies" Src="~/Movies.ascx" %>
<!DOCTYPE html PUBLIC "-//W3C//DTD XHTML 1.1//EN"
 "http://www.w3.org/TR/xhtml11/DTD/xhtml11.dtd">
<html xmlns="http://www.w3.org/1999/xhtml" >
<head id="Head1" runat="server">
    <title>Show User Control Cache</title>
</head>
<body>
    <form id="form1" runat="server">
    <div>

    Page Time:
    <%= DateTime.Now.ToString("T") %>
    <hr />

    <user:Movies
        id="Movies1"
        Runat="server" />

    </div>
    </form>
</body>
</html>
```

You can use the following attributes with an <%@ OutputCache %> directive declared in a User Control:

- ▶ **Duration**—The amount of time in seconds that the rendered content of the User Control is cached.

- ▶ **Shared**—Enables you to share the same cached version of the User Control across multiple pages.

- ▶ **VaryByParam**—Enables you to create different cached versions of a User Control, depending on the values of one or more query string or form parameters. You can specify multiple parameters by supplying a semicolon-delimited list of query string or form parameter names.

- ▶ **VaryByControl**—Enables you to create different cached versions of a User Control, depending on the value of a control. You can specify multiple controls by supplying a semicolon-delimited list of control IDs.

- ▶ **VaryByCustom**—Enables you to specify a custom string used by a custom cache policy. (You also can supply the special value browser, which causes different cached versions of the control to be created when the type and major version of the browser differs.)

Because each User Control that you add to a page can have different caching policies, and because you can nest User Controls with different caching policies, you can build pages that have fiendishly complex caching policies. There is nothing wrong with doing this. In fact, you should take advantage of this caching functionality whenever possible to improve the performance of your applications.

> **WARNING**
>
> Be careful when setting properties of a cached User Control. If you attempt to set the property of a User Control programmatically when the content of the control is served from the cache, you get a `NullReference` exception. Before setting a property of a cached control, first check whether the control actually exists like this:

```
if (myControl != null)
  myControl.SomeProperty = "some value";
```

Sharing a User Control Output Cache

By default, instances of the same User Control located on different pages do not share the same cache. For example, if you add the same Movies User Control to more than one page, then the contents of each user control is cached separately.

If you want to cache the same User Control content across multiple pages, then you need to include the Shared attribute when adding the <%@ OutputCache %> directive to a User Control. For example, the modified Movies User Control in Listing 25.23 includes the Shared attribute.

LISTING 25.23   SharedMovies.ascx

```
<%@ Control Language="C#" ClassName="SharedMovies" %>
<%@ OutputCache Duration="600" VaryByParam="none" Shared="true" %>

User Control Time:
<%= DateTime.Now.ToString() %>

<asp:GridView
    id="grdMovies"
    DataSourceID="srcMovies"
    Runat="server" />

<asp:SqlDataSource
    id="srcMovies"
```

```
ConnectionString="<%$ ConnectionStrings:Movies %>"
SelectCommand="SELECT Title,Director FROM Movies"
Runat="server" />
```

Using the Shared attribute is almost always a good idea. You can save a significant amount of server memory by taking advantage of this attribute.

Manipulating a User Control Cache Programmatically

When you include an `<%@ OutputCache %>` directive in a User Control, you can modify programmatically how the User Control is cached. The User Control CachePolicy property exposes an instance of the ControlCachePolicy class, which supports the following properties:

▶ **Cached**—Enables you to enable or disable caching.

▶ **Dependency**—Enables you to get or set a cache dependency for the User Control.

▶ **Duration**—Enables you to get or set the amount of time (in seconds) that content is cached.

▶ **SupportsCaching**—Enables you to check whether the control supports caching.

▶ **VaryByControl**—Enables you to create different cached versions of the control, depending on the value of a control.

▶ **VaryByParams**—Enables you to create different cached versions of the control, depending on the value of a query string or form parameter.

The ControlCachePolicy class also supports the following methods:

▶ **SetExpires**—Enables you to set the expiration time for the cache.

▶ **SetSlidingExpiration**—Enables you to set a sliding expiration cache policy.

▶ **SetVaryByCustom**—Enables you to specify a custom string used by a custom cache policy. (You also can supply the special value browser, which causes different cached versions of the control to be created when the type and major version of the browser differs.)

For example, the User Control in Listing 25.24 uses a sliding expiration policy of one minute. When you specify a sliding expiration policy, a User Control is cached just as long as you continue to request the User Control within the specified interval of time.

LISTING 25.24   SlidingUserCache.ascx

```
<%@ Control Language="C#" ClassName="SlidingUserCache" %>
<%@ OutputCache Duration="10" VaryByParam="none" %>
<script runat="server">

    void Page_Load()
    {
```

LISTING 25.24   Continued

```
        CachePolicy.SetSlidingExpiration(true);
        CachePolicy.Duration = TimeSpan.FromMinutes(1);
    }

</script>


User Control Time:
<%= DateTime.Now.ToString("T") %>
```

The CD that accompanies this book includes a page named ShowSlidingUserCache.aspx, which contains the SlidingUserCache control. If you keep requesting this page and do not let more than 1 minute pass between requests, then the User Control isn't dropped from the cache.

Creating a User Control Cache File Dependency

You can use the CacheControlPolicy.Dependency property to create a dependency between a cached User Control and a file (or set of files) on the file system. When the file is modified, the User Control is dropped from the cache automatically and reloaded with the next page request.

For example, the User Control in Listing 25.25 displays all the movies from the Movies.xml file in a GridView control. Notice that the User Control includes a Page_Load() handler that creates a dependency on the Movies.xml file.

LISTING 25.25   MovieFileDependency.ascx

```
<%@ Control Language="C#" ClassName="MovieFileDependency" %>
<%@ OutputCache Duration="9999" VaryByParam="none" %>
<script runat="server">

    void Page_Load()
    {
        CacheDependency depend = new CacheDependency(MapPath("~/Movies.xml"));
        this.CachePolicy.Dependency = depend;
    }
</script>
User Control Time:
<%= DateTime.Now.ToString("T") %>
<hr />


<asp:GridView
    id="grdMovies"
    DataSourceID="srcMovies"
    Runat="server" />
```

```
<asp:XmlDataSource
    id="srcMovies"
    DataFile="Movies.xml"
    Runat="server" />
```

The CD that accompanies this book includes a page named ShowMovieFileDependency, which displays the MovieFileDependency User Control (see Figure 25.9). If you open the page, then the User Control is automatically cached until you modify the Movies.xml file.

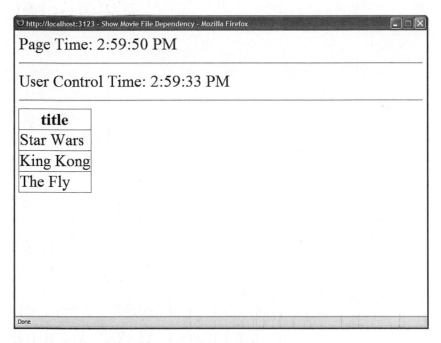

FIGURE 25.9   Displaying a User Control with a file dependency.

Caching Dynamically Loaded User Controls

You can load a User Control dynamically by using the Page.LoadControl() method. You can cache dynamically loaded User Controls in the same way that you can cache User Controls declared in a page. If a User Control includes an <%@ OutputCache %> directive, then the User Control will be cached regardless of whether the control was added to a page declaratively or programmatically.

However, you need to be aware that when a cached User Control is loaded dynamically, the ASP.NET Framework automatically wraps the User Control in an instance of the PartialCachingControl class. Therefore, you need to cast the control returned by the Page.LoadControl() method to an instance of the PartialCachingControl class.

For example, the page in Listing 25.26 dynamically adds the Movies User Control in its Page_Load() event handler. The Page_Load() method overrides the default cache duration specified in the User Control's <%@ OutputCache %> directive. The cache duration is changed to 15 seconds (see Figure 25.10).

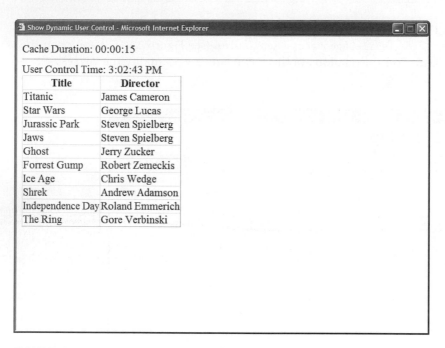

FIGURE 25.10   Programmatically caching a User Control.

LISTING 25.26   ShowDynamicUserControl.aspx

```
<%@ Page Language="C#" %>
<!DOCTYPE html PUBLIC "-//W3C//DTD XHTML 1.1//EN"
"http://www.w3.org/TR/xhtml11/DTD/xhtml11.dtd">
<script runat="server">

    void Page_Load()
    {
        // Load the control
        PartialCachingControl cacheMe =
        ➥(PartialCachingControl)Page.LoadControl("Movies.ascx");

        // Change cache duration to 15 seconds
        cacheMe.CachePolicy.SetExpires(DateTime.Now.AddSeconds(15));

        // Add control to page
        PlaceHolder1.Controls.Add(cacheMe);
```

```
            // Display control cache duration
            lblCacheDuration.Text = cacheMe.CachePolicy.Duration.ToString();
        }
</script>
<html xmlns="http://www.w3.org/1999/xhtml" >
<head id="Head1" runat="server">
    <title>Show Dynamic User Control</title>
</head>
<body>
    <form id="form1" runat="server">
    <div>

    Cache Duration:
    <asp:Label
        id="lblCacheDuration"
        Runat="server" />
    <hr />

    <asp:PlaceHolder
        id="PlaceHolder1"
        Runat="server" />

    </div>
    </form>
</body>
</html>
```

In Listing 25.26, the default cache duration is modified by modifying the
PartialCachingControl's CachePolicy property. This property returns an instance of the
same ControlCachePolicy class described in the two previous sections of this chapter.

You can refer to the User Control contained with an instance of the
PartialCachingControl class by using the class's CachedControl property. Normally, this
property returns the value Nothing (null) because when the User Control is cached, it is
never actually created.

Using DataSource Caching

Instead of caching at the page or User Control level, you can cache at the level of a
DataSource control. Three of the four standard ASP.NET DataSource controls—the
SqlDataSource, ObjectDataSource, and XmlDataSource controls—include properties that
enable you to cache the data that the DataSource control represents (The LinqDataSource
control does not support caching).

One advantage of using the DataSource controls when caching is that the DataSource controls can reload data automatically when the data is updated. For example, if you use a SqlDataSource control to both select and update a set of database records, then the SqlDataSource control is smart enough to reload the cached data after an update.

The DataSource controls are also smart enough to share the same data across multiple pages. For example, when using the SqlDataSource control, a unique entry is created in the Cache object for each combination of the following SqlDataSource properties: SelectCommand, SelectParameters, and ConnectionString. If these properties are identical for two SqlDataSource controls located on two different pages, then the two controls share the same cached data.

> **NOTE**
>
> DataSource caching does not work with LINQ to SQL queries. To learn about caching LINQ to SQL queries, see Chapter 18.

In this section, you learn how to use the SqlDataSource, ObjectDataSource, and XmlDataSource controls to cache data. You learn how to set either an absolute or sliding expiration policy. Finally, you learn how to create a cache key dependency that you can use to expire the cache programmatically.

Using an Absolute Cache Expiration Policy

When you use an absolute cache expiration policy, the data that a DataSource represents is cached in memory for a particular duration of time. Using an absolute cache expiration policy is useful when you know that your data does not change that often. For example, if you know that the records contained in a database table are modified only once a day, then there is no reason to keep grabbing the same records every time someone requests a web page.

> **WARNING**
>
> When caching with the SqlDataSource control, the SqlDataSource control's DataSourceMode property must be set to the value DataSet (the default value) rather than DataReader.

The page in Listing 25.27 displays a list of movies that are cached in memory. The page uses a SqlDataSource control to cache the data.

LISTING 25.27   DataSourceAbsoluteCache.aspx

```
<%@ Page Language="C#" %>
<!DOCTYPE html PUBLIC "-//W3C//DTD XHTML 1.1//EN"
  "http://www.w3.org/TR/xhtml11/DTD/xhtml11.dtd">
<html xmlns="http://www.w3.org/1999/xhtml" >
<head id="Head1" runat="server">
    <title>DataSource Absolute Cache</title>
</head>
<body>
    <form id="form1" runat="server">
    <div>

    <asp:GridView
        id="grdMovies"
        DataSourceID="srcMovies"
        Runat="server" />

    <asp:SqlDataSource
        id="srcMovies"
        EnableCaching="True"
        CacheDuration="3600"
        SelectCommand="SELECT * FROM Movies"
        ConnectionString="<%$ ConnectionStrings:Movies %>"
        Runat="server" />

    </div>
    </form>
</body>
</html>
```

In Listing 25.27, two properties of the SqlDataSource control related to caching are set. First, the EnableCaching property is set to the value True. Next, the CacheDuration property is set to the value 3,600 seconds (1 hour). The movies are cached in memory for a maximum of 1 hour. If you don't supply a value for the CacheDuration property, the default value is Infinite.

It is important to understand that there is no guarantee that the SqlDataSource control will cache data for the amount of time specified by its CacheDuration property. Behind the scenes, DataSource controls use the Cache object for caching. This object supports scavenging. When memory resources become low, the Cache object automatically removes items from the cache.

You can test whether the page in Listing 25.27 is working by opening the page and temporarily turning off your database server. You can turn off SQL Server Express by opening the SQL Configuration Manager located in the Microsoft SQL Server 2005 program group and stopping the SQL Server service (see Figure 25.11). If you refresh the page, the data is displayed even though the database server is unavailable.

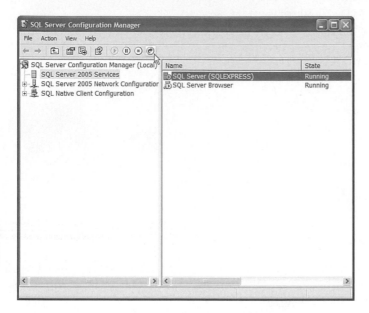

FIGURE 25.11   The SQL Configuration Manager.

Using a Sliding Cache Expiration Policy

If you need to cache a lot of data, then it makes more sense to use a sliding expiration policy rather than an absolute expiration policy. When you use a sliding expiration policy, data remains in the cache as long as the data continues to be requested within a certain interval.

For example, imagine that you have been asked to rewrite the Amazon website with ASP.NET. The Amazon website displays information on billions of books. You couldn't cache all this book information in memory. However, if you use a sliding expiration policy, then you can cache the most frequently requested books automatically.

The page in Listing 25.28 illustrates how you can enable a sliding cache expiration policy. The cache duration is set to 15 seconds. As long as no more than 15 seconds pass before you request the page, the movies are kept cached in memory.

LISTING 25.28   DataSourceSlidingCache.aspx

```
<%@ Page Language="C#" %>
<!DOCTYPE html PUBLIC "-//W3C//DTD XHTML 1.1//EN"
"http://www.w3.org/TR/xhtml11/DTD/xhtml11.dtd">
<script runat="server">
```

```
        protected void srcMovies_Selecting(object sender,
        ➥SqlDataSourceSelectingEventArgs e)
        {
            lblMessage.Text = "Selecting data from database";
        }
    </script>
    <html xmlns="http://www.w3.org/1999/xhtml" >
    <head id="Head1" runat="server">
        <title>DataSource Sliding Cache</title>
    </head>
    <body>
        <form id="form1" runat="server">
        <div>

        <p>
        <asp:Label
            id="lblMessage"
            EnableViewState="false"
            Runat="server" />
        </p>

        <asp:GridView
            id="grdMovies"
            DataSourceID="srcMovies"
            Runat="server" />

        <asp:SqlDataSource
            id="srcMovies"
            EnableCaching="True"
            CacheExpirationPolicy="Sliding"
            CacheDuration="15"
            SelectCommand="SELECT * FROM Movies"
            ConnectionString="<%$ ConnectionStrings:Movies %>"
            OnSelecting="srcMovies_Selecting"
            Runat="server" />

        </div>
        </form>
    </body>
    </html>
```

Notice that the page in Listing 25.28 includes a srcMovies_Selecting() event handler. This handler is called only when the movies are retrieved from the database rather than from memory. In other words, you can use this event handler to detect when the movies are dropped from the cache (see Figure 25.12).

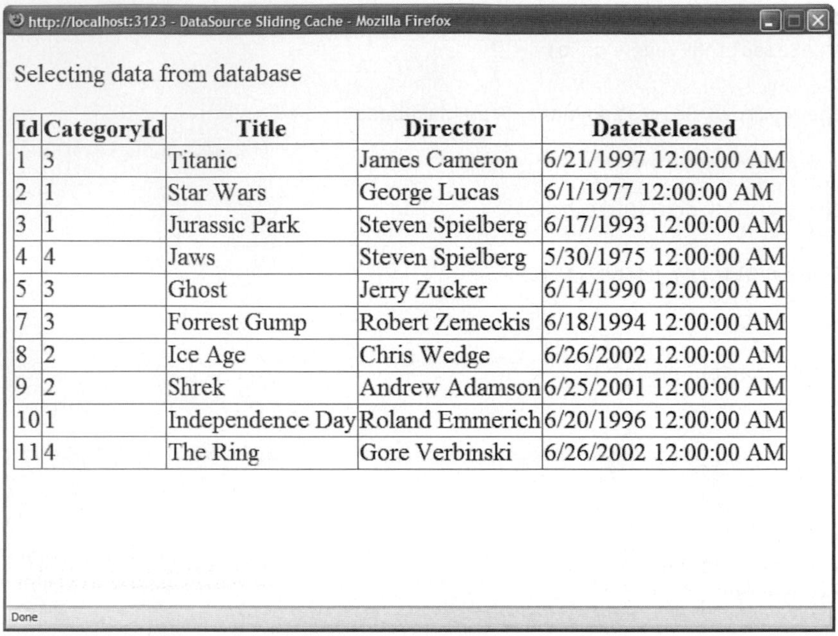

Id	CategoryId	Title	Director	DateReleased
1	3	Titanic	James Cameron	6/21/1997 12:00:00 AM
2	1	Star Wars	George Lucas	6/1/1977 12:00:00 AM
3	1	Jurassic Park	Steven Spielberg	6/17/1993 12:00:00 AM
4	4	Jaws	Steven Spielberg	5/30/1975 12:00:00 AM
5	3	Ghost	Jerry Zucker	6/14/1990 12:00:00 AM
7	3	Forrest Gump	Robert Zemeckis	6/18/1994 12:00:00 AM
8	2	Ice Age	Chris Wedge	6/26/2002 12:00:00 AM
9	2	Shrek	Andrew Adamson	6/25/2001 12:00:00 AM
10	1	Independence Day	Roland Emmerich	6/20/1996 12:00:00 AM
11	4	The Ring	Gore Verbinski	6/26/2002 12:00:00 AM

FIGURE 25.12 Using a sliding expiration policy with a `DataSource` control.

Caching with the `ObjectDataSource` Control

The `ObjectDataSource` control supports the same caching properties as the `SqlDataSource` control. You can cache the data that an `ObjectDataSource` control represents by setting its `EnableCaching`, `CacheDuration`, and (optionally) `CacheExpirationPolicy` properties.

NOTE

Multiple `ObjectDataSource` controls can share the same cached data. To share the same cache, the `ObjectDataSource` controls must have identical `TypeName`, `SelectMethod`, and `SelectParameters` properties.

For example, the page in Listing 25.29 uses an `ObjectDataSource` control to represent the `Movies` database table. The `ObjectDataSource` is bound to a component named `Movie` that includes a method named `GetMovies()` that returns all of the records from the Movies database table.

LISTING 25.29 `ShowObjectDataSourceCaching.aspx`

```
<%@ Page Language="C#" %>
<!DOCTYPE html PUBLIC "-//W3C//DTD XHTML 1.0 Transitional//EN"
"http://www.w3.org/TR/xhtml1/DTD/xhtml1-transitional.dtd">
```

```
<script runat="server">

    protected void srcMovies_Selecting(object sender,
    ➥ObjectDataSourceSelectingEventArgs e)
    {
        lblMessage.Text = "Selecting data from component";
    }
</script>
<html xmlns="http://www.w3.org/1999/xhtml" >
<head id="Head1" runat="server">
    <title>Show ObjectDataSource Caching</title>
</head>
<body>
    <form id="form1" runat="server">
    <div>

    <asp:Label
        id="lblMessage"
        EnableViewState="false"
        Runat="server" />
    <br /><br />

    <asp:GridView
        id="grdMovies"
        DataSourceID="srcMovies"
        Runat="server" />

    <asp:ObjectDataSource
        id="srcMovies"
        EnableCaching="true"
        CacheDuration="15"
        TypeName="Movie"
        SelectMethod="GetMovies"
        OnSelecting="srcMovies_Selecting"
        Runat="server" />

    </div>
    </form>
</body>
</html>
```

The ObjectDataSource control in Listing 25.29 includes an event handler for its Selecting event. The event handler displays a message in a Label control. Because the Selecting event is not raised when data is retrieved from the cache, you can use this method to determine when data is retrieved from the cache or the Movie component.

The Movie component is contained in Listing 25.30.

LISTING 25.30   Movie.cs

```csharp
using System;
using System.Data;
using System.Data.SqlClient;
using System.Web.Configuration;

public class Movie
{
    public static DataTable GetMovies()
    {
        string conString = WebConfigurationManager.ConnectionStrings["Movies"].
        ➥ConnectionString;
        SqlDataAdapter dad = new SqlDataAdapter("SELECT Title,Director FROM
        ➥Movies", conString);
        DataTable movies = new DataTable();
        dad.Fill(movies);
        return movies;
    }
}
```

Notice that the GetMovies() method returns a DataTable. When using the
ObjectDataSource control, you can cache certain types of data but not others. For
example, you can cache data represented with a DataSet, DataTable, DataView, or collection. However, you cannot cache data represented by a DataReader. If you attempt to bind
to a method that returns a DataReader, then an exception is thrown.

Caching with the XmlDataSource Control

Unlike the SqlDataSource and ObjectDataSource controls, the XmlDataSource control has
caching enabled by default. The XmlDataSource automatically creates a file dependency on
the XML file that it represents. If the XML file is modified, the XmlDataSource control
automatically reloads the modified XML file.

For example, the page in Listing 25.31 contains an XmlDataSource control that represents
the Movies.xml file. If you modify the Movies.xml file, then the contents of the files are
automatically reloaded.

LISTING 25.31   ShowXmlDataSourceCaching.aspx

```aspx
<%@ Page Language="C#" %>
<!DOCTYPE html PUBLIC "-//W3C//DTD XHTML 1.0 Transitional//EN"
 "http://www.w3.org/TR/xhtml1/DTD/xhtml1-transitional.dtd">
<html xmlns="http://www.w3.org/1999/xhtml" >
```

```
<head id="Head1" runat="server">
    <title>Show XmlDataSource Caching</title>
</head>
<body>
    <form id="form1" runat="server">
    <div>

    <asp:GridView
        id="grdMovies"
        DataSourceID="srcMovies"
        Runat="server" />

    <asp:XmlDataSource
        id="srcMovies"
        DataFile="Movies.xml"
        Runat="server" />

    </div>
    </form>
</body>
</html>
```

25

Creating a `DataSource` Control Key Dependency

Imagine that your web application has multiple pages that display different sets of records from the Movies database table. However, you have one page that enables a user to enter a new movie. In that case, you need some method of signaling to all your `DataSource` controls that the Movies database table has changed.

You can create a key dependency between the `DataSource` controls in your application and an item in the cache. That way, if you remove the item from the cache, all the `DataSource` controls will reload their data.

The page in Listing 25.32 contains a `SqlDataSource` control that displays the contents of the Movies database table. The `SqlDataSource` caches its data for an infinite duration.

LISTING 25.32   DataSourceKeyDependency.aspx

```
<%@ Page Language="C#" %>
<!DOCTYPE html PUBLIC "-//W3C//DTD XHTML 1.1//EN"
"http://www.w3.org/TR/xhtml11/DTD/xhtml11.dtd">
<script runat="server">

    protected void srcMovies_Selecting(object sender,
    ➥SqlDataSourceSelectingEventArgs e)
```

LISTING 25.32   Continued

```
    {
        lblMessage.Text = "Selecting data from database";
    }
</script>

<html xmlns="http://www.w3.org/1999/xhtml" >
<head id="Head1" runat="server">
    <title>DataSource Key Dependency</title>
</head>
<body>
    <form id="form1" runat="server">
    <div>

    <p>
    <asp:Label
        id="lblMessage"
        EnableViewState="false"
        Runat="server" />
    </p>

    <asp:GridView
        id="grdMovies"
        DataSourceID="srcMovies"
        Runat="server" />

    <asp:SqlDataSource
        id="srcMovies"
        EnableCaching="True"
        CacheDuration="Infinite"
        CacheKeyDependency="MovieKey"
        SelectCommand="SELECT * FROM Movies"
        ConnectionString="<%$ ConnectionStrings:Movies %>"
        OnSelecting="srcMovies_Selecting"
        Runat="server" />

    <br /><br />
    <a href="AddMovieDataSourceKeyDependency.aspx">Add Movie</a>

    </div>
    </form>
</body>
</html>
```

Notice that the `SqlDataSource` control in Listing 25.32 includes a `CacheKeyDependency` property that has the value `MovieKey`. This property creates a dependency between the DataSource control's cached data and an item in the cache named `MovieKey`.

The `Global.asax` file in Listing 25.33 creates the initial `MovieKey` cache item. The value of the cache item doesn't really matter. In Listing 25.33, the `MovieKey` cache item is set to the current date and time.

LISTING 25.33   Global.asax

```
<%@ Application Language="C#" %>
<script runat="server">

    void Application_Start(object sender, EventArgs e)
    {
        HttpContext context = HttpContext.Current;
        context.Cache.Insert(
            "MovieKey",
            DateTime.Now,
            null,
            DateTime.MaxValue,
            Cache.NoSlidingExpiration,
            CacheItemPriority.NotRemovable,
            null);
    }
</script>
```

The page in Listing 25.34 contains a `DetailsView` control that enables you to insert a new record. Notice that the `DetailsView` control's `ItemInserted` event is handled. When you insert a new record, the `MovieKey` item is reinserted into the cache and every DataSource control that is dependent on this key is reloaded automatically.

LISTING 25.34   AddMovieDataSourceKeyDependency.aspx

```
<%@ Page Language="C#" %>
<!DOCTYPE html PUBLIC "-//W3C//DTD XHTML 1.0 Transitional//EN"
"http://www.w3.org/TR/xhtml1/DTD/xhtml1-transitional.dtd">
<script runat="server">

    protected void dtlMovie_ItemInserted(object sender,
    ➥DetailsViewInsertedEventArgs e)
    {
        Cache.Insert("MovieKey", DateTime.Now);
        Response.Redirect("~/DataSourceKeyDependency.aspx");
    }
```

LISTING 24.34   Continued

```
</script>
<html xmlns="http://www.w3.org/1999/xhtml" >
<head id="Head1" runat="server">
    <title>Add Movie Key Dependency</title>
</head>
<body>
    <form id="form1" runat="server">
    <div>

    <h1>Add Movie</h1>

    <asp:DetailsView
        id="dtlMovie"
        DefaultMode="Insert"
        DataSourceID="srcMovies"
        AutoGenerateRows="false"
        AutoGenerateInsertButton="true"
        OnItemInserted="dtlMovie_ItemInserted"
        Runat="server">
        <Fields>
        <asp:BoundField
            DataField="Title"
            HeaderText="Title:" />
        <asp:BoundField
            DataField="Director"
            HeaderText="Director:" />
        </Fields>
    </asp:DetailsView>

    <asp:SqlDataSource
        id="srcMovies"
        ConnectionString="<%$ ConnectionStrings:Movies %>"
        InsertCommand="INSERT Movies (Title, Director)
            VALUES (@Title, @Director)"
        Runat="server" />

    </div>
    </form>
</body>
</html>
```

Using Data Caching

Behind the scenes, all the various caching mechanisms included in the ASP.NET Framework use the Cache object. In other words, the Cache object is the fundamental mechanism for all caching in the ASP.NET Framework.

One instance of the Cache object is created for each ASP.NET application. Any items you add to the cache can be accessed by any other page, control, or component contained in the same application (virtual directory).

In this section, you learn how to use the properties and methods of the Cache object. You learn how to add items to the cache, set cache expiration policies, and create cache item dependencies.

Using the Cache Application Programming Interface

The Cache object exposes the main application programming interface for caching. This object supports the following properties:

- ▶ **Count**—Represents the number of items in the cache.

- ▶ **EffectivePrivateBytesLimit**—Represents the size of the cache in kilobytes.

The Cache object also supports the following methods:

- ▶ **Add**—Enables you to add a new item to the cache. If the item already exists, this method fails.

- ▶ **Get**—Enables you to return a particular item from the cache.

- ▶ **GetEnumerator**—Enables you to iterate through all the items in the cache.

- ▶ **Insert**—Enables you to insert a new item into the cache. If the item already exists, this method replaces it.

- ▶ **Remove**—Enables you to remove an item from the cache.

For example, the page in Listing 25.35 displays all the items currently contained in the cache (see Figure 25.13).

LISTING 25.35   EnumerateCache.aspx

```
<%@ Page Language="C#" %>
<!DOCTYPE html PUBLIC "-//W3C//DTD XHTML 1.0 Transitional//EN"
"http://www.w3.org/TR/xhtml1/DTD/xhtml1-transitional.dtd">
<script runat="server">

    public class CacheItem
    {
        private string _key;
        private object _value;
```

25

LISTING 25.35   Continued

```
        public string Key
        {
            get { return _key; }
        }

        public string Value
        {
            get { return _value.ToString(); }
        }

        public CacheItem(string key, object value)
        {
            _key = key;
            _value = value;
        }
    }

    void Page_Load()
    {
        ArrayList items = new ArrayList();
        foreach (DictionaryEntry item in Cache)
            items.Add(new CacheItem(item.Key.ToString(),item.Value));

        grdCache.DataSource = items;
        grdCache.DataBind();
    }
</script>
<html xmlns="http://www.w3.org/1999/xhtml" >
<head id="Head1" runat="server">
    <style type="text/css">
        .grid td, .grid th
        {
            padding:5px;
        }
    </style>
    <title>Enumerate Cache</title>
</head>
<body>
    <form id="form1" runat="server">
    <div>

    <asp:GridView
        id="grdCache"
        CssClass="grid"
```

```
        Runat="server" />

    </div>
    </form>
</body>
</html>
```

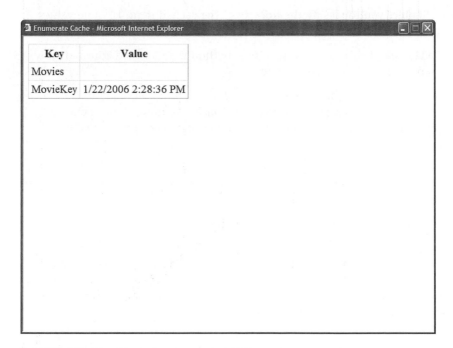

FIGURE 25.13   Displaying the cache's contents.

The page in Listing 25.35 displays only items that have been added to the cache by the methods of the Cache object. For example, it does not display a list of pages that have been output cached. Output cached pages are stored in the internal cache (the secret cache maintained by the ASP.NET Framework).

Adding Items to the Cache

You can add items to the cache by using the Insert() method. There are several overloaded versions of the Insert() method. The maximally overloaded version of the Insert() method accepts the following parameters:

▶ **key**—Enables you to specify the name of the new item.

▶ **value**—Enables you to specify the value of the new item.

▶ **dependencies**—Enables you to specify one or more cache dependencies, such as a file, key, or SQL dependency.

▶ **absoluteExpiration**—Enables you to specify an absolute expiration time for the cached item. If you don't need to specify a value for this property, use the static field `Cache.NoAbsoluteExpiration`.

▶ **slidingExpiration**—Enables you to specify a sliding expiration interval for the cached item. If you don't need to specify a value for this property, use the static field `Cache.NoSlidingExpiration`.

▶ **priority**—Enables you to specify the priority of the cached item. Possible values are `AboveNormal`, `BelowNormal`, `Default`, `High`, `Low`, `Normal`, and `NotRemovable`.

▶ **onRemoveCallback**—Enables you to specify a method that is called automatically before the item is removed from the cache.

When using the cache, it is important to understand that items that you add to the cache might not be there when you attempt to retrieve the item in the future. The cache supports scavenging. When memory resources become low, items are automatically evicted from the cache.

Before using any item that you retrieve from the cache, you should always check whether the item is `Nothing` (null). If an item has been removed, then you'll retrieve `Nothing` when you attempt to retrieve it from the cache in the future.

You can add almost any object to the cache. For example, you can add custom components, `DataSets`, `DataTables`, `ArrayLists`, and `Lists` to the cache.

You shouldn't add items to the cache that depend on an external resource. For example, it does not make sense to add a `SqlDataReader` or a `FileStream` to the cache. When using a `SqlDataReader`, you need to copy the contents of the `SqlDataReader` into a static representation such as an `ArrayList` or `List` collection.

Adding Items with an Absolute Expiration Policy

When you insert items in the cache, you can specify a time when the item will expire. If you want an item to remain in the cache for an extended period of time, then you should always specify an expiration time for the item.

The page in Listing 25.36 illustrates how you can add an item to the cache with an absolute expiration policy. The item is added to the cache for 1 hour.

LISTING 25.36   ShowAbsoluteExpiration.aspx

```
<%@ Page Language="C#" Trace="true" %>
<%@ Import Namespace="System.Data" %>
<%@ Import Namespace="System.Data.SqlClient" %>
<%@ Import Namespace="System.Web.Configuration" %>
<!DOCTYPE html PUBLIC "-//W3C//DTD XHTML 1.0 Transitional//EN"
"http://www.w3.org/TR/xhtml1/DTD/xhtml1-transitional.dtd">
<script runat="server">
```

```
    void Page_Load()
    {
        // Get movies from Cache
        DataTable movies = (DataTable)Cache["Movies"];

        // If movies not in cache, recreate movies
        if (movies == null)
        {
            movies = GetMoviesFromDB();
            Cache.Insert("Movies", movies, null, DateTime.Now.AddHours(1),
            ➥Cache.NoSlidingExpiration);
        }

        grdMovies.DataSource = movies;
        grdMovies.DataBind();
    }

    private DataTable GetMoviesFromDB()
    {
        Trace.Warn("Getting movies from database");
        string conString = WebConfigurationManager.ConnectionStrings
        ➥["Movies"].ConnectionString;
        SqlDataAdapter dad = new SqlDataAdapter("SELECT Title,Director FROM
        ➥Movies", conString);
        DataTable movies = new DataTable();
        dad.Fill(movies);
        return movies;
    }
</script>
<html xmlns="http://www.w3.org/1999/xhtml" >
<head id="Head1" runat="server">
    <title>Show Absolute Expiration</title>
</head>
<body>
    <form id="form1" runat="server">
    <div>

    <asp:GridView
        id="grdMovies"
        Runat="server" />

    </div>
    </form>
</body>
</html>
```

25

The first time the page in Listing 25.36 is requested, nothing is retrieved from the cache. In that case, a new DataTable is created that represents the Movies database table. The DataTable is inserted into the cache. The next time the page is requested, the DataTable can be retrieved from the cache and there is no need to access the database.

The DataTable will remain in the cache for 1 hour or until memory pressures force the DataTable to be evicted from the cache. In either case, the logic of the page dictates that the DataTable will be added back to the cache when the page is next requested.

Tracing is enabled for the page in Listing 25.36 so that you can see when the Movies database table is loaded from the cache and when the table is loaded from the database. The GetMoviesFromDB() method writes a Trace message whenever it executes (see Figure 25.14).

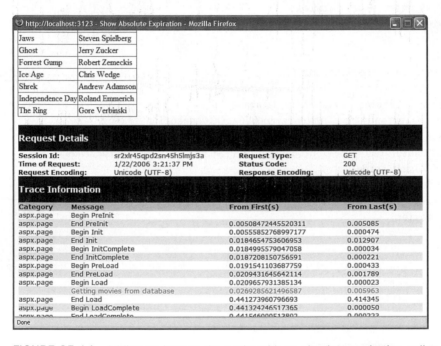

FIGURE 25.14   Adding an item to the cache with an absolute expiration policy.

Adding Items with a Sliding Expiration Policy

When you specify a sliding expiration policy, items remain in the cache just as long as they continue to be requested within a specified interval of time. For example, if you specify a sliding expiration policy of 5 minutes, then the item remains in the Cache just as long as no more than 5 minutes pass without the item being requested.

Using a sliding expiration policy makes sense when you have too many items to add to the cache. A sliding expiration policy keeps the most requested items in memory and the remaining items are dropped from memory automatically.

The page in Listing 25.37 illustrates how you can add a DataSet to the cache with a sliding expiration policy of 5 minutes.

LISTING 25.37   ShowSlidingExpiration.aspx

```
<%@ Page Language="C#" Trace="true" %>
<%@ Import Namespace="System.Data" %>
<%@ Import Namespace="System.Data.SqlClient" %>
<%@ Import Namespace="System.Web.Configuration" %>
<!DOCTYPE html PUBLIC "-//W3C//DTD XHTML 1.0 Transitional//EN"
"http://www.w3.org/TR/xhtml1/DTD/xhtml1-transitional.dtd">
<script runat="server">

    void Page_Load()
    {
        // Get movies from Cache
        DataSet movies = (DataSet)Cache["Movies"];

        // If movies not in cache, recreate movies
        if (movies == null)
        {
            movies = GetMoviesFromDB();
            Cache.Insert("Movies", movies, null, Cache.NoAbsoluteExpiration,
            ➥TimeSpan.FromMinutes(5));
        }

        grdMovies.DataSource = movies;
        grdMovies.DataBind();
    }

    private DataSet GetMoviesFromDB()
    {
        Trace.Warn("Getting movies from database");
        string conString = WebConfigurationManager.ConnectionStrings
        ➥["Movies"].ConnectionString;
        SqlDataAdapter dad = new SqlDataAdapter("SELECT Title,Director FROM
        ➥Movies", conString);
        DataSet movies = new DataSet();
        dad.Fill(movies);
        return movies;
    }
</script>
<html xmlns="http://www.w3.org/1999/xhtml" >
<head id="Head1" runat="server">
    <title>Show Sliding Expiration</title>
</head>
```

25

LISTING 25.37   Continued

```
<body>
    <form id="form1" runat="server">
    <div>

    <asp:GridView
        id="grdMovies"
        Runat="server" />

    </div>
    </form>
</body>
</html>
```

In Listing 25.37, when the DataSet is added to the cache with the Insert() method, its absoluteExpiration parameter is set to the value Cache.NoAbsoluteExpiration, and its slidingExpiration parameter is set to an interval of 5 minutes.

Adding Items with Dependencies

When you add an item to the Cache object, you can make the item dependent on an external object. If the external object is modified, then the item is automatically dropped from the cache.

The ASP.NET Framework includes three cache dependency classes:

▶ **CacheDependency**—Enables you to create a dependency on a file or other cache key.

▶ **SqlCacheDependency**—Enables you to create a dependency on a Microsoft SQL Server database table or the result of a SQL Server 2005 query.

▶ **AggregateCacheDependency**—Enables you to create a dependency using multiple CacheDependency objects. For example, you can combine file and SQL dependencies with this object.

The CacheDependency class is the base class. The other two classes derive from this class. The CacheDependency class supports the following properties:

▶ **HasChanged**—Enables you to detect when the dependency object has changed.

▶ **UtcLastModified**—Enables you to retrieve the time when the dependency object last changed.

The CacheDependency object also supports the following method:

▶ **GetUniqueID**—Enables you to retrieve a unique identifier for the dependency object.

> **NOTE**
>
> You can create a custom cache dependency class by deriving a new class from the base CacheDependency class.

The `SqlCacheDependency` class is discussed in detail in the final section of this chapter. In this section, I want to show you how you can use the base `CacheDependency` class to create a file dependency on an XML file.

The page in Listing 25.38 creates a dependency on an XML file named `Movies.xml`. If you modify the `Movies.xml` file, the cache is reloaded with the modified file automatically.

LISTING 25.38   ShowFileDependency.aspx

```
<%@ Page Language="C#" Trace="true" %>
<%@ Import Namespace="System.Data" %>
<%@ Import Namespace="System.Data.SqlClient" %>
<!DOCTYPE html PUBLIC "-//W3C//DTD XHTML 1.0 Transitional//EN"
"http://www.w3.org/TR/xhtml1/DTD/xhtml1-transitional.dtd">
<script runat="server">

    void Page_Load()
    {
        DataSet movies = (DataSet)Cache["Movies"];
        if (movies == null)
        {
            Trace.Warn("Retrieving movies from file system");
            movies = new DataSet();
            movies.ReadXml(MapPath("~/Movies.xml"));
            CacheDependency fileDepend = new
            ➥CacheDependency(MapPath("~/Movies.xml"));
            Cache.Insert("Movies", movies, fileDepend);
        }
        grdMovies.DataSource = movies;
        grdMovies.DataBind();
    }
</script>
<html xmlns="http://www.w3.org/1999/xhtml" >
<head id="Head1" runat="server">
    <title>Show File Dependency</title>
</head>
<body>
    <form id="form1" runat="server">
    <div>

    <asp:GridView
```

25

LISTING 25.38   Continued

```
            id="grdMovies"
            Runat="server" />

    </div>
    </form>
</body>
</html>
```

Specifying Cache Item Priorities

When you add an item to the Cache, you can specify a particular priority for the item. Specifying a priority provides you with some control over when an item gets evicted from the Cache. For example, you can indicate that one cached item is more important than other cache items so that when memory resources become low, the important item is not evicted as quickly as other items.

You can specify any of the following values of the CacheItemPriority enumeration to indicate the priority of a cached item:

- ▶ AboveNormal

- ▶ BelowNormal

- ▶ Default

- ▶ High

- ▶ Low

- ▶ Normal

- ▶ NotRemovable

For example, the following line of code adds an item to the cache with a maximum absolute expiration time and a cache item priority of NotRemovable:

```
Cache.Insert("ImportantItem", DateTime.Now, null, DateTime.MaxValue,
Cache.NoSlidingExpiration, CacheItemPriority.NotRemovable, null);
```

Configuring the Cache

You can configure the size of the cache by using the web configuration file. You specify cache settings with the cache element. This element supports the following attributes:

- ▶ **disableMemoryCollection**—Enables you to prevent items from being removed from the cache when memory resources become low.

- ▶ **disableExpiration**—Enables you to prevent items from being removed from the cache when the items expire.

▶ **privateBytesLimit**—Enables you to specify the total amount of memory that can be consumed by your application and its cache before items are removed.

▶ **percentagePhysicalMemoryUsedLimit**—Enables you to specify the total percentage of memory that can be consumed by your application and its cache before items are removed.

▶ **privateBytesPollTime**—Enables you to specify the time interval for checking the application's memory usage.

Notice that you can't set the size of the cache directly. However, you can specify limits on the overall memory that your application consumes, which indirectly limits the size of the cache.

By default, both the `privateBytesLimit` and `percentPhysicalMemoryUsedLimit` attributes have the value 0, which indicates that the ASP.NET Framework should determine the correct values for these attributes automatically.

The web configuration file in Listing 25.39 changes the memory limit of your application to 100,000 kilobytes and disables the expiration of items in the cache.

LISTING 25.39   Web.Config

```
<configuration>
    <system.web>
      <caching>
        <cache privateBytesLimit="100000" disableExpiration="true"/>
      </caching>
    </system.web>
</configuration>
```

The page in Listing 25.40 displays your application's current private bytes limit (see Figure 25.15):

LISTING 25.40   ShowPrivateBytesLimit.aspx

```
<%@ Page Language="C#" %>
<!DOCTYPE html PUBLIC "-//W3C//DTD XHTML 1.0 Transitional//EN"
"http://www.w3.org/TR/xhtml1/DTD/xhtml1-transitional.dtd">
<script runat="server">

    void Page_Load()
    {
        lblPrivateBytes.Text = Cache.EffectivePrivateBytesLimit.ToString("n0");
    }
</script>
<html xmlns="http://www.w3.org/1999/xhtml" >
<head id="Head1" runat="server">
```

25

LISTING 25.40   Continued

```
    <title>Show Private Bytes Limit</title>
</head>
<body>
    <form id="form1" runat="server">
    <div>

    Effective Private Bytes Limit:
    <asp:Label
        id="lblPrivateBytes"
        Runat="server" />

    </div>
    </form>
</body>
</html>
```

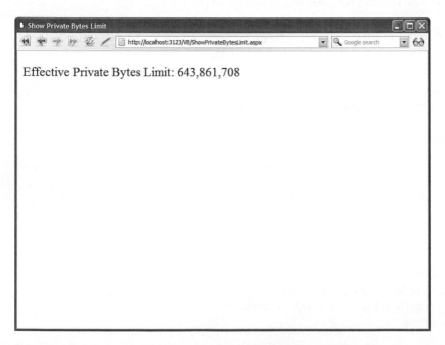

FIGURE 25.15   Displaying the maximum application and cache size.

Using SQL Cache Dependencies

One of the most powerful features supported by the ASP.NET Framework is SQL cache dependencies. This feature enables you to reload cached database data automatically whenever the data in the underlying databases changes.

There is a tradeoff when you use either an absolute or sliding cache expiration policy. The tradeoff is between performance and stale data. For example, if you cache data in memory for 20 seconds, then the data that is displayed on your web pages might be 20 seconds out of date.

In the case of most applications, displaying slightly stale data does not really matter. For example, if you are building a discussion forum, then everyone can live with the fact that new posts might not appear immediately.

However, there are certain types of applications in which you cannot afford to display any stale data at all. For example, if you are creating a stock trading website or an auction website, then every second might count.

The ASP.NET Framework's support for SQL cache dependencies enables you to take advantage of caching but minimize stale data. When you use a SQL cache dependency, you can automatically detect when data has changed in the underlying database and refresh the data in the cache.

The ASP.NET Framework supports two types of SQL cache dependencies: Polling and Push. You can use Polling SQL cache dependencies with any recent version of Microsoft SQL Server, including Microsoft SQL Server 2005 Express, Microsoft SQL Server 2000, and Microsoft SQL Server 7.0. The second type of cache dependency, Push SQL cache dependency, works with only Microsoft SQL Server 2005 or Microsoft SQL Server 2005 Express because it requires the SQL Server 2005 Service Broker.

You can use either type of SQL cache dependencies with Page Output Caching, DataSource Control Caching, and Data Caching. The following sections examine each scenario.

Using Polling SQL Cache Dependencies

A Polling SQL cache dependency is the most flexible type of SQL cache dependency, and I recommend that you use Polling rather than Push SQL cache dependencies for most applications. You can use a Polling SQL cache dependency to detect any type of modification to a database table.

Behind the scenes, a Polling SQL cache dependency uses a database trigger. When a table is modified, the trigger fires and a row in a database table named AspNet_SqlCacheTablesForChangeNotification is updated to record the fact that the table has been changed.

The ASP.NET Framework uses a background thread to poll this database table for changes on a periodic basis. If there has been a change, then any item in the cache that is dependent on the database table is dropped from the cache.

If you use a Polling SQL cache dependency, then you can eliminate the majority of your database traffic. Unless a database table changes, the only traffic between your web server and the database server is the query that checks for changes in the AspNet_SqlCacheTablesForChangeNotification table.

Because a Polling SQL cache dependency must poll the database for changes, an item cached with a SQL Polling cache dependency won't be dropped from the cache immediately after there is a change in the database. The polling interval determines the staleness of your cached data. You can configure the polling interval to be any value you need.

Configuring Polling SQL Cache Dependencies

Before you can use a Polling SQL cache dependency, you must perform two configuration steps:

1. Enable SQL cache dependencies for a database and one or more database tables.
2. Configure SQL cache dependencies in your web configuration file.

Let's examine each of these steps.

Configuring a Database for Polling SQL Cache Dependencies   You can configure a SQL Server database to support Polling SQL cache dependencies by using a class in the framework named the SqlCacheDependencyAdmin class. This class has the following methods:

▶ **DisableNotifications**—Enables you to disable a database for Polling SQL cache dependencies; removes all tables and stored procedures used by Polling SQL cache dependencies.

▶ **DisableTableForNotification**—Enables you to disable a particular database table for Polling SQL cache dependencies.

▶ **EnableNotifications**—Enables a database for Polling SQL cache dependencies by adding all the necessary database objects.

▶ **EnableTableForNotifications**—Enables a particular database table for Polling SQL cache dependencies.

▶ **GetTablesEnabledForNotifications**—Enables you to retrieve all tables enabled for Polling SQL cache dependencies.

You should not use the SqlCacheDependencyAdmin class in an ASP.NET page because calling the methods of this class requires database permissions to create tables, stored procedures, and triggers. For security reasons, the ASP.NET process should not be given these permissions. Instead, you should use the SqlCacheDependencyAdmin class in a command-line tool.

The ASP.NET Framework includes a command-line tool named aspnet_regsql that enables you to configure a database to support Polling SQL cache dependencies. This tool works with Microsoft SQL Server 7.0, Microsoft SQL Server 2000, and Microsoft SQL Server 2005. Unfortunately, the aspnet_regsql command-line tool does not work with a local instance of Microsoft SQL Server 2005. (But we'll fix this limitation in a moment.)

The aspnet_regsql tool is located in the following folder:

```
c:\Windows\Microsoft.NET\Framework\v2.0.50727
```

NOTE

If you open the SDK Command Prompt from the Microsoft .NET Framework SDK Program group, then you do not need to navigate to the Microsoft.NET folder to execute the `aspnet_regsql` command-line tool.

Executing the following command enables the Pubs database for SQL cache dependencies:

```
aspnet_regsql -C "Data Source=localhost;Integrated Security=True;Initial
Catalog=Pubs" -ed
```

This command creates the AspNet_SqlCacheTablesForChangeNotification database table and adds a set of stored procedures to the database specified in the connection string.

After you enable a database, you can enable a particular table for SQL cache dependencies with the following command:

```
aspnet_regsql -C "Data Source=localhost;Integrated Security=True;Initial
Catalog=Pubs" -et -t Titles
```

This command enables the Titles database table for SQL cache dependencies. It creates a new trigger for the Titles database table and adds a new entry in the AspNet_SqlCacheTablesForChangeNotification table.

Unfortunately, you cannot use the standard `aspnet_regsql` tool to enable a local SQL Server 2005 Express database for Polling SQL cache dependencies. The `aspnet_regsql` tool does not allow you to use the `AttachDBFileName` parameter in the connection string.

To get around this limitation, I've written a custom command-line tool named `enableNotifications` that works with a local SQL Express database. This tool is included on the CD that accompanies this book.

To use the `enableNotifications` tool, you need to open a command prompt and navigate to the folder that contains your local SQL Express database table. Next, execute the command with the name of the database file and the name of the database table that you want to enable for Polling SQL cache dependencies. For example, the following command enables the Movies database table located in the `MyDatabase.mdf` database:

```
enableNotifications "MyDatabase.mdf" "Movies"
```

The `enableNotifications` tool works only with a local instance of Microsoft SQL Server Express 2005. You cannot use the tool with other versions of Microsoft SQL Server.

WARNING

When using the `enableNotifications` tool, you must navigate to the same folder as the database that you want to enable for Polling SQL cache dependencies.

Configuring an Application for Polling SQL Cache Dependencies   After you set up a database to support Polling SQL cache dependencies, you must configure your application to poll the database. You configure Polling SQL cache dependencies with the `sqlCacheDependency` subelement of the caching element in the web configuration file.

For example, the file in Listing 25.41 causes your application to poll the AspNet_ SqlCacheTablesForChangeNotification table every 5 seconds (5000 milliseconds) for changes.

LISTING 25.41   Web.Config

```
<configuration>

  <connectionStrings>
    <add name="Movies" connectionString="Data Source=.\SQLEXPRESS;
      AttachDbFilename=¦DataDirectory¦MyDatabase.mdf;Integrated Security=True;
User Instance=True" />
  </connectionStrings>

  <system.web>
    <caching>
      <sqlCacheDependency enabled="true" pollTime="5000">
        <databases>
          <add
            name="MyDatabase"
            connectionStringName="Movies" />
        </databases>
      </sqlCacheDependency>
    </caching>
  </system.web>
</configuration>
```

Using Polling SQL Cache Dependencies with Page Output Caching

After you configure Polling SQL cache dependencies, you can use a SQL dependency with Page Output Caching. For example, the page in Listing 25.42 is output cached until you modify the Movies database table.

LISTING 25.42   PollingSQLOutputCache.aspx

```
<%@ Page Language="C#" %>
<%@ OutputCache Duration="9999" VaryByParam="none"
  SqlDependency="MyDatabase:Movies" %>
<!DOCTYPE html PUBLIC "-//W3C//DTD XHTML 1.0 Transitional//EN"
  "http://www.w3.org/TR/xhtml1/DTD/xhtml1-transitional.dtd">
<html xmlns="http://www.w3.org/1999/xhtml" >
```

```
<head id="Head1" runat="server">
    <title>Polling SQL Output Cache</title>
</head>
<body>
    <form id="form1" runat="server">
    <div>

    <%- DateTime.Now.ToString("T") %>
    <hr />

    <asp:GridView
        id="grdMovies"
        DataSourceID="srcMovies"
        Runat="server" />

    <asp:SqlDataSource
        id="srcMovies"
        ConnectionString="<%$ ConnectionStrings:Movies %>"
        SelectCommand="SELECT Title, Director FROM Movies"
        Runat="server" />

    </div>
    </form>
</body>
</html>
```

The page in Listing 25.42 includes an `<%@ OutputCache %>` directive with a `SqlDependency` attribute. The value of the `SqlDependency` attribute is the name of the database enabled for SQL dependencies in the web configuration file, followed by the name of a database table.

If you open the page in Listing 25.42 in your browser and click your browser's Reload button multiple times, then you'll notice that the time displayed does not change. The page is output cached (see Figure 25.16).

However, if you modify the Movies database, then the page is dropped from the cache automatically (within 5 seconds). The next time you click the Reload button, the modified data is displayed.

If you want to make a page dependent on multiple database tables, then you can assign a semicolon-delimited list of database and table names to the `SqlDependency` attribute.

NOTE

You also can use Polling SQL cache dependencies with an `<%@ OutputCache %>` directive included in a User Control. In other words, you can use Polling SQL cache dependencies with Partial Page Caching.

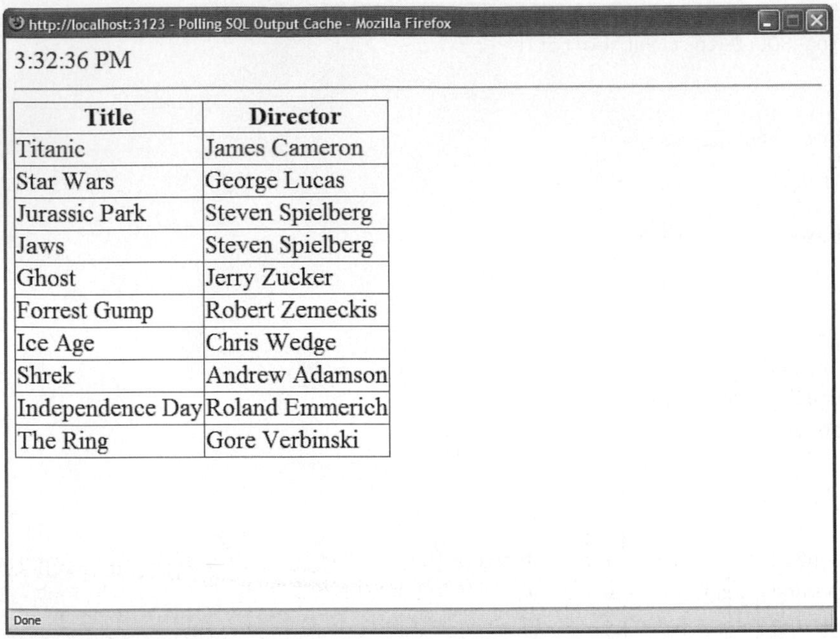

FIGURE 25.16   Using Page Output Caching with a Polling SQL cache dependency.

Using Polling SQL Cache Dependencies with DataSource Caching

You can use Polling SQL cache dependencies with both the SqlDataSource and ObjectDataSource controls by setting the SqlCacheDependency property. For example, the page in Listing 25.43 caches the output of a SqlDataSource control until the Movies database table is modified.

LISTING 25.43   PollingSQLDataSourceCache.aspx

```
<%@ Page Language="C#" %>
<!DOCTYPE html PUBLIC "-//W3C//DTD XHTML 1.0 Transitional//EN"
"http://www.w3.org/TR/xhtml1/DTD/xhtml1-transitional.dtd">
<script runat="server">

    protected void srcMovies_Selecting(object sender,
    ➥SqlDataSourceSelectingEventArgs e)
    {
        lblMessage.Text = "Retrieving data from database";
    }
</script>
<html xmlns="http://www.w3.org/1999/xhtml" >
<head id="Head1" runat="server">
    <title>Polling SQL DataSource Cache</title>
</head>
```

```
<body>
    <form id="form1" runat="server">
    <div>

    <asp:Label
        id="lblMessage"
        EnableViewState="false"
        Runat="server" />
    <hr />

    <asp:GridView
        id="grdMovies"
        DataSourceID="srcMovies"
        Runat="server" />

    <asp:SqlDataSource
        id="srcMovies"
        ConnectionString="<%$ ConnectionStrings:Movies %>"
        SelectCommand="SELECT Title, Director FROM Movies"
        EnableCaching="true"
        SqlCacheDependency="MyDatabase:Movies"
        OnSelecting="srcMovies_Selecting"
        Runat="server" />

    </div>
    </form>
</body>
</html>
```

In Listing 25.43, the SqlDataSource control includes both an EnableCaching property and a SqlCacheDependency property. A database name and table name are assigned to the SqlCacheDependency property. (The database name must correspond to the database name configured in the <sqlCacheDependency> section of the web configuration file.)

If you need to monitor multiple database tables, you can assign a semicolon-delimited list of database and table names to the SqlCacheDependency property.

Using Polling SQL Cache Dependencies with Data Caching

You also can use Polling SQL cache dependencies when working with the Cache object. You represent a Polling SQL cache dependency with the SqlCacheDependency object.

For example, the page in Listing 25.44 creates a SqlCacheDependency object that represents the Movies database table. When a DataTable is added to the Cache object, the DataTable is added with the SqlCacheDependency object.

LISTING 25.44   PollingSQLDataCache.aspx

```
<%@ Page Language="C#" Trace="true" %>
<%@ Import Namespace="System.Data" %>
<%@ Import Namespace="System.Data.SqlClient" %>
<%@ Import Namespace="System.Web.Configuration" %>
<!DOCTYPE html PUBLIC "-//W3C//DTD XHTML 1.0 Transitional//EN"
"http://www.w3.org/TR/xhtml1/DTD/xhtml1-transitional.dtd">
<script runat="server">

    void Page_Load()
    {
        DataTable movies = (DataTable)Cache["Movies"];
        if (movies == null)
        {
            movies = GetMoviesFromDB();
            SqlCacheDependency sqlDepend = new SqlCacheDependency("MyDatabase",
            ➥"Movies");
            Cache.Insert("Movies", movies, sqlDepend);
        }
        grdMovies.DataSource = movies;
        grdMovies.DataBind();
    }


    private DataTable GetMoviesFromDB()
    {
        Trace.Warn("Retrieving data from database");
        string conString = WebConfigurationManager.ConnectionStrings
        ➥["Movies"].ConnectionString;
        SqlDataAdapter dad = new SqlDataAdapter("SELECT Title,Director FROM
        ➥Movies", conString);
        DataTable movies = new DataTable();
        dad.Fill(movies);
        return movies;
    }
</script>
<html xmlns="http://www.w3.org/1999/xhtml" >
<head id="Head1" runat="server">
    <title>Polling SQL Data Cache</title>
</head>
<body>
    <form id="form1" runat="server">
    <div>

    <asp:GridView
        id="grdMovies"
```

```
        Runat="server" />

    </div>
    </form>
</body>
</html>
```

In Listing 25.44, an instance of the `SqlCacheDependency` class is created. A database name and table name are passed to the constructor for the `SqlCacheDependency` class. This class is used as a parameter with the `Cache.Insert()` method when the `DataTable` is added to the Cache.

> **NOTE**
>
> If you need to create dependencies on multiple database tables, then you need to create multiple `SqlCacheDependency` objects and represent the multiple dependencies with an instance of the `AggregateCacheDependency` class.

Using Push SQL Cache Dependencies

When using Microsoft SQL Server 2005, you have the option of using Push SQL cache dependencies rather than Polling SQL cache dependencies. Microsoft SQL Server 2005 includes a feature called query notifications, which use the Microsoft SQL Server 2005 Service Broker in the background. The Service Broker can automatically send a message to an application when data changes in the database.

> **WARNING**
>
> You can create two types of databases with SQL Server Express: a Local or a Server database. You should not use Push dependencies with a Local database. You should use Push dependencies only with a Server database.
>
> You cannot create new Server databases when using Visual Web Developer. You can create a Server database by using the full version of Visual Studio 2008 or by downloading Microsoft SQL Server Management Studio Express from the Microsoft MSDN website (msdn.microsoft.com).

The advantage of using Push dependencies rather than Polling dependencies is that your ASP.NET application does not need to continuously poll your database for changes. When a change happens, your database is responsible for notifying your application of the change.

Now the bad news. There are significant limitations on the types of queries that you can use with Push dependencies. Here are some of the more significant limitations:

▶ The query must use two-part table names (for example, dbo.Movies instead of Movies) to refer to tables.

- ▶ The query must contain an explicit list of column names (you cannot use *).

- ▶ The query cannot reference a view, derived table, temporary table, or table variable.

- ▶ The query cannot reference large object types such as Text, NText, and Image columns.

- ▶ The query cannot contain a subquery, outer join, or self join.

- ▶ The query cannot use the DISTINCT, COMPUTE, COMPUTE BY, or INSERT keywords.

- ▶ The query cannot use many aggregate functions including AVG, COUNT(*), MAX, and MIN.

This is not a complete list of query limitations. For the complete list, refer to the Creating a Query for Notification topic in the SQL Server 2005 Books Online or the MSDN website (msdn.Microsoft.com).

For example, the following simple query won't work:

```
SELECT * FROM Movies
```

This query won't work for two reasons. First, you cannot use the asterisk (*) to represent columns. Second, you must supply a two-part table name. The following query, on the other hand, will work:

```
SELECT Title, Director FROM dbo.Movies
```

You can use Push SQL cache dependencies with stored procedures. However, each SELECT statement in the stored procedure must meet all the requirements just listed.

Configuring Push SQL Cache Dependencies

You must perform two configuration steps to enable Push SQL cache dependencies:

- ▶ You must configure your database by enabling the SQL Server 2005 Service Broker.

- ▶ You must configure your application by starting the notification listener.

In this section, you learn how to perform both of these configuration steps.

WARNING

Unfortunately, when a Push SQL cache dependency fails, it fails silently, without adding an error message to the Event Log. This makes the situation especially difficult to debug. I recommend that after you make the configuration changes discussed in this section that you restart both your web server and database server.

Configuring a Database for Push SQL Cache Dependencies   Before you can use Push SQL cache dependencies, you must enable the Microsoft SQL Server 2005 Service Broker. You can check whether the Service Broker is activated for a particular database by executing the following SQL query:

```
SELECT name, is_broker_enabled FROM sys.databases
```

If the Service Broker is not enabled for a database, then you can enable it by executing an ALTER DATABASE command. For example, the following SQL command enables the Service Broker for a database named MyMovies:

```
ALTER DATABASE MyMovies SET ENABLE_BROKER
```

Finally, the ASP.NET process must be supplied with adequate permissions to subscribe to query notifications. When an ASP.NET page is served from Internet Information Server, the page executes in the context of the NT Authority\NETWORK SERVICE account (in the case of Microsoft Windows Server 2003 or Vista) or the ASPNET account (in the case of other operating systems such as Windows XP).

Executing the following SQL command provides the local ASPNET account on a server named YOURSERVER with the required permissions:

```
GRANT SUBSCRIBE QUERY NOTIFICATIONS TO "YOURSERVER\ASPNET"
```

When you request an ASP.NET page when using the Visual Web Developer web server, an ASP.NET page executes in the security context of your current user account. Therefore, when using a file system website, you'll need to grant SUBSCRIBE QUERY NOTIFICATIONS permissions to your current account.

25

> **NOTE**
>
> Push SQL cache dependencies do not use the SQL Server 2005 Notification Services.

Configuring an Application for Push SQL Cache Dependencies   Before you can receive change notifications in your application, you must enable the query notification listener. You can enable the listener with the Global.asax file in Listing 25.45.

LISTING 25.45   Global.asax

```
<%@ Application Language="C#" %>
<%@ Import Namespace="System.Data.SqlClient" %>
<%@ Import Namespace="System.Web.Configuration" %>
<script runat="server">

    void Application_Start(object sender, EventArgs e)
    {
        // Enable Push SQL cache dependencies
        string conString = WebConfigurationManager.ConnectionStrings
        ➥["MyMovies"].ConnectionString;
        SqlDependency.Start(conString);
    }
</script>
```

The `Application_Start` handler executes once when your application first starts. In Listing 25.45, the `SqlDependency.Start()` method is called with a connection string to a SQL Express server database named MyMovies.

> **WARNING**
>
> The code in Listing 25.45 is commented out in the `Global.asax` file on the CD that accompanies this book so that it won't interfere with all the previous code samples discussed in this chapter. You'll need to remove the comments to use the code samples in the following sections.

Using Push SQL Cache Dependencies with Page Output Caching

You can use Push SQL cache dependencies when caching an entire ASP.NET page. If the results of any SQL command contained in the page changes, then the page is dropped automatically from the cache.

The `SqlCommand` object includes a property named the `NotificationAutoEnlist` property. This property has the value `True` by default. When `NotificationAutoEnlist` is enabled, a Push cache dependency is created between the page and the command automatically.

For example, the page in Listing 25.46 includes an `<%@ OutputCache %>` directive that includes a `SqlDependency` attribute. This attribute is set to the special value `CommandNotification`.

LISTING 25.46   PushSQLOutputCache.aspx

```
<%@ Page Language="C#" %>
<%@ OutputCache Duration="9999" VaryByParam="none"
  SqlDependency="CommandNotification" %>
<!DOCTYPE html PUBLIC "-//W3C//DTD XHTML 1.0 Transitional//EN"
  "http://www.w3.org/TR/xhtml1/DTD/xhtml1-transitional.dtd">
<html xmlns="http://www.w3.org/1999/xhtml" >
<head id="Head1" runat="server">
    <title>Push SQL Output Cache</title>
</head>
<body>
    <form id="form1" runat="server">
    <div>

    <%= DateTime.Now.ToString("T") %>
    <hr />

    <asp:GridView
        id="grdMovies"
        DataSourceID="srcMovies"
```

```
            Runat="server" />

        <asp:SqlDataSource
            id="srcMovies"
            ConnectionString="<%$ ConnectionStrings:MyMovies %>"
            SelectCommand="SELECT Title, Director FROM dbo.Movies"
            Runat="server" />

    </div>
    </form>
</body>
</html>
```

The page in Listing 25.46 includes a SqlDataSource control that retrieves all the records from the Movies database table. Notice that the SqlDataSource control uses a SQL query that explicitly lists column names and uses a two-part table name. These are requirements when using Push dependencies.

The page in Listing 25.46 displays the current time. If you request the page in your browser, and refresh the page, the time does not change. The time does not change until you modify the Movies database table.

WARNING

The page in Listing 25.46 connects to a Server database named MyMovies. You should not use Push dependencies with a Local SQL Express database. The page uses a database table named Movies, which was created with the following SQL command:

```
CREATE TABLE Movies
(
  Id int IDENTITY NOT NULL,
  Title nvarchar(100) NOT NULL,
  Director nvarchar(50) NOT NULL,
  EntryDate datetime NOT NULL DEFAULT GetDate()
)
```

WARNING

You cannot use Push SQL cache dependencies with an <%@ OutputCache %> directive included in a User Control. In other words, you cannot use Push SQL cache dependencies with Partial Page Caching.

Using Push SQL Cache Dependencies with DataSource Caching

You also can use Push SQL cache dependencies with both the `SqlDataSource` and `ObjectDataSource` controls by setting the `SqlCacheDependency` property. When using Push rather than Polling dependencies, you need to set the `SqlCacheDependency` property to the value `CommandNotification`.

For example, the page in Listing 25.47 contains a `SqlDataSource` control that has both its `EnableCaching` and `SqlDependency` properties set.

LISTING 25.47   PushSQLDataSourceCache.aspx

```
<%@ Page Language="C#" %>
<!DOCTYPE html PUBLIC "-//W3C//DTD XHTML 1.0 Transitional//EN"
"http://www.w3.org/TR/xhtml1/DTD/xhtml1-transitional.dtd">
<script runat="server">

    protected void srcMovies_Selecting(object sender,
    ➥SqlDataSourceSelectingEventArgs e)
    {
        lblMessage.Text = "Retrieving data from database";
    }
</script>
<html xmlns="http://www.w3.org/1999/xhtml" >
<head id="Head1" runat="server">
    <title>Push SQL DataSource Cache</title>
</head>
<body>
    <form id="form1" runat="server">
    <div>

    <asp:Label
        id="lblMessage"
        EnableViewState="false"
        Runat="server" />
    <hr />

    <asp:GridView
        id="grdMovies"
        DataSourceID="srcMovies"
        Runat="server" />

    <asp:SqlDataSource
        id="srcMovies"
        ConnectionString="<%$ ConnectionStrings:MyMovies %>"
        SelectCommand="SELECT Title, Director FROM dbo.Movies"
```

```
            EnableCaching="true"
            SqlCacheDependency="CommandNotification"
            OnSelecting="srcMovies_Selecting"
            Runat="server" />

    </div>
    </form>
</body>
</html>
```

In Listing 25.47, the `SqlDataSource` control includes a `Selecting` event handler. Because this event is raised when the data cannot be retrieved from the cache, you can use this event to determine when the data is retrieved from the cache or the database server (see Figure 25.17).

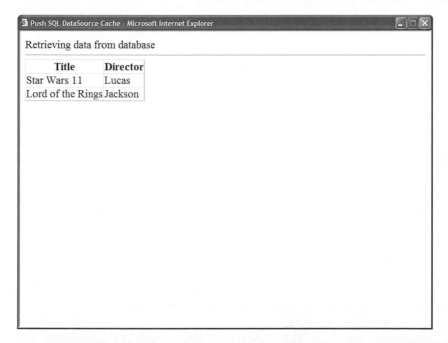

FIGURE 25.17   Using Push SQL cache dependencies with a `DataSource` control.

> **WARNING**
>
> The page in Listing 25.47 connects to a Server database named MyMovies. You should not use Push dependencies with a Local SQL Express database. The page uses a database table named Movies, which was created with the following SQL command:
>
> ```
> CREATE TABLE Movies
>     (
> ```

```
    Id int IDENTITY NOT NULL,
    Title nvarchar(100) NOT NULL,
    Director nvarchar(50) NOT NULL,
    EntryDate datetime NOT NULL DEFAULT GetDate()
)
```

Using Push SQL Cache Dependencies with Data Caching

You can use Push SQL cache dependencies when working with the Cache object. You represent a Push SQL cache dependency with an instance of the SqlCacheDependency class.

For example, in the Page_Load() handler in Listing 25.48, a DataTable is added to the cache that represents the contents of the Movies database table. The DataTable is displayed in a GridView control.

LISTING 25.48   PushSQLDataCache.aspx

```
<%@ Page Language="C#" Trace="true" %>
<%@ Import Namespace="System.Data" %>
<%@ Import Namespace="System.Data.SqlClient" %>
<%@ Import Namespace="System.Web.Configuration" %>
<!DOCTYPE html PUBLIC "-//W3C//DTD XHTML 1.0 Transitional//EN"
"http://www.w3.org/TR/xhtml1/DTD/xhtml1-transitional.dtd">
<script runat="server">

    void Page_Load()
    {
        DataTable movies = (DataTable)Cache["Movies"];
        if (movies == null)
        {
            Trace.Warn("Retrieving data from database");
            string conString = WebConfigurationManager.ConnectionStrings
            ➥["MyMovies"].ConnectionString;
            SqlDataAdapter dad = new SqlDataAdapter("SELECT Title,Director FROM
            ➥dbo.Movies", conString);
            SqlCacheDependency sqlDepend = new SqlCacheDependency(dad.SelectCommand);
            movies = new DataTable();
            dad.Fill(movies);

            Cache.Insert("Movies", movies, sqlDepend);
        }
        grdMovies.DataSource = movies;
        grdMovies.DataBind();
```

```
    }
</script>
<html xmlns="http://www.w3.org/1999/xhtml" >
<head id="Head1" runat="server">
    <title>Push SQL Data Cache</title>
</head>
<body>
    <form id="form1" runat="server">
    <div>

    <asp:GridView
        id="grdMovies"
        Runat="server" />

    </div>
    </form>
</body>
</html>
```

Notice that an instance of the `SqlCacheDependency` class is created. A `SqlCommand` object is passed to the constructor for the `SqlCacheDependency` class. If the results of the `SqlCommand` changes, then the `DataTable` will be dropped automatically from the cache.

The order of the commands here is important. You need to create the `SqlCacheDependency` object before you execute the command. If you call the `Fill()` method before you create the `SqlCacheDependency` object, then the dependency is ignored.

WARNING

The page in Listing 25.48 connects to a Server database named MyMovies. You should not use Push dependencies with a Local SQL Express database. The page uses a database table named Movies, which was created with the following SQL command:

```
CREATE TABLE Movies
(
  Id int IDENTITY NOT NULL,
  Title nvarchar(100) NOT NULL,
  Director nvarchar(50) NOT NULL,
  EntryDate datetime NOT NULL DEFAULT GetDate()
)
```

Summary

In this chapter, you learned how to improve the performance of your ASP.NET applications by taking advantage of caching. In the first part of this chapter, you learned how to use each of the different types of caching technologies supported by the ASP.NET Framework.

First, you learned how to use Page Output Caching to cache the entire rendered contents of a page. You learned how to create different cached versions of the same page when the page is requested with different parameters, headers, and browsers. You also learned how to remove pages programmatically from the Page Output Cache. Finally, we discussed how you can define Cache Profiles in a web configuration file.

Next, you learned how to use Partial Page Caching to apply different caching policies to different regions in a page. You learned how to use post-cache substitution to dynamically inject content into a page that has been output cached. You also learned how to use User Controls to cache different areas of a page.

We also discussed how you can cache data by using the different `DataSource` controls. You learned how to enable caching when working with the `SqlDataSource`, `ObjectDataSource`, and `XmlDataSource` controls.

Next, you learned how to use the `Cache` object to cache items programmatically. You learned how to add items to the cache with different expiration policies and dependencies. You also learned how to configure the maximum size of the cache in the web configuration file.

Finally, we discussed SQL cache dependencies. You learned how to use SQL cache dependencies to reload database data in the cache automatically when the data in the underlying database changes. You learned how to use both Polling and Push SQL cache dependencies with Page Output Caching, DataSource Caching, and the `Cache` object.

CHAPTER 26

Localizing Applications for Multiple Languages

You can localize an ASP.NET website so that it supports multiple languages and cultures. For example, you might need to create both an English language and Spanish language version of the same website.

One approach to localization is to simply create multiple copies of the same website and translate each copy into a different language. This is a common approach when building ASP Classic (or even ASP.NET 1.1) websites. The problem with this approach is it creates a website maintenance nightmare. Whenever you need to make a change to the website—no matter how simple—you must make the change in each copy of the website.

When building ASP.NET applications, you do not need to create multiple copies of a website to support multiple languages. Instead, you can take advantage of resource files. A resource file contains language-specific content. For example, one resource file might contain a Spanish version of all the text in your website, and a second resource file might contain the Indonesian version of all the text in your website.

In this chapter, you learn how to localize ASP.NET applications. First, you learn how to set the culture of the current page. You learn how to use both the `Culture` and `UICulture` properties. You also learn how to detect users' preferred languages automatically through their browser settings.

Next, local resources are explored. A local resource contains content that is scoped to a particular file such as an ASP.NET page. You learn how to use both implicit and explicit resource expressions.

This chapter also examines global resources. A global resource contains content that can be used in any page within an application. For example, you can place the title of your website in a global resource file.

Finally, the ASP.NET `Localize` control is discussed. You learn how to use this control in your pages to localize big chunks of page text.

Setting the Current Culture

Two main properties of the `Page` class have an effect on localization:

▶ UICulture

▶ Culture

The `UICulture` property is used to specify which resource files are loaded for the page. The resource files can contain all the text content of your pages translated into a particular language. You can set this property to any standard culture name. This property is discussed in detail during the discussion of using local and global resources later in this chapter.

The `Culture` property, on the other hand, determines how strings such as dates, numerals, and currency amounts are formatted. It also determines how values are compared and sorted. For example, by modifying the `Culture` property, you can display dates with language-specific month names such as January (English), Januar (German), or Enero (Spanish).

Both the `UICulture` and `Culture` properties accept standard culture names for their values. Culture names follow the RFC 1766 and RFC 3066 standards maintained by the Internet Engineering Task Force (IETF). The IETF website is located at www.IETF.org.

Here are some common culture names:

▶ de-DE = German (Germany)

▶ en-US = English (United States)

▶ en-GB = English (United Kingdom)

▶ es-MX = Spanish (Mexico)

▶ id-ID = Indonesian (Indonesia)

▶ zh-CN = Chinese (China)

Notice that each culture name consists of two parts. The first part represents the language code and the second part represents the country/region code. If you specify a culture name and do not provide a country/region code—for example, en—then you have specified something called a *neutral culture*. If you provide both a language code and a country/region code—for example, en-US—then you have specified something called a *specific culture*.

NOTE

You can view the culture names supported by the .NET Framework by looking up the entry for the `CultureInfo` class in the Microsoft .NET Framework SDK documentation. It's a really long list.

The `Culture` property must always be set to a specific culture. This makes sense because, for example, different English speakers use different currency symbols. The `UICulture` property, on the other hand, can be set to either a neutral or specific culture name. Text written in Canadian English is pretty much the same as text written in U.S. English.

You can set the `UICulture` and `Culture` properties to the same value or different values. For example, if you are creating an online store, then you might want to set the `UICulture` property to the value `de-DE` to display German product descriptions. However, you might want to set the `Culture` property to the value `en-US` to display product prices in United State currency amounts.

Setting a Culture Manually

You can set either the `UICulture` or `Culture` properties by using the `<%@ Page %>` directive. For example, the page in Listing 26.1 sets both properties to the value `id-ID` (Indonesian).

LISTING 26.1   `Bagus.aspx`

```
<%@ Page Language="C#" Culture="id-ID" UICulture="id-ID" %>
<!DOCTYPE html PUBLIC "-//W3C//DTD XHTML 1.1//EN"
"http://www.w3.org/TR/xhtml11/DTD/xhtml11.dtd">
<script runat="server">

    void Page_Load()
    {
        lblDate.Text = DateTime.Now.ToString("D");
        lblPrice.Text = (512.33m).ToString("c");
    }
</script>
<html xmlns="http://www.w3.org/1999/xhtml" >
<head id="Head1" runat="server">
    <title>Bagus</title>
</head>
<body>
    <form id="form1" runat="server">
    <div>

    Today's date is:
    <br />
```

LISTING 26.1   Continued

```
    <asp:Label
        id="lblDate"
        Runat="server" />

    <hr />
    The price of the product is:
    <br />
    <asp:Label
        id="lblPrice"
        Runat="server" />

    </div>
    </form>
</body>
</html>
```

The page in Listing 26.1 displays a date and a currency amount. Because the Culture property is set to the value id-ID in the <%@ Page %> directive, both the date and currency amount are formatted with Indonesian cultural conventions (see Figure 26.1).

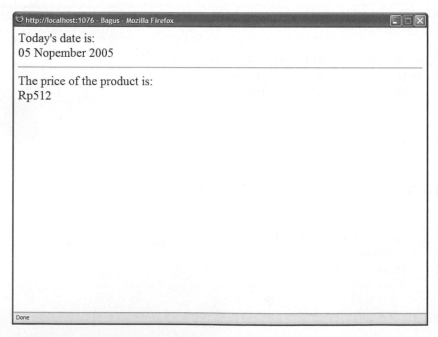

FIGURE 26.1   Displaying a localized date and price.

The date is displayed like this:

05 November 2005

The currency amount is displayed as an Indonesian Rupiah amount like this:

Rp512

NOTE

Setting the Culture does not actually convert a currency amount. Setting a particular culture only formats the currency as appropriate for a particular culture. If you need to convert currency amounts, then you need to use a Web service: Conversion rates change minute by minute. See, for example, www.xmethods.com.

Instead of using the `<%@ Page %>` directive to set the `Culture` or `UICulture` properties, you can set these properties programmatically. For example, the page in Listing 26.2 enables you to select a particular culture from a drop-down list of cultures (see Figure 26.2).

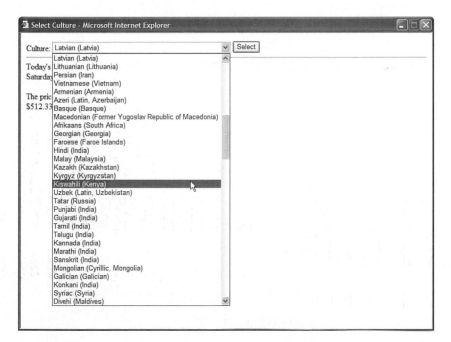

FIGURE 26.2   Selecting a culture from a `DropDownList` control.

LISTING 26.2 SelectCulture.aspx

```
<%@ Page Language="C#" %>
<!DOCTYPE html PUBLIC "-//W3C//DTD XHTML 1.1//EN"
"http://www.w3.org/TR/xhtml11/DTD/xhtml11.dtd">
<script runat="server">
    protected void btnSelect_Click(object sender, EventArgs e)
    {
        Culture = ddlCulture.SelectedValue;
    }

    void Page_PreRender()
    {
        lblDate.Text = DateTime.Now.ToString("D");
        lblPrice.Text = (512.33m).ToString("c");
    }
</script>
<html xmlns="http://www.w3.org/1999/xhtml" >
<head id="Head1" runat="server">
    <title>Select Culture</title>
</head>
<body>
    <form id="form1" runat="server">
    <div>

    <asp:Label
        id="lblCulture"
        Text="Culture:"
        AssociatedControlID="ddlCulture"
        Runat="server" />

    <asp:DropDownList
        id="ddlCulture"
        DataTextField="DisplayName"
        DataValueField="Name"
        DataSourceID="srcCultures"
        Runat="server" />

    <asp:Button
        id="btnSelect"
        Text="Select"
        Runat="server" OnClick="btnSelect_Click" />


    <asp:ObjectDataSource
```

```
            id="srcCultures"
            TypeName="System.Globalization.CultureInfo"
            SelectMethod="GetCultures"
            Runat="server">
            <SelectParameters>
                <asp:Parameter Name="types" DefaultValue="SpecificCultures" />
            </SelectParameters>
        </asp:ObjectDataSource>

        <hr />

        Today's date is:
        <br />
        <asp:Label
            id="lblDate"
            Runat="server" />

        <br /><br />

        The price of the product is:
        <br />
        <asp:Label
            id="lblPrice"
            Runat="server" />

        </div>
        </form>
</body>
</html>
```

The `DropDownList` control in Listing 26.2 is bound to an `ObjectDataSource` control, which retrieves a list of all the culture names supported by the .NET Framework. The culture names are retrieved during a call to the `GetCultures()` method of the `CultureInfo` class.

When you click the button to select a culture, the `btnSelect_Click()` method executes and assigns the name of the selected culture to the page's `Culture` property. When you select a new culture, the formatting applied to the date and currency amount changes.

Several websites on the Internet display a page that requires the user to select a language before entering the main website. For example, the Federal Express website (www.FedEx.com) requires you to select a country before entering the website.

You can take advantage of the `Profile` object to store a user's preferred culture. That way, a user needs to select a culture only once and the culture is then used any time the user returns to your website in the future. The page in Listing 26.3 illustrates this approach.

LISTING 26.3   SelectCultureProfile.aspx

```
<%@ Page Language="C#" %>
<!DOCTYPE html PUBLIC "-//W3C//DTD XHTML 1.1//EN"
"http://www.w3.org/TR/xhtml11/DTD/xhtml11.dtd">
<script runat="server">

    protected override void InitializeCulture()
    {
        Culture = Profile.UserCulture;
        UICulture = Profile.UserUICulture;
    }


    protected void btnSelect_Click(object sender, EventArgs e)
    {
        Profile.UserCulture = ddlCulture.SelectedValue;
        Profile.UserUICulture = ddlCulture.SelectedValue;
        Response.Redirect(Request.Path);
    }


    void Page_PreRender()
    {
        lblDate.Text = DateTime.Now.ToString("D");
        lblPrice.Text = (512.33m).ToString("c");
    }
</script>
<html xmlns="http://www.w3.org/1999/xhtml" >
<head id="Head1" runat="server">
    <title>Select Culture Profile</title>
</head>
<body>
    <form id="form1" runat="server">
    <div>

    <asp:Label
        id="lblCulture"
        Text="Culture:"
        AssociatedControlID="ddlCulture"
        Runat="server" />

    <asp:DropDownList
        id="ddlCulture"
        DataTextField="DisplayName"
        DataValueField="Name"
        DataSourceID="srcCultures"
```

```
            Runat="server" />

        <asp:Button
            id="btnSelect"
            Text="Select"
            Runat="server" OnClick="btnSelect_Click" />


        <asp:ObjectDataSource
            id="srcCultures"
            TypeName="System.Globalization.CultureInfo"
            SelectMethod="GetCultures"
            Runat="server">
            <SelectParameters>
                <asp:Parameter Name="types" DefaultValue="SpecificCultures" />
            </SelectParameters>
        </asp:ObjectDataSource>

        <hr />

        Today's date is:
        <br />
        <asp:Label
            id="lblDate"
            Runat="server" />

        <br /><br />

        The price of the product is:
        <br />
        <asp:Label
            id="lblPrice"
            Runat="server" />

        </div>
        </form>
    </body>
    </html>
```

You should notice two things about the page in Listing 26.3. First, notice that the culture is set in the InitializeCulture() method. This method overrides the InitializeCulture() method of the base Page class and sets the UICulture and Culture properties by using the Profile object.

Second, notice that the btnSelect_Click() handler updates the properties of the Profile object and redirects the page back to itself. This is done so that the InitializeCulture() method executes after a user changes the selected culture.

The page in Listing 26.3 uses the Profile defined in the web configuration file contained in Listing 26.4.

LISTING 26.4   Web.Config

```
<configuration xmlns="http://schemas.microsoft.com/.NetConfiguration/v2.0">
  <system.web>
    <anonymousIdentification enabled="true"/>

    <profile>
      <properties>
        <add
          name="UserCulture"
          defaultValue="en-US" />
        <add
          name="UserUICulture"
          defaultValue="en"/>
      </properties>
    </profile>
  </system.web>
</configuration>
```

Notice that the web configuration file in Listing 26.4 includes an anonymousIdentification element. Including this element causes a profile to be created for a user even if the user has not been authenticated.

Automatically Detecting a Culture

In the previous section, you learned how to set the UICulture and Culture properties by allowing the user to select a particular culture from a DropDownList control. Instead of requiring users to select their culture, you can automatically detect users' cultures through their browser settings.

Whenever a browser makes a request for a web page, the browser sends an Accept-Language header. The Accept-Language header contains a list of the user's preferred languages.

You can set your preferred languages when using Microsoft Internet Explorer or Mozilla Firefox by selecting the menu option Tools, Internet Options and clicking the Languages button. You can then create an ordered list of your preferred languages (see Figure 26.3). When using Opera, select the menu option Tools, Preferences and click the Details button (see Figure 26.4).

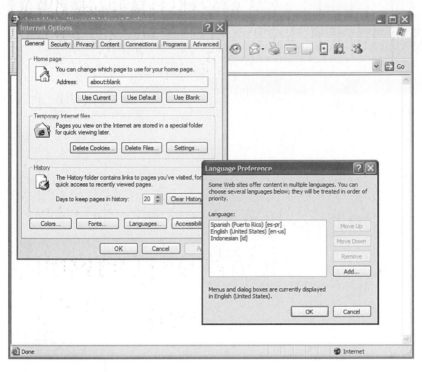

FIGURE 26.3   Setting your preferred language with Internet Explorer.

26

FIGURE 26.4   Setting your preferred language with Opera.

You can retrieve the value of the Accept-Language header by using the `Request.UserLanguages` property. For example, the page in Listing 26.5 displays a list of the languages retrieved from a browser's Accept-Language header (see Figure 26.5).

FIGURE 26.5   Displaying a browser's language settings.

LISTING 26.5   ShowAcceptLanguages.aspx

```
<%@ Page Language="C#" %>
<!DOCTYPE html PUBLIC "-//W3C//DTD XHTML 1.1//EN"
"http://www.w3.org/TR/xhtml11/DTD/xhtml11.dtd">
<script runat="server">

    void Page_Load()
    {
        bltAcceptLanguages.DataSource = Request.UserLanguages;
        bltAcceptLanguages.DataBind();
    }

</script>
<html xmlns="http://www.w3.org/1999/xhtml" >
<head id="Head1" runat="server">
    <title>Show Accept Languages</title>
</head>
<body>
```

```
    <form id="form1" runat="server">
    <div>

    <asp:BulletedList
        id="bltAcceptLanguages"
        Runat="server" />

    </div>
    </form>
</body>
</html>
```

If you want to set the `Culture` or `UICulture` properties automatically by detecting the browser's Accept-Language header, then you can set either of these properties to the value auto. For example, the page in Listing 26.6 automatically displays the date and currency amount according to the user's preferred language.

LISTING 26.6   SelectCultureAuto.aspx

```
<%@ Page Language="C#" Culture="auto:en-US" UICulture="auto:en-US"%>
<!DOCTYPE html PUBLIC "-//W3C//DTD XHTML 1.1//EN"
"http://www.w3.org/TR/xhtml11/DTD/xhtml11.dtd">
<script runat="server">

    void Page_PreRender()
    {
        lblDate.Text = DateTime.Now.ToString("D");
        lblPrice.Text = (512.33m).ToString("c");
    }
</script>
<html xmlns="http://www.w3.org/1999/xhtml" >
<head id="Head1" runat="server">
    <title>Select Culture Auto</title>
</head>
<body>
    <form id="form1" runat="server">
    <div>

    Today's date is:
    <br />
    <asp:Label
        id="lblDate"
        Runat="server" />

    <br /><br />
```

LISTING 26.6   Continued

```
    The price of the product is:
    <br />
    <asp:Label
        id="lblPrice"
        Runat="server" />

    </div>
    </form>
</body>
</html>
```

In the <%@ Page %> directive in Listing 26.6, both the Culture and UICulture attributes are set to the value auto:en-US. The culture name that appears after the colon enables you to specify a default culture when a language preference cannot be detected from the browser.

> **WARNING**
>
> Don't assume that all values of the Accept-Language header retrieved from a browser are valid culture names. Most browsers enable users to enter a "user-defined" language, which may or may not be valid.

Setting the Culture in the Web Configuration File

Rather than set the Culture and UICulture properties in each page, you can set these properties once in the web configuration file. Typically, you should take this approach because it makes your website easier to maintain.

The web configuration file in Listing 26.7 sets both the Culture and UICulture properties to the value de-DE (German).

LISTING 26.7   Web.Config

```
<configuration xmlns="http://schemas.microsoft.com/.NetConfiguration/v2.0">
<system.web>

  <globalization
    culture="de-DE"
    uiCulture="de-DE" />

</system.web>
</configuration>
```

The web configuration file in Listing 26.7 sets the Culture and UICulture for all pages to the value de-DE (German).

If you prefer, you can use the value auto in the web configuration file if you want the culture to be automatically detected based on the value of the browser Accept-Language header. If you need to override the configuration settings in the web configuration file in a particular page, then you can simply set the Culture and UICulture properties in the page.

Culture and ASP.NET Controls

The value of the Culture property automatically has an effect on the rendering behavior of ASP.NET controls such as the Calendar control. For example, Listing 26.8 uses the ASP.NET Calendar control to display a calendar (see Figure 26.6).

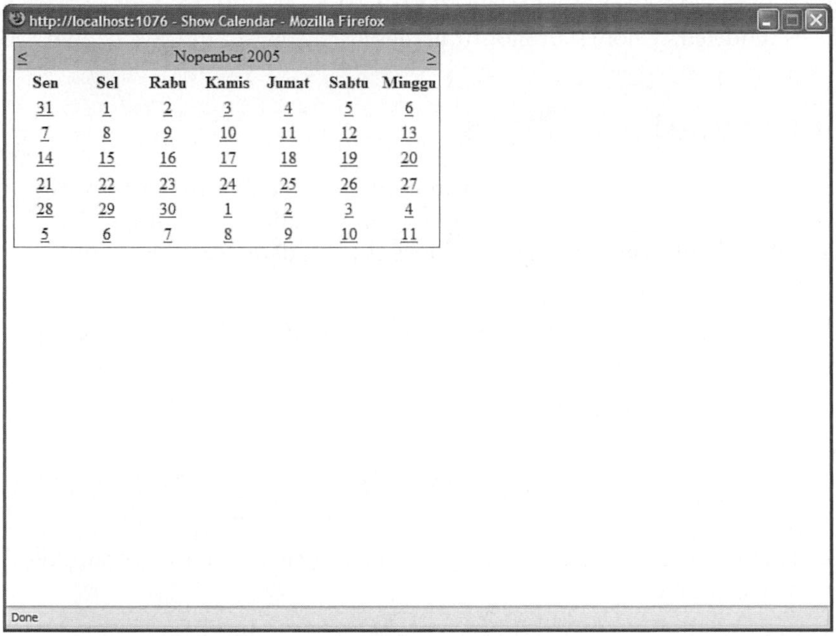

FIGURE 26.6   Displaying a localized Calendar control.

LISTING 26.8   ShowCalendar.aspx

```
<%@ Page Language="C#" Culture="id-ID" %>
<!DOCTYPE html PUBLIC "-//W3C//DTD XHTML 1.1//EN"
"http://www.w3.org/TR/xhtml11/DTD/xhtml11.dtd">
<html xmlns="http://www.w3.org/1999/xhtml" >
<head id="Head1" runat="server">
    <title>Show Calendar</title>
</head>
<body>
    <form id="form1" runat="server">
    <div>
```

LISTING 26.8   Continued

```
    <asp:Calendar
        id="Calendar1"
        Runat="server" />

    </div>
    </form>
</body>
</html>
```

The Culture attribute in the <%@ Page %> directive is set to the value id-ID (Indonesian). When the calendar is rendered, Indonesian month names are displayed in the calendar.

Using the CultureInfo Class

The CultureInfo class contains information about more than 150 different cultures. You can use the methods of this class in your code to retrieve information about a specific culture and use the information when formatting values such as dates, numbers, and currency amounts.

To represent a culture with the CultureInfo class, you can instantiate the class by passing a culture name to the class constructor like this:

```
Dim culture As New CultureInfo("de-DE")
```

You can also use any of the following methods of the CultureInfo class to retrieve information about a culture or cultures:

- ▶ **CreateSpecificCulture**—Enables you to create a CultureInfo object by supplying the name of a specific culture.

- ▶ **GetCultureInfo**—Enables you to create a CultureInfo object by supplying an identifier, culture name, or CompareInfo and TextInfo object.

- ▶ **GetCultureInfoByIetfLanguageTag**—Enables you to create a CultureInfo object efficiently by supplying a culture name.

- ▶ **GetCultures**—Enables you to retrieve an array of cultures.

The CultureInfo class lives in the System.Globalization namespace. Before you can use the CultureInfo class, you need to import this namespace.

Using the CultureInfo Class to Format String Values

To this point, the culture has been set at the level of an individual ASP.NET page or the level of an entire ASP.NET application. However, you might need to take advantage of locale-specific formatting at a more granular level. You can use the CultureInfo class to format a particular value independent of the Culture set for the page.

When you use the `ToString()` method to format dates, times, numbers, and currency amounts, you can supply an additional parameter that formats the value in accordance with a specific culture. For example, the page in Listing 26.9 formats two sets of date and time values.

LISTING 26.9   ToStringCulture.aspx

```
<%@ Page Language="C#" %>
<%@ Import Namespace="System.Globalization" %>
<!DOCTYPE html PUBLIC "-//W3C//DTD XHTML 1.1//EN"
"http://www.w3.org/TR/xhtml11/DTD/xhtml11.dtd">
<script runat="server">

    void Page_Load()
    {
        // Get German Culture Info
        CultureInfo gCulture = new CultureInfo("de-DE");

        // Use culture when formatting strings
        lblGermanDate.Text = DateTime.Now.ToString("D", gCulture);
        lblGermanPrice.Text = (512.33m).ToString("c", gCulture);

        // Get Indonesian Culture Info
        CultureInfo iCulture = new CultureInfo("id-ID");

        // Use culture when formatting strings
        lblIndonesianDate.Text = DateTime.Now.ToString("D", iCulture);
        lblIndonesianPrice.Text = (512.33m).ToString("c", iCulture);
    }
</script>
<html xmlns="http://www.w3.org/1999/xhtml" >
<head id="Head1" runat="server">
    <title>ToString Culture</title>
</head>
<body>
    <form id="form1" runat="server">
    <div>

    <h1>German</h1>

    Today's date is:
    <br />
    <asp:Label
        id="lblGermanDate"
        Runat="server" />
```

LISTING 26.9   Continued

```
    <br /><br />

    The price of the product is:
    <br />
    <asp:Label
        id="lblGermanPrice"
        Runat="server" />


    <h1>Indonesian</h1>

    Today's date is:
    <br />
    <asp:Label
        id="lblIndonesianDate"
        Runat="server" />

    <br /><br />

    The price of the product is:
    <br />
    <asp:Label
        id="lblIndonesianPrice"
        Runat="server" />


    </div>
    </form>
</body>
</html>
```

The first date and time is formatted with German cultural conventions, and the second date and time is formatted with Indonesian cultural conventions (see Figure 26.7). Notice that two `CultureInfo` objects, corresponding to two cultures, are created in the `Page_Load()` method.

Comparing and Sorting String Values

Different cultures follow different conventions when comparing and sorting string values. If you need to compare or sort string values in your code, then you should use the `String.Compare()` method and optionally supply the method with an instance of the `CultureInfo` object.

FIGURE 26.7   Formatting with the ToString() method.

The String.Compare() method returns one of the following values:

- Negative Integer—The first string is less than the second string.

- Zero—The first string is equal to the second string.

- Positive Integer—The first string is greater than the second string.

For example, the following conditional compares two strings, using the current culture set for the page:

```
if (String.Compare("Hello", "Hello") == 0)
  lblResult.Text = "The strings are the same!";
```

The following conditional uses a specific culture to perform a string comparison:

```
if (String.Compare("Hello", "Hello", true, new CultureInfo("de-DE")) == 0)
  lblResult.Text = "The strings are the same!";
```

In this case, the first two parameters passed to the String.Compare() method are the strings being compared. The third parameter indicates whether the comparison performed should be case sensitive or not. Finally, the last parameter represents a CultureInfo object.

Creating Local Resources

If you need to modify the text (or other content) in a page depending on a user's language, then you can take advantage of resource files. Each resource file can contain page text translated into a particular language.

The ASP.NET Framework supports two types of resource files: local and global resources. In this section, you learn how to use local resources. A local resource is scoped to a particular file such as an ASP.NET page.

Explicit Localization Expressions

The page in Listing 26.10 is a very simple page. It contains a button labeled "Click Here!" and displays the text "Thank You!" after you click the button.

LISTING 26.10   SimplePage.aspx

```
<%@ Page Language="C#" %>
<!DOCTYPE html PUBLIC "-//W3C//DTD XHTML 1.1//EN"
"http://www.w3.org/TR/xhtml11/DTD/xhtml11.dtd">
<script runat="server">

    protected void btnSubmit_Click(object sender, EventArgs e)
    {
        lblMessage.Visible = true;
    }
</script>
<html xmlns="http://www.w3.org/1999/xhtml" >
<head id="Head1" runat="server">
    <title>Simple Page</title>
</head>
<body>
    <form id="form1" runat="server">
    <div>

    <asp:Button
        id="btnSubmit"
        Text="Click Here!"
        OnClick="btnSubmit_Click"
        Runat="server" />

    <br /><br />

    <asp:Label
        id="lblMessage"
        Text="Thank You!"
```

```
            Visible="false"
            Runat="server" />

      </div>
      </form>
</body>
</html>
```

The page in Listing 26.10 displays the same text regardless of the language of the user visiting the page. If you want to display text in different languages for different users, then you need to make a few modifications to the page.

The page in Listing 26.11 is a localizable version of the same page.

LISTING 26.11   LocalizablePage.aspx

```
<%@ Page Language="C#" UICulture="auto" %>
<!DOCTYPE html PUBLIC "-//W3C//DTD XHTML 1.1//EN"
"http://www.w3.org/TR/xhtml11/DTD/xhtml11.dtd">
<script runat="server">

    protected void btnSubmit_Click(object sender, EventArgs e)
    {
        lblMessage.Visible = true;
    }
</script>
<html xmlns="http://www.w3.org/1999/xhtml" >
<head id="Head1" runat="server">
    <title>Localizable Page</title>
</head>
<body>
    <form id="form1" runat="server">
    <div>

    <asp:Button
        id="btnSubmit"
        Text="<%$ Resources:ClickHere %>"
        OnClick="btnSubmit_Click"
        Runat="server" />

    <br /><br />

    <asp:Label
        id="lblMessage"
        Text="<%$ Resources:ThankYou %>"
        Visible="false"
```

LISTING 26.11   Continued

```
        Runat="server" />

    </div>
    </form>
</body>
</html>
```

Two types of changes were made to the page in Listing 26.11. First, notice that the <%@
Page %> directive includes a UICulture attribute that is set to the value auto. When a user
requests the page, a resource file that matches the user's preferred browser language is
loaded automatically.

> **NOTE**
>
> Don't confuse the Page UICulture property with the Page Culture property. The
> UICulture property determines which resource files are loaded for the page. The
> Culture property, on the other hand, determines how date, number, and currency val-
> ues are formatted.

Second, notice that both the Button and Label controls have been modified. The Button
control is declared like this:

```
<asp:Button
    id="btnSubmit"
    Text="<%$ Resources:ClickHere %>"
    OnClick="btnSubmit_Click"
    Runat="server" />
```

The value of the Text property is a resource expression. This resource expression retrieves
the value of an entry named ClickHere from the loaded resource file. This resource expression is considered to be an *explicit* resource expression because the property is explicitly set
to the value of a particular resource entry.

After you localize a page, you can associate a resource file with the page. All the resource
files that you want to associate with a page must be added to a special folder named
App_LocalResources. You create the App_LocalResources folder in the same folder as the
page that you want to localize. For example, if the page is located in the root of your
application, then you would add the App_LocalResources folder to the root folder.

You associate a resource file in the App_LocalResources folder with a particular page by
using the following file naming convention:

```
page name.[culture name].resx
```

For example, all the following resource files are associated with the
LocalizablePage.aspx page:

```
LocalizablePage.aspx.resx
LocalizablePage.aspx.es-PR.resx
LocalizablePage.aspx.es.resx
```

The first resource file is the default resource file. If none of the other resource files match the user's language settings, then the contents of the default resource file are used.

The second resource file name includes the specific culture name es-PR (Puerto Rican Spanish). If a user's browser is set to Puerto Rican Spanish, then the contents of this resource file are loaded.

Finally, the third resource file name includes the neutral culture name es (Spanish). If a user's preferred language is Spanish, but not Puerto Rican Spanish, then the contents of this resource file are loaded.

You create a resource file when using Visual Web Developing by right-clicking an App_LocalResources folder, selecting Add New Item, and selecting Assembly Resource file. Visual Web Developer automatically displays an editor for the resource file. The editor enables you to enter name and value pairs. For example, the LocalizablePage.aspx.es.resx resource file contains the two name/value pairs in Listing 26.12.

LISTING 26.12   App_LocalResources\LocalizablePage.aspx.es.resx

Name	Value
ClickHere	chasque aquí
ThankYou	¡Gracias!

Behind the scenes, resource files are XML files. You can open a resource file in Notepad and edit its contents. The ASP.NET Framework dynamically compiles resource files into assemblies in the background.

Implicit Localization Expressions

As an alternative to using explicit localization expressions, you can use an implicit localization expression. An implicit localization expression enables you to localize multiple control properties with one resource key.

The page in Listing 26.13 uses implicit localization expressions.

LISTING 26.13   LocalizablePageImplicit.aspx

```
<%@ Page Language="C#" UICulture="auto" %>
<!DOCTYPE html PUBLIC "-//W3C//DTD XHTML 1.1//EN"
"http://www.w3.org/TR/xhtml11/DTD/xhtml11.dtd">
<script runat="server">

    protected void btnSubmit_Click(object sender, EventArgs e)
    {
```

LISTING 26.13   Continued

```
            lblMessage.Visible = true;
    }
</script>
<html xmlns="http://www.w3.org/1999/xhtml" >
<head id="Head1" runat="server">
    <title>Localizable Page Implicit</title>
</head>
<body>
    <form id="form1" runat="server">
    <div>

    <asp:Button
        id="btnSubmit"
        meta:resourceKey="btnSubmit"
        Text="Click Me!"
        ToolTip="Click to show message"
        OnClick="btnSubmit_Click"
        Runat="server" />

    <br /><br />

    <asp:Label
        id="lblMessage"
        meta:resourceKey="lblMessage"
        Text="Thank You!"
        Visible="false"
        Runat="server" />

    </div>
    </form>
</body>
</html>
```

Notice that both the Button and Label control include a meta:resourceKey property. The value of this property represents a resource key in a local resource file.

For example, the resource file in Listing 26.14 contains three entries.

LISTING 26.14   App_LocalResources\LocalizablePageImplicit.aspx.es.resx

Name	Value
btnSubmit.Text	chasque aquí
btnSubmit.ToolTip	Chasque aquí para demostrar el mensaje
lblMessage.Text	¡Gracias!

The first two entries set the Text and ToolTip properties of the btnSubmit control. The third entry sets the value of the Text property of the lblMessage property.

> **WARNING**
>
> When you are ready to start localizing a page, always create a default localization file (for example, LocalizablePageImplicit.aspx.resx). If you don't create a default localization file, other culture-specific localization files are ignored.

There are two advantages to using implicit localization expressions over using explicit localization expressions. First, implicit expressions enable you to override multiple control properties by associating a single resource key with the control.

Second, by taking advantage of implicit localization expressions, you can more easily localize an existing website. You simply need to add the meta:resourceKey attribute to any control that you need to localize.

Using Local Resources with Page Properties

You can use resource expressions when setting page properties such as the page title. For example, the page in Listing 26.15 uses an explicit resource expression to set the page title.

LISTING 26.15   PageExplicit.aspx

```
<%@ Page Language="C#" UICulture="auto" %>
<!DOCTYPE html PUBLIC "-//W3C//DTD XHTML 1.1//EN"
    "http://www.w3.org/TR/xhtml11/DTD/xhtml11.dtd">
<html xmlns="http://www.w3.org/1999/xhtml" >
<head id="Head1" runat="server">
    <title><asp:Literal Text="<%$ Resources:Title %>" runat="Server" /></title>
</head>
<body>
    <form id="form1" runat="server">
    <div>

    <h1>Page Explicit Localization</h1>


    </div>
    </form>
</body>
</html>
```

26

In Listing 26.15, the page title is created with a `Literal` control. The `Literal` control contains an explicit resource expression for the value of its `Text` property.

You also can use implicit resource expressions when setting the page title. This approach is illustrated by the page in Listing 26.16.

LISTING 26.16   PageImplicit.aspx

```
<%@ Page Language="C#" UICulture="auto" meta:resourceKey="page" %>
<!DOCTYPE html PUBLIC "-//W3C//DTD XHTML 1.1//EN"
    "http://www.w3.org/TR/xhtml11/DTD/xhtml11.dtd">
<html xmlns="http://www.w3.org/1999/xhtml" >
<head id="Head1" runat="server">
    <title>Page Title</title>
</head>
<body>
    <form id="form1" runat="server">
    <div>

    <h1>Page Implicit Localization</h1>

    </div>
    </form>
</body>
</html>
```

Notice that the `<%@ Page %>` directive includes a `meta:resourceKey` attribute. If a local resource includes a `page.Title` entry, then the value of this entry is used for the title displayed by the page.

Retrieving Local Resources Programmatically

If you need to retrieve a local resource in your page code, then you can use the `GetLocalResourceObject()` method. For example, the page in Listing 26.17 grabs a welcome message from a resource file. The welcome message is used to format some text, and then the formatted text is displayed in a `Label` control.

LISTING 26.17   ProgramLocal.aspx

```
<%@ Page Language="C#" %>
<!DOCTYPE html PUBLIC "-//W3C//DTD XHTML 1.1//EN"
"http://www.w3.org/TR/xhtml11/DTD/xhtml11.dtd">
<script runat="server">
```

```
    void Page_Load()
    {
        string welcomeMessage = (string)GetLocalResourceObject("welcomeMessage");
        lblMessage.Text = String.Format(welcomeMessage, "Steve");
    }

</script>
<html xmlns="http://www.w3.org/1999/xhtml" >
<head id="Head1" runat="server">
    <title>Program Local Resource</title>
</head>
<body>
    <form id="form1" runat="server">
    <div>

    <asp:Label
        id="lblMessage"
        Runat="server" />

    </div>
    </form>
</body>
</html>
```

Notice that the result returned from the `GetLocalResourceObject()` must be cast to a string value. As the method name implies, the method returns an object and not a string value.

The resource file associated with the page in Listing 26.17, named `ProgramLocal.aspx.es.resx`, is contained in Listing 26.18.

LISTING 26.18   `App_LocalResources\ProgramLocal.aspx.es.resx`

Name	Value
welcomeMessage	Welcome {0} to our website!

If someone's browser is set to Spanish as the preferred language, and the user requests the page, then the welcome message is retrieved from this resource file, the name Steve is added to the string, and the result is displayed in the browser (see Figure 26.8).

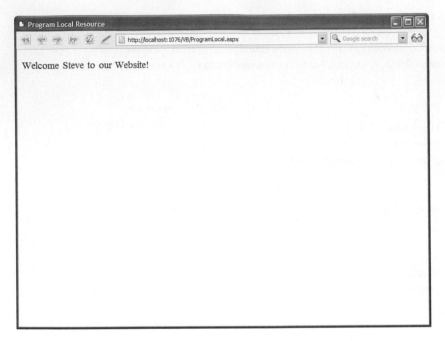

FIGURE 26.8   Retrieving a local resource programmatically.

You also can retrieve local resources in a component. Within a component, use the shared
HttpContext.GetLocalResourceObject() method. For example, the component in
Listing 26.19 grabs the entry named ClickHere from the local resource file that corre-
sponds to the page named LocalizablePage.aspx.

LISTING 26.19   LocalComponent.cs

```
using System;
using System.Web;

public class LocalComponent
{
    public static string getResource()
    {
        return (string)HttpContext.GetLocalResourceObject("~/LocalizablePage.aspx",
"ClickHere");
    }
}
```

Creating Global Resources

A local resource is scoped to a particular page. A global resource, on the other hand, can be used by any page in an application. Any localized content that you need to share among multiple pages in your website should be added to a global resource file.

You create global resource files by adding the files to a special folder named App_GlobalResources. This folder must be located in the root of your application.

For example, the file in Listing 26.20 is a global resource file.

LISTING 26.20   App_GlobalResources\Site.resx

Name	Value
Title	My website
Copyright	Copyright © 2006 by the Company

The page in Listing 26.21 uses the entries from the global resource file (see Figure 26.9).

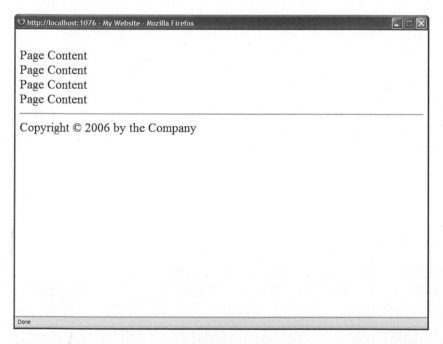

FIGURE 26.9   Displaying global resource entries.

LISTING 26.21   ShowGlobalPage.aspx

```
<%@ Page Language="C#" %>
<!DOCTYPE html PUBLIC "-//W3C//DTD XHTML 1.1//EN"
    "http://www.w3.org/TR/xhtml11/DTD/xhtml11.dtd">
<html xmlns="http://www.w3.org/1999/xhtml" >
<head id="Head1" runat="server">
    <title>
    <asp:Literal
        id="ltlTitle"
        Text="<%$ Resources:Site,Title %>"
        Runat="Server" />
    </title>
</head>
<body>
    <form id="form1" runat="server">
    <div>

    <br />Page Content
    <br />Page Content
    <br />Page Content
    <br />Page Content

    <hr />
    <asp:Literal
        id="ltlCopyright"
        Text="<%$ Resources:Site,Copyright %>"
        Runat="Server" />

    </div>
    </form>
</body>
</html>
```

Just as you can with a local resource file, you can localize a global resource file by adding culture names to the filename. For example, the page in Listing 26.22 is localized to Spanish.

LISTING 26.22   App_GlobalResources\Site.es.resx

Name	Value
Title	Mi Website
Copyright	Copyright © 2006 de la compañía

If you modify the `UICulture` attribute contained in the `<%@ Page %>` directive in Listing 26.21 to the value `es`, then the resource file in Listing 26.22 will be used with the page. Alternatively, you can set `UICulture` to the value `auto` and change your browser's language settings.

Retrieving Global Resources Programmatically

You can retrieve a global resource entry programmatically from any page by using the `GetGlobalResourceObject()` method. For example, the page in Listing 26.23 grabs the Title entry from the Site resource file and displays the value of the entry in a `Label` control.

LISTING 26.23   ProgramGlobal.aspx

```
<%@ Page Language="C#" UICulture="auto" %>
<!DOCTYPE html PUBLIC "-//W3C//DTD XHTML 1.1//EN"
"http://www.w3.org/TR/xhtml11/DTD/xhtml11.dtd">
<script runat="server">

    void Page_Load()
    {
        lblMessage.Text = (string)GetGlobalResourceObject("Site", "Title");
    }
</script>
<html xmlns="http://www.w3.org/1999/xhtml" >
<head id="Head1" runat="server">
    <title>Program Global</title>
</head>
<body>
    <form id="form1" runat="server">
    <div>

    <asp:Label
        id="lblMessage"
        Runat="server" />

    </div>
    </form>
</body>
</html>
```

The `GetGlobalResourceObject()` method requires two parameters: the name of the resource class and the name of an entry. The resource class corresponds to the global resource filename.

Using Strongly Typed Localization Expressions

The ASP.NET Framework automatically converts global resources into compiled classes behind the scenes. This enables you to use strongly typed expressions when working with global resources in your code.

When you create a resource, a new class is added automatically to the Resources namespace. The class exposes all the entries of the resource file as properties.

For example, the page in Listing 26.24 retrieves the Title entry from the Site global resource file (Site.resx and its culture-specific variations).

LISTING 26.24   ProgramGlobalTyped.aspx

```
<%@ Page Language="C#" UICulture="auto" %>
<!DOCTYPE html PUBLIC "-//W3C//DTD XHTML 1.1//EN"
"http://www.w3.org/TR/xhtml11/DTD/xhtml11.dtd">
<script runat="server">

    void Page_Load()
    {
        lblMessage.Text = Resources.Site.Title;
    }
</script>
<html xmlns="http://www.w3.org/1999/xhtml" >
<head id="Head1" runat="server">
    <title>Program Global Typed</title>
</head>
<body>
    <form id="form1" runat="server">
    <div>

    <asp:Label
        id="lblMessage"
        Runat="server" />

    </div>
    </form>
</body>
</html>
```

Notice that you can use the following expression magically to refer to the Title entry in the Site resource file:

```
lblMessage.Text = Resources.Site.Title
```

Using the Localize Control

The ASP.NET Framework includes a control named the Localize control. This control is included in the Framework to make it easier to localize big chunks of text in a page.

For example, the page in Listing 26.25 uses the Localize control in the body of the page.

LISTING 26.25 ShowLocalizeControl.aspx

```
<%@ Page Language="C#" UICulture="auto" %>
<!DOCTYPE html PUBLIC "-//W3C//DTD XHTML 1.1//EN"
    "http://www.w3.org/TR/xhtml11/DTD/xhtml11.dtd">
<html xmlns="http://www.w3.org/1999/xhtml" >
<head id="Head1" runat="server">
    <title>Show Localize Control</title>
</head>
<body>
    <form id="form1" runat="server">
    <div>

    <asp:Localize
        ID="locBodyText"
        meta:resourceKey="locBodyText"
        Runat="server">
        Here is the page body text
    </asp:Localize>

    <br /><br />

    <asp:Literal
        ID="ltlBodyText"
        runat="server">
        Here is some literal text
    </asp:Literal>

    </div>
    </form>
</body>
</html>
```

The Localize control is very similar to the Literal control (it derives from the Literal control). In SourceView, there is nothing that distinguishes the two controls. The difference between the Localize control and Literal control is apparent only in DesignView.

Unlike the Literal control, the contents of the Localize control can be edited directly on the Designer surface in DesignView (see Figure 26.10).

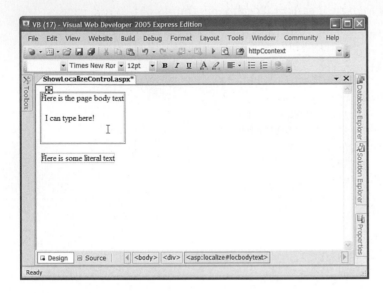

FIGURE 26.10   Using the Localize control in Design View.

Summary

In this chapter, you learned how to localize websites for different languages and culture. In the first section, you learned how to use the Culture and UICulture properties to set the current culture for the page. You also learned how to set these properties automatically by detecting a browser's preferred language settings.

Next, you learned how to create local resource files that you can apply to particular pages (and other files). You learned how to use both explicit and implicit localization expressions. You also saw how you can programmatically retrieve local resource entries in your code.

You then studied the topic of global resource files, which contain entries that can be used within any page in a website. You learned to use explicit resource expressions with global resources and how to retrieve global resource entries programmatically.

Finally, you had a brief look at the ASP.NET Localize control. You learned how to use this control to localize big chunks of text in a page.

CHAPTER 27

Working with the HTTP Runtime

This chapter tackles a number of advanced topics by digging deeper into the mechanics of how an ASP.NET page is processed. In this first section, you learn how to create a custom `BuildProvider`. A `BuildProvider` is a .NET class that generates source code from a file automatically. You learn how to create a custom `BuildProvider` that builds custom data access components automatically.

Next, you learn how to create a custom `ExpressionBuilder`. An `ExpressionBuilder` is responsible for parsing an expression into code. For example, when you use the `<%$ ConnectionStrings:MyDatabase %>` syntax to refer to a connection string, you are using the `ConnectionStringExpressionBuilder` in the background. In this chapter, you learn how to build a custom `ExpressionBuilder` that looks up values from an XML file.

You also learn how to work with HTTP Handlers. An HTTP Handler is a .NET class that executes whenever a request is made for a file at a certain path. For example, you can use a custom HTTP Handler to retrieve an image from a database table whenever someone requests a file with the extension `.gif` or `.jpeg`.

Finally, you learn how to create custom HTTP Modules. An HTTP Module is a .NET class that executes with each and every request. For example, you can implement a custom authentication system by creating a custom HTTP Module. You also can use a custom HTTP Module to create a custom logging module.

Creating a Custom `BuildProvider`

When you write an ASP.NET page and save the page to your computer's file system, the ASP.NET page gets compiled dynamically into a .NET class in the background. The page is compiled dynamically by a `BuildProvider`.

The ASP.NET Framework includes a number of `BuildProviders`. Each `BuildProvider` is responsible for compiling a file with a particular extension that is located in a particular type of folder. For example, there are `BuildProviders` for Themes, Master Pages, User Controls, and Web Services.

When a `BuildProvider` builds, it builds a new class in the Temporary ASP.NET Files folder. Any class added to the folder becomes available to your application automatically. When you use Visual Web Developer, any public properties and methods of the class appear in Intellisense.

You can create your own `BuildProviders`. This can be useful in a variety of different scenarios. For example, imagine that you find yourself building a lot of ASP.NET pages that display forms. You can tediously build each ASP.NET page by hand by adding all the necessary form and validation controls. Alternatively, you can create a new `BuildProvider` that takes an XML file and generates the form pages for you automatically.

Or, imagine that you are spending a lot of time building data access components. For example, every time you need to access a database table, you create a new component that exposes properties that correspond to each of the columns in the database table. In this case, it would make sense to create a custom `BuildProvider` that generates the data access component automatically.

Creating a Simple `BuildProvider`

Let's start by creating a really simple `BuildProvider`. The new `BuildProvider` will be named the `SimpleBuildProvider`. Whenever you create a file that has the extension `.simple`, the `SimpleBuilderProvider` builds a new class with the same name as the file in the background. The dynamically compiled class also includes a single method named `DoSomething()` that doesn't actually do anything.

The `SimpleBuildProvider` is contained in Listing 27.1.

LISTING 27.1   App_Code\CustomBuildProviders\SimpleBuildProvider.cs

```
using System;
using System.Web.Compilation;
using System.CodeDom;
using System.IO;

namespace AspNetUnleashed
{
    public class SimpleBuildProvider : BuildProvider
```

```
    {
        public override void GenerateCode(AssemblyBuilder ab)
        {
            string fileName = Path.GetFileNameWithoutExtension(this.VirtualPath);
            string snippet = "public class " + fileName + @"
                {
                    public static void DoSomething(){}
                }";
            ab.AddCodeCompileUnit(this, new CodeSnippetCompileUnit(snippet));
        }


    }
}
```

All `BuildProviders` must inherit from the base `BuildProvider` class. Typically, you override the `BuildProvider` class `GenerateCode()` method. This method is responsible for generating the class that gets added to the Temporary ASP.NET Files folder.

An instance of the `AssemblyBuilder` class is passed to the `GenerateCode()` method. You add the class that you want to create to this `AssemblyBuilder` by calling the `AssemblyBuilder.AddCodeCompileUnit()` method.

In Listing 27.1, a `CodeSnippetCompileUnit` is used to represent the source code for the class. Any code that you represent with the `CodeSnippetCompileUnit` is added, verbatim, to the dynamically generated class. This approach is problematic.

Unfortunately, you can use the `SimpleBuildProvider` in Listing 27.1 only when building a C# application. It doesn't work with a Visual Basic .NET application. Because the code represented by the `CodeSnippetCompileUnit` is C# code, using the `SimpleBuildProvider` with a Visual Basic .NET application would result in compilation errors. The `SimpleBuildProvider` would inject C# code into a Visual Basic .NET assembly.

The proper way to write the `SimpleBuildProvider` class would be to use the `CodeDom`. The `CodeDom` enables you to represent .NET code in a language neutral manner. When you represent a block of code with the `CodeDom`, the code can be converted to either C# or Visual Basic .NET code automatically. You learn how to use the `CodeDom` when we build a more complicated `BuildProvider` in the next section. For now, just realize that we are taking a shortcut to keep things simple.

When you add the `SimpleBuildProvider` to your project, it is important that you add the file to a separate subfolder in your App_Code folder and you mark the folder as a separate code folder in the web configuration file. For example, in the sample code on the CD that accompanies this book, the `SimpleBuildProvider` is located in the App_Code\ CustomBuildProviders folder.

You must add a `BuildProvider` to a separate subfolder because a `BuildProvider` must be compiled into a different assembly than the other code in the App_Code folder. This makes sense because a `BuildProvider` is actually responsible for compiling the other code in the App_Code folder.

The web configuration file in Listing 27.2 defines the CustomBuildProviders folder and registers the `SimpleBuildProvider`.

LISTING 27.2 Web.Config

```
<configuration>
    <system.web>

      <compilation>
        <codeSubDirectories>
          <add directoryName="CustomBuildProviders"/>
        </codeSubDirectories>
        <buildProviders>
          <add extension=".simple" type="AspNetUnleashed.SimpleBuildProvider" />
        </buildProviders>
      </compilation>

    </system.web>
</configuration>
```

The web configuration file in Listing 27.2 associates the `SimpleBuildProvider` with the file extension `.simple`. Whenever you add a file with the `.simple` extension to the App_Code folder, the `SimpleBuildProvider` automatically compiles a new class based on the file.

> **NOTE**
>
> Build Providers execute at different times depending on the type of folder. Build Providers associated with the App_Code folder execute immediately after a new file is saved. (Oddly, the Build Provider executes twice.) Build Providers associated with the Web or App_Data folders execute when a file is requested.

For example, adding the file in Listing 27.3 to your App_Code folder causes the `SimpleBuildProvider` to create a new class named `Mike`.

LISTING 27.3 App_Code\Mike.simple

```
Hello!
Hello!
Hello!
```

The actual content of the file that you create doesn't matter. The `SimpleBuildProvider` ignores everything about the file except for the name of the file.

You can see the new file created by the `SimpleBuildProvider` by navigating to the Sources_App_Code folder contained in the folder that corresponds to your application in the Temporary ASP.NET Files folder. The contents of the auto-generated file are contained in Listing 27.4.

LISTING 27.4 `mike.simple.72cecc2a.cs`

```
#pragma checksum "C:\Chapter27\Code\CS\App_Code\Mike.simple" "{406ea660-64cf-4c82-
b6f0-42d48172a799}" "AD2E00BE337DD88E4E4B07F6B4580617"
public class Mike
{
  public static void DoSomething(){}
}
```

Any class added to the Temporary ASP.NET Files folder is available in your application automatically. For example, the page in Listing 27.5 uses the `Mike` class.

LISTING 27.5 `ShowSimpleBuildProvider.aspx`

```
<%@ Page Language="C#" %>
<!DOCTYPE html PUBLIC "-//W3C//DTD XHTML 1.0 Transitional//EN"
"http://www.w3.org/TR/xhtml1/DTD/xhtml1-transitional.dtd">
<script runat="server">

    void Page_Load()
    {
        Mike.DoSomething();
    }
</script>
<html xmlns="http://www.w3.org/1999/xhtml" >
<head id="Head1" runat="server">
    <title>Show SimpleBuildProvider</title>
</head>
<body>
    <form id="form1" runat="server">
    <div>

    </div>
    </form>
</body>
</html>
```

27

The Mike class appears in Intellisense. For example, if you type **Mike** followed by a period, the DoSomething() method appears (see Figure 27.1).

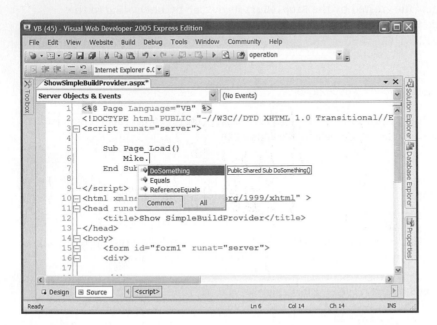

FIGURE 27.1   Using a BuildProvider to generate a class dynamically.

Creating a Data Access Component BuildProvider

In the previous section, we created a simple but useless BuildProvider. In this section, we create a complicated but useful BuildProvider. The DataBuildProvider generates a data access component automatically from an XML file. For example, if you add the XML file in Listing 27.6 to your project, then the DataBuildProvider generates the class in Listing 27.7 automatically.

LISTING 27.6   App_Code\Movie.data

```
<Movies>
  <add name="Title" />
  <add name="Director" />
  <add name="BoxOfficeTotals" type="Decimal" />
</Movies>
```

LISTING 27.7   movie.data.72cecc2a.cs

```csharp
#pragma checksum "C:\Documents and Settings\Steve\My Documents\ASP.NET 3.5
  Unleashed\Chapter27\Code\CS\App_Code\Movie.data" "{406ea660-64cf-4c82-b6f0-
  42d48172a799}" "2E0F31E6B8F9D4B8687F94F0305E6D15"
//———————————————————————————————————
// <auto-generated>
//     This code was generated by a tool.
//     Runtime Version:2.0.50727.1378
//
//     Changes to this file may cause incorrect behavior and will be lost if
//     the code is regenerated.
// </auto-generated>
//———————————————————————————————————

namespace Data {
    using System;

    public partial class Movie {

        private string _Title;
        private string _Director;
        private Decimal _BoxOfficeTotals;

        public Movie() {
        }

        public virtual string Title {
            get {
                return this._Title;
            }
            set {
                this._Title = value;
            }
        }

        public virtual string Director {
            get {
                return this._Director;
            }
            set {
                this._Director = value;
            }
        }

        public virtual Decimal BoxOfficeTotals {
```

27

LISTING 27.7   Continued

```
        get {
            return this._BoxOfficeTotals;
        }
        set {
            this._BoxOfficeTotals = value;
        }
    }

    /// <summary>Returns List of Movie</summary>
    public static System.Collections.Generic.List<Movie>
    ➥Select(System.Data.SqlClient.SqlConnection con) {
        System.Collections.Generic.List<Movie> results = new
        ➥System.Collections.Generic.List<Movie>();
        System.Data.SqlClient.SqlCommand cmd = new System.Data.SqlClient.
        ➥SqlCommand();
        cmd.Connection = con;
        string cmdText = "SELECT Title,Director,BoxOfficeTotals FROM Movies";
        cmd.CommandText = cmdText;
        System.Data.SqlClient.SqlDataReader reader = cmd.ExecuteReader();
        int counter;
        for (counter = 0; reader.Read(); counter = (counter + 1)) {
            Movie record = new Movie();
            record.Title = ((string)(reader["Title"]));
            record.Director = ((string)(reader["Director"]));
            record.BoxOfficeTotals = ((Decimal)(reader["BoxOfficeTotals"]));
            results.Add(record);
        }
        return results;
    }

    /// <summary>Returns List of Movie</summary>
    public static System.Collections.Generic.List<Movie> Select(string
    ➥connectionStringName) {
        System.Collections.Generic.List<Movie> results = new
        ➥System.Collections.Generic.List<Movie>();
        System.Configuration.ConnectionStringSettings conStringSettings =
        ➥System.Web.Configuration.WebConfigurationManager.ConnectionStrings
        ➥[connectionStringName];
        string conString = conStringSettings.ConnectionString;
        System.Data.SqlClient.SqlConnection con = new
        ➥System.Data.SqlClient.SqlConnection();
        con.ConnectionString = conString;
        try {
            con.Open();
```

```
                    results = Movie.Select(con);
                }
                finally {
                    con.Close();
                }
                return results;
            }
        }
    }
}
```

The XML file in Listing 27.6 contains the name of a database table (Movies) and a list of columns from the database table. When you add the file in Listing 27.6 to your project, the class in Listing 27.7 is generated automatically.

The data access component in Listing 27.7 contains a property that corresponds to each of the columns listed in the `Movie.data` file. Furthermore, each property has the data type specified in the `Movie.data` file.

Notice, furthermore, that the Movie data access component includes two `Select()` methods. You can retrieve all the records from the Movies database table in two ways: by passing an open `SqlConnection` object to the `Select()` method or by passing the name of a connection string defined in the web configuration file to the `Select()` method.

The page in Listing 27.8 illustrates how you can use the Movie data access component within an ASP.NET page (see Figure 27.2).

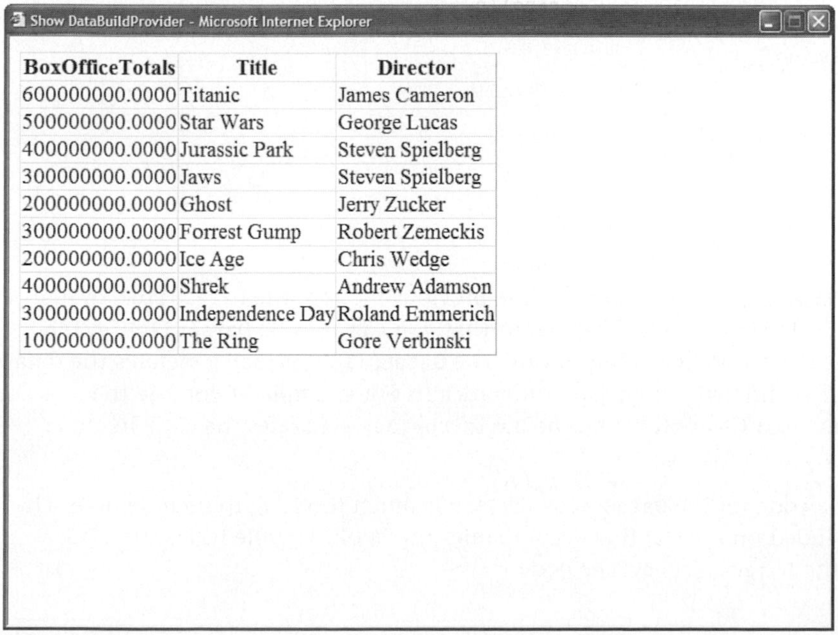

BoxOfficeTotals	Title	Director
600000000.0000	Titanic	James Cameron
500000000.0000	Star Wars	George Lucas
400000000.0000	Jurassic Park	Steven Spielberg
300000000.0000	Jaws	Steven Spielberg
200000000.0000	Ghost	Jerry Zucker
300000000.0000	Forrest Gump	Robert Zemeckis
200000000.0000	Ice Age	Chris Wedge
400000000.0000	Shrek	Andrew Adamson
300000000.0000	Independence Day	Roland Emmerich
100000000.0000	The Ring	Gore Verbinski

27

FIGURE 27.2   Displaying data returned by a dynamically generated data access component.

LISTING 27.8   ShowDataBuildProvider.aspx

```
<%@ Page Language="C#" %>
<!DOCTYPE html PUBLIC "-//W3C//DTD XHTML 1.0 Transitional//EN"
"http://www.w3.org/TR/xhtml1/DTD/xhtml1-transitional.dtd">

<script runat="server">

    void Page_Load()
    {
        grdMovies.DataSource = Data.Movie.Select("Movies");
        grdMovies.DataBind();
    }

</script>

<html xmlns="http://www.w3.org/1999/xhtml" >
<head id="Head1" runat="server">
    <title>Untitled Page</title>
</head>
<body>
    <form id="form1" runat="server">
    <div>

    <asp:GridView
        id="grdMovies"
        Runat="server" />

    </div>
    </form>
</body>
</html>
```

Unlike the `SimpleBuildProvider` created in the previous section, the `DataBuildProvider` uses the `CodeDom` to represent code. This means that you can use the `DataBuildProvider` in both Visual Basic .NET and C# applications. The `DataBuildProvider` generates the data access component in different languages automatically. For example, if you use the `DataBuildProvider` in a C# application, the `BuildProvider` generates the code in Listing 27.6 in C#.

Unfortunately, the code for the `DataBuildProvider` is much too long to include here. The entire code is included on the CD that accompanies the book. The file in Listing 27.9 contains part of the `DataBuildProvider` code.

LISTING 27.9   DataBuildProvider.cs (Partial)

```csharp
using System;
using System.Collections.Generic;
using System.Web.Compilation;
using System.CodeDom;
using System.Xml;
using System.IO;
using System.Web.Hosting;

namespace AspNetUnleashed
{
    public class DataBuildProvider : BuildProvider
    {
        string _className;

        public override void GenerateCode(AssemblyBuilder ab)
        {
            // Load the XML file
            XmlDocument xmlData = new XmlDocument();
            xmlData.Load(HostingEnvironment.MapPath(this.VirtualPath));

            // Generate code from XML document
            CodeCompileUnit dataCode = GetDataCode(xmlData);

            // Add the code
            ab.AddCodeCompileUnit(this, dataCode);
        }

        private CodeCompileUnit GetDataCode(XmlDocument xmlData)
        {
            // Add class
            _className = Path.GetFileNameWithoutExtension(this.VirtualPath);
            CodeTypeDeclaration dataType = new CodeTypeDeclaration(_className);
            dataType.IsPartial = true;

            // Add constructor
            AddConstructor(dataType);

            // Add properties
            AddProperties(dataType, xmlData);

            // Add Select method
            AddSelect(dataType, xmlData);

            // Add Select with conString overload
```

LISTING 27.9   Continued

```
                AddSelectConString(dataType, xmlData);

                // Create namespace
                CodeNamespace dataNS = new CodeNamespace("Data");

                // Add class to namespace
                dataNS.Types.Add(dataType);

                // Create code unit
                CodeCompileUnit dataCode = new CodeCompileUnit();

                // Add namespace to code unit
                dataCode.Namespaces.Add(dataNS);

                // Add default namespaces
                dataNS.Imports.Add(new CodeNamespaceImport("System"));

                return dataCode;
            }
        }
}
```

The DataBuildProvider's GenerateCode() method loads a .data file into an XmlDocument.
Notice that the VirtualPath property represents the path of the file that is being built. For
example, if you add a file named Products.data to your project, then the VirtualPath
property would represent the path to the Products.data file.

Next, the code for the data access component is created from the XML file by the
GetDataCode() method. The GetDataCode() method makes heavy use of the CodeDom to
generate the code in a language-neutral manner.

Working with the CodeDom is a strange and tedious experience. You must build up a block
of code by building a code tree. In Listing 27.9, a CodeCompileUnit named dataCode is
created. A CodeNamespace named dataNS that represents a namespace is created and added
to the CodeCompileUnit. And, a CodeTypeDeclaration named datatype that represents a
class is added to the namespace. After the class is created, the methods and properties are
added to the class block by block.

Creating a Custom **ExpressionBuilder**

An ExpressionBuilder class generates one expression from another expression. Typically, you use an ExpressionBuilder to look up a particular value given a particular key.

The ASP.NET Framework includes the following ExpressionBuilder classes:

- ▶ **AppSettingsExpressionBuilder**—Retrieves values from the appSettings section of the web configuration file.

- ▶ **ConnectionStringsExpressionBuilder**—Retrieves values from the connectionStrings section of the web configuration file.

- ▶ **ResourceExpressionBuilder**—Retrieves values from resource files.

The ConnectionStringsExpressionBuilder has been used throughout this book whenever a connection string has needed to be retrieved.

You use the following syntax when working with an ExpressionBuilder:

```
<%$ ConnectionStrings:MyDatabase %>
```

The <%$ and %> tags are used to mark an expression that should be parsed by an ExpressionBuilder. The prefix ConnectionStrings is mapped to the particular ExpressionBuilder class that is responsible for parsing the expression.

ExpressionBuilders must always be used with control properties. For example, you cannot display a connection string in a page like this:

```
<%$ ConnectionStrings:MyDatabase %>
```

Instead, you must display the connection string like this:

```
<asp:Literal
  Id="ltlConnectionString"
  Text='<%$ ConnectionStrings:MyDatabase %>'
  Runat="server" />
```

You can create a custom ExpressionBuilder when none of the existing ExpressionBuilder classes do what you need. For example, you might want to store your application settings in a custom section of the web configuration file. In that case, you might want to create a custom ExpressionBuilder that grabs values from the custom configuration section.

27

Creating a Lookup ExpressionBuilder

In this section, you learn how to extend the ASP.NET Framework by building a custom ExpressionBuilder class. We'll create a Lookup ExpressionBuilder that looks up string values from an XML file.

The LookupExpressionBuilder class is contained in Listing 27.10.

LISTING 27.10   App_Code\LookupExpressionBuilder.cs

```
using System;
using System.CodeDom;
using System.Web.UI;
using System.ComponentModel;
using System.Web.Compilation;
using System.Xml;
using System.Web.Hosting;
using System.Web.Caching;

namespace AspNetUnleashed
{
    public class LookupExpressionBuilder : ExpressionBuilder
    {
        public override CodeExpression GetCodeExpression(BoundPropertyEntry entry,
        ➥object parsedData, ExpressionBuilderContext context)
        {
            CodeTypeReferenceExpression refMe = new
            ➥CodeTypeReferenceExpression(base.GetType());
            CodePrimitiveExpression expression = new
            ➥CodePrimitiveExpression(entry.Expression);
            return new CodeMethodInvokeExpression(refMe, "GetEvalData", new
            ➥CodeExpression[] { expression });
        }

        public override object EvaluateExpression(object target, BoundPropertyEntry
        ➥entry, object parsedData, ExpressionBuilderContext context)
        {
            return GetEvalData(entry.Expression);
        }

        public override bool SupportsEvaluate
        {
            get
            {
                return true;
```

```
            }
        }

        public static string GetEvalData(string expression)
        {
            XmlDocument lookupDoc =
            ➥(XmlDocument)HostingEnvironment.Cache["Lookup"];
            if (lookupDoc -- null)
            {
                lookupDoc = new XmlDocument();
                string lookupFileName = HostingEnvironment.MapPath
                ➥("~/Lookup.config");
                lookupDoc.Load(lookupFileName);
                CacheDependency fileDepend = new CacheDependency(lookupFileName);
                HostingEnvironment.Cache.Insert("Lookup", lookupDoc, fileDepend);
            }

            string search = String.Format("//add[@key='{0}']", expression);
            XmlNode match = lookupDoc.SelectSingleNode(search);
            if (match != null)
                return match.Attributes["value"].Value;
            return "[no match]";
        }

    }
}
```

Before you can use the LookupExpressionBuilder class, you need to register it
in the web configuration file. The web configuration file in Listing 27.11 includes an
<expressionBuilders> section that registers the LookupExpressionBuilder class for the
prefix lookup.

LISTING 27.11 Web.Config

```
<configuration>
  <system.web>
    <compilation>
      <expressionBuilders>
        <add expressionPrefix="lookup"
            type="AspNetUnleashed.LookupExpressionBuilder" />
      </expressionBuilders>
    </compilation>
  </system.web>
</configuration>
```

27

The LookupExpressionBuilder uses an XML file named Lookup.config to contain a data-base of lookup values. This file contains key and value pairs. A sample Lookup.config file is contained in Listing 27.12.

LISTING 27.12   Lookup.config

```
<lookup>
  <add key="WelcomeMessage" value="Welcome to our Web site!" />
  <add key="Copyright" value="All content copyrighted by the company." />
</lookup>
```

Finally, the page in Listing 27.13 uses the LookupExpressionBuilder. It contains a Literal control that displays the value of a lookup expression named WelcomeMessage (see Figure 27.3).

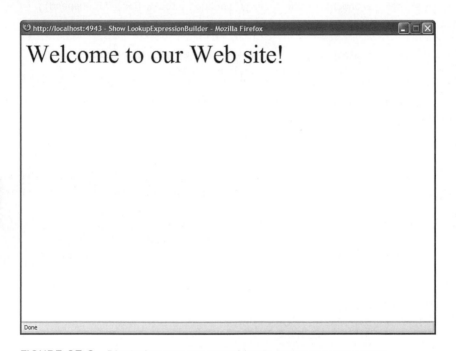

FIGURE 27.3   Displaying text generated by an ExpressionBuilder.

LISTING 27.13   ShowLookupExpressionBuilder.aspx

```
<%@ Page Language="C#" %>
<!DOCTYPE html PUBLIC "-//W3C//DTD XHTML 1.0 Transitional//EN"
  "http://www.w3.org/TR/xhtml1/DTD/xhtml1-transitional.dtd">
<html xmlns="http://www.w3.org/1999/xhtml" >
<head id="Head1" runat="server">
    <title>Show LookupExpressionBuilder</title>
```

```
</head>
<body>
    <form id="form1" runat="server">
    <div>

    <asp:Literal ID="Literal1"
        Text="<%$ lookup:WelcomeMessage %>"
        runat="Server" />

    </div>
    </form>
</body>
</html>
```

You create a custom ExpressionBuilder by inheriting a new class from the base ExpressionBuilder class. The ExpressionBuilder class has the following methods:

▶ **GetCodeExpression**—Returns the code that is used to evaluate an expression.

▶ **EvaluateExpression**—Evaluates the expression in the case of no-compile ASP.NET pages.

▶ **ParseExpression**—Returns a parsed version of the expression.

The ExpressionBuilder class also supports the following property:

▶ **SupportsEvaluate**—When true, the ExpressionBuilder can be used in no-compile ASP.NET pages.

When you use an ExpressionBuilder in a normal ASP.NET page, the ExpressionBuilder returns code that is integrated into the compiled ASP.NET page. The GetCodeExpression() method returns a block of code that is injected into the compiled ASP.NET page class that gets created in the Temporary ASP.NET Files folder.

Because an ExpressionBuilder might be used with either a Visual Basic .NET or C# ASP.NET page, the code returned by the GetCodeExpression() method must be language neutral. This means that you must represent the code that gets executed with the CodeDom.

In Listing 27.11, the GetCodeExpression() method returns an instance of the CodeMethodInvokeExpression class. This class represents an expression that invokes a class method. In this case, the CodeMethodInvokeExpression class is used to represent the expression LookupExpressionBuilder.GetEvalData(). In other words, the ExpressionBuilder adds code to the compiled ASP.NET page class that invokes the GetEvalData() method contained in Listing 27.10.

As an alternative to creating a normal ASP.NET page, you can create something called a *no-compile* ASP.NET page. A no-compile ASP.NET page is not compiled dynamically. You create a no-compile ASP.NET page by adding the following attribute to a <%@ Page %> directive:

```
<%@ Page CompilationMode="Never" %>
```

27

> **NOTE**
>
> No-compile ASP.NET pages are discussed in Chapter 1, "Overview of the ASP.NET Framework."

If you want an `ExpressionBuilder` to work with no-compile ASP.NET pages, then you must return the value `True` from the `ExpressionBuilder.SupportsEvaluate` property and implement the `EvaluateExpression()` method. The `EvaluateExpression` is executed at runtime when the no-compile ASP.NET page is requested. In Listing 27.11, the `EvaluateExpression()` method simply calls the `GetEvalData()` method.

Creating HTTP Handlers

An HTTP Handler is a .NET class that executes whenever you make a request for a file at a certain path. Each type of resource that you can request from an ASP.NET application has a corresponding handler.

For example, when you request an ASP.NET page, the `Page` class executes. The `Page` class is actually an HTTP Handler because it implements the `IHttpHandler` interface.

Other examples of HTTP Handlers are the `TraceHandler` class, which displays application-level trace information when you request the `Trace.axd` page and the `ForbiddenHandler` class, which displays an Access Forbidden message when you attempt to request source code files from the browser.

You can implement your own HTTP handlers. For example, imagine that you want to store all your images in a database table. However, you want use normal HTML `<img>` tags to display images in your web pages. In that case, you can map any file that has a `.gif` or `.jpeg` extension to a custom image HTTP handler. The image HTTP handler can retrieve images from a database automatically whenever an image request is made.

Or imagine that you want to expose an RSS feed from your website. In that case, you can create a RSS HTTP Handler that displays a list of blog entries or articles hosted on your website.

You can create an HTTP Handler in two ways. You can either create something called a Generic Handler, or you can implement the `IHttpHandler` interface in a custom class. This section explores both methods of creating an HTTP Handler.

Creating a Generic Handler

The easiest way to create a new HTTP Handler is to create a Generic Handler. When you create a Generic Handler, you create a file that ends with the extension `.ashx`. Whenever you request the `.ashx` file, the Generic Handler executes.

You can think of a Generic Handler as a very lightweight ASP.NET page. A Generic Handler is like an ASP.NET page that contains a single method that renders content to the browser. You can't add any controls declaratively to a Generic Handler. A Generic Handler also doesn't support events such as the Page `Load` or Page `PreRender` events.

In this section, we create a Generic Handler that dynamically generates an image from a string of text. For example, if you pass the string `Hello World!` to the handler, the handler returns an image of the text `Hello World!`.

The Generic Handler is contained in Listing 27.14.

LISTING 27.14   `ImageTextHandler.ashx`

```csharp
<%@ WebHandler Language="C#" Class="ImageTextHandler" %>


using System;
using System.Web;
using System.Drawing;
using System.Drawing.Imaging;

public class ImageTextHandler : IHttpHandler
{

    public void ProcessRequest(HttpContext context)
    {
        // Get parameters from querystring
        string text = context.Request.QueryString["text"];
        string font = context.Request.QueryString["font"];
        string size = context.Request.QueryString["size"];

        // Create Font
        Font fntText = new Font(font, float.Parse(size));

        // Calculate image width and height
        Bitmap bmp = new Bitmap(10, 10);
        Graphics g = Graphics.FromImage(bmp);
        SizeF bmpSize = g.MeasureString(text, fntText);
        int width = (int)Math.Ceiling(bmpSize.Width);
        int height = (int)Math.Ceiling(bmpSize.Height);
        bmp = new Bitmap(bmp, width, height);
        g.Dispose();

        // Draw the text
        g = Graphics.FromImage(bmp);
        g.Clear(Color.White);
        g.DrawString(text, fntText, Brushes.Black, new PointF(0, 0));
        g.Dispose();
```

LISTING 27.14   Continued

```
        // Save bitmap to output stream
        bmp.Save(context.Response.OutputStream, ImageFormat.Gif);
    }

    public bool IsReusable
    {
        get
        {
            return true;
        }
    }

}
```

The `ImageTextHandler` in Listing 27.14 includes one method and one property. The `ProcessRequest()` method is responsible for outputting any content that the handler renders to the browser.

In Listing 27.14, the image text, font, and size are retrieved from query string fields. You specify the image that you want to return from the handler by making a request that looks like this:

```
/ImageTextHandler.ashx?text=Hello&font=Arial&size=30
```

Next, a bitmap is created with the help of the classes from the System.Drawing namespace. The bitmap is actually created twice. The first one is used to measure the size of the bitmap required for generating an image that contains the text. Next, a new bitmap of the correct size is created, and the text is drawn on the bitmap.

After the bitmap has been created, it is saved to the `HttpResponse` object's `OutputStream` so that it can be rendered to the browser.

The handler in Listing 27.14 also includes an `IsReusable` property. The `IsReusable` property indicates whether the same handler can be reused over multiple requests. You can improve your application's performance by returning the value `True`. Because the handler isn't maintaining any state information, there is nothing wrong with releasing it back into the pool so that it can be used with a future request.

The page in Listing 27.15 illustrates how you can use the `ImageTextHandler.ashx` file. This page contains three HTML `<img>` tags that pass different query strings to the handler (see Figure 27.4).

LISTING 27.15   ShowImageTextHandler.aspx

```
<%@ Page Language="C#" %>
<!DOCTYPE html PUBLIC "-//W3C//DTD XHTML 1.0 Transitional//EN"
  "http://www.w3.org/TR/xhtml1/DTD/xhtml1-transitional.dtd">
```

```
<html xmlns="http://www.w3.org/1999/xhtml" >
<head id="Head1" runat="server">
    <title>Show ImageTextHandler</title>
</head>
<body>
    <form id="form1" runat="server">
    <div>

    <img src="ImageTextHandler.ashx?text=Some Text&font=WebDings&size=42" />
    <br />
    <img src="ImageTextHandler.ashx?text=Some Text&font=Comic Sans MS&size=42" />
    <br />
    <img src="ImageTextHandler.ashx?text=Some Text&font=Courier New&size=42" />

    </div>
    </form>
</body>
</html>
```

FIGURE 27.4   Displaying text images with an HTTP Handler.

Implementing the `IHttpHandler` Interface

The big disadvantage of a Generic Handler is that you cannot map a Generic Handler to a particular page path. For example, you cannot execute a Generic Handler whenever someone requests a file with the extension `.gif`.

If you need more control over when an HTTP Handler executes, then you can create a class that implements the IHttpHandler interface.

After you create a class that For example, the class in Listing 27.16 represents an Image HTTP Handler. This handler retrieves an image from a database table and renders the image to the browser.

LISTING 27.16   App_Code\ImageHandler.cs

```
using System;
using System.Web;
using System.Data;
using System.Data.SqlClient;
using System.Web.Configuration;

namespace AspNetUnleashed
{
    public class ImageHandler : IHttpHandler
    {
        const string connectionStringName = "Images";

        public void ProcessRequest(HttpContext context)
        {
            // Don't buffer response
            context.Response.Buffer = false;

            // Get file name
            string fileName = VirtualPathUtility.GetFileName(context.Request.Path);

            // Get image from database
            string conString = WebConfigurationManager.ConnectionStrings
            ➥[connectionStringName].ConnectionString;
            SqlConnection con = new SqlConnection(conString);
            SqlCommand cmd = new SqlCommand("SELECT Image FROM Images WHERE
            ➥FileName=@FileName", con);
            cmd.Parameters.AddWithValue("@fileName", fileName);
            using (con)
            {
                con.Open();
                SqlDataReader reader = cmd.ExecuteReader(CommandBehavior.
                ➥SequentialAccess);
                if (reader.Read())
                {
                    int bufferSize = 8040;
                    byte[] chunk = new byte[bufferSize];
                    long retCount;
```

```
            long startIndex = 0;
            retCount = reader.GetBytes(0, startIndex, chunk, 0, bufferSize);
            while (retCount == bufferSize)
            {
                context.Response.BinaryWrite(chunk);

                startIndex += bufferSize;
                 retCount = reader.GetBytes(0, startIndex, chunk, 0,
                 ➥bufferSize);
            }
            byte[] actualChunk = new Byte[retCount - 1];
            Buffer.BlockCopy(chunk, 0, actualChunk, 0, (int)retCount - 1);
            context.Response.BinaryWrite(actualChunk);
        }
    }

    }

    public bool IsReusable
    {
        get { return true; }
    }
  }
}
```

implements the IHttpHandler interface, you need to register the class in the web configuration file. The web configuration file in Listing 27.17 includes an httpHandlers section that associates the .gif, .jpeg, and .jpg extensions with the Image handler.

LISTING 27.17   Web.Config

```
<configuration>
  <connectionStrings>
    <add name="Images"
      connectionString="Data Source=.\SQLExpress;Integrated
          Security=True;AttachDBFileName=¦DataDirectory¦ImagesDB.mdf;
          User Instance=True"/>
  </connectionStrings>
    <system.web>

      <httpHandlers>
        <add path="*.gif" verb="*"
          type="AspNetUnleashed.ImageHandler" validate="false" />
        <add path="*.jpeg" verb="*"
          type="AspNetUnleashed.ImageHandler" validate="false" />
        <add path="*.jpg" verb="*"
```

LISTING 27.17   Continued

```
            type="AspNetUnleashed.ImageHandler" validate="false" />
    </httpHandlers>

    </system.web>
</configuration>
```

When you register a handler, you specify the following four attributes:

- ▶ **path**—Enables you to specify the path associated with the handler. You can use wildcards in the path expression.

- ▶ **verb**—Enables you to specify the HTTP verbs, such as GET or POST, associated with the handler. You can specify multiple verbs in a comma-separated list. You can represent any verb with the * wildcard.

- ▶ **type**—Enables you to specify the name of the class that implements the handler.

- ▶ **validate**—Enables you to specify whether the handler is loaded during application startup. When true, the handler is loaded at startup. When false, the handler is not loaded until a request associated with the handler is made. This second option can improve your application's performance when a handler is never used.

The page in Listing 27.18 uses the ImageHandler to render its images. The page enables you to upload new images to a database named ImagesDB. The page also displays existing images (see Figure 27.5).

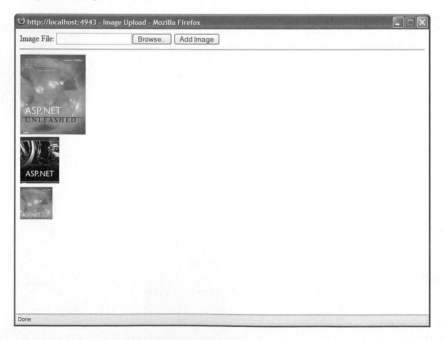

FIGURE 27.5   Displaying images with the ImageHandler.

LISTING 27.18   ImageUpload.aspx

```
<%@ Page Language="C#" %>
<!DOCTYPE html PUBLIC "-//W3C//DTD XHTML 1.0 Transitional//EN"
"http://www.w3.org/TR/xhtml1/DTD/xhtml1-transitional.dtd">
<script runat="server">

    protected void btnAdd_Click(object sender, EventArgs e)
    {
        if (upFile.HasFile)
        {
                srcImages.Insert();
        }
    }
</script>
<html xmlns="http://www.w3.org/1999/xhtml" >
<head id="Head1" runat="server">
    <style type="text/css">
        .fileList li
        {
            margin-bottom:5px;
        }
    </style>
    <title>Image Upload</title>
</head>
<body>
    <form id="form1" runat="server">
    <div>

    <asp:Label
        id="lblFile"
        Text="Image File:"
        AssociatedControlID="upFile"
        Runat="server" />
    <asp:FileUpload
        id="upFile"
        Runat="server" />
    <asp:Button
        id="btnAdd"
        Text="Add Image"
        OnClick="btnAdd_Click"
        Runat="server" />
    <hr />

    <asp:GridView
        id="grdImages"
```

LISTING 27.18   Continued

```
        DataSourceID="srcImages"
        AutoGenerateColumns="false"
        ShowHeader="false"
        GridLines="None"
        Runat="server">
        <Columns>
        <asp:ImageField
            DataImageUrlField="FileName"
            DataAlternateTextField="FileName" />
        </Columns>
    </asp:GridView>

    <asp:SqlDataSource
        id="srcImages"
        ConnectionString="<%$ ConnectionStrings:Images %>"
        SelectCommand="SELECT FileName FROM Images"
        InsertCommand="INSERT Images (FileName,Image) VALUES (@FileName,@FileBytes)"
        Runat="server">
        <InsertParameters>
            <asp:ControlParameter Name="FileName" ControlID="upFile"
            ➥PropertyName="FileName" />
            <asp:ControlParameter Name="FileBytes" ControlID="upFile"
            ➥PropertyName="FileBytes" />
        </InsertParameters>
    </asp:SqlDataSource>

    </div>
    </form>
</body>
</html>
```

Registering Extensions with Internet Information Server

The web server included with Visual Web Developer maps all requests to the ASP.NET Framework. For example, if you create an HTTP Handler that handles requests for .gif files, then you don't have to do anything special when using the handler with the Visual Web Developer web server.

Internet Information Server, on the other hand, does not map all requests to the ASP.NET Framework. In particular, it does not map requests for .gif files to ASP.NET. If you want to use a special extension for a handler, then you must configure Internet Information Server to map that extension to the ASP.NET Framework.

If you are serving your pages with Internet Information Server 6.0 (included with Windows Server 2003), then you can create something called a *wildcard application mapping.* A wildcard application mapping enables you to map all page requests to an application such as the ASP.NET Framework. Follow these steps to configure a wildcard mapping for ASP.NET:

1. Open Internet Information Services by selecting Start, Control Panel, Administrative Tools, Internet Information Services.

2. Open the property sheet for a particular website or virtual directory.

3. Open the Application Configuration dialog box by selecting the Directory tab and clicking the Configuration button.

4. Select the Mappings tab.

5. Click the Insert button at the bottom of the Mappings tab to open the Add/Edit Application Extension Mapping dialog box (see Figure 27.6).

6. In the Executable field, enter the path to the ASP.NET ISAPI DLL. (You can copy and paste this path from the Application Mapping for the .aspx extension.)

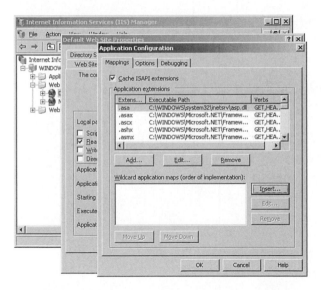

FIGURE 27.6   Adding a wildcard application mapping.

After you complete these steps, all requests made for any type of file are handled by the ASP.NET Framework. If you make a request for a .gif image, then any handlers that you have registered in the web configuration file for the .gif extension will execute.

Earlier versions of Internet Information Server, such as the version included with Microsoft Windows XP, do not support wildcard application mappings. You must map each file extension that you want to associate with the ASP.NET Framework one by one. Follow these steps to map the .gif extension to the ASP.NET Framework:

1. Open Internet Information Services by selecting Start, Control Panel, Administrative Tools, Internet Information Services.

2. Open the property sheet for a particular website or virtual directory.

3. Open the Application Configuration dialog box by selecting the Directory tab and clicking the Configuration button.

4. Select the Mappings tab (see Figure 27.7).

5. Click the Add button to open the Add/Edit Application Extension Mapping dialog box.

6. In the Executable field, enter the path to the ASP.NET ISAPI DLL. (You can copy and paste this path from the Application Mapping for the `.aspx` extension.)

7. In the Extension field, enter **`.gif`**.

FIGURE 27.7   Adding an application mapping.

After you complete these steps, requests for `.gif` images are handled by the ASP.NET Framework. If you have registered an HTTP handler for the `.gif` extension in the web configuration file, then the HTTP Handler will execute whenever someone makes a request for a `.gif` file.

Creating an Asynchronous HTTP Handler

When you create an HTTP Handler by creating either a Generic Handler or implementing the IHttpHandler interface, you are creating a synchronous handler. In this section, you learn how to create an asynchronous handler.

The advantage of creating an asynchronous handler is scalability. The ASP.NET Framework maintains a limited pool of threads that are used to service requests. When the ASP.NET

Framework receives a request for a file, it assigns a thread to handle the request. If the ASP.NET Framework runs out of threads, the request is queued until a thread becomes available. If too many threads are queued, then the framework rejects the page request with a 503 Server Too Busy response code.

If you execute an HTTP Handler asynchronously, then the current thread is released back into the thread pool so that it can be used to service another page request. While the asynchronous handler is executing, the ASP.NET framework can devote its attention to handling other requests. When the asynchronous handler completes its work, the framework reassigns a thread to the original request and the handler can render content to the browser.

> **NOTE**
>
> You can configure the ASP.NET thread pool with the httpRuntime element in the web configuration file. You can modify the appRequestQueueLimit, minFreeThreads, and minLocalRequestFreeThreads attributes to control how many requests the ASP.NET Framework queues before giving up and sending an error.

You create an asynchronous HTTP handler by implementing the IHttpAsyncHandler interface. This interface derives from the IHttpHandler interface and adds two additional methods:

▶ **BeginProcessRequest**—Called to start the asynchronous task.

▶ **EndProcessRequest**—Called when the asynchronous task completes.

For example, the file in Listing 27.19 contains an asynchronous handler that grabs an RSS feed from the Microsoft MSDN website.

27

LISTING 27.19   App_Code\RSSHandler.cs

```
using System;
using System.Web;
using System.Net;
using System.IO;

namespace AspNetUnleashed
{
    public class RSSHandler : IHttpAsyncHandler
    {
        private HttpContext _context;
        private WebRequest _request;

        public IAsyncResult BeginProcessRequest(HttpContext context, AsyncCallback
        ➡cb, object extraData)
        {
            // Store context
```

LISTING 27.19   Continued

```csharp
        _context = context;

        // Initiate call to RSS feed
        _request = WebRequest.Create
            ("http://msdn.microsoft.com/asp.net/rss.xml");
        return _request.BeginGetResponse(cb, extraData);
    }

    public void EndProcessRequest(IAsyncResult result)
    {
        // Get the RSS feed
        string rss = String.Empty;
        WebResponse response = _request.EndGetResponse(result);
        using (response)
        {
            StreamReader reader = new StreamReader(response.GetResponseStream());
            rss = reader.ReadToEnd();
        }
        _context.Response.Write(rss);
    }

    public bool IsReusable
    {
        get { return true; }
    }

    public void ProcessRequest(HttpContext context)
    {
        throw new Exception("The ProcessRequest method is not implemented.");
    }
    }
}
```

The handler in Listing 27.19 implements both the `BeginProcessRequest()` and `EndProcessRequest()` methods required by the `IHttpAsyncHandler` interface.

The `BeginProcessRequest()` method uses the `WebRequest` class to request the page that contains the RSS headlines from the MSDN website. The `WebRequest.BeginGetResponse()` method is used to retrieve the remote page asynchronously.

When the `BeginGetResponse()` method completes, the handler's `EndProcessRequest()` method is called. This method retrieves the page and renders the contents of the page to the browser.

Before you can use the RSSHandler, you need to register it in your web configuration file. The web configuration file in Listing 27.20 includes an <httpHandlers> section that registers the RSSHandler and associates the handler with the .rss extension.

LISTING 27.20 Web.Config

```
<configuration>
    <system.web>

      <httpHandlers>
        <add path="*.rss" verb="*" type="AspNetUnleashed.RSSHandler"/>
      </httpHandlers>

    </system.web>
</configuration>
```

After you register the RSSHandler, you can execute the handler by making a request for any file that ends with the extension .rss. If you have a news reader, such as SharpReader, then you can enter a path like the following in the reader's address bar:

http://localhost:2026/YourApp/news.rss

The page in Listing 27.21 contains a GridView and XmlDataSource control. The XmlDataSource control calls the RssHandler to retrieve the headlines that are displayed in the GridView control (see Figure 27.8).

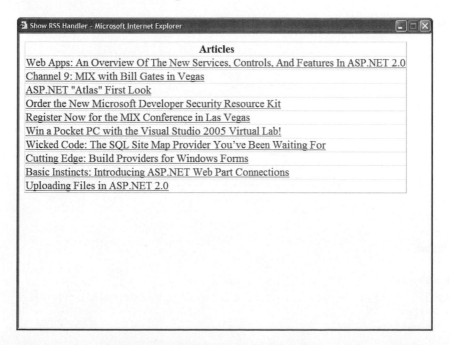

27

FIGURE 27.8   Retrieving an RSS feed asynchronously.

LISTING 27.21   ShowRSSHandler.aspx

```
<%@ Page Language="C#" %>
<%@ Import Namespace="System.IO" %>
<!DOCTYPE html PUBLIC "-//W3C//DTD XHTML 1.0 Transitional//EN"
"http://www.w3.org/TR/xhtml1/DTD/xhtml1-transitional.dtd">
<script runat="server">

    void Page_Load()
    {
        string pagePath = Request.Url.OriginalString;
        string rssPath = Path.ChangeExtension(pagePath, ".rss");
        srcRSS.DataFile = rssPath;
    }
</script>
<html xmlns="http://www.w3.org/1999/xhtml" >
<head id="Head1" runat="server">
    <title>Show RSS Handler</title>
</head>
<body>
    <form id="form1" runat="server">
    <div>

    <asp:GridView
        id="grdRSS"
        DataSourceID="srcRSS"
        AutoGenerateColumns="false"
        Runat="server">
        <Columns>
        <asp:TemplateField HeaderText="Articles">
        <ItemTemplate>
            <asp:HyperLink
                id="lnkRSS"
                Text='<%# XPath("title") %>'
                NavigateUrl='<%# XPath("link") %>'
                Runat="server" />
        </ItemTemplate>
        </asp:TemplateField>
        </Columns>
    </asp:GridView>

    <asp:XmlDataSource
        id="srcRSS"
        XPath="//item"
        Runat="server" />
```

```
        </div>
    </form>
</body>
</html>
```

Working with HTTP Applications and HTTP Modules

Whenever you request an ASP.NET page, the ASP.NET Framework assigns an instance of the HttpApplication class to the request. This class performs the following actions in the following order:

1. Raises the BeginRequest event.

2. Raises the AuthenticateRequest event.

3. Raises the AuthorizeRequest event.

4. Calls the ProcessRequest() method of the Page class.

5. Raises the EndRequest event.

The entire page execution lifecycle happens during the fourth step. For example, the Page Init, Load, and PreRender events all happen when the Page class ProcessRequest() method is called.

The HttpApplication object is responsible for raising application events. These application events happen both before and after a page is executed.

You might want to handle one of the application events for several reasons. For example, you might want to implement a custom authentication scheme. In that case, you would need to handle the AuthenticateRequest event to identify the user.

Or you might want to create a custom logging module that tracks the pages that your website users visit. In that case, you might want to handle the BeginRequest event to record the pages being requested.

If you want to handle HttpApplication events, there are two ways to do it. You can create a Global.asax file, or you can create one or more custom HTTP Modules.

Creating a Global.asax File

By default, the ASP.NET Framework maintains a pool of HttpApplication objects to service incoming page requests. A separate HttpApplication instance is assigned to each request.

If you prefer, you can create a custom HttpApplication class. That way, an instance of your custom class is assigned to each page request.

You can create custom properties in your derived class. These properties can be accessed from any page, control, or component. You also can handle any application events in your custom HttpApplication class.

You create a custom HttpApplication class by creating a special file named Global.asax in the root of your application. Every application can have only one of these files.

For example, the Global.asax file in Listing 27.22 can be used to track the number of page requests made for any page.

LISTING 27.22   Global.asax

```
<%@ Application Language="C#" %>
<%@ Import Namespace="System.Data" %>
<%@ Import Namespace="System.Data.SqlClient" %>
<%@ Import Namespace="System.Web.Configuration" %>
<script runat="server">

    private string _conString;
    private SqlConnection _con;
    private SqlCommand _cmdSelect;
    private SqlCommand _cmdInsert;

    public override void Init()
    {
        // initialize connection
        _conString = WebConfigurationManager.ConnectionStrings["Log"].
        ➥ConnectionString;
        _con = new SqlConnection(_conString);

        // initialize select command
        _cmdSelect = new SqlCommand("SELECT COUNT(*) FROM Log WHERE Path=@Path",
        ➥_con);
        _cmdSelect.Parameters.Add("@Path", SqlDbType.NVarChar, 500);

        // initialize insert command
        _cmdInsert = new SqlCommand("INSERT Log (Path) VALUES (@Path)", _con);
        _cmdInsert.Parameters.Add("@Path", SqlDbType.NVarChar, 500);
    }

    public int NumberOfRequests
    {
        get
        {
```

```
            int result = 0;
            _cmdSelect.Parameters["@Path"].Value = Request.
            ➥AppRelativeCurrentExecutionFilePath;
            try
            {
                _con.Open();
                result = (int)_cmdSelect.ExecuteScalar();
            }
            finally
            {
                _con.Close();
            }
            return result;
        }
    }

    void Application_BeginRequest(object sender, EventArgs e)
    {
        // Record new request
        _cmdInsert.Parameters["@Path"].Value = Request.
        ➥AppRelativeCurrentExecutionFilePath;
        try
        {
            _con.Open();
            _cmdInsert.ExecuteNonQuery();
        }
        finally
        {
            _con.Close();
        }
    }
}
</script>
```

The Global.asax page in Listing 27.23 handles the Application BeginRequest()
event. You can handle any application event by following the naming pattern
Application_*EventName* where *EventName* is the name of the *HttpApplication* event.

In Listing 27.23, the Application_BeginRequest() handler is used to record the path of
the page being requested. A SqlCommand object is used to record the page path to a database table named Log.

The Global.asax file also extends the base HttpApplication class with a custom property
named NumberOfRequests. This property retrieves the number of requests made for the
page at the current path.

Finally, the `Global.asax` includes an `Init()` method that overrides the base `HttpApplication`'s `Init()` method. In Listing 27.23, the `Init()` method is used to initialize the `SqlConnection` and two `SqlCommand` objects used in the `Global.asax` file.

The `Init()` method is called when the class represented by the `Global.asax` is initialized. It is called only once, when the class is first created.

> **WARNING**
>
> The same instance of the `HttpApplication` object is re-used for multiple page requests (although never for multiple page requests at the same time). Any value that you assign to a property in a `Global.asax` file is maintained over the multiple page requests.

The page in Listing 27.23 displays the value of the custom property exposed by the `Global.asax` file (see Figure 27.9). Notice that the `ApplicationInstance` property is used to refer to the instance of the `HttpApplication` class associated with the page. Because the `Global.asax` file is compiled dynamically in the background, any properties that you declare in the `Global.asax` file are exposed as strongly typed properties.

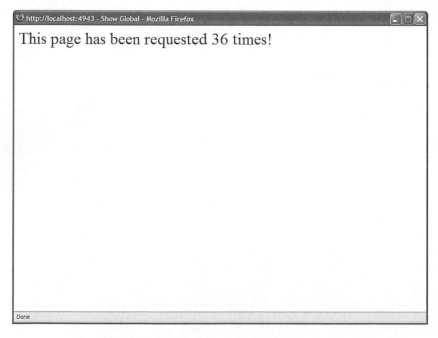

FIGURE 27.9   Displaying the `NumberOfRequests` property.

LISTING 27.23   ShowGlobal.aspx

```
<%@ Page Language="C#" %>
<!DOCTYPE html PUBLIC "-//W3C//DTD XHTML 1.0 Transitional//EN"
"http://www.w3.org/TR/xhtml1/DTD/xhtml1-transitional.dtd">
<html xmlns="http://www.w3.org/1999/xhtml" >
<head id="Head1" runat="server">
    <title>Show Global</title>
</head>
<body>
    <form id="form1" runat="server">
    <div>

    This page has been requested
    <%= this.ApplicationInstance.NumberOfRequests %>
    times!

    </div>
    </form>
</body>
</html>
```

Creating Custom HTTP Modules

An HTTP Module is a .NET class that executes with each and every page request. You can use an HTTP Module to handle any of the `HttpApplication` events that you can handle in the `Global.asax` file.

Behind the scenes, the ASP.NET Framework uses HTTP Modules to implement many of the standard features of the framework. For example, the ASP.NET Framework uses the `FormsAuthenticationModule` to implement Forms authentication and the `WindowsAuthenticationModule` to implement Windows authentication.

Session state is implemented with an HTTP Module named the `SessionStateModule`. Page output caching is implemented with an HTTP Module named the `OutputCacheModule`, and the `Profile` object is implemented with an HTTP Module named the `ProfileModule`.

When a new instance of an `HttpApplication` class is created, the `HttpApplication` loads all of the HTTP Modules configured in the web configuration file. Each HTTP Module subscribes to one or more `HttpApplication` events. For example, when the `HttpApplication` object raises its `AuthenticateRequest` event, the `FormsAuthenticationModule` executes its code to authenticate the current user.

In this section, we create a simple authentication HTTP Module. The HTTP Module doesn't allow you to request a page unless you include the proper query string with the request. The code for the custom HTTP Module is contained in Listing 27.24.

27

LISTING 27.24   App_Code\QueryStringAuthenticationModule.cs

```csharp
using System;
using System.Web;

namespace AspNetUnleashed
{
    public class QueryStringAuthenticationModule : IHttpModule
    {
        public void Init(HttpApplication app)
        {
            app.AuthorizeRequest += new EventHandler(AuthorizeRequest);
        }

        private void AuthorizeRequest(Object sender, EventArgs e)
        {
            // Get context
            HttpApplication app = (HttpApplication)sender;
            HttpContext context = app.Context;

            // If the request is for Login.aspx, exit
            string path = context.Request.AppRelativeCurrentExecutionFilePath;
            if (String.Compare(path, "~/login.aspx", true) == 0)
                return;

            // Check for password
            bool authenticated = false;
            if (context.Request.QueryString["password"] != null)
            {
                if (context.Request.QueryString["password"] == "secret")
                    authenticated = true;
            }

            // If not authenticated, redirect to login.aspx
            if (!authenticated)
                context.Response.Redirect("~/Login.aspx");
        }

        public void Dispose() { }
    }
}
```

The class in Listing 27.25 implements the IHttpModule interface. This interface includes two methods:

▶ **Init**—Enables you to subscribe to HttpApplication events.

▶ **Dispose**—Enables you to clean up any resources used by the HTTP Module.

In Listing 27.25, the Init() method adds an event handler for the HttpApplication AuthorizeRequest event. When the HttpApplication raises the AuthorizeRequest event, the HTTP Module's AuthorizeRequest() method executes.

The AuthorizeRequest() method checks for a password=secret query string. If the query string does not exist, then the user is redirected to the Login.aspx page. (The method also checks whether the user is requesting the Login.aspx page to avoid a vicious circle.)

Before you can use the QueryStringAuthenticationModule, you must register the HTTP Module in the web configuration file. The web configuration file in Listing 27.25 includes an <httpModules> section that registers the module.

LISTING 27.25   Web.Config

```
<configuration>
    <system.web>

      <httpModules>
        <add name="QueryStringAuthenticationModule"
             type="AspNetUnleashed.QueryStringAuthenticationModule"/>
      </httpModules>

    </system.web>
</configuration>
```

After you register the HTTP Module, if you attempt to request any page without including the password=secret query string, then you are redirected to the Login.aspx page. (If the Login.aspx page doesn't exist, you receive a 404 - Not Found error message.)

Summary

In this chapter, you learned how to extend the ASP.NET Framework by extending different parts of the HTTP Runtime. In the first section, you learned how to create a custom BuildProvider. For example, you learned how to create a BuildProvider that dynamically generates a data access component from an XML file.

Next, you explored the topic of ExpressionBuilders. You learned how to use an ExpressionBuilder to automatically replace one expression with another. For example, we created a custom ExpressionBuilder that enables you to look up a value from an XML file.

The topic of HTTP Handlers was also explored. You learned two methods of creating custom HTTP Handlers. You learned how to create a Generic Handler, and you learned how to create an HTTP Handler by implementing the `IHttpHandler` interface. You also saw how you can improve the scalability of your ASP.NET applications by implementing asynchronous HTTP Handlers.

Finally, you learned two methods of handling applicationwide events. You learned how to create a custom `HttpApplication` by creating a `Global.asax` file. You also learned how to handle application events by implementing a custom HTTP Module.

CHAPTER 28

Configuring Applications

In this chapter, you learn how to configure your ASP.NET applications. In the first section, you are provided with an overview of the different sections contained in a web configuration file. You also learn how to modify web configuration files by using both the Web Site Administration Tool and the ASP.NET Microsoft Management Console Snap-In.

Next, you learn how to manipulate configuration settings programmatically with the Configuration API. We discuss how you can both retrieve and modify configuration settings. You also learn how to work with configuration settings located at a remote website.

You also learn how to add custom configuration sections to the web configuration file. You learn how to register custom configuration sections and interact with custom configuration sections with the Configuration API.

Finally, we discuss the very important topic of protecting your configuration files. You learn how to encrypt different sections of a configuration file so that they cannot be read by human eyes. You also learn how you can deploy an encrypted configuration file from one server to another.

Overview of Website Configuration

ASP.NET uses a hierarchical system of configuration. At the top of the hierarchy is the Machine.config file. This file contains all the default configuration settings for ASP.NET applications and all other types of applications built with the .NET Framework.

The `Machine.config` file is located at the following path:

`C:\WINDOWS\Microsoft.NET\Framework\v2.0.50727\CONFIG\Machine.config`

This same folder also contains a `Web.config` file. The `Web.config` file contains settings specific to ASP.NET applications. The `Web.config` file overrides particular settings in the `Machine.config` file.

NOTE

The `\CONFIG` folder includes the following six files:

▶**Machine.config**—Contains the actual configuration settings.

▶**Machine.config.default**—Contains the default values for all configuration settings.

▶**Machine.config.comments**—Contains comments on each configuration setting.

▶**Web.config**—Contains the actual configuration settings.

▶**Web.config.default**—Contains the default values for all configuration settings.

▶**Web.config.comments**—Contains comments on each configuration setting.

Only the `Machine.config` and `Web.config` files are actually used. The other files are there for the purpose of documentation.

You can place a `Web.config` file in the root folder of a website, such as the wwwroot folder. A `Web.config` file located in the root folder of a website contains settings that apply to all applications contained in the website.

You also can place a `Web.config` file in the root of a particular application. In that case, the `Web.config` file has application scope.

Finally, you can place a `Web.config` file in an application subfolder. In that case, the `Web.config` file applies to all pages in that folder and below.

When an ASP.NET application starts, this hierarchy of configuration files is merged and cached in memory. A file dependency is created between the cached configuration settings and the file system. If you make a change to any of the configuration files in the hierarchy, the new configuration settings are loaded into memory automatically.

When an ASP.NET page reads a configuration setting, the setting is read from memory. This means that the ASP.NET Framework can read configuration settings, such as connection strings, very efficiently.

Furthermore, when you make a change to a configuration setting, you don't need to stop and restart an application manually for the new setting to take effect. The ASP.NET Framework reloads the cached configuration settings automatically when the configuration settings are changed on the file system. (The one exception to this is modifications to the `processModel` section.)

> **WARNING**
>
> Modifying most configuration settings results in an application restart. Any data stored using the cache or in-process Session state is lost and must be reloaded. You can get around this issue by using external configuration files. See the section "Placing Configuration Settings in an External File" later in this chapter.

The configuration files are XML files. You can modify configuration settings by opening the Machine.config file or a Web.config file and modifying a setting in Notepad. Alternatively, you can change many of the configuration settings (but not all) by using either the Web Site Administration Tool or the ASP.NET Microsoft Management Console Snap-In.

Using the Web Site Administration Tool

If you are using Visual Web Developer (or Visual Studio .NET), then you can modify certain configuration settings with the Web Site Administration Tool. This tool provides you with a form interface for making configuration changes (see Figure 28.1).

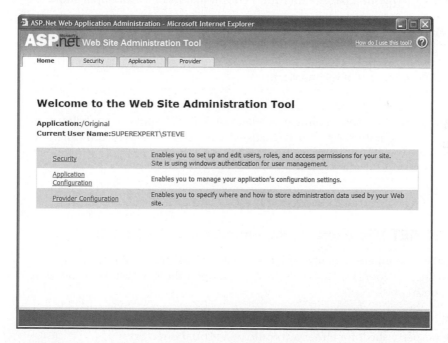

FIGURE 28.1   Opening the Web Site Administration Tool.

You open the Web Site Administration Tool by selecting the menu option Website, ASP.NET Configuration. Selecting this option opens a browser window that contains the tool.

The Web Site Administration Tool has the following four tabs:

▶ **Home**—This tab contains links to the other tabs.

▶ **Security**—This tab enables you to configure authentication, authorization, and the Role Manager.

▶ **Application**—This tab enables you to create and manage application settings, configure SMTP settings, and enable application tracing, debugging, and error pages. You also can use this tab to take your application offline.

▶ **Provider**—This tab enables you to select a provider for Membership and the Role Manager.

Under the Application tab, you can click the link to take your application offline. When you click this link, the following httpRuntime element is added to your web configuration file:

```
<httpRuntime enable="false" />
```

This setting causes the Application Domain associated with the ASP.NET application to refuse any requests. When an application is offline, all requests result in a 404—Not Found error message. You might want to take your application offline, for example, to prevent people from requesting pages while you perform updates to your application.

NOTE

You also can take an ASP.NET application offline by adding a file with the name app_offline.htm to the root of your application.

The Web Site Administration Tool is implemented as an ASP.NET application. Behind the scenes, it uses the Configuration API that is discussed later in this chapter. You can view the entire source code for the Web Site Administration Tool by navigating to the following folder:

```
C:\WINDOWS\Microsoft.NET\Framework\v2.0.50727\ASP.NETWebAdminFiles
```

Using the ASP.NET Microsoft Management Console Snap-In

You also can make configuration changes with the ASP.NET Microsoft Management Console (MMC) Snap-In tool (see Figure 28.2). You can open the ASP.NET MMC Snap-In by following these steps:

1. Open Internet Information Services from Start, Control Panel, Administrative Tools.
2. Open the property sheet for either a website or a virtual directory.
3. Select the ASP.NET tab.
4. Click the Edit Configuration (or Edit Global Configuration) button.

The ASP.NET MMC Snap-In includes the following tabs:

▶ **General**—Enables you to configure connection strings and application settings.

▶ **Custom Errors**—Enables you to configure custom error pages.

▶ **Authorization**—Enables you to configure authorization rules.

▶ **Authentication**—Enables you to configure Forms, Windows, or Passport authentication.

▶ **Application**—Enables you to configure application settings such as application-wide Master Pages and Themes.

▶ **State Management**—Enables you to configure Session state.

▶ **Locations**—Enables you to apply configuration settings to a particular folder or page.

Behind the scenes, the ASP.NET MMC Snap-In uses the Configuration API to make changes to web configuration files.

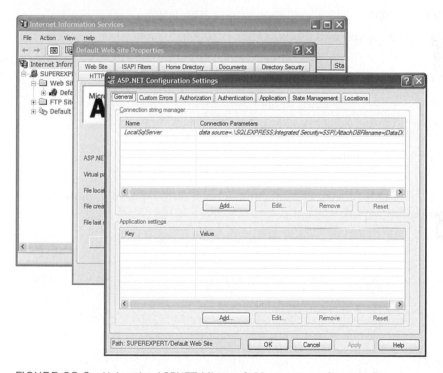

FIGURE 28.2   Using the ASP.NET Microsoft Management Console Snap-In.

ASP.NET Configuration Sections

All the configuration sections in the `Machine.config` or `Web.config` file related to ASP.NET are contained in the `<system.web>` section group. Here is a complete list of the 36 ASP.NET configuration sections and a brief explanation of the purpose of each section:

▶ **anonymousIdentification**—Enables you to configure anonymous user identification, which is used, for example, by the `Profile` object. See Chapter 24, "Maintaining Application State."

▶ **authentication**—Enables you to configure authentication. See Chapter 23, "Using ASP.NET Membership."

▶ **authorization**—Enables you to configure authorization. See Chapter 23.

▶ **browserCaps**—Enables you to configure the lookup of browser capabilities.

▶ **caching**—Enables you to configure caching. See Chapter 25, "Caching Application Pages and Data."

▶ **clientTarget**—Enables you to configure aliases for different clients (browsers).

▶ **compilation**—Enables you to configure how ASP.NET applications are compiled. For example, you can specify whether an application is compiled in debug mode.

▶ **customErrors**—Enables you to configure custom error pages.

▶ **deployment**—Enables you to specify whether an ASP.NET application is deployed in retail mode.

▶ **deviceFilters**—Enables you to configure device filters.

▶ **globalization**—Enables you to configure the Culture, UICulture, and other attributes related to building multi-lingual web applications. See Chapter 26, "Localizing Applications for Multiple Languages."

▶ **healthMonitoring**—Enables you to configure Health Monitoring. See the final section of this chapter.

▶ **hostingEnvironment**—Enables you to configure ASP.NET application properties such as the application idle timeout.

▶ **httpCookies**—Enables you to configure how cookies are sent to the browser. See Chapter 24.

▶ **httpHandlers**—Enables you to configure HTTP Handlers. See Chapter 27, "Working with the HTTP Runtime."

▶ **httpRuntime**—Enables you to configure properties of the HTTP Runtime, such as the number of threads maintained in the thread pool.

▶ **httpModules**—Enables you to configure HTTP Modules. See Chapter 27.

▶ **identity**—Enables you to configure the identity of the ASP.NET application account.

▶ **machineKey**—Enables you to configure encryption keys used by Membership and Session state. See Chapter 23 and Chapter 24.

▶ **membership**—Enables you to configure ASP.NET Membership. See Chapter 23.

▶ **mobileControls**—Enables you to configure adapters used with ASP.NET mobile controls.

▶ **pages**—Enables you to configure page properties such as the website Master Page and Theme. See Chapter 5, "Designing Websites with Master Pages," and Chapter 6, "Designing Websites with Themes."

▶ **processModel**—Enables you to configure the ASP.NET process.

▶ **profile**—Enables you to configure the Profile object. See Chapter 24.

▶ **roleManager**—Enables you to configure the Role Manager. See Chapter 23.

▶ **securityPolicy**—Enables you to map security policy files to trust levels.

▶ **sessionPageState**—Enables you to configure how mobile devices store Session state.

▶ **sessionState**—Enables you to configure Session state. See Chapter 24.

▶ **siteMap**—Enables you to configure Site Maps. See Chapter 20, "Using Site Maps."

▶ **trace**—Enables you to configure page and application tracing.

▶ **trust**—Enables you to configure Code Access Security (CAS) for an ASP.NET application.

▶ **urlMappings**—Enables you to remap page requests to new pages. See Chapter 21, "Advanced Navigation."

▶ **webControls**—Enables you to specify the location of client-script files used by web controls.

▶ **webParts**—Enables you to configure Web Parts. See Part VIII, "Custom Control Building."

▶ **webServices**—Enables you to configure web services.

▶ **xhtmlConformance**—Enables you to configure the level of XHTML conformance of the XHTML rendered by web controls.

Applying Configuration Settings to a Particular Path

By default, the settings in a Machine.config or Web.config file are applied to all pages in the same folder and below. However, if you have the need, you can also apply configuration settings to a particular path. For example, you can apply configuration settings to a particular subfolder or even a particular page.

You apply configuration settings to a particular path by using the <location> element. For example, the web configuration file in Listing 28.1 enables password-protection for a single file named Secret.aspx.

28

LISTING 28.1   Web.config

```
<configuration >

  <system.web>
    <authentication mode="Forms" />
  </system.web>

  <location path="Secret.aspx">
    <system.web>
      <authorization>
        <deny users="?" />
      </authorization>
    </system.web>
  </location>

</configuration>
```

If you attempt to request the Secret.aspx page, you are redirected to the Login.aspx page. However, none of the other files in the same application are password protected by the configuration file.

The <location> element must be added as an immediate child of the <configuration> element. You can't, for example, add the <location> element within a <system.web> element. You must surround the <system.web> element with the <location> element.

> **NOTE**
>
> You can create the web configuration file in Listing 28.1 by selecting the menu option Website, Add New Item, and selecting the Web Configuration File template. Alternatively, you can add the appSettings section by using either the Web Site Administration Tool or the ASP.NET MMC Snap-In. Both tools enable you to enter values for the appSettings section through a user-friendly interface.

Locking Configuration Settings

You can lock configuration settings so that they cannot be overridden at a lower level in the configuration hierarchy. For example, you might want to require that no application running on your production server execute in debug mode. In that case, you can lock the debug configuration setting in a website Web.config file, the root Web.config file, or the Machine.config file.

You can lock a configuration setting in multiple ways. The Web.config file in Listing 28.2 illustrates how you can lock a setting by using the allowOverride="false" attribute of the <location> element.

LISTING 28.2 Web.config

```
<configuration >

  <location allowOverride="false">
    <system.web>
      <compilation debug="false" />
    </system.web>
  </location>

</configuration>
```

TIP

As an alternative to locking the compilation section to prevent a production website being deployed in debug mode, you can take advantage of the deployment element. Adding the following element to the system.web section of the machine.config disables debug mode, enables remote custom errors, and disables trace:

```
<deployment retail="true" />
```

The configuration file in Listing 28.2 locks the compilation element. If you attempt to add a configuration file that sets the debug attribute to the value true, and the configuration file is located below the configuration file in Listing 28.2, then an exception is raised (see Figure 28.3).

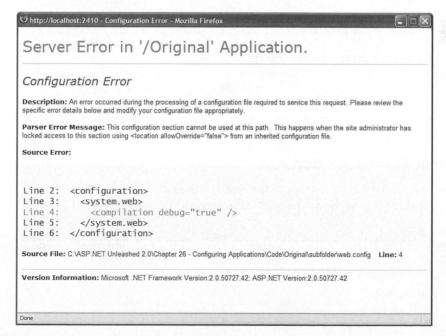

FIGURE 28.3   Attempting to override a locked configuration section.

One problem with the configuration file in Listing 28.2 is that it locks the entire compilation element. If you attempt to change any attribute of the compilation element at a lower level in the configuration hierarchy, then an exception is raised.

You can add any of the following attributes to a particular configuration element to lock either the entire element or one or more of its attributes:

- **lockAllAttributesExcept**—Enables you to lock all attributes except those listed as the value of this attribute. You can specify multiple attributes to exclude in a comma-delimited list.

- **lockAllElementsExcept**—Enables you to lock all child elements of the current element except those listed as the value of this attribute. You can specify multiple elements to exclude in a comma-delimited list.

- **lockAttributes**—Enables you to lock multiple attributes. You can specify the attributes to lock in a comma-delimited list.

- **lockElements**—Enables you to lock multiple child elements. You can specify the child elements to lock in a comma-delimited list.

- **lockItem**—Enables you to lock the current element.

For example, the web configuration file in Listing 28.3 locks the debug attribute, and only the debug attribute, of the <compilation> element.

LISTING 28.3   Web.config

```
<configuration >


  <system.web>
    <compilation debug="false" lockAttributes="debug" />
  </system.web>


</configuration>
```

Adding Custom Application Settings

You can add custom configuration settings to the web configuration file easily by taking advantage of the appSettings section. The appSettings section contains a list of key and value pairs.

For example, the web configuration file in Listing 28.4 contains a welcome message and a copyright notice.

LISTING 28.4   Web.config

```
<configuration>
  <appSettings>
    <add key="welcome" value="Welcome to our Web site!" />
```

```
        <add key="copyright" value="Copyright (c) 2007 by the company" />
    </appSettings>
</configuration>
```

You can retrieve values from the appSettings section either programmatically or declaratively. The page in Listing 28.5 illustrates both approaches (see Figure 28.4).

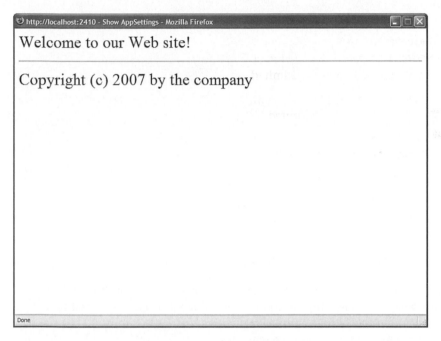

FIGURE 28.4   Displaying values from the appSettings configuration section.

LISTING 28.5   ShowAppSettings.aspx

```
<%@ Page Language="C#" %>
<%@ Import Namespace="System.Web.Configuration" %>
<!DOCTYPE html PUBLIC "-//W3C//DTD XHTML 1.0 Transitional//EN"
"http://www.w3.org/TR/xhtml1/DTD/xhtml1-transitional.dtd">
<script runat="server">

    void Page_Load()
    {
        lblWelcome.Text = WebConfigurationManager.AppSettings["welcome"];
    }

</script>
<html xmlns="http://www.w3.org/1999/xhtml" >
```

LISTING 28.5   Continued

```
<head id="Head1" runat="server">
    <title>Show AppSettings</title>
</head>
<body>
    <form id="form1" runat="server">
    <div>

    <asp:Label
        id="lblWelcome"
        Runat="server" />

    <hr />

    <asp:Literal
        id="ltlCopyright"
        Text="<%$ AppSettings:copyright %>"
        Runat="server" />

    </div>
    </form>
</body>
</html>
```

In Listing 28.5, the welcome message is retrieved programmatically from the `WebConfigurationManager.AppSettings` property. The value retrieved is assigned to a `Label` control. Notice that the `System.Web.Configuration` namespace must be imported before you can use the `WebConfigurationManager` class.

You retrieve the copyright notice declaratively by using `AppSettingsExpressionBuilder`. The following expression is used to retrieve the value of the copyright key:

```
<%$ AppSettings: copyright %>
```

Placing Configuration Settings in an External File

You can place particular configuration sections in an external file. You might want to do this for a couple of reasons. First, you can make a configuration file more manageable by dividing it into multiple files. Also, when you place configuration information in a separate file, you can prevent application restarts when you change a configuration setting.

Every configuration element includes a `configSource` attribute. You can assign a path to a file as the value of the `configSource` attribute.

For example, the web configuration file in Listing 28.6 uses the `configSource` attribute in its `<appSettings>` element.

LISTING 28.6 Web.config

```
<configuration>
  <appSettings configSource="appSettings.config" />
</configuration>
```

The `appSettings` are stored in the external file in Listing 28.7.

LISTING 28.7 appSettings.config

```
<appSettings>
  <add key="message" value="Hello World!" />
</appSettings>
```

Normally, modifying a web configuration file results in your ASP.NET application restarting. Any data stored in `Session` state or the `Cache` object is lost.

However, the `appSettings` section is declared in the `Machine.config` file with a `restartOnExternalChanges="false"` attribute. This attribute prevents your application from restarting when a change is made to the `appSettings` section in an external configuration file. If you modify the file in Listing 28.6, for example, your application won't restart.

NOTE

The CD that accompanies this book includes a page named `ShowAppStartTime.aspx`, which displays the time that the current ASP.NET application started. You can use this file to detect when a modification made to a web configuration file caused an application restart. (The application start time is retrieved in the `Application_Start()` event handler in the `Global.asax` file.)

28

Using the Configuration API

The Configuration API enables you to retrieve and modify configuration settings. You can use the Configuration API to modify web configuration files on the local machine or a remote machine.

If you are responsible for maintaining a large number of websites, the Configuration API can make your life much easier. You can build administrative tools that enable you to make configuration changes quickly to multiple applications. You can use the

Configuration API in an ASP.NET page, or you can build command-line tools or Windows Forms applications that use the Configuration API.

The Configuration API is exposed by the WebConfigurationManager class (located in the System.Web.Configuration namespace). This class supports the following properties:

- **AppSettings**—Exposes all the settings from the appSettings section.

- **ConnectionStrings**—Exposes all the settings from the connectionStrings section.

The WebConfigurationManager also supports the following methods:

- **GetSection**—Retrieves a configuration section relative to the current page or a supplied virtual path.

- **GetWebApplicationSection**—Retrieves a configuration section from the current web application root web configuration file.

- **OpenMachineConfiguration**—Retrieves a Machine.config file on either the local machine or a remote server.

- **OpenMappedMachineConfiguration**—Retrieves a Machine.config file by using a particular file mapping.

- **OpenMappedWebConfiguration**—Retrieves a web configuration file by using a particular file mapping.

- **OpenWebConfiguration**—Retrieves a Web.config file on either the local machine or a remote server.

Almost every configuration section in the web configuration file has a corresponding class in the .NET Framework that represents the configuration section. These classes provide you with a strongly typed representation of each configuration section.

For example, corresponding to the <authentication> section in the web configuration file, there is a System.Web.Configuration.AuthenticationSection class. Corresponding to the <pages> section in the web configuration file, there is a System.Web.Configuration.PagesSection class. Each of these classes expose properties that correspond to all the attributes you can set in the web configuration file.

Reading Configuration Sections from the Current Application

When an ASP.NET application starts, the application merges all the configuration settings in the configuration hierarchy to create one representation of the configuration settings. A particular configuration setting might have different values at different levels in the hierarchy. You can use the methods of the WebConfigurationManager class to get the value of a configuration setting at any level in the hierarchy.

The `WebConfigurationManager.GetWebApplicationSection()` method always retrieves a configuration setting from the application root `Web.config` file. For example, the page in Listing 28.8 displays whether debugging is enabled.

LISTING 28.8   `ShowConfigApp.aspx`

```
<%@ Page Language="C#" %>
<%@ Import Namespace="System.Web.Configuration" %>
<!DOCTYPE html PUBLIC "-//W3C//DTD XHTML 1.0 Transitional//EN"
"http://www.w3.org/TR/xhtml1/DTD/xhtml1-transitional.dtd">
<script runat="server">

    void Page_Load()
    {
        CompilationSection section = (CompilationSection)WebConfigurationManager.
        ➥GetWebApplicationSection("system.web/compilation");
        lblDebug.Text = section.Debug.ToString();
    }
</script>
<html xmlns="http://www.w3.org/1999/xhtml" >
<head id="Head1" runat="server">
    <title>Show Config App</title>
</head>
<body>
    <form id="form1" runat="server">
    <div>

    Debug Mode:
    <asp:Label
        id="lblDebug"
        Runat="server" />

    </div>
    </form>
</body>
</html>
```

The `GetWebApplication()` method returns an object. You must cast the value returned by this method to a particular configuration section type. In Listing 28.8, the value returned by this method is cast to an instance of the `CompilationSection` type.

Realize that you will get the same result when the page in Listing 28.8 is located in different subfolders. For example, debugging might not be enabled in a root configuration file, but it might be enabled in a configuration file in a particular subfolder. However, if you call the GetWebApplicationSection() method, the method always returns the configuration setting for the application root Web.config file.

If you want to get the value of a configuration setting relative to the folder in which the page executes, then you can use the GetSection() method instead of the GetWebApplicationSection() method. The page in Listing 28.9 is located in a subfolder. The page displays the value of the debug setting retrieved from both the GetWebApplicationSection() method and the GetSection() method (see Figure 28.5).

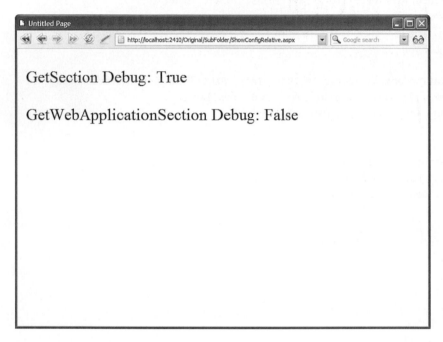

FIGURE 28.5   Retrieving a configuration setting with the GetSection() and GetWebApplicationSection() methods.

LISTING 28.9   SubFolder\ShowConfigRelative.aspx

```
<%@ Page Language="C#" %>
<%@ Import Namespace="System.Web.Configuration" %>
<!DOCTYPE html PUBLIC "-//W3C//DTD XHTML 1.0 Transitional//EN"
"http://www.w3.org/TR/xhtml1/DTD/xhtml1-transitional.dtd">
<script runat="server">

    void Page_Load()
    {
```

```
        CompilationSection section =
(CompilationSection)WebConfigurationManager.GetSection("system.web/compilation");
        lblDebug1.Text = section.Debug.ToString();

        section = (CompilationSection)WebConfigurationManager.
        ➥GetWebApplicationSection("system.web/compilation");
        lblDebug2.Text = section.Debug.ToString();
    }

</script>
<html xmlns="http://www.w3.org/1999/xhtml" >
<head id="Head1" runat="server">
    <title>Show Config Relative</title>
</head>
<body>
    <form id="form1" runat="server">
    <div>

    GetSection Debug:
    <asp:Label
        id="lblDebug1"
        Runat="server" />

    <br /><br />

    GetWebApplicationSection Debug:
    <asp:Label
        id="lblDebug2"
        Runat="server" />

    </div>
    </form>
</body>
</html>
```

When you request the page in Listing 28.9, different values are displayed by the GetSection() method and GetWebApplicationSection() method. The method displays the configuration setting relative to the current directory. The second method displays the configuration setting from the application root Web.config file.

If you want to retrieve the value of a configuration setting for a particular path, then you can use the overload of the GetSection() method that accepts a path parameter. The page in Listing 28.10 iterates through all the immediate subfolders contained in the current application and displays whether debugging is enabled (see Figure 28.6).

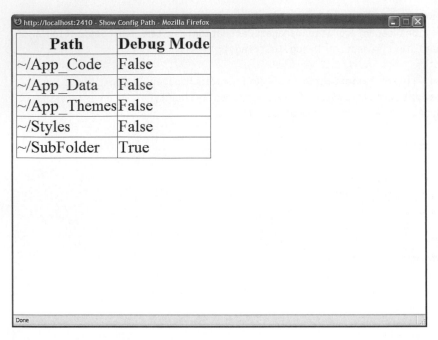

FIGURE 28.6   Displaying configuration settings for each subfolder in an application.

LISTING 28.10   ShowConfigPath.aspx

```
<%@ Page Language="C#" %>
<%@ Import Namespace="System.IO" %>
<%@ Import Namespace="System.Web.Configuration" %>
<%@ Import Namespace="System.Collections.Generic" %>
<!DOCTYPE html PUBLIC "-//W3C//DTD XHTML 1.0 Transitional//EN"
"http://www.w3.org/TR/xhtml1/DTD/xhtml1-transitional.dtd">
<script runat="server">

    void Page_Load()
    {
        Dictionary<string, bool> results = new Dictionary<string, bool>();
        DirectoryInfo rootDir = new DirectoryInfo(Request.PhysicalApplicationPath);
        DirectoryInfo[] dirs = rootDir.GetDirectories();
        foreach (DirectoryInfo dir in dirs)
        {
            string path = "~/" + dir.Name;
            CompilationSection section = (CompilationSection)
            ➡WebConfigurationManager.GetSection("system.web/compilation", path);
            results.Add(path, section.Debug);
        }
        grdResults.DataSource = results;
```

```
            grdResults.DataBind();
    }
</script>
<html xmlns="http://www.w3.org/1999/xhtml" >
<head id="Head1" runat="server">
    <title>Show Config Path</title>
</head>
<body>
    <form id="form1" runat="server">
    <div>

    <asp:GridView
        id="grdResults"
        AutoGenerateColumns="false"
        Runat="server">
        <Columns>
        <asp:BoundField DataField="Key" HeaderText="Path" />
        <asp:BoundField DataField="Value" HeaderText="Debug Mode" />
        </Columns>
    </asp:GridView>

    </div>
    </form>
</body>
</html>
```

Opening a Configuration File

If you want to open a particular configuration file, then you can use one of the Open methods exposed by the WebConfigurationManager class. For example, the page in Listing 28.11 uses the OpenMachineConfiguration() method to open the Machine.config file and displays the default value for the authentication mode setting.

LISTING 28.11   ShowConfigMachine.aspx

```
<%@ Page Language="C#" %>
<%@ Import Namespace="System.Web.Configuration" %>
<!DOCTYPE html PUBLIC "-//W3C//DTD XHTML 1.0 Transitional//EN"
"http://www.w3.org/TR/xhtml1/DTD/xhtml1-transitional.dtd">
<script runat="server">

    void Page_Load()
    {
        Configuration config = WebConfigurationManager.OpenMachineConfiguration();
```

28

LISTING 28.11   Continued

```
        AuthenticationSection section = (AuthenticationSection)config.GetSection
        ➥("system.web/authentication");
        lblMode.Text = section.Mode.ToString();
    }
</script>
<html xmlns="http://www.w3.org/1999/xhtml" >
<head id="Head1" runat="server">
    <title>Show Config Machine</title>
</head>
<body>
    <form id="form1" runat="server">
    <div>

    Authentication Mode Default Value:
    <asp:Label
        id="lblMode"
        Runat="server" />

    </div>
    </form>
</body>
</html>
```

You can use the `WebConfigurationManager` class to display configuration information for other websites located on the same server. For example, the page in Listing 28.12 displays a list of all the virtual directories contained in the default website. You can select a virtual directory and view the authentication mode associated with the virtual directory (see Figure 28.7).

LISTING 28.12   ShowConfigSites.aspx

```
<%@ Page Language="C#" %>
<%@ Import Namespace="System.Web.Configuration" %>
<%@ Import Namespace="System.DirectoryServices" %>
<%@ Import Namespace="System.Collections.Generic" %>
<!DOCTYPE html PUBLIC "-//W3C//DTD XHTML 1.0 Transitional//EN"
"http://www.w3.org/TR/xhtml1/DTD/xhtml1-transitional.dtd">

<script runat="server">

    const string sitePath = "IIS://localhost/W3SVC/1/ROOT";

    void Page_Load()
    {
```

```
            if (!Page.IsPostBack)
            {
                dropVDirs.DataSource = GetVirtualDirectories();
                dropVDirs.DataBind();
            }
        }

        private List<String> GetVirtualDirectories()
        {
            List<String> dirs = new List<string>();
            DirectoryEntry site = new DirectoryEntry(sitePath);
            DirectoryEntries vdirs = site.Children;

            foreach (DirectoryEntry vdir in vdirs)
            {
                if (vdir.SchemaClassName == "IIsWebVirtualDir")
                {
                    string vPath = vdir.Path.Remove(0, sitePath.Length);
                    dirs.Add(vPath);
                }
            }
            return dirs;
        }

        protected void btnSelect_Click(object sender, EventArgs e)
        {
            Configuration config = WebConfigurationManager.OpenWebConfiguration
            ➥(dropVDirs.SelectedValue);
            AuthenticationSection section = (AuthenticationSection)config.GetSection
            ➥("system.web/authentication");
            lblAuthenticationMode.Text = section.Mode.ToString();
        }
</script>
<html xmlns="http://www.w3.org/1999/xhtml" >
<head id="Head1" runat="server">
    <title>Show Config Sites</title>
</head>
<body>
    <form id="form1" runat="server">
    <div>

    <asp:Label
        id="lblVirtualDirectory"
        Text="Virtual Directory:"
        AssociatedControlID="dropVDirs"
        Runat="server" />
```

LISTING 28.12   Continued

```
    <asp:DropDownList
        id="dropVDirs"
        Runat="server" />
    <asp:Button
        id="btnSelect"
        Text="Select"
        OnClick="btnSelect_Click"
        Runat="server" />

    <hr />

    Authentication Mode:
    <asp:Label
        id="lblAuthenticationMode"
        Runat="server" />

    </div>
    </form>
</body>
</html>
```

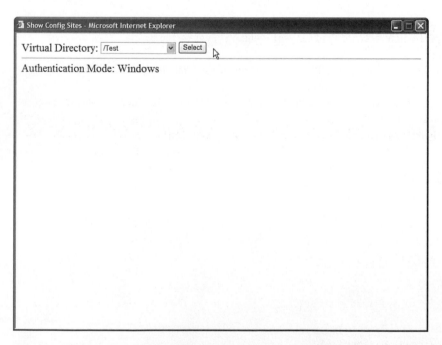

FIGURE 28.7   Displaying configuration information for any application hosted on a server.

The list of virtual directories is retrieved with the classes from the `System.DirectoryServices` namespace. When you select a virtual directory, the `OpenWebConfiguration()` method is called with the path to the virtual directory to get the configuration information.

> **WARNING**
>
> Before you can use the classes from the `System.DirectoryServices` namespace, you must add a reference to the `System.DirectoryServices.dll` assembly. In Visual Web Developer, select the menu option Website, Add Reference.

Opening a Configuration File on a Remote Server

You can use the `WebConfigurationManager` class to open `Machine.config` or `Web.config` files located on remote web servers. However, before you can do this, you must perform one configuration step. You must enable the remote server to accept remote configuration connections by executing the following command from a command prompt:

```
aspnet_regiis -config+
```

To disable remove configuration connections, execute the following command:

```
aspnet_regiis -config-
```

The `aspnet_regiis` tool is located in the following path:

```
C:\WINDOWS\Microsoft.NET\Framework\v2.0.50727\aspnet_regiis.exe
```

> **NOTE**
>
> If you open the SDK Command Prompt, then you don't need to navigate to the Microsoft.NET folder to execute the `aspnet_regiis` tool.

After you make this modification to a remote server, you can retrieve (and modify) configuration settings on the remote server by using one of the Open methods exposed by the `WebConfigurationManager` class. For example, the page in Listing 28.13 contains a form that enables you to enter a server, username, and password. When you submit the form, the page connects to the remote server and retrieves its `Machine.config` file. The page displays the current value of the remote server's authentication mode (see Figure 28.8).

28

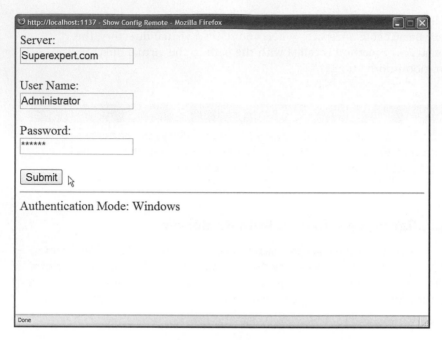

FIGURE 28.8   Changing configuration settings for a remote server.

LISTING 28.13   ShowConfigRemote.aspx

```csharp
<%@ Page Language="C#" %>
<%@ Import Namespace="System.Web.Configuration" %>
<!DOCTYPE html PUBLIC "-//W3C//DTD XHTML 1.0 Transitional//EN"
"http://www.w3.org/TR/xhtml1/DTD/xhtml1-transitional.dtd">
<script runat="server">

    protected void btnSubmit_Click(object sender, EventArgs e)
    {
        try
        {
            Configuration config = WebConfigurationManager.
            ➥OpenMachineConfiguration(null, txtServer.Text, txtUserName.Text,
            ➥txtPassword.Text);
            AuthenticationSection section = (AuthenticationSection)config.
            ➥GetSection("system.web/authentication");
            lblAuthenticationMode.Text = section.Mode.ToString();
        }
        catch (Exception ex)
        {
            lblAuthenticationMode.Text = ex.Message;
        }
```

```
        }
</script>
<html xmlns="http://www.w3.org/1999/xhtml" >
<head id="Head1" runat="server">
    <title>Show Config Remote</title>
</head>
<body>
    <form id="form1" runat="server">
    <div>

    <asp:Label
        id="lblServer"
        Text="Server:"
        AssociatedControlID="txtServer"
        Runat="server" />
    <br />
    <asp:TextBox
        id="txtServer"
        Runat="server" />
    <br /><br />
    <asp:Label
        id="lblUserName"
        Text="User Name:"
        AssociatedControlID="txtUserName"
        Runat="server" />
    <br />
    <asp:TextBox
        id="txtUserName"
        Runat="server" />
    <br /><br />
    <asp:Label
        id="lblPassword"
        Text="Password:"
        AssociatedControlID="txtPassword"
        Runat="server" />
    <br />
     <asp:TextBox
        id="txtPassword"
        TextMode="Password"
        Runat="server" />
    <br /><br />
    <asp:Button
        id="btnSubmit"
        Text="Submit"
        OnClick="btnSubmit_Click"
        Runat="server" />
```

28

LISTING 28.13   Continued

```
    <hr />

    Authentication Mode:
    <asp:Label
        id="lblAuthenticationMode"
        Runat="server" />

    </div>
    </form>
</body>
</html>
```

You can use the page in Listing 28.13 even when the web server is located in some distant part of the Internet. You can enter a domain name or IP address in the server field.

Using the Configuration Class

When you use one of the WebConfigurationManager Open methods—such as the OpenMachineConfiguration() or OpenWebConfiguration() methods—the method returns an instance of the Configuration class. This class supports the following properties:

- **AppSettings**—Returns the appSettings configuration section.

- **ConnectionStrings**—Returns the connectionStrings configuration section.

- **EvaluationContext**—Returns an instance of the ContextInformation class that enables you to determine the context of the configuration information.

- **FilePath**—Returns the physical file path to the configuration file.

- **HasFile**—Returns True when there is a file that corresponds to the configuration information.

- **Locations**—Returns a list of locations defined by the configuration.

- **NamespaceDeclared**—Returns True when the configuration file includes a name-space declaration.

- **RootSectionGroup**—Returns the root section group.

- **SectionGroups**—Returns the child section groups contained by this configuration.

- **Sections**—Returns the child sections contained by this configuration.

The Configuration class also supports the following methods:

- **GetSection**—Enables you to return the specified configuration section.

- **GetSectionGroup**—Enables you to return the specified configuration section group.

▶ **Save**—Enables you to save any configuration changes.

▶ **SaveAs**—Enables you to save the configuration as a new file.

A configuration file contains two basic types of entities: section groups and sections. For example, the <system.web> element in a configuration file represents a section group. The <system.web> section group contains child sections such as the <authentication> and <httpRuntime> sections.

You can use the Configuration.RootSectionGroup property to get the primary section group in a configuration file. You can use the SectionGroups property to return all of a section group's child section groups and the Sections property to return all of a section group's child sections.

For example, the page in Listing 28.14 recursively displays the contents of the Machine.config file in a TreeView control (see Figure 28.9).

FIGURE 28.9   Displaying all configuration sections from the system.web configuration section group.

LISTING 28.14   ShowConfigContents.aspx
```
<%@ Page Language="C#" %>
<%@ Import Namespace="System.Web.Configuration" %>
<!DOCTYPE html PUBLIC "-//W3C//DTD XHTML 1.0 Transitional//EN"
"http://www.w3.org/TR/xhtml1/DTD/xhtml1-transitional.dtd">
<script runat="server">
```

LISTING 28.14   Continued

```
    void Page_Load()
    {
        // Add first node
        TreeNode parentNode = new TreeNode("configuration");
        TreeView1.Nodes.Add(parentNode);

        // Start from the root section group
        Configuration config = WebConfigurationManager.OpenMachineConfiguration();

        // Show child section groups
        AddChildSectionGroups(parentNode, config.RootSectionGroup);

        // Show child sections
        AddChildSections(parentNode, config.RootSectionGroup);
    }

    private void AddChildSectionGroups(TreeNode parentNode,
    ➥ConfigurationSectionGroup parentConfigSectionGroup)
    {
        foreach (ConfigurationSectionGroup configSectionGroup in
        ➥parentConfigSectionGroup.SectionGroups)
        {
            TreeNode childNode = new TreeNode(configSectionGroup.SectionGroupName);
            parentNode.ChildNodes.Add(childNode);
            AddChildSectionGroups(childNode, configSectionGroup);
            AddChildSections(childNode, configSectionGroup);
        }
    }

    private void AddChildSections(TreeNode parentNode, ConfigurationSectionGroup
    ➥parentConfigSectionGroup)
    {
        foreach (ConfigurationSection configSection in
        ➥parentConfigSectionGroup.Sections)
        {
            TreeNode childNode = new TreeNode
            ➥(configSection.SectionInformation.Name);
            parentNode.ChildNodes.Add(childNode);
        }
    }
</script>
<html xmlns="http://www.w3.org/1999/xhtml" >
<head id="Head1" runat="server">
    <title>Show Config Contents</title>
```

```
</head>
<body>
    <form id="form1" runat="server">
    <div>

    <asp:TreeView
        id="TreeView1"
        Runat="server" />

    </div>
    </form>
</body>
</html>
```

Modifying Configuration Sections

You can use the WebConfigurationManager class not only when opening a configuration file to read the values of various configuration settings but to modify existing configuration settings or add new ones.

The Configuration class supports two methods for saving configuration information: the Save() and SaveAs() methods. For example, the page in Listing 28.15 enables you to turn on and off debugging for an application (see Figure 28.10).

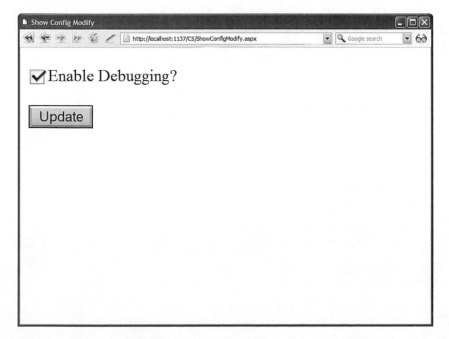

FIGURE 28.10   Modifying the value of the Debug configuration setting.

LISTING 28.15   `ShowConfigModify.aspx`

```
<%@ Page Language="C#" %>
<%@ Import Namespace="System.Web.Configuration" %>
<!DOCTYPE html PUBLIC "-//W3C//DTD XHTML 1.0 Transitional//EN"
"http://www.w3.org/TR/xhtml1/DTD/xhtml1-transitional.dtd">
<script runat="server">

    void Page_Load()
    {
        if (!Page.IsPostBack)
        {
            Configuration config = WebConfigurationManager.OpenWebConfiguration
            ➥(Request.ApplicationPath);
            CompilationSection section = (CompilationSection)config.GetSection
            ➥("system.web/compilation");
            chkDebug.Checked = section.Debug;
        }
    }


    protected void btnUpdate_Click(object sender, EventArgs e)
    {
        Configuration config = WebConfigurationManager.OpenWebConfiguration
        ➥(Request.ApplicationPath);
        CompilationSection section = (CompilationSection)config.GetSection
        ➥("system.web/compilation");
        section.Debug = chkDebug.Checked;
        config.Save(ConfigurationSaveMode.Modified);
    }
</script>
<html xmlns="http://www.w3.org/1999/xhtml" >
<head id="Head1" runat="server">
    <title>Show Config Modify</title>
</head>
<body>
    <form id="form1" runat="server">
    <div>

    <asp:CheckBox
        id="chkDebug"
        Text="Enable Debugging?"
        Runat="server" />
    <br /><br />
    <asp:Button
        id="btnUpdate"
        Text="Update"
```

```
        OnClick="btnUpdate_Click"
        Runat="server" />

    </div>
    </form>
</body>
</html>
```

The page in Listing 28.15 loads the application root `Web.config` file with the help of the `OpenWebConfiguration()` method. (The `Nothing` parameter causes the root `Web.config` file to be loaded.) Next, the value of the `Compilation.Debug` property is modified. Finally, the `Save()` method is called to save this change.

When you call the `Save()` method, you can pass a `ConfigurationSaveMode` parameter to the method. This parameter can have the following values:

▶ **Full**—Saves all configuration settings, regardless of whether they have been modified.

▶ **Minimal**—Saves only those configuration settings that are different from their inherited value.

▶ **Modified**—Saves only those configuration settings that have been modified.

To use the `Save()` or `SaveAs()` methods, the account associated with the page must have `Write` permissions for the folder where the configuration file is saved. By default, when pages are served from Internet Information Server, ASP.NET pages execute in the security context of the NT Authority\NETWORK SERVICE account (in the case of Windows Server 2003 or Vista) or the ASPNET account (in the case of other operating systems). By default, neither of these accounts have permissions to save configuration changes.

NOTE

To make things more confusing, when pages are served from the web server included with Visual Web Developer, the pages are always served in the security context of the current user.

28

There are multiple ways that you can get around this permission problem. First, remember that you can use many of the methods of the `WebConfigurationManager` class from a console application or a Windows Forms application. If you build this type of application, then you can sidestep these security issues.

Another option is to enable per-request impersonation for your ASP.NET application. When impersonation is enabled, an ASP.NET page executes within the security context of the user making the page request. If the user account has permissions to write to the file system, then the page has permissions to write to the file system.

The web configuration file in Listing 28.16 enables impersonation.

LISTING 28.16   Web.config

```
<configuration>
    <system.web>
      <identity impersonate="true" />
    </system.web>
</configuration>
```

If you add the configuration file in Listing 28.16 to the same folder that contains the file in Listing 28.15, then you will be able to make modifications to configuration files.

> **WARNING**
>
> Most changes to a configuration file result in an application restart. When an ASP.NET application restarts, all data stored in memory is blown away. For example, all data cached in the Cache object or Session state is lost.

Provisioning a New Website

When you are provisioning new websites, you often need to create a new virtual directory. The Configuration API doesn't provide you with any help here. However, you can create new virtual directories (and applications) by taking advantage of the classes in the System.DirectoryServices namespace. These classes enable you to use Active Directory Services Interface (ADSI) to modify properties of Internet Information Server.

> **NOTE**
>
> You also can manipulate Internet Information Server properties by using Windows Management Instrumentation (WMI). For more information, see the topic "Using WMI to Configure IIS" at the Microsoft MSDN website (msdn.microsoft.com).

Before you can use the classes from the System.DirectoryServices namespace, you need to add a reference to the System.DirectoryServices.dll assembly. In Visual Web Developer, select the menu option Website, Add Reference, and select System.DirectoryServices.dll.

For example, the page in Listing 28.17 enables you to provision a new ASP.NET application (see Figure 28.11). The page creates a new virtual directory and a new application. The page also creates a new web configuration file in the virtual directory that contains the default language and debug settings you specify.

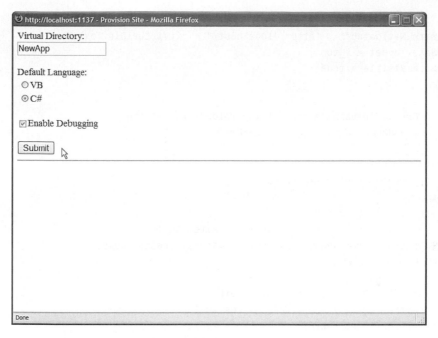

FIGURE 28.11   Creating a new ASP.NET application.

LISTING 28.17   ProvisionSite.aspx

```
<%@ Page Language="C#" %>
<%@ Import Namespace="System.IO" %>
<%@ Import Namespace="System.DirectoryServices" %>
<%@ Import Namespace="System.Web.Configuration" %>
<!DOCTYPE html PUBLIC "-//W3C//DTD XHTML 1.0 Transitional//EN"
"http://www.w3.org/TR/xhtml1/DTD/xhtml1-transitional.dtd">

<script runat="server">

    const string wwwroot = @"c:\Inetpub";
    const string sitePath = @"IIS://localhost/W3SVC/1/ROOT";

    protected void btnSubmit_Click(object sender, EventArgs e)
    {
        string newFolder = Path.Combine(wwwroot, txtVirtualDir.Text);

        CreateVirtualDirectory(newFolder, txtVirtualDir.Text, txtVirtualDir.Text);
        CreateConfiguration(txtVirtualDir.Text);

        // Show link to new site
```

28

LISTING 28.17   Continued

```
        lnkNewSite.NavigateUrl = "http://localhost/" + txtVirtualDir.Text;
        lnkNewSite.Target = "_top";
        lnkNewSite.Visible = true;
    }

    private void CreateVirtualDirectory(string folderPath, string
    ➥virtualDirectoryName, string appFriendlyName)
    {
        // Create new Folder
        Directory.CreateDirectory(folderPath);

        // Create Virtual Directory
        DirectoryEntry vRoot = new DirectoryEntry(sitePath);
        DirectoryEntry vDir = vRoot.Children.Add(virtualDirectoryName,
        ➥"IIsWebVirtualDir");
        vDir.CommitChanges();
        vDir.Properties["Path"].Value = folderPath;
        vDir.Properties["DefaultDoc"].Value = "Default.aspx";
        vDir.Properties["DirBrowseFlags"].Value = 2147483648;
        vDir.CommitChanges();
        vRoot.CommitChanges();

        // Create Application (Isolated)
        vDir.Invoke("AppCreate2", 1);
        vDir.Properties["AppFriendlyName"].Value = appFriendlyName;
        vDir.CommitChanges();
    }

    private void CreateConfiguration(string virtualPath)
    {
        // Open configuration
        Configuration config = WebConfigurationManager.OpenWebConfiguration("/" +
        ➥virtualPath);

        // Set language and debug setting
        CompilationSection section = (CompilationSection)config.GetSection
        ➥("system.web/compilation");
        section.DefaultLanguage = rdlLanguage.SelectedItem.Text;
        section.Debug = chkDebug.Checked;

        // Save configuration
        config.Save(ConfigurationSaveMode.Modified);
    }
</script>
```

```
<html xmlns="http://www.w3.org/1999/xhtml" >
<head id="Head1" runat="server">
    <title>Provision Site</title>
</head>
<body>
    <form id="form1" runat="server">
    <div>

    <asp:Label
        id="lblVirtualDir"
        Text="Virtual Directory:"
        AssociatedControlID="txtVirtualDir"
        Runat="server" />
    <br />
    <asp:TextBox
        id="txtVirtualDir"
        Runat="server" />
    <br /><br />
    <asp:Label
        id="lblLanguage"
        Text="Default Language:"
        AssociatedControlID="rdlLanguage"
        Runat="server" />
    <asp:RadioButtonList
        id="rdlLanguage"
        Runat="server">
        <asp:ListItem Text="VB" Selected="True" />
        <asp:ListItem Text="C#" />
    </asp:RadioButtonList>
    <br />
    <asp:CheckBox
        id="chkDebug"
        Text="Enable Debugging"
        Runat="server" />
    <br /><br />
    <asp:Button
        id="btnSubmit"
        Text="Submit"
        OnClick="btnSubmit_Click"
        Runat="server" />

    <hr />
    <asp:HyperLink
        id="lnkNewSite"
        Visible="false"
        Text="Go to New Site"
```

28

LISTING 28.17   Continued

```
        Runat="server" />

    </div>
    </form>
</body>
</html>
```

To use the page in Listing 28.17, you'll need adequate permissions. You can enable per-request impersonation by adding the file in Listing 28.16 to the same folder as the page in Listing 28.17.

NOTE

Internet Information Server includes several sample ADSI scripts. Look in your Inetpub\AdminScripts folder.

Creating Custom Configuration Sections

You can add custom configuration sections to a web configuration file. You can use a custom configuration section to store whatever information you want.

For example, if you need to manage a large number of database connection strings, then you might want to create a custom database connection string configuration section. Or, if you want to follow the Provider Model and implement a custom provider, then you need to create a custom configuration section for your provider.

You create a custom configuration section by inheriting a new class from the base ConfigurationSection class. For example, the class in Listing 28.18 represents a simple custom configuration section.

LISTING 28.18   App_Code\DesignSection.cs

```
using System;
using System.Configuration;
using System.Drawing;

namespace AspNetUnleashed
{
    public class DesignSection : ConfigurationSection
    {
        [ConfigurationProperty("backcolor", DefaultValue = "lightblue", IsRequired
        ➥= true)]
        public Color BackColor
        {
```

```
        get { return (Color)this["backcolor"]; }
        set { this["backcolor"] = value; }
    }

    [ConfigurationProperty("styleSheetUrl", DefaultValue =
    ➥"~/styles/style.css", IsRequired = true)]
    [RegexStringValidator(".css$")]
    public string StyleSheetUrl
    {
        get { return (string)this["styleSheetUrl"]; }
        set { this["styleSheetUrl"] = value; }
    }

    public DesignSection(Color backcolor, string styleSheetUrl)
    {
        this.BackColor = backcolor;
        this.StyleSheetUrl = styleSheetUrl;
    }

    public DesignSection()
    {
    }
  }
}
```

The class in Listing 28.18 represents a Design configuration section. This section has two properties: `BackColor` and `StyleSheetUrl`.

Notice that both properties are decorated with `ConfigurationProperty` attributes. The `ConfigurationProperty` attribute is used to map the property to an element attribute in the configuration file. When you declare the `ConfigurationProperty` attribute, you can use the following parameters:

- **Name**—Enables you to specify the name of the attribute in the configuration file that corresponds to the property.

- **DefaultValue**—Enables you to specify the default value of the property.

- **IsDefaultCollection**—Enables you to specify whether the property represents the default collection of an element.

- **IsKey**—Enables you to specify whether the property represents a key for a collection of configuration elements.

- **IsRequired**—Enables you to specify whether this property must have a value.

- **Options**—Enables you to use flags to specify the values of the above options.

28

You also can use validators when defining configuration properties. For example, in Listing 28.18, the RegexStringValidator is used to check whether the value of the StyleSheetUrl property ends with a .css extension.

You can use the following validators with configuration properties:

▸ **CallbackValidator**—Enables you to specify a custom method to use to validate a property value.

▸ **IntegerValidator**—Enables you to validate whether a property value is an integer value (System.Int32).

▸ **LongValidator**—Enables you to validate whether a property value is a long value (System.Int64).

▸ **PositiveTimeSpanValidator**—Enables you to validate whether a property value is a valid time span.

▸ **RegexStringValidator**—Enables you to validate a property value against a regular expression pattern.

▸ **StringValidator**—Enables you to validate a property value that represents a string against a minimum length, maximum length, and list of invalid characters.

▸ **SubClassTypeValidator**—Enables you to validate whether the value of a property is inherited from a particular class

▸ **TimeSpanValidator**—Enables you to validate a property value that represents a time span against a minimum and maximum value.

WARNING

When you use validators such as the RegexStringValidator, make sure that you provide a property with a default value by using the DefaultValue parameter with the ConfigurationProperty attribute.

After you create a custom configuration section, you need to register it in a configuration file before you can use it. The web configuration file in Listing 28.19 adds the DesignSection configuration section to the system.web section.

LISTING 28.19   Web.config

```
<configuration>
  <configSections>
    <sectionGroup name="system.web">
    <section
        name="design"
        type="AspNetUnleashed.DesignSection"
        allowLocation="true"
```

```
          allowDefinition="Everywhere"/>
      </sectionGroup>
    </configSections>
    <system.web>
      <design
        backcolor="red"
        styleSheetUrl="~/styles/style.css"/>
    </system.web>
</configuration>
```

You are not required to add a custom configuration section to any particular configuration section group. For that matter, you are not required to add a custom configuration section to any configuration section group at all.

After you register a custom configuration section, you can use it just like any of the standard configuration sections. You can use the methods of the `WebConfigurationManager` class to retrieve and modify the custom section.

For example, the page in Listing 28.20 uses the custom configuration section just created to retrieve the page background color and style sheet (see Figure 28.12).

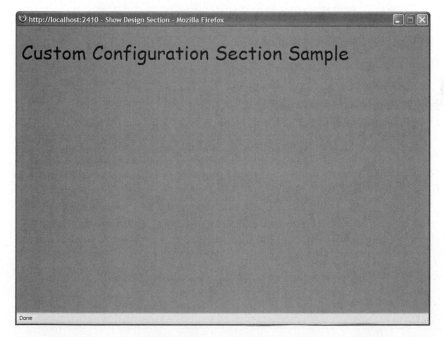

FIGURE 28.12   Using the custom configuration section to modify the page style and background color.

28

LISTING 28.20   ShowDesignSection.aspx

```
<%@ Page Language="C#" %>
<%@ Import Namespace="AspNetUnleashed" %>
<%@ Import Namespace="System.Web.Configuration" %>
<!DOCTYPE html PUBLIC "-//W3C//DTD XHTML 1.0 Transitional//EN"
"http://www.w3.org/TR/xhtml1/DTD/xhtml1-transitional.dtd">
<script runat="server">

    void Page_Load()
    {
        // Get configuration
        DesignSection section = (DesignSection)WebConfigurationManager.
        ➥GetWebApplicationSection("system.web/design");

        // Set Background Color
        htmlBody.Attributes["bgcolor"] = System.Drawing.ColorTranslator.ToHtml
        ➥(section.BackColor);

        // Set style sheet
        HtmlLink link = new HtmlLink();
        link.Href = section.StyleSheetUrl;
        link.Attributes.Add("rel", "stylesheet");
        link.Attributes.Add("type", "text/css");
        Page.Header.Controls.Add(link);
    }
</script>
<html xmlns="http://www.w3.org/1999/xhtml" >
<head id="Head1" runat="server">
    <title>Show Design Section</title>
</head>
<body id="htmlBody" runat="server">
    <form id="form1" runat="server">
    <div>

    <h1>Custom Configuration Section Sample</h1>

    </div>
    </form>
</body>
</html>
```

Creating a Configuration Element Collection

A configuration element can contain a collection of child elements. For example, if you need to create a custom configuration section to configure a provider, then you use child elements to represent the list of providers.

The class in Listing 28.21 represents a configuration section for a `ShoppingCart`. The configuration section includes three properties: `MaximumItems`, `DefaultProvider`, and `Providers`. The `Providers` property represents a collection of shopping cart providers.

LISTING 28.21   App_Code\ShoppingCartSection.cs
_____

```
using System;
using System.Configuration;

namespace AspNetUnleashed
{
    public class ShoppingCartSection : ConfigurationSection
    {
        [ConfigurationProperty("maximumItems", DefaultValue = 100, IsRequired =
        ➥true)]
        public int MaximumItems
        {
            get { return (int)this["maximumItems"]; }
            set { this["maximumItems"] = value; }
        }

        [ConfigurationProperty("defaultProvider")]
        public string DefaultProvider
        {
            get { return (string)this["defaultProvider"]; }
            set { this["defaultProvider"] = value; }
        }

        [ConfigurationProperty("providers", IsDefaultCollection = false)]
        public ProviderSettingsCollection Providers
        {
            get { return (ProviderSettingsCollection)this["providers"]; }
        }

        public ShoppingCartSection(int maximumItems, string defaultProvider)
        {
            this.MaximumItems = maximumItems;
            this.DefaultProvider = defaultProvider;
        }
```

LISTING 28.21   Continued

```
        public ShoppingCartSection()
        {
        }
    }
}
```

The Providers property returns an instance of the ProviderSettingsCollection class.
This class is contained in the System.Configuration namespace.

The web configuration file in Listing 28.22 illustrates how you can use the
ShoppingCartSection.

LISTING 28.22   Web.config

```
<configuration>
  <configSections>
    <sectionGroup name="system.web">
      <section
        name="shoppingCart"
        type="AspNetUnleashed.ShoppingCartSection"
        allowLocation="true"
        allowDefinition="Everywhere" />
    </sectionGroup>
</configSections>
<system.web>

  <shoppingCart
    maximumItems="50"
    defaultProvider="SqlShoppingCartProvider">
    <providers>
      <add
        name="SqlShoppingCartProvider"
        type="AspNetUnleashed.SqlShoppingCartProvider" />
      <add
        name="XmlShoppingCartProvider"
        type="AspNetUnleashed.XmlShoppingCartProvider" />
    </providers>
  </shoppingCart>

</system.web>
</configuration>
```

The ShoppingCartSection class takes advantage of an existing class in the .NET Framework: the ProviderSettingsCollection class. If you have the need, you can create a custom configuration element collection class.

The AdminUsersSection class in Listing 28.23 enables you to represent a list of users. The class includes a property named Users that exposes an instance of the AdminUsersCollection class. The AdminUsersCollection represents a collection of configuration elements. The AdminUsersCollection class is also defined in Listing 28.23.

LISTING 28.23   App_Code\AdminUsersSection.cs

```csharp
using System;
using System.Configuration;

namespace AspNetUnleashed
{
    public class AdminUsersSection : ConfigurationSection
    {
        [ConfigurationProperty("", IsDefaultCollection = true)]
        public AdminUsersCollection Users
        {
            get { return (AdminUsersCollection)this[""]; }
        }

        public AdminUsersSection()
        {
        }
    }

    public class AdminUsersCollection : ConfigurationElementCollection
    {
        protected override ConfigurationElement CreateNewElement()
        {
            return new AdminUser();
        }

        protected override object GetElementKey(ConfigurationElement element)
        {
            return ((AdminUser)element).Name;
        }

        public AdminUsersCollection()
        {
            this.AddElementName = "user";
        }
    }
```

28

LISTING 28.23   Continued

```
    public class AdminUser : ConfigurationElement
    {
        [ConfigurationProperty("name", IsRequired = true, IsKey = true)]
        public string Name
        {
            get { return (string)this["name"]; }
            set { this["name"] = value; }
        }

        [ConfigurationProperty("password", IsRequired = true)]
        public string Password
        {
            get { return (string)this["password"]; }
            set { this["password"] = value; }
        }
    }
}
```

Notice that the ConfigurationProperty attribute that decorates the Users property sets the name of the configuration attribute to an empty string. It also marks the property as representing the section's default collection. These options enable you to avoid having to create a subtag for the user collection. The user collection appears immediately below the main <adminUsers> section tag.

The web configuration file in Listing 28.24 illustrates how you can use the AdminUsersSection class.

LISTING 28.24   Web.config

```
<configuration>
<configSections>
  <sectionGroup name="system.web">
    <section
      name="adminUsers"
      type="AspNetUnleashed.AdminUsersSection"
      allowLocation="true"
      allowDefinition="Everywhere" />
  </sectionGroup>
</configSections>
<system.web>

  <adminUsers>
    <user name="Bob" password="secret" />
    <user name="Fred" password="secret" />
```

```
    </adminUsers>

</system.web>
</configuration>
```

The ASP.NET page in Listing 28.25 displays all the users from the adminUsers section in a BulletedList control (see Figure 28.13).

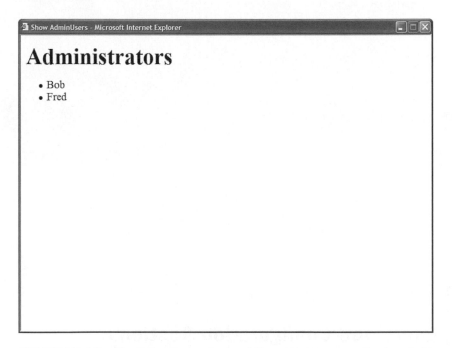

FIGURE 28.13   Displaying the contents of the adminUsers section in a BulletedList control.

LISTING 28.25   ShowAdminUsersSection.aspx

```
<%@ Page Language="C#" %>
<%@ Import Namespace="AspNetUnleashed" %>
<%@ Import Namespace="System.Web.Configuration" %>
<!DOCTYPE html PUBLIC "-//W3C//DTD XHTML 1.0 Transitional//EN"
"http://www.w3.org/TR/xhtml1/DTD/xhtml1-transitional.dtd">
<script runat="server">

    void Page_Load()
    {
        // Get configuration
        AdminUsersSection section = (AdminUsersSection)WebConfigurationManager.
        ➥GetWebApplicationSection("system.web/adminUsers");
```

28

LISTING 28.25   Continued

```
        // Bind section to GridView
        bltAdminUsers.DataSource = section.Users;
        bltAdminUsers.DataBind();
    }
</script>
<html xmlns="http://www.w3.org/1999/xhtml" >
<head id="Head1" runat="server">
    <title>Show AdminUsersSection</title>
</head>
<body>
    <form id="form1" runat="server">
    <div>

    <h1>Administrators</h1>
    <asp:BulletedList
        id="bltAdminUsers"
        DataTextField="Name"
        Runat="server" />

    </div>
    </form>
</body>
</html>
```

Creating Encrypted Configuration Sections

If you need to protect sensitive information stored in a configuration file, you can encrypt the information. For example, you should always encrypt the connectionStrings section of a configuration file to prevent your database connection strings from being stolen by evil hackers.

You can encrypt just about any section in the web configuration file. You can encrypt any of the sections in the system.web section group with the sole exception of the processModel section. You also can encrypt a custom configuration section.

The .NET Framework uses the Provider model for encrypting configuration sections. The Framework ships with two ProtectedConfigurationProviders: the RsaProtectedConfigurationProvider and the DpapiProtectedConfigurationProvider.

The RsaProtectedConfigurationProvider protect sensitive information stored in a configuration file, you can encrypt is the default provider. It uses the RSA algorithm to protect a configuration section. The RSA algorithm uses public key cryptography. It depends on the fact that no one has discovered an efficient method to factor large prime numbers.

The second provider, the `DpapiProtectedConfigurationProvider`, uses the Data Protection API (DPAPI) to encrypt a configuration section. The DPAPI is built into the Windows operating system (Microsoft Windows 2000 and later). It uses either Triple-DES or AES (the United States Government–standard encryption algorithm) to encrypt data.

The `RsaProtectedConfigurationProvider` is the default provider, and it is the one that you should almost always use. The advantage of the `RsaProtectedConfigurationProvider` is that this provider supports exporting and importing encryption keys. This means that you can move an application that contains an encrypted configuration file from one web server a new web server. For example, you can encrypt a configuration section on your development web server and deploy the application to a production server.

If you use the `DpapiProtectedConfigurationProvider` to encrypt a configuration section, on the other hand, then you cannot decrypt the configuration section on another web server. If you need to move the configuration file from one server to another, then you need to first decrypt the configuration file on the source server and re-encrypt the configuration file on the destination server.

WEB STANDARDS NOTE

The .NET Framework uses the World Wide Web Consortium (W3C) recommendation for encrypting XML files. This recommendation is located at www.w3.org/TR/2002/REC-xmlenc-core-20021210.

You can use encryption not only with configuration files, but also with other XML files. To learn more about encrypting XML files, look up the `EncryptedXml` class in the Microsoft .NET Framework SDK Documentation.

Encrypting Sections with the `aspnet_regiis` tool

The easiest way to encrypt a section in the web configuration file is to use the `aspnet_regiis` command-line tool. This tool is located at the following path:

```
C:\WINDOWS\Microsoft.NET\Framework\v2.0.50727\aspnet_regiis.exe
```

NOTE

You don't need to navigate to the Microsoft.NET directory to execute the `aspnet_regiis` tool if you open the SDK Command Prompt.

If you want to encrypt a particular section of a configuration file, then you can use the `-pef` option when executing the `aspnet_regiis` tool. For example, the following command encrypts the `connectionStrings` section of a configuration file located in a folder named MyWebApp:

```
aspnet_regiis -pef connectionStrings c:\Websites\MyWebApp
```

28

If you prefer, rather than specify the location of a web application by its file system path, you can use its virtual path. The following command encrypts the `connectionStrings` section of a configuration file located in a virtual directory named /MyApp:

```
aspnet_regiis -pe connectionStrings -app /MyApp
```

Notice that the `-app` option is used to specify the application's virtual path.

You can decrypt a configuration section by using the `-pdf` option. The following command decrypts a configuration file located in a folder named MyWebApp:

```
aspnet_regiis -pdf connectionStrings c:\Websites\MyWebApp
```

You also can decrypt a configuration section by specifying a virtual directory. The following command uses the `-pd` option with the `-app` option:

```
aspnet_regiis -pd connectionStrings -app /MyApp
```

When you encrypt a configuration section, you can specify the `ProtectedConfigurationProvider` to use to encrypt the section. The `Machine.config` file configures two providers: the `RsaProtectedConfigurationProvider` and the `DataProtectionConfigurationProvider`. The `RsaProtectedConfigurationProvider` is used by default.

If you execute the following command, then the `connectionStrings` section is encrypted with the `DataProtectionConfigurationProvider`:

```
aspnet_regiis -pe connectionStrings -app /MyApp -prov
➥ProtectedConfigurationProvider
```

Notice that this command includes a `-prov` option that enables you to specify the `ProtectedConfigurationProvider`.

Encrypting Sections Programmatically

Instead of using the `aspnet_regiis` tool to encrypt configuration sections, you can use the Configuration API. Specifically, you can encrypt a configuration section by calling the `SectionInformation.ProtectSection()` method.

For example, the ASP.NET page in Listing 28.26 displays all the sections contained in the `system.web` section group in a `GridView` control. You can click Protect to encrypt a section, and you can click UnProtect to decrypt a section (see Figure 28.14).

LISTING 28.26   EncryptConfig.aspx

```
<%@ Page Language="C#" %>
<%@ Import Namespace="System.Web.Configuration" %>
<%@ Import Namespace="System.Collections.Generic" %>
```

```
<!DOCTYPE html PUBLIC "-//W3C//DTD XHTML 1.0 Transitional//EN"
"http://www.w3.org/TR/xhtml1/DTD/xhtml1-transitional.dtd">
<script runat="server">

    void Page_Load()
    {
        if (!Page.IsPostBack)
            BindSections();
    }


    protected void grdSections_RowCommand(object sender, GridViewCommandEventArgs e)
    {
        int rowIndex = Int32.Parse((string)e.CommandArgument);
        string sectionName = (string)grdSections.DataKeys[rowIndex].Value;
        if (e.CommandName == "Protect")
            ProtectSection(sectionName);
        if (e.CommandName == "UnProtect")
            UnProtectSection(sectionName);
        BindSections();
    }


    private void ProtectSection(string sectionName)
    {
        Configuration config = WebConfigurationManager.OpenWebConfiguration
        ➥(Request.ApplicationPath);
        ConfigurationSection section = config.GetSection(sectionName);
        section.SectionInformation.ProtectSection
        ➥("RsaProtectedConfigurationProvider");
        config.Save(ConfigurationSaveMode.Modified);
    }


    private void UnProtectSection(string sectionName)
    {
        Configuration config = WebConfigurationManager.OpenWebConfiguration
        ➥(Request.ApplicationPath);
        ConfigurationSection section = config.GetSection(sectionName);
        section.SectionInformation.UnprotectSection();
        config.Save(ConfigurationSaveMode.Modified);
    }


    private void BindSections()
    {
        Configuration config = WebConfigurationManager.OpenWebConfiguration
        ➥(Request.ApplicationPath);
        List<SectionInformation> colSections = new List<SectionInformation>();
```

28

LISTING 28.26   Continued

```
        foreach (ConfigurationSection section in
        ➥config.SectionGroups["system.web"].Sections)
            colSections.Add(section.SectionInformation);
        grdSections.DataSource = colSections;
        grdSections.DataBind();
    }

</script>
<html xmlns="http://www.w3.org/1999/xhtml" >
<head id="Head1" runat="server">
    <title>Encrypt Config</title>
</head>
<body>
    <form id="form1" runat="server">
    <div>

    <asp:GridView
        id="grdSections"
        DataKeyNames="SectionName"
        AutoGenerateColumns="false"
        OnRowCommand="grdSections_RowCommand"
        Runat="server" >
        <Columns>
        <asp:ButtonField ButtonType="Link" Text="Protect" CommandName="Protect" />
        <asp:ButtonField ButtonType="Link" Text="UnProtect" CommandName=
        ➥"UnProtect" />
        <asp:CheckBoxField DataField="IsProtected" HeaderText="Protected" />
        <asp:BoundField DataField="SectionName" HeaderText="Section" />
        </Columns>
    </asp:GridView>

    </div>
    </form>
</body>
</html>
```

When you click the Protect link, the grdSection_RowCommand() event handler executes and calls the ProtectSection() method. This method calls the SectionInformation. ProtectSection() method to encrypt the selected section. Notice that the name of a ProtectedConfigurationProvider is passed to the ProtectSection() method.

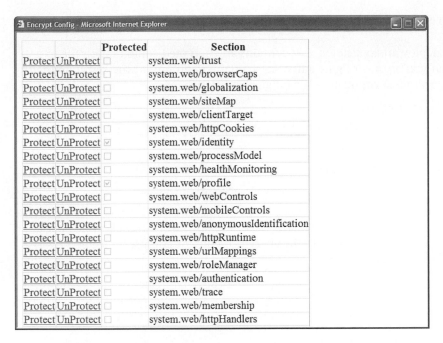

	Protected	Section
Protect UnProtect	☐	system.web/trust
Protect UnProtect	☐	system.web/browserCaps
Protect UnProtect	☐	system.web/globalization
Protect UnProtect	☐	system.web/siteMap
Protect UnProtect	☐	system.web/clientTarget
Protect UnProtect	☐	system.web/httpCookies
Protect UnProtect	☑	system.web/identity
Protect UnProtect	☐	system.web/processModel
Protect UnProtect	☐	system.web/healthMonitoring
Protect UnProtect	☑	system.web/profile
Protect UnProtect	☐	system.web/webControls
Protect UnProtect	☐	system.web/mobileControls
Protect UnProtect	☐	system.web/anonymousIdentification
Protect UnProtect	☐	system.web/httpRuntime
Protect UnProtect	☐	system.web/urlMappings
Protect UnProtect	☐	system.web/roleManager
Protect UnProtect	☐	system.web/authentication
Protect UnProtect	☐	system.web/trace
Protect UnProtect	☐	system.web/membership
Protect UnProtect	☐	system.web/httpHandlers

FIGURE 28.14   Encrypting and decrypting configuration sections.

WARNING

The page in Listing 28.26 saves the configuration file. By default, the ASPNET and NETWORK SERVICE accounts do not have permission to write to the file system. If you want the page in Listing 28.26 to execute within the security context of the user requesting the page, then you can enable per-request impersonation by adding the configuration file in Listing 28.16 to the root of your application.

Deploying Encrypted Web Configuration Files

If you need to copy an encrypted configuration file from one server to a new server, then you must copy the keys used to encrypt the configuration file to the new server. Otherwise, your application can't read encrypted sections of the configuration file on the new server.

WARNING

You can't copy an encrypted configuration file from one server to another when you are using the DpapiProtectedConfigurationProvider. This section assumes that you are using the RsaProtectedConfigurationProvider.

By default, the RsaProtectedConfigurationProvider uses a public/private key pair stored in a key container named NetFrameworkConfigurationKey. This key container is located at the following path:

28

```
\Documents and Settings\All Users\Application Data\Microsoft\Crypto\RSA\MachineKeys
```

If you want to deploy an application that contains an encrypted configuration file to a new server, then you must configure a new key container and import the key container to the new server. You must complete five configuration steps:

1. Create a new key container.
2. Configure your application to use the new key container.
3. Export the keys from the origin server.
4. Import the keys on the destination server.
5. Grant access to the key container to your ASP.NET application.

You need to perform this sequence of configuration steps only once. After you have set up both servers to use the same encryption keys, you can copy ASP.NET applications back and forth between the two servers and read the encrypted configuration sections. Let's examine each of these steps one by one.

First, you need to create a new key container because the default key container, the NetFrameworkConfigurationKey key container, does not support exporting both the public and private encryption keys. Execute the following command from a command prompt:

```
aspnet_regiis -pc "SharedKeys" -exp
```

This command creates a new key container named SharedKeys. The -exp option is used to make any keys added to the container exportable.

After you create the new key container, you must configure your application to use it. The web configuration file in Listing 28.27 configures RsaProtectedConfigurationProvider to use the SharedKeys key container.

LISTING 28.27   Web.config

```
<configuration>
  <configProtectedData
    defaultProvider="MyProtectedConfigurationProvider">
    <providers>
    <add
      name="MyProtectedConfigurationProvider"
      type="System.Configuration.RsaProtectedConfigurationProvider"
      cspProviderName=""
      useMachineContainer="true"
      useOAEP="false"
      keyContainerName="SharedKeys" />
    </providers>
  </configProtectedData>
```

```
    <connectionStrings>
      <add
        name="Movies"
        connectionString="Data Source=DataServer;Integrated Security=true;
          Initial Catalog=MyDB" />
    </connectionStrings>
</configuration>
```

Notice that the configuration file in Listing 28.27 includes a configProtectedData section. This section is used to configure a new ProtectedConfigurationProvider named MyProtectedConfigurationProvider. This provider includes a keyContainerName attribute that points to the SharedKeys key container.

The next step is to export the keys contained in the SharedKeys key container to an XML file. You can export the contents of the SharedKeys key container by executing the following command:

```
aspnet_regiis -px "SharedKeys" keys.xml -pri
```

Executing this command creates a new XML file named keys.xml. The -pri option causes both the private and public key—and not only the public key—to be exported to the XML file.

WARNING

The XML key file contains very secret information (the keys to the kingdom). After importing the XML file, you should immediately destroy the XML file (or stick the XML file on a CD and lock the CD away in a safe location).

After you create the keys.xml file on the origin server, you need to copy the file to the destination server and import the encryption keys. Execute the following command on the destination server to create a new key container and import the encryption keys:

```
aspnet_regiis -pi "SharedKeys" keys.xml
```

The final step is to grant access to the key container to your ASP.NET application. By default, a page served from Internet Information Server executes within the security context of either the NT Authority\NETWORK SERVICE account (Windows 2003 Server or Vista) or the ASPNET account (other operating systems). You can grant access to the SharedKeys key container to the ASPNET account by executing the following command:

```
aspnet_regiis -pa "SharedKeys" "ASPNET"
```

Executing this command modifies the ACLs for the SharedKeys key container so that the ASPNET account has access to the encryption keys.

28

After you complete this final step, you can transfer ASP.NET applications with encrypted configuration files back and forth between the two servers. An application on one server can read configuration files that were encrypted on the other server.

> **NOTE**
>
> As an alternative to using the `aspnet_regiis` tool, you can transfer encryption keys with the help of the `RsaProtectedConfigurationProvider` class. The `RsaProtectedConfigurationProvider` class contains methods for exporting and importing keys to and from XML files programmatically.

Summary

This chapter was devoted to the topic of configuration. In the first section, you were provided with an overview of the configuration sections used by the ASP.NET Framework. You learned how to lock configuration sections to prevent sections from being modified. You also learned how to place configuration sections in external files.

Next, we tackled the topic of the Configuration API. You learned how to read and modify configuration files programmatically. You also learned how to provision new ASP.NET applications by creating new virtual directories and configuration files.

You also learned how to create custom configuration sections. You learned how to create both simple custom configuration sections and custom configuration sections that contain custom collections of configuration elements.

Finally, we discussed the topic of encryption. You learned how to encrypt a configuration section by using the `aspnet_regiis` command-line tool. You also learned how to encrypt configuration sections programmatically. In the final section, you also learned how to deploy encrypted configuration files from a development server to a production server.

PART VIII

Custom Control Building

IN THIS PART

Building Custom Controls

In this chapter, you learn how to extend the ASP.NET Framework by building custom controls. You learn how to create controls in exactly the same way as Microsoft developed the standard ASP.NET controls such as the TextBox and Button controls.

Overview of Custom Control Building

You must answer two questions before writing a custom control:

▶ What type of control do I want to write?

▶ From what class do I inherit?

The two basic types of controls are fully rendered and composite controls. When you build a fully rendered control, you start from scratch. You specify all the HTML content that the control renders to the browser.

When you create a composite control, on the other hand, you build a new control from existing controls. For example, you can create a composite AddressForm control from existing TextBox and RequiredFieldValidator controls. When you create a composite control, you bundle together existing controls as a new control.

The second question that you must address is the choice of the base control for your new control. You can inherit a new control from any existing ASP.NET control. For example, if you want to create a better GridView control, then you can inherit a new control from the `GridView` control and add additional properties and methods to your custom `GridView` control.

Typically, when building a basic control, you inherit your new control from one of the following base classes:

- ▶ `System.Web.UI.Control`
- ▶ `System.Web.UI.WebControls.WebControl`
- ▶ `System.Web.UI.WebControls.CompositeControl`

The `CompositeControl` class inherits from the `WebControl` class, which inherits from the `Control` class. Each of these base classes adds additional functionality.

The base class for all controls in the ASP.NET Framework is the `System.Web.UI.Control` class. Every control, including the `TextBox` and `GridView` controls, ultimately derives from this control. This means that all the properties, methods, and events of the `System.Web.UI.Control` class are shared by all controls in the Framework.

All Web controls inherit from the base `System.Web.UI.WebControls.WebControl` class. The difference between the `Control` class and `WebControl` class is that controls that derive from the `WebControl` class always have opening and closing tags. Because a `WebControl` has an opening and closing tag, you also get more formatting options. For example, the `WebControl` class includes `BackColor`, `Font`, and `ForeColor` properties.

For example, the ASP.NET `Literal` control inherits from the base `Control` class, whereas the `Label` control inherits from the base `WebControl` class. The `Repeater` control inherits from the base `Control` class, whereas the `GridView` control (ultimately) inherits from the `WebControl` class.

Finally, the `System.Web.UI.WebControls.CompositeControl` should be used as the base class for any composite control. The `CompositeControl` automatically creates a naming container for its child controls. It also includes an overridden `Controls` property that forces child controls to appear in Design view.

Building Fully Rendered Controls

Let's start by creating a simple fully rendered control. When you create a fully rendered control, you take on the responsibility of specifying all the HTML content that the control renders to the browser.

The file in Listing 29.1 contains a fully rendered control that derives from the base `Control` class.

LISTING 29.1   `FullyRenderedControl.cs`

```
using System.Web.UI;


namespace myControls
{
```

```
    public class FullyRenderedControl : Control
    {
        private string _Text;

        public string Text
        {
            get { return _Text; }
            set { _Text = value; }
        }

        protected override void Render(HtmlTextWriter writer)
        {
            writer.Write(_Text);
        }
    }
}
```

NOTE

Add the control in Listing 29.1 to your App_Code folder. Any code added to the
App_Code folder is compiled dynamically.

The control in Listing 29.1 inherits from the base `Control` class, overriding the base
class `Render()` method. The control simply displays whatever value that you assign to
its `Text` property. The value of the `Text` property is written to the browser with the
`HtmlTextWriter` class's `Write()` method.

The file in Listing 29.2 illustrates how you can use the new control in a page.

LISTING 29.2   ShowFullyRenderedControl.aspx

```
<%@ Page Language="C#" %>
<%@ Register TagPrefix="custom" Namespace="myControls" %>
<!DOCTYPE html PUBLIC "-//W3C//DTD XHTML 1.0 Transitional//EN"
"http://www.w3.org/TR/xhtml1/DTD/xhtml1-transitional.dtd">
<html xmlns="http://www.w3.org/1999/xhtml" >
<head id="Head1" runat="server">
    <title>Show Fully Rendered Control</title>
</head>
<body>
    <form id="form1" runat="server">
    <div>

    <custom:FullyRenderedControl
```

LISTING 29.2   Continued

```
        ID="FullyRenderedControl1"
        Text="Hello World!"
        runat="Server" />

    </div>
    </form>
</body>
</html>
```

NOTE

In Listing 29.2, the custom control is registered in the page through use of the <%@
Register %> directive. Alternatively, you can register the control for an entire website
by registering the control in the <pages> section of the web configuration file.

If you open the page in Listing 29.2 in a browser and select View Source, you can see the
HTML rendered by the control. The control simply renders the string "Hello World!".

Rather than inherit from the base Control class, you can create a fully rendered control by
inheriting a new control from the base WebControl class. When inheriting from the
WebControl class, you override the RenderContents() method instead of the Render()
method.

For example, the control in Listing 29.3 contains a simple fully rendered control that
inherits from the WebControl class.

LISTING 29.3   FullyRenderedWebControl.cs

```csharp
using System.Web.UI;
using System.Web.UI.WebControls;

namespace myControls
{
    public class FullyRenderedWebControl : WebControl
    {
        private string _Text;

        public string Text
        {
            get { return _Text; }
            set { _Text = value; }
        }

        protected override void RenderContents(HtmlTextWriter writer)
```

```
        {
            writer.Write(_Text);
        }
    }
}
```

The page in Listing 29.4 illustrates how you can use the new control (see Figure 29.1). Notice that the BackColor, BorderStyle, and Font properties are set. Because the control in Listing 29.3 derives from the base WebControl class, you get these properties for free.

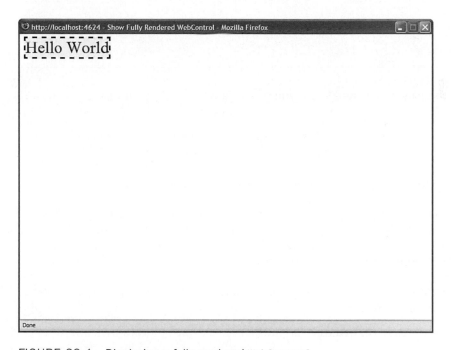

FIGURE 29.1   Displaying a fully rendered WebControl.

LISTING 29.4   ShowFullyRenderedWebControl.aspx

```
<%@ Page Language="C#" %>
<%@ Register TagPrefix="custom" Namespace="myControls" %>
<!DOCTYPE html PUBLIC "-//W3C//DTD XHTML 1.0 Transitional//EN"
"http://www.w3.org/TR/xhtml1/DTD/xhtml1-transitional.dtd">
<html xmlns="http://www.w3.org/1999/xhtml" >
<head id="Head1" runat="server">
    <title>Show Fully Rendered WebControl</title>
</head>
<body>
    <form id="form1" runat="server">
    <div>
```

LISTING 29.4   Continued

```
    <custom:FullyRenderedWebControl
        ID="FullyrenderedWebControl1"
        Text="Hello World"
        BackColor="Yellow"
        BorderStyle="Dashed"
        Font-Size="32px"
        Runat="Server" />

    </div>
    </form>
</body>
</html>
```

After opening the page in Listing 29.4, if you select View Source in your browser, you can see the rendered output of the control. It looks like this:

```
<span id="FullyrenderedWebControl1" style="display:inline-block;background-
color:Yellow;border-style:Dashed;font-size:32px;">Hello World</span>
```

A WebControl, unlike a control, renders an enclosing <span> tag by default.

Understanding the HtmlTextWriter Class   When you create a fully rendered control, you use the HtmlTextWriter class to write the HTML content to the browser. The HtmlTextWriter class was specifically designed to make it easier to render HTML. Here is a partial list of the methods supported by this class:

▶ **AddAttribute()**—Adds an HTML attribute to the tag rendered by calling RenderBeginTag().

▶ **AddStyleAttribute()**—Adds a CSS attribute to the tag rendered by a call to RenderBeginTag().

▶ **RenderBeginTag()**—Renders an opening HTML tag.

▶ **RenderEndTag()**—Renders a closing HTML tag.

▶ **Write()**—Renders a string to the browser.

▶ **WriteBreak()**—Renders a <br /> tag to the browser.

You can call the AddAttribute() or the AddStyleAttribute() method as many times as you want before calling RenderBeginTag(). When you call RenderBeginTag(), all the attributes are added to the opening HTML tag.

The methods of the HtmlTextWriter class can use the following enumerations:

▶ **HtmlTextWriterTag**—Contains a list of the most common HTML tags.

▶ **HtmlTextWriterAttribute**—Contains a list of the most common HTML attributes.

▶ **HtmlTextWriterStyle**—Contains a list of the most Cascading Style Sheet attributes.

When using the methods of the HtmlTextWriter class, you should strive to use these enumerations to represent HTML tags and attributes. If a particular tag or attribute is missing from one of the enumerations, you can pass a string value instead.

For example, the control in Listing 29.5 renders a table of HTML colors by using an HTML table (see Figure 29.2). Notice that the RenderContents() method takes advantage of the methods of the HtmlTextWriter class to render the HTML table.

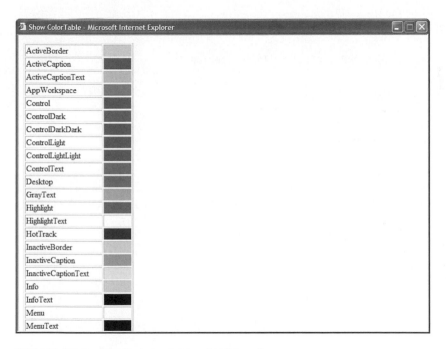

FIGURE 29.2   Displaying a table of HTML colors.

LISTING 29.5   ColorTable.cs

```
using System;
using System.Web.UI;
using System.Web.UI.WebControls;
using System.Drawing;

namespace myControls
{
    public class ColorTable : WebControl
    {
```

LISTING 29.5   Continued

```
    protected override void RenderContents(HtmlTextWriter writer)
    {
        // Get list of colors
        KnownColor[] colors = (KnownColor[])Enum.GetValues(typeof(KnownColor));

        // Render opening table tag
        writer.AddAttribute(HtmlTextWriterAttribute.Border, "1");
        writer.RenderBeginTag(HtmlTextWriterTag.Table);

        // Render table body
        foreach (KnownColor colorName in colors)
        {
            writer.RenderBeginTag(HtmlTextWriterTag.Tr);

            // Render first column
            writer.RenderBeginTag(HtmlTextWriterTag.Td);
            writer.Write(colorName);
            writer.RenderEndTag();

            // Render second column
            writer.AddAttribute(HtmlTextWriterAttribute.Width, "50px");
            writer.AddAttribute(HtmlTextWriterAttribute.Bgcolor,
            ➥colorName.ToString());
            writer.RenderBeginTag(HtmlTextWriterTag.Td);
            writer.Write(" ");
            writer.RenderEndTag();

            writer.RenderEndTag();
        }

        // close table
        writer.RenderEndTag();
    }
  }
}
```

You should notice a number of things about the control in Listing 29.5. First, notice that
the AddAttribute() method is called to add the table border attribute. When the
RenderBeginTag() method is called, the table border attribute is added to the opening
table tag.

Furthermore, notice that you do not specify the tag when calling the `RenderEndTag()` method. This method automatically closes the last tag opened with the `RenderBeginTag()` method.

> **NOTE**
>
> The CD that accompanies this book includes a `ShowColorTable.aspx` page that you can open in your browser to view the rendered output of the `ColorTable` control.

The control in Listing 29.6, the `DropShadow` control, illustrates how you can use the `AddStyleAttribute()` method of the `HtmlTextWriter` class to add Cascading Style Sheet attributes to an HTML tag.

LISTING 29.6   DropShadow.cs

```
using System.Web.UI;
using System.Web.UI.WebControls;

namespace myControls
{
    public class DropShadow : WebControl
    {
        private string _Text;

        public string Text
        {
            get { return _Text; }
            set { _Text = value; }
        }

        protected override void RenderContents(HtmlTextWriter writer)
        {
            writer.AddStyleAttribute(HtmlTextWriterStyle.Filter,
            ➥"dropShadow(color=#AAAAAA,offX=3,offY=3);width:500px");
            writer.RenderBeginTag(HtmlTextWriterTag.Div);
            writer.Write(_Text);
            writer.RenderEndTag();
        }
    }
}
```

The control in Listing 29.6 renders a drop shadow behind whatever text you assign to the control's `Text` property (see Figure 29.3). The drop shadow is created with the help of an Internet Explorer `DropShadow` filter.

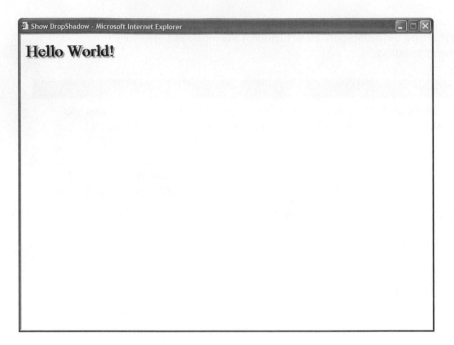

FIGURE 29.3   Displaying a drop shadow with the DropShadow control.

Notice that the Filter attribute is added to the <div> tag with a call to the AddStyleAttribute() method. The AddStyleAttribute() method works just like the AddAttribute() method, except that the AddStyleAttribute() method adds a CSS attribute instead of an HTML attribute.

WEB STANDARDS NOTE

Filters are an Internet Explorer extension to the Cascading Style Sheet standard. They don't work with Firefox or Opera. Firefox has its own extensions to Cascading Style Sheets with its -moz style rules.

Specifying the Containing WebControl Tag   By default, a WebControl renders an HTML <span> tag around its contents. You can specify a different tag by overriding the WebControl's TagKey property.

For example, the control in Listing 29.7 renders its contents within an HTML <div> tag.

LISTING 29.7   Glow.cs

```
using System.Web.UI;
using System.Web.UI.WebControls;
```

```
namespace myControls
{
    public class Glow : WebControl
    {
        private string _Text;

        public string Text
        {
            get { return _Text; }
            set { _Text = value; }
        }

        protected override HtmlTextWriterTag TagKey
        {
            get
            {
                return HtmlTextWriterTag.Div;
            }
        }

        protected override void AddAttributesToRender(HtmlTextWriter writer)
        {
            writer.AddStyleAttribute(HtmlTextWriterStyle.Filter,
            ➥"glow(Color=#ffd700,Strength=10)");
            base.AddAttributesToRender(writer);
        }

        protected override void RenderContents(HtmlTextWriter writer)
        {
            writer.Write(_Text);
        }

        public Glow()
        {
            this.Width = Unit.Parse("500px");
        }

    }
}
```

The control in Listing 29.7 displays a glowing effect around any text that you assign to its Text property. The control takes advantage of the Internet Explorer Glow filter to create the glow effect (see Figure 29.4).

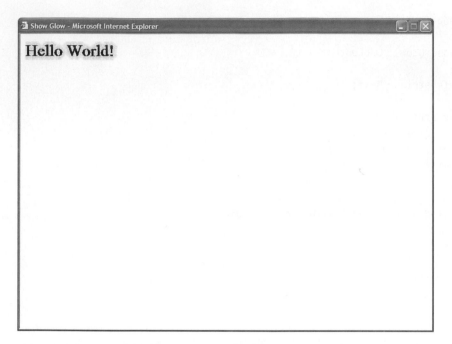

FIGURE 29.4   Displaying glowing text with the Glow control.

Notice that the control overrides the base WebControl's TagKey property. Because the over-ridden property returns a <div> tag, the WebControl renders a <div> tag.

> **NOTE**
>
> There are several methods you can use to modify the tag rendered by a WebControl. You can override the TagName property instead of the TagKey property. The TagName property enables you to specify an arbitrary string for the tag. (It doesn't limit you to the HtmlTextWriterTag enumeration.) You also can specify the tag rendered by a WebControl in the WebControl's constructor. Finally, you can override a WebControl's RenderBeginTag() and RenderEndTag() methods and completely customize the opening and closing tags.

Furthermore, you should notice that the control in Listing 29.7 overrides the AddAttributesToRender() method. If you override this method, then you can add HTML or CSS attributes to the opening HTML tag rendered by the control. When overriding this method, be careful to call the base AddAttributesToRender() method or the standard control attributes, such as the control ID, won't be rendered.

Building Composite Controls

If you don't want to start from scratch when building a custom control, you can build a composite control. When you create a composite control, you create a new control from existing controls.

Every ASP.NET control has a `Controls` property that represents all of its child controls. If you add child controls to a control, then the child controls are automatically rendered when the parent control is rendered.

When you create a composite control, you typically override a control's `CreateChildControls()` method. This method is called when a control builds its collection of child controls.

For example, the control in Listing 29.8 combines a `TextBox` control and `RequiredFieldValidator` control.

LISTING 29.8   RequiredTextBox.cs

```csharp
using System;
using System.Web.UI.WebControls;

namespace myControls
{
    public class RequiredTextBox : CompositeControl
    {
        private TextBox input;
        private RequiredFieldValidator validator;

        public string Text
        {
            get
            {
                EnsureChildControls();
                return input.Text;
            }
            set
            {
                EnsureChildControls();
                input.Text = value;
            }
        }

        protected override void CreateChildControls()
        {
            input = new TextBox();
            input.ID = "input";
            this.Controls.Add(input);

            validator = new RequiredFieldValidator();
            validator.ID = "valInput";
            validator.ControlToValidate = input.ID;
            validator.ErrorMessage = "(Required)";
```

29

LISTING 29.8   Continued

```
            validator.Display = ValidatorDisplay.Dynamic;
            this.Controls.Add(validator);
        }
    }
}
```

Notice that the control in Listing 29.8 inherits from the base `CompositeControl` class. Furthermore, rather than override the base control's `RenderContents()` method, the control overrides the base control's `CreateChildControls()` method.

You should notice one other special thing in Listing 29.8. Notice that the `EnsureChildControls()` method is called in both the `Get` and `Set` methods of the `Text` property. The `EnsureChildControls()` method forces the `CreateChildControls()` method to be called. However, it prevents the `CreateChildControls()` method from being called more than once.

The Text property gets or sets a property of a child control (the TextBox control). If you attempt to use the Text property before the `CreateChildControls()` method is called, then you receive a null reference exception. The child controls must be created before you can access any of the child control properties.

The page in Listing 29.9 illustrates how you can use the `RequiredTextBox` control in a page.

LISTING 29.9   ShowRequiredTextBox.aspx

```
<%@ Page Language="C#" Trace="true" %>
<%@ Register TagPrefix="custom" Namespace="myControls" %>
<!DOCTYPE html PUBLIC "-//W3C//DTD XHTML 1.0 Transitional//EN"
"http://www.w3.org/TR/xhtml1/DTD/xhtml1-transitional.dtd">
<script runat="server">

    protected void btnSubmit_Click(object sender, EventArgs e)
    {
        lblResults.Text = txtUserName.Text;
    }
</script>
<html xmlns="http://www.w3.org/1999/xhtml" >
<head id="Head1" runat="server">
    <title>Show RequiredTextBox</title>
</head>
<body>
    <form id="form1" runat="server">
    <div>

    <asp:Label
```

```
            ID="lblUserName"
            Text="User Name:"
            AssociatedControlID="txtUserName"
            Runat="server" />

        <custom:RequiredTextBox
            ID="txtUserName"
            Runat="Server" />

        <br />

        <asp:Button
            ID="btnSubmit"
            Text="Submit"
            Runat="server" OnClick="btnSubmit_Click" />

        <hr />

        <asp:Label
            id="lblResults"
            Runat="server" />

        </div>
        </form>
</body>
</html>
```

The page in Listing 29.9 has tracing enabled. If you look at the control tree for the page, you see that the `RequiredTextBox` control includes both a `TextBox` and `RequiredFieldValidator` control as child controls.

Building Hybrid Controls

In practice, you rarely build pure composite controls. In most cases in which you override a control's `CreateChildControls()` method, you also override the control's `RenderContents()` method to specify the layout of the child controls.

For example, the control in Listing 29.10 represents a `Login` control. In the control's `CreateChildControls()` method, two `TextBox` controls are added to the control's collection of child controls.

LISTING 29.10 Login.cs

```
using System;
using System.Web.UI;
using System.Web.UI.WebControls;
```

LISTING 29.10   Continued

```csharp
namespace myControls
{
    public class Login : CompositeControl
    {
        private TextBox txtUserName;
        private TextBox txtPassword;

        public string UserName
        {
            get
            {
                EnsureChildControls();
                return txtUserName.Text;
            }

            set
            {
                EnsureChildControls();
                txtUserName.Text = value;
            }
        }

        public string Password
        {
            get
            {
                EnsureChildControls();
                return txtPassword.Text;
            }

            set
            {
                EnsureChildControls();
                txtPassword.Text = value;
            }
        }

        protected override void CreateChildControls()
        {
            txtUserName = new TextBox();
            txtUserName.ID = "txtUserName";
            this.Controls.Add(txtUserName);

            txtPassword = new TextBox();
```

```csharp
        txtPassword.ID = "txtPassword";
        txtPassword.TextMode = TextBoxMode.Password;
        this.Controls.Add(txtPassword);
    }

    protected override void RenderContents(HtmlTextWriter writer)
    {
        writer.RenderBeginTag(HtmlTextWriterTag.Tr);

        // Render UserName Label
        writer.RenderBeginTag(HtmlTextWriterTag.Td);
        writer.AddAttribute(HtmlTextWriterAttribute.For, txtUserName.ClientID);
        writer.RenderBeginTag(HtmlTextWriterTag.Label);
        writer.Write("User Name:");
        writer.RenderEndTag(); // Label
        writer.RenderEndTag(); // TD

        // Render UserName TextBox
        writer.RenderBeginTag(HtmlTextWriterTag.Td);
        txtUserName.RenderControl(writer);
        writer.RenderEndTag(); // TD

        writer.RenderEndTag();
        writer.RenderBeginTag(HtmlTextWriterTag.Tr);

        // Render Password Label
        writer.RenderBeginTag(HtmlTextWriterTag.Td);
        writer.AddAttribute(HtmlTextWriterAttribute.For, txtPassword.ClientID);
        writer.RenderBeginTag(HtmlTextWriterTag.Label);
        writer.Write("Password:");
        writer.RenderEndTag(); // Label
        writer.RenderEndTag(); // TD

        // Render Password TextBox
        writer.RenderBeginTag(HtmlTextWriterTag.Td);
        txtPassword.RenderControl(writer);
        writer.RenderEndTag(); // TD

        writer.RenderEndTag(); // TR
    }

    protected override HtmlTextWriterTag TagKey
    {
        get
        {
            return HtmlTextWriterTag.Table;
```

29

LISTING 29.10   Continued

```
            }
        }

    }
}
```

In Listing 29.10, the `RenderContents()` method is overridden in order to layout the two `TextBox` controls. The `TextBox` controls are rendered within an HTML table (see Figure 29.5). Notice that each `TextBox` is rendered by calling the `RenderControl()` method.

FIGURE 29.5   Performing layout with an HTML table.

The default `RenderContents()` method simply calls the `RenderControl()` method for each child control. If you override the `RenderContents()` method, you have more control over the layout of the control.

The `Login` control in Listing 29.10 uses an HTML table for layout. From a web standards perspective, using HTML tables for layout is frowned upon. The modified `Login` control in Listing 29.11 uses <div> tags instead of a <table> tag for layout.

LISTING 29.11   LoginStandards.cs

```
using System;
using System.Web.UI;
```

```csharp
using System.Web.UI.WebControls;

namespace myControls
{
    public class LoginStandards : CompositeControl
    {
        private TextBox txtUserName;
        private TextBox txtPassword;

        public string UserName
        {
            get
            {
                EnsureChildControls();
                return txtUserName.Text;
            }

            set
            {
                EnsureChildControls();
                txtUserName.Text = value;
            }
        }

        public string Password
        {
            get
            {
                EnsureChildControls();
                return txtPassword.Text;
            }

            set
            {
                EnsureChildControls();
                txtPassword.Text = value;
            }
        }

        protected override void CreateChildControls()
        {
            txtUserName = new TextBox();
            txtUserName.ID = "txtUserName";
            this.Controls.Add(txtUserName);

            txtPassword = new TextBox();
```

LISTING 29.11   Continued

```
            txtPassword.ID = "txtPassword";
            txtPassword.TextMode = TextBoxMode.Password;
            this.Controls.Add(txtPassword);
        }

        protected override void RenderContents(HtmlTextWriter writer)
        {
            writer.AddStyleAttribute("float", "left");
            writer.RenderBeginTag(HtmlTextWriterTag.Div);
            writer.AddStyleAttribute(HtmlTextWriterStyle.Padding, "3px");
            writer.RenderBeginTag(HtmlTextWriterTag.Div);
            writer.AddAttribute(HtmlTextWriterAttribute.For, txtUserName.ClientID);
            writer.RenderBeginTag(HtmlTextWriterTag.Label);
            writer.Write("User Name:");
            writer.RenderEndTag();
            writer.RenderEndTag();

            writer.AddStyleAttribute(HtmlTextWriterStyle.Padding, "3px");
            writer.RenderBeginTag(HtmlTextWriterTag.Div);
            writer.AddAttribute(HtmlTextWriterAttribute.For, txtPassword.ClientID);
            writer.RenderBeginTag(HtmlTextWriterTag.Label);
            writer.Write("Password:");
            writer.RenderEndTag();
            writer.RenderEndTag();
            writer.RenderEndTag();

            writer.AddStyleAttribute("float", "left");
            writer.RenderBeginTag(HtmlTextWriterTag.Div);
            writer.AddStyleAttribute(HtmlTextWriterStyle.Padding, "3px");
            writer.RenderBeginTag(HtmlTextWriterTag.Div);
            txtUserName.RenderControl(writer);
            writer.RenderEndTag();

            writer.AddStyleAttribute(HtmlTextWriterStyle.Padding, "3px");
            writer.RenderBeginTag(HtmlTextWriterTag.Div);
            txtPassword.RenderControl(writer);
            writer.RenderEndTag();
            writer.RenderEndTag();

            writer.Write("<br style='clear:left' />");
        }

        protected override HtmlTextWriterTag TagKey
        {
```

```
        get
        {
            return HtmlTextWriterTag.Div;
        }
    }
    }
}
```

The control in Listing 29.11 works quite nicely in all recent browsers (Internet Explorer 6, Firefox 1, Opera 8) without requiring an HTML table for layout (see Figure 29.6).

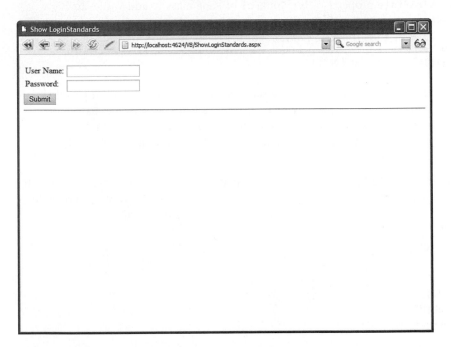

FIGURE 29.6   Performing CSS layout.

> **NOTE**
>
> Microsoft does not have the luxury of using <div> tags for layout. Because Microsoft must support very old browsers that have limited or no support for Cascading Style Sheets (HTML 3.2 browsers), the standard controls must rely on HTML tables for layout.

View State and Control State

The standard ASP.NET controls retain the values of their properties across postbacks. For example, if you change the text displayed by a Label control, the Label control will continue to display the new text even if you repeatedly post the page containing the Label control back to the server.

The ASP.NET Framework takes advantage of a hidden form field named __VIEWSTATE to preserve the state of control properties across postbacks. If you want your controls to preserve the values of their properties, then you need to add the values of your control properties to this hidden form field.

The ASP.NET Framework supports two methods of preserving values across postbacks. You can take advantage of either View State or Control State.

Supporting View State

You can use the ViewState property of the Control or Page class to add values to View State. The ViewState property exposes a dictionary of key and value pairs. For example, the following statement adds the string Hello World! to View State:

```
ViewState("message") = "Hello World!"
```

Technically, you can add an instance of any serializable class to View State. In practice, however, you should add only simple values to View State, such as Strings, DateTimes, and Integers. Remember that anything that you add to View State must be added to the hidden __VIEWSTATE form field. If this field gets too big, it can have a significant impact on your page's performance.

The control in Listing 29.12 has two properties, named Text and ViewStateText. The first property does not use View State, and the second property does use View State. The value of the ViewStateText property is preserved across postbacks automatically.

LISTING 29.12 ViewStateControl.cs

```csharp
using System;
using System.Web;
using System.Web.UI;
using System.Web.UI.WebControls;

namespace myControls
{
    public class ViewStateControl : WebControl
    {
        private string _text;

        public string Text
        {
            get { return _text; }
            set { _text = value; }
        }
```

```
    public string ViewStateText
    {
        get
        {
            if (ViewState["ViewStateText"] == null)
                return String.Empty;
            else
                return (string)ViewState["ViewStateText"];
        }
        set { ViewState["ViewStateText"] = value; }
    }

    protected override void RenderContents(HtmlTextWriter writer)
    {
        writer.Write("Text: " + Text);
        writer.WriteBreak();
        writer.Write("ViewStateText: " + ViewStateText);
        writer.WriteBreak();
    }

    }
}
```

Notice that the `ViewStateText` property uses the Control's `ViewState` collection to preserve whatever value is assigned to the `ViewStateText` property across postbacks. When you add a value to the `ViewState` collection, the value is stuffed into the hidden __VIEWSTATE form field automatically.

WARNING

View State is loaded after the Page `InitComplete` event, and View State is saved after the Page `PreRenderComplete` event. This means that you should not attempt to retrieve a value from View State before or during the `InitComplete` event. You also should not attempt to add a value to View State after the `PreRenderComplete` event.

The page in Listing 29.13 includes the `ViewStateControl`. The text `Hello World!` is assigned to both control properties in the `Page_Load()` handler. However, if you post the page back to itself by clicking the button, only the value of the `ViewStateText` property is preserved across postbacks.

LISTING 29.13　ShowViewState.aspx

```
<%@ Page Language="C#" %>
<%@ Register TagPrefix="custom" Namespace="myControls" %>
<!DOCTYPE html PUBLIC "-//W3C//DTD XHTML 1.0 Transitional//EN"
```

LISTING 29.13   Continued

```
"http://www.w3.org/TR/xhtml1/DTD/xhtml1-transitional.dtd">
<script runat="server">

    void Page_Load()
    {
        if (!Page.IsPostBack)
        {
            ViewStateControl1.Text = "Hello World!";
            ViewStateControl1.ViewStateText = "Hello World!";
        }
    }

</script>
<html xmlns="http://www.w3.org/1999/xhtml" >
<head runat="server">
    <title>Show View State</title>
</head>
<body>
    <form id="form1" runat="server">
    <div>

    <custom:ViewStateControl
        id="ViewStateControl1"
        Runat="server" />

    <asp:Button
        id="btnSubmit"
        Text="Submit"
        Runat="server" />

    </div>
    </form>
</body>
</html>
```

Supporting Control State

The ASP.NET Framework includes a feature named Control State. Control State is very similar to View State. Just like View State, any values that you add to Control State are preserved in the hidden __VIEWSTATE form field. However, unlike View State, Control State cannot be disabled. Control State is intended to be used only for storing crucial information across postbacks.

Control State was introduced to address a problem that developers encountered in the first version of the ASP.NET Framework. You can disable View State for any control by assigning the value False to a control's EnableViewState property. Often, this is a very good idea for performance reasons. However, disabling View State also made several controls nonfunctional.

For example, by default a GridView control retains the values of all the records that it displays in View State. If you display 500 database records with a GridView control, then by default all 500 records are stuffed into the hidden __VIEWSTATE form field. To improve performance, you might want to disable View State for the GridView.

However, a GridView uses the __VIEWSTATE form field to remember crucial information required for the proper functioning of the control, such as the current page number and the currently selected row. You don't want the GridView to forget this critical information even when View State is disabled.

The concept of Control State was introduced enable you to save critical information in the hidden __VIEWSTATE form field even when View State is disabled. Microsoft makes it slightly more difficult to use Control State because they don't want you to overuse this feature. You should use it only when storing super critical information.

For example, the control in Listing 29.14 includes two properties named ViewStateText and ControlStateText. View State is used to preserve the value of the first property, and Control State is used to preserve the value of the second property.

LISTING 29.14   ControlStateControl.cs

```
using System;
using System.Web;
using System.Web.UI;
using System.Web.UI.WebControls;

namespace myControls
{

    public class ControlStateControl : WebControl
    {

        private string _controlStateText;

        public string ViewStateText
        {
            get
            {
                if (ViewState["ViewStateText"] == null)
                    return String.Empty;
                else
                    return (string)ViewState["ViewStateText"];
```

29

LISTING 29.14   Continued

```
                    }
             set { ViewState["ViewStateText"] = value; }
          }

          public string ControlStateText
          {
             get { return _controlStateText; }
             set { _controlStateText = value; }
          }

          protected override void OnInit(EventArgs e)
          {
             Page.RegisterRequiresControlState(this);
             base.OnInit(e);
          }

          protected override object SaveControlState()
          {
             return _controlStateText;
          }

          protected override void LoadControlState(object savedState)
          {
             _controlStateText = (string)savedState;
          }

          protected override void RenderContents(HtmlTextWriter writer)
          {
             writer.Write("ViewStateText: " + ViewStateText);
             writer.WriteBreak();
             writer.Write("ControlStateText: " + ControlStateText);
             writer.WriteBreak();
          }

      }
}
```

Notice that the control in Listing 29.14 overrides the base Control class's OnInit(),
SaveControlState(), and LoadControlState() methods. In the OnInit() method, the
RegisterRequiresControlState() method is called to indicate that the control needs to
take advantage of Control State.

The SaveControlState() and LoadControlState() methods are responsible for saving and
loading the Control State. Notice that Control State is saved as an object. The object is serialized by the ASP.NET Framework into the hidden __VIEWSTATE form field automatically.

The page in Listing 29.15 illustrates the difference between View State and Control State. In the Page_Load() handler, the value Hello World! is assigned to both properties of the ControlStateControl. Notice that the control has View State disabled. However, if you click the button and post the page back to itself, the value of the ControlStateText property is not lost.

LISTING 29.15   ShowControlState.aspx

```aspx
<%@ Page Language="C#" %>
<%@ Register TagPrefix="custom" Namespace="myControls" %>
<!DOCTYPE html PUBLIC "-//W3C//DTD XHTML 1.0 Transitional//EN"
"http://www.w3.org/TR/xhtml1/DTD/xhtml1-transitional.dtd">
<script runat="server">

    void Page_Load()
    {
        if (!Page.IsPostBack)
        {
            ControlStateControl1.ViewStateText = "Hello World!";
            ControlStateControl1.ControlStateText = "Hello World!";
        }
    }

</script>
<html xmlns="http://www.w3.org/1999/xhtml" >
<head id="Head1" runat="server">
    <title>Show Control State</title>
</head>
<body>
    <form id="form1" runat="server">
    <div>

    <custom:ControlStateControl
        id="ControlStateControl1"
        EnableViewState="false"
        Runat="server" />

    <asp:Button
        id="btnSubmit"
        Text="Submit"
        Runat="server" />

    </div>
    </form>
</body>
</html>
```

29

Processing Postback Data and Events

The ASP.NET Framework is built around web forms. ASP.NET controls pass information from the browser to the server by submitting a form to the server. This process of posting a form back to the server is called a *postback*.

When an ASP.NET page processes a form that has been posted back to the server, two types of information can be passed to the controls in the page. First, if a control initiates a postback, then a server-side event can be raised when the form is posted to the server. For example, if you click a Button control, then a Click event is raised on the server when the form containing the Button is posted back to the server. This event is called a *postback event*.

Second, the form data contained in the web form can be passed to a control. For example, when you submit a form that contains a TextBox control, the form data is passed to the TextBox control when the web form is submitted to the server. This form data is called the *postback data*.

When building a custom control, you might need to process either postback data or a postback event. In this section, you learn how to implement the required control interfaces for processing postbacks.

Handling Postback Data

If your control needs to process form data submitted to the server, then you need to implement the IPostbackDataHandler interface. This interface includes the following two methods:

- **LoadPostData()**—Receives the form fields posted from the browser.

- **RaisePostDataChangedEvent()**—Enables you to raise an event indicating that the value of a form field has been changed.

For example, the control in Listing 29.16 is a simple TextBox control. It implements the IPostbackDataHandler interface to preserve the state of an input field across postbacks.

LISTING 29.16   CustomTextBox.cs

```
using System;
using System.Web.UI;
using System.Web.UI.WebControls;

namespace myControls
{
    public class CustomTextBox : WebControl, IPostBackDataHandler
    {
        public event EventHandler TextChanged;

        public string Text
```

```
        {
            get
            {
                if (ViewState["Text"] == null)
                    return String.Empty;
                else
                    return (string)ViewState["Text"];
            }

            set { ViewState["Text"] = value; }
        }

        protected override void AddAttributesToRender(HtmlTextWriter writer)
        {
            writer.AddAttribute(HtmlTextWriterAttribute.Type, "text");
            writer.AddAttribute(HtmlTextWriterAttribute.Value, Text);
            writer.AddAttribute(HtmlTextWriterAttribute.Name, this.UniqueID);
            base.AddAttributesToRender(writer);
        }

        protected override HtmlTextWriterTag TagKey
        {
            get
            {
                return HtmlTextWriterTag.Input;
            }
        }

        public bool LoadPostData(string postDataKey, System.Collections.
        ➥Specialized.NameValueCollection postCollection)
        {
            if (postCollection[postDataKey] != Text)
            {
                Text = postCollection[postDataKey];
                return true;
            }
            return false;
        }

        public void RaisePostDataChangedEvent()
        {
            if (TextChanged != null)
                TextChanged(this, EventArgs.Empty);
        }
    }
}
```

29

The `LoadPostData()`Receives the form fields posted from the browser method in Listing 29.16 is passed a collection of all the form fields posted to the server. The `postDataKey` represents the name of the field that corresponds to the current control.

> **NOTE**
>
> If the name of a form field rendered by a control does not match the name of the control, then you need to notify the page containing the control to pass the form data to the control. You can call the `Page.RegisterRequiresPostBack()` method inside (or before) the control's `PreRender()` event to notify the page that the control is interested in receiving the postback data. In other words, if you discover that your control's `LoadPostData()` method is never being called, then call the `Page.RegisterRequiresPostBack()` method in your control.

If the value of the form field has changed—in other words, it does not match the current value of the control's `Text` property—then the `Text` property is updated and the method returns the value `True`. Otherwise, the method returns the value `False`.

When the `LoadPostData()` method returns `True`, the `RaisePostDataChangedEvent()` method is executed. Typically, you implement this method to raise a change event. In Listing 29.16, this method is used to raise the `TextChanged` event, indicating that the contents of the `TextBox` have been changed.

The page in Listing 29.17 illustrates how you can use the custom `TextBox` control in a page (see Figure 29.7).

LISTING 29.17   ShowCustomTextBox.aspx

```
<%@ Page Language="C#" %>
<%@ Register TagPrefix="custom" Namespace="myControls" %>
<!DOCTYPE html PUBLIC "-//W3C//DTD XHTML 1.0 Transitional//EN"
"http://www.w3.org/TR/xhtml1/DTD/xhtml1-transitional.dtd">
<script runat="server">

    protected void CustomTextBox1_TextChanged(object sender, EventArgs e)
    {
        lblResults.Text = CustomTextBox1.Text;
    }
</script>
<html xmlns="http://www.w3.org/1999/xhtml" >
<head id="Head1" runat="server">
    <title>Show CustomTextBox</title>
</head>
<body>
    <form id="form1" runat="server">
```

```
    <div>

    <custom:CustomTextBox
        id="CustomTextBox1"
        OnTextChanged="CustomTextBox1_TextChanged"
        Runat="server" />

    <asp:Button id="btnSubmit"
        Text="Submit"
        Runat="server" />

    <hr />

    <asp:Label
        id="lblResults"
        Runat="server" />

    </div>
    </form>
</body>
</html>
```

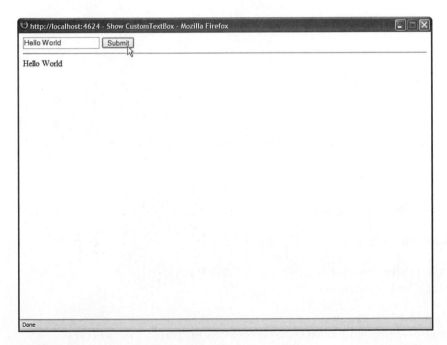

FIGURE 29.7   Handling postback data.

The custom TextBox control works in a very similar manner as the standard ASP.NET TextBox control. The control preserves its state across postbacks and it raises a TextChanged event when its contents have been modified.

> **NOTE**
>
> You will discover that you need to implement the IPostbackDataHandler interface quite often when building custom JavaScript controls. A common method of passing data from a JavaScript control back to the server is to use a hidden form field. You can process the contents of the hidden form field by using the IPostBackDataHandler interface.

Handling Postback Events

Only one control in a page at a time can cause a form to be submitted back to the server. When a control initiates a postback, the control can raise a postback event.

To process a postback event, you need to implement the IPostBackEventHandler interface. This interface includes a single method:

▶ **RaisePostBackEvent()**—Called on the server when a control initiates a postback.

The control in Listing 29.18 illustrates how you can implement the IPostBackEventHandler interface.

LISTING 29.18   CustomLinkButton.cs

```
using System;
using System.Web.UI;
using System.Web.UI.WebControls;

namespace myControls
{
    public class CustomLinkButton : WebControl, IPostBackEventHandler
    {
        public event EventHandler Click;

        private string _Text;

        public string Text
        {
            get { return _Text; }
            set { _Text = value; }
        }

        protected override void AddAttributesToRender(HtmlTextWriter writer)
        {
```

```
        string eRef = Page.ClientScript.GetPostBackClientHyperlink(this,
        ➥String.Empty);
        writer.AddAttribute(HtmlTextWriterAttribute.Href, eRef);
        base.AddAttributesToRender(writer);
    }

    protected override HtmlTextWriterTag TagKey
    {
        get
        {
            return HtmlTextWriterTag.A;
        }
    }

    protected override void RenderContents(HtmlTextWriter writer)
    {
        writer.Write(_Text);
    }


    public void RaisePostBackEvent(string eventArgument)
    {
        if (Click != null)
            Click(this, EventArgs.Empty);
    }
    }
}
```

The control in Listing 29.18 is a simple custom LinkButton control. It works very much like the standard ASP.NET LinkButton control. When you click the link rendered by the control on the browser, the form containing the control is posted back to the server and the RaisePostBackEvent() method is called. In Listing 29.18, the RaisePostBackEvent() method simply raises the Click event.

Notice that the Page.ClientScript.GetPostBackClientHyperlink() method is called in the control's AddAttributesToRender() method. The GetPostBackClientHyperLink() method returns the JavaScript that initiates the form postback in the browser. When this method is called in Listing 29.18, it returns the following JavaScript:

```
javascript:__doPostBack('CustomLinkButton1','')
```

The __doPostBack() JavaScript method calls the client-side form submit() method, which causes the form to be submitted back to the web server. (You can see all this by selecting View Source in your web browser.)

> **NOTE**
>
> There is a closely related method to the GetPostBackClientHyperLink()
> method named the GetPostBackEventReference() method. The
> GetPostBackClientHyperLink() method includes the "JavaScript:" prefix,
> whereas the GetPostBackEventReference() does not.

The page in Listing 29.19 demonstrates how you can use the custom LinkButton in an ASP.NET page.

LISTING 29.19 ShowCustomLinkButton.aspx

```
<%@ Page Language="C#" %>
<%@ Register TagPrefix="custom" Namespace="myControls" %>
<!DOCTYPE html PUBLIC "-//W3C//DTD XHTML 1.0 Transitional//EN"
"http://www.w3.org/TR/xhtml1/DTD/xhtml1-transitional.dtd">
<script runat="server">

    protected void CustomLinkButton1_Click(object sender, EventArgs e)
    {
        lblResults.Text = txtUserName.Text;
    }
</script>
<html xmlns="http://www.w3.org/1999/xhtml" >
<head id="Head1" runat="server">
    <title>Show CustomLinkButton</title>
</head>
<body>
    <form id="form1" runat="server">
    <div>

    <asp:Label
        id="lblUserName"
        Text="User Name:"
        AssociatedControlID="txtUserName"
        Runat="server" />
    <asp:TextBox
        id="txtUserName"
        Runat="server" />

    <br /><br />

    <custom:CustomLinkButton
        id="CustomLinkButton1"
        Text="Submit"
```

```
        OnClick="CustomLinkButton1_Click"
        runat="server" />

    <hr />

    <asp:Label
        id="lblResults"
        EnableViewState="false"
        Runat="server" />

    </div>
    </form>
</body>
</html>
```

The page in Listing 29.19 contains a TextBox control and the custom LinkButton control. When you click the LinkButton, the form is posted back to the server. The Click handler displays the value of the TextBox control's Text property in a Label control (see Figure 29.8).

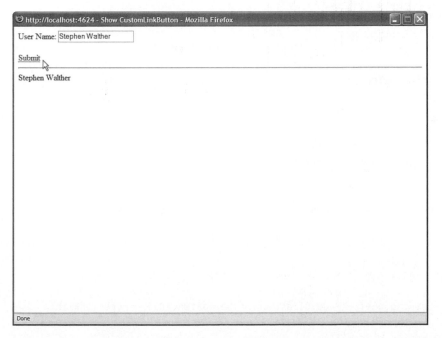

FIGURE 29.8   Using the CustomLinkButton control.

Passing Postback Event Arguments   When you call the GetPostBackClientHyperLink() method, you can supply the method with an optional argument. The argument is passed from the browser to the server when a postback is initiated. The value of the argument is passed to the RaisePostBackEvent() method on the server.

Imagine, for example, that you want to create a custom pager control that you could use with the GridView control. You want the custom control to display a list of page numbers you can click to navigate to a particular page of records displayed by a GridView.

> **NOTE**
>
> The ASP.NET 3.5 Framework includes a DataPager control. However, it works only with the ListView control.

To create this control, you need to render multiple links that initiate a postback event. Each link needs to pass the correct page number.

Listing 29.20 contains the custom pager control.

LISTING 29.20   Pager.cs

```
using System;
using System.Web.UI;
using System.Web.UI.WebControls;

namespace myControls
{
    public class Pager : WebControl, IPostBackEventHandler
    {
        string _controlToPage;

        public string ControlToPage
        {
            get { return _controlToPage; }
            set { _controlToPage = value; }
        }

        protected override void RenderContents(HtmlTextWriter writer)
        {
            GridView grid = GetControlToPage();

            for (int i = 0; i < grid.PageCount; i++)
            {
                string eRef = Page.ClientScript.GetPostBackClientHyperlink(this,
                ➥i.ToString());
                writer.Write("[");
                if (i == grid.PageIndex)
                    writer.AddStyleAttribute(HtmlTextWriterStyle.FontWeight, "bold");
                writer.AddAttribute(HtmlTextWriterAttribute.Href, eRef);
                writer.RenderBeginTag(HtmlTextWriterTag.A);
                writer.Write("{0}", i + 1);
```

```
            writer.RenderEndTag();
            writer.Write("] ");
        }
    }

    private GridView GetControlToPage()
    {
        if (String.IsNullOrEmpty(_controlToPage))
            throw new Exception("Must set ControlToPage property");
        return (GridView)Page.FindControl(_controlToPage);
    }

    public void RaisePostBackEvent(string eventArgument)
    {
        GridView grid = GetControlToPage();
        grid.PageIndex = Int32.Parse(eventArgument);
    }
    }
}
```

In Listing 29.20, the `RenderContents()` method renders the page numbers. Each page number is rendered as a link. When you click a link, the associated `GridView` control changes the page that it displays (see Figure 29.9).

The `href` attribute for each link is created by calling the `GetPostBackClientHyperLink()` method. The page number is passed as an argument to this method. When the pager is rendered to the browser, the following series of links is rendered:

```
[<a href="javascript:__doPostBack('Pager1','0')" style="font-weight:bold;">1</a>]
[<a href="javascript:__doPostBack('Pager1','1')">2</a>]
[<a href="javascript:__doPostBack('Pager1','2')">3</a>]
[<a href="javascript:__doPostBack('Pager1','3')">4</a>]
```

When you click a page number link, the corresponding page number is posted back to the server. The `RaisePostBackEvent()` method receives the page number and changes the page displayed by its associated `GridView`.

The page in Listing 29.21 illustrates how you can use the pager control to navigate to different pages of records displayed by a `GridView` control.

LISTING 29.21   `ShowPager.aspx`

```
<%@ Page Language="C#" %>
<%@ Register TagPrefix="custom" Namespace="myControls" %>
<!DOCTYPE html PUBLIC "-//W3C//DTD XHTML 1.0 Transitional//EN"
"http://www.w3.org/TR/xhtml1/DTD/xhtml1-transitional.dtd">
<html xmlns="http://www.w3.org/1999/xhtml" >
```

29

LISTING 29.21   Continued

```
<head id="Head1" runat="server">
    <title>Show CustomPager</title>
</head>
<body>
    <form id="form1" runat="server">
    <div>

    <asp:GridView
        id="GridView1"
        DataSourceID="srcMovies"
        AllowPaging="true"
        PageSize="3"
        PagerSettings-Visible="false"
        Runat="server" />

    <custom:Pager
        id="Pager1"
        ControlToPage="GridView1"
        Runat="server" />

    <asp:SqlDataSource
        id="srcMovies"
        ConnectionString="Data Source=.\SQLExpress;Integrated Security=True;
            AttachDbFileName=¦DataDirectory¦MyDatabase.mdf;User Instance=True"
        SelectCommand="SELECT Id,Title,Director FROM Movies"
        Runat="server" />

    </div>
    </form>
</body>
</html>
```

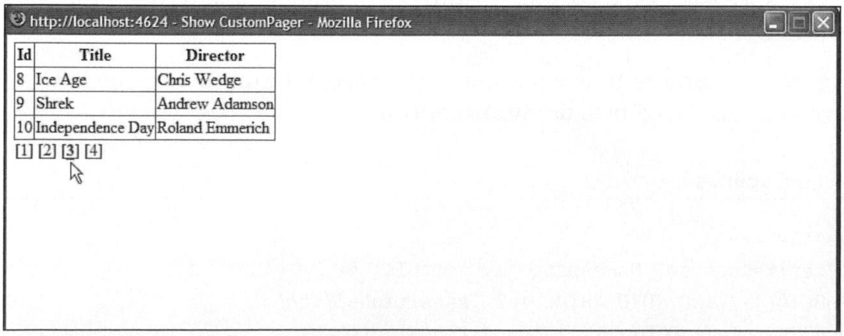

FIGURE 29.9   Using the Pager control.

Using Postback Options   Postbacks are more complicated than you might think. A postback can involve cross-page posts, validation groups, and programmatic control of control focus. To implement these advanced features in a custom control, you need to be able to specify advanced postback options.

You specify advanced postback options by taking advantage of the `PostBackOptions` class. This class has the following properties:

- ▶ **ActionUrl**—Enables you to specify the page where form data is posted.

- ▶ **Argument**—Enables you to specify a postback argument.

- ▶ **AutoPostBack**—Enables you to add JavaScript necessary for implementing an AutoPostBack event.

- ▶ **ClientSubmit**—Enables you to initiate the postback through client-side script.

- ▶ **PerformValidation**—Enables you to specify whether validation is performed (set by the `CausesValidation` property).

- ▶ **RequiresJavaScriptProtocol**—Enables you to generate the `JavaScript:` prefix.

- ▶ **TargetControl**—Enables you to specify the control responsible for initiating the postback.

- ▶ **TrackFocus**—Enables you to scroll the page back to its current position and return focus to the control after a postback.

- ▶ **ValidationGroup**—Enables you to specify the validation group associated with the control.

Imagine that you need to create a form that enables users to place a product order. However, imagine that you want to create an advanced options check box. When someone clicks the advanced options check box, the current form data is submitted to a new page that includes a more complex form.

The `AdvancedCheckBox` control in Listing 29.22 supports cross-page posts. When you click the check box, the form data is submitted to the page indicated by its `PostBackUrl` property.

> **NOTE**
>
> Cross-page posts are covered during the discussion of `Button` controls in Chapter 2, "Using the Standard Controls."

29

LISTING 29.22 `AdvancedCheckBox.cs`

```
using System;
using System.Web.UI;
using System.Web.UI.WebControls;
```

LISTING 29.22   Continued

```csharp
namespace myControls
{
    public class AdvancedCheckBox : WebControl
    {
        private string _Text;
        private string _PostBackUrl;

        public string Text
        {
            get { return _Text; }
            set { _Text = value; }
        }

        public string PostBackUrl
        {
            get { return _PostBackUrl; }
            set { _PostBackUrl = value; }
        }

        protected override void AddAttributesToRender(HtmlTextWriter writer)
        {
            PostBackOptions options = new PostBackOptions(this);
            options.ActionUrl = _PostBackUrl;

            string eRef = Page.ClientScript.GetPostBackEventReference(options);

            writer.AddAttribute(HtmlTextWriterAttribute.Onclick, eRef);
            writer.AddAttribute(HtmlTextWriterAttribute.Name, this.UniqueID);
            writer.AddAttribute(HtmlTextWriterAttribute.Type, "checkbox");


            base.AddAttributesToRender(writer);
        }

        protected override void RenderContents(HtmlTextWriter writer)
        {
            if (!String.IsNullOrEmpty(_Text))
            {
                writer.AddAttribute(HtmlTextWriterAttribute.For, this.ClientID);
                writer.RenderBeginTag(HtmlTextWriterTag.Label);
                writer.Write(_Text);
                writer.RenderEndTag();
            }
        }
```

```
        protected override HtmlTextWriterTag TagKey
        {
            get
            {
                return HtmlTextWriterTag.Input;
            }
        }
    }
}
```

In the `AddAttributesToRender()` method in Listing 29.22, an instance of the `PostBackOptions` class is created. The `ActionUrl` property is modified to support cross-page posts. The instance of the `PostBackOptions` class is passed to the `GetPostBackEventReference()` method to generate the JavaScript for initiating the postback.

The page in Listing 29.23 illustrates how you can use the `AdvancedCheckBox` control to submit form data to a new page when you click the check box (see Figure 29.10). Notice that the `AdvancedCheckBox` control's `PostBackUrl` property is set to the value `ShowAdvancedOptions.aspx`. When you click the check box, the form data is posted to this page.

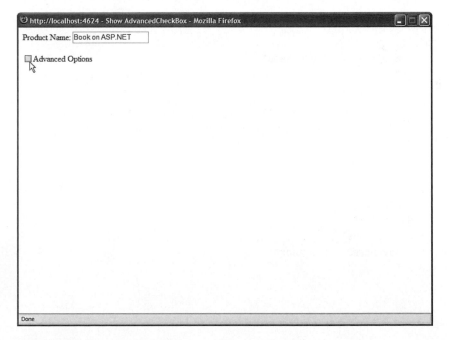

FIGURE 29.10   Using the `AdvancedCheckBox` control.

LISTING 29.23   ShowAdvancedCheckBox.aspx

```
<%@ Page Language="C#" %>
<%@ Register TagPrefix="custom" Namespace="myControls" %>
<!DOCTYPE html PUBLIC "-//W3C//DTD XHTML 1.0 Transitional//EN"
"http://www.w3.org/TR/xhtml1/DTD/xhtml1-transitional.dtd">
<script runat="server">

    public string ProductName
    {
        get { return txtProductName.Text; }
    }
</script>
<html xmlns="http://www.w3.org/1999/xhtml" >
<head id="Head1" runat="server">
    <title>Show AdvancedCheckBox</title>
</head>
<body>
    <form id="form1" runat="server">
    <div>

    <asp:Label
        id="lblProductName"
        Text="Product Name:"
        AssociatedControlID="txtProductName"
        Runat="server" />

    <asp:TextBox
        id="txtProductName"
        Runat="server" />

    <br /><br />

    <custom:AdvancedCheckBox
        id="AdvancedCheckBox1"
        Text="Advanced Options"
        PostBackUrl="AdvancedOptions.aspx"
        Runat="server" />

    </div>
    </form>
</body>
</html>
```

Working with Control Property Collections

When you build more complex controls, you often need to represent a collection of items. For example, the standard ASP.NET DropDownList control contains one or more ListItem controls that represent individual options in the DropDownList. The GridView control can contain one or more DataBoundField controls that represent particular columns to display.

In this section, we build several controls that represent a collection of items. We build multiple content rotator controls that randomly display HTML content, as well as a server-side tab control that renders a tabbed view of content.

Using the ParseChildren Attribute

When building a control that contains a collection of child controls, you need to be aware of an attribute named the ParseChildren attribute. This attribute determines how the content contained in a control is parsed.

When the ParseChildren attribute has the value True, then content contained in the control is parsed as properties of the containing control. If the control contains child controls, then the child controls are parsed as properties of the containing control. (The attribute really should have been named the ParseChildrenAsProperties attribute.)

When the ParseChildren attribute has the value False, then no attempt is made to parse a control's child controls as properties. The content contained in the control is left alone.

The default value of the ParseChildren attribute is False. However, the WebControl class overrides this default value and sets the ParseChildren attribute to the value to True. Therefore, you should assume that ParseChildren is False when used with a control that inherits directly from the System.Web.UI.Control class, but assume that ParseChildren is True when used with a control that inherits from the System.Web.UI.WebControls. WebControl class.

Imagine, for example, that you need to create a content rotator control that randomly displays content in a page. There are two ways of creating this control, depending on whether ParseChildren has the value True or False.

The control in Listing 29.24 illustrates how you can create a content rotator control when ParseChildren has the value False.

LISTING 29.24   ContentRotator.cs

```
using System;
using System.Web.UI;
using System.Web.UI.WebControls;

namespace myControls
{
```

29

LISTING 29.24   Continued

```
[ParseChildren(false)]
public class ContentRotator : WebControl
{
    protected override void AddParsedSubObject(object obj)
    {
        if (obj is Content)
            base.AddParsedSubObject(obj);
    }

    protected override void RenderContents(HtmlTextWriter writer)
    {
        Random rnd = new Random();
        int index = rnd.Next(this.Controls.Count);
        this.Controls[index].RenderControl(writer);
    }
}

public class Content : Control
{
}
}
```

The file in Listing 29.24 actually contains two controls: a ContentRotator control and a Content control. The ContentRotator control randomly selects a single Content control from its child controls and renders the Content control to the browser. This all happens in the control's RenderContents() method.

Notice that the ParseChildren attribute has the value False in Listing 29.24. If you neglected to add this attribute, then the Content controls would be parsed as properties of the ContentRotator control and you would get an exception.

NOTE

The AddParsedSubObject() method is discussed in the next section.

The page in Listing 29.25 illustrates how you can use the ContentRotator and Content controls (see Figure 29.11).

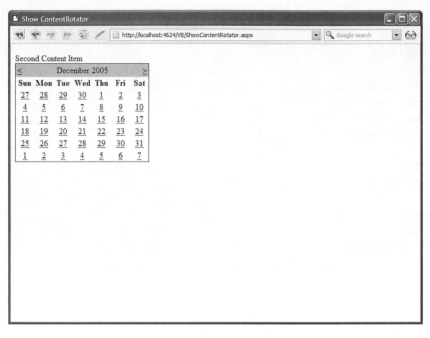

FIGURE 29.11   Randomly displaying content with the ContentRotator control.

LISTING 29.25   ShowContentRotator.aspx

```
<%@ Page Language="C#" %>
<%@ Register TagPrefix="custom" Namespace="myControls" %>
<!DOCTYPE html PUBLIC "-//W3C//DTD XHTML 1.0 Transitional//EN"
"http://www.w3.org/TR/xhtml1/DTD/xhtml1-transitional.dtd">
<html xmlns="http://www.w3.org/1999/xhtml" >
<head id="Head1" runat="server">
    <title>Show ContentRotator</title>
</head>
<body>
    <form id="form1" runat="server">
    <div>

    <custom:ContentRotator
        id="ContentRotator1"
        Runat="server">
        <custom:Content
            id="Content1"
            Runat="server">
            First Content Item
        </custom:Content>
```

LISTING 29.25   Continued

```
        <custom:Content
            id="Content2"
            Runat="server">
            Second Content Item
            <asp:Calendar
                id="Calendar1"
                Runat="server" />
        </custom:Content>
        <custom:Content
            id="Content3"
            Runat="server">
            Third Content Item
        </custom:Content>
    </custom:ContentRotator>

    </div>
    </form>
</body>
</html>
```

If `ParseChildren` is not set to the value `False`, then you need to add a property to your control that corresponds to the child controls contained in the control. For example, the control in Listing 29.26 includes an `Items` property that represents the `Item` controls contained in the control.

LISTING 29.26   ItemRotator.cs

```
using System;
using System.Collections;
using System.Web.UI;
using System.Web.UI.WebControls;
using System.ComponentModel;

namespace myControls
{
    [ParseChildren(true, "Items")]
    public class ItemRotator : CompositeControl
    {
        private ArrayList _items = new ArrayList();

        [Browsable(false)]
        public ArrayList Items
        {
            get { return _items; }
```

```
        }

        protected override void CreateChildControls()
        {
            Random rnd = new Random();
            int index = rnd.Next(_items.Count);
            Control item = (Control)_items[index];
            this.Controls.Add(item);
        }
    }

    public class Item : Control
    {

    }
}
```

In Listing 29.26, the second value passed to the `ParseChildren` attribute is the name of a control property. The contents of the `ItemRotator` are parsed as items of the collection represented by the specified property.

Unlike the `ContentRotator` control, the controls contained in the `ItemRotator` control are not automatically parsed into child controls. After the `CreateChildControls()` method executes, the `ItemRotator` control contains only one child control (the randomly selected `Item` control).

The page in Listing 29.27 illustrates how you can use the `ItemRotator` control to randomly display page content.

LISTING 29.27 `ShowItemRotator.aspx`

```
<%@ Page Language="C#" Trace="true" %>
<%@ Register TagPrefix="custom" Namespace="myControls" %>
<!DOCTYPE html PUBLIC "-//W3C//DTD XHTML 1.0 Transitional//EN"
"http://www.w3.org/TR/xhtml1/DTD/xhtml1-transitional.dtd">
<html xmlns="http://www.w3.org/1999/xhtml" >
<head id="Head1" runat="server">
    <title>Show ItemRotator</title>
</head>
<body>
    <form id="form1" runat="server">
    <div>

    <custom:ItemRotator
        id="ItemRotator1"
        Runat="server">
```

LISTING 29.27   Continued

```
        <custom:item ID="Item1" runat="server">
            First Item
        </custom:item>
        <custom:item ID="Item2" runat="server">
            Second Item
            <asp:Calendar
                id="Calendar1"
                Runat="server" />
        </custom:item>
        <custom:item ID="Item3" runat="server">
            Third Item
        </custom:item>
    </custom:ItemRotator>

    </div>
    </form>
</body>
</html>
```

There is no requirement that the contents of a control must be parsed as controls. When building a control that represents a collection of items, you can also represent the items as objects. For example, the ImageRotator control in Listing 29.28 contains ImageItem objects. The ImageItem class does not represent a control.

LISTING 29.28   ImageRotator.cs

```
using System;
using System.Collections;
using System.Web.UI;
using System.Web.UI.WebControls;
using System.ComponentModel;

namespace myControls
{
    [ParseChildren(true, "ImageItems")]
    public class ImageRotator : WebControl
    {
        private ArrayList _imageItems = new ArrayList();

        public ArrayList ImageItems
        {
            get
```

```
            {
                return _imageItems;
            }
        }

        protected override void RenderContents(HtmlTextWriter writer)
        {
            if (_imageItems.Count > 0)
            {
                Random rnd = new Random();
                ImageItem img = (ImageItem)_imageItems[rnd.Next
                ➥(_imageItems.Count)];
                writer.AddAttribute(HtmlTextWriterAttribute.Src, img.ImageUrl);
                writer.AddAttribute(HtmlTextWriterAttribute.Alt, img.AlternateText);
                writer.RenderBeginTag(HtmlTextWriterTag.Img);
                writer.RenderEndTag();
            }
        }
    }

    public class ImageItem
    {
        private string _imageUrl;
        private string _alternateText;

        public string ImageUrl
        {
            get { return _imageUrl; }
            set { _imageUrl = value; }
        }

        public string AlternateText
        {
            get { return _alternateText; }
            set { _alternateText = value; }
        }
    }
}
```

Notice that the ImageItem class is just a class. It does not derive from the base Control class. Because the ImageItem class does nothing more than represent a couple of properties, there is no reason to make it a full-blown control.

The page in Listing 29.29 illustrates how you can use the `ImageRotator` control to display different images randomly.

LISTING 29.29 `ShowImageRotator.aspx`

```
<%@ Page Language="C#" Trace="true" %>
<%@ Register TagPrefix="custom" Namespace="myControls" %>
<!DOCTYPE html PUBLIC "-//W3C//DTD XHTML 1.0 Transitional//EN"
"http://www.w3.org/TR/xhtml1/DTD/xhtml1-transitional.dtd">
<html xmlns="http://www.w3.org/1999/xhtml" >
<head id="Head1" runat="server">
    <title>Show ImageRotator</title>
</head>
<body>
    <form id="form1" runat="server">
    <div>

    <custom:ImageRotator
        id="ImageRotator1"
        Runat="server">
        <custom:ImageItem ImageUrl="Image1.gif" AlternateText="Image 1" />
        <custom:ImageItem ImageUrl="Image2.gif" AlternateText="Image 2" />
        <custom:ImageItem ImageUrl="Image3.gif" AlternateText="Image 3" />
    </custom:ImageRotator>

    </div>
    </form>
</body>
</html>
```

The page in Listing 29.29 has tracing enabled. If you look in the Control Tree section, you see that the `ImageRotator` control does not contain any child controls (see Figure 29.12).

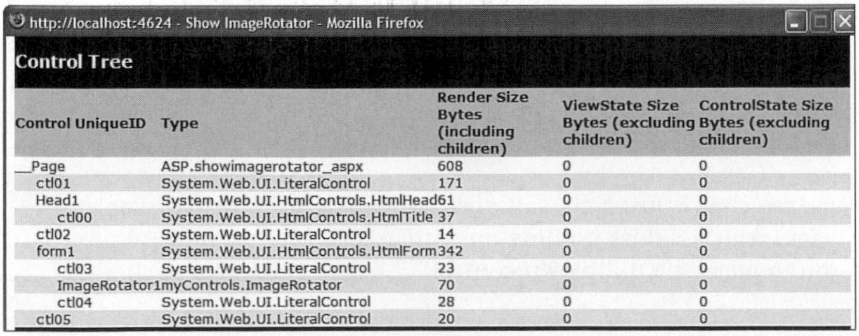
http://localhost:4624 - Show ImageRotator - Mozilla Firefox

Control Tree

Control UniqueID	Type	Render Size Bytes (including children)	ViewState Size Bytes (excluding children)	ControlState Size Bytes (excluding children)
__Page	ASP.showimagerotator_aspx	608	0	0
ctl01	System.Web.UI.LiteralControl	171	0	0
Head1	System.Web.UI.HtmlControls.HtmlHead	61	0	0
ctl00	System.Web.UI.HtmlControls.HtmlTitle	37	0	0
ctl02	System.Web.UI.LiteralControl	14	0	0
form1	System.Web.UI.HtmlControls.HtmlForm	342	0	0
ctl03	System.Web.UI.LiteralControl	23	0	0
ImageRotator1	myControls.ImageRotator	70	0	0
ctl04	System.Web.UI.LiteralControl	28	0	0
ctl05	System.Web.UI.LiteralControl	20	0	0

FIGURE 29.12 The `ShowImageRotator.aspx` page control tree.

Using the `AddParsedSubObject()` Method

When the `ParseChildren` attribute has the value `false`, the contents of a control are automatically added to the control's collection of child controls (represented by the `Controls` property). It is important to understand that all content contained in the control, even carriage returns and spaces, are added to the controls collection.

Any content contained in a control that does not represent a server-side control is parsed into a `Literal` control. In some cases, you might want to allow only a certain type of control to be added to the `Controls` collection.

The `AddParsedSubObject()` method is called as each control is added to the Controls collection. By overriding the `AddParsedSubObject()` method, you can block certain types of controls—such as `Literal` controls—from being added to the `Controls` collection.

For example, the `ContentRotator` control in Listing 29.20 overrides the base `AddParsedSubObject()` method and prevents anything that is not a `Content` control from being added to the `ContentRotator Controls` collection. If you removed the `AddParsedSubObject()` method from this control, then all of the carriage returns and spaces between the `Content` controls would be added to the `Controls` collection as `Literal` controls.

Using a `ControlBuilder`

The `AddParsedSubObject()` method enables you to specify which parsed controls get added to a Controls collection. Sometimes, you must take even more control over the parsing of a control.

When the ASP.NET Framework parses a page, the Framework uses a special type of class called a `ControlBuilder` class. You can modify the way in which the content of a control is parsed by associating a custom `ControlBuilder` with a control.

Here's a list of the most useful methods supported by the `ControlBuilder` class:

- ▶ **`AllowWhiteSpaceLiterals()`**—Enables you to trim white space from the contents of a control.

- ▶ **`AppendLiteralString()`**—Enables you trim all literal content from the contents of a control.

- ▶ **`GetChildControlType()`**—Enables you to specify how a particular tag gets parsed into a control.

The `GetChildControlType()` method is the most useful method. It enables you to map tags to controls. You can use the `GetChildControlType()` method to map any tag to any control.

For example, the file in Listing 29.30 contains a `ServerTabs` control that renders multiple tabs (see Figure 29.13). Each tab is represented by a `Tab` control.

29

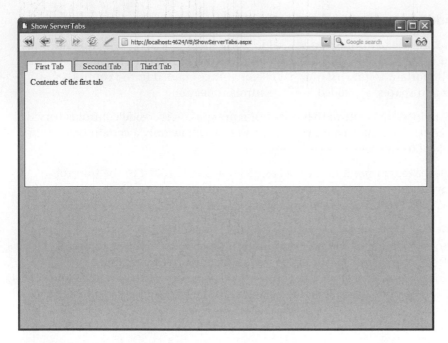

FIGURE 29.13   Using the ServerTabs control.

LISTING 29.30   ServerTabs.cs

```csharp
using System;
using System.Collections;
using System.Web.UI;
using System.Web.UI.WebControls;

namespace myControls
{
    [ControlBuilder(typeof(ServerTabsBuilder))]
    [ParseChildren(false)]
    public class ServerTabs : WebControl, IPostBackEventHandler
    {
        public int SelectedTabIndex
        {
            get
            {
                if (ViewState["SelectedTabIndex"] == null)
                    return 0;
                else
                    return (int)ViewState["SelectedTabIndex"];
            }
```

```
    set
    {
        ViewState["SelectedTabIndex"] = value;
    }
}

protected override void RenderContents(HtmlTextWriter writer)
{
    for (int i = 0; i < this.Controls.Count; i++)
    {
        ServerTab tab = (ServerTab)this.Controls[i];
        string eRef = Page.ClientScript.GetPostBackClientHyperlink(this,
        ➥ i.ToString());

        if (SelectedTabIndex == i)
            writer.AddAttribute(HtmlTextWriterAttribute.Class, "tab
            ➥ selectedTab");
        else
            writer.AddAttribute(HtmlTextWriterAttribute.Class, "tab");
        writer.RenderBeginTag(HtmlTextWriterTag.Div);
        writer.AddAttribute(HtmlTextWriterAttribute.Href, eRef);
        writer.RenderBeginTag(HtmlTextWriterTag.A);
        writer.Write(tab.Text);
        writer.RenderEndTag(); // A
        writer.RenderEndTag(); // Tab DIV
    }
    writer.Write("<br style='clear:both' />");

    writer.AddAttribute(HtmlTextWriterAttribute.Class, "tabContents");
    writer.RenderBeginTag(HtmlTextWriterTag.Div);
    this.Controls[SelectedTabIndex].RenderControl(writer);
    writer.RenderEndTag(); // Tab Contents DIV
}

protected override void AddParsedSubObject(object obj)
{
    if (obj is ServerTab)
        base.AddParsedSubObject(obj);
}

protected override HtmlTextWriterTag TagKey
{
    get
    {
        return HtmlTextWriterTag.Div;
```

LISTING 29.30   Continued

```
            }
        }

        public void RaisePostBackEvent(string eventArgument)
        {
            SelectedTabIndex = Int32.Parse(eventArgument);
        }
    }

    public class ServerTabsBuilder : ControlBuilder
    {
        public override Type GetChildControlType(string tagName, IDictionary attribs)
        {
            if (String.Compare(tagName, "tab", true) == 0)
                return typeof(ServerTab);
            else
                return null;
        }
    }

    public class ServerTab : Control
    {
        private string _Text;

        public string Text
        {
            get { return _Text; }
            set { _Text = value; }
        }
    }
}
```

Notice that the ServerTabs class is decorated with a ControlBuilder attribute. This attribute associates the ServerTabs control with a ControlBuilder class named ServerTabsBuilder.

The ServerTabsBuilder class overrides the base ControlBuilder GetChildControlType() method. The overridden method maps the <tab> tag to the Tab control. Because of this mapping, you do not need to use a prefix or use the runat="server" attribute when declaring a tab within the ServerTabs control.

The page in Listing 29.31 illustrates how you can use the ServerTabs control.

LISTING 29.31   ShowServerTabs.aspx

```
<%@ Page Language="C#" %>
<%@ Register TagPrefix="custom" Namespace="myControls" %>
<!DOCTYPE html PUBLIC "-//W3C//DTD XHTML 1.0 Transitional//EN"
"http://www.w3.org/TR/xhtml1/DTD/xhtml1-transitional.dtd">
<html xmlns="http://www.w3.org/1999/xhtml" >
<head id="Head1" runat="server">
    <style type="text/css">
        html
        {
            background-color:silver;
        }
        .tab
        {
            float:left;
            position:relative;
            top:1px;
            background-color:#eeeeee;
            border:solid 1px black;
            padding:0px 15px;
            margin-left:5px;
        }
        .tab a
        {
            text-decoration:none;
        }
        .selectedTab
        {
            background-color:white;
            border-bottom:solid 1px white;
        }
        .tabContents
        {
            border:solid 1px black;
            background-color:white;
            padding:10px;
            height:200px;
        }
    </style>
    <title>Show ServerTabs</title>
</head>
<body>
    <form id="form1" runat="server">
    <div>
```

29

LISTING 29.31   Continued

```
<custom:ServerTabs
    ID="ServerTabs1"
    Runat="Server">
    <tab Text="First Tab">
      Contents of the first tab
    </tab>
    <tab Text="Second Tab">
      Contents of the second tab
    </tab>
    <tab Text="Third Tab">
      Contents of the third tab
    </tab>
</custom:ServerTabs>

</div>
</form>
</body>
</html>
```

The `ControlBuilder` enables you to declare instances of the `Tab` control by using the `<tab>` tag instead of using a `<custom:Tab runat="server">` tab.

Creating a Better Designer Experience

Up to this point, we've ignored the Design view experience. In other words, we've ignored the question of how our custom controls appear in the Visual Web Developer or Visual Studio .NET Design view.

You can modify the appearance of your control in Design view in two ways. You can apply design-time attributes to the control, or you can associate a `ControlDesigner` with your control. We'll explore both methods in this section.

Applying Design-Time Attributes to a Control

Design-time attributes enable you to modify how control properties appear in Design view. Some attributes are applied to the control itself, whereas other attributes are applied to particular properties of a control.

Here is the list of the design-time attributes you can apply to a control:

▶ **DefaultEvent**—Enables you to specify the default event for a control. When you double-click a control in Visual Web Developer or Visual Studio .NET, an event handler is automatically created for the default event.

▶ **DefaultProperty**—Enables you to specify the default property for a control. When you open the Property window for a control, this property is highlighted by default.

▶ **PersistChildren**—Enables you to specify whether child controls or properties are persisted as control attributes or control contents.

▶ **ToolboxData**—Enables you to specify the tag added to a page when a control is dragged from the Toolbox.

▶ **ToolboxItem**—Enables you to block a control from appearing in the Toolbox.

Here is the list of design-time attributes you can apply to a control property:

▶ **Bindable**—Enables you to indicate to display a Databindings dialog box for the property.

▶ **Browsable**—Enables you to block a property from appearing in the Properties window.

▶ **Category**—Enables you to specify the category associated with the property. The property appears under this category in the Properties window.

▶ **DefaultValue**—Enables you to specify a default value for the property. When you right-click a property in the Properties window, you can select Reset to the return the property to its default value.

▶ **Description**—Enables you to specify the description associated with the property. The description appears in the Properties window when the property is selected.

▶ **DesignerSerializationVisibility**—Enables you to specify how changes to a property are serialized. Possible values are `Visible`, `Hidden`, and `Content`.

▶ **Editor**—Enables you to specify a custom editor for editing the property in Design view.

▶ **EditorBrowsable**—Enables you to block a property from appearing in Intellisense.

▶ **NotifyParentProperty**—Enables you to specify that changes to a subproperty should be propagated to the parent property.

▶ **PersistenceMode**—Enables you to specify whether a property is persisted as a control attribute or control content. Possible values are `Attribute`, `EncodedInnerDefaultProperty`, `InnerDefaultProperty`, and `InnerProperty`.

▶ **TypeConverter**—Enables you to associate a custom type converter with a property. A type converter converts a property between a string representation and a type (or vice versa).

The `Editor` attribute enables you to associate a particular editor with a property. Certain types in the Framework have default editors. For example, a property which represents a `System.Drawing.Color` value is automatically associated with the `ColorEditor`. The `ColorEditor` displays a color picker (see Figure 29.14). To view the list of editors included

29

in the .NET Framework, look up the `UITypeEditor` class in the .NET Framework SDK Documentation.

The `MovieView` control contained in Listing 29.32 illustrates how you can use several of these attributes. The control displays a single movie.

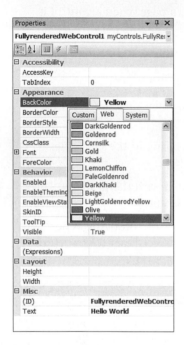

FIGURE 29.14   Using the `ColorEditor` to pick a color.

LISTiNG 29.32   MovieView.cs

```csharp
using System;
using System.Web.UI;
using System.Web.UI.WebControls;
using System.ComponentModel;

namespace myControls
{
    [DefaultProperty("Title")]
    public class MovieView : WebControl
    {

        private string _title = "Movie Title";
        private string _description = "Movie Description";
```

```csharp
        [Category("Movie")]
        [Description("Movie Title")]
        public string Title
        {
            get { return _title; }
            set { _title = value; }
        }


        [Category("Movie")]
        [Description("Movie Description")]
        public string Description
        {
            get { return _description; }
            set { _description = value; }
        }



        protected override void RenderContents(HtmlTextWriter writer)
        {
            writer.RenderBeginTag(HtmlTextWriterTag.H1);
            writer.Write(_title);
            writer.RenderEndTag();

            writer.Write(_description);
        }

        protected override HtmlTextWriterTag TagKey
        {
            get
            {
                return HtmlTextWriterTag.Div;
            }
        }
    }
}
```

The page in Listing 29.33 contains the MovieView control. Open the page in Design view to see the effect of the various design-time attributes. For example, notice that a category and description are associated with both the Title and Description properties in the Properties window (see Figure 29.15).

FIGURE 29.15   The MovieView control in Design view.

LISTING 29.33   ShowMovieView.aspx

```
<%@ Page Language="C#" %>
<%@ Register TagPrefix="custom" Namespace="myControls" %>
<!DOCTYPE html PUBLIC "-//W3C//DTD XHTML 1.0 Transitional//EN"
"http://www.w3.org/TR/xhtml1/DTD/xhtml1-transitional.dtd">
<html xmlns="http://www.w3.org/1999/xhtml" >
<head id="Head1" runat="server">
    <title>Show MovieView</title>
</head>
<body>
    <form id="form1" runat="server">
    <div>

    <custom:MovieView
        id="MovieView1"
        Runat="server" />

    </div>
    </form>
</body>
</html>
```

Creating Control Designers

You can modify the appearance of your custom controls in Design view by creating a `ControlDesigner`. The ASP.NET Framework enables you to implement a number of fancy features when you implement a `ControlDesigner`. This section focuses on just two of these advanced features.

First, you learn how to create a `ContainerControlDesigner`. A `ContainerControlDesigner` enables you to drag and drop other controls from the Toolbox onto your control in Design view.

You also learn how to add Smart Tags (also called Action Lists) to your control. When a control supports Smart Tags, a menu of common tasks pop up above the control in Design view.

Creating a Container `ControlDesigner`

If you associate a custom control with a `ContainerControlDesigner`, then you can add child controls to your control in Design view. For example, the file in Listing 29.34 contains a `GradientPanel` control. This control displays a gradient background behind its contents (see Figure 29.16).

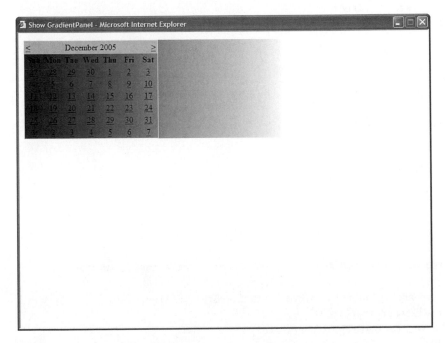

FIGURE 29.16   Displaying the `GradientPanel` control.

29

LISTING 29.34   GradientPanel.cs

```csharp
using System;
using System.Web.UI;
using System.Web.UI.WebControls;
using System.Web.UI.Design;
using System.ComponentModel;
using System.Drawing;

namespace myControls
{
    [Designer(typeof(GradientPanelDesigner))]
    [ParseChildren(false)]
    public class GradientPanel : WebControl
    {
        private GradientDirection _direction = GradientDirection.Horizontal;
        private Color _startColor = Color.DarkBlue;
        private Color _endColor = Color.White;

        public GradientDirection Direction
        {
            get { return _direction; }
            set { _direction = value; }
        }

        public Color StartColor
        {
            get { return _startColor; }
            set { _startColor = value; }
        }

        public Color EndColor
        {
            get { return _endColor; }
            set { _endColor = value; }
        }

        protected override void AddAttributesToRender(HtmlTextWriter writer)
        {
            writer.AddStyleAttribute(HtmlTextWriterStyle.Filter, this.
            ➥GetFilterString());
            base.AddAttributesToRender(writer);
        }
```

```
    public string GetFilterString()
    {
        return String.Format("progid:DXImageTransform.Microsoft.Gradient
        ➥(gradientType={0},startColorStr={1},endColorStr={2})",
        ➥_direction.ToString("d"), ColorTranslator.ToHtml(_startColor),
        ➥ColorTranslator.ToHtml(_endColor));
    }


    public GradientPanel()
    {
        this.Width = Unit.Parse("500px");
    }


    protected override HtmlTextWriterTag TagKey
    {
        get
        {
            return HtmlTextWriterTag.Div;
        }
    }
}


public enum GradientDirection
{
    Vertical = 0,
    Horizontal = 1
}


public class GradientPanelDesigner : ContainerControlDesigner
{
    protected override void AddDesignTimeCssAttributes(System.Collections.
    ➥IDictionary styleAttributes)
    {
        GradientPanel gPanel = (GradientPanel)this.Component;
        styleAttributes.Add("filter", gPanel.GetFilterString());
        base.AddDesignTimeCssAttributes(styleAttributes);
    }
}
}
```

29

The `GradientPanel` control uses an Internet Explorer filter to create the gradient background. The filter is applied in the `AddAttributesToRender()` method. You can set the `StartColor`, `EndColor`, and `Direction` properties to control the appearance of the gradient background.

Notice that the GradientPanel control is decorated with a ControlDesigner attribute. This attribute associates the GradientPanelDesigner class with the GradientPanel control.

The GradientPanelDesigner is also included in Listing 29.34. One method is overridden in the GradientPanelDesigner class. The AddDesignTimeCssAttributes() method is used to apply the gradient background in Design view.

> **WARNING**
>
> The file in Listing 29.34 doesn't compile unless you add a reference to the System.Design.dll assembly to your application. You can add the necessary reference by selecting the menu option Website, Add Reference and selecting the System.Design assembly.

The page in Listing 29.35 illustrates how you can declare the GradientPanel in a page. However, to understand the effect of the ContainerControlDesigner, you need to open the page in Design view in either Visual Web Developer or Visual Studio .NET.

LISTING 29.35   ShowGradientPanel.aspx

```
<%@ Page Language="C#" %>
<%@ Register TagPrefix="custom" Namespace="myControls" %>
<!DOCTYPE html PUBLIC "-//W3C//DTD XHTML 1.0 Transitional//EN"
"http://www.w3.org/TR/xhtml1/DTD/xhtml1-transitional.dtd">
<html xmlns="http://www.w3.org/1999/xhtml" >
<head id="Head1" runat="server">
    <title>Show GradientPanel</title>
</head>
<body>
    <form id="form1" runat="server">
    <div>

    <custom:GradientPanel
        id="GradientPanel1"
        Runat="server">
        <asp:Calendar
            ID="Calendar1"
            runat="server" />
    </custom:GradientPanel>

    </div>
    </form>
</body>
</html>
```

When you open the page in Listing 29.35 in Design view, you can drag other controls from the toolbox onto the `GradientPanel` control. For example, if you drag a `Calendar` control onto the `GradientPanel` control, the `Calendar` control is added automatically to the control collection of the `GradientPanel` (see Figure 29.17).

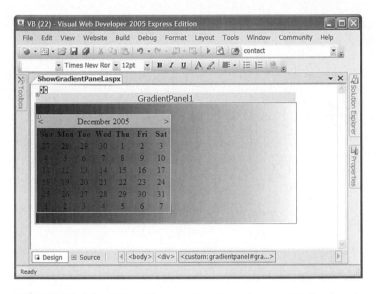

FIGURE 29.17   Editing the `GradientPanel` control in Design view.

Adding Smart Tasks

If you add a `GridView` control to a page when you are in Design view, you'll notice that a menu of common tasks appears above the `GridView`. For example, you can select a Smart Task to enable sorting or paging.

You can add your own Smart Tasks to a custom control by inheriting a new class from the base `DesignerActionList` class.

For example, the file in Listing 29.36 contains three classes. It contains a custom control, named the `SmartImage` control, which enables you to rotate and mirror images. It also contains a `ControlDesigner`. Finally, it contains a `DesignerActionList` class that contains two Smart Tasks.

LISTING 29.36   `SmartImage.cs`

```
using System;
using System.Web.UI;
using System.Web.UI.WebControls;
using System.Web.UI.Design;
```

LISTING 29.36   Continued

```csharp
using System.ComponentModel;
using System.ComponentModel.Design;

namespace myControls
{
    [Designer(typeof(SmartImageDesigner))]
    public class SmartImage : WebControl
    {
        string _imageUrl;
        string _alternateText;
        int _rotation = 0;
        bool _mirror = false;

        public string ImageUrl
        {
            get { return _imageUrl; }
            set { _imageUrl = value; }
        }

        public string AlternateText
        {
            get { return _alternateText; }
            set { _alternateText = value; }
        }

        public int Rotation
        {
            get { return _rotation; }
            set { _rotation = value; }
        }

        public bool Mirror
        {
            get { return _mirror; }
            set { _mirror = value; }
        }

        protected override HtmlTextWriterTag TagKey
        {
            get
            {
                return HtmlTextWriterTag.Img;
            }
        }
```

```csharp
    private string GetFilterString()
    {
        string _mirrorValue = "0";
        if (_mirror)
            _mirrorValue = "1";

        return String.Format("progid:DXImageTransform.Microsoft.
        ➥BasicImage(Rotation={0},Mirror={1})", _rotation, _mirrorValue);
    }

    protected override void AddAttributesToRender(HtmlTextWriter writer)
    {
        writer.AddStyleAttribute(HtmlTextWriterStyle.Filter, this.
        ➥GetFilterString());
        writer.AddAttribute(HtmlTextWriterAttribute.Src, _imageUrl);
        writer.AddAttribute(HtmlTextWriterAttribute.Alt, _alternateText);


        base.AddAttributesToRender(writer);
    }
}

public class SmartImageDesigner : ControlDesigner
{
    public override DesignerActionListCollection ActionLists
    {
        get
        {
            DesignerActionListCollection actionLists = new
            ➥DesignerActionListCollection();
            actionLists.AddRange(base.ActionLists);
            actionLists.Add(new SmartImageActionList(this));
            return actionLists;
        }
    }
}

public class SmartImageActionList : DesignerActionList
{

    private DesignerActionItemCollection items;
    private SmartImageDesigner _parent;

    public SmartImageActionList(SmartImageDesigner parent)
        : base(parent.Component)
```

29

LISTING 29.36   Continued

```
    {
        _parent = parent;
    }

    public void Rotate()
    {
        TransactedChangeCallback toCall = new TransactedChangeCallback(DoRotate);
        ControlDesigner.InvokeTransactedChange(this.Component, toCall,
        ➥"Rotate", "Rotate image 90 degrees");
    }

    public void Mirror()
    {
        TransactedChangeCallback toCall = new TransactedChangeCallback(DoMirror);
        ControlDesigner.InvokeTransactedChange(this.Component, toCall,
        ➥"Mirror", "Mirror Image");
    }

    public override DesignerActionItemCollection GetSortedActionItems()
    {
        if (items == null)
        {
            items = new DesignerActionItemCollection();
            items.Add(new DesignerActionMethodItem(this, "Rotate", "Rotate
            ➥Image", true));
            items.Add(new DesignerActionMethodItem(this, "Mirror", "Mirror
            ➥Image", true));
        }
        return items;
    }

    public bool DoRotate(object arg)
    {
        SmartImage img = (SmartImage)this.Component;
        img.Rotation += 1;
        if (img.Rotation > 3)
            img.Rotation = 0;
        _parent.UpdateDesignTimeHtml();
        return true;
    }

    public bool DoMirror(object arg)
    {
        SmartImage img = (SmartImage)this.Component;
        img.Mirror = !img.Mirror;
```

```
            _parent.UpdateDesignTimeHtml();
            return true;
        }
    }
}
```

The SmartImage control takes advantage of an Internet Explorer filter named the BasicImage filter. This filter enables you to manipulate images by rotating, mirroring, and changing the opacity of images. In Listing 29.36, the filter is applied in the AddAttributesToRender() method.

The SmartImage control is associated with a ControlDesigner named the SmartImageDesigner through the control's Designer attribute. The SmartImageDesigner class overrides the base class's ActionLists property to expose a custom DesignerActionList.

The DesignerActionList is the final class declared in Listing 29.36. This class contains four methods named Rotate(), DoRotate(), Mirror(), and DoMirror(). The GetSortedActionItems() method exposes the Rotate and Mirror actions.

When all is said and done, the custom ActionList enables you to display Rotate and Mirror Smart Tags for the SmartImage control in Design view. When you open a page in the browser after clicking the Rotate action in Design view, the image is rotated (see Figure 29.18).

FIGURE 29.18   Adding Smart Tags to a control.

29

NOTE

You can view the SmartImage control by opening the ShowSmartImage.aspx page included on the CD that accompanies this book.

WARNING

Sadly, although you could rotate the monkey while in Design view in the previous version of Visual Web Developer, in this version the rotated monkey does not appear until you view the page in a browser.

Summary

In this chapter, you learned how to build basic controls in the ASP.NET Framework. First, you learned how to create both fully rendered and composite controls. You also learned how to combine the features of fully rendered and composite controls by creating hybrid controls.

You also learned how to preserve the values of control properties in View State. You learned the difference between View State and Control State and how to use both features of the framework.

Next, you learned how to handle postback data and events. You saw how you can process form data submitted to the server. You also learned how you can raise a server-side event that is initiated by a postback.

This chapter examined the topic of building controls that represent a collection of items. You learned how to use the ParseChildren attribute to parse the inner content of a control in different ways. You also learned how to alter the parsing of a control's content by overriding the AddParsedSubObject() method and by creating custom ControlBuilders.

Finally, you saw two methods of modifying the appearance of a control in Design view. You learned how to apply design-time attributes to a control and its properties. You also learned how to associate a ControlDesigner with a custom control.

Building Templated Databound Controls

The ASP.NET Framework is a framework. If you don't like anything about the framework, you always have the option of extending it. In particular, if you discover that the standard databound controls in the framework don't do everything you need, you can create a custom databound control.

In this chapter, you learn how to create custom controls that work like the ASP.NET GridView, DetailsView, ListView, and FormView controls. In the first part of this chapter, you learn how to create controls that support templates. You learn how to implement controls that support both standard templates and two-way databinding templates. You also learn how to supply a control with a default template.

The last part of this chapter is devoted to the topic of databound controls. You learn about the new base control classes included in the framework that were supplied to make it easier to create custom databound controls. We create a custom templated databound control.

Creating Templated Controls

A template enables you to customize the layout of a control. Furthermore, a template can contain expressions that are not evaluated until runtime.

The ASP.NET Framework supports two types of templates. First, you can create a one-way databinding template. You use a one-way databinding template to display data items. In a one-way databinding template, you use the Eval() expression to display the value of a data item.

Second, you have the option of creating a two-way databinding template. A two-way databinding template can be used not only to display data items, but also to update data items. You can use the Bind() expression in a two-way databinding template to both display a data item and extract the value of a data item.

Typically, you use templates with a databound control. For example, the ListView, GridView, Repeater, DataList, FormView, and DetailsView controls all support an ItemTemplate that enables you to format the data items that these controls display. However, you can use a template even when you are not displaying a set of data items. For example, the Login control supports a LayoutTemplate that enables you to customize the appearance of the Login form.

This part of this chapter concentrates on creating nondatabound controls that support templates. In the next part of this chapter, you learn how to use templates with databound controls.

Implementing the ITemplate Interface

You create a one-way databinding template by adding a property to a control that returns an object that implements the ITemplate interface. The ITemplate interface includes one method:

▶ **InstantiateIn**—Instantiates the contents of a template in a particular control.

You are not required to implement the InstantiateIn() method yourself. The ASP.NET Framework creates the method for you automatically. You call the InstantiateIn method in your control to add the contents of a template to your control.

For example, the control in Listing 30.1 represents an article. The Article control includes a template named ItemTemplate. The ItemTemplate is used to lay out the elements of the article: the title, author, and contents.

LISTING 30.1   Article.cs

```
using System;
using System.Web;
using System.Web.UI;
using System.Web.UI.WebControls;

namespace myControls
{
    public class Article : CompositeControl
    {

        private string _title;
        private string _author;
        private string _contents;
```

```
        private ITemplate _itemTemplate;

        public string Title
        {
            get { return _title; }
            set { _title = value; }
        }

        public string Author
        {
            get { return _author; }
            set { _author = value; }
        }

        public string Contents
        {
            get { return _contents; }
            set { _contents = value; }
        }

        [TemplateContainer(typeof(Article))]
        [PersistenceMode(PersistenceMode.InnerProperty)]
        public ITemplate ItemTemplate
        {
            get { return _itemTemplate; }
            set { _itemTemplate = value; }
        }

        protected override void CreateChildControls()
        {
            _itemTemplate.InstantiateIn(this);
        }
    }

}
```

Notice that the Article control contains a property named ItemTemplate that returns an object that implements the ITemplate interface. Notice that this property is decorated with two attributes: a TemplateContainer and a PersistenceMode attribute.

The TemplateContainer attribute is used to specify the type of control that will contain the template. In the case of the Article control, the template will be contained in the Article control itself. Therefore, the Article control's type is passed to the TemplateContainer attribute.

The `PersistenceMode` attribute indicates how a property is persisted in an ASP.NET page. The possible values are `Attribute`, `EncodedInnerDefaultProperty`, `InnerDefaultProperty`, and `InnerProperty`. We want to declare the `ItemTemplate` like this:

```
<custom:Article
  runat="server">
  <ItemTemplate>
  ... template contents ...
  </ItemTemplate>
</custom:Article>
```

Because we want to declare the `ItemTemplate` inside the `Article` control, the `PersistenceMode` attribute needs to be set to the value `InnerProperty`.

The `Article` control overrides the base `WebControl` class's `CreateChildControls()` method. The `ItemTemplate` is added as a child control to the `Article` control. Any controls contained in the template become child controls of the current control.

The page in Listing 30.2 illustrates how you can use the `Article` control and its `ItemTemplate`.

LISTING 30.2   ShowArticle.aspx

```
<%@ Page Language="C#" %>
<%@ Register TagPrefix="custom" Namespace="myControls" %>
<!DOCTYPE html PUBLIC "-//W3C//DTD XHTML 1.0 Transitional//EN"
"http://www.w3.org/TR/xhtml1/DTD/xhtml1-transitional.dtd">
<script runat="server">

    void Page_Load()
    {
        Article1.Title = "Creating Templated Databound Controls";
        Article1.Author = "Stephen Walther";
        Article1.Contents = "Blah, blah, blah, blah...";
        Article1.DataBind();
    }

</script>
<html xmlns="http://www.w3.org/1999/xhtml" >
<head id="Head1" runat="server">
    <title>Show Article</title>
</head>
<body>
    <form id="form1" runat="server">
    <div>
```

```
      <custom:Article
          id="Article1"
          Runat="server">
          <ItemTemplate>

          <h1><%# Container.Title %></h1>
          <em>By <%# Container.Author %></em>
          <br /><br />
          <%# Container.Contents %>

          </ItemTemplate>
      </custom:Article>

      </div>
      </form>
</body>
</html>
```

When you open the page in Listing 30.2, the contents of the ItemTemplate are displayed (see Figure 30.1).

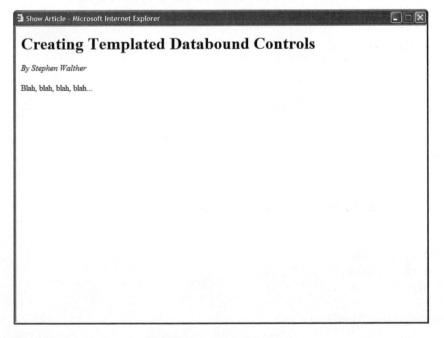

FIGURE 30.1   Using a template to display an article.

In the Page_Load() method, the Title, Author, and Contents properties of the article are set. Notice that these properties are used within databinding expressions within the Article control's ItemTemplate. For example, the value of the Title property is displayed with the following databinding expression:

```
<%# Container.Title %>
```

The Container keyword refers to the current *binding container*. In this case, the binding container is the Article control itself. Therefore, you can refer to any property of the Article control by using the Container keyword.

Notice that the Article control's DataBind() method is called at the end of the Page_Load() method. Don't forget to call this method when you include databinding expressions in a template. If you don't call this method, then the databinding expressions are never evaluated and displayed.

Creating a Default Template

The previous section discussed the ITemplate interface's InstantiateIn() method. Normally, you don't implement the InstantiateIn() method; you let the ASP.NET Framework do it for you. However, if you want to supply a control with a default template, then you need to implement this method.

The modified Article control in Listing 30.3 includes a default template for the ItemTemplate. The default template is used when an ItemTemplate is not supplied.

LISTING 30.3   ArticleWithDefault.cs

```csharp
using System;
using System.Web;
using System.Web.UI;
using System.Web.UI.WebControls;

namespace myControls
{

    public class ArticleWithDefault : CompositeControl
    {

        private string _title;
        private string _author;
        private string _contents;

        private ITemplate _itemTemplate;

        public string Title
        {
```

```csharp
            get { return _title; }
            set { _title = value; }
        }

        public string Author
        {
            get { return _author; }
            set { _author = value; }
        }

        public string Contents
        {
            get { return _contents; }
            set { _contents = value; }
        }

        [TemplateContainer(typeof(ArticleWithDefault))]
        [PersistenceMode(PersistenceMode.InnerProperty)]
        public ITemplate ItemTemplate
        {
            get { return _itemTemplate; }
            set { _itemTemplate = value; }
        }

        protected override void CreateChildControls()
        {
            if (_itemTemplate == null)
                _itemTemplate = new ArticleDefaultTemplate();
            _itemTemplate.InstantiateIn(this);
        }
    }

    public class ArticleDefaultTemplate : ITemplate
    {
        public void InstantiateIn(Control container)
        {
            Label lblTitle = new Label();
            lblTitle.DataBinding += new EventHandler(lblTitle_DataBinding);

            Label lblAuthor = new Label();
            lblAuthor.DataBinding += new EventHandler(lblAuthor_DataBinding);

            Label lblContents = new Label();
            lblContents.DataBinding += new EventHandler(lblContents_DataBinding);
```

30

LISTING 30.3   Continued

```
            container.Controls.Add(lblTitle);
            container.Controls.Add(new LiteralControl("<br />"));
            container.Controls.Add(lblAuthor);
            container.Controls.Add(new LiteralControl("<br />"));
            container.Controls.Add(lblContents);
        }


        void lblTitle_DataBinding(object sender, EventArgs e)
        {
            Label lblTitle = (Label)sender;
            ArticleWithDefault container = (ArticleWithDefault)lblTitle.
            ➥NamingContainer;
            lblTitle.Text = container.Title;
        }


        void lblAuthor_DataBinding(object sender, EventArgs e)
        {
            Label lblAuthor = (Label)sender;
            ArticleWithDefault container = (ArticleWithDefault)lblAuthor.
            ➥NamingContainer;
            lblAuthor.Text = container.Author;
        }


        void lblContents_DataBinding(object sender, EventArgs e)
        {
            Label lblContents = (Label)sender;
            ArticleWithDefault container = (ArticleWithDefault)lblContents.
            ➥NamingContainer;
            lblContents.Text = container.Contents;
        }


    }


}
```

The control in Listing 30.3 is very similar to the control created in the previous section. However, notice that the CreateChildControls() method has been modified. The new version of the CreateChildControls() method tests whether there is an ItemTemplate. If there is no ItemTemplate, an instance of the ArticleDefaultTemplate class is created.

The ArticleDefaultTemplate class, which is also included in Listing 30.3, implements the ITemplate interface. In particular, the class implements the InstantiateIn() method. The instantiateIn() method creates all the controls that will appear in the template.

In Listing 30.3, three `Label` controls are created that correspond to the `Title`, `Author`, and `Contents` properties. Notice that the `DataBinding` event is handled for all three of these `Label` controls. When the `DataBind()` method is called, the `DataBinding` event is raised for each child control in the `Article` control. At that time, the values of the `Title`, `Author`, and `Contents` properties are assigned to the `Text` properties of the `Label` controls.

The page in Listing 30.4 illustrates how you can use the modified `Article` control.

LISTING 30.4 ShowArticleWithDefault.aspx

```
<%@ Page Language="C#" %>
<%@ Register TagPrefix="custom" Namespace="myControls" %>
<!DOCTYPE html PUBLIC "-//W3C//DTD XHTML 1.0 Transitional//EN"
"http://www.w3.org/TR/xhtml1/DTD/xhtml1-transitional.dtd">
<script runat="server">

    void Page_Load()
    {
        ArticleWithDefault1.Title = "Creating Templated Databound Controls";
        ArticleWithDefault1.Author = "Stephen Walther";
        ArticleWithDefault1.Contents = "Blah, blah, blah, blah...";
        ArticleWithDefault1.DataBind();
    }

</script>
<html xmlns="http://www.w3.org/1999/xhtml" >
<head id="Head1" runat="server">
    <title>Show Article with Default Template</title>
</head>
<body>
    <form id="form1" runat="server">
    <div>

    <custom:ArticleWithDefault
        id="ArticleWithDefault1"
        Runat="server" />

    </div>
    </form>
</body>
</html>
```

The `ArticleWithDefault` control in Listing 30.4 does not include an `ItemTemplate`. When the page is displayed in a browser, the contents of the `ItemTemplate` are supplied by the `ArticleDefaultTemplate` class (see Figure 30.2).

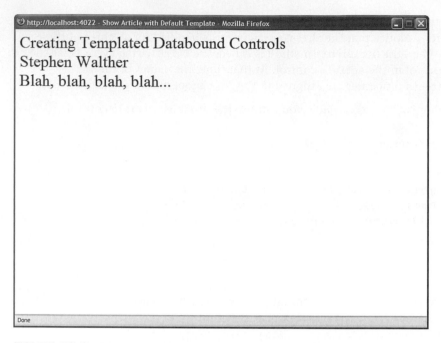

FIGURE 30.2   Displaying an article with a default template.

Supporting Simplified Databinding

The databinding expressions used in the previous two sections might seem a little odd. For example, we used the following databinding expression to refer to the Title property:

```
<%# Container.Title %>
```

When you use a databinding expression with one of the standard ASP.NET controls, such as the GridView control, you typically use a databinding expression that looks like this:

```
<%# Eval("Title") %>
```

Why the difference? The standard ASP.NET controls support a simplified databinding syntax. If you want to support this simplified syntax in your custom controls, then you must implement the IDataItemContainer interface.

The IDataItemContainer includes the following three properties, which you are required to implement:

- ▶ **DataItem**—Returns the value of the data item.
- ▶ **DataItemIndex**—Returns the index of the data item from its data source.
- ▶ **DisplayIndex**—Returns the index of the data item as it is displayed in a control.

Typically, you implement the `IDataItemContainer` when creating a databound control. For example, you wrap up each record retrieved from a database table in an object that implements the `IDataItemContainer` interface. That way, you can use a simplified databinding expression to refer to the value of a particular database record column.

In this section, we create a nondatabound control that supports the simplified databinding syntax. The control is named the `Product` control, and it is included in Listing 30.5.

LISTING 30.5   `Product.cs`

```csharp
using System;
using System.Web;
using System.Web.UI;
using System.Web.UI.WebControls;

namespace myControls
{
    public class Product : CompositeControl
    {
        private ITemplate _itemTemplate;
        private ProductItem _item;

        public string Name
        {
            get
            {
                EnsureChildControls();
                return _item.Name;
            }
            set
            {
                EnsureChildControls();
                _item.Name = value;
            }
        }

        public Decimal Price
        {
            get
            {
                EnsureChildControls();
                return _item.Price;
            }
            set
            {
                EnsureChildControls();
```

LISTING 30.5 Continued

```csharp
                _item.Price = value;
            }
        }

        [TemplateContainer(typeof(ProductItem))]
        [PersistenceMode(PersistenceMode.InnerProperty)]
        public ITemplate ItemTemplate
        {
            get { return _itemTemplate; }
            set { _itemTemplate = value; }
        }

        protected override void CreateChildControls()
        {
            _item = new ProductItem();
            _itemTemplate.InstantiateIn(_item);
            Controls.Add(_item);
        }
    }

    public class ProductItem : WebControl, IDataItemContainer
    {
        private string _name;
        private decimal _price;

        public string Name
        {
            get { return _name; }
            set { _name = value; }
        }

        public decimal Price
        {
            get { return _price; }
            set { _price = value; }
        }

        public object DataItem
        {
            get
            {
                return this;
            }
        }
```

```
        public int DataItemIndex
        {
            get { return 0; }
        }

        public int DisplayIndex
        {
            get { return 0; }
        }
    }


}
```

The file in Listing 30.5 actually contains two classes: the `Product` and the `ProductItem` class. The `Product` control includes an `ItemTemplate` property. Notice that the `TemplateContainer` attribute that decorates this property associates the `ProductItem` class with the `ItemTemplate`.

In the `CreateChildControls()` method, the `ItemTemplate` is instantiated into the `ProductItem` class. The `ProductItem` class, in turn, is added to the controls collection of the `Product` class.

The `ProductItem` class implements the `IDataItemContainer` interface. Implementing the `DataItemIndex` and `DisplayIndex` properties is a little silly because there is only one data item. However, you are required to implement all the properties of an interface.

The page in Listing 30.6 illustrates how you can use the `Product` control with the simplified databinding syntax.

LISTING 30.6   ShowProduct.aspx

```
<%@ Page Language="C#" %>
<%@ Register TagPrefix="custom" Namespace="myControls" %>
<!DOCTYPE html PUBLIC "-//W3C//DTD XHTML 1.0 Transitional//EN"
"http://www.w3.org/TR/xhtml1/DTD/xhtml1-transitional.dtd">

<script runat="server">

    void Page_Load()
    {
        Product1.Name = "Laptop Computer";
        Product1.Price = 1254.12m;
        Product1.DataBind();
    }

</script>
```

LISTING 30.6   Continued

```
<html xmlns="http://www.w3.org/1999/xhtml" >
<head id="Head1" runat="server">
    <title>Show Product</title>
</head>
<body>
    <form id="form1" runat="server">
    <div>

    <custom:Product
        id="Product1"
        Runat="Server">
        <ItemTemplate>
        Name: <%# Eval("Name") %>
        <br />
        Price: <%# Eval("Price", "{0:c}") %>
        </ItemTemplate>
    </custom:Product>

    </div>
    </form>
</body>
</html>
```

Notice that the `Eval()` method is used in the `Product` control's `ItemTemplate`. For example, the expression `Eval("Name")` is used to display the product name. If you prefer, you can still use the `Container.Name` syntax. However, the `Eval()` syntax is more familiar to ASP.NET developers.

Supporting Two-Way Databinding

Two-way databinding is a feature that was introduced with the ASP.NET 2.0 Framework. Two-way databinding enables you to extract values from a template. You can use a two-way databinding expression not only to display the value of a data item, but also to update the value of a data item.

You create a template that supports two-way databinding expressions by creating a property that returns an object that implements the `IBindableTemplate` interface. This interface inherits from the `ITemplate` interface. It has the following two methods:

- ▶ **InstantiateIn**—Instantiates the contents of a template in a particular control.

- ▶ **ExtractValues**—Returns a collection of databinding expression values from a template.

For example, the `ProductForm` control in Listing 30.7 represents a form for editing an existing product. The control includes a property named `EditItemTemplate` that represents a two-way databinding template.

LISTING 30.7   ProductForm.cs

```csharp
using System;
using System.Web;
using System.Web.UI;
using System.Web.UI.WebControls;
using System.ComponentModel;
using System.Collections.Specialized;

namespace myControls
{

    public class ProductForm : CompositeControl
    {
        public event EventHandler ProductUpdated;

        private IBindableTemplate _editItemTemplate;
        private ProductFormItem _item;
        private IOrderedDictionary _results;

        public IOrderedDictionary Results
        {
            get { return _results; }
        }

        public string Name
        {
            get
            {
                EnsureChildControls();
                return _item.Name;
            }
            set
            {
                EnsureChildControls();
                _item.Name = value;
            }
        }

        public decimal Price
        {
            get
            {
                EnsureChildControls();
                return _item.Price;
            }
```

LISTING 30.7   Continued

```
        set
        {
            EnsureChildControls();
            _item.Price = value;
        }
    }

    [TemplateContainer(typeof(ProductFormItem), BindingDirection.TwoWay)]
    [PersistenceMode(PersistenceMode.InnerProperty)]
    public IBindableTemplate EditItemTemplate
    {
        get { return _editItemTemplate; }
        set { _editItemTemplate = value; }
    }

    protected override void CreateChildControls()
    {
        _item = new ProductFormItem();
        _editItemTemplate.InstantiateIn(_item);
        Controls.Add(_item);
    }

    protected override bool OnBubbleEvent(object source, EventArgs args)
    {
        _results = _editItemTemplate.ExtractValues(_item);
        if (ProductUpdated != null)
            ProductUpdated(this, EventArgs.Empty);
        return true;
    }
}

public class ProductFormItem : WebControl, IDataItemContainer
{
    private string _name;
    private decimal _price;

    public string Name
    {
        get { return _name; }
        set { _name = value; }
    }

    public decimal Price
    {
```

```
            get { return _price; }
            set { _price = value; }
        }

        public object DataItem
        {
            get { return this; }
        }

        public int DataItemIndex
        {
            get { return 0; }
        }

        public int DisplayIndex
        {
            get { return 0; }
        }


    }
}
```

You should notice two special things about the `EditItemTemplate` property. First, notice that the property returns an object that implements the `IBindableTemplate` interface. Second, notice that the `TemplateContainer` attribute that decorates the property includes a `BindingDirection` parameter. You can assign one of two possible values to `BindingDirection`: `OneWay` and `TwoWay`.

The `ProductForm` includes an `OnBubbleEvent()` method. This method is called when a child control of the `ProductForm` control raises an event. For example, if someone clicks a `Button` control contained in the `EditItemTemplate`, the `OnBubbleEvent()` method is called.

In Listing 30.7, the `OnBubbleEvent()` method calls the `EditItemTemplate`'s `ExtractValues()` method. This method is supplied by the ASP.NET Framework because the `EditItemTemplate` is marked as a two-way databinding template.

The `ExtractValues()` method returns an `OrderedDictionary` collection that contains name/value pairs that correspond to each of the databinding expressions contained in the `EditItemTemplate`. The `ProductForm` control exposes this collection of values with its `Results` property. After the values are extracted, the control raises a `ProductUpdated` event.

The page in Listing 30.8 illustrates how you can use the `ProductForm` control to update the properties of a product.

LISTING 30.8 ShowProductForm.aspx

```
<%@ Page Language="C#" %>
<%@ Register TagPrefix="custom" Namespace="myControls" %>
<!DOCTYPE html PUBLIC "-//W3C//DTD XHTML 1.0 Transitional//EN"
"http://www.w3.org/TR/xhtml1/DTD/xhtml1-transitional.dtd">

<script runat="server">

    void Page_Load()
    {
        if (!Page.IsPostBack)
        {
            ProductForm1.Name = "Laptop";
            ProductForm1.Price = 433.12m;
            ProductForm1.DataBind();
        }
    }

    protected void ProductForm1_ProductUpdated(object sender, EventArgs e)
    {
        lblName.Text = ProductForm1.Results["Name"].ToString();
        lblPrice.Text = ProductForm1.Results["Price"].ToString();
    }
</script>

<html xmlns="http://www.w3.org/1999/xhtml" >
<head id="Head1" runat="server">
    <title>Show ProductForm</title>
</head>
<body>
    <form id="form1" runat="server">
    <div>

    <custom:ProductForm
        id="ProductForm1"
        Runat="server" OnProductUpdated="ProductForm1_ProductUpdated">
        <EditItemTemplate>

        <asp:Label
            id="lblName"
            Text="Product Name:"
            AssociatedControlID="txtName"
            Runat="server" />
        <asp:TextBox
            id="txtName"
```

```
                  Text='<%# Bind("Name") %>'
                  Runat="server" />
           <br /><br />
           <asp:Label
               id="lblPrice"
               Text="Product Price:"
               AssociatedControlID="txtPrice"
               Runat="server" />
           <asp:TextBox
               id="txtPrice"
               Text='<%# Bind("Price") %>'
               Runat="server" />
           <br /><br />
           <asp:Button
               id="btnUpdate"
               Text="Update"
               Runat="server" />

        </EditItemTemplate>
    </custom:ProductForm>

    <hr />
    New Product Name:
    <asp:Label
        id="lblName"
        Runat="server" />

    <br /><br />

    New Product Price:
    <asp:Label
        id="lblPrice"
        Runat="server" />

    </div>
    </form>
</body>
</html>
```

In the Page_Load() method in Listing 30.8, the ProductForm Name and Price properties are set. Next, the DataBind() is called in order to cause the ProductForm control to evaluate its databinding expressions.

Notice that the ProductForm control's EditItemTemplate includes Bind() expressions instead of Eval() expressions. You use Bind() expressions in a two-way databinding template.

The EditItemTemplate includes a Button control. When you click the Button control, the ProductForm control's OnBubbleEvent() method executes, the values are retrieved from the EditItemTemplate, and the ProductUpdated event is raised.

The page in Listing 30.8 handles the ProductUpdated event and displays the new values with two Label controls (see Figure 30.3).

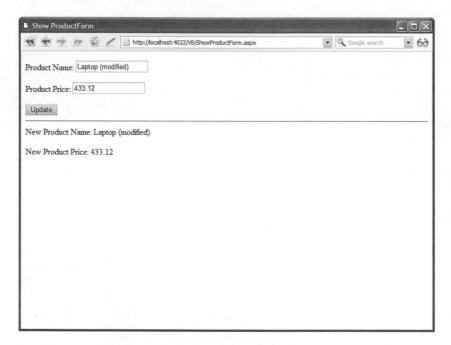

FIGURE 30.3   Using a two-way databinding template.

Creating Templated Databound Controls

In this section, you learn how to build templated databound controls. A databound control can be bound to a DataSource control such as the SqlDataSource or ObjectDataSource controls.

The ASP.NET Framework provides you with a number of base classes that you can use when creating a custom databound control. So, let's look at some tables and figures. Table 30.1 lists the base control classes for all the standard ASP.NET databound controls. Figure 30.4 displays the inheritance hierarchy of all the new databound controls in the ASP.NET Framework. Typically, you inherit from one of the leaf nodes. You create a control that derives from the base CompositeDataBoundControl, HierarchicalDataBoundControl, or ListControl class.

This chapter concentrates on inheriting new controls from the base CompositeDataBoundControl class. This is the easiest base class to use when you want to display one or more database records and use templates.

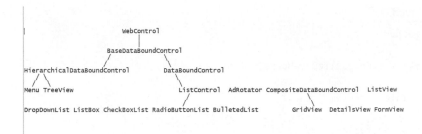

FIGURE 30.4   Databound control inheritance hierarchy.

> **NOTE**
>
> You learned how to create controls that inherit from the base `ListControl` class in Chapter 10, "Using List Controls."

TABLE 30.1   Base Databound Control Classes

Control	Base Control
ListView	DataBoundControl
GridView, DetailsView, FormView	CompositeDataBoundControl
Menu, TreeView	HierarchicalDataBoundControl
DropDownList, ListBox RadioButtonList, CheckBoxList, BulletedList	ListControl
DataList, DataGrid	BaseDataList
Repeater	Control

Creating a `DivView` Control

Let's start simple. In this section, we create a custom databound control named the `DivView` control. The `DivView` control displays a set of data items (database records) in HTML <div> tags.

The `DivView` control inherits from the base `CompositeDataBoundControl` class and overrides a single method of the base class. The `DivView` control overrides the base class's `CreateChildControls()` method.

The `DivView` control is contained in Listing 30.9.

LISTING 30.9   DivView.cs

```
using System;
using System.Collections;
using System.Web;
using System.Web.UI;
using System.Web.UI.WebControls;
```

30

LISTING 30.9   Continued

```
namespace AspNetUnleashed
{
    public class DivView : CompositeDataBoundControl
    {
        private ITemplate _itemTemplate;

        [TemplateContainer(typeof(DivViewItem))]
        [PersistenceMode(PersistenceMode.InnerProperty)]
        public ITemplate ItemTemplate
        {
            get { return _itemTemplate; }
            set { _itemTemplate = value; }
        }

        protected override int CreateChildControls(IEnumerable dataSource, bool
        ➥dataBinding)
        {
            int counter = 0;
            foreach (object dataItem in dataSource)
            {
                DivViewItem contentItem = new DivViewItem(dataItem, counter);
                _itemTemplate.InstantiateIn(contentItem);
                Controls.Add(contentItem);
                counter++;
            }
            DataBind(false);
            return counter;
        }

        protected override HtmlTextWriterTag TagKey
        {
            get
            {
                return HtmlTextWriterTag.Div;
            }
        }
    }


    public class DivViewItem : WebControl, IDataItemContainer
    {
        private object _dataItem;
        private int _index;
```

```
        public object DataItem
        {
            get { return _dataItem; }
        }

        public int DataItemIndex
        {
            get { return _index; }
        }

        public int DisplayIndex
        {
            get { return _index; }
        }

        protected override HtmlTextWriterTag TagKey
        {
            get
            {
                return HtmlTextWriterTag.Div;
            }
        }

        public DivViewItem(object dataItem, int index)
        {
            _dataItem = dataItem;
            _index = index;
        }

    }
}
```

The `DivView` control supports an `ItemTemplate` that is used to format each of its data
items. You are required to supply an `ItemTemplate` when you use the `DivView` control.

All the work happens in the `CreateChildControls()` method. Notice that this is not the
same `CreateChildControls()` method that is included in the base `System.Web.UI.Control`
class. The `DivView` control overrides the `CompositeDataBounControl`'s
`CreateChildControls()` method.

The `CreateChildControls()` method accepts the following two parameters:

▶ **dataSource**—Represents all the data items from the data source.

▶ **dataBinding**—Represents whether the `CreateChildControls()` method is called
  when the data items are being retrieved from the data source.

The `CreateChildControls()` method is called every time that the `DivView` control renders its data items. When the control is first bound to a `DataSource` control, the `dataSource` parameter represents the data items retrieved from the `DataSource` control. After a postback, the `dataSource` parameter contains a collection of null values, but the correct number of null values.

After a postback, the contents of the data items can be retrieved from View State. As long as the correct number of child controls is created, the Framework can rebuild the contents of the databound control.

You can use the `dataBinding` parameter to determine whether the data items from the data source actually represent anything. Typically, the `dataBinding` parameter has the value `True` when the page first loads and the value `False` after each postback.

Notice that the `DataBind()` method is called after the child controls are created. You must call the `DataBind()` method when a template includes databinding expressions. Otherwise, the databinding expressions are never evaluated.

The page in Listing 30.10 illustrates how you can bind the `DivView` control to a `SqlDataSource` control.

LISTING 30.10   ShowDivView.aspx

```
<%@ Page Language="C#" %>
<%@ Register TagPrefix="custom" Namespace="AspNetUnleashed" %>
<!DOCTYPE html PUBLIC "-//W3C//DTD XHTML 1.0 Transitional//EN"
    "http://www.w3.org/TR/xhtml1/DTD/xhtml1-transitional.dtd">
<html xmlns="http://www.w3.org/1999/xhtml" >
<head id="Head1" runat="server">
    <style type="text/css">
        .movies
        {
            width:500px;
        }
        .movies div
        {
            border:solid 1px black;
            padding:10px;
            margin:10px;
        }
    </style>
```

```
        <title>Show DivView</title>
    </head>
    <body>
        <form id="form1" runat="server">
        <div>

        <custom:DivView
            id="lstMovies"
            DataSourceID="srcMovies"
            CssClass="movies"
            Runat="Server">
            <ItemTemplate>
            <h1><%# Eval("Title") %></h1>
            Director: <%# Eval("Director") %>
            </ItemTemplate>
        </custom:DivView>


        <asp:SqlDataSource
            id="srcMovies"
            ConnectionString="<%$ ConnectionStrings:Movies %>"
            SelectCommand="SELECT Title, Director FROM Movies"
            Runat="server" />

        <br />
        <asp:LinkButton
            id="lnkReload"
            Text="Reload"
            Runat="server" />

        </div>
        </form>
    </body>
</html>
```

In Listing 30.10, the `SqlDataSource` control represents the Movies database table. The `DivView` control includes an `ItemTemplate` that formats each of the columns from this database table (see Figure 30.5).

30

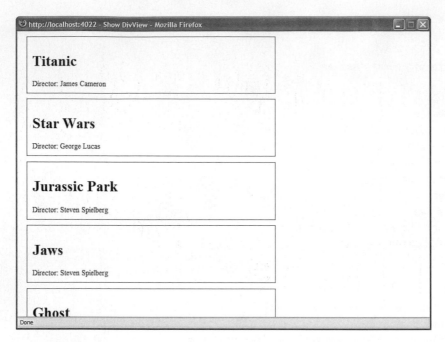

FIGURE 30.5 Displaying database records with the DivView control.

Summary

This chapter was devoted to the topic of building templated databound controls. In the first part, you learned how to support templates in your custom controls. You learned how to create templates that support both one-way and two-way databinding expressions. You also learned how to create a default template for a control.

The second half of this chapter focused on the topic of building databound controls. You learned how to create a simple DivView control that displays the records from a database table in a series of HTML <div> tags.

PART IX

ASP.NET AJAX

IN THIS PART

Using Server-Side ASP.NET AJAX

Microsoft ASP.NET is a dying technology. It received its death blow on February 18, 2005 when Jesse James Garrett published his article "Ajax: A New Approach to Web Applications." All that is left is the long, slow goodbye.

All the previous chapters in this book were about ASP.NET. ASP.NET is the present. This chapter, and the two that follow, are about the future. The future is Ajax. In this chapter and the next, you learn about server-side ASP.NET AJAX. In the chapter that follows, you learn about client-side ASP.NET AJAX.

In this chapter, you learn about Microsoft's primary server-side AJAX control: the UpdatePanel control. This control enables you to easily retrofit existing ASP.NET applications with Ajax functionality. You use the UpdatePanel control to update content in a page without posting the entire page back to the web server. You also learn about two controls that support the UpdatePanel control: the Timer control and the UpdateProgress control.

> **NOTE**
>
> You'll notice in this chapter that I switch between Ajax and AJAX. Jesse James Garrett insists that Ajax should be spelled Ajax (initial-capped), and Microsoft insists that the word should be spelled AJAX (all capped, like a proper acronym). Because Mr. Garrett coined the word, I'll use his preferred spelling, Ajax, when not referring to a Microsoft product name.

The Ajax Vision

ASP.NET is a *server-side* technology for building web applications. Almost all the work happens on the web server and not the web browser. Whenever you perform an action in an ASP.NET page—such as clicking a button or sorting a GridView—the entire page must be posted back to the web server. Any significant action on a page results in a postback.

If you think about it, this is incredibly inefficient. When you perform a postback in an ASP.NET page, the entire page must be transported across the Internet from browser to server. Next, the .NET class that corresponds to the page must re-render the entire page again from scratch. Finally, the finished page must be sent back across the Internet to the browser. This whole long, slow, agonizing process must occur even if you are updating a tiny section of the page.

Using a server-side technology such as ASP.NET results in a bad user experience. Every time a user performs some action on a page, the universe temporarily freezes. Whenever you perform a postback, the browser locks, the page jumps, and the user must wait patiently twiddling his thumbs while the page gets reconstructed. All of us have grown accustomed to this awful user experience. However, we would never design our desktop applications in the same way.

When the members of the ASP.NET team invented ASP.NET in the late 1990s, there was good reason to embrace the server side. Getting a page that was written in JavaScript to work consistently across different browsers, and even across different versions of the same browser, was very difficult. The server side was safe and reliable.

However, we've reached a tipping point. Web developers are discovering that if they want to build truly great applications, they need to leave the safety of the server side and enter the wilds of the client side. Google has hacked out a path for us by creating several proof-of-concept web applications that demonstrate that you can build reliable, user-friendly, web applications that execute entirely in the browser without the need for postbacks.

Google Docs (http://docs.google.com) demonstrates that you can build Microsoft Office better than Office by building it as a web application. Google Docs enables you to save your documents, spreadsheets, and presentations on a central server so that they don't get lost and can be accessed anywhere. Furthermore, Google Docs enables people to collaborate on documents and spreadsheets over the Internet, which is something that you just cannot do in Microsoft Office.

Google Suggest (http://www.google.com/webhp?complete=1&hl=en) was the Google application that convinced me that the future is Ajax. Google Suggest works like the normal Google home page, except for the fact that the Google Suggest page offers suggestions as you type. While you are typing, Google Suggest looks up matching words from its database and shows them to you in real time (before seeing Google Suggest, I would have thought this violated the laws of physics).

Finally, Google Gmail (http://gmail.google.com) is the application that started all the excitement about Ajax. Gmail is an email client that works very much like a desktop email application. Jesse James Garrett credits Google Gmail for inspiring him to coin the word *Ajax*.

> **NOTE**
>
> It is ironic that Google Gmail, an email web client, is the application that got everyone excited about Ajax because the technology behind Ajax was invented by Microsoft in support of its email web client. Microsoft invented AJAX to support its web client for Microsoft Exchange Server. You can read about the invention of the technology behind Ajax in the following blog post:
>
> http://msexchangeteam.com/archive/2005/06/21/406646.aspx

An Ajax application is a client-side web application written using native browser technologies such JavaScript and the DOM. A pure Ajax application is a web application that consists of a single page and performs all its communications with the web server through web service calls.

> **NOTE**
>
> Applications that use client-side technologies such as Flash, Flex, Java applets, and Silverlight don't count as Ajax applications because these are proprietary technologies. An Ajax application must use native browser technologies.

Unlike a server-side web application, an Ajax application can be very responsive to user interaction. If a user clicks a button in a server-side web application, the button Click event doesn't actually happen until the page gets posted back to the server. In a server-side application, the button Click event gets shifted in time and space. In a client-side Ajax application, on the other hand, the button Click event happens when it happens: right on the browser.

In an Ajax application, the user interface layer is located in the browser (where it should be). The business logic and data access layers are located on the server. The user interface layer accesses the business logic layer through web services.

In this section, I've tried to convey to you the Ajax vision. I've tried to explain why I am excited about Ajax and why I think most web applications will be written as Ajax applications in the future. Unfortunately, however, the ideal does not completely intersect with the real, and we have not quite reached the point where we can build pure Ajax applications. But we are very close.

> **NOTE**
>
> To learn more about Ajax, I recommend that you visit the Ajaxian.com website and go to the Ajaxian conferences.

Server-Side Ajax versus Client-Side Ajax

Microsoft has a complicated relationship with Ajax. On the one hand, the company wants to provide its existing ASP.NET developers with an easy way to implement Ajax functionality without having to learn JavaScript. On the other hand, Microsoft recognizes that the future is on the client. Therefore, it wants to provide web developers with the tools they need to build pure client-side Ajax applications. For these reasons, Microsoft has both a server-side Ajax framework and a client-side Ajax framework.

If you want to retrofit an existing ASP.NET application to take advantage of Ajax, you can take advantage of Microsoft's server-side Ajax framework. To take advantage of the server-side framework, you don't need to write a single line of JavaScript code. You can continue to build ASP.NET pages with server-side controls in the standard way. You learn how to take advantage of the server-side Ajax framework in this chapter.

The advantage of the server-side framework is that it provides existing ASP.NET developers with a painless method of doing Ajax. The disadvantage of the server-side framework is that it doesn't escape all the problems associated with a server-side framework. You still have to run back to the server whenever you perform any client-side action.

The Microsoft client-side Ajax framework (which we discuss in Chapter 33, "Using Client-Side ASP.NET Ajax") embraces the client side. When building applications with the Microsoft client-side Ajax framework, you must build the application by using JavaScript. The advantage of building applications with the client-side framework is that you can build very rich and responsive web applications. You can build web applications with the same rich interactivity as a desktop application. The disadvantage is that Microsoft's client-side framework is currently not fully baked.

Debugging Ajax Applications

Before we start discussing the Microsoft AJAX frameworks, you need to be aware of two crucial debugging tools. Debugging Ajax applications presents challenges not present in a normal server-side application. If an Ajax call fails, you won't necessarily know. You need a way of monitoring the Ajax calls that happen between the browser and server.

The first tool is called Fiddler. You can download this tool (for free) at http://www. fiddler2.com. Fiddler enables you to view HTTP requests and responses, including Ajax calls. Fiddler works by installing itself as a proxy between your web browser and the rest of the universe. You can use Fiddler with Internet Explorer, Mozilla Firefox, Opera, Safari, and just about any other browser.

After you install Fiddler, you can launch the tool by selecting the menu option Tools, Fiddler2 from within Microsoft Internet Explorer. After Fiddler launches, every browser request and response is recorded in the Fiddler Web Sessions pane. You can click a request and then click the Session Inspector tab to see the full request and response (see Figure 31.1).

31

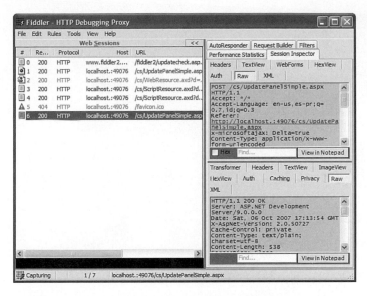

FIGURE 31.1   Using Fiddler to inspect an Ajax request and response.

NOTE

If you can't get Fiddler to capture page requests from localhost, try adding a period directly after localhost in the browser address bar. For example, make a request that looks like this:

http://localhost.:6916/Original/Feedback.aspx

If you are using Microsoft Vista, you might need to disable IPv6 support. In Fiddler, select the menu option Tools, Fiddler Options, and uncheck the Enable IPv6 check box.

The other critical Ajax debugging tool is Firebug, which is a free Firefox extension. You can download Firebug by launching Firefox and selecting the menu option Tools, Add-ons. Next, click the Get Extensions link. Finally, enter **Firebug** into the search box and follow the installation instructions.

Firebug, like Fiddler, enables you to monitor Ajax calls, but it enables you to do much more. After you install Firebug, you enable it by selecting the menu option Tools, Firebug and unchecking Disable Firebug. After Firebug is enabled, you can click the green check box at the bottom right of the Firefox browser to open Firebug (see Figure 31.2).

Firebug has several very useful features for debugging JavaScript applications. For example, it enables you to set breakpoints in JavaScript scripts, inspect DOM elements, and determine which CSS rules apply to which elements in a page. Right now, however, I want you to notice that you can use Firebug to monitor Ajax requests and responses. If you click the Net tab and the XHR tab, then every Ajax call will appear in the Firebug window. You can click a particular Ajax request to see the full request and response interaction between browser and server.

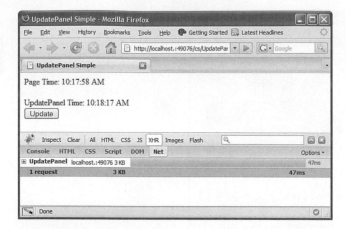

FIGURE 31.2   Using Firebug in Mozilla Firefox.

Using the UpdatePanel Control

Microsoft's server-side AJAX framework consists of one main control: the UpdatePanel control. The UpdatePanel control enables you to update a portion of a page without updating the entire page. In other words, it enables you to perform partial-page rendering.

Let's start with a super-simple example of a page that uses the UpdatePanel control. The page in Listing 31.1 contains a ScriptManager control and an UpdatePanel control. The UpdatePanel control contains a single Button control. When you click the button, only the content contained in the UpdatePanel control is refreshed (see Figure 31.3).

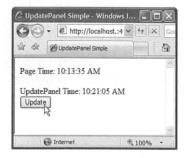

FIGURE 31.3   Using the UpdatePanel control.

LISTING 31.1   UpdatePanelSimple.aspx

```
<%@ Page Language="C#" %>
<!DOCTYPE html PUBLIC "-//W3C//DTD XHTML 1.0 Transitional//EN"
"http://www.w3.org/TR/xhtml1/DTD/xhtml1-transitional.dtd">
<html xmlns="http://www.w3.org/1999/xhtml">
<head runat="server">
    <title>UpdatePanel Simple</title>
```

```
    </head>
    <body>
        <form id="form1" runat="server">

        <asp:ScriptManager ID="ScriptManager1" runat="server" />

        Page Time: <%= DateTime.Now.ToString("T") %>
        <br /><br />

        <asp:UpdatePanel
            id="up1"
            runat="server">
            <ContentTemplate>
            UpdatePanel Time: <%= DateTime.Now.ToString("T") %>
            <br />
            <asp:Button
                id="btn"
                Text="Update"
                runat="server" />
            </ContentTemplate>
        </asp:UpdatePanel>

        </form>
    </body>
</html>
```

The page in Listing 31.1 displays the current time both inside and outside the UpdatePanel control. When you click the button, only the time within the UpdatePanel control is refreshed.

Let's look at a more realistic example that just begs for some Ajax (see Figure 31.4). The page in Listing 31.2 does not use any of the ASP.NET AJAX controls. It contains two cascading DropDownList controls. The first DropDownList enables you to pick a state, and the second DropDownList enables you to pick a city. The list of cities changes depending on the state selected.

FIGURE 31.4   A page with cascading DropDownList controls.

LISTING 31.2   CascadingDropDownsNoAjax.aspx

```
<%@ Page Language="C#" %>
<!DOCTYPE html PUBLIC "-//W3C//DTD XHTML 1.0 Transitional//EN"
"http://www.w3.org/TR/xhtml1/DTD/xhtml1-transitional.dtd">
<html xmlns="http://www.w3.org/1999/xhtml">
<head runat="server">
    <title>Cascading DropDownList Controls</title>
</head>
<body>
    <form id="form1" runat="server">
    <div>

    <asp:Label
        id="lblState"
        Text="State:"
        AssociatedControlID="ddlState"
        Runat="server" />
    <asp:DropDownList
        id="ddlState"
        DataSourceID="srcState"
        DataTextField="State"
        DataValueField="State"
        AutoPostBack="true"
        Runat="server" />
    <asp:SqlDataSource
        id="srcState"
        ConnectionString='<%$ ConnectionStrings:con %>'
        SelectCommand="SELECT State FROM State
            ORDER BY State"
        Runat="server" />


    <br /><br />


    <asp:Label
        id="Label1"
        Text="City:"
        AssociatedControlID="ddlCity"
        Runat="server" />
    <asp:DropDownList
        id="ddlCity"
        DataSourceID="srcCity"
        DataTextField="City"
        AutoPostBack="true"
        Runat="server" />
```

```
    <asp:SqlDataSource
        id="srcCity"
        ConnectionString='<%$ ConnectionStrings:con %>'
        SelectCommand="SELECT City FROM City
            WHERE State=@State
            ORDER BY City"
        Runat="server">
        <SelectParameters>
            <asp:ControlParameter Name="State" ControlID="ddlState" />
        </SelectParameters>
    </asp:SqlDataSource>

    </div>
    </form>
</body>
</html>
```

When you select a state using the first DropDownList control, there is a click, and the page posts back to itself in order to populate the second DropDownList control with matching cities. Clearly, the user experience here is less than optimal. All work must stop while the page performs a postback.

Let's fix up this page with some Ajax. The page in Listing 31.3 is exactly the same as the page in Listing 31.2, except for two changes. First, the page now contains a ScriptManager control. Second, and more importantly, the DropDownList controls in Listing 31.3 are wrapped inside an UpdatePanel control.

LISTING 31.3   CascadingDropDownsAjax.aspx

```
<%@ Page Language="C#" %>
<!DOCTYPE html PUBLIC "-//W3C//DTD XHTML 1.0 Transitional//EN"
"http://www.w3.org/TR/xhtml1/DTD/xhtml1-transitional.dtd">
<html xmlns="http://www.w3.org/1999/xhtml">
<head id="Head1" runat="server">
    <title>Cascading DropDownList Controls</title>
</head>
<body>
    <form id="form1" runat="server">
    <div>

    <asp:ScriptManager
        id="sm1"
        Runat="server" />

    <asp:UpdatePanel
        id="UpdatePanel1"
```

LISTING 31.3   Continued

```
        Runat="server">
        <ContentTemplate>

    <asp:Label
        id="lblState"
        Text="State:"
        AssociatedControlID="ddlState"
        Runat="server" />
    <asp:DropDownList
        id="ddlState"
        DataSourceID="srcState"
        DataTextField="State"
        DataValueField="State"
        AutoPostBack="true"
        Runat="server" />
    <asp:SqlDataSource
        id="srcState"
        ConnectionString='<%$ ConnectionStrings:con %>'
        SelectCommand="SELECT State FROM State
            ORDER BY State"
        Runat="server" />


    <br /><br />


    <asp:Label
        id="Label1"
        Text="City:"
        AssociatedControlID="ddlCity"
        Runat="server" />
    <asp:DropDownList
        id="ddlCity"
        DataSourceID="srcCity"
        DataTextField="City"
        AutoPostBack="true"
        Runat="server" />
    <asp:SqlDataSource
        id="srcCity"
        ConnectionString='<%$ ConnectionStrings:con %>'
        SelectCommand="SELECT City FROM City
            WHERE State=@State
            ORDER BY City"
```

```
        Runat="server">
        <SelectParameters>
            <asp:ControlParameter Name="State" ControlID="ddlState" />
        </SelectParameters>
    </asp:SqlDataSource>

    </ContentTemplate>
    </asp:UpdatePanel>

    </div>
    </form>
</body>
</html>
```

In Listing 31.3, when you select a new state with the first DropDownList control, matching cities are displayed in the second DropDownList control. However, there is no click and there is no noticeable postback. The browser doesn't freeze, and the page does not jump. Everything happens smoothly and professionally through the magic of Ajax.

The ScriptManager control in Listing 31.3 is used to add the necessary JavaScript scripts to enable Ajax. Anytime you create a page that uses Ajax, regardless of whether you are doing server-side or client-side Ajax, you'll add a ScriptManager control to the page.

> **NOTE**
>
> If you select the AJAX Web Form template instead of the normal Web Form template from the Website, Add New Item menu option, then you get the ScriptManager control automatically.
>
> Another option is to pick the AJAX Master Page template, which also includes the ScriptManager control. If you use the AJAX Master Page, you don't need to add the ScriptManager control to individual content pages.

The UpdatePanel control is the control that is doing all the Ajax work here. It hijacks the normal postback that would happen when you select a new item in the first DropDownList control. The UpdatePanel hijacks the normal postback and performs a "sneaky" postback to grab the new content in the background.

Let's look at another page that takes advantage of the UpdatePanel control. The page in Listing 31.4 represents a simple customer feedback form (see Figure 31.5). The page contains a FormView control and a GridView control. The FormView control is used to render the insert form, and the GridView control is used to display previous customer responses. You can sort the contents of the GridView in order of the different columns.

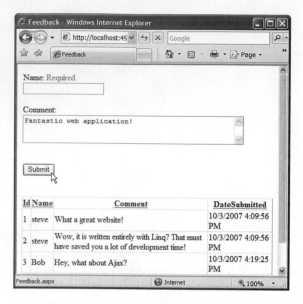

FIGURE 31.5   Entering customer feedback into an Ajax-enabled form.

LISTING 31.4   Feedback.aspx

```
<%@ Page Language="C#" %>
<!DOCTYPE html PUBLIC "-//W3C//DTD XHTML 1.0 Transitional//EN"
"http://www.w3.org/TR/xhtml1/DTD/xhtml1-transitional.dtd">
<html xmlns="http://www.w3.org/1999/xhtml">
<head runat="server">
    <title>Feedback</title>
</head>
<body>
    <form id="form1" runat="server">
    <div>

    <asp:ScriptManager
        id="sm1"
        Runat="server" />


    <asp:UpdatePanel
        id="up1"
        Runat="server">
        <ContentTemplate>

    <asp:FormView
        id="frmFeedback"
        DataSourceId="srcFeedback"
```

```
        DefaultMode="Insert"
        Runat="server">
        <InsertItemTemplate>

        <asp:Label
            id="lblName"
            Text="Name:"
            AssociatedControlID="txtName"
            Runat="server" />
        <asp:RequiredFieldValidator
            id="valName"
            Text="Required"
            ControlToValidate="txtName"
            Runat="server" />
        <br />
        <asp:TextBox
            id="txtName"
            Text='<%# Bind("Name") %>'
            Runat="server" />
        <br /><br />
        <asp:Label
            id="lblComment"
            Text="Comment:"
            AssociatedControlID="txtComment"
            Runat="server" />
        <asp:RequiredFieldValidator
            id="valComment"
            Text="Required"
            ControlToValidate="txtComment"
            Runat="server" />
        <br />
        <asp:TextBox
            id="txtComment"
            Text='<%# Bind("Comment") %>'
            TextMode="MultiLine"
            Columns="50"
            Rows="3"
            Runat="server" />
        <br /><br />
        <asp:Button
            id="btnSubmit"
            Text="Submit"
            CommandName="Insert"
            Runat="server" />
        </InsertItemTemplate>
    </asp:FormView>
```

LISTING 31.4   Continued

```
    <br /><br />

    <asp:GridView
        id="grdFeedback"
        DataSourceID="srcFeedback"
        AllowSorting="true"
        Runat="server" />

    </ContentTemplate>
    </asp:UpdatePanel>


    <asp:SqlDataSource
        id="srcFeedback"
        ConnectionString='<%$ ConnectionStrings:con %>'
        SelectCommand="SELECT Id,Name,Comment,DateSubmitted
            FROM Feedback"
        InsertCommand="INSERT Feedback (Name,Comment)
            VALUES (@Name,@Comment)"
        Runat="server" />

    </div>
    </form>
</body>
</html>
```

Because the UpdatePanel control in Listing 31.4 contains both the FormView and GridView, you can interact with the page without performing a single postback. When you submit the form, the form data is submitted back to the server using Ajax. When you sort the columns in the GridView, the sorted rows are retrieved from the server through an Ajax call.

The UpdatePanel control has six important properties:

▶ **ChildrenAsTriggers**—Gets or sets a Boolean value that indicates whether child controls should trigger an asynchronous postback automatically.

▶ **ContentTemplateContainer**—Gets the container for the UpdatePanel control's ContentTemplate. You can add controls to the ContentTemplate programmatically using this property.

▶ **IsInPartialRendering**—Gets a Boolean value indicating whether the UpdatePanel is being rendered in response to an asynchronous postback.

▶ **RenderMode**—Gets or sets a value that indicates whether the contents of an UpdatePanel should be enclosed in an HTML <div> or <span> tag. Possible values are Block (the default) and Inline.

▶ **Triggers**—Gets a list of controls that trigger the UpdatePanel to perform either an asynchronous or synchronous postback.

▶ **UpdateMode**—Gets or sets a value indicating when the content of the UpdatePanel is updated. Possible values are Always (the default) and Conditional.

The UpdatePanel also supports the following single important method:

▶ **Update()**—Causes the UpdatePanel to update its contents.

You learn how to take advantage of these properties and methods in the following sections.

Specifying UpdatePanel Triggers

By default, an UpdatePanel hijacks any postbacks that any of its child controls performs. For example, if a Button control is contained in an UpdatePanel, the UpdatePanel will hijack the button Click event and perform an Ajax call instead of the normal postback.

You can cause an UpdatePanel to refresh its contents from a control located outside of the UpdatePanel by specifying a trigger. For example, the page in Listing 31.5 contains a Button control outside of an UpdatePanel that causes the UpdatePanel to refresh its content.

LISTING 31.5   TriggerUpdatePanel.aspx

```
<%@ Page Language="C#" %>
<!DOCTYPE html PUBLIC "-//W3C//DTD XHTML 1.0 Transitional//EN"
"http://www.w3.org/TR/xhtml1/DTD/xhtml1-transitional.dtd">
<html xmlns="http://www.w3.org/1999/xhtml">
<head runat="server">
    <title>Trigger Update Panel</title>
</head>
<body>
    <form id="form1" runat="server">
    <div>

    <asp:ScriptManager
        id="sm1"
        Runat="server" />

    Page Time: <%= DateTime.Now.ToString("T") %>
    <br />
    <asp:Button
        id="btnUpdate"
        Text="Update"
        Runat="server" />

    <asp:UpdatePanel
        id="up1"
        Runat="server">
```

LISTING 31.5   Continued

```
    <Triggers>
        <asp:AsyncPostBackTrigger
            ControlID="btnUpdate"
            EventName="Click" />
    </Triggers>
    <ContentTemplate>

    Update Panel Time: <%= DateTime.Now.ToString("T") %>

    </ContentTemplate>
</asp:UpdatePanel>

</div>
</form>
</body>
</html>
```

The UpdatePanel in Listing 31.5 includes a Triggers sub-element that contains a single AsyncPostBackTrigger. This trigger points to the Button control located outside of the UpdatePanel named btnUpdate. Because the UpdatePanel contains this trigger, clicking the Button control causes the UpdatePanel to refresh its contents.

If you want, you can prevent the UpdatePanel from refreshing its contents unless you have explicitly created a trigger. If you set the UpdatePanel control's ChildrenAsTriggers property to the value false, you must explicitly create a trigger to update the contents of the UpdatePanel.

The UpdatePanel supports two types of triggers: AsyncPostBackTrigger and PostBackTrigger. The AsyncPostBackTrigger causes an asynchronous (Ajax) postback. The PostBackTrigger causes a normal entire-page postback.

You'll rarely use a PostBackTrigger. The only situation in which it makes sense to use a PostBackTrigger is when you need to mix buttons that cause asynchronous postbacks and normal postbacks in the same UpdatePanel control. For example, because you cannot perform a file upload without performing a normal entire-page postback, if a file-upload button is contained in an UpdatePanel, you need to create a PostBackTrigger for the file-upload button.

Nesting UpdatePanel Controls

One UpdatePanel can contain another UpdatePanel. In fact, you can nest UpdatePanels to your heart's content, just like Russian nesting dolls.

Nesting UpdatePanel controls is useful when you want to control how much of a page gets refreshed during an asynchronous postback. Sometimes, you might need to update only a tiny portion of a page, and other times you might need to update the entire page.

For example, the page in Listing 31.6 contains two nested UpdatePanels. The outer UpdatePanel contains a DropDownList, FormView, and ListView control. The inner UpdatePanel contains only the ListView control (see Figure 31.6).

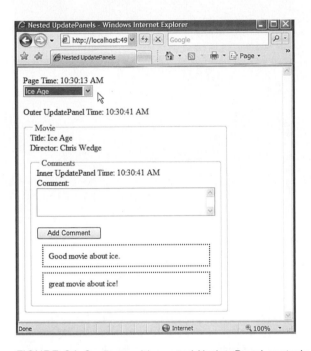

FIGURE 31.6   Page with nested UpdatePanel controls.

LISTING 31.6   NestedUpdatePanels.aspx

```
<%@ Page Language="C#" %>
<!DOCTYPE html PUBLIC "-//W3C//DTD XHTML 1.0 Transitional//EN"
"http://www.w3.org/TR/xhtml1/DTD/xhtml1-transitional.dtd">
<html xmlns="http://www.w3.org/1999/xhtml">
<head runat="server">
    <title>Nested UpdatePanels</title>
    <style type="text/css">
        fieldset
        {
            padding: 10px;
        }
        .comment
        {
            padding: 10px;
            border: dotted 2px black;
```

LISTING 31.6   Continued

```
                margin: 10px;
            }
        </style>
</head>
<body>
    <form id="form1" runat="server">
    <div>

    <asp:ScriptManager
        id="sm1"
        Runat="server" />

    Page Time: <%= DateTime.Now.ToString("T") %>
    <br />

    <asp:DropDownList
        id="ddlMovie"
        DataSourceID="srcMovies"
        DataValueField="Id"
        DataTextField="Title"
        AutoPostBack="true"
        Runat="server" />
    <asp:SqlDataSource
        id="srcMovies"
        ConnectionString='<%$ ConnectionStrings:con %>'
        SelectCommand="SELECT Id, Title FROM Movie"
        Runat="server" />

    <br /><br />

    <asp:UpdatePanel ID="upOuter" UpdateMode="Conditional" runat="server">
    <Triggers>
        <asp:AsyncPostBackTrigger ControlID="ddlMovie" />
    </Triggers>
    <ContentTemplate>

    Outer UpdatePanel Time: <%= DateTime.Now.ToString("T") %>
    <br />

    <asp:FormView
        id="frmMovie"
        DataSourceID="srcMovie"
        Runat="server">
        <ItemTemplate>
        <fieldset>
```

```
<legend>Movie</legend>
Title: <%# Eval("Title") %>
<br />
Director: <%# Eval("Director") %>

<asp:UpdatePanel ID="upInner" runat="server">
<ContentTemplate>
<asp:ListView
    id="lstMovieComments"
    DataSourceID="srcMovieComments"
    InsertItemPosition="FirstItem"
    Runat="server">
    <LayoutTemplate>
        <fieldset>
        <legend>Comments</legend>
        Inner UpdatePanel Time: <%= DateTime.Now.ToString("T") %>
        <div id="itemContainer" runat="server">
        </div>
        </fieldset>
    </LayoutTemplate>
    <ItemTemplate>
        <div class="comment">
        <%# Eval("Comment") %>
        </div>
    </ItemTemplate>
    <InsertItemTemplate>
    <asp:Label
        id="lblComment"
        Text="Comment:"
        AssociatedControlID="txtComment"
        Runat="server" />
    <br />
    <asp:TextBox
        id="txtComment"
        Text='<%# Bind("Comment") %>'
        TextMode="MultiLine"
        Columns="40"
        Rows="3"
        Runat="server" />
    <br />
    <asp:Button
        id="btnInsert"
        Text="Add Comment"
        CommandName="Insert"
        Runat="server" />
    </InsertItemTemplate>
```

LISTING 31.6   Continued

```
            </asp:ListView>
            </ContentTemplate>
            </asp:UpdatePanel>
            <asp:SqlDataSource
                id="srcMovieComments"
                ConnectionString='<%$ ConnectionStrings:con %>'
                SelectCommand="SELECT Id, Comment
                    FROM MovieComment
                    WHERE MovieId=@MovieId"
                InsertCommand="INSERT MovieComment (Comment,MovieId)
                    VALUES (@Comment,@MovieId)"
                Runat="server">
                <SelectParameters>
                    <asp:ControlParameter Name="MovieId" ControlID="ddlMovie" />
                </SelectParameters>
                <InsertParameters>
                    <asp:ControlParameter Name="MovieId" ControlID="ddlMovie" />
                </InsertParameters>
            </asp:SqlDataSource>
            </fieldset>
            </ItemTemplate>
        </asp:FormView>
        </ContentTemplate>
        </asp:UpdatePanel>
        <asp:SqlDataSource
            id="srcMovie"
            ConnectionString='<%$ ConnectionStrings:con %>'
            SelectCommand="SELECT Id, Title, Director
                FROM Movie
                WHERE Id=@Id"
            Runat="server">
            <SelectParameters>
                <asp:ControlParameter Name="Id" ControlID="ddlMovie" />
            </SelectParameters>
        </asp:SqlDataSource>

        </div>
        </form>
</body>
</html>
```

When you select a movie by using the DropDownList control, the entire page is updated. When you add a new comment to the movie with the ListView control, on the other hand, only the comments portion of the page is updated.

There are two UpdatePanel controls. The first UpdatePanel control has an ID of upOuter. It includes a trigger that points to the DropDownList control used to select a movie. Notice that this UpdatePanel control has its UpdateMode property set to the value Conditional. If the UpdateMode property was not set to this value, the outer UpdatePanel would refresh its content when the Add Comment button contained in the inner UpdatePanel control was clicked.

The inner UpdatePanel is named upInner. This UpdatePanel surrounds the ListView used to display the form for adding and displaying movie comments. When you add a new movie comment, only the comments area of the page is updated and not the entire page.

The page, the outer UpdatePanel, and the inner UpdatePanel all display the current time. When you select a new movie, the time displayed by both the outer and inner UpdatePanel—but not the page—changes. When you add a new comment, only the time displayed by the inner UpdatePanel changes.

In general, for performance reasons, you should place the smallest possible area that you need to update inside of an UpdatePanel control. The larger the area contained in an UpdatePanel, the more content that must be passed across the Internet when the UpdatePanel is updated. By nesting UpdatePanel controls, you have more granular control over the content that gets updated in a page.

Updating UpdatePanels Programmatically

The UpdatePanel control includes an Update() method. You can use this method to update the content of an UpdatePanel programmatically during an asynchronous postback.

Two properties determine when an UpdatePanel control updates its contents: UpdateMode and ChildrenAsTriggers. If you set the UpdateMode property to the value Conditional and you set ChildrenAsTriggers to the value false (and you don't define any triggers), the only way to update an UpdatePanel control's content is by calling the Update() method.

For example, the page in Listing 31.7 enables you to search movies by title. The page contains two UpdatePanel controls. The first UpdatePanel control contains a TextBox control and a Button control. The second UpdatePanel control contains a GridView control. When you click the button, the Button Click event is raised on the server through an asynchronous postback. The second UpdatePanel that contains the GridView of results is updated if, and only if, any results are found that match the search query.

LISTING 31.7   UpdateUpdatePanel.aspx

```
<%@ Page Language="C#" %>
<!DOCTYPE html PUBLIC "-//W3C//DTD XHTML 1.0 Transitional//EN"
"http://www.w3.org/TR/xhtml1/DTD/xhtml1-transitional.dtd">
<script runat="server">
    protected void btnSearch_Click(object sender, EventArgs e)
    {
        ArrayList results = Movie.Search(txtSearch.Text);
```

LISTING 31.7   Continued

```
        if (results.Count > 0)
        {
            grdResults.DataSource = results;
            grdResults.DataBind();
            upResults.Update();
        }
    }
</script>
<html xmlns="http://www.w3.org/1999/xhtml">
<head runat="server">
    <title>Update UpdatePanel</title>
</head>
<body>
    <form id="form1" runat="server">
    <div>

    <asp:ScriptManager
        id="sm1"
        Runat="server" />

    <asp:UpdatePanel
        id="upSearch"
        Runat="server">
        <ContentTemplate>
        <asp:TextBox
            id="txtSearch"
            Runat="server" />
        <asp:Button
            id="btnSearch"
            Text="Search"
            OnClick="btnSearch_Click"
            Runat="server" />
        </ContentTemplate>
    </asp:UpdatePanel>

    <asp:UpdatePanel
        id="upResults"
        UpdateMode="Conditional"
        Runat="server">
        <ContentTemplate>
        Results Time: <%= DateTime.Now.ToString("T") %>
        <br />
        <asp:GridView
            id="grdResults"
```

```
            runat="server" />
        </ContentTemplate>
    </asp:UpdatePanel>

    </div>
    </form>
</body>
</html>
```

UpdatePanels and JavaScript

You must take special care when using JavaScript with UpdatePanel controls. If you use the standard methods of the `ClientScriptManager` class for working with JavaScript, they will fail when called during an asynchronous request.

For example, I often use the `Page.ClientScript.RegisterStartupScript()` method from my server-side code to inject a JavaScript script into a page dynamically. The page in Listing 31.8 contains a button labeled Delete All Files. When you click the button, and the `FileHelper.DeleteAll()` method returns `true`, then a JavaScript alert box displays the message "All Files Deleted Successfully!" (see Figure 31.7).

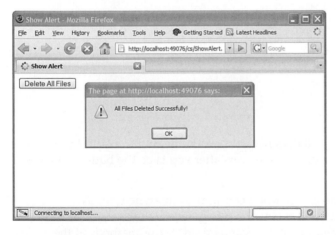

FIGURE 31.7   Displaying a JavaScript alert.

LISTING 31.8   ShowAlert.aspx

```
<%@ Page Language="C#" %>
<!DOCTYPE html PUBLIC "-//W3C//DTD XHTML 1.0 Transitional//EN"
"http://www.w3.org/TR/xhtml1/DTD/xhtml1-transitional.dtd">
<script runat="server">

    protected void btnDeleteAll_Click(object sender, EventArgs e)
```

LISTING 31.8   Continued

```
        {
            if (FileHelper.DeleteAll() == true)
            {
                string script = @"alert('All Files Deleted Successfully!');";
                Page.ClientScript.RegisterStartupScript(this.GetType(), "filesDeleted",
                ➥script, true);
            }
        }
    }
</script>
<html xmlns="http://www.w3.org/1999/xhtml">
<head runat="server">
    <title>Show Alert</title>
</head>
<body>
    <form id="form1" runat="server">
    <div>

    <asp:Button
        id="btnDeleteAll"
        Text="Delete All Files"
        OnClick="btnDeleteAll_Click"
        Runat="server" />

    </div>
    </form>
</body>
</html>
```

Unfortunately, the page in Listing 31.8 does not work when the Button control is wrapped in an UpdatePanel. The JavaScript alert never appears after you click the button. The page fails silently.

If you need to inject JavaScript into a page when performing an asynchronous postback, you need to take advantage of the methods exposed by the ScriptManager class. The ScriptManager class duplicates all the standard JavaScript methods of the ClientScriptManager class, including the following:

▶ **RegisterArrayDeclaration()**—Enables you to add a JavaScript array to the page.

▶ **RegisterClientScriptBlock()**—Enables you to add an inline JavaScript script right after the opening <form> tag.

▶ **RegisterClientScriptInclude()**—Enables you to add a JavaScript <script src=""> tag to a page.

▶ **RegisterClientScriptResource()**—Enables you to add a reference to a JavaScript file embedded in an assembly.

▶ **RegisterExpandoAttribute()**—Enables you to register a tag expando.

▶ **RegisterOnSubmitStatement()**—Enables you to register a JavaScript script that is executed when the form is submitted.

▶ **RegisterStartupScript()**—Enables you to add an inline JavaScript script right before the closing <form> tag.

The page in Listing 31.9 demonstrates how you can add JavaScript from the server to a page when performing an asynchronous postback.

LISTING 31.9   ShowAlertUpdatePanel.aspx

```
<%@ Page Language="C#" %>
<!DOCTYPE html PUBLIC "-//W3C//DTD XHTML 1.0 Transitional//EN"
"http://www.w3.org/TR/xhtml1/DTD/xhtml1-transitional.dtd">
<script runat="server">

    protected void btnDeleteAll_Click(object sender, EventArgs e)
    {
        if (FileHelper.DeleteAll() == true)
        {
            string script = @"alert('All Files Deleted Successfully!');";
            ScriptManager.RegisterStartupScript(this, this.GetType(),
            ➥"filesDeleted", script, true);
        }
    }
</script>
<html xmlns="http://www.w3.org/1999/xhtml">
<head id="Head1" runat="server">
    <title>Show Alert UpdatePanel</title>
</head>
<body>
    <form id="form1" runat="server">
    <div>

    <asp:ScriptManager
        id="sm1"
        Runat="server" />

    <asp:UpdatePanel id="up1" runat="server">
    <ContentTemplate>
    UpdatePanel Time: <%= DateTime.Now.ToString("T") %>
    <br />
    <asp:Button
        id="btnDeleteAll"
        Text="Delete All Files"
```

LISTING 31.9   Continued

```
        OnClick="btnDeleteAll_Click"
        Runat="server" />

    </ContentTemplate>
    </asp:UpdatePanel>

    </div>
    </form>
</body>
</html>
```

In Listing 31.9, the Button control is wrapped in an UpdatePanel. When you click the button, the `ScriptManager.RegisterStartupScript()` method is used to add the JavaScript alert to the page dynamically.

UpdatePanel Server-Side Page Execution Lifecycle

It is important to understand that a server-side page goes through its normal page execution lifecycle when you perform an asynchronous postback. The Page `PreInit`, `Init`, `Load`, and `PreRender` events are raised for an asynchronous postback in just the same way as these events are raised for a normal postback.

The page in Listing 31.8 logs each server event and displays the log in a BulletedList control (see Figure 31.8).

FIGURE 31.8   Viewing an asynchronous postback's server lifecycle.

LISTING 31.10   ServerLifecycle.aspx

```
<%@ Page Language="C#" %>
<!DOCTYPE html PUBLIC "-//W3C//DTD XHTML 1.0 Transitional//EN"
"http://www.w3.org/TR/xhtml1/DTD/xhtml1-transitional.dtd">
<script runat="server">
```

```
    public ArrayList _log = new ArrayList();

    void Page_PreInit()
    {
        _log.Add("PreInit " + sm1.IsInAsyncPostBack);
    }

    void Page_Init()
    {
        _log.Add("Init " + sm1.IsInAsyncPostBack);
    }

    void Page_Load()
    {
        _log.Add("Load " + sm1.IsInAsyncPostBack);
    }

    void Page_PreRender()
    {
        _log.Add("PreRender " + sm1.IsInAsyncPostBack);

        // Show Lifecycle log
        bltLog.DataSource = _log;
        bltLog.DataBind();
    }
</script>

<html xmlns="http://www.w3.org/1999/xhtml">
<head runat="server">
    <title>Server Lifecycle</title>
</head>
<body>
    <form id="form1" runat="server">
    <div>

    <asp:ScriptManager
        id="sm1"
        runat="server" />

    <asp:UpdatePanel
        id="up1"
        runat="server">
        <ContentTemplate>
        <asp:Button
            id="btnLog"
            Text="Show Server Page Lifecycle"
```

LISTING 31.11   Continued

```
    <div>
        <asp:ScriptManager ID="ScriptManager1" runat="server" />

        <asp:UpdatePanel ID="up1" runat="server">
        <ContentTemplate>
            <asp:Button ID="btnAsync" Text="Async Postback" runat="server" />
        </ContentTemplate>
        </asp:UpdatePanel>
        <asp:Button ID="Button1" Text="Normal Postback" runat="server" />

        <br /><br />
        <textarea id="TraceConsole" cols="60" rows="10"></textarea>

    </div>
    </form>
</body>
<script type="text/javascript">

  Sys.Application.add_init(application_init);

  function application_init()
  {
    Sys.Debug.trace("Application.Init");

    var prm = Sys.WebForms.PageRequestManager.getInstance();
    prm.add_initializeRequest( prm_initializeRequest );
    prm.add_beginRequest( prm_beginRequest );
    prm.add_pageLoading( prm_pageLoading );
    prm.add_pageLoaded( prm_pageLoaded );
    prm.add_endRequest( prm_endRequest );
  }

  function pageLoad()
  {
    Sys.Debug.trace("Application.Load");
  }

  function prm_initializeRequest()
  {
    Sys.Debug.trace("PageRequestManager.initializeRequest");
  }

  function prm_beginRequest()
  {
```

<
<
</bod
</htm

Wher
Bulle
IsInA
a nor

The p
initia
event
async

NC

No
Pr
pro

Upd

A pag
lifecy
happ

▶

▶

▶

▶

```
    Sys.Debug.trace("PageRequestManager.beginRequest");
  }

  function prm_pageLoading()
  {
    Sys.Debug.trace("PageRequestManager.pageLoading");
  }

  function prm_pageLoaded()
  {
    Sys.Debug.trace("PageRequestManager.pageLoaded");
  }

  function prm_endRequest()
  {
    Sys.Debug.trace("PageRequestManager.endRequest");
  }

  function pageUnload()
  {
    alert("Application.Unload");
  }

</script>
</html>
```

Notice that because we are discussing client-side events, we have moved over into the JavaScript world. The script in Listing 31.11 has to be written in JavaScript because it executes within the browser and not on the server.

NOTE

When using `Sys.Debug.trace()` with Internet Explorer, you must add a `<textarea>` to your page with an ID of `TraceConsole` to view the trace messages. When using Mozilla Firefox with the Firebug extension, on the other hand, you can simply use the Firebug console to view the trace messages.

Different information is available during each client-side event. You can access the event information by reading the properties of the second parameter passed to the event handler. What follows is the event information passed to each event handler.

InitializeRequestEventArgs   Passed to the `PageRequestManager.initializeRequest` event handler. Supports the following properties:

▶ **cancel**—Enables you to cancel the current asynchronous postback

▸ **postBackElement**—The element that caused the asynchronous postback

▸ **request**—The request object used to perform the asynchronous postback

BeginRequestEventArgs   Passed to the `PageRequestManager.beginRequest` event handler. Supports the following properties:

▸ **postBackElement**—The element that caused the asynchronous postback

▸ **request**—The request object used to perform the asynchronous postback

PageLoadingEventArgs   Passed to the `PageRequestManager.pageLoading` event handler. Supports the following properties:

▸ **dataItems**—The data items registered with the `ScriptManager. RegisterDataItem()` method

▸ **panelsDeleting**—The array of UpdatePanel elements being deleted

▸ **panelsUpdating**—The array of UpdatePanel elements being updated

PageLoadedEventArgs   Passed to the `PageRequestManager.pageLoaded` event handler. Supports the following properties:

▸ **dataItems**—The data items registered with the `ScriptManager. RegisterDataItem()` method

▸ **panelsCreated**—The array of UpdatePanel elements created

▸ **panelsUpdated**—The array of UpdatePanel elements updated

ApplicationLoadEventArgs   Passed to the `Application.load` event handler. Supports the following properties:

▸ **components**—The array of components created since the last time the `Application.load` event was raised

▸ **isPartialLoad**—Indicates whether the page is executing in the context of an asynchronous postback

EndRequestEventArgs   Passed to the `PageRequestManager.endRequest` event handler. Supports the following properties:

▸ **dataItems**—The data items registered with the `ScriptManager. RegisterDataItem()` method

▸ **error**—The error, if any, that occurred during the asynchronous postback

▸ **errorHandled**—Enables you to suppress the error

▸ **response**—The response associated with the asynchronous postback

> **NOTE**
>
> You can detect whether a page is executing within the context on an asynchronous post-back within client code by using the `PageRequestManager.isInAsyncPostBack` property.

The page in Listing 31.12 illustrates how you can take advantage of these event properties. The page contains two UpdatePanel controls. During an asynchronous call, the border of the active UpdatePanel turns the color orange. When the asynchronous call completes, the border of the updated UpdatePanel turns green.

> **NOTE**
>
> Later in this chapter, you learn how to use the UpdateProgress control to display an UpdatePanel's progress. The method described in this section of handling client events directly is useful when you want to display a custom progress indicator.

LISTING 31.12   UpdatePanelCustomProgress.aspx

```
<%@ Page Language="C#" %>
<!DOCTYPE html PUBLIC "-//W3C//DTD XHTML 1.0 Transitional//EN"
"http://www.w3.org/TR/xhtml1/DTD/xhtml1-transitional.dtd">
<script runat="server">

    protected void btnSubmit_Click(object sender, EventArgs e)
    {
        System.Threading.Thread.Sleep(2000); // sleep 2 seconds
    }

</script>
<html xmlns="http://www.w3.org/1999/xhtml">
<head runat="server">
    <title>UpdatePanelCustomProgress</title>
    <style type="text/css">
        .normal
        {
            width:300px;
            padding:10px;
            margin:10px;
            border: solid 4px black;
        }

        .updating
        {
            width:300px;
            padding:10px;
```

LISTING 31.12   Continued

```
            margin:10px;
            border: solid 4px orange;
        }

        .updated
        {
            width:300px;
            padding:10px;
            margin:10px;
            border: solid 4px green;
        }
    </style>
</head>
<body>
    <form id="form1" runat="server">

    <asp:ScriptManager ID="ScriptManager1" runat="server" />

    <div id="panelContainer">
    <asp:UpdatePanel id="up1" UpdateMode="Conditional" runat="server">
    <ContentTemplate>
        <%= DateTime.Now.ToString("T") %>
        <asp:Button
            id="btnSubmit1"
            Text="Submit 1"
            OnClick="btnSubmit_Click"
            Runat="server" />
    </ContentTemplate>
    </asp:UpdatePanel>

    <asp:UpdatePanel id="up2" UpdateMode="Conditional" runat="server">
    <ContentTemplate>
        <%= DateTime.Now.ToString("T") %>
        <asp:Button
            id="btnSubmit2"
            Text="Submit 2"
            OnClick="btnSubmit_Click"
            Runat="server" />
    </ContentTemplate>
    </asp:UpdatePanel>
    </div>
    </form>
    <script type="text/javascript">
    var prm = Sys.WebForms.PageRequestManager.getInstance();
```

```
    prm.add_beginRequest(prm_beginRequest);
    prm.add_pageLoaded(prm_pageLoaded);

    function prm_beginRequest(sender, args)
    {
        var container = args.get_postBackElement().parentNode;
        container.className = 'updating';
    }

    function prm_pageLoaded(sender, args)
    {
        var panelsCreated = args.get_panelsCreated();
        for (var k=0;k<panelsCreated.length;k++)
            panelsCreated[k].className = 'normal';

        var panelsUpdated = args.get_panelsUpdated();
        for (var k=0;k<panelsUpdated.length;k++)
            panelsUpdated[k].className = 'updated';
    }

    </script>
</body>
</html>
```

When the page in Listing 31.12 first loads in your browser, the PageRequestManager pageLoaded event is raised and the prm_pageLoaded event handler executes. This event handler assigns a default CSS class (named normal) to each of the UpdatePanel controls in the page. The list of UpdatePanels is retrieved from the PageLoadedEventArgs. panelsCreated property.

If you click the first button, the border around the first button turns orange until the asynchronous postback completes and the border turns green. The same thing happens when you click the second button.

When you click a button, the PageRequestManager beginRequest event is raised and the border around the button turns orange. After the response is returned from the server, the PageRequestManager pageLoaded event is raised and the border around the button turns green. The list of updated UpdatePanels is retrieved from the PageLoadedEventArgs.updated property.

What happens if you click both buttons in rapid succession? In that case, you are attempting to perform two simultaneous asynchronous postbacks. Unfortunately, the UpdatePanel does not support multiple simultaneous asynchronous postbacks. By default, the last postback performed will abort all previous postbacks.

NOTE

I was, quite bluntly, flabbergasted when I learned that multiple UpdatePanel controls cannot perform an asynchronous postback at the same time. This is a very disappointing limitation of the Microsoft AJAX Framework.

Canceling the Current Asynchronous Postback

As you learned in the previous section, you can perform at most one asynchronous postback in a page at a time. By default, the last postback wins. If you initiate a new postback while a previous postback is being processed, the previous postback is aborted.

If you want to reverse this logic, and give precedence to the first postback over future postbacks, you can cancel every postback that occurs after the first postback until the first postback completes. The page in Listing 31.13 illustrates how to cancel an asynchronous postback in the event handler for the `PageRequestManager.initializeRequest` event (see Figure 31.10).

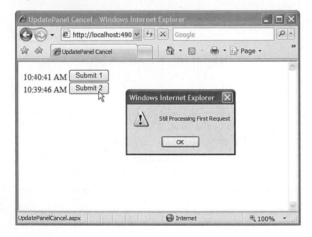

FIGURE 31.10   Canceling an asynchronous postback.

LISTING 31.13   UpdatePanelCancel.aspx

```csharp
<%@ Page Language="C#" %>
<!DOCTYPE html PUBLIC "-//W3C//DTD XHTML 1.0 Transitional//EN"
"http://www.w3.org/TR/xhtml1/DTD/xhtml1-transitional.dtd">
<script runat="server">

    protected void btnSubmit_Click(object sender, EventArgs e)
    {
        System.Threading.Thread.Sleep(3000); // sleep 3 seconds
    }
</script>
<html xmlns="http://www.w3.org/1999/xhtml">
<head runat="server">
```

31

```
        <title>UpdatePanel Cancel</title>
</head>
<body>
    <form id="form1" runat="server">
    <asp:ScriptManager ID="ScriptManager1" runat="server" />

    <asp:UpdatePanel ID="up1" UpdateMode="Conditional" runat="server">
    <ContentTemplate>
        <%= DateTime.Now.ToString("T") %>
        <asp:Button
            id="btnSubmit1"
            Text="Submit 1"
            OnClick="btnSubmit_Click"
            Runat="server"/>
    </ContentTemplate>
    </asp:UpdatePanel>

    <asp:UpdatePanel ID="up2" UpdateMode="Conditional" runat="server">
    <ContentTemplate>
        <%= DateTime.Now.ToString("T") %>
        <asp:Button
            id="btnSubmit2"
            Text="Submit 2"
            OnClick="btnSubmit_Click"
            Runat="server" />
    </ContentTemplate>
    </asp:UpdatePanel>

    </form>
    <script type="text/javascript">

    var prm = Sys.WebForms.PageRequestManager.getInstance();
    prm.add_initializeRequest( prm_initializeRequest );

    function prm_initializeRequest(sender, args)
    {
        if (prm.get_isInAsyncPostBack())
        {
            alert('Still Processing First Request');
            args.set_cancel(true);
        }
    }
    </script>

</body>
</html>
```

Using similar logic, you can always give precedence to one UpdatePanel over another. Listing 31.14 contains client-script that always gives precedence to the btnSubmit1 button over any other button that causes an asynchronous postback in the page. (The entire page is included on the CD that accompanies this book.)

LISTING 31.14   UpdatePanelPrecedence.aspx

```
<script type="text/javascript">


    var prm = Sys.WebForms.PageRequestManager.getInstance();
    prm.add_initializeRequest( prm_initializeRequest );

    var prevPostBackElementId;

    function prm_initializeRequest(sender, args)
    {
        if (prm.get_isInAsyncPostBack())
        {
            if (prevPostBackElementId == 'btnSubmit1')
            {
                alert('Still Processing btnSubmit1 Request');
                args.set_cancel(true);
            }
        }
        prevPostBackElementId = args.get_postBackElement().id;
    }
</script>
```

If you click the second button (btnSubmit2) immediately after clicking the first button (btnSubmit1), the second asynchronous postback is canceled.

Aborting the Previous Asynchronous Postback

You can explicitly abort a previous asynchronous postback by using the PageRequestManager abortPostBack() method. Explicitly aborting a postback is useful when you want to associate a Cancel button with an asynchronous postback (see Figure 31.11).

For example, the page in Listing 31.15 contains two buttons. The first button retrieves your fortune. The oracle, however, is slow. It takes 3 seconds for the oracle to deliver a new fortune. If you want to cancel the new fortune during these 3 seconds, you can click the Cancel button.

FIGURE 31.11   Aborting an asynchronous postback with a Cancel button.

> **WARNING**
>
> Aborting an asynchronous postback does not actually stop any work that has been started on the server. Aborting simply causes the Page Request Manager to ignore any response returned from the server. If you want to cancel a long-running process on the server, you need to perform another asynchronous call which performs logic that explicitly halts the long-running process.

LISTING 31.15   UpdatePanelAbort.aspx

```csharp
<%@ Page Language="C#" %>
<!DOCTYPE html PUBLIC "-//W3C//DTD XHTML 1.0 Transitional//EN"
"http://www.w3.org/TR/xhtml1/DTD/xhtml1-transitional.dtd">
<script runat="server">

    protected void btnGetFortune_Click(object sender, EventArgs e)
    {
        System.Threading.Thread.Sleep(3000); // wait 3 seconds
        lblFortune.Text = String.Format("At {0:T}, the oracle says: ",
        ➥DateTime.Now);
        Random rnd = new Random();
        switch (rnd.Next(4))
        {
            case 0:
                lblFortune.Text += "You're doomed!";
                break;
            case 1:
                lblFortune.Text += "Good luck is around the corner.";
```

LISTING 31.15   Continued

```
                    break;
            case 2:
                lblFortune.Text += "Don't leave home.";
                    break;
            case 3:
                lblFortune.Text += "Buy stock today.";
                    break;
        }
    }
</script>
<html xmlns="http://www.w3.org/1999/xhtml">
<head runat="server">
    <title>UpdatePanel Abort</title>
</head>
<body>
    <form id="form1" runat="server">
    <div>
        <asp:ScriptManager ID="ScriptManager1" runat="server" />

        <asp:UpdatePanel ID="up1" runat="server">
        <ContentTemplate>
            <asp:Button
                id="btnGetFortune"
                Text="Get Fortune"
                OnClick="btnGetFortune_Click"
                Runat="server" />
            <asp:Button
                id="btnCancel"
                Text="Cancel"
                Enabled="false"
                Runat="server" />
                <br />
                <asp:Label ID="lblFortune" runat="server" />
        </ContentTemplate>
        </asp:UpdatePanel>

    </div>
    </form>
    <script type="text/javascript">

    var prm = Sys.WebForms.PageRequestManager.getInstance();
    prm.add_initializeRequest(prm_initializeRequest);

    function prm_initializeRequest(sender, args)
```

```
    {
        if (args.get_postBackElement().id == 'btnCancel')
        {
            prm.abortPostBack();
            alert("Fortune Aborted!");
        }
        else
        {
            $get('btnCancel').disabled = false;
        }
    }
    </script>
</body>
</html>
```

Passing Additional Information During an Asynchronous Postback

You can pass additional items from the web server to the web browser during an asynchronous postback. Passing additional items is useful when the area that you need to update on a page does not fall into a neat little rectangle. For example, you might want to update a page's title or a page's meta tags based on the results of an asynchronous query.

The page in Listing 31.16 contains a DetailsView control that you can use to navigate the contents of the Movie database table. The DetailsView control is contained inside of an UpdatePanel control so that a postback does not happen when you navigate to a new movie.

LISTING 31.16   UpdatePanelDataItem.aspx

```
<%@ Page Language="C#" %>
<!DOCTYPE html PUBLIC "-//W3C//DTD XHTML 1.0 Transitional//EN"
"http://www.w3.org/TR/xhtml1/DTD/xhtml1-transitional.dtd">
<script runat="server">

    protected void dtlMovie_DataBound(object sender, EventArgs e)
    {
        string movieTitle = (string)DataBinder.Eval(dtlMovie.DataItem, "Title");

        if (sm1.IsInAsyncPostBack)
        {
            sm1.RegisterDataItem(Head1, movieTitle);
        }
        else
        {
            Head1.Title = movieTitle;
```

LISTING 31.16   Continued

```
                hTitle.InnerHtml = movieTitle;
        }
    }
</script>
<html xmlns="http://www.w3.org/1999/xhtml">
<head id="Head1" runat="server">
    <title>UpdatePanel DataItem</title>
</head>
<body>
    <form id="form1" runat="server">
    <div>

    <asp:ScriptManager
        id="sm1"
        Runat="server" />

    <h1 id="hTitle" runat="server"></h1>


    <asp:UpdatePanel
        id="upSearch"
        Runat="server">
        <ContentTemplate>

        <asp:DetailsView
            id="dtlMovie"
            DataSourceID="srcMovies"
            AllowPaging="true"
            Runat="server" OnDataBound="dtlMovie_DataBound" />

        </ContentTemplate>
    </asp:UpdatePanel>

    <asp:SqlDataSource
        id="srcMovies"
        ConnectionString='<%$ ConnectionStrings:con %>'
        SelectCommand="SELECT Id,Title,Director FROM Movie"
        Runat="server" />

    </div>
    </form>
    <script type="text/javascript">

    var prm = Sys.WebForms.PageRequestManager.getInstance();
```

```
    prm.add_pageLoaded( prm_pageLoaded );

    function prm_pageLoaded(sender, args)
    {
        if (prm.get_isInAsyncPostBack())
        {
            var movieTitle = args.get_dataItems()['Head1'];
            // assign browser title bar
            document.title = movieTitle;
            // assign heading
            $get('hTitle').innerHTML = movieTitle;
        }
    }
    </script>
</body>
</html>
```

When you navigate to a new movie, both the browser title bar and the page heading are updated to display the title of the new movie (see Figure 31.12). The title and heading are updated by passing a data item that represents the movie title during the asynchronous postback.

FIGURE 31.12   Updating a page's header and title asynchronously.

Handling UpdatePanel Errors Gracefully

Sometimes things go terribly wrong. The Internet gets clogged, an application's database server goes down, and so on. How do you recover from these types of errors gracefully in an Ajax application?

By default, if an error occurs during an asynchronous postback, a JavaScript alert box appears that displays an error message. This is a jarring experience in a production application.

You have several options for avoiding this default experience: You can configure a custom error page, you can handle the error on the server side, or you can handle the error on the client side. Let's examine each of these options.

First, if you configure a custom error page for your application, then by default the custom error page applies to asynchronous postback errors. You enable a custom error page by adding the following element to the system.web section of your web configuration file:

```
<customErrors mode="On" defaultRedirect="ErrorPage.aspx" />
```

This element enables a custom error page for both local and remote requests. Any unhandled exceptions in any page cause the browser to be redirected to a page named ErrorPage.aspx.

The page in Listing 31.17 throws an exception when you click the button located in the UpdatePanel control. If you open the page in Listing 31.15 with a custom error page enabled, the browser is redirected to the ErrorPage.aspx page automatically.

LISTING 31.17   UpdatePanelError.aspx

```
<%@ Page Language="C#" %>
<!DOCTYPE html PUBLIC "-//W3C//DTD XHTML 1.0 Transitional//EN"
"http://www.w3.org/TR/xhtml1/DTD/xhtml1-transitional.dtd">
<script runat="server">

    protected void btnSubmit_Click(object sender, EventArgs e)
    {
        throw new Exception("Server Error");
    }
</script>
<html xmlns="http://www.w3.org/1999/xhtml">
<head runat="server">
    <title>UpdatePanel Error</title>
</head>
<body>
    <form id="form1" runat="server">

    <asp:ScriptManager
        id="sm1"
        Runat="server" />

    <asp:UpdatePanel
        id="up1"
        runat="server">
        <ContentTemplate>

        <asp:Button
```

```
            id="btnSubmit"
            Text="Submit"
            OnClick="btnSubmit_Click"
            Runat="server" />

        </ContentTemplate>
    </asp:UpdatePanel>

    </form>
</body>
</html>
```

You can disable custom error pages in the case of an asynchronous postback by adding an AllowCustomErrorRedirect attribute to the ScriptManager tag, like this:

```
<asp:ScriptManager
    id="sm1"
    AllowCustomErrorsRedirect="false"
    Runat="server" />
```

Instead of redirecting the user to an error page, you can customize the error message that the user sees. You can customize the error on both the server and the client.

On the server, you can handle the ScriptManager control's AsyncPostBackError event to customize the error message transmitted to the client. For example, the page in Listing 31.18 modifies the error message to be a generic one.

LISTING 31.18   UpdatePanelErrorServer.aspx

```
<%@ Page Language="C#" %>
<!DOCTYPE html PUBLIC "-//W3C//DTD XHTML 1.0 Transitional//EN"
"http://www.w3.org/TR/xhtml1/DTD/xhtml1-transitional.dtd">
<script runat="server">

    protected void btnSubmit_Click(object sender, EventArgs e)
    {
        throw new Exception("Server Error");
    }

    protected void sm1_AsyncPostBackError(object sender,
    ➥AsyncPostBackErrorEventArgs e)
    {
        sm1.AsyncPostBackErrorMessage = "A server error occurred";
    }
</script>
<html xmlns="http://www.w3.org/1999/xhtml">
```

LISTING 31.18   Continued

```
<head id="Head1" runat="server">
    <title>UpdatePanel Error Server</title>
</head>
<body>
    <form id="form1" runat="server">

    <asp:ScriptManager
        id="sm1"
        OnAsyncPostBackError="sm1_AsyncPostBackError"
        Runat="server" />

    <asp:UpdatePanel
        id="up1"
        runat="server">
        <ContentTemplate>

        <asp:Button
            id="btnSubmit"
            Text="Submit"
            OnClick="btnSubmit_Click"
            Runat="server" />

        </ContentTemplate>
    </asp:UpdatePanel>

    </form>
</body>
</html>
```

The page in Listing 31.18 cloaks the actual server-side error message with a generic message. The error message displayed by the page is still not very professional. Most likely, you'll want to customize the error message even more when the error is displayed on the client.

The page in Listing 31.19 illustrates how you can customize an error message on the client. The page displays an error message directly above the UpdatePanel when an asynchronous postback fails (see Figure 31.13).

FIGURE 31.13   Customizing a client-side error message.

LISTING 31.19   UpdatePanelErrorClient.aspx

```
<%@ Page Language="C#" %>
<!DOCTYPE html PUBLIC "-//W3C//DTD XHTML 1.0 Transitional//EN"
"http://www.w3.org/TR/xhtml1/DTD/xhtml1-transitional.dtd">
<script runat="server">

    protected void btnSubmit_Click(object sender, EventArgs e)
    {
        throw new Exception("Server Error");
    }

    protected void sm1_AsyncPostBackError(object sender,
    ➡AsyncPostBackErrorEventArgs e)
    {
        sm1.AsyncPostBackErrorMessage = "A server error occurred";
    }
</script>
<html xmlns="http://www.w3.org/1999/xhtml">
<head id="Head1" runat="server">
    <title>UpdatePanel Error Server</title>
    <style type="text/css">

    .errorMessage
    {
        background-color: Yellow;
        color: Red;
    }

    </style>
</head>
<body>
    <form id="form1" runat="server">
```

LISTING 31.19   Continued

```
    <asp:ScriptManager
        id="sm1"
        OnAsyncPostBackError="sm1_AsyncPostBackError"
        Runat="server" />

    <span id="spanError" class="errorMessage"></span>

    <asp:UpdatePanel
        id="up1"
        runat="server">
        <ContentTemplate>

        <asp:Button
            id="btnSubmit"
            Text="Submit"
            OnClick="btnSubmit_Click"
            Runat="server" />

        </ContentTemplate>
    </asp:UpdatePanel>

    </form>
    <script type="text/javascript">

    var prm = Sys.WebForms.PageRequestManager.getInstance();
    prm.add_endRequest( prm_endRequest );

    function prm_endRequest(sender, args)
    {
        var spanError = $get("spanError");
        if (args.get_error())
        {
            args.set_errorHandled(true);
            spanError.innerHTML = "Could not complete your request";
        }
        else
        {
            spanError.innerHTML = "";
        }
    }

    </script>
</body>
</html>
```

Before leaving this section, I need to mention one last property supported by the ScriptManager control that is related to errors: the `AsyncPostBackTimeOut` property. This property determines the amount of time in seconds before an asynchronous postback times out. The default value is 90 seconds. You might want to set this value to a briefer duration.

UpdatePanel Performance

The UpdatePanel hides the normal page postback by performing an asynchronous (sneaky) postback. Even though you can use the UpdatePanel to trick your users into believing that a postback is not occurring, it is important that you do not trick yourself.

You can use either of the two debugging tools discussed earlier in this chapter to view the Ajax request and response that occur during an asynchronous postback. For example, Listing 31.20 contains a typical Ajax request, and Listing 31.21 contains a typical Ajax response.

LISTING 31.20   Ajax Request

```
sm1=up1%7CgrdFeedback&__EVENTTARGET=grdFeedback&__EVENTARGUMENT=Sort%24Name&__VIEWS
TATE=%2FwEPDwUKLTk4MzMyODc2MQ9kFgICAw9kFgICAw9kFgJmD2QWBAIBDzwrAAoBAA8WBB4LXyFEYXRh
Qm91bmRnHgtfIUl0ZW1Db3VudGZkFgJmD2QWBGYPDxYCHgdWaXNpYmxlaGRkAgIPDxYCHwJoZGQCAw88KwA
NAgAPFgQfAGcfAQIEZAwUKwAEFggeBE5hbWUFAklkHgpJc1JlYWRPbmx5aB4EVHlwZRkrAR4JRGF0YUZpZW
xkBQJJZBYIHwMFBE5hbWUfBGgfBRkrAh8GBQROYW1lFggfAwUHQ29tbWVudB8EaB8FGSsCHwYFB0NvbW1lb
nQWCB8DBQ1EYXRlU3VibWl0dGVkHwRoHwUZKVxTeXN0ZW0uRGF0ZVRpbWUsIG1zY29ybGliLCBWZXJzaW9u
PTIuMC4wLjAsIEN1bHR1cmU9bmV1dHJhbCwgUHVibGljS2V5VG9rZW49Yjc3YTVjNTYxOTM0ZTA4OR8GBQ1
EYXRlU3VibWl0dGVkFgJmD2QWCgIBD2QWCGYPDxYCHgRUZXh0BQE0ZGQCAQ8PFgIfBwUFU3RldmVkZA-
ICDw8WAh8HBRJIZXJ1IGlzIG15IGNvbW1lbnRkZAIDDw8WAh8HBRQxMC8zLzIwMDcgNDo1MjowNCBQTWRk-
AgIPZBYIZg8PFgIfBwUBM2RkAgEPDxYCHwcFA0JvYmRkAgIPDxYCHwcFFUhleSwgd2hhdCBhYm91dCBBamF
4P2RkAgMPDxYCHwcFFDEwLzMvMjAwNyA0OjE5OjI1IFBNZGQCAw9kFghmDw8WAh8HBRExZGQCAQ8PFgIfB-
wUFc3RldmVkZAICDw8WAh8HBRVXaGF0IGEgZ3J1YXQgd2Vic210ZSFkZAIDDw8WAh8HBRQxMC8zLzIwMD-
cgNDowOTo1NiBQTWRkAgQPZBYIZg8PFgIfBwUBMmRkAgEPDxYCHwcFBXN0ZXZlZGQCAg8PFgIfBwVaV293L
CBpdCBpcyB3cml0dGVuIGVudGlyZWx5IHdpdGggTGlucT8gVGhhdCBtdXN0IGhhdmUgc2F2ZWQgeW91IGEg
bG90IG9mIGRldmVsb3BtZW50IHRpbWUhZGQCAw8PFgIfBwUUMTAvMy8yMDA3IDQ6MDk6NTYgUE1kZA-
IFDw8WAh8CaGRkGAIFC2dyZEZlZWRiYWNrDzwrAAkCBAUHQ29tbWVudAgCAWQFC2ZybUZlZWRiYWNrDx-
QrAAdkZAICZGQWAGRkuZs7yL%2Fem%2BLQG%2FRqUcYBa9aTsI4%3D&frmFeedback%24txtName=&frmFe
edback%24txtComment=&__EVENTVALIDATION=%2FwEWCALS%2BMLfAgKVvojNBgKio6JkAp7t15OBAtnw
1uUHApCu1%2B4GAoKl7PcLAoGY7eABIj9XtltK55e8Og9%2BNK4DglwM43M%3D&
```

LISTING 31.21   Ajax Response

```
2124¦updatePanel¦up1¦


    <table cellspacing="0" border="0" id="frmFeedback"
      style="border-collapse:collapse;">
    <tr>
        <td colspan="2">
```

LISTING 31.21   Continued

```html
      <label for="frmFeedback_txtName" id="frmFeedback_lblName">Name:</label>
      <span id="frmFeedback_valName" style=
        "color:Red;visibility:hidden;">Required</span>
      <br />
      <input name="frmFeedback$txtName" type="text" id="frmFeedback_txtName" />
      <br /><br />
      <label for="frmFeedback_txtComment" id=
        "frmFeedback_lblComment">Comment:</label>
      <span id="frmFeedback_valComment" style=
        "color:Red;visibility:hidden;">Required</span>
      <br />
      <textarea name="frmFeedback$txtComment" rows="3" cols="50"
        id="frmFeedback_txtComment"></textarea>
      <br /><br />
      <input type="submit" name="frmFeedback$btnSubmit" value="Submit"
        onclick="javascript:WebForm_DoPostBackWithOptions
        (new WebForm_PostBackOptions(&quot;frmFeedback$btnSubmit&quot;,
        &quot;&quot;, true, &quot;&quot;, &quot;&quot;, false, false))"
          id="frmFeedback_btnSubmit" />
      </td>
    </tr>
</table>

    <br /><br />

    <div>
    <table cellspacing="0" rules="all" border="1" id="grdFeedback"
          style="border-collapse:collapse;">
      <tr>
        <th scope="col"><a href="javascript:__
                     doPostBack('grdFeedback','Sort$Id')">Id</a></th>
                     <th scope="col"><a href="javascript:__doPostBack
                     ('grdFeedback','Sort$Name')">Name</a></th><th
                       scope="col">
                     <a href="javascript:__doPostBack
                     ('grdFeedback','Sort$Comment')">Comment</a></th>
                     <th scope="col"><a href="javascript:__doPostBack
                     ('grdFeedback','Sort$DateSubmitted')">
                      DateSubmitted</a></th>
      </tr><tr>
        <td>3</td><td>Bob</td><td>Hey, what about Ajax?
                    </td><td>10/3/2007 4:19:25 PM</td>
      </tr><tr>
        <td>1</td><td>steve</td><td>What a great website!
                    </td><td>10/3/2007 4:09:56 PM</td>
```

```
        </tr><tr>
            <td>2</td><td>steve</td><td>Wow, it is written entirely
                        with Linq? That must have saved you a lot of
                        development time!</td><td>10/3/2007 4:09:56 PM</td>
        </tr><tr>
            <td>4</td><td>Steve</td><td>Here is my comment
                        </td><td>10/3/2007 4:52:04 PM</td>
        </tr>
    </table>
</div>
```

¦0¦hiddenField¦__EVENTTARGET¦¦0¦hiddenField¦__EVENTARGUMENT¦¦1264¦hidden-
Field¦__VIEWSTATE¦/wEPDwUKLTk4MzMyODc2MQ9kFgICAw9kFgICAw9kFgJmD2QWBAIBDzwrAAoBAA8WB
B4LXyFEYXRhQm91bmRnHgtfIUl0ZW1Db3VudGZkFgJmD2QWBGYPDxYCHgdWaXNpYmxlaGRkAgIPDxYCH-
wJoZGQCAw88KwANAgAPFgQfAGcfAQIEZAwUKwAEFggeBE5hbWUFAklkHgpJc1JlYWRPbmx5aB4EVHlwZRkr
AR4JRGF0YUZpZWxkBQJJZBYIHwMFBE5hbWUfBGgfBRkrAh8GBQROYW1lFggfAwUHQ29tbWVudB8EaB8FGSs
CHwYFB0NvbW1lbnQWCB8DBQ1EYXRl1U3VibWl0dGVkVkHwRoHwUZKVxTeXN0ZW0uRGF0ZVRpbWUsIG1zY29ybG
liLCBWZXJzaW9uPTIuMC4wLjAsIEN1bHR1cmU9bmV1dHJhbCwgUHVibGljS2V5VG9rZW49Yjc3YTVjNTYx-
OTM0ZTA4OR8GBQ1EYXRl1U3VibWl0dGVkFgJmD2QWCgIBD2QWCGYPDxYCHgRUZXh0BQEzZGQCAQ8PFgIfB-
wUDQm9iZGQCAg8PFgIfBwUVSGV5LCB3aGF0IGFib3V0IEFqYXg/ZGQCAw8PFgIfBwUUMTAvMy8yMDA3IDQ6
MTk6MjUgUE1kZAICD2QWCGYPDxYCHwcFATFkZAIBDw8WAh8HBQVzdGV2ZWRkAgIPDxYCHwcFFVdoYXQgYS-
BncmVhdCB3ZWJzaXRlIWRkAgMPDxYCHwcFFDEwLzMvMjAwNyA0OjA5OjU2IFBNZGQCAw9kFghmDw8WAh8HB
QEyZGQCAQ8PFgIfBwUFc3RldmVkZAICDw8WAh8HBVpXb3csIGl0IGlzIHdyaXR0ZW4gZW50aXJlbHkgd2l0
aCBMaW5xPyBUaGF0IG11c3QgaGF2ZSBzYXZlZCB5b3UgYSBsb3Qgb2YgZGV2ZWxvcG1lbnQgdGltZS-
FkZAIDDw8WAh8HBRQxMC8zLzIwMDcgNDowOTo1NiBQTWRkAgPZBYIZg8PFgIfBwUBNGRkAgEPDxYCHwcF-
BVN0ZXZlZGQCAg8PFgIfBwUSSGVyZSBpcyBteSBjb21tZW50ZGQCAw8PFgIfBwUUMTAvMy8yMDA3IDQ6NTI
6MDQgUE1kZAIFDw8WAh8CaGRkGAIFC2dyZZlZWRiYWNrDzwrAAkCBAUETmFtZZQgCAWQFC2ZybUZlZWRiY-
WNrDxQrAAdkZAICZGQWAGRkVKO/p/Z+TKr7wPvuagKWmQ2FfIY=¦96¦hiddenField¦__EVENTVALIDA-
TION¦/wEWCAKuyYyNBQKVvojNBgKio6JkAp7t150BAtnw1uUHApCu1+4GAoKl7PcLAoGY7eABqkyic8N4ML
Im8nwM1bpWblCsXyA=¦0¦asyncPostBackControlIDs¦¦¦0¦postBackControlIDs¦¦¦4¦updatePan-
elIDs¦¦tup1¦0¦childUpdatePanelIDs¦¦¦3¦panelsToRefreshIDs¦¦up1¦2¦asyncPostBackTime-
out¦¦90¦13¦formAction¦¦Feedback.aspx¦8¦pageTitle¦¦Feedback¦46¦arrayDeclaration¦Page
_Validators¦document.getElementById("frmFeedback_valName")¦49¦arrayDeclaration¦Page
_Validators¦document.getElementById("frmFeedback_valComment")¦139¦scriptBlock¦Scrip
tPath¦/Original/ScriptResource.axd?d=pGcnA3xf7SUaukdr-behbvslg2hOq48wA9WuXk0fdM20
k9xho9i9m9JZzVPbP2-5l3cHqVSeROczjHZXGFjpag2&t=633231592768281250¦367¦scriptBlock¦
ScriptContentWithTags¦{"text":"\r\n\u003c!—\r\nvar Page_ValidationActive =
false;\r\nif (typeof(ValidatorOnLoad) == \"function\") {\r\n   ValidatorOn-
Load();\r\n}\r\n\r\nfunction ValidatorOnSubmit() {\r\n   if (Page_ValidationAc-
tive) {\r\n   return ValidatorCommonOnSubmit();\r\n   }\r\n   else {\r\n
return true;\r\n   }\r\n}\r\n// —\u003e\r\n","type":"text/javascript"}¦90¦onSub-
mit¦¦if (typeof(ValidatorOnSubmit) == "function" && ValidatorOnSubmit() == false)
return false;¦21¦expando¦document.getElementById('frmFeedback_valName')['controltovalidate']¦"frmFeedback_txtName"¦39¦expando¦document.getElementById('frmFeedback_va
lName')['evaluationfunction']¦"RequiredFieldValidatorEvaluateIsValid"¦2¦expando¦doc
ument.getElementById('frmFeedback_valName')['initialvalue']¦""¦24¦expando¦docu-

```
ment.getElementById('frmFeedback_valComment')['controltovalidate']¦"frmFeedback_txt
Comment"¦39¦expando¦document.getElementById('frmFeedback_valComment')['evaluation-
function']¦"RequiredFieldValidatorEvaluateIsValid"¦2¦expando¦document.getElement-
ById('frmFeedback_valComment')['initialvalue']¦""¦78¦scriptDispose¦up1¦Array.remove
(Page_Validators, document.getElementById('frmFeedback_valName'));¦81¦scriptDis-
pose¦up1¦Array.remove(Page_Validators, document.getElementById('frmFeedback_
valComment'));¦
```

The Ajax request and response in Listing 31.20 and Listing 31.21, respectively, were captured using Fiddler after sorting by the Name column in the Feedback.aspx page.

I'm including the full request and response traffic to make a point. No one would describe either the request or response as tiny. A lot of text must be passed back and forth from the browser to the server and back again when an UpdatePanel control refreshes its content.

A big chunk of both the request and response consists of ViewState. ViewState is passed to the server during an asynchronous postback, just like it is passed during a normal postback. The server-side page executes just like it executes during a normal postback. Therefore, the server-side page needs the ViewState to execute correctly.

In order to improve the performance of asynchronous postbacks performed by an UpdatePanel, consider disabling ViewState for the controls contained within the UpdatePanel. Every ASP.NET control has an EnableViewState property. You can always set this property to the value False in order to disable ViewState.

The following table compares the size of the asynchronous request and response with the GridView control's ViewState enabled and disabled:

Ajax Request/Response Size

	ViewState Enabled	ViewState Disabled
Request	2,066	1,067
Response	5,720	4,719

As the table clarifies, you save about a thousand bytes for both the request and response by disabling ViewState.

The disadvantage of disabling ViewState for a control such as a GridView is that it forces the GridView to make a new database call whenever you sort or page the GridView. However, one easy way to reduce the load on your database server is to take advantage of caching. If you cache all the records displayed by the GridView on the server, and disable ViewState, then you reduce your network traffic and you don't place any additional load on your database server.

NOTE

To learn more about caching, see Chapter 25, "Caching Application Pages and Data."

When working with the UpdatePanel, you should never forget that the server-side page undergoes its normal page execution lifecycle whenever an asynchronous postback occurs. If you perform an expensive database lookup in your Page_Load() method, that lookup will occur with each asynchronous call to your server.

You can avoid performing unnecessary server-side work during an asynchronous postback by taking advantage of the ScriptManager control's IsInAsyncPostBack property. You can use this property to detect whether the page is executing in the context of a normal postback or an asynchronous postback.

Using the Timer Control

The ASP.NET AJAX Timer control enables you to refresh an UpdatePanel (or the entire page) on a timed basis. The Timer control has one important property:

▶ **Interval**—The amount of time, in milliseconds, between Tick events. The default value is 60,000 (1 minute).

The Timer control raises a Tick event every so many milliseconds, depending on the value of its Interval property.

If you don't associate the Timer control with an UpdatePanel, the Timer posts the entire page back to the server performing a normal postback. For example, the page in Listing 31.22 posts the entire page back to the server every 2 seconds.

LISTING 31.22   TimerPage.aspx

```
<%@ Page Language="C#" %>
<!DOCTYPE html PUBLIC "-//W3C//DTD XHTML 1.0 Transitional//EN"
"http://www.w3.org/TR/xhtml1/DTD/xhtml1-transitional.dtd">
<html xmlns="http://www.w3.org/1999/xhtml">
<head runat="server">
    <title>Timer Page</title>
</head>
<body>
    <form id="form1" runat="server">
    <div>
    <asp:ScriptManager ID="ScriptManager1" runat="server" />

    <asp:Timer ID="Timer1" Interval="2000" runat="server" />

    The time is <%= DateTime.Now.ToString("T") %>

    </div>
    </form>
</body>
</html>
```

A more typical use of the Timer control is to refresh an UpdatePanel control's content on a timed basis. For example, the page in Listing 31.23 displays a random quotation every 2 seconds (see Figure 31.14).

FIGURE 31.14   Refreshing the control content using Timer control.

LISTING 31.23   TimerQuote.aspx

```
<%@ Page Language="C#" %>
<%@ Import Namespace="System.Collections.Generic" %>
<!DOCTYPE html PUBLIC "-//W3C//DTD XHTML 1.0 Transitional//EN"
"http://www.w3.org/TR/xhtml1/DTD/xhtml1-transitional.dtd">
<script runat="server">

    protected void Page_Load(object sender, EventArgs e)
    {
        List<string> quotes = new List<string>();
        quotes.Add("A fool and his money are soon parted");
        quotes.Add("A penny saved is a penny earned");
        quotes.Add("An apple a day keeps the doctor away");

        Random rnd = new Random();
        lblQuote.Text = quotes[rnd.Next(quotes.Count)];
    }
</script>
<html xmlns="http://www.w3.org/1999/xhtml">
<head id="Head1" runat="server">
    <title>Timer Quote</title>
</head>
<body>
    <form id="form1" runat="server">
    <div>
    <asp:ScriptManager ID="ScriptManager1" runat="server" />

    <asp:Timer ID="Timer1" Interval="2000" runat="server" />
```

```
    Page Time: <%= DateTime.Now.ToString("T") %>

    <fieldset>
    <legend>Quote</legend>
    <asp:UpdatePanel ID="up1" runat="server">
    <Triggers>
        <asp:AsyncPostBackTrigger ControlID="Timer1" EventName="Tick" />
    </Triggers>
    <ContentTemplate>
        <asp:Label ID="lblQuote" runat="server" />
    </ContentTemplate>
    </asp:UpdatePanel>
    </fieldset>

    </div>
    </form>
</body>
</html>
```

Notice that the Timer control in Listing 31.23 is configured as a trigger for the UpdatePanel control. When the Timer raises its Tick event, the UpdatePanel control refreshes its content by performing an asynchronous postback and grabbing a new quotation to display.

The final example of the Timer control is contained in Listing 31.24. In this example, a Timer control is used to refresh a discussion forum's messages every 5 seconds. If you leave your browser window open, you'll see new messages as they are posted by other members of the forum (see Figure 31.15).

FIGURE 31.15   Database messages being updated asynchronously.

LISTING 31.24   TimerMessages.aspx

```csharp
<%@ Page Language="C#" %>
<!DOCTYPE html PUBLIC "-//W3C//DTD XHTML 1.0 Transitional//EN"
"http://www.w3.org/TR/xhtml1/DTD/xhtml1-transitional.dtd">
<html xmlns="http://www.w3.org/1999/xhtml">
<head runat="server">
    <title>Timer Messages</title>
    <style type="text/css">

    .message
    {
        margin-left: 20px;
        font-style:italic;
    }

    </style>
</head>
<body>
    <form id="form1" runat="server">

    <asp:ScriptManager ID="sm1" runat="server" />

    <asp:Timer ID="Timer1" Interval="5000" runat="server" />

    <asp:UpdatePanel ID="up1" runat="server">
    <Triggers>
        <asp:AsyncPostBackTrigger ControlID="Timer1" EventName="Tick" />
    </Triggers>
    <ContentTemplate>
    Last Refresh <%= DateTime.Now.ToString("T") %>
    <hr />
    <asp:ListView
        id="lstMessages"
        DataSourceID="srcMessages"
        Runat="server">
        <LayoutTemplate>
            <div id="itemContainer" runat="server">
            </div>
        </LayoutTemplate>
        <ItemTemplate>
            <div>
                Posted by <%# Eval("PostedBy") %>
                <div class="message">
                <%# Eval("Post") %>
                </div>
```

```
            </div>
        </ItemTemplate>
    </asp:ListView>
    </ContentTemplate>
    </asp:UpdatePanel>

    <asp:ObjectDataSource
        id="srcMessages"
        TypeName="Message"
        SelectMethod="Select"
        Runat="server" />

    </form>
</body>
</html>
```

The page in Listing 31.24 contains a ListView that gets refreshed every 5 seconds. Be aware that each and every person who has this page open in a browser will cause a database call to be made every 5 seconds. This data is an excellent candidate for caching.

Using the UpdateProgress Control

The very last control that we need to examine in this chapter is the UpdateProgress control. This control enables you to display a progress indicator while an UpdatePanel is updating its content.

During a normal postback, the browser displays its progress in downloading new content by spinning an icon or displaying a progress bar. During an asynchronous postback, on the other hand, there is no visual indication of progress. You can use the UpdateProgress control to give the users some sense that something is happening during an asynchronous postback.

> **NOTE**
>
> In the next chapter, we examine an alternative method of displaying UpdatePanel progress. You learn how to use the UpdatePanelAnimation control to display an animation while an UpdatePanel's content is being refreshed.

The page in Listing 31.25 illustrates how to use the UpdateProgress control. If you click the button, an animation spins while the asynchronous postback is performed (see Figure 31.16).

FIGURE 31.16   Viewing a spinning asynchronous progress indicator.

LISTING 31.25   ShowUpdateProgress.aspx

```
<%@ Page Language="C#" %>
<!DOCTYPE html PUBLIC "-//W3C//DTD XHTML 1.0 Transitional//EN"
"http://www.w3.org/TR/xhtml1/DTD/xhtml1-transitional.dtd">
<script runat="server">

    protected void btnSubmit_Click(object sender, EventArgs e)
    {
        System.Threading.Thread.Sleep(5000);
    }
</script>
<html xmlns="http://www.w3.org/1999/xhtml">
<head runat="server">
    <title>Show UpdateProgress</title>
    <style type="text/css">
    .progress
    {
        font-family:Arial;
        position: absolute;
        background-color:lightyellow;
        border:solid 2px red;
        padding:5px;
    }
    </style>
</head>
<body>
    <form id="form1" runat="server">
    <div>
        <asp:ScriptManager ID="ScriptManager1" runat="server" />
        <asp:UpdatePanel ID="up1" runat="server">
        <ContentTemplate>
            <%= DateTime.Now.ToString("T") %>
            <asp:Button
                id="btnSubmit"
                Text="Submit"
```

```
                Runat="server" OnClick="btnSubmit_Click" />
        </ContentTemplate>
        </asp:UpdatePanel>
        <asp:UpdateProgress
            ID="progress1"
            AssociatedUpdatePanelID="up1"
            runat="server">
            <ProgressTemplate>
                <div class="progress">
                <asp:Image
                    id="imgProgress"
                    ImageUrl="~/Images/Progress.gif"
                    Runat="server" />
                    Retrieving content...
                </div>
            </ProgressTemplate>
        </asp:UpdateProgress>

    </div>
    </form>
</body>
</html>
```

When you click the button in Listing 31.25, the response is delayed for 5 seconds so you have a chance to see the progress indicator. The delay simulates a network delay.

> **NOTE**
>
> Several websites enable you to generate fancy animator progress indicator icons. Here is the address to one of my favorites:
>
> http://www.ajaxload.info

The UpdateProgress control supports the following three properties:

- ▶ **AssociatedUpdatePanelID**—The UpdateProgress control displays progress for this UpdatePanel control.

- ▶ **DisplayAfter**—The amount of time, in milliseconds, before the UpdateProgress control displays content. The default is 500 milliseconds (half a second).

- ▶ **DynamicLayout**—When this property is set to true (the default), the UpdateProgress control is initially hidden with the Cascading Style Sheet attribute display:none. When this property is set to false, the UpdateProgress control is hidden with the Cascading Style Sheet attribute visibility:hidden.

Summary

In this chapter, you learned how to use the primary server-side ASP.NET AJAX control: the UpdatePanel control. The bulk of this chapter was devoted to discussing the different features of this control. You learned how to specify triggers for an UpdatePanel. You also learned about how the UpdatePanel control participates in a page's server-side and client-side page execution lifecycle. We also examined how you can handle errors gracefully when using the UpdatePanel control.

In the final parts of this chapter, you learned how to use two controls that support the UpdatePanel control. First, you learned how to use the Timer control to refresh an UpdatePanel on a timed basis. Second, you learned how to use the UpdateProgress control to give the user something to watch during an UpdatePanel control's asynchronous postback.

Using the ASP.NET AJAX Control Toolkit

The ASP.NET AJAX Control Toolkit consists of 34 server-side Ajax controls that you can use in your ASP.NET applications. You can take advantage of the controls to create website special effects such as animations, rounded corners, and modal pop-ups. The controls also can be used for more serious applications such as implementing auto-complete and masked edit text fields.

The controls in the ASP.NET AJAX Control Toolkit are Ajax controls in the broad sense of the word *Ajax*. All the Toolkit controls use client-side JavaScript. However, most of the controls do not perform asynchronous postbacks. So, they are Ajax controls in the sense that they take advantage of a lot of JavaScript.

Almost all the controls in the Toolkit are extender controls. The controls extend the functionality of existing ASP.NET controls, such as the standard TextBox and Panel controls, with new functionality. Almost all the Toolkit controls have a `TargetControlID` property that you use to point to a control to extend.

In the first part of this chapter, you learn how to install and use the Toolkit controls in an ASP.NET application. Next, you are provided with a brief overview of each of the 34 controls. Finally, we examine six of the controls in more detail: We discuss the `AutoComplete` control, the `DragPanel` control, the `FilteredTextBox` control, the `MaskedEdit` control, the `Animation` control, and the `UpdatePanelAnimation` control.

Using the ASP.NET AJAX Control Toolkit

The ASP.NET AJAX Control Toolkit is not included with the ASP.NET 3.5 Framework. The Toolkit is being continuously updated. A new release of the Toolkit is available every couple months.

The Toolkit is maintained as a project at Microsoft CodePlex. You can download the latest release of the ASP.NET AJAX Control Toolkit at the following location:

```
http://www.codeplex.com/AtlasControlToolkit
```

When you download the Toolkit, you have the choice of either (1) downloading the controls and the source code or (2) downloading the controls only. You'll need to unzip the download onto your hard drive.

As part of the download, you get a sample website that demonstrates each of the Toolkit controls. You can open the sample website by launching Visual Web Developer, selecting the menu option File, Open Website, and browsing to the SampleWebSite folder in the unzipped download.

The ASP.NET AJAX Control Toolkit is not installed in the Global Assembly Cache. You must copy the AjaxControlToolkit.dll assembly from the /Bin folder of the SampleWebSite to the /Bin folder in your application. There are multiple ways to do this:

▶ **Copy the assembly by hand.** You can simply copy the AjaxControlToolkit.dll assembly from the SampleWebSite /Bin folder to a /Bin folder located in a new website.

▶ **Add an assembly reference.** Follow these steps:

  1. Within Visual Web Developer, select the menu option Website, Add Reference.

  2. Select the Browse tab.

  3. Browse to the AjaxControlToolkit.dll assembly located in the SampleWebSite /Bin folder.

▶ **Add the Toolkit to your Toolbox (see Figure 32.1).** You can add the ASP.NET AJAX Control Toolkit to the Visual Web Developer Toolbox by following these steps:

  1. Within Visual Web Developer, create a new ASP.NET page.

  2. Right-click in the Toolbox window and select the menu option Add Tab. Create a new tab named Toolkit.

  3. Right-click under the new tab and select the menu option Choose Items.

  4. Click the Browse button located at the bottom of the .NET Framework Components tab.

  5. Browse to the /Bin folder of the SampleWebSite and select the AjaxControlToolkit.dll assembly.

6. When you drag a control from the Toolbox onto a page, the AjaxControlToolkit.dll is copied to the Website /Bin folder automatically.

FIGURE 32.1   Adding the ASP.NET AJAX Control Toolkit to the Toolbox.

The majority of the controls in the ASP.NET AJAX Control Toolkit are extender controls. Visual Web Developer provides additional designer features for working with extender controls. For example, if you add a standard TextBox control to the Designer, an Add Extender link will appear in the Common TextBox Tasks dialog box (see Figure 32.2).

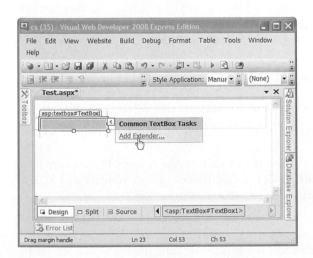

FIGURE 32.2   The Add Extender task.

If you click the Add Extender link, a dialog box appears that enables you to pick an extender that can be applied to the TextBox control (see Figure 32.3). Different extenders appear for different controls. For example, because you can apply a ConfirmButton extender to a Button control but not a TextBox control, the ConfirmButton extender only appears when you click Add Extender for the Button control.

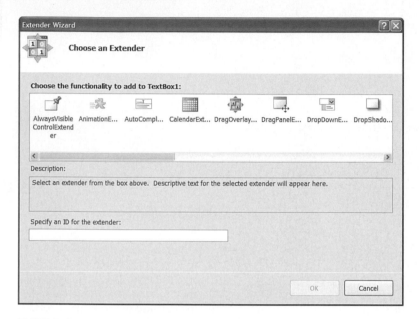

FIGURE 32.3   Selecting an extender control.

When you extend a control, additional properties appear for the control being extended in the extended control's Properties window. For example, if you extend a TextBox control with the AutoComplete extender, the AutoComplete extender control's properties appear when you open the TextBox control's Properties window (see Figure 32.4).

Overview of the Toolkit Controls

As I write this chapter, the ASP.NET AJAX Control Toolkit contains 34 controls. By the time you read this, the Toolkit might contain even more controls because the Toolkit is updated so frequently.

In this section, I provide you with a brief overview of each of the current Toolkit controls. I recommend that you open the ASP.NET AJAX Control Toolkit sample website and experiment with the controls while reading this chapter.

▶ **Accordion**—The Accordion control enables you to create a Microsoft Outlook–like expanding and collapsing menu. The Accordion control can contain one or more AccordionPane controls. One AccordionPane can be selected at a time. The selected pane is expanded, and the other panes are collapsed.

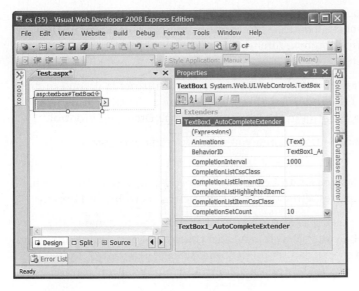

FIGURE 32.4   Viewing extender control properties.

▶ **AlwaysVisibleControl**—The `AlwaysVisibleControl` enables you to display content that is fixed at one location in the browser window even when you scroll the window. The control works like the `position:fixed` Cascading Style Sheet attribute. However, unlike the CSS attribute, the `AlwaysVisibleControl` works with Microsoft Internet Explorer 6.0.

▶ **Animation**—The `Animation` control enables you to add fancy animation effects to your website. For example, you can move, resize, and fade elements in a page. We examine the `Animation` control in detail in the section "Using the Animation Control."

▶ **AutoComplete**—The `AutoComplete` control enables you to display suggestions as a user types text into a text field. We discuss this control in detail in the section "Using the AutoComplete Control" (this control is used in the sample application described in the last chapter of this book).

▶ **Calendar**—The `Calendar` control displays a pop-up calendar next to a TextBox. It enables you to select a year, month, and date by clicking dates in a pop-up calendar.

▶ **CascadingDropDown**—The `CascadingDropDown` control enables you to make the list of items displayed in one `DropDownList` control dependent on the list of items displayed in another `DropDownList` control. The `DropDownList` items are updated by performing an asynchronous postback.

▶ **CollapsiblePanel**—The `CollapsiblePanel` control enables you to hide or display content contained in a Panel control. When you click its header, the content either appears or disappears.

▶ **ConfirmButton**—The `ConfirmButton` control enables you to display a confirmation dialog box when a user clicks a button. The confirmation dialog box can be the default JavaScript confirmation box. Alternatively, you can associate a modal dialog box with the `ConfirmButton` control.

▶ **DragPanel**—The `DragPanel` control enables you to create a panel that you can drag with your mouse around the page. It enables you to create a virtual floating window. We discuss the `DragPanel` control in the section "Using the DragPanel Control."

▶ **DropDown**—The `DropDown` control enables you to create a SharePoint-style drop-down menu.

▶ **DropShadow**—The `DropShadow` control enables you to add a drop shadow to a Panel control. You can set properties of the drop shadow, such as its width and opacity.

▶ **DynamicPopulate**—The `DynamicPopulate` control enables you to dynamically populate the contents of a control, such as a Label control, by performing an asynchronous call to the server. You can set up the `DynamicPopulate` control so that the asynchronous request is triggered by another control such as a Button control.

▶ **FilteredTextBox**—The `FilteredTextBox` control enables you to prevent certain characters from being entered into a TextBox. The `FilteredTextBox` is discussed in the section "Using the FilteredTextBox Control."

▶ **HoverMenu**—The `HoverMenu` displays a pop-up menu when you hover over another control.

▶ **ListSearch**—The `ListSearch` control enables you to perform an incremental search against the items in either a ListBox or DropDownList control.

▶ **MaskedEdit**—The `MaskedEdit` control forces a user to enter a certain pattern of characters into a TextBox control. The `MaskedEdit` control is discussed in the section "Using the MaskedEdit Control."

▶ **ModalPopup**—The `ModalPopup` control enables you to display a modal pop-up. When the modal pop-up appears, the remainder of the page is grayed out, preventing you from interacting with the page.

▶ **MutuallyExclusiveCheckBox**—The `MutuallyExclusiveCheckBox` control enables you to treat a set of `CheckBox` controls like a set of `RadioButton` controls. Only one `CheckBox` can be selected at a time.

▶ **NoBot**—The `NoBot` control attempts to prevent spam robots from posting advertisements to your website. The control attempts to detect whether a human or robot is posting content.

▶ **NumericUpDown**—The `NumericUpDown` control enables you to display up and down buttons next to a TextBox control. When you click the up and down buttons, you can cycle through a set of numbers or other items such as month names or flavors of ice cream.

▶ **PagingBulletedList**—The `PagingBulletedList` control enables you to display different content depending on the bullet clicked in a `BulletedList` control.

▶ **PasswordStrength**—The `PasswordStrength` control enables you to display a pop-up box that indicates the security strength of a password as a user selects a new password (this control is used in the sample application described in the last chapter of this book).

▶ **PopupControl**—The `PopupControl` displays a pop-up window.

▶ **Rating**—The `Rating` control enables you to rate an item on a scale (this control is used in the sample application described in the last chapter of this book).

▶ **ReorderList**—The `ReorderList` enables you to render an interactive list of items that supports reordering through drag and drop.

▶ **ResizableControl**—The `ResizableControl` enables you to resize images and other content contained on a web page.

▶ **RoundedCorners**—The `RoundedCorners` control enables you to add rounded corners around an element on a page.

▶ **Slider**—The `Slider` control enables you to create either a horizontal or vertical slider for selecting a particular value in a range of values.

▶ **SlideShow**—The `SlideShow` control displays a slide show of images. The control can render Next, Previous, Play, and Stop buttons.

▶ **Tabs**—The `Tabs` control enables you to create a tabbed interface. Switching tabs does not require a postback.

▶ **TextBoxWatermark**—The `TextBoxWatermark` control enables you to display background text inside of a TextBox control. When focus is given to the TextBox, the background text disappears.

▶ **ToggleButton**—The `ToggleButton` control enables you to customize the appearance of a `CheckBox` control. Instead of displaying a check box, you can display a thumbs-up or thumbs-down image.

▶ **UpdatePanelAnimation**—The `UpdatePanelAnimation` control enables you to display an animation while the UpdatePanel is performing an asynchronous postback. We discuss the `UpdatePanelAnimation` control in the section "Using the UpdatePanelAnimation Control."

▶ **ValidatorCallout**—The `ValidatorCallout` control can be used with any of the standard ASP.NET validation controls to create a callout effect when there is a validation error.

In the following sections, we examine six of the controls in more detail: the `AutoComplete` control, the `DragPanel` control, the `FilteredTextBox` control, the `MaskedEdit` control, the `Animation` control, and the `UpdatePanelAnimation` control.

Using the `AutoComplete` Control

The one control I use most often from the ASP.NET AJAX Control Toolkit is the `AutoComplete` control. The `AutoComplete` control enables you to convert a standard ASP.NET TextBox control into something resembling a combo box. As you enter text into the TextBox control, a list of matching options is displayed beneath the control (see Figure 32.5).

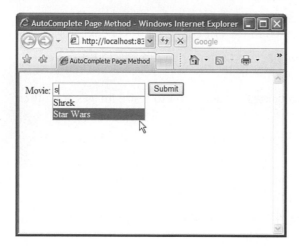

FIGURE 32.5   Using the `AutoComplete` extender control.

The cool thing about the `AutoComplete` control is that it retrieves the matching options from the web server, using an Ajax call, while you type. You can use the `AutoComplete` control to efficiently search through a database of billions of items because the entire database of items never needs to be downloaded to the browser.

The `AutoComplete` control is smart enough to cache items on the client. If you enter the same text into a TextBox that you enter previously, the `AutoComplete` control can grab the suggestions from its cache instead of performing another Ajax call to retrieve the same information.

In this section, you learn how to use the `AutoComplete` extender control. You learn how to expose the items displayed by the `AutoComplete` control from a web method contained in the same page as the `AutoComplete` control and from a web method exposed by a separate web service. Finally, you learn how to associate hidden values (such as primary keys) with each item displayed by the `AutoComplete` control.

Using the `AutoCompleteExtender` with a Page Method

If you don't need to use suggestions in more than one page, it makes sense to expose the list of auto-complete suggestions from a page method. You can create a web method that is a static method on a page.

32

NOTE

When creating pages that use the ASP.NET AJAX Control Toolkit, you should create an AJAX Web Form instead of a normal Web Form. An AJAX Web Form includes a `ScriptManager` control automatically. Select Website, Add New Item, AJAX Web Form.

For example, the page in Listing 32.1 contains an `AutoComplete` extender control. The control is used to display movie title suggestions while the user enters a movie title into a TextBox control.

LISTING 32.1   AutoCompletePageMethod.aspx

```
<%@ Page Language="C#" %>
<%@ Register TagPrefix="ajax" Namespace="AjaxControlToolkit"
 Assembly="AjaxControlToolkit"  %>
<%@ Import Namespace="System.Linq" %>
<!DOCTYPE html PUBLIC "-//W3C//DTD XHTML 1.0 Transitional//EN"
 "http://www.w3.org/TR/xhtml1/DTD/xhtml1-transitional.dtd">
<script runat="server">
    [System.Web.Services.WebMethod]
    public static string[] GetSuggestions(string prefixText, int count)
    {
        MyDatabaseDataContext db = new MyDatabaseDataContext();
        return db.Movies
            .Where( m => m.Title.StartsWith(prefixText) )
            .OrderBy( m => m.Title )
            .Select( m => m.Title)
            .Take(count)
            .ToArray();
    }

    protected void btnSubmit_Click(object sender, EventArgs e)
    {
        lblSelectedMovieTitle.Text = txtMovieTitle.Text;
    }
</script>
<html xmlns="http://www.w3.org/1999/xhtml">
<head runat="server">
    <title>AutoComplete Page Method</title>
</head>
<body>
    <form id="form1" runat="server">
    <div>

    <asp:ScriptManager ID="sm1" runat="server" />
```

LISTING 32.1   Continued

```
    <asp:Label
        id="lblMovieTitle"
        Text="Movie:"
        AssociatedControlID="txtMovieTitle"
        Runat="server" />
    <asp:TextBox
        id="txtMovieTitle"
        AutoComplete="off"
        Runat="server" />
    <ajax:AutoCompleteExtender
        id="ace1"
        TargetControlID="txtMovieTitle"
        ServiceMethod="GetSuggestions"
        MinimumPrefixLength="1"
        runat="server" />
    <asp:Button
        id="btnSubmit"
        Text="Submit"
        OnClick="btnSubmit_Click"
        Runat="server" />

    <br /><br />

    <asp:Label
        id="lblSelectedMovieTitle"
        runat="server" />

    </div>
    </form>
</body>
</html>
```

In Listing 32.1, the `AutoComplete` extender control is declared like this:

```
    <ajax:AutoCompleteExtender
        id="ace1"
        TargetControlID="txtMovieTitle"
        ServiceMethod="GetSuggestions"
        MinimumPrefixLength="1"
        runat="server" />
```

The `TargetControlID` property refers to the control that is being extended. In this case, the `AutoComplete` extender is being used to extend a TextBox control named `txtMovieTitle` with auto-complete functionality.

> **NOTE**
>
> Notice that the extended TextBox includes an `AutoComplete="off"` attribute. This attribute is necessary to disable the built-in browser auto-complete for Internet Explorer and Firefox. Realize that there is an important difference between `AutoComplete="off"` and `AutoComplete="false"`.

The `MinimumPrefixLength` property represents the number of characters that must be entered before suggestions are displayed. The default value for this property is 3. I've changed the default to 1 so that suggestions appear immediately after you start typing.

The `ServiceMethod` property refers to the name of a web method. In this case, the web method is defined in the same page as the `AutoComplete` control as a static page method. The `GetSuggestions()` method looks like this:

```
[System.Web.Services.WebMethod]
public static string[] GetSuggestions(string prefixText, int count)
{
    MyDatabaseDataContext db = new MyDatabaseDataContext();
    return db.Movies
        .Where( m => m.Title.StartsWith(prefixText) )
        .OrderBy( m => m.Title )
        .Select( m => m.Title)
        .Take(count)
        .ToArray();
}
```

Notice that the `GetSuggestions()` method is declared as a static method—this is a requirement. Furthermore, notice that the method is decorated with the `WebMethod` attribute.

The `GetSuggestions()` method must have `prefixText` and `count` parameters. The `prefixText` parameter represents the text entered into the TextBox being extended so far. The `count` parameter represents the number of suggestions to return.

The `GetSuggestions()` method returns matching movie titles from the Movie database table. A LINQ to SQL query is used to retrieve movie records that start with the prefix text.

> **NOTE**
>
> To learn more about LINQ to SQL, see Chapter 18, "Data Access with LINQ to SQL."

Using the **AutoCompleteExtender** with a Web Service Method

If you prefer, you can retrieve the auto-complete suggestions from a separate web service instead of a page method. For example, the web service in Listing 32.2, the FileService web service, retrieves a list of matching filenames from the file system.

LISTING 32.2   FileService.asmx

```
<%@ WebService Language="C#" Class="FileService" %>

using System;
using System.Web;
using System.Web.Services;
using System.Web.Services.Protocols;
using System.IO;
using System.Linq;

[WebService(Namespace = "http://tempuri.org/")]
[WebServiceBinding(ConformsTo = WsiProfiles.BasicProfile1_1)]
[System.Web.Script.Services.ScriptService]
public class FileService  : System.Web.Services.WebService {

    [WebMethod]
    public string[] GetSuggestions(string prefixText, int count)
    {
        DirectoryInfo dir = new DirectoryInfo("c:\\windows");
        return dir
            .GetFiles()
            .Where( f => f.Name.StartsWith(prefixText) )
            .Select( f => f.Name )
            .ToArray();
    }

}
```

The web service in Listing 32.2 includes a web method named GetSuggestions() that returns a list of filenames that match the prefix text passed to the web method. A LINQ query is used to return the matching results.

Notice that the FileService class is decorated with a ScriptService attribute. This attribute is required when exposing a web method to an Ajax request. If you don't include the ScriptService attribute, the web service cannot be called from the client side.

The page in Listing 32.3 contains an AutoComplete extender control that calls the web service.

LISTING 32.3   AutoCompleteWebService.aspx

```
<%@ Page Language="C#" %>
<%@ Register TagPrefix="ajax" Namespace="AjaxControlToolkit"
 Assembly="AjaxControlToolkit"  %>
<!DOCTYPE html PUBLIC "-//W3C//DTD XHTML 1.0 Transitional//EN"
```

```
    "http://www.w3.org/TR/xhtml1/DTD/xhtml1-transitional.dtd">
<script runat="server">
    protected void btnSubmit_Click(object sender, EventArgs e)
    {
        lblSelectedFileName.Text = txtFileName.Text;
    }
</script>
<html xmlns="http://www.w3.org/1999/xhtml">
<head runat="server">
    <title>Show AutoComplete Web Service</title>
</head>
<body>
    <form id="form1" runat="server">
    <div>

    <asp:ScriptManager ID="sm1" runat="server" />

    <asp:Label
        id="lblFileName"
        Text="File Name:"
        AssociatedControlID="txtFileName"
        Runat="server" />
    <asp:TextBox
        id="txtFileName"
        AutoComplete="off"
        Runat="server" />
    <ajax:AutoCompleteExtender
        id="ace1"
        TargetControlID="txtFileName"
        ServiceMethod="GetSuggestions"
        ServicePath="~/FileService.asmx"
        MinimumPrefixLength="1"
        runat="server" />
    <asp:Button
        id="btnSubmit"
        Text="Submit"
        OnClick="btnSubmit_Click"
        Runat="server"/>

    <br /><br />

    <asp:Label
        id="lblSelectedFileName"
        runat="server" />
```

LISTING 32.3   Continued

```
        </div>
        </form>
</body>
</html>
```

As you enter text into the TextBox rendered by the page in Listing 32.3, a list of matching filenames is retrieved by calling the GetSuggestions() method declared in the web service. The AutoComplete control is declared like this:

```
<ajax:AutoCompleteExtender
    id="ace1"
    TargetControlID="txtFileName"
    ServiceMethod="GetSuggestions"
    ServicePath="~/FileService.asmx"
    MinimumPrefixLength="1"
    runat="server" />
```

The AutoComplete control is declared with values assigned to its ServiceMethod and ServicePath properties. ServicePath represents the path to the web service.

> **NOTE**
>
> The web service used with the AutoComplete control must be located in the same domain as the calling page. Using the Microsoft AJAX Framework, you can't make Ajax requests across domains (other Ajax Frameworks don't have this limitation).

Using Text and Value Pairs with the AutoCompleteExtender

In the previous two sections, you saw how you can use the AutoComplete control to display suggestions as you enter text into a TextBox control. For example, you saw how you can display matching movie titles as you type. After entering a title in the TextBox, you might want to retrieve the entire movie database record.

However, you run into a problem here. The GetSuggestions() method retrieves the movie titles from the database and not the movie IDs. You need the movie ID to do a lookup for the matching movie database record. You need some way of retrieving both the movie title and movie ID when using the AutoComplete control.

The AutoComplete control includes a static method named CreateAutoCompleteItem() that returns a single string that represents a text and value pair. You can use this method when returning a string array from the GetSuggestions() method to include a primary key with each suggestion.

A TextBox control, however, can represent only a single value. In order to represent the ID of the selected movie, you need to add a hidden form field to your page. You can update the value of the hidden field whenever a user selects a new suggestion.

The page in Listing 32.4 illustrates how you can retrieve the primary key associated with the suggestion that a user selects when using the AutoComplete control.

LISTING 32.4   AutoCompleteTextValue.aspx

```
<%@ Page Language="C#" %>
<%@ Register TagPrefix="ajax" Namespace="AjaxControlToolkit"
 Assembly="AjaxControlToolkit"  %>
<%@ Import Namespace="System.Collections.Generic" %>
<%@ Import Namespace="System.Linq" %>
<!DOCTYPE html PUBLIC "-//W3C//DTD XHTML 1.0 Transitional//EN"
 "http://www.w3.org/TR/xhtml1/DTD/xhtml1-transitional.dtd">
<script runat="server">
    [System.Web.Services.WebMethod]
    public static string[] GetSuggestions(string prefixText, int count)
    {
        MyDatabaseDataContext db = new MyDatabaseDataContext();
        List<Movie> movies = db.Movies
            .Where( m => m.Title.StartsWith(prefixText) )
            .OrderBy( m => m.Title )
            .Take(count)
            .ToList();
        return movies
            .Select( m => AutoCompleteExtender.CreateAutoCompleteItem(
                m.Title, m.Id.ToString()))
            .ToArray();
    }


    protected void btnSubmit_Click(object sender, EventArgs e)
    {
        lblSelectedMovieTitle.Text = txtMovieTitle.Text;
        lblSelectedMovieId.Text = ace1Value.Value;
    }
</script>
<html xmlns="http://www.w3.org/1999/xhtml">
<head id="Head1" runat="server">
    <title>AutoComplete Page Method</title>
    <script type="text/javascript">

    function ace1_itemSelected(sender, e)
    {
        var ace1Value = $get('<%= ace1Value.ClientID %>');
        ace1Value.value = e.get_value();
    }

    </script>
```

LISTING 32.4   Continued

```
</head>
<body>
    <form id="form1" runat="server">
    <div>

    <asp:ScriptManager ID="sm1" runat="server" />

    <asp:Label
        id="lblMovieTitle"
        Text="Movie:"
        AssociatedControlID="txtMovieTitle"
        Runat="server" />
    <asp:TextBox
        id="txtMovieTitle"
        AutoComplete="off"
        Runat="server" />
    <ajax:AutoCompleteExtender
        id="ace1"
        TargetControlID="txtMovieTitle"
        ServiceMethod="GetSuggestions"
        MinimumPrefixLength="1"
        OnClientItemSelected="ace1_itemSelected"
        FirstRowSelected="true"
        runat="server" />
    <asp:HiddenField
        id="ace1Value"
        Runat="server" />
    <asp:Button
        id="btnSubmit"
        Text="Submit"
        OnClick="btnSubmit_Click"
        Runat-"server" />

    <br /><br />

    Title:
    <asp:Label
        id="lblSelectedMovieTitle"
        runat="server" />

    <br /><br />
```

```
    Primary Key:
    <asp:Label
        id="lblSelectedMovieId"
        runat="server" />


    </div>
    </form>
</body>
</html>
```

Several aspects of the page in Listing 32.4 require explanation. Let's start with the GetSuggestions() web method. This method is declared like this:

```
[System.Web.Services.WebMethod]
public static string[] GetSuggestions(string prefixText, int count)
{
    MyDatabaseDataContext db = new MyDatabaseDataContext();
    List<Movie> movies = db.Movies
        .Where( m => m.Title.StartsWith(prefixText) )
        .OrderBy( m => m.Title )
        .Take(count)
        .ToList();
    return movies
        .Select( m => AutoCompleteExtender.CreateAutoCompleteItem(
            m.Title, m.Id.ToString()))
        .ToArray();
}
```

The GetSuggestions() web method consists of two LINQ queries. The first LINQ query, a LINQ to SQL query, retrieves matching movies from the database. The second LINQ query, a standard LINQ query, calls the AutoCompleteExtender.CreateAutoCompleteItem() method for each movie. This method combines the movie Title and Id into a single string.

The AutoComplete extender is declared in the page with an associated HiddenField control, like this:

```
<ajax:AutoCompleteExtender
    id="ace1"
    TargetControlID="txtMovieTitle"
    ServiceMethod="GetSuggestions"
    MinimumPrefixLength="1"
    OnClientItemSelected="ace1_itemSelected"
    FirstRowSelected="true"
```

32

```
          runat="server" />
    <asp:HiddenField
        id="ace1Value"
        Runat="server" />
```

The AutoComplete extender control includes an OnClientItemSelected property. When a new suggestion is selected, the ace1_itemSelected() JavaScript method executes.

The ace1_itemSelected() method updates the value of the HiddenField with the value of the selected suggestion. This JavaScript method looks like this:

```
function ace1_itemSelected(sender, e)
{
    var ace1Value = $get('<%= ace1Value.ClientID %>');
    ace1Value.value = e.get_value();
}
```

The second parameter passed to the JavaScript method includes a value property that represents the primary key of the selected suggestion. The primary key is assigned to the HiddenField so that it can be read when the page is posted back to the server.

When you select a movie and click the Submit button, both the title of the selected movie and the primary key associated with the selected movie are displayed in Label controls (see Figure 32.6).

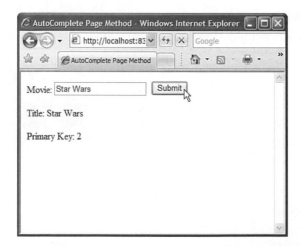

FIGURE 32.6   Selecting a primary key value with auto-complete.

Using the DragPanel Control

The DragPanel extender control enables you to create a virtual window for your web application. The DragPanel can be used to extend the Panel control so that you can drag the Panel around the page.

The DragPanel extender has the following properties:

- ▶ **TargetControlID**—The ID of the Panel control to drag.

- ▶ **DragHandleID**—The ID of the control that the user clicks to drag the Panel control.

The page in Listing 32.5 contains a GridView that lists the current movies in the Movie database table. When you click the Add Movie link, a draggable window appears that contains a form for inserting a new movie (see Figure 32.7).

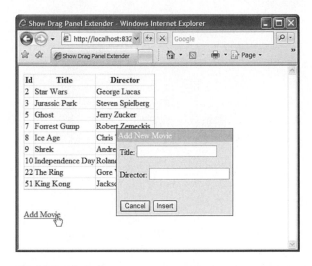

FIGURE 32.7   A virtual pop-up window created with the DragPanel control.

LISTING 32.5   ShowDragPanel.aspx

```
<%@ Page Language="C#" %>
<%@ Register TagPrefix="ajax" Namespace="AjaxControlToolkit"
 Assembly="AjaxControlToolkit"  %>
<!DOCTYPE html PUBLIC "-//W3C//DTD XHTML 1.0 Transitional//EN"
 "http://www.w3.org/TR/xhtml1/DTD/xhtml1-transitional.dtd">
<html xmlns="http://www.w3.org/1999/xhtml">
<head runat="server">
    <title>Show Drag Panel Extender</title>
    <style type="text/css">

    .pnlAdd
    {
        display: none;
        border: solid 1px black;
        background-color: #eeeeee;
    }
```

LISTING 32.5   Continued

```
    .pnlDrag
    {
        background-color: #cccccc;
        color: White;
        cursor:move;
        padding: 3px;
    }

    .pnlContents
    {
        padding: 5px;
    }

    </style>
</head>
<body>
    <form id="form1" runat="server">
    <div>

    <asp:ScriptManager id="sm1" Runat="server" />

    <asp:GridView
        id="grdMovies"
        DataSourceID="srcMovies"
        Runat="server" />

    <asp:Panel ID="pnlAdd" CssClass="pnlAdd" runat="server">
        <asp:Panel ID="pnlDrag" CssClass="pnlDrag" runat="server">
        Add New Movie
        </asp:Panel>
        <div class="pnlContents">
        <asp:FormView
            ID="frmMovie"
            DataSourceID="srcMovies"
            DefaultMode="Insert"
            runat="server">
        <InsertItemTemplate>

        <asp:Label
            id="lblTitle"
            AssociatedControlID="txtTitle"
            Text="Title:"
            Runat="server" />
        <asp:TextBox
```

```
            id="txtTitle"
            Text='<%# Bind("Title") %>'
            Runat="server" />


        <br /><br />


        <asp:Label
            id="lblDirector"
            AssociatedControlID="txtDirector"
            Text="Director:"
            Runat="server" />
        <asp:TextBox
            id="txtDirector"
            Text='<%# Bind("Director") %>'
            Runat="server" />


        <br /><br />


        <asp:Button
            id="btnCancel"
            Text="Cancel"
            CommandName="Cancel"
            Runat="server" />
        <asp:Button
            id="btnInsert"
            Text="Insert"
            CommandName="Insert"
            Runat="server" />


        </InsertItemTemplate>
        </asp:FormView>
        </div>
</asp:Panel>
<ajax:DragPanelExtender
        id="dpe1"
        TargetControlID="pnlAdd"
        DragHandleID="pnlDrag"
        Runat="server" />

<br /><br />

<a
    href="javascript:void(0)"
    onclick="$get('pnlAdd').style.display='block';">Add Movie</a>
```

LISTING 32.5   Continued

```
    <asp:ObjectDataSource
        id="srcMovies"
        TypeName="Movie"
        SelectMethod="Select"
        InsertMethod="Insert"
        Runat="server" />

    </div>
    </form>
</body>
</html>
```

In Listing 32.5, the DragPanel extender control is declared like this:

```
<ajax:DragPanelExtender
    id="dpe1"
    TargetControlID="pnlAdd"
    DragHandleID="pnlDrag"
    Runat="server" />
```

Both the TargetControlID and DragHandleID properties point at Panel controls. The outer Panel, named pnlAdd, is the Panel that gets dragged. The inner Panel, named pnlDrag, is the Panel that you click to drag the outer Panel control.

When you first open the page, the Panel does not appear. The Cascading Style Sheet rule associated with the Panel hides the Panel with display:none. The page includes the following link that displays the draggable Panel:

```
<a
    href="javascript:void(0)"
    onclick="$get('pnlAdd').style.display='block';">Add Movie</a>
```

The $get() method is an alias for the document.getElementById() method. When you click the link, the display style for the pnlAdd Panel is set to block and the Panel and its contents appear.

Using the FilteredTextBox Control

The FilteredTextBox extender control enables you to prevent users from entering the wrong type of content into a TextBox. You can use the FilteredTextBox extender control, for example, to create a TextBox that only accepts numbers.

The page in Listing 32.6 illustrates how to use the FilteredTextBox control. The page contains two TextBox controls. The first TextBox accepts only numbers. The second TextBox accepts lowercase letters, underscores, and exclamation marks.

LISTING 32.6   ShowFilteredTextBox.aspx

```
<%@ Page Language="C#" %>
<%@ Register TagPrefix="ajax" Namespace="AjaxControlToolkit"
 Assembly="AjaxControlToolkit"  %>
<!DOCTYPE html PUBLIC "-//W3C//DTD XHTML 1.0 Transitional//EN"
 "http://www.w3.org/TR/xhtml1/DTD/xhtml1-transitional.dtd">
<html xmlns="http://www.w3.org/1999/xhtml">
<head runat="server">
    <title>Show Filtered TextBox</title>
</head>
<body>
    <form id="form1" runat="server">
    <div>
        <asp:ScriptManager ID="ScriptManager1" runat="server" />

        <asp:Label
            id="lblNumeric"
            Text="Enter a Number:"
            AssociatedControlID="txtNumeric"
            Runat="server" />
        <br />
        <asp:TextBox
            id="txtNumeric"
            Runat="server" />
        <ajax:FilteredTextBoxExtender
            id="fte1"
            TargetControlID="txtNumeric"
            FilterType="Numbers"
            Runat="server" />

        <br /><br />

        <asp:Label
            id="lblProductCode"
            Text="Enter a Product Code:"
            AssociatedControlID="txtProductCode"
            Runat="server" />
        <br />
        <asp:TextBox
            id="txtProductCode"
            Runat="server" />
        <ajax:FilteredTextBoxExtender
            id="fte2"
            TargetControlID="txtProductCode"
            FilterType="LowercaseLetters,Custom"
```

32

LISTING 32.6   Continued

```
            FilterMode="ValidChars"
            ValidChars="_!"
            Runat="server" />
        <br />
        (A product code can contain only lower-case characters,
        underscores, exclamation marks, and no spaces)

    </div>
    </form>
</body>
</html>
```

You specify the type of characters that a TextBox extended with the FilteredTextBox control accepts by setting the FilterType property. This property accepts the following constants: Numbers, LowercaseLetters, UppercaseLetters, and Custom. You can assign more than one of these constants to the FilterType property by separating the constants with a comma.

If at least one of the FilterType constants is Custom, you can create either a list of valid characters or list of invalid characters for the filter. The second FilteredText control in Listing 32.6 has its FilterMode property set to the value ValidChars. The ValidChars property lists two valid characters (_ and !) that a user can enter in addition to lowercase letters.

Using the MaskedEdit Control

The MaskedEdit extender control renders a user interface that guides you as to what type of input a TextBox control accepts. For example, you can use the MaskedEdit control to force a user to enter a date, a number, or a currency amount in a certain format.

The page in Listing 32.7 includes a movie date released field. This field requires a date in the format mm/dd/yyyy. The MaskedEdit control is used to enforce that format (see Figure 32.8).

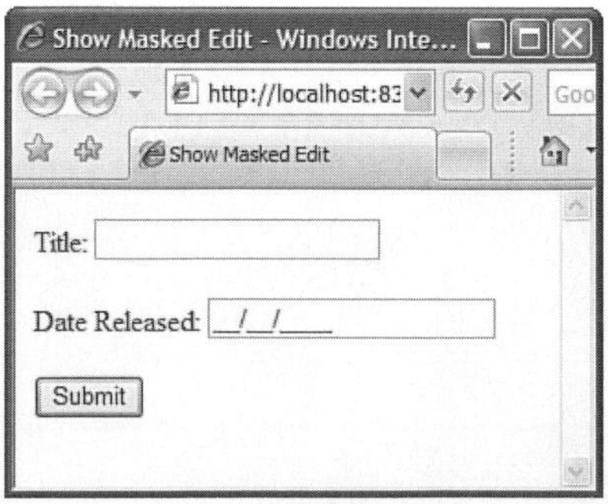

FIGURE 32.8   Using the MaskedEdit control when entering a date.

LISTING 32.7   ShowMaskedEdit.aspx

```
<%@ Page Language="C#" %>
<%@ Register TagPrefix="ajax" Namespace="AjaxControlToolkit"
 Assembly="AjaxControlToolkit"  %>
<!DOCTYPE html PUBLIC "-//W3C//DTD XHTML 1.0 Transitional//EN"
 "http://www.w3.org/TR/xhtml1/DTD/xhtml1-transitional.dtd">
<html xmlns="http://www.w3.org/1999/xhtml">
<head runat="server">
    <title>Show Masked Edit</title>
</head>
<body>
    <form id="form1" runat="server">
    <div>
        <asp:ScriptManager ID="ScriptManager1" runat="server" />

        <asp:Label
            id="lblTitle"
            Text="Title:"
            AssociatedControlID="txtTitle"
            Runat="server" />
        <asp:TextBox
            id="txtTitle"
            Runat="server" />

        <br /><br />

        <asp:Label
            id="lblDateReleased"
            Text="Date Released:"
            AssociatedControlID="txtDateReleased"
            Runat="server" />
        <asp:TextBox
            id="txtDateReleased"
            Runat="server" />
        <ajax:MaskedEditExtender
            id="me1"
            TargetControlID="txtDateReleased"
            Mask="99/99/9999"
            MaskType="Date"
            runat="Server" />

        <br /><br />

        <asp:Button
            id="btnSubmit"
```

LISTING 32.7   Continued

```
            Text="Submit"
            Runat="server" />


    </div>
    </form>
</body>
</html>
```

The `MaskedEdit` control has three important properties:

▶ **TargetControlID**—The TextBox to extend.

▶ **Mask**—The mask to apply to the TextBox.

▶ **MaskType**—The type of mask to apply. Possible values are `None`, `Number`, `Date`, `Time`, and `DateTime`.

The `TargetControlID` and `Mask` properties are required. You should also set the `MaskType` property if you want the resulting text to be formatted correctly.

The `Mask` property accepts a character pattern. You can use the following special characters:

▶ 9—Only a numeric character

▶ L—Only a letter

▶ $—Only a letter or a space

▶ C—Only a custom character (case sensitive)

▶ A—Only a letter or a custom character

▶ N—Only a numeric or custom character

▶ ?—Any character

▶ /—Date separator

▶ :—Time separator

▶ .—Decimal separator

▶ ,—Thousands separator

▶ \—Escape character

▶ {—Initial delimiter for repetition of masks

▶ }—Final delimiter for repetition of masks

The final two special characters listed are curly braces. They enable you to specify how many times a character is allowed to be repeated. For example, you can use the following

TextBox and `MaskedEdit` controls to force someone to enter a social security number in the format 555-55-5555:

```
<asp:TextBox
    id="txtSSN"
    Runat="server" />
<ajax:MaskedEditExtender
    id="MaskedEditExtender1"
    TargetControlID="txtSSN"
    Mask="9{3}-9{2}-9{4}"
    runat="Server" />
```

The character pattern 9{3} requires the user to enter three numbers in a row.

> **NOTE**
>
> The ASP.NET AJAX Control Toolkit also includes a MaskedEditValidator control that accompanies the `MaskedEdit` control. You can take advantage of the MaskedEditValidator control to provide the user with validation error messages when a user enters the wrong type of value into a TextBox extended with the `MaskedEdit` control.

Using the `Animation` Control

The Microsoft ASP.NET AJAX Control Toolkit includes a rich, declarative animation framework. You can use this framework to create animation special effects in your pages. For example, you can fade, move, and resize elements in a page. These animations are created without the benefit of Flash or Silverlight. The effects are written entirely in JavaScript.

Several of the Toolkit controls support the animation framework. For example, earlier in this chapter, we discussed the `AutoComplete` extender control. You can use the animation framework to create an animation when the list of suggestions appear and disappear. For instance, you might want the list of suggestions to fade in and out of view.

> **NOTE**
>
> Microsoft's animation framework holds a huge debt to Script.aculo.us. The Script.aculo.us framework was the first popular animation framework written with JavaScript. To learn more about Script.aculo.us, visit http://Script.aculo.us.

In this section, you learn about the `Animation` extender control. This control enables you to target one or more elements in a page and play an animation. The page in Listing 32.8 uses the `Animation` control to move a Panel control into the center of the page and then fade it out.

LISTING 32.8   ShowAnimationSimple.aspx

```
<%@ Page Language="C#" %>
<%@ Register TagPrefix="ajax" Namespace="AjaxControlToolkit"
 Assembly="AjaxControlToolkit"  %>
<!DOCTYPE html PUBLIC "-//W3C//DTD XHTML 1.0 Transitional//EN"
 "http://www.w3.org/TR/xhtml1/DTD/xhtml1-transitional.dtd">
<html xmlns="http://www.w3.org/1999/xhtml">
<head runat="server">
    <title>Show Animation Simple</title>
    <style type="text/css">

    #pnl
    {
        position:absolute;
        padding:3px;
        background-color: #eeeeee;
        border:solid 1px black;
    }

    </style>
</head>
<body>
    <form id="form1" runat="server">
    <div>
        <asp:ScriptManager ID="ScriptManager1" runat="server" />

        <asp:Panel
            ID="pnl"
            runat="server">
            <h3>I feel so animated!</h3>
        </asp:Panel>

        <ajax:AnimationExtender
            ID="ae1"
            TargetControlID="pnl"
            runat="server">
            <Animations>
            <OnLoad>
                <Sequence>
                <Move
                    Horizontal="300"
                    Vertical="300"
                    Duration="1"
                    Fps="20" />
                <FadeOut
```

```
                    Duration="1"
                    Fps="20" />
               </Sequence>
             </OnLoad>
            </Animations>
        </ajax:AnimationExtender>

    </div>
    </form>
</body>
</html>
```

In Listing 32.8, the `Animation` control targets a Panel control named `pnl`. The Panel control is moved to the center of the page and then is faded out.

NOTE

Notice that the page in Listing 32.8 includes an inline style that sets several style attributes of the Panel control. In particular, the Panel control is given an absolute position. This is a requirement when using the Move animation.

When you create an animation, you must specify the event that triggers the animation. You can use any of the following events:

- ▶ **OnLoad**—Animation plays when the page loads.

- ▶ **OnClick**—Animation plays when the target control is clicked.

- ▶ **OnMouseOver**—Animation plays when you move your mouse over the target.

- ▶ **OnMouseOut**—Animation plays when you move your mouse away from the target.

- ▶ **OnHoverOver**—Animation plays when you hover your mouse over the target (stops any `OnHoverOut` animation).

- ▶ **OnHoverOut**—Animation plays when you hover your mouse away from the target (stops any `OnHoverOver` animation).

In the page in Listing 32.8, the animation starts as soon as the page loads.

An animation can consist of a set of animation effects that play in sequence or play in parallel. In Listing 32.8, the animation plays in sequence. First, the Panel was moved and then it was faded.

The ability to play animations in parallel is powerful because it provides you with a method of composing more complex animations out of simpler ones. For example, the Panel contained in the page in Listing 32.9 fades into view at the same time as it grows in size.

32

LISTING 32.9   ShowAnimationComposite.aspx

```
<%@ Page Language="C#" %>
<%@ Register TagPrefix="ajax" Namespace="AjaxControlToolkit"
 Assembly="AjaxControlToolkit"  %>
<!DOCTYPE html PUBLIC "-//W3C//DTD XHTML 1.0 Transitional//EN"
 "http://www.w3.org/TR/xhtml1/DTD/xhtml1-transitional.dtd">
<html xmlns="http://www.w3.org/1999/xhtml">
<head id="Head1" runat="server">
    <title>Show Animation Composite</title>
    <style type="text/css">

    #pnl
    {
        display:none;
        position:absolute;
        width:1px;
        height:1px;
        left:200px;
        top:200px;
        padding:3px;
        background-color: #eeeeee;
        border:solid 1px black;
    }

    </style>
</head>
<body>
    <form id="form1" runat="server">
    <div>
        <asp:ScriptManager ID="ScriptManager1" runat="server" />

        <asp:Button
            id="btn"
            Text="Play"
            OnClientClick="return false;"
            Runat="server" />

        <asp:Panel
            ID="pnl"
            runat="server">
            <h3>I feel so animated!</h3>
        </asp:Panel>

        <ajax:AnimationExtender
            ID="ae1"
```

```
                    TargetControlID="btn"
                    runat="server">
                    <Animations>
                    <OnClick>
                      <Sequence AnimationTarget="pnl">
                        <EnableAction
                            AnimationTarget="btn"
                            Enabled="false" />
                        <StyleAction
                            Attribute="display"
                            Value="block"/>
                        <Parallel>
                        <FadeIn
                            Duration="1"
                            Fps="20" />
                        <Scale
                            Duration="1"
                            Fps="20"
                            ScaleFactor="30.0"
                            Center="true" />
                        </Parallel>
                      </Sequence>
                    </OnClick>
                    </Animations>
                </ajax:AnimationExtender>

        </div>
        </form>
</body>
</html>
```

When you click the button rendered by the page in Listing 32.9, the following animations play:

▶ **EnableAction**—This animation is used to disable the button that started the animation.

▶ **StyleAction**—This animation is used to display the Panel control. When the page first opens, the Panel control has a style of display:none.

▶ **FadeIn**—This animation is used to fade the Panel into view.

▶ **Scale**—This animation is used to grow the Panel into view.

Notice that the FadeIn and Scale animations are contained in a <Parallel> tag. This tag causes these two animation effects to play simultaneously.

The animation framework supports the following types of animations:

- **Parallel Animation**—Plays a set of animations in parallel.

- **Sequence Animation**—Plays a set of animations in sequence.

- **Condition Animation**—Plays an animation when a JavaScript expression evaluates to `true`; otherwise, it plays another animation (the `else` clause).

- **Case Animation**—Plays one animation from a list of animations depending on the evaluation of a JavaScript expression.

- **Fade Animation**—Plays either a fade-in or fade-out animation.

- **FadeIn Animation**—Plays a fade-in animation.

- **FadeOut Animation**—Plays a fade-out animation.

- **Pulse Animation**—Plays fade-in and fade-out animations in rapid succession.

- **Discrete Animation**—Plays an animation by setting a property of the target element to a sequence of values.

- **Interpolated Animation**—Plays an animation by changing a property gradually between a range of values represented by `startValue` and `endValue`.

- **Color Animation**—Plays an animation by changing a property gradually between a range of values represented by a start color and an end color.

- **Length Animation**—Plays an animation by changing a property gradually between a range of values representing a start and end unit of length.

- **Move Animation**—Plays an animation by moving an element (either relatively or absolutely) across the page.

- **Resize Animation**—Plays an animation by resizing an element by changing the element's width and height.

- **Scale Animation**—Plays an animation by resizing an element by using a scale factor.

- **Enable Action**—An action that disables or enables an element on the page (such as a Button control).

- **Hide Action**—An action that hides an element by setting `display:none`.

- **Style Action**—An action that applies a style attribute to an element.

- **Opacity Action**—An action that modified the transparency of an element.

- **Script Action**—An action that executes a JavaScript script.

To learn more about the properties that you can use with each of these different types of animations, refer to the Animation Reference included with the ASP.NET AJAX Control Toolkit SampleWebSite website.

Using the `UpdatePanelAnimation` Control

The final Toolkit control that we need to discuss in this chapter is the
`UpdatePanelAnimation` extender control. This control can play an animation both when
an `UpdatePanel` is initiating an asynchronous postback and when postback results are
returned from the web server.

Performing some type of animation while an `UpdatePanel` is performing an asynchronous
postback provides the user with a way to know that your web application hasn't frozen.
The animation indicates that some work is being done in the background.

> **NOTE**
>
> In the previous chapter, we discussed the UpdateProgress control, which enables you
> to display a busy wait indicator while an UpdatePanel is performing an asynchronous
> postback. In my opinion, playing an animation seems like a less intrusive method of
> indicating UpdatePanel control progress.

The page in Listing 32.10 demonstrates how you can use the `UpdatePanelAnimation`
control to create a yellow fade effect while an `UpdatePanel` is performing an update.

LISTING 32.10   ShowUpdatePanelAnimation.aspx

```
<%@ Page Language="C#" %>
<%@ Register TagPrefix="ajax" Namespace="AjaxControlToolkit"
 Assembly="AjaxControlToolkit"  %>
<!DOCTYPE html PUBLIC "-//W3C//DTD XHTML 1.0 Transitional//EN"
 "http://www.w3.org/TR/xhtml1/DTD/xhtml1-transitional.dtd">
<script runat="server">

    protected void btnSubmit_Click(object sender, EventArgs e)
    {
        System.Threading.Thread.Sleep(2000);
        lblSelectedColor.Text = txtFavoriteColor.Text;
    }
</script>

<html xmlns="http://www.w3.org/1999/xhtml">
<head runat="server">
    <title>Show UpdatePanel Animation</title>
</head>
<body>
    <form id="form1" runat="server">
    <div>
        <asp:ScriptManager ID="ScriptManager1" runat="server" />
```

LISTING 32.10   Continued

```
<%-- First Update Panel --%>

<asp:UpdatePanel ID="up1" runat="server">
<ContentTemplate>

<asp:Label
    id="lblFavoriteColor"
    Text="Enter Your Favorite Color:"
    Runat="server" />
<asp:TextBox
    id="txtFavoriteColor"
    Runat="server" />
<asp:Button
    id="btnSubmit"
    Text="Submit"
    Runat="server" OnClick="btnSubmit_Click" />

</ContentTemplate>
</asp:UpdatePanel>
<ajax:UpdatePanelAnimationExtender
    id="upae1"
    TargetControlID="up1"
    runat="server">
<Animations>
    <OnUpdating>
    <Color
        Duration="0.5"
        Fps="20"
        Property="style"
        PropertyKey="backgroundColor"
        StartValue="#FFFFFF"
        EndValue="#FFFF90" />

    </OnUpdating>
    <OnUpdated>
    <Color
        Duration="1"
        Fps="20"
        Property="style"
        PropertyKey="backgroundColor"
        StartValue="#FFFF90"
        EndValue="#FFFFFF" />
    </OnUpdated>
</Animations>
```

```
        </ajax:UpdatePanelAnimationExtender>

        <p> </p>

        <%-- Second Update Panel --%>
        <asp:UpdatePanel ID="up2" runat="server">
        <ContentTemplate>

        You selected:
        <asp:Label
            id="lblSelectedColor"
            Runat="server" />

        </ContentTemplate>
        </asp:UpdatePanel>
        <ajax:UpdatePanelAnimationExtender
            id="UpdatePanelAnimationExtender1"
            TargetControlID="up2"
            runat="server">
        <Animations>
            <OnUpdating>
            <Color
                Duration="0.5"
                Fps="20"
                Property="style"
                PropertyKey="backgroundColor"
                StartValue="#FFFFFF"
                EndValue="#FFFF90" />

            </OnUpdating>
            <OnUpdated>
            <Color
                Duration="3"
                Fps="20"
                Property="style"
                PropertyKey="backgroundColor"
                StartValue="#FFFF90"
                EndValue="#FFFFFF" />
            </OnUpdated>
        </Animations>
        </ajax:UpdatePanelAnimationExtender>

    </div>
    </form>
</body>
</html>
```

The page in Listing 32.10 contains two UpdatePanel controls. The first UpdatePanel control contains a form that asks you to enter your favorite color. When you submit the form, the color that you entered appears in a Label control that is contained in the second UpdatePanel control.

The yellow fade effect is applied to both UpdatePanel controls. When you submit the form, the background colors of both UpdatePanel controls fade to yellow. Then, gradually, the background colors fade back to white.

There are two good reasons to use a yellow fade effect in the page in Listing 32.10. First, this animation effect is used with the first UpdatePanel to show that work is being done. During an asynchronous postback, a user cannot look at the browser progress bar to detect progress. You need to provide the user with some indication of work.

The second UpdatePanelAnimation control is used to apply a yellow fade effect to the UpdatePanel that displays the value that the user entered into the form. The other reason to use a yellow fade effect is to highlight the areas of a page that have been updated. Because Ajax enables you to quietly update different regions of a page, you need some way of drawing a user's attention to the areas that have been updated. The UpdatePanelAnimation control provides you with an easy way to grab the user's attention and focus it on areas of the page that have been changed.

> **NOTE**
>
> The yellow fade effect was invented and popularized by Matthew Linderman at 37 signals. You can read the original description of this technique at the following address:
>
> http://www.37signals.com/svn/archives/000558.php

Summary

This chapter provided you with an overview of the ASP.NET AJAX Control Toolkit. In the first part of this chapter, you were provided with a brief overview of each of the 34 controls currently contained in the Toolkit. Next, we focused on six of the controls: the AutoComplete control, the DragPanel control, the FilteredTextBox control, the MaskedEdit control, the Animation control, and the UpdatePanelAnimation control.

You learned how to use the AutoComplete control to display auto-complete suggestions while a user is entering text into a TextBox. You learned how to expose the suggestions from a web method contained in a page and a web method contained in a separate web service. You also learned how to associate a primary key value with each suggestion.

Next, we examined the DragPanel control. You learned how to use the DragPanel control to create a pop-up, draggable virtual window.

We then looked at two controls that can be used to restrict user input into a TextBox. You learned how to use the `FilteredTextBox` control to allow only certain characters to be entered in a TextBox. You also learned how to use the `MaskedEdit` control to provide a user interface that indicates the type of content a TextBox accepts.

Finally, we explored the topic of animation. You were provided with an overview of the rich, declarative animation framework included with the ASP.NET AJAX Control Toolkit. You also learned how to play an animation while an `UpdatePanel` control is performing an asynchronous postback.

32

Using Client-Side ASP.NET AJAX

This chapter is about the future of building web applications. In this chapter, you learn how to build "pure" Ajax applications that execute on the browser instead of the server.

In the first part of this chapter, you learn how Microsoft has extended JavaScript so that the JavaScript language more closely resembles .NET languages such as C# and VB.NET. You also learn how Microsoft has added useful debugging and tracing support to JavaScript.

Next, we get to the heart of client-side AJAX. You learn how to perform Ajax calls from the browser to the server. You learn how to call both web methods exposed by a web service and web methods exposed by a page. We also discuss how you can call three built-in services included with the AJAX Framework. You learn how to work with the Authentication, Role, and Profile services.

Finally, you learn how to create client-side AJAX controls and behaviors. You learn how to add client-side controls and behaviors to an AJAX page both programmatically and declaratively.

Making JavaScript Look Like C#

Let me start by saying that there is nothing wrong with JavaScript the language. It is not a toy language. It is not a limited language. JavaScript simply has it roots in a different programming language family than other languages you are familiar with, such as C# and VB.NET.

> **NOTE**
>
> For a great, quick introduction to JavaScript the language, I recommend that you read "A re-introduction to JavaScript" at http://developer.mozilla.org/en/docs/A_re-introduction_to_JavaScript.

JavaScript is an object-oriented programming language. In fact, one could argue that it is more object-oriented than languages such as C# and VB.NET. In a language such as C#, you make a distinction between classes (Aristotelian forms) and objects (Aristotelian matter). An object is an instance of a class, but a class does not exist in its own right.

In JavaScript, classes do not exist. The only thing that exists are objects (everything is matter). Objects are not related to one another by being instances of the same class. Instead, one object can be related to another object when one object is the prototype for another object.

Another major difference between JavaScript and C# is that JavaScript is a dynamic language. The type of a variable can change at any moment during runtime. When JavaScript code is executed, a String might transform into an Integer and back again. The C# language, on the other hand, is statically typed. Once declared, a String is a String and it can never be anything else.

In the past, I believe that there were two reasons that JavaScript was not taken very seriously as a programming language. First, it seemed to be a dead language. If it was evolving, no one was paying attention. This situation changed when Mozilla Firefox was introduced into the world. New versions of JavaScript have been popping up in new releases of Firefox. It is no coincidence that the inventor of JavaScript, Brendan Eich, is now the CTO of Mozilla.

Second, for a number of years, JavaScript was primarily used to create cheesy special effects on web pages or obnoxious advertisements that floated across web pages. All the excitement over Ajax, however, has caused developers to reexamine JavaScript as a language. Developers have learned that JavaScript is a much more flexible and powerful language than originally thought.

For example, Douglas Crockford writes the following in "A Survey of the JavaScript Programming Language" (http://javascript.crockford.com/survey.html):

> When JavaScript was first introduced, I dismissed it as being not worth my attention. Much later, I took another look at it and discovered that hidden in the browser was an excellent programming language. My initial attitudes were based on the initial positioning of JavaScript by Sun and Netscape. They made many misstatements about JavaScript in order to avoid positioning JavaScript as a competitor to Java. Those misstatements continue to echo in the scores of badly written JavaScript books aimed at the dummies and amateurs market.

> **NOTE**
>
> Several good articles on the evolution of the perception of JavaScript as a toy language to a real language can be found at the Ajaxian website (www.ajaxian.com).

So, it is with mixed feelings that I describe Microsoft's attempts to make JavaScript work more like C#. On the one hand, I really don't think the language needs improving. On the other hand, one of the best features of JavaScript is that you can easily extend it. So, if Microsoft can make JavaScript work more like C#, and be more palatable to .NET developers, who can blame them?

Using the Microsoft AJAX Library

The supporting code for the client-side Microsoft AJAX Framework is contained in a single JavaScript file named MicrosoftAjax.js. This file is included in a page automatically when you add an ASP.NET ScriptManager control to a page. If you add an AJAX Web Form to a website within Visual Web Developer, the page contains the ScriptManager control automatically (see Figure 33.1).

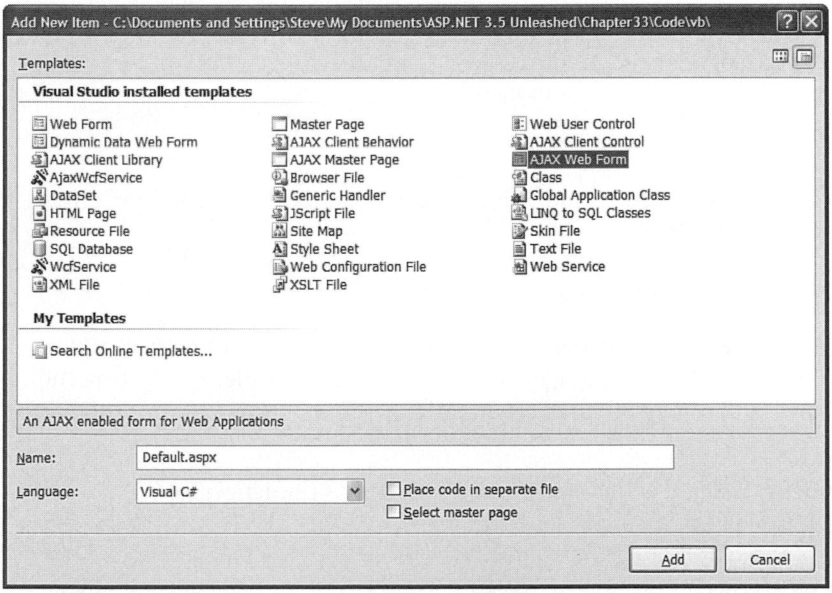

FIGURE 33.1   Adding an AJAX Web Form with Visual Web Developer.

> **NOTE**
>
> By default, the ScriptManager adds references to both the MicrosoftAjax.js and
> MicrosoftAjaxWebForms.js files. The MicrosoftAjaxWebForms.js file contains the
> JavaScript code for supporting the `UpdatePanel` control. If you are not using the
> `UpdatePanel` control, you can assign the value `false` to the ScriptManager control's
> `EnablePartialRendering` property and the MicrosoftAjaxWebForms.js file will no
> longer be included.

If you want to look at the contents of the MicrosoftAjax.debug.js file, you can open it
from the Microsoft folder on the CD that accompanies this book.

The MicrosoftAjax.js file has a debug version and a release version. The release version is
minimized and has debugging code removed so that it can be downloaded faster to a web
browser. The size of the release version of the Microsoft AJAX Library is a trim 83KB. The
size of the debug version is 325KB.

> **NOTE**
>
> For good reason, people worry about the size of AJAX libraries. The Microsoft AJAX
> Library is extremely tiny. For the sake of comparison, the size of the release version of
> the Microsoft AJAX Library is only about double the size of a typical picture that is dis-
> played on the home page of *The New York Times* website (www.nytimes.com).
> Furthermore, it is important to remember that a browser caches a JavaScript file
> across multiple pages and multiple visits to the same website.

All the functionality we discuss in the following sections is contained in the JavaScript
code in the MicrosoftAjax.js file.

Creating an AJAX Client Library

Before we do anything else, we need to discuss how you create an external JavaScript file
and reference it in an AJAX Web Form page. You create a JavaScript file by selecting the
menu option Website, Add New Item and selecting the AJAX Client Library option (see
Figure 33.2).

For example, the file in Listing 33.1 contains a single JavaScript function called
sayMessage() that displays a JavaScript alert with a message.

LISTING 33.1   myLibrary.js

```
/// <reference name="MicrosoftAjax.js"/>


function sayMessage()
{
```

```
    alert("Hello World!");
}
if(typeof(Sys) !== "undefined") Sys.Application.notifyScriptLoaded();
```

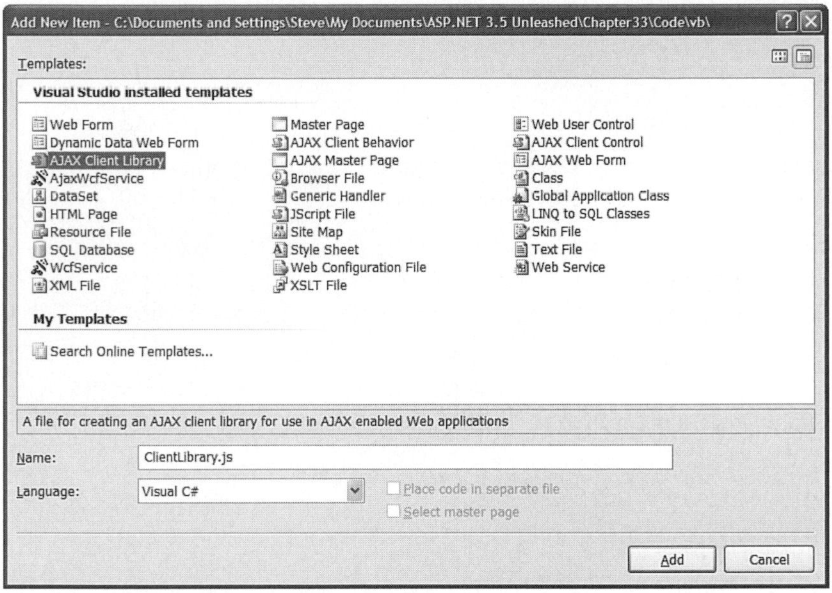

FIGURE 33.2   Creating an AJAX Client Library with Visual Web Developer.

You should notice two special things about this file. First, at the top of the file is a comment. The significance of this comment will be explained in the next section.

Second, at the bottom of the file is a conditional that checks whether a namespace named Sys exists. If it does exist, the Application.notifyScriptLoaded() method is called. You should add this conditional to the bottom of every external JavaScript file that you use with the ASP.NET AJAX Framework. The notifyScriptLoaded() method is used to tell the Framework that the external JavaScript file has been successfully loaded.

The check for the Sys namespace enables you to use the JavaScript file in applications that do not use the ASP.NET AJAX Framework. If the Sys namespace doesn't exist, the application is not an ASP.NET AJAX application and there is no point in calling the notifyScriptLoaded() method.

After you create an external JavaScript file, you can use it in an ASP.NET AJAX–enabled page by creating a script reference. The page in Listing 33.2 illustrates how you add a script reference to the myLibrary.js library.

LISTING 33.2   ShowMyLibrary.aspx

```
<%@ Page Language="C#" %>
<html xmlns="http://www.w3.org/1999/xhtml">
<head runat="server">
    <title>Show myLibrary</title>
    <script type="text/javascript">

      function pageLoad()
      {
        sayMessage();
      }

    </script>
</head>
<body>
    <form id="form1" runat="server">
    <div>
        <asp:ScriptManager ID="ScriptManager1" runat="server">
        <Scripts>
            <asp:ScriptReference Path="~/myLibrary.js" />
        </Scripts>
        </asp:ScriptManager>
    </div>
    </form>
</body>
</html>
```

The page in Listing 33.2 contains a ScriptManager control that contains a `<Scripts>` sub-element. A reference to the myLibrary.js JavaScript library is contained in this sub-element.

The page also contains a client-side `pageLoad` event handler. This event handler calls the `sayMessage()` function we defined in the external JavaScript file.

Taking Advantage of JavaScript Intellisense

One huge advantage of using Visual Web Developer to write client-side AJAX applications is its support for Intellisense for JavaScript. The Intellisense appears both for built-in JavaScript objects and methods and for JavaScript libraries you write.

Visual Web Developer will attempt to infer the data type of a JavaScript variable. This is quite an accomplishment considering that JavaScript is a dynamic language and a variable might change its data type at any time at runtime.

For example, suppose you assign a string to a variable and declare it like this:

```
var message = "hello world";
```

Visual Web Developer will pop up with a list of all the string methods and properties when you type the variable name followed by a period (see Figure 33.3).

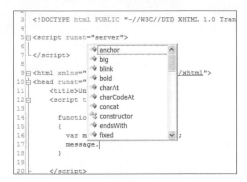

FIGURE 33.3   Viewing Visual Web Developer JavaScript Intellisense.

Visual Web Developer can even detect whether you are attempting to work with a DOM element and will show the appropriate properties and methods.

> **NOTE**
>
> The exact list of properties and methods displayed by Intellisense for a DOM element depends on your Validation settings (select the menu option Tools, Options, Text Editor, HTML, Validation). By default, Visual Web Developer is configured to validate against the XHTML 1.0 Transitional standard. Because the innerHTML property is not supported by that standard, you won't get the innerHTML property in Intellisense. If, however, you target Internet Explorer 6.0 for validation, the innerHTML property appears.

When you create a new AJAX Client Library file, as we did in the previous section, the top of the file includes the following comment:

```
/// <reference name="MicrosoftAjax.js"/>
```

This strange-looking comment has a very important purpose. It enables Visual Web Developer to provide Intellisense for the Microsoft AJAX Library. For example, if you type Sys.Browser, you'll see all the properties of the Browser object contained in the Sys namespace (see Figure 33.4). The Browser object is defined in the MicrosoftAjax.js file.

You can provide Intellisense for a client library that you create. To add Intellisense to your libraries, you simply need to add XML comments to your JavaScript code (just like you would for C# or VB.NET code). For example, the client library in Listing 33.3 contains a method named addNumbers() that adds two numbers together. Notice that XML comments are used to describe the function and the two parameters.

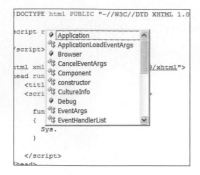

FIGURE 33.4   Displaying Intellisense for an external library.

LISTING 33.3   mathLib.js

```
/// <reference name="MicrosoftAjax.js"/>


function addNumbers(firstNumber, secondNumber)
{
/// <summary>Adds 2 numbers</summary>
/// <param name="firstNumber" type="Number">The first number</param>
/// <param name="secondNumber" type="Number">The second number</param>
/// <returns type="Number">The sum of numbers</returns>

    return firstNumber + secondNumber;
}


if(typeof(Sys) !== "undefined") Sys.Application.notifyScriptLoaded();
```

There is one important difference between how you add XML comments to JavaScript and how you add comments to C# or VB.NET. Notice that the comment appears within the function and not above the function. This is a requirement.

After you add XML comments to a client library, the comments appear when you use the library. The comments appear in a page when you use the library in a page, and they appear in a separate client library when you add a reference the original library. For example, the file in Listing 33.4 contains a reference (at the top of the file) to the MathLib.js file. If you start typing the name of the addNumbers() function, Intellisense will appear (see Figure 33.5).

LISTING 33.4   referMathLib.js

```
/// <reference name="MicrosoftAjax.js"/>
/// <reference path="mathLib.js"/>
```

```
var num = addNumbers(1, 2);

if(typeof(Sys) !== "undefined") Sys.Application.notifyScriptLoaded();
```

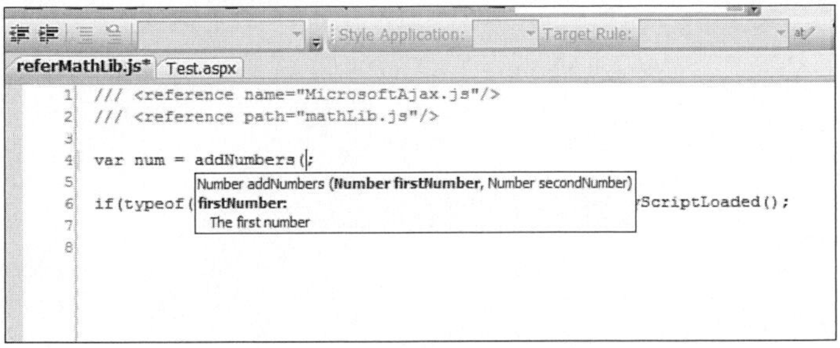

FIGURE 33.5   Generating Intellisense with XML comments.

Notice that the reference to the MicrosoftAjax.js library uses the `name` attribute and that the reference to the mathLib.js library uses the `path` attribute. The MicrosoftAjax.js library is compiled as an embedded resource into the System.Web.Extensions.dll assembly. When a library is embedded in an assembly, you use the library name instead of its path.

> **NOTE**
>
> For more information about JavaScript XML comments, see http://weblogs.asp.net/ bleroy/archive/2007/04/23/the-format-for-javascript-doc-comments.aspx.

Working with Classes

As discussed previously, the JavaScript language does not have classes. In the JavaScript universe, everything is an object.

In order to make JavaScript look more like C#, Microsoft has extended JavaScript in such a way that you can pretend that the JavaScript language has classes. That way, you can use familiar C# language constructs such as interfaces and class inheritance.

The file in Listing 33.5 demonstrates how you create a class by using the Microsoft AJAX Library.

LISTING 33.5   MyClass.js

```
/// <reference name="MicrosoftAjax.js"/>

var MyClass = function()
{
    this._message = 'Hello World';
    this._animal = function() {alert("wow")};
```

LISTING 33.5   Continued

```
};

MyClass.prototype =
{
    get_message: function()
    {
        return this._message;
    },

    set_message: function(value)
    {
        this._message = value;
    },

    sayMessage: function()
    {
        alert(this._message);
    },

    yellMessage: function()
    {
        alert(this._message + '!');
    }
};

MyClass.registerClass('MyClass');

if (typeof(Sys) !== 'undefined') Sys.Application.notifyScriptLoaded();
```

In JavaScript, you create a particular type of object by creating a constructor function. Just like in C# or VB.NET, a constructor function is typically used to initialize the fields of the object being created. The following code declares the constructor function for MyClass:

```
var MyClass = function()
{
    this._message = 'Hello World';
};
```

This constructor initializes a single private field named _message. The underscore is used to mark the field as a private field.

> **NOTE**
>
> By convention, when building an ASP.NET AJAX application, you name private members of an object with a leading underscore. Any field, property, or method of an object that has a name starting with an underscore does not appear in Intellisense.
>
> Strictly speaking, these object members are not truly private. From the point of view of the JavaScript language, there is no difference between an object member named _message and an object member named message. Calling alert(obj._message) will show the value of the private _message field.
>
> The JavaScript language does support truly private fields if you are willing to do some work (see http://www.crockford.com/javascript/private.html).

Next, the public methods and properties of the class are defined by specifying a prototype object for the class. The following code causes all MyClass objects to include a property named message and two methods named sayMessage() and yellMessage():

```
MyClass.prototype =
{
    get_message: function()
    {
        return this._message;
    },

    set_message: function(value)
    {
        this._message = value;
    },

    sayMessage: function()
    {
        alert(this._message);
    },

    yellMessage: function()
    {
        alert(this._message + '!');
    }
};
```

Notice how you define a property. The message property is defined by creating a set_message() property setter and a get_message() property getter. The version of JavaScript included with Internet Explorer does not support true properties. So, properties are simulated by creating setter and getter methods.

33

> **NOTE**
>
> Getters and setters were added to the JavaScript language in version 1.5. Because Internet Explorer does not support this feature, the getters and setters must be simulated with methods.

The two methods are declared in a straightforward manner. Both the sayMessage() and yellMessage() methods access the private _message field. The sayMessage() method displays the message in a JavaScript alert. The yellMessage() method tacks an exclamation mark at the end of the message before displaying it.

Finally, the class is registered with the ASP.NET AJAX Framework with the following call to the registerClass() method:

```
MyClass.registerClass('MyClass');
```

This syntax here is a little odd. Notice that the registerClass() method is called on the class itself and that the name of the class is passed to the method. It all seems very circular. How can MyClass have a registerClass() method when it hasn't even been registered yet?

It all makes sense when you realize that MyClass is actually a function. Remember, MyClass is the constructor function for creating MyClass objects. The AJAX Library extends the JavaScript Function object so that it includes a registerClass() method. Therefore, the registerClass() statement isn't really circular because the registerClass() method of the Function object is being called.

> **NOTE**
>
> The registerClass() method is a method of the Type object. However, the Type object is simply an alias for the built-in JavaScript Function object. In the AJAX Library, this is accomplished with the following lines of code:
>
> ```
> // Alias Function as Type
> window.Type = Function;
> ```

After you define a class, you can use it in pages and other external JavaScript files (client libraries). The page in Listing 33.6 creates an instance of the MyClass class in the pageLoad handler, assigns a value to the message property, and calls the yellMessage() method.

LISTING 33.6   ShowMyClass.aspx

```
<%@ Page Language="C#" %>
<!DOCTYPE html PUBLIC "-//W3C//DTD XHTML 1.0 Transitional//EN"
 "http://www.w3.org/TR/xhtml1/DTD/xhtml1-transitional.dtd">
<html xmlns="http://www.w3.org/1999/xhtml">
<head runat="server">
    <title>Show MyClass</title>
    <script type="text/javascript">
```

```
    function pageLoad()
    {
      var obj = new MyClass();
      obj.set_message("Good Day");
      obj.yellMessage();
    }

    </script>
</head>
<body>
    <form id="form1" runat="server">
    <div>
        <asp:ScriptManager ID="ScriptManager1" runat="server">
        <Scripts>
            <asp:ScriptReference Path="~/MyClass.js" />
        </Scripts>
        </asp:ScriptManager>
    </div>
    </form>
</body>
</html>
```

When using the `MyClass` object, you get full Intellisense. The private `_message` field is hidden and the public methods are displayed (see Figure 33.6).

FIGURE 33.6   Viewing `MyClass` members.

Working with Inheritance

If you use the `registerClass()` method to simulate creating .NET classes on the client, you can take advantage of something that resembles class inheritance. You can create a derived class that inherits from a base class. The derived class can override and extend the properties and methods of the base class.

For example, the client library in Listing 33.7 includes a `Product` class and a `Laptop` class. The `Laptop` class inherits from the `Product` class and overrides two of the base class properties.

LISTING 33.7   Product.js

```
/// <reference name="MicrosoftAjax.js"/>


// Define Computer
var Computer = function()
{
    this._price = 500.00;
};

Computer.prototype =
{
    get_name: function()
    {
        return "Computer";
    },

    get_price: function()
    {
        return this._price;
    }
};

Computer.registerClass("Computer");

// Define Laptop
var Laptop = function()
{
    Laptop.initializeBase(this);
};

Laptop.prototype =
{
    // Overrides base method
    get_name: function()
    {
        return "Laptop";
    },

    // Override and extend base method
    get_price: function()
    {
        return Laptop.callBaseMethod(this, "get_price") * 2;
    }
};
```

```
Laptop.registerClass("Laptop", Computer);
if (typeof(Sys) !== 'undefined') Sys.Application.notifyScriptLoaded()
```

The Computer class (the base class) is registered with the following statement:

```
Computer.registerClass("Computer");
```

The Laptop class (the derived class) is registered with the following statement:

```
Laptop.registerClass("Laptop", Computer);
```

The second parameter passed to the registerClass() method represents a base class. This register statement causes the Laptop class to inherit from the Product class.

Notice that the Laptop class includes a call to initializeBase() in its constructor function. This call is necessary to initialize the fields in the base class constructor function. In this case, if you neglect to call the initializeBase() method, the _price field won't be initialized.

The Laptop class contains two properties that override properties of the base Product class. The first property simply overrides the get_name() property. The second property, the get_price() property, also overrides the base property. However, this property calls the base property with the callBaseMethod() method so that the base price can be doubled (laptop computers always cost double the price of a normal computer).

The page in Listing 33.8 illustrates how you can use the Laptop class.

LISTING 33.8   ShowProduct.aspx

```
<%@ Page Language="C#" %>
<!DOCTYPE html PUBLIC "-//W3C//DTD XHTML 1.0 Transitional//EN"
 "http://www.w3.org/TR/xhtml1/DTD/xhtml1-transitional.dtd">
<html xmlns="http://www.w3.org/1999/xhtml">
<head runat="server">
    <title>Show Product</title>
    <script type="text/javascript">

      function pageLoad()
      {
        var myLapTop = new Laptop();
        var message = String.format("The {0} costs {1}",
            myLapTop.get_name(), myLapTop.get_price().localeFormat("c"));
        alert( message  );
      }

    </script>
</head>
<body>
```

LISTING 33.8   Continued

```
    <form id="form1" runat="server">
    <div>
        <asp:ScriptManager ID="ScriptManager1" runat="server">
        <Scripts>
            <asp:ScriptReference Path="~/Product.js" />
        </Scripts>
        </asp:ScriptManager>
    </div>
    </form>
</body>
</html>
```

In the pageLoad() method, an instance of the Laptop class is created. Next, the static String.Format() method is used to build a string from the name and price properties of Laptop. Finally, the string is displayed in a JavaScript alert.

NOTE

The Microsoft AJAX Library also supports creating interfaces and enumerations. To learn more, see the Microsoft .NET Framework SDK documentation.

Working with Namespaces

In the .NET Framework, namespaces are used to group related classes. For example, all the classes related to working with the file system are located in the System.IO namespace. This is done for the purposes of documentation and to prevent naming collisions. If a class appears in the System.IO namespace, you know that is has something to do with file access. Different namespaces can have classes with the very same name.

JavaScript does not explicitly support namespaces. The AJAX Library extends the JavaScript language so that you can simulate namespaces. For example, the page in Listing 33.9 registers a new namespaces named MyNamespace and adds a class named MyClass to the MyNamespace.

LISTING 33.9   Namespaces.js

```
/// <reference name="MicrosoftAjax.js"/>


Type.registerNamespace("MyNamespace");


MyNamespace.MyClass = function()
{
  this._message = "Fantastic!";
};
```

```
MyNamespace.MyClass.prototype =
{
    sayMessage: function()
    {
        alert(this._message);
    }
};


MyNamespace.MyClass.registerClass("MyNamespace.MyClass");


if (typeof(Sys) !== 'undefined') Sys.Application.notifyScriptLoaded();
```

The new namespace is created by calling the static `Type.registerNamespace()` method. Notice that when the class is registered with the `registerClass()` method, the fully qualified name of the class is used (`MyNamespace.MyClass` instead of `MyClass`).

The page in Listing 33.10 demonstrates how you can use the `MyNamespace` namespace when working with a class.

LISTING 33.10   ShowNamespaces.aspx

```
<%@ Page Language="C#" %>
<!DOCTYPE html PUBLIC "-//W3C//DTD XHTML 1.0 Transitional//EN"
 "http://www.w3.org/TR/xhtml1/DTD/xhtml1-transitional.dtd">
<html xmlns="http://www.w3.org/1999/xhtml">
<head runat="server">
    <title>Show Namespaces</title>
    <script type="text/javascript">

      function pageLoad()
      {
        var myClass = new MyNamespace.MyClass();
        myClass.sayMessage();
      }

    </script>
</head>
<body>
    <form id="form1" runat="server">
    <div>
        <asp:ScriptManager ID="ScriptManager1" runat="server">
        <Scripts>
            <asp:ScriptReference Path="~/Namespaces.js" />
        </Scripts>
        </asp:ScriptManager>
    </div>
```

LISTING 33.10   Continued

```
    </form>
</body>
</html>
```

In Listing 33.10, an instance of the `MyClass` class is created in the `pageLoad()` method. The instance of the class is created by using the namespace-qualified name of the class: `MyNamespace.MyClass()`.

Retrieving DOM Elements

One of the most common operations you perform when building Ajax applications is retrieving DOM elements. For example, you might need to grab a `span` element from a page and modify its `innerHTML`. In a typical JavaScript application, you would use the `document.getElementById()` method to grab the DOM element, like this:

```
var span = document.getElementById("mySpan");
span.innerHTML = "Hello World!";
```

The Microsoft AJAX Library introduces a shortcut method you can use instead of the `document.getElementById()` method. You can use the `$get()` method, like this:

```
var span = $get("mySpan");
span.innerHTML = "Hello World!";
```

Alternatively, if you want to write really condensed code, you can use the `$get()` method, like this:

```
$get("mySpan").innerHTML = "Hello World!";
```

When calling `$get()`, you can pass a second parameter that represents the DOM element to search. For example, the following statement returns the `mySpan` element contained in the `myDiv` element:

```
var myDiv = $get("myDiv");
$get("mySpan", myDiv).innerHTML = "Hello World!";
```

Be careful when calling either `$get()` or `document.getElementById()` because they are expensive operations in terms of performance. It is better to use `$get()` to grab a reference to a DOM element and assign it to a variable once than to use `$get()` multiple times to work with the same DOM element.

> **NOTE**
>
> The Prototype framework (a popular, non-Microsoft AJAX framework) first introduced the `$()` function as an alias for `document.getElementById()`. Originally, Microsoft used `$()` instead of `$get()` as well. However, Microsoft wanted developers to be able to mix Prototype applications with Microsoft AJAX applications so it changed the name of the function to `$get()`.

Handling DOM Events

One of the biggest pains associated with writing client-side applications has to do with handling DOM events (for example, handling a client-side Button click event). The problem is that Microsoft Internet Explorer does not follow W3C standards. Therefore, you always end up writing a lot of extra code to make sure your application works with Internet Explorer and standards-compliant browsers such as Firefox and Opera.

The Microsoft AJAX Library provides an abstraction layer that smoothes over the difference between browsers. You handle a DOM event either with the $addHandler() shortcut or the $addHandlers() shortcut.

For example, the page in Listing 33.11 contains an <input type="button"> element. In the pageLoad() method, the doSomething method is wired to the Button click event with the help of the $addHandler() shortcut. The doSomething() method simply displays an alert box with the message "Hello World!".

LISTING 33.11   ShowAddHandler.aspx

```
<%@ Page Language="C#" %>
<!DOCTYPE html PUBLIC "-//W3C//DTD XHTML 1.0 Transitional//EN"
 "http://www.w3.org/TR/xhtml1/DTD/xhtml1-transitional.dtd">
<html xmlns="http://www.w3.org/1999/xhtml">
<head runat="server">
    <title>Show AddHandler</title>
    <script type="text/javascript">

      function pageLoad()
      {
        $addHandler( $get("btn"), "click", doSomething);

        Sys.Application.add_disposing(appDispose);
      }

      function doSomething()
      {
        alert("Hello World!");
      }

      function appDispose()
      {
        $removeHandler( $get("btn"), "click", doSomething);
      }

    </script>
</head>
<body>
```

LISTING 33.11   Continued

```
    <form id="form1" runat="server">
    <asp:ScriptManager ID="ScriptManager1" runat="server" />

    <input id="btn" type="button" value="Do Something" />

    </form>
</body>
</html>
```

The $addHandler() shortcut accepts three parameters: the DOM element, the name of the event to handle, and a reference to the method to execute.

If you need to wire up multiple event handlers to the same element, you can use the $addHandlers() method. The $addHandlers() method accepts a list of event handlers for its second parameter. For example, the page in Listing 33.12 handles a <div> element's mouseover and mouseout events. The background color of the <div> element changes from white to yellow (see Figure 33.7).

FIGURE 33.7   Handling the mouseover and mouseout events.

LISTING 33.12   ShowAddHandlers.aspx

```
<%@ Page Language="C#" %>
<!DOCTYPE html PUBLIC "-//W3C//DTD XHTML 1.0 Transitional//EN"
 "http://www.w3.org/TR/xhtml1/DTD/xhtml1-transitional.dtd">
<html xmlns="http://www.w3.org/1999/xhtml">
<head runat="server">
    <title>Show AddHandlers</title>
    <style type="text/css">
        .glow
        {
            background-color:yellow;
        }
    </style>
```

```
    <script type="text/javascript">

      var divHover;

      function pageLoad()
      {
        divHover = $get("divHover");
        $addHandlers( divHover, {mouseover:addGlow, mouseout:removeGlow} );

        Sys.Application.add_disposing(appDispose);
      }

      function addGlow()
      {
        Sys.UI.DomElement.addCssClass(divHover, "glow");
      }

      function removeGlow()
      {
        Sys.UI.DomElement.removeCssClass(divHover, "glow");
      }

      function appDispose()
      {
        $clearHandlers( divHover );
      }

    </script>
</head>
<body>
    <form id="form1" runat="server">
    <asp:ScriptManager ID="ScriptManager1" runat="server" />

    <div id="divHover">

        <h1>Hover Here!</h1>

    </div>
    </form>
</body>
</html>
```

When you are wiring up DOM event handlers, it is important to unwire the event handlers when you are done using them. Unfortunately, Internet Explorer exhibits bad memory leaks when you create references between JavaScript objects and DOM objects.

You can avoid these memory leaks by calling either the $removeHandler or $clearHandlers() shortcut method.

In Listing 33.11, the $removeHandler() method is used to remove the doSomething() handler from the Button click event. In Listing 33.12, the $clearHandlers() method is used to remove all the handlers from divHover's <div> element. In both cases, the method is called within an application-disposing event handler.

NOTE

The application-disposing event is raised whenever the user moves from the current page. For example, disposing is raised when the user refreshes the browser, navigates to a new page, or closes the browser window.

Retrieving DOM Event Information

When you are writing a normal JavaScript application, retrieving information about an event is just as difficult as wiring up a handler for a client-side event. Again, Internet Explorer represents event information in a completely different way than Firefox or Opera. The Microsoft AJAX Library, once again, enables you to smooth over the differences between the different browsers.

If you create an event handler with the Microsoft AJAX Library, event information is passed to the event handler as a parameter. In particular, an instance of the Sys.UI.DomEvent class is passed to the event handler.

The Sys.UI.DomEvent class has a number of useful properties:

- **altKey**—Returns true when the Alt key is pressed.

- **button**—Returns a value from the Sys.UI.MouseButton enumeration: leftButton, middleButton, or rightButton.

- **charCode**—Returns the code for the key pressed that raised the event. Use the Sys.UI.Key enumeration to compare the charCode against the particular types of keys, such as the Backspace, Tab, and Enter.

- **clientX**—Returns the horizontal position of the mouse relative to the client area of the browser window, excluding the scroll bars.

- **clientY**—Returns the vertical position of the mouse relative to the client area of the browser window, excluding the scroll bars.

- **ctrlKey**—Returns true when the Ctrl key is pressed.

- **offsetX**—Returns the horizontal position of the mouse relative to the element that raised the event.

- **offsetY**—Returns the vertical position of the mouse relative to the element that raised the event.

- ▸ **screenX**—Returns the horizontal position of the mouse relative to the entire screen.

- ▸ **screenY**—Returns the vertical position of the mouse relative to the entire screen.

- ▸ **shiftKey**—Returns `true` when the Shift key is pressed.

- ▸ **target**—Returns the original element that raised the event (as distinct from the element associated with the event handler).

- ▸ **type**—Returns the name of the event (for example, `click`).

The `Sys.UI.DomEvent` class also has two useful methods:

- ▸ **preventDefault**—Stops the default action associated with the event.

- ▸ **stopPropagation**—Stops the event from bubbling up to its parent element.

The `preventDefault` method is especially useful. If you want to prevent the default event associated with performing an action, then you can call this method to cancel it. For example, if you add a `<button>` tag to a page, and you don't want a postback to happen when you click the button, then call the `preventDefault()` method.

The page in Listing 33.13 illustrates how you can use the `DomEvent` class to determine the target of an event. The page contains a simple menu of food items. When you click an item, the selected item appears in a `<span>` tag (see Figure 33.8).

FIGURE 33.8   Selecting a menu item.

Each menu item is contained in a `<span>` tag. The `<span>` tags are contained in a `<div>` tag. A single event handler is wired up to the `<div>` tag's `click` event. When you click a menu item, the selected menu item is detected with the help of the `DomEvent` class's `target` property.

LISTING 33.13   ShowDOMEvent.aspx

```
<%@ Page Language="C#" %>
<!DOCTYPE html PUBLIC "-//W3C//DTD XHTML 1.0 Transitional//EN"
 "http://www.w3.org/TR/xhtml1/DTD/xhtml1-transitional.dtd">
<html xmlns="http://www.w3.org/1999/xhtml">
<head runat="server">
```

LISTING 33.13   Continued

```
    <title>Show DOM Event</title>
    <style type="text/css">
        #divMenu
        {
            padding: 5px;
        }
        #divMenu span
        {
            margin: 4px;
            padding: 3px;
            border:solid 1px black;
            background-color: #eeeeee;
        }
    </style>
    <script type="text/javascript">

      function pageLoad()
      {
        $addHandler( $get("divMenu"), "click", selectMenuItem );
        Sys.Application.add_disposing(appDispose);
      }

      function selectMenuItem(e)
      {
        if (e.target.tagName === "SPAN")
            $get("spanSelection").innerHTML = e.target.innerHTML;
      }

      function appDispose()
      {
        $clearHandlers( $get("divMenu") );
      }

    </script>
</head>
<body>
    <form id="form1" runat="server">
    <asp:ScriptManager ID="ScriptManager1" runat="server" />

    <div id="divMenu">

        <span>Cheeseburger</span>
```

```
        <span>Milkshake</span>

        <span>French fries</span>

    </div>

    <br /> You selected:
    <span id="spanSelection"></span>

    </form>
</body>
</html>
```

Creating Callbacks and Delegates

In the previous sections, you learned how to handle DOM events and retrieve event information by using the $addHandler() method. This method of wiring up an event handler, however, has a serious limitation: It doesn't enable you to pass additional information to the event handler.

The ASP.NET AJAX Library includes two methods you can use to pass additional information to event handlers:

▶ Function.createCallback(method, context)

▶ Function.createDelegate(instance, method)

Calling the createCallback() method creates a method that passes an additional context parameter to an event handler. You can pass anything you want as the context parameter. For example, the context parameter could be a simple string or it could be a reference to a component.

Calling the createDelegate() method does not pass any additional parameters to the event handler. However, it changes the meaning of this in the handler. Normally, if you use this in an event handler, it refers to the DOM element that raised the event. The createDelegate() method enables you to change this to refer to anything you like.

The difference between createCallback() and createDelegate() is illustrated by the page in Listing 33.14 (see Figure 33.9). The page contains four buttons, named btnHandler, btnCallback, btnDelegate, and btnHandlers. The page also contains four event handlers, named doSomething1(), doSomething2(), doSomething3(), and doSomething4(). Different parameters are passed to the different event handlers, depending on how the handlers are wired up to the buttons.

FIGURE 33.9   Executing a callback handler.

LISTING 33.14   ShowDelegates.aspx

```
<%@ Page Language="C#" %>
<!DOCTYPE html PUBLIC "-//W3C//DTD XHTML 1.0 Transitional//EN"
 "http://www.w3.org/TR/xhtml1/DTD/xhtml1-transitional.dtd">
<html xmlns="http://www.w3.org/1999/xhtml">
<head runat="server">
    <title>Show Delegates and Callbacks</title>
    <script type="text/javascript">

      function pageLoad()
      {
        // Use $addHandler
        $addHandler($get("btnHandler"), "click", doSomething);

        // Use createCallback
        var callback = Function.createCallback(doSomething2, "apple");
        $addHandler($get("btnCallback"), "click", callback);

        // Use createDelegate
        var delegate = Function.createDelegate("apple", doSomething3);
        $addHandler($get("btnDelegate"), "click", delegate);

        // Use $addHandlers
        $addHandlers($get("btnHandlers"), {click: doSomething4}, "apple");
      }

      function doSomething(event)
      {
        alert( [this.id, event.type] );
      }
```

```
        function doSomething2(event, context)
        {
          alert( [this.id, event.type, context] );
        }

        function doSomething3(event)
        {
          alert( [this, event.type] );
        }

        function doSomething4(event)
        {
          alert( [this, event.type] );
        }

    </script>
</head>
<body>
    <form id="form1" runat="server">
    <asp:ScriptManager ID="ScriptManager1" runat="server" />

    <input id="btnHandler" type="button" value="Handler" />
    <input id="btnCallback" type="button" value="Callback" />
    <input id="btnDelegate" type="button" value="Delegate" />
    <input id="btnHandlers" type="button" value="Handlers" />

    </form>
</body>
</html>
```

If you click either of the first two buttons, then *this* refers to the button clicked. If you click either of the second two buttons, then *this* refers to the string "apple" since "apple" was passed to the createDelegate() method and the $addHandlers() shortcut.

Notice that the $addHandlers() shortcut, when you pass a final argument that represents the context, does the same thing as calling the createDelegate() method. The advantage of $addHandlers() is that you can use this shortcut to wire up multiple methods to events at a time.

In real-world scenarios, you won't change this to refer to a string; you'll change this to refer to the client-side control or behavior associated with the event handler. Within an event handler, you'll want to refer to the properties and methods of the client-side control or behavior associated with the event.

Debug and Release AJAX Libraries

Two versions of the MicrosoftAjax.js file contain the AJAX Library: the release version and the debug version. The release version of the library is minimized to its smallest possible size. All inessential code and comments have been stripped.

The debug version, on the other hand, is quite readable. It contains comments on each of the methods. Furthermore, the debug version contains additional code intended to inform you when you are misusing a method. When you call a method using the release version of the library, all the parameters passed to the method are validated (the type and number of parameters are validated).

You will want to use the release version of the AJAX Library for a production application and the debug version only while actively developing an application. The easiest way to switch between the release and debug versions of the script is to switch between debug and release mode in the web configuration file. The same setting you use to control whether server-side code is compiled in debug or release mode controls whether the debug or release version of the AJAX Library is served.

To switch to debug mode, find or add the compilation element in the `system.web` section of the web.config file and assign the value `true` to its `debug` attribute, like this:

```
<compilation debug="true">
```

Alternatively, you can control whether the debug or release version of the AJAX Library is used by modifying the `ScriptMode` property of the ScriptManager control. This property has the following four possible values:

- **Auto**—This is the default value. Use the compilation setting from the Web.config file.
- **Debug**—Use debug scripts.
- **Inherit**—Same as `Auto`.
- **Release**—Use release scripts.

Declaring a ScriptManager control in a page like this forces the debug version of the AJAX Library to be used:

```
<asp:ScriptManager ID="ScriptManager1" ScriptMode="Debug" runat="server" />
```

Debugging Microsoft AJAX Applications

The last topic we need to examine in this section is debugging. There are two ways that you can debug a client-side ASP.NET AJAX application: You can display trace messages, and you can use the Visual Web Developer debugger.

The Microsoft AJAX Library includes a Sys.Debug class. You can use this class to output trace messages and break into the Visual Web Developer debugger. The Sys.Debug class supports the following methods:

- **assert**—Enables you to evaluate a JavaScript expression. If the expression returns false, a message is displayed in the debugger and the trace console and you are prompted to break into the debugger.

- **clearTrace**—Enables you to clear all messages from the trace console.

- **fail**—Enables you to display a message in the debugger and the trace console and break into the debugger.

- **trace**—Enables you to output a message to the debugger and trace console.

- **traceDump**—Enables you to dump all properties of an object to the debugger and trace console.

These methods output trace messages to two different consoles. The debugger console is the Visual Web Developer debugger console that appears when you execute an application in debug mode. Right-click a page in the Solution Explorer window and select the menu option Set as Start Page. Select the menu option Debug, Start Debugging (F5), and the messages will appear in the debugger console Output window (see Figure 33.10).

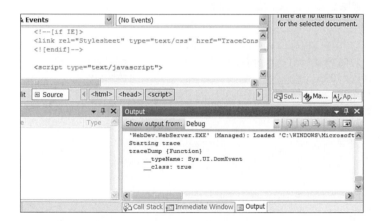

FIGURE 33.10   Viewing trace messages in the console's Output window.

The trace console works in different ways, depending on whether you are using Microsoft Internet Explorer or Mozilla Firefox. If you are using Firefox and you have the Firebug extension installed, trace messages sent to the trace console appear in the Firebug console (see Figure 33.11).

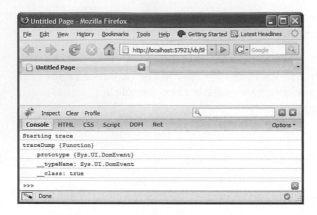

FIGURE 33.11   Viewing trace output in the Firebug console.

If you are using Internet Explorer and you want to view messages sent to the trace console, you need to add a <textarea> element to your page with the ID TraceConsole. All trace messages will be sent to this text area.

The page in Listing 33.15 demonstrates how to use the trace() and traceDump() methods.

LISTING 33.15   ShowDebug.aspx

```
<%@ Page Language="C#" %>
<!DOCTYPE html PUBLIC "-//W3C//DTD XHTML 1.0 Transitional//EN"
 "http://www.w3.org/TR/xhtml1/DTD/xhtml1-transitional.dtd">
<html xmlns="http://www.w3.org/1999/xhtml">
<head runat="server">
    <title>Untitled Page</title>
    <style type="text/css">
        #TraceConsole
        {
            display:none;
        }
    </style>
    <!—[if IE]>
    <link rel="Stylesheet" type="text/css" href="TraceConsole.css" />
    <![endif]—>

    <script type="text/javascript">

      function pageLoad()
      {
        Sys.Debug.trace("Starting trace");
        Sys.Debug.traceDump( Sys.UI.DomEvent );
      }
```

```
        </script>
    </head>
    <body>
        <form id="form1" runat="server">
        <div>
            <asp:ScriptManager ID="ScriptManager1" runat="server" />

            <textarea id="TraceConsole"></textarea>
        </div>
        </form>
    </body>
</html>
```

The page in Listing 33.15 hides the TraceConsole `<textarea>` by default. However, it includes an Internet Explorer conditional comment. If you are using Internet Explorer, an external style sheet named TraceConsole is loaded. This style sheet displays the `<textarea>` and gives the console a fixed position at the bottom of the page (so that the Internet Explorer trace console will kind of look like the Firebug console, as shown in Figure 33.12).

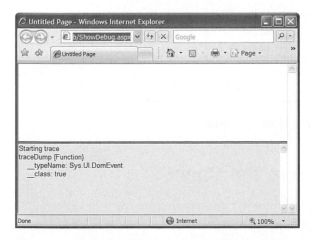

FIGURE 33.12   Viewing trace messages in a fake Internet Explorer console.

You can also use the Visual Web Developer debugger when debugging ASP.NET AJAX applications. You can use the debugger to set breakpoints and step through your JavaScript code, line by line, just like you do for your C# code. You can set breakpoints both on a page and in external JavaScript files.

In order for debugging to work, you need to set two properties of Internet Explorer. Select the menu option Tools, Internet Options and then select the Advanced Tab. Make sure the option Disable Script Debugging (Internet Explorer) and the option Disable Script Debugging (Other) are both unchecked.

You can use either the `Sys.Debug.assert()` method or the `Sys.Debug.fail()` method to break into the debugger while running your JavaScript code. Alternatively, you can set breakpoints by double-clicking in the left-hand gutter of the main window in Source view (see Figure 33.13).

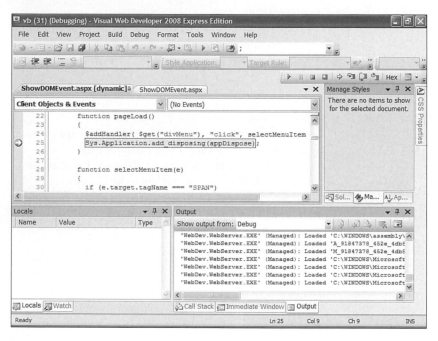

FIGURE 33.13   Setting breakpoints in Visual Web Developer.

Calling Web Services from the Client

The heart of Ajax is the ability to send and retrieve information from the web server without needing to post a page back to the web server. Ajax is all about performing "sneaky" postbacks.

The vision behind a pure Ajax application is that it should consist of a single page. All updates to the single page after it has been loaded should be performed by calling web services. You should never need to perform a postback because any postback results in a bad user experience (the page jumps and the universe freezes).

The ASP.NET AJAX Library provides support for calling web services directly from the client (the web browser). In this section, you learn two methods of exposing a web method to an AJAX page. You learn how to call a web method from a separate web service, and you learn how to call a web method exposed by the page itself. Finally, we examine three specialized web services exposed by the ASP.NET AJAX Framework: the Authentication service, the Role service, and the Profile service.

Calling an External Web Service

Let's start simple. We'll create a Quotation web service that randomly returns a quotation from a list of quotations. Next, we'll create an AJAX page that contains a button. When you click the button, a random quotation will be displayed in a <span> tag (see Figure 33.14).

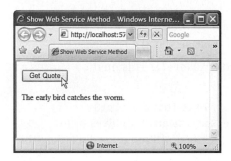

FIGURE 33.14   Retrieving a random quotation from the server.

The first step is to create the web service. The web service is contained in Listing 33.16.

LISTING 33.16   QuotationService.asmx

```
<%@ WebService Language="C#" Class="QuotationService" %>

using System;
using System.Web;
using System.Web.Services;
using System.Web.Services.Protocols;
using System.Web.Script.Services;
using System.Collections.Generic;

[WebService(Namespace = "http://tempuri.org/")]
[WebServiceBinding(ConformsTo = WsiProfiles.BasicProfile1_1)]
[ScriptService]
public class QuotationService  : System.Web.Services.WebService
{

    [WebMethod]
    public string GetQuote()
    {
        List<string> quotes = new List<string>();
        quotes.Add("The fool who is silent passes for wise.");
```

LISTING 33.16   Continued

```
        quotes.Add("The early bird catches the worm.");
        quotes.Add("If wishes were true, shepherds would be kings.");
        Random rnd = new Random();
        return quotes[rnd.Next(quotes.Count)];
    }


}
```

You create the file in Listing 33.16 by selecting the menu option Website, Add New Item and choosing the Web Service item.

The web service contains a single web method named GetQuote(). This method returns a single quotation from a list of quotations as a string.

There is only one thing special about this web service. Notice that a ScriptService attribute is applied to the web service class (the ScriptService attribute lives in the System.Web.Script.Services namespace). You must add this attribute in order to call the web service from an AJAX page.

Now that we have created the web service, we can call it from an AJAX page. The page in Listing 33.17 calls the web service in order to display a random quotation.

LISTING 33.17   ShowWebServiceMethod.aspx

```
<%@ Page Language="C#" %>
<!DOCTYPE html PUBLIC "-//W3C//DTD XHTML 1.0 Transitional//EN"
  "http://www.w3.org/TR/xhtml1/DTD/xhtml1-transitional.dtd">
<html xmlns="http://www.w3.org/1999/xhtml">
<head runat="server">
    <title>Show Web Service Method</title>
    <script type="text/javascript">

      function pageLoad()
      {
        $addHandler( $get("btnGet"), "click", getQuote );
      }

      function getQuote()
      {
        QuotationService.GetQuote(getQuoteSuccess, getQuoteFail);
      }

      function getQuoteSuccess(result)
      {
        $get("spanQuote").innerHTML = result;
      }
```

```
        function getQuoteFail(error)
        {
          alert(error.get_message());
        }

    </script>
</head>
<body>
    <form id="form1" runat="server">
    <div>
        <asp:ScriptManager ID="ScriptManager1" runat="server">
        <Services>
            <asp:ServiceReference
                InlineScript="true"
                Path="~/Services/QuotationService.asmx" />
        </Services>
        </asp:ScriptManager>

        <input id="btnGet" type="button" value="Get Quote" />
        <br /><br />
        <span id="spanQuote"></span>

    </div>
    </form>
</body>
</html>
```

You should note several things in this page. To begin, notice that the ScriptManager control contains a `<Services>` element that includes a reference to the QuotationService web service. Adding this reference causes a proxy class for the QuotationService web service to be generated automatically.

The ScriptReference control has two properties: `Path` and `InlineScript`. You use the `Path` property to provide the path to the web service. The `InlineScript` property accepts the value `true` or `false`. When the value is `true`, the web service proxy is added inline to the page. When the value is `false`, a separate request must be made to grab the proxy class from the server (the browser can cache the proxy and use it for multiple pages). If you plan to use the web service in only one page, you should assign the value `true` to `InlineScript`. If you plan to use the web service in multiple pages, you should assign the value `false`.

WARNING

You can only call web services located in the same domain as the AJAX page. You can't call a web service located in another domain.

In the `pageLoad()` method, a button is wired up to the `getQuote()` method. When you click the button, the `getQuote()` method executes and calls the remote web service. The web service is called with the following line of code:

```
QuotationService.GetQuote(getQuoteSuccess, getQuoteFail);
```

The `QuotationService` class is the proxy class that is generated automatically by the ServiceReference included the ScriptManager control. The proxy class includes a method that corresponds to each of the remote web methods exposed by the web service. In this case, the `getQuote()` method is called.

When you call a web method, you can pass a reference to both a success and a fail method. If the web method call is successful, the success method is called. Otherwise, the fail method is called.

In Listing 33.17, if the `getQuote()` method is successful, the quotation is displayed in a `<span>` tag in the body of the page. This is accomplished with the `getQuoteSuccess()` method:

```
function getQuoteSuccess(result)
{
   $get("spanQuote").innerHTML = result;
}
```

The parameter passed to `getQuoteSuccess()` method represents whatever was returned by the web service. In this case, the result is a string that represents the quotation.

If the call to the web service fails, the following `getQuoteFailure()` method is called:

```
function getQuoteFail(error)
{
   alert(error.get_message());
}
```

This method simply displays an alert with the error message. The `error` parameter is an instance of the `Sys.Net.WebServiceError` class. This class supports the following properties:

- ▶ **exceptionType**—Returns a string representation of the exception type.
- ▶ **message**—Returns the error message from the server.
- ▶ **stackTrace**—Returns the stack trace from the server.
- ▶ **statusCode**—Returns an HTTP status code (for example, 500 for an Internal Server Error).
- ▶ **timedOut**—Returns `true` if the call to the web service timed out.

Calling a Static Page Method

If you are not planning to call a web method from multiple pages, there is no reason to perform all the work of creating a separate web service. Instead, you can expose a static method from the same AJAX page that is calling the web method.

For example, the page in Listing 33.18 includes a server method named GetQuote(). The server GetQuote() method is called by a client method named GetQuote().

LISTING 33.18   ShowPageMethod.aspx

```
<%@ Page Language="C#" %>
<%@ Import Namespace="System.Collections.Generic" %>
<!DOCTYPE html PUBLIC "-//W3C//DTD XHTML 1.0 Transitional//EN"
 "http://www.w3.org/TR/xhtml1/DTD/xhtml1-transitional.dtd">
<script runat="server">

    [System.Web.Services.WebMethod]
    public static string GetQuote()
    {
        List<string> quotes = new List<string>();
        quotes.Add("The fool who is silent passes for wise.");
        quotes.Add("The early bird catches the worm.");
        quotes.Add("If wishes were true, shepherds would be kings.");
        Random rnd = new Random();
        return quotes[rnd.Next(quotes.Count)];
    }

</script>
<html xmlns="http://www.w3.org/1999/xhtml">
<head runat="server">
    <title>Show Page Method</title>
    <script type="text/javascript">

      function pageLoad()
      {
        $addHandler( $get("btnGet"), "click", getQuote );
      }

      function getQuote()
      {
       PageMethods.GetQuote(getQuoteSuccess, getQuoteFail);
      }

      function getQuoteSuccess(result)
      {
```

LISTING 33.18   Continued

```
        $get("spanQuote").innerHTML = result;
      }

      function getQuoteFail(error)
      {
        alert(error.get_message());
      }
    </script>
</head>
<body>
    <form id="form1" runat="server">
    <asp:ScriptManager
        ID="ScriptManager1"
        EnablePageMethods="true"
        runat="server" />

    <input id="btnGet" type="button" value="Get Quote" />
    <br /><br />
    <span id="spanQuote"></span>
    </form>
</body>
</html>
```

You must do one special thing before you can expose web methods from a page. You must assign the value true to the ScriptManager control's EnablePageMethods property.

In Listing 33.18, the server GetQuote() method is called with the following line of code:

```
PageMethods.GetQuote(getQuoteSuccess, getQuoteFail);
```

Just like in the previous section, when you call a page method, you can supply both a success and failure handler.

You might be wondering where the PageMethods class comes from. This class is generated in the page automatically when you expose a page method. The class will always be called PageMethods. The class will contain a proxy client method that corresponds to each server page method.

Editing Movies with AJAX

In this section, I want to present you with a more complicated (and realistic) example of calling server web methods from the client. In this section, we create a page that can be used to edit the Movie database table. The page enables you to add new movies to the database and display all the existing movies (see Figure 33.15). Both operations are performed through AJAX calls so that a postback is never necessary.

FIGURE 33.15   Displaying and inserting database records with AJAX.

The EditMovies.aspx page is contained in Listing 33.19.

LISTING 33.19   EditMovies.aspx

```
<%@ Page Language="C#" %>
<!DOCTYPE html PUBLIC "-//W3C//DTD XHTML 1.0 Transitional//EN"
 "http://www.w3.org/TR/xhtml1/DTD/xhtml1-transitional.dtd">
<html xmlns="http://www.w3.org/1999/xhtml">
<head runat="server">
    <title>Edit Movies</title>
    <script type="text/javascript">

      function pageLoad()
      {
        $addHandler($get("btnAdd"), "click", addMovie);
        bindMovies();
      }

      function bindMovies()
      {
        MovieService.SelectAll(selectAllSuccess);
      }

      function addMovie()
      {
        var movieToAdd =
```

LISTING 33.19   Continued

```
                {
                    Title: $get("txtTitle").value,
                    Director: $get("txtDirector").value
                };

            MovieService.Insert(movieToAdd, addMovieSuccess);
        }

        function addMovieSuccess()
        {
            bindMovies();
        }

        function selectAllSuccess(results)
        {
            var sb = new Sys.StringBuilder()
            var movie;
            var row;
            for (var i=0;i < results.length; i++)
            {
                movie = results[i];
                row = String.format("{0} directed by {1}<br />",
                        movie.Title, movie.Director);
                sb.appendLine(row);
            }
            $get("divMovies").innerHTML = sb.toString();
        }
    </script>
</head>
<body>
<form runat="server">
<asp:ScriptManager ID="ScriptManager1" runat="server">
<Services>
    <asp:ServiceReference
        InlineScript="true"
        Path="~/Services/MovieService.asmx" />
</Services>
</asp:ScriptManager>

<fieldset>
<legend>Add Movie</legend>

<label for="txtTitle">Title:</label>
<input id="txtTitle" />
```

```
<br /><br />

<label for="txtTitle">Director:</label>
<input id="txtDirector" />

<br /><br />

<input id="btnAdd" type="button" value="Add Movie" />

</fieldset>

<div id="divMovies"></div>

</form>
</body>
</html>
```

The page in Listing 33.19 calls an external web service named MovieService. The two web methods from MovieService are SelectAll() and Insert(). The SelectAll() method is called to get the current list of movies. This method is called when the page first loads and it is called after a new movie is inserted. The list of movies is displayed in a <div> element with the following code:

```
function selectAllSuccess(results)
{
  var sb = new Sys.StringBuilder()
  var movie;
  var row;
  for (var i=0;i < results.length; i++)
  {
      movie = results[i];
      row = String.format("{0} directed by {1}<br />",
         movie.Title, movie.Director);
      sb.appendLine(row);
  }
  $get("divMovies").innerHTML = sb.toString();
}
```

This code iterates through the list of Movie objects returned by the web service. A single string that represents all the movies is built with a StringBuilder object. Finally, the contents of the StringBuilder are displayed in a <div> tag.

The Insert() web method is called to add a new movie to the database. The body of the page contains a simple form for gathering the movie title and director. When you click the Add Movie button, the following method is called:

```
function addMovie()
{
  var movieToAdd =
      {
          Title: $get("txtTitle").value,
          Director: $get("txtDirector").value
      };

    MovieService.Insert(movieToAdd, addMovieSuccess);
}
```

The addMovie() method creates a new Movie object named movieToAdd. The movieToAdd
object represents the values that the user entered into the <input> elements of txtTitle
and txtDirector. Finally, the movieToAdd object is passed to the Insert() method
exposed by the MovieService web service proxy.

The MovieService web service used by the page is contained in Listing 33.20.

LISTING 33.20   MovieService.asmx

```
<%@ WebService Language="C#" Class="MovieService" %>

using System;
using System.Web;
using System.Web.Services;
using System.Web.Services.Protocols;
using System.Collections.Generic;
using System.Linq;
using System.Data.Linq;
using System.Web.Script.Services;

[WebService(Namespace = "http://tempuri.org/")]
[WebServiceBinding(ConformsTo = WsiProfiles.BasicProfile1_1)]
[ScriptService]
public class MovieService   : System.Web.Services.WebService
{
    [WebMethod]
    public List<Movie> SelectAll()
    {
        MyDatabaseDataContext db = new MyDatabaseDataContext();
        return db.Movies.ToList();
    }

    [WebMethod]
    public int Insert(Movie movieToAdd)
    {
```

```
            MyDatabaseDataContext db = new MyDatabaseDataContext();
            db.Movies.InsertOnSubmit(movieToAdd);
            db.SubmitChanges();
            return movieToAdd.Id;
        }

}
```

Notice that you can pass objects back and forth between an AJAX page and a web service. The AJAX page passes a `Movie` object to the web service's `Insert()` method. The web service's `SelectAll()` method returns a collection of `Movie` objects. These objects are seamlessly passed back and forth between the client world and the server world.

Using the Authentication Service

The Microsoft AJAX Library includes three built-in web services. In this section, we examine the first of these built-in web services: the Authentication service.

The Authentication service works with ASP.NET Form authentication. You can use it with the ASP.NET membership framework to authenticate users using one of the ASP.NET membership providers. The two providers included with the ASP.NET framework are SqlMembershipProvider (authenticates users against a database of usernames and passwords) and ActiveDirectoryMembershipProvider (authenticates users against the Active Directory).

Before you can use the Authentication service, you need to make two configuration changes to your web configuration file. First, you need to enable Forms authentication (the default form of authentication is Windows). Find the `<authentication>` element in the `<system.web>` section and modify it to look like this:

```
<authentication mode="Forms"/>
```

Second, you need to enable the Authentication service because it is disabled by default. If your web configuration file does not already contain a `<system.web.extensions>` element, you will need to add one. Add it outside of the `<system.web>` section. The `<system.web.extensions>` element must contain an `<authenticationService>` element that looks like this:

```
<system.web.extensions>
    <scripting>
        <webServices>
            <authenticationService enabled="true"/>
        </webServices>
    </scripting>
</system.web.extensions>
```

33

> **NOTE**
>
> The <authenticationService> element includes a requireSSL attribute in case you want to require an encrypted connection when logging in to the server.

Finally, if you want to create one or more users, you can use the Website Administration Tool. Select the menu option Website, ASP.NET Configuration and then select the Security tab. Click the Create User link to create a new user.

> **NOTE**
>
> To learn more about the ASP.NET membership providers, see Chapter 23, "Using ASP.NET Membership."

The page in Listing 33.21 demonstrates how you can call the Authentication service from an AJAX page. The page contains a login form that you can use to authenticate against the SqlMembershipProvider. If you log in successfully, you get to see the secret message (see Figure 33.16).

FIGURE 33.16   Authenticating and seeing the secret message.

> **NOTE**
>
> If you want to try the ShowLogin.aspx page on the CD, a valid username and password are Steve and secret#, respectively.

LISTING 33.21   ShowLogin.aspx

```
<%@ Page Language="C#" %>
<!DOCTYPE html PUBLIC "-//W3C//DTD XHTML 1.0 Transitional//EN"
 "http://www.w3.org/TR/xhtml1/DTD/xhtml1-transitional.dtd">
```

```
<script runat="server">

    [System.Web.Services.WebMethod]
    public static string GetSecretMessage()
    {
        return "Time is a fish";
    }

</script>
<html xmlns="http://www.w3.org/1999/xhtml">
<head runat="server">
    <title>Show Login</title>
    <script type="text/javascript">

      function pageLoad()
      {
        $addHandler( $get("btnLogin"), "click", login);
      }

      function login()
      {
        Sys.Services.AuthenticationService.login
            (
                $get("txtUserName").value,
                $get("txtPassword").value,
                false,
                null,
                null,
                loginSuccess,
                loginFail
            );
      }

      function loginSuccess(isAuthenticated)
      {
        if (isAuthenticated)
            PageMethods.GetSecretMessage(getSecretMessageSuccess);
        else
            alert( "Log in failed" );
      }

      function loginFail()
      {
            alert( "Log in failed" );
      }
```

LISTING 33.21   Continued

```
        function getSecretMessageSuccess(message)
        {
          $get("spanMessage").innerHTML = message;
        }


    </script>
</head>
<body>
    <form id="form1" runat="server">
    <asp:ScriptManager
        ID="ScriptManager1"
        EnablePageMethods="true"
        runat="server" />

    <fieldset>
    <legend>Login</legend>

        <label for="txtUserName">User Name:</label>
        <input id="txtUserName" />

        <br /><br />

        <label for="txtUserName">Password:</label>
        <input id="txtPassword" type="password" />

        <br /><br />
        <input id="btnLogin" type="button" value="Login" />

    </fieldset>

    The secret message is:
    <span id="spanMessage"></span>

    </form>
</body>
</html>
```

The page in Listing 33.21 contains a simple Login form. When you click the Login button, the login() method executes and calls the following method:

```
Sys.Services.AuthenticationService.login
    (
```

```
            $get("txtUserName").value,
            $get("txtPassword").value,
            false,
            null,
            null,
            loginSuccess,
            loginFail
        );
```

The `AuthenticationService.login()` method accepts the following parameters:

- ▶ **userName**—The username to authenticate.

- ▶ **password**—The password to authenticate.

- ▶ **isPersistent**—Determines whether a session or persistent cookie is created after successful authentication.

- ▶ **customInfo**—Not used.

- ▶ **redirectUrl**—The page to which the user is redirected after successful authentication.

- ▶ **loginCompletedCallback**—The method to call when the web service call completes.

- ▶ **failedCallback**—The method to call when the web service call fails.

- ▶ **userContext**—Additional information to pass to the `loginCompletedCallback` or `failedCallback` method.

If the web service call to the Authentication service is successful, the following method is called:

```
function loginSuccess(isAuthenticated)
{
  if (isAuthenticated)
      PageMethods.GetSecretMessage(getSecretMessageSuccess);
  else
      alert( "Log in failed" );
}
```

It is important to understand that this method is called both when the user is successfully authenticated and when the user is not successfully authenticated. This method is called when the Authentication web service call is successful.

The first parameter passed to the method represents whether or not the user is successfully authenticated. If the user is authenticated, the secret message is grabbed from the server and displayed in a <span> element in the body of the page. Otherwise, a JavaScript alert is displayed that informs the user that the login was a failure.

> **WARNING**
>
> Don't ever put secret information in your JavaScript code. Anyone can always view all your JavaScript code. If you have secret information that you only want authenticated users to view, don't retrieve the information from the server until the user is authenticated successfully.

Notice that we were not required to create the Authentication web service. The Authentication web service is built in to the AJAX framework.

Using the Role Service

The second of the built-in application services included with ASP.NET AJAX is the Role service. This service enables you to retrieve the list of roles associated with the current user.

For example, you might want to display different content and provide different functionality to different users depending on their roles. A member of the Administrators role can edit a record, but a member of the Public role can only view a record.

To use the Role service, you need to make two configuration changes to your web configuration file. First, you need to enable the Role service. You can enable the Role service by adding the following <roleService> element to the <system.web.extensions> section of your web.config file:

```
<system.web.extensions>
    <scripting>
        <webServices>
            <authenticationService enabled="true"/>
            <roleService enabled="true"/>
        </webServices>
    </scripting>
</system.web.extensions>
```

Second, you need to enable ASP.NET roles. You enable roles by adding the following element to the <system.web> section of your web configuration file:

```
<roleManager enabled="true" />
```

After you make these configuration changes, roles are enabled for both the server and the client. You can create new roles, as well as associate the roles with users, by using the Website Administration Tool. Select the menu option Website, ASP.NET Configuration and then select the Security tab. Click the Create or Manage Roles link to create a new role and associate it with a user.

Now that we have everything configured, we can create an AJAX page that takes advantage of the Role service. The page in Listing 33.22 displays whether or not a user is a member of the Painters and Plumbers roles.

LISTING 33.22   ShowRoles.aspx

```
<%@ Page Language="C#" %>
<!DOCTYPE html PUBLIC "-//W3C//DTD XHTML 1.0 Transitional//EN"
 "http://www.w3.org/TR/xhtml1/DTD/xhtml1-transitional.dtd">
<html xmlns="http://www.w3.org/1999/xhtml">
<head runat="server">
    <title>Show Roles</title>
    <script type="text/javascript">

    function pageLoad()
    {
      Sys.Services.AuthenticationService.login
          (
              "Steve",
              "secret#",
              false,
              null,
              null,
              loginSuccess
          );
    }

    function loginSuccess(isAuthenticated)
    {
      if (isAuthenticated)
          loadRoles();
      else
          alert("Log in failed!");
    }

    function loadRoles()
    {
      Sys.Services.RoleService.load(loadRolesSuccess, loadRolesFail);
    }

    function loadRolesSuccess()
    {
      var isPlumber = Sys.Services.RoleService.isUserInRole("Plumber");
      $get("spanPlumber").innerHTML = isPlumber;

      var isPainter = Sys.Services.RoleService.isUserInRole("Painter");
      $get("spanPainter").innerHTML = isPainter;
    }

    function loadRolesFail(error)
```

LISTING 33.22   Continued

```
        {
            alert("Could not load roles!");
        }

    </script>
</head>
<body>
    <form id="form1" runat="server">
    <div>
        <asp:ScriptManager ID="ScriptManager1" runat="server" />

        Is Plumber: <span id="spanPlumber"></span>

        <br /><br />

        Is Painter: <span id="spanPainter"></span>

    </div>
    </form>
</body>
</html>
```

In the pageLoad() method in Listing 33.22, the Authentication service is called to authenticate a user named Steve. When the Authentication web service call completes, and the user is authenticated successfully, the following loadRoles() method is called:

```
function loadRoles()
{
  Sys.Services.RoleService.load(loadRolesSuccess, loadRolesFail);
}
```

The RoleService.load() method loads all the roles for the current user. The method accepts two parameters: the method to call if the web service call is successful, and the method to call if the web service call fails.

If the RoleService.load() method completes successfully, the following method is called:

```
function loadRolesSuccess()
{
  var isPlumber = Sys.Services.RoleService.isUserInRole("Plumber");
  $get("spanPlumber").innerHTML = isPlumber;

  var isPainter = Sys.Services.RoleService.isUserInRole("Painter");
  $get("spanPainter").innerHTML = isPainter;
}
```

This method uses the `RoleService.isUserInRole()` method to detect whether the current user is a member of the Plumber and Painter roles. This information is displayed in two `<span>` tags contained in the body of the page (see Figure 33.17).

FIGURE 33.17   Displaying a user's roles.

The `RoleService` class also includes a `roles` property. You can call `Sys.Services.RoleService.get_roles()` to get a list of all roles associated with the current user.

Using the Profile Service

The final built-in application service we need to discuss is the Profile service. The Profile service enables you to store information associated with a user across multiple visits to a web application. You can use the Profile service to store any type of information you need. For example, you can use the Profile service to store a user shopping cart.

> **NOTE**
>
> We discussed the ASP.NET `Profile` object in Chapter 24, "Maintaining Application State."

Before you use the Profile service, you must enable it for both the server and the client. On the server side, you need to enable and define the profile. The following `<profile>` element, which you should add to the `<system.web>` section of the web.config file, enables the `Profile` object and defines two properties named `pageViews` and `backgroundColor`:

```
<anonymousIdentification enabled="true"/>
<profile enabled="true">
<properties>
```

```
        <add
            name="pageViews"
            type="Int32"
            defaultValue="0"
            allowAnonymous="true" />
        <add
            name="backgroundColor"
            defaultValue="yellow"
            allowAnonymous="true" />
</properties>
</profile>
```

Notice the <anonymousIdentification> element. This element causes anonymous users to be tracked by a cookie. If you don't include the <anonymousIdentification> element, only authenticated users can modify profile properties. Both the pageViews and backgroundColor properties include an allowAnonymous="true" property so that anonymous users can modify these properties.

If you want to restrict the profile to authenticated users, remove the <anonymousIdentification> element. In that case, you will need to use the Authentication service to authenticate a user before you modify the user's profile properties.

You must perform an additional configuration step on the server to enable an AJAX page to access a user profile. You must add a <profileService> element to the <system.web.extensions> section of the web configuration file, like this:

```
<system.web.extensions>
    <scripting>
        <webServices>
            <profileService
                enabled="true"
                readAccessProperties="pageViews,backgroundColor"
                writeAccessProperties="pageViews" />
        </webServices>
    </scripting>
</system.web.extensions>
```

You must enable the Profile service before you can use it. It is disabled by default.

Notice that the <profileService> element includes both a readAccessProperties and a writeAccessProperties attribute. These attributes are used to expose a comma-separated list of Profile properties that can be read and written from the client. You can read the backgroundColor profile property, but you cannot modify it. The pageViews property, on the other hand, can be read and modified.

Now that we have the profile configured on the server, we can use it in an AJAX page. The page in Listing 33.23 keeps count of the number of times a particular user has requested the page. Each time a user requests the page, the count increments by one and the total count is displayed in the body of the page (see Figure 33.18).

FIGURE 33.18   Updating page views with the Profile service.

Furthermore, the page in Listing 33.23 is displayed using the background color defined in the profile. If you modify the profile background color, the page background color is also modified.

LISTING 33.23   ShowProfile.aspx

```
<%@ Page Language="C#" %>
<!DOCTYPE html PUBLIC "-//W3C//DTD XHTML 1.0 Transitional//EN"
 "http://www.w3.org/TR/xhtml1/DTD/xhtml1-transitional.dtd">
<html id="html1" xmlns="http://www.w3.org/1999/xhtml">
<head runat="server">
    <title>Show Profile</title>
    <script type="text/javascript">

    function pageLoad()
    {
      // Increment page views
      Sys.Services.ProfileService.properties.pageViews ++;

      // Save profile
      Sys.Services.ProfileService.save(["pageViews"], saveSuccess);

      // Show page views
      $get("spanPageViews").innerHTML =
         Sys.Services.ProfileService.properties.pageViews;

      // Change background color
      var backgroundColor = Sys.Services.ProfileService.properties
      ➥["backgroundColor"];
      $get("html1").style.backgroundColor = backgroundColor;
    }

    function saveSuccess(countOfPropertiesSaved)
    {
      Sys.Debug.trace("Profile properties saved: " + countOfPropertiesSaved);
```

LISTING 33.23   Continued

```
        }

    </script>
</head>
<body>
    <form id="form1" runat="server">
    <div>
        <asp:ScriptManager ID="ScriptManager1" runat="server">
            <ProfileService
                LoadProperties="pageViews,backgroundColor" />
        </asp:ScriptManager>

        Your total page views:
        <span id="spanPageViews"></span>
    </div>
    </form>
</body>
</html>
```

The page in Listing 33.23 loads the current user's profile properties when the page first loads. Notice that the ScriptManager control includes a <ProfileService> sub-element. The <ProfileService> sub-element includes a LoadProperties attribute that contains a comma-separated list of profile properties to load when the page loads.

> **NOTE**
>
> If you want to load profile properties after a page loads, you can use the Sys.Services. ProfileService.load() method to load them through a web service call.

The pageLoad method increments the total page views with the following line of code:

```
Sys.Services.ProfileService.properties.pageViews ++;
```

Notice that you can access profile properties on the client just like you can on the server. Profile properties are automatically exposed through the Sys.Services. ProfileService.properties property. You even get Intellisense for the client-side profile properties.

After the pageViews profile property is modified, it is saved back to the server with the following line of code:

```
Sys.Services.ProfileService.save(["pageViews"], saveSuccess);
```

The first parameter to the ProfileService.save() method represents a JavaScript array of profile property names to save back to the server. The second parameter is a method that gets called when the web service call completes.

33

NOTE

As an alternative to supplying a list of property names to the `ProfileService.save()` method, you can pass the value `null`. When you pass the value `null`, all profile properties are saved.

The `saveSuccess()` method gets called when the profile properties are saved to the server. This method looks like this:

```
function saveSuccess(countOfPropertiesSaved)
{
  Sys.Debug.trace("Profile properties saved: " + countOfPropertiesSaved);
}
```

A count of the profile properties that got saved on the server successfully is passed to this method. The `saveSuccess()` method simply writes the count to the debug and trace console.

After updating the total page views, the `pageLoad` method displays the page views in a `<span>` element in the body of the page. Finally, the `pageLoad()` method changes the background color of the page to the value of the profile `backgroundColor` property.

Creating Custom AJAX Controls and Behaviors

In this final part of this chapter, you learn how to create custom AJAX controls and behaviors. AJAX controls and behaviors are some of the most exciting features of the Microsoft AJAX Framework. Unfortunately, they are also some of the features that are least developed.

In the following sections, you learn how to create custom AJAX controls and behaviors. You also learn how to launch AJAX controls and behaviors from server-side controls.

Creating AJAX Controls

In the Ajax world, an AJAX control is the equivalent of an ASP.NET control. However, whereas an ASP.NET control executes on the server and renders content to the browser, an AJAX control executes entirely in the browser. An AJAX control is built entirely from JavaScript and DOM elements.

WARNING

You can build an AJAX control that works with all major modern browsers, including Microsoft Internet Explorer, Mozilla Firefox, Opera, and Safari. However, browser compatibility is entirely up to you. The version of JavaScript supported by Firefox is different from the version of JavaScript supported by Internet Explorer. There are substantial differences in how the DOM is implemented in different browsers.

When using Visual Web Developer, you create an AJAX control by selecting the menu option Website, Add New Item and selecting the AJAX Client Control template. When you create a new control, you start with the control skeleton in Listing 33.24.

LISTING 33.24   ClientControl.js

```
/// <reference name="MicrosoftAjax.js"/>


Type.registerNamespace("myControls");


myControls.ClientControl = function(element)
{
    myControls.ClientControl.initializeBase(this, [element]);
}

myControls.ClientControl.prototype =
{
    initialize: function()
    {
        myControls.ClientControl.callBaseMethod(this, 'initialize');
        // Add custom initialization here
    },

    dispose: function()
    {
        //Add custom dispose actions here
        myControls.ClientControl.callBaseMethod(this, 'dispose');
    }
}
myControls.ClientControl.registerClass('myControls.ClientControl', Sys.UI.Control);

if (typeof(Sys) !== 'undefined') Sys.Application.notifyScriptLoaded();
```

Like the JavaScript classes we created earlier in this chapter, an AJAX control consists of a constructor function and a set of methods defined in the control's prototype.

If you look at the second-to-last line in the skeleton, you will notice that an AJAX control inherits from the base Sys.UI.Control class. For this reason, in the constructor function, it is important to call initializeBase() so that the base Sys.UI.Control class get initiated.

Notice that a parameter is passed to the constructor function (and to the initializeBase() method). This parameter represents the DOM element with which the AJAX control is associated. You can use the base Sys.UI.Control class's get_element() method to retrieve the DOM element within any of the control methods.

The control has two methods: `initialize()` and `dispose()`. You use the `initialize()` method to build up the control's DOM elements and wire up the control's event handlers. You use the `dispose()` method to unwire the event handlers to prevent memory leaks.

Let's go ahead and create a really simple AJAX control: a Glow control. When you hover your mouse over the control, its background color changes to yellow. The Glow control is contained in Listing 33.25.

LISTING 33.25   Glow.js

```
/// <reference name="MicrosoftAjax.js"/>


Type.registerNamespace("myControls");


myControls.Glow = function(element)
{
    myControls.Glow.initializeBase(this, [element]);

    // initialize fields
    this._text = "Glow Control";
    this._backgroundColor = "yellow";
}

myControls.Glow.prototype =
{
    initialize: function()
    {
        myControls.Glow.callBaseMethod(this, 'initialize');

        // Wire-up delegates to element events
        $addHandlers
            (
                this.get_element(),
                {
                    mouseover: this._onMouseOver,
                    mouseout: this._onMouseOut
                },
                this
            );
    },

    dispose: function()
    {
        // Unwire delegates
        $clearHandlers(this.get_element());
        myControls.Glow.callBaseMethod(this, 'dispose');
```

LISTING 33.25   Continued

```
    },

    _onMouseOver: function()
    {
        this.get_element().style.backgroundColor = this._backgroundColor;
    },

    _onMouseOut: function()
    {
        this.get_element().style.backgroundColor = "";
    },

    get_text: function()
    {
        return this._text;
    },

    set_text: function(value)
    {
        this._text = value;
        this.get_element().innerHTML = value;
    },

    get_backgroundColor: function()
    {
        return this._backgroundColor;
    },

    set_backgroundColor: function(value)
    {
        this._backgroundColor = value;
    }
}
myControls.Glow.registerClass('myControls.Glow', Sys.UI.Control);

if (typeof(Sys) !== 'undefined') Sys.Application.notifyScriptLoaded();
```

A single parameter is passed to the Glow control's constructor function. This parameter represents the DOM element to which the Glow control will be attached.

In the Glow control's constructor function, two private fields named _text and _backgroundColor are initialized with default values. If you don't modify the control's properties, the control contains the text "Glow Control" and changes its background color to yellow when you hover over it.

The control's prototype object contains an `initialize()` method that is used to set up the mouseover and mouseout event handlers for the control. The delegates are created and wired up to the mouseover and mouseout events with the following lines of code:

```
// Wire-up delegates to element events
$addHandlers
    (
        this.get_element(),
        {
            mouseover: this._onMouseOver,
            mouseout: this._onMouseOut
        },
        this
    );
```

If you hover your mouse over the DOM element associated with the control, the `_onMouseOver()` method is called. If you move your mouse away from the control, the `_onMouseOut()` method is called.

Notice that a final context argument, `this`, is passed to the `$addHandlers()` shortcut. This final argument changes the meaning of `this` within the `_onMouseOver()` and `_onMouseOut()` methods. Normally, within these event handlers, `this` would refer to the DOM element that raised the mouseout or mouseover event. Passing a final context argument to the `$addhandlers()` shortcut changes the meaning of `this` to refer to the client control instead of the DOM element.

The `_onMouseOver()` event handler contains the following code:

```
_onMouseOver: function()
{
  this.get_element().style.backgroundColor = this._backgroundColor;
}
```

The `get_element()` method returns the DOM element associated with the control. The backgroundColor of the DOM element is changed to the value of the control's private `_backgroundColor` field.

The page in Listing 33.26 illustrates one way you can use the Glow control in an AJAX page.

LISTING 33.26   ShowGlowControl.aspx

```
<%@ Page Language="C#" %>
<!DOCTYPE html PUBLIC "-//W3C//DTD XHTML 1.0 Transitional//EN"
 "http://www.w3.org/TR/xhtml1/DTD/xhtml1-transitional.dtd">
<html xmlns="http://www.w3.org/1999/xhtml">
<head runat="server">
    <title>Show Glow Control</title>
    <script type="text/javascript">
```

33

LISTING 33.26   Continued

```
      function pageLoad()
      {
        $create
            (
                myControls.Glow,
                {text: "Hello", backgroundColor: "orange"},
                null,
                null,
                $get("div1")
            );
      }

    </script>
</head>
<body>
    <form id="form1" runat="server">
    <div>
        <asp:ScriptManager ID="ScriptManager1" runat="server">
        <Scripts>
            <asp:ScriptReference Path="~/Glow.js" />
        </Scripts>
        </asp:ScriptManager>

        <div id="div1"></div>

    </div>
    </form>
</body>
</html>
```

In Listing 33.26, the Glow control is created in the pageLoad() method with the following $create() shortcut:

```
$create
(
    myControls.Glow,
    {text: "Hello", backgroundColor: "orange"},
    null,
    null,
    $get("div1")
);
```

The $create() shortcut accepts the following parameters:

▶ **type**—The type of control or behavior to create.

▶ **properties**—A set of property values used to initialize the control.

▶ **events**—A set of event handlers used to initialize the control.

▶ **references**—A set of references to other components used to initialize the control.

▶ **element**—The DOM element associated with the control.

In Listing 33.26, the Glow control is associated with a <div> element named div1. The $create() shortcut transforms the <div> element into an AJAX client control. If you hover your mouse over the <div> element, the background color of the <div> element changes to orange.

Calling the $create() shortcut to create an instance of an AJAX control might seem like a crazy amount of work to instantiate a control in a page. What if you have dozens of controls in a page? In that case, would you need to call the $create() method dozens of times? (I feel exhausted just thinking about it.)

You can create server-side controls simply by declaring the control in a page. It seems like you should be able to do the very same thing when creating client-side AJAX controls. I want to declare an AJAX control, not create it programmatically. We address this issue in the next section.

Launching a Client-Side Control from the Server

Two chapters ago, I wrote that ASP.NET is a dead technology. The server side is the past; the client side is the future. If we want responsive applications, they need to be client-side applications.

However, in the brave new world of Ajax, there is still a place for ASP.NET server-side controls. An ASP.NET server-side control can be used as a launch device (like the booster rockets on the space shuttle) to lift JavaScript code from the server to the client.

Once we have reached escape velocity, it is important that an application continue to execute on the client. Just as it is incredibly expensive and time consuming to move back and forth from earth to orbit and orbit to earth, an AJAX page should not keep posting back to the server. An ASP.NET server control has done all the work it should ever do after it renders its contents once.

In this section, you learn how to create a server-side control that launches the AJAX client-side control we created in the previous section. Actually, we create two different server-side controls that do the same thing. First, we create an AJAX user control and then we create an AJAX custom control.

Creating a Server-Side AJAX User Control   One way to create a server-side control that launches a client-side AJAX control is to create a server-side user control. To make this work, you must implement the System.Web.UI.IScriptControl interface when you create the user control.

NOTE

We discussed user controls in Chapter 7, "Creating Custom Controls with User Controls."

The user control in Listing 33.27 launches the client-side Glow control.

LISTING 33.27   Glow.ascx

```
<%@ Control Language="C#" ClassName="Glow" %>
<%@ Implements Interface="System.Web.UI.IScriptControl" %>
<%@ Import Namespace="System.Collections.Generic" %>
<script runat="server">

    private string _Text = "Glow Control";
    private string _BackgroundColor = "orange";

    public string Text
    {
        get { return _Text; }
        set { _Text = value; }
    }

    public string BackgroundColor
    {
        get { return _BackgroundColor; }
        set { _BackgroundColor = value; }
    }

    public IEnumerable<ScriptReference> GetScriptReferences()
    {
        ScriptReference sref = new ScriptReference("Glow.js");
        List<ScriptReference> colSRefs = new List<ScriptReference>();
        colSRefs.Add( sref );
        return colSRefs;
    }

    public IEnumerable<ScriptDescriptor> GetScriptDescriptors()
    {
        ScriptControlDescriptor des = new ScriptControlDescriptor
        ➥("myControls.Glow", this.ClientID);
        des.AddProperty("text", _Text);
        des.AddProperty("backgroundColor", _BackgroundColor);
        List<ScriptDescriptor> colDes = new List<ScriptDescriptor>();
        colDes.Add( des );
        return colDes;
```

```
    }

    protected override void OnPreRender(EventArgs e)
    {
        ScriptManager.GetCurrent(Page).RegisterScriptControl(this);
        base.OnPreRender(e);
    }


    protected override void Render(HtmlTextWriter writer)
    {
        ScriptManager.GetCurrent(Page).RegisterScriptDescriptors(this);
        base.Render(writer);
    }

</script>

<div id='<%= this.ClientID %>'></div>
```

The IScriptControl interface has two methods that you must implement:

▶ **GetScriptReferences()**—Returns a list of JavaScript files required by the client-side control.

▶ **GetScriptDescriptors()**—Returns a list of $create() shortcuts for instantiating the client-side control.

The GetScriptReferences() method is implemented like this:

```
public IEnumerable<ScriptReference> GetScriptReferences()
{
    ScriptReference sref = new ScriptReference("Glow.js");
    List<ScriptReference> colSRefs = new List<ScriptReference>();
    colSRefs.Add( sref );
    return colSRefs;
}
```

This method creates a single ScriptReference that represents the Glow.js JavaScript file. Because our simple Glow client-side control has no other JavaScript file dependencies, we don't need to perform any other work.

The GetScriptDescriptors() method looks like this:

```
public IEnumerable<ScriptDescriptor> GetScriptDescriptors()
{
    ScriptControlDescriptor des = new ScriptControlDescriptor("myControls.Glow",
    ➥this.ClientID);
    des.AddProperty("text", _Text);
```

```
    des.AddProperty("backgroundColor", _BackgroundColor);
    List<ScriptDescriptor> colDes = new List<ScriptDescriptor>();
    colDes.Add( des );
    return colDes;
}
```

This method creates a single ScriptControlDescriptor. When the control renders the ScriptControlDescriptor, it looks like this:

```
$create(myControls.Glow, {"backgroundColor":"orange","text":"Glow Control"}, null,
null, $get("Glow1"));
```

Notice that the user control's OnPreRender() and Render() methods are overridden. In the OnPreRender() method, the user control is registered with the ScriptManager control. The Render() method causes the user control's ScriptDescriptors ($create() shortcuts) to be rendered.

Finally, notice that the user control contains a single <div> element that looks like this:

```
<div id='<%= this.ClientID %>'></div>
```

This <div> element is rendered to the browser. The $create() shortcut transforms the <div> element into a client-side Glow control.

Listing 33.28 illustrates how you can use the user control in an AJAX page.

LISTING 33.28   ShowUserControlGlow.aspx

```
<%@ Page Language="C#" %>
<%@ Register TagPrefix="user" TagName="Glow" Src="~/Glow.ascx" %>
<!DOCTYPE html PUBLIC "-//W3C//DTD XHTML 1.0 Transitional//EN"
 "http://www.w3.org/TR/xhtml1/DTD/xhtml1-transitional.dtd">
<html xmlns="http://www.w3.org/1999/xhtml">
<head runat="server">
    <title>Show User Control Glow</title>
</head>
<body>
    <form id="form1" runat="server">
    <div>
        <asp:ScriptManager ID="ScriptManager1" runat="server" />

        <user:Glow
            ID="Glow1"
            Text="The First One"
            BackgroundColor="red"
            runat="server" />

        <br /><br />
```

```
        <user:Glow
            ID="Glow2"
            Text="The Second One"
            BackgroundColor="yellow"
            runat="server" />

    </div>
    </form>
</body>
</html>
```

Notice that there is absolutely no code (client side or server side) in the AJAX page in Listing 33.28. Two instances of the Glow user control are declared with different Text and BackgroundColor properties. When the page is rendered, the following two $create() shortcuts are rendered automatically (you can see these statements by selecting View Source in your browser):

```
Sys.Application.add_init(function() {
  $create(myControls.Glow, {"backgroundColor":"red","text":"The First One"}, null,
null, $get("Glow1"));
});
Sys.Application.add_init(function() {
  $create(myControls.Glow, {"backgroundColor":"yellow","text":"The Second One"},
null, null, $get("Glow2"));
});
```

Creating a Server-Side AJAX Custom Control   Another option for launching a client-side control from the server side is to create a custom server-side control. When creating a custom server-side control, you can implement the IScriptControl interface just like we did in the previous section. Alternatively, you can derive a custom control from the base ScriptControl class.

The control in Listing 33.29 illustrates how you can launch the client-side Glow control by deriving a server-side control from the ScriptControl class.

LISTING 33.29   App_Code\Glow.cs

```
using System;
using System.Web.UI;
using System.Web.UI.WebControls;
using System.Collections.Generic;

namespace MyControls
{
public class Glow : ScriptControl
```

LISTING 33.29   Continued

```
{
    private string _Text = "Glow Control";
    private string _BackgroundColor = "orange";

    public string Text
    {
        get { return _Text; }
        set { _Text = value; }
    }

    public string BackgroundColor
    {
        get { return _BackgroundColor; }
        set { _BackgroundColor = value; }
    }

    protected override IEnumerable<ScriptReference> GetScriptReferences()
    {
        ScriptReference sref = new ScriptReference("Glow.js");
        List<ScriptReference> colSRefs = new List<ScriptReference>();
        colSRefs.Add(sref);
        return colSRefs;
    }

    protected override IEnumerable<ScriptDescriptor> GetScriptDescriptors()
    {
        ScriptControlDescriptor des = new ScriptControlDescriptor
        ➡("myControls.Glow", this.ClientID);
        des.AddProperty("text", _Text);
        des.AddProperty("backgroundColor", _BackgroundColor);
        List<ScriptDescriptor> colDes = new List<ScriptDescriptor>();
        colDes.Add(des);
        return colDes;
    }
}
}
```

The ScriptControl class is an abstract class. It has two methods that you must implement:

▶ **GetScriptReferences()**—Returns a list of JavaScript files required by the client-side control.

▶ **GetScriptDescriptors()**—Returns a list of $create() shortcuts for instantiating the client-side control.

These methods should look familiar because they are the same methods you are required to implement when implementing the `IScriptControl` interface.

Notice that you are not required to call the `RegisterScriptControl()` and `RegisterScriptDescriptors()` methods like we did in the previous section. The base `ScriptControl` class calls these methods for us automatically.

The page in Listing 33.30 illustrates how you can use the server-side Glow control in an AJAX page.

LISTING 33.30   ShowCustomControlGlow.aspx

```
<%@ Page Language="C#" %>
<%@ Register TagPrefix="custom" Namespace="MyControls" %>
<!DOCTYPE html PUBLIC "-//W3C//DTD XHTML 1.0 Transitional//EN"
 "http://www.w3.org/TR/xhtml1/DTD/xhtml1-transitional.dtd">
<html xmlns="http://www.w3.org/1999/xhtml">
<head runat="server">
    <title>Show Custom Control Glow</title>
</head>
<body>
    <form id="form1" runat="server">
    <asp:ScriptManager ID="ScriptManager1" runat="server" />

        <custom:Glow
            ID="Glow1"
            Text="The First One"
            BackgroundColor="red"
            runat="server" />

        <br /><br />

        <custom:Glow
            ID="Glow2"
            Text="The Second One"
            BackgroundColor="yellow"
            runat="server" />

    </form>
</body>
</html>
```

The page in Listing 33.30 has two instances of the Glow control. Notice, once again, that the page does not contain any server-side or client-side control. The AJAX client-side control was launched completely declaratively.

Creating Client-Side Behaviors

Client-side behaviors are closely related to client-side controls. Like a client-side control, a client-side behavior executes entirely within the browser. A client-side behavior is cobbled together out of JavaScript and DOM elements.

Whereas a DOM element can be associated with only a single client-side control, it can be associated with multiple client-side behaviors. You can use client-side behaviors to layer multiple features onto a single DOM element.

> **NOTE**
>
> Almost the entire ASP.NET AJAX Control Toolkit was implemented as client-side behaviors. For example, the AutoComplete extender renders a client-side behavior that adds auto-complete functionality to a TextBox control.

In this section, we create a HelpBehavior client-side behavior. This behavior adds a pop-up help box to an <input> element (see Figure 33.19). The source code for the HelpBehavior is contained in Listing 33.31.

FIGURE 33.19   Using the HelpBehavior behavior.

LISTING 33.31   HelpBehavior.js

```
/// <reference name="MicrosoftAjax.js"/>


Type.registerNamespace("myControls");


myControls.HelpBehavior = function(element)
{
    myControls.HelpBehavior.initializeBase(this, [element]);
```

```
    // Initialize fields
    this._text = "Help Text...";
    this._helpBox = null;

}

myControls.HelpBehavior.prototype =
{
    initialize: function()
    {
        myControls.HelpBehavior.callBaseMethod(this, 'initialize');

        // Initialize help box
        this._initializeHelpBox();

        // Wire-up delegates
        $addHandlers
            (
                this.get_element(),
                {
                    focus: this._onFocus,
                    blur: this._onBlur
                },
                this
            );
    },

    _initializeHelpBox: function()
    {
        // Create div element for help box
        this._helpBox = document.createElement("DIV");

        // Hard code a bunch of inline styles
        this._helpBox.style.display = "none";
        this._helpBox.style.position = "absolute";
        this._helpBox.style.width = "100px";
        this._helpBox.style.backgroundColor = "lightyellow";
        this._helpBox.style.border = "solid 1px black";
        this._helpBox.style.padding = "4px";
        this._helpBox.style.fontSize = "small";
        this._helpBox.innerHTML = this._text;

        // Position box right below input element
        var bounds = Sys.UI.DomElement.getBounds(this.get_element());
        Sys.UI.DomElement.setLocation(this._helpBox, bounds.x, bounds.y +
        ➥bounds.height);
```

LISTING 33.31   Continued

```
        // Append box to body
        document.body.appendChild(this._helpBox);
    },

    dispose: function()
    {
        $clearHandlers(this.get_element());
        myControls.HelpBehavior.callBaseMethod(this, 'dispose');
    },

    _onFocus: function()
    {
        this._helpBox.style.display = "";
    },

    _onBlur: function()
    {
        this._helpBox.style.display = "none";
    },

    get_text: function()
    {
        return this._text;
    },

    set_text: function(value)
    {
        this._text = value;
    }

}
myControls.HelpBehavior.registerClass('myControls.HelpBehavior', Sys.UI.Behavior);

if (typeof(Sys) !== 'undefined') Sys.Application.notifyScriptLoaded();
```

Notice that the skeleton for HelpBehavior.js looks almost exactly the same as the skeleton for an AJAX client-side control. You create a client-side behavior in the same way you create a client-side control. You declare a constructor function to generate a class. In the class prototype, you create both an initialize() and a dispose() method.

The only difference between a client-side control and a client-side behavior is the base class. A client-side behavior inherits from the Sys.UI.Behavior class instead of the Sys.UI.Control class.

After you create a behavior, you can use the `$create()` shortcut to instantiate the behavior and associate it with a DOM element. The page in Listing 33.32 illustrates how you can use the HelpBehavior with an `<input>` element.

LISTING 33.32   ShowHelpBehavior.aspx

```
<%@ Page Language="C#" %>
<!DOCTYPE html PUBLIC "-//W3C//DTD XHTML 1.0 Transitional//EN"
 "http://www.w3.org/TR/xhtml1/DTD/xhtml1-transitional.dtd">
<html xmlns="http://www.w3.org/1999/xhtml">
<head runat="server">
    <title>Show Help Box</title>
    <script type="text/javascript">

    function pageLoad()
    {
      $create
          (
              myControls.HelpBehavior,
              {text:"Enter your first name"},
              null,
              null,
              $get("txtFirstName")
          );

      $create
          (
              myControls.HelpBehavior,
              {text:"Enter your last name."},
              null,
              null,
              $get("txtLastName")
          );
    }

    </script>
</head>
<body>
    <form id="form1" runat="server">
    <div>
        <asp:ScriptManager ID="ScriptManager1" runat="server">
        <Scripts>
            <asp:ScriptReference Path="~/HelpBehavior.js" />
        </Scripts>
        </asp:ScriptManager>
```

33

LISTING 33.32   Continued

```
        <label for="txtFirstName">First Name:</label>
        <input id="txtFirstName" />

        <br /><br />

        <label for="txtLastName">Last Name:</label>
        <input id="txtLastName" />

    </div>
    </form>
</body>
</html>
```

When you move focus between the first name and last name input boxes, different help messages are displayed.

Launching a Client-Side Behavior from the Server

In the same way that you can launch a client-side control from the server, you can launch a client-side behavior from the server. A server-side control that launches a behavior is called an *extender* control.

> **NOTE**
>
> The extenders in the AJAX Control Toolkit ultimately derive from the `ExtenderControl` class. However, the Toolkit uses an intermediate base class named the `ExtenderControlBase` class. This intermediate class is included in the source code download of the AJAX Control Toolkit.

You can create an extender control in one of two ways: You can implement the `IExtenderControl` interface, or you can derive a control from the base `ExtenderControl` class. The control in Listing 33.33 illustrates how you can create a new extender control by inheriting from the `ExtenderControl` class.

LISTING 33.33   HelpExtender.cs

```
using System;
using System.Web.UI;
using System.Web.UI.WebControls;
using System.Collections.Generic;

namespace MyControls
{
```

```
[TargetControlType(typeof(TextBox))]
public class HelpExtender: ExtenderControl
{
    private string _Text = "Help Text...";

    public string Text
    {
        get { return _Text; }
        set { _Text = value; }
    }

    protected override IEnumerable<ScriptReference> GetScriptReferences()
    {
        ScriptReference sref = new ScriptReference("~/HelpBehavior.js");
        List<ScriptReference> colSRefs = new List<ScriptReference>();
        colSRefs.Add(sref);
        return colSRefs;
    }

    protected override IEnumerable<ScriptDescriptor> GetScriptDescriptors
    (
      Control targetControl
    )
    {
        ScriptControlDescriptor des = new ScriptControlDescriptor
        ➥("myControls.HelpBehavior", TargetControlID);
        des.AddProperty("text", _Text);
        List<ScriptDescriptor> colDes = new List<ScriptDescriptor>();
        colDes.Add(des);
        return colDes;
    }
}
}
```

The extender control in Listing 33.33 derives from the base `ExtenderControl` class. The `ExtenderControl` class is an abstract class. You must implement the following two methods:

▶ **GetScriptReferences()**—Returns a list of JavaScript files required by the client-side behavior.

▶ **GetScriptDescriptors()**—Returns a list of `$create()` shortcuts for instantiating the client-side behavior.

These are the same methods you would need to implement for a client-side control. The one difference is that the `ExtenderControl.GetScriptDescriptors()` method, unlike the `ScriptControl.GetScriptDescriptors()` method, has the target control passed to it.

Notice that the extender control in Listing 33.33 includes the following class-level attribute:

```
[TargetControlType(typeof(TextBox))]
```

This attribute restricts the type of control to which you can apply the extender control. In particular, this attribute prevents you from applying the extender control to anything other than a TextBox control.

NOTE

Unfortunately, an extender control must be applied to a server-side control. You cannot use an HTML element as the target of an extender control. For this reason, when building pure client-side AJAX applications, I would stick with the server-side `ScriptControl` class as a launch vehicle for both client-side controls and behaviors.

The page in Listing 33.34 demonstrates how you can use the HelpExtender control to extend the functionality of two TextBox controls.

LISTING 33.34   ShowHelpExtender.aspx

```
<%@ Page Language="C#" %>
<%@ Register TagPrefix="custom" Namespace="MyControls" %>
<!DOCTYPE html PUBLIC "-//W3C//DTD XHTML 1.0 Transitional//EN"
 "http://www.w3.org/TR/xhtml1/DTD/xhtml1-transitional.dtd">
<html xmlns="http://www.w3.org/1999/xhtml">
<head runat="server">
    <title>Show Help Extender</title>
</head>
<body>
    <form id="form1" runat="server">
    <div>
        <asp:ScriptManager ID="ScriptManager1" runat="server" />

        <asp:Label
            id="lblFirstName"
            Text="First Name:"
            AssociatedControlID="txtFirstName"
            Runat="server" />
        <asp:TextBox
            id="txtFirstName"
            Runat="server" />
        <custom:HelpExtender
            id="he1"
```

```
            TargetControlID="txtFirstName"
            Text="Enter your first name."
            Runat="server" />

        <br /><br />

        <asp:Label
            id="lblLastName"
            Text="Last Name:"
            AssociatedControlID="txtLastName"
            Runat="server" />
        <asp:TextBox
            id="txtLastName"
            Runat="server" />
        <custom:HelpExtender
            id="he2"
            TargetControlID="txtLastName"
            Text="Enter your last name."
            Runat="server" />

    </div>
    </form>
</body>
</html>
```

When you move focus between the two TextBox controls rendered by the page in Listing 33.34, the different help boxes appear.

Summary

This chapter was about the future. Times are changing. People are demanding more interactivity and responsiveness from their web applications. The future is Ajax.

In the first part of this chapter, you learned how to take advantage of the features of the Microsoft AJAX Library. You learned how to make JavaScript feel more like C#. In particular, you learned how to use the methods of the Microsoft AJAX Library to create classes and namespaces. You also learned how to debug a client-side AJAX application.

In the next part of this chapter, you learned how to call web services from the browser. You learned how to call a web method in an external web service. You also learned how to call a static web method exposed from a server-side page. We also discussed the three built-in web services included with the Microsoft AJAX Framework: the Authentication service, the Role service, and the Profile service.

In the final part of this chapter, you learned how to create AJAX client-side controls and behaviors. You learned how to create AJAX controls and behaviors programmatically by using the `$create()` shortcut. You also learned how to launch a client-side control and client-side behavior from the server side by building server-side `ScriptControl` and `ExtenderControl` classes.

PART X
Sample Application

IN THIS PART

Building a Code Sample Website

The goal of this final chapter is to present an entire ASP.NET 3.5 application that takes advantage of many of the new features of the .NET 3.5 Framework. In this chapter, we build a code sample website that also includes a simple blog.

There are two motivations behind this chapter. First, most of the code samples in this book are very brief. The code samples are intended to illustrate a particular point in the fewest lines of code possible. There are challenges, however, that you do not encounter until you build a full-blown web application. My hope is that you can apply the lessons I learned while building this application to an application you are building (in other words, learn from my pain).

The second motivation for writing this chapter is to tie together many of the technologies discussed in this book. This is a long book. Not many people read it from end to end (I thank the crazy few readers who manage to do it). My hope is that you'll study the application presented in this chapter and become more interested in new .NET 3.5 technologies such as LINQ to SQL and the ASP.NET AJAX Extensions. (You might even use the `VirtualPathProvider` class someday.)

In the first part of this chapter, I provide you with a walk-through of the pages contained in the sample application. Next, we examine more closely how different features of the website are implemented. In particular, we examine how data access and form validation are implemented in the sample website. We also discuss the Ajax features of the sample site. Finally, we discuss how the website enables "live" code samples.

> **NOTE**
>
> The entire code sample website is included on the CD that accompanies this book. The source code for the sample website is included in both C# and VB.NET.
>
> The sample website database is preloaded with the code listings from the first three chapters of this book.

Overview of the Sample Website

The primary purpose of the website is to act as a code sample website for .NET code. Anyone who visits the website can post a new code sample entry. A code sample entry can consist of one or more code sample files. The author of the code sample entry can provide a description of each of the files. Furthermore, the author can add one or more tags to the code samples to categorize and describe their purpose.

Visitors to the website can browse the existing code sample entries. They can rate code samples when they view them. Furthermore, they can copy the code samples so they can use the samples in their own applications.

The website also includes a simple blog. The administrator of the website can post blog entries about the code samples or about any other topic. Visitors to the website can add comments to a blog entry.

The website exposes both an ATOM and RSS feed. If someone wants to subscribe to the blog, that person can subscribe to either the ATOM or RSS feed.

The home page of the website displays a code cloud and a list of recent blog entries (see Figure 34.1). The code cloud consists of a distinct list of all the code entry tags. The more code entries that share a tag, the larger the tag appears in the code cloud. In the figure, you'll notice that a lot of code samples are related to validation. If you click a tag in the code cloud, you are transferred to a page that contains a list of code samples associated with the tag.

The home page also contains a list of three recent blog entries. A summary of each blog entry appears in the home page. You can click a blog entry to view the full entry.

In this section, you are provided with a walkthrough (with lots of screen shots) of the process of adding both blog entries and code entries.

Creating Blog Entries

Only a member with the Administrators role can post new blog entries. If you want to add a new blog entry, you must log in by clicking the Login link that appears at the top of every page.

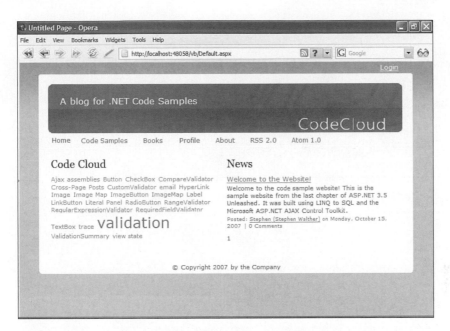

FIGURE 34.1   The home page of the sample website.

NOTE

I'm set up as the administrator for the website by default. If you log in using the user-name **Stephen** and password **secret**, you will be logged in as an administrator.

You can create a new administrator account (and delete the Stephen account) by using the Website Administration Tool. After opening the sample site in Visual Web Developer, select the menu option Website, ASP.NET Configuration. When the Website Administration Tool opens, select the Security tab to manage users and roles.

After you log in, you can post a new blog entry by clicking the {Add Blog Entry} link that appears under the current list of blog entries on the home page. Clicking this link transfers you to the page displayed in Figure 34.2.

When you create a new blog post, you complete the following fields:

▶ **Title**—The title of the blog post.

▶ **Introduction Text**—The introduction text appears on the home page of the website as a summary of a blog entry. The introduction text is also used by the ATOM and RSS feeds.

▶ **Post**—The full blog entry post.

▶ **Is Pinned**—When this box is checked, the blog entry appears before all other blog entries on the home page.

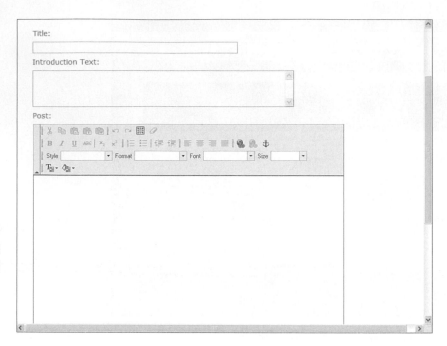

FIGURE 34.2   Adding a new blog entry.

Notice that the input field for entering a blog post uses a rich text editor. The sample website uses the open source FCKeditor. You can download the FCKeditor from www.fckeditor.net. The FCKeditor displays a rich editor in the case of Internet Explorer and Firefox. A plain text editor is displayed when the page is requested using the Opera browser.

If you attempt to submit the form without completing a required field, validation errors are displayed using callouts (see Figure 34.3). Validation errors are not displayed until you actually click the Next button.

After you successfully complete the form for adding a new blog entry and click the Next button, you are redirected to a page that you can use to tag the new blog entry (see Figure 34.4). You can add as many tags to a blog entry as you desire. The tags enable users to cross-navigate among related blog entries. Blog entries that share the same tags are linked.

The TextBox for adding a new tag uses the AJAX Control Toolkit AutoComplete Extender control. As you type, matching tags are retrieved from the database. Using the AutoComplete extender makes it more likely that you'll use the same tags for multiple blog posts.

When you are done adding all your tags, you can click the Finish button to finish the process of adding a new blog entry. You are redirected to the finished blog entry that the world sees.

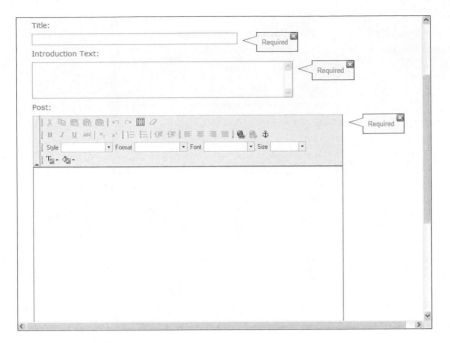

FIGURE 34.3   Receiving validation errors when submitting the Blog form.

FIGURE 34.4   Tagging a blog entry.

After you create a blog entry, you always have the option of editing or deleting the entry. To edit or delete a blog entry, log in to the website using an Administrator account, navigate to the blog entry page, and click either the {Edit} or {Delete} link.

Creating Code Sample Entries

The main purpose of the code sample website is to enable people to post new code samples, browse existing code samples, and rate code samples. Any registered user can post a new code sample entry at the website.

Before you can post a new code sample, you must navigate to the main code sample page. Click the Code Samples link that appears at the top of any page. You'll see the page in Figure 34.5.

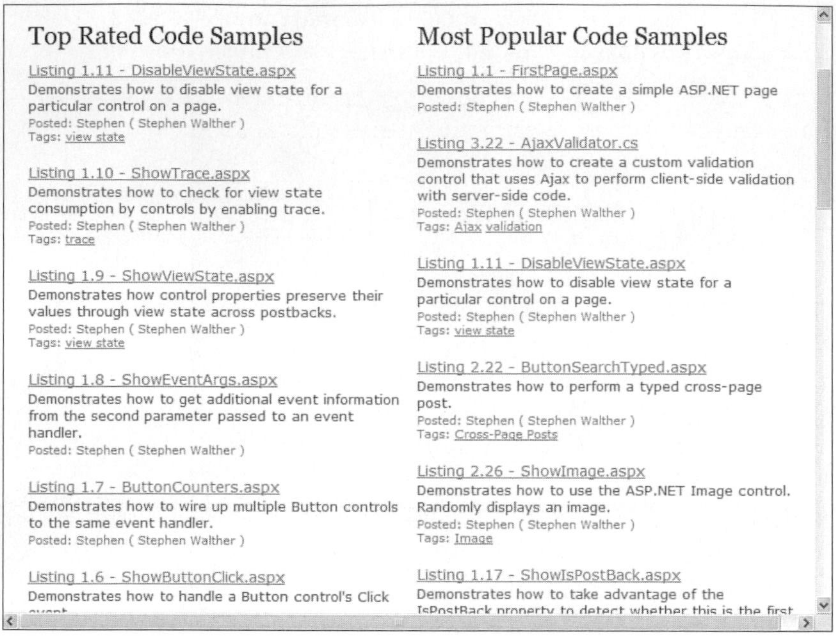

FIGURE 34.5   The main code sample page.

The main code sample page displays a list of the top ten highest rated code samples, the top ten most viewed code samples, and the top ten most recent code samples. At the bottom of the page, you can click the Add New Code Sample link to add a new code sample.

After you click the Add New Code Sample link, you see the form in Figure 34.6. A code sample entry can contain one more code samples. Typically, a code sample consists of multiple files. The form in Figure 34.6 enables you to provide a description of the entire code sample entry.

After you provide a description for the code sample entry and click Next, you are redirected to a page that you can use to associate one or more code samples with the code sample entry (see Figure 34.7). For example, you might want to create both a VB.NET and C# version of a code sample.

If you click the Add Code Sample link, you can add a new code sample. The form for adding a new code sample contains the following fields:

▶ **File Name**—The name of the code sample file (for example, SamplePage.aspx).

▶ **File Language**—The programming language used for the code sample.

▶ **Description**—The description of the code sample.

▶ **Code**—The actual source code of the code sample.

▶ **Enable Try It**—When this box is checked, the code sample can be executed "live" from the website. This field appears only for users in the Administrators role.

▶ **Try It Code**—The code executed when a code sample is executed "live" from the website. This field appears only for users in the Administrators role.

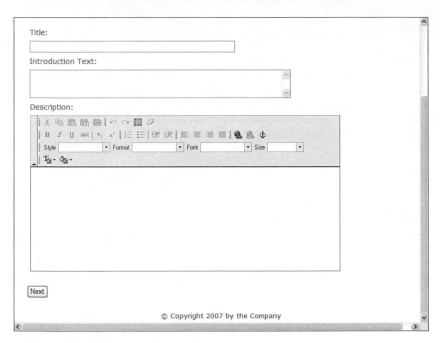

FIGURE 34.6   Form for adding a new code sample entry.

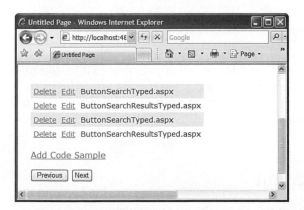

FIGURE 34.7   Managing code samples associated with a code sample entry.

The last two fields require some explanation. If you are a member of the Administrators role, you can enable users to execute a code sample. When you check the Enable Try It check box, a Try It link appears with the code sample that a user can click to run the code sample (see Figure 34.8).

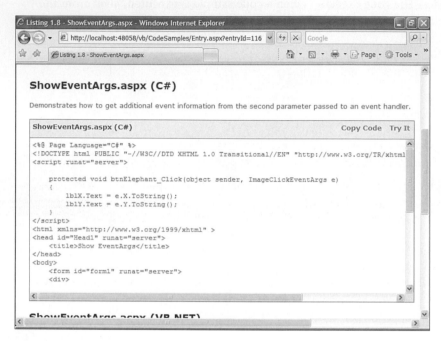

FIGURE 34.8   Viewing a code sample with a Try It link.

Because, most likely, you'll want to use a different database connection with the code that gets executed when a user clicks Try It, there is a separate text field that you can use to enter the Try It code. The source code entered into the Try It Code text field is never displayed to the public.

After you submit a code sample, you can click Next to move to a page that enables you to tag a code sample entry. You can associate a maximum of three tags with any code sample entry. The tags appear in the code cloud. They also appear at the bottom of each code entry to provide visitors to the website with a way to navigate between related code samples.

Data Access and Validation

In this section, you learn how data access and form validation are implemented for the sample website. Data access and form validation are implemented by taking advantage of new features of the .NET 3.5 Framework.

Using LINQ to SQL

All data access performed by the sample website is performed using LINQ to SQL. No explicit SQL code was written. Taking advantage of LINQ to SQL enabled me to dramatically reduce the amount of time and code required to build the website.

> **NOTE**
>
> LINQ to SQL is discussed in detail in Chapter 18, "Data Access with LINQ to SQL."

Normally, when performing data access from a web application, you need to write an entire data access layer to bridge the divide between your application and your database. By taking advantage of LINQ to SQL, I could avoid writing a data access layer. Instead, I could concentrate on the real task that I needed to accomplish: writing the data access queries.

I used the Object Relational Designer to create my LINQ entities (see Figure 34.9). I ran into one issue when using the Designer. Several of the website database tables include a DateCreated column. This column has a default value generated by the SQL GetDate() function. However, the Object Relational Designer did not pick up on this fact and I received errors when performing inserts and updates. To work around this problem, I had to manually update the DateCreated property for each entity in the Object Relational Designer. Within the Object Relational Designer, you can select a property of an entity and modify that property in the Properties window. In the case of the DateCreated property, I had to assign the value True to the Auto Generated Value property (see Figure 34.10).

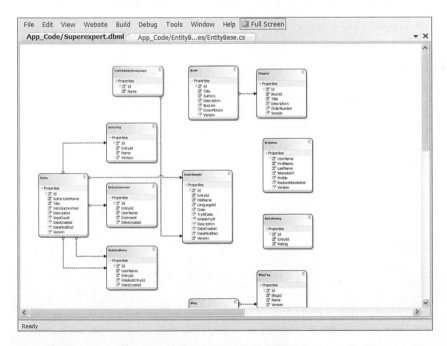

FIGURE 34.9   Using the Object Relational Designer.

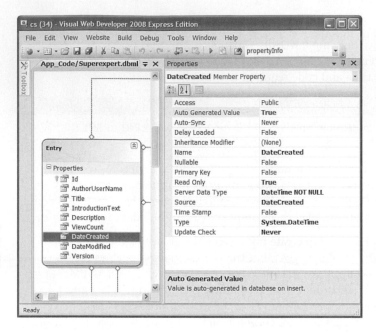

FIGURE 34.10   Modifying the `DateCreated` Auto Generated Value property.

I created a separate partial class for each entity. I added the LINQ to SQL queries that I needed to the partial class. For example, Listing 34.1 contains some of the code for the partial `CodeSample` entity.

LISTING 34.1   CodeSample.cs (Partial)

```
public partial class CodeSample : EntityBase<CodeSample>
{
    public IEnumerable<CodeSample> SelectByEntryId(int entryId)
    {
        return Table.Where( s => s.EntryId == entryId );
    }

    partial void OnCreated()
    {
        this.LanguageId = -1;
    }
}
```

Notice that the class is declared as a partial class. The other half of the partial class is generated by the Object Relational Designer. You can find the Designer-generated half of the `CodeSample` partial class in the Superexpert.Designer.cs file in the App_Code folder.

The preceding partial class contains a method named `SelectByEntryId`. This method executes a LINQ to SQL query that returns all code samples associated with a certain `entryId`. The `Table` property used within the method is a property exposed by the base class (we discuss this base class in the next section).

Notice that the class also includes an `OnCreated()` method. Unfortunately, you can't add a constructor to a LINQ to SQL partial class because the Object Relational Designer already creates a constructor. However, you can create the equivalent of a class constructor by handling the `OnCreated()` event. In the case of the `CodeSample` class, the `OnCreated()` event is used to provide a default value for the `CodeSample.LanguageId` property.

> **NOTE**
>
> All the entity partial classes can be found in the App_Code\Entities folder on the CD.

Handling Common Database Operations

When building the LINQ to SQL queries for the sample application, I noticed that I ended up writing almost the exact same queries for each entity. For example, I needed to write Select, Insert, Update, and Delete queries for both the `Blog` and the `CodeSample` entities. Whenever you find yourself writing duplicate code, you should stop yourself and determine whether there is a way to make the code more generic. In this case, I took advantage of a custom entity base class.

All the entity partial classes derive from the base `EntityBase` class. This class contains generic `Get`, `Select`, `Update`, `Delete`, and `Insert` methods. It also contains generic methods for sorting and paging database data.

For example, the `Blog` partial class is declared like this:

```
public partial class Blog : EntityBase<Blog>
```

Because the `Blog` class derives from the `EntityBase` class, it includes methods such as `Get`, `Select`, `Insert`, `Update`, and `Delete` for free. It inherits all the properties and methods of the `EntityBase` class (the `EntityBase` class is located in the App_Code\EntityBaseClasses folder).

> **NOTE**
>
> We discuss the EntityBase class in more detail in the last part of Chapter 18.

Creating a Single Insert and Update Form

The sample application includes forms for inserting and updating blog entries, inserting and updating code sample entries, and inserting and updating individual code samples. All the forms in the sample application follow the same pattern. A FormView that contains a single EditItemTemplate is used for displaying the form for both inserting and updating the form data.

For example, the page used for inserting and updating a blog entry is contained in Listing 34.2.

LISTING 34.2   Edit.aspx

```csharp
<%@ Page Language="C#" MasterPageFile="~/Design/MasterPage.master"
  Title="Blog Post" %>
<script runat="server">

    /// <summary>
    /// Add default values for new blog entry
    /// </summary>
    protected void srcBlog_Updating
    (
      object sender,
      ObjectDataSourceMethodEventArgs e
    )
    {
        // If new blog entry, add user name
        Blog newBlog = (Blog)e.InputParameters[1];
        if (newBlog.Id == 0)
        {
            newBlog.AuthorUserName = User.Identity.Name;
        }
    }


    /// <summary>
    /// If no problems, then redirect to blog tags page
    /// </summary>
    protected void srcBlog_Updated(object sender, ObjectDataSourceStatusEventArgs e)
    {
        if (e.Exception == null)
        {
            Blog newBlog = (Blog)e.ReturnValue;
            Response.Redirect("~/Admin/BlogTags/Edit.aspx?blogId=" + newBlog.Id);
        }
    }


    /// <summary>
    /// If there was a problem, keep the form in edit mode
    /// and show validation errors
    /// </summary>
    protected void frmBlog_ItemUpdated(object sender, FormViewUpdatedEventArgs e)
    {
        if (e.Exception != null)
        {
            e.KeepInEditMode = true;
```

```
                e.ExceptionHandled = true;
                ValidationUtility.ShowValidationErrors(this, e.Exception);
            }
        }

</script>
<asp:Content ID="Content1" ContentPlaceHolderID="cphMain" Runat="Server">

<asp:UpdatePanel ID="up1" runat="server">
<ContentTemplate>
<asp:FormView
        id="frmBlog"
        DataSourceID="srcBlog"
        DataKeyNames="Id,Version"
        DefaultMode="Edit"
        OnItemUpdated="frmBlog_ItemUpdated"
        Width="100%"
        Runat="server">
        <EditItemTemplate>

        <div class="field">
            <div class="fieldLabel">
            <asp:Label
                id="lblTitle"
                Text="Title:"
                AssociatedControlID="txtTitle"
                Runat="server" />
            </div>
            <div class="fieldValue">
            <asp:TextBox
                id="txtTitle"
                Text='<%# Bind("Title") %>'
                Columns="60"
                Runat="server" />
            </div>
            <div class="fieldValue">
            <super:EntityCallOutValidator
                id="valTitle"
                PropertyName="Title"
                Runat="server" />
            </div>
        </div>

        <div class="field">
            <div class="fieldLabel">
            <asp:Label
```

LISTING 34.2   Continued

```
                id="lblIntroductionText"
                Text="Introduction Text:"
                AssociatedControlID="txtIntroductionText"
                Runat="server" />
        </div>
        <div class="fieldValue">
        <asp:TextBox
                id="txtIntroductionText"
                Text='<%# Bind("IntroductionText") %>'
                TextMode="MultiLine"
                Columns="60"
                Rows="4"
                Runat="server" />
        </div>
        <div class="fieldValue">
        <super:EntityCallOutValidator
                id="valIntroductionText"
                PropertyName="IntroductionText"
                Runat="server" />
        </div>
    </div>

    <div class="field">
        <div class="fieldLabel">
        <asp:Label
                id="lblPost"
                Text="Post:"
                AssociatedControlID="txtPost"
                Runat="server" />
        </div>
        <div class="fieldValue">
        <fck:FCKeditor
                id="txtPost"
                BasePath="~/FCKEditor/"
                ToolbarSet="Superexpert"
                Value='<%# Bind("Post") %>'
                Width="600px"
                Height="600px"
                runat="server" />
        </div>
        <div class="fieldValue">
        <super:EntityCallOutValidator
                id="EntityCallOutValidator1"
                PropertyName="Post"
                Runat="server" />
```

```
                    </div>
            </div>

            <div class="field">
                <div class="fieldLabel">
                </div>
                <div>
                <asp:CheckBox
                    id="chkIsPinned"
                    Text="Is Pinned"
                    Checked='<%# Bind("IsPinned") %>'
                    Runat="server" />
                </div>
            </div>

            <div class="field">
                <div class="fieldLabel">
                </div>
                <div>
                <asp:Button
                    id="btnNext"
                    CommandName="Update"
                    Text="Next"
                    Runat="server" />
                </div>
            </div>

            </EditItemTemplate>
        </asp:FormView>
    </ContentTemplate>
</asp:UpdatePanel>

<super:EntityDataSource
    id="srcBlog"
    TypeName="Blog"
    SelectMethod="Get"
    UpdateMethod="Save"
    OnUpdating="srcBlog_Updating"
    OnUpdated="srcBlog_Updated"
    Runat="Server">
    <SelectParameters>
        <asp:QueryStringParameter Name="id" QueryStringField="blogId" />
    </SelectParameters>
</super:EntityDataSource>

</asp:Content>
```

34

The page in Listing 34.2 contains a `FormView` control bound to a `DataSource` control. The `FormView` control contains a single EditItemTemplate template. Notice that it does not include an InsertItemTemplate, even though the `FormView` is used both for inserting new blog entries and editing existing blog entries. By using a single template, you reduce the amount of code you must write and maintain by half.

> **NOTE**
>
> Most of the pages in the sample application use a `DataSource` control named the `EntityDataSource` control. We discussed the `EntityDataSource` control in Chapter 18. This control is derived from the `ObjectDataSource` control and provides default values for some of the `ObjectDataSource` control's properties. The `EntityDataSource` control is contained in the App_Code\EntityBaseClasses folder on the CD.

The `DataSource` control includes a select QueryStringParameter that grabs an `id` value from the query string. The `DataSource` control calls the `Get()` method to grab an instance of the `Blog` entity when the page is first requested.

The `Get()` method is a method of the `EntityBase` class. It looks like this:

```
public static T Get(int? id)
{
  if (id == null)
    return new T();

  return Table.Single(GetDynamicGet(id.Value));
}
```

When a null ID is passed to the `Get()` method, it simply returns a new instance of the entity (in this case, the `Blog` entity). If the `id` parameter does have a value, on the other hand, the entity with a matching ID is retrieved from the database with the help of the `GetDynamicGet()` method.

Therefore, if you request the page in Listing 34.2 without passing an `id` parameter in the query string, a form that represents a new `Blog` entry is displayed. Otherwise, if you do pass an `id` parameter, a form for editing the existing `Blog` entity is displayed.

Handling Form Validation

The sample application discussed in this chapter does not use any of the standard ASP.NET validation controls. Validation is handled at the entity level. In other words, validation is performed in the business logic layer, where validation should be performed, instead of the user interface layer.

The `EntityBase` class includes an abstract (`MustInherit`) method named `Validate()`. Each of the entities implements this abstract method. All the validation logic is contained in the entity's `Validation()` method.

For example, Listing 34.3 contains the `Validation()` method used by the `Blog` entity.

LISTING 34.3   Blog.cs (Partial)

```csharp
public partial class Blog : EntityBase<Blog>
{
    /// <summary>
    /// Where all validation happens
    /// </summary>
    protected override void Validate()
    {
        // Required fields
        if (!ValidationUtility.SatisfiesRequired(Title))
            ValidationErrors.Add("Title", "Required");
        if (!ValidationUtility.SatisfiesRequired(IntroductionText))
            ValidationErrors.Add("IntroductionText", "Required");
        if (!ValidationUtility.SatisfiesRequired(Post))
            ValidationErrors.Add("Post", "Required");
    }
}
```

The `Validate()` method takes advantage of the ValidationUtility to check for several required fields. If any of the validation checks fails, an error message is added to the entity's `ValidationErrors` collection.

> **NOTE**
>
> We discuss the ValidationUtility in Chapter 18. The ValidationUtility contains additional methods for validating property values against regular expressions stored in the web configuration file.

If you look closely at the `EditItemTemplate` contained in the FormView in Listing 34.2, you'll notice that `EntityCallOutValidator` controls are associated with each TextBox. For example, the following `EntityCallOutValidator` control is associated with the `txtTitle` TextBox:

```
<super:EntityCallOutValidator
    id="valTitle"
    PropertyName="Title"
    Runat="server" />
```

When the `ValidationUtility.ShowValidationErrors()` method is called in the `frmBlog_ItemUpdated()` event handler, any validation error that matches the value of an `EntityCallOutValidator` control's `PropertyName` property is displayed.

The advantage of placing your validation logic in your business logic layer is that your validation logic is applied automatically wherever you use the entity. For example, if the `Blog` entity is used in multiple pages (or even multiple applications), you don't need to rewrite the very same validation logic.

> **NOTE**
>
> The traditional advantage of placing your validation logic in the user interface layer is responsiveness. You don't need to perform a postback to view validation error messages. However, Ajax is blurring this traditional divide between server and client. All the forms used in the sample application use the `UpdatePanel` control in order to make the forms more responsive.

Taking Advantage of Ajax

The sample application discussed in this chapter takes advantage of the Microsoft server-side AJAX controls. The `UpdatePanel` control is used with almost all the forms for inserting and editing data. The sample application also takes advantage of the ASP.NET AJAX Control Toolkit. Two controls from the Toolkit, the `AutoCompleteExtender` and the `Rating` control, are used to create a more interactive experience.

Using the UpdatePanel Control

Almost all the `FormView` controls used in the sample application are wrapped in an `UpdatePanel` control. When you submit a form, a disruptive postback is not performed. Instead, a sneaky postback is performed in the background by the `UpdatePanel` control.

The overall user experience is improved by the `UpdatePanel` control. For example, the `UpdatePanel` control creates the illusion that the validation error messages are being generated on the client when, in fact, the validation error messages are being generated by the server.

> **NOTE**
>
> We discuss the `UpdatePanel` control in detail in Chapter 31, "Using Server-Side ASP.NET AJAX."

However, using the `UpdatePanel` control made debugging the sample application more difficult. The `UpdatePanel` control prevents normal error messages from being displayed in the browser. Furthermore, because an `UpdatePanel` control times out, stepping through code with the Visual Web Developer debugger in a page that contains an `UpdatePanel` is difficult.

My recommendation is that you don't add `UpdatePanel` controls to a web application until after it is fully debugged.

Using the ASP.NET AJAX Control Toolkit

The sample application uses two controls from the ASP.NET AJAX Control Toolkit: the `AutoCompleteExtender` control and the `Rating` control.

> **NOTE**
>
> The ASP.NET AJAX Control Toolkit is discussed in Chapter 32, "Using the ASP.NET AJAX Control Toolkit."

The `AutoCompleteExtender` control can be used to extend a TextBox control so that suggestions appear while you type (like in Google Suggest). The suggestions are retrieved from a web method. The web method can be defined in the page that contains the `AutoCompleteExtender` control, or the web method can be defined in a separate web service.

The `AutoCompleteExtender` control is used in multiple pages within the sample application. For example, it is used both in the page for editing blog tags (see Figure 34.11) and in the page for editing code sample tags. Listing 34.4 is extracted from the page for editing blog tags.

FIGURE 34.11   Receiving auto-complete suggestions as you type.

LISTING 34.4   Admin\BlogTags\Edit.aspx (Partial)

```
<asp:TextBox
    id="txtTag"
    AutoComplete="Off"
    Text='<%# Bind("Name") %>'
    Runat="server" />
<ajaxToolkit:AutoCompleteExtender
    ID="AutoCompleteExtender1"
    ServiceMethod="GetSuggestions"
    TargetControlID="txtTag"
    MinimumPrefixLength="1"
    Runat="server" />
```

Notice that the TextBox control in Listing 34.4 includes an `AutoComplete="Off"` attribute. This attribute disables the built-in browser auto-complete (for Internet Explorer and Firefox) so that it does not interfere with the Ajax auto-complete.

In Listing 34.4, the `AutoCompleteExtender` is associated with the TextBox control through its `TargetControlID` property. The `MinimumPrefixLength` property configures the control to start displaying suggestions as soon as you type at least one character into the TextBox control. Finally, the `AutoCompleteExtender` control is set up to retrieve its suggestions from a web method named `GetSuggestions()`. This method is declared in the same page as the `AutoCompleteExtender` control. The code for the `GetSuggestions()` method is contained in Listing 34.5.

LISTING 34.5   Admin\BlogTags\Edit.aspx (Partial)

```
[System.Web.Services.WebMethod]
public static string[] GetSuggestions(string prefixText, int count)
{
    return BlogTag.GetSuggestions(prefixText, count);
}
```

When a web method is declared in a page, it must be declared as a static method. Furthermore, it must be decorated with the `WebMethod` attribute.

The `GetSuggestions()` method in Listing 34.5 calls the `GetSuggestions()` method of the `BlogTag` entity to get existing blog tags that match the prefix from the database. The `BlogTag.GetSuggestions()` method is contained in Listing 34.6.

LISTING 34.6   BlogTag.cs (Partial)

```
public partial class BlogTag : EntityBase<BlogTag>
{
    public static string[] GetSuggestions(string prefixText, int count)
    {
        return Table.Where( t => t.Name.StartsWith(prefixText) )
            .Select(t => t.Name).Distinct().Take(count).ToArray();
    }
}
```

The other control from the ASP.NET AJAX Control Toolkit used in the sample application is the `Rating` control. This control is used to enable users to rate the quality of a code sample (see Figure 34.12).

The `Rating` control is declared with the following attributes in the CodeSamples\ Entry.aspx page:

```
<ajaxToolkit:Rating
    ID="Rating1"
```

```
    BehaviorID="RatingBehavior1"
    CurrentRating="2"
    MaxRating="5"
    StarCssClass="ratingStar"
    WaitingStarCssClass="savedRatingStar"
    FilledStarCssClass="filledRatingStar"
    EmptyStarCssClass="emptyRatingStar"
    runat="server"
    style="float:left"
    Tag='<%# Eval("Id") %>'
    OnChanged="Rating1_Changed" />
```

FIGURE 34.12   Rating a code sample.

When a user clicks the Rating control and selects a rating, the Rating control raises its Changed event. The Changed event is handled by the following event handler:

```
    protected void Rating1_Changed(object sender, RatingEventArgs e)
    {
        EntryRating.Insert( new EntryRating(){EntryId=Int32.Parse(e.Tag),
            Rating = Int32.Parse(e.Value)} );
    }
```

This event handler inserts a new EntryRating entity into the database that represents the user rating. The second parameter passed to this method is an instance of the RatingEventArgs class. Two properties of this class are used when inserting the new record: Value and Tag. The Value property represents the rating the user selected. The Tag property can represent any information you want to associate with the rating. When the Rating control is declared, the code sample Entry.Id is assigned to the tag.

> **NOTE**
>
> The Rating control performs a normal server postback when you select a particular rating.

Using the VirtualPathProvider Class

The VirtualPathProvider class was introduced into the ASP.NET 2.0 Framework. Not many people know about this class. The VirtualPathProvider class can be used to abstract the location of an ASP.NET file away from the file system.

I want visitors to the code sample website to be able to try the code samples "live." Someone browsing the code samples should be able to click a Try It link and execute a code sample (see Figure 34.13).

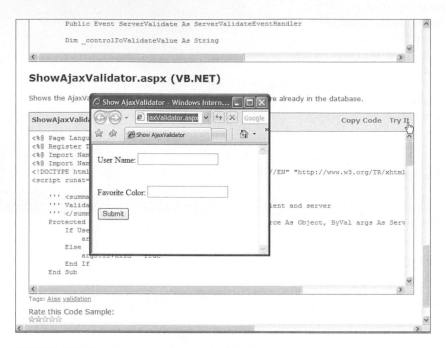

FIGURE 34.13   Trying a code sample "live."

In the sample application, code samples are stored in a database table. In order to get the Try It functionality to work, the application must be able to execute code samples directly from the database. This is exactly what the VirtualPathProvider class enables you to do. The code sample application takes advantage of the VirtualPathProvider class to execute ASP.NET pages directly from a database table.

The VirtualPathProvider class hijacks a particular file system path. Any path that starts with a directory named /virtual is passed to VirtualPathProvider. For example, when you click the Try It link next to a code sample, a request for a page at the following location is sent to the server:

```
/virtual/codesample/166/ShowAjaxValidator.aspx
```

Because this path starts with a directory named /virtual, the request gets routed to the VirtualPathProvider class, which grabs the file from the TryItCode column in the CodeSample database table. The file gets dynamically compiled by the ASP.NET Framework and served as a normal ASP.NET page.

> **NOTE**
>
> The `VirtualPathProvider` class is discussed in detail in Chapter 21, "Advanced Navigation."

Summary

The goal of this chapter was to demonstrate how you can take advantage of several of the new features of the ASP.NET 3.5 Framework when building a web application. In this chapter, you were presented with an overview of a complex application written with ASP.NET 3.5. You learned about the code sample application.

In the first part of this chapter, you learned how data access and form validation are implemented in the sample application. My hope is that studying this application will convince you to stop writing SQL queries and start writing LINQ queries.

In the second part of this chapter, you learned how the sample application takes advantage of the new server-side Ajax features introduced into the ASP.NET 3.5 Framework. You learned how the sample application uses the `UpdatePanel` control to create more responsive forms. We also discussed two controls from the ASP.NET AJAX Control Toolkit used in the sample application: the `AutoCompleteExtender` and `Rating` controls.

Finally, we discussed one of the more obscure and overlooked classes contained in the ASP.NET Framework: the `VirtualPathProvider` class. You learned how the sample application uses the `VirtualPathProvider` class to execute ASP.NET pages directly from a database table.

34

Index

Symbols

A

B

How can we make this index more useful? Email us at indexes@samspublishing.com

F

Guestbook component, 786

Guestbook.cs file, 786

guestbooks, displaying, 785-788

H

HandleError.aspx page, 399-400

HandleErrors.aspx page, 788-790

handling events. *See* events

HasChanged property (CacheDependency class), 1346

HasChildNodes property (SiteMapNode class), 1051

HasFile property

    Configuration class, 1468

    FileUpload control, 182

HashPasswordForStoringInConfigFile() method, 1173

HasKeys property (HttpCookie class), 1230

head tag, 257

HeaderContent.aspx file, 256

HeaderImageUrl property (BoundField), 520

headers

    HeaderContent.aspx file, 256

    MetaContent.aspx file, 257

    varying output cache by, 1298-1299

HeaderStyle property

    BoundField, 520

    DataList control, 653

    DetailsView control, 596

HeaderTemplate property (TemplateField), 541

HeaderTemplate templates, 228, 624, 641

HeaderText property

    BoundField, 520

    DetailsView control, 596

    ValidationSummary control, 167

    Wizard control, 228

healthMonitoring section (web.config file), 1448

HelloWorld component, 688-690

HelloWorld.cs file, 688

HelpBehavior.js file, 1762-1764

HelpExtender class, 1766-1767

hide action animations, 1688

hiding Login control from authenticated users, 1111-1116

hierarchical DataBound controls

    Menu, 345

    Movies.xml page, 347-348

    ShowHierarchicalDataBound.aspx page, 345-347

    TreeView, 345

highlighting

    rows, 542-544

    validation errors

        ShowSetFocusOnError.aspx page, 131-132

        ShowValidators.aspx page, 133-134

        ValidationImage.aspx page, 130

HighlightRows.aspx page, 543-544

HorizontalAlign property (Panel control), 116

Host property (SmtpClient class), 13

hostingEnvironment section (web.config file), 1448

HotSpot classes, 108

HotSpotMode property (ImageMap control), 113

HotSpots property (ImageMap control), 113

HoverMenu control, 1662

HoverNodeStyle object, 1032

HTML controls, 21-23

HtmlControls.aspx page, 22

HtmlEncode property (BoundField), 520

HtmlEncode() method, 914-915

HtmlMeta controls, 258

HtmlTextWriter class

    drop shadows, rendering, 1507

    HTML color table, rendering, 1505-1506

    methods, 1504-1505

HtppContext object, 713

HTTP Handlers, 1420

    anonymous HTTP Handlers, 1430-1433

        IHttpAsyncHandler interface, 1431

        RSSHandler.cs file, 1431

I

L

M

N

How can we make this index more useful? Email us at indexes@samspublishing.com

How can we make this index more useful? Email us at indexes@samspublishing.com

S

How can we make this index more useful? Email us at indexes@samspublishing.com

How can we make this index more useful? Email us at indexes@samspublishing.com

X-Y-Z

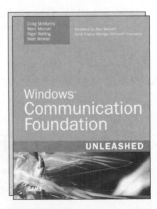